*International Directory of*

# COMPANY
# HISTORIES

*International Directory of*

# COMPANY HISTORIES

## VOLUME 37

*Editor*
**Tina Grant**

## ST. JAMES PRESS

AN IMPRINT OF THE GALE GROUP

DETROIT • NEW YORK • SAN FRANCISCO
LONDON • BOSTON • WOODBRIDGE, CT

## STAFF

Tina Grant, *Editor*

Miranda H. Ferrara, *Project Manager*

Erin Bealmear, Christa Brelin, Joann Cerrito, Steve Cusack,
Kristin Hart, Melissa Hill, Margaret Mazurkiewicz, Carol Schwartz,
Christine Tomassini, Michael J. Tyrkus, *St. James Press Editorial Staff*

Peter M. Gareffa, *Managing Editor, St. James Press*

**Library of Congress Catalog Number: 89-190943**

**British Library Cataloguing in Publication Data**

International directory of company histories. Vol. 37
I. Tina Grant
338.7409

ISBN 1-55862-442-2

Printed in the United States of America
Published simultaneously in the United Kingdom

St. James Press is an imprint of The Gale Group

Cover photograph: Tel Aviv Stock Exchange trading floor
(courtesy: The Tel Aviv Stock Exchange Ltd.)

10 9 8 7 6 5 4 3 2 1

# CONTENTS _____

## Company Histories

# PREFACE

The St. James Press series *The International Directory of Company Histories (IDCH)* is intended for reference use by students, business people, librarians, historians, economists, investors, job candidates, and others who seek to learn more about the historical development of the world's most important companies. To date, *IDCH* has covered over 4,850 companies in 37 volumes.

## Inclusion Criteria

Most companies chosen for inclusion in *IDCH* have achieved a minimum of US$50 million in annual sales and are leading influences in their industries or geographical locations. Companies may be publicly held, private, or nonprofit. State-owned companies that are important in their industries and that may operate much like public or private companies also are included. Wholly owned subsidiaries and divisions are profiled if they meet the requirements for inclusion. Entries on companies that have had major changes since they were last profiled may be selected for updating.

The *IDCH* series highlights 10% private and nonprofit companies, and features updated entries on approximately 45 companies per volume.

## Entry Format

Each entry begins with the company's legal name, the address of its headquarters, its telephone, toll-free, and fax numbers, and its web site. A statement of public, private, state, or parent ownership follows. A company with a legal name in both English and the language of its headquarters country is listed by the English name, with the native-language name in parentheses.

The company's founding or earliest incorporation date, the number of employees, and the most recent available sales figures follow. Sales figures are given in local currencies with equivalents in U.S. dollars. For some private companies, sales figures are estimates and indicated by the abbreviation *est*. The entry lists the exchanges on which a company's stock is traded and its ticker symbol, as well as the company's NAIC codes.

Entries generally contain a *Company Perspectives* box which provides a short summary of the company's mission, goals, and ideals, a *Key Dates* box highlighting milestones in the company's history, lists of *Principal Subsidiaries, Principal Divisions, Principal Operating Units, Principal Competitors,* and articles for *Further Reading.*

American spelling is used throughout *IDCH*, and the word ''billion'' is used in its U.S. sense of one thousand million.

## Sources

Entries have been compiled from publicly accessible sources both in print and on the Internet such as general and academic periodicals, books, annual reports, and material supplied by the companies themselves.

## Cumulative Indexes

*IDCH* contains three indexes: the **Index to Companies**, which provides an alphabetical index to companies discussed in the text as well as to companies profiled, the **Index to Industries**, which allows researchers to locate companies by their principal industry, and the **Geographic Index**, which lists companies alphabetically by the country of their headquarters. The indexes are cumulative and specific instructions for using them are found immediately preceding each index.

## Suggestions Welcome

Comments and suggestions from users of *IDCH* on any aspect of the product as well as suggestions for companies to be included or updated are cordially invited. Please write:

The Editor
*International Directory of Company Histories*
St. James Press
27500 Drake Rd.
Farmington Hills, Michigan 48331-3535

## ABBREVIATIONS FOR FORMS OF COMPANY INCORPORATION

| | |
|---|---|
| A.B. | Aktiebolaget (Sweden) |
| A.G. | Aktiengesellschaft (Germany, Switzerland) |
| A.S. | Atieselskab (Denmark) |
| A.S. | Aksjeselskap (Denmark, Norway) |
| A.Ş. | Anomin Şirket (Turkey) |
| B.V. | Besloten Vennootschap met beperkte, Aansprakelijkheid (The Netherlands) |
| Co. | Company (United Kingdom, United States) |
| Corp. | Corporation (United States) |
| G.I.E. | Groupement d'Intérêt Economique (France) |
| GmbH | Gesellschaft mit beschränkter Haftung (Germany) |
| H.B. | Handelsbolaget (Sweden) |
| Inc. | Incorporated (United States) |
| KGaA | Kommanditgesellschaft auf Aktien (Germany) |
| K.K. | Kabushiki Kaisha (Japan) |
| LLC | Limited Liability Company (Middle East) |
| Ltd. | Limited (Canada, Japan, United Kingdom, United States) |
| N.V. | Naamloze Vennootschap (The Netherlands) |
| OY | Osakeyhtiöt (Finland) |
| PLC | Public Limited Company (United Kingdom) |
| PTY. | Proprietary (Australia, Hong Kong, South Africa) |
| S.A. | Société Anonyme (Belgium, France, Switzerland) |
| SpA | Società per Azioni (Italy) |

## ABBREVIATIONS FOR CURRENCY

| | | | |
|---|---|---|---|
| DA | Algerian dinar | M$ | Malaysian ringgit |
| A$ | Australian dollar | Dfl | Netherlands florin |
| Sch | Austrian schilling | Nfl | Netherlands florin |
| BFr | Belgian franc | NZ$ | New Zealand dollar |
| Cr | Brazilian cruzado | N | Nigerian naira |
| R | Brazilian Real | NKr | Norwegian krone |
| C$ | Canadian dollar | RO | Omani rial |
| RMB | Chinese renminbi | P | Philippine peso |
| COL | Colombian Peso | PLN | Polish Zloty |
| DKr | Danish krone | Esc | Portuguese escudo |
| E£ | Egyptian pound | Ru | Russian ruble |
| EUR | Euro Dollars | SRls | Saudi Arabian riyal |
| Fmk | Finnish markka | S$ | Singapore dollar |
| FFr | French franc | R | South African rand |
| DM | German mark | W | South Korean won |
| HK$ | Hong Kong dollar | Pta | Spanish peseta |
| HUF | Hungarian forint | SKr | Swedish krona |
| Rs | Indian rupee | SFr | Swiss franc |
| Rp | Indonesian rupiah | NT$ | Taiwanese dollar |
| IR£ | Irish pound | B | Thai baht |
| L | Italian lira | £ | United Kingdom pound |
| ¥ | Japanese yen | $ | United States dollar |
| W | Korean won | B | Venezuelan bolivar |
| KD | Kuwaiti dinar | K | Zambian kwacha |
| LuxFr | Luxembourgian franc | | |

# International Directory of

# COMPANY HISTORIES

# **▲ADAMS**GOLF™

# Adams Golf, Inc.

**300 Delaware Avenue, Suite 572**
**Wilmington, Delaware 19801**
**U.S.A.**
**Telephone: (302) 427-5892**
**Fax: (972) 673-9200**
**Web site: http://www.adamsgolf.com**

*Public Company*
*Incorporated:* 1987
*Employees:* 243
*Sales:* $54.00 million (1999)
*Stock Exchanges:* NASDAQ
*Ticker Symbol:* ADGO
*NAIC:* 33992 Sporting and Athletic Goods Manufacturing

Adams Golf, Inc. designs, manufactures, and markets golf clubs domestically and internationally. Adams Golf also operates a custom-fitting operation comprising more than 300 golf professionals who are certified to custom fit clubs through a network of more than 100 accounts. Nearly all of the company's revenues are derived from the sale of golf clubs, primarily from Adams Golf's signature line of Tight Lies fairway woods. The company also sells Tight Lies drivers, SC Series Titanium drivers, and Faldo Series wedges. World-recognized professional golfers Nick Faldo and Tom Watson represent the Adams Golf brand. Internationally, the company sells its product line primarily in the United Kingdom, Japan, and Canada.

## *Origins*

A one-time field engineer for Corning Glass, Barney Adams founded Adams Golf. After leaving Corning Glass, Adams earned a reputation in turnaround management, spending much of the 1970s and the early 1980s in northern California's Silicon Valley, where he helped troubled companies regain their footing. Eventually, Adams' experience with helping others manage their companies fed his desire to start his own company. One passion dovetailed with another in 1987, when he was able to combine his entrepreneurial inclinations and his love for the game of golf. Adams convinced six investors to financially support his dream, enabling him to invest $50,000 in a defunct

golf club business named Dave Pelz Golf. Located in Abilene, Texas, the acquired company was immediately given Adams' name and began operating as a component supplier and contract manufacturer.

After moving the company to Richardson, Texas, in 1991, Adams altered its business approach. In 1992, he established Adams Golf's custom-fitting operation. The change shaped the company into a tailor-made supplier of golf clubs. Variables such as the length and stiffness of the club shaft, the placement of the head relative to the shaft, and the club's weight distribution were each adjusted to conform to the unique characteristics of a particular individual, taking into account the golfer's physical attributes and the peculiarity of his or her swing. The company started the custom-fitting process by measuring the customer to determine shaft length and head placement. Next, the customer used ten different club sets to establish which type of clubs worked best, a trial-and-error analysis that typically revealed one club set to yield superior performance results. The chosen clubs were then used as the foundation for the remainder of the fitting process. "We call it harmonic club fitting," Adams explained in a May 13, 1994 interview with *Dallas Business Journal*.

Adams began selling his custom-designed clubs at Hank Haney Golf Ranch, a McKinney, Texas golf resort run by Hank Haney, a highly regarded professional instructor. The business was successful, attracting a handful of customers whose satisfaction spurred Adams Golf's modest growth. As word passed of the company's custom-fitting operation from one golfer to another, Adams earned a solid reputation within a small circle of the golfing community, but he had no illusions about his company's stature within the multi-billion-dollar golf equipment industry. "We're not a big success," Adams conceded to the *Dallas Business Journal* on May 13, 1994. "We're embryonic," he added. Within the national landscape of high-profile, high-finance golf equipment corporations, Adams Golf was a nonentity. In 1994, the company was hoping to collect $500,000 in sales, putting Adams Golf in a different league than the industry's leaders, whose annual revenue totals were 1,000 times greater.

As Adams Golf entered the mid-1990s, Adams was content with his company remaining a diminutive yet respected participant in the golf equipment market. The resources at his disposal left no genuine hope for much else: Adams Golf was supported primarily by word-of-mouth advertising, with the company's capital devoted to designing its golf clubs rather than to funding promotional activities. The company also lacked the resources for a major sponsorship deal with a professional golfer, a marketing strategy embraced by all premier golf equipment companies. Between 30 and 40 golfers on the professional tour used Adams Golf's clubs by 1994, but none were paid to do so and, consequently, their choice of clubs could not be used to promote Adams' company. Partly out of choice and partly because of the financial realities he faced, Adams centered his focus on a limited customer base, hoping that his attention to quality and the word-of-mouth advertising it promoted would one day lift his company out of obscurity.

### 1995 Debut of Tight Lies

In 1994 Adams' long-term objectives were to sell between 2,000 and 2,500 clubs a year and to increase the company's distribution network to include as many as 125 golf outlets. His expectations soon grew much grander. In the fall of 1995, Adams Golf introduced the invention of its founder, a fairway wood called Tight Lies. The Tight Lies fairway wood featured an upright trapezoidal head shape—"upside down" in relation to the shape of conventional club heads—a shallow face, and a low center of gravity. These attributes made the club an ideal replacement for shots that typically required a "long iron," an iron club with a flattened face designed to hit longer distances. Long iron shots were the bane of many golfers, particularly for amateurs who found it difficult to control the flight of a ball hit with a long iron. As had been his practice, Adams relied on word of mouth to support the sales of his new club, but he soon realized that he had a revolutionary golf club on his hands. Adams stepped up his marketing efforts, placing advertisements in newspapers and magazines. He used telemarketing. He paid for a 30-minute infomercial, using every medium of advertising he could think of. "It was a once-in-a-lifetime product," Hank Haney explained in a June 4, 1998 *Knight-Ridder/Tribune Business News* article, adding "It's so far superior to anything that was out there at the time."

After the introduction of the Tight Lies fairway wood and the groundswell of attention it attracted, the years of anonymity were over for Adams Golf. In the golf equipment industry, product innovation served as the overriding catalyst for growth. Any new club or ball perceived by the public as having the capability to

take strokes off a golf score created an intense wave of curiosity, which usually translated into an equally powerful desire to buy the product. Innovation had helped catapult start-up golf manufacturers into the industry's elite. Adams, who had played the game for more than 40 years, was well aware of the massive fortunes a technological breakthrough could deliver. Whether his company's small stature was preferred or not, Adams found the potential for growth irresistible—the "once-in-a-lifetime" opportunity that Haney had referred to.

What emerged after the introduction of the original Tight Lies was a company clamoring to develop the marketing, administrative, and manufacturing abilities to support the swelling popularity of its new fairway wood. The introduction of the product helped the company surpass the $1-million-in-sales mark in 1995. From there, the company's sales growth occurred at a vigorous pace, entirely because of the golfing public's fascination with Tight Lies. As the movement behind Adams Golf's signature product intensified and the company's marketing efforts matured, the market reaction to the fairway wood began to become evident. Sales shot up to $3.5 million in 1996 and in 1997, after the Tight Lies infomercial aired, sales exploded to $36.7 million. Adams, who had 18 employees the year Tight Lies was introduced, found himself with a workforce of 250 three years later. Although the company continued to pale against competitors such as Callaway Golf Co., which collected nearly $850 million in annual sales, Adams faced a point in the company's development where he had to shape Adams Golf into the type of company that could compete against the likes of Callaway Golf.

### Late 1990s Growth

As Adams faced the daunting task of taking on the industry's stalwart concerns, he could at least take solace in launching such a bid in a favorable economic climate. Driven largely by innovations, the golf equipment market grew at a 13 percent annual rate between 1993 and 1998, developing into a business worth $2.7 billion in revenue each year. Clubs made of titanium, golf balls proven to fly longer—anything perceived to make a difference over 18 holes of golf—found receptive consumers whose spending habits were invigorated by a robust economy. However, to consider Adams Golf as a legitimate rival to the industry's largest companies required profound changes to the company's way of doing business.

To successfully complete the enormous evolutionary step from a regional concern to one of the industry's leading companies, Adams Golf needed to address its approach internationally and to assume a more aggressive position domestically. In its new posture, the company would need to take on the trappings of a typical golf equipment heavyweight. "If you're not prepared to play in their game, you're kidding yourself," Adams acknowledged in his June 4, 1998 interview with *Knight-Ridder/Tribune Business News*. Internationally, the company had yet to eclipse $1 million in sales by 1997, but the push to drive up sales abroad was on. During the first six months of 1998, the company reached agreements with 33 distributors whose territory encompassed 39 countries. Touting itself as a major golf equipment company also required a sponsorship deal with a high-profile touring professional, the financial reality of which had long eluded the company and still—in 1998— seemed to be beyond Adams Golf's financial ability. In May

**Key Dates.**

**1987:** Barney Adams acquires Dave Pelz Golf.
**1992:** Company establishes a custom-fitting operation.
**1995:** Tight Lies fairway wood is released, triggering explosive growth.
**1998:** Professional golfer, Nick Faldo, joins the company.
**1999:** New product introductions and a sponsorship deal with Tom Watson highlight the year.
**2000:** Adams Golf Japan, Inc. is formed as a subsidiary to oversee operations in Asia.

1998, however, the company scored a coup of sorts, forming what it called a lifetime relationship with Nick Faldo.

As far as professional golfers, Adams would have been hard-pressed to affiliate his company with a more renowned figure than Nick Faldo. Faldo had won scores of U.S. and international championships during his career, including three Masters Tournaments and three British Open Championships, ranking as the world's best golfer for a one-and-a-half-year period between 1993 and 1994. Faldo's long-term affiliation with the company represented an enormous boon to the Adams Golf brand name, a deal that was made possible by giving Faldo an ownership stake in the company, royalty payments, and hiring him as an active participant in the future development of the company's product line. In August 1999, Adams Golf gained another high-profile professional emissary when it signed a five-year sponsorship deal with Tom Watson. Winner of five British Open Championships, two Masters Tournaments, and a U.S. Open Championship, Watson, like Faldo, was expected to be actively involved in product development.

Although animated revenue growth and the association of an internationally prominent professional with his company were bright spots in the company's transformation, Adams also suffered the low points of his company's accelerated growth curve. Profits were essentially nonexistent throughout the 1990s, casting a pall on the company's otherwise strident success during the latter half of the decade. In July 1998, the company's lackluster profitability became an evident weakness when Adams converted to public ownership. Adams Golf's initial public offering of stock, however, was deemed necessary, raising nearly $100 million to help the company develop the infrastructure and the products to compete against much larger rivals.

Adams Golf concluded the 1990s by broadening its product line and strengthening its international operations. In January 1999, the company countered criticism that it was a one-product company by introducing SC Series Titanium drivers and Faldo Series wedges, the first product line designed with the input of Nick Faldo. In a bid to leverage the popularity of its mainstay Tight Lies fairway woods, Adams Golf released the Tight Lies Tour line and the Tight Lies 2 line of fairway woods in June and October, respectively. The Tight Lies family of clubs was extended further with the introduction of the Tight Lies 2 driver in January 2000, incorporating the same technology used in the fairway woods. Against the backdrop of the product debuts, the company assumed greater control over the prosecution of its

international business. In early 1999, Adams Golf acquired the golf club distribution business of its exclusive distributor in the United Kingdom, a company called Dimensions in Sport, Ltd.. The acquisition was renamed Adams Golf U.K., Ltd. and organized as a wholly owned subsidiary of Adams Golf. A similar desire for greater overseas control prompted the company to sever its relationship with its distributor in Asia. Adams Golf Japan, Inc. was formed in early 2000 as a subsidiary to manage the activities formerly conducted by the independent distributor.

As Adams Golf prepared for the future, much remained to be determined concerning the company's ability to effectively compete against much larger foes. The extension of the company's product line had reduced its dependence on the Tight Lies fairway woods, which accounted for 96 percent of sales in 1998. In 1999, fairway woods generated 63 percent of sales, with drivers—previously a nonexistent product category—accounting for 32 percent of sales. Nevertheless, Adams Golf felt the brunt of competitive pressures in 1999, as a lower volume of fairway wood sales contributed to an annual decline in overall sales from $84.6 million to $54 million, one year after the company had registered a 131 percent increase in sales. "It's been whirlwind, it's been roller-coaster, it's been tiring," Adams remarked in a January 25, 1999 interview with *Brandweek*. "It took me 11 years to become an overnight success," he continued. "In the last year, I've aged another 11 years." To successfully survive in the upper tier of the golf equipment market, Adams needed to replicate the success he recorded with Tight Lies in other product categories. The objective required substantial resources and the art of innovation, the prerequisites of Adams Golf's future success.

### *Principal Subsidiaries*

Adams Golf, Ltd.; Adams Golf Direct Response, Ltd.; Adams Golf Holding Corp.; Adams Golf GP Corp.; Adams Golf Management Corp.; Adams Golf RAC Corp.; Adams Golf IP, L.P.; Adams Golf Foreign Sales Corporation (Barbados); Adams Golf U.K., Ltd.; Adams Golf Japan, Inc.

### *Principal Competitors*

Taylor Made Golf Company, Inc.; Fortuna Brands, Inc.; Callaway Golf Company.

### *Further Reading*

Allen, James C., "Golf Club Maker Bets on Excellence," *Dallas Business Journal,* May 13, 1994, p. B1.
Alm, Richard, "Texas-Based Golf Club Company's Sales Soar; Plans Expansion," *Knight-Ridder/Tribune Business News,* June 4, 1998.
Cunningham, Michael, "Strike Force," *BC Business,* March 2000, p. 77.
Hill, J. Dee, "Adams Begins Review," *ADWEEK Southwest,* July 26, 1999, p. 8.
——, "Adams Goes Straight," *ADWEEK Southwest,* March 13, 2000, p. 9.
Stogel, Chuck, "On Shaky Grounds," *Brandweek,* January 25, 1999, p. 26.
Wells, Garrison, "Golf Stocks Hit Rough Year," *Knight-Ridder/Tribune Business News,* October 8, 1998.

—Jeffrey L. Covell

# Allders plc

Centre Tower, The Whitgift Centre
Croydon, Surrey CR9 1WE
United Kingdom
Telephone: +44-20 8929 5500
Fax: +44-20 8929 5505
Web site: http://www.allders.co.uk

*Public Company*
*Founded:* 1862
*Employees:* 7,364
*Sales:* £510.55 million ($732.49 million)
*Stock Exchanges:* London
*Ticker Symbol:* ADS
*NAIC:* 452110 Department Stores

England's fourth largest department store group, Allders plc, operates 40 department stores under the Allders Department Store and Allders-At-Home names, with nearly three million square feet of retail floor space. The company's 20 Allders Department Stores—located chiefly in England's High Streets and shopping malls—feature the full complement of typical department store items, with an emphasis on furniture and home furnishings. In an attempt to expand beyond its traditional appeal to middle-income, middle-aged consumers, Allders has boosted its clothing range in the late 1990s, adding a number of fashionable brand names, including Adidas, Calvin Klein, Timberland, and DKNY, among others, but also by introducing a number of its own labels. New Allders clothing labels include Hydrogen, featuring sportswear aimed at the executive shopper, and Act3 and A-Grade, aimed at the youth fashions market. Other new Allders-owned brand names include Cooks & Co. and Episode and encompass the company's aim to offer consumers leading-edge fashions at low prices. Most of the company's clothing is manufactured in the United Kingdom, with some accessories and materials supplied from Hong Kong and India. Supporting its new fashion lines, Allders has launched a national advertising campaign designed to give the company a new look among consumers. In addition to its department stores, Allders has also taken a page from the American retail market by opening its own warehouse-store concept, the home furnishings specialist

Allders-At-Home. Primarily located in extra-urban and "edge-of-town" commercial districts, the Allders-At-Home chain, introduced in the mid-1990s, has grown to represent nearly half of Allders's total property portfolio. In addition to its physical stores, Allders is moving to capture a share of the Internet consumer budget, launching a full-service on-line wedding gift and registry boutique in October 2000. The company plans to expand its Internet commerce activities with two more on-line boutique sites as early as 2001. Led by CEO Harvey Lipsith, Allders, formerly part of conglomerate Hanson Plc, trades on the London Stock Exchange and posted revenues of nearly £511 in 1999. The subject of a failed acquisition attempt by larger rival House of Fraser in 1999, Allders itself approached smaller retail group Bentalls. When that acquisition fell through as well, Allders opened its £150 million war chest to purchase four stores from the struggling C&A retail group. Most observers—including Allders itself—continued to expect a consolidation of the United Kingdom's retail industry in the face of increasing economic globalization and the rapid growth of an Internet-based economy.

### Department Store Pioneer in the 19th Century

The first Allders department store was opened by Joshua Allder in Croydon, in the southeast of England, in 1862. The Allders name soon was found on other retail locations, remaining primarily in its southeast region. By the end of the 1920s, however, the Allders stores had come under the ownership of the growing retail group, United Drapery Stores, which nevertheless kept the Allders brand name for its department stores.

United Drapery Stores began a push to become the United Kingdom's largest retail group at the end of World War II, as the British economy, spurred by the need to reconstruct after the ravages of the war, joined much of the rest of the western world for an extended period of strong growth. United Drapery Stores, later the UDS Group, began adding to its collection of retail signage, adding such store names as Claude Alexander, Richard Shops, and Fifty Shilling Tailors.

By the 1960s, UDS Group had succeeded in taking the lead as the United Kingdom's top retailer, with a 1,300-strong empire of retail shops. The end of the postwar economic boom, which collapsed abruptly in the early 1970s after the Arab Oil

Embargo, not only sent oil prices spiraling upward, but introduced an extended period of high inflation and recession that dramatically depressed the United Kingdom's retail market, while also encouraging consumers to change their shopping and buying habits. The UDS Group, however, had been too slow in recognizing and responding to the changes in the retail market. The UDS Group soon found itself burdened by too many retail store concepts—selling everything from shoes to clothing and other goods—that proved poorly adapted to the new retail climate. As the company's fortunes dwindled in the late 1970s, its independence was more and more threatened.

Meanwhile, the UDS Group had entered a new retail arena, that of the duty-free shop, when it acquired the license to open and operate the shop at London's Heathrow airport. Attached to its Allders department store division, and later operated as Allders International, the UDS Group rapidly built up its network of duty-free shops around the world. By the end of the 1980s, Allders International had taken second place behind market leader Duty Free Shoppers Group Ltd. The concept of duty-free goods—exempted from import, excise, and sales taxes—proved highly successful as the numbers of international travelers booked steady increases in the late 1970s and early 1980s. A feature on many cruise ships since the 1930s, duty-free first came to international air travel at Ireland's Shannon airport, a major refueling site for transatlantic flights. The rising rate of international travel during the 1960s and 1970s helped the duty-free shop to become commonplace not only in the world's airports, but also in its harbors, border train stations, and other border crossings. Allders International joined in the drive to take the duty-free shop worldwide, and by the end of the 1980s, most of its duty-free revenues was generated outside of the United Kingdom and more than 75 percent was generated outside of the European Community zone.

If UDS Group saw success with its duty-free shops, the rest of its retail store empire was crumbling fast. By the early 1980s, the company was placed on the auction block. Winning the battle to take over the UDS Group was the fast-growing conglomerate Hanson Trust, led by Lord Hanson, in 1983. The Hanson Trust had by then already gained nationwide popularity for its aggressive growth. Its continued growth in the 1980s became for many the perfect illustration of Thatcher-era free market capitalism, as Hanson swallowed up not only a vast

array of international companies, but also a number of the United Kingdom's largest companies in the first half of the 1980s, including battery manufacturer Berec (later renamed as British Ever Ready), London Brick, and Imperial Group, as well as the UDS Group.

Hanson Trust's commitment to its shareholders above all else was widely applauded in the 1980s as the conglomerate rapidly gutted its acquisitions—eliminating management, slashing payrolls, eliminating research & development and other ''unprofitable'' investments, while also selling off its acquisitions' assets—in search of quick profits and low investments. As the decade wore on, Lord Hanson's short-term approach to business helped him to become one of the United Kingdom's most admired businessmen. The UDS Group was given the same treatment as Hanson's other acquisitions of the period, as Hanson broke apart the retail empire. By the end of the 1980s, what had once been the United Kingdom's largest retail group had been eviscerated of all but the Allders department store group and its Allders International subsidiary of duty-free shops.

### Staying Afloat in the 1990s

Leading the conversion of the Hanson Trust's retail acquisition was Harvey Lipsith, who had served as Hanson's finance director before being placed in charge of restructuring the UDS Group into what was then renamed the Allders Group. The economic downturn at the end of the 1980s, brought on by the stock market crash of 1987 and the collapse of the building market, led Hanson Trust to join another economic trend of the decade—in 1989, the conglomerate agreed to spin off its Allders retail division in a management buyout led by Lipsith. For £150 million, Lipsith gained control of the group's six department stores as well as its high-performance chain of duty-free shops.

Lipsith began adding more stores to the Allders chain, while also launching the Allders name on a new concept. As much of the revenues generated at the Allders department stores traditionally came through its sales of beds, oriental rugs, and other home furnishings, the company decided to turn its expertise in this market to a new retailing concept being brought over from the United States, that of the warehouse ''category killer.'' In 1993, Allders launched its Allders-At-Home home furnishings warehouse stores. Unlike its department stores, typically located in England's High Street urban shopping districts, the Allders-At-Home stores joined the growing ranks of extra-urban ''edge of town'' retailers, attracted by the lower rents and the growing suburban consumer base. By 1993, the company operated 12 department stores and six Allders-At-Home stores.

As the worst effects of the recession began to subside in the early 1990s, Allders looked for funding to repay the debt from its management buyout and to continue its expansion. In 1993, the company went public, taking a listing on the London Stock Exchange. The initial public offering, worth £175, helped absorb the company's debt and also gave it the capital to expand its portfolio of store properties.

### Focusing on the United Kingdom for the 21st Century

By then, Allders International was seeing the writing on the wall: the opening of the European Community's borders in

## Key Dates:

**1862:** Joshua Allder opens first department store.
**1927:** United Drapery Stores (UDS) acquires Allders.
**1974:** Company launches Allders International duty-free store division.
**1983:** UDS is acquired by Hanson Trust.
**1989:** Allders is spun off in management buyout.
**1992:** Allders-At-Home stores debut.
**1993:** Allders goes public on London Stock Exchange.
**1996:** Company sells off Allders International, and buys eight Owen Owen stores.
**1997:** The A3 private label is launched.
**1998:** Company acquires 11 new stores; launches A-Grade and other private labels.
**1999:** Acquisition by House of Fraser fails.
**2000:** Company fails in attempt to acquire Bentalls; buys four stores from C&A; launches on-line wedding gifts site.

1992 effectively removed the need for duty-free shops, since no duties were charged among member countries. By 1995, proposals were being made to eliminate the EC's duty-free shops altogether. Despite protests from duty-free retailers and airports—which pocketed as much as 50 percent and more of store revenues—the end of the duty-free shop in the European zone was proclaimed for 1999.

Allders chose not to wait that long, and announced its intention to sell its 128-strong network of duty-free shops. First approached by SwissAir—which sought to develop its retail network, duty-free or not—Allders was quickly caught up in a bidding war, as newly privatized BAA, which held the monopoly on England's airports, placed a bid on the Allders International operations as well and suggested that it might evict Allders International's stores from its airports if the bid was not successful. However, after SwissAir topped the BAA bid with one worth £160 million, BAA dropped out of the bidding, and Allders International was sold to SwissAir in 1996.

Allders promptly turned over a large share of the sale to its shareholders—who also were rewarded as the stock market welcomed the "simplified" Allders—then took the rest on a buying spree. In 1996, the company bought eight stores from the Owen Owen chain for about £23 million. This purchase was followed by seven more stores, bought for £3.8 million from bankrupt furniture chain Maples, in 1997. While the former Owen Owen stores were refurbished and converted to Allders Department Stores, the Maples stores were placed under the Allders-At-Home banner. Meanwhile, the "simplified" U.K.-oriented Allders was greeted warmly by stock market analysts.

Allders continued to add new stores during 1998, including seven Allders-At-Home stores and four new Allders department stores, giving the company a total of 38 retail locations, including its Croydon flagship—and largest—store. In 1998, the company also stepped up an effort to rejuvenate its image among shoppers, started in 1997 with the launch of its first private label, A3. In 1998, Allders launched a second label,

A-Grade, and announced plans to roll out more labels, including the plus-sized range, Anagram, and the Hydrogen range of "executive" sportswear. These brand rollouts were accompanied by the introduction of a new variety of popular fashion labels in the Allders Department Stores, as the company brought in such brand names as DKNY, Calvin Klein, Timberland, Adidas, and others.

Allders nearly gave up its independence in 1999, however. In May of that year, the company announced that it had entered—and broken off—talks with House of Fraser that would have seen the larger retailer acquire Allders Plc. After House of Fraser's stock slipped, the two companies ended their acquisition discussion, while reserving the possibility of reaching agreement in the future. Both companies agreed that the United Kingdom's retail industry, challenged by increasing numbers of discounters on one end and the blossoming of Internet-based commerce on the other, was ripe for consolidation.

Mid-sized Allders admitted that in the coming consolidation it could easily be prey for its larger competitors or predator itself for its smaller rivals. Indeed, in the first half of 2000, the company showed its predator side, announcing that it had amassed a war chest of some £100 million. The company appeared ready to take its war chest on the war path, when it made acquisition overtures to the Bentalls chain of eight department store. Those talks ended without success, however.

In August 2000, Allders made a deal with real estate and building group Minerva to sell its flagship Croydon store and lease a new, larger store in a new shopping center. The sale netted Allders some £50 million, a portion of which the company promptly spent, buying up four department stores from the C&A store chain in October 2000. At the same time, Allders moved to stake a position in the growing Internet-based retail scene, opening its first full-scale commercial web site. The site, devoted to wedding registry and gift sales, was expected to be joined by two more commercial sites in the year 2001. Nonetheless, the company continued to assert that consolidation in its sector was inevitable; it remained to be seen whether the Allders name would be able to ride out the coming consolidation wave.

### Principal Competitors

Arcadia Group plc; ASDA Group Limited; Debenhams plc; The Great Universal Stores plc; House of Fraser plc; James Beattie plc; John Lewis Partnership plc; Marks and Spencer plc; Matalan plc; N Brown Group plc; Next plc; Selfridges Plc; Storehouse plc.

### Further Reading

Bethell, James, "Optimistic Allders Increases Profits," *Independent*, December 13, 1994, p. 32.
Cowdy, Hannah, "UK's Allders Says Could Raise 100 mln stg for Buys," *Reuters*, May 31, 2000.
Osborne, Alistair, "Allders Plc—Acquisition," *RNS*, October 20, 2000.
——, "Allders Raises BP100 Million War Chest," *Guardian*, June 1, 2000.
——, "Merger 'Inevitable' Claims Allders," *Daily Telegraph*, December 1, 1999.

—M.L. Cohen

# AmeriSource Health Corporation

300 Chester Field Parkway
Malvern, Pennsylvania 19355
U.S.A.
Telephone: (610) 727-7000
Fax: (610) 727-3600
Web site: http://www.amerisource.com

*Public Company*
*Incorporated:* 1985 as Alco Health Services Corp.
*Employees:* 3,200
*Sales:* $9.8 billion
*Stock Exchanges:* New York
*Ticker Symbol:* AAS
*NAIC:* 422210 Drugs and Druggists' and Sundries
   Wholesalers

AmeriSource Health Corporation, formerly known as Alco Health Services Corporation, is the fourth largest wholesale distributor of pharmaceuticals and related healthcare products and services in the United States, through its wholly-owned subsidiary AmeriSource Corporation. AmeriSource operates a national network of 20 distribution facilities that supplies brand-name prescription drugs, generic drugs, over the counter healthcare products, cosmetics and fragrances, and medical/surgical supplies. The company serves hospitals, independent and chain drugstores, pharmacy departments of supermarkets and mass merchandisers, nursing homes, clinics, and physicians. AmeriSource also provides a line of health and beauty products and a growing number of support services to its retailing customers.

### Building a Network of Drug Wholesalers: 1977–85

In August 1985, the company that would become AmeriSource was incorporated as Alco Health Services and held an initial public stock offering of 4.7 million shares. The history of the predecessor Alco Health Services can be traced to 1977, when a diversified conglomerate, the Alco Standard Corporation, entered the pharmaceutical-distribution business by purchasing The Drug House, a major wholesaler operating in Pennsylvania and Delaware.

Alco Standard was the brainchild of entrepreneur Tinkham Veale II, who had built a multimillion-dollar conglomerate on the principle of corporate partnership. Veale sought to acquire healthy, owner-managed companies in the $5 million to $10 million range. He allowed each company practically full autonomy, while providing support in legal and tax matters. When Alco Standard was incorporated in 1960, it was a modest $5 million chemical company. By 1968, sales were $140 million, coming from 52 subsidiaries with products ranging from stamped metal parts to wax paper.

Shortly after Alco Standard's acquisition of The Drug House, the company began to build a network of drug wholesalers. In early 1978, Duff Brothers of Chattanooga, Tennessee, was acquired, and later that year Marsin Medical Supply Company of Philadelphia, Pennsylvania, was purchased. Geer Drug, with annual sales of about $45 million, was acquired in 1979. Headquartered in Charleston, South Carolina, Geer foreshadowed an expansive drive southward. By the early 1980s, Alco Standard's pharmaceutical distribution network was the third largest in the nation.

Alco Standard soon made other acquisitions of pharmaceutical wholesalers, including Kauffman-Lattimer of Columbus, Ohio; Smith-Higgins of Johnson City, Tennessee; Strother Drug of Virginia; and Brown Drug, which operated in South Dakota, Iowa, and Minnesota. At the same time, the drug industry itself was undergoing intense change. Healthcare expenditures in the United States were on the uptrend, amounting to about ten percent of the gross national product by 1985. As the population grew older, the healthcare industry promised continued growth.

### Alco Health Services Grows as an Independent Operation

In 1985, Alco Standard's drug-distribution operations were spun off into a separate company, Alco Health Services Corporation. Alco Standard retained approximately 60 percent of the new company's stock. The new company continued to use Alco Standard's administrative functions on a fee basis. Alco Health was led by John H. Kennedy as chairman and Joseph B. Churchman as president.

**Company Perspectives:**

*A nationwide warehouse network, national accounts and dozens of value-added programs strengthen our proven performance in serving customers through our strong local organization. We deliver superior local service to customers while maintaining a low cost operating structure, enabling us to achieve superior returns on committed capital.*

Shortly after Alco Health began to operate independently, it acquired the Valdosta Drug Company of Valdosta, Georgia, with $22 million in annual sales, and the $100-million-a-year Meyers and Company of Tiffin, Ohio. These two acquisitions helped push Alco's sales over the $1 billion mark.

In the early 1980s, drug wholesalers found new ways to support the independent drug retailers that comprised nearly 60 percent of their business. Wholesalers offered more non-drug products, like hospital supplies and health and beauty aids. Alco Health sought to strengthen its independent customers by sharing its own primary strength-marketing. By offering services like in-store merchandising and group advertising, wholesalers could help their customers compete with the growing drugstore chains. Alco Health introduced its retail support program in 1982. Support like customized price stickers gave a boost to those independent druggists who participated. A year later, Alco introduced a complete line of medical equipment for home use, from wheelchairs to disposable syringes under the Total Home Health Care program, which provided independent retailers the marketing support they needed for such products, through direct-to-customer delivery and accounting assistance.

Computer services provided by the wholesaler included management-information reports, automated retail accounts-receivable systems, and shelf labels for automated inventory control. By 1985, Alco Health was marketing an in-pharmacy computer system based on an IBM personal computer that was capable of being used for total store automation.

At the same time, wholesalers including Alco Health began to develop the business of large drugstore chains and mass merchandisers. In 1981, 25 percent of all wholesalers' business was to drugstore chains, up from 15 percent in 1971. The opportunity arose because of the reluctance of manufacturers to maintain the costly sales force needed for direct selling to chains. The trend continued throughout the 1980s. By 1985, chain drugstores and mass merchandisers made up 18 percent of Alco Health's annual revenues.

Sales to hospitals also increased in the early 1980s, as health-care facilities attempted to lower their costs by reducing their pharmaceutical inventories. Alco was able to provide rapid, often same-day, service to many facilities. By 1985, 24 percent of Alco Health's sales were to hospitals.

During the latter half of the 1980s, Alco Health continued to grow at a tremendous rate. In 1986, further acquisitions included L.S. DuBois Son and Company of Paducah, Kentucky; Pennington Drug of Joplin, Missouri; Mississippi Drug of Jackson, Mississippi; and MD Pharmaceuticals of Dothan, Alabama, adding $300 million in annual revenues. Archer Drug of

Little Rock, Arkansas, and Michiana Merchandising of Mishawaka, Indiana, were also purchased.

In 1987, Alco Health reorganized several of its operating units. Smith-Higgins, Valdosta Drug, MD Pharmaceuticals, Mississippi Drug, and Duff Brothers were combined to make up the southeastern region of Alco Health. Geer Drug and Strother Drug were combined to eliminate overlap. Management of the new units remained in the hands of regional managers, and their territories were enlarged considerably.

Alco Health's marketing strategy, which focused on three areas—independent druggists, hospitals, and chain drugstores and mass merchandisers—remained constant throughout the 1980s. A major boost to the third segment came in 1987, when Alco Health was selected as the primary wholesale supplier to 1,000 of the Revco chain's 2,000 drugstores. In 1988 revenues passed $2 billion.

John F. McNamara, formerly chief operating officer, became president of Alco Health in 1987. McNamara came to the company in 1981 when Kauffman-Lattimer was acquired. Kennedy remained chairman until August 1988, when previously retired Ray Mundt returned temporarily to oversee changes in Alco Health's ownership. Mundt previously had served as president of Alco Standard and on the Alco Health board of directors.

### Management-Led Buyout Leads to AmeriSource: 1998

In early 1988, a management group attempted a leveraged buyout of Alco Health, offering $26 per share to take the company private. Shortly thereafter, in June, McKesson Corp., formerly Foremost-McKesson, the largest drug wholesaler in the country with 28 percent of the national market, offered $30 per share, or $508 million, for Alco Health. The deal, however, fell through three months later when the Federal Trade Commission (FTC) ruled against the acquisition on antitrust grounds. Alco Health was still 49-percent owned by its former parent, Alco Standard Corporation. Alco Health explored options with its investment banker, Drexel Burnham Lambert.

In November 1988, a group of investors, which included Citicorp Venture Capital Ltd. and a group of Alco management-level employees, proposed a cash tender offer for Alco Health's shares at $31 per share. A holding company, AHSC Holdings Corporation, was set up to handle the acquisition. The proposal was accepted and when the tender offer expired at the end of December 1988, AHSC Holdings owned 92 percent of Alco Health's stock. The merger allowed for the conversion of the remaining equity into debentures due in the year 2004. Alco Health continued its normal daily operations during the transition of ownership. John F. McNamara led the company as chairman, CEO, and president from 1989.

### New Challenges and Opportunities in the 1990s

The early 1990s provided new challenges and opportunities to Alco Health Services and pharmaceutical wholesalers in general. The drug market continued its expansion, fueled by an aging population and its need for health care. The trend in pharmaceutical distribution was toward fewer competitors handling a greater market share. From 1979 to 1990, the number of

U.S. drug wholesalers decreased from 150 to 90, while the role of middlemen increased. The top five companies, including Alco Health, handled about half of the business nationwide. As the field of suitable acquisitions thinned out, and as the pharmaceutical-distribution field became a battle of the giants, Alco Health placed greater emphasis on internal expansion.

In July 1994, Alco Health, one of America's top five pharmaceutical wholesalers, changed its name to AmeriSource Health Corporation. The company aimed to increase its business by driving unnecessary costs out of its distribution system and repositioning itself as a unified source of products and programs nationally. Many of the company's divisions, which until then had maintained their original identity, became part of the AmeriSource family. The company, now located in Malvern, Pennsylvania, continued to acquire other companies throughout the latter half of the 1990s: in 1995, Liberty Drug Systems, the North Carolina-based provider of pharmacy software and hardware and Newbro Drug Co. of Idaho Falls; in 1996, Gulf Distribution Inc.; and in 1997, the equity interests of Walker Drug Company LLC. AmeriSource also aimed to tighten its relationship with its retail customers via a nationwide telemarketing program instituted in 1995. However, in 1996, several of those customers were less than satisfied. In a case later dismissed in District Court, several retail pharmacies claimed that AmeriSource had conspired to deprive them of discounts offered by HMOs, hospitals, and mail order pharmacies.

In 1997, AmeriSource made national news as it joined again with McKesson, this time as part of a proposed merger. The U.S. District Court blocked the move, as it did a similar move that year to merge Bergen Brunswig and Cardinal Health. Both mergers would have reshaped the distribution picture across the United States. All four companies argued that they sought consolidation in a move to make themselves more efficient and cut prices. However, the FTC claimed that the mergers were the companies' "chosen means to remove their incentives to cut prices." The drug wholesalers, according to the FTC, had so many distribution centers that they were forced to cut prices to keep products off their shelves.

AmeriSource responded to the Court's decision by turning its attention to local objectives, signing on new customers, attempting to control costs, and investing in new marketing initiatives cumulatively known as "disease state management." "At the end of the day," according to R. David Yost, president and chief executive officer of the company, in a 1998 *Drug Store News* article, "we maintain that wholesaling is a local business. . . . In our vision for the future, we see the community pharmacy playing a key role. . . . We see the pharmacist of the future being totally involved in customers' healthcare management and being paid for it."

To this end, AmeriSource, introduced value-added programs in the late 1990s, such as MedAssess, a disease state management program to help pharmacists monitor clients' regimens, and the Diabetes Shoppe, a program designed to train the pharmacist to train the diabetic. Other programs included: Family Pharmacy, American Health Packaging, Health Services Plus, and ECHO, the company's proprietary software system. In 1999, the company purchased a substantial share of ADDS Telepharmacy Solutions, Inc., a leading provider of e-commerce medications management.

The company continued to grow in size and reputation in 1999 and 2000. In 1999, AmeriSource purchased C.D. Smith Healthcare, a leading regional wholesale pharmaceutical distributor, and gained a contract with the Department of Veterans Affairs to provide services to its more than 500 pharmacies. In 2000, it purchased Pharmacy Healthcare Solution, a pharmacy consulting company. The company became a "preferred provider" in 1999 of both the Pharmacy Providers Service Corporation, representing 1,200 independent pharmacies, and Premier, Inc., the nation's largest alliance of hospitals and healthcare systems in the United States.

### Principal Subsidiaries

AmeriSource Corporation; C.D. Smith Healthcare, Inc.

### Principal Competitors

Bergen Brunswig Corporation; Cardinal Health, Inc.; McKesson Corporation.

### Further Reading

"AmeriSource Shifts Management to Focus on Three Key Channels," *Drug Store News,* April 5, 1999, p. 3.
Binzen, Peter, "One Leveraged Buyout Has Paid Off, and It Keeps On Growing," *Philadelphia Inquirer,* December 12, 1994, p. D3.
Heller, Al, "Formidable Four Move Ahead Separately, Optimistically," *Drug Store News,* September 21, 1998, p. 11.
Roller, Kim, "AmeriSource Trade Show Leaves All 'Energized' for the Real World," *Drug Store News,* August 28, 2000, p. 16.
Werner, Thomas, " 'Without Negatives': That's How Alco Health Services' Chief Describes its Business," *Barron's,* April 13, 1987.

—Thomas M. Tucker
—updated by Carrie Rothburd

# ANNTAYLOR

## AnnTaylor Stores Corporation

142 West 57th Street
New York, New York 10019
U.S.A.
Telephone: (212) 541-3300
Fax: (212) 541-3379
Web site: http://www.anntaylor.com

*Public Company*
*Incorporated:* 1988
*Employees:* 7,980
*Sales:* $1.08 billion (2000)
*Stock Exchanges:* New York
*Ticker Symbol:* ANN
*NAIC:* 44812 Women's Clothing Stores

Through its wholly owned subsidiary, AnnTaylor Inc., Ann-Taylor Stores Corporation is a retailer of women's apparel, with stores in major downtown city locations and shopping malls across the United States. Noted for its classic, tailored designs for career women, AnnTaylor strives to provide what it refers to as ''a head to toe concept of dressing with an edited assortment of tasteful, fashion-updated classic apparel and accessories in a one-stop shopping environment.'' Having faced several challenges in the early 1990s, in the form of falling sales and management shakeups, the company regained its poise in the latter half of the 1990s.

### The 1950s–70s: From College Town Boutique to Manhattan

The original AnnTaylor store was founded in New Haven, Connecticut, in 1954, by Robert Liebskind. Interestingly, there was never an actual Ann Taylor; the name was simply selected to characterize the target customer. The company's line of classic clothing became popular and eventually new shops were opened primarily in such eastern college towns as New Haven, Providence, Boston, Cambridge, and Georgetown. In 1977, Liebskind sold his stores to Garfinckel, Brooks Brothers, Miller

& Rhodes Corporation (known as Garfinckels). Under new management, AnnTaylor stores began to spread rapidly during the late 1970s.

During this time, AnnTaylor began showcasing the work of Perry Ellis, who designed clothing for the AnnTaylor label; AnnTaylor also had exclusive contracts with Marimeko and other cutting-edge, upscale designers. The stores eventually began to offer European fashions, as management found that loyal AnnTaylor customers were generally willing to spend a little more for unique, less conservative styles but still less likely to pay the prices or risk the fashion statements available in designer boutiques. Moreover, by refraining from carrying a wide variety of designer labels and brands offered by department stores, AnnTaylor had less competition and thus more pricing flexibility; the company could also produce fast reactions to fashion trends and regional needs.

The value of AnnTaylor's name as a brand increased steadily, and the stores became increasingly popular. The flagship store for the company, on 57th Street in Manhattan, featured a chic restaurant on the third floor. The AnnTaylor customer during this time was characterized as a new breed of well-dressed career women who favored classic fabrics in fashionable designs. Describing a 1978 AnnTaylor catalog, one writer for *Working Woman* magazine noted that the catalog showed ''a duo of well-dressed working women ganging up on a would-be mugger, hitting him with their AnnTaylor purses. The message: The AnnTaylor woman might wear silk and cashmere, but watch out—she's taken karate.''

### The 1980s: A Series of New Owners and Management

In 1981, AnnTaylor, as part of Garfinckels, was acquired by Allied Stores Corporation and quickly became the most profitable among the group of Allied retailers, outperforming even Brooks Brothers and Bonwit Teller. Allied subsequently unloaded unprofitable subsidiaries and further polished its core stores' image of upscale, high-profile specialty and department stores. In 1983, Sally Frame Kasaks, who had started in the fashion industry as a salesperson, was named president of the

**Company Perspectives:**

*Our purpose is to provide our clients with a fashion right wardrobing experience with quality products, service, and shopping environment that are relevant to her lifestyle needs; our associates with a work environment that is inspiring, compassionate and learning-orients, emphasizing high standards of excellence; our shareholders with a solid and growing investment; our world with a company culture committed to improving quality of life for women and celebrating their accomplishments.*

company, and she served in that capacity until 1985, when she left to join Talbots and, eventually, Abercrombie & Fitch.

A new president and CEO, Mark Shulman, faced new challenges. A Canadian financier, Robert Campeau, was attracted by Allied's cache of healthy, upscale stores with recognizable names. In 1986, his Campeau Corporation made an overture to acquire Allied but was rebuffed. Campeau was tiny compared with Allied; it had 1985 revenues of $153 million, while Allied reported $4.1 billion for the same year. Nevertheless, in the leveraged buyout-crazed 1980s, it was not hard for Campeau to get financial backing. After securing $3 billion in credit, Campeau launched a hostile takeover of Allied. The final price for the deal was more than $5 billion by some estimates, and Campeau had to sell off many of Allied's units to pay for the purchase, retaining only the best performers, like Brooks Brothers and AnnTaylor. By the end of 1987, more than $1 billion of Allied's holdings had been sold off, and Campeau was able to pay down some of its debts.

Although it was ahead of schedule on debt payments, Campeau was still feeling the effects of the transaction, earning only $44 million in the first three quarters of 1987. Moreover, its interest payments for that same time period were $244 million. Thus some analysts were surprised when Campeau quickly set its sights on Federated Department Stores, Inc., a giant holding company of department stores then three times the size of Allied. With more than $4 billion in fresh loans, Campeau initiated a similar takeover, again increasing the initial per-share offer, until the final cost for Federated reached $6.6 billion. Campeau sold off Brooks Brothers to a British department store to get cash for its debts and for Federated stock. Although Campeau vowed he would not sell AnnTaylor, the retailer was put on the block by June 1988, when Campeau claimed that AnnTaylor's spot in specialty retailing no longer complemented Campeau's department store holdings. At the time, AnnTaylor had 100 stores nationwide and accounted for eight percent of Allied's $3.96 billion in sales in 1988. AnnTaylor was the last of Allied's specialty stores. Proceeds from the sale would go toward Allied's bank debt, as well as for Federated stock.

It was not hard to find a buyer for AnnTaylor. Joseph E. Brooks, formerly the chief executive officer of Lord & Taylor, led a group of investors that included Merrill Lynch Capital Partners, Inc. and some of AnnTaylor's management. The price paid was $430 million, which, to some observers, seemed a tad

high for a company that, like many companies in the women's apparel industry, had recently reported flat earnings. In fact, although AnnTaylor had more than 36 percent annual growth in both earnings and sales between 1983 and 1987, its earnings seemed to have peaked in 1986. Expectations soared, however, now that Brooks was in charge.

Brooks was noted for making Lord & Taylor over into an upscale store offering classic merchandise. Under his leadership, Lord & Taylor had expanded from 19 to 46 units and sales had quadrupled. Brooks moved quickly at AnnTaylor, bringing in a new management team, some of whom had been with him at Lord & Taylor, including his son, Thomas H.K. Brooks, who was named AnnTaylor's president. Faced with staggering interest payments and a tricky debt-to-equity load, the company focused on rapid expansion and cost-cutting tactics.

### 1990s: Hard Times in the Industry; Instability at Home

By 1991, AnnTaylor had spread as far from its East Coast roots as Jackson, Mississippi, and now boasted 58 new outlets and a total of 176 stores. With new stores helping to boost sales, Brooks felt confident enough to make bids for Saks Fifth Avenue and Bloomingdale's. He was outbid for Saks, however, and the $1 billion he offered for Bloomingdale's failed to tempt its owners, Federated Stores. With the debt load still pressuring AnnTaylor to perform, the company's buyout bosses proposed a public offering of AnnTaylor stock. The industry was limping and a stock offering seemed a good way to raise equity enough to tide AnnTaylor over the rough spots. Despite the fact that AnnTaylor was not faring well in same-store sales, the indication of a retail store's ability to increase stock, the offering went well. Seven million shares were sold at $26 per share, providing the cash flow necessary to continue planned expansions.

The offering also increased AnnTaylor's burden to perform well in sales and earnings growth, however, and it was in the face of such pressures that some decisions were made that would eventually prove detrimental to the company. The new management decided that the typical AnnTaylor customer of 1990 was not as affluent as its earlier clientele had been, and, in an effort to broaden its appeal and cut expenses, the company began using fabrics of lesser quality for the first time.

Management also opted to end AnnTaylor's long and profitable relationship with Joan & David shoes, a product that had accounted for roughly 14 percent of AnnTaylor's sales for 30 years and had a fine reputation of its own, pulling many customers into AnnTaylor stores. AnnTaylor began offering its own line of shoes instead, at about half the price. Early reviews of these shoes bordered on snide, and earnings and revenues became weak. Stock collapsed and some stockholders sued, alleging misrepresentation of the facts by the prospectus that accompanied the public offering.

Then, in December 1991, Joseph E. Brooks abruptly announced his retirement from his position as chairman. His son, Thomas Brooks, had quit the presidency just as suddenly a few weeks earlier, as had Gerald H. Blum, the company's vice-chairman. With their company suddenly being run by a committee, stockholders and investors became anxious. The company

## Key Dates:

**1954:** Robert Liebskind opens the first AnnTaylor store in New Haven, Connecticut.
**1977:** Liebskind sells his stores to Garfinckel, Brooks Brothers, Miller & Rhodes Corporation.
**1981:** AnnTaylor, as part of Garfinckel, is acquired by Allied Stores Corporation.
**1983:** Sally Frame Kasaks becomes president of the company.
**1985:** Mark Shulman replaces Kasaks as chief executive officer.
**1987:** The Campeau Corporation enacts a hostile takeover of Allied Stores.
**1988:** The Campeau Corporation sells AnnTaylor to Merrill Lynch Capital Partners, Inc. and some of AnnTaylor's management.
**1991:** AnnTaylor goes public.
**1992:** Sally Frame Kasaks returns to head AnnTaylor.
**1996:** AnnTaylor buys Cygne's stock in its joint ventures; J. Patrick Spainhour and Patricia DeRosa replace Kasaks.

had lost about two-thirds of its market value since going public in 1991 and was losing its most loyal customers daily. That year, AnnTaylor lost $15.8 million on sales of $438 million.

In February 1992, AnnTaylor wooed former president Sally Frame Kasaks back. Her first action, like Brooks's, was to install a solid management team. Kasaks chose a primarily female management staff, composed of seasoned veterans of the specialty retail trade. Kasaks then worked to reestablish Ann-Taylor's reputation for high-quality clothing, getting rid of the cheap synthetic fabrics and overseeing a new autumn line of clothes that borrowed heavily from popular and costly designs of Donna Karan and Ralph Lauren. Four months after Kasaks rejoined AnnTaylor, the company's same-store sales were up ten percent.

After reassuring the customer of the quality of AnnTaylor merchandise, Kasaks sought a strategy for keeping prices reasonable. Toward that end, she explored several manufacturing options, finally reaching an agreement with Cygne Designs for the manufacture of apparel through a joint venture called CAT. A private-label company with factory contracts mainly overseas, Cygne worked with AnnTaylor to produce items made to specification more cheaply and quickly. As a result, what few designer labels the AnnTaylor stores stocked nearly disappeared, and lines of casual and weekend clothes were added, as were lines of petite sizes and whole new lines meant to attract younger women.

By her own admission, Kasaks worked hard to stay in touch with suppliers and customers. "This is very much a business of relationships," she was quoted as saying in a 1995 *Chain Store Executive* article, adding "And as a symbol of this business, I need to stay out there." Thus she visited on average 100 stores a year, refused to fly first class on business trips "because it is something that most AnnTaylor customers do not do on a

regular basis," and tried to see that overseas factories maintained responsible manufacturing and production practices.

Sales at new stores opened in 1993 grew an impressive 13.6 percent by March 1994, and the Merrill Lynch Capital Partners and other affiliates still holding 52 percent of AnnTaylor's stock prepared to make another public offering. During the first six months of 1994, same-store sales grew 10.6 percent, while other popular specialty stores, such as The Gap and Nordstrom's, were reporting gains of less than half that amount. By year's end, the company's sales had increased considerably to $659 million with earnings of $32 million, as formerly loyal customers began to return to AnnTaylor, and analysts were hailing AnnTaylor as being "back on track." A new fragrance line was introduced, five freestanding shoe and accessory stores were opened, and a mail-order catalog was launched in 1994. Kasaks also expanded AnnTaylor's traditional career offerings to include casual clothes, denims, and petites. The company updated its systems and controls for supplying stores with merchandise. It opened a new business, AnnTaylor Loft, intended to have greater appeal to younger customers with its more fashionable, less basics-oriented approach.

The Loft was also an attempt to compete with discount apparel stores, the most potent threat to apparel specialty stores at that time because of the price deflation they caused in the moderate and lower priced lines. By early 1995, AnnTaylor was feeling this threat as it was forced to cut prices by ten to 15 percent. The board, in an attempt to maintain the company's growth, tripled its capital-spending budget as plans were undertaken for further aggressive expansion. By the end of the year, however, AnnTaylor's spectacular comeback was being labeled a flop. The spring line, which included cropped t-shirts and leather jackets in an attempt to woo the younger customer, had not sold well.

Kasaks attributed the company's sales problems to the difficult retail environment, but others attributed them to Kasaks herself. Known for her mercurial disposition, she had ostensibly shaken up more than one staff meeting. More than a dozen executives, including the company's senior vice-president and general merchandising manager, had resigned as AnnTaylor's stock dipped from its December 1994 high of almost $45 to a low of $10 in October 1995. The company became unable to meet the conditions of its loans.

In April 1996, two shareholders filed a class action suit accusing the company of concealing its financial problems and hiding inventory. In September 1996, in an effort to salvage its ailing principal supplier, AnnTaylor bought Cygne's 60 percent stake in CAT and Cygne's AnnTaylor Woven Division. After 14 straight months of declining sales and losses or lower profits in five of six quarters, Kasaks resigned under pressure from the board in August 1996, replaced by J. Patrick Spainhour, former chief financial officer of Donna Karan International, as chief executive, and Particia DeRosa, former president of Gap Kids, as president and chief operating officer.

In 1997, AnnTaylor invested heavily in advertising for its fall line of clothes, the more conservatively stylish, businesslike attire with which it had made its name. Sales remained sluggish through most of 1997, when sales for the entire company fell

? 1 percent. By 1998, however, the company seemed to have solidified its comeback. For this, AnnTaylor had its loyal customer base to thank, who, according to at least one analyst in the *Milwaukee Journal Sentinel,* kept coming back to browse the racks even after styles disappointed them. Sales for the year increased to $912 million, yielding profits of $39.3 million.

Sales at AnnTaylor continued to improve, albeit slowly, throughout 1999 and into 2000, when there was talk of a company buyout by May Department Stores. The company's share price continued to be volatile throughout this period, reaching an April 1999 high of about $53, but dropping as low as about $15 in early 2000. By mid-2000, when AnnTaylor offered a new Internet shopping service to customers, the future of the company was still far from certain.

### Principal Subsidiaries

AnnTaylor Inc.

### Principal Divisions

AnnTaylor Loft; Anntaylor.com; AnnTaylor Factory Stores.

### Principal Competitors

The Gap Inc.; Liz Claiborne Inc.; Donna Karan International Inc.

### Further Reading

"Brooks Group Gets AnnTaylor for $430 Million," *Women's Wear Daily,* November 30, 1988, pp. 1, 26.

Caminiti, Susan, "How to Win Back Customers," *Fortune,* June 14, 1993, p. 118.

Coleman, Lisa, "Welcome Back," *Forbes,* August 17, 1992, p. 124.

Colodny, Mark, "Mr. Ann Taylor," *Fortune,* March 11, 1991, p. 105.

Contavski, Vicki, "Who'll Mind the Store?," *Forbes,* December 9, 1991, p. 16.

Donahue, Christine, "AnnTaylor Turns Barbara Bush into a Fashion Plate," *Adweek's Marketing Index,* September 4, 1989, p. 31.

Furman, Phyllis, "Fashionable AnnTaylor to Sell Stock," *Crain's New York Business,* March 25, 1991, pp. 3, 34.

Jeresky, Laura, "Rags to Riches," *Forbes,* April 15, 1991, p. 42.

Mahar, Maggie, "Mission Impossible?," *Working Woman,* December 1993, pp. 60–68.

McNally, Pamela, "The AnnTaylor Footwear Formula," *Footwear News,* August 1, 1994, p. S6.

McNish, Jacquie, "Campeau Plans to Sell Allied's AnnTaylor Unit," *Wall Street Journal,* June 16, 1988, p. 10.

Power, William, "Soaring AnnTaylor May Need Some Caution as Accessory," *Wall Street Journal,* April 15, 1994.

Steinhauer, Jennifer, "Can AnnTaylor Dust Itself Off?," *New York Times,* December 2, 1995, p. 35.

——, "In a Surprise, AnnTaylor's Chief Resigns," *New York Times,* August 24, 1996, p. 35.

Trachtenberg, Jeffrey, "AnnTaylor Plans Expansion to Pay $37 Million in Interest from Buy-Out," *Wall Street Journal,* May 11, 1989, p. A4.

Wachs Book, Esther, "The Treachery of Success," *Forbes,* September 12, 1994, pp. 88–90.

Wilson, Marianne, "Reinventing AnnTaylor," *Chain Store Age Executive,* January 1995, pp. 26–45.

Zinn, Laura, "Trouble Stalks the Aisles at AnnTaylor," *Business Week,* December 9, 1991, p. 38.

—Carol I. Keeley
—updated by Carrie Rothburd

# Arandell Corporation

---

N82 W13118 Leon Road
Menominee Falls, Wisconsin 53051
U.S.A.
Telephone: (262) 255-4400
Fax: (262) 255-8218
Web site: http://www.arandell.com

Private Company
*Incorporated:* 1922 as R & L Service Inc.
*Employees:* 600
*Sales:* $170 million (1998 est.)
*NAIC:* 323110 Commercial Lithographic Printing;
323119 Other Commercial Printing

---

Arandell Corporation is one of the nation's leading printers of upscale catalogs. Its customers include many department store chains, including Saks Fifth Avenue, R.H. Macy & Co., Lord & Taylor, and the May Department Stores. It also handles the catalog printing of Coach Leather, Warner Brothers, and many others. It is one of the five largest catalog printers in North America, and one of the few companies that owns the large and sophisticated equipment needed to produce high-quality color catalogs. Its services include not only printing but mailing of finished catalogs. The company has its own post office on the premises of its corporate offices in Menominee Falls. It ships out printed catalogs on average of more than 80 truckloads a day. It also works with its customers on database management, targeting mailing lists so catalogs reach only the most likely consumers. Arandell also assists its customers with website development and electronic commerce.

### Early History

Arandell Corporation was formed from the merger of two southeastern Wisconsin printers. That area of the country had a strong tradition of printing. Wisconsin was a major paper producer, and also had abundant water. These factors made printing easy and economical. In the 19th century, Milwaukee attracted many immigrant lithographers from Germany who found work printing beer bottle labels at the city's many large breweries.

The two companies that became Arandell Corp. both started in the area around the same time. One company, founded in 1922 as a sheet-fed printer of labels for brewers and for sausagemakers, was first known as R & L Service Inc. In 1949, a man named F. Edward Treis purchased an interest in R & L and became chairman and president of the company. In 1953 Treis changed the name of the company from R & L to its phonetic equivalent, Arandell. The second company was the E.F. Schmidt Company, founded in Milwaukee in 1923.

By the mid-1950s, E.F. Schmidt was one of a small core of specialized sheet-fed lithographers in Milwaukee, each of which held onto a particular market niche. Schmidt was renowned for making calendars. Its calendar business spread through the Midwest in the 1950s and 1960s, and then on to New York. Its customers were mainly large corporations, which ordered vast print runs of imprinted calendars as gifts to employees and clients. Some of Schmidt's prominent corporate customers were General Electric and Pan American Airways.

In the mid-1970s, Schmidt was one of only a handful of manufacturers in the United States that had such sophisticated equipment as wire binders and plastic binders to produce quality calendars. Since few other companies had made this technological investment, Schmidt had few competitors. The company made a major technological transition in the 1970s, switching from sheet-fed equipment to the so-called web process, which uses giant rolls of paper. This transition entailed the construction of a new plant, which the company built in nearby Menominee Falls, Wisconsin. The company's success had attracted potential buyers, but the printer remained in the hands of the founding Schmidt family, with Harold Schmidt as president, and another Schmidt brother as chairman.

### Merger and New Market in the 1980s

E.F. Schmidt balanced out its calendar business, which peaked in the fall, by printing corporate annual reports in the spring. This gave the company two busy seasons, but in the intervening months, it scrambled to pick up any kind of work it could get. Despite this, the company continued to grow in the late 1970s, adding a second web press in 1978. But that year,

Harold Schmidt died, and the company's remaining management faced an uncertain future. The calendar market had begun to shrink. The giving of fancy corporate gift calendars became less common, and more and more calendars were printed by private publishers who made small runs of calendars with special interest topics (butterflies, cats, etc.). This was not a market Schmidt could compete in, because the commercial calendars generally had a much smaller press run. These could be made profitably by a small sheet-fed printing house, not by a company with the large-scale web printing capabilities of Schmidt. Also, the company's two major products, calendars and annual reports, gave the firm two busy cycles and two uncertain and slow periods. A steady year-round business would have been more suitable. So after Harold Schmidt's death, the company began to look for a new market.

Just after Harold Schmidt died, the company's vice-president, Robert Burrington, got a call from a major paper manufacturer who was doing a survey to determine printing needs in the upcoming 1980s. Burrington agreed to participate, as long as he could see the results. What he saw convinced him that upscale catalog printing was going to be the next boom in the industry. With a growing population of affluent but busy young people, the direct mail market was expected to grow. Catalog printing was similar to the fine calendar printing Schmidt was versed in, and it required large runs that would keep Schmidt's equipment busy all year round. So Burrington actively pursued the catalog market. He looked first to Dallas, a city that housed several upscale mail-order businesses, including the Horchow Collection and Neiman-Marcus. Burrington hired a Dallas-area printing salesman to spearhead Schmidt's campaign. The salesman, David Mixon, arranged to use existing film from a previous catalog and do a mock run for several potential Dallas clients. Schmidt flew representatives from the potential client companies to Menominee Falls to see the mock print run, and show them firsthand what a quality job Schmidt was capable of. This strategy was a big success, and within a year, Schmidt was printing catalogs for Horchow, Neiman-Marcus, and several other Texas department store chains. Then the company began trawling the New York market for similar business.

Catalog printing required specialized printing skills. Customers required exact color reproduction, so that the green pants in the catalog were the same green as the ones in the store or warehouse. E.F. Schmidt had proven it could move into the catalog market, but it needed money to buy new equipment if it was going to pursue customers nationwide. The Schmidt family decided to look for a merger to give the company cash for expansion. Though E.F. Schmidt at that time had sales of

around $20 million, its buyer, Arandell, turned out to be a much smaller company with sales of only around $6 million. However, Arandell outbid other larger competitors in order to get in on Schmidt's growing catalog business. The sale took place in 1981, and the merged company became known as Arandell-Schmidt Corporation. The new corporation continued E.F. Schmidt's drive to capture the catalog market. Robert Burrington, Schmidt's vice-president, stayed on in direct marketing, and members of Arandell's Treis family became president and chief operating officer.

By 1985, Arandell-Schmidt had an impressive roster of catalog customers. The most renowned names in department stores all did their catalog printing at Arandell, including Bergdorf Goodman, Saks Fifth Avenue, Macy's, Bullock's, Bloomingdales, and Lord & Taylor. The company got 75 percent of its sales revenues from catalogs. Most of the rest of its business was in brochures for companies like Chrysler and Volkswagen. Less than five percent of its business was calendars. The company shed its annual reports business almost completely, since producing them in springtime interfered with the rest of Arandell's work. Sales grew enormously. The year after the merger, annual sales were $24 million. The next year, they had risen to $38 million, and by 1984 the company was bringing in $52 million. Arandell continued to invest in new equipment. By the mid-1980s, it operated five web presses as well as three sheet-fed presses. The production expansion had cost the firm around $13 million, and included the construction of new buildings to house the equipment. The company also opened a mailing department in the mid-1980s, allowing it to not only print but distribute the catalogs. It also invested in ink-jet addressing equipment, so it could print consumer addresses directly on the finished catalogs. To handle growing nationwide sales, Arandell opened regional offices across the country. By 1985, the company had offices in San Francisco, Dallas, New York City, Minneapolis, Detroit, Chicago, Los Angeles, and Kansas City.

### *Stock Offering Doesn't Happen*

Sales at Arandell continued to rise quickly. Sales for fiscal 1987 were over $70 million, and in May 1987 the company announced that it would make an initial public stock offering. Its growth curve was exceptional, and likely to be smiled on by Wall Street, and the company could use the money raised to reduce its debt. Stock in the private company was held by owners and top executives. F. Edward Treis, who had built up Arandell since 1949, held over 80 percent of the stock. Another large block, totaling over 13 percent, was held by the firm's executive vice-president of finance, George Kaiser. Kaiser and Treis planned to sell substantial portions of their holdings, so that after the offering, about 30 percent of the company's stock would be in public hands. But on October 19, 1987, the stock market crashed. Members of the Treis family, including F. Edward Treis and his sons Donald, Edward, and James, along with other managers, decided to cancel the stock offering. Abruptly, three top executives quit the firm. George Kaiser resigned, along with Larry Vorbrich, who had been head of marketing. Then Robert Burrington, who had spearheaded the company's shift into the upscale catalog market, left Arandell to take a position with a competitor. Donald Treis took over the presidency of the company from his father, and Arandell continued to operate as a private firm.

**Key Dates:**

**1922:** Company founded as R & L Service Inc. in Milwaukee.
**1923:** E.F. Schmidt Co. founded.
**1949:** F. Edward Treis becomes chairman and president of R & L.
**1953:** Name changed to Arandell Corp.
**1981:** Arandell purchases E.F. Schmidt. Co.
**1987:** Company announces it will go public, but then withdraws.

The early 1990s were not as booming a time for the catalog industry as the 1980s had been. Sales at Arandell did not move up much between 1989 and 1990, hovering at just over $82 million. An increase in the postal rate made catalog mailings more costly. As a result, retailers searched for ways to hone their databases in order to eliminate costly mailings to consumers who were unlikely to buy. Arandell's customers had been placing catalog orders three months in advance, but the time shortened to one month in the early 1990s, as client companies struggled to refine their mailing lists.

Though the recession years of the early 1990s proved more difficult for the company than earlier years, Arandell persisted in its pursuit of the upscale catalog market. By 1994, the company had decided it needed more capacity, and it invested over $10 million in new equipment. It bought a new web press, as well as new bindery equipment. This was the single biggest equipment purchase Arandell had ever made. The new technology increased the firm's capacity by 60 percent, allowing it to go after bigger customers and to offer bigger press runs to its current clients. While some other area printers had been swallowed up by bigger competitors, Arandell aimed to become bigger itself, and keep itself privately owned.

Two years later, Arandell upgraded its bindery equipment by installing new computer software, making Arandell one of the most automated binderies in the United States. It was putting out over 300 million catalogs a year by that time, and its customers included new names such as Toys 'R' Us, American Express, Amway, and Cartier. To serve customers who were manipulating their mailing lists to target specific populations, the company's sophisticated equipment was able to print different versions of catalogs simultaneously.

The company continued to innovate in the late 1990s and beyond. Its postal system continued to grow in size and sophistication. In 2000, Arandell's director of postal systems was honored by the U.S. Postal Service for new programs he had implemented at the company. Arandell used an advanced tracking system to make sure its catalogs arrived on time, and it also established an Internet-based information system that allowed its customers to share tracking and other information with the Postal Service. Also in 2000, Arandell began using an Internet-based work-flow management system to help its customers follow the status of their catalog orders. Customers had often needed to visit the printing plant at odd hours to check on press runs, and last-minute changes or equipment failures could be disastrous. The new technology allowed customers to access the status of their jobs in real time from their desktop computer. Customers could also use the new system to receive proposals, make changes, and track their print job at all stages of development. The company remained in the hands of the Treis family into the 2000s. Donald Treis continued as president, his brother James was vice-president for marketing and sales, and patriarch F. Edward Treis remained chairman and chief executive officer.

### *Principal Competitors*

R.R. Donnelley and Sons; Quebecor Printing.

### *Further Reading*

Foran, Pat, "Arandell-Schmidt Keeps Its Profitable Presses Rolling Through Pivotal Year," *Business Journal-Milwaukee,* April 11, 1988, p. 3S.

Johnston, Peter, "Boom, Baby, Boom," *Graphic Arts Monthly,* August 1985, pp. 80–84.

Kirchen, Rich, "Printer Adds $10 Million in Equipment," *Business Journal-Milwaukee,* January 8, 1994, p. 1.

Krenn, Mike, "Industry Leaves Firm Imprint," *Milwaukee Journal,* December 21, 1986.

Kueny, Barbara, "Presses at Milwaukee-Area Printers Ready to Roll Out of Recession," *Business Journal-Milwaukee,* May 27, 1991, p. S32.

Metzner, Julie Hill, "Arandell-Schmidt Doubles Sales by Tapping New Markets," *Business Journal-Milwaukee,* October 14, 1985, p. 18.

Skolnik, Rayna, "Coddling Customers 24 Hours a Day," *Sales & Marketing Management,* December 9, 1985, p. 38.

"Three Printers Choose Software to Update Bindery," *Graphic Arts Monthly,* November 1996, p. 38.

Wojahn, Ellen, "Stop the Presses," *Inc.,* January 1986, p. 97.

—A. Woodward

# Association des Centres Distributeurs E. Leclerc

52 rue Camille Desmoulins
92451 Issy-les-Moulineaux
France
Telephone: (+33) 1 46 62 51 00
Fax: (+33) 1 46 62 51 26
Web site: http://www.e-leclerc.com

*Private Cooperative*
*Incorporated:* 1949
*Employees:* 67,000
*Sales:* EUR 25 billion ($22 billion)(1999 est.)
*NAIC:* 445110 Supermarkets and Other Grocery (Except Convenience) Stores

Retailing powerhouse Association des Centres Distributeurs E. Leclerc, France's second-largest distribution group (after the Carrefour-Promodes merger of August 2000), is a private cooperative grouping nearly 500 members and their 358 "hypermarkets" (vast warehouses selling everything from traditional grocery items to car parts, home appliances and other department store-style goods) and 143 supermarkets. The Leclerc group also oversees a network of 472 gas stations; 200 jewelry stores (the Manège à Bijoux, France's largest seller of gold jewelry); nearly 140 cafeterias; nearly 100 travel agencies; some 70 automobile service centers; more than 60 stores dedicated to hardware and/or gardening supplies; and some 50 "Cultural Centers" featuring books, videos and DVDs, compact discs, and computers and computer supplies and equipment. Many of these specialty shops are located under the same roof or within the same park complex as the group's hypermarkets. However, the Leclerc banner is also featured on a number of smaller independent specialty stores, primarily clothing stores, but also furniture and perfume stores. Despite its dominance of the French market, Leclerc is barely present internationally, with under 15 stores across Spain, Portugal, and Poland, and plans to open stores in Italy. In order to counter the increasing consolidation of the French retail market, Leclerc has entered a cooperation agreement with fellow cooperative distribution group Système U, which primarily operates supermarkets. The company is led by founder's son Edouard-Michel Leclerc, while the founder himself, Edouard Leclerc, remains active in planning group strategy.

### Getting the Retail Religion in the 1950s

Edouard Leclerc abandoned his studies for the catholic priesthood in 1949 and opened a small grocery store in Landerneau, in the north of France. From the start, Leclerc's vision of retailing included something of a social component, offering consumers wholesale-level prices in an era when the word discount had not yet entered the French shopping vocabulary. Leclerc's pricing policies quickly brought him into conflict with other local merchants–both grocers and department stores—as well as their industrial suppliers. As Leclerc's retail competitors launched a "dumping" campaign, selling products below costs, while setting higher prices for Leclerc himself, they encouraged their suppliers either to refuse to deliver goods to Leclerc's store or to force him to charge fixed prices for their goods.

Leclerc fought back, however, showing a battling spirit that would characterize the company particularly in the 1980s; in 1953, he succeeded in seeing the passage of new legislation, the so-called Pinay Law, which prohibited the singling out of individual retailers and the setting of fixed prices. With the commercial battleground leveled, Leclerc set about building his retail empire.

Among the features of Leclerc's early organization was his commitment to the advancement of his employees. Leclerc employees were encouraged to rise through the ranks and then were given help to raise financing needed to leave and found their own Leclerc-branded stores. Leclerc himself—and later, other Leclerc store owners—acted as "godparent" to the new store, providing financial guarantees for the new owner. The willingness to fund the growth of new business, rather than solely expand one's own holdings, was to become a prominent feature of the Leclerc group, where no single store owner—including Edouard Leclerc himself—was allowed to own more than two stores.

By 1958, the Leclerc name was found on more than 50 stores. In that year, a group of managers from a local company joined together to open a Leclerc store in Grenoble. The following year, Leclerc opened its first store in the Paris region, in Issy-les-Moulineaux, later to become the site of the Leclerc headquarters. Meanwhile, Leclerc continued to push for changes in the French retail and distribution market. In 1960, the group launched a campaign to circumvent the distribution monopolies then in place, organizing protests by farmers in Paris to demand the right to sell directly to Leclerc, without having to go through a third-party. The Leclerc initiative once again brought about new legislation. This in turn led to the creation in 1962 of a group-purchasing association among Leclerc store owners, the forerunner to the reorganization of the group as a cooperative at the end of the decade.

The growth of the supermarket concept in the mid-1960s led to a distinctly French creation: the hypermarket. Grouping traditional supermarket fare under the same roof as items normally found in department stores, the hypermarket quickly caught on among French consumers. Edouard Leclerc was the first in the Leclerc group to explore this new territory, expanding his Landerneau store into the first Leclerc hypermarket. It was only fitting for Leclerc to extend its product assortment, as the group continued to pressure the various distribution monopolies for the right to enter previously restricted territory. The group's next target was the dairy industry, long controlled by a number of dairy cooperatives. In the early 1960s, the Leclerc association joined together with several of France's dairy farmers in a drive to set up direct purchasing organizations for the farmer's milk and dairy products.

The number of Leclerc stores grew quickly in the 1960s. However, dissension was growing among the ranks of store owners. The disagreements came to a head in 1969, when a group of 95 Leclerc store owner-operators, led by Jean-Pierre Le Roch, left the Leclerc group and set up a new supermarket cooperative—ITM Entreprises—which grew to become one of France's largest distribution groups under the Intermarché and Bricomarché banners. Where the Le Roch group pursued a separate supermarket and specialty store concept, the Leclerc group focused instead on building its single-brand Leclerc hypermarkets and supermarkets. In 1970, the remaining Le-

clerc store owners reorganized their association as the cooperative Groupement d'Achat des Centres E. Leclerc, or GALEC.

### Monopoly Buster in the 1970s and 1980s

In 1972, the first legislation designed to restrict the growth of the hypermarket trend in France—inspired in an attempt to protect the small merchant as the larger retail groups captured a greater and greater share of the retail market—threatened the growth of the Leclerc cooperative. The legislation required that all proposed new retail surfaces be granted authorization and agree to a number of conditions, such as funding unrelated infrastructure constructions (municipal swimming pools and the like) in the communities they sought to enter. The Leclerc group fought back, decrying the new system's discrimination against, ironically, the small merchant, who was required to take on an even greater financial burden in order to build a new store. Existing merchants were also able to use the new legislation to protect their retail territory. Yet a number of Leclerc's members proceeded to flout the new legislation, building new hypermarkets without waiting for the required authorization, often with the support of local consumer groups and unions.

Leclerc's battling spirit continued throughout the 1970s. In the mid-1970s, Leclerc turned its attention to new fronts. The first, the monopoly on fish distribution, which saw all of the nation's fish processed through a central facility at Rungis, in Paris, and took a high margin on sales to distributors. In 1975, Leclerc began organizing its own direct-purchasing facilities in cooperation with a number of independent fishing groups.

Meanwhile, with gas and oil prices soaring in the wake of the Arab Oil Embargo, Leclerc attacked a new monopoly, that of the gasoline market controlled by Total and Elf in France. In 1976, Leclerc began opening its own gasoline stations, making purchases from independent oil companies outside of France, and cutting the price on a liter of gas. The company's imposition on this market helped force down the exorbitant price of gasoline in France.

In the late 1970s, Leclerc continued to look for ways to gain its independence from the country's distribution monopolies. In 1978 the group bought up a slaughtering facility in Brittany, then built a pork processing facility, France's largest, while also opening a salted meats plant to supply up to one-third of the cooperatives needs. During this period, a growing number of the Leclerc cooperatives' members were converting their stores to the hypermarket concept; by the early 1980s, the Leclerc name included more than 100 hypermarkets across France.

Joining the company in 1979 was Leclerc's son, Edouard-Michel, who became co-chairman in 1982. The younger Leclerc helped energize Leclerc's battling spirit, taking the cooperative head-to-head with still more distribution monopolies in the 1980s. Among the protected retail segments attacked by Leclerc during the decade were those of clothing, sporting goods, perfume, and cosmetics and other ''para-pharmacy'' goods, such as vitamins. The cooperative also gained entry into the gold jewelry market by creating the gold jewelry manufacturing company DEVINLEC, offering the group's own designs in its Manèges à Bijoux boutiques (usually located in the hypermarket shopping center) at prices up to 60 percent lower than those of its competition. Similarly, the group was able to enter the hitherto protected travel agency market by forming a joint-venture with Groupe Bolloré, known as Leclerc Voyages. Leclerc's legal battles—and successes—helped break up a number of retail monopolies, lowering prices on a wide variety of products. The company also circumvented the monopoly governing the nation's credit card system by installing its own server network to handle credit card transactions. The company also added its own network of automobile service centers to its hypermarket complexes, growing to 150 centers in the early 1990s.

### Recapturing Momentum for the 21st Century

The recession of the early 1990s brought a new competitor to the French retailing scene; deep discounters, such as Germany's Lidl and Aldi, began invading the French market, slashing prices with a range of generic goods. Leclerc was forced to respond, introducing its own range of deep-discounted items. The company also created its own brand of clothing, Tissaia, in 1991. By then, the company had turned to a new sector, opening its first automotive service center along the French autoroute system, previously controlled entirely by the big multinational oil companies.

If the company's French network continued to grow, its moves into the international front were less successful. Hampering the company's international growth was the cooperative formula that had built its success in France; opening a new store in another country required that a current cooperative member install himself in that country and train management staff capable of expanding the Leclerc name into the rest of the country. Nonetheless, the group opened its first stores in Poland and Portugal in 1995. Meanwhile, one member's attempt to bring the Leclerc format to the United States, opening a hypermarket in Baltimore, failed, going bankrupt after only three years.

More alarming for the company was the tightening of the "anti-hypermarket" regulations, resulting in a near-ban on all new hypermarket construction in the country in the mid-1990s. The new laws, which reduced the authorization requirement to include all stores of 300 square meters or more, effectively ended the possibility for Leclerc to continue its internal growth in France. Yet its weakness on the international front left it in a delicate position, particularly compared to its integrated competitors, such as Carrefour, Promodes, Casino, and others.

Leclerc continued to maintain its leadership of the French market through most of the decade, in part because of the successful launch of its Cultural Centers, which sold books, videos and compact discs, and computers and computer equipment and supplies. Its position was also secured, moreover, by the continued success of its jewelry sales, which captured the leadership in gold sales in France by mid-decade.

However, in the late 1990s, Leclerc had to fight to recapture the leading edge in retailing. In 1997, it launched its own label, the Marque Repere, countering the private labels introduced by its competitors. By the end of the decade, the Marque Repere range of some 800 items accounted for more than 20 percent of store sales. The company also continued its slow international growth, opening four more stores in Portugal, Spain and Poland.

Yet a number of new difficulties confronted the group as it turned toward the new century. The takeover of Carrefour by rival retailer Promodes sent Leclerc plunging to the number two position in the country and placed it at a distinct disadvantage, both in terms of purchasing power and marketing and advertising clout, as it settled into the shadows of the new global retailing behemoth. Unable to increase its number of French hypermarkets, the cooperative instead was faced with a growing number of members who, looking forward to retiring, became tempted to sell their locations to Leclerc's capital-ready competitors. The group was able to circumvent—at least temporarily—this danger by insisting that all members sign a pact giving the Leclerc company the first right of purchase.

Meanwhile, a new law introduced on the French retail scene effectively ended one of Leclerc's favorite practices by prohibiting stores from taking losses on some of their items. Yet the company, approaching its 50th anniversary, was able to perform an end-run around this new restriction, by offering rebates on purchases of certain items. This promotion enabled the company to boost its market share for the first time in several years. At the same time, the company moved to shore up its negotiating position by forming a cooperation agreement with another northern France independent cooperative group, Système U. The two cooperatives agreed to jointly form a buying center, Lucie, in 1999.

As it entered the 21st century, Leclerc remained a primary force on the French retail scene. Yet its position as only number 22 among the world's top retailers left it vulnerable in an increasingly global economy. In 2000, the company began to eye new means of encouraging its international expansion. Adopting a licensing approach, the company looked for international partnerships to open new Leclerc franchises. A first such agreement was made in Portugal, with the purchasing cooperative Elos. A similar agreement was being pursued in Italy. After 50 years of bringing lower prices to the French consumer, Leclerc hoped to be able to do the same for the rest of the world.

### Principal Divisions

Scapnor; Scadif; Scapest; Scarmor; Scaouest; Socamaine; Scachap; Scaso; Scalandes; Socamil; Lecasud; Socara; Scacentre; Scanormande; Scapalsace; Scapartois; Kermene; DEVINLEC; Cefilec; E.Leclerc Voyages; Edel Banque; Siplec; Scapauto; Unilec; Sofilec.

### Principal Competitors

Carrefour S.A; Casino Guichard S.A.; Castorama S.A.; E.Leclerc; Guyenne et Gascogne S.A.; Lidl & Schwarz Stiftung; METRO AG; Pinault-Printemps-Redoute S.A.; Royal Ahold N.V.

### Further Reading

Budget, Antoine, "Leclerc veut relancer le débat sur le prix unique du livre," *Les Echos*, January 27, 2000, p. 22.
Courage, Sylvain, "Le système Leclerc résistera-t-il à Carrefour?" *Capital*, October 2000, p. 64.
Markides, Constantinos, "Strategic Innovation in Established Companies," *Sloan Management Review*, March 22, 1998, p. 31.
Meignan, Géraldine, "La pub 'provoc' de Leclerc," *L'Expansion*, April 27, 2000, p. 22.
Peyrani, Béatrice, "Un fils de pub nommé Leclerc," *L'Expansion*, August 29, 1996, p. 68.

—M.L. Cohen

# Auchan

**200 rue de la Recherche**
**59650 Villeneuve d'Ascq Cedex**
**France**
**Telephone: (+33) 3 20 67 62 22**
**Fax: (+33) 3 20 67 62 55**
**Web site: http://www.auchan.com**

*Private Company*
*Incorporated:* 1961
*Employees:* 116,413
*Sales:* EUR 22 billion ($18.8 billion) (1999)
*NAIC:* 445110 Supermarkets and Other Grocery (Except Convenience) Stores

Auchan is one of the world's top retail and distribution groups with more than EUR 22 billion in revenues each year. Privately owned by the founding Mulliez family—the more than 300 members of which hold 85 percent of the company's shares—Auchan also has long held a policy of opening its shares to its employees, who own 15 percent of the company (and some of whom have become millionaires through their stockholdings). The Auchan empire is based on the group's 211 "hypermarkets"—vast stores that combine traditional supermarkets with a department store concept in huge spaces ranging upward to 100,000 square feet—and its smaller supermarkets. The group's stores trade primarily under the Auchan (hypermarket) and Atac (supermarket) banners in France, where the group posts some 70 percent of sales, but also under other names on the international scene, primarily in Spain, Portugal, and Italy. In the late 1990s, the group has extended its interests to include South America, Central Europe, and the Far East, particularly Thailand and China. The company is less present in the United States, operating a sole hypermarket in Houston, Texas. The Auchan group also acts as an umbrella for a number of other Mulliez family-owned retail operations, including the Leroy Merlin DIY (do-it-yourself) chain, the second largest in the French market; the restaurant group Flunch; clothing, under the Kiabi store banner; appliances, electronics, and computers through 50 Boulanger stores; the Tapis-St. Maclou chain of flooring and carpets; as well as the original Mulliez family company, the Phildar chain of clothing, textiles, and sewing and knitting supplies. Auchan is led by Christophe Dubrulle, cousin to founder Gerard Mulliez—who, after building his home next to the company's northern France headquarters, remains active in planning the group's strategy.

### Inheriting the Retail Gene in the 1960s

The Mulliez family founded its first company, Phildar, in 1903. At first a manufacturer of textiles, Phildar turned to the retail sector in 1946, when it trademarked the company name and began to develop its Phildar brand name of textiles and knitting and sewing supplies. The company turned toward franchising to expand its distribution network, licensing the first Phildar franchise store in 1956. Phildar grew to become one of the largest textiles distributors in the world—by the end of the 20th century the company's network included 1,500 stores.

Yet Phildar also was manufacturing another product: Gerard Mulliez, one of French retailing's major retailing figures in the 20th century. A self-proclaimed autodidact, Mulliez never completed high school, but instead went to work, at first in manufacturing, becoming a foreman in the family's textile dye shop before managing the company's knitting factory. At the start of the 1960s, Mulliez decided to go into business for himself. In 1961, Mulliez, then 29 years old, opened his first store, a grocery, in Roubaix, in a neighborhood known as the "haut champs" (or high fields). Pronounced "oh-cham," this first retail location soon gave its name to what was to become the Auchan retail empire.

Mulliez's first store failed, however. Yet, rescued by his family, Mulliez determined to stay in retailing. Taking his inspiration from Edouard Leclerc, the former priest turned founder of the E. Leclerc retail chain, Mulliez—himself a devout Catholic—adopted Leclerc's discount, self-service supermarket formula. Cutting prices throughout his store, Mulliez soon began to attract a new clientele. By the mid-1960s, the company was ready to expand, taking French retailing to an entirely new level.

In 1967, Mulliez opened the first of a new retailing concept—the so-called "hypermarket." Combining the product assortment of a typical supermarket with the range of goods found in department stores—everything from musical recordings to furniture, household appliances, and automobile parts—the hypermarket format was quickly emulated throughout France, growing to mammoth stores of up to 100,000 square feet, as large as several football playing fields. The first Auchan hypermarket opened near the Mulliez family's base, in Tourcoing/Roncq in 1967.

The Auchan format was an instant success—in its first year the company posted sales of FFr 70 million and profits of some FFr 300,000. Mulliez quickly began building the Auchan name into one of the country's top retailers. In this, he was helped by a number of factors, from economic to political. The collapse of the long postwar economic boom in France, as the country slipped into the recession brought on by the Arab Oil Embargo, encouraged consumers to seek out Auchan's discount formula. The introduction of a variety of company-owned brands—some 200 in all—which were priced significantly lower than competing national and international brand name products, helped drive store sales as well. Consumers were also attracted to the modern appeal of these large self-service stores, to the detriment of the country's large class of small boutique shops.

Politicians of the time also greeted the rise of the hypermarket as a way to fight the rampant inflation that was cutting deeply into the country's economy in the 1970s. The large-scale purchasing power of Auchan and rivals such as E. Leclerc, Carrefour, Docks de France, and Casino enabled these stores to maintain relatively low prices. In the 1980s, the transfer of a great deal of planning authority from the national level to the local and regional levels made it possible for communities to clear away a number of planning codes and other obstacles that had prevented the growth of the hypermarket formula. Eager to reap the benefits of the tax revenues and employment opportunities offered by the new huge commercial centers, communities welcomed the new hypermarkets. By the mid-1970s, Auchan's annual sales had topped FFr 2 billion.

Mulliez, who had at first clung to his family's northern France base, launched a new strategy toward the end of the 1970s to transform Auchan into one of the country's top na-

tional retailers. In 1977, Auchan began to extend its network of hypermarkets across the country. Yet Mulliez avoided raising capital on the public market; instead, the company, like its competitors, was able to take advantage of the staggered payment structure (up to three months for paying suppliers), using its huge cash flow to finance its expansion. At the same time Auchan began offering stock to its employees, thereby giving them a share of the company. While criticism aimed at the company pointed to the low wages earned by many of its employees, a number of Auchan's employees nonetheless became quite wealthy, as the average share price (agreed upon each year by the extended Mulliez family) increased from a starting point of just FFr 12 francs to more than FFr 500 francs by the late 1990s.

### National and International Growth in the 1980s

With the encouragement of local authorities, France's retailing landscape turned more and more toward the construction of large commercial centers located on the outskirts of the country's cities and towns. Auchan joined this trend, expanding its number of hypermarkets across the country. At the same time, the company was developing other store formats, including standard supermarkets and smaller grocers, which were located in the country's smaller communities or in urban locations. By the mid-1980s, Auchan had grown to annual sales of more than FFr 20 billion.

By then, the Mulliez family had becoming something of a retail empire in France. While Gerard Mulliez built the Auchan chain, other family members were encouraged to explore their own retail initiatives. The flooring and carpeting company, founded by cousin Gonzague Mulliez in 1963, had risen to become France's leading specialist in this category, with 160 large-format stores at the end of the 1990s. Another retail concept, launched by Patrick Mulliez in 1978, was the discount clothing chain Kiabi, which grew to a fashion giant, posting FFr 7.8 billion in sales through more than 170 stores across Europe. Another success story was the company's acquisition of DIY and home decoration chain Leroy Merlin, founded in 1923. After acquiring half of Leroy Merlin in 1979, the Auchan group took full control by 1981 and built up its network to more than 100 stores across France and Europe. Meanwhile, the company was enjoying huge success with its Decathlon sporting goods chain, created by family member Michel Leclerc, restaurant group Flunch, and then the electronics and home appliance chain Boulanger, acquired in 1986.

Nevertheless, the Auchan chain continued to drive the family's fortunes, as Auchan began to expand onto the international market in the 1980s. The company opened its first store in Saragosse, Spain—under the Alcampo banner—in 1981, building up that chain to nearly 40 hypermarkets and 90 supermarkets by the end of the 1990s. At the end of the 1980s, Auchan looked toward another southern European market, Italy, where it initiated a partnership with that country's IFIL. Auchan also joined the rush into retailing's Mecca—the vast United States market. The company opened several hypermarkets, but by the end of the 1990s remained with only one in operation, in Houston, Texas—the American consumer had proven reluctant to adopt the huge hypermarket format, which often required a mile of walking for a single shopping trip.

## Key Dates:

**1961:** Gerard Mulliez opens first Auchan store.
**1967:** First Auchan hypermarket is established.
**1977:** Company begins employee stock distribution program; launches national expansion.
**1981:** First international store opens in Spain.
**1989:** First store in Italy is opened, and a hypermarket in Houston, Texas, opens for business.
**1996:** Company initiates hostile takeover of Docks de France, as well as of Pao de Açucar (Portugal); opens first Poland store.
**1997:** Auchan enters Mexico, Thailand, and Argentina.
**1998:** Company enters Hungary.
**1999:** Company launches new Auchan brand name product range.

### *Consolidating in the 1990s*

Auchan was facing constraints at home, too. Faced with dwindling sales as the result of the deep economic recession that gripped France during much of the 1990s, Auchan was confronted with a growing backlash against its core hypermarket format. In the early 1990s, more and more voices were calling for limits on the rate of hypermarket expansion, and, by the mid-1990s, legislation had been passed that effectively stopped the building of new hypermarkets in France. Similar legislation began to appear in Spain and other countries as well.

Auchan, which had built up an empire of 80 hypermarkets, for annual sales worth FFr 64 billion, had taken a position as France's sixth largest distribution group. Yet Auchan's internal expansion in its home market was now severely limited. Only a handful of permits for new hypermarket construction were being granted each year. In addition, the company was under pressure from its larger competitors, particularly Carrefour, Casino, and market leader Leclerc, which enjoyed greater economies of scale. As a result, Auchan felt it had no choice but to make the "defensive" move of launching a hostile takeover of close competitor, and publicly listed, Docks de France, with its chain of Mammouth hypermarkets and Atac supermarkets, as well as 500 U.S.-based Lil'Champ convenience stores. This last chain, heavily in debt, was sold off in 1997.

The highly publicized takeover battle, a rarity in the French business world, sent Docks de France seeking a "white knight" in England—an even greater rarity in France. At last, however, Auchan had managed to gain majority control of Docks de France and, in 1997, completed its takeover. The takeover enabled Auchan to double in size, securing its position among France's top retailers. Despite the company's assurances that it would maintain the integrity of Docks de France, Auchan quickly began to dismantle the Docks de France organization, converting its Mammouth signage to Auchan, and then reorganized the entire company along format segments, keeping for the time being the Atac supermarket chain.

The integration of the Docks de France organization took nearly two years to complete and resulted in a new Auchan weighing in at more than FFr 147 billion in sales per year. The company's new size enabled it to pursue continued international expansion—soon after the Docks de France takeover, the company performed a similar takeover of Portugal's Pao de Açucar, giving it a new leading position in that market. In the late 1990s, the company targeted new strategic growth areas: in Central Europe, starting in Poland in 1996; in Italy, where in 1998 it strengthened its partnership agreement and launched a new phase of Gruppo Auchan openings; in the vast Asian market, beginning with the opening of stores in Thailand in 1997 and China in 1999; and the Latin American market, including the launch of Auchan stores in Argentina and Mexico. Back home, Auchan was refining its hypermarket concept in line with new consumer trends. The company abandoned its more than 200 brand names—which had ceased to be identified with Auchan by its shoppers—in favor of a single discount Auchan brand. The company similarly launched a new in-house clothing label, replacing its former multilabel offering.

Gerard Mulliez retired from day-to-day control of the empire he had founded in 1996. But the Mulliez family remained in full control of its group of companies—taking Mulliez's spot was cousin Christophe Dubrulle. Like the rest of the Mulliez family, Dubrulle had worked his way up through the family-owned ranks, beginning with a simple laborer's job before succeeding to positions as department head, store manager, and, finally, director of the Leroy Merlin chain, before being brought into Auchan as Mulliez's heir apparent. Gerard Mulliez nonetheless pledged to remain active in charting his family's empire's growth into the new century. Indeed, Mulliez had retired to the home he built for himself—right next door to the Auchan headquarters.

### *Principal Subsidiaries*

Leroy Merlin; Boulanger; Decathlon; Kiabi; Phildar; Flunch; Tapis Saint-Maclou.

### *Principal Competitors*

Carrefour S.A; Casino Guichard S.A.; Castorama S.A.; E. Leclerc; Guyenne et Gascogne S.A.; Lidl & Schwarz Stiftung; METRO AG; Pinault-Printemps-Redoute S.A.; Royal Ahold N.V.

### *Further Reading*

Gay, Pierre-Angel, "Auchan, qui achève l'absorption de Docks de France, va faire une pause," *Les Echos,* June 8, 1998, p. 20.
——, "En retard sur ses concurrents, Auchan relance sa politique de marque propre," *Les Echos,* February 10, 1999, p. 18.
——, "Le nouvel Auchan abat ses cartes," *Les Echos,* September 30, 1996, p. 19.
Phillipon, Thierry, and Christophe Bouchet, "Auchan: Ce mystérieux M. Mulliez," *Nouvel Observateur,* July 4, 1996, p. 58.

—M.L. Cohen

BANG & OLUFSEN

# Bang & Olufsen Holding A/S

Peter Bangs Vej 15
Struer DK-7600
Denmark
Telephone: +45-96-84-11-22
Fax: +45-96-84-11-44
Web site: http://www.bang-olufsen.com

*Public Company*
*Incorporated:* 1925
*Employees:* 2,783
*Sales:* DKK 3.4 billion ($397.78 million) (2000)
*Stock Exchanges:* Copenhagen
*Ticker Symbol:* BO-B.CO
*NAIC:* 551112 Offices of Other Holding Companies;
    33431 Audio and Video Equipment Manufacturing;
    33421 Telephone Apparatus Manufacturing; 334519
    Other Measuring & Controlling Device Manufacturing

Bang & Olufsen Holding A/S (B&O) is a leading consumer electronics firm, manufacturing a complete line of technologically sophisticated, sleekly designed stereos, speakers, televisions, and telephones. The company sells its products in 40 countries through a network of more than 2,000 stores that are partly owned by the company. Renowned for its attention to design and leading-edge technology, the company represents a singular force in the multibillion-dollar consumer electronics industry.

### B&O Begins with an Experiment

Peter Boas Bang and Svend Anreas Gron Olufsen grew up in era of swift technological innovation. Both were born around the time Guglielmo Marconi's made his 1901 transmittal of long-wave radio signals across the Atlantic Ocean in, a historic achievement that set the stage both youths' experiments with radios. At age 10, Peter Bang read about the world's first live radio transmission, Enrico Caruso's performance at New York's Metropolitan Opera in 1910. Soon after, he began his first experiments with radio, eventually leading him to pursue

an engineering degree at the Electrotechnical School in Århus, Denmark. After earning his degree in 1924, Bang moved to the United States, where the flourishing radio industry had 600 commercial broadcasting stations and so presented fertile ground for exploring his interests. In the United States, Bang worked at a service station and at a radio manufacturing plant, but he soon felt entrepreneurial urges again. After six months, Bang returned to Denmark, intent on starting his own business.

Back in Denmark, Svend Olufsen was busy building his own radio. Olufsen also liked to experiment with electricity and chemistry and had attended the Electrotechnical School at the same time as Bang, also earning an engineering degree. Olufsen began his radio experiments at his family's Quistrup estate, occupying a room in the attic where he started building a mains receiver, a radio that required neither accumulators nor the batteries needed to recharge them. While he was away at boarding school and later at the Electrotechnical School, Bang had written frequently to his father asking for money to pay for more batteries. Bang's mains receiver would be the prototype upon which Olufsen's experiments would be based.

At Quistrup, Olufsen's mains receiver was half finished when Bang returned from the United States. Olufsen needed help, and his former classmate was uniquely qualified to provide it. Bang left Copenhagen and traveled to the countryside in the west to the Olufsens' Quistrup. There, in the attic that would serve as B&O's first laboratory, Bang and Olufsen worked together on the mains receiver, a nest of thick copper wire and insulated cables that stretched from one side of the room to the other. The pair used the money Olufsen's mother received for selling the farm's eggs to finance their endeavor. Before long, Bang achieved his entrepreneurial dreams. In 1925, Bang and Olufsen, with the backing of their fathers, formed a limited company funded with DKK 10,000.

After traveling to Copenhagen, where the necessary papers were drawn up, naming Bang's father, Camillo Cavour Bang, as B&O's first chairman of the board, the two radio aficionados returned to Quistrup. Bang moved into the attic, putting his bed in the same room as the mains receiver. Bang and Olufsen hired the cowman's daughter as the company's sole employee, whose first task each morning was to wake up Bang 15 minutes before the

**Company Perspectives:**

*At the threshold of a new century, Bang & Olufsen's reputation remains second-to-none in the global market for leading-edge audio & video products. Little wonder that New York's Museum of Modern Art arranged a 39-piece special exhibition of Bang & Olufsen products in 1978—an honor only given to three other companies during the 20th century.*

company's day officially began. The company's first product was the B&O Eliminator, a device—an aggregate—that connected a battery receiver to the mains to produce noise-free current.

B&O grew quickly. By 1927, the activities in the attic had spread throughout the estate and spilled onto the lawns, where B&O Eliminators were assembled by a staff of 30. Quistrup could no longer accommodate the growth of the company's payroll and the sprawl of the manufacturing operations, forcing Bang and Olufsen to establish a new site for the company's headquarters. Their fathers, who together owned 20 percent of the company, remained unconvinced that radio would last, so they stipulated that the new factory be designed as a school building in case radio proved a fleeting fancy. In 1927, B&O moved into its new factory, and the company soon began development of a new radio.

### The Five Lamper Debuts in 1929

By 1929, the company had completed the design of its breakthrough radio, the "Five Lamper," and its peripheral "Type D" loudspeaker. Powered from the mains, the Five Lamper only required connection to an electrical outlet for operation. It was the company's first signal success, embodying the two characteristics that would define B&O's success in the decades to follow: style and technology. The Five Lamper was a technological marvel, displaying what would become a signature trait of B&O's products. The Five Lamper was also the first radio encased in a walnut cabinet, exuding elegance in design that drew its inspiration from the Danish furniture industry. For B&O, the combination of style and technology would prove to be a potent formula for success, becoming the foundation upon which all of its subsequent products were based.

The Five Lamper established B&O in the Danish market, securing a leading and lasting position for the West Jutland company, far removed from the hub of activity in Copenhagen. Strong sales and a sleek design at a time when radios were clunky and cumbersome set B&O apart, establishing a reputation that the company would solidify during the 1930s. During that decade, B&O introduced new products, including a radio gramophone in 1930 and several new radio models (Radio 5 RGF, Hyperbo 5 RGF, and Beolit 39). These products notwithstanding, the years preceding World War II were most notable for less tangible results. The 1930s saw B&O strengthen its image as a design-oriented, technology-driven company. It was a company that proclaimed itself as "The Danish Hallmark of Quality," registered as the company's slogan in 1931, and a company that bore a "pregnant B" inspired by the Bauhaus school of design as part of its corporate logo, trademarked in 1932.

The outbreak of World War II cast a pall over the future of B&O just as the company had taken a firm hold on the Danish market. Denmark was largely defenseless against the onrush of the German Blitzkrieg, and within seven months of the war's start, the country was occupied by German troops. Not surprisingly, raw materials became hard to come by, particularly radio tubes, but Bang and Olufsen had anticipated the war's arrival and had begun increasing their stock of essential parts as far back as 1935. Consequently, B&O was able to retain its full workforce during the first few years of the war, a rare feat for Danish manufacturing companies. Ultimately, however, B&O paid a price for its resilience and, specifically, for its resistance. In January 1945, the Germans bombed B&O's factory, targeting the building because the company had refused to collaborate and because a number of B&O employees were suspected Danish Resistance members. Construction of a new factory began the day after the bombing and was completed in early 1946, but it took another year before full production was resumed.

### A Pan-European Strategy Takes Shape in the 1960s

As B&O recovered from the turmoil of the 1940s, it enjoyed a brief respite before another portentous event clouded the company's future. After introducing electric shavers into the market in 1946—a diversification spawned from the scarcity of raw materials during World War II—B&O started manufacturing televisions and tape recorders, fleshing out its product line as it honed its skills in design. Beginning in the 1950s, the company began soliciting the help of Denmark's renowned architects and designers, drawing from the pool of talent that had made the Danish furniture industry an influential force in design. The effect of the company's collaboration with the country's leading designers became evident during the latter half of the 1950s, as B&O radios, televisions, and tape recorders earned high praise for their aesthetic appeal. At the same time, by the end of the 1950s, the company's prospects for survival appeared grim. A little more than a decade after rebuilding its factory, the company again faced the considerable might of the Germans, a face-off that few industry observers believed B&O could withstand.

B&O's concerns stemmed from the 1957 Treaty of Rome, which spawned the European Economic Community. Tariffs, duties, and customs were relaxed between member countries, leading to the consensus that the Danish radio industry, comprising approximately 20 small companies, would be subsumed by the superior strength of the much larger German manufacturers. The looming threat of much stiffer competition forced B&O to rethink its strategy, prompting the company to leverage its esteemed design expertise and its experience selling semiprofessional, high-fidelity equipment to the United States as the basis for its new approach. The company decided to sacrifice its leading market position in Denmark in order to concentrate on the much larger European market, forsaking dominance in a small market for a small share of a bigger market. In accordance with the new business focus, the company began to develop an entirely new line of stereo products that catered to the high end of the market, an approach evident in the slogan adopted during the 1960s: "B&O—for those who discuss taste and quality before price."

B&O's efforts to penetrate the European market bore fruit with the introduction of the Beomaster 900. The Beomaster 900 did to Europe what the Five Lamper had done to Denmark 30

<table>
<tr><td colspan="2">

**Key Dates:**

</td></tr>
<tr><td>**1925.**</td><td>Bang & Olufsen is formed as a limited company.</td></tr>
<tr><td>**1929:**</td><td>Introduction of the Five Lamper secures Bang & Olufsen's presence in the Danish market.</td></tr>
<tr><td>**1962:**</td><td>Concerted push into European markets begins.</td></tr>
<tr><td>**1975:**</td><td>Beomaster 1900 becomes best-selling product for next 20 years.</td></tr>
<tr><td>**1980:**</td><td>Company revenues drop due to Asian competition and internal corporate problems.</td></tr>
<tr><td>**1991:**</td><td>New management team spearheads recovery.</td></tr>
</table>

years earlier: the transistorized radio became a success throughout Europe, and despite the company's fears, its share of the Danish market did not diminish. The Treaty of Rome had forced many of the Danish manufacturers out of business, leaving B&O in a position to strengthen its domestic lead. By the time Beomaster 900 was introduced, B&O was ready to secure a presence in the then-developing market for high-fidelity systems. The company wanted to establish the standard by which all stereo systems would measured, an ideal that was realized with the Beolab 5000 series. Featuring a sensitive tuner, a powerful amplifier, and linear controls instead of knobs, the Beolab 5000 became B&O's second European success, spawning more affordable versions, Beomaster 1200 and Beomaster 3000.

Having established itself as a genuine contender in the vast European market, B&O spent the late 1960s restructuring its operations to conform to its new market orientation. The company established subsidiaries that replaced a network of agents that had previously carried out the international distribution. The reorganization included the formation of Bomark in 1970, which created an international marketing department responsible for coordinating all of the company's marketing activities. Previously, the company had taken whatever advertising it had created for the Danish market and used it to support its foreign marketing efforts, changing it only slightly to reflect cultural and market differences. The new system regarded the Danish market as only one of many markets, driving the company's evolution toward becoming a multinational concern. B&O marketing adopted the company's new perspective, as advertising campaigns became specifically tailored for the nuances of individual markets amid divergent cultures.

After the success of Beolab 5000, B&O next prodded its engineers and designers to develop a complete array of stereo components. The first product to make its debut was Beogram 4000, a turntable introduced in 1972 featuring a tangential arm that reproduced a recording in the same way in which it had been made. The record player was designed to target a different, much larger market segment, music lovers rather than the more exclusive retinue of technology-focused customers. Advanced technology, always an integral aspect of B&O's products, was not forsaken, but hidden beneath the surface, as the company's products earned a new distinction of exterior simplicity. This quality was first evident in Beomaster 1900, a system introduced in 1975 that market a turning point in the evolution of the B&O product line. For the next 20 years, Beomaster 1900 would be the company's best-selling product.

### Problems in the 1980s Are Resolved in the 1990s

This success notwithstanding, the 1980s proved to be a difficult decade for B&O, as the company struggled to beat back fierce competition from its Asian rivals. Although external pressures played their part, the company also fell victim to internal problems, problems of its own making that B&O's management was slow to acknowledge. The company's distributors lost faith in the B&O product line, and revenues began to slip. Initially, B&O tried to arrest its slide by narrowing its market focus on its wealthiest customers, but in the process the company's products lost some of their integrity, as substance was sacrificed for style. The company also tried to restore loyalty within its distributor ranks by staging seasonal product launches in exotic locations, but the effort failed. B&O's fundamental problem had to do with the decentralization that followed the company's full-fledged foray into international markets. The subsidiaries, by the 1980s, had become separate fiefdoms, which led to overspending, high costs, and superfluous bureaucratization. At the same time, the company had lost the ability to react nimbly to changing market conditions.

Before the end of the decade, B&O became a cash-strapped enterprise. The need for capital led to a strategic alliance with Koninklijke Philips Electronics N.V., the Dutch consumer electronics conglomerate, but the capital gained from the investment was soon drained. Rudderless and ailing financially, B&O entered the 1990s in crisis mode.

Salvation arrived in May 1991, when B&O's board of directors installed a new management team, led by Anders Knutsen. Knutsen's first task was to cut costs, an objective fulfilled by laying off employees, streamlining operations, and paring away excess layers of management. Knutsen also implemented a new strategic plan known as ''Break Point 1993,'' which addressed the problems born of the company's earlier decentralization. Knutsen reintroduced centralized management and made the company more responsive to the demands of its customers. Stocks of finished products and parts were removed from many of B&O's subsidiaries, as Knutsen transformed B&O from a company geared for mass production into an enterprise organized to fulfill customers' orders. The changes sparked a turnaround, refreshing the spirit and resharpening the focus that had predicated B&O's success.

At the end of the 1990s, B&O approached its 75th anniversary as a unique competitor in the consumer electronics industry. The company's attention to design and its long record of technological advancements remained the qualities that set the B&O name apart. With sales nearing the half-billion-dollar mark by the century's end, B&O promised to figure as a prominent force in the years ahead, as a new generation of high-technology stereos, speakers, and televisions, and telephones continued the legacy established by Peter Bang and Svend Olufsen.

### Principal Subsidiaries

Bang & Olufsen Medicom A/S; Bang & Olufsen Telecom A/S; Bang & Olufsen Technology A/S; Bang & Olufsen Power-House A/S; Bang & Olufsen America, Inc.

### Principal Competitors

Bose Corporation; Harman International Industries, Inc.; Matsushita Electric Industrial Co., Ltd.

### Further Reading

Baeb, Eddie, ''Bang & Olufsen Marching to Its Own Drummer,'' *Crain's Chicago Business,* October 30, 2000, p. 9.

''Bang & Olufsen Divest Shareholding in Baan NV,'' *M2 Communications Ltd.,* January 4, 2000.

Bang, Jens, *From Vision to Legend,* Denmark: Bang & Olufsen, 1999.

''Business Diary: Agreements: Visteon Automotive,'' *Crain's Detroit Business,* June 21, 1999.

Carnoy, David, ''Bang for the Buck,'' *Fortune,* May 1, 2000, p. 362.

''Harvey Electronics, Inc. Announces Opening of Bang & Olufsen Showroom in Greenwich, Connecticut,'' *Business Wire,* October 18, 2000.

''Toys for the Ear,'' *Boston Herald,* December 5, 1999, Sunday Magazine Section.

—Jeffrey L. Covell

# Banner Aerospace, Inc.

45025 Aviation Drive, Suite 400
Dulles, Virginia 20166
U.S.A.
Telephone: (703) 478-5790
Fax: (703) 478-5795
Web site: http://www.banner.com

*Wholly Owned Subsidiary of The Fairchild Corporation*
*Incorporated:* 1956 as Banner Hardware Jobbing Co.
*Employees:* 375
*Sales:* $101 million (2000)
*NAIC:* 54171 Research and Development in the Physical,
    Engineering, and Life Sciences; 336412 Aircraft
    Engine and Engine Parts Manufacturing; 336413
    Other Aircraft Parts and Auxiliary Equipment
    Manufacturing

Banner Aerospace, Inc. overhauls and distributes rotable aircraft parts—components that are meant to be recycled. Its products include flight data recorders, avionics, and defense and space equipment. Banner sells its products to commercial airlines, air cargo carriers, original equipment manufacturers, and other distributors. About one-third of its sales are made internationally. The company had kept a low profile until the mid-1980s, when Jeffrey J. Steiner assumed control and began using it as an investment and takeover vehicle. In the latter half of that decade, Banner's rapid-fire, junk-bond-financed acquisitions earned it a reputation as "the KKR (Kohlberg, Kravis, Roberts and Co.) of public companies." Banner focused on its core businesses after its circle of finance collapsed with the aviation industry slowdown of the early 1990s.

### Origins

Although Banner Aerospace is legally a successor to Burbank Aircraft Supply, Inc., its history can more accurately be traced through Banner Industries, Inc.. According to *Moody's Industrial Manual,* the original Banner Hardware Jobbing Co. was incorporated in 1956. Its name was abbreviated to Banner Industries in 1960, and the firm was reincorporated in 1970 under that name. Samuel J. Krasney is credited with saving Banner Industries from bankruptcy in 1968 and slowly building the Cleveland company into a major player in the secondary aerospace parts industry. While Krasney planned to grow through acquisition, many of his early purchases proved to be missteps. Patterson Industries, Inc. was acquired in 1968 and divested in 1973; Misceramic Tile, Inc. was bought in 1969 and sold four years later; and Advance Foundry was purchased in 1969 and sold in 1975.

### Success in the 1970s

The 1970s brought better fortunes. The 1972 acquisition of Thompson Aircraft Tire Corp. established Banner as the exclusive distributor of Japanese-made Bridgestone aircraft tires. By the mid-1980s, tires and retreads contributed one-fifth of the company's annual sales, and Thompson ranked as the largest independent retreader of aircraft tires in the world. In 1973 Banner bought Burbank Aircraft Supply, Inc., a subsidiary that would grow to become the group's largest revenue generator. The California-based company ranked as one of the most important distributors of aircraft fasteners, fittings, and electrical components in the global aircraft industry. Krasney's methodical acquisition strategy proved successful, and the group ended the 1970s with record earnings.

During the early 1980s, forays into manufacturing and trucking proved poorly timed. The company's trucking subsidiary, Lee Way Holding Co., fell into Chapter 11 bankruptcy in 1985. This transport company had been formed through the 1977 merger of the newly acquired Lovelace Truck Service, Inc. with Commercial Motor Freight, Inc. (acquired in 1969). The deregulation of the interstate trucking industry was cited as the cause of the subsidiary's failure. Throughout the early 1980s, the $100 million company was unable to surpass 1979's earnings record of $5 million. In 1982, Banner dipped into the red, and Thomas Jaffe of *Forbes* speculated that Banner's difficulties made it a prime takeover candidate.

The company's financial difficulties also took a heavy toll on CEO Krasney. After three rounds of heart surgery, Krasney decided to rid himself of the problematic company. He reduced his stake in Banner from 38 percent to 28 percent in 1983 with the sale of 400,000 shares to the venture capital fund Warburg, Pincus Capital Corp. Although he still remained active in the company, Krasney sold most of his remaining interest in Banner two years later to Jeffrey J. Steiner for $15 million. Steiner also picked up Warburg, Pincus's shares, raising his stake to 39 percent by mid-1988.

### A Raider Takes Over in 1985

Steiner brought a cosmopolitan air to Banner. Born in Austria, he spoke four languages and maintained residences in London, Paris, St. Tropez, Palm Beach, and New York. As a child during World War II, Steiner had fled with his Jewish father and Turkish mother from Austria to his mother's homeland. He later earned a degree in textile engineering from Britain's Bradford Institute of Technology. After graduation, he planned to work in the United States for one year, then go home to his family's textile business. Plans changed when the young sales trainee at Texas Instruments quickly advanced through the corporate ranks to become president of subsidiaries in France, Mexico, and Switzerland. By the time he was 25, Steiner had earned a position on Texas Instruments' management committee.

After ten years at Texas Instruments, Steiner returned to Europe to found Cedec S.A., a turnkey engineering firm headquartered in Paris. Steiner began dabbling in investing on the side, concentrating primarily on the European energy market in the 1970s. Then, in 1981, he decided to cash out of Europe and try his hand at the American investment scene. Banner proved to be the opportunity he was looking for.

As chairman and CEO, Steiner oversaw financing and acquisition planning from his Manhattan office, while Krasney continued to make a significant contribution to Banner's day-to-day activities as vice-chairman and chief operating officer in Cleveland. A hard-working risk-taker, Steiner took his cues from corporate raiders like Carl Icahn and Nelson Peltz. In partnership with Icahn in the early 1980s, Steiner amassed stakes in Marshall Field, Uniroyal Co., and Phillips Petroleum Co. According to *Business Week,* Steiner hoped his Banner Industries would grow like "Peltz's Triangle Industries Inc., which [had] built a $3 billion empire using Drexel financing to buy old-line industrials it then tries to fix up." Through Banner, Steiner began, in the words of Robert McGough of *Financial World,* to "trade subsidiaries like a stockbroker with a blind account."

Steiner, who was elected chairman and chief executive officer late in 1985, acquired Solair Inc., a broad-based aircraft

equipment supplier with about $10 million in annual sales, by the end of 1986. The new leader took Banner into the world of junk-bond financing in 1987 with the acquisition of Rexnord Automation Inc., a diversified manufacturer of oil pipeline and refining equipment, water pollution control systems, and aerospace fasteners. The total $825 million price tag dwarfed Banner's $149 million annual sales, but Drexel Burnham Lambert prepared a successful financing package. Krasney candidly acknowledged to *Crain's Cleveland Business* that he "never in a thousand years would have done something this big."

Within less than two years, Steiner liquidated $825 million worth of Rexnord's assets, including the subsidiary's research and development operations, Bellofram Corp., Mathews Conveyor Co., Railway Maintenance Equipment Co., and Fairfield Manufacturing Co. in order to meet Banner's $3.2 million monthly interest charges. Steiner also cut a deal with former employer Texas Instruments Inc. for the divestment of Rexnord Automation Inc., raising $65 million with this transaction alone. The sales recouped Rexnord's purchase price, yet allowed Banner to retain 40 percent of Rexnord's earning power. Steiner characterized his strategy to *Financial World* as "a combination of industrial restructuring and LBOs."

The acquisitions spree powered a 39 percent growth rate from 1984 to 1989, ranking Banner among *Fortune*'s 25 fastest-growing companies. By 1989, Steiner increased Banner's net worth fourfold to $160 million and the firm had amassed more than $1 billion in assets. Annual sales volume tripled from $128 million in 1985 to $433 million in 1989, and net income multiplied to about $50 million. Although $525 million in debt was retired during the period, the company was still highly leveraged, with about $620 million in outstanding junk bonds.

Instead of using Banner's cash flow to settle these obligations, Steiner continued to leverage the company's borrowing power to finance new deals. Banner acquired Indianapolis-based rival PT Components late in 1988 for an estimated $175 million cash. Steiner merged the formerly privately held PT Components—one of the leading manufacturers of power transmission parts in the United States—with Rexnord's mechanical power division and sold about 60 percent of the resulting Rexnord Corp.'s shares to outside investors.

### Joining Fairchild in 1989

Banner acted as white knight to Fairchild Industries in 1989 when it rescued the company from a year-long hostile assault from the Carlyle Group, a Washington, D.C., merchant bank. The $265 million cash transaction increased Banner's consolidated annual revenues by more than 100 percent to almost $1 billion. The merged companies underwent a complicated reshuffling in the ensuing months. Banner Industries and Fairchild were united under the name the Fairchild Corporation in 1990. Although Fairchild was the larger of the two, the "new" Fairchild was legally considered a successor to Banner Industries.

Throughout all of the mergers, the Banner name was not retired: Steiner reorganized Banner Industries' Aerospace Distribution Group as Banner Aerospace, Inc. in 1990. This "new" company's legal predecessor and primary subsidiary was Bur-

## Key Dates:

**1968:** Samuel J. Krasney saves Banner Industries, Inc. from bankruptcy.
**1973:** Banner buys Burbank Aircraft Inc.
**1982:** Trucking industry troubles dip Banner into red ink.
**1985:** Jeffrey J. Steiner takes control of Banner Industries, using it as a vehicle for leveraged buyouts.
**1990:** Banner's aerospace division restructured as a subsidiary of The Fairchild Corporation.
**1994:** Steiner engineers a turnaround at Banner Aerospace, Inc.
**1999:** The Fairchild Corporation buys Banner Aerospace's remaining shares.

bank Aircraft Supply. Samuel J. Krasney was named Banner Aerospace's CEO, president, and chairman.

The Fairchild deal became the capstone of a precarious pyramid of leverage that began to crumble in the early 1990s. Defense cutbacks, increased competition, and general economic difficulties depressed the aviation industry. The downturn cut into cash flow when both Banner and Fairchild needed it most. By late 1990, Banner/Fairchild's cash flow barely covered its expenses. In August 1990 Fairchild sold about 53 percent of Banner Aerospace's equity to outside investors. Fairchild divested other subsidiaries to raise the funds needed to meet its debt payments.

Banner Aerospace's sales and earnings increased from $218.59 million and $15.98 million in 1990 to $264.44 million and $19.03 million in 1991, but began to decline in 1992. Sales declined to $205.12 million by 1994 and Banner lost a total earnings of $14.84 million in 1993 and 1994. The closure of two subsidiaries—Banner Aeronautical Corp. and Aero International Inc.—accounted for $11 million of that deficit. Banner also blamed intense price competition for its red ink.

After a quarter-century with Banner in Cleveland, Samuel Krasney retired in September 1993. The firm's 17-person headquarters was moved to Chantilly, Virginia, and Krasney was succeeded by Jeffrey Steiner, who engineered a quick turnaround in 1994. Banner squeaked out of its losing position with a $475,000 profit and an optimistic outlook in fiscal 1995.

### Focusing in the Mid-1990s

As part of its comeback, Banner began to focus on rotables, and divested non-core businesses. It sold Austin Jet Corp. and AJ Aerospace Services Inc. to an outside investor in January 1995. It also sold Barcel Wire & Cable Corp. to that unit's CEO. To reduce costs, Burbank Aircraft Supply's warehouse and distribution operations were relocated to Salt Lake City beginning in late 1995. Boosted by a strong fourth quarter performance, Banner was able to report a 29 percent sales increase in the 1996 fiscal year; net income was $1.6 million on revenues of $287.9 million.

Banner acquired Harco, Inc., a precision fasteners distributor based in El Segundo, California, with annual sales of about

$30 million, from The Fairchild Corporation in March 1996 for about $27 million in stock. This brought Fairchild's holding in Banner from 47 percent to 58 percent. After the acquisition, Harco's president, Tucker Nason, was named CEO of Banner's largest subsidiary, Burbank Aircraft Supply, Inc..

Nine months after buying Harco, Banner added another fastener distributor to its portfolio. St. Louis-based P.B. Herndon Company had annual sales of $20 million when it was acquired in January 1997. The next month, Banner announced a rights offering to raise $28 million for debt reduction and future acquisitions. At the same time, Banner was acquiring another Fairchild subsidiary, the Scandinavian Bellyloading Company. This $2 million business specialized in on-board cargo loading systems for narrow-body airliners.

Strategic acquisitions and recovery of the aviation industry helped lift Banner's earnings by 375 percent in the 1997 fiscal year. Net income was $7.5 million on sales of $389.1 million, about a third of which were derived overseas. Long-term contracts with several major airlines were credited with improving profits internally.

Banner sold its Hardware Group and PacAero chemicals unit to AlliedSignal in January 1998. The New Jersey-based maker of components for the automotive and aerospace industries gave Banner $345 million worth of stock for the units, which extended its aircraft parts line. Banner planned to spend half the money to reduce debt. AlliedSignal expected annual revenues of $250 million from the acquisitions—equal to what Banner expected from its own remaining units.

The divestment left Banner Aerospace with rotables and engine groups. The sale of its Hardware Group pushed income for the 1998 fiscal year to $81.5 million; sales for the year were $420.3 million. Another significant divestment was announced in December 1998: Solair Inc. was being acquired by Kellstrom Industries, a reseller of aircraft and engines. It had accounted for 30 percent of Banner's revenues; Kellstrom, which had annual sales of about $180 million, agreed to pay about $60 million for Solair, which manufactured coffee makers as well as landing gear.

By the late 1990s, Fairchild's shareholding in Banner Aerospace had risen to 85 percent. On December 3, 1998, a merger of the two companies was announced. They both already shared the same CEO and chairman: Jeffrey J. Steiner. Fairchild formally acquired the outstanding stock on April 8, 1999.

### Principal Subsidiaries

DAC International, Inc.; Georgetown Jet Center, Inc.; Matrix Aviation, Inc.; NASAM, Inc.; Professional Aircraft Accessories, Inc.; Professional Aviation Associates, Inc.

### Principal Divisions

Avionics; Rotables; Repair and Overhaul; Defense and Space.

### Principal Competitors

Air Ground Equipment Services; Duncan Aviation; Honeywell; Litton; Rockwell Collins; Stevens Aviation.

### *Further Reading*

Ashyk, Loretta, "Just Like Any Guy?" *Crain's Cleveland Business,* March 9, 1987, p. 1.

Giesen, Lauri, "Banner Sells off Rexnord R&D Unit to Pay Down Debt," *Metalworking News,* July 13, 1987, p. 4.

Gordon, Mitchell, "Put Out the Pennants," *Barron's,* April 28, 1986, p. 54.

Jaffe, Thomas, "Happy Landing," *Forbes,* October 21, 1985, p. 210.

Jones, Sam L., "Fastener Industry Riveted by Sudden Talk of Mergers," *Metalworking News,* October 31, 1988, p. 1.

Livingston, Sandra, "Banner to Take Over Fairchild," *Cleveland Plain Dealer,* May 9, 1989, p. 1D.

McGough, Robert, "Banner Industries: Do Your Homework," *Financial World,* October 16, 1990, p. 20.

Phillips, Stephen, "Banner Aerospace to Relocate," *Cleveland Plain Dealer,* August 12, 1993, p. 1E.

"PT Components Acquired by Banner Industries," *Industrial Distribution,* September 1988, p. 15.

Sabath, Donald, "Banner Aerospace Loss Due to Air-Transport Woes," *Cleveland Plain Dealer,* May 27, 1993, p. F2.

Schiller, Zachary, and Kathleen Deveny, "The Next Takeover Artist You Meet Could Be Jeff Steiner," *Business Week,* February 9, 1987, p. 33.

Taub, Stephen, "The KKR of Public Companies?" *Financial World,* March 21, 1989, p. 14.

—April Dougal Gasbarre
—updated by Frederick C. Ingram

# Boca Resorts, Inc.

**501 East Camino Real**
**Boca Raton, Florida 33432**
**U.S.A.**
**Telephone: (561) 447-5300**
**Fax: (561) 447-5315**
**Web site: http://www.bocaresortsinc.com**

*Public Company*
*Incorporated:* 1996
*Employees:* 4,772
*Sales:* $421.5 million (2000)
*Stock Exchanges:* New York
*Ticker Symbol:* RST
*NAIC:* 711211 Sports Teams and Clubs; 711310
    Promoters of Performing Arts, Sports, and Similar
    Events with Facilities; 721110 Hotels (Except
    Casinos); 713940 Fitness and Recreational Sports
    Centers

Boca Resorts Inc. owns and operates six world-class hotels: Boca Raton Resort & Club; the Radisson Bahia Mar Beach Resort and the Hyatt Regency Pier 66 in Fort Lauderdale, Florida; The Registry Resort and the Edgewater Beach Hotel in Naples, Florida; and the Arizona Biltmore Resort & Spa in Phoenix, Arizona. Beyond the luxury accommodations and amenities, each hotel has its own distinctive: history, one-of-a-kind location, or rich, natural surroundings. Boca Resorts also owns the Florida Panthers hockey team, the National Car Rental Center, home ice for the team, Incredible Ice Skating Rinks, and the Miami Arena. Billionaire H. Wayne Huizenga owns 98 percent of Boca Resorts.

### *Early 1990s Sporting Origins*

Boca Resorts originated as Florida Panthers Holdings when the National Hockey League (NHL) awarded H. Wayne Huizenga the franchise for the Florida Panthers hockey team. Huizenga had built his fortune on two highly successful companies, Waste Management, of which he was co-founder, and Blockbuster Video, which he headed during its period of greatest growth. Huizenga secured a $45 million loan to purchase the franchise, and the company put together a team in time to play in the 1993–94 hockey season. The Florida Panthers played at the Miami Arena, home court for the Miami Heat basketball team.

Although Huizenga promised the NHL that he would build a new arena for the Panthers, it was also in the financial interests of the company to have its own arena. At the Miami Arena the Heat held exclusive rights to advertising revenues and luxury suites and paid only $13,500 per game to play there. The Panthers paid $30,000 per game plus 7 percent of ticket revenues for games that exceeded $250,000 in sales; during the first season, ticket revenues averaged $355,000 per game.

The Broward County Commissioners approved the plan for a tax-funded arena in Sunrise in June 1996. Under the agreement, the Panthers received 95 percent of revenue from ticket and merchandise sales and advertising signage and all of the revenue from 50 luxury skyboxes and 2,400 club seats. The team also received the first $14 million in operating profits and 80 percent of additional profits for managing the arena. Construction on the $185-million facility began in 1997.

The future financial success of the team depended on a new arena because Florida Panthers Holdings operated at loss. With revenues of $33.3 million, the company lost $11.1 million on operations in fiscal year ending September 30, 1996. Amortization of the cost of the franchise and interest expense resulted in an actual loss of $25.5 million. The loss was due in part to the doubling of player salaries, from a total of $10.2 million in the team's first season to $20.1 million in the 1995–96 season, but was mitigated by participation in the playoffs, which earned a $3.3-million profit. To be sure that the Panthers and the Marlins received adequate airplay in the future, Huizenga acquired 50 percent of SportsChannel Florida Associates.

Huizenga took Florida Panthers Holdings public in November 1996, seeking funds to pay debt and to cover losses. At $10 per share, Huizenga offered 4.6 million shares to private investors for a minimum purchase of 100 shares. The general public could buy a minimum of one share as Huizenga fostered fan ownership as a novelty, purchased for emotional satisfaction

**Company Perspectives:**

*We are in the business of marketing a one-of-a-kind experience. We specialize in catering to guests, individuals, and groups, with customized service. Our combination of exceptional service and unique locations had earned our resorts a reputation as superior destinations, ideal for business and pleasure.*

rather as a serious investment. Trading started at $11.50 per share but ended the day at $11.12 due to the emotional nature of investor interest as more than 8,000 fans purchased one to ten shares. Under the NHL franchise agreement, Huizenga retained a 51 percent ownership of the team. The offering raised $67.3 million after expenses.

### Huizenga Changes Direction After IPO

The Florida Panthers became the second professional sports team to be publicly owned without unrelated investments. However, when Florida Panthers Holdings stock remained stagnant after the public offering, Huizenga decided to diversify the company into a sports, leisure, and entertainment conglomerate to attract serious investors. In December 1996 the company purchased two premier Fort Lauderdale hotels, the Hyatt Regency Pier 66 Resort and Marina and the Radisson Bahia Mar Beach Resort and Marina. Both stood out because they were on the Intercoastal Waterway, minutes from beaches and Fort Lauderdale's Las Olas Boulevard. Huizenga and some business associates held an 80 percent interest in the hotels, and Rahn Properties, which managed the hotel, owned the other 20 percent. Florida Panthers Holdings acquired ownership from Huizenga and Rahn Properties through a stock and cash transaction valued at $125 million. The diversification boosted the company's stock to $17 per share.

Through a private sale of stock in January 1997, Florida Panthers Holdings raised $68.2 million for further acquisitions. The private placement at $27.75 per share led to an increase in publicly traded shares to $30.62 per share. The stock rate was equivalent to three times the actual value of the company. Investors trusted Huizenga and expected his new endeavor to do well because as cofounder of Waste Management and chairman of Blockbuster Entertainment, he led those companies during their greatest growth.

Huizenga continued to expand the company's holdings. Florida Panthers Holdings purchased the renowned Boca Raton Resort and Club near West Palm Beach, Florida, for $325 million in stock and cash. Facilities at the 298-acre included a golf club and two golf courses, a marina, and a private beach. The purchase involved development plans, such as the state-of-the art conference center, then under construction.

Florida Panthers Holdings as a sports business acquired Florida ice-skating facilities. In January 1997 the Panthers bought Incredible Ice, a state-of-the-art, interactive ice-skating facility in Coral Springs, Florida, for $13 million in stock, cash, and debt assumption. The 75,000-square-foot facility housed two full-size ice rinks, spectator seating, training rooms, a

sports bar, and a retail store. The following summer the company acquired the lease to operate the Gold Coast Ice Arena in Pompano Beach, the practice rink for the Panthers and also home ice for the Gold Coast Minor Hockey League and the FGC Figure Skating Club.

Florida Panthers Holdings continued to add luxury resorts to its investments. In August 1997 the company acquired controlling interest in the Registry Hotel at Pelican Bay in Naples, Florida, a 474-room, four-star hotel considered one of the state's top ten resorts. The following December the company gained a majority interest in the prestigious Arizona Biltmore for $288.5 million in stock, cash, and debt assumption. The work of Frank Lloyd Wright inspired the design of the 1929 luxury resort at the base of Squaw Peak.

The Boca Raton's $46 million, 140,000-square-foot conference center opened in January 1998, allowing the hotel to serve more than one large group simultaneously. The presence of the meeting center lowered the hotel's rating from five to four stars, but it attracted a record number of conferences. The company planned further expansions and renovation at an anticipated cost of $55 million.

The company also planned a Country Pursuits Centre near the Everglades National Park as a response to growing interest in adventure tourism. The center would offer lessons in fly-fishing, shooting, hunting with dogs, and falconry, hunting wild fowl and game with falcons, though no killing would be allowed. Zoning issues with the county and the water district, however, delayed completion of the project.

In April 1998 Florida Panthers Holdings bought the Edgewater Beach Hotel, a four-star, all-suite hotel in Naples, for $41.2 million. The company began constructing a golf course to serve guests at both the Edgewater and The Registry and acquired complete ownership of The Registry in July. The company also purchased a golf course in Plantation for use of guests of the Bahia Mar and Pier 66 hotels, but zoning restrictions held up planned renovations.

### Panthers Attain Profitability in 1998

As revenues from hotels covered losses from the hockey team, Florida Panthers Holdings recorded its first profit for fiscal year ending June 30, 1998. On revenue of $293.3 million, the company realized a net income of $1.3 million. This compared to fiscal 1997 revenues of $54.3 million and losses of $10.3 million. The Panthers became more profitable as the team sold out all home games for the 1996–97 and 1997–98 seasons, but player salaries rose $18.7 million. Losses from the hockey team reached $20.4 million in fiscal 1998, while acquisitions caused revenues from leisure and recreation businesses to jump from $17.6 million in 1997 to $252.6 million in fiscal 1998. The company expected increased revenue from the new hockey arena to improve the hockey team's profitability.

The new Panthers hockey arena in Sunrise opened as the 872,000-square-foot, multipurpose National Car Rental Center in October 1998. National Car Rental, a subsidiary of Huizenga's Republic Industries, was awarded the naming rights for the arena for $25 million to be paid incrementally over ten years. In its first year, the center hosted 150 events, including

## Key Dates:

**1992:** H. Wayne Huizenga is awarded hockey franchise and forms team to begin play in 1993–94 season.

**1993:** The Florida Panthers hockey team plays first season.

**1996:** Company is incorporated, makes its initial public offering of stock, and begins acquiring luxury hotels.

**1999:** Huizenga changes the company name to reflect primary focus of operating luxury hotels and resorts and announces plans to sell hockey team.

sell-out concerts by the Rolling Stones, Neil Diamond, and 'N Sync, attended by a total of more than $1 million people.

The new arena did improve the profitability of the hockey team. The Panthers sold 15,500 season tickets to the team's 41 home games, for an overall increase of 4,000 spectators per game. It held 19,500 seats, 4,500 more than the Miami Arena, and also had 70 luxury skyboxes. The facility increased entertainment and sports revenues for fiscal 1999 more than 50 percent, to $62.6 million, while operating expenses increased less than 10 percent. Overall, Florida Panthers Holdings had a net income of $5.4 million.

The new arena did not increase the stock price of Florida Panthers Holdings as Huizenga had hoped. The company's stock held at $10 per share, in part because of a general decline in the value of hotel stocks. Another private offering of stock in February 1999 raised $40.3 million, selling four million shares at $10.25 per share. The company also permitted existing investors to buy one share for every ten owned. The offering raised $16 million, but Huizenga wanted to raise $30 million to pay short-term debt from the acquisition of the Arizona Biltmore. With improved profitability of the new arena, rumors began to circulate that Huizenga might sell the hockey team to pay debt, and shift his focus to luxury resorts.

### Strategies for Growth

Florida Panthers Holdings pursued internal growth, building on the strengths of its distinguished hotels. Huizenga planned to spread the Boca Raton's excellence to the company's other properties and to develop the resort's Premier Club concept at the other hotels. Premier Club members paid an initiation fee and annual dues for use of the resort facilities.

The company also initiated several capital improvement projects, including guest rooms at The Hyatt Pier 66 ($8.4 million), renovation of the 27,000 square foot club house, an upgraded golf course, redesigned by Raymond Floyd, and a new three-par golf course. Renamed Grande Oaks Golf Club, the facility reopened in June 1999. The company also completed a new golf course, designed by Rees Jones, for patrons of the two hotels in Naples. In September the Arizona Biltmore finished a new, $12-million wing, adding 122 luxury rooms and an Olympic-size swimming pool. New construction at the Boca Raton Resort encompassed 114 luxury suites with a view of the marina, additional boat slips, and new retail space.

Florida Panthers Holdings did increase both profits and bookings through a strategy to improve sales and reduce overhead by replacing outside management companies at the Pier 66, Bahia Mar, and the Arizona Biltmore with its own employees. The company also raised the 60 percent occupancy rate at the Arizona Biltmore after it increased expenditures for marketing to $4.4 million, compared to less than $1 million previously, and added sales representatives in major U.S. cities and advertisements in Canada and Europe.

In September 1999 Florida Panthers Holdings changed its name to Boca Resorts to reflect the company's emphasis on luxury resort and conference accommodations. Shortly after, the company announced its interest in selling the hockey team, as predicted, and also considered unsolicited offers to buy the Arizona Biltmore.

Boca Resorts planned to maintain its focus on internal growth rather than acquisitions, continuing to renovate hotel facilities and add new services. Boca Resorts expected to begin construction on a new luxury spa, a golf club house, and a casual restaurant in 2000. In February 2000 Boca Resorts introduced the Premier Club concept at the Edgewater and The Registry hotels, requiring members to pay a $45,000 initiation fee plus $2,300 in annual dues, and an additional $5,000 per year for use of tennis and golf facilities. The company also instituted online, real-time room reservations.

Revenues for fiscal 2000 reached $421.5 million, garnering net income of $13.5 million. Much of the increase was due to increases in the average daily rate for hotel rooms, increased occupancy, and increased availability, as well as higher occupancy at the Arizona Biltmore. The Panthers reached the first round of the Stanley Cup playoffs, generating an additional $1.2 million in ticket sales, but this only offset an overall decrease in sports and entertainment revenues compared to fiscal 1999.

### Principal Subsidiaries

Florida Panthers Hockey Club, Ltd.; Arena Operating Company, Ltd.; Decoma Miami Associates, Ltd. (78%).

### Principal Competitors

Hyatt Corporation; Marriott International, Inc.; Starwood Hotels and Resorts Worldwide, Inc.; Wyndham International, Inc.

### Further Reading

Commisso, Marco, ''Boca Raton, Fla., Resort Has Helped Transform Once-Sleepy Town,'' *Knight-Ridder/Tribune Business News*, August 7, 1997.

Corbett, Peter, ''Phoenix-Area Resort is in Talks to be Sold,'' *Knight-Ridder/Tribune Business News*, April 4, 2000.

Corbett, Sue, ''Broward, Team Could Gain if Panthers Move,'' *Miami Herald*, March 4, 1994, p. 1A.

Fakler, John T, ''Boca Resorts' Plan for Wilderness Center Bogs Down,'' *South Florida Business Journal*, April 14, 2000, p. 4B.

''Florida Panthers Holdings, Inc. Closes on The Registry Hotel in Naples,'' *PR Newswire*, August 12, 1997.

Goodman, Cindy Krischer, ''Florida-Based Resort Firm to Drop Hockey Team's Name,'' *Knight-Ridder/Tribune Business News*, September 15, 1999.

——. ''Panthers Stock Leaps After Promo on CNN,'' *Miami Herald*, January 24, 1997, p. 1C.

Grimm, Fred, ''Panthers Fan not Cheering Stock Prices,'' *Miami Herald*, May 19, 1998, p. 1BR.

Hilton, Lisette, ''Boca Raton Resort is Going to the Dogs—Fishy Stuff, Too,'' *South Florida Business Journal,* August 14, 1998, p. 7A.

Jackson, Barry, ''Balancing the Book on the Panthers' Finances '96 Playoff Ride Profitable, but Losses Still Top $11 Million,'' *Miami Herald*, November 17, 1996, p. 7C.

——, ''Cats Revenue to Soar; Spending Won't,'' *Miami Herald*, May 9, 1998, p. 2D.

Kay, Julie, ''Arena Officially Named for Car Rental Company,'' *Miami Herald*, July 15, 1998, p. 1BR.

Magenheim, Henry, ''Huizenga Group to Buy Boca Raton Resort & Club,'' *Travel Weekly*, March 27, 1997, p. 31.

Muellner, Alexis, ''Will Sale of the Panthers Boost Boca Resorts' Stock?'' *South Florida Business Journal*, November 12, 1999, p. 18.

Ostrowski, Jeff, ''Wayne's Shopping Spree—Billions and Billions in Just 7 Months,'' *South Florida Business Journal*, January 31, 1997, p. 14A.

Rafinski, Karen, ''It's official: Florida Panthers Will Make Sunrise New Home,'' *Miami Herald*, June 5, 1996, p. 2B.

Rodgers, Jodi, and Alexis Muellner, ''Panthers' Business Plan: Diversify, Pump up Resort Jewels,'' *South Florida Business Journal*, November 6, 1998, p. 20A.

—Mary Tradii

# Boston Scientific Corporation

**1 Boston Scientific Place**
**Natick, Massachusetts 01760-1537**
**U.S.A.**
**Telephone: (508) 650-8000**
**Fax: (508) 647-2200**
**Web site: http://www.bsci.com**

*Public Company*
*Incorporated:* 1979
*Employees:* 13,500
*Sales:* $2.84 billion (1999)
*Stock Exchanges:* New York
*Ticker Symbol:* BSX
*NAIC:* 339112 Surgical and Medical Instrument
   Manufacturing

Boston Scientific Corporation is a pioneer in providing medical devices for less invasive surgical procedures. As improvements in medical imaging made such procedures more practical, the company established itself as a leader in coronary stents and stent systems. After going public in 1992 the company grew tremendously through acquisitions, with revenue reaching $2.84 billion in 1999. Toward the end of the decade, however, the company began experiencing such problems as product recalls and a financial scandal that caused its stock to fall out of favor with Wall Street.

### Early History: 1969–79

Boston Scientific Corporation was founded in 1979 by John Abele and Peter Nicholas, who met while watching their children play soccer. Nicholas, a Wharton M.B.A., had worked for pharmaceutical company Ely Lilly & Co. since 1968. Nicholas was mainly interested in management; Abele was more technically oriented. He had majored in philosophy and physics at Amherst and had been employed selling medical devices for Advanced Instruments, Inc. In 1968 Abele met Itzak Bentov, inventor of a steerable catheter that was used in less invasive surgical procedures. With financial backing from Cooper Labo-

ratories, Abele began marketing the device through Medi-Tech, Inc., a company in which Abele had acquired an equity interest. In 1969 Medi-Tech introduced its first products, a family of steerable catheters that were used in some of the first less invasive procedures.

By the time Abele and Nicholas met, Cooper Laboratories wanted to sell the medical device company. Abele and Nicholas founded Boston Scientific Corporation for the purpose of acquiring Medi-Tech, Inc. The two men received $500,000 in bank financing and raised another $300,000.

In its first year Boston Scientific reported revenues of about $2 million. Its first products included catheters for gall bladder surgery. The early 1980s marked a period of active marketing, new product development, and organizational growth. The company focused on catheters and other products that could be used as alternatives to traditional surgery. As medical imaging techniques improved, less invasive procedures became more feasible. The catheters allowed doctors to perform surgical procedures through little incisions. Such procedures were also much less expensive. The company soon expanded its line of catheter-based devices to include heart, vascular, respiratory, gastrointestinal, and urological applications.

### Capital Needs Affect Growing Private Company: 1980s

By 1983 sales were $16 million. To meet the company's voracious working capital needs, Abele and Nicholas sold a 20-percent interest in Boston Scientific to Abbott Laboratories in return for $21 million, which Abbott would pay over the next four years. The company needed large amounts of working capital, because of the long lead-time between product development and product marketing. In addition, the medical devices that Boston Scientific made required approval by the U.S. Food and Drug Administration (FDA), a process that typically took several years. As a result, the company lost $900,000 in 1988 on sales of nearly $100 million. After learning how to shorten the approval time from the FDA, Boston Scientific again became profitable, earning $23.5 million on sales of $159 million. In 1991 sales reached $230 million, with earnings of $42 million.

### Going Public and Acquisitions: 1992–2000

Boston Scientific went public in May 1992 with an initial public offering (IPO) of 23.5 million shares priced at $17 a share that raised $400 million in capital. Following the IPO, co-founders Nicholas and Abele and their families owned two-thirds of the firm's stock. Nicholas was in charge of the firm's management; Abele had removed himself from day-to-day operations around 1990. Abbott Laboratories sold its shares back to Boston Scientific at the time of the IPO.

The company had four operating divisions: Medi-Tech, which specialized in radiology; Mansfield, for cardiology; Microvasive Endoscopy for gastroenterology; and Microvasive Urology. Boston Scientific would typically introduce a device for use in less critical places, such as the urinary tract, then apply it to higher-risk situations, such as those in cardiology. This helped speed up development of new products. The company posted 40 percent revenue growth for the first half of 1992, while earnings for the same period grew by 28 percent compared to the same period in 1991. For the year, Boston Scientific had revenue of $315 million.

In 1993 sales reached $380 million, while net income rose to nearly $70 million. Between 1994 and 1995 sales rose from $449 million to $1.2 billion, as the company began an aggressive four-year program of strategic acquisitions. International sales accounted for about one-third of the firm's 1995 revenue.

Beginning in fall 1994, Boston Scientific acquired nine companies over a 16-month period, spending about $2.5 billion. During this period it acquired several companies that made niche products that could be marketed worldwide. It paid $400 million for Meadox Medicals Inc., an Oakland, New Jersey-based producer of blood vessel replacement devices. Heart Technology Inc. of Redmond, Washington, was acquired for $450 million; it made surgical tools to unclog arteries. By acquiring Meadox, Boston Scientific gained graft technology that would have taken five years to develop. Heart Technology's single product, Rotablator, was a catheter with a spinning diamond bit that cleaned out clogged arteries. Rotablator's sales had skyrocketed from zero in 1993 to $80 million in 1995.

At the end of 1995 Boston Scientific's market capitalization had grown to $8.5 billion, compared to $1.5 billion at the end of 1994. Its workforce had grown from 2,000 to 8,000 employees. Its product line increased from 3,000 to 8,000 items. With the help of Andersen Consulting, the company was developing a global systems project that would standardize business practices for the firm and its new acquisitions.

In the latter half of the 1990s, trends supporting demand for medical devices included political pressures to develop new cost-effective technology; demand for fast, effective, and safe procedures; and a broad international market. The FDA responded to pressure reduce its review time for certain types of new devices to 90 to 120 days instead of 18 months or more. Boston Scientific's main business, products for interventional cardiology, served a $3-billion global market that was expected to grow at least 15 percent annually. Its other markets, neurointerventional medicine and endoscopy, were each growing at 15 to 20 percent annually. At the end of 1996 the company had a direct sales force in 17 countries and distributors in 85 additional countries. Its strategy was to acquire or develop niche products and market them worldwide. Foreign sales accounted for 38 percent of Boston Scientific's revenue in 1996 and were expected to reach 50 percent in the next couple of years.

Reviewing Boston Scientific's performance in its January 13, 1997 issue, *Medical Economics* asked the then-rhetorical question, "What could go wrong with such a success story?" Unfortunately for Boston Scientific and its investors, the correct answer was, "Plenty."

### Growth and Setbacks: 1997–2000

Boston Scientific continued to grow through acquisitions in 1997. Target Therapeutics, Inc. made products used to treat patients with strokes, including microcatheters and microcoil products used in to the small blood vessels of the brain, heart, and extremities. A new coil that Target developed received FDA approval in 1995; it offered a relatively safe and cost-effective treatment for patients with brain aneurysms. Boston Scientific acquired Target Therapeutics for about $1.1 billion in stock in 1997. The acquisition gave Boston Scientific immediate leadership in neurosurgical products and a line or products to treat aneurysms, and expanded its overseas sales.

By mid-1997 Boston Scientific's rapid growth rate was expected to level off at about 25 percent annually. The company announced it would spend $300 million to upgrade five manufacturing facilities. In addition, it was incurring significant costs in integrating more than a dozen acquisitions made since late 1994. According to *Forbes,* Boston Scientific's main product line—balloons for angioplasty—were becoming a commodity. Surgeons were showing a preference for balloons with stents attached to keep arteries open. While Boston Scientific marketed such devices in Europe, it did not sell them in the United States. The U.S. market leader in this area was Johnson & Johnson, and Medtronic, another competitor, received approval for its stent-balloon combination in June 1997.

Boston Scientific's stock took two significant tumbles during 1997. One occurred when its first-quarter profits failed to meet Wall Street's expectations; stock fell 33 percent. The second occurred after the company warned that its third-quarter earnings would also fall short. In September 1997 it fell 17 percent, from around $76 a share to around $63. For 1997, Boston Scientific had revenue of $1.87 billion and earnings of $139.3 million.

**Key Dates:**

**1969:** Medi-Tech Inc., partially owned by John Abele, introduces its first products, a family of steerable catheters.
**1979:** Boston Scientific is founded by John Abele and Peter Nicholas for the purpose of acquiring Medi-Tech, Inc.
**1992:** Boston Scientific makes first public stock offering.
**1994:** Boston Scientific begins a string of acquisitions that will raise revenue to $2.84 billion in 1999.

In mid-1998 Boston Scientific announced it would spend $2.1 billion to acquire Schneider Worldwide, the vascular devices unit of Pfizer, Inc. Schneider sold surgical stents and artery-clearing devices used in balloon angioplasty. The acquisition was Boston Scientific's largest to date and gave the company a major position in the growing cardiovascular stent market. For 1997, Schneider had worldwide sales of $330 million. It was headquartered near Zurich, Switzerland, and had 2,200 employees worldwide, about 1,200 of whom were in the United States.

In October 1998 Boston Scientific announced a recall of its coronary stent delivery system called "NIR on Ranger with Sox." The company had received more than 100 reports of balloon leakage in the system. The product began shipping in August 1998 to 200 hospitals and medical centers in the United States. By the time of the recall, about 36,000 systems had been shipped and an estimated 25,000 were in use. The recall raised regulatory concerns at the FDA, which had not been notified of manufacturing changes in the stent system. The system had been developed with business partner Medinol Ltd., based in Tel Aviv, Israel.

In November 1998 the company announced it had found about $45 million of "questionable sales" at its Japanese subsidiary for the current year, and an additional $40 million of "improper sales" in previous years. The announcement, coupled with the firm's product recall, pushed Boston Scientific's stock down 11 percent to around $46. The stock had reached a high of $81 in August prior to the recall. For 1998 Boston Scientific reported revenue of $2.23 billion and a net loss of $264 million.

In February 1999 Boston Scientific announced it would cut about 2,000 jobs in 1999 as part of its restructuring following its recent string of acquisitions. About 1,500 of the eliminated positions would affect Schneider employees. The company also expected to spend about $62 million on severance costs.

At the end of 1998 rumors surfaced that James R. Tobin would succeed Peter Nicholas as Boston Scientific's CEO. Tobin resigned in December 1998 as CEO of Biogen Inc., a biotechnology company. Tobin was named CEO of Boston Scientific in March 1999 and assumed the position in June, replacing Peter Nicholas, who remained as chairman. Tobin's assignment essentially was to turn the company around. Over the next 14 months he would eliminate 1,900 jobs and close manufacturing operations in three states. During this period

Boston Scientific's stock would lose about two-thirds of its value—fallout from the product recalls and Japanese scandal. To help finance its acquisition of Schneider Worldwide, Boston Scientific raised $500 million through a secondary stock offering in mid-1999.

Following its five-year string of acquisitions, Boston Scientific was organized into six divisions. EP Technologies specialized in cardiac electrophysiology. Medi-Tech was a leading developer and supplier of minimally invasive and surgical devices for peripheral vascular disease management, including balloon catheters and metallic stents. Microvasive Urology manufactured diagnostic and therapeutic products for endourology for stone management, incontinence, and prostate disease. Microvasive Endoscopy focused on providing devices and services for gastrointestinal endoscopic procedures. Boston Scientific Scimed Inc. was the company's primary cardiology unit. Target Therapeutics was a leader in neuro endovascular intervention, manufacturing medical devices to treat the brain and other hard-to-reach parts of the body in a minimally invasive manner.

In June 1999 the company received a new patent covering a process for injecting genes into the heart that would allow it to enter the gene therapy field. The process could stimulate the formation of blood vessels and would be used to treat patients with serious heart problems. The patent originated in gene research conducted by CardioGene Therapeutics Inc., which Boston Scientific acquired in July 1998.

In August 1999 Boston Scientific recalled two of its medical laser system used in treating heart disease, the Rotablator RotaLink Advancer and RotaLink Plus systems. The systems employed a high-speed drill that used a blade to clear plaque from a clogged artery. After the company received complaints that the system's brake failed to stop the drill from moving through the artery after it had already cleared the blockage, it issued a voluntary recall. The company had sold about $60 million worth of the Rotablator systems in the first half of 1999 and expected no further sales for the rest of the year.

For 1999 the company reported revenue of $2.84 billion and net income of $371 million. Revenues for the first half of 2000 were expected to suffer from a lack of new products. In the latter half of 2000 the company was planning to introduce a gold-plated stent. Analysts noted that Boston Scientific was lagging behind its two major competitors, Guidant Corporation and Medtronic Inc., in introducing new stents, which typically had one-year life cycles.

Between July 1999 and February 2000 the company's stock price fell by 57 percent, from around $46 to $19 a share. In 2000, Tobin created a new business unit focused solely on heart stents and stent-delivery systems. These had been manufactured by the company's Minneapolis-based Scimed division, which would continue to provide cardiologists with products such as balloon catheters, guide wires, and guide catheters. In addition, Tobin announced he would be naming a chief technology officer to the newly created position.

In March 2000 Boston Scientific received FDA approval to resume marketing its NIR on Ranger with Sox coronary stents, after solving the leakage problems.

In July 2000 Boston Scientific continued its reorganization, cutting 1,000 positions in Minnesota, Washington, and Massachusetts, while adding 100 employees to its Miami operation and 800 jobs to company plants in Ireland. In Miami, some 300 jobs involving the production of biopsy forceps would be transferred to a lower-cost foreign contract manufacturer, while 400 positions for workers making guidewires were added. About 850 workers were dismissed from the company's Watertown, Massachusetts, plant. Facilities in Plymouth, Minnesota, which employed about 750 workers, and Redmond, Washington, with about 350 employees, were to be closed. One of the Watertown sites became the headquarters to the company's Medi-Tech division, which developed vascular surgery and radiology products. The reorganization was expected to save about $70 million in 2001 and $145 million in 2002.

Difficulties between Boston Scientific and Medinol Ltd., its key supplier of coronary stents, led to delayed product launches, according to some analysts. As a result, the company's stock plunged more than $7 in one day in July 2000 to close at $18.5625. Also affecting the stock price were the company's lower-than-expected second-quarter sales and a poor outlook for the rest of 2000. Boston Scientific subsequently entered negotiations to acquire Medinol Ltd., of which it already owned part, as a means of becoming more competitive with rival companies that already made their own stents.

Meanwhile, the episode of fraudulent sales reports for the period from January 1997 through June 1998 from Boston Scientific Japan was resolved with the Securities and Exchange Commission, whose report chastised the company for lacking effective controls at the time.

The year 2000 and those leading up to it were difficult for Boston Scientific. Product recalls and new competitors led to the loss of the company's market-leading position in its key product line, coronary stents and stent systems. Difficulties with its primary supplier of stents added to the company's woes. Its stock fell out of favor with Wall Street, resulting in a significant reduction in the firm's market capitalization. As investors wait for Boston Scientific to return to its leadership position, the company faces multiple challenges.

### Principal Divisions

EP Technologies; Medi-Tech; Microvasive Urology; Microvasive Endoscopy; Scimed; Target Therapeutics.

### Principal Competitors

Cook, Inc.; Johnson & Johnson (Cordis Unit); EndoSonics; Medtronic Inc.; Guidant Corp.; Arterial Vascular Engineering Inc.; Human Genome Sciences; GenVec Inc.; Spectranetics Corp.

### Further Reading

"Boston Scientific Corp.," *Insiders' Chronicle,* November 2, 1992, p. 3.
"Boston Scientific Corp. Closing 350-Employee Redmond Location," *Puget Sound Business Journal,* July 14, 2000, p. 15.
Bray, Hiawatha, "Acquisitive Boston Scientific Corp. to Purchase Target Therapeutics, Inc.," *Knight-Ridder/Tribune Business News,* January 21, 1997.
Kerber, Ross, "Natick, Mass.-Based Medical Device Maker to Cut 2,000 Jobs Worldwide," *Knight-Ridder/Tribune Business News,* February 11, 1999.
Koenig, Bill, "Bloomington, Ind., Medical Device Maker Files Patent-Infringement Suits," *Knight-Ridder/Tribune Business News,* March 22, 1999.
Lutton, Christine, "Growth Spurt," *Forbes,* July 1, 1996, p. 16.
Mangan, Doreen, "Why Medical-Device Stocks Belong in Your Portfolio," *Medical Economics,* January 13, 1997, p. 55.
McDonald, Duff J., "Cashing in on the Best New Multinationals," *Money,* May 1996, p. 136.
McLaughlin, Tim, "SEC Order Raps Boston Scientific for False Sales," *Reuters,* August 21, 2000.
McMenamin, Brigid, "An Odd Couple," *Forbes,* October 17, 1994, p. 58.
Mullich, Joe, "Online Recruiting Gets Scientific," *InternetWeek,* July 10, 2000, p. 46.
Padley, Karen, "Plymouth, Minn., Medical Device Firm's Workers Staying Put So Far," *Knight-Ridder/Tribune Business News,* October 20, 1998.
Pascavis, Travis, "Boston Scientific's Stock is Cheap for a Reason," *Morningstar.com,* July 18, 2000.
Peltz, Michael, et al., "Buttressing Balance Sheets," *Institutional Investor,* January 1993, p. 55.
"Pffft," *Forbes,* July 28, 1997, p. 248.
Sohmer, Slade, "Emerging as a Global Sales Success," *Sales & Marketing Management,* May 2000, p. 124.
Solo, Sally, "Boston Scientific," *Fortune,* April 5, 1993, p. 97.
Stevens, Tim, "Multiplication by Addition," *Industry Week,* July 1, 1996, p. 20.
Woods, Jenny, "Week in Review," *Minneapolis-St. Paul City Business,* July 21, 2000, p. 39.

—David P. Bianco

## Bristol-Myers Squibb Company

# Bristol-Myers Squibb Company

**345 Park Avenue**
**New York, New York 10154-0037**
**U.S.A.**
**Telephone: (212) 546-4000**
**Fax: (212) 546-4020**
**Web site: http://www.bms.com**

*Public Company*
*Incorporated:* 1900 as Bristol-Myers Company
*Employees:* 54,500
*Sales:* $20.22 billion (1999)
*Stock Exchanges:* New York
*Ticker Symbol:* BMY
*NAIC:* 325412 Pharmaceutical Preparations
    Manufacturing; 32562 Toilet Preparations
    Manufacturing

Bristol-Myers Squibb Company is comprised of four core businesses: pharmaceuticals, consumer products, medical devices, and nutritional products. It is the third largest pharmaceutical company in the world, and its offerings include cardiovascular and anti-cancer drugs, anti-infective agents, drugs for treating the central nervous system, diagnostic imaging agents, and dermatological products. The consumer products division markets well-known brands such as Clairol and Excedrin, and the company's medical devices division serves the orthopedics market with products such as artificial hip and knee replacements, while also supplying various items needed for ostomy procedures, wound and burn care, and other surgical specialties. The company came to be known as Bristol-Myers Squibb in the late 1980s, when Bristol-Myers Company and the Squibb Corporation merged. At that time, competitive pressure and the increasing cost of research led many pharmaceutical firms to seek business partners in order to survive.

### The Early Years: 1887–1920

Bristol-Myers was originally founded in 1887 by two former fraternity brothers, William McLaren Bristol and John Ripley Myers. They each invested $5,000 in the Clinton Pharmaceutical Company—a failing drug manufacturer based in New York—and their small operation began selling medical preparations by horse and buggy to local doctors and dentists. For the first few years, the company struggled due to insufficient capital and the new owners' lack of understanding of how drugs were made. The firm relocated from Clinton to Syracuse, New York in 1889 to improve its shipping capability, and then moved again ten years later to Brooklyn, New York for easier access to its expanding base of customers in Pennsylvania and New England.

In 1898, the company's name was changed to Bristol, Myers Company. One year later, John Ripley Myers died. To help the company grow, the firm increased its sales force, referred to as "detail men," and began shifting its attention from physicians to wholesale and retail druggists, who were increasingly being recognized as primary suppliers of medication.

In 1900, the firm incorporated and again modified its name, replacing the comma between Bristol and Myers with a hyphen. The same year, Bristol-Myers Company made its first profit, and entered the market for specialty products. Sales of such Bristol-Myers items as Sal Hepatica (a laxative mineral salt) and Ipana toothpaste (the first such product to contain a disinfectant) grew rapidly between 1903 and 1905.

Strong demand caused several changes in the company's operation, including the creation of an export department to handle international orders, and the opening of new manufacturing facilities in Hillside, New Jersey. In 1915, Henry Bristol, William Bristol's oldest son, became the company's general manager. Henry was later joined in 1928 by his brothers, William Jr. and Lee, who handled manufacturing and advertising, respectively.

### The 1920s to 1960s: Steady Growth and Acquisitions

During the recession that followed World War I, the company discontinued its line of "ethical," or prescription, drugs to focus production instead on its two best-selling specialty products, as well as other toiletries, antiseptics, and cough syrups. It was then that Bristol-Myers also moved its offices to its present location in Manhattan. The shift in product focus was accompa-

## Company Perspectives:

*Our company's mission is to extend and enhance human life by providing the highest quality health and personal care products. To our customers, we pledge excellence in everything we make and market, providing you with the safest, most effective and highest-quality products. We promise to improve our products through innovation, diligent research and development, and an unyielding commitment to be the very best.*

nied by a new emphasis on advertising directed toward consumers rather than doctors and dentists. Bristol-Myers sponsored a radio show featuring a group called the Ipana Troubadours, and introduced the slogan "Ipana for the Smile of Beauty; Sal Hepatica for the Smile of Health."

In 1928, the company became a part of Drug, Inc., a large, newly formed holding company that produced proprietary drugs and other medications, while also operating a large retail chain. Bristol-Myers continued to grow and advertised heavily during the Great Depression, launching several new and successful consumer products. Other operations affiliated with Drug, Inc. did not fare nearly as well, however, and the holding company disbanded in 1933.

Upon the outbreak of World War II, Bristol-Myers again became a manufacturer of ethical pharmaceuticals. It mass produced penicillin for the Allied armed forces through its Bristol Laboratories subsidiary, which had previously been acquired under the name of Cheplin Laboratories. Bristol Laboratories' experience in the process of fermentation—which was required to make its primary product, acidophilus milk—was easily converted to the manufacture of the antibiotics. This led to the firm's formal re-entry into the ethical drug arena, and enabled it to take advantage of the growing demand for antibiotics after the war.

The company continued to grow over the next decade, assisted by television advertisements. In 1957, Henry Bristol became chair of the board and was succeeded as president and chief executive officer by Fredric N. Schwartz, the former head of Bristol Laboratories. Assisted by Gavin K. MacBain, the company's treasurer (who later assumed the position of chairperson), Schwartz acquired several smaller, well-managed companies in growing industries. The new subsidiaries grew quickly with help from Bristol-Myers' research and marketing expertise. These acquisitions included Clairol, a maker of hair coloring products, purchased in 1959; Drackett, a household products manufacturer, acquired in 1965; and Mead Johnson, a producer of infant formula and children's vitamins, purchased in 1967. At the time of the acquisition, Clairol had already made marketing history as a result of the popular advertising campaign "Does she or doesn't she? Hair color so natural only her hairdresser knows for sure!"

### The 1970s and 1980s: New Management and New Products

Richard Gelb, the son of Clairol's founder, reluctantly joined Bristol-Myers after the acquisition to head the Clairol operation. Gelb was given a wide berth in managing Clairol, and he did so well that he was promoted to executive vice-president and then to president under chairman Gavin MacBain. Gelb became president just as Bristol-Myers's growth was flattening out. A string of new-product failures during the late 1960s had drained finances and depressed stock value. In 1972, Gelb was appointed chair and CEO. He initiated a comeback over the next decade by spending $400 million advertising the company's most popular brands, and by expanding its line of health care products. This growth was accomplished in part through the acquisitions of Zimmer Manufacturing Company, a producer of orthopedic and surgical products, in 1972; and Unitek Corporation, a dental equipment supplier, in 1978.

Under Gelb's leadership, Bristol-Myers was able to shift gears quickly in response to market changes. When concern over the use of fluorocarbons threatened the spray deodorant market in the mid-1970s, the company increased advertising of its Ban roll-on deodorant. This strategy vaulted Ban into the top-selling spot, and increased the sales of all other roll-on products by 75 percent in one year.

Soon thereafter, however, the company suffered a major marketing setback with its Clairol products. In 1977, the National Cancer Institute reported a link between an ingredient used in hair colorants, 2–4 DAA, and cancer in laboratory animals. Bristol-Myers disputed these findings at first, but later introduced a new line of hair coloring products which was reformulated and did not include 2–4 DAA as an ingredient. The decision eventually helped the company overcome the effects of the bad press it had received.

Bristol-Myers' continued attention toward health-care research was also a major factor in its resurgence. Beginning in the late 1970s, the company began to use cash generated by its consumer-products business to fund the research and development of additional drugs beyond its antibiotics and synthetic penicillins. Several new areas were explored, including cardiovascular agents and anticancer drugs.

At the time, Bristol-Myers was the only pharmaceutical company to invest in anticancer drugs, because growth potential appeared small. The company obtained the marketing rights to several anti-cancer drugs developed by the National Institutes of Health and other research institutions, universities, and drug companies, and was well positioned when that market took off. Between 1974 and 1980, Bristol-Myers launched 11 new drugs for treatment of cancer and other diseases. Although none of these products were breakthrough drugs, they contributed over $200 million in sales to the company by 1980. This growth occurred despite the company's relatively small research budget.

The company was already an experienced marketer of over-the-counter (OTC) analgesics. Its Excedrin and Bufferin brands had accounted for one-quarter of the total market for nonprescription pain relievers until the early 1960s, when an OTC version of Johnson & Johnson's Tylenol—a non-aspirin product—took a significant percentage of Bristol-Myers's market share away. In the mid-1970s, Bristol-Myers challenged Johnson & Johnson with Datril, a non-aspirin product priced lower than Tylenol. Johnson & Johnson responded quickly, lowering the price of Tylenol.

## Key Dates:

**1887:** William McLaren Bristol and John Ripley Myers invest in the Clinton Pharmaceutical Company.

**1900:** The company changes its name to Bristol-Myers Company.

**1915:** Henry Bristol, William Bristol's oldest son, becomes general manager.

**1928:** The company becomes a part of Drug, Inc.; William Bristol Jr. and Lee Bristol become head of manufacturing and advertising, respectively.

**1933:** The holding company disbands.

**1957:** Henry Bristol becomes chair of the board; Fredric N. Schwartz becomes president and chief executive officer.

**1959:** Bristol-Myers acquires Clairol.

**1967:** Bristol-Myers acquires Mead Johnson.

**1972:** Richard Gelb is appointed chair and chief executive officer.

**1983:** The company introduces tamper-resistant packaging for its capsule products.

**1984:** Bristol-Myers builds a multimillion-dollar research facility in Wallingford, Connecticut.

**1989:** Bristol-Myers merges with Squibb Corporation; Gelb becomes chief executive.

**1994:** Major reorganization; worldwide revenues total $11.4 billion.

In 1981, Bristol-Myers settled a series of ten-year-old antitrust suits alleging that Bristol-Myers and Beecham Group, a British pharmaceutical company, had improperly obtained a patent on the antibiotic ampicillin. The suits also accused the firms of engaging in restrictive licensing practices, which had resulted in excessive charges to hospitals, wholesalers, and retailers.

The following year, a series of product-tampering incidents occurred involving various over-the-counter analgesic products, including Bristol-Myers's Excedrin capsules. The company responded to new Food and Drug Administration (FDA) regulations in 1983 with tamper-resistant packaging for its capsule products.

In 1984, Bristol-Myers signed an agreement with Upjohn, which enabled it to introduce Nuprin, a new nonprescription form of ibuprofen pain reliever. With the agreement, Bristol-Myers again gained the means to take on Tylenol once again. It also pitted the firm against American Home Products, which already sold a pain reliever under the Anacin brand, and was planning to launch a new ibuprofen-based product called Advil.

At this time, Bristol-Myers entered the market for drugs used to treat anxiety and depression. The company licensed the rights to products manufactured by foreign firms, while continuing to invest heavily in its own pharmaceutical research and development. The firm had reorganized its internal research operations and, in 1984, built a multimillion-dollar research facility in Wallingford, Connecticut. Two years later, Bristol-Myers received FDA approval to market its own tranquilizer

product, BuSpar, which did not produce many of the negative side effects of other antidepressant drugs already on the market.

In 1986, the firm became enmeshed in the complex acquisition of Genetic Systems Corporation (GSC), a Seattle-based biotechnology company. GSC was founded in 1980 by a group of entrepreneurial microbiologists who teamed up with Syntex Corporation, a drug company, to manufacture and market tests for sexually transmitted diseases. Three years later, the partners formed another venture, Oncogen, to manufacture products for cancer treatment, and in 1985, they offered Bristol-Myers an opportunity to invest in the operation. Later that year, a Bristol-Myers competitor—Eli Lilly & Company—acquired Hybridtech, a leading producer of monoclonal antibodies. Bristol-Myers then negotiated an agreement with GSC management to buy GSC and Oncogen, unaware that GSC had negotiated a similar deal with Syntex two months before. After threatening a lawsuit, Syntex elected to withdraw its offer for GSC in exchange for a $15 million compensation package provided by Bristol-Myers and for marketing rights to selected GSC and Oncogen products. Bristol-Myers sold GSC to Sanofi, a French pharmaceutical firm, in 1990.

In June 1986, a second incident of tampering with capsule-type pain relief products caused two deaths in the Seattle area. This incident led Bristol-Myers to recall its Excedrin capsules nationwide. It soon withdrew all of its nonprescription capsule products from the market, including Comtrex, a cold relief medication. The capsules were replaced with the caplet, a specially coated, capsule-shaped pill. With this action, Bristol-Myers became the second company in its industry, after Johnson & Johnson, to end the sale of OTC medication in capsule form.

In an attempt to establish a stronger position in the field of coronary care, Bristol-Myers negotiated an agreement in March 1987 to acquire SciMed Life Systems, a manufacturer of coronary balloon angioplasty catheters and other disposable products for treating cardiovascular disease. Two months later, Bristol-Myers withdrew its offer after SciMed was sued by Eli Lilly & Company for patent infringement.

Meanwhile, Bristol-Myers continued to grow as a manufacturer of prescription pharmaceuticals, lessening its dependence on consumer products by focusing on acquired immune deficiency syndrome (AIDS) research. Because both cancer and AIDS research were virology-based, this area was a natural fit for the company. In 1987, Bristol-Myers obtained an exclusive license to produce and test two new AIDS drugs, dideoxyadenosine (DDA) and dideoxyinosine (DDI). It also received FDA approval to test an experimental AIDS vaccine on humans.

In 1989, the company negotiated an agreement with Gerber Products Company to manufacture and market Gerber Baby Formula directly to U.S. consumers. Controversial advertising for this product touched off a boycott of the company's line of formula products, however. A group of pediatricians felt that Bristol-Myers was attempting to discourage breastfeeding, and attempting to compromise physicians' influence in baby formula selection.

In November 1989, Bristol-Myers merged with Squibb Corporation. Squibb had been established in 1858 and was among the oldest U.S. pharmaceutical companies. Over half of Squibb's sales were generated by pharmaceuticals, and the company also owned a profitable cosmetic business. Furthermore, the two firms had similar corporate cultures. The merger also brought together two chief executives, Bristol Myers' Gelb and Richard M. Furlaud of Squibb, who had been friends for 25 years and had discussed the idea of a merger occasionally over the previous three years.

## The 1990s: Jockeying to Become the Top Pharmaceutical Company Worldwide

As part of the merger agreement, Richard Gelb became chairman and chief executive officer of the combined company, while Furlaud, his counterpart at Squibb, became president and headed up the company's pharmaceutical business. Squibb benefited from Bristol-Myers' biomedical research capabilities and its established presence in consumer health products. That market was becoming increasingly important to Squibb, since several competitors were already negotiating agreements to market their prescription drugs in OTC forms to consumers. In Squibb, Bristol-Myers obtained a new source of prescription drugs with strong sales potential, particularly in the cardiovascular area, and a sizable budget to add to its own continuing research operation.

The merger was not without tension, unfortunately. By December 1990, 2,000 employees—four percent of the total workforce—had been laid off, and Bristol planned to close 60 pharmaceutical plants worldwide. Closings of 6 of 18 consumer products plants were scheduled through 1993. Nevertheless, the merger gave Bristol an important worldwide presence, thanks to Squibb's strong position in Europe, the world's largest drug market.

As it entered the 1990s, Bristol-Myers Squibb's goal was to achieve the top spot in world pharmaceutical sales by the year 2001. The company received FDA approval for its cholesterol-lowering drug, Pravachol, in 1991. Bristol-Myers Squibb also had several other drugs in various stages of development: Videx, used to fight AIDS, and Taxol, an anticancer drug made from the bark of the pacific yew tree, among others. The FDA gave the company the go-ahead in early 1993 to market Taxol to ovarian cancer patients. In February 1993, however, the U.S. Subcommittee on Regulation, Business Opportunities, and Energy accused Bristol-Myers Squibb and several other pharmaceutical companies of overpricing, pointing to Taxol's price of six to eight thousand dollars per complete treatment. The company maintained that the price was not excessive, and declined to supply the subcommittee with the data used to set the price.

Despite the controversy, by the end of the first quarter of 1993, sales at Bristol-Myers Squibb had increased four percent, or $2.8 billion. By the end of the year, worldwide revenues totaled $11.4 billion. In 1993, two committees of the U.S. Food and Drug Administration gave the go-ahead to new uses of two of the company's existing products: Capoten, for use by patients who had suffered a heart attack, and Megace, for treatment of anorexia and HIV-related weight loss. In 1995, Bristol-Myers introduced Glucophage, the first new class of drugs to be used in almost 20 years in the U.S. to treat people with adult-onset diabetes. The drug increased the effectiveness of the insulin a person produced, and thus helped control blood glucose levels

without causing hypoglycemia. Bristol-Myers also continued research into Zerit, a new remedy for people with HIV infections.

In January 1993, Bristol signed a contract with Mead Johnson, establishing a joint venture to produce and sell Enfamil and Enfapro infant formulas in Guangzhou, China. Nevertheless, the main focus of research at Bristol-Myers Squibb remained in anti-cancer drugs. Company scientists sought to develop drugs that kill cancerous cells with fewer side effects in the patient. Its first success in this area came in 1994, when the company succeeded in locating a semi-synthetic source of paclitaxel, the critical ingredient of Taxol, in the taxus baccata plant.

Led by Charles A. Heimbold, Jr., the company's newest chief executive, the company also undertook a major reorganization of its international consumer business in 1994 as part of its goal of continued global expansion. It created three business units: one overseeing the company's consumer business in Japan; a second overseeing consumer businesses in Canada, Europe, the Middle East, and Latin America, as well as Clairol business in the U.S.; and a third overseeing consumer and nutritional markets in the Far East. It also made several acquisitions in the mid- to late 1990s. In 1994, it purchased the remaining shares of UPSA, a French pharmaceutical group that specialized in pain treatment, in which Bristol had had a minority share since 1990. In 1995, it acquired Calgon Vestal Laboratories from Merck and Co., Inc., which it added to its ConvaTec division. In 1997, it sold off its Linvatec subsidiary, which manufactured arthroscopy products and powered instruments, to CONMED.

New discoveries continued through the rest of the nineties. In 1996, Genzyme Transgenics Corp., working with Bristol-Myers, announced the birth of a genetically altered goat, which carried the gene for an anticancer drug. Beginning in 1996, Bristol-Myers scientists collaborated with BioServe Technologies, a NASA-funded non-profit, to explore the use of space for developing commercial products. Crew members aboard Discovery shuttles tested rates of fungal and bacterial fermentation in weightlessness, medicinal plant growth, and x-ray crystallography. In 1997, Bristol-Myers' Mead Johnson subsidiary, working with Cytyc Corporation, co-promoted Cytyc's ThinPrep Pap Test, shown to be more effective than the conventional smear in diagnosing women's health problems.

The future of Bristol-Myers Squibb Company at the turn of the century was dependent upon continued product leadership on an international basis in each of its highly competitive core businesses, as well as a continuing commitment to research and develop new products. Several forces—including an aging population, an increasing percentage of women in the full-time workforce, and a growing number of nontraditional households—were expected to create needs that would have a strong influence on the company's consumer products business. The company took a slight hit in 1998, when after years of litigation, it settled upon the final cost of its breast implant product and prescription drug pricing liability—approximately $400 and $500 million to be paid out to injured or overcharged consumers. In 2000, as a wave of consolidation swept the pharmaceutical industry, the company, with about $20 billion in annual sales, downplayed the need to merge, but would not rule it out. In September, it announced that it would sell its Clairol operations and Zimmer orthopedics implants to concentrate on its core pharmaceutical business. "We are not looking back or standing still," one company officer noted in the *Los Angeles Times* in April 2000, adding "We are looking at all our options with great intensity."

### Principal Subsidiaries

Apothecon, Inc.; Bristol-Myers Squibb Manufacturing; Clairol Incorporated; Convatec Limited; Matrix Essentials, Inc.; Mead Johnson & Company; Westwood-Squibb Pharmaceuticals, Inc.; Zimmer, Inc.

### Principal Competitors

Aventis S.A., Glaxo Wellcome, Merck & Co., Inc.

### Further Reading

*Bristol-Myers Company Special Report: The Next Century,* New York: Bristol-Myers Company, 1987.

"Bristol-Myers Squibb Announces New Organization for Consumer Businesses," *PR Newswire,* May 9, 1994.

"Bristol-Myers Squibb Gets an Okay on Taxol," *Chemical Marketing Reporter,* January 4, 1993, p. 3.

"Bristol-Myers Squibb Reports Results," *PR Newswire,* April 21, 1993.

"Drug Setback May Make Bristol-Myers a Takeover Target," *Los Angeles Times,* April 21, 2000, p. C1.

Frazier, Lynne McKenna, "Bristol-Myers Squibb to Sell Warsaw, Indiana-based Orthopedic Implant Firm," *News-Sentinel,* September 27, 2000.

Hager, Bruce, "Marriage Becomes Bristol-Myers Squibb," *Business Week,* December 3, 1990, pp. 138–39.

"Nielsen Signs Agreement with Bristol-Myers Squibb Company," *PR Newswire,* Feburary 22, 1994.

—Sandy Schusteff
—updated by Marinell Landa and Carrie Rothburd

# Buderus

## Buderus AG

Sophienstrasse 30-32
D-35576 Wetzlar
Germany
Telephone: (49)(6441) 418-0
Fax: (49) (6441) 418-1901
Web site: http://www.buderus.de

*Public Company*
*Incorporated:* 1731 as Friedrichshütte, Johann Wilhelm
   Buderus I
*Employees:* 9,577
*Sales:* DM 3.41 billion ($1.74 billion) (1998–99)
*Stock Exchanges:* Frankfurt/Main
*Ticker Symbol:* BUD.ETR
*NAIC:* 333414 Heating Equipment (Except Warm Air
   Furnaces) Manufacturing; 331111 Iron and Steel
   Mills; 331513 Steel Foundries (Except Investment);
   331221 Rolled Steel Shape Manufacturing; 33634
   Motor Vehicle Brake System Manufacturing; 32731
   Cement Manufacturing; 32739 Other Concrete
   Product Manufacturing

Buderus AG is the holding company for the German Buderus concern, best known for three main divisions producing steel, cast iron pipe systems, and heating systems. The Heating Products division, Buderus Heiztechnik, produces furnaces, burners, boilers, solar heating systems, and heating control systems and supplies. This division operates five production facilities in Germany and two in the Netherlands; it distributes its products through more than 45 German sales offices and through subsidiaries and licensed wholesalers worldwide. The company's Castings division, Buderus Guss, makes cast iron pipes, as well as castings for automotive and other precision applications. Buderus Guss is also active in the fields of waste water treatment systems and drainage technology. It operates five production facilities in Germany, as well as one in Austria. The company's Special Steel Products division, Edelstahlwerke Buderus, produces high-quality steel products such as rolled steel, closed-die forgings, and other forged materials. It operates

a major production facility in Wetzlar, Germany, and a second location in Pont Salomon, France, as well as 28 warehouses and 48 sales offices throughout the world. The heating products division accounts for about two-thirds of the group's total sales, the Castings division for about 19 percent, and the Special Steel Products division for 17 percent. One-third of Buderus' total sales come from abroad.

### Foundations in the 18th Century

On March 14, 1731, a dream came true for Johann Wilhelm Buderus. That day an administrator at the Friedrichshütte iron works made a down payment and became the official lessee of the business (located in central-western Germany near the river Lahn and north of Frankfurt) owned by Count von Solms-Laubach. Having envisioned the day he would take over the Friedrichshütte, Buderus had invested heavily in the iron works and owned most of its operating capital by 1729. Shortly after being awarded the new title ''Hochgräflicher und Herrrschaftlicher Hüttenmodiator,'' he married for the second time (his first wife having died at age 30 when delivering her fifth child.) His new wife, a daughter of a priest who also served a countess, gave Buderus a leg up in society via access to people in upper-class positions. However, the new business and marriage were not enough to secure a fortune for Buderus. Over the next two decades, Buderus and the foundry were challenged by rising exploration and production costs of ore, rising wages for iron workers, and the bureaucracy involved with out-of-county exports. Plagued by worries about feeding his 13-member family, Buderus continued to negotiate with the county administration to keep the lease price down over the years and concentrated on the production of raw iron since there was not much demand for his cast iron products. On June 23, 1753, Johann Wilhelm Buderus died at age 63, little realizing the enduring success of his business.

After his sudden death, his wife, Elisabeth Magdalena, managed the family business and secured its existence through many challenges, including destructive floods and storms, as well as months of ''daily robbery'' during the Seven Years' War. Later, the founder's youngest son Johann Wilhelm Buderus II took over the business. The financial backing Buderus II obtained through

46

his diplomatic talent and a marriage to the daughter of a wealthy iron works owner enabled him to bring the Friedrichshütte though a severe economic downturn in the 1770s.

### A Family Dispute in the 19th Century

The three sons of Johann Wilhelm Buderus II—Friedrich Andreas, Christian Wilhelm, and Georg Carl Theodor—reorganized the family business and received equal shares in the Sozietät J.W. Buderus Söhne in the early 1800s. However, the oldest two died as early as 1833 at ages 25 and 26; thus the youngest, Georg Carl Theodor Buderus, together with his three nephews and other family members, managed and expanded the Buderus company during the 19th century, moving its main presence to the area around the river Lahn, which flowed southwest to the Rhine. By 1835 the Buderus company operated five iron works, producing cast-iron furnaces, ovens, cookware, and irons.

It was in that year that a dispute arose among the heirs. The cause was a request by Friedrich Buderus to formally and fairly divide the company's assets between family members. Georg Buderus II, the oldest of the three nephews, vigorously resisted this endeavor to secure the family's unity and was—at first—successful. However, after the company's worth was established in 1838, a new agreement between the three family groups was negotiated, giving each group one-third of the shares. The agreement included a clause stipulating that no shareholder would initiate any adverse acquisitions or leases or run any businesses on the side. After Georg Buderus I death in 1840, Friedrich Buderus again insisted on redistributing the shares in the company according to the assets owned by each heir. His two brothers finally gave in to avoid further disputes.

From 1841 on Friedrich Buderus held $8/18$ of the company's shares while his brothers Georg and Richard held $5/18$ each. However, the deal left a bitter aftertaste. His brothers came to his help when Friedrich got into trouble after breaching his contract by acquiring a company without consulting them. However, when he refused to repay his debt and conducted several other business transactions not allowed by the agreement, they lost their trust and patience. In 1870 the Sozietät J.W. Buderus Söhne was dissolved. Friedrich Buderus founded his own company, L. Fr. Buderus zu Audenschmiede, which was later managed by his son who died in 1919 with no heirs. With their remaining assets Georg II and Richard Buderus moved headquarters to the Hedwigshütte, located at the Main-Weser railroad near Lollar which was acquired in 1861 and later

became one of the main locations for the company. The Offene Handelsgesellschaft (OHG) Gebrüder Buderus zur Main-Weser-Hütte bei Lollar was incorporated on January 1, 1870, and was a major player in the economic upswing caused by the foundation of the German Empire.

### Industrialization and Expansion Begins in 1864

In the middle of the 19th century, with industrialization well underway, a new technology for blast furnaces operated in iron works started replacing the old processes. Traditionally, these furnaces were powered by charcoal, but this was gradually being replaced by coke as the new fuel. In 1864 the first coke-powered blast furnace started operations at the Main-Weser-Hütte iron works.

Six years later, in order to secure supplies of raw material, Buderus moved to the German town of Wetzlar on the river Lahn where the company was also operating ore mines in the surrounding areas. The newly-built iron works and foundry was also close to a railroad connection that made it possible to ship products quickly to such German cities and industrial centers as Cologne, Frankfurt, Koblenz, Giessen, and Kassel. It took two years to build the new facilities on a property near the Wetzlar train station between two railroad lines. Named after the mother of Georg and Richard Buderus, the Sophienhütte started operating its first blast-furnace in 1872. A second one started production in the following year.

In 1878 the Buderus brothers had a breakthrough. For the first time the cast iron made by OHG Gebrüder Buderus, was able to compete with the English and Scottish brands that dominated the German market. The new iron quality made the production of very thin cast iron possible. Buderus also started making modern coal-fueled room furnaces.

### Buderus Becomes Public Company in 1884

Financial demands to secure the further dynamic growth of the company and an ever-expanding number of family members called for a new legal entity. On March 13, 1884 Buderus was transformed into a public company—the Aktiengesellschaft Buderus'sche Eisenwerke. All shares and leading positions were held by Buderus family members. At that time the company owned six iron works with five blast furnaces, two foundries, and several other production facilities. However, with its focus narrowed on the production of raw iron, the company slid into a serious crisis in the following years when competition and price pressures for raw iron became tougher, and debt from investments in new iron ore mines and modernization of the blast furnaces weighed heavily on the balance sheets. Buderus decided to sell two of its iron works to get out of debt. The Hirzenhain iron works was sold in 1891 to Hugo Buderus—the second leading figure of the Buderus family after Georg Buderus III. Hugo Buderus took advantage of the crisis situation, acquiring the profitable facility with cash he obtained through an advantageous marriage and leaving the company with other less profitable facilities. In 1895 Georg Buderus III agreed to sell the Main-Weser iron works and died shortly thereafter.

However, Buderus was able to survive only with the financial support of a bank consortium. Within one year, the last Buderus

## Key Dates:

**1731:** Johann Wilhelm Buderus leases the iron works and foundry Friedrichshütte.
**1807:** Sozietät J.W. Buderus Söhne is founded.
**1870:** OHG Gebrüder Buderus zur Main-Weser-Hütte bei Lollar is incorporated.
**1899:** Buderus shares are traded for the first time at the stock exchanges in Frankfurt and Berlin.
**1911:** Buderus's own distribution company for heating products is established.
**1917:** Buderus starts producing stainless steel.
**1935:** Hessen-Nassauischer Hüttenverein merges with Buderus.
**1956:** Friedrich Flick KG in Dusseldorf takes over majority of Buderus shares.
**1965:** Buderus is integrated into the Flick concern.
**1981:** The last blast-furnace for raw iron ceases production.
**1987:** Buderus becomes a management holding company with five operating companies.
**1992:** Metallgesellschaft acquires majority of Buderus shares.
**1994:** Buderus becomes independent again.

family member left the executive board of directors. In April 1899 the banks placed part of the Buderus shares at the stock exchanges in Frankfurt and Berlin. Only a few days after the company had decided to raise its capital in 1900, construction started for a new foundry for iron pipes in Wetzlar. To further diversify its product range, Buderus also erected a cement production facility in Wetzlar in 1899. In the following decades a strong emphasis was placed on the production of iron cast products and several foundries were acquired and expanded.

Heating technology became one of Buderus hallmarks around the turn of the 19th century. In 1898 the first Buderus patent for a cast-iron furnace was registered. The Main-Weser iron works and foundry became an independent company in 1895; Buderus acquired the renamed Eisenwerke Lollar AG in 1905 and became a major manufacturer of cast-iron heating products. As early as 1908, the company established a testing facility for furnaces and radiators. In 1911 Buderus established its own distribution company for heating products and supplies, the Buderus'sche Handelsgesellschaft m.b.H. By 1912 the distribution network extended throughout all of Germany and some neighboring countries.

### World Wars and an Unfriendly Takeover

When World War I broke out, Buderus was integrated into the German war industry. By the end of 1915 two new Siemens-Martin furnaces started producing steel at the Sophienhütte. Two years later Buderus also started making stainless steel. In 1920 the Stahlwerke Buderus-Röchling AG was founded. The joint venture with steel maker Röchlingsche Eisen- und Stahlwerke based in Völklingen leased the Buderus steel works and erected new facilities to further process the steel. In 1924 the company was renamed Röchling-Buderus AG.

Because of its broad product range, government-subsidized job programs in the construction industry, and a sustainable financial strategy, Buderus survived the Great Depression and the economic turmoil in Germany afterwards. In the early 1930s the Hessen-Nassauischer Hüttenverein, a family business and the second largest company in the iron industry in the Lahn-Dill region met with financial trouble and finally merged with Buderus in 1935. This transaction included the takeover of an iron works in Oberscheld, six iron foundries, and extensive properties of iron ore mines. Beginning in the late 1930s, the German government put more and more restrictions on business activities until eventually Buderus was forced to produce war supplies again. In September 1944 the iron works in Wetzlar were bombed, and because of severe damages the blast-furnaces ceased raw-iron production.

After World War II ended, the German state of Hessen took steps to put the raw materials and power generation sectors under government control. In 1947 all Buderus production facilities in these industries in the state were administrated by a state government trustee. An agreement was finally reached in 1954 under which Buderus was given a maximum share of 26 percent in the Berghütte which was organized as the Hessische Berg- und Hüttenwerke AG in 1952.

After World War II the company started making consumer products again, including ovens, furnaces, iron-cast radiators, cookware, sheet metal for roofs, and plows. In 1953 the new Buderus subsidiary Omnical GmbH began making steel furnaces for central heating systems. With the postwar construction boom fading, Buderus decided to focus even more on more refined products. In 1955 the company took over the majority of Munich-based Krauss-Maffei AG. Three years later Buderus acquired a majority share in the Burger Eisenwerke AG, a leading manufacturer of heating systems and ovens with the brand name "Juno."

In March 1955 the value of Buderus shares at the Frankfurt stock exchange jumped up 232.5 percent. Insiders and experts speculated that someone was systematically buying Buderus shares, and some suggested German steel magnate Friedrich Flick as a possible driving force. On July 4, 1956, the Friedrich Flick KG in Dusseldorf announced that it had acquired the majority of Buderus shares. Nine years later the company was integrated into the Flick empire when Flick's iron works Metallhüttenwerke Lübeck GmbH merged with Buderus'sche Eisenwerke. In 1965 Buderus took over the 50 percent stake of Röchlingsche Eisen- und Stahlwerke in the Röchling-Buderus AG which was renamed Edelstahlwerke Buderus AG. In the same year Buderus was able to buy back the 74 percent stake of the State of Hessen in the iron works Berghütte.

### New Technologies, Markets, and Shareholders in the 1970s and Beyond

After the expansion years of the 1950s and 1960s, the 1970s were a period of technological and organizational restructuring for Buderus. With a process of concentration underway in the German iron and steel industry, the company decided to divest its activities in iron mining and production. Buderus subsidiaries Burger Eisenwerke and Hessische Berg- und Hüttenwerke were merged with the parent company which was renamed

Buderus AG in 1977. The company's last blast-furnace ceased production in 1981. At the same time, the oil crisis of the 1970s and the rising concern about environmental pollution accelerated the search for cleaner and more efficient heating technology. In 1977 Buderus introduced a new heating product series under the "Ecomatic" brand name, based on a new-low temperature technology. Combining the words "economic" and "automatic" in its name the new furnace was made from new materials that extended product life. The connected heating systems were equipped with energy saving electronic control systems that reduced the water temperature in the boiler depending on outside temperature or even room temperature. In addition the new technology used cleaner and more efficient burner technology that cut down fuel use and emissions. All together the new designs used 12 to 15 percent less energy.

After Friedrich Flick's son Friedrich Karl Flick publicly announced that he intended to sell his private industrial shareholdings for tax reasons in December 1985, Feldmühle Nobel AG, the successor to the Friedrich Flick Industrieverwaltung KGaA, became Buderus' new parent company. This transaction was followed by a restructuring program, initiated by the company's new CEO Wolfgang Laaf. Buderus AG became the management holding company of five independent operating companies: Buderus Heiztechnik GmbH (heating technology), Buderus Bau- und Abwassertechnik GmbH (construction and waste water technology), Buderus Kundenguß GmbH (customized foundry products), Buderus Küchentechnik GmbH (ovens), and Buderus Sell GmbH (airplane kitchens and supplies).

Still, Buderus continued to struggle until 1988. That year a new executive board of directors was established and a new strategy defined. Beginning in 1989 Buderus sold off its unprofitable subsidiaries and started reorganizing and expanding its distribution network. After the reunification of Germany, the company was extended into the former East Germany. Buderus Handel GmbH, a subsidiary in Berlin, organized sales in eastern Germany and Metallverarbeitung Neukirchen, a traditional metal processing firm in Saxony, was acquired in 1991.

The 1990s brought Buderus back its independence. In January 1992 the German industrial holding concern Metallgesellschaft acquired Buderus. However, the group slid into a financial crisis one year later and decided to sell its Buderus shares. The 79.9 percent of the company's share capital held by Metallgesellschaft was publicly offered in June 1994. German banks Commerzbank and Dresdner Bank, and construction group Bilfinger + Berger based in Mannheim, became new major Buderus shareholders. The rest of the company's shares were widely spread among several thousand shareholders.

During the 1990s Buderus also expanded abroad. The company's first foreign subsidiary was founded in Austria in November 1989. Next, Buderus Italia S.r.l. was founded in March 1992 with the takeover of two Italian wholesale firms. Buderus Chauffage SA, a subsidiary in France, followed in 1993. In the same year the company acquired Nefit Fasto B.V., a leading Dutch manufacturer of wall-mounted heating technology. The year 1999 marked the 100th anniversary year of the first placement of Buderus shares on the Frankfurt and Berlin stock exchanges. In that year the company sold its five millionth cast iron furnace. The fact that Buderus was one of the oldest public stock companies in Germany was honored with a special monograph dedicated to the history of Buderus shares.

### Principal Subsidiaries

Buderus Heiztechnik GmbH; Buderus Nefit Holding B.V. (Netherlands); Nefit Fasto B.V. (Netherlands); Sieger Heizsysteme GmbH; Buderus Technika Grzewcza sp.z o.o. (Poland); Ferroknepper Buderus S.A. (Luxembourg); Buderus Austria Heiztechnik Ges.mbh (Austria); Buderus Hydronic Systems Inc. (United States); Buderus Guss GmbH; Tiroler Röhren- und Metallwerke AG (Austria); Guss Komponenten GmbH (Austria); Edelstahlwerke Buderus AG (Germany); Deville Rectification S.A. (France); Buderus Specialty Steel Corp. (United States).

### Principal Divisions

Heating Products; Castings; Special Steel Products.

### Principal Competitors

Vaillant Corp.; Viessmann Werke GmbH & Co.; Pont-à-Mousson S.A.; Georg Fischer Ltd.; ThyssenKrupp AG; Böhler-Uddeholm AG.

### Further Reading

*75 Jahre Edelstahlwerke: Buderus AG, 1920–1995*, Wetzlar, Germany: Edelstahlwerke Buderus AG, 1995, 55 p.

"Buderus seit 100 Jahren an der Börse notiert," *Frankfurter Allgemeine Zeitung*, April 10, 1999, p. 18.

"Der Baukonzern Bilfinger + Berger engagiert sich bei Buderus," *Frankfurter Allgemeine Zeitung*, July 14, 1994, p. 17.

Haus, Rainer, *Die Buderus-Aktie—ein Wertpapier im Wandel der Zeit*, Wetzlar, Germany: Buderus Aktiengesellschaft, 2000, 98 p.

"Heizungstechnik wird zur tragenden Säule," *Frankfurter Allgemeine Zeitung*, October 15, 1993, p. 20.

*Vom Ursprung und Werden der Buderus'schen Eisenwerke Wetzlar*, Munich, Germany: F. Bruckmann KG, 1938.

—Evelyn Hauser

# C-CUBE

# C-Cube Microsystems, Inc.

**1778 McCarthy Boulevard**
**Milpitas, California 95035**
**U.S.A.**
**Telephone: (408) 490-8000**
**Fax: (408) 490-8132**
**Web site: http://www.c-cube.com**

*Public Company*
*Incorporated:* 1988
*Employees:* 600
*Sales:* $250 million (2000 est.)
*Stock Exchanges:* NASDAQ
*Ticker Symbol:* CUBE
*NAIC:* 334413 Semiconductor and Related Device
   Manufacturing

C-Cube Microsystems, Inc. provides enabling silicon technology for image compression and the digital video market. During the 1990s the company pioneered the MPEG digital video standard. For three consecutive years C-Cube was named the world's top supplier of MPEG digital silicon by *Dataquest*. In 1995 the company received an Emmy award for technical achievement in digital audio-visual.

### 1988–94: Developing Semiconductor Products

C-Cube Microsystems was established as a California corporation in July 1988. Its co-founders were the president and CEO, Edmund Sun, who had previously started Weitek Corp.; Alexandre Balkanski, who once chaired the video standards group MPEG (Moving Picture Experts Group); the executive vice-president in charge of marketing, Alain Rossman, who had co-founded Radius Inc.; and Jim Rafferty, co-founder of Cricket Software. The company received financial backing of $13 million from the venture capitalist firm Hambrecht & Quist and from Japan's Kubota Ltd., a farm equipment manufacturer. Financial support also came from JAFCO America Ventures, raising the overall investment in the company to $15.7 million.

At first, the firm wasn't certain what kinds of products it would produce. Originally, the founders intended to design high-speed microprocessors. However, a survey of potential customers revealed a strong demand for solutions to image compression.

The company began shipping its first product in early 1990, a single-chip encoder/decoder (codec) for the proposed Joint Photographic Experts Group (JPEG) standard, which was endorsed by the world's largest standard-setting groups, the International Standards Organization (ISO) and the Consultative Committee on Telecommunications Technology (CCITT). The chip could compress images by 10:1 with no visible degradation and up to 100:1 with varying degrees of degradation. Later in the year C-Cube claimed the chip could compress images by 50 times without degradation. Expected applications included digital cameras and VCRs, color printers and scanners, and high-speed image transmission for local-area networks, modems, and color facsimile systems. It was a unique product that was at least a year ahead of the competition. The product incorporated six patents held by C-Cube. Praising the chip, *Microprocessor Report* noted, "It's an exciting and significant advance."

Other proprietary compression algorithms that were being proposed at the time included Intel Corp.'s DVI algorithm and Philips Consumer Electronics' CD-I algorithm. The introduction of C-Cube's monolithic processor, however, brought the industry closer to supporting worldwide, vendor-independent standards. In fact, C-Cube's chip was introduced before a still-motion standard was approved, although the company maintained that all of the technical issues regarding the standard had been resolved.

As early as 1990, the company was predicting that by 1995 its products would be at the core of multimedia PCs and consumer electronics, as computers, television, and communications all began to converge. They envisioned C-Cube products as being instrumental in converting the consumer market from analog to digital.

The company announced plans in 1990 to introduce an AT-based image-compression board for developers that would contain C-Cube's CL550 processor to compress and decompress

## Company Perspectives:

*C-Cube recognizes that it takes an industry to establish the critical infrastructure that enables digital video to penetrate applications worldwide. Through strategic relationships with content owners, hardware and software technology providers, systems manufacturers and standards bodies, C-Cube has brought the necessary industry players together to lay the foundation for the conversion of the home from analog to digital video.*

TGA files by 25 times without loss of image quality. By the end of 1990 the company had about 70 employees. It was pursuing joint ventures in Japan to develop products using the CL550 processor. Potential applications included inserting the chip into still cameras to allow pictures to be taken digitally instead of on film. The chip also made it possible to edit video on desktop computers. The chip was also seen as enhancing the development of video telephony.

In 1991 the JPEG standard received additional industry support, as other companies announced products employing the standard and using C-Cube's CL550 chip. The products included a multimedia workstation from Fluent Machines Inc., PC image-compression boards from Lead Technologies Inc., a PC media compression board from VideoLogic Inc., a video-editing system from Avid Technology Inc., and a full-motion video board from New Media Graphics Corp.

In September 1991 William O'Meara was named president and CEO of C-Cube. He was formerly president and CEO of Headland Technology, an affiliate of LSI Logic Corp., and was described by *Fortune* as "a veteran semiconductor industry executive."

C-Cube and Chips and Technologies Inc. partnered to produce a JPEG Video Development Kit for original equipment manufacturers (OEMs) and developers. The $4,000 kit included the CL550 processor and Chips and Technologies' PC Video window-controller chip on an AT board. The kit, which was scheduled to ship in February 1992, was expected to allow a standard JPEG video-capture method to emerge quickly.

In May 1992 C-Cube announced the immediate availability of production quantities of the first single-chip MPEG decoder. Dubbed the CL450, it was developed in cooperation with Philips and was used in a Philips demonstration of full-screen full-motion video from a CD-ROM. The CL450 and CL450i were compatible with Philips' CD-I format and the MPEG standard for full motion and color video. They were expected to be used in compact disk-based video systems and compact disk-interactive (CD-I) consumer electronics, including Karaoke machines. C-Cube's overall sales in 1992 were about $19 million.

In 1993 C-Cube entered into an agreement with Texas Instruments Inc. to exchange video and audio compression circuit technology. The agreement allowed both firms to develop derivative products utilizing the other's current and future MPEG decoder and JPEG coder/decoder products. Applications included digital cable TV, direct broadcast satellite TV, compact disc, and high definition TV. Previously, Texas Instrument had focused on audio technology, while C-Cube was known for its video circuits. The agreement also gave C-Cube access to TI's production capacity. C-Cube did not have its own fabrication facility and was using four foundries in the United States and Japan. C-Cube also entered into a similar agreement with chipmaker Advanced Micro Devices to gain access to its production facilities.

In 1993 C-Cube became a supplier of VLSI circuits and encoders/decoders for the receiving devices of Thomson Consumer Electronics' Digital Satellite System (DSS), which was to receive programming from DirecTV. C-Cube's VLSI circuits would implement the MPEG compression/decompression algorithm, making it possible to have four to eight times the number of channels than was allowed by the current analog DBS systems. C-Cube encoders would be used in satellite uplink equipment, with the decoder chips in RCA receivers.

For 1993–94 C-Cube chips would be used in the new wave of video players from Sony, JVC, Samsung, and others, that would use CD-ROMs instead of cassettes or laser disks. In Japan the chips were being used in video jukeboxes sold by JVC and used in Karaoke bars. JVC expected to sell $1 billion worth of the jukeboxes annually. Around this time co-founder Edward Sun left the company to start a business in Taiwan that would build Karaoke machines using C-Cube chips.

In fall 1993 C-Cube introduced the first real-time MPEG-1 video encoder. The CL4000 graphics coprocessor was capable of performing real-time video encoding or decoding and was compatible with both MPEG and JPEG standards. The chip's high level of integration was expected to reduce the price of multimedia authoring systems to less than $4,000 within two years. The coprocessor contained 1.2 million transistors, giving it the power to perform real-time MPEG encoding or decoding. Multiple CL4000s could be employed together to encode larger, high-resolution images.

For 1993 C-Cube reported an 80 percent increase in revenues to $24 million. The company was clearly the leader in the video compression market. Its customers included Thomson Consumer Electronics, Scientifica Atlanta, Philips, and Compression Labs in the broadcast market. In the consumer electronics market its customers included JVC, Commodore, Goldstar, Samsung, and 3DO. The video compression market was expected to grow so rapidly that C-Cube predicted its revenue would double every year and that it would be able to spend 35 percent of its revenue on research and development. One key to C-Cube's continued market dominance was its access to the wafer fabrication facilities of Texas Instruments and Advanced Micro Devices.

### 1994–99: Going Public

In 1994 C-Cube reincorporated as a Delaware corporation. It made its initial public offering (IPO) of stock in April 1994, selling some 2.4 million shares at an initial price of $15 per share. Prior to the IPO the company had raised about $38 million from investors. Among the investors was venture capital firm Sequoia Capital, whose Don Valentine had become C-Cube's chairman.

---

**Key Dates:**

**1988:** C-Cube Microsystems, Inc. is established as a California corporation.
**1990:** The company ships its first product, a single-chip encoder/decoder for image compression.
**1994:** C-Cube goes public.
**1996:** C-Cube acquires DiviCom, a maker of integrated circuits for set-top boxes.
**2000:** DiviCom merges with Harmonic, Inc.; C-Cube Microsystems continues as a semiconductor provider to the digital video market.

---

In April 1994 C-Cube announced it would introduce the first multimode video decoder chip for shipment later in the year. The CL9100, RISC-based integrated circuit (IC) could decode four video compression algorithms: MPEG-2 (both simple and main profile), DigiCipher II, and MPEG-1. It also supported all standards, including NTSC, PAL, and film, so that cable box manufacturers could use the single chip to implement the most widely accepted compression systems.

In fall 1994 C-Cube introduced a new chip, the CL480V/CD, that was expected to reduce the price of video compact disc players from $400 to less than $250. The consumer electronics chip could also enable PC video CD add-in cards for less than $300. By 1995 some 22 consumer electronic companies were relying on C-Cube's chips to build video CD players.

For the broadcast market, C-Cube introduced the CLM4700 family of real-time MPEG-2 encoders at the end of 1994. These devices would allow broadcasters to incorporate digital compression in their delivery, whether cable, telephone, or direct broadcast. MPEG-2 was now seen as the principal enabler for digital TV, and it was widely accepted as the industry standard.

In early 1995 C-Cube formed a new business unit to concentrate on growing the market for JPEG video compression devices. The firm noted that the MPEG market, in which it held a leadership position, was becoming more crowded with software-based solutions, chips from the Far East and Europe, and new competitors. Up to this time JPEG was being used primarily for high-end digital video editing, high-end copiers, Postscript printers, newspaper wirephoto transmission, medical imaging, and security applications.

During the year C-Cube introduced a second-generation MPEG-2 CLM4400 encoder chip based on its VideoRISC architecture. The chip reduced the number of required encoding devices to four, which would enable customers to pack more data streams over existing bandwidth. The company also introduced a CLM4550 MPEG-1 encoder for real-time communications and authoring for games and entertainment. The firm's new CL480PC System Decoder combined MPEG audio and video decoders on a single chip and integrated them with other logic circuits in a multimedia PC design, thus bringing MPEG decoding to laptop computers and multimedia desktop PCs.

Also in 1995 C-Cube entered the video telephony market by developing the CLM4200, a video encoder/decoder (codec). Its first customer for the chip was PictureTel, which planned to use the chip in a group video conferencing system currently under development. In August 1995 C-Cube's stock rose ten percent in one day to around $44 a share, after the company announced it would sell video decoder chips to Sony Corp. and Sharp Electronics. C-Cube was supplying more than 20 consumer electronics companies with chips for use in a new generation of digital video machines. Utilizing C-Cube's technology, up to 74 minutes of video data could be stored on one compact disk. So far, the biggest market for video compact disks was Asia, where the Karaoke craze was fueling demand.

For 1995, C-Cube's stock rose 558 percent. For the first nine months of 1995 the company's profits rose 437 percent to $16 million, while revenue jumped 140 percent to $74 million for nine months. Co-founder Alexandre Balkanski had become C-Cube's CEO. By mid-1996 the stock was in the low $30s following a market correction that affected many technology stocks. Also in 1995 the company received an Emmy award for its MPEG-2 technology contribution to digital television.

In 1996 C-Cube faced challenges from IBM and LSI Logic to its dominance of the MPEG-2 video decoder market. Both companies introduced video codecs aimed at the broadcast market for real-time broadcast encoding. At the spring 1996 meeting of the National Association of Broadcasters (NAB) in Las Vegas, C-Cube introduced three chipsets. Its seven-chip CLM4740 MPEG-2 device targeted direct broadcast satellite, digital or wireless cable, and wide-screen enhanced definition television (EDTV) applications. Its two-chip CLM4440 video authoring device was the first MPEG-1 advanced videoCD decoder to integrate NTCS and PAL standards. At least three OEMs planned to announce PC add-in boards for creating video content based on the CLM4440 multimedia authoring chipset at the NAB exhibition. A third new product, the CLM4720 storage encoder, was designed to format video for storage on video file servers for video-on-demand, local television advertising insertions, and broadcast automation applications.

In 1996 C-Cube acquired DiviCom Inc., in which C-Cube had taken a 5.4 percent ownership interest when it was founded in 1993. DiviCom manufactured integrated circuits for set-top boxes. As a subsidiary of C-Cube, it would become the leading provider of MPEG-2 encoding products and systems for digital video broadcasting. C-Cube's semiconductor division would continue to supply digital video IC's for both consumer electronics and communication products. For 1996 C-Cube reported revenues of $320 million, compared to $125 million in 1995.

C-Cube's new low-cost MPEG-1 video decoder, the CLM4111, promised to bring true video processing to PCs. When added to a PC, the CLM4111 let users capture, edit, store, and communicate with digital video. PC users could thus create high-quality MPEG videos for presentations, training videos, and communications on the Internet.

With digital videodiscs (DVDs) expected to hit U.S. and worldwide consumer markets in 1997, C-Cube introduced a new single-chip decoder for DVD video players and on-card solutions for PCs. It also introduced a process that enabled a 133-minute movie to be encoded in real-time on a single DVD. Later in the year the company introduced SecureView, a copy-protection chip designed to prevent unauthorized copying of movies that were recorded in the DVD format. SecureView was expected to lower the cost of DVD hardware for consumers and to encourage Hollywood studios to make more titles available in the DVD format. During the year C-Cube also introduced its ZiVA DVD decoder, which was considered the first MPEG-2 audio/video product to be recognized as Dolby Digital 6-Channel compliant.

In mid-1997 C-Cube introduced a new reference design that would support a new class of PC peripherals known as MVP, or MPEG video peripherals, for the consumer market. Peripheral manufacturers Avermedia and Videonics announced they would develop MVPs using C-Cube's reference design. MVPs had the potential to bring high-quality still and full-motion video capture capabilities to a new audience of consumers. The MVPs were powered by C-Cube's VideoRISC MPEG processor.

Later in 1997 C-Cube launched its DVx IC, the first single-chip codec for MPEG-2. Up to this time MPEG-2 codecs had relied on three to 12 ICs. The new chip was expected to reduce the costs of video editing and production and allow consumers to do MPEG-based video editing on PCs equipped with a recordable digital versatile disc (DVD) drive. Among the first customers for the DVx codec were JVC, DiviCom, Optibase, Vela Research, Comsat Laboratories, and Optivision.

C-Cube followed up in 1998 with its DVxpress series, a family of MPEG-2 encoder/decoder (codec) products targeted at digital broadcast, professional studio, post production, and content authoring applications. The MPEG-2 editing environment was considered compatible with most digital editing technologies. In the fall C-Cube introduced DVxpress-MX, a codec that allowed studio and broadcast production and editing users to have all-digital video production. For the first time, MPEG and digital video could co-exist in the same environment and be used together.

Later in the year C-Cube entered into an alliance designed to provide cable TV operators with an interoperable digital system. The four firms involved in the strategic alliance were C-Cube and its subsidiary DiviCom, along with Japan's Pioneer Electronics and Europe's Canal+. The alliance with Canal+ was considered something of a surprise, because its biggest silicon supplier for set-top boxes was C-Cube's biggest rival, STMicroelectronics. In Europe, Canal+ had about 1.8 million set-top boxes installed for interactive television applications such as Web browsing and home shopping.

For 1998 C-Cube reported revenues of $351.8 million and net income of $46.3 million, compared to 1997 revenues of $337 million and net income of $44.3 million.

In January 1999 C-Cube acquired the communication technology, patents, and personnel of TV/COM International, which was part of the Mindport Group Inc. of San Diego. The acquisition gave C-Cube strategic communication technologies for interactive cable and satellite digital set-top boxes. The next month C-Cube won a contract from Canal+ to supply it with set-top box digital video chipsets. Canal+ was one of Europe's largest digital pay-TV services. C-Cube subsequently announced it would also supply set-top box chipsets for Germany's KirchGroup for use on German Pay TV. During the year C-Cube continued to actively pursue the European set-top box market. In fall 1999 C-Cube introduced an improved high-definition chip for video production and broadcast called the DVxHD.

## Divestiture and Spin-Off: 2000

Until May 2, 2000, C-Cube consisted of two divisions, C-Cube Semiconductor and DiviCom. At the close of business on May 2, the semiconductor division was spun off as a stand-alone entity with the temporary name of C-Cube Semiconductor Inc. The next day, the remainder of C-Cube Microsystems—essentially DiviCom—was merged into Harmonic, Inc., a Sunnyvale, California-based maker of digital fiber-optic systems. The acquisition of DiviCom by Harmonic was valued at $1.7 billion. Following the merger, C-Cube Semiconductor Inc. re-acquired the name C-Cube Microsystems, Inc. Umesh Padval, who had been president of C-Cube Semiconductor since 1998, became president and CEO of C-Cube Microsystems.

With the sale of DiviCom, which provided open solutions for digital television and was C-Cube's systems integration business, C-Cube Microsytems became a pure semiconductor company with a strong presence in the digital video market. C-Cube expected to build on its strength of designing and manufacturing silicon solutions for DVD and digital VHS players, personal video recorders, digital set-top boxes, video production equipment, and television broadcasting systems.

C-Cube was enjoying explosive growth in its DVD chipsets. In September 2000 it announced it was the first chip supplier to surpass the ten million unit mark in silicon shipments for the worldwide DVD market. The DVD market began in 1997, and in 1999 C-Cube shipped nearly four million DVD chips, more than all DVD industry shipments in 1998. For 1999 the company claimed about 30 percent market share and was named the world's top supplier of DVD silicon.

## Principal Competitors

ESS Technology, Inc.; LSI Logic Corp.; Zoran Corp.; Sony Electronics, Inc.; STMicroelectronics, Inc.; Conexant Systems, Inc.; Oak Technology, Inc.

## Further Reading

Anderson, James A., ''More than Instinct Alone,'' *Black Enterprise,* December 1997, p. 51.

Brown, Peter, ''C-Cube Continues Along the DVxpress,'' *Electronic News,* May 3, 1999, p. 23.

——, ''Route Canal for C-Cube,'' *Electronic News,* February 8, 1999, p. 50.

''C-Cube DVx Chip Debuts,'' *Television Digest,* August 25, 1997, p. 13.

''C-Cube Microsystems,'' *Business Journal-San Jose,* September 30, 1991, p. 21.

Cataldo, Anthony, ''C-Cube Lines up PictureTel for New Video Codec,'' *Electronic News (1991),* May 1, 1995, p. 22.

——, ''C-Cube, LSI Logic: Tale of Two MPEGs,'' *Electronic News,* September 26, 1994, p. 76.

Davey, Tom, ''C-Cube on a Roll with MPEG-2 Chips for PC Video Production,'' *PC Week,* April 15, 1996, p. 10.

Dickson, Glen, ''C-Cube Unveils New Set-Top Chips,'' *Broadcasting & Cable,* December 9, 1996, p. 112.

''Fortune Visits 25 Cool Companies,'' *Fortune,* Autumn 1993, p. 56.

Fusaro, Roberta, "C-Cube: Favorable Buzz," *Computerworld,* August 3, 1998, p. 82.

Glitman, Russell, "C-Cube Proving to be a Gem in the Land of Silicon," *PC Week,* June 11, 1990, p. 121.

Greenberg, Herb, "The Little Chipmaker that (Probably) Won't," *Fortune,* March 3, 1997, p. 36.

McConnell, Chris, "Chip Maker C-Cube Microsystems," *Broadcasting & Cable,* May 2, 1994, p. 51.

Miner, Nicola, "C-Cube to Bring MPEG Decoding to Laptops," *InfoWorld,* April 24, 1995, p. 48.

Reis, Charles, "C-Cube's MPEG-2 Comes of Age," *Advanced Imaging,* November 1998, p. 66.

Rosen, Carol, "C-Cube Becomes the King of Compression," *Electronic Business Buyer,* April 1994, p. 66.

Rothman, Matt, "C-Cube Microsystems Inc.: Snapping Tiny Pictures," *California Business,* December 1990, p. 10.

Schonfield, Erick, "Getting in Real Early on Digital Video," *Fortune,* February 5, 1996, p. 136.

Young, Jeffrey, "Pirate's Best Friend," *Forbes,* March 10, 1997, p. 164.

—David P. Bianco

# The Canadian Broadcasting Corporation (CBC)

250 Lanark Avenue
P.O. Box 3220, Station C
Ottawa, Ontario K1Y 1E4
Canada
Telephone: (613) 724-1200
Fax: (613) 724-5725
Web site: http://www.cbc.radio-canada.ca

*Government-Owned Company*
*Founded:* 1936
*Employees:* 7,650
*Sales:* US$348 million (2000)
*NAIC:* 51312 Television Broadcasting; 51311 Radio
   Broadcasting

The Canadian Broadcasting Corporation (CBC) is Canada's public broadcaster. Created by an Act of Parliament in 1936, the government owned company provides services in both of Canada's official languages, English and French. All told, the CBC operates two television networks, four radio networks, a cable television service, an international shortwave radio service and a commercial-free audio service. CBC operates approximately 100 radio and television stations across Canada.

### Background

To understand the role that CBC plays in Canada, it is important to first understand the three uniquely Canadian issues that have played a major role in its creation and growth. First, Canada is a country with a large landmass and relatively low population, distributed unevenly, with the majority living in the South, within 100 miles of the U.S. border. Canada's remote northern communities are separated from the southern population by mountains, tundra, rough terrain, and by hostile weather conditions throughout several months of the year. Consequently, Canada has always striven to develop communication structures to connect these widely separated communities. Throughout its history, CBC has responded to the challenge of providing services and programming to all Canadians, regardless of location. Second, since Canada has two official languages, French and English, the CBC provides services in two languages. In addition, since many of Canada's northern Aboriginal peoples speak neither English nor French, CBC has made programming available in Aboriginal languages. Finally, the need to present programming with Canadian content has played a major role in CBC's development. Canada has always struggled to maintain its own identify separate from that of its larger neighbor to the south. From the earliest days of the CBC's history, Canadians have demanded that the broadcaster provide Canadian news, sports, cultural broadcasts and other national content.

### CBC's Early Years: 1919–36

CBC's roots stem back to 1919, when Canada's first licensed radio station, the Marconi station XWA, began experimental broadcasts. Throughout the 1920s, many radio stations sprung up across the country. However, stations tended to be situated in larger cities while smaller, isolated communities received no service. National programming and content was limited. Distribution from east to west was costly. Only a few frequencies were uniquely Canadian, and there was ongoing interference with large Mexican and U.S. stations. Public discontent increased steadily.

Consequently, in 1928, the government-commissioned Aird Report recommended establishing a publicly owned and funded network that would provide coast to coast service and would provide Canadian content. Implementation was delayed until 1932, when the Canadian Radio Broadcasting Act was passed establishing the Canadian Radio Broadcasting Commission (CRBC).

Within four years, the CRBC acquired radio stations, broadcast Canadian content in two languages, and solved many of the previous problems. However, the Commission was handicapped by limited funding, limited authority, and by organizational challenges. In 1936, a new Broadcasting Act was passed, creating the CBC to replace the CRBC. The CBC was to be publicly owned but modeled along the lines of a private corporation.

### Prewar and War Years: 1936–45

In 1936, the CBC took over the CRBC's staff and facilities. Initially, only 49 percent of the population were being served,

## Company Perspectives:

*As Canada's public broadcaster, the CBC provides services in English and in French, and is accountable to all Canadians. The CBC: tells Canadian stories reflecting the reality and the diversity of our country; informs Canadians about news and issues of relevance and interest; supports Canadian arts and culture; builds bridges among Canadians, between regions and the two linguistic communities.*

and areas around Toronto, Montreal, Winnipeg, Saskatoon, and Edmonton were experiencing interference from outside of Canada. By 1939, the CBC had addressed the problems by building four high-powered regional transmitters situated in strategic spots across Canada.

In 1937, an international conference involving Canada, the United States, Mexico, and Cuba resulted in an agreement for the redistribution of North American frequencies. Canada gained 11 clear channels and the shared use of 43 lower-power channels—thereby eliminating most of the former problems created by outside interference.

As the decade ended, national coverage was close to 90 percent. The national network had grown to 34 stations with optional programming on another 26. Studies were underway to examine service provision in difficult reception areas in remote regions of British Columbia. Regional farm broadcasts were available in both official languages, and school broadcasts were underway in several regions.

In 1939, the CBC performed its biggest broadcasting task to date—daily coverage, in two languages, of the Royal Tour of Canada. During this time, the CBC observed the experimental television that was underway in several countries, including Canada. When World War II broke out in 1939, worldwide development of television slowed to accommodate wartime priorities. However, wartime requirements were the impetus for the expansion of radio broadcasting.

In 1939, CBC implemented a small overseas unit of one technician and one reporter. In cooperation with England's BBC network, this unit began two-way broadcasting to Canadian troops in Britain as well as broadcasting wartime programming to Canadian listeners at home. During the war years, this small unit increased in size and was first among the wartime broadcasters to use mobile equipment to make on the spot recordings. The CBC's recordings were often used by the BBC and by movie newsreel companies.

Meanwhile, at home, the CBC News Service was established in 1941 to bring regional programming to the country. Many of these initial programs were war related, but others were of more lasting nature. CBC won its first international programming awards at this time, in competition at Ohio State University.

Despite the short supply of technical equipment during wartime, the CBC managed to extend or improve coverage in communities in Northern British Columbia, Ontario, and New Brunswick. In 1944, the Toronto transmitter was linked with 34 private stations to form a second English network called the Dominion. The original English network was renamed the Trans-Canada.

Wartime also brought CBC into international shortwave broadcasting. The CBC International Service, operated by the CBC but financed separately, was officially opened in 1945. Services were in seven languages and were beamed to Europe, Latin America, and the Caribbean.

### Postwar Era: 1945–75

With the end of World War II, the CBC obtained a loan from the Federal government and pursued a number of urgent capital projects intended to improve radio service across the country. Over the course of the next two decades, CBC radio service expanded to include programming for the two millions square miles in Canada's north. Programming was made available in French, English, Inuit dialects, and a selection of Indian languages.

In the early 1950s, the CBC International Service began broadcasting to Canadian forces in England and Korea, and later to Canadian service men and women situated in France and Germany. In 1968, all International Service operations were an important part of CBC, and a system was implemented for emergency broadcasting in case of a national emergency.

During the same period, television broadcasting was underway. In 1949, a Canadian television service was authorized. By 1962, the role of television was such that in 1962, the Dominion and Trans-Canada networks consolidated into one network with 160 outlets—both CBC and private. In 1969, color television was introduced in Canada, and CBC was given authorization for a C$15 million first stage conversion. By the early 1970s, much of CBC's television programming was in color.

In Canada's centennial year, 1967, the CBC broadcast 1,500 hours of Centennial programming, in addition to building and operating a C$10 million broadcasting center at Expo '67 in Montreal. Also in 1967, the CBC became the official broadcaster for the Pan-American Games in Winnipeg. By the end of the decade, CBC was providing television coverage to 96.6 percent of Canadians, and satellite coverage was in the planning stages. Moreover, the Canadian Radio-Television Commission (CRTC) had been established to regulate and license the broadcasting industry.

### A Period of Challenge and Growth: 1975–2000

As CBC personality Knowlton Nash observed in his book *The Microphone Wars*, the 1960s heralded in a period of turmoil for CBC—turmoil that would reoccur for decades and reach national proportions. As Canada struggled with a shaky economy, budgetary cutbacks were commonplace among all government-funded entities. The CBC was no exception. Like many companies during this time, the CBC was faced with the need to do more with less. Meanwhile, periodic labor disputes disrupted service provision, and internal conflicts took their toll on morale and productivity. A group of CBC radio and television personalities, known as ''The Seven Day Rebels'' battled

## Key Dates:

**1936:** The Canadian Broadcasting Act creates the CBC.

**1941:** The company establishes a news service.

**1952:** The Canadian TV network CBC begins operations.

**1966:** Color TV is introduced in Canada.

**1968:** Canadian Radio-Television Commission (CRTC) is established as the regulatory and licensing authority.

**1977:** CBC installs broadcast facilities in the House of Commons.

**1981:** CBC introduces closed captioning on Canadian TV programs.

**1984:** CBC stereo networks start 24-hour broadcasting and supplementary cable distribution.

**1986:** CBC's 50th anniversary is acknowledged by a commemorative postage stamp.

**1995:** CBC is granted a license to operate a new digital audio music service.

**1997:** The Minister of Canadian Heritage announces five years of stable funding for CBC.

so bitterly with CBC management that John Diefenbaker, Leader of the Opposition, called for an emergency debate in the House of Commons. In his official request, Diefenbaker wrote, "I do not think that there has ever been a matter that in such a short time has brought about so much antagonism in all parts of Canada." The call for debate was rejected, but the Prime Minister called for an investigation.

Meanwhile at the CBC, life went on, and the public broadcaster continued to provide services. In 1972, the Report of the Special Senate Committee, chaired by Senator Keith Davey, offered a voice of confidence in CBC radio. Davey noted that "CBC radio was a national medium in a country unable to support a national press." In that same year, the CRTC issued network licenses to CBC for the first time.

Also in the early 1970s, the CRTC introduced Canadian content regulations, stipulating that 60 percent of private and public television programming on the network had to be Canadian. Two years later, the CRTC invited proposals for the future development of pay television. In 1972, CBC contracted for three channels with the newly launched Anik-1 satellite, developed by the Telesat Corporation (now Telesat Canada). This brought new or improved broadcasting services to 99 percent of Canadians, including many of the remote communities above the 60th parallel.

Throughout the remainder of the 1970s, CBC activities included the opening of La Maison de Radio-Canada in Montreal; the introduction of a new CBC logo or symbol based on "C" for Canada; the opening of French and English FM stereo networks; and the opening of a Global Network. CBC was the host broadcaster for the Summer Olympics held in Montreal in 1976. Later in the decade, CBC designed and installed broadcast facilities in the House of Commons. Live TV coverage commenced from the House of Commons in 1979. Also during

this time, CBC began operating its first production facilities in the North in the Northwest Territories town of Yellowknife.

The 1980s brought about other significant events in the CBC's history. In 1980, the CBC Knowledge Network was established, and in 1981 the CBC introduced closed captioning for the hearing impaired on Canadian television programs. The network was also asked to manage the installation of a telecommunications system called OASIS in Parliamentary offices.

During this time, the CBC received a highly critical report from a government commission known as the Cultural Policy Review Committee. According to *The Microphone Wars,* the Applebaum-Hébert report recommended diverse changes with grave implications for the future of CBC. The Canadian government did not implement the recommendations but it did announce a broadcast strategy for Canada, emphasizing the need for a stronger CBC.

However, in 1984, a national election brought about a change in government. The newly elected Prime Minister Brian Mulroney announced massive budget cuts to CBC, cuts that, according to Knowlton Nash, far exceeded cuts made to other government-funded bodies. These cuts forced staff layoffs, the discontinuing of programming, and the introduction of commercials to content that had previously been commercial-free. Despite what appeared to be a lack of support from the Mulroney government, public support for the CBC remained high. In 1986, a commemorative postage stamp was issued to mark CBC's 50th anniversary.

Also in 1986, the Federal Task Force on Broadcasting Policy (Caplan/Sauvageau) published recommendations supporting CBC's role as public broadcaster and recommending increased financing to pay for enhanced services and programming. Most of these recommendations were not acted upon.

Despite a much smaller operating budget, CBC operations continued. Ten new specialty channels were licensed by CRTC; The Cabinet approved the development of the CBC Broadcast Centre Development in Toronto and also approved the CBC license application to operate an English all-news channel (Newsworld.)

In 1990 the CBC published a corporate vision entitled Mission, Values, Goals and Objectives, and CBC Engineering began working on the development of Digital Audio Broadcasting. In 1991, a new Broadcasting Act was passed, removing wording that defined the CBC's role in fostering national unity. Fearing that the provision was a constraint on freedom of expression and that the former wording might pave the way for propaganda distribution, legislators replaced the wording with, "contribute to shared national consciousness and identity."

In 1994, the CBC and Power Broadcasting Inc. partnered to launch two new specialty channels to the United States (Trio and Newsworld International), and in 1995, CBC was licensed to operate a new digital audio music service known as Galaxie.

1997 was a year of good news and new growth for the CBC. The Minister of Canadian Heritage announced stable funding for the CBC for a five-year period. CBC Radio received an additional $10 million dollars per year, and Radio Canada

International received stable funding of $15.5 million annually. During this time, English Information Radio Service was renamed "Radio One," and the Stereo Service "Radio Two." CBC's French radio services were renamed Première Chaîne and Chaîne culturelle. Galaxie, a pay audio service was launched, and the CBC enriched content to bring its English Television prime-time content almost 100 percent Canadian. The year 1997 also brought a significant change to CBC management processes. The board of directors approved Project Evolution, an integrated management system called SAP (Systems/Applications/Products). Under the SAP program, administrative functions were streamlined and made more efficient.

In 1998, the CBC provided 700 hours of programming at the Nagano Olympics. Partnered with Sympatico Internet Provider and the Stentor group of phone companies, the CBC offered instant access to Olympic results via the Internet. The International Olympic Committee awarded CBC, in partnership with NetStar, the broadcast rights to the next five Olympic Games. In April 1998, the CBC was awarded an honorary Golden Rose from the Montreaux Festival, recognizing the quality of its programs.

Not all news was good, however. Canada's Heritage Minister announced that CBC would no longer be guaranteed access to the Canadian Television Fund after the year 2000. Most alarmingly for CBC, the CRTC announced intentions to hold a serious of public consultations prior to renewing CBC's license in 1999. Since the licenses for CBC's Radio and Television networks, its 24 TV stations, RDI, and Newsworld, were up for renewal at the same time, the outcome was critical.

In response, the CBC invited feedback from the Canadian public. When the CRTC held the planned public consultation sessions, most of the 600 participants expressed strong support for the CBC. The CBC itself received 54,500 letters and emails offering support, suggestions, and feedback. As the year neared its end, CBC won an Emmy in the technical category from the National Academy of Television Arts and Science in the United States.

New Year's Day, 2000, found CBC services uninterrupted with no Y2K problems in evidence. In early January, the CBC received word that the CRTC had renewed all its licenses for a seven-year term. However, the CRTC imposed certain conditions on television programming that would create additional expenditures of $50 million. CBC management opted not to appeal the decision. At the beginning of the new century, the CBC appeared to be fairy stabilized following the traumatic years that went before. CEO and President, Robert Rabinovitch announced plans to create a Reengineering Task Force, a body that would examine all aspects of CBC's operations with an eye on refocusing resources on programming.

### Principal Divisions

CBC Radio One; CBC Radio Two; La Radio de Radio-Canada; La Chaîne culturelle FM; CBC Newsworld; Le Réseau de l'information (RDI); Radio Canada International; Galaxie.

### Principal Competitors

CanWest Global Communications Corp.; Rogers Communications Inc.; Shaw Communications Inc.

### Further Reading

*CBC: A Brief History of the Canadian Broadcasting Corporation*, Ottawa: CBC Public Relations, 1976.

Manera, Anthony, *A Dream Betrayed: The Battle for CBC*, Toronto: Stoddart Publishing, 1996.

Nash, Knowlton, *Cue the Elephant!: Backstage Tales at the CBC*, Ontario: McClelland & Stewart, 1997.

——, *The Microphone Wars: A History of Triumph and Betrayal at the CBC*, Ontario: McClelland & Stewart, 1998.

*Our Commitment to Canadians: The CBC's Strategic Plan*, Ottawa: CBC, 1999.

Skene, Wayne, *Fade to Black: A Requiem of the CBC*, Vancouver: Douglas & McIntyre, 1994.

—June Campbell

# Cap Gemini Ernst & Young

Place de l'Etoile
11 rue de Tilsitt
75017 Paris
France
Telephone: (+33) 1 47 54 50 00
Fax: (+33) 1 42 27 32 11
Web site: http://www.capgemini.com

*Public Company*
*Incorporated:* 1967 as Sogeti (Société pour la gestion de l'entreprise et le traitement de l'informatique)
*Employees:* 57,000
*Sales:* EUR 7.7 billion ($7 billion) (1999)
*Stock Exchanges:* Euronext Paris
*Ticker Symbol:* CAP.012533
*NAIC:* 541511 Custom Computer Programming Services; 541513 Computer Facilities Management Services; 541512 Computer Systems Design Services

Cap Gemini Ernst & Young is one of the world's heavyweights in the information technology services industry. Created from the August 2000 merger of France's Cap Gemini S.A. and the IT consulting division of Ernst & Young, the new group employs more than 57,000 people worldwide and generated some EUR 7.7 billion in pro forma combined sales in 1999. Led by founder and chairman Serge Kampf and CEO Geoff Unwin, Cap Gemini Ernst & Young operates in three core areas: software development and systems integration, worth 51 percent of the company's annual sales; information systems consulting and management, which adds some 23 percent of revenue; and the management of information systems, which also generates 23 percent of the company's sales. Cap Gemini Ernst & Young is quoted on the Euronext stock exchange.

### Birth of an Industry in the 1960s

Serge Kampf received degrees in law and economics but turned his attention instead to the newly developing computer industry in the early 1960s. Working as a salesman for French computer systems manufacturer Bull, Kampf quickly made his

mark, becoming director of the company's Grenoble region operations. After Bull was sold to GE, however, Kampf left the company. After a brief stint in the commercial export department of an industrial baker, Kampf decided to go into business on his own. Despite a personal aversion to computers—he would admit to *Time* in 1991 that he had a "holy aversion" to them—Kampf recognized the growth potential of the computer industry. Instead of turning to the hardware side, Kampf instead determined to make his mark on the nascent software side, reasoning the large and international corporations would inevitably turn to experts to help implement and manage their information technology needs.

With a handful of partners, Kampf founded the Société pour la gestion de l'entreprise et le traitement de l'informatique, or Sogeti, in 1967. The company joined a myriad of computer services companies, most of which focused on the Paris market. Yet Kampf stuck to his Grenoble roots, recognizing that that region and other provincial markets remained largely underserved by the IT industry.

Sogeti met with almost immediate success, posting more than FFr 1.5 million in revenues by the end of its first year, while building up a staff of some 20 employees. The company was also already profitable—with net profits FFr 60,000 worth more than four percent of its sales. Kampf also weathered a management crisis in the company's first year, surviving a power struggle among the founding partners to take majority control of Sogeti. The company's policy of targeting its local market paid off with a growing number of contracts with corporations and government bodies, as these began to adopt computer technology for their management and data storage needs. One such large contract took Sogeti to Switzerland, where the company opened its first subsidiary operation in 1968. By the end of 1969, Sogeti's sales had topped FFr 4.2 million, and its payroll had swelled to 49.

From the start, Kampf, who held 84 percent of the company's shares, led Sogeti on a program of partnerships and mergers with others in the industry. An early partnership was set up with Gemini Computer Systems in 1969, giving the U.S.-based company's French operations a 20 percent share of Sogeti. Before that partnership was dissolved after only a year, Kampf also attempted to bring in a major player in the French IT industry, CAP. However, CAP refused to join the then unknown Kampf and his company.

---

### Company Perspectives:

*Cap Gemini Ernst & Young benefits from a balanced geographic coverage that will permit it to pursue a global strategic offensive around the following axes: an operational approach centered on large international companies and based on Ernst & Young's expertise in this area (an approach known as account-centric); a policy of strong alliances with the major players in the market, permitting the new group to bring its clients quick solutions adapted to the changes related to the Net economy; an ambitious human resources program designed to attract and retain the best people by offering them attractive opportunities for professional advancement; a systematic capitalization on expertise in both the sector services.*

---

Sogeti's growing treasury—the company refused to pay out dividends—enabled it to turn its attention to growth by acquisition. In 1970, the company acquired rival Solame, and then a 52 percent controlling interest in Sorgas. Sogeti then joined in with a group of partner companies to form Euroinfor. Meanwhile, the company had also pursued a policy of maintaining close proximity with its growing list of customers, opening branch offices throughout France, beginning with Lyon in 1969. By 1972, Sogeti had offices in more than 12 French cities, plus a growing network in Switzerland through its Sogeti Suisse subsidiary. The company's Parisian office opened in 1979. A strong factor in the company's growth was its policy of decentralized management, giving the manager of each office a large degree of autonomy—and financial incentive—while guiding the company's overall strategy from its Grenoble headquarters.

By 1973 company's sales had topped FFr 52 million. Payroll had grown to nearly 650. That year, however, saw the company make a dramatic change in its position in the French IT market. After gaining some 15 percent of CAP—the company that had snubbed him a few years earlier—Kampf led Sogeti on a hostile takeover of its larger rival, building up a position, combined with Kampf's 15 percent, of 49 percent of CAP by the end of 1973. As CAP largest single shareholder, Sogeti placed pressure on its other shareholders to gain full control—which it did after a bitter battle in June 1974. The new company, dubbed Cap Sogeti, was quickly joined by another major acquisition, that of Gemini Computer Systems in September 1974. After merging the three companies, the new group took on a new name in January 1975, that of Cap Gemini Sogeti.

### Growing into the 1980s

The new group had become one of the French IT industry's largest, with sales topping FFr 226 million and nearly 2,000 employees. The company continued its dual growth strategy of internal expansion—opening new branches across France and launching new foreign subsidiaries, offices, and partnerships in London in 1973, Washington, D.C., in 1978, and Spain in 1979—and growth by acquisition through purchasing shares in such rivals as Bossard in 1976 and Sesa in 1982. By the end of 1982, Cap Gemini Sogeti had passed the FFr 1 billion mark.

If Cap Gemini Sogeti remained a largely European company—with its primary focus on its domestic market—it was beginning to nurture global ambitions. At the beginning of the 1980s, the company began to make its first moves into the all-important United States IT market, making a number of acquisitions that were then regrouped as subsidiary Cap Gemini America in 1986. By then, the company's official language had already turned to English—marking its global ambitions. The company had also gone public and was listed on the Paris Exchange in 1985, providing fuel for its future growth in the rapidly developing IT market of the 1980s.

By the end of the 1980s, Cap Gemini Sogeti had secured a position as the world's fifth-largest IT services company. The company had made particularly strong advances across Europe, making acquisitions in (West) Germany, Italy, Denmark, Sweden, and Finland to bolster its presence throughout the European Community. The company also continued to add to its U.S. presence, including the acquisition of Merit Systems in 1989. By then, the addition of full control of France's Sesa in 1987 had enabled the company's sales to leap to more than FFr 4 billion. The company made a new jump in 1990 when it acquired the United Kingdom's Hoskyns Group. Led by Geoff Unwin, the Hoskyns Group was one of the leading European IT services companies, and the IT leader in the United Kingdom. That purchase, for $345 million, helped push Cap Gemini Sogeti's annual revenues past the FFr 9 billion mark in 1990. Total payroll was now nearly 16,500.

### Global Leader in the 1990s

The Hoskyns acquisition inaugurated Cap Gemini Sogeti's most ambitious expansion to date, joining more than 20 other acquisitions into the mid-1990s. In order to fuel its expansion, Kampf decided to abandon the company's long-cherished independence, selling a 34 percent stake to German industrial giant Daimler-Benz. The 1991 sale, for a total of more than $750 million, gave Daimler-Benz the right to acquire majority control of Cap Gemini Sogeti by 1995. The deal was supposed to aid Cap Gemini Sogeti in its push to build up its market share in the United States, where the company held only one percent of the market, compared to its seven percent share of the European market. It also gave the company deeper pockets with which to pursue its continued expansion.

Yet Cap Gemini was hard hit by the worldwide recession, as momentum across the computer industry slowed in the wake of the Persian Gulf War and the economic uncertainty across Europe and the United States. In 1992, the company posted its first-ever loss of FFr 72 million on revenues of FFr 11.88 billion. Its losses mounted still higher for the following year, reaching nearly FFr 430 million, while revenues slipped back to FFr 11.03 billion. The company was at last forced to call into question its decentralized approach. In 1993, Cap Gemini Sogeti launched a companywide reorganization that regrouped the company's operations around seven strategic business areas. It was hoped the new organization would enable the company to benefit from increasing cooperation across its far-flung operations as business areas began to share expertise, resources, and clients. The company also shed some of its underperforming units, including its German subsidiary Cap Debis, with revenues of FFr 1.1 billion created from the Daimler-Benz share

## Key Dates:

**1967:** Sogeti is founded.
**1973:** Sogeti launches a hostile takeover of CAP.
**1974:** Company acquires Gemini Computer Systems.
**1975:** Sogeti, CAP, and Gemini merge to form Cap Gemini Sogeti.
**1982:** Cap Gemini Sogeti tops FFr 1 billion in revenues.
**1984:** English becomes official company language.
**1992:** Cap Gemini Sogeti posts first net loss in company's history.
**1993:** Net losses reach FFr 429 million; company launches "Genesis" restructuring plan.
**1995:** Company returns to profitability.
**1996:** Company's name is changed to Cap Gemini S.A.
**2000:** Cap Gemini acquires Ernst & Young Technology for $11 billion and changes name to Cap Gemini Ernst & Young.

acquisition (Debis was Daimler-Benz's IT subsidiary). The reorganization, dubbed "Genesis," cost the company more than $100 million, but began to bear fruit by 1994. After reducing its losses to FFr 94 million that year, the company returned to the black in 1995, posting net profits of FFr 52 million on revenues of FFr 11.3 billion.

The choice of the name Genesis for the company's 1990s reorganization pointed the way to a new name as well. In 1996, the company dropped its founding company's name, and became known simply as Cap Gemini S.A. The following year, in what resembled yet another rebirth for the company, Daimler-Benz, rather than increasing its stake to majority control of Cap Gemini, instead moved to divest its shareholding, restoring Cap Gemini its independence. The partnership, hit at its outset by the recession, had never quite jelled. With the arrival of a new head at Daimler-Benz, who performed an about-face of his predecessor's diversification strategy, the two sides agreed to a divorce.

Newly independent Cap Gemini returned its attention to its expansion, acquiring full control of Groupe Bossard in 1997. It also began capitalizing on a new matter of concern across the computer industry—the so-called Y2K bug, which rendered computers and computer software incapable of recognizing the date change into the year 2000. Cap Gemini released its own successful bug-fixing software in 1996 and became a leader in the worldwide race to protect computers—and the societies that depended on them—from a vast meltdown at the beginning of the next century. The company also benefited from the run-up to the launch of the new common European currency, the Euro, and the need to reprogram computer systems for the new currency.

At the same time, the company began to look to a new means of asserting itself on the global marketplace, that of strategic partnerships with other computer industry heavyweights. As such, Cap Gemini concluded marketing and technology deals with such giants as Oracle Corp., Cisco Systems, ICL, Microsoft, and others. Meanwhile, Cap Gemini continued in its struggle to assert itself in the U.S. market. Despite its ambitious acquisition program begun at the start of the 1990s, Cap Gemini remained a bit player in the key U.S. market, dominated by the likes of IBM and EDS. While the company had enjoyed strong growth through the last half of the 1990s—in the four years since 1996, Cap Gemini nearly doubled its revenues, reaching EUR 4.3 billion (FFr 28.3 billion)—its U.S. presence remained limited.

The company took new steps toward improving its U.S. position and building itself as a global IT services heavyweight for the new century. In April 1999, Cap Gemini acquired New Jersey-based Beechwood, which specialized in providing IT services to the telecommunications industry. Yet it was the following year, in June 2000, that Cap Gemini scored its biggest coup yet. In June 2000, the company announced that it had agreed to purchase Ernst & Young Technology, the IT consultancy operations of Ernst & Young for $11 billion. The merger, which combined Ernst & Young Technology's 18,000 employees with the nearly 40,000 Cap Gemini employees, created the EUR 7.7 billion (sales) IT services giant Cap Gemini Ernst & Young. At the same time, Serge Kampf, who remained the company's chairman, took a first, albeit tentative move, to relinquishing the company he had built into one of the industry's top IT services specialists when he appointed Geoff Unwin as the newly enlarged company's CEO. While analysts hoped for a name change, or at least a shortening of the company's name, Cap Gemini Ernst & Young looked forward to staking a fresh claim to a major position in the world's IT market.

### Principal Subsidiaries

Cap Gemini America Inc.: CGS Holdings Ltd. (U.K.); Gemini Consulting AB (Sweden); Gemini Consulting A.S. (Norway); Gemini Consulting Holding Ltd. (U.K.); Gemini Consulting Iberia S.A. (Spain); Gemini Consulting S.A.; Gemini Management Consulting Spa (Italy); Immobilière Les Fontaines; SCI Paris Etoile; TDI GmbH.

### Principal Competitors

AGENCY.COM Ltd.; American Management Systems Inc.; Icon Medialab International AB; Andersen Consulting Inc.; iGATE Capital Corp.; Atos S.A.; iXL Enterprises; Bull; Keane, Inc.; CIBER Inc.; Logica; CMG PLC.; Perot Systems Corp.; EDS; Razorfish Inc.; Renaissance Worldwide Inc.; Sapient Corp.; Sema Group plc; IBM Corporation.

### Further Reading

Gaston-Breton, Tristan, *La saga Cap Gemini*, Paris: 1999.
Noguchi, Yuki, "Cap Gemini Spins off Va. Consulting Unit," *Washington Post*, August 15, 2000, p. E3.
Ricciuti, Mike and Erich Luening, "New Deals Help Consulting Giant Break into U.S.," *CNET News.com*, March 8, 2000.
Rudolph, Barbara, "Serge Kampf, Founder and Chairman of Cap Gemini Sogeti," *Time International*, October 21, 1991, p. 57.
Tillier, Alan, "Cap Gemini Celebrates Its Divorce," *European*, July 3, 1997, p. 20.
——, "Cap Gemini Raises Funds for Shakeup," *Newsbytes News Network*, March 11, 1998.
——, "Oracle, Gemini Launch Wireless Net Portal," *Reuters Business Report*, January 11, 2000.

—M.L. Cohen

# Carmike Cinemas, Inc.

1301 First Avenue
Columbus, Georgia 31901-2109
U.S.A.
Telephone: (706) 576-3400
Fax: (706) 576-2812
Web site: http://www.carmike.com

*Public Company*
*Incorporated:* 1982
*Employees:* 11,068
*Sales:* $486.93 million (1999)
*Stock Exchanges:* New York
*Ticker Symbol:* CKE
*NAIC:* 512131 Motion Picture Theaters (Except Drive-Ins); 722213 Snack and Nonalcoholic Beverage Bars

Carmike Cinemas, Inc. is one of the largest movie theater chains in the United States, with 2,850 screens in 36 states. Carmike's theaters are located mainly in smaller cities, where they are frequently the only movie venues in town. By operating primarily in these secondary markets, Carmike has avoided, in large part, the rugged competition for city and suburban viewers engaged in by most other big movie exhibitors. Nearly all of the company's theaters are multi-screen facilities, and their highest concentration is in the South and the Midwest, although expansion has been taking place in just about every part of the country. Declining revenues caused by industrywide overbuilding, as well as a weak season for films, caused the company financial problems in the summer of 2000. That August, Carmike filed for Chapter 11 bankruptcy protection.

## 1960s Roots

Carmike's swift rise to prominence among movie exhibitors was the work of the Patrick family, a clan with a history in the theater business. Company chairman Carl Patrick, Sr., was an executive with Martin Theaters, a Columbus, Georgia-based chain owned by another family. In 1969 Martin was purchased by Atlanta tycoon J.B. Fuqua, and it became part of Fuqua

Industries. Although Patrick initially wanted his two sons, Michael and Carl, Jr., to stay away from the movie theater industry, Michael had other ideas.

While still a student at Georgia State University, Michael Patrick worked at the Rialto Theater in Atlanta, taking tickets and making popcorn. Shortly after that he accepted a job with Martin. Eventually, Carl, Sr., became president of Fuqua Industries, while Michael worked his way up to head of the company's movie theater division. When Fuqua decided to shed the division in 1982, the father and son team took hold of the theater chain in a leveraged management buyout. They then named the new company Carmike, a combination of the first names of brothers Carl, Jr. (who became a director, but remained uninvolved in company operations) and Michael.

With Carl, Sr., as chairman and chief executive, and Michael running the company's operations as president, Carmike embarked on a program of expansion at a time when many theater chains were holding back, fearful that movie-going was giving way to home video and cable television. In 1983 Carmike acquired Video Independent Theatres, Inc., adding 85 screens to the 265-screen base with which it had emerged from the Martin buyout. The company grew by building new theaters as well, adding 27 screens in 1982 and 18 in 1983 through its own construction projects. Carmike's strategy was clear from the outset. Patrick sought out smaller cities that he believed were underserved by movie theaters. Upon finding a good candidate, he then either purchased and expanded the existing theater or built a new multi-screen facility, often adjacent to the local mall. Using this method, Carmike expanded quickly throughout the South.

Carmike's management has credited a great deal of the company's success to I.Q. Zero, its unique computer system. Early on, Patrick realized that the small markets in which he was operating would not allow him much slack in controlling operating costs. To address this problem, he commissioned some Columbus, Georgia, friends to create a hardware and software package that would allow Carmike management to monitor the expenses and revenue of each Carmike theater to the most minute detail. The result was I.Q. Zero, a system unlike any other that exists in the industry. At the end of each business day, I.Q. Zero sends box office, concessions, and other types of information to company headquarters in Columbus. Using I.Q. Zero, the company can access sales figures for a particular size of a particular brand of candy at one theater in Tennessee with the touch of a button. I.Q. Zero is also capable of alerting theater managers when their sales per person ratio has fallen below acceptable levels as determined by top management. By providing this kind of information, I.Q. Zero has helped Carmike keep a tight rein on costs by substituting technology for management personnel wherever possible.

### IPO and Continuing Growth in the Mid-1980s

The company's growth spurt continued unchecked through the middle of the 1980s. Although no existing theater chains were acquired in 1984 or 1985, Carmike built 55 new screens of its own during those two years. The year 1986 was an especially eventful one for Carmike. That year, the company acquired Essantee Theatres, Inc., adding 209 screens to its growing empire. In addition, 54 new screens were constructed. The Patricks took Carmike public in October 1986, with an initial over-the-counter stock offering, although the Patrick family retained about three-fourths of the company's voting stock. In the mid-1990s, the family held roughly 59 percent of the company's stock.

The company also met with some challenges in 1986. Like many of its competitors, Carmike split markets to keep the upper hand in negotiations with movie studios for the rights to show new pictures. When this practice was ultimately deemed illegal, Carmike ended up paying a $325,000 fine for an antitrust violation. In spite of the scrutiny of regulators, Carmike carried on with its strategy of finding smaller-sized cities in which it could have a virtual monopoly on first-run movies; the company was able to attain that status in some 60 percent of the markets in which it operated. The other key element in Carmike's approach was to show movies with the broadest possible appeal, carefully avoiding anything that could be construed as an art film.

By 1987 Carmike was earning $3 million on revenue of $84 million. The company continued to add screens by the dozen, and by 1988 the chain consisted of 670 screens in 216 movie theaters in 135 cities, still mostly located in the South, where it had already become the biggest movie exhibitor in the region. Nationally, Carmike was fifth largest in terms of number of screens by this time. While the four theater chains that remained larger—General Cinema, United Artists Theatre Circuit, Cineplex Odeon, and AMC Entertainment—continued to butt heads with each other over the movie-going dollars generated by

America's major population centers, Carmike sailed along by itself, opening multi-screen complexes in smaller markets, of which there seemed to be an endless supply.

Carmike brought another existing chain, the 116-screen Consolidated Theaters, Inc., into the fold in 1989, while adding another 35 screens of its own construction. Patrick also took his first vacation since launching the company. The company continued to prosper, with revenues approaching the $100 million mark, by bringing Hollywood's biggest, most mainstream movies into the sleepy towns of Middle America. Because it maintained monopoly or near-monopoly positions in most of its markets, Carmike was able to negotiate better rates from movie distributors than could many of its competitors. Patrick was in a position, according to the *Wall Street Journal*'s Anita Sharpe, to tell Hollywood, "Either you play Carmike Cinemas or Blockbuster Video." The company found savings in other areas as well. Its small town costs for constructing new theaters ran less than half of what such projects cost in prime suburban locations. In addition, although ticket prices were lower at Carmike Cinemas than in big market theaters, Carmike's high-tech systems allowed it to expand the chain without adding large numbers of home office employees.

### More Than 1,000 Screens by the Mid-1990s

As the 1990s began, Carmike's approach still ran contrary to that of its major competitors: although they were trying to become "leaner and meaner," Carmike was still looking for new turf. Consequently, the 154 existing screens the company acquired in 1990 came from two of its biggest rivals, Cineplex Odeon and United Artists. On top of that, 24 new screens were constructed. With nearly 1,000 total screens in about 175 different markets, Carmike was established as a major force in the movie theater industry. Meanwhile, Hollywood studios were emphasizing the kinds of films that Carmike's customers favored—action movies featuring big-name stars. The Rambo-type movies went over especially well at the many Carmike theaters located near military facilities.

Over the next couple of years, Carmike picked up additional screens cast off by the likes of American Multi Cinema (AMC). Its biggest single leap in size came in 1991 with the addition of 353 screens in the form of a joint venture with Excellence Theaters. Carmike bought out its partners in that project two years later. By 1992 the company was operating 1,400 movie screens, twice the number it had in its possession only three years earlier, and posting revenues of $172 million. After buying out its joint venture partners in the Eastwynn Theatres chain (formerly called Excellence) in 1993, Carmike was probably the third largest movie chain in the country, trailing only United Artists and AMC. The company also absorbed Manos Enterprises, a chain with 80 movie screens. That year, the company's revenue jumped to $242 million. As the chain continued to expand, Patrick and his team found ways to wring even more savings out of the I.Q. Zero system. The system took over yet more tasks formerly performed by humans, allowing management to reduce corporate overhead costs to a mere 2.5 percent of operating revenues, down from the four percent level the company had maintained for several years.

By the middle of 1993, Carmike had established a presence in 23 states in the South, Southwest, and Midwest. The com-

## Key Dates:

**1982:** Carl Patrick, Sr., and son buy movie theater division of Fuqua Industries, name it Carmike.
**1983:** Carmike acquires 85-screen Video Independent Theaters chain.
**1986:** Acquisition of 209-screen Essantee Theaters chain; initial public stock offering.
**1989:** Consolidated Theaters, with 116 screens, is purchased.
**1991:** Joint venture with Excellence Theaters adds 353 screens.
**1995:** Ongoing expansion puts Carmike on top of U.S. cinema chains in number of screens.
**1997:** Carmike and Wal-Mart form joint venture to build family entertainment centers.
**2000:** Carmike files for Chapter 11 bankruptcy protection.

pany's 388 theaters contained a total of 1,560 screens. Again in 1994, Carmike picked up screens from other chains, built theaters of its own, and had a record year in just about every category. During 1994 the company acquired 178 screens from Cinema World, bought another 48 screens from General Cinema, and built five new complexes holding 43 screens. Carmike also added 15 new screens to complexes already in operation. Part of the financing for all of this growth came from a public offering of $58 million worth of newly issued common stock, after which the Patricks still held the majority of voting interest in the company.

Buoyed by its five new acquisitions between the beginning of 1994 and the middle of 1995, Carmike narrowed the size gap between itself and industry leader United Artists considerably. By July 1995, the company had 2,223 screens in its empire, less than 100 screens fewer than the number operated by United Artists, and by the end of the year it had added enough more to take the number one position for itself. Many movie industry analysts considered Carmike the best-managed theater chain in the country during the early 1990s. The company's ability to churn out profits year after year while its competitors struggled to streamline and stem their losses seemed to support this opinion.

Meanwhile, Carmike's success in getting Middle America to come to the movies made Patrick something of a guru among Hollywood executives. Top managers at entertainment companies such as Disney, Twentieth Century Fox, and Time Warner frequently turned to Patrick for projections about how certain films would do at the box office. Mogul Ted Turner consulted Patrick before his Turner Broadcasting System bought production companies New Line Cinema and Castle Rock Entertainment. By knowing the tastes of his small-town audience, Patrick was occasionally even able to make hits out of movies that were poorly received in big cities.

### Expansion in the Mid-1990s and Bankruptcy in 2000

Carmike's expansion continued in 1996, and the following year it entered into a joint venture with Wal-Mart Stores, Inc. to create what were dubbed "family entertainment centers."

These combined a movie multiplex with a skating rink, a video arcade, and a restaurant, and occupied structures left vacant by closed Wal-Mart stores. The new complexes were given the name "The Hollywood Connection." Carmike had originated the concept at a site in its home base of Columbus, Georgia, and the first jointly owned facility was opened in late 1997 in Goshen, Indiana. Three others were slated for Valparaiso, Indiana; Dekalb, Illinois; and Salt Lake City, Utah, with the latter to be solely owned by Carmike.

The company's position as leader in its industry was drawing notice, and competitors began building theaters in the smaller markets that were its stronghold. The entire movie exhibition business was on a building binge, with the new trend toward stadium seating, larger screens, and digital sound systems upping the ante for new theaters. In many prime markets, cinema chains built all-new "megaplexes" to replace their multiplexes. Some of the latter were converted to second-run discount houses, while others were closed. With new theaters impinging on Carmike's territory, some of the company's older sites began to lose audience share, and it was forced to further ramp up construction to replace these outdated multiplexes.

In July of 1998 Carmike reached an agreement with the U.S. Justice Department to make its 516 theaters barrier free in accordance with the Americans With Disabilities Act. The ruling had come after a Des Moines, Iowa woman lodged a complaint about accessibility at Carmike's three theaters in that city. Earlier, the company had settled a lawsuit by an obese woman who could not fit in the standard seats at a Nashville Carmike Theater and had been refused permission to bring in her own chair.

Also during 1998, Carmike competitors Regal Cinemas and Act III merged to create the largest theater chain in the United States, while Loews Cineplex Entertainment's merger with Cineplex Odeon pushed it into the number two slot. Near the end of the year, Carmike received an infusion of capital from Goldman Sachs, which invested $55 million to buy 16 percent of the company. It also was borrowing heavily from lenders, money that would be used to build the more than 300 additional screens that were planned for 1999.

The aggressive building campaigns of theater chains were supportable so long as Hollywood kept pumping out hits. But the 2000 movie season was not a strong one, with no massive blockbuster to perk up ticket sales industrywide as *Titanic* and *Star Wars* had once done. There was also an unanticipated effect of the chains' recent overbuilding, and the resultant wider availability of new films to audiences. Because film distributors took a higher percentage of the gross receipts during a movie's opening weeks, exhibitors found that their profits were declining even for the big hits, which could more easily be viewed by the bulk of the audience before they could take their cut.

Carmike had now posted two consecutive years of annual losses, and the added strain of weak summer ticket sales caused problems in managing its massive debt load. As a result, the company filed for bankruptcy protection on August 8, 2000. Observers noted that Carmike was in much better shape than several other cinema chains that had recently filed for bankruptcy, and in fact the company listed nearly $200 million more in assets than it did liabilities. It had previously announced cutbacks in expansion, with only 88 new screens planned for the year.

The future for Carmike, and the motion picture exhibition business in general, had clouded over in the late 1990s. The industry had reached a point of market saturation that was causing a shakeout of major proportions. Further hurdles, such as the expected conversion to digital projection systems from film and the shortened theatrical lifespan of new releases, might cause further bloodletting. Carmike's track record was a good one, however, and its experienced management team appeared capable of bringing the company back to health.

### Principal Subsidiaries

Wooden Nickel Pub, Inc.; Eastwynn Theatres, Inc.; Military Services, Inc. (80%).

### Principal Competitors

AMC Entertainment, Inc.; Century Theatres LP; Cinemark USA, Inc.; GC Companies, Inc.; Loews Cineplex Entertainment Corp.; National Amusements, Inc.; Regal Cinemas, Inc.; United Artists Theatre Circuit, Inc.

### Further Reading

Barrett, William P., "A Wal-Mart for the Movies," *Forbes,* August 22, 1988, pp. 60–61.

Blickstein, Jay, "Small-Town Dixie Chain on Exhib Fast Track," *Variety,* March 30, 1992, p. 51.

"Box Office Bonanza," *Forbes,* March 27, 1993, p. 19.

Byrne, Harlan, "Carmike Cinemas: *Jurassic Park* Could Help It Have a Dino-Mite Year," *Barron's,* June 28, 1993, pp. 39–40.

"Georgia-Based Carmike Cinemas Drops to Second Place in Theaters," *KRTBN Knight-Ridder Tribune Business News,* January 21, 1998.

Goldsmith, Jill, "Exhib Carmike Turns Page to Chapter 11," *Daily Variety,* August 9, 2000, p. 1.

Hawkins, Chuck, "The Movie Mogul Who Thinks Small," *Business Week,* July 2, 1990, p. 37.

"Now Playing, Carmike," *Forbes,* March 27, 1995, pp. 160–61.

Parets, Robin Taylor, "Leaders & Success: Carmike's Michael Patrick," *Investor's Business Daily,* July 24, 1997, p. A1.

Peers, Martin, "Carmike's Profits Off," *Daily Variety,* February 4, 1998, p. 8.

Pendleton, Jennifer, "Chain Sees Possibilities in Midst of Recession," *Variety,* March 30, 1992, p. 51.

Reingold, Jennifer, "Carmike Cinemas: It Always Plays in Peoria," *Financial World,* March 14, 1995, pp. 20–22.

Sharpe, Anita, "Last Picture Show," *Wall Street Journal,* July 12, 1995, p. A1.

Sherer, Paul M., and Carrick Mollenkamp, "A Thriller with a Touch of Horror—Critics Pan Carmike Cinemas' Surprise Bankruptcy Filing," *Asian Wall Street Journal,* September 7, 2000, p. 22.

Walters, Nolan, "Columbus, Ga.-Based Carmike Cinemas to Become More Accessible to Disabled," *KRTBN Knight-Ridder Tribune Business News,* July 1, 1998.

—Robert R. Jacobson
—updated by Frank Uhle

# Carriage Services, Inc.

**1300 Post Oak Boulevard**
**Suite 1500**
**Houston, Texas 77056**
**U.S.A.**
**Telephone: (281) 556-7400**
**Fax: (281) 556-7401**
**Web site: http://www.carriageservices.com**

*Public Company*
*Incorporated:* 1991
*Employees:* 2,769
*Sales:* $168.5 million (1999)
*Stock Exchanges:* New York
*Ticker Symbol:* CSV
*NAIC:* 81221 Funeral Homes; 81222 Cemeteries and
   Crematories

Carriages Services, Inc. is the fastest-growing publicly traded funeral and cemetery service company in the United States. Since its inception, Carriage Services has grown at a rapid rate by acquiring local funeral homes and cemeteries. By 2000, in fact, the company had become the fourth largest player in the consolidating "death care market," owning and operating more than 180 funeral homes and 40 cemeteries in 30 states. The company provides an array of services to the deceased and their families: removing and preparing remains; selling caskets and urns; hosting memorials, visitations, and ceremonies; providing transportation services; performing burials; and maintaining cemetery grounds.

### Entrepreneurial Beginnings: 1991

Melvyn Payne and Mark Duffey jointly founded Carriage Services, Inc. in 1991. Although neither had experience in the death care industry, they saw lucrative opportunities to be gained by buying and operating funeral homes and cemeteries. Payne had worked previously as a management consultant for J. Howard Marshall II (the Houston oil tycoon who became famous for marrying model Anna Nicole Smith). Payne had acquired a solid reputation for successfully turning around troubled companies, but he and Duffey were ready to set out on their own. "We wanted to be our own boss," Payne told the *Houston Chronicle*. Their first entrepreneurial attempts were less than triumphant, however, as their oil-field boat supply business and rent-to-own companies quickly collapsed. The third time proved the charm, though, when they launched Carriage Services in 1991. Payne would serve as the company's chief executive officer, with Duffey as its chairman and president.

Carriage Services entered the death care market during a period of massive consolidation in the field. This trend actually had begun in the early 1960s, when Robert Waltrip (who had inherited a funeral home from his father in the 1950s) began to apply the principles of service chains such as Holiday Inn to funeral homes. Waltrip founded Service Corporation International in 1962 and began to acquire "mom and pop" funeral homes across the country. Two years after he took his company public in 1969, Waltrip purchased Kinney Services, then the largest funeral home business in the United States. Service Corporation International grew at a phenomenal rate thereafter. As other companies took note of Waltrip's stunning success, they followed his business model. By the time Payne and Duffey founded Carriage Services, several large companies were gaining an ever-increasing share of the death care business through takeovers of smaller operations.

In an ironic twist, Carriage Services received much of its initial financing from a unit of Service Corporation, Provident Services, which extended Carriage Services more than $30 million in loan commitments. Carriage Services took the funds and began to purchase local funeral homes and cemeteries. Sales increased from $1.8 million to $11.3 million between 1992 and 1993, as Payne and Duffey's enterprise built a network of funeral homes.

### Dynamic Growth in the Middle to Late 1990s

By 1996, Carriage Services had grown to include 60 funeral homes in 13 states. Its revenues had increased steadily as well—from $18.4 million in 1994 to $24.2 million in 1995. But the company was still a minor player in the industry, paling in comparison with titans like Service Corporation, which owned 2,700 funeral homes, generated $1.8 billion in annual revenue, and had international holdings in Australia, Britain, and France. Carriage Services hoped to compete at this level, but recognized that it would need to expand further to be able to do so. In an effort to fund further acquisitions, Payne and Duffey took their company public in August of 1996, selling 3.4 million shares of Carriage Service stock in an initial public offering (IPO). The company needed the extra capital because "competition in the acquisition market [was] intense, and prices paid for funeral homes and cemeteries [had] increased substantially in recent years," Carriage Services noted in its investor prospectus. Using the money generated by the IPO, Carriage Services planned to grow aggressively, aiming to spend more than $100 million on acquisitions in 1997 alone.

Carriage Services' faith in the death care market was well founded. As *Investor's Business Daily* explained, "the funeral industry [was] inherently more stable than other industries." For obvious reasons, death is a recession-proof business, but demographic trends indicated that it was also one on the verge of an unprecedented boom. Approximately 2.3 million Americans died every year during the latter part of the 20th century, but as the gigantic baby boom generation grew old, the death care industry stood to make a killing. Analysts predicted that annual deaths would increase 85 percent between 1992 and 2040.

Moreover, most industry insiders predicted that the funeral business's consolidation was far from complete and that there was still plenty of room for upstarts such as Carriage Services to expand. As of August 1996, the four largest companies—Service Corporation International, The Loewen Group, Stewart Enterprises, and Equity Corporation—controlled only a combined eight percent of the market. An executive for The Loewen Group declared to *Investor's Business Daily* that "the market could get to 40 percent to 50 percent consolidated," but even that figure indicated that there would still be room for smaller players. Indeed, despite the best efforts of these giants, funeral services remained "a fragmented industry dominated by independent operators," Susan Little, an analyst with Raymond James & Associates Inc., told the *Mergers & Acquisitions Report.*

The nature of the industry, however, made even small efforts at consolidation difficult. In the years prior to Carriage Services' public stock offering, the lowest-hanging fruit—regional funeral home chains—had, in large part, been plucked. But more than 20,000 small, family-owned funeral homes and cemeteries remained independent, and many were resistant to the overtures of the industry leaders (who often sought to make wholesale personnel and policy changes in their new acquisitions). Carriage Services believed that it was uniquely positioned to approach this market and to bring the highest quality local death care providers into its fold. Part of Carriage Services' appeal was financial. The

company provided often cash-strapped businesses with management and cooperative purchasing resources. Under Carriage Services' umbrella, individual funeral homes could purchase products at lower rates than they could obtain on their own, and they were able to pool resources with other Carriage Services-owned homes in their area. For example, five funeral homes all acquired by Carriage Services in one geographic area could share a fleet of cars. Carriage Services also offered businesses an incentive-based compensation system and the broadest stock-ownership plan in the industry.

Even more important, though, was the security that Carriage Services could offer local funeral homes. As Melvyn Payne explained to the *Wall Street Transcript,* Carriage Services strove to retain a "corporate family environment." According to the *Mergers & Acquisitions Report,* most funeral homes had been family-owned for two or three generations. At the end of the 20th century, these owners were facing a crisis of "succession and planning," as their intended heirs often wanted to go into other businesses. Although these funeral homes wanted the benefits offered by a consolidator, they also were concerned about maintaining the reputation and continuity of their business. But to be able to offer security to these local operators, Carriage Services had to ensure that it was protected from being taken over itself. To this end, Carriage Services had created two classes of stock—A and B—during its IPO. Class A shares were sold on the open market, while Class B shares (which carried ten times the voting power of Class A ones) remained mostly in the hands of company officers and directors. By ensuring its long-term integrity in this fashion, Carriage Services was able to present itself as a stable force to skittish local operators. Funeral homes "are joining us for our style, our entrepreneurial culture," Payne told the *Houston Chronicle.* "And they don't want to do that if three months from now we'd want to sell our company to anybody." Moreover, when Carriage Services bought a local funeral home, it did not replace staff or implement new policies.

Carriage Services' strategy was successful. In 1997, the company spent a total of $118 million on acquisitions, purchasing 21 funeral homes and four cemeteries between January and June alone. Early that year, Carriage Services made an important deal when it bought CNM, a California corporation that owned and operated ten Wilson & Kratzer funeral homes in Alameda and Contra Costa Counties in northern California. With this transaction, Carriage Services became the fifth largest publicly traded funeral services company. In July, Carriage Services merged with Forest Lawn/Evergreen Management Corporation of Panama City, Florida, and gained several funeral homes and cemeteries in Florida and Alabama. By the close of 1997, Carriage Services had achieved sales of $77.4 million, and it reported the first net profit in its history—$4.3 million. These results were particularly impressive given that 1997 was a bad year for the death industry as a whole. Analysts attributed this fact in large part to the weather. More people die during the winter than any other time of the year, and the winter of 1997 was unusually mild.

Carriage Services maintained its rapid growth rate in 1998, purchasing a total of 48 funeral homes and seven cemeteries. The company did begin to focus on the profitability of its acquisitions, however, rather than simply on the number of new businesses it bought. In the process, Carriage Services became

---

**Key Dates:**

**1991:** Melvyn Payne founds Carriage Services Inc. with Mark Duffey.
**1996:** Carriage Services becomes a publicly traded company.
**1997:** Carriage Services acquires Forest Lawn/Evergreen Management Corporation.

---

the fourth largest purveyor of death care services. Carriage Services also acted to ensure the continued quality of its operations in 1998 when it acquired Sessions Group, Inc., a company specializing in leadership development for employees and management in the death care industry. By incorporating Sessions into its family of businesses, Carriage Services was able to host ongoing training programs and implement service improvements. Similarly, Carriage Services launched the Carriage Family Survey in 1998, a "report card" to evaluate customer satisfaction levels. With operations in 30 states, 1998 revenues exceeding $116 million, and the year's profits topping $9.5 million, Carriage Services truly had become a national leader.

Carriage Services' positive results in 1998 were aided by outside factors as well. The Midwest and New England suffered a particularly harsh winter, which increased the number of deaths in the United States that year. Moreover, as analyst Steven Saltzman commented in the January 21, 1998 issue of the *Houston Chronicle,* the prominent coverage given to Princess Diana's funeral late in 1997 "showed how much people get out of the experience of watching or attending a funeral." Diana-mania survived the princess, as many people were inspired to have "a more lavish send-off instead of a minimal service, as most people expect they want." Carriage Services also received a boost from the troubles of a rival. The Loewen Group continued to suffer under the fallout from a 1995 lawsuit in which a Mississippi jury imposed a $500 million dollar damage award against the company because of its business practices. Loewen eventually negotiated an $85 million settlement, an amount that represented a full year's earnings. Because of this revenue hit, the company was unable to keep pace in 1997 and 1998 with Carriage Services.

### Gains, Struggles, and Challenges: 1999 and Beyond

The death care industry continued to undergo major changes in 1999 when Service Corporation acquired rival consolidator Equity Corporation, whose 1997 sales reached $135.1 million. Together the two companies boasted 3,600 funeral homes, 500 cemeteries, and 175 crematoria worldwide. In order to complete the merger, though, the Federal Trade Commission required Service Corporation to divest assets in 14 markets. The company complied, and it sold seven funeral homes and 12 cemeteries to Carriage Services. With this acquisition, Carriage Services gained a presence in Oregon and added a fourth cemetery to its Texas holdings.

Although Carriage Services had reaped gains from the merger of Service Corporation and Equity, it also suffered from some of its consequences. Service Corporation's buying spree

had left that company overextended. Some of its most recent holdings underperformed, and the company staggered under a weight of debt and the burden of integrating its far-flung operations. In January of 2000, Service Corporation instituted cost-cutting plans, as it sought to reduce its workforce and shed some funeral homes and cemeteries. Unfortunately for the rest of the death care industry, Service Corporation's troubles undermined the entire sector. Investors avoided the industry, and the stock prices of the major consolidators tumbled. Without access to capital markets, Carriage Services had limited opportunities to make additional purchases. "I hope Service Corporation can get their ship righted so the equity markets will open to all of us," Payne told the *Houston Chronicle* on January 14, 2000.

Despite these difficulties, Carriage Services performed well in 1999. Its sales rose to $168.5 million, with a net income of $10.7 million. The aging—and subsequent expiration—of the baby boom generation presented Carriage Services with future growth potential. But it also presented challenges. The company—like its competitors—would have to negotiate what *Harper's Magazine* termed the "under-ritualization" of the baby boomers. In the future, companies such as Carriage Services would be dealing with a population that was not only living longer, but that had been weaned on the industry exposés of muckraking authors such as Jessica Mitford and tended to express a preference (at least in surveys) for spending less on funerals. Already the percentage of Americans who chose to be cremated—by far the cheapest (and thus least profitable to funeral homes) way to dispose of human remains—had increased from four percent to 21 percent between 1963 and 1997. However, Carriage Services was resourceful. Taking an "if you can't beat them, join them" attitude, the company moved aggressively to cater to those who chose cremation, adding expensive urns and memorial markers to its product lines. The company also announced that acquisitions would remain a centerpiece of its future plans.

### Principal Competitors

Service Corporation International; Stewart Enterprises, Inc.; The Loewen Group Inc.

### Further Reading

Boisseau, Charles, "Leader in Profit Growth Emerges from Coffin Corner," *Houston Chronicle,* May 17, 1998.
"CEO Interviews: Melvyn Pain, Chairman and CEO Discusses the Outlook for Carriage Services Inc.," *Wall Street Transcript,* July 15, 1997.
"Consolidation Continues in 'Death Care' Industry," *Mergers & Acquisitions Report,* August 5, 1996.
"Death Watch," *Houston Chronicle,* January 21, 1998.
Gessel, Chris, "Investor's Corner Growth, Consolidation Fuels Funeral Stocks," *Investor's Business Daily,* June 24, 1996.
Moreno, Jenalia, "SCI's Cost-Cutting Includes Local Jobs," *Houston Chronicle,* January 14, 2000.
Newman, Judith, "At Your Disposal: The Funeral Industry Prepares for Boom Times," *Harper's Magazine,* November 1, 1997.
Springer, John, "2 Family-Owned Firms in Bristol Merge with a National Company," *Hartford Courant,* July 4, 1996.

—Rebecca Stanfel

# The Carsey-Werner Company, L.L.C.

**4024 Radford Avenue**
**Studio City, California 91604**
**U.S.A.**
**Telephone: (818) 655-5598**
**Fax: (818) 655-5930**
**Web site: http://www.carseywerner.com**

*Private Company*
*Founded:* 1981
*Employees:* 130
*Sales:* $199.00 million (1999)
*NAIC:* 51211 Motion Picture and Video Production;
   51212 Motion Picture and Video Distribution

Founded in 1981 by programming veterans Marcy Carsey and Tom Werner, the Carsey-Werner Company, L.L.C. is one of the few remaining independent television production studios in Hollywood. Creating sitcoms is the heart of the company, which is valued at more than $1 billion. Its top-rated television shows include such hits as the *Cosby Show, Roseanne,* and *3rd Rock From the Sun.* Carsey-Werner has enjoyed success on each of the top four broadcast networks, and during one stretch in 1988–89 became the first studio of any size to take the first three slots in the annual rankings. Over the years, the company has created its own distribution arm and film operation, and also became a partner in Oxygen Media, which integrates television and Internet content targeted at women.

### Background

Marcy Carsey graduated with a degree in English from the University of New Hampshire in the mid-1960s with a vague interest in acting. She moved to New York and used her job as a tour guide at NBC to become a production assistant for the *Tonight Show,* based in New York at the time. It was there she met an associate producer who became her future husband, writer John Carsey. She also worked as a program supervisor at William Esty Advertising before moving to Los Angeles with her husband, who had been hired to write for *Rowan and Martin's Laugh-In.* She went to work as a story analyst for

Tomorrow Entertainment, becoming executive story editor, then accepted a job at ABC-TV in 1974 to serve as a general program executive assigned to comedy programming. Carsey systematically rose through the ranks of the network. In 1976 she was named vice-president of Prime Time Comedy and Variety Programs, then in 1979 became senior vice-president of Prime Time Series, responsible for the creation, development, and supervision of all prime time series on the network.

Carsey's future partner, Tom Werner, graduated from Harvard in 1971 and worked as a documentary filmmaker for two years before taking a position in ABC-TV's planning and development department. He was manager of Prime Time Program Development, East Coast in 1975 when he met Carsey. She was Director of Comedy Programming at the time and hired him as manager of Comedy Programming. They worked so well together that for the sake of convenience they set up shop in the same office. Their collaboration helped to produce hit shows from the period that included *Taxi, Soap, Dynasty,* and *Barney Miller.*

One of their most popular shows, *Mork and Mindy,* was created by the pair while on a flight to New York where scheduling meetings were to be held. With the goal of coming up with an eight o'clock hit for the network, Carsey and Werner worked out a tentative comedy to star Robin Williams, a little known stand-up comic, who had impressed them with a guest appearance on *Happy Days* in which he played an alien. They decided to team Williams with Pam Dawber, who had done an earlier pilot for them. Footage from *Happy Days* episodes was cobbled together to make a presentation. Management, however, balked at the idea. Even though the series was little more than a tentative concept, Carsey jeopardized her reputation and position by insisting that the project be produced. The show became a hit and the reputation of both Carsey and Werner was only enhanced in the industry.

### Early 1980s Company Origins

In November 1980, dissatisfied with a change in management, Carsey left ABC, took out a second mortgage on her home, and started her own production company. Werner succeeded her as head of series television, but less than a year later he was persuaded to join her as an independent producer, forming the Carsey-Werner Production Company in 1981.

The existence of Carsey-Werner was immediately threatened in its first year by a writers' strike and an actors' strike. The company then produced a number of pilots that failed. Its first series to reach the air was *Oh, Madeline!,* starring Madeline Kahn, that ran on ABC during the 1983–84 season. The company also produced a made-for-television movie, *Single Bars, Single Women,* based on a Dolly Parton song. Financially, however, Carsey-Werner was suffering. Networks and studios offered production deals, but Carsey and Werner valued their independence and decided to persevere. Their company desperately needed a hit, a show that would run long enough to become a viable product for syndication, where the profits could be made.

Although the numbers have changed since the early 1980s when Carsey-Werner began to independently produce television shows, the fundamental economics have not. Bill Carter in a 1996 article for the *New York Times* describes the reality for production companies: "All series are produced at a deficit because networks do not pay enough in license fees to cover the costs of making a show. A typical episode of a half-hour comedy costs between $500,000 and $600,000 to produce and runs a deficit of $100,000 to $200,000. Without a big bankroll, it is almost impossible to absorb those deficits while waiting for the payoff that a big hit brings: the hundred of millions of dollars that can be made in syndication.''

The breakout hit for Carsey-Werner was the *Cosby Show.* In the early 1980s Bill Cosby was a well-known and popular stand-up comedian with a couple of fairly successful television series to his credit, but to the networks he was deemed risky. Carsey-Werner believed in Cosby, and its confidence was rewarded with a show that, beginning in 1984, became a consistent ratings leader. Eventually it would reap close to an unprecedented $1 billion in syndication money. With the success of the *Cosby Show,* more offers were made to Carsey-Werner, but by now the company's existence was assured.

Another personality that Carsey and Werner believed in was a comedienne they discovered on the *Tonight Show:* Roseanne Barr. The producers considered her for roles in all of their shows under development. Finally they decided to take a chance and develop a series around Roseanne. The result was another hit show that would run for many years, providing the profits in syndication that would subsidize Carsey-Werner efforts that proved less popular with the public, such as *Chicken Soup* (1989). Another hit show of the 1980s for Carsey-Werner was the *Cosby Show* spin-off *A Different World,* which aired on NBC beginning in 1987. The following season, 1988–89, the company would accomplish the unprecedented feat of produc-

ing the year's three highest rated shows: *Cosby* at number one, followed by *Roseanne* and *A Different World.*

Carsey and Werner were given an opportunity by CBS in the late 1980s to run all of the network's programming. They declined, again preferring to keep their independence and the ability to shop their ideas to all of the networks. That flexibility had proven to be critical in more than one situation. Carsey-Werner was able to place the *Cosby Show* with NBC after ABC had rejected the idea. Later, NBC would reject *Roseanne,* and the company was able to turn to ABC. In the 1990s Carsey-Werner hits *Cybill* and *3rd Rock From the Sun* would also be rejected by the first network to which the shows were offered, only to be picked up by a rival. If Carsey-Werner had been tied to an exclusive deal with one network, almost all of its hit shows might never have been produced.

A key addition to the Carsey-Werner management team was Stuart Glickman, who became chief executive officer in 1987. Originally a trial lawyer, Glickman became involved in the entertainment industry in 1968 when he became Assistant Counsel for American International Pictures. In 1970 he became director of business affairs for CBS Television. Glickman then worked as an entertainment lawyer for 15 years, providing legal and business advice to top companies and talents, including Carsey-Werner. After becoming the CEO, Glickman expanded on the company's production success with a mandate to create a diversified, global entertainment company with multiple revenue streams. He oversaw the creation of a distribution operation, reacquiring Carsey-Werner's library of shows from Viacom, then brokered a number of innovative syndication deals. He helped to create Carsey-Werner Moving Pictures, to position the company to produce feature films. According to *Variety,* Glickman helped turn Carsey-Werner into a "tiny powerhouse.''

Carsey-Werner endured a lull in the early 1990s. Shows that failed to succeed were *Grand* (1990), *Davis Rules* (1991), *Frannie's Turn* (1993), a Bill Cosby update of the Groucho Marx quiz show *You Bet Your Life* (1993), and *She TV (1994).* At one point Carsey-Werner had only one hit show running, *Roseanne.* Fortunes were revived with *Grace Under Fire* in 1993 and *Cybill* in 1994. Then Carsey and Werner looked to a past success, *Mork and Mindy,* to create one of their most popular sitcoms, *3rd Rock From the Sun.*

The concept for the show, "aliens on a field trip,'' was given to the husband-wife writing team of Bonnie and Terry Turner, who shaped it into a vehicle that would allow for wry observations about the human condition. To star in the show Carsey-Werner brought in film veteran John Lithgow, and Jane Curtin, famous from her days with *Saturday Night Live.* With the show in development, another tempting offer was made to Carsey and Werner, this time from the head of Disney-ABC, Michael Eisner, who wanted the producing team to take over the network's troubled entertainment division. Rather than abandon the shows they had in development, they turned down the offer. A year later, in 1996, one of those shows, *3rd Rock,* would begin to air on NBC and become an immediate hit. Two other shows that premiered in 1996, however, did not succeed: *Townies* and *Cosby,* the latter of which was an attempt (same stars in a different situation) to recapture the magic that had launched

## Key Dates:

**1981:** Carsey-Werner Company is formed.
**1984:** The *Cosby Show* becomes first hit show for Carsey-Werner.
**1987:** Stuart Glickman is named chief executive officer.
**1989:** Carsey-Werner takes top three slots in television rankings for the season.
**1996:** Carsey-Werner sitcom *3rd Rock From the Sun* begins run on NBC.
**1998:** Carsey-Werner partners with Oprah Winfrey and Geraldine Laybourne to create Oxygen Media.

the production company a decade earlier. In 1998 Carsey-Werner scored another success with *That 70s Show* for the Fox network, giving the company the distinction of having placed hits with the four largest broadcast networks.

At a time when most of the few remaining independent producers joined forces with a studio or network, Carsey-Werner maintained its independence throughout the 1990s, managing its profits carefully and using its money to expand its business, as Glickman steered the company "in an industry increasingly hostile to non-vertically integrated companies," in the words of *Variety*. A major part of the company's formula was to offer ownership stakes to key personnel. Generally that meant the star of the show, such as Bill Cosby, who became even wealthier through his association with Carsey-Werner. According to Richard Zoglin in a 1996 *Time* article, "Carsey and Werner have also become experts in a more conventional TV game: appeasing stars with big egos. Both Roseanne and Brett Butler, the star of *Grace Under Fire*, have driven out a succession of writers and producers with whom they've clashed over scripts. *Cybill* executive producer Jay Daniel has just been ousted after a falling out with star Cybill Shepherd—she had been trying to assert more control over her series, reportedly even fighting for more close-ups as shows are being edited. Some criticize the team for invariably caving in to the stars in these disputes. One producer claims that Carsey-Werner is particularly inhospitable to writers, who are seen as expendable. The duo reply that they're just doing what is best for the show."

Despite individual success, and the wealth that came with it, both Carsey and Werner remained unassuming, preferring to keep their lives private. They continued to share an office and were known to choose the commissary over expensive restaurants. Werner did indulge himself in 1991 when he purchased the San Diego Padres baseball team, a venture that proved disastrous and lasted only three years. In the summer of 2000 he became fodder for gossip columnists when he began a bi-coastal romantic relationship with *Today Show* star Katie Couric.

In an effort to stay in the forefront of a rapidly changing media landscape, Carsey, Werner, and company president Caryn Mandabach created an entity known as Carsey-Werner-Mandabach, which formed a partnership with Oprah Winfrey and Geraldine Laybourne (formerly with Nickelodeon and Disney) to create Oxygen Media. The new company, announced with much fanfare in 1998, was conceived as an integration of

Internet web sites and a cable television channel targeted at women. On the television side of Oxygen, Carsey-Werner-Mandabach planned to use its three-year, $325 million budget to produce programming for themed blocks of time. Weekday prime time, for instance, would feature the comedy-oriented Oxygen Tent from six to eight p.m., consisting of live and taped comedy sketches and a mix of other material, followed from eight to ten p.m. by Pure Oxygen, in which the emphasis would be on women's real stories, augmented by a live online presence via chat rooms and surveys.

Launched in February 2000, Oxygen had trouble finding room on basic-service cable packages. Whereas other new channels were paying cable systems to carry their programming, Oxygen asked for 19 cents for each subscriber. By July only 13 million of the country's more than 70 million cable homes were able to receive Oxygen, providing too few viewers to be counted by the Nielsen ratings service, a serious shortfall, since advertising rates are based on those numbers. Oxygen's five-year plan called for a budget of $450 million, but only $300 million had been raised. Online, Oxygen quickly dropped two of its shopping-related sites, opting to steer away from direct sales. Moreover, Oxygen's viewers did not respond well to its initial offering of low-budget television programming that consisted of too many people "talking on couches." Two of its shows were soon taken out of production: the morning news show and "Trackers," a teenage gab-fest. Whereas most new channels filled out their schedules with popular, previously-aired material, Oxygen was further hampered by the unavailability of the Carsey-Werner library until 2002. Oxygen officials remained optimistic, however, insisting that the media company always expected that it would have to find a successful formula. The company received encouraging news August 2000 when, for the first time, women, Oxygen's target audience, outnumbered men online.

The fortune of Carsey-Werner's core business, in the meantime, was mixed in 2000. The company's attempt to break into animation, *God, the Devil and Bob,* was pulled from NBC after only four episodes, unable to compete opposite ABC's hit quiz show, *Who Wants to be a Millionaire?* The company did add a major new star, however, when it announced in May that Steve Martin had signed a production deal. Perhaps most important of all to Carsey-Werner's future may have been the announcement in June that its CEO of 13 years, Stuart Glickman, would be leaving the company to "explore new business and investment opportunities." The company's fall production plans had just been concluded, with the return to network television of *That 70s Show* and *3rd Rock From the Sun,* plus the addition of a new comedy, *Don't Ask.* "I wanted to wait for an orderly time when all things were done," Glickman explained to *Variety,* adding "I feel like I'm leaving the company in good shape." Glickman also agreed to help in the search for his replacement.

### Principal Divisions

Carsey-Werner Distribution; Carsey-Werner Moving Pictures.

### Principal Competitors

Sony Pictures Entertainment; Fox Entertainment; Time Warner Entertainment.

### *Further Reading*

Carter, Bill, ''Cadillac-Sized Hits by the VW of Producers,'' *New York Times,* January 22, 1996, pp. C1, C4.

Miller, Jill Young, ''The Web Grows up as Females Catch up to Male Users,'' *Atlanta Constitution,* August 14, 2000, p. D1.

''Oxygen is Closing Sites for Shopping, Consumer-Service,'' *Wall Street Journal,* June 26, 2000, p. A42.

''Oxygen Media Revamps Shows, Seeks Respect,'' *Wall Street Journal,* July 21, 2000, p. B1.

Post, Tom, ''The Convergence Gamble,'' *Forbes,* February 22, 1999, pp. 112–117.

Schneider, Michael, ''C-W Vet Glickman Ankles CEO Post,'' *Variety,* June 2, 2000, p. 1.

Swasy, Alecia, ''Speaking of Success, In a Woman's Voice,'' *New York Times,* August 13, 2000, p. 6.

Tyrer, Thomas, ''Independent Carsey-Werner Readies for Mega-Merger Future,'' *Electronic Media,* October 2, 1995, pp. 1, 20.

Zoglin, Richard, ''Midas Touch,'' *Time,* September 23, 1996, pp. 69–79.

—Ed Dinger

# Championship Auto Racing Teams, Inc.

**755 W. Big Beaver Road, Suite 800**
**Troy, Michigan 48084**
**U.S.A.**
**Telephone: (248) 362-8800**
**Fax: (248) 362-8810**
**Web site: http://www.cart.com**

*Public Company*
*Incorporated:* 1978
*Employees:* 83
*Sales:* $68.8 million (1999)
*Ticker Symbol:* MPH
*Stock Exchanges:* New York
*NAIC:* 711212 Racetracks; 71132 Promoters of Performing Arts, Sports, and Similar Events without Facilities

Championship Auto Racing Teams, Inc. (CART) sanctions open-wheel "Indy Car" races, primarily in the United States. These custom-built, single-occupant cars can reach speeds of more than 240 miles an hour. CART sponsors more than 40 races per year, which make up three series. These consist of the premier Fedex Championship series, the Datsun Indy Lights Championship series, and the Toyota Atlantic Championship series. CART was founded by a group of driving teams that broke away from the United States Auto Club (USAC) in 1978, and the organization has since become the leading American sanctioning body for Indy Car races. CART has recently patched up its strained relationship with USAC successor the Indy Racing League, allowing its drivers to resume competition in the prestigious Indianapolis 500, which a CART team won in 2000. CART also operates a merchandising and licensed products subsidiary.

## Beginnings

CART's roots go back to the early years of the 20th century, when automobile racing (and the automobile itself) was in its infancy. Races of specially built high-speed cars drew crowds as soon as the idea was originated, with the first race held at Indianapolis Speedway in 1911. In 1955 the United States Auto Club (USAC) was formed to serve as the sanctioning body for races of the type of custom-built, open-wheel cars that were used at Indianapolis.

By the mid-1970s, with expenses rising and having only token representation on the USAC board of directors, a group of team owners began to push for greater control of the organization. When USAC refused their request for more input, 18 owners broke away and created their own sanctioning organization. Championship Auto Racing Teams, Inc. was formed in November of 1978, with owner U.E. "Pat" Patrick chosen as president. A total of 24 ownership shares were distributed to members of the group, with several (including Patrick and Roger Penske) receiving more than one.

In March of 1979 the first CART-sanctioned race was run. Gordon Johncock won the nationally televised 150-mile event at Phoenix International Raceway. During its first year in operation, CART produced a total of 13 races. These were organized separately from a series run by USAC, which bitterly resented the breakaway group. The antagonistic USAC refused six CART teams entry into the Indianapolis 500 that year, relenting only after CART filed a lawsuit.

During its first year, CART also signed a deal with PPG Industries to sponsor the 1980 CART World Series, beginning a relationship that would continue for many years. On the technical side, CART team Hall Racing introduced an innovative car during the year that utilized what was called "ground effects." The aerodynamically designed vehicle was literally sucked to the ground by the creation of a low-pressure area beneath it, giving it better stability and traction.

Following a successful first season, the new organization's events grew in popularity, with several additional races added to the schedule over the next decade. Top drivers such as Rick Mears (who won the first championship series, as well as back-to-back championships in 1981 and 1982), Mario Andretti, Al Unser, and Al Unser, Jr., won titles during the 1980s, with Bobby Rahal becoming the first to achieve $1 million in yearly earnings in 1986. Initially, USAC and CART both declared separate national racing champions, but this was resolved in 1982, when the

## Company Perspectives:

*The Company's mission is to build America's premier open-wheel series—our core business—into a major U.S. sports and entertainment business. Subsequently, the Company will "export" the Series to international markets through television and by racing in a limited number of major international markets. The Company will apply innovative strategies across a number of related businesses to achieve its mission. However, everything that the Company does must be evaluated on the basis of its contribution to the core business. We must achieve the mission in a manner that provides value to our key stakeholders—promoters, sponsors, licensees, race teams, drivers, media partners and shareholders—and provides our fans with a sense of pride and "ownership" in the Series. As a public company, we must provide competitive returns and growth to our shareholders.*

groups agreed to recognize a common winner. USAC continued to sponsor the Indianapolis 500, but it had few other races of consequence, while CART's schedule typically featured 15 or more races in major markets around the United States and Canada. Unlike USAC, which favored an oval racetrack, CART races were run on several different types of courses, which required that its drivers be skilled in each racing style. Speedways such as Indianapolis, shorter oval courses, temporary road courses created in the downtown areas of large cities, and existing roadways were all used for different CART races.

### A Restructured Board from 1989

Conflict surfaced in 1989 when the CART board voted to remove Chairman John Frasco and President John Caponigro. The two executives were accused of favoring the teams of Roger Penske and Pat Patrick to the detriment of less influential members. Frasco had been chairman since 1980, and Caponigro had been in office less than a year. Following this action, CART's board was restructured to include everyone who held one or more of the 24 ownership shares. John Capels took the reins as transitional leader and chief operating officer until July of 1990, when William Stokkan was named CEO. Stokkan previously had headed the licensing and merchandising arm of Playboy Enterprises, Inc.

CART was increasing its purses at this time, with a record $1 million given out in 1989 at the Detroit Grand Prix. In 1991 the company's first overseas event debuted, the Gold Coast CART Grand Prix, held in Surfer's Paradise, Australia. That year the company also signed a four-year broadcasting contract with cable sports network ESPN. In technical matters, 1992 saw Ford re-enter the open-wheel racing field with its first series of new Indy Car engines in 21 years. Recent CART races had been dominated by Chevrolet's Ilmor engines, which had won 60 of 63 races, but Ford was able to take five of the first 16 that it entered. Other new engines were introduced by Mercedes-Benz and Honda over the next several seasons.

CART vehicles were completely custom-built, with the cost of running a racing team as high as $10 million per year. Most

teams lost money, with all relying heavily upon corporate sponsorships to remain afloat. A typical car and driver were plastered with the logos of as many as several dozen sponsors, which might include automotive companies like PPG, Valvoline, and Texaco, as well as the ubiquitous Marlboro, Budweiser, and Miller Lite. Teams were often owned by former drivers, such as Foyt and Paul Newman, or wealthy racing fans like David Letterman and Bruce McCaw.

The early 1990s saw CART experiment with a seven-member board, which was abandoned after 18 months when the larger one was reinstated. CEO Stokkan was replaced in 1994 by Andrew Craig, formerly of ISL Marketing. Craig was charged with restructuring and revitalizing CART, which had begun to lose ground against the marketing success of NASCAR-sanctioned stock-car racing. Soon after taking charge, Craig faced a crisis when a major new rift arose between CART and the sponsors of the Indianapolis 500. Tony George, whose family had run the Indianapolis race for several generations, announced new rules for qualifying to run and new technical specifications. CART's response was to remove its teams from the event and create a new $1 million race, the U.S. 500, that would be held on the same day at a speedway in Brooklyn, Michigan. For his part George announced the creation of the Indy Racing League (IRL), which was to sponsor a series of races that were intended to steal some of CART's thunder.

Results of the first skirmishes were mixed, with the primarily rookie field at Indianapolis generating reduced fan interest, though the race itself was hailed as an exciting one, and the tickets sold out. George also successfully sued CART to prohibit its use of the expression "Indy Cars" when referring to its vehicles. CART took up the name "Champ Cars" instead, which it claimed had often been used in the past. After a second year of sponsoring a race the same weekend as Indianapolis, CART scrapped its head-to-head anti-Indy strategy, but its teams continued to avoid Indianapolis and other IRL races. The rules George had created for IRL qualification required a substantially different vehicle, one that was not turbo-charged, used a different chassis, and was slower, though also less expensive to build. CART maintained that technology should lead the way, and that car designs should not be limited in ways that prevented them reaching the maximum possible safe speed.

In January of 1997 the company formed CART Licensed Products (CLP), a merchandising and licensing subsidiary that was a joint venture with Robert E. Hollander. One of the most visible elements of NASCAR's success had been the cross-promotion of its brand through the selling of collectible toys and clothing and by the use of its drivers as advertising pitchmen. CART hoped to follow this same path with the newly created CLP. The company also signed an agreement with Federal Express Corporation to sponsor CART's championship race series for three years beginning with the 1998 season. On the track, CART teams continued to make technical breakthroughs, with a record qualifying speed of slightly more than 240 miles per hour reached in September.

### 1998 IPO and Acquisition of Two New Race Series

In early 1998, CART made its initial public offering on the New York Stock Exchange. Each of the company's original 24

## Key Dates:

**1978:** CART is formed by a breakaway group of U.S. Auto Club team owners.
**1979:** First CART-sanctioned race is held in Phoenix, Arizona.
**1986:** Bobby Rahal wins $1 million for the year, first CART driver to top this mark.
**1989:** CART president and chairman is fired; Board is expanded to include all shareholders.
**1991:** First overseas race takes place in Australia.
**1996:** CART teams boycott Indianapolis 500, stage U.S. 500 race in Michigan instead.
**1998:** CART-sanctioned racing begins in Japan.
**2000:** Return to Indianapolis 500; CEO Andrew Craig is replaced by Bobby Rahal.

shares also was exchanged for 400,000 new ones. Sales of stock gave CART enough cash to purchase two additional race series, which were to be used as training grounds for new drivers. These were the Dayton Indy Lights Championship series and the Toyota Atlantic Championship series, each of which consisted of approximately a dozen races per year. CART also added new races to its FedEx Championship series in Houston, Texas and in Japan. The latter was CART's third foreign venture, the second having come in 1997 when a race was added in Rio de Janeiro, Brazil. The FedEx series also included two races in Canada. In July, tragedy struck at a race in Michigan when parts from an out-of-control car flew into the grandstand and killed three spectators, though the vehicle's driver sustained only minor injuries. The next year's racing season saw two more fatalities, both drivers who died in separate accidents.

Addressing concerns that CART drivers consisted almost exclusively of white males, in 1999 the organization announced its African-American Development Program, as well as newly increased efforts to recruit women. CART had also for some time been seeing declining attendance and television viewership, which seemed due at least in part to the absence of its teams from the hugely popular Indianapolis 500. Bowing to the inevitable, the company began talks with the IRL to resolve the two organizations' differences. The company also purchased the remaining interest in CART Licensed Products during the year. The FedEx Championship series now consisted of 20 races, with the most recent addition being in Chicago.

The year 2000 saw dramatic changes for CART. The talks with the IRL were successful, and a CART team entered and won that year's Indianapolis 500. At about the same time, CEO Andrew Craig was fired by the organization's board and replaced on an interim basis by retired driving champion Bobby

Rahal. CART owners reportedly had been dissatisfied with Craig's performance for some time.

After nearly 20 years in business, Championship Auto Racing Teams, Inc. remained the premier sponsor of open-wheel racing in the United States. Having faced a number of difficulties during the 1990s, the organization was getting back on track by addressing the challenge to its audience base posed by stock car racing and by focusing on improving diversity among its drivers. Most important, perhaps, it had made amends with the backers of the Indianapolis 500, allowing its drivers to compete again in the most famous race in America.

### Principal Subsidiaries

CART Licensed Products, Inc.; CART Properties, Inc.

### Principal Competitors

Indy Racing League; International Hot Rod Association; National Association for Stock Car Auto Racing; National Hot Rod Association; National Muscle Car Association; Professional SportsCar Racing; SCCA Pro Racing; United States Auto Club.

### Further Reading

Barkholz, David, "CART Races Toward IPO, But Team Owners Will Steer," *Automotive News,* January 12, 1998, p. 26J.

*CART FedEx Championship Series 2000 Media Guide,* Troy, Mich.: Championship Auto Racing Teams, Inc., 2000.

Glick, Shav, "CART to Deal with Diversity in Its Meeting," *Los Angeles Times,* January 8, 1990, p. 14.

——, "Changing Gears—Indy Racing League Has Its Own Cars, Tracks and Schedule and Has Even Taken the Name Indy Car from Rivals at CART," *Los Angeles Times,* January 22, 1997, p. C1.

Hampton, William J., "Gentlemen, Start Your Selling," *Business Week,* May 5, 1988, p. 86.

Helyar, John, "Dueling Indy Car Circuits Set to Rumble," *Wall Street Journal,* March 1, 1996, p. B8.

——, "Racing Fans Are the Losers as Indy Feud Goes in Circles," *Wall Street Journal,* May 23, 1997, p. B6.

Kerwin, Kathleen, and Bill Koenig, "Gentlemen, Start Your Grudge Match," *Business Week,* May 27, 1996, p. 70.

Melilli, Denise, "A Shift in Leadership: Unhappiness with Craig Puts Rahal in Driver's Seat," *Crain's Cleveland Business,* June 26, 2000, p. G7.

——, "Driving for Diversity: CART Program Out to Widen Participant Spectrum," *Crain's Cleveland Business,* June 21, 1999, p. G8.

——, "The Race for Dominance: CART Looks to Share NASCAR's Marketing Success," *Crain's Cleveland Business,* June 21, 1999, p. G12.

Nauss, Donald W., "Indy 500: Revving Up for War," *Los Angeles Times,* May 21, 1996, p. A1.

—Frank Uhle

# Chateau Communities, Inc.

6160 South Syracuse Way
Greenwood Village, Colorado 80111
U.S.A.
Telephone: (303) 874-3305
Fax: (303) 741-3715
Web site: http://www.chateaucomm.com

*Public Company*
*Incorporated:* 1993
*Employees:* 1,183
*Sales:* $192.2 million (1999)
*Stock Exchanges:* New York
*Ticker Symbol:* CPJ
*NAIC:* 521190 Lessors of Other Real Estate Properties;
525930 Real Estate Investment Trusts; 531311
Residential Property Managers

An owner, manager, and developer of manufactured home communities in the United States, Chateau Communities, Inc. is the country's largest self-managed, self-administered real estate investment trust (REIT). As a REIT, the company owns and manages 165 properties (with 51,000+ homes), while it manages-only another 44 communities (with 9,700 homes). All told, Chateau Communities serves about 130,000 residents. Though Chateau has properties in 34 states, its greatest presence is in the states of Florida and Michigan. The company was formed in 1997, when Chateau Properties merged with ROC Communities.

### Chateau and ROC in a Favorable Market

Based in southeastern Michigan, in Clinton Township, Chateau Properties had owned, managed, and developed mobile/manufactured home communities in Michigan and Florida since 1966. ROC Communities was founded in 1979 in Englewood, Colorado, to own and manage mobile home parks and grew to include properties in Florida, Georgia, Indiana, Colorado, Montana, and Wyoming.

The merger of the two companies occurred at a time of renewed interest in manufactured homes as a housing alterna-

tive. While mobile home parks had proliferated in America in the 1970s, with half of new housing starts in 1972 being manufactured home sites, the industry had overbuilt and the parks did not begin to fill until the mid-1980s. By the early 1990s, manufactured homes rebounded as a new form of affordable housing. Manufactured homes differed from mobile homes in that they tended to move only once, from the factory to the homesite. Better construction of the prefabricated homes and more pleasant surroundings, with amenities, graceful landscaping, and the look of permanent homes, transformed manufactured home communities into a desirable housing alternative.

Chateau Estates and ROC Communities sought to capitalize on the growing demand for manufactured homesites and on new investor interest through separate public offerings of stock in 1993. Manufactured home communities became an attractive investment on Wall Street due to their stability. The cost of relocating a mobile/manufactured home resulted in low resident turnover while the low cost of operations and the low rate of loan defaults made the industry a fairly low-risk investment. Wall Street's support for manufactured home communities spawned consolidation within the industry as well as new manufactured housing developments.

### History of Chateau

Originally named Chateau Estates, Chateau Properties, Inc. incorporated prior to an initial public offering in late 1993 in conjunction with a merger with two other companies. To Chateau Estates' 20 properties in Florida and Michigan, Mass Manufactured Home Group added six properties in western Michigan and Intercoastal Communities, Inc. added 17 properties in Florida. With a total of 15, 261 homesites at 33 properties, the merger placed Chateau Properties among the largest manufactured home community operators in the country. The company organized as a REIT and operated primarily under the newly formed CP Partnership Limited. Operation as a trust allowed for tax-free revenues as long as the company distributed at least 95 percent of net income to shareholders.

Through the offering of 5.7 million shares of stock, at $20 per share, Chateau Properties raised $110 million which al-

## Company Perspectives:

*The company's mission is to create valued residential relationships by providing a welcoming environment, quality products and resident services in attractive settings, in partnership with our residents, employees, and shareholders.*

lowed the company to acquire and expand several manufactured home communities. In January 1994 the company acquired a 129-site community in Spring Lake Township, Michigan, adjacent to the company's Country Estates property. The $2.5 million acquisition of Forest Lake involved land already zoned for additional homesites. Expansion began in June, adding 37 homesites for single and multi-section manufactured homes. The company also added 63 new homesites at Chateau Anchor Bay, for a total 1,213 sites there. In July Chateau Properties acquired Lake in the Hills, a 238-site community in Auburn Hills, Michigan, for $7.3 million.

Chateau Properties began a $1 million expansion of its premier manufactured home community, Chateau of Grand Blanc. Amenities at the property included a community center with banquet facilities, a games room, and a fitness center while outdoor facilities included a swimming pool, baseball diamond, volleyball and basketball courts, and two playgrounds. To the existing 337 homesites, the expansion added 78 sites for multi-section homes on lots from 5,000 to 6,000 square feet, the largest homesites in the company.

Expansion outside of Michigan involved the acquisition of properties in Minnesota, North Dakota, and Florida. In September 1994 Chateau Properties purchased seven mobile home parks from NHD of Minneapolis for $44 million. The transaction yielded the company two properties in Fargo and one in Grand Forks, North Dakota, and four properties in Minneapolis, for a combined total of 2,116 sites. Chateau Properties purchased two all-adult communities in Florida in 1995. Del Tura, in North Fort Myers, featured 1,343 homesites which surrounded a 27-hole golf course. In September Chateau Properties purchased the Hidden Valley manufactured home community in Lake Buena Vista, with 303 occupied homesites. The company paid $6.1 million for Hidden Valley, a transaction which comprised $2.6 million in cash and $3.5 million in Operating Partnership units of stock. By July 1996, when Chateau Properties announced the merger agreement with ROC Communities, Chateau Properties owned and managed 44 properties with 19,594 homesites in four states.

### History of ROC

Like Chateau, ROC Communities had also gone public in 1993. The principal owners of Clayton Homes, Inc., the largest producer of manufactured homes in the United States, and ROC Properties formed ROC Communities earlier that year. Prior to the public offering of stock, 6.3 million shares for $19.25 per share, ROC Communities acquired ROC Properties. At that time the company owned seven communities and managed 77 communities for a fee. Immediately after the stock offering, ROC Communities acquired 20 fee-managed properties from

affiliated limited partnerships for $62.1 million and 20 fee-managed properties from The Windsor Corporation for $57 million. By the end of 1993 ROC Communities acquired an additional eight communities from unaffiliated sellers for a total investment of $34 million. The company offered the property owners cash or the tax-deferred option of a stock transaction. ROC Communities continued to manage 37 properties.

ROC Communities utilized funds from a secondary offering of stock to further growth. In 1994 the company grew to 62 properties in 23 states through the acquisitions of 14 manufactured home communities for $95 million. Approximately $32 million of that investment went to the purchase of five communities in California, a new market for the company. The following year ROC Communities purchased six properties for $35 million, bringing the total number of homesites to 18,078. In 1995 the National Manufactured Housing Congress voted ROC Communities the National Manufactured Home Community Operator of the Year for the third consecutive year.

ROC Communities expanded through acquisition and new development in 1996. In January the company acquired a 354-site home park in Cincinnati; the 52-acre property cost $9.75 million. The following April the company purchased a 235-site community in Albion, New York, for $4 million. The property consisted of 117 acres with 55 new homesites approved for construction, plus an additional 50 acres for future expansion. Four additional acquisitions involved 2,275 homesites, bringing the company's total properties to 72 with 20,940 homesites.

In a joint venture with McStain Enterprises of Boulder, Colorado, ROC Communities developed an 87-acre manufactured home community in Longmont, Colorado. Long View Park accommodated 401 homesites on lots which averaged 5,000 square feet and rented for $285 to $380 per month. Home prices ranged from $58,900 to $75,000. Financing through a personal property loan enabled a buyer to purchase a manufactured home with a minimum $3,000 down payment and about $150 in fees. The premium, factory-built homes included 2-by-6 metal construction, R-19 rated insulation for heating and cooling efficiency, better carpet and appliances, decks, and enhanced landscaping. Amenities at Long View Park included a 3,000 square foot clubhouse, built in a rustic style with logs and stone, a playground, a swimming pool, and 15 acres of parks and green spaces.

### The 1997 Merger

ROC Communities and Chateau Properties announced their agreement to merge in July 1996, but competition in the industry delayed the transaction. The two companies planned a merger of equals, an equal stock swap rather than one company acquiring the other. In 1995, Chateau Properties revenues reached $62 million and net $5.3 million profit, while ROC Communities garnered $51.5 million and net $11.5 million. Plans for the merger attracted two unsolicited offers from companies which sought to acquire Chateau Properties. Chicago Real estate magnate Sam Zell's Manufactured Home Communities (MHC) made a tender offer of $26 per share, while Sun Communities of Farmington Hills, Michigan, made a similar offer. After Chateau Properties rejected both offers, MHC tried to block the merger, valued at $21 per share in a tax-free stock swap. During the delay, the two companies formed a joint venture to develop seven new communities with 2,900 homesites.

In early 1997 shareholders at both Chateau Properties and ROC Communities voted in favor of the merger. In accordance with an adjusted agreement, shareholders at ROC Communities received 1.042 shares of stock in Chateau Properties, later renamed Chateau Communities. Leadership changes placed Gary P. McDaniel, CEO of ROC Communities, as CEO of Chateau Communities, while C.G. Kellogg, president and CEO of Chateau Properties became president of the new entity. John Boll, chairman of the board of Chateau Properties, became chairman of the board of the Chateau Communities. The companies consolidated their main offices in Englewood, CO, while two division offices remained in Clinton Township and Atlanta. The merger created the largest company to provide sites for manufactured homes, with 128 owned and 32 managed properties, a combined total of 49,593 sites in 30 states.

The newly formed company pursued growth through acquisition, development of new sites at existing communities, and the inception of supplemental business activities. The company organized older, smaller manufactured home parks, which provided as few as 100 homesites, under a new subsidiary, N'Tandem Trust. In late 1997 the company purchased four properties in the suburbs south of Boston, for $20 million, obtaining 640 sites and 150 potential sites. The company completed the development of 509 homesites, adding 354 to its core portfolio of active, usable sites. At the end of 1997, Chateau Communities recorded 93.6 percent occupancy of the core portfolio.

The company formed another new subsidiary, Community Sales, Inc. in order to provide services to existing and potential residents. Community Sales provided real estate agent services to act as broker or agent in the buying and selling of new and pre-owned manufactured homes. One goal of the programs was to facilitate resident turnover in pre-owned manufactured homes at company properties. In 1997, the first year in operation, Community Sales sold 415 homes and brokered 800 home purchases.

In January 1998 Chateau Communities issued $100 million in securities to pay debt and for working capital and new acquisitions. The company acquired six mobile home parks and one recreational vehicle (RV) park and, shortly afterward, leased seven manufactured home communities and two RV parks. The 16 properties, located in Connecticut (4), Florida

(10), and South Carolina (2), comprised a total of 2,333 homesites, 1,359 RV sites, and 125 potential expansion sites. The transactions represented a $40 million investment of cash and Operating Partnership units. Continued acquisitions involved five communities in the area of South Bend, Indiana, and one in Mount Morris, Michigan, an aggregate total of 1,521 homesites plus 536 potential expansion sites purchased for $36.7 million. The company purchased an additional ten communities in Michigan and two in North Carolina, a $79 million investment for 3,036 homesites and 381 expansion sites. By the end of April, Chateau Communities owned and managed 165 properties with 50,690 homesites and fee-managed 32 properties with 6,600 homesites.

With Maryland home developer R. Wayne Newsome, Chateau Communities developed a manufactured home community near Baltimore, called New Colony Village. The company planned to develop approximately 300 homesites and introduced two-story manufactured homes, built in accordance with Housing and Urban Development (HUD) codes. Priced from $130,000 to $140,000, the homes featured one car garages, porches, and, for the first time in the industry, optional basements. The venture completed 100 homesites in 1998, during which time Chateau Communities became its sole owner. More than half of residents at the gated community paid $400 per month for rent. Designed for families, amenities included a day care center and a general store. The National Manufactured Housing Congress voted New Colony Village the Best New Land-Lease Community while Chateau Communities became National Manufactured Home Community Operator of the Year for the sixth consecutive year.

### 1999: New Businesses and Developments

In 1999 Chateau Properties stepped away from acquisition as a growth strategy. The company viewed 8,000 of 25,000 manufactured home communities as potential acquisitions, based on the number of homes in each community, on the quality of each community and its amenities, and on the company's preference for metropolitan locations. The company acquired only two properties in 1999, both of which fit the portfolio of N'Tandem Trust, then holding a total of 31 properties.

As acquisition opportunities declined Chateau Communities initiated the Business Development unit to explore new areas of growth. The Business Development unit sought avenues of growth in existing business by providing new services to the company's community residents. By the end of 1999 approximately half of the company's properties offered shed storage rental, a total of 610 sheds which averaged $33 per month rent. Chateau Communities began to test market services which catered to its elderly clientele, such as prescription delivery, home health services, and rental of medical equipment, walkers, and wheelchairs. The company introduced Brinks security system at ten communities and Community Sales Inc. began to offer home financing and homeowners' insurance. In addition to 587 homes sales, and 1,273 brokered sales, the subsidiary arranged 863 home loans, with fees averaging $1,600 fee per transaction.

Continuing operations in 1999 related to the completion of 525 homesites at existing properties as well as 420 "greenfield" development homesites, including 44 at New Colony

Village. At a new development at Onion Creek in Austin, Texas, homesites sat amidst rolling hills and mature trees. Antelope Ridge, near Colorado Springs, featured mountain views from its multi-section, two-car garage homes. The covenant-controlled community also included parks, playgrounds, a swimming pool, and a clubhouse. Company-wide occupancy remained steady at 93.2 percent and Funds From Operations increased 11.3 percent. Revenues increased 9.4 percent, from $173 million in 1998 to $189.4 million in 1999, while earnings increased from $26.8 million to $34.6 million. Assets neared $1 billion in 1999.

The company's plans for the future involved investment in new property developments for manufactured homesites. Chateau Communities acquired a development property in Michigan and invested $16 million in nine joint ventures to develop new manufactured home communities. The company planned an assisted-living manufactured home community at its Colony Cove property in Florida, scheduled to open in 2001. With 130,000 residents at the end of 1999, the company set a goal to serve 200,000 residents by 2002.

### Principal Subsidiaries

Community Sales, Inc.; CP Limited Partnership; N'Tandem Trust.

### Principal Competitors

Commercial Assets, Inc.; Manufactured Home Communities, Inc.; Sun Communities, Inc.

### Further Reading

Allen, George F., "Upscale Manufactured Home Communities? Really!," *Journal of Property Management*, March-April 1999, p. 46.

Burgess, Robert. "Chateau Expands Portfolio in 2 States," *Denver Post*, April 14, 1998, p. C1.

"Chateau Communities Sets Deal," *Wall Street Journal*, March 18, 1998, p. B14.

"Chateau Properties Approves Merger With ROC Communities," *PR Newswire*, February 11, 1997.

Craig, Charlotte W., "Michigan's Chateau Properties Joins Colorado Home-Site Provider," *Knight-Ridder/Tribune Business News*, July 19, 1996.

Gargaro, Paul, "Home Free . . . Almost," *Crain's Detroit Business*, September 30, 1996, p. 2.

——, "May the Better Offer Win," *Crain's Detroit Business*, August 26, 1996, p. 2.

——, "SEC Filing Next Step in Chateau Bid," *Crain's Detroit Business*, September 16, 1996, p. 3.

——, "Sun Continues to Rise," *Crain's Detroit Business*, November 11, 1996, p. 2.

Graham, Sandy, "Factory Housing Built to Last," *Denver Rocky Mountain News*, December 19, 1999, p. 3G.

Halliday, Jean, "Keeping Tabs," *Crain's Detroit Business*, November 29, 1993, p. 32.

Holt, Nancy, "Trashing a Trailer-Park Image—Manufactured Housing Tries to Boost Its Stature," *Wall Street Journal*, April 7, 1999, p. B12.

Moore, Paula, "Trailer Park REITs Win Favor of Analysts," *Denver Business Journal*, November 19, 1999, p. 6A.

"New Phase of Project Planned," *Crain's Detroit Business*, March 28, 1994.

Raabe, Steve, "Preassembled Homes Aim for 'Country-Club Living'," *Denver Post*, January 30, 1996, p. C3.

"ROC Communities Buys NY Property," *Denver Post*, April 30, 1996, p. C3.

Rudnitsky, Howard, "New Life for Old Mobile Home Parks," *Forbes*, November 7, 1994, p. 44.

Wood, Christopher, "Real Estate Trusts Are On a Roll: ROC Seeks $125 Mil. for Prefab Housing," *Denver Business Journal*, June 11, 1993, p. 3.

—Mary Tradii

# THE CHILDREN'S
# PLACE

## The Children's Place Retail Stores, Inc.

915 Secaucus Road
Secaucus, New Jersey 07094
U.S.A.
Telephone: (201) 558-2400
Fax: (201) 558-2841
Web site: http://www.childrensplace.com

*Public Company*
*Incorporated:* 1969
*Employees:* 3,700
*Sales:* $421.5 million (2000)
*Stock Exchanges:* NASDAQ
*Ticker Symbol:* PLCE
*NAIC:* 44813 Children's and Infants' Clothing Stores

The Children's Place Retail Stores Inc. operates a chain of children's clothing stores across most of the United States. Its products are designed for children aged newborn to 12. It sells under its own "The Children's Place" brand name. In the competitive children's retail market, The Children's Place offers prices significantly lower than principal brand name competitors. Most of the chain's stores are in malls, with a mix of upscale and more down-market sites. A pair of entrepreneurs started the company on the east coast, and it gradually spread west and south. By the year 2000 The Children's Place had close to 400 stores in 42 states, with plans to expand rapidly. In 1981, the founders sold it to the retail empire of Federated Department Stores. The company is now publicly owned, with about a third of the stock in the hands of CEO Ezra Dabah and his family.

### An Entrepreneurial Venture in the 1970s

The first Children's Place store was opened by two 1965 graduates of Harvard Business School, David Pulver and Clinton Clark. Pulver and Clark both agreed that they did not want to go to work for big corporations, but it took them several years to decide what kind of business they would like to run. Some of the options they first considered were opening auto repair shops or marketing special meltable crayons. Eventually they focused

on opening a children's department store. Both men had children and thought they knew something of what children wanted, so they decided to put this expertise to work. Pulver and Clark opened The Children's Place in Hartford, Connecticut, in 1969. The store sold toys as well as clothing and accessories, a product mix described by Clark in a February 1, 1982 profile in *Forbes* as "everything for everyone." This strategy was not particularly successful; many lines were unprofitable. Pulver and Clark spent three years adjusting the product mix and learning how to run the store before The Children's Place made money. They chose to focus on medium-priced children's sportswear, along with some name-brand kids' clothing. Pulver and Clark expanded, opening more stores in the east. After ten years, The Children's Place had blossomed into a chain of 34 stores. Revenues were growing at close to 50 percent annually, and profits were growing by a third.

The Children's Place had little direct competition at first. Its stores were primarily located in malls. Consumers could buy children's clothing at mall anchor department stores such as J.C. Penney and Sears, but The Children's Place was generally the only small mall shop selling children's wear exclusively. The chain galloped along, nearly doubling to 65 stores by 1981. Sales were over $50 million. Pulver and Clark took the chain public in 1981, and were apparently besieged by merger offers. The two founders were willing to sell the company, but they did not want to stay on and run it under a corporate boss. In 1982, they sold The Children's Place to Federated Department Stores. Federated was a large chain store conglomerate with sales of around $6 billion. It ran such well-known department stores such as Bloomingdale's and I. Magnin. Pulver and Clark's deal with Federated called for them to train replacements to run The Children's Place, so their association with the retail chain ended soon after the sale.

### Ups and Downs in the 1980s

The chain's growth continued under new ownership. From 1982 to 1986, The Children's Place added on average 20 stores a year, spreading mostly through malls across the northeast and midwest. But under Federated, the chain was no longer as profitable as it had been in its early years. The store sold a mix

**Company Perspectives:**

*At The Children's Place, we are committed to creating a true lifestyle brand for kids. We are proud of what we have achieved and very excited about our future. Our success to date is due to our steadfast commitment to our core values: Quality that our customers have come to expect: Service on our customers' terms; style that fits our customers' needs; prices that won't strain our customers' budgets.*

of brand-name clothes and some private label, but its sales were hurt by discounters offering comparable goods at cheaper prices. A new chain, Kids 'R' Us, an offshoot of the mass-market toy store chain Toys 'R' Us, also provided new competition. In 1985, The Children's Place lost money, and then stayed in the red for 1986 and 1987.

Federated had made some changes to the chain, remodeling a few stores after a new prototype in 1984, and then progressively remodeling others for the more updated look. The parent company built a new warehouse to handle The Children's Place goods, and hired new staff, anticipating growing the chain to 300 stores by 1990. However, The Children's Place seemed to lose its uniqueness. It lost out to discounters, but it was not as upscale as some of its department store competitors. It lacked guidance from Federated, and this was made worse in 1988, when the Federated conglomerate was bought by a Canadian company, Campeau Corp. Already a small piece of a big firm, The Children's Place was even farther from the center of operations after the sale of Federated. The Children's Place lost $12 million in 1988, and Campeau decided to sell it. It went on the block along with a sister chain it had started in 1986, The Accessory Place. This was another mall-based chain, selling accessories to girls and young women.

By 1988, The Children's Place had grown to 161 stores. Campeau hoped to get bids of $75 million for the chain, in tandem with The Accessory Place, but no buyers were willing to shell out that much. Eventually the two chains together went for $28 million. The purchaser was an investor group led by Morris Dabah, the head of the apparel corporation Gitano Group. Dabah's investor group bought the two chains from Federated, then sold The Accessory Place the next day for $6 million. The chief executive position at The Children's Place was then taken over by Ezra Dabah, who was also president of E.J. Gitano, Gitano Group's children's division. He had a solid background in children's merchandising, extensive contacts with manufacturers, and was a father of five himself.

### Under Ezra Dabah in the 1990s

Ezra Dabah was enthusiastic about running The Children's Place. He knew the company had not been well managed under Federated, but he was sure the chain had great potential. It was still the only national children's specialty chain to be found principally in malls. Its main competitor, Kids 'R' Us, was primarily in strip malls or the kind of edge-of-town retail areas where big box stores were found. The mall locale of the Children's Place chain gave it a unique identity. And Dabah be-

lieved that children's apparel was a market poised for immense growth. Dabah quickly initiated plans to get the chain back on its feet. He opened two new prototype stores, planning to build other new ones on the same model. These had a bright, open floor plan with walls accented by floral wallpaper; a toddler play area; revamped fitting rooms, including one for handicapped children; video monitors; and colorful posters and props. Unprofitable stores were shut down, layers of management cut, and the merchandise mix was reconsidered. Dabah preferred to go with an upscale image. Ninety percent of the clothing was branded, with labels like Gloria Vanderbilt, Bugle Boy, OshKosh, and Gitano. By late 1989, Dabah was able to claim that The Children's Place would turn a profit that year. Expenses were down, and inventory was turning over faster.

Dabah also announced that the chain would continue to grow. In an article in *WWD* for September 18, 1989, Dabah revealed plans to add 20 to 30 stores in 1990, and eventually bring the chain up to 400 to 500 stores. Direct competitors were considered the department stores that frequently anchored malls, such as J.C. Penney and Macy's. Price was not to be the main draw at The Children's Place. "The big come-on," Dabah declared to *WWD*, "will be the merchandise itself."

Nevertheless, The Children's Place remained financially troubled. Between 1990 and 1992, the company lost $60 million. Store closings outnumbered openings, bringing the total number in the chain to only 90. The investor group that had bought the firm filed for Chapter 11 in November 1993, along with Ezra Dabah and three other members of his family. The Dabah's Gitano Group was not doing well, either. It filed for bankruptcy in 1994. The Children's Place had trouble meeting its payments, and finally agreed in 1993 to an out-of-court settlement restructuring its debts. This allowed the firm to remain in business. Three years later, the company was still not financially sound, and it brought in two outside firms to help it handle its debt. These were Saunders Karp & Megrue (SKM), which took a stake of over 30 percent in The Children's Place, and Nomura Holding America, which took a smaller stake of around nine percent. The Dabah family continued to hold the remaining stock.

By 1997, the company had changed its marketing thrust somewhat. Instead of offering high-priced brand-name merchandise, it sold good quality but value-priced children's clothing under its own brand name, Children's Place. This gave it more of a competitive edge against the many retailers it was up against in the children's market. These newcomers included Gap Kids, Baby Gap, and Old Navy, all offshoots of The Gap; Limited Too, a children's version of the long-standing mall-based The Limited chain; and Gymboree, a nationwide chain of children's clothing stores. The Children's Place continued to vie for market share with J.C. Penney, Sears, and other mall department stores, as well as Kids 'R' Us. The Children's Place set the price of its private label clothing at 20 to 30 percent below most of its mall-based competitors. Its Children's Place brand was sold exclusively in its own stores. In 1997, the company vaunted its new, improved image to attract investors for an initial public offering (IPO). By then it had grown to include 130 stores. Sales in 1996 of $122 million had given the firm a slim $1.65 million in profit, but for 1997 the figures were better, with net income of over $30 million on sales of around $144 million.

## Public Company in the Late 1990s and After

The Children's Place hoped to raise $70 million with its IPO. In fact it raised $50 million, which went to pay off debt. SKM, which had taken a stake in the company in 1996 to help turn its finances around, sold off its holdings in the IPO. More than 40 percent of the stock remained in the hands of CEO Ezra Dabah, and the company's board in total held almost 80 percent. The publicly traded shares started out at $14, and soon reached a high of over $16. But unseasonably warm weather depressed fall sales, and a month after the September IPO, The Children's Place announced that it would have lower than expected results for that quarter. The stock plunged, and shareholders sued.

However, a year later, the stock was performing well, and the company seemed back on track. Though the company faced stiff competition from Gap Kids, Gymboree, and others, its lower pricing set its stores apart. The chain kept up its expansion, moving west and south. In 1998 it had 180 stores and looked forward to opening many more. Its stated goal was to have 800 stores by 2004. By 2000, the chain's growth seemed more assured than at any time in its recent past. Over the three years since the public offering, sales rose 44 percent, topping $400 million, and earnings also climbed by over 15 percent. The Children's Place opened 84 stores in 1999, and planned 100 more openings in 2000. Analysts in various publications agreed that The Children's Place had at last found itself a unique niche. A retail analyst quoted in *Crain's New York Business* (May 3, 1999) claimed "There's not another concept out there like them. . . . The clothes offer great value, and they're fashionable." Another industry expert quoted in *Business Week* (May 29, 2000) echoed this, declaring the chain's stores "have a real and unique niche." Ezra Dabah, quoted in the same article, crowed that "We do well where our competitors cannot." The secret was the mix of fashion and low pricing. The Children's Place could open stores in fancy upscale malls, where they fit in because of the bright look of the décor. But its stores did well too in more cost-conscious malls and retail strips, because the clothes were priced for value. Dabah's long experience in children's clothing apparently allowed him to keep costs down. Another analyst interviewed in the *Crain's New York Business* article mentioned above declared, "Most companies go to the factories and say, 'I want a pair of jeans for $5.' Ezra negotiates every single element. He goes in and says, 'I'll pay this price for the zipper and use this kind of stitch.' In the end, he comes out with good quality at a great price."

Good quality at a great price was almost a universal retailer's dream. As long as Dabah could continue to manage this for The Children's Place brand, prospects at the chain looked bright. Children's clothing was expected to be a hot growth industry in the 2000s, as the "baby boomlet" ensured that children were a growing percentage of the population.

The chain planned to expand its number of stores, moving south into the Sunbelt and farther west as well. It also found more locations by increasing the number of stores within one city. It often clustered more stores near an existing location, or near its competitors' stores. And when moving into Portland, Oregon, for example, it opened not one store but five within months of each other. With room to grow and at last a seemingly reliable retail formula, The Children's Place looked forward to becoming an even bigger player within the children's clothing market in the years to come.

### Principal Competitors

Gymboree Corporation; J.C. Penney Company, Inc.; Kids 'R' Us; Gap Kids.

### Further Reading

Auerbach, Jonathan, "Children's Place Seeks Out-of-Court Settlement," *Daily News Record,* February 26, 1993, p. 10.

"Campeau's Federated Sets $30 Million Sale of Children's Place," *Wall Street Journal,* November 10, 1988, p. B12.

Chanko, Kenneth M., "Gitano Makes Deal for Children's Place," *Discount Store News,* January 23, 1989, p. 1.

"Children's Place: Hey, Good-Looking," *Business Week,* May 29, 2000, p. 190.

Cuccio, Angela, "The Children's Place: Born Again," *WWD,* September 18, 1989, p. 4.

Denitto, Emily, "Kids Apparel Retailer Survives El Nino as Stock Recovers Allure," *Crain's New York Business,* July 13, 1998, p. 4.

Fitzgerald, Beth, "Stocks Plunge at Children's Place Apparel Stores," *Knight-Ridder/Tribune Business News,* October 15, 1997.

Forman, Ellen, "Secret Memo Gives Details of $7.4M Loss at Children's Place," *Daily News Record,* August 1, 1988, p. 3.

Gault, Ylonda, "Third Time's the Charm," *Crain's New York Business,* May 3, 1999, p. 3.

Goldfield, Robert, "Kid's Clothing Chain to Open Local Stores," *Business Journal-Portland,* March 17, 2000, p. 3.

Moin, David, "Children's Place Is Growing Up," *WWD,* August 24, 1998, p. 18.

Reeves, Scott, "Niches Can Get Crowded," *Barron's,* September 29, 1997, p. 39.

Rohmann, Laura, "Golf Is Boring, Anyway," *Forbes,* February 1, 1982, pp. 104–05.

"The Children's Place Sizes Up New Sites," *Shopping Center World,* July 1998, p. 26.

Wilson, Marianne, "A Second Childhood," *Chain Store Age Executive,* October 1989, pp. 21–23.

—A. Woodward

# The Chubb Corporation

15 Mountain View Road, P.O. Box 1615
Warren, New Jersey 07061
U.S.A.
Telephone: (908) 903-2000
Fax: (908) 580-3402
Web site: http://www.chubb.com

*Public Company*
*Incorporated:* 1882 as Chubb & Son
*Employees:* 11,900
*Sales:* $6.7 billion (1999)
*Stock Exchanges:* New York
*Ticker Symbol:* CB
*NAICs:* 52321 Security and Commodity Exchanges;
    524113 Direct Life Insurance Carriers; 52413
    Reinsurance Carriers; 524114 Direct Health and
    Medical Insurance Carriers; 23311 Land Subdivision
    and Land Development; 551112 Offices of Other
    Holding Companies; 524126 Direct Property and
    Casualty Insurance Carriers; 524128 Other Direct
    Insurance (Except Life); 52519 Other Insurance
    Funds

The Chubb Corporation is best known as a provider of specialty insurance policies for upscale clients, both individuals and organizations. The Chubb Corporation operates as a holding company for an internationally diversified group of companies whose core business is in commercial, personal property and casualty insurance. The company also used to do business in health and life insurance, real estate development, consulting, and financial subsidiaries, but exited these areas in the early 1990s. What distinguishes Chubb from its competitors is its focus on niche products—such as policies covering liability for corporate officers and directors, or insuring stage productions—which account for more than one third of its property and casualty revenues. In the mid-1990s, the company was the fourth largest insurer in the United States, and among the top 15 worldwide.

## *Steady Growth During the First 75 Years*

Chubb was formed over a century ago with the partnership of Thomas Chubb—a New York underwriter of cargo and ship insurance—and his son, Percy Chubb. The two formed Chubb & Son, in 1882. Their venture was initially funded with $100,000 collected in $1,000 portions from each of 100 prominent merchants. Soon after its formation, Chubb & Son was one of the 100 founders of the New York Marine Underwriters (NYMU). Chubb first operated as a representative of NYMU and Sea Insurance Company Limited of England. In 1901, NYMU, Chubb's principal property and casualty affiliate, was reorganized as Federal Insurance Company.

During its first 40 years of business, Chubb & Son grew quickly, acting as an agent for several insurers. The company established itself as a respected underwriter of insurance for ships and cargo. During the 1920s, the company explored new areas. In 1921, Chubb & Son began to represent U.S. Guarantee Company. Through that company, Chubb began to underwrite fidelity, surety, and casualty insurance. In 1923, Chubb opened its first branch in Chicago. In March 1929, Chubb and another transportation insurance agent—the Marine Office of America—organized the Associated Aviation Underwriters, the largest aviation insurance-underwriting group in the United States. Seven companies represented by Chubb and eight insurers represented by the Marine Office joined to form the association.

During the Depression, Chubb's growth slowed as the insurance industry suffered. Nevertheless, in April 1930, Chubb & Son bought a 9,000-square-foot plot in Manhattan to house its companies and allow room for expansion. In 1939, Chubb founded Vigilant Insurance Company, a wholly owned fire and marine subsidiary. During World War II, the economy recovered, and Chubb & Son's business began to grow more quickly.

In December 1941, Chubb gave employees with more than six months of service their first Christmas bonuses. The workers each received half of their bonus in cash, and half in the form of war bonds. Also in December 1941, Chairman Charles A. Seibert, a 55-year veteran of the company, announced his retire-

> ### Company Perspectives:
>
> *Chubb has always been known for its appetite for risk and its innovative approaches to satisfying customers' needs. These traits have enabled us to grow and prosper over the decades. However, we are also known for our financial strength and fairness and speed in paying claims–qualities that are very important to our customers. We are committed to protecting this financial strength by accepting only prudent risks and leaving the reckless gambles to our competitors.*

ment. The company acquired The Colonial Life Insurance Company of America in 1957, and, in 1959, Chubb & Son reincorporated under the laws of New York.

### Reorganization and Acquisitions: Late 1960s–80s

The Chubb Corporation saw many changes in the late 1960s. In 1967, the company's management formed The Chubb Corporation to act as a holding company. Chubb & Son became a wholly owned subsidiary of The Chubb Corporation, as did Chubb & Son's subsidiaries. The property and casualty companies within the Chubb group of insurance companies fell under the management of Chubb & Son, the branch responsible for the company's domestic property and casualty insurance companies and U.S. branches of foreign insurers. The primary property and casualty insurance company managed by Chubb & Son remained Federal Insurance Company.

In July 1967, Chubb acquired Pacific Indemnity Corporation of Los Angeles. In November 1967, Pacific Indemnity president and chief executive officer Carl Fisher was elected senior vice-president and director of Chubb. In January 1969, First National City Corporation—later to become Citicorp—agreed to acquire The Chubb Corporation. In April 1969, however, the two corporations confirmed that the Department of Justice was examining the antitrust implications of the merger. Later that month, the two companies agreed to postpone the merger until the summer of 1969 in order to allow the Department of Justice to complete its study of the transaction. On June 13, 1969, the Department of Justice announced its intention to bring suit to bar the acquisition. Three hours later, First National City Corporation canceled the planned merger.

In September 1969, William M. Rees, then president of The Chubb Corporation, was elected chief executive officer and became responsible for all operations excluding investment. Investment responsibilities and general corporate policy and development remained with Chairman Percy Chubb II.

In 1970, Chubb acquired Bellemead Development Corporation, a Delaware real estate company with land holdings primarily in New Jersey and Florida. This acquisition was Chubb's first major move into the real estate field. Chubb confirmed that its real estate consultants placed a value of more than $25 million on Bellemead's properties if sold individually on the open market.

In 1971, Chubb acquired United Life & Accident Insurance Company and founded Chubb Custom Market. Chubb Custom Market became involved heavily in the entertainment industry. The subsidiary specialized in insurance for the film industry, and insured such movies as *E.T.: The Extra-Terrestrial, Tootsie, The Verdict,* and *Missing.* When Dustin Hoffman developed laryngitis and was unable to perform for three days during the filming of *Tootsie,* Chubb covered the additional expense. In addition to insuring films, Chubb Custom Market provides entertainment coverage for television productions, special entertainment events, and Broadway shows. In 1983, Chubb insured 75 percent of the productions on Broadway. Chubb's coverage was popular because of its comprehensive nature, which included theft, injuries, and equipment failure.

On June 9, 1971, American Financial Corporation, a Cincinnati, Ohio-based financial holding company, sold 875,000 shares of Chubb stock to Salomon Brothers in a transaction valued at more than $54 million. American Financial had begun to acquire the stock in 1969 and had planned to attempt a buyout of Chubb. Salomon Brothers resold the shares, which represented a 14 percent stake in Chubb, to the public later in the day. In 1973, Chubb, through the international division of Chubb & Son, joined First National City Corporation's subsidiary, FNC Comercio, in buying a majority interest in Companhia de Seguros Argos Fluminense, a Brazilian multiple-line insurance company.

The Chubb Corporation formed Chubb Life Insurance Company of America in 1978 to serve as an intermediate holding company for life insurance subsidiaries. In 1981, the company began to consolidate the activities of The Colonial Life Insurance Company of America and United Life & Accident Insurance Company at Chubb Life's headquarters in Concord, New Hampshire. This consolidation was completed in 1984.

In 1983, The Chubb Corporation completed and relocated to a new head office on 185 acres in Warren, New Jersey. The following year, Chubb focused its efforts on growth in its international division. The company sought to increase its international property and casualty insurance business and to expand its worldwide coverage for U.S. multinationals. The company's strategy for distinguishing itself was not to offer universal contracts or pre-formulated programs, but instead to create policies tailored to meet the needs of its clients. Chubb set a goal of maintaining 20 percent annual growth of its international business. Also in 1984, Chubb acquired Volunteer State Life Insurance Company of Chattanooga, Tennessee, and discontinued its money-losing medical-malpractice insurance policies.

During the summer of 1987, a nine-person delegation from the People's Republic of China spent two days at the company's Warren, New Jersey headquarters. The company's relations with China dated to before World War II, when Chubb owned and operated the Cathay Insurance Company. The delegation, consisting of government officials and representatives from the People's Insurance Company of China, studied Chubb's safety and loss control problems. Also in 1987, Chubb acquired Sovereign Corporation, a life insurance holding company. Profits were significantly lower that year due to higher catastrophe losses from the Chicago rainstorms, Edmonton tornadoes, and a hurricane in Bermuda.

## Key Dates:

**1882:** Thomas and Percy Chubb form Chubb & Son.

**1901:** Chubb's principal property and casualty affiliate reorganizes as Federal Insurance Company.

**1923:** Chubb opens its first branch in Chicago.

**1939:** Chubb founds Vigilant Insurance Company.

**1957:** The company acquires The Colonial Life Insurance Company of America.

**1959:** Chubb & Son reincorporates under the laws of New York.

**1967:** The company's management forms The Chubb Corporation to act as a holding company for Chubb & Son and its subsidiaries; Chubb acquires Pacific Indemnity Corporation.

**1970:** Chubb acquires Bellemead Development Corporation.

**1971:** Chubb acquires United Life & Accident Insurance Company and founds Chubb Custom Market.

**1978:** The Chubb Corporation forms Chubb Life Insurance Company of America.

**1983:** The Chubb Corporation relocates its head office in Warren, New Jersey.

**1984:** Chubb acquires Volunteer State Life Insurance Company.

**1987:** Chubb acquires Sovereign Corporation.

**1993:** Chubb adds offices in Birmingham, Reading, and Manchester.

**1998:** Chubb sells a substantial portion of its Bellemead Development portfolio and forms Chubb Re.

**1999:** Chubb purchases Executive Risk Inc.

### Specialties and International Expansion:
### Late 1980s through Mid-1990s

Through a New York firm called Good Weather International Incorporated, Chubb began advertising rain insurance in ten states in May 1988. Drought insurance was also offered to Midwestern farmers by the Chubb subsidiary, Federal Insurance Company. Chubb usually reserved the authority to approve each policy that its independent agents sold, but in this case Good Weather was given the authority to approve Chubb policies. Because rain insurance was a small part of Chubb's business—Chubb issued $5 million of coverage to approximately 200 farmers in 1987—the company set a total limit of $30 million of coverage.

Response was moderate until early June, when lack of rain threatened farmers with the most serious drought in over 50 years. On June 14 and June 15, 1988, Good Weather received over 6,600 applications seeking $275 million worth of coverage, and applications kept coming after the deadline. While farmers worried about the drought, Good Weather and Chubb worried about the flood of applications. The figures were not totaled until the end of June. In the confusion, agents had signed up at least $350 million of coverage for nearly 9,000 farmers. The drought continued, and, on July 15th, Chubb notified 7,616 farmers that they had been denied coverage. In a goodwill effort, Chubb offered to return double the original premiums to

farmers who had applied on June 14th or 15th. The effort was unsuccessful and by 1991, many lawsuits filed by those farmers remained unresolved. After this experience, Chubb decided to discontinue drought insurance.

In July 1988, Dean R. O'Hare, chairman and chief executive officer of The Chubb Corporation and Federal Insurance Company since May, was elected chairman and chief executive officer of Chubb & Son. In August 1988, Chubb agreed to let American National General Agencies Incorporated (ANGA) take over its entertainment insurance underwriting responsibilities on the East Coast. Headquartered in Los Angeles as a wholesale entertainment insurance broker, ANGA branched into New York to assume the underwriting function for production risks through Chubb Custom Market.

In 1989, Chubb took great measures to reestablish a positive corporate image. This time, its efforts were successful, and 1989 was a good year for the company overall. In April 1989, Chubb Life Insurance of America joined The Geese Theatre Company, a non-profit touring theater group working exclusively in prisons, in establishing a theater residency program in Concord, New Hampshire. Chubb generated more good press later that year when it won the Insurance Marketing Communications Association Special Award from members. The competition was mounted to recognize and award superior marketing communications work in the property and casualty industry.

Hurricane Hugo and the California earthquake had a significant impact on Chubb's 1989 domestic earnings, however. Although earnings still increased, the catastrophes took a substantial bite out of profits. International operations continued to contribute greatly to the company's financial success, and revenues from international operations that year approached $500 million, about 12.5 percent of the year's $4 billion total. Chubb worked to increase its international activities and set a goal of generating 25 percent of total revenue from international operations by the year 2000.

The softening of the property and casualty insurance market in the early 1990s affected Chubb less than some of its competitors. The company's focus on specialty products helped Chubb outperform the industry through those years. Chubb had showed great improvement in life and health insurance during 1989, and anticipated that earnings would continue to increase as group health operating conditions improved. At $4.2 billion, earnings for 1990 reached a new high, setting the company's fifth consecutive year of record earnings. The success was attributed to conservative underwriting, a large network of branch offices (71 with plans to open four more), and a solid balance sheet. With the failure of many large financial institutions shaking public confidence in the late 1980s, a clear ability to cover liabilities with liquid assets became essential to maintaining a reliable reputation; Chubb fulfilled this requirement well.

At the same time, a downturn in the economy and unfavorable regulatory conditions began to reveal potential vulnerabilities in Chubb's real estate and commercial insurance businesses. Commercial overbuilding in the 1980s glutted the market, and regulatory scrutiny following the Savings and Loan bank failures led banks to curtail real estate lending. Unable to counteract these changes, Chubb's real estate holdings and development ventures began to lose money. Chubb said in its 1990 annual report that it saw these market conditions as more than a cyclical downturn, and that it would begin to view real estate holdings as long-term investments. The company predicted that conditions in the real estate market would even worsen as companies economized on space as a result of consolidating and downsizing their operations. In fact, Chubb reported a steady decline in net income from real estate after 1989, and a loss of about $2 million a year in 1993 and 1994.

Simultaneously, potential changes in environmental and healthcare regulations initiated by the Clinton administration and state legislatures presented challenges for Chubb and the insurance industry in general. On the environmental side, uncertainties relating to toxic waste and asbestos claims made on policies written decades earlier posed an increasingly large threat to profitability. Chubb began to lobby actively for regulatory reform, hoping to narrow the widening judicial interpretations of such regulations as Superfund toxic waste clean-up rules. In 1994, Chubb settled its most costly asbestos exposure claim from an insurance policy issued in 1956 to Fibreboard Corporation by Pacific Indemnity Corporation, a Chubb subsidiary.

New legislation in New York and New Jersey significantly changed the way the company would handle health insurance in that region. The legislation created community-based rating and limited restrictions on pre-existing conditions. Whereas other insurers left that market, Chubb restructured its offerings, encouraging clients to move to managed health care policies, and remained effective in the region, which accounted for 80 percent of Chubb's group health business.

In the mid-1990s, Chubb increased its international expansion and accelerated the growth of its domestic network. The company's London branch, at the center of the world insurance market, had doubled in size since its formation in the early 1980s. In 1993, Chubb added offices in Birmingham, Reading, and Manchester to take advantage of profitable opportunities in more local business. When the company determined that London lacked the service-oriented insurance products required for that city's growing affluent population, it focused upon personal insurance—which represented 23 percent of Chubb's total business. In Germany, the new opportunities created by the formation of the European Community and the deregulation of the European insurance industry led Chubb to promote its commercial lines. As a commercial powerhouse, Germany provided an attractive new market for foreign insurers.

In 1994, premiums from international business passed 20 percent of the total, approaching the company's goal of 25 percent for the year 2000. Chubb opened offices in Beijing, Hamburg, Munich, London, and Glasgow. In the United States, Chubb opened a new office in Fresno, California. By 1995, the company, which had 20 domestic branches in 1965, had grown to 89 branches worldwide. The company estimated hiring 1,300 new underwriters a year for the next five years. Some analysts questioned if quality operations could be maintained at such a high growth rate in a soft market, but by 1999, the number of offices worldwide was 132.

## A Narrower Focus in the Late 1990s

Chubb's gains were impressive, particularly in light of the fact that the early to mid-1990s were hard years for property and casualty insurers. With too many companies chasing too little business, and premiums that had stagnated at 1987 levels, the industry was rocked in 1994 by a series of underwriting losses: the California earthquake, snowstorms in the Northeast, flooding in the south and west United States, and a series of environmental clean-up claims. Insurers paid out $15 billion in disasters in 1994 alone, leading the industry as a whole to institute a 4.9 percent premium hike in 1994 and a 6.6 hike in 1995.

Over the next several years, Chubb began to shed some of its businesses, following a trend in the insurance industry to concentrate on a single segment. Chubb chose to focus on its property and casualty lines. In 1996, it severed its 114-year relationship with Sun Alliance, the United Kingdom's largest insurer, as part of this refocusing. In 1998, it sold a substantial portion of its Bellemead Development portfolio to PW/MS Acquisition for $737 million, and its life insurance business to the Jefferson-Pilot Corporation for $875 million. It used proceeds from the sales to buy back about 30 percent of the company's outstanding shares during 1997 through 1999.

Chubb made news repeatedly in 1997 for having issued President Clinton a personal-liability umbrella policy in the early 1990s and for later assuming half of the legal costs of his defense in the suit brought against him by Paula Jones. Some argued that the president appeared to be receiving preferential treatment from Chubb and State Farm, who paid the other half of his legal costs, but both companies insisted that they were paying his defense costs as a matter of policy.

Chubb also was noted for its leadership in tackling issues unique to the nascent-online publishing industry. Beginning in 1997, it began to offer multimedia coverage—liability insurance for the multimedia business. Such coverage, as defined by Chubb, included the unauthorized use of ideas, an area not touched upon by normal liability insurance—for example, the stealing of someone's videogame scenario.

The company continued to grow through new ventures and acquisition throughout the late 1990s. In 1998, in a move to enter the global reinsurance market, it formed Chubb Re, Inc. and became a low-cost reinsurance provider. In December, it purchased a 28 percent stake in Hiscox, the integrated Lloyd's of London insurer. Chubb also expanded its umbrella liability policy, offering liability insurance for food processors, suppliers, and franchisers. In 1999, it purchased Executive Risk Inc., the third largest insurer of executives and directors in a $750 million stock deal.

Unfortunately for Chubb, the commercial and property insurance markets continued to struggle through hard times. The industry's overcapacity created a bad pricing environment for insurers and slowed revenue growth, and the strength of the company's personal and specialty lines were not sufficient to counterbalance its losses in standard commercial insurance in 1998 and 1999. Announced earnings for 1998 were short of expectations, despite rate increases in commercial premiums, and stock prices tumbled. To make matters worse, catastrophic losses were heavy in both 1998 and 1999 as a result of Hurricane Floyd, which caused the largest number of claims from a single event in the company's history.

Chubb set itself the task of turning its standard commercial lines around in the year 2000, by continuing its "pricing and pruning" strategy of premium increases, while continuing to grow in its personal and specialty businesses. Analysts as a group, however, were positive that the company, with its solid history and experience, would pull through its hard times. In January 2000, *Fortune* magazine named the company to its list of "The 100 Best Companies to Work for in America." In August 2000, Chubb received an operating license to open a branch in Shanghai, which the company estimated would bring in about $200 million in business each year. Despite mid-year rumors that the company was ripe for a takeover, the company insisted it was not for sale.

### *Principal Subsidiaries*

Federal Insurance Co.; Vigilant Insurance Co.; Great Northern Insurance Co.; Pacific Indemnity Co.; Northwestern Pacific Indemnity Co.; Texas Pacific Indemnity Co.; Executive Risk Indemnity Inc.; Quadrant Indemnity Co.; Chubb Custom Insurance Co.; Chubb Insurance Co. of New Jersey; Chubb National Insurance Co.; Chubb Atlantic Indemnity, Ltd.; Chubb Insurance Co. of Australia, Ltd.; Chubb Insurance Co. of Canada; Chubb Insurance Co. of Europe; Chubb Argentine de Seguros, S.A.; Chubb do Brasil Companhis de Seguros (Brazil); Chubb de Colombia Compañia de Seguros S.A.; Chubb de Chile Compañia de Seguros Generales S.A.; Chubb de Mexico, Compania de Seguros, S.A. de C.V.; Chubb de Venezuela Compania de Seguros C.A.; PT Asuransi Chubb Indonesia; Chubb Custom Market, Inc.; Chubb Multinational Managers, Inc.; Foundation Reinsurance (PCC) Ltd.; Chubb Re, Inc.; Personal Lines Insurance Brokerage, Inc.; Bellemead Development Corp.; Chubb Capital Corp.; Chubb Asset Managers, Inc.; Chubb Computer Services, Inc.; The Chubb Institute, Inc.

### *Principal Competitors*

Aetna Life and Casualty Co.; State Farm Insurance Companies; The St. Paul Companies; American International Group, Inc.

### *Further Reading*

"Chubb Vanguard Swoops in Ahead of WTO Accession," *South China Morning Post,* October 2, 2000, p. 3.

"Chubb Corporation: It's an Ill, Dry Wind," *Economist,* September 3, 1988, p. 76.

Fefer, Mark D., "Chubb: How to Win in a Land of Losers," *Fortune,* August 23, 1993, p. 80.

Gallagher, Kathleen, "Industry Problems Make Insurer's Stock Undervalued," *Milwaukee Journal Sentinel,* February 14, 1999, Business p. 4.

Hutton, Cynthia, "How Chubb Got Soaked on Drought Insurance," *Fortune,* September 12, 1988, p. 10.

"Insuring Stage Productions Can Be a Titanic Expense," *Tampa Tribune,* April 16, 1997, p. 7.

"Is the President Getting Special Insurance Treatment for the Paula Jones Lawsuit?," *Insight on the News,* July 21, 1997, p. 24.

Kirk, Don, "Germany Imports New Style Market," *Business Insurance,* November 7, 1994, p. 35.

Liscio, John, "Chubb Corp.," *Barron's,* December 28, 1987, pp. 33–34.

Mack, Gracian, "At the Top of His Game," *Black Enterprise,* March 1995, pp. 84–87.

Moreau, Dan, "Chubb Thinks Small, But All Its Little Pieces Add Up," *Kiplinger's,* May 1995, pp. 38–40.

—Leslie C. Halpern
—updated by Katherine Smethurst and Carrie Rothburd

# Cleco Corporation

2030 Donahue Ferry Road
Pineville, Louisiana 71360-5226
U.S.A.
Telephone: (318) 484-7400
Toll Free: (800) 622-6537
Fax: (318) 484-7465
Web site: http://www.cleco.com

Public Company
Incorporated: 1934
Employees: 1,416
Sales: $754 million (2000)
Stock Exchanges: New York
Ticker Symbol: CNL
NAIC: 221112 Fossil Fuel Electric Power Generation;
221122 Electric Power Distribution; 48621 Pipeline
Transportation of Natural Gas

Cleco Corporation, which employs over 1,400 people, is a major provider of electricity and related services to customers in Louisiana. Structured as a holding company, it operates in three core businesses: the Cleco Utility Group, Cleco Midstream Resources LLC, and Utility Construction & Technology Solutions LLC (known as Utilitech Solutions). The Cleco Utility Group provides electrical services for about 246,000 residents and businesses. Cleco Midstream Resources, a regional energy services consortium, develops and operates power-generating plants and invests in and helps maintain natural gas pipelines, providing energy for other companies and agencies with their own electric utility systems. UtiliTech Solutions offers line construction and engineering services for various third-party distributors of electricity, including both private and publicly owned utility companies. With a partial ownership of four major electrical plants, Cleco can generate over 1,300 megawatts of power for consumption by its central Louisiana customers.

## 1914–25: An Independent Ice and Electrical Plant in Bunkie

Cleco's origin can be traced back to 1914, when, in Bunkie, Louisiana, a small group of businessmen built an ice plant using a 50-kilowatt generator both to light the facility and manufacture the ice. At the time, ice was an essential good because it was used in most households as the sole means of preserving perishable foods. It was a greater necessity than either indoor plumbing or electricity, conveniences still decades away from reaching much of rural America. Until local ice manufacturing became feasible, it had to be harvested from frozen lakes in the North, stored in insulated buildings, and shipped to the South by boat, a costly method that encouraged the proliferation of local, independent ice plants. Because the ice-making process required the use of gasoline or diesel generators and electric motors, in many areas of the country electric companies had their beginning in the ice business. Plants began using their excess power to provide electricity for nearby homes and businesses, and over time the demand for electricity began outstripping the demand for ice.

## 1926–40: Surviving the Depression

The plant in Bunkie remained private and independent for over a decade, providing ice and electrical power to customers only in that town. However, in 1926 businessman Wiley Corl started up the Louisiana Ice & Utilities Company and began buying small, south-central Louisiana ice and electric utility companies, including the Bunkie plant. The company also ran dairy operations and marketed its products under the Blu-Ribon name. Corl soon faced tough going because of the economic devastation ushered in by the stock market crash of 1929, and in that year he sold the company to Floyd Woodcock, a Philadelphia businessman. In 1933, unable to pay off its debts, Louisiana Ice & Utilities was forced into bankruptcy. Had it not been for Woodcock's business acumen, the insolvent company might have become extinct, but in 1934 he reorganized it as the Louisiana Ice & Electric Company and steered it through the difficult Depression years. Woodcock brought several years of experience to the task, having been involved in operating public utilities since the early 1920s. He also seemed to have an uncanny sense of how to build a successful utility system despite the hard times, and he played an important part in helping the industry grow and prosper. Under his tutelage, by 1935 Louisiana Ice & Electric was able to begin paying dividends on its capital stock.

At Bunkie, in 1938, the company completed building and placed in operation the Rea Station, its first power plant. Its main units were 1,000-kilowatt generators powered by natural gas, the fuel of choice because of large gas reserves available in the area. At the time, it was the largest gas-fueled electric producing plant in the country. In was also in 1938 that Frank Hugh Coughlin joined Louisiana Ice & Electric as vice president and general manager. Like Woodcock, he brought years of experience to the job, including a decade of service with the Southwest Utilities Corporation of Texas.

### 1941–50: Wartime and Postwar Demand Spurs Growth

Coughlin helped Woodcock guide the company through the challenging years of World War II, when, because of the sudden burgeoning of military camps in the area, the demand for electricity rapidly increased. Within 50 miles of Alexandria, eleven training camps were home to about a half million soldiers and airmen. These installations needed huge amounts of power, not all of which could be provided by Louisiana Ice & Electric. Even though by 1941 additional generators increased the capacity of the Rea Station to 5,700 kilowatts, which was supplemented by another 900 kilowatts produced by a small Pineville plant, the company had to tap into the reserves of other systems in order to meet the military's needs and those of the communities that grew as a result of the influx of workers. In 1945, reflecting the fact that Louisiana Ice & Electric had

evolved into the major provider of electrical power in its area, the company changed its name to Central Louisiana Electric Company, Inc.

In 1947, when Woodcock vacated the presidency of Cleco to become chairman of the board, Coughlin succeeded him in that office. One of the main challenges facing Coughlin was to meet the growing demand for rural electrification, something that had been promoted under Franklin D. Roosevelt's Rural Electrification Administration (REA) in the 1930s. Although the war slowed the progress of rural electrification somewhat, by 1945 Cleco was serving 5,432 rural customers. In 1948, to help the expansion, the company formed its first subsidiary, Louisiana Rural Electric Company. Its function was to use REA funds to provide electrical lines and service for sparsely populated, rural areas. Under its aegis, Cleco's rural customer base grew to 35,000 by 1960. It was also in 1948 that the company put the first two 7,500-kilowatt electrical generators on line at its new Coughlin Power Station, the first plant in the nation to place its turbine generators outside, exposed to the elements. Construction would continue at the site until 1966, when the older units went offline, replaced by two new units that could generate up to 334,000 kilowatts of electrical power.

### 1951–65: Expansion and Consolidation

In 1951, in a major expansion, Cleco merged with Gulf Public Service Company, Inc. (GPS), a company that had been formed and incorporated in 1944 and, through a 1946 merger with Louisiana Public Utilities, had grown much larger than Cleco. The GPS-Cleco merger, joining the properties and management of both companies, more than doubled the size of Cleco and increased its operating revenues by 70 percent. The move required the interconnection of their power lines and ambitious new construction. Steps taken included increasing the capacity of the Coughlin Station and the building of a new plant, the Teche Station, which first went on line in 1953. Moreover, because GPS had also produced and distributed natural gas and water, Cleco entered new markets. The company formed two subsidiaries to handle the demand for gas—South Louisiana Production Company, Inc., started up in 1955 and Louisiana Intrastate Gas Corporation, followed the next year. As its gas customer base expanded, eventually producing almost 30 percent of Cleco's annual sales, the company sold off its ice, dairy, and other nonutility businesses.

Besides tremendous growth, the 1950s saw Cleco's involvement in important initiatives. For example, it participated in studies of atomic energy as a potential source of electrical power and helped begin a program of selling and interchanging reserve energy with the Tennessee Valley Authority. In the next decade, the company undertook a major marketing campaign that stressed the tremendous value and convenience of electricity. In addition to selling power that was rapidly dropping in cost, Cleco advertised and sold home appliances. Although it also marketed natural gas, the company's stress was on electricity, and one of its major themes was total electric living as evidenced in Gold Medallion Homes, which were entirely powered by electricity. The campaign brought a steady increase in sales, even as electric rates continued to decline. It was a relatively tranquil period for Cleco, despite some violent re-

## Key Dates:

**1914:** Louisiana Ice & Utilities is created in Bunkie, Louisiana.

**1926:** Wiley Corl helps form Louisiana Ice & Utilities Company.

**1929:** Floyd Woodcock buys the utility company.

**1933:** Depression forces company into bankruptcy.

**1934:** Woodcock reorganizes the system as Louisiana Ice & Electric Company.

**1938:** The company's first power plant, the Rea Station, commences operations in Bunkie.

**1945:** Louisiana Ice & Electric is renamed Central Louisiana Electric Company, Inc.

**1946:** Hugh Coughlin succeeds Woodcock as president.

**1951:** Cleco merges with Gulf Public Service Company, Inc.

**1959:** Company sells last nonutility property.

**1966:** W. Donner Rodemacher becomes Cleco's president.

**1968:** Company goes public with common stock traded on the NYSE.

**1978:** ENERGY is organized as parent company of Cleco.

**1981:** Cleco separates from ENERGY.

**1985:** William F. Terbot is elected Cleco president and CEO.

**1986:** Dolet Hills Unit 1 goes into commercial operation and new company headquarters in Pineville centralizes Cleco's management.

**1998:** Company changes name from Central Louisiana Electric Company to Cleco Corporation.

**1999:** Cleco reorganizes as holding company.

**2000:** Cleco creates Cleco ConnexUs, an Internet Service Provider.

minders that nature could and would periodically disrupt the calm. In 1964, Hurricane Hilda roared into Louisiana, just as Hurricane Audrey had done in 1957, causing both loss of life and power outages that in some places lasted several days. However, the company's emergency response time and equipment had improved by the 1960s and Hilda proved far less disruptive than Audrey.

### 1966–84: Going Public and Reorganizing

In 1966 Coughlin advanced to the chairmanship of Cleco's board, and W. Donner Rodemacher assumed the company's presidency. Rodemacher had come to Cleco through its merger with Gulf Public Service. As treasurer and then president, he helped prepare Cleco for going public, which it did in 1968. Through his 12-year tenure as president, Rodemacher also oversaw the company's continued expansion, especially its growth in the industrial power sector and the development of its relatively small subsidiaries into major companies. There were problems, however, especially during the 1970s when the industry was adversely impacted by double-digit interest rates and the Arab Oil Embargo, which quickly drove Cleco's fuel costs up, as much as 73 percent in a single year. The company had no choice but to increase its rates. Although not as cheap as it had been, electricity was still a good bargain, even if, as the com-

pany's new philosophy stressed, it needed to be conserved and used as effectively as possible. Despite the increased cost, the demand for electricity continued to grow, and Cleco continued to grow with it. In 1975, it put Rodemacher Unit 1 on line near Boyce, Louisiana. The 455,000-kilowatt unit, costing $75 million, became the largest gas-fired unit in Cleco's system and was designed to meet customer demands while the company sought alternative fuel solutions to the problem of the increasing cost of oil and gas.

During the 1970s Cleco cycled through some reorganizing moves that were the result of rapid growth of its subsidiaries involved in the oil and natural gas businesses. In 1978, in order to accommodate the operations of both its utility and nonutility businesses, the company formed Central Louisiana Energy Corporation (ENERGY), a holding company for both Cleco and its various subsidiaries. Three years later, Cleco separated from ENERGY to become an independent electric utility, headed by James M. Henderson, who had been elected Cleco's president in 1978. He oversaw the start-up of important new programs designed to help the utility increase its efficiency, including some streamlining of billing and service procedures. While Henderson held the office, Cleco put on line its first major alternative-fuel generator, Rodemacher Power Station Unit 2. Jointly owned by Cleco and two other companies, this 523,000-kilowatt unit, which began operating in 1982, was fueled by coal mined in Gillette, Wyoming, and shipped to Louisiana by rail. Coal proved more economical to use than natural gas, and during the first three years of the unit's operation, it saved Cleco's customers over $55 million.

### 1985–2000: Fuel Diversification, Acquisitions, and Restructuring

Cleco continued its fuel diversification program through the petroleum industry's recession that hit the Gulf states very hard in the mid-1980s. Although the price of both natural gas and oil plummeted, the risk of future market volatility was great enough to encourage greater reliance on coal, including lignite, a low-grade type of coal found in northwest Louisiana. That was the fuel chosen for the company's jointly owned Dolet Hills Power Station, Units 1 and 2. Unit 1, a 640,000-kilowatt generator, went on line in 1986, the year after Henderson retired and Cleco's presidency passed to William F. Terbot. By then Cleco was servicing over 192,000 customers in 25 parishes in Louisiana. It had also reached a power generating capacity of 1,361 million kilowatts and had centralized its operations at new headquarters in Pineville, Louisiana.

Over the next 14 years Cleco maintained steady growth, expanding its customer base to about 246,000 by the end of the century. During the 1990s, its revenue increased from $334 million in 1990 to $768.2 million in 1999. Significantly, from 1998 to 1999, Cleco's revenue grew by $253 million, an increase of 48 percent. Acquisitions, additional power production, and restructuring spurred growth through the decade.

In 1992, the presidency of Cleco passed to Gregory L. Nesbitt, who had joined the company in 1980. During his tutelage, Cleco began reorganizing, streamlining its operations, and making preparations for anticipated deregulation of electric utilities by federal and state agencies. The streamlining began in 1993, with plans to improve operations and offer better, lower cost services to customers. In 1995, Cleco began operating a customer call center 24 hours a day, seven days a week and consolidated 25 customer service offices into ten regional offices. At the same time, the company was negotiating the purchase of Teche Electric Cooperative, Inc., a move that was finalized in 1997, significantly increasing Cleco's customer base.

In 1998, the company officially changed its name from Central Louisiana Electric Company to Cleco Corporation and began implementing its plans to reorganize as a holding company, a move completed in 1999, the year in which David Eppler succeeded Nesbitt as Cleco's president and CEO. The restructuring allowed Cleco to separate its regulated and nonregulated operations into distinct subsidiaries. Under its corporate umbrella, Cleco began managing its principal subsidiaries: Cleco Utility Group, Inc., a regulated utility company; Cleco Midstream Resources LLC, Cleco's wholesale power and natural gas production and sales business; UtiliTech Solutions, which provided engineering and line construction services; and Cleco Support Group LLC, which provided various services for the other subsidiaries.

The reorganization achieved a necessary flexibility, including the ability to create new or spin-off subsidiaries as technological advances made them feasible. Such is the case with Cleco ConnexUs, an Internet service provider, which Cleco established in 2000. Cleco also planned greater expansion through continued partnering with other companies, jointly undertaking additional, power plant building ventures. For example, in March of 2000, Cleco Midstream Resources entered into a partnership with Calpine, an independent power company. Under the agreement, the partners would build and operate a 1,000-megawatt, natural gas-fired power plant scheduled to commence commercial operation near Eunice, Louisiana, in June 2002. In the summer of 2000, Cleco Midstream also entered a 50 percent partnership agreement with Southern Energy Inc., with which it plans to build a 700-megawatt power plant at Perryville, in northeast Louisiana. Such moves were designed to meet the ever increasing energy demands that Cleco faced at the close of the century and would continue to face thereafter.

### *Principal Subsidiaries*

Utility Construction & Technology Solutions LLC (Utilitech); Cleco Utility Group Inc.; Cleco Midstream Resources LLC; ClecoConnexUs.

### *Principal Competitors*

American Electric Power Company, Inc.; Entergy Corporation; Southern Company.

### *Further Reading*

"Calpine, Cleco Enter Project," *Oil Daily*, March 7, 2000.

Campanella, Frank W., "Spelling Relief: Rate Boost Helps Central Louisiana to a Smart Rebound in Earnings," *Barron's*, August 3, 1987, p. 39.

"Cleco Corporation Teams with Southern Energy Inc: to Develop Power Plant in Northeast Louisiana," *PR Newswire*, July 31, 2000.

Core, Gael, "Open Markets? Open a Warehouse," *Computerworld*, May 19, 1997, p. 63.

Donaldson, Gary Alan, *A History of Louisiana's Rural Electric Cooperatives, 1937–1983*, Ann Arbor, Mich.: University Microfilms International, 1984.

Springer, Neil, "Mfr. Pressure Shapes Louisiana Rate Hike Plan," *Energy User News*, June 10, 1985, p. 9.

Troy, Alan A., *Louisiana Electric Utilities*, Baton Rouge, La.: Louisiana Department of Natural Resources, 1994.

—John W. Fiero

# Cleveland Indians Baseball Company, Inc.

Jacobs Field
2401 Ontario Street
Cleveland, Ohio 44115
U.S.A.
Telephone: (216) 420-4200
Fax: (216) 420-4430
Web site: http://www.indians.com

*Private company*
*Employees:* 1,897 (1998)
*Sales:* $151.7 million (1998)
*NAIC:* 711211 Sports Teams and Clubs

An original member of the American League, the Cleveland Indians Baseball Company, Inc. is one of baseball's most enduring teams. Since moving into a new stadium, Jacobs Field, in 1994, the Indians have become one the most successful teams in baseball, and boast a record for consecutive regular-season sellouts. By the beginning of the new century the value of the franchise is second only to the New York Yankees in Major League Baseball.

## Origins

Cleveland has had a big league baseball team since 1871. The Forest Citys played in the National Association from 1871 to 1875, when the National League was formed. Cleveland began play in the National League in 1879, becoming known as the Spiders in 1889. Cleveland became home to what many consider the worst ball club in the history of the game. The 1899 Spiders had the misfortune of being owned by Frank DeHaas Robison, who, after purchasing the St. Louis Browns, out of spite transferred the best Spiders to his new team. Cleveland won only 20 games, losing 134. Attendance was so sparse that after July most Spider games were played on the road. The team disbanded at the end of the season.

## A New Century, A New League

The Western League, a minor circuit eager to challenge the Nationals, changed its name to the American League in 1900,

and looked to expand to larger cities for its first season in 1901. Cleveland was a perfect fit, and a franchise was sold to a group of local investors. A coal baron named Charley Somers became the official owner of the new team. Known briefly as the Blues, then the Bronchos, the team then became known as the Naps, named after their star player Napolean Lajoie. When Somers' finances soured, Lajoie was traded away after the 1914 season, and a new name for the team was needed.

According to popular legend the Cleveland franchise became known as the Indians in honor of a Native American named Louis Sockalexis who had played briefly for the old Spiders in the 1890s. This explanation, however, is more likely to be a justification after the fact than reality. The Cleveland newspapers fielded fan suggestions that included Foresters, Some Runners, Tornadoes, Commodores, Rangers, Sixers, Speeders, and Harmonics, but Indians was not among the published nicknames. The talk of baseball that year was the miracle Boston Braves. When the sportswriters settled on the Cleveland Indians as the team's new name, it was more likely an allusion to the Boston ball club's use of the nickname Braves than to Sockalexis who played only 94 games in the city. Newspapers were reporting the team's new "temporary" name well before the first mention of a connection to Sockalexis. Then it was recalled that the team had been referred to briefly as the Indians when Sockalexis had made an initial splash with the team. Unfortunately, Sockalexis was more troubled than talented, appearing only in twenty-one and seven games his last two seasons in baseball. After years of hard drinking, he died of a heart attack at the age of 41. Despite Sockalexis's personal troubles, the belief that the Indians were named in tribute to him is deeply held by the ball club and many of its fans. What is not in doubt is that the temporary nickname proved enduring.

In 1916 when Somers was in danger of losing the Indians to the bank, American League President Ban Johnson and a few of Somers' friends met at a Chicago bar to discuss the situation. For no apparent reason, Johnson decided that Sunny Jim Dunn should become the next owner, despite the fact that Dunn could only come up with $15,000. His partner in an Iowa construction business, Paddy McCarthy, thought he could add another $15,000. The bartender offered to kick in $10,000, and he, too, joined the growing consortium. Numerous other investors were solicited until Dunn had $500,000 to purchase the Cleveland team and bail out Somers.

### Team Successes and Failures

The Cleveland Indians would know both tragedy and triumph in 1920. On August 17, star shortstop Ray Chapman was hit in the left temple by a pitch, and died twelve hours later without regaining consciousness. He is the only major league baseball player to die from an accident on the field. The team rebounded, however, and won the American League pennant, edging out the Chicago White Sox, who were forced to finish the 1920 season without eight of their best players following a gambling scandal that tainted the 1919 World Series. The Indians then defeated the Brooklyn Dodgers in the World Series to win the team's first championship.

With the emergence of the New York Yankees in the 1920s, the Indians rarely challenged first place for the next generation. Businessman and president of the Cleveland Chamber of Commerce, Alva Bradley became the front man for a group of investors that bought the team in 1928. He is reported to have said, ''I'm the perfect man to own the Indians—I know nothing about baseball!'' He was certainly true to his word. He alienated fans by banning radio broadcasts in 1933. He changed managers so often that Cleveland became known as ''the Graveyard of Managers.'' Only once under Bradley's ownership, in 1940, did the Indians seriously threaten to win the American League. The team lost the championship to Detroit by one game.

Even the construction of a new ballpark didn't help the franchise. After playing its entire history in League Park, which had been built for the Spiders in 1891, the Indians moved into cavernous Cleveland Stadium on July 31, 1932. With 76,000 seats it was easily the largest baseball facility in the country. After drawing 80,000 for its opening game, the Indians saw attendance drop dramatically. Playing the entire 1933 season in the Stadium, the Indians averaged less than 6,000 fans a game. The following year, to save money, the team returned to League Park for all but Sunday games and holidays.

Following the 1941 season, the Indians were once again in need of a new manager. The youngest member of the team, 24-year-old shortstop Lou Boudreau, wrote to Bradley to express his interest in the job. With nothing to lose, Bradley invited the player to meet the board of directors. Boudreau, a University of Illinois Physical Education graduate with future plans for coaching, spoke to Bradley and his backers. Only one, George Martin, chairman of the board of Sherwin-Williams paints, voted for Boudreau. He liked the young man's confidence and good looks, and argued that the move would spark debate and possibly ticket sales. The board voted again, but this time with a

unanimous result. Boudreau was hired as the new player-manager of the Cleveland Indians, much to the surprise of everyone in baseball, not the least of whom were his teammates.

The ''Boy Manager'' took over the team in 1942 and wasted no time in showing that he had a lot to learn. International events, however, worked in his favor. America was plunged into World War II, and baseball teams had to scramble to find able-bodied players. Boudreau was exempt from the draft because of arthritic ankles. He was one of the stars of the American League and popular with fans, so there was no thought to replace him as manager, despite less than stellar results. Only twice did the Indians post winning records under Boudreau from 1942 to 1946.

### Post-World War II Becomes
### a Golden Era for Indians

Another change in ownership after the war precipitated a golden era for the Cleveland Indians. On June 21, 1946 the club was sold for $1.6 million to Bill Veeck, Jr., as part of a ten-member syndicate. The son of a baseball executive, Veeck was a self-described hustler eager to run a baseball team in his own way, after years of working for the conservative ownership of the Chicago Cubs. He circulated with the fans to learn what they wanted; he had the public address system fixed; he promised to put Indians' games on the radio, even if he had to give away the rights; he had the women's rest rooms cleaned every two innings; he even allowed fans to keep baseballs that were hit into the stands, an act of generosity foreign to the previous ownership. Veeck ran his team in a manner that was not only ahead of its time, but peculiar to his personality. He might present an orchestra to entertain the fans before the game, or fireworks and circus acts after the game. He gave away nylons or orchids on Ladies Day. He brought in flagpole sitters. He gave away livestock. He gave away used cars. He answered his own phone and took any call that came through to his office. He stood at the turnstiles and shook countless hands. And the fans loved him. The Indians topped one million in attendance for the first time in 1946. The following season, now playing exclusively at the Stadium, they drew more than 1.5 million, second in the American League, despite finishing a distant fourth in the standings.

Veeck would do anything to improve his team or draw a crowd, even if it was controversial. Only 11 weeks after African-American baseball player Jackie Robinson broke baseball's color barrier with the National League Dodgers, Veeck signed 23-year-old Larry Dolby. Robinson, who was 28, had been prepared for Brooklyn by playing a year with the Dodgers' minor league team in Montreal, as well as going through spring training in 1947; but two days after signing, Dolby was playing for the Indians. Although the move was lauded in most quarters, signing Dolby was hardly without controversy. Teammates were distant, a situation not helped when Dolby was unable to eat or room with the team on the road. Opposing players and fans were not above hurling racial epithets. Even umpires were hostile. The best that could be said for Dolby's first year with the Indians, in which he batted only 32 times, was that he endured it.

Veeck had no doubts about keeping Dolby, who he felt certain would become a star player. Who he didn't care for was his young player-manager. But when word leaked to the press

---

### Key Dates:

**1901:** Cleveland begins play in the American League.
**1915:** Team becomes known as the Indians.
**1920:** Indians win first World Series.
**1946:** Franchise sold to Bill Veeck, Jr.
**1948:** Indians win second World Series.
**1986:** Indians sold to Richard Jacobs.
**1994:** Jacobs Field opens for play.
**2000:** Indians sold to Lawrence J. Dolan.

---

that Veeck was trying to trade Boudreau to the St. Louis Browns, he was smart enough to embrace the ensuing controversy. Even though the deal had fallen through, he milked it for every drop of publicity before announcing at a press conference, ''Since the people are against trading Lou Boudreau, then I shout fervently that he will not be traded.''

In 1948 Boudreau was motivated to produce his best season. He was named the Most Valuable Player in the American League as he led the Indians to their first World Series title in 28 years. It was a magical year for the team, as it drew more than 2.6 million fans, a Cleveland record that would not be broken until 1995. Although the Indians would remain one of the top teams in the American League for the next several seasons, 1948 would prove to be the pinnacle of achievement for the Cleveland Indians in the twentieth century.

After the 1949 season Veeck was sued for divorce by his wife and was forced to sell the team to pay for the settlement. Over the next 35 years the Indians would undergo numerous changes in ownership. The team enjoyed a stellar regular season in 1954, winning an American League record 111 games, only to lose to the Giants in the World Series. The Indians would field several competitive teams after that, but would be relegated for long stretches to the bottom half of the American League standings. Attendance in the decaying Stadium never approached the levels that Cleveland had reached under Veeck's leadership. Financially strapped, the Indians were poorly positioned to operate in the costly new era of free agent players that began in the 1970s. Over the years, rumors circulated that the team would be relocated to Seattle, Atlanta, New Orleans, and other cities. During these years, the Indians could boast of one achievement, at least: in 1974 it became the first major league team to hire an African-American manager, Frank Robinson.

### A New Beginning in 1986

In 1986 the Indians were sold to real estate developer Richard Jacobs for $35 million. Although improvement on the field was not realized immediately, the new management team invested heavily in player development and scouting, as well as marketing. The Indians endured setbacks, such as losing a club

record 105 games in 1991; but the most devastating moment since the death of Ray Chapman occurred during spring training in 1993 when a boating accident took the lives of pitchers Tim Crews and Steve Olin, and severely injured Bob Ojeda. The final year in Cleveland Stadium was played with a pall cast over it, although the team played well in the second half of the season.

The Indians opened Jacobs Field, a state-of-the-art facility that ushered in a new era of excellence, in 1994. The team was in contention when a players' strike ended the 1994 season, and in 1995 the Indians continued its stellar play, finishing the year with baseball's best mark. The team advanced to its first World Series since 1954, but lost to the Atlanta Braves. As the Indians began to string together five consecutive Division championships, and another World Series appearance, it set attendance records. The 1948 mark was finally broken in 1995 when 2.8 million fans attended Indians' games. The following year the team would break three million and begin a consecutive regular-season sellout streak that would stretch into the next century.

In 1998 the Indians became the first independent publicly traded Major League Baseball team when an IPO raised $60 million. The stock did not, however, perform well. It opened at $15 and soon dropped below $10. As successful as the Indians were, the club still reported a net loss in 1998 of $2.5 million. After Jacobs announced in May 1999 that he intended to sell the team, the stock rose to a level above $20.

In November 1999 the club announced that the team had been sold for $323 million to Ohio lawyer Lawrence J. Dolan. It was the largest amount ever paid for a baseball team, eclipsing the $311 million paid for the Los Angeles Dodgers. According to the *Wall Street Journal* the price would have been higher if the Indians played in a larger television market. Broadcast revenues for 1998 were only $19 million, compared to the Yankees' $50 million. The sale was approved in January 2000 by Major League Baseball. Shareholders of the Indians voted their approval of the deal the following month. On February 15, 2000, Dolan and family trusts assumed ownership of the team, delisted it from the NASDAQ, and took the company private once again.

### Principal Competitors

Cincinnati Reds; Pittsburgh Pirates; Detroit Tigers.

### Further Reading

Pietruska et al., *Baseball: The Biographical Encyclopedia,* Kingston, N.Y.: Total Sports, 2000.
Pluto, Terry, *Our Tribe,* New York: Simon & Schuster, 1999.
Thorn et al., *Total Baseball,* Kingston, N.Y.: Total Sports, 1999.
Walker, Sam, ''Attorney Set to Buy Cleveland Indians in $320 Million Deal,'' *Wall Street Journal,* November 5, 1999, p. B2.

—Ed Dinger

# Columbus McKinnon Corporation

**140 Audubon Parkway**
**Amherst, New York 14228-1197**
**U.S.A.**
**Telephone: (716) 689-5400**
**Fax: (716) 680-5598**
**Web site: http://www.cmworks.com**

*Public Company*
*Incorporated:* 1929
*Employees:* 4,350
*Sales:* $736.3 (2000)
*Stock Exchanges:* NASDAQ
*Ticker Symbol:* CMCO
*NAIC:* 333120 Construction Machinery Manufacturing;
    333923 Overhead Traveling Crane, Hoist, and
    Monorail System Manufacturing

With a history that spans more than a hundred years, Columbus McKinnon Corporation has made its reputation on the manufacture of chains and hoists. Since going public in 1996 the Amherst, New York-based company has attempted to expand its business through an aggressive program of acquisitions to include the full range of material handling products and services. A stagnant stock price and a string of poor financial results, however, has led to discontent among some shareholders, forcing management to consider selling all or part of the company. Columbus McKinnon employs 4,350 at 76 locations in 14 countries.

### 1875 Origins

When Columbus McKinnon was incorporated in 1929, two different yet complimentary lines of business were brought together: chains and hoists. The hoist component of Columbus McKinnon dates back to the creation of Chicago's Moore Manufacturing Company in 1875. Moore focused much of its attention on the railroad industry, in particular sliding doors and door hangers for freight cars, but by 1889 the company, now known as Moore Manufacturing and Foundry Company and headquar-

tered in Milwaukee, turned increasingly to hoists, trolleys, and cranes. In 1899 S.H. Chisholm became president of the company, which now became known as the Chisholm and Moore Manufacturing Company. Over the next 30 years Chisholm Moore would develop a line of high speed hoists and hand chain hoists. During the 1920s the company began to offer electric wire rope hoists and electric cranes. In 1928 Chisholm Moore was acquired by the Columbus McKinnon Chain Company.

The making of chain was a craft and until the mid-19th century was mostly produced in small shops, predominantly in England. Created around the turn of the 20th century, the Columbus Chain Company, located in Columbus, Ohio, was one of the earliest American suppliers of fire welded chain. The company had been founded by employees of the Hayden Iron Company, which since 1825 had been producing harness hardware but also manufactured coil chain.

The McKinnon half of Columbus McKinnon derives from Canadian-born Lachlan Ebenezer McKinnon. He went from hardware clerk to store owner when in 1878 he became a partner in an Ontario business called McKinnon and Mitchell Hardware. The business focused on saddle and wagon hardware. A four-man shop in the back of the store produced wagon gears and a patented adjustable dash. In 1887 McKinnon created a Buffalo subsidiary, the McKinnon Dash Company. He branched out into the manufacture of any number of products that made use of metal, including suspender buckles, as well as bicycles and chains. It was his nephew, Archie McKinnon, who was primarily responsible for McKinnon Dash's entry into the chain making business. He applied the technique of electric welding to chain in 1905. At least with the smaller sizes of chain, electric welding would replace fire welding. In 1909 the McKinnon Chain Company was formed, using the electric welding process to produce coil, ladder and ''sugar'' chain, donkey and horse trace chain, lorry and plough trace chain, as well as tire chain for cars and trucks.

In 1917 McKinnon Chain merged with the Columbus Chain Company. In Canada it was known as McKinnon Columbus, and in America it was known as Columbus McKinnon. Either way it was a good fit for both companies. McKinnon brought superior technology, and Columbus brought a better grasp of

## Company Perspectives:

*We will focus on products of the absolutely highest quality so that they will produce economically measurable benefits and superior value to our customers. We will continue to seek new products and product lines both by development and acquisition. We will edge our way into new markets as against revolutionary diversification. We will stay close to our customers and serve them as we would like to be served by doing exactly what we said we would do. We will continually strive to provide a climate that allows each of us to perform to the maximum of our abilities as individuals, and makes us, collectively, a good citizen of our communities. Because we believe profits flow from doing all things well, we will continually try to do everything we do well.*

the American market. The parent company of McKinnon Chain changed its name to McKinnon Industries, and shifted its focus from horses to automotive products. By 1922 McKinnon decided to sell its share of the chain business to the Columbus interests. Two years later L.E. McKinnon died, and in 1929 McKinnon Industries would be purchased by General Motors of Canada.

Shortly after McKinnon Industries sold its chain interests, the business of Columbus McKinnon began to suffer. Its fortunes were revived in 1925 when one of the board members, Julius Stone, decided to buy the company. Stone was a self-educated son of German immigrants who had worked as a telegraph operator, coal miner, brakeman, and fireman before he became a manufacturer of motorized fire engines in Columbus, Ohio. Among his friends in his lifetime, Stone could count Orville Wright and Albert Einstein. He was a longtime trustee of Ohio State University, also located in Columbus. No matter how deep his ties to the city, however, when he took control of Columbus McKinnon Chain Company, he recognized that the electric welded chain made in New York was in greater demand than the fire welded chain made in Ohio, and in 1927 he moved the company's headquarters to Tonawanda, New York. By 1931 the Columbus plant was shut down and eight of its 125 forges were moved to Tonawanda. It wouldn't be until the 1950s that fire welded chain would be completely phased out.

Columbus McKinnon was the sole supplier of the electric welded chain that was used by Chisholm Moore and by the Wright Hoist Manufacturing Company. When a competitor, American Chain Company, bought Wright and the Ford Chain Block Company, Stone felt the need to respond. He purchased Chisholm Moore in 1928, thus joining the manufacture of chains and hoists under one company that the following year would became known as Columbus McKinnon Corp. It was the same year that would usher in the Great Depression.

### The 1930s: Challenge, Innovation, and Expansion

Columbus McKinnon, like most businesses, had its share of struggles during the 1930s. One employee was quoted as saying that in 1932, "if an order for a piece of chain came in, everyone

could celebrate." Nevertheless the company made a number of significant improvements in its product lines. In 1931 Columbus McKinnon introduced the first aluminum hoist. In 1933 the company was responsible for one of the most important contributions to the manufacture of chain when it produced the first alloy chain, which would prove to be lighter, stronger, and more resistant to high temperatures than the wrought iron chain it would soon replace in lifting slings. Another new product that helped Columbus McKinnon survive the Depression was the Evans Carloading Hoist, which prevented damage to automobiles as they were loaded into railroad box cars. The company also introduced an electric hand chain hoist, which would be greatly improved when it employed the new alloy chain. In fact, the chain and hoist businesses that came together under Columbus McKinnon seemed to spur one another to innovate and improve. The hoist business would need better chain for a new design, and the chain business would find a way to supply that need. The result was increasingly lighter and efficient hoists. To better coordinate the development of new products, Columbus McKinnon would in 1939 create a separate Research and Development unit.

The first Columbus McKinnon facility to be built abroad was a factory in South Africa in 1935. The company had for years been exporting chain for use in the mines of South Africa. When Stone heard that a British competitor was thinking of building a local plant, he was quick to act. He traveled to South Africa and established McKinnon Chain S.A. near Johannesburg. The new company produced tire chain and ladder chain for the gold mines, anchor chain and trek chain for the oxen.

### The War Years

Columbus McKinnon would play a prominent role during World War II, but not under the direction of Stone. He was one of the many "one-dollar-a-year" men who went to work for the government during the crisis. The company supplied the Air Force with countless hand hoists. It also supplied both the Navy and Air Force with vast quantities of tie-down chain. Columbus McKinnon was the only company, in fact, that could meet the government's specification for the strength of military chain.

After the war and through the 1950s Columbus McKinnon grew steadily and solidified its position as one of the most respected manufacturers of chain and hoist. It also made a concerted effort to expand its presence in Europe. Head of product development, Bill Devonshire was picked by Stone to set up a distribution network throughout Europe. Within 20 years Columbus McKinnon products would be available in over 70 countries through more than 100 distributors.

Columbus McKinnon also began to establish affiliations with foreign manufacturers. In Australia, Pitt Waddell Bennett Chains Ltd. was formed to make chain using Columbus McKinnon machinery. In Great Britain a similar arrangement was set up with Wheway Watson Ltd. By the mid-1970s Columbus McKinnon would have subsidiaries and affiliates in Canada, South Africa, Zambia, Australia, England, and France.

In North America, meanwhile, Columbus McKinnon opened a Product Development and Engineering center in Tonawanda in 1959. A plant in St. Catharines, Ontario, was built in 1966 to produce both hoists and chain. A hoist factory was opened in Damascus, Virginia, in 1969. A plant that opened in Manatee, Florida, in 1970 was dedicated to the production of Columbus McKinnon chainmaking equipment. In 1971 a Lexington, Tennessee, plant was built to produce carbon chain.

In June 1974 Columbus McKinnon purchased Acquired Engineered Products of MeKees Rocks, Pennsylvania, in what was planned to be a series of acquisitions. It wouldn't be until the mid-1990s, however, that the company would truly engage in an aggressive pattern of mergers and acquisitions, a strategy that was intended to enlarge the scope of Columbus McKinnon beyond the mere manufacture of chains and hoists.

### Late-1990s Bring Expansion and Turmoil

After the 1995 acquisition of three companies—Cady Lifters, Inc., which produced pallet lifters and crane forks; Endor, a Mexican manufacturer of hoists; and Lift-Tech, a Michigan manufacturer of chain hoists—Columbus McKinnon, in order to fuel further expansion, went public in February 1996 at $15 per share and began trading on the NASDAQ exchange. Later in the year, Columbus McKinnon bought Yale International, makers of a variety of material handling products in addition to hoists. Early in 1998 Columbus McKinnon bought Danish Univeyor A/S, an international company that designed, developed, and implemented material handling applications for a number of industries. In addition to providing hoists that worked vertically, Columbus McKinnon was now positioning itself to move materials horizontally throughout a facility, a function that many companies were choosing to outsource and what had become a tempting $2 billion a year domestic market.

In March 1998 Columbus McKinnon purchased LICO Inc., a company that designed and built large conveyor systems that were predominantly used on automotive assembly lines. Using a new revolving credit line of $300 million, Columbus McKinnon paid $155 million for LICO. The one drawback of LICO was its dependence on automakers and the uncertainty when large projects might be put up to bid. Columbus McKinnon also moved to add cranes to its mix of material handling products. In August 1998 the company purchased Abell-Howe Crane division of Abell-Howe Co.

The momentum of Columbus McKinnon was checked, however, when volatility in the automotive industry had an adverse effect on the company. In late August 1998 management warned investors that second quarter profits would fall short of expectations. Columbus McKinnon's stock dropped 12 percent, to a level barely above its initial $15 price per share. The company instituted a hiring freeze and cut back on discretionary spending, but despite these cost-savings measures it was difficult to continue an aggressive pattern of growth with a low stock price that would make it difficult to pay for further acquisitions by using shares. Management was also reluctant to issue new shares when the company's stock was valued so low.

Columbus McKinnon continued to make acquisitions, albeit on a smaller scale. In December 1998 it purchased a French firm, Societe D'Exploitation des Raccords Gautier (SERG) for $2.94 million. SERG produced swivel joints and rotary unions, and helped Columbus McKinnon to expand its industrial components business. In February 1999 the company purchased Camlok Lifting Clamps Limited and the Tigrip product line from German manufacture Schmidt-Krantz & Co. for $6.3 million. The transaction provided Columbus McKinnon with plate clamps, crane weighers, and other products that complimented the company's line of hoists. In March 1999 Columbus McKinnon purchased Texas-based G.L. International, a crane builder, for $20.6 million in stock and an assumption of $10.9 million in debt. Columbus McKinnon also announced that it was now in a position to create a network for crane manufacturers, a venture it planned to call CraneMart. Members would be able to command lower prices on essential products, such as steel, by combining forces. In May 1999 Columbus McKinnon solidified its position in this sector by paying $6.6 million to purchase Washington Equipment Co., an Illinois crane manufacturer.

The day after management announced the Washington Equipment deal, on 7 May 1999, the company was caught off guard by an announcement that a group of shareholders wanted to replace the board and look into selling the company. Metropolitan Capital Advisors, a New York City investor group headed by Jeffrey Schwarz, owned 8.5 percent of Columbus McKinnon's stock. Although Schwarz conceded that management had done a good job running the company, he said he was concerned that increased sales and profits had not lifted the stock's price. Schwarz's group had first suggested that management consider selling the company in August 1997, and again in a pair of meetings in March 1999. With all eight directors' seats up for election at an August 16 annual meeting, a proxy fight for control of the company was now underway. Management contended that the dissident's strategy was shortsighted and vowed to resist the takeover.

Columbus McKinnon was not the first company to be pressured to sell by Schwarz and Metropolitan. In fact, Columbus McKinnon's purchase of Yale International in 1996 was the result of Metropolitan's efforts. The following year the group forced the sale of Raymond Corp, and in 1998 followed the same strategy to pressure surgical equipment maker Circon Corp. into a deal with Maxxim Medical Inc. In all of these cases, stock prices rose and Metropolitan pocketed significant profits. Even when the group failed to force a New Orleans bank, Meritrust, to sell, it still was able to take advantage of an inflated stock price.

Columbus McKinnon management, led by CEO Timothy Tevens, did not disguise its belief that Schwarz was nothing less than a stock manipulator with no long-term interest in the health of the company. It sued Metropolitan, contending that the group had not properly notified the Securities and Exchange Commission of its plans. Metropolitan countersued, and both sides began to actively court shareholders to support them in the upcoming vote, all the while firing salvos at one another through the press. Unfortunately for management, financial results reported in July were flat. A major factor was the automotive-dependent LICO unit (now known as Automatic Systems, Inc. or ASI), which was the victim of the lingering effects of a labor strike against General Motors.

Management of Columbus McKinnon won the August proxy fight with 78 percent of the vote, and enjoyed a spike in the price of its stock. By October, however, the price dropped 22 percent, and Schwarz renewed his efforts to force a sale of the company. When management announced its second quarter results on October 27, 1999, investors were stunned to learn that earnings had been so poor that instead of 50 cents a share, the actual earnings were a mere four cents a share. Without issuing an early warning of the results, management all but insured that the company's stock would be battered. Again the major culprit was LICO, the acquisition of which Schwarz was calling a major blunder. His views were gaining support among shareholders that had to this point been loyal to management, which was now forced to announce that it would be willing to sell or at least restructure the business.

The investment banker that had helped Columbus McKinnon go public, Bear, Stearns & Co., was hired to advise the company on how to maximize shareholder value, likely presenting options that could very well include a sale or merger. Third quarter results reported in January 2000 were again disappointing, but the numbers for the ASI unit was better than expected. To buy time, management postponed its annual meeting. In July Columbus McKinnon announced higher than expected results, fueled in great part by a further rebound by ASI. The second quarter results announced in October showed an even more dramatic improvement. Profits for the quarter exceeded the previous year's second quarter by 758 percent. Sales for ASI were up 21.7 percent from the prior year. The price of the company's stock, however, rose only modestly. Management continued to work with Bear Stearns to increase shareholder value, leaving open the possibility that it might still sell all or part of the company. In the meantime, in spite of uncertainty, the company continued to stay the course and try to grow its business.

## Principal Subsidiaries

Abell-Howe Crane, Inc.; Automatic Systems, Inc.; Univeyor A/S; Washington Equipment Company; Yale Industrial Products, Inc.

## Principal Competitors

Cascade Corp.; FKI plc.; Ingersoll-Rand Corp.

## Further Reading

Bridger, Chet, "Columbus McKinnon Shareholders Renew Fight to Sell Firm," *Buffalo News,* October 26, 1999, p. E5.

"Columbus McKinnon Acquires European Plate Clamp Manufacturer and Product Line," *PR Newswire,* February 18, 1999, p. 1.

"Columbus McKinnon Sues to Halt Attempt to Oust Board, Sell," *Wall Street Journal,* May 27, 1999, p. B14.

"Columbus McKinnon Suing Dissident Stockholder Group," *Buffalo News,* May 27, 1999, p. D14.

"Columbus McKinnon Up for Sale," *Warehousing Management,* January/February 2000, p. 7.

Madore, James T., "Amherst Firm Buys Michigan Producers of Chain Hoists," *Buffalo News,* November 18, 1995, p. A9.

Montgomery, Robert L. Jr., "Columbus McKinnon Corporation Acquires Univeyor A/S of Denmark," *PR Newswire,* January 9, 1998, p. 1.

"One Hundred Years at CM," Amherst: Columbus McKinnon Corp., 1975.

Robinson, David, "Columbus McKinnon Buys Danish Company in Move into Full Materials Handling Systems," *Buffalo News,* January 10, 1998, p. B11.

——, "Columbus McKinnon Buys LICO Inc. Conveyor Firm Acquired for $155 Million," *Buffalo News,* March 12, 1998, p. D1.

——, "Columbus McKinnon Buys Manufacturing Firm in France," *Buffalo News,* December 15, 1998, p. E6.

——, "Columbus McKinnon Stock Plunges to All-Time Low" *Buffalo News,* October 27, 1999, p. E1.

——, "Columbus McKinnon Takes Business in New Directions," *Buffalo News,* October 4, 1998, p. B11.

——, "How Long Will Shareholders of McKinnon Stay Patient," *Buffalo News,* October 31, 1999, p. B9.

——, "Stockholder Group Seeks to Sell Columbus McKinnon," *Buffalo News,* May 7, 1999, p. C5.

Williams, Fred O., and David Robinson, "Team of Advisers to Resist Takeover of Columbus McKinnon Corp.," *Buffalo News,* May 8, 1999, p. A7.

Williams, Fred O., "Columbus McKinnon Buys Crane Maker for $6.6 Million," *Buffalo News,* May 6, 1999, p. D1.

——, "Columbus McKinnon's Profits Decline 50%," *Buffalo News,* January 26, 2000, p. C4.

—Ed Dinger

# Cominco Ltd.

**500-200 Burrard Street**
**Vancouver, British Columbia V6C 3L7**
**Canada**
**Telephone: (604) 682-0611**
**Fax: (604) 685-3019**
**Web site: http://www.cominco.com**

*Public Company*
*Incorporated:* 1906 as Consolidated Mining & Smelting
    Company of Canada, Ltd
*Employees:* 4,142
*Sales:* C$1.64 billion (1999)
*Stock Exchanges:* Toronto New York
*Ticker Symbol:* CLT
*NAIC:* 212231 Mining Lead-Zinc Bearing Ores; 212233
    Mining Copper Bearing Ores; 331410 Smelting and
    Refining of Nonferrous Metals (Except Aluminum);
    325313 Fertilizers, Chemical and Manufacturing

Incorporated in Canada in 1906, Cominco Ltd. has emerged as a leading integrated zinc and copper producer. With mines in Canada, the United States, Chile, and Peru, Cominco is the world's largest producer of zinc concentrate as well as the fourth-largest zinc metal refiner. Additionally, Cominco produces lead, silver, gold, germanium, and indium. The company's head office is situated in Vancouver, British Columbia, Canada, while it oversees subsidiaries worldwide. Teck Corporation is the largest single shareholder with 44 percent of Cominco's Common Shares.

### The Beginning: 1850–1900

Cominco's history reaches back to the Gold Rush in the second half of the 19th century. Thousands of placer prospectors flocked to the unexplored wilderness that was later to become the Province of British Columbia. (Placer refers to a gravel deposit containing particles of gold). Although the Gold Rush ended after ten years, it hastened the proclamation of the Colony of British Columbia in 1858 and influenced the development of trails throughout the region.

The newly created trails made it possible for the remaining prospectors to move further afield. Before long, placer gold was discovered in various parts of the Kootenay region in southeastern British Columbia. Soon after, steamboat service along the upper Columbia River made it easier for miners, prospectors, and others to reach the area.

Despite these transportation enhancements, mining activity was limited until the coming of the railways 20 years later. It was difficult to move the heavy, bulky ore mined in the Kootenays to the early smelters that were situated in the U.S. states of Montana and Washington. It was clear that cheap railway transportation was the key to success. In 1871, the Canadian government commissioned the Canadian Pacific Railway (CPR) to build a railway across Canada. To the south, the United States was developing a similar national railway system.

From 1875 to the beginning of the new century, no new gold fields were discovered in British Columbia, and gold mining was soon surpassed by silver, lead, and coal mining. Mining companies desperately awaited the coming of railway transportation to the Kootenay mines, but the wait was a long one. According to ''The Cominco Story,'' published in the company periodical *The Orbit* in June 1988, both the Canadian and U.S. national railways were riddled with corruption and scandals leading to inevitable delays in construction. These delays lead to an influx of competing spur lines and affiliated businesses coming in from the United States. This competition ultimately resulted in the CPR acquiring a company that was later to become Cominco Ltd.

In 1891, the U.S.-owned Le Roi Mining & Smelting Company set the wheels in motion by deciding that the mines near Rossland, British Columbia, required a local smelter. The company enlisted the aid of Fredrick Augustus Heinze, a U.S. promoter, gambler, and visionary whose credentials included building a smelter in Butte, Montana. During the four years of Heinze's involvement, he succeeded in building the smelter at Trail, British Columbia, and in transferring control of the mines and utilities from American to Canadian and British interests. In 1896, Heinze incorporated his new company, British Columbia Smelting and Refining Company Limited, in the State of New Jersey. Due to Heinze's propensity for deal making, his busi-

---

**Company Perspectives:**

*We are committed to achieving above-average returns for our shareholders through improvements to existing operations, strategic acquisitions and divestitures; promoting the health and safety of our employees: protecting the environment; and contributing positively to the sustainable future of the communities in which we operate.*

---

ness interests now included the smelter, mining interests, railway lines, railway charters, and associated land grants.

A year later, Heinze put the company up for sale. The CPR had no interest in the mines and mining activities but desperately wanted control of the railway lines that Heinze owned. However, the sale was a package deal. The CPR hired Walter Hull Aldridge, a smelter manager from Montana, to negotiate with Heinze on their behalf. Under Aldridge's leadership, the CPR bought Heinze's company, including the mining interests that proved to be a source of profit for the next 88 years.

After Aldridge took over in 1898, the smelter was known as the Canadian Smelting Works and was officially owned by the British Columbia Southern Railway, a CPR subsidiary. Canadian Smelting Works later became the Consolidated Mining and Smelting Company of Canada, Limited, which was renamed Cominco Ltd. in 1966.

### Early Growth: 1900–35

Within two years, Aldridge had doubled the smelter's capacity, the CPR had improved its rail facilities, and other railway companies had built track providing the first rail connection for mines in the region. By 1901, Aldridge had installed three lead blast furnaces that were supplied with custom ore from the surrounding mines. The bullion was shipped to San Francisco for refining, then the refined lead was sold in Eastern Canada and the Far East. This represented the company's first move overseas.

In time, Aldridge negotiated with CPR executives and with the owners of the mines that supplied ore to the smelter to join the mines and smelter into one company with one management. In 1906, The Consolidated Mining and Smelting Company of Canada, Limited was incorporated as a subsidiary of the CPR.

In 1908, Consolidated leased the Sullivan Mine in East Kootenay. The Sullivan was a rich source of lead, silver, and zinc, but had been unprofitable to operate, as there was limited need for zinc, and the ore was a complicated mixture of minerals that was difficult to smelt. Anticipating that the metallurgical problems could be solved, Aldridge looked for solutions. By 1910, the Sullivan had become the largest source of lead in Canada. In 1913, Consolidated obtained complete ownership of the Sullivan, a mine that was to become the company's mainstay for years to come.

Relying on a slow and expensive method of hand picking, the mines could produce 50 tons of lead a day by 1916. The zinc-rich ore fragments were regarded as waste. However,

World War I created a need for zinc for munitions. Consolidated contracted with the Imperial Munitions Board to produce 35 tons of zinc daily. Production costs were high, and Aldridge knew that in postwar years, the cost would be prohibitive. Consequently, Consolidated hired Randolphe "Ralph" William Diamond, a prominent metallurgist from Ontario, to head up the company's milling operations and to conduct testing on the Sullivan ore. Diamond developed a process that permitted use of lower-grade ore and simplified hand sorting. The plant expanded to handle 600 tons daily.

Shortly after, Diamond developed "differential flotation," a process that would have an impact on the entire industry. Differential flotation allowed minerals to "float" by sticking to bubbles formed in certain mixtures of chemicals and oils. The bubbles formed a surface froth, which could then be skimmed off, separating the mineral from the rest of the mixture. This process indicated a major step for Consolidated. The company could now mine the Sullivan on a worldwide scale. By 1923, the company had built a new concentrator near Kimberley, British Columbia. By 1924, the lead output had risen by 64 percent. Consolidated's general manager, S.G. Blaylock, wrote in the 1924 Annual Report: "The year just past has been one of more than ordinary importance in the life of the Company."

By the latter part of the decade, environmental pollution became a concern. Emissions of sulphur dioxide ($SO_2$) contaminated the valley and extended to lands along the Columbia River in Washington State. Damage to vegetation and land was severe. In 1927, an International Joint Commission assessed damages at $350,000. Additional damages of $78,000 were awarded in 1941. To prevent further damage, Consolidated explored alternative uses for sulphuric acid, which it was producing in small quantities from the $SO_2$. This led to the development of chemical fertilizers and to diversification into a new business. Also during this time, Consolidated contracted to purchase phosphate rock from a company in Garrison, Montana, the first step towards acquiring an American subsidiary company.

Consolidated's operation was suitable for producing fertilizers that could be used in the Canadian Prairies and marketed to other countries. By 1930, three sulphuric acid plants were operating and construction of a fertilizer complex had started. The fertilizers were marketed under the name Elephant Brand.

On October 29, 1929, the stock market crash heralded the Great Depression, and during that time there was limited market for fertilizers. Thus, Consolidated looked for other uses for the gases. It developed a process to manufacture elemental sulphur by the reduction of sulphur dioxide with coke. This process continued until 1943. Consolidated curtailed some of its activities during the Great Depression, including exploration, marketing, and sales efforts in fertilizers. By 1935, it was evident that grain growing could not continue without the use of fertilizers, and Consolidated again turned to the Prairie fertilizer market.

### Exploration and Expansion: 1930–45

In the third decade of the 20th century, Consolidated entered a period of exploration. Interest in northern exploration lead to the establishment of an aviation service to transport personnel and supplies to properties in northern Canada. Cominco's air

## Key Dates:

**1902:** Cominco's predecessor builds the world's first electrolytic lead refinery at Trail, British Columbia.
**1906:** The Consolidated Mining & Smelting Company of Canada Limited is incorporated as a subsidiary of the Canadian Pacific Railway Co. Inc.
**1909:** The Sullivan mine begins production under Cominco's ownership.
**1925:** Company pioneers aircraft prospecting in the Northwest Territories.
**1931:** Company initiates fertilizer production plants as a pollution control measure at the Trail mine.
**1944:** Company completes the Brilliant Dam in British Columbia to supply electricity for wartime production.
**1961:** Cominco American discovers the Magmont lead deposit in Missouri.
**1966:** Company name is changed to Cominco Ltd.
**1977:** Cominco initiates a 20-year, C$1 billion dollar project to modernize the Sullivan Mine and Trail Operations.
**1986:** Teck Corporation acquires significant stake in Cominco Ltd. from Canadian Pacific.
**1996:** Cominco celebrates its 90th anniversary.

service was one of several regional services that were later consolidated to form the Canadian Pacific Airlines.

Much of the northern exploration enjoyed only limited success. As S.G. Blaylock, the company's general manager once remarked, "Three things are necessary to find a mine: brains, guts and luck." During the 1930s and 1940s, Consolidated worked a number of gold mines across Canada. However, only the Con in the Northwest Territories proved to be a winner. The Con became the first gold mine that went into production in the Northwest Territories, and it was a profitable source for 50 years until it was sold in 1986. Further exploration lead to the discovery of the Campbell Shear Zone that came into production in 1956.

As the century progressed, sophisticated mining technology, combined with changing needs, made it profitable to mine various other minerals. During World War II, Allied requirements led to opening two new mines in British Columbia to provide tungsten for armor-piercing shells and to provide coal for the smelter in Trail. Increased need for mercury, used in bomb detonators, led to the operation of the Pinchi mine. The Pinchi was later closed but remained a Cominco property.

During World War II, Cominco contracted with the British Government to supply zinc and lead. Later, because of its experience in fertilizer production, Consolidated acquired authorization to build nitric acid and ammonium nitrate plants near Calgary, Alberta. Nitric acid and ammonium nitrate were used in explosives. While the plants were being constructed, a new explosive was developed that did not require ammonium nitrate. Consolidated consequently switched the plants over to the production of fertilizer grade nitrogen. In making the transi-

tion, Consolidated developed a new means of prilling ammonium nitrate that had a worldwide impact on the industry. (Prilling is the process of atomizing and cooling molten liquids to form a bead).

In 1942, Consolidated was selected to produce large quantities of heavy water required for the war effort. Heavy water, consisting of two deuterium atoms instead of two hydrogen atoms, was thought to be useful in the control of neutron particles resulting from atomic fission. Consolidated was chosen because it already had an electrolytic hydrogen plant, a natural concentrator of heavy water. The company shipped 100 pounds of heavy water a month to Ohio. In 1945, the plant began supplying heavy water to a uranium facility owned by the Canadian government. Also that year, Consolidated mourned the death of S.G. Blaylock, general manager and later chairman of the company.

### Postwar Years: 1945–80

The postwar years proved to be the most active of Consolidated's history. Technological advances made it possible to operate previously unprofitable mines, such as the Bluebell lead-zinc mine. The Bluebell became the largest lead-zinc mine in the province and remained operational for 20 years. Other major Consolidated mines going into operation during this time included the H.B. zinc-lead mine at Salmo, British Columbia, and the Pine Point zinc-lead mine in the Northwest Territories.

Beginning in the 1950s, Consolidated branched out aggressively into new domestic and international markets. The Canada Metal Company (a lead fabricating firm) and National Hardware Specialties Limited (a die casting company) were among the best-known operations. In 1962, Consolidated and the company's agents in Calcutta formed Cominco Binani Zinc Ltd. to build an electrolytic zinc smelter and refinery and a sulphuric acid by-product plant in southern India. Cominco Binani Zinc Ltd. experienced difficult beginnings, due to local and international economic conditions but would ultimately reach full production in 1969. In 1964, Consolidated and Mitsubishi Metal Mining Company in Japan joined to construct a lead smelter to be supplied with concentrates from Cominco operations. More than one million tonnes [a unit of metric measurement similar to an Imperial ton] of lead concentrate had been shipped to Mitsubishi Cominco in the late 1990s. Also in 1964, Consolidated acquired Western Canada Steel Limited, which would be a part of its family until 1988 when Consolidated restructured and sold the company.

In 1966, Consolidated established Cominco American Incorporated. The American subsidiary had its roots in Montana Phosphate Products Company (MPP), a small company that had been supplying phosphate rock to Trail. MPP obtained phosphate leases in the area and also discovered a lead deposit with zinc and copper at Salem, Missouri. After incorporation, Cominco American combined with another Cominco venture, Cominco Products Inc., bringing all of the company's mining, exploration, and fertilizer activities together in the United States.

Also in 1966, Consolidated began exploring opportunities in Australia. The company first established the Cominco Australian Pty Ltd. as a holding company with Cominco Exploration

Pty Ltd. as a wholly-owned subsidiary. Later, in 1971, Cominco would obtain an interest in Aberfoyle Ltd., an Australian mining company. By 1977, Cominco had reorganized Aberfoyle's many small companies under the umbrella of Aberfoyle Limited.

Other international explorations and operations included activities along the Iberian Peninsula, resulting in a 47 percent interest in Exploración Minera International (España) S.A. Later, Cominco teams discovered zinc-lead-copper deposits in north central Spain.

In 1968, Consolidated, having officially changed its name to Cominco Ltd., along with Canadian Pacific Investments Ltd. formed Fording Coal Limited to develop coal deposits in southeastern British Columbia. Cominco sold its interests to Canadian Pacific in 1985.

### Turbulent Times: 1980–90

For Cominco, the 1980s was a period of economic turmoil, riddled with gains and losses, the startup of new operations, and the closure of others—as well as a change in majority ownership. The slumping U.S. economy resulted in a gigantic drop in Cominco's net earnings in 1980 and 1981. High interest rates combined with a reduced demand for consumer goods led to lowered prices for metals. In 1982, the company recorded its first loss since 1932. The situation worsened; by the end of 1985, Cominco was more than C$1.0 billion in debt.

Still, there were triumphs. In 1984, the company completed the first phase of the Trail modernization program, initiated in 1977. This included construction of the world's first zinc pressure leaching plant and a new lead smelter feed plant. Operations commenced at three new mines: the world's northernmost mine, the Polaris zinc-lead mine in the Northwest Territories; the Highland Valley Copper mine (50 percent interest), a mine which has become the second largest copper mine in the world; and Buckhorn open pit gold mine in Nevada. The most significant event of the decade, however, was widely regarded as the production of the Red Dog mine in Alaska. An engineering triumph, the mine was and remained one of the world's largest zinc-lead mines.

To reduce debt, Cominco sold its interest in a number of non-core assets and mines, including the Con gold mine, Cominco's first mining operation in the north. At the same time, Cominco's parent company, the Canadian Pacific Railway, sold its 52.5 percent stake in Cominco. Nunachiaq Inc., a holding company for a consortium comprised of Teck Corporation, Metallgesellschaft AG, and M.I.M. Holdings Company purchased 29.5 percent interest. The remaining shares were sold publicly. By 1987, Cominco was in the black and by 1988, debt was down to C$344 million.

### Better Times: 1990s and Beyond

The 1990s ushered in a period of prosperity. In fact, the year 1990 saw the discovery of two new depositions: the drill hole hit mineralization at the Cerattepe copper-gold deposit in Tur-

key and the Pebble copper-gold deposit in Alaska. In 1994, Quebrada Blanca copper mine began production, and the Kudz Ze Kayah zinc deposit was discovered in the Yukon. A year later, in 1995, Cominco found major new ore reserves at Red Dog. CESL Engineering announced a breakthrough in copper and nickel hydrometallurgy, and the company bought the Cajamarquilla zinc refinery in Peru. In 1996, as Cominco celebrated its 90th birthday, the company commenced a production rate increase project at Red Dog.

In 1998, net profits dipped, but the following year Cominco enjoyed consolidated net earnings of C$159 million, a C$182 million improvement over the previous year. Trail, Cajamarquilla, Red Dog, Polaris, and Quebrada Blanca mines achieved record production, while zinc contained in concentrate rose to a new record of 728,000 tonnes of zinc. In 1999, Cominco Ltd.'s operations in British Columbia won two civic awards and one award for mine safety. Cominco Ltd. commenced the new millennium in a position of strength and stability.

### Principal Subsidiaries

Cominco Engineering Services Ltd.; Highland Valley Copper (50%); Cominco American Inc. (United States); Cominco Alaska Inc. (United States); Glenbrook Nickel Company (United States); Lake Minerals Corporation (United States); Minera Cominco Chile Ltda (Chile); Cia, Minera Constelación, S.A. de C.V. (Mexico); Cominco Madençilik Sanayai A.S. (Turkey); Cominco (Peru) S.R.L. (Peru); Refinería de Cajamarquilla S.A. (Peru; 82%).

### Principal Operating Units

Red Dog Mine; Trail Operations; Sullivan Mine; Polaris Mine; Refinería de Cajamarquilla.

### Principal Competitors

Inco Limited; Noranda Inc.; WMC Ltd.

### Further Reading

Bradner, Tim, "Cominco Tests New Ore Processing," *Alaska Journal of Commerce,* September 24, 2000, p. 11.
"Cominco Begins Sullivan Layoffs," *American Metal Market,* October 2, 200, p. 6.
"Cominco Posts Stellar Results," *Northern Miner,* February 13, 2000, p. 1.
"Nature's Gifts to the People," Vancouver: Cominco Ltd., 2000.
*Orbit: Cominco's Magazine,* Vancouver: Cominco Ltd., 2000.
"Red Dog Drives Cominco Rise," *American Metal Market,* May 2000, p. 7.
"Red Dog to Optimize Mill," *Canadian Mining Journal,* April 2000, p. 7.
"Responsible Mine Development," Vancouver: Cominco Ltd.
*Shared Values, Common Goals, Exceptional Results: The Red Dog Mine Story,* Vancouver: Cominco Ltd., 1998.
"Trail's 100th Anniversary," *Canadian Mining Journal,* October 1996, p. 4.

—June Campbell

# Cumulus Media Inc.

111 East Kilbourn Avenue, Suite 2700
Milwaukee, Wisconsin 53202
U.S.A.
Telephone: (414) 615-2800
Fax: (414) 615-2880
Web site: http://www.cumulus.com

*Public Company*
*Incorporated:* 1997
*Employees:* 4,000
*Sales:* $180 million (1999)
*Stock Exchanges:* NASDAQ
*Ticker Symbol:* CMLS
*NAIC:* 513112 Radio Stations

Since it was established in 1997, Cumulus Media Inc. has focused on acquiring clusters of radio stations in small and medium-size markets. In its brief history it once owned or had pending more than 300 radio stations. However, a series of events in early 2000 depressed the company's stock price and made it difficult for Cumulus to finance all of its pending acquisitions. It restructured some acquisitions, swapping stations where necessary, which left it with 271 stations in 54 markets at last count. That made it the second largest radio company behind Clear Channel Communications, Inc. in terms of number of stations owned, and seventh in terms of revenue.

### Acquiring Radio Stations: 1997

Following the passage of the Telecommunications Act of 1996, which changed radio stations ownership rules among other things, Cumulus Media, Inc. was founded in 1997 in Milwaukee by Lew Dickey, Jr., and Richard Weening. They received financial backing from a group of institutional investors that included the State of Wisconsin Investment Board, NationsBank Capital Corporation, Heller Equity Capital Corporation, and Quaestus Management Corporation. Northwestern Mutual Life Insurance Co. subsequently joined the investor group. The company was established for the purpose of acquiring and developing radio station clusters in medium-size and smaller cities across the United States. Operations commenced on May 22, 1997.

Prior to co-founding Cumulus, Dickey had started the Stratford Research Co., Inc., a consulting and market research firm for radio and television broadcasters. He was a nationally known consultant on radio strategy and the author of the 1994 book, *The Franchise: Building Radio Brands,* which was published by the National Association of Broadcasters. From 1996 to 1998 Dickey served as president and CEO of Midwestern Broadcasting Inc., which operated two radio stations in Toledo, Ohio, that were subsequently acquired by Cumulus. He would serve as Cumulus's vice-chairman.

Weening, on the other hand, helped establish Cumulus through Quaestus, a private equity investment and advisory firm of which he was chairman and CEO. He had prior experience as a CEO and investor in book and magazine publishing, radio broadcasting, online services, and electronic commerce software and services. Before launching Quaestus in 1989, he had established two successful information and publishing companies. In March 1998 he assumed the role of executive chairman at Cumulus, with Dickey as vice-chairman.

### Going Public and Aggressive Acquisitions: 1998–99

Cumulus became a public company with an initial public offering (IPO) on June 26, 1998. The company sold 7.6 million shares at an opening price of $14. Cumulus also sold $125 million of preferred stock and $160 million of senior subordinated bonds, raising a total of $391 million. Some $280 million of the proceeds were earmarked to cover the cost of pending acquisitions and to reduce outstanding debt.

At the time it went public, Cumulus owned or was in the process of buying 167 radio stations, including 119 FM and 48 AM stations. The company's acquisition strategy had been to build station clusters in small to mid-size markets, mainly in the Midwest, Southeast, Southwest, and Northeast. In July 1998 Cumulus acquired its first radio stations on the East Coast, when it acquired WQCB-FM and WBZN-FM in Bangor, Maine, for $6.4 million from Castle Broadcasting. The same month it acquired its sixth station in Myrtle Beach, South Carolina, WSEA-FM, for $1.3 million.

In its first 17 months, Cumulus acquired 207 stations, creating the first small-market-only radio conglomerate. Following the company's IPO, its stock fell from $14 to less than $5 on October 9, 1998, then rebounded to around $10 at the beginning of November. The firm's long-term debt had reached $422 million. Some radio executives familiar with small markets thought that Cumulus was overpaying to buy top stations in markets that did not have a great upside potential. As of November 1998 its biggest market was Toledo, which was ranked 76th. The company's strategy was to acquire four FM and two AM stations in each market. It preferred to buy two of the top four performing stations in a market, then two of the next four, all with mainstream formats. As Cumulus consolidated its stations and improved ad sales and on-air quality, it hoped to attract national advertisers. It also planned to improve the operating profit margins of its stations, and in 1998 raised them from around 10–20 percent to more than 30 percent. For 1998 Cumulus reported revenue of $98.8 million, with broadcast cash flow of $26.6 million. Its cash-flow margin reached 27 percent.

For the first quarter of 1999, Cumulus reported a 216 percent increase in broadcast cash flow compared to the same quarter in 1998 and a 155 percent increase in net broadcast revenue. However, the company's quarterly loss increased from $5.3 million in the first quarter of 1998 to $10.1 million in the first quarter of 1999. With 232 stations in 44 markets, Cumulus claimed to be the third largest radio company in the United States in terms of number of stations owned.

In November 1999 Cumulus paid $26.5 million to Duke Broadcasting for three radio stations in Jonesboro, Arkansas, including the market's two largest FM stations and a full-service news/talk AM station. Jonesboro, located near Memphis, Tennessee, was a newly ranked market at 271st in the United States. The acquisition also included Duke's Southern Outdoor Advertising, marking Cumulus's first venture in outdoor advertising.

Before the end of the month Cumulus made a $242 million deal with Connoisseur Communications of Greenwich, Connecticut, for 35 radio stations. The stations were located in Canton and Youngstown, Ohio; Flint, Saginaw-Bay City, and Muskegon, Michigan; Rockford and the Quad Cities, Illinois; Evansville, Indiana; and Waterloo Cedar Falls, Iowa. With 299 stations owned or pending, Cumulus ranked second to Clear Channel Communications, Inc. in terms of number of stations owned. Following the acquisition, Cumulus would have stations in 58 markets. In November the company's stock rose above $40 a share, more than three times the IPO price.

In December Cumulus spent $51 million to acquire eight Oregon and California radio stations from McDonald Media Group and another station in Santa Barbara, California, from Pacific Coast Communications. It was the company's first acquisition of stations on the West Coast. Meanwhile, back in Wisconsin it was announced that football team Green Bay Packers radio network would switch affiliations in some markets to stations owned by Milwaukee-based Cumulus. For 1999 Cumulus reported $180 million in revenue and $46.7 million broadcast cash flow.

### Financial Challenges in 2000

In January 2000 the Federal Communications Commission (FCC) announced it had flagged for public comment Cumulus's pending acquisition of Connoisseur Communications. The agency was especially concerned with markets in Waterloo-Cedar Falls, Iowa; Flint, Michigan; Evansville, Indiana; the Quad Cities; and Rockford, Illinois. In March Cumulus acquired The Advisory Board, Inc., which conducted sales training programs for the radio industry under the name The Lytle Organization.

In the biggest radio industry consolidation to date, Clear Channel Communications acquired AMFM Inc. for $23 billion. As part of the deal, Clear Channel was required to sell 72 of its radio stations. Cumulus announced it would purchase a group of those stations, including four stations in Harrisburg, Pennsylvania; three stations in Cedar Rapids, Iowa; three stations in Shreveport, Louisiana; and one station in Melbourne, Florida. Cumulus expected to pay about $159 million for the 11 Clear Channel stations.

However, Cumulus's stock took a tumble in the first quarter of 2000, losing about two-thirds of its value. Affecting the stock price were rumors of accounting improprieties over the company's annual audit after it restated its earnings for the first three quarters of 1999. As a result, class-action lawsuits were filed against Cumulus charging the company with artificially inflating revenue and profit in 1999. In March vice-chairman Lew Dickey took over the job of president of Cumulus Broadcasting, the company's primary operating subsidiary, from William Bungeroth. It was also disclosed that chief financial officer Richard Bonick, Jr., had left the company in January 2000.

Cumulus needed to raise nearly $300 million to finance pending acquisitions, a task made more difficult by the company's sagging stock price. The company announced it would restructure other pending acquisitions and sell some non-core businesses to reduce its debt load. The company had debt of $285 million, which could increase to as much as $650 million to pay for all of the pending acquisitions. The company had yet to close on acquisitions totaling $584 million in 36 markets, including 11 stations from Clear Channel and 35 stations from Connoisseur Communications.

In April the company issued revised annual reports for 1998 and 1999. Its net loss for 1999 was revised from $20.8 million to $13.6 million. Its net loss for 1998 was restated from $13.7 million to $8 million, after the company found a $4.9 million tax benefit that had been underreported.

The company's stock fell below $9 in April. After its accounting firm, PricewaterhouseCoopers, resigned on April 24, Cumulus needed to restore the confidence of Wall Street analysts and investors. The company was also in the process of expanding and training the advertising sales staffs at its more

| **Key Dates:** |
| --- |
| **1996:** The Telecommunications Act of 1996 removes ownership restrictions on radio stations. |
| **1997:** Cumulus Media, Inc. is founded in Milwaukee by Lewis W. Dickey, Jr., and Richard Weening, with financial backing from institutional investors. |
| **1998:** Cumulus Media goes public on June 26. |

than 300 radio stations. In May it hired a new CFO, Martin Gausvik, as well as a new auditor, KPMG LLP. Gausvik had previous experience as a financial executive at Jacor Communications and Latin Communications Group.

Pending acquisitions involving Clear Channel and Connoisseur Communications were both restructured. Connoisseur agreed to extend the closing of the $242 million deal until the third or fourth quarter of 2000. Clear Channel agreed to renegotiate the sale of 11 stations to Cumulus. The original cash payment of $147.5 million was reduced to about $36.6 million. In addition, Cumulus would swap 20 stations in four markets and a five-station cluster in Chattanooga, Tennessee. Later in the year, though, Cumulus failed to close on four of the stations in Harrisburg, Pennsylvania.

In June 2000 Lew Dickey was named president and CEO of Cumulus Media. His brother, John W. Dickey, was promoted to executive vice-president of Cumulus Media. The management realignment marked the end of the firm's ''acquisition-intensive start-up stage,'' according to executive chairman Weening. The company had made more than 100 acquisitions since 1997, resulting in clusters in 60 U.S. markets. Management would now begin to devote ''all of our energies toward making Cumulus a premier operating company in the industry,'' said Weening.

The company began to implement two restructuring programs. It planned to consolidate its headquarters and finance operations in Atlanta, Georgia, by October 1, 2000. Facilities in Milwaukee and Chicago would be vacated. Some 500 positions throughout the company were eliminated between April and August, some of them through attrition in the sales force and by cutting part-time air staff. The company also discontinued the operations of Cumulus Internet Services. As a result of these changes, the company took a one-time charge of $9.3 million for the second quarter of 2000.

Additional station swaps were made between Cumulus and Clear Channel later in the year. In September 2000 it was announced that Cumulus would swap 45 stations in eight markets for four stations in Harrisburg, Pennsylvania, and $55 million in cash. To this point Cumulus had swapped 105 stations in 18 markets with Clear Channel in exchange for 11 stations in five Clear Channel markets and $222 million in cash. Following these deals Cumulus would own or have under contract 225 radio stations, compared to 321 in March 2000.

As early as May 2000 executive chairman Richard Weening admitted, ''We grew too fast. These are the growing pains of a company that came together very quickly.'' While analysts agreed that the company's radio station properties remained

quite valuable, it nevertheless faced a number of challenges. With its stock trading at 52-week lows in September 2000 and its Moody's Investor Service's rating dropped from stable to negative, Cumulus needed to restore investor confidence. It was felt that this could be accomplished by closing on pending acquisitions and posting two or three quarters of strong cash flow. As it stood, however, the company was heavily in debt and short of cash to pay for previously announced acquisitions.

### *Principal Subsidiaries*

Cumulus Broadcasting, Inc.

### *Principal Competitors*

Clear Channel Communications, Inc.; Cox Radio, Inc.; Infinity Broadcasting Corp.; Citadel Communications Corp.; Emmis Communications Corp.; Saga Communications, Inc.; Radio One, Inc.

### *Further Reading*

Bachman, Katy, ''Clouds over Cumulus,'' *Mediaweek,* March 20, 2000, p. 6.

——, ''Wall Street Remains Cautious on Cumulus,'' *Mediaweek,* March 27, 2000, p. 4.

Brown, Sara, ''Cumulus Taking Itself Public,'' *Broadcasting & Cable,* April 13, 1998, p. 64.

''Cumulus Media Inc.'s Stock Price Perked up Last Tuesday,'' *Broadcasting & Cable,* May 15, 2000, p. 72.

''Dickey Moves Cumulus to Atlanta,'' *Mediaweek,* June 12, 2000, p. 5.

Furrell, Greg, ''Cumulus Binge Continues,'' *Mediaweek,* July 27, 1998, p. 29.

''IPO Update: Cumulus Media Inc.,'' *Broadcasting & Cable,* July 6, 1998, p. 64.

Jones, Tim, ''Fall of Milwaukee-Based Media Empire Shows Perilous Flip Side of Buying Frenzy,'' *Knight-Ridder/Tribune Business News,* May 26, 2000.

Kirchen, Rich, ''Cumulus Cancels Purchase of Four Stations in Pa,'' *Mediaweek,* July 31, 2000, p. 8.

Kirchen, Rich, ''Cumulus Goes Up-Market,'' *Business Journal-Milwaukee,* May 12, 2000, p. 26.

——, ''Cumulus Likes Small Towns in a Big Way,'' *Broadcasting & Cable,* November 2, 1998, p. 33.

——, ''Dark Clouds Cast Uncertainty over Cumulus,'' *Business Journal-Milwaukee,* March 24, 2000, p. 9.

——, ''Dispelling the Clouds,'' *Mediaweek,* September 11, 2000, p. 16.

Rathbun, Elizabeth A., ''Cumulus' Auditor Jumps Ship,'' *Broadcasting & Cable,* May 1, 2000, p. 12.

——, ''Cumulus' 'Minor' Misallocations,'' *Broadcasting & Cable,* March 27, 2000, p. 47.

——, ''Cumulus: Pie in the Sky?,'' *Broadcasting & Cable,* December 6, 1999, p. 58.

Saxe, Frank, ''Storm Clouds Gather over Cumulus Media,'' *Billboard,* April 1, 2000, p. 98.

Torpey-Kemph, Anne, ''Cumulus Rebuilds, Names New CFO,'' *Mediaweek,* May 22, 2000, p. 44.

Turner, Lance, ''Cumulus Accumulating,'' *Arkansas Business,* November 22, 1999, p. 30.

——, ''Strange Bedfellows,'' *Arkansas Business,* July 31, 2000, p. 34.

''What's Latin for Tanking?,'' *Broadcasting & Cable,* March 20, 2000, p. 14.

''WTMJ-AM,'' *Business Journal-Milwaukee,* December 31, 1999, p. 19.

—David P. Bianco

# Current, Inc.

1005 East Woodmen Road
Colorado Springs, Colorado 80920
U.S.A.
Telephone: (719) 594-4100
Fax: (719) 531-2329
Web site: http://www.currentcatalog.com

*Wholly Owned Subsidiary of Taylor Corporation*
*Incorporated:* 1947
*Employees:* 1,250
*Sales:* $231 million (1997)
*NAIC:* 323119 Other Commercial Printing; 454110
Electronic Shopping and Mail-order Houses; 511191
Greeting Card Publishers; 511199 All Other
Publishers

Current, Inc. sells social expression gifts, greeting cards, stationery, and a variety of related items by direct mail-order catalog and through the company's web site. Current manufactures many gift items and prints all paper products at its facilities in Colorado Springs. Paper products include everyday note cards, greeting cards for every holiday and occasion, gift wrap, stationery, rolled address labels, and related stationery items. Gift items include toys, women's and children's clothing, household decorative items, and household gadgets. Current mails 35 million catalogs to about six million customers annually.

### From a 1940s Cottage Industry to a Leader in Direct Mail-Order Marketing

Current, Inc. originated as Looart Press, a greeting card and stationery company started by Orin and Mariam Loo in 1947. A Swedish artist and lithographer, Orin worked at Hallmark Cards in Kansas City for ten years before moving his family to Colorado Springs for the cooler climate and a change. After a year as art director at a local stationery firm, Orin gathered his savings and borrowed $2,000 from his father-in-law to start his own company. He designed ten Christmas cards, which he displayed in a simple, black photo album from Woolworth's and presented for

sale to card shop owners in Colorado Springs. His second year in business Orin expanded the line to 17 card designs and generated $7,000 in sales. He also marketed Christmas cards to local companies and printed their names inside the cards.

The early years of the business were a constant struggle. The Loos operated the business from their home with a printing press in the basement. Orin used the family sunroom for an art studio and office and Mariam filled orders at the dining room table. Orin sought outside investment and finally managed to obtain a $5,000 bank loan to keep the business going. In 1950 Orin sold a 40 percent interest in the business to Danforth Killips, an investment banker in Evanston, Illinois.

Mariam started the mail-order end of the business in 1950 while trying to find a market for Orin's boxed note paper, called Post-a-Notes. She decided to try promoting card and stationery sales as a fund-raising activity for nonprofit organizations by offering the products at a low wholesale rate. Mariam mailed product samples to more than 400 church groups, primarily women's groups. The response was enthusiastic and the company's mail-order business took shape. Mariam added decorated recipe cards and designs to the note paper, eventually developing four designs each. She used an outside printer and boxed the orders at home. The Loo children delivered the orders to the post office after school.

The stationery and direct mail-order businesses grew and by 1960 the Loos regained complete ownership of the company. The two operations continued to operate from the Loo home until 1960, when they relocated operations for the first time. The Loos' two sons, Dusty and Gary, joined the company in 1962 and 1964, respectively. Current added new products, such as post cards, personalized stationery, calendars, posters, children's storybooks and coloring books, as well as gift items and home decorations, with many items being produced by the company. Continued growth required two more moves, until the company settled into new headquarters on Stone Road in 1968. The company expanded that facility twice within three years, adding 45,000 square feet of space for manufacturing and warehouse facilities, including a four-color press for in-house production. The executive offices were relocated to the new addition and the original offices were used for an art studio and a data processing center. Current invested $765,000 in the facility upgrade and $500,000 on new equipment.

### Renaming the Company in 1967

The structure of the company changed after Orin Loo retired in 1967. The two companies merged and the mail-order business took the name Current, Inc. Mariam chose the name for its implication of being contemporary. Looart Press became a holding company for the Current brand and mail-order business, forming two divisions, Looart Retail Products Division and Current Direct Mail Order Products. Eventually, the company dropped Looart and used only the Current name. The company also changed through the 1970 acquisition of American Stationery Company of Peru, Indiana. The addition of more than 40 direct mail-order products, including personalized stationery, Christmas cards, and related items, nearly doubled Current's annual sales.

When Mariam retired in 1970, her children persuaded her to write a cookbook for the company's mail-order catalog. Using her own family recipes, she wrote *Mariam B. Loo's Family Favorites*. The cookbook sold more than 600,000 copies, prompting Mariam to write another cookbook. She rented a test kitchen from a local cooking teacher whom she hired to test recipes. After a visit to the test kitchens of Betty Crocker and *Sunset* magazine, Mariam added two more home economists and two more test kitchens where new recipes were created for more than a dozen more cookbooks over the next decade. The cookbooks featured economical, family cooking; titles included *Meals of Many Lands*, with recipes that children could prepare. Mariam also designed 17 recipe calendars.

By the late 1970s the company required additional operating space and constructed a new facility on Woodmen Road on 112 acres. Completed in 1979, by 1981 Current doubled the warehouse space. The company set up a fast and efficient order-filling system involving 4,000 feet of conveyer belts that transported shipping boxes to employees who filled the orders from computer-generated order forms.

The company grew dramatically in the early 1980s. In 1981 Current opened its first retail store in Phoenix, OWLS Stores, Inc.; the fourth store opened in the company's home city, Colorado Springs, in 1985. Hoping to broaden its customer base beyond women over 30 with children, Current doubled its product offering in the 1984 Christmas catalog to more than 800 items, most of them produced by Current. New products involved license agreements to use Crayola and Cabbage Patch Kids themes. The company purchased a new six-color press, which printed more than 1.4 million sheets of various paper products each week. In 1986 Current began a successful new enterprise, selling checks to consumers by direct mail.

The company mailed six different full-color catalogs each year to more than six million customers. Current's method of catalog distribution was based on the purchasing history of each customer. Low volume customers received fewer catalogs each year than high-volume customers. The system also matched product offerings in each catalog to a customer's product preferences. With more than 1,000 employees, Current filled more than three million orders per year, most just before Christmas when the company employed about 1,500 workers. With annual sales at more than $100 million, Current had become the largest direct mail marketer of greeting cards, stationery, gifts, and related products. Current's unusually low prices, for a direct mail marketer, suggested unseen potential for other mail-order businesses.

### New Ownership in the Late 1980s

The company continued its successful growth during its first years under new ownership. The Loo family sold Current to American Can in late 1986 for $114 million. Barely more than a year later, that company sold Current to Deluxe Check Printers for $180 million. Deluxe expected the market for checks to slow, being a mature business, and sought to diversify into similar businesses. Current, Inc. formed the Consumer Specialty Products Division at the company, renamed Deluxe Corporation.

During Current's first full year under Deluxe, 1989, sales increased 18 percent to $187.7 million. During that year Current distributed 43 million catalogs to more than six million customers. In 1989 the company received 6.4 million customer orders, resulting in the shipment of more than 59 million units. Current produced about two-thirds of its product line, 2,000 different items, with all greeting cards, gift wrap, and other printed products produced in-house. In 1989 Current received an award from the Shop-at-Home Directory for overall customer satisfaction.

National economic matters challenged Current's profitability. The company averted a potentially slow holiday shopping season as national recession threatened in 1990. Current reduced the minimum order from 16 units to 12 units and sought new customers through customer list rentals and newspaper advertising. The company also added new paper stock, new products, and new product designs. Sales increased 16 percent despite the recession. By 1991 and 1992 the recession quickened and sales growth dropped significantly, although overall sales did not decline. Income did decline, however, due to a postal increase in February 1991. The company reduced the size and weight of its catalogs as well as the number of catalogs mailed by fine-tuning its target marketing. Sales promotions also helped to increase revenues and unit sales.

Areas of growth included new specialty products, such as an unusual line of greeting cards, Say Anything Cards. School Matters featured teaching aids and classroom rewards. A major area of growth involved direct mail checks. Current was the largest supplier of direct mail checks, with more than 20 check styles, such as the popular Elvis check set introduced in 1993. In 1994, the company added a line of checks for small businesses.

Deluxe's ownership of Current affected Current in a variety of ways. Deluxe purchased Paper Direct, a direct mail marketer of paper and software to desktop publishers, and combined printing and order fulfillment operations with Current operations at the Woodmen facility. Sales at Current slowed while expenses rose, including the cost of paper and newspaper insert advertising, and a ten percent increase in postal rates. In an attempt to improve profitability, Deluxe initiated an employee buyout in February 1995, offering incentive packages to 550 salaried employees. Several hourly employees and 93 salaried employees, including two vice-presidents, accepted the buyout. A year later Deluxe laid off 26 employees at Current's marketing department. Some manufacturing positions were eliminated when Deluxe discontinued production on unprofitable products, but losses continued.

Deluxe reported decreasing earnings for 1995, prompting the company to reevaluate its operations. In 1996, the Deluxe board approved the sale of Current's "social expressions" mail-order business, as the company's focus shifted to providing bank-related financial services. Deluxe intended to keep the direct mail check business, which continued to grow and complemented the company's original check printing operations. Deluxe packaged Current with Paper Direct for sale, taking a $112 million write-off for the lower book value of these companies, based on an outside evaluation.

Deluxe received four unsatisfactory bids and took the companies off the market in early 1997. The difficulty in obtaining an attractive offer related to the inconsistent profitability of the two companies in recent years, primarily Paper Direct's losses, and the overlap of Current's check printing and social expressions operations in facilities and personnel. Deluxe began to separate the check printing and social expressions operations in preparation for a future sale, leaving Current with approximately 1,000 permanent employees, 1,250 when combined with Paper Direct employees. Deluxe took a $140 million write-down in October 1997, valuing Current for its assets only.

Current was in a kind of exile, as the parent company did not want to invest in Current but wanted it to remain profitable as an attractive purchase for another company. Jon Medved left the company as CEO and chairman in 1995, creating a void in leadership until Lee Meyer, a long-time Current employee, was appointed president of both Current and Paper Direct in July 1997. In the meantime sales dropped to $231 million for the two companies combined, a loss of $4.2 million. Although most of the sales originated with Current, all of the losses originated with Paper Direct. Meyer implemented several cost-cutting measures and improved sales. Profits improved at Current, but remained elusive at Paper Direct. After a potential sale of the two companies fell through in July 1998, Deluxe considered selling Paper Direct separately from Current, but faced the problem of overlapping operations in manufacturing and order entry.

### Another New Parent Company in the Late 1990s

In December 1998, the Taylor Corporation purchased both Current's social expressions business and Paper Direct. Deluxe retained Current's check printing division, renamed Direct Checks Unlimited, and Current became the second largest company at the Taylor Corporation, a privately held company. Founded by Glen Taylor in 1975, the Taylor Corporation comprised more than 70 specialty printing and mail-order businesses located in North America, Europe, and Australia. Glen Taylor, who owned 87 percent of the company, was known for buying printing and direct mail companies with the potential to be made profitable. Each company operated under its own name and generated an estimated combined sales of $1 billion for the Taylor Corporation.

Based in North Mankato, Minnesota, Current's new parent company brought new executive management to Current, with Mike Lloyd as president. Lloyd immediately initiated new cost controls, such as the layoff of 140 employees, including many who had been with the company for several years. Lloyd then had to establish positive relationships with the managers and employees who remained. He reinstated Current's previous practice of quarterly manager meetings, beginning with a discussion in which managers determined core company values: trust, communication, accountability, clear focus, the value of people, and teamwork. Lloyd also instituted semi-annual meetings with employees and an open-door policy, encouraging employees to approach him with their concerns and comments. Lloyd moved his office to the main floor of company headquarters at Woodmen Road.

In August 1999 Taylor Corporation acquired Artistic Direct, Inc., formerly Artistic Greetings, and combined part of the company with Current. Artistic Direct's main business involved rolled address labels sold through newspaper inserts. The combination of Artistic Direct and Current's address label business made Current the second largest manufacturer of rolled address labels in the country. Taylor Corporation consolidated label operations with Current, creating 100 new jobs, and combined Artistic Direct's mail-order business with another Taylor-owned company.

Lloyd implemented a number of strategies to improve business operations at Current. The company invested in Current's Internet site, leading to an increase in customer orders, which accounted for five percent of 1999 sales. The company added new products, such as women's and children's clothing and children's toys, to attract younger customers. A new line of greeting cards and gifts involved Christian themes. Current returned to the business of printing and distributing personalized checks, this time for other vendors. Capital improvements included a $500,000 rewire and upgrades to Current's call center and structural improvements at the Woodmen Road headquarters. The company planned to build a 200,000-square-foot manufacturing center in Colorado Springs.

### *Principal Competitors*

Lillian Vernon Corporation; Fingerhut Companies, Inc.

### *Further Reading*

"American Can Acquires Looart," *Wall Street Journal,* December 31, 1986, p. 18.

Bean, Joanne, "Check It Out—Current Splits Businesses," *Colorado Springs Gazette-Telegraph,* July 23, 1997, p. B1.

——, "Current Considers Split Sale/Parent Company Is Rethinking Its Strategy to Market Social Expressions Division and Paper Direct," *Colorado Springs Gazette-Telegraph,* August 1, 1998, Bus. Sec., p. 1.

——, "Current Firm Up for Grabs/Bidding Reopens After Deal for Springs Catalog Business Fizzles," *Colorado Springs Gazette-Telegraph,* July 10, 1998, Bus. Sec., p. 1.

——, "Current Living Life in Limbo, Still for Sale," *Colorado Springs Gazette-Telegraph,* April 27, 1997, p. F1.

——, "Current Off Bidding Block/Parent Company Says Offers for Catalog Business Were Too Low," *Colorado Springs Gazette-Telegraph,* April 22, 1997, p. D1.

——, "Current Will Dominate Address Label Market After Artistic Deal," *Colorado Springs Gazette-Telegraph,* August 31, 1999, Bus. Sec. p. 1.

——, "Current Won't Reveal Buyer," *Colorado Springs Gazette-Telegraph,* April 24, 1998, Bus. Sec., p. 1.

——, "Keeping the Workplace Current," *Colorado Springs Gazette-Telegraph,* November 14, 1999, Bus. Sec., p. 1.

——, "President of Current Resigns/Medved's Move Not Expected," *Colorado Springs Gazette-Telegraph,* June 27, 1995, p. D1.

Crosi, Jerome R., "Current Inc., Started Small, But Grew Big; Springs Mail-Order Firm Has $100 Million in Sales," *Rocky Mountain Business Journal,* January 28, 1985, p. 4.

"Current Managers to Resign as Taylor Corp Takes Over," *Colorado Springs Gazette-Telegraph,* December 11, 1998, p. BUS1.

"Deluxe Closes $180 Million Purchase," *Wall Street Journal,* January 5, 1988, p. 8.

"Deluxe Cuts Selling Price/Tax Writeoffs Trims $110 from What's Expected When Two Springs Businesses Are Divested," *Colorado Springs Gazette-Telegraph,* January 2, 1997, p. E6.

Heilman, Wayne, "Orin Loo, Springs Philanthropist, Founder of Current, Inc., Dies at 97/Self-Made Millionaire Fondly Remembered," *Colorado Springs Gazette-Telegraph,* October 5, 1996, p. A1.

Hirschman, Dave, "After a Buyout, Current Adapts to Marketplace," *Colorado Springs Gazette-Telegraph,* June 2, 2000, p. BUS1.

Mallory, Jim, "Springs Business Honoree: Gary Loo," *Denver Post,* October 26, 1996, p. D3.

Melrose, Frances, "Card Firm Is Family Success Tale," *Rocky Mountain News,* May 11, 1981, p. 15.

Raylesberg, Iris, "Colorado Springs Paper Plant Taking Part in 'Greening' of America," *Colorado Springs Business Journal,* April 8, 1994, p. 11.

—Mary Tradii

# DePuy Inc.

**700 Orthopaedic Drive**
**Warsaw, Indiana 46581-0988**
**U.S.A.**
**Telephone: (219) 267-8143**
**Toll Free: (800) 366-8143**
**Fax: (219) 267-7196**
**Web site: http://www.depuy.com**

*Wholly Owned Subsidiary of Johnson & Johnson*
*Incorporated:* 1895
*Employees:* 3,220
*Sales:* $770.2 million (1997)
*NAIC:* 339112 Surgical and Medical Instrument
    Manufacturing (pt)

DePuy Inc., a Johnson & Johnson company since 1998, is a leading designer, manufacturer, and distributor of orthopaedic devices and supplies. Founded in 1895, DePuy is the world's oldest orthopaedic company, and it operates through five distinct divisions—DePuy Orthopaedics, DePuy ACE, DePuy AcroMed, DePuy CMW, and DePuy International. DePuy Orthopaedics, which produces hip and extremity implants, knee implants, environmental protection products, and surgical equipment, is the company's core, accounting for more than half of its total revenues. DePuy Orthopaedics' joint replacement products, such as its pioneering AML Total Hip System and LCS Total Knee System, have been particularly successful. DePuy ACE produces specialty orthopaedic trauma products, and DePuy AcroMed has made great strides in the lucrative spinal implants and instruments market. DePuy CMW produces bone cement. DePuy's global arm—DePuy International—also has grown tremendously as the company seeks to expand its overseas sales.

### A More Comfortable Splint: 1895–1965

Traveling pharmaceutical salesman Revra DePuy founded DePuy Manufacturing in 1895 in Warsaw, Indiana, to produce a fiber splint he had devised to set broken bones. Prior to DePuy's innovation, splints were made from uncomfortable and cumbersome pieces of hard wood resembling barrel staves. DePuy's alternative sold well, and the company gradually added slings, neck collars, and braces to its product offerings.

After DePuy's death in 1921, the company changed hands a number of times. DePuy's widow, Winifred, ran the business by herself until 1924, when she married Herschel Leiter, who had previously been a salesman with the company. The couple ran DePuy for the next 25 years. In 1926, former DePuy salesman (and Revra DePuy's first hire) Justin O. Zimmer made overtures about buying the business but was rebuffed. In response, Zimmer launched a rival orthopaedic company, Zimmer Manufacturing, which would become DePuy's greatest business rival and a leader in the orthopaedics field.

Leiter assumed sole control of DePuy upon Winifred's death in 1949. He married Amrette Webb Ailes shortly thereafter. Leiter's death in 1950 threw the company into a state of near-crisis, as Leiter had promised to leave control of the company to its salesmen but actually bequeathed it to his new wife instead. An ownership battle raged until 1951 when Amrette and her new husband, former Bell Telephone executive Harry Hoopes, prevailed. For the next 14 years, the Hoopeses ran the company as their personal fief. Although DePuy continued to post annual profits, Amrette and Harry were suspected of diverting company funds for their own purposes. DePuy's products—which by this time included soft goods, splints, bone plates, and screws—remained popular (1950 sales alone hit $3.2 million), but the company made few capital investments and Zimmer Manufacturing soon surpassed it as the industry leader.

### Changes in Ownership: 1965–74

In 1965 DePuy was sold to a group of investors led by Bill Weaver of Brown Brothers Harriman & Co. of New York. The deal was engineered by DePuy's executive vice-president, Keaton Landis. "I was pretty much running [the company] anyway," Landis told the author of *One Hundred Years of Orthopaedic Excellence.* "I wanted it placed with someone with business sense who would make it grow, rather than bleed it." The investor group selected Landis as DePuy's new president and gave him the formidable task of turning the company around. As a company executive noted in *One Hundred Years of Orthopae-*

dic Excellence, "We had gotten way behind in the orthopedic business. . . . The orthopedic industry was beginning to take off, and Zimmer was four times larger than we were." DePuy's new owners pledged to invest in new product research and development and Landis immediately increased DePuy's sales force.

DePuy changed ownership again in 1968, when Bio-Dynamics, Inc., a blood diagnostic business, acquired it. The transaction was beneficial to both parties; Bio-Dynamics needed a substantial sales force such as DePuy's, and DePuy was in dire need of capital. "We were underfinanced and we wanted to continue the growth pattern," Robert Williams, who was named president of DePuy in 1969, told the author of *One Hundred Years of Orthopaedic Excellence*. Bio-Dynamics financed DePuy's 1968 acquisition of the exclusive rights to market a hip replacement invented by Dr. Maurice Müller. This transaction enabled DePuy to enter the emerging and highly lucrative replacement segment of the orthopaedics market.

Major replacement surgeries were not possible until the late 1960s, when methyl methacrylate (a cement that holds artificial bones in place) was approved by the Food and Drug Administration (FDA) and became widely available. When DePuy gained the exclusive rights to market the Müller Total Hip, the company changed its image from a "soft goods" orthopaedic firm (selling rib belts, collars, braces, and some pins and wires) to a pioneer in the nascent joint replacement market, with profitable results. DePuy did not, however, abandon its established soft goods business. In 1968 the company purchased the Jackson, Michigan-based Kellogg Industries, a garment and

equipment manufacturer. DePuy transferred its soft goods production to Jackson, thereby freeing its Warsaw factory to concentrate on manufacturing total hip replacements.

### A New Era: 1974–90

Bio-Dynamics sold DePuy in 1974 to Boehringer Mannheim Companies, a privately held German pharmaceutical giant that was itself controlled by the holding company Corange, Ltd. (DePuy was not the only orthopaedic company in transition; arch-rival Zimmer was acquired by the Bristol-Myers Co. in 1972.) Under its new ownership, DePuy flourished, taking advantage of the resources and autonomy Boehringer offered. DePuy's primary achievement during this decade was its development (along with Dr. Charles Engh) of an artificial hip, the Anatomic Medullary Locking stem, that was the first to incorporate biological fixation (the attachment of hip prostheses by human tissue rather than artificial fixants such as methyl methacrylate). In 1977 DePuy began marketing the product under the brand name AML, which quickly became one of the company's best-selling items and remained a flagship product into the 21st century.

In 1979 the company gained the rights to use a new technology—a method of sintering a porous surface to orthopaedic implants, thereby allowing human tissue to be more effectively fixed—devised by Canadian Oxygen, Ltd. Marketed as Porocoat Porous Coating, the process became essential to DePuy's artificial joint business and boosted sales. In 1980 DePuy introduced its LCS Total Knee System, an artificial knee that used mobile (rather than fixed) bearings to duplicate more closely the mechanics of a healthy human knee.

During the 1980s, DePuy also benefited from the continued expansion of the U.S. healthcare industry. James Lent, who had accrued considerable industry experience as the president of Johnson & Johnson's orthopaedic division, took over as company president in 1985 after Robert Williams's retirement. Williams's tenure had been a successful one, during which DePuy grew from ten to 300 employees. 1985 revenues alone topped $95 million. Lent oversaw a period of even greater expansion, as DePuy introduced a slew of new products, including the AMK Total Knee System, the Global Total Shoulder System, and the Solution System.

Lent also pushed the venerable company to diversify its focus beyond orthopaedic products and joint replacements. To achieve this goal DePuy teamed up with E.I. duPont de Niemours and Co. (DuPont) to combine DuPont's superior research, development, and engineering divisions with DePuy's established position in the orthopaedic products market. This DePuy DuPont partnership, inaugurated in 1989, led to DePuy's production of environmental protection devices, such as Life Liner gloves. These glove liners were made from Kevlar and protected healthcare workers from possibly dangerous cuts and needle sticks.

### New Strategies in Era of Managed Care: The Early 1990s

Lent changed offices in 1990, becoming DePuy's chairman and chief executive officer. Mike McCaffrey, also formerly at Johnson & Johnson's orthopaedics division, succeeded Lent as

## Key Dates:

**1895:** Revra DePuy founds DePuy Manufacturing in Warsaw, Indiana.

**1921:** Revra DePuy dies; his wife Winifred takes control of the company.

**1949:** Winifred dies, and passes control of company to her second husband, Herschel Leiter; Herschel Leiter marries Amrette Webb Ailes.

**1950:** Leiter dies.

**1951:** Amrette Leiter marries Harry Hoopes; the couple run DePuy jointly.

**1965:** A group of investors, led by Bill Weaver, purchases DePuy from the Hoopeses.

**1968:** DePuy is acquired by Bio-Dynamics; DePuy enters hip replacement sector; DePuy purchases Kellogg Industries.

**1974:** DePuy is acquired by Boehringer Mannheim Companies (owned by Corange Ltd.).

**1987:** DePuy forms a partnership with E.I. duPont de Niemours and Co.

**1990:** Boehringer Mannheim purchases Charles F. Thackray Ltd.

**1992:** DePuy forms alliance with Genentech, Inc.; DePuy acquires the Rotek Company.

**1993:** DePuy enters into a joint venture with Biedermann Motech dubbed DePuy Motech.

**1994:** Corange purchases ACE Medical Products and forms new company, DePuy ACE Medical Co.

**1996:** DePuy acquires Landanger-Camus; Corange announces an IPO for DePuy.

**1998:** Roche Holding Ltd. purchases Corange in a transaction that includes DePuy; DePuy acquires AcroMed Corp., thereby becoming the world's second largest spinal implant company; Johnson & Johnson purchases DePuy from Roche.

president. McCaffrey continued Lent's diversification efforts, but was faced with a new obstacle—massive changes in the U.S. healthcare industry. After the boom years of the 1970s and 1980s, the American healthcare landscape changed radically in the early 1990s with the advent of managed care companies, which used their size to negotiate bulk rates for medical treatment so as to contain costs. *Health Industry Today* succinctly explained the situation: "Buying groups, product standardization, and health care reform, led by the managed care movement, have chewed deeply into manufacturers' profit margins. The days of double-digit growth are gone, probably forever."

DePuy rushed to adapt, accelerating the pace of its diversification into new markets and products. As the *Indianapolis Business Journal* noted, DePuy's "strategy feature[d] a blizzard of acquisitions and joint ventures [to] extend DePuy's reach in domestic and foreign markets and expand its product line." By expanding, DePuy planned to achieve cost savings through greater economies of scale and to make itself a better fit for large health care buyers who preferred "one stop shopping" for products. As part of this plan, DePuy acquired the Rotek Corporation in 1992. After the purchase, DePuy broadened Rotek's roster of environ-

mental protection products (which already included the Vacu-Mix bowl and Sterile View hoods and helmets), adding more Sterile View items, Repel and Life Liner Glove Liners (designed in conjunction with DuPont), and the Opti-Con family of products. In 1992 DePuy also teamed up with biotechnology leader Genentech, Inc. to produce orthopaedic devices that incorporated Transforming Growth Factor Beta, a protein that can impact bone tissue growth and regeneration.

In 1993 DePuy ventured into the fastest-growing segment of the orthopaedics market, spinal implants, forming a joint venture with Biedermann Motech, a German manufacturer of such devices. The product of this collaboration—DePuy Motech Inc.—developed, manufactured, and marketed spinal implants. DePuy again broke new ground in 1994, as Boehringer Mannheim acquired ACE Medical Company, a manufacturer of orthopaedic products for the surgical repair of trauma injuries, and placed it under DePuy's control (where it was renamed DePuy ACE Medical Co.). With 1993 sales exceeding $35 million, ACE offered DePuy access to the lucrative trauma products market. In 1994, DePuy added yet another company to its family of businesses when it purchased Orthopedic Technology for $46.2 million. A manufacturer of external braces for sports medicine, Orthopedic Technology also bolstered DePuy's position in the "soft goods" market.

During this period, DePuy looked to expand abroad as well. In April of 1990, Boehringer Mannheim had acquired Charles F. Thackray Limited of Leeds, England. Since 1963, Thackray had been one of the largest manufacturers of total hip replacements in the world and had distributorships and sales staffs in 100 countries. Indeed, Thackray sold 18 percent of all replacement joints worldwide, making it an excellent platform from which DePuy could increase its international reach. In November of 1991, DePuy made Thackray its international headquarters and rechristened it DePuy International Ltd. William Tidmore (who would go on to replace Mike McCaffrey as DePuy's president in 1994) was named the new entity's first president. "From our base in Leeds, we plan to develop our business and to extend out market share . . . in Europe and other international markets," Tidmore explained in *DePuy Ink* (a company publication) in 1992.

Throughout the first half of the 1990s, DePuy created a bevy of subsidiaries to further its global growth, establishing operations in France and New Zealand in 1990, in Australia and South Korea in 1991, in Germany, Italy, Japan and Spain in 1992, and in Portugal and India in 1994. DePuy also made major changes to its distribution system in Latin America. These efforts yielded tremendous results. International sales had accounted for only five percent of total sales in 1984, but represented 35 percent of DePuy's sales by 1995.

### Rapid Growth in the Mid-1990s

DePuy's pace of expansion quickened further in the mid-1990s. Corange partially spun off DePuy in 1996, selling 15.8 percent of the company in an initial public stock offering that raised $258 million (funds that DePuy earmarked for future acquisitions). Michael Dorner was installed as DePuy's newest president the same year.

Flush with capital, DePuy bought Landanger-Camus, the leading French manufacturer of hip implants and one of that nation's primary distributors of orthopaedic devices and supplies, in 1997, As James Lent explained in a company press release, "The acquisition enhance[d] [DePuy's] position as #2 in the worldwide hip market . . . and provided a launching pad for further consolidation in Europe."

Another major change occurred that year as well. Roche Holding Ltd., one of the world's largest drug companies, purchased Corange for $11 billion. Roche, however, was more interested in Corange's diagnostics business than in DePuy's orthopaedic interests, and analysts predicted that Roche would quickly sell off this part of its new acquisition. Nonetheless, DePuy's position in the global orthopaedics market was impressive. By May of 1997, DePuy controlled a 17 percent share of the $7.3 billion orthopaedic market, second only to its old nemesis Zimmer.

In 1998 DePuy made a major acquisition when it purchased the Cleveland, Ohio-based AcroMed Corp. for $325 million. AcroMed was the world's second largest producer of spinal implants (with sales in 1997 of more than $90 million) and provided DePuy with the opportunity to command a greater share of that quickly growing market (which DePuy had initially entered with the formation of DePuy Motech in 1993). AcroMed not only manufactured a line of lucrative spinal implants, but had recently invented the Brantigan I/F Cage, a carbon-fibre reinforced spinal fusion cage, and had the AcroFlex artificial disk in development. AcroMed was renamed DePuy AcroMed and became known as the world's second largest spinal implant company.

### A Johnson & Johnson Company: 1998 and Beyond

DePuy itself was bought by Johnson & Johnson for $3.5 billion in November 1998. Johnson & Johnson then merged its own orthopaedic business, Johnson & Johnson Professional, into DePuy, creating the world's largest orthopaedic products company, formally known as "DePuy, Inc., a Johnson & Johnson Company." James Lent was selected to lead the combined operations, which were integrated rather seamlessly (aided by the fact that DePuy's top two executives were Johnson & Johnson veterans and that the two companies' product lines complemented rather than competed with one another).

Under Johnson & Johnson's guidance, DePuy shuttered its DePuy OrthoTech subsidiary in July of 2000. According to the *Stockton Record,* Johnson & Johnson planned to focus primar-

ily on orthopaedic implants and spinal and trauma products, and it wanted to scuttle its soft goods arm. DePuy continued to form alliances with other companies—especially in the realm of orthobiologics (tissue engineering for orthopaedics). In July of 2000, DePuy reached a distribution agreement with Etex Corporation for Etex alpha BSM (bone substitute material), which might prove useful for treating fractures and bone voids. The following month, DePuy obtained the exclusive marketing rights to Biotty, Bio-Technology General Corp.'s proprietary product for the treatment of knee pain associated with osteoarthritis.

DePuy's future prospects looked bright. The company had diversified to the point that 50 percent of its sales in 1999 occurred outside the United States. By actively pursuing the emerging field of orthobiologics, DePuy was laying claim to cutting-edge technology for the future. Furthermore, as the massive baby boomer generation aged, DePuy could look forward to a growing market for its orthopaedic implants.

### Principal Divisions

DePuy Orthopaedics; DePuy ACE; DePuy AcroMed; DePuy CMW; DePuy International.

### Principal Competitors

Biomet, Inc.; Bristol-Myers Squibb Company; Exactech, Inc.; Medtronic Sofamor Danek, Inc.; Orthofix International N.V.; OrthLogic Corp.

### Further Reading

"DePuy Orthopaedics Inc: From Barrel Staves to High-Tech Hips," *Machine Design,* September 23, 1999.
"DePuy to Buy AcroMed," *Financial Post,* March 21, 1998.
Eckert, Toby, "1997 Indiana 100: DePuy Plots Strategy to Survive the Challenges of Managed Care," *Indianapolis Business Journal,* May 19, 1997.
Fujii, Reed, "Employees of Tracy, Calif.-Based Sports Medicine Company Laid Off," *Stockton Record,* July 8, 2000.
"It All Started with a More Comfortable Splint," *South Bend Tribune,* July 26, 1998.
Lamirand, Bob, *One Hundred Years of Orthopaedic Excellence,* Warsaw, Ind.: DePuy Inc., 1995.
"Numbers Remain Impressive in a Mature Hip and Knee Market," *Health Industry Today,* March 1, 1998.

—updated by Rebecca Stanfel

*Don Massey Cadillac*

# Don Massey Cadillac, Inc.

---

**40475 Ann Arbor Road**
**Plymouth, Michigan 48170**
**U.S.A.**
**Telephone: (734) 453-7500**
**Fax: (734) 453-6680**
**Web site: http://www.donmasseycadillac.com**

*Private Company*
*Incorporated:* 1961
*Employees:* 1,525
*Sales:* $979.9 million (1998)
*NAIC:* 44111 New Car Dealers; 44112 Used Car Dealers;
  81111 Automotive Mechanical and Electrical Repair
  and Maintenance

---

Don Massey Cadillac, Inc. operates one of the top auto dealership groups in the United States, as well as the world's number one Cadillac dealership at its home base of Plymouth, Michigan. Six of Massey's other locations are also ranked among the top 40 Cadillac showrooms in the world. Massey dealers also sell Rolls-Royces, Bentleys, Buicks, Oldsmobiles, Pontiacs, Chevrolets, and Hondas. The company's 17 dealerships are located in Michigan, Colorado, Kentucky, Florida, North Carolina, California, Tennessee, and Texas. Don Massey Cadillac has been owned since inception by the company's founder and namesake, who continues to serve as its president and CEO.

### Early Years

Don Massey was born in Lawrenceburg, Tennessee, just before the start of the Great Depression, and got his first taste of the automobile business at 14, when he worked for a summer at a Dodge dealership in Jacksonville, Florida. A decade later, married and living in Michigan, he entered the business full-time when he took a job selling used cars at a Wayne, Michigan, Desoto/Plymouth dealership. Massey was a natural salesman, and soon moved to a better job at nearby Paul McGlone Chevrolet, where he was promoted to Assistant Used Car Manager within a year, then was named General Manager a year after that.

Massey's tenure coincided with McGlone becoming the number one Chevrolet dealership in the world from 1958 to 1960.

In 1960 Massey was warned by his doctor that his health would deteriorate if he continued to maintain his heavy work load and bad eating habits. Deciding that he had no choice but to retire, he quit his job. However, after several months of relaxing and eating properly he found that he had improved enough to go back to work. This time he opened his own used car lot in Wayne, and the business was such a success that he was able to retire for good just five years later. Thinking he had sold his last car, he gave up the lot and moved to neighboring Plymouth, Michigan.

Massey quickly discovered that retirement didn't agree with him. As a way to stave off boredom, he decided to buy ''a little store that sold a couple hundred Oldsmobiles and fifty-sixty Cadillacs per year.'' He told *Automobile Dealer Magazine,* ''I thought that it would be the perfect retirement. . . . I'd work three to four hours a day, and take it easy, take care of my health. Well, I got here January 1, 1967, and a blizzard dropped three to four feet of snow right on top of us. While I was digging out to do inventory on New Year's Day, I sold seven cars. I don't recall getting home before nine o'clock any evening since.'' Within a few years Don Massey Cadillac had become the top-selling Cadillac dealership in the world, a position it would consistently retain. The company later branched out to sell Rolls-Royces and Bentleys as well.

Massey's sales ability was legendary. While working for McGlone Chevrolet, he once reportedly went in for a doctor appointment and ended up selling cars to the physician, the nurse, and the receptionist. On another occasion, when he was buying a house, he leased two cars to his realtor, sold a car to the home's former owner, and also sold three to his realtor's partners. Massey discussed his sales philosophy with *Automobile Dealer Magazine.* ''I think that a lot of salespeople are actually afraid that they are going to sell a car. Many salespeople walk up to a customer believing they are not going to sell that customer a car. Well, I believe that a customer is sold when they walk in. If we don't unsell them, they are going to leave in one of our cars. You have to take the time to acquaint yourself with the customer.'' His approach was not aggressive. ''I don't go straight for the wallet. I walk up, I talk to the customer, I try to get to know them and I listen [but] I never let them feel hurried, rushed, or pressured. . . . Many times I show them something that's more fitting to their needs and desires than what they were initially interested in. Usually, I make a friend.''

### Expansion in the 1980s

In 1981 Massey acquired the second dealership in what would eventually become a string of 20. Capitol Cadillac of Lansing, Michigan, 70 miles west of Plymouth, had been in business for many years, but its owners wanted to sell out. They contacted Massey, who made the drive over to Lansing and quickly decided to buy it. Some problems were encountered with integrating the second dealership into the organization, but ultimately both were able to function well together.

Several years later, Massey's wife Joyce was seriously injured in an automobile accident in Colorado. Massey stayed with her while she was undergoing a lengthy recuperation in a hospital near Denver. One day he experienced a minor problem with the rear end of the Chevy van he was using to transport her wheelchair, and he took it to a local Cadillac dealership for repair. He declared to the staff that he would rather pay a Cadillac dealer to fix it than have it worked on under warranty at a Chevrolet dealership, diplomatically omitting the fact that he had also gone there to satisfy his curiosity about how the place was run. After several hours the service manager reported, to Massey's surprise, that they could find nothing wrong with the vehicle. Explaining again what the problem was, and offering advice on how to diagnose and correct it, Massey went off to lunch with the dealer, whom he had befriended. Upon their return the service manager reported once again that there was nothing wrong with the van. Massey immediately turned to the dealer and said, ''Sir, why don't you sell me this place?'' The man was surprised at the sudden offer, but Massey told him that he thought the staff's poor work was tarnishing his reputation, and noted that the dealer looked like someone to whom this would be disagreeable. The man seemed to be taken aback by his bluntness, so Massey quickly left to rejoin his wife at the hospital. Several hours later, the dealer appeared, carrying his financial records. The sale was finalized in the spring of 1986.

Over the next decade other Cadillac dealerships were purchased around the country, including ones in Littleton, Colorado; Memphis and Nashville, Tennessee; Orlando, Florida; and Charlotte, North Carolina. In the latter city, Massey acquired two Cadillac/Oldsmobile dealerships that had been owned by golfer Arnold Palmer. At the same time Palmer also sold him a Chevrolet, Buick, and Geo dealership in Cave City, Kentucky,

and a Quincy, California, showroom that carried the full line of General Motors products. Later, other acquisitions were made in Englewood, Colorado; Downey, California; and Dallas and Houston, Texas.

Massey also opened three Saturn dealerships in the Detroit area after General Motors began to manufacture this new nameplate. The first debuted in the fall of 1990, with the other two appearing over the next several years. Also in Detroit, Massey purchased a local competitor, Dreisbach & Sons Cadillac, renaming it Massey Cadillac. Dreisbach was the only Cadillac dealership still located within the Motor City. In the fall of 1995 Massey Cadillac's Nashville dealership also opened a separate Honda showroom, the company's first association with a Japanese nameplate.

### A Philosophy of Minimal Interference

Massey's acquisitions were not micromanaged from above, but were generally allowed to operate much as they had previously done, so long as they were profitable. Personnel changes were kept to a minimum, with the exception of the departing dealer/owner who would be replaced by a new general manager. Massey tried to find a person for this position within the ranks of existing staff, if possible. Commenting on his acquisition philosophy, he told *Automobile Dealer Magazine,* ''In Cadillac, we already know we've got the right cars, so if we've got a reasonable location and if we've got the right people, we're going to win.''

Massey's salesmanship and personal involvement extended to the company's advertising, with the owner himself reading copy for radio commercials in his distinctive southern drawl. His down-home style proved a hit with listeners in the growing Detroit metropolitan area, which the town of Plymouth had become a part of in the decades since Massey first set up shop there. Other promotional efforts were as low-key, and included cosponsoring a Plymouth-area ice sculpture contest and holding a free barbecue cookout at the dealership on the Fourth of July. While waiting to have a car serviced at Massey's Plymouth dealership, a customer could get free coffee, a shoeshine, and even a haircut. The company's flagship store, which displayed 14 vehicles under a U-shaped skylight, also ran the New York Stock Exchange ticker above the entrance to the service department.

Offers to buy his company began to appear in 1998, as Don Massey neared the age of 70. One which was nearly consummated involved American Public Automotive Group of Indianapolis, Indiana of Indianapolis, Indiana, which offered a reported $300 million. The deal fell through, and American Public subsequently declared bankruptcy. Late in the year General Motors Corp. reached a deal with Massey to purchase all three of his Saturn dealerships. GM was reportedly seeking to create a group of 50 to 75 dealerships which could be spun off as a publicly owned company. The automaker also bought a Cadillac showroom in Ann Arbor, Michigan, from Massey in early 1999, but GM's offer to purchase the rest of the company's holdings was rejected. By this time Massey's annual sales were approaching the $1 billion mark.

At the beginning of the 21st century, Don Massey Cadillac remained one of the most successful auto dealer groups in the

---

### Key Dates:

**1961:** Don Massey opens a used car lot in Wayne, Michigan.
**1966:** Massey "retires," then buys a Cadillac dealership in Plymouth, Michigan.
**1981:** Company purchases Capitol Cadillac in Lansing, Michigan.
**1990:** First Saturn dealership opens.
**1998:** Massey sells its three Saturn dealerships to General Motors.
**1999:** Cadillac dealership is sold to GM; offer to buy entire company is turned down.

---

United States. With its owner at an age when many would retire, and with no designated successor in place, the company could go in either of several directions. But whatever its future held, Don Massey and the company he had founded had made their mark as leaders in the field of selling cars.

### Principal Subsidiaries

Don Massey Cadillac, Inc.; Capitol Cadillac Corporation; Don Massey Buick, Inc.; Massey Cadillac, Inc.; Crest Cadillac, Inc.; Massey Chevrolet, Inc.; Arngar, Inc.; PMO Motors of Kentucky; Joy Agency, Inc.; Massey Enterprises, Inc.

### Principal Competitors

AutoNation, Inc.; Avis Ford; CarMax Group; Hendrick Automotive Group; Mel Farr Automotive Group; Phil Long Automotive Group, Inc.; The Meade Group; Troy Motors, Inc.

### Further Reading

"Cadillac Dealer's Toughest Foe Soon Will Be His Own Dealership," *Detroit News*, January 17, 1996, p. B3.
Crain, Keith, "Holiday Retailing is a Picnic for the Cadillac King," *Crain's Detroit Business*, July 12, 1999, p. 6.
Roscoe, Michael, "The Extended Forecast . . . More Cadillacs!," *Automobile Dealer Magazine*, July/August 1996, pp. 20–28.
Roush, Matt, "Don Massey Buys Dreisbach & Sons Cadillac," *Crain's Detroit Business*, January 8, 1996, p. 3.
Sedgwick, David, "Dealer Pushes Cadillac Style," *Detroit News*, October 28, 1991, p. 7F.
——, "GM Bids for Big Dealer: Massey Heads $1 Billion Empire," *Automotive News*, February 15, 1999, p. 1.
——, "Massey: Selling His Stores?," *Automotive News*, November 16, 1998, p. 4.

—Frank Uhle

# Edelbrock Corporation

**2700 California Street**
**Torrance, California 90503**
**U.S.A.**
**Telephone: (310) 781-2222**
**Toll Free: (800) 416-8626**
**Fax: (310) 782-3828**
**Web site: http://www.edelbrock.com**

*Public Company*
*Incorporated:* 1938
*Employees:* 691
*Sales:* $121.17 million (2000)
*Stock Exchanges:* NASDAQ
*Ticker Symbol:* EDEL
*NAIC:* 336399 All Other Motor Vehicle Parts
 Manufacturing

Edelbrock Corporation manufactures and markets specialty performance automotive and motorcycle parts. Under the Edelbrock and QwikSilver brand names, the company sells intake manifolds, carburetors, camshafts, cylinder heads, exhaust systems, shock absorbers, and other components to used-vehicle owners seeking to improve the performance and efficiency of their cars and motorcycles. As such, Edelbrock Corp. competes in the automotive and motorcycle aftermarket, a market segment comprising parts that are purchased by consumers after they purchase their cars or motorcycles. Edelbrock Corp. operates its own sand-cast aluminum foundry in San Jacinto, California, and manufacturing, distribution, and warehouse facilities in Torrance, California. The two most important product lines in terms of revenue are high-performance carburetors and intake manifolds. In 1999, carburetors and manifolds accounted for 68 percent of total sales. Although the company's stock is traded on the NASDAQ National Market, the Edelbrock family owns nearly 50 percent of the company. Vic Edelbrock, Jr., the son of Edelbrock Corp.'s founder, has served as chairman, chief executive officer, and president since 1962.

## Origins

Edelbrock Corp.'s long-time position in the performance parts industry was established by Vic Edelbrock, Sr., a Kansas native with a passion for modified, high-performance, "hot rod" vehicles. Born in a small farming community in Wichita in 1913, Edelbrock began working full time at age 14, when his school days were cut short by a fire that razed his father's grocery store. Edelbrock was thrust into the position of having to help support his family. He found a job at an auto repair shop, where he first developed his skills as an automotive mechanic. Several years later, after the Great Depression had descended upon the nation, Edelbrock joined in the great exodus west, attracted, like thousands of Midwesterners, by promise of prosperity in California.

At age 18, Edelbrock arrived in California in 1931 to live with his brother. Two years later, Edelbrock married and soon went into business with his wife's brother. The pair opened a repair shop on Wilshire Boulevard in Beverly Hills, and, despite the bleak economic times, the business quickly flourished. After a year, in 1934, Edelbrock opened his own shop on the corner of Venice and Hoover in Los Angeles and, again, enjoyed a steady stream of customers. Edelbrock moved his shop three more times during the 1930s, with his reputation as an expert mechanic traveling with him. Edelbrock became a fixture within the regional racing community, working on cars during the day and spending his weekends racing at Muroc Dry Lake, the future site of Edwards Air Force Base. His stature within the circle of Los Angeles racing enthusiasts grew significantly after 1938, the year he bought a 1932 Ford roadster. The 1932 roadster became a proving ground on wheels for Edelbrock's product designs, a litmus test for the performance-enhancing automotive parts he would test at the dry lakes located 80 miles northeast of Los Angeles.

When Edelbrock bought the Ford roadster, he began designing a custom manifold, an automotive component used to direct fuel to the engine's cylinders. At first, he teamed up with a partner, Tommy Thickston, to develop the "Thickston" manifold, but Edelbrock was dissatisfied with the result. He designed his own, the "Slingshot" manifold, the first product to bear the Edelbrock name. As he would with other aftermarket parts,

Edelbrock tested his new manifold by racing with it at Muroc. He drove his modified 1932 roadster out to the dry lakes, removed the fenders and windshield, and then put them back on when he was finished racing. Using his Ford roadster to test the performance of his custom parts proved to be a marketing boon. At Murac, Edelbrock was a consistent winner, driving at speeds in excess of 120 miles per hour before the war. Competitors and onlookers soon learned of his Slingshot manifold, creating a rush of excitement and scores of new customers. Edelbrock built roughly 100 Slingshots during the course of the next three years, further etching the Edelbrock name into the minds of the racing community.

When the United States entered World War II, Edelbrock stopped racing and applied his talents to the prosecution of the war. Although the turn of events represented an interruption to Edelbrock's burgeoning business, the experience he gained during the war years exposed him to the capabilities of a wide array of machining tools. Edelbrock spent time welding at the Long Beach shipyards in Southern California and hand fabricating parts for aircraft. When the war ended, he turned his attention back to racing and to resuming the development of his business interests. He purchased his first building for his company in Hollywood and opened a machine shop and auto repair facility.

### Postwar Growth

Considering his love for racing, which had turned to midget car racing after the war, Edelbrock's auto repair business was always more of a performance parts shop than a repair shop. His company's first catalog, printed in 1946 and destined to become a marketing staple for the company throughout the century, declared as much, with "Edelbrock Power and Speed Equipment" emblazoned across the front cover. Edelbrock competed in midget races as often as six nights a week, touring throughout the Southern California racing circuit and showcasing his high-performance auto parts. To support his efforts on the track, Edelbrock bought one of the performance industry's first engine dynamometers in 1949, which enabled him to substantiate his racing results with data and point to measurable performance gains. Along with the dynamometer, the Edelbrock Equipment

Company, as the company was then called, also gained its first purpose-built facility in 1949. Containing 5,000 square feet, the building housed a small machine shop, repair bays, the engine dynamometer, a stock room, and office space, giving Edelbrock the space and the capabilities to flesh out his catalog of performance parts.

The company hit its stride during the 1950s, as Edelbrock focused all of his attention on fabricating components designed to add power and speed to automobiles. The company's parts were purchased by competitive racers and car hobbyists alike— by anyone who wanted to increase vehicle performance. Within this cross-section of mechanical sophisticates, the Edelbrock name was regarded with trust and respect, enjoying brand strength that could be applied to a host of products. The company's production selection broadened beyond its signature intake manifolds to include aluminum cylinder heads, flywheels, pistons, camshafts, adjustable tappets, and other parts. During this period of product expansion, Edelbrock parts appeared on the cover of magazines such as *Hot Rod*.

### 1962: From One Generation to Another

One era of leadership gave way to another when Vic Edelbrock died of cancer in 1962 at the age of 49. His son, 26-year-old O. Vic Edelbrock, Jr., inherited the Edelbrock legacy and the reins of command. The transition was smoothed considerably by the presence of the company's long-serving employees and support management, individuals who had started working for Vic, Sr., in the 1930s. Under his son's management—a tenure that would stretch into the 21st century—the company continued its leadership role in the design and development of performance parts. Vic, Jr., personified the company's esteem within the high-performance aftermarket industry, serving as the president of the Specialty Equipment Marketing Association from 1971 to 1974, but he did not earn the post because of his company's size. Relative to the industry's largest concerns, Edelbrock was a small company known more for its attention to product design and development than for its market dominance. The company remained as such during the first two decades of Vic, Jr.'s, leadership, content with catering to the needs of a specific and small clientele. A more ambitious Edelbrock Corp. emerged during the 1980s, as the company broadened its product selection and pursued a larger segment of the aftermarket.

Although Edelbrock Corp. continued to deliver automotive components sought after by racing enthusiasts, the company widened its target customer base to include those who frequented aftermarket retail shops for purposes other than racing. There existed a market segment of car owners who merely wanted to increase the performance of the efficiency of their vehicles, and Edelbrock Corp. tailored its strategic focus to address the needs of such customers. The company's product selection increased to include camshaft kits, valve train parts, exhaust systems, engine accessories, fuel system parts, and other performance parts. As a whole, Edelbrock Corp.'s product line represented what the company called its "Total Power Package" line. Customers could purchase components piecemeal, until they ultimately acquired the Edelbrock power package. The switch in strategy was significant, embellishing on the hot rod clientele with which the company had established its reputation. Although the Edelbrock name still registered as a

**Key Dates:**

**1938:** Vic Edelbrock, Sr., develops the Slingshot manifold.
**1946:** First product catalog is released.
**1962:** Vic Edelbrock, Jr., assumes control over the company.
**1994:** Edelbrock Corp. completes its initial public offering of stock.
**1995:** QwikSilver II, Inc. is acquired.
**1998:** Company introduces its first line of shock absorbers.
**2000:** Company enters the import aftermarket.

trustworthy choice for the aftermarket connoisseurs, the more inclusive market approach addressed a larger customer base, delivering a discernible boost to the company's financial totals.

Once the extension of the company's product line proved successful, Edelbrock Corp. began to develop the infrastructure to support the aggrandizement of the Edelbrock brand name. In 1987, the company moved its headquarters to Torrance, California, after spending 20 years in El Segundo, California. From there, Edelbrock Corp. made a move toward vertically integrating its operations, building its own sand-cast aluminum foundry in 1990. What followed was the continued extension of the company's product line, as the Edelbrock brand name was leveraged to support the sales of carburetors, aluminum cylinder heads, aluminum water pumps, and fuel-injected manifolds. The company manufactured approximately half of its own products, contracting with domestic manufacturers for the rest.

The latter half of the 1990s witnessed substantial physical expansion and strategic diversification, growth that for the first time in the company's history came under the eye of the investing public. In October 1994, Edelbrock Corp. completed its initial public offering of stock, raising $21 million for the expansion of its operations and the purchase of new equipment. The proceeds were put to use several months later when the company constructed a new 37,000-square-foot building in Torrance that expanded its exhaust products division, a producer of mufflers, tailpipes, and other exhaust related products. New construction also included the addition of a 15,000-square-foot building in San Jacinto, California, which was dedicated to warehouse space for the aluminum foundry.

As Edelbrock Corp. stepped up production capacity of its nearly 60-year-old automotive aftermarket business, the company also took its first steps into a new market. In 1994, the company began making a line of intake manifolds and aluminum cylinder heads for Harley Davidson motorcycles. The foray into the motorcycle aftermarket was strengthened with the March 1995 acquisition of QwikSilver II, Inc., an Apple Valley, California-based manufacturer of carburetors for Harley Davidson motorcycles. The $500,000 acquisition fleshed out the company's line so that it could offer a complete Harley Davidson aftermarket package. By the end of the company's fiscal

1995, revenues were up 26 percent to $67 million, an increase attributable, in large part, to the diversification into the motorcycle aftermarket.

Edelbrock pressed ahead with increasing manufacturing capacity following the QwikSilver acquisition. A new 45,000-square-foot building was constructed next to the company's exhaust facility in December 1996, followed by the construction of two smaller facilities located next to the foundry in San Jacinto. One of the new buildings, a 15,000-square-foot structure, became the new home for the QwikSilver business formerly based in Apple Valley.

In May 1998, Edelbrock Corp. entered another new market, introducing a line of aftermarket shock absorbers. Production of the shock absorbers was housed in the recently constructed building next to the company's exhaust manufacturing site in Torrance.

By the end of the 1990s, the company's aggressive expansion and willingness to enter new markets enabled it to reach a significant financial milestone. In 1999, the company eclipsed the $100-million-in-sales mark, posting $109 million in sales. Perhaps more important, the expansion and new product introductions had not tarnished the company's profit performance. Net income growth demonstrated encouraging vitality during the latter half of the decade, increasing from $6.4 million in 1996 to $8 million in 2000, when sales reached $121 million, more than twice the total recorded five years earlier. Further robust financial growth was expected in the years ahead, with the company basing much of its optimism on anticipated growth in the import aftermarket. In June 2000, Edelbrock Corp. acquired the exclusive rights to manufacture and sell internal engine, exhaust, and suspension components under the Edelbrock and JG name to the import aftermarket, providing a new substantial area of growth for the years ahead.

### Principal Subsidiaries

Edelbrock Foundry Corp.; Edelbrock II, Inc.

### Principal Competitors

Holley Performance Products, Inc.; Federal-Mogul Corporation; Rancho Industries; Harley Davidson, Inc.; S & S Cycle, Inc.

### Further Reading

"Edelbrock Corp. Reports Record Sales and Earnings for Fiscal Fourth Quarter and Year 2000," *Business Wire*, September 6, 2000, p. 0054.
Fine, Howard, "Slow But Steady Growth for Auto Parts Firm Edelbrock," *Los Angeles Business Journal*, February 15, 1999, p. 21.
Glover, Kara, "Sales Zooming for Car-Parts Specialist," *Los Angeles Business Journal*, July 24, 1995, p. 1.
Schonfeld, Erick, "Erector Sets for Hog and Car Lovers," *Fortune*, October 30, 1995, p. 227.

—Jeffrey L. Covell

# Edison Schools Inc.

**521 Fifth Avenue**
**New York, New York 10175**
**U.S.A.**
**Telephone: (212) 419-1600**
**Fax: (212) 973-0571**
**Web site: http://www.edisonschools.com**

*Public Company*
*Incorporated:* 1999
*Employees:* 3,868
*Sales:* $224.58 million (2000)
*Stock Exchanges:* NASDAQ
*Ticker Symbol:* EDSN
*NAIC:* 541611 Administrative Management and General
    Management Consulting Services; 61111 Elementary
    and Secondary Schools

Edison Schools Inc. is the leading for-profit manager of public schools in the United States. In July 2000 it was running 108 schools in 21 states, operating them under local school districts or charter-school boards. In return for administering these schools, Edison receives per-pupil funding generally comparable to that spent on other public schools in the same area.

### Launching the Edison Project: 1991–95

Christopher Whittle, a publishing entrepreneur who, in 1990, had introduced a commercial-sponsored television news program—entitled ''Channel One''—for high school students, established the Edison Project in 1991. It was funded by Whittle Communications L.P., in which Time Warner Inc., Philips Electronics N.V., and Associated Newspapers Holdings P.L.C. held the major stakes. The ambitious Edison Project endeavor aimed to design a new education system that would provide a better education than public schools. These for-profit schools would charge as tuition the average cost per pupil in public schools, but one-fifth of all students would receive full scholarships. The plan originally called for 200 ''campuses'' combining day care and pre-elementary education by the fall of 1996, at a cost

approaching $2.5 billion to $3 billion. One additional age group would be added each year. Whittle hoped to expand to 1,000 campuses, with an enrollment of two million students attending through high school, soon after the new millennium. His project also planned to contract services for public and private schools.

The Edison Project received instant credibility when it hired Benno C. Schmidt, Jr., president of Yale University, to become president and chief executive officer of the enterprise. ''The reason this hasn't been done before,'' Schmidt told the press on reaching his decision in May 1992, ''is that thing is a matter of D-Day dimensions. Only someone with a high tolerance for risk would even be willing to contemplate it.'' A blue-ribbon panel of educators and entrepreneurs already had been established by Whittle to explore every aspect of education and how to redesign American schools.

The concept developed leaned strongly on electronic technology, with all students supplied with a personal computer linked, by video-satellite network, to their teachers, other Edison schools, libraries, lecturers, newscasts, and interactive town halls. Textbooks would be online, with students taking home a two-page printout of the day's lessons instead of a backpack of books.

By 1993 Whittle Communications was in financial difficulty, and as a result the Edison Project dropped its private school approach, vowing instead to seek contracts from local school districts or state-sanctioned charter school boards to teach students in existing buildings. After more drastic economies, the company sold Channel One to K-III Communications Corp. in 1994 for about $240 million. This enabled Whittle Communications to avoid bankruptcy but effectively liquidated it by early 1995, following the sale of other divisions and properties.

The Edison Project was spun off as a separate venture, but Time Warner, which had lost $120 million of its $185 million investment in Whittle Communications, dropped out. Philips and Associated Newspapers, although declining to invest more money, stayed on as equal partners with Whittle, who had pledged to put up an additional $24 million. These funds were sorely needed, for, although the project had spent $40 million by the fall of 1994, it was in need of $25 million to $50 million more to buy computers, wire classrooms, hire teachers, and bring its first schools into operation by the fall of 1995. Only two contracts had been signed: to run a public school in Mount Clemens, Michigan, and a charter school in Boston. Schmidt reportedly tried to oust Whittle as chairman, without success.

The Edison Project was rescued from liquidation at the eleventh hour in December 1994, when Whittle sold his Manhattan East Side townhouse, his apartment in the Central Park West landmark Dakota building, a mansion in his native Tennessee, and most of his art collection. The $15 million infusion was initially applied to keeping the company afloat long enough to find a new partner to replace Philips and Associated Newspapers. In February 1995 the Sprout Group—the venture capital arm of Donaldson, Lufkin and Jenrette Securities Corp.—agreed to invest $12 million. Schmidt and two friends put up another $3 million. Whittle controlled or owned 75 percent of the stock but, at Sprout's insistence, had to step aside temporarily as chairman of the venture. Whittle replaced Schmidt as president in 1997 and chief executive officer in 1998, with Schmidt replacing Whittle as chairman in 1997. By midsummer 1999 the Edison project had raised $232 million from private placements, including capital from J.P. Morgan Investment Corp.

### Making Progress: 1996–98

When the academic year 1995–96 began, Edison was operating four schools: the ones in Boston and Mount Clemens, as well as schools in Wichita, Kansas and Sherman, Texas. The number expanded to 12 for the 1996–97 year and 25 for the 1997–98 year, when 13,000 children were enrolled in Edison-operated schools. By the beginning of the 1998–99 school year, the company doubled its scope, raising the number of schools operated to 51. Encouraging initial results were reported in the schools, which followed an educational plan that called for a school day at least one hour longer than usual and a school year of at least 200 days instead of the usual 180. The project also provided an Edison-owned computer in each student's home—linked to the company's local and national school networks—and reading and mathematics curricula developed by Johns Hopkins University and the University of Chicago, respectively. Most students were chosen through a lottery system.

By the end of the 1996–97 school year the Edison Project could point to some educational achievements. All but one of the eight local authorities that had extended contracts had expanded their relationships with the company. At the Dodge-Edison Elementary School in a poor part of Wichita, fifth graders raised their reading performance from the 46th to the 59th percentile nationwide, and from 35th to 64th in mathematics. Another survey reported that Edison kindergarten and first

grade students greatly exceeded students in a control group at two sites. Music, art and physical fitness were being taught every day, according to an Edison executive, and all students were studying Spanish, beginning in kindergarten. Critical observers, however, claimed problems with providing special education services at some Edison sites, difficulty in adapting to the company's complex design at others, and differing interpretations of the project's early test results.

Most of the administrators and teachers Edison was hiring were not union members. Interviewed by A.J. Vogl for *Across the Board,* company vice-president John Chubb said in 1998 that teachers were being paid initially "whatever they would've been making on a district scale . . . plus 8 percent to 10 percent for the extra time." Each year after that, he added, compensation was determined by merit increases and bonuses. Where hired by a charter board, Edison had complete freedom to establish compensation, but where answering to a public school district, compensation was constrained by whatever agreements had been worked with the district or with a union, if the teachers were organized. He conceded that teacher turnover was 24 percent, compared with about 15 percent for public schools.

Chubb called Edison's provision of a home computer to students crucial because it enhanced parent participation. Before taking a computer home, parents had to spend six hours of training at the school. Pupils also had access to computers in the classroom. "You want [the children] interacting, working with one another, learning from one another, using computers on a team or project basis," Chubb explained. "But then, if children go home and write their papers on a yellow pad or in a loose-leaf notebook, their computers are never going to be integral to their lives." Chubb said that parents supported the longer school day—eight hours for third grade and up—because it relieved them of much of the burden of after-school care and baby-sitting. He added that in the elementary schools, 90 minutes were being devoted to reading and 60 minutes to mathematics each day. Chubb said that the longer, 205-day school year was "attractive to working parents who need to find quality activities for their kids" and added that "disadvantaged children . . . tend to fall back more in the summer than middle-class kids, who tend to have academic reinforcement in the summer."

### Mixed Report Card: 1999–2000

At the beginning of the 1999–2000 academic year, Edison was in charge of 79 schools in 16 states and the District of Columbia, mostly under contract with traditional school districts but about 30 percent with organizations authorized to run charter schools. The company was receiving an average of about $5,500 per pupil, the same amount allotted, on average, to publicly run schools. In a November 1999 article appearing in the *Wall Street Journal,* Thomas Toch wrote that several Edison schools had failed, some had indeed poorly served special education students, many of the company's teachers had failed to apply its technology effectively, and most of the new schools that had opened in the fall of 1999 lacked books and supplies because of errors that resulted in Edison firing the entire purchasing staff. Cost-cutting had reduced the school year by ten days and led to scaling back the home computer program to begin in third grade instead of kindergarten. Because of low state spending, Edison had found it could not profitably operate schools in much of the South, California, and the Rocky Mountain states.

Nevertheless, Toch concluded that Edison students were performing better than others with similar backgrounds, that student attendance was generally high, and that dropout rates were low. Student achievement in basic subjects was being surveyed each month. Principals were being awarded performance-based bonuses by the company, and principals and teachers deemed to be doing poorly were being quickly fired. "Whatever Edison's flaws," he summed up, "the mostly disadvantaged kids on Edison's campuses are by and large in more attractive, safer schools with higher standards, more resources and a greater sense of purpose than the traditional public schools most would otherwise attend."

According to a *Time* article by John Greenwald published in March 2000, Edison was focusing on installing pride and discipline in its students, 60 percent of whom came from families with incomes below the poverty line. The company, he said, was only spending about 16 cents per dollar on administrative costs, compared with 20 to 30 cents for the typical school. (In a later *Washington Post* interview, however, Whittle gave the figure of 21 percent for Edison.) Greenwald reported Whittle's claims that Edison students had raised their results on standardized tests by an average of five percent a year and quoted Whittle as saying, "We either make it or don't make it on the basis of test scores."

By the beginning of the 2000–2001 school year, Edison Schools had signed contracts to run 30 more schools, including three low-performing ones in Baltimore taken over by the state of Maryland—this contract being the first the company had signed with a state government. Independent studies were said to have shown greater parental involvement and satisfaction with Edison schools than comparable neighboring public ones. The company reported that test scores among its students at 40 schools had risen by an average of seven percent during the previous school year.

On the other hand, a survey of the 1,100-student Boston Renaissance Charter School, which Edison started in 1995, found that examination scores had generally declined between 1996 and 1999. An evaluation of an Edison-run elementary school in Miami reported poorer than average results compared with students from neighboring schools. Minnesota state educators said that students at three Edison schools in Minneapolis and Duluth were scoring at or below average in reading and mathematics. A charter school study commissioned by the state of Michigan, where Edison was running more than 20 schools, was reported to have shown Edison schools trailing the others. An analysis of Edison test scores by teachers' unions, from data provided by state education officials, reported poor results in California and mixed ones in Colorado, Kansas, and Michigan, compared with similar schools. Edison officials also acknowledged a staff turnover rate of 18 percent.

While educators debated the Edison Project's academic performance, prospective investors were looking at an unpromising bottom line. Revenue from educational services grew from zero in fiscal 1995 (the year ended June 30, 1995) to $11.77 million in fiscal 1996 and $38.56 million in fiscal 1997. Edison had a net loss, however, of $14.13 million in fiscal 1997, $10.1 million in 1996, and $11.42 million in 1997. In fiscal 1998, revenues almost doubled again, to $69.41 million, but the project's net loss grew correspondingly, to $21.92 million. Revenues once again almost doubled in fiscal 1999, to $132.76 million, but the net loss for the year more than doubled to $49.43 million, a sum that included a $22 million charge to reissue stock options.

Despite this consistent red ink, the company, as Edison Schools Inc., announced in August 1999 its intention to issue an initial public offering of stock. The prospectus made for queasy reading, even stating, "We are not certain when we will become profitable, if at all." Edison was seeking to sell $172.5 million worth of common stock to the public, after which, according to Diane Brady of *Business Week*, "both Whittle and Schmidt are expected to walk away with millions." She concluded that the offering deserved a grade of D-. Edison Schools subsequently settled in November for net receipts of $109.7 million by selling 6.8 million shares at $18 a share. Earlier, during the summer, the company had sold a $30 million, 5.8 percent stake to Microsoft Corp. cofounder Paul Allen, through Allen's Vulcan Ventures, Inc.

Edison Schools had revenue of $224.58 million in fiscal 2000 and incurred a net loss of $36.59 million for the fiscal year. Company debt rose to $36.28 million, compared with $2.83 million in fiscal 1996. Officers and directors owned 49 percent of Edison's Class A common stock at the end of fiscal 2000, with Whittle holding 12 percent through his personally owned corporation, WSI Inc. He controlled about 30 percent of the voting shares.

### Principal Competitors

Bright Horizons Family Solutions Inc.; Nobel Learning Communities Inc.; TesseracT Group.

### Further Reading

Applebome, Peter, "For-Profit Education Venture to Expand," *New York Times*, June 2, 1997, p. 12.
——, "A Venture on the Brink: Do Education and Profits Mix?," *New York Times*, Sec. 1, October 30, 1994, p. 28.
Brady, Diane, "Chris Whittle's New IPO Deserves a D-," *Business Week*, September 6, 1999, p. 40.
Campanile, Carl, "A Mixed Report Card for Edison," *New York Post*, August 19, 2000, p. 2.

Carton, Barbara, "Edison Project Is Given New Financing in Move Reducing Role of Its Founder," *Wall Street Journal,* May 17, 1995, p. B7.

"The Education of Chris Whittle," *Psychology Today,* September/October 1997, pp. 31–33, 78.

Frauenheim, Ed, "Virtual Schoolhouse," *Village Voice Education Supplement,* August 1995, pp. 3–4, 22.

Greenwald, John, "School for Profit," *Time,* March 20, 2000, pp. 56–57.

Mathews, Jay, "New School of Thought: Making Education Pay," *Washington Post,* April 19, 2000, pp. E1, E4.

Sanchez, Rene, "Edison School Project Growing Slowly," *Washington Post,* August 22, 1997, p. A3.

Sontag, Deborah, "Yale President Quitting to Lead National Private-School Venture," *New York Times,* May 26, 1992, pp. A1, B8.

Stout, Hilary, "Whittle Lays Out Plans to Establish For-Profit Schools," *Wall Street Journal,* May 17, 1991, p. A10.

Symonds, William C., "For-Profit Schools," *U.S. News & World Report,* February 7, 2000, pp. 66, 72.

Tanner, Adam, "Edison Project's Future Hinges on Financing," *Christian Science Monitor,* December 22, 1994, p. 9.

Toch, Thomas, "Manager's Journal: Whittling Away the Public School Monopoly," *Wall Street Journal,* November 15, 1999, p. A50.

Trimble, Vance H., *An Empire Undone: The Wild Rise and Hard Fall of Chris Whittle,* New York: Carol Publishing, 1995.

Vogl, A.L., "Let There Be Light," *Across the Board,* May 1998, p. 39 and continuation.

Walsh, Mark, "Edison Project Spares No Cost in Wooing Prospective Clients," *Education Week,* October 14, 1998, pp. 1, 16.

—Robert Halasz

# Electric Lightwave, Inc.

4400 N.E. 77th Avenue
Vancouver, Washington 98662
U.S.A.
Telephone: (360) 816-3000
Fax: (360) 816-0998
Web site: http://www.eli.net

*Public Subsidiary*
*Incorporated:* 1990
*Employees:* 1,182
*Sales:* $187 million (1999)
*Stock Exchanges:* NASDAQ
*Ticker Symbol:* ELIX
*NAIC:* 513310 Wired Telecommunications Carriers

Since it was established in 1990, Electric Lightwave, Inc. has focused on providing alternative telecommunications access and services. It began as a competitive access provider (CAP), linking its business customers to their long-distance services. It later gained regulatory approval in certain western states to become a competitive local exchange carrier (CLEC). Since 1998 the company has been an integrated communications provider (ICP), offering high-volume business clients a full complement of telecommunications services.

### *Offering Alternative Access to Business Clients: 1990–93*

Electric Lightwave was incorporated on July 18, 1990, as a Delaware company by Citizens Utilities Co., which was headquartered in Stamford, Connecticut. The company's plan was to become a profitable alternative telecommunications provider for medium-sized metropolitan areas. It would provide companies with private access to their long-distance services over its own fiber-optic network, thus bypassing the local exchange networks. This took place before deregulation made such alternatives commonplace.

Before Citizens Utilities decided to invest in the idea, the two entrepreneurs who devised the business plan for the com-

pany—John Warta and Earl Kamsky—presented it to Portland [Oregon] General Electric (PGE), which declined to participate. Once Citizens Utilities became a major investor, Electric Lightwave was incorporated, with Warta as president and CEO and Kamsky as vice-president. The company began hiring its first employees in September 1990 and began construction of its first Metropolitan Area Network (MAN) in Portland, Oregon the next month. Citizens Utilities had net income of $93.7 million on revenue of $356 million in fiscal 1990 and provided the financing for Electric Lightwave's fiber-optic construction as well as any legal battles that might arise involving state regulatory agencies and local telephone utilities.

Electric Lightwave began providing service in Portland on January 1, 1991. In the second quarter of 1991 it began construction on its second MAN in Seattle, which became operative in December 1991, following approval from the Washington Utilities and Transportation Commission (WUTC). At that time local dial tone service in Seattle was provided by U.S. West Inc. and GTE Northwest Inc. Electric Lightwave provided commercial customers with fiber-optic connections to their long-distance carriers. Since its service bypassed local dial tone providers, the telephone utilities were concerned that it would eventually open up competition for local dial tone service.

In early 1992 Electric Lightwave sought authority in Washington and Oregon to offer point-to-point service to its commercial customers. The company was targeting high-volume communications customers such as software companies and travel reservation services as well as hospitals and financial institutions. Such a service would only allow a customer's different locations to communicate with each other. Calls outside the system would still require going through the local telephone utility, through a process known as switching.

At this point, Electric Lightwave was not seeking to provide switched services. Both U.S. West and GTE Northwest were opposed to Electric Lightwave's plans, but in March 1992 Electric Lightwave gained an important regulatory victory when Oregon's Public Utility Commission granted the company authority to provide dedicated inter-exchange services. It marked the first time commercial telephone customers in Oregon would have a source other than their local telephone utility

<table>
<tr><td>

**Company Perspectives:**

*Electric Lightwave continues to grow as technology and legislation alter the future of the telecommunications industry. The company's business strategy focuses on broadening its MAN (metropolitan area network) cities and cluster markets by offering a full range of telecommunications services to medium and large businesses. Electric Lightwave will also continue to assert itself on the West Coast with the completion of the largest SONET ring in the Western United States—a ring that interconnects seven western states. As it continues its expansion to extend services across the country, Electric Lightwave intends to have a market presence in every metropolitan area east of the Rockies.*

</td></tr>
</table>

to provide such services. Under the ruling, Electric Lightwave was able only to provide point-to-point or point-to-multipoint services, and only locations served by different exchanges could be linked in the dedicated line service. At this point the Oregon PUC could not grant authority for dedicated service within an exchange area, because of Oregon statutes.

In early 1993 Electric Lightwave began a $120 million expansion to extend its private fiber-optic networks to nine cities over three years. The company's strategy was to find mid-sized cities with companies that needed the services it provided. By the end of 1993 it planned to operate in Phoenix, Sacramento, and Salt Lake City, in addition to Portland and Seattle. San Diego was targeted for 1994, but no other cities had been decided on yet. Subsequently, Las Vegas was added to the list.

By March 1993 Electric Lightwave had laid about 60 miles of fiber-optic cable in the Sacramento area. It was noted that the city had a growing high-tech community. Electric Lightwave would be the third company offering fiber-optic cable access to businesses in Sacramento; the other two were Pacific Bell and Phoenix FiberLink, both of which opposed Electric Lightwave's entry into the market. In Salt Lake City the company planned to build a 35-mile fiber-optic loop, and construction on a 140-mile fiber-optic loop in Phoenix was to begin during the first quarter of 1993.

For 1991 and 1992 the company had about 30 employees and grew to about 60 employees in early 1993. The planned expansion was expected to add 100 to 150 more employees by the end of 1993. Meanwhile, parent company Citizens Utilities—Electric Lightwave's source of financing—continued to grow, reporting revenue of $600 million and net income of $115 million in fiscal 1992. For 1992 Electric Lightwave had revenue of about $2 million.

Warta left Electric Lightwave in 1993 to start up another fiber-optic and microwave communications company called PacWest Network. A noncompete agreement prevented him from operating in the same cities as Electric Lightwave. He was succeeded as president and CEO at Electric Lightwave by Al Rymarz. Within the year Earl Kamsky and the other minority shareholders who helped found the company also had departed.

## Competing for Local Telephone Service: 1994–96

By early 1994 Electric Lightwave had asked regulators in Washington for authority to compete with local telephone utilities and provide local phone service to businesses. Back in April 1993 Washington regulators had granted Electric Lightwave and Teleport Communications Group authority to offer private line and data services within local exchange services.

In March 1994 Electric Lightwave, which was not a regulated utility, received permission from the California Public Utilities Commission to sell its high-speed fiber-optic data transmission services to Sacramento businesses. Existing providers Pacific Bell and Phoenix FiberLink complained that the corporate market that Electric Lightwave was going after was their most lucrative business and that it supported their less lucrative consumer telephone services. Electric Lightwave planned to undercut existing prices by about ten percent. It would provide business customers with an alternative local telecommunications link to their long-distance carriers. At the time Electric Lightwave entered the Sacramento market, Pacific Bell had a 300-mile local fiber-optic network in place and was planning to spend $94 million to build an all-digital fiber-optic network in Sacramento. The other competitor, Phoenix FiberLink, had entered the Sacramento market in 1992 and had laid about 60 miles of fiber-optic cable. Sacramento was the fifth city in which Electric Lightwave would compete, after Portland, Seattle, Salt Lake City, and Phoenix.

In Phoenix, U.S. West had a monopoly on local telephone service. In 1994 Electric Lightwave and Phoenix FiberLink both began offering competitive access to business customers located in downtown Phoenix. Both built six-mile fiber-optic loops in the downtown area to give business customers an alternative link to their long-distance carriers.

In March 1994 Electric Lightwave became the first company west of the Mississippi River to be authorized to provide competitive local exchange (dial tone) service to its customers. It won such authorization in the state of Washington. Statutory changes in Oregon and Utah already allowed competitive access providers (CAP) to offer such service. In November 1994 it also became the first company to provide competitive, facilities-based telecommunications services in the state of Washington. During the year the company opened full-service offices in Sacramento and in Salt Lake City, Utah. Additional offices were opened in Phoenix in 1995; Boise, Idaho, in May 1997; and Spokane, Washington, in November 1998.

In mid-1994 the company announced plans to expand into another 24 cities—all of them mid-sized cities in the Rocky Mountain states and the Far West—as well as to start offering conventional local telephone service in competition with local monopolies such as U.S. West and GTE. The company had about 110 employees but would have to greatly expand its workforce if it began offering local dial tone service. Also in 1994 Electric Lightwave opened videoconferencing facilities in Portland and Seattle that could connect with any similar system in 146 U.S. cities and 21 other countries.

Dave Sharkey joined Electric Lightwave as president and CEO in August 1994, replacing Al Rymarz. Known as a marketing specialist, Sharkey was previously an executive with

---

**Key Dates:**

**1990:** Electric Lightwave is incorporated to provide alternative telecommunications services.

**1991:** Electric Lightwave begins providing service to business customers in Portland, Oregon and Seattle, Washington.

**1993:** Targets Phoenix, Sacramento, and Salt Lake City for its next metropolitan area networks (MAN).

**1994:** Becomes the first company west of the Mississippi River to be authorized to provide competitive local exchange (dial tone) service to its customers.

**1997:** Becomes a public company with an initial public offering (IPO) on the NASDAQ exchange.

**1998:** Agrees to purchase bandwidth on Qwest Communications' 9,000-mile-long fiber-optic route for $122 million.

**2000:** Completes its western SONET network of more than 3,200 miles at a cost of $131 million.

---

Mobile Media, Inc., a radio common carrier provider, and worked in technical operations and sales and marketing at New Jersey Bell Telephone and AT&T. In 1997 he became chief operating officer of Electric Lightwave.

In November 1994 Electric Lightwave requested permission from the Oregon PUC to compete against U.S. West and GTE Northwest Inc. for local dial tone service in Portland and other nearby communities. Electric Lightwave was the first company to ask to compete with the monopoly utilities. Legislation permitting such competition was passed in Oregon in 1993. It was up to the PUC to determine if such competition was in the public interest. The PUC also had to work out the technical and policy issues that were involved.

In August 1995 Electric Lightwave won approval from the Utah Public Service Commission to provide telephone service to customers throughout the state. Up to this time U.S. West had a monopoly on telephone service in Utah. Electric Lightwave would have to negotiate interconnection contracts with U.S. West regarding how they would use each other's lines. Electric Lightwave planned to offer service to business customers only, not residential service. By March 1996, however, U.S. West had failed to negotiate an interconnection agreement with Electric Lightwave. When Electric Lightwave appealed to the Utah PSC to force U.S. West into an agreement, the two companies succeeded in reaching an agreement following two weeks of intense negotiations. A year later, though, Electric Lightwave accused U.S. West of dragging its feet and failing to follow interconnection orders. In mid-1997 it sued U.S. West, charging it with failure to comply with the federal antitrust provisions in the Telecommunications Act of 1996 and for providing insufficient interconnection services. The lawsuit alleged that U.S. West's actions had resulted in disconnects, busy signals, blocked calls, and other problems—all of which contributed to an image of unreliability for the alternative provider.

Meanwhile, in California Electric Lightwave had built more than 100 miles of fiber-optic cable in the Sacramento area. As of

January 1, 1996, it would be able to offer local telephone service to business customers in competition with Pacific Bell, which already had built a much larger fiber-optic system in the state capital. In May it purchased a telephone system at Mather Field from the U.S. Air Force and was installing more fiber-optic cable in the Sacramento area. The company also had established an office for data services in Los Angeles and was planning to establish a similar office in San Francisco in 1998. During the year it also signed an interconnect agreement with Pacific Bell.

In 1996 Electric Lightwave signed the largest and most comprehensive strategic alliance in the United States with Arizona's Salt River Project (SRP), which gave Electric Lightwave access to SRP's vast fiber-optic network in the Phoenix metropolitan area. For 1996 the company reported revenue of $31.3 million and a net loss of $29.4 million.

### Going Public and Subsequent Growth: 1997–2000

Electric Lightwave went public with an initial public offering (IPO) in November 1997. The company sold eight million shares and raised $128 million, which would be used to finance expansion plans for the build-out of its existing market clusters and interconnection of its longhaul routes. Following the IPO Citizens Utilities owned more than 80 percent of the company and controlled some 97 percent of the combined voting power of its common stock. Citizens Utilities reported revenue of $1.4 billion for its fiscal year ending September 30, 1997. For 1997 Electric Lightwave reported revenue of $61 million and a net loss of $33.9 million.

In June 1998 Electric Lightwave signed a $122 million contract with Qwest Communications to purchase bandwidth on Qwest's national fiber optic network. Qwest owned a 9,000-mile-long fiber-optic route and planned to double it in 1999, providing access to 130 cities that accounted for 80 percent of all voice and data traffic in the United States. The agreement enabled Electric Lightwave to bring its services to major metropolitan areas throughout the country by the end of 1998.

In July 1998 Electric Lightwave announced that it was evolving from a competitive access provider (CAP) and a competitive local exchange carrier (CLEC) to become an integrated communications provider (ICP). It planned to offer a complete communications package to its customers, including local and long-distance services, national data networks, and videoconferencing, among other services. It also offered direct access to the Internet and Web hosting services. The company had about 2,500 miles of fiber routes, metropolitan area networks in six Western cities, and data-only networks in other cities.

In 1998 Electric Lightwave opened a sales office in Las Vegas. By 1999 it planned to finish a switching facility that would allow it to offer local and long distance calling plans to area businesses. Additional fiber routes were under construction to connect Las Vegas with Los Angeles, Salt Lake City, Boise, and Portland. The company also announced plans in August 1998 to build a SONET (synchronous optical network) ring that would connect fiber networks operating in 83 West Coast cities. The project would expand the Internet backbone and relieve congestion on the Internet. In 1999 Electric Lightwave began offering data and Internet access services in 14 major metropolitan areas across the United States.

In April 1999 Electric Lightwave and Touch America agreed to give each other access to portions of their fiber networks. Both companies operated in the northwest and were in the process of expanding their networks. Under the agreement Electric Lightwave would gain greater access to markets in Minnesota, Montana, North Dakota, and Wyoming. Touch America had a 10,000-mile network and was planning to add another 2,000 miles.

Electric Lightwave made a similar deal with IXC Communications Inc. of Austin, Texas. Electric Lightwave gained access to fiber links that IXC was building between Salt Lake City and Denver and between Denver and Dallas. During 1999 Electric Lightwave became involved in another dispute with U.S. West involving reciprocal compensation for Internet-related traffic. Complaints filed against U.S. West in Arizona, Utah, Oregon, and Idaho were all resolved in Electric Lightwave's favor by early 2000.

During 1999 Electric Lightwave closed its Voice Solution division, which marketed prepaid phone services and videoconferencing services. In other cost-cutting measures, the company closed six eastern retail sales offices and consolidated them in Dallas. Later in the year the company rolled out a radio and print advertising campaign targeting business customers. In October the company named Rudy J. Graf as vice-president and CEO. Graf was also president and COO of parent company Citizens Utilities. Sharkey remained president and COO and retained day-to-day control of Electric Lightwave. Parent company Citizens Utilities was in the process of divesting its gas, electric, and water and wastewater treatment businesses. The parent company planned to focus exclusively on telecommunications ventures. For 1999 Electric Lightwave reported record revenue of $187 million as well as its largest net loss, $133.5 million.

Electric Lightwave completed its western SONET network of more than 3,200 miles in mid-2000, at a cost of $131 million. By enabling the company to replace leased capacity lines with its own fiber, the new longhaul fiber-optic network would help Electric Lightwave reduce its operating costs. It also would improve the speed and reliability experienced by customers. With the completion of the SONET, Electric Lightwave had more than 6,300 route miles of fiber-optic cable, including its metropolitan area networks (MAN).

Although Electric Lightwave's goal was to become profitable, for the first six months of 2000 it reported a net loss of $70.1 million on revenue of $117.4 million, compared with revenue of $84.3 million and a net loss of $68.2 million for the first six months of 1999. In its second quarter report, the company told investors that it was running out of money for operating leases, working capital, capital expenditures, and debt service. Although Electric Lightwave only had $46 million left of its $400 million credit line, it noted that its parent company

Citizens Utilities would continue to finance its cash requirements until other financing was in place.

### Principal Competitors

GST Telecommunications, Inc.; U.S. West; Pacific Bell; GTE Corp.; AT&T Local Services; MCI WorldCom Inc.; NEXTLINK Communications Inc.

### Further Reading

Baker, M. Sharon, "WUTC Ruling Clears Way for Local Fiber-Optic Nets," *Puget Sound Business Journal,* May 7, 1993, p. 5.
"A Bigger Digital Footprint," *Telephony,* June 29, 1998.
Brown, Craig, "Vancouver, Wash.-Based Communications Firm Cuts Marketing Jobs," *Knight-Ridder/Tribune Business News,* August 25, 1999.
Bucholtz, Chris, "High Expectations: Electric Lightwave Accuses US West of Inadequate Customer Support," *Telephony,* July 14, 1997, p. 16.
"Electric Lightwave," *Oregon Business,* May 1994, p. 56.
"Electric Lightwave Inc.," *Business Journal-Portland,* January 14, 2000, p. 5.
"Electric Lightwave Inc.," *Puget Sound Business Journal,* December 23, 1991, p. 21.
"Electric Lightwave Ruling," *Business Journal Serving Phoenix & the Valley of the Sun,* November 5, 1999, p. 92.
Fahys, Judy, "Local Telephone Competition Delayed in Utah," *Knight-Ridder/Tribune Business News,* March 14, 1996.
——, "Utah Monopoly to End for US West," *Knight-Ridder/Tribune Business News,* August 18, 1995.
Havranek, Sharon, "Michael Morey," *Sacramento Business Journal,* September 5, 1997, p. 24.
Larson, Mark, "Big Firms to Get Choice of Local Phone Service," *Business Journal Serving Greater Sacramento,* August 28, 1995, p. 6.
——, "Third Runner Joins Fiber-Optic Race," *Business Journal Serving Greater Sacramento,* March 28, 1994, p. 1.
Lindstrom, Annie, "Regional CLECs Plant Fiber Stakes in the Ground," *America's Network,* September 1, 1998, p. 62.
Marks, Anita, "Departed Warta Sues Citizens Over Conflicts at Electric Lightwave Inc.," *Business Journal-Portland,* September 9, 1994, p. 2.
——, "Electric Lightwave Readies Expansion Worth $120 Million," *Business Journal-Portland,* March 1, 1993, p. 1.
——, "Electric Lightwave's Upstart Plan Ignites Phone Service Turf Battle," *Business Journal-Portland,* January 27, 1992, p. 1.
——, "ELI Hopes to Go Tone-to-Tone Vs. US West, GTE," *Business Journal-Portland,* November 11, 1994, p. 1.
McMillan, Dan, "A Billion-Dollar Label Change," *Business Journal-Portland,* July 24, 1998, p. 14.
——, "Lightwave's Parent to Be More Attentive," *Business Journal-Portland,* December 3, 1999, p. 3.
——, "We're Low on Dough, Says Electric Lightwave," *Business Journal-Portland,* September 22, 2000, p. 1.
O'Shea, Dan, "Light Years," *Telephony,* July 19, 1999.
Rendleman, John, "Internet Opens Throttle," *PC Week,* August 31, 1998, p. 18.
Rivenburgh, John, "Paving the Way for Phase 2 SONET Deployment," *Telephony,* June 14, 1993, p. 40.

—David P. Bianco

# eToys, Inc.

**2850 Ocean Park Boulevard, Suite 225**
**Santa Monica, California 90405**
**U.S.A.**
**Telephone: (310) 664-8100**
**Fax: (310) 663-8101**
**Web site: http://www.etoys.com**

*Public Company*
*Incorporated:* 1997
*Employees:* 1,000
*Sales:* $151 million (2000)
*Stock Exchanges:* NASDAQ
*Ticker Symbol:* ETYS
*NAIC:* 45112 Hobby, Toy, and Game Shops; 45411
    Electronic Shopping and Mail-Order Houses

eToys Inc. is a leading on-line retailer of children's products. Its emphasis is toys, but it aims to sell parents a vast array of things that their children might want or need. Its entire product line comprises more than 100,000 stock-keeping units of products such as children's books, videos, music, and software, as well as toys. Its broad range of toy products includes such mass-market items as Barbie dolls, as well as less-well-known items for more specialized tastes. In total, eToys carries over 750 brands. eToys' goods are sold exclusively on the Internet. Its web site catalogs its vast holdings, and shoppers can use the site's advanced search capabilities to find items by a variety of strategies. For example, consumers can search eToys for toys of a specific color, or ask for suggestions for products designed for children of a particular age. The site regularly lists updated suggestions of Bestsellers, Birthday Gifts Made Easy, Favorites by Age, and 200 under $20. The eToys site also allows shoppers to sign up for a birthday reminder service. The company notifies shoppers by e-mail three weeks in advance of a child's birthday, and appends a list of gifts appropriate for that age. The site also provides a Wish List service. Children or their parents can use it to e-mail friends and family members lists of the gifts they most hope for. Children can also visit the eToys web site to play

computer games, through the site's Play@eToys service. Other web site features offer tips, advice, and product ideas to parents.

Besides the company's headquarters in Santa Monica, California, eToys maintains regional headquarters in San Francisco; Danville, Virginia; and London, England. It ships goods out of one east coast and one west coast warehouse. eToys operates a related web site, etoys.co.uk, to offer its goods and services to customers in the United Kingdom.

### Disney Executive Turns to Internet Toy Sales

eToys Inc. was founded by Edward C. Lenk, known as Toby. Lenk was born in Boston in 1961 and graduated with a degree in economics from Bowdoin College, Maine, in 1983. From Bowdoin he went to Harvard Business School, where he earned his MBA in 1987. Lenk held a variety of positions in the 1980s. He worked in Washington as a health policy researcher and later was a consultant for a firm called LEK Partnership. In 1991 he joined Walt Disney, where he became vice president for strategic planning, overseeing growth of Disney's theme parks. Lenk's career at Disney lasted only five years. By the summer of 1996, Lenk was bored with climbing the corporate ladder. He quit to go into business for himself. He wanted to get in on the Internet craze, but wasn't sure what kind of business he wanted to start. Then, while Christmas shopping for his niece and nephew, it occurred to Lenk that the hectic pace and desperate atmosphere of the late December toy store was something the world might very well do without. He decided to create a virtual toy store. His first proposal to investors was for a web site that would sell high-priced toys to wealthy consumers. This idea failed to get backing, and Lenk thought about ways to refine his plan. He came back with a proposal to outdo traditional toy stores by offering a huge selection on-line, of everything from mass-market toys to the kind of fancy, high-priced toys he had first considered.

No one else yet had a toy store on-line. Being first to the market is always considered a business advantage, and investors began shoving money at Lenk. He collected over $15 million from the venture capital firm Sequoia and other venture capital firms, plus $250,000 in seed capital from a web business incubator called Idealab. He raised money from friends at Disney as well. eToys seemed to be in the position Amazon.com had been in when it became the first on-line bookstore. Lenk was sure that the giant mass-market toy retailer Toys 'R' Us would soon start its own web site, and he rushed to get eToys going before that happened. In March 1997, eToys went on line.

Getting the site going was very expensive. Merely putting the site up on the web would not guarantee customers, so Lenk spent $3 million to become a so-called anchor tenant of America Online (AOL). This gave eToys a promotional space on AOL's portal for two years. He signed a similar deal with another popular Internet portal, Yahoo! He enlisted 5,000 other web sites to spread the eToys name, offering a 25 percent commission on sales to any site that referred customers. He stocked his California warehouse with goods from more than 350 different manufacturers.

eToys expected competition from Toys 'R' Us, but in fact that company waited almost a year before it began offering goods on-line. In the meantime, eToys faced competition in cyberspace from the bookseller Amazon.com. Amazon had basically pioneered web-based retailing, building the business model others strove to emulate. After its first success with books, it began branching into other areas, including toys and music. In October 1998, eToys formed a marketing partnership with three other web retailers to promote each other's sites. The other members of the group were CD-Now, Reel.com, and Cyberian Outpost. By promoting each other's sites and sharing customer lists, the four hoped to counter some of the impact of Amazon's dominance.

eToys ran through its cash quickly. It ended its first fiscal year $2.3 million in debt. Losses were even steeper the next year, yet the firm continued to attract investors. By 1998 it had raised approximately $2 billion, although eToys was admittedly far from turning a profit. Investors seemed to excuse the company's poor finances, because eToys was building a market for itself. The toy industry in total had sales of $22 billion a year, and eToys was the first to take aim at this huge market from the Internet. Estimated total revenues from on-line toy sales across the industry for 1998 were only $40 million, far less than consumers were spending on books, music, and entertainment ($1,300 million), apparel ($300 million), food and wine ($200 million) or even on-line car sales ($70 million). Yet the growth rate from 1997 was more than 300 percent for toys, higher than almost all other categories tracked, according to a survey in *Fortune* published February 1, 1999.

### 1998's e-Christmas

Christmas 1998 was the first time the Internet was a significant force in the yearly American shopping ritual. eToys prepared by spending even more money on advertising, using print and television ads for the first time. Its advertising campaign featured the tag line: "We bring the toy store to you," hoping to

emphasize the convenience of at-home shopping versus the crowded scramble at the mall. The most popular toy of the year was a talking creature called the Furby, which shortsighted retailers had underpurchased for the season, creating a wide demand. eToys held on-line sweepstakes to give away free Furbies, attracting thousands of potential customers. The company also made every effort to keep customers satisfied. It offered free upgrades from regular to express shipping for some, and gave out $5 coupons to mollify customers whose desired goods were out of stock. Operating out of a single warehouse near the Los Angeles airport, eToys shipped out 95 percent of its Christmas orders within 24 hours. The massive warehouse employed hundreds of people to pick, pack, check, and wrap orders. Sales for the fourth quarter of 1998 soared to more than 20 times that of 1997, and overall some 3.4 million people visited the eToys site. eToys surpassed the Toys 'R' Us site easily. The Toys 'R' Us web site drew few customers, and it was only able to offer half the merchandise that eToys had.

### Initial Public Offering in 1999

With this successful Christmas behind it, eToys decided to go public. Its IPO was first valued at $115 million and underwritten by the venerable investment firms Goldman, Sachs & Co., Merrill Lynch, and others. The company cheerfully hoped to raise money by the sale, even as it advised that operating losses and negative cash flow were likely to continue. The IPO was first announced in March, but it was delayed when eToys decided to purchase a company that marketed goods for babies, BabyCenter Inc. BabyCenter's stockholders ended up with about a 15 percent share of the merged companies, and the IPO was put off so this deal could be cemented. The public offering finally took place at the end of May 1999. The results were astonishing. The stock began at $20 a share, and by the end of the first day, it had risen to $77. The company, which had consistently lost money and had revenues at that point of only $30 million, ended up worth on paper $7.7 billion. This made it worth over 30 percent more than Toys 'R' Us, although that company was a profitable national chain with annual sales of over $11 billion.

With the enormously successful public offering behind it, eToys began to prepare for increasing competition. This came from two directions. eToys had always had an eye on Toys 'R' Us, expecting that company to rush to the web and do on-line what it already did in its nationwide stores. However, the Toys 'R' Us web site had proved disappointing, and it did not do well over the 1998 Christmas toy season. In April 1999 Toys 'R' Us relaunched its web site. It spun its Internet operations off as a separate company and announced plans to invest $80 million in it. Meanwhile, Amazon.com also put the pressure on eToys. In July 1999 it opened a whole new toy section on its web site. With its huge customer base of an estimated 10 million people, Amazon's CEO believed his company was already the top marketer of children's goods on-line. Amazon had leveraged its name recognition and customer base to become the leading music and video seller on-line, squeezing out sites like CD-Now. It seemed possible that it could do the same thing with toys.

### A Place for Kids' Stuff

eToys believed it could match Amazon by presenting itself not so much as a toy store as a place for kids' stuff. That meant it would sell maternity wear and strollers (through its BabyCenter affiliation), books, toys, and perhaps sporting goods, so that parents could go to the site looking for anything their kids might need. By September 1999 eToys had announced that it had 80,000 children's book titles available for sale through its site. It hyped its new bookstore by arranging on-line interviews with notable children's authors, and it made sample pages of some 400 books available for on-line browsing. Then it teamed up with television talk show hostess Rosie O'Donnell. O'Donnell began a ''Rosie's Readers'' children's book club on her show, and eToys tied in with her with a special ''Rosie's Readers'' portion of its web site. Part of the proceeds of eToys' Rosie's Readers sales went to O'Donnell's charitable foundation.

To prepare for the Christmas season, eToys began running advertising on television and in parenting magazines. The ads differed from its previous year's campaign, which had emphasized the convenience of on-line shopping versus going out to the toy store. The 1999 ads tried to portray the company as uniquely able to help parents meet the needs of children. One ad showed a mother looking at fish in a rock pool with her son. Next the mother was shown typing ''fish'' into eToys' web site. The tag line ran, ''Where will you find the perfect gift for your child? EToys. Where great ideas come to you.'' The campaign cost eToys $20 million, which represented a significant portion of the company's total revenues. The soft tone of the advertising sought to convey a new, broader image of the company. eToys was not just another place to shop for toys, but a parent's ally in finding the best for a child.

Also to prepare for Christmas, eToys outsourced some of its order fulfillment to Fingerhut, a catalog company that had built a new business niche for itself helping out fledgling on-line retailers. Sales for the holiday season burgeoned, rising 366 percent over 1998's figures. And 99 percent of the company's orders were fulfilled on time. But this left one percent, or thousands of individual orders, arriving after Christmas. eToys blamed Fingerhut, though Fingerhut denied that its warehouse had been the problem. The company's stock, which had actually started to fall in November, plummeted after December. Shares that had sold for as much as $86 fell to $5 before beginning to inch back up.

Although the company had done nothing but lose money since its inception, only now did investors seem troubled by

that. The costs of running an on-line business had not fallen enough to allow eToys to make more money than it had to spend. CEO Lenk was sure the company would be profitable by 2003, when he predicted the business would reach a big enough market to take advantage of some economies of scale. In the meantime, eToys continued to spend money. It built two new warehouses, giving it an east coast as well as a west coast presence for the first time. And to run its warehouses, the company hired the former logistics manager from the computer dealer Gateway. eToys also searched for ways to use its customer lists to find consumers who would go for more of its higher margin toys. And the company put out a private label eToys line of toys ready for Christmas 2000. These goods promised the company a profit margin of close to 75 percent.

Although investor confidence in so-called dot-com companies had fallen dramatically since eToys' IPO, the company had no intention of trying to move off the Internet in any way, such as partnering with a traditional bricks-and-mortar retailer. Lenk's experience at Disney had shown him that the proper family-friendly attitude could keep loyal customers for years. He hoped to make his company's web site into a similar family-focused area, offering comprehensive service and goods that no other retailer could match. Though the high costs of running an on-line business seemed formidable, Lenk was sure he had a quality product. He believed it would take only a few more years before eToys fulfilled its promise.

### Principal Subsidiaries

BabyCenter.com.

### Principal Competitors

Toys 'R' Us, Inc.; KB Toys; Amazon.com, Inc.; Wal-Mart Stores, Inc.

### Further Reading

Andrews, Whit, ''Four Web Retailers Join Forces in Effort to Cross-Promote Sites,'' *Internet World,* October 19, 1998, p. 5.

Armstrong, Larry, ''This Toy War Is No Game,'' *Business Week,* August 9, 1999, pp. 86–87.

Bannion, Lisa, '' 'Tis the Season for eToys' $20 Million Blitz,'' *Wall Street Journal,* September 27, 1999, p. B10.

Bryant, Adam, ''A Lot of Play-Dough,'' *Newsweek,* May 31, 1999, p. 54.

Kelly, Erin, ''The Last E-Store on the Block,'' *Fortune,* September 18, 2000, pp. 214–20.

Maughan, Shannon, ''Children's Books Look Rosie,'' *Publishers Weekly,* October 18, 1999, p. 12.

Sellers, Patricia, ''Inside the First E-Christmas,'' *Fortune,* February 1, 1999, pp. 71–73.

Weintraub, Arlene, ''He's Not Playing,'' *Business Week,* July 24, 2000, pp. 93–96.

''With Early-Bird Web-Site and Portal Deals, Former Disney Executive Seeks to Pre-Empt Toys 'R' Us,'' *Inc.,* October 1998.

—A. Woodward

# Euronext Paris S.A.

39, rue Cambon
75039 Paris, Cedex 01
France
Telephone: (+33) 1 49-27-10-00
Fax: (+33) 1 49-27-11-71
Web site: http://www.euronext.com/fr/

*Subsidiary of Euronext N.V.*
*Incorporated:* 1724 as Bourse de Paris; 1991 as Société
   des Bourses Françaises; 1999 as ParisBourse S.A.
*Employees:* 1,008
*Sales:* EUR 723 billion ($700 billion) (1999)
*NAIC:* 523210 Securities and Commodity Exchanges

Euronext Paris S.A. is the French partner exchange to the Euronext N.V. stock exchange created in September 2000 by the mergers of the Paris, Amsterdam, and Brussels stock exchanges. Euronext Paris, renamed after the merger from ParisBourse S.A., brings its more than 1,200 member firms, worth some EUR 723 billion in total transactions in 1999, to Euronext to create an exchange powerhouse to rival European leaders the London Stock Exchange and the Deutsche Börse. In total, Euronext N.V., holding company for the three partner exchanges, boasts listings of nearly 2,000 member firms, making it Europe's second largest exchange after London. The Euronext Amsterdam, Euronext Brussels, and Euronext Paris exchanges link trading services across the Euronext Paris-developed NCS electronic trading system, enabling the new stock exchange to join forces without the need for a common trading floor. The company's clearing and settlement are unified under the Clearnet platform originally developed by ParisBourse, and settlements are processed through Euroclear. The streamlining of transactions to a single source is expected to bring not only some EUR 50 million in cost savings per year to Euronext, but also reduce the cost of trading to its European customers, who often pay up to ten times the amount charged to U.S. traders. Euronext Paris is headed by Chairman Jean-François Théodore, who also serves as CEO and chairman for Euronext N.V. The company intends to extend its network of exchanges to other European exchanges, such as Milan and Madrid. Analysts expect to see continued mergers among the many European stock exchanges, resulting in just one or two stock exchanges capable of rivaling the New York Stock Exchange.

## 18th-Century Beginnings

The Paris stock exchange—or bourse, as European stock exchanges came to be known—was among the youngest of Europe's exchanges when it was created by royal decree in 1724. The Bourse de Paris inherited nonetheless several centuries of French trading activity. As early as 1572, King Charles IX announced regulations governing the country's ''couratiers'' (which gave way to ''courtiers,'' French for broker), establishing practices such as the obligatory separation of a broker's personal affairs from his dealings with his clients.

Toward the end of that century, the kingdom's first major bourse was established in Lyon, focused on money changing—the many dukes, counts, and princes, as well as the king himself, had long held a practice of coining their own money. Money changing moved to Paris at the beginning of the 17th century, where the Pont-aux-Changes served as a gathering point for moneychangers. In 1639, the role and function of the kingdom's moneychangers, called ''Agents de change,'' were defined by royal decree. The moneychangers were then organized within a Compagnie des Agents de Change and granted exclusive authority to perform money changing duties.

An investment scandal at the beginning of the 18th century led to the creation of an official bourse in Paris in 1724. The new bourse, which opened in the rue Vivienne, granted exclusive rights to negotiate trading to the Compagnie des Agents de Change. The Paris bourse was to become instrumental in raising funds for the French war effort, as well as its colonial expansion. By the end of the century, however, the bourse had fallen into disarray and scandal and was closed in September 1795. One month later, the bourse reopened, with 25 new agents de change granted the monopoly on all transactions.

After taking power in the early 19th century, the new emperor Napoleon had the bourse moved to the royal palace. In 1806, a competition was opened to design a new home for the

Parisian bourse. The competition was won by Théodore
Brongniart; construction began in 1808. The completed building was inaugurated in November 1826 and became the permanent home for the Paris stock exchange. At its opening, the
exchange boasted some 26 listed stocks. By the end of the 19th
century—and despite a number of stock market crashes—the
number of listed stocks had grown to more than 1,000.

The Wall Street crash, the beginning of the Great Depression, and finally the outbreak of the Second World War were to
sink the Paris exchange into a long troubled period. As one
government official was reported to say: "I'd close the exchange and lock up the brokers." Nevertheless, the Paris exchange was to prove instrumental in helping to rebuild the
French economy after the end of the war.

### A European Leader in the 1990s

A series of measures helped to win new confidence in the
Paris exchange, such as the end of a double tax on stock
dividends in the mid-1960s, and the creation of the COB (Commission des Opérations de Bourse), a watchdog body set up in
1967 as the French version of the Securities and Exchange
Commission. The installment of a regulatory body helped to
instill confidence in the exchange by new generations of investors and, in particular, private investors. A new law, voted in
1978, giving tax deductions to private investors, also helped to
stimulate a growing interest in the stock market. Another incentive to individual investors was the Paris Bourse's unique "reglement mensuel" or monthly settlement, which permitted investors to defer as much as 80 percent of the cost of their stock
purchases until the first of the next month after the purchase.
This system enabled investors with limited means to join in the
stock market, despite criticism that the system encouraged
speculation—investors were granted, in effect, free credit for
their market transactions. The "reglement mensuel" was abol-
ished in September 2000, to bring the Paris exchange in line
with its European neighbors.

At the beginning of the 1980s, the Paris exchange lost a large
part of its value. A wave of nationalization carried out by the
new Socialist government led by Mitterand transformed a number of France's largest public companies into government-run
entities, thereby removing them from the Paris bourse. In response, the Bourse de Paris created a new market, called the
Second Marché, to encourage mid-sized companies to join the
stock market. The Second Marché, which also served as a
springboard for larger corporations before joining the bourse's
Premier Marché, enabled the Paris Bourse to boost the number
of its quoted companies, and the Paris exchange became one of
Europe's most prominent.

In the mid-1980s, the Bourse de Paris joined the movement
toward electronic trading, when it introduced its own computerized transaction system, called CAC, ending traditional floor
trading. The new CAC system linked trading in France's regional exchanges in Lyon, Bordeaux, Lille, Marseille, Nancy,
and Nantes exchanges with the larger Paris exchange, as the
first step toward creating a single entity, the Société des Bourses
Françaises.

Following the market crash of October 1987, the Bourse de
Paris introduced new changes. Most prominent of these was the
ending of the long-held monopoly by the Agents de Change in
1988. Abolishing this monopoly opened trading to foreign investors for the first time, while also opening the exchange to
banks and other financial bodies. Three years later, the Société
des Bourses Françaises was officially created when the six
regional exchanges were merged into the Paris exchange. The
regional exchanges were now operated as commercial branches
of the main Paris bourse.

These moves enabled the Paris bourse to take on greater
stature among the European and world stock exchanges in the
1990s, attracting increasing numbers of both foreign and domestic institutional investors. At the same time, a growing
number of international corporations began to seek listings on
the Paris exchange. In the mid-1990s the Bourse de Paris
introduced an upgraded version of its CAC software, giving it
some of the most sophisticated trading software among worldwide stock exchanges.

The growing number of high-technology stocks, which often
presented different financial portraits and requirements from traditional stocks, led the Bourse de Paris to introduce a new market,
called the Nouveau Marché, devoted to the new breed of stock.
The Nouveau Marché enabled the Paris bourse to go into competition against high-tech leader NASDAQ and more recent rival,
AIM, set up by the London Stock Exchange in 1995.

Competition among the European exchanges was slated to
heat up, however, as the European Community headed toward
the creation of the Euro currency. As countries battled to determine the site of the new currency's financial center, the stock
exchanges also began to jockey for position to become the
preeminent exchange of the new Europe. The creation of the
Deutsche Börse, gathering a number of regional German exchanges under the main Frankfurt exchange, and then an agreement to partner with the Zurich exchange—fourth largest in
Europe—sparked a wave of market mergers and partnerships in
the late 1990s. Paris responded by reaching a partnership with
the Swiss exchange.

While talk turned to the creation of a single European
exchange—through the merger of the Amsterdam, Brussels,
Frankfurt, London, Madrid, Milan, Paris, and Zurich exchanges, the battle to become the "bourse of Europe" quickly
came down to a race among the London, Paris, and Deutsche
bourses. Yet the French exchange was quickly outpaced by its
German and English rivals—in 1998, the London and Deutsche
exchanges announced their intention to merge and form the
giant IX exchange. The merged exchange was to be some three
times larger than its Parisian relative. While the Paris exchange
had been offered a place in the new exchange, it was only in a

minority capacity—just 20 percent of the proposed new exchange, as opposed to the 40 percent to be held by each of the London and German exchanges. Insulted and angered, Jean-François Théodore announced an offer to the Amsterdam, Brussels, Milan, and Madrid exchanges to join the Bourse de Paris in their own merger. The following year, Société des Bourses Françaises changed its name to ParisBourse S.A.

While Milan and Madrid declined the offer, negotiations began among the Paris, Amsterdam, and Brussels exchanges. By March 2000, the three exchanges announced their intention to merge into a new entity, Euronext. With the holding company Euronext N.V. located in the Netherlands, the new entity was to act as parent to three subsidiary exchanges, Euronext Amsterdam, Euronext Brussels, and Euronext Paris. The three exchanges were to share a common trading "floor," using the Paris exchanges perfected NCS trading system, while both clearing and settlement activities were streamlined into single bodies for all three exchanges.

The announcement of Euronext—which extended an invitation to the London exchange, as well as began talks over a partnership with the New York Stock Exchange—spurred the proposed IX partners to step up the pace of their own negotiations. By summer 2000, however, it became apparent that the London and German partners were not able to agree, and the IX exchange project collapsed.

The Euronext merger went ahead as scheduled, and the new multicountry exchange, the first in the world, came into being in September 2000. Rivaling the London exchange in terms of market capitalization, worth some $2.3 trillion, Euronext became the most important exchange in the so-called "Eurozone" (the United Kingdom had not yet agreed to convert to the new currency), giving it the potential clout to attract more and more of the continent's largest corporations. The new exchange also announced its plans to extend its trading hours to 20:00 hours GMT in the year 2001, bringing the exchange in line with the NYSE operations. At the same time, Euronext N.V. acknowledged its plans to make its own public offering—on the Euronext exchange, of course.

As Euronext turned toward its first full year of trading, it continued to make overtures for new mergers and partners, particularly to the Milan and Madrid exchanges. The exchange had also entered into merger negotiations with the smaller Luxembourg exchange. At the same time, Euronext left open its invitation to the London Stock Exchange, which by then had come under a hostile takeover attack by the owners of the Swedish exchange. Meanwhile, Euronext pursued negotiations toward the creation of a larger exchange partnership—the so-called Global Equity Market, or GEM, to be formed by the New York, Euronext, Sydney, Hong Kong, Sao Paulo, Toronto, and Tokyo exchanges, which promised to enable 24-hour global trading. As the economy had gone global during the 1990s, the world's stock exchanges were expected to follow. Euronext, as first out of the gate, appeared likely to play a prominent role in the creation of the next century's investment landscape.

### Principal Subsidiaries

Euronext Amsterdam N.V.; Euronext Brussels S.A.; Euronext Paris S.A.

### Principal Competitors

New York Stock Exchange; London Stock Exchange; Deutsche Börse; Tokyo Stock Exchange.

### Further Reading

Clary, Isabelle, "Euronext Says Merger Offer with LSE Still on Table," *Reuters,* May 18, 2000.
——, "Euronext Seeks NYSE Ties That Would Rival IX-NASDAQ," *Reuters,* May 16, 2000.
Grose, Thomas K., "A European Super Market," *Time International,* April 3, 2000, p. 43.
Zwick, Steve, "The Emperor's New Pipes," *Time International,* October 2, 2000, p. 58.
——, "Euronext Plans Longer Trading Hours in 2001," *Reuters,* May 31, 2000.
——, "What About the Others?," *Economist,* July 25, 1998.

—M.L. Cohen

# Eurotunnel Group

**Cheriton Parc**
**Cheriton High Street**
**Folkestone, Kent CT19 4QS**
**United Kingdom**
**Telephone: (1303) 273-300**
**Fax: (1303) 282-026**
**Web site: http://www.eurotunnel.com**

*Public Company*
*Incorporated:* 1986
*Employees:* 3,400
*Sales:* £654.38 million (1999)
*Stock Exchanges:* London Paris
*Ticker Symbol:* ETLB.L (London) 12537.PA (Paris)
*NAIC:* 23412 Bridge and Tunnel Construction; 482111
Line-Haul Railroads; 48821 Support Activities for
Rail Transportation

The Eurotunnel Group includes Eurotunnel plc, which, through its Eurotunnel subsidiaries, was established to design, finance, construct, and operate a 31-mile tunnel that links France and England beneath the English Channel. The tunnel, or ''Chunnel,'' was completed in 1993 and opened to passenger traffic in 1994. Although the ambitious tunnel project was beset from the start with cost overruns, construction problems, and delays, the finished product stands as an impressive monument to mankind's technological and engineering prowess.

On June 20, 1993, the first passenger train traveled through the tunnel beneath the English Channel, marking the completion of the largest private engineering project in history. The 31-mile tunnel, 23.5 miles of which is under 150 feet of water, linked for the first time the countries of England and France. The completed tunnel was the culmination of seven years of business problems, controversial political disputes, and engineering setbacks. For example, many U.K. citizens resented the fact that England would no longer be an island. Further, investors and contractors argued about who would pay for the major cost overruns even as the Chunnel opened for business. Never-

theless, many Eurotunnel employees, contractors, and associates involved in building and financing the tunnel looked back on the project as the achievement of a lifetime. Le Shuttle has a 54 percent share of the market for car shuttles; Eurotunnel also leads the freight shuttle market (39 percent). More than eight million passenger cars and 800,000 trucks pass through the Chunnel ever year; independent freight trains and Eurostar passenger trains also use it.

### Origins

Whereas Eurotunnel was incorporated in 1985 for the purpose of building a ''fixed link'' between England and France, the concept of bridging the English channel was an old one. In 1751, for example, the Amiens Academy in France conducted a competition that awarded participants for offering innovative ways to cross the English Channel. Since that time, engineers and politicians presented numerous alternatives to the traditional ferry system, but none of the ideas ever progressed to the construction phase due to enormous financial and complicated engineering hurdles. One ambitious construction program actually advanced to the tunneling stage in 1974, but the initiative was abandoned soon after it had begun.

Despite the failure of this construction program, support for the idea continued to mount. In 1978, a group of British and French contractors revisited the 1974 effort to see where the project had failed. Further, in September of 1981 English Prime Minister Margaret Thatcher and French President Mitterand announced that they would join forces to finance new studies for a fixed link across the English Channel. Subsequently, a consortium of five French and five British contractors, along with five banks, proposed a scheme to finance and construct a tunnel connecting Paris and London. That group, which was initially headed by former diplomat Sir Nicholas Henderson, was the start of Eurotunnel. The French contractors involved in the project included Bouygues SA, Dumes SA, Societe Auxiliaire d'Entrepreses SA, Societe Generale d'Entrepreses, and Spie Batignolles SA. The English contractors included Balfour Beatty Construction Ltd., Costain Civil Engineering Ltd., Tarmac Construction Ltd., Taylor Woodrow Construction Ltd., and Wimpey International Ltd.

Although the original Channel Tunnel Group, as it called itself, was not the only consortium interested in building the tunnel across the English Channel, they were perhaps the most organized. Because the consortium comprised an experienced team of contractors and financiers, such as National Westminster Bank, they easily won the contract when the French and British governments invited groups to bid on the massive project in April 1985. The Channel Tunnel Group was selected to head the project the following January; in addition, the two governments signed an agreement that authorized the company to operate the tunnel for 55 years. After the Channel Tunnel Group was awarded the project, the contractors joined to form Transmanche-Link (TML), the company that would actually build the tunnel. Likewise, the group that would oversee the completion and operation of the Chunnel formed Eurotunnel plc, which became a public company in July of 1986.

The Eurotunnel Group was formed on August 13, 1986. It consisted of Eurotunnel plc and its French counterpart, Eurotunnel SA. (Shares of the two companies are ''twinned'' together.) Lord Pennock served as chairman of Eurotunnel plc until September 1986, when Alastair Morton assumed control. Morton cochaired the Eurotunnel Group with Andre Benard, who became chairman of the French holding company Eurotunnel SA in February 1987.

The chief purpose of separating the construction from the management aspects of the Chunnel project was to restrict the contractors' access to the bank's financial resources, forming a sort of checks and balances arrangement designed to avoid conflicts of interest. Unfortunately, this effort was less than successful. Before the arrangement was finalized, all members agreed on the terms of a contract that effectively allowed TML—which constituted the contractors—to circumvent the restrictions imposed by its financiers. Further, the agreement failed to provide Eurotunnel—which was supposed to oversee the operations—representation by independent management. ''In the files of the French Treasury is a memorandum that argues with passion . . . that in no circumstances should the contract for the construction . . . be signed while the contractors were still majority shareholders and Eurotunnel did not have independent management,'' Morton explained in the May 2, 1994, *Engineering News Record*. ''But it did happen, and there was trouble ever after that.''

One of the high points of the Chunnel project came in July 1987, when England and France signed an historic treaty approving the connection between the two countries. Despite this diplomatic triumph, Eurotunnel lacked the cash necessary to fund the massive US$7 billion-plus project. In fact, the group of financiers involved in the project had raised only about US$500 million in 1986 and they had planned to make a second public stock offering in November of 1987. To their dismay, the U.S. stock market crashed in October of that year; nevertheless, they went ahead with the offering. In what one Eurotunnel executive called a miracle, the project collected more than 100,000 shareholders almost overnight and boosted Eurotunnel's coffers by about US$1.5 billion.

### Breaking Ground in 1988

Once the investment capital had been secured, TML began boring the tunnel from an existing service tunnel in the United Kingdom. About three months later a French tunnel-boring machine began grinding its way toward England. The concept was to bore a 31-mile link 150 feet below the English Channel that consisted of three tunnels—two rail tunnels and a smaller service tunnel. When completed, passenger shuttles and trains would be able to travel through the tunnels at speeds of 90 miles per hour and higher. Instead of boarding a ferry for a one-and-one-half-hour ride across the channel, passengers could make the trip in about 30 minutes. The project would offer new opportunities to commuters living in either England or France. For example, a sales representative in Britain also could cover a territory in France. Similarly, a resident of Calais, where the tunnel emerges in France, could go to dinner and a movie in London and return home by late evening. Further, freight carriers, including over-the-road trucking companies, could benefit from the underwater tunnel.

Despite all of these high hopes for the completed project, fundamental construction problems arose early. As a result, tunneling fell behind schedule, particularly from the United Kingdom's end, and bitter disputes over money and project control erupted between several different parties. Most early differences were eventually smoothed out through renegotiation of contract payments and management changes. In May of 1989, American Jack Lemley was hired as the chief executive of TML. When he arrived in Europe, he was surprised to find virtually independent construction teams operating on each side of the channel. Under his direction, TML gradually unified its contractors on either side of the English Channel, reduced several unnecessary project costs, and reaffirmed their plan to meet the original construction schedule. Despite these significant gains in management, setbacks continued to plague Eurotunnel throughout the construction phase.

A particularly disastrous setback involved the complications caused by a 5.4-meter-wide tunnel boring machine striking bad ground, in spite of the fact that decades of soil studies found the area stable. The state-of-the-art, computer-controlled machine, which was specially designed for the tunnel project, was capable only of boring through compact chalk. The bad patch of ground into which it drilled caused moisture to seep into the machine's electrical systems and devastated its specialized concrete lining system. Eurotunnel was forced to invest heavily to compensate for the mishap, and this and other setbacks contrib-

---

### Key Dates:

**1751:** Napoleonic engineers seriously contemplate ways of bridging *La Manche*.
**1974:** A tunnel under the English Channel is started, but abandoned.
**1981:** Britain and France finance studies for a fixed link.
**1986:** Eurotunnel Group is formed.
**1987:** A second public stock offering raises $1.5 billion.
**1990:** Workers digging from each side of the Channel finally meet.
**1994:** The Chunnel is officially inaugurated.
**1995:** Eurotunnel suspends interest payments on $8 billion of junior debt.
**1996:** A fire suspends freight service and depresses share price further.
**1997:** A debt restructuring is finalized.

---

uted to another major dispute regarding the method of payment that Eurotunnel had agreed to use to compensate TML contractors who fixed equipment. The end result was a US$2.5 billion lawsuit filed by TML against Eurotunnel and a lengthy court battle that raged through most of the construction phase in the late 1980s and early 1990s.

In addition to disputes with its sister company, Eurotunnel was also burdened by frustrating intervention from government agencies. Leading the bureaucratic assault was the Intergovernmental Commission (IGC), an oversight body focusing on safety requirements made up of civil servants from both France and the United Kingdom. In one instance, early in the project TML had asked for the IGC's approval to install standard 600-millimeter doors in the passenger car trains. The request became mired in red tape at the IGC, so TML went ahead and ordered the doors in an effort to keep up with its construction schedule. After the doors had been built, the IGC decided to mandate 700-millimeter doors. This change caused a nearly nine-month delay in the project and cost Eurotunnel a staggering US$70 million to rectify. Similarly, although the Chunnel was designed using seismic criteria used for nuclear power plants, the IGC decided midway through the construction process to increase the relevant design factor fourfold. Furthermore, the IGC decided in the final stages of the project to require the installation of an advanced electronic anti-terrorist system.

Such poorly executed mandates contributed to huge cost overruns and construction delays on the tunnel project. Whereas in 1988 Eurotunnel had set a target opening date of May 1993, one year later the completion date was pushed back to June. By February 1992, TML, mired in uncontrollable delays, abandoned the May projection altogether. Later that year, TML estimated that the tunnel would be in operation by December, although that date was eventually postponed as well. As bureaucratic and engineering setbacks proliferated, the relationship between TML and Eurotunnel became more strained. For its part, Eurotunnel was in a double bind because it was trying to facilitate cooperation between a demanding consortium of contractors at TML on one side and a powerful group of financiers on the other, while at the same time struggling to overcome

bureaucratic hurdles. Suspicion and mistrust gradually permeated the entire business relationship, to the point that Eurotunnel unsuccessfully sought an injunction to stop TML's work on the tunnel.

In Morton's estimation, much of the problem stemmed from TML's heavy influence that it had negotiated in the original agreement with Eurotunnel. "[Eurotunnel] had to wrest control of the project from the contractor [TML] . . . without intervening in its responsibility . . . for the design-build commission and guarantee," Morton recalled in the May 2, 1994, *Engineering News Record*. "The continuous dilemma of what exactly was the contractor's position [relating to] the client . . . and what exactly was both the capability and responsibility of the client has been the drama of the tunnel." While Eurotunnel took exception to TML's grab for power, TML executives blamed construction difficulties in part on Eurotunnel's inexperience in overseeing large construction projects. Despite these internal disputes, Eurotunnel and TML rose to the challenge of finding the money to pay for cost overruns and completing the tunnel on a reasonable timetable.

### Breakthrough in 1990

Indeed, as construction costs escalated, Eurotunnel scrambled to amass the world's largest syndicate of investors and financial institutions, which included 220 banks throughout the world. Using virtually no public funds, Eurotunnel had raised US$13.5 billion in capital by 1994 and was working to secure at least another US$1.5 billion. Meanwhile, TML shifted into high gear during the early 1990s in an effort to overcome bureaucratic and engineering hurdles and meet its ambitious construction schedule. TML eventually broke tunnel-boring speed records, advancing more than 1,400 feet in just one week. TML and Eurotunnel celebrated the official breakthrough of the service tunnel on December 1, 1990. The historic event—French and English workmen punching through a rock wall to join hands below the English Channel—was televised throughout the world. The celebration was repeated in May 1991 when the north tunnel was completed, and again in June when the south shafts were joined.

TML and Eurotunnel spent 1992 and 1993 getting the tunnels and related amenities finished. That effort entailed, among other activities, installing electrical and communications equipment, finishing 150 cross passages between the service and rail tunnels, and constructing terminals on each side of the channel. The first passenger train traveled through the tunnel in May of 1993, and the official opening was slated for May 6, 1994. As TML put the finishing touches on the Chunnel and Eurotunnel scrambled to raise more funds, the two groups nevertheless continued to battle each other in the courts. Initially, TML was hesitant to give up full control of the Chunnel to its sister company, but after a series of negotiations involving TML, Eurotunnel, and major investors, an agreement to transfer control from TML to Eurotunnel was reached. Eurotunnel took full control of the project beginning late in 1993 and conducted final tests on the system with the help of TML in 1994. Overall, the project had taken 99 months from start to finish, 15,000 workers were involved, and 11 giant tunnel-boring machines were used.

The Chunnel was officially inaugurated on May 8, 1994. It soon began providing limited passenger service and was almost fully operational after several months. The system was designed to accommodate 2,500 foot long shuttle trains that traveled at 90 miles per hour. Cars and buses pulled onto large wagons on the train, and passengers were allowed to move about on the wagons during the ride through the Chunnel. Truck drivers pulled their rigs onto more rudimentary wagons and traveled separately from their vehicles. Interspersed with those shuttles, moreover, were high-speed trains that also could run on Britain's and continental Europe's railway systems. The train system lived up to its promise of moving passengers between London and Paris in three hours, and between the continents in about 35 minutes. In part because of cost overruns, Eurotunnel began charging rates of US$240 to US$460 per passenger, depending on the time of year, for a round trip. That compared to about US$90 for a one-and-one-half-hour ferry trip.

When the Chunnel opened in 1994, critics condemned Eurotunnel and the other parties involved in the project for creating an expensive, undesirable, and unnecessary transport system. The project was indeed expensive; originally expected to cost US$7.5 billion, expenditures had increased to US$15 billion by 1994 and then to a staggering US$23 billion by early 1995. Eurotunnel was left grappling with a cash crunch, and angry creditors began pressuring the company to pay its bills. Fortunately for Eurotunnel, by 1995 the Chunnel was beginning to live up to its originators' claims of being a viable system of transportation. In fact, by February of that year the Chunnel had snapped up an impressive 20 to 25 percent of the cross-channel freight market. Furthermore, the service was competing aggressively with airlines serving the London/Paris and London/Belgium routes. Although the Chunnel's profit potential remained unproven going into the mid-1990s, its status as an engineering marvel of the 20th century was undeniable.

### Digging for Profits in 1995

Two factors kept Eurotunnel from posting a profit in the 1990s. It carried a massive debt burden leftover from the construction of the tunnel. In addition, the two main ferry companies, the Peninsular & Oriental Steam Navigation Co. plc (P&O) and Stena-Sealink, lowered prices and increased their Channel crossings to 80 a day. Airlines, though, generally lost market share on competing routes.

Eurotunnel suspended interest payments on £5.3 billion ($8 billion) of junior debt in September 1995 as they reached £2 million ($3 million) a day. A long process of renegotiating the debt ensued. "What has to happen is a sharing of the pain," said Morton in the *New York Times*.

Meanwhile, the company introduced more populist pricing to compete with the ferries. The British government approved a high-speed rail link between London and Kent in March 1996, and Eurotunnel began breaking even—apart from financing costs—that same month.

Robert Malpas took over as Eurotunnel plc chairman in November 1996. Morton, his predecessor, had arranged a $19 billion debt-equity swap with 225 banks and 750,000 share-

holders by mid-October. Morton had reason to tell the *Financial Times*, "We have arrived at the end of the beginning."

The proverbial light at the end of the tunnel was obscured by smoke on November 18, 1996, when a fire broke out in the Chunnel. Although its pressurized service tunnel worked properly, it took two hours to lay a fire hose. In the wake of the incident, commercial freight shuttle services were canceled until June 1997. Eurotunnel's share prices fell further; the company lost £642 million in 1996 before taxes, although it limited its operating loss to just £33 million, from £200 million the previous year.

Eurotunnel retreated from price competition with the ferry companies in March 1997. P&O and Stena could not obtain regulatory approval to merge their cross-Channel operations for the peak summer season, giving Eurotunnel a respite from what would have been a powerful joint venture.

In November 1997, Eurotunnel's lenders agreed to restructure £8.7 billion ($14.8 billion) of the company's debt. The number of banks involved had fallen to 174 after it stopped paying interest on its junior debt; American banks had raised their interest in the Chunnel from four to 25 percent. Eurotunnel Group gave 45.5 percent of its equity to the banks, which eliminated £1 billion of the debt and charged a lower interest rate on the remainder. Such a debt-equity swap was probably the only way for Eurotunnel to avoid bankruptcy, which likely would have been an even messier proposition than the two years of negotiations that led to the new debt deal. Small shareholders demanded the concession to operate the Chunnel be extended beyond 2052 in order for the debt rescheduling to proceed; Eurotunnel was given the right to operate the tunnel until 2086.

At the end of 1999, Eurotunnel submitted a feasibility study for a second, drive-through tunnel under the Channel. The study had been mandated in 1986. The group aimed to be profitable by 2004. Interest charges, however, continued to wipe out Eurotunnel's operating profit (£91 million) in the first half of 2000. A net loss of £75 million was posted. The company's retail operations were devastated by the abolition of duty-free sales, worth about £50 million a year, on June 30, 1999. Freight traffic increased and higher fares for cars and buses helped compensate. Still, Deutsche Bank forecast Eurotunnel would see a full-year loss of a £100 million for 2000.

### Principal Subsidiaries

Eurotunnel plc; Eurotunnel SA.

### Principal Competitors

Peninsular & Oriental Steam Navigation Co. plc; Stena Line.

### Further Reading

Barnard, Bruce, "Questions on Ferry Merger Provide Some Relief to Cash-Starved Eurotunnel," *Journal of Commerce*, June 12, 1997, p. 3B.

Cave, Andrew, "Eurotunnel Appoints New Chief Ahead of Debts Deal," *Daily Telegraph*, City Sec., July 25, 1996, p. 23.

"The Channel Battle," *Corporate Location, Channel Tunnel Region Supplement*, 1994, pp. 25–31.

"The Chunnel's Chances," *Fortune,* December 21, 1987, p. 9.

" 'Chunnel' Operator Faces Crunch Getting Its Finances in Order," *Los Angeles Times,* May 23, 1994, p. D8.

Croft, Jane, "Eurotunnel Hedges Loan Exposure; Deal Covers Two-Thirds of Junior Debt," *Financial Times,* Companies & Finance, August 11, 2000, p. 20.

——, "Eurotunnel Offsets Loss of Duty Free," *Financial Times,* Companies & Finance, July 25, 2000, p. 28.

Darnton, John, "Chunnel's Money Crisis Is Growing," *New York Times,* September 15, 1995, p. D1.

Davidson, Andrew, "Sir Alastair Morton," *Management Today,* October 1994, pp. 50–54.

Downer, Stephen, "So Far, Eurotunnel a Ferry Good Thing," *Advertising Age,* May 2, 1994, p. 39.

"EDMS Helps Channel Chunnel Project," *IMC Journal,* November/December 1994, pp. 8–11.

"Eurotunnel Makes Concession Extension Key to Restructuring Deal," *AFX News,* April 24, 1997.

"Eurotunnel Plan Avoids Bankruptcy," *New York Times,* November 27, 1997, p. D4.

"Eurotunnel to Withdraw from Cross-Channel Price-Cutting Battle," *AFX News,* February 6, 1997.

Fairweather, Virginia, "The Channel Tunnel: Larger than Life, and Late," *Civil Engineering,* May 1994, pp. 42–46.

Ferrabee, James, "Confident Chunnel Man," *Gazette,* February 8, 1995, p. D7.

Harper, Keith, "Chunnel to Tighten Safety Procedures," *Journal of Commerce,* November 25, 1998, p. 15A.

Healy, Tim, "Kent Firm Sees Light at End of Tunnel," *Seattle Times,* October 31, 1990, p. 1D.

Laushway, Ester, "Paris: Chunnel Vision," *Europe: Magazine of the European Community,* May 1994, pp. 43–45.

Levine, Joshua, "Chunnel Vision," *Forbes,* February 14, 1990, p. 146.

Lewis, William, "The Chunnel Has Stimulated Huge Capital Spending," *Financial Times,* Survey of Kent: Land, Sea and In the Air, March 15, 1996, p. 12.

Lincoln, Lori, " 'Chunnel' to Open in Late Summer '93: Tunnel Rail Service Will Link Britain, Continent," *Travel Weekly,* April 9, 1992, p. E3.

McCabe, Aileen, "Man Behind English Channel Tunnel Bows Out," *Gazette* (Montreal), November 1, 1996, p. C2.

Nankivell, Neville, "Channel Tunnel Facing Contract Dateline," *Financial Post,* March 27, 1993, p. 18.

Reina, Peter, "After 99 Months' Work Channel Tunnel Prepares for Trains," *Engineering News Record,* May 2, 1994, pp. 22–26.

Stewart, Toy, "Luxury, Calm, and Speed: It's the Chunnel Train," *Business Week,* November 14, 1994, p. 143.

—Dave Mote
—updated by Frederick C. Ingram

# FiberMark

## FiberMark, Inc.

161 Wellington Road
Brattleboro, Vermont 05302
U.S.A.
Telephone: (802) 257-9365
Fax: (802) 257-5900
Web site: http://www.fibermark.com

*Public Company*
*Incorporated:* 1989 as Specialty Paperboard, Inc.
*Employees:* 1,562
*Sales:* $325.3 million (1999)
*Stock Exchanges:* New York
*Ticker Symbol:* FMK
*NAIC:* 32213 Paperboard Mills

FiberMark, Inc. is a leading producer of specialty fiber-based materials (paper, synthetic, and composite) serving industrial and consumer needs worldwide. With ten production facilities in the United States and Europe, the company's three divisions focus on niche markets where components or finished products for industrial and consumer applications are manufactured. FiberMark's customers usually purchase the company's products in roll or sheet form, converting it later into finished products.

Materials manufactured by FiberMark are grouped into four product families: filter media, tape base and label material, technical specialties, and cover materials for home, school, and office use. A few of the end uses of FiberMark's wide variety of products include: fuel filters in automobiles or air filters in airplane passenger cabins; vacuum cleaner bags; backing materials for masking tapes or tapes used for checkbook and memo pads; self-adhesive and garment labels; base materials for sandpaper, photographic, printing and graphic arts, wallpaper, and flooring overlay; electrical/electronic applications, such as printed circuit boards; and disposable medical drapes, garments and linens.

### Early Years: 1861–1961

FiberMark adopted its present name in 1997, but the company traces its history to 1861, when two young brothers, Alfred Wells Case and Albert Willard Case, began making paper as Case Brothers, Inc. in South Manchester, Connecticut. This area of Connecticut was one of the important paper producing centers of 19th century America, and a second paper mill was subsequently built in East Hartford. The brothers had learned the papermaking trade while employed by Charles Bunce, one of the first paper manufacturers in the area. Until the Civil War, paper was not made from wood pulp, but from linen or cotton rags or a mixture of those fibers. With capital of just $135, Alfred and Albert Case set up a mill that produced washed cotton waste needed for the manufacture of gun cotton (similar to gunpowder) used by the Union Army during the Civil War.

At the end of the war, the Case brothers began a specialized papermaking operation and soon became a leader in the manufacture of pressboard, or paperboard, a strong, highly glazed paper product, used at the time as album board, shoe board, and binder board. The brothers invented several methods for laminating paperboard and increasing its density. They also developed a new type of cylinder machine that produced paperboard in a continuous process. True Connecticut Yankees, they ran an efficient, innovative, highly skilled operation. When a fire severely damaged their three-story frame factory in 1875, they put the mill back into operation within 40 days.

For the next century, Case Brothers continued to flourish in Connecticut as the New England paper industry reached its peak. In 1878 the company won first prize for its pressed paper at the International Paris Exposition, competing with paper manufacturers from throughout Europe, and achieved another success at the Melbourne, Australia, Exhibition of 1880. Specialty paperboard products continued to be refined and developed, and the company, which remained in the family, became very successful.

### Brattleboro and Boise Cascade: 1961–89

Exactly a century after its founding, Case Brothers expanded its operations to Brattleboro, Vermont. The company's new, modern manufacturing facility was built to meet the growing demand for Case Brothers' product lines, particularly pressboard. The 200,000 square-foot plant was the first new multicylinder paper mill built in New England in 50 years and the only plant that had ever been designed exclusively for making

## Company Perspectives:

*With its versatile manufacturing and technical capabilities and strong service orientation, FiberMark holds leadership positions in its core markets. Using a wide range of fibers and raw materials, including glass, rayon and other synthetic fibers, cotton denim, wood pulp, and recovered paper, the company's manufacturing capabilities comprise paper-making, nonwoven production, including synthetic web technology (meltblown) and wet-laid nonwoven; saturating; coating; embossing; and other converting processes.*

pressboard products. In addition to pressboard, the new Brattleboro plant manufactured specialty industrial materials such electrical insulation.

Leading figures in the company at the time of its expansion to Brattleboro were Wells Case Dennison, president, and vice-president Robert Case Dennison, both direct descendants of Albert Willard Case. As the successful Brattleboro operation became the core business of Case Brothers, the decision was made to close the company's older mills in Connecticut. In 1973, ground was broken in Brattleboro for construction of a new administrative building as the company began to consolidate its entire business there.

Meanwhile, in 1967, the paper industry giant Boise Cascade Corporation purchased Case Brothers. Case offered a strategic fit with Boise's existing office materials business since pressboard was primarily a cover material for office supplies used in filing and binding. For Case Brothers, Boise offered capital and people resources that the company needed in order to expand. Case management hoped to find a company with a similar management philosophy, and they found it with Boise.

The company, now Boise's Specialty Paperboard Division, entered an aggressive expansion period. Over two decades, Boise made several acquisitions and sales aimed at consolidating its paperboard activities. In 1977, Latex Fiber Industries and Payne-Jones, Inc. were acquired from Uniroyal. This major purchase consisted of two paperboard mills in Beaver Falls, New York, (Lewis and Latex), one in Brownville, New York, and the Payne-Jones specialized coating and finishing facility in Lowville, New York. In 1983, Boise acquired the Mississquoi Mill in Sheldon Springs, Vermont. (Boise sold Payne-Jones, Inc. in 1987 and, after shutting down the Brownville mill in 1988, sold it in 1989.)

Under Boise's auspices, the company enjoyed continued market growth and undertook major facility upgrades. Through acquisition of complementary manufacturing companies and continued facility enhancements, the division developed new capabilities, including coating, embossing, and saturating, that allowed its manufactured materials to be substituted for other materials such as textiles, leathers, rubber, and plastics. By 1972, Specialty Paperboard was reputed to be the largest producer in the world of paper pressboard and employed some 300 persons.

The division also took a leadership role in environmental matters when, in December 1972, it became one of the first

manufacturers in Vermont to comply with government water treatment regulations. After investing in an $850,000 water treatment facility, Specialty Paperboard was able to completely recycle water from the Connecticut River, which supplied the firm with about one million to 1.75 million gallons of water each day. The purpose of the system was to make possible the reuse of water solids left over from the manufacturing process. The state's water resources commissioner regarded the company's cooperation in meeting environmental standards ''fantastic,'' according to the Brattleboro *Reformer* (December 14, 1972).

### Emerging as Specialty Paperboard: 1989–97

In June 1989, in a leveraged buyout by management that included K. Peter Norrie, a former executive vice-president of Boise Cascade's Paper Group; A. Ben Groce, general manager of the Specialty Paperboard Division; and Jack Sherman, who became chief financial officer (CFO). With the help of private investment firm McCown, De Leeuw & Co., the company became a private, independently held company, headquartered in Brattleboro, with the name Specialty Paperboard, Inc. When it was incorporated in 1989, Specialty Paperboard had revenues of $120 million. Boise Cascade, which had decided to divest itself of its non-core businesses, retained a 30 percent share in the company.

Specialty Paperboard then entered the most challenging period in its history. The United States was in the midst of an economic recession, and the company's assets were heavily leveraged. Management consolidated Specialty Paperboard's operations into a few facilities in order to reduce debt and focus on the company's most profitable manufacturing and marketing segments. In 1991, the Mississquoi Mill was sold.

The company went public in 1993 on the NASDAQ Exchange, trading under the symbol SPBI, simultaneously buying out Boise Cascade's remaining shares. By this time, Specialty Paperboard was concentrating almost exclusively on paper products using recycled fiber and office waste products, primarily (60 percent) for sale to the office products industry. The remainder of its business was evenly divided between the sale of gaskets, principally to the automobile industry, and latex-reinforced materials for albums and book covers. During the early 1990s, widespread market interest in recycled materials peaked as new government standards went into effect, and the company responded by developing even more materials with significant recovered material content.

The year 1993 was a particularly momentous one for Specialty Paperboard. In addition to launching its initial public offering, the company, according to the Keene (N.H.) *Sentinel*, was forced to shut down briefly during the summer when its major customers, under pressure from office supply superstores, cut back on orders. By December of that year, however, Specialty Paperboard was up and running seven days a week, 24-hours a day, and shipping 100 tons of product each day. The company, with revenues of $80 million, was now employing some 250 persons.

The management team that had led the 1989 leveraged buyout underwent some important changes during the early 1990s. Both A. Ben Groce and Jack Sherman left the company,

**Key Dates:**

**1861:** Case Brothers, Inc. is founded in South Manchester, Connecticut; another mill added later in East Hartford.
**1961:** Case Brothers builds Brattleboro mill.
**1967:** Boise Cascade purchases Case Brothers.
**1989:** Leveraged buyout by management; company becomes Specialty Paperboard, Inc.
**1993:** Specialty Paperboard, Inc. goes public on NASDAQ.
**1997:** Name of company changed to FiberMark, Inc.; company moves to New York Stock Exchange.

but K. Peter Norrie remained as chairman. Bruce Moore, who had served as general manager of the Latex Fiber Products Division, became vice-president and CFO in December 1990. Alex Kwader, who had been a senior vice-president of the company, serving as general manager of the Pressboard Products Division, became president and CEO in 1991. Moore and Kwader continued to serve in those roles through the 1990s.

Beginning in 1994, Specialty Paperboard initiated a targeted acquisitions strategy that significantly expanded the company's product offerings. In July 1994, the company acquired Endura Products Division from W.R. Grace & Co. for $24.5 million. Seeking also to concentrate its focus on specific profitable niche markets, the company sold the assets of its Lewis Mill, as well as its gasket business, to Armstrong World Industries, Inc. in 1995 for approximately $14 million.

By 1996, the company had become a leading manufacturer of specialty fiber-based materials for a number of industrial and consumer applications. Key products included: pressboard used in filing products and report covers for office and school use, filtration materials for car and truck engines, insulation materials for power transformers and printed circuit boards, and saturated base materials for masking tapes and book covers.

On November 1, 1996, Specialty Paperboard announced its most ambitious purchase to date: the acquisition of Custom Papers Group, Inc. (CPG) and Arcon Coating Mills, both manufacturers of specialty paper products. CPG operated five paper mills and manufactured a diverse group of specialty papers for industrial and technical markets, including filtration products for internal combustion engines, electrical insulating paper used in the manufacture of power distribution transformers, mat boards for picture mounting applications, base paper for industrial abrasive/sanding products, and photographic packaging materials. Arcon manufactured colored binding and stripping tapes and edge cover materials sold primarily to the office products, checkbook, and book binding markets. Since many of Arcon's products were already being combined with Specialty Paperboard's pressboard cover materials for book and report covers and other office supplies, this purchase was a particularly complementary one.

The two acquisitions, which totaled some $130 million, were financed through a $100 million offering of ten-year non-amortizing senior notes. In a company announcement of these purchases, Kwader predicted they would "effectively double the revenues of our company and provide synergies that will add to our overall profitability."

His confidence proved justified. Sales shot up from $124 million in 1996 to $325.3 million in 1999. From 1993, when Specialty Paperboard went public, through December 1999, sales had increased 306 percent. Over the same period, the company achieved a 25 percent compound annual growth rate, excluding extraordinary events. Moreover, 1999 marked the seventh consecutive year of record earnings as well as sales growth for FiberMark. According to *Better Investing* (March 1998), the company's success during this period could be attributed "primarily to management's ability to consolidate acquisitions and deliver greater profitability."

### *FiberMark: A New Look, A Broader Vision*

In April 1997, the company changed its name. Announcing the new corporate identity, Kwader remarked, "The name FiberMark more accurately reflects our consolidated businesses and the fact that we are leaders in the manufacture and conversion of specialty fiber-based materials." By the late 1990s, as its product line expanded, the company was indeed using a wide array of raw materials to formulate its products, including virgin hardwood and softwood pulp, secondary wood fiber from pre- and post-consumer waste, secondary cotton fiber from the apparel industry, synthetic fibers (nylon, polyester and fiberglass), and synthetic latex. Significantly, as FiberMark continued to acquire businesses in other markets with very demanding technical requirements, the use of recovered material content in its products began to decline.

As the new century began, management continued to pursue a focused strategy of making selective acquisitions in niche markets, rationalizing production capacity, and building a global customer base. According to its strategic plan, FiberMark expected to realize revenues exceeding $1 billion by 2005–2007. The company was also poised to extend its leadership in specialty fiber-based materials by diversifying geographically and operationally, while focusing on value-added opportunities within specialty fiber-based materials markets.

For FiberMark to meet its ambitious strategic objectives, major acquisitions would have to continue to play a critical role. Beginning in 1994, the company completed five significant acquisitions, all of which soon added to the bottom line. A key move was the purchase of a German company, Steinbeis Gessner GmbH & Co., in 1997, for $43 million. Renamed FiberMark Gessner, the division made filter media for automotive applications, vacuum bag filter materials, abrasives and masking tape base materials for pressure sensitive tapes and carrier tapes for electronic components. FiberMark Gessner immediately began to play a significant role in the company as a whole. In May 1999, all worldwide filter-media business, accounting for almost 45 percent of FiberMark's sales, was consolidated under Gessner's leadership. Gessner's strategic and marketing-planning process, using a combination of market and customer-specific objectives, provided a model that FiberMark adapted for company-wide use.

In August 1999, FiberMark acquired a second major German company: Papierfabriek Lahnstein GmbH, another leader in complementary niche markets for specialty fiber-based materials, including security papers and base materials for wall coverings and self-adhesive labels. Purchased from its publicly-held Swiss parent company Sihl AG, Lahnstein was acquired for approximately $22 million. It had net revenues in 1998 of approximately $31.8 million and in 1999, of $39 million. Renamed FiberMark Lahnstein, the company, headquartered near Frankfurt, brought new markets to FiberMark as well as new technologies and products. One such product was a weather-resistant synthetic-content material for labels used in outdoor settings that prints well and can be bar-coded.

Meanwhile, in order to streamline operations, FiberMark's management closed the Owensboro, Kentucky, facility in January 1998, the Beaver Falls, New York, plant in January 1999, and expected to cease manufacturing operations at the Hughesville, New Jersey, mill by December 31, 2000. Production at each of these plants was consolidated in other domestic FiberMark facilities. With the closing of the Hughesville mill, the company would operate nine facilities in the United States and Europe.

New fiber-based products continued to be developed as FiberMark moved into the 21st century. Among them were, lighter-weight and embossed cover stocks; food board for containers used by fast-food outlets; a synthetic sheet to replace cloth in certain tape applications; new media that enables auto filters to provide higher performance; and a new nonwoven base for wall coverings that, among other attributes, is dry-strippable and will not shrink.

### Principal Divisions

Durable Specialties Division; FiberMark Gessner GmbH & Co. and Filter Media Division (Germany); Technical & Office Products Division.

### Principal Operating Units

Filter Media North America; FiberMark Lahnstein (Germany).

### Principal Competitors

Ahlstrom Filtration, Inc.; Kimberly Clark Corp.; Arjo Wiggins Appleton PLC; International Paper Co.

### Further Reading

"Case Brothers Comes to Brattleboro," *Brattleboro Daily Reformer,* July 11, 1961.
"FiberMark, Inc. A Stock to Study," *Better Investing,* March 1998 pp. 7, 97–100.
Marcel, Joyce, "Paper Chase Leads FiberMark Around the World," *Vermont Business Magazine,* November 1999.
Ogden, Marianne, "Boise Sells Plant," *Brattleboro Daily Reformer,* April 11, 1989, p. 1.
Poole, William, "Boise Cascade Leads in State," *Brattleboro Daily Reformer,* December 14, 1972, p.5.

—Margery M. Heffron

# *Fimalac* S.A.

# Fimalac S.A.

97, rue de Lille
75007 Paris
France
Telephone: (+33) 1 47 53 61 50
Fax: (+33) 1 45 55 45 96
Web site: http://www.fimalac.com

*Public Company*
*Incorporated:* 1996 as Financière Marc de Lacharrière
S.A.
*Employees:* 10,003
*Sales:* EUR 1.58 billion ($1.4 billion)
*Stock Exchanges:* Euronext Paris
*NAIC:* 551112 Offices of Other Holding Companies;
551114 Corporate, Subsidiary, and Regional
Managing Offices

French holding company Fimalac S.A. (named for founder and financier Marc Ladreit de Lacharrière) wants to transform itself into a global "business-to-business" services Internet company. As such, the group has abandoned a number of its original investments—including magazine publishing and real estate—to refocus itself around three main axes. The first sector is credit rating services, through its Fitch IBCA holding, which accounted for 17 percent of Fimalac's revenues in 1999. In 2000, Fimalac boosted its credit rating division with the acquisitions of Duff & Phelps Credit Rating and the BankWatch unit of Canadian publisher Thomson. The company's credit rating segment is also a driving force behind the company's growing Internet-based activity. Handtools and automotive and garage parts, tools, and equipment is the company's largest division, established through Fimalac's surprise—and hostile—takeover of Facom S.A. in 1999 and boosted by the FFr 3.6 billion acquisition of Autodistribution, a specialist provider of parts for the automotive aftermarket in that same year. The Facom component contributed 45 percent of Fimalac's 1999 revenues. Fimalac's third major area of operations revolves around its industrial holdings, which include its CLAL-MSX subsidiary and the related Engelhardt-CLAL joint venture, which produce

metal alloys; LBC, the world's number two provider of chemical storage facilities and services, with more than two million cubic meters of storage space. LBC, for Lille Bonnières Colombes, was one of the original Fimalac holdings. The company's industrial and manufacturing segment also includes Secap, a maker of postage and franking machines and other office-related equipment. Long criticized as a mishmash of unrelated activities, Fimalac's attempt to reposition itself as a "business-to-business" provider with an Internet focus (the group claims as much as 50 percent of its revenues will be generated through Internet sales in the year 2000) also seeks to boost the value of its stock by enabling the company to be assessed for the worth of its holdings, rather than as a holding company (the company estimated its share price to be as much as EUR 50 per share too low in 1999). Such a revaluation would at least benefit Marc Ladreit de Lacharrière, the company's founder, chairman, president, CEO, and holder of nearly 88 percent of the company's shares.

## *Holding Financial Clout in the 1990s*

The formation of holding company Fimalac S.A., for Financière Marc de Lacharrière, in 1991 was merely a consecration of nearly 20 years of financial investments for its founder Marc Ladreit de Lacharrière. A member of France's former nobility (who, although stripped of their aristocratic status after the French revolution nonetheless remained influential in the country's political and financial circles), de Lacharrière was something of a maverick in his youth—after founding, then selling the highly successful teenage fashion magazine *Mademoiselle,* de Lacharrière joined the Ecole Nationale d'Administration (ENA), the breeding ground of France's political (and financial) elite. Yet de Lacharrière soon surprised his peers, who included future political leaders and economic kingpins, such as Louis Schweitzer, later named as head of the government-owned automaker, Renault, by refusing to join the French civil service directly upon his graduation—something unheard of among ENA graduates.

Instead, de Lacharrière rejoined the commercial world, first joining the banking industry, with the Banque de Suez (later the Banque Indosuez). In 1976, de Lacharrière left the Banque de

**Key Dates:**

**1991:** Marc Ladreit de Laccharière acquires publicly listed Lille Bonnières et Colombes (LBC).
**1992:** Company acquires Sofres.
**1993:** Acquires IBCA; Sofres acquires Secodip.
**1996:** LBC acquires two other publicly quoted de Laccharière holding companies, renames as Fimalac S.A.; IBCA acquires Quest insurance ratings provider.
**1997:** Fimalac defines new "business to business" strategy, divests its publishing and real estate holdings, agrees to merge Sofres into Taylor Nelson AGB; IBCA acquires Fitch's Investors Services, renaming it Fitch IBCA.
**1999:** Fimalac takes over Facom S.A.; Fitch IBCA acquires Duff & Phelps and BankWatch.
**2000:** Fimalac announces intention to boost its Internet-based business.

Suez to become financial director of French cosmetics powerhouse L'Oréal. De Lacharrière went on to a brilliant career at L'Oréal, rising to the number two position in less than ten years, when he was named vice-president in 1984.

Yet Lacharrière already had begun leading a double life before joining L'Oréal—that of financier. One of de Lacharrière's first investments was that of publisher Editions Masson, which de Lacharrière bought in 1973. Publishing was to continue to be one of de Lacharrière's main "hobby" interests, as his holdings grew to include publishing group Valmonde and such diverse titles as the weekly *Le Journal des Finances, Valeurs Actuelles,* and the high-brow intellectual magazine *Revue des Deux Mondes,* originally launched in 1829.

De Lacharrière's investment interests continued throughout his career at L'Oréal at the same time that he was helping that company capture one of the world-leading positions in the cosmetics industry (and generating a personal fortune as reward for his part in L'Oréal's success). However, de Lacharrière's personal fortunes were aided by his outside investment interests as well. During the 1980s, a number of de Lacharrière's investments hit the jackpot, as it were, as he received the benefits of such events as the hostile takeover of insurance group Victoire by the Banque Suez. While his interests in Centenaire Blanzy— fused into Fimalac in the late 1990s—also were generating strong dividends, de Lacharrière built up a strong real estate portfolio that was to provide the basis for his group's Sefimeg subsidiary. At the same time, de Lacharrière also served as an administrator for acquisition-hungry Crédit Lyonnaise, a position he was to hold until 1993.

### Financier to Internet Industrialist for the 21st Century

At the beginning of the 1990s, de Lacharrière once again surprised his peers when he resigned from L'Oreal at the age of 50 to devote his attentions to his growing financial holdings. One of de Lacharrière's first moves as a newly "free-lance"

financier was the takeover of Lille Bonnières et Colombes (LBC), one of France's leading chemical storage services providers. The LBC takeover also gave de Lacharrière a publicly quoted company to run.

During the first half of the 1990s, de Lacharrière continued to build up his interests, grouping his various holdings under a number of publicly listed holding companies, including LBC, Alspi, Comptoir Lyon Alemand Louyot, Centenaire Blanzy (in which de Lacharrière built up controlling interest in the late 1990s), and Clal, the specialty metals and alloys producer.

In 1992, de Lacharrière decided to launch his growing portfolio into a new direction, and he acquired controlling stakes in France's Sofres, a public research company, and followed that acquisition with the takeover of Secodip, making Sofres the leading market research company in France. After Sofres was acquired by Taylor Nelson AGB (creating Taylor Nelson Sofres Plc), de Laccharière's share of the new company, one of the world leaders, remained at 11 percent.

Meanwhile, de Laccharière had brought his interest to bear in another new area, when his holding company acquired International Banking and Credit Analysis (IBCA), a London-based bond ratings firm with a specialty in the banking sector, in 1993. IBCA, founded in 1978 by Robin Monro Davis, who continued to lead the company after its acquisition, was the only non-American ratings firm admitted as a Nationally Recognized Statistical Rating Organization (NRSRO) by the Securities and Exchange Commission. With the Sofres and IBCA acquisitions, de Lacharrière had correctly recognized the growing trend toward such information services, a market that was to see a full boom by the mid-1990s. Under de Lacharrière's control, both IBCA and Sofres grew to become leaders in their sectors, expanding their range of services as well as building their position through acquisitions. Following the acquisitions of these interests, de Lacharrière sold off his stake in Editions Masson.

Often described as a "mishmash" of "bric-a-brac," de Lacharrière's varied holdings—based on a "cascade" model of publicly quoted holding companies that had been popular among French financiers in the 1980s—had grown to more than FFr 8 billion in revenues. In the mid-1990s, however, de Lacharrière joined a growing trend toward unified holdings. The first stage of the creation of a new, simplified investment structure was taken in 1996, when the Lille Bonnières et Colombes holding absorbed the Alspi and Clal vehicles to create the single Fimalac S.A. (which stood for Financière Marc de Lacharrière) holding company. The simplification of de Lacharrière's holding company's and Fimalac's structure continued into 1998, when Centenaire Blanzy (by then de Lacharrière had built up more than 85 percent of that group's voting rights) was merged into Fimalac. These dealings led to complaints from the various minority shareholders in de Lacharrière's holdings; de Lacharrière was criticized for "juggling" with his companies and employees without consulting his minority shareholders.

The lack of transparency among de Lacharrière's holdings and the lack of focus among Fimalac's business areas meanwhile continued to depress the group's stock price, as the Paris stock market remained wary of diversified holding companies.

In part in response to this situation, de Lacharrière and Fimalac devised a new strategy designed to clarify the holding company's direction. Beginning in 1997, the company identified its future focus as that of a "business to business" company. As such Fimalac began divesting itself of various interests, including its Sefimeg real estate group, sold to fellow financier François Pinault, followed by the sales of its Valmonde publishing holdings, and then its interests in the market research sector, through its shares of Sofres.

The redirection of the company continued through 1998, as Fimalac pared down to a new core of holdings, including its Clal precious metals and alloys transformation unit, which produced specialty metals for applications ranging from dentistry to jewelry (and which accounted for some 65 percent of revenues in 1998), the Secap-Anfa business machines group, and Fimalac's LBC chemical storage arm. If Fimalac maintained a strong industrial component to its holdings, its attention also had been drawn to the rapidly growing "information age." In 1996, Fimalac's IBCA ratings company moved into the largely protected—because of the heavy cost of start-up investments—American market with the acquisition of American insurance rating company Quest. Then the company moved to claim a place among the top three ratings companies worldwide, behind Moody's and Standard and Poor, when it acquired the United States' Fitch Investors' Services, for US$175 million.

The renamed ratings company, Fitch IBCA, continued to drive Fimalac's growth into 1999, when the company added two more North American companies, bond rater Duff & Phelps, and then bank ratings company BankWatch, formerly part of Canada's Thomson publishing group. Yet in mid-1999, de Laccharière added a new dimension to the company when it launched a hostile takeover for France's hand tool and automotive aftermarket leader Facom S.A. An unusual move for de Laccharière, the Facom takeover proceeded on a more or less friendly basis after Fimalac raised its purchase offer. De Laccharière then put friend Alain Gomez, former head of French electronics giant Thomson S.A. in place as CEO of Facom.

By 2000, de Laccharière and Fimalac, in a continuing quest to boost the company's stock market valuation, were proclaiming their conversion to the religion of the "new Internet economy"; by the end of the year 2000, the company expected some 50 percent of its sales to come through the Internet, driven not only by the strong on-line services offerings of its Fitch IBCA subsidiary but also by Facom's strong internet presence. But Fimalac promised to go further, as de Laccharière announced his company's readiness to invest whatever funds necessary to build its share of revenues provided through the Internet, including an interest in acquiring businesses directly involved in the booming "e-business" sector in the early years of the new century.

### *Principal Subsidiaries*

CLAL-MSX S.A.; CLAL US Eurl; Engelhard-CLAL SAS (50%); Facom S.A. (93.75%); Financière SECAP S.A.; LBC S.A.; Minerais & Engrais S.A.; Rhenameca S.A.; SEFI SNC; Fimalac Inc. (U.S.A.); Fitch IBCA Inc.

### *Principal Competitors*

Cookson Group plc; Dun & Bradstreet Corp.; Emerson Electric Co.; GATX Corp; Inco Limited; Invensys PLC; Johnson Matthey PLC; Metals USA Inc.; Moody's Corp; Neopost S.A.; Rio Algom Ltd; Robert Bosch GmbH; Ryerson Tull Inc; Saint-Gobain S.A.; Snap-On Inc.

### *Further Reading*

Gay, Pierre-Angel, "Fimalac cherche à convaincre la Bourse de son ancrage dans la 'nouvelle économie,' " *Les Echos,* April 27, 2000, p. 28.

Jacquin, Jean-Baptiste, "Fimalac To Acquire BankWatch Unit from the Thomson Corporation," *Canadian Corporate News,* October 19, 2000.

——, "Les ennuis de Marc Ladreit de Lacharrière," *L'Expansion,* May 15, 1996, p. 12.

——, "Moi, un raider ? Surtout ne le dites à personne," *L'Expansion,* May 27, 1999, p. 88.

——, "Opération nettoyage dans les holdings," *L'Expansion,* June 27, 1996, p. 24.

——, "The Would-Be King of Credit Ratings," *Economist,* August 16, 1997.

Marcial, Gene G., "A Buy Rating on This Bond-Rater?," *Business Week,* March 29, 1999, p. 180.

—M.L. Cohen

# First Albany Companies Inc.

**30 South Pearl Street**
**Albany, New York 12207-0052**
**U.S.A.**
**Telephone: (518) 447-8500**
**Toll Free: (800) 462-6242**
**Fax: (518) 447-8663**
**Web site: http://www.fac.com**

*Public Company*
*Incorporated:* 1953 as First Albany Corporation
*Employees:* 870
*Sales:* $248.7 million (1999)
*Stock Exchanges:* NASDAQ
*Ticker Symbol:* FACT
*NAIC:* 52232 Financial Transactions Processing, Reserve,
     and Clearing House Activities; 52311 Investment
     Banking and Securities Dealing; 52312 Securities
     Brokerage; 52392 Portfolio Management; 52393
     Investment Advice; 52591 Open-End Investment
     Funds

First Albany Companies Inc., acting through its subsidiaries, conducts a full-service investment banking and brokerage business. These activities include securities brokerage for institutional customers and market making and trading of corporate, government, and municipal securities. First Albany also underwrites and distributes municipal and corporate securities, provides securities clearance activities for other brokerage firms, and offers financial advisory services to its customers, including serving as investment manager, making investment decisions, and providing research, statistical analysis, and continuous supervision of portfolios. It also provides venture capital and merchant banking services to firms in the high-technology sector.

### Privately Owned Brokerage and Financial Services Firm: 1953–85

First Albany Corporation was founded in 1953 by Daniel V. McNamee, Jr., a lawyer who also had become a vice-president of his father-in-law's investment brokerage business in Albany, New York. The company established a financial services department in the 1970s, with three units: financial planning, limited partnerships, and insurance. By the time McNamee died in 1977, First Albany had offices in 11 cities in upstate New York and New England, a specialty in selling municipal bonds to the public, and annual revenues of about $7 million. He was succeeded as head of the firm by his son George, who had become president in 1975.

Seeking to attract funds from institutional clients and convinced that the United States would have to rebuild its military forces in the post-Vietnam era, the younger McNamee, in 1979, began concentrating on defense stocks. First Albany sponsored seminars and research reports on military technologies for its institutional clients, and a team of its analysts established five categories for further investigation: lasers, precision guided missiles and electronic guidance systems, high-speed integrated circuits, defense manufacturing technology and advanced strategic metals, and nuclear materials. When the Reagan administration came into office in 1981 and began sponsoring a major military buildup, First Albany's research started to bring in clients—not only institutional investors but also underwriting business for defense-related companies seeking to go public. "The trick in the research business is to differentiate yourself," a money manager told Pamela Sherrid of *Business Week* in 1983. "By looking at small companies that no one else is, First Albany has made its name."

McNamee was ably supported by Hugh Johnson, senior vice-president and director of equity services. By 1981 Johnson was respected enough in the financial community to rate an interview in *Barron's,* where he warned investors to "hunker down" and avoid speculative investments in the face of a recessionary business climate and bear market but continued to recommend certain defense stocks. He also cast a favorable eye on telecommunications companies that were investing in information technology.

First Albany, in 1981, had 20 offices and was a member of the New York Stock Exchange, the American Stock Exchange, and various regional exchanges. Its revenues rose from $24.37 million in fiscal 1982 (the year ended September 30, 1982) to $58.37

## Company Perspectives:

*We will now be directing our efforts and capital to research-driven investment banking, capital markets, and venture capital operations. This positions First Albany as one of the only employee-owned public companies remaining in the securities industry with a pure institutional focus.*

million in fiscal 1986. Net income rose from $79,000 to $3.26 million over this period. It became, as First Albany Companies, a public company in 1985 and was operating 24 offices in five states the following year. Of its fiscal 1986 revenues, securities commissions accounted for 38 percent; interest (mainly from financing of customer margin loans, securities lending activities, and securities owned), 22 percent; principal transactions (trading in stocks, bonds, options, government securities, bank certificates of deposit, mortgage-based securities, and corporate obligations), 17 percent; investment banking, 14 percent; and clearing revenues, five percent. Its retail business accounted for 74 percent of revenues and institutional for only nine percent. Now also a member of the National Association of Securities Dealers, Inc., First Albany was making a market (acting as a specialist or "broker's broker") for 73 common stock or other equity securities quoted on the NASDAQ market.

First Albany was engaged principally in providing brokerage services to retail clients through its sales force, which had grown from about 60 to 164 over the previous five years. Many of these so-called Investment Executives had joined the company after previous association with large securities firms, and First Albany believed that they were receiving higher compensation for similar levels of production than their counterparts with many of these firms. In addition to selling these clients stocks, bonds, mutual funds, and other investment products, First Albany also made available to selected clients specialized financial services. The Financial Planning Department advised clients on a variety of interrelated financial matters, including investment portfolio review, tax management, insurance analysis, education, and retirement planning and estate analysis. Financial planners prepared detailed reports for clients, with specific recommendations aimed at accumulating wealth and reaching financial goals. First Albany also offered a range of retirement plans, fixed and variable annuities, and life and health insurance programs. In addition, it offered various tax-advantaged investments to its clients, usually in the form of limited partnership interests in real estate, oil and gas drilling, and similar ventures.

### Expanding Its Scope: 1986–95

Over the next five years First Albany expanded into three more states and more than doubled the number of securities for which it was serving as market maker. Revenues reached $72.58 million in fiscal 1991, with net income of $2.29 million. Principal transactions were now the chief source of revenue, accounting for 39 percent, followed by securities commissions, at 27 percent. Institutional business had become much more important to the firm, accounting for 29 percent of revenue, compared with 56 percent for retail.

First Albany won favorable mention as an underwriter in 1989 from the business periodical *Forbes,* which rated 70 percent of its new stock issues between 1982 and 1987 as outperforming Standard & Poor's index of 500 stocks, a ratio higher than any other investment bank surveyed. Nine of the ten were selling in 1989 at more than their offering price. "You make your reputation by the deals you don't do," McNamee explained to Richard L. Stern of *Forbes.* "We turn away a lot of deals, and some of them turn up at other firms," he added. Johnson also continued to earn respect from the business press, including *Fortune,* whose Andrew Serwer interviewed him for the publication's first issue of 1990. Johnson, he wrote, predicted, "In 1982, on the eve of the great bull market . . . that stocks would climb and urged investors to sign on. In 1987, just prior to the October crash, he warned them it was time to bail out." In the interview, Johnson correctly forecast a recession and advised readers to keep half their portfolios in high-quality bonds. When he recommended particular stocks, Johnson proved to be on target as well. In early 1993 Edward A. Wyatt of *Barron's* wrote of First Albany, "Last year, the firm's picks gained 27.5 percent, handsomely outperforming all the major stock issues."

First Albany Asset Management Corp. was formed in 1991 as a subsidiary with two acquired mutual funds: Investors' Preference Fund for Income and Investors' Preference N.Y. Tax Free Fund, both bond funds purchased from Dollar Dry Dock Savings Bank of New York City, with combined assets of $58.8 million. First Albany also formed a four-person division that fiscal year to sell high-yield securities, and a new venture to provide financial and merger services for banks, savings institutions, and other financial companies, mainly in the Northeast. By the end of fiscal 1995, First Albany's total revenues had reached $123.1 million. Its net income for the year was $3.35 million. That year the firm moved its investment banking arm from Albany to Boston and increased its research, institutional sales, and corporate finance units to 90 people, half of them in Boston. Among the local companies that First Albany helped bring public were Cambridge-based Project Software & Development Inc., Westborough-based Applix Inc., Lexington-based CP Clare Corp., and Natick-based Natural MicroSystems Corp. In all, the firm underwrote three initial public offerings in 1993, six in 1994, and six in 1995, with an emphasis on technology companies.

Also in fiscal 1995, First Albany added an institutional municipal risk-trading operation in which certain inventory positions are hedged by highly liquid future contracts. In addition, that year the company formed a strategic alliance with META Group, Inc., by which it turned over to the latter responsibility for research and analysis of developments and trends in information technology.

### Focus on High-Technology Investments: 1998–2000

By 1998 First Albany was focusing on three niche segments other than technology expected to provide exceptional investment opportunities: energy, financial institutions, and health care. That year, the parent company formed First Albany Enterprise Funding, Inc. as a private equity investment company whose business was to provide venture capital and merchant banking services to firms in the high-technology sector. Investment banking accounted for 13 percent of First Albany's revenues of $248.7 million in (calendar year) 1999. Its activities in that field included underwritings, initial and secondary offerings, advisory services, mergers and acquisitions, and private placements.

Principal transactions remained First Albany's largest revenue earner in 1999, with 28.9 percent of the total. These transactions included making a market in 193 common stocks quoted on NASDAQ. Also included were trades in tax-exempt and (beginning in 1999), taxable municipal bonds and taxable debt obligations, including U.S. Treasury bills, notes, and bonds; U.S. government agency notes and bonds; bank certificates of deposit; mortgage-backed securities; and corporate obligations. Securities commissions accounted for 28.5 percent of revenue and interest income for 24.7 percent. The firm's net income was only $413,000 in 1999 after taking a pretax loss of $7.2 million attributed primarily to a decline in book value of the investment portfolio. First Albany had 33 offices in 12 states at the end of 1999.

Brokerage services to private clients accounted for about half of First Albany's 1999 revenue, but in May 2000 the firm agreed to sell its Private Client Group to First Union Securities, Inc. for $100 million. This sale reduced First Albany by about 90,000 accounts, 200 brokers, and $11.4 billion in managed assets. Eighteen offices remained in 11 states: California, Connecticut, Florida, Illinois, Massachusetts, Minnesota, New Jersey, New York, Pennsylvania, Texas, and Virginia. McNamee announced that the firm would henceforth focus on investment banking, capital markets, and venture capital operations.

F.A. Technology Ventures, the First Albany venture capital arm aimed at launching high-technology businesses, had $70 million in its coffers by August 2000, when it received $50 million in investment from the state of New York's pension fund. Some of the revenue from the sale to First Union also was expected to go to this unit, which was to focus on investing in companies in the Northeast and, especially upstate New York. Based in Albany and Boston, the fund was to focus on information technology, such as software and Internet businesses, and on energy technology, especially new generating processes, transmission, and energy storage devices. First Albany Enterprise, the company's prior venture fund, was managing about $11 million in investments. First Albany Asset Management, the mutual fund subsidiary, had $590 million under management at the end of 1999.

Among the companies in the Albany area receiving financial backing from First Albany in 2000 were Tech Valley Communications of Albany, a new telecommunications firm; PowerAdz.com of Rensselaer, a Web site developer for newspapers; and MapInfo Corp. of North Greenbush, a mapping software developer. McNamee was chairman and a founder of Plug Power Inc. of Latham, an energy provider, and chief executive officer of Mechanical Technology Inc. of Colonie, an incubator for other technology companies. Described as a technology geek and outside-the-box thinker, McNamee told Kenneth Aaron of the *Albany Times-Union,* ''This is the greatest period of technological opportunities since the 1890s.'' McNamee owned 15.3 percent of First Albany's common stock in April 2000. Alan P. Goldberg, president since 1989 and co-chief executive officer since 1992, held 11.6 percent. An employee stock ownership plan owned 22.2 percent.

### *Principal Subsidiaries*

First Albany Asset Management Corporation; First Albany Corporation; First Albany Enterprise Funding, Inc.

### *Principal Divisions*

Equity; Municipal; Taxable Fixed Income.

### *Principal Competitors*

Goldman Sachs and Co.; Merrill Lynch and Company Inc.; PaineWebber Inc.; United Asset Management Corp.

### *Further Reading*

Aaron, Kenneth, ''High-Tech Man for All Seasons,'' *Albany Times-Union,* July 2, 2000, pp. D1 and continuation.

Ballman, Barbara, ''First Albany Subsidiary Buys Mutual Funds to Boost Earnings,'' *Capital District Business Review,* July 22, 1991, p. 2.

Barry, David G., ''First Albany Sees Technology Investments Start to Pay Off,'' *Boston Business Journal,* January 12, 1996, p. 7.

Bruno, Nicholas J., ''Reps. Sell Insurance as Fin. Service,'' *National Underwriter: Life & Health/Financial Services,* August 13, 1990, pp. 7-8.

Byrne, Harlan S., ''First Albany Cos.,'' *Barron's,* August 3, 1992, p. 32.

''D.V. McNamee Jr., Founder and Head of Banking Concern,'' *New York Times,* November 1, 1977, p. 40.

''First Union Corp.,'' *Wall Street Journal,* May 10, 2000, p. C19.

Mattox, Kerri P., ''First Albany Arm Takes Ventures Lead,'' *Albany Times-Union,* August 2, 2000, p. E1.

——, ''New Venture Capital Fund Raising Money,'' *Albany Times-Union,* June 17, 2000, p. B12.

Noble, Kenneth B., ''First Albany's Defense Stock Niche,'' *New York Times,* June 7, 1981, Sec. 3, p. 13.

Serwer, Andrew, ''Warnings of a Bear Market,'' *Fortune,* January 1, 1990, pp. 28–29.

Sherrid, Pamela, ''Military Options,'' *Forbes,* March 28, 1983, pp. 192, 194.

Stern, Richard L., and Charles M. Bartlett, Jr., ''But the Client Is Delighted,'' *Forbes,* April 3, 1989, pp. 130, 132.

Welling, Kathryn M., ''Hunker Down,'' *Barron's,* October 12, 1981, pp. 9, 32–34.

——, ''Investing in a Cold Climate,'' *Barron's,* October 5, 1992, pp. 8–9, 23.

Wyatt, Edward A., ''Local Talent,'' *Barron's,* January 11, 1993, p. 16.

—Robert Halasz

# Franklin Covey Company

2200 West Parkway Boulevard
Salt Lake City, Utah 84119
U.S.A.
Telephone: (801) 975-1776
Toll Free: (888) 833-1776
Fax: (801) 977-1431
Web site: http://www.franklincovey.com

*Public Company*
*Incorporated:* 1983 as Franklin Institute, Inc.
*Employees:* 4,165
*Sales:* $554.9 million (1999)
*Stock Exchanges:* New York
*Ticker Symbol:* FC
*NAIC:* 61143 Professional and Management Development
Training

Franklin Covey Company, formerly known as the Franklin Quest Co., is a leading provider of time management training seminars and products, including the well-known line of Franklin Planner books. The firm's clients include 82 of the Fortune 100 companies and more than two-thirds of the Fortune 500 companies, as well as thousands of other companies and governmental agencies at all levels. The company has also created pilot partnerships with schools systems across the United States, teaching the "7 Habits" to both administrators and teachers from kindergarten to college. The company's offerings are based on its comprehensive "Franklin System," which is designed to help individuals identify goals and prioritize tasks, as well as the 7 Habits as outlined and explained in Stephen R. Covey's *The 7 Habits of Highly Effective People*. The company has sales offices on four continents and operates more than 130 retail stores worldwide. Its products, including books, audio tapes and CDs, and software programs, are available in 32 languages. Franklin Covey markets over 1.5 million books and trains in excess of 750,000 seminar participants annually.

## 1981–91: Foundation and Early Growth

Franklin Institute, Inc., the forerunner of Franklin Covey Co., was incorporated in 1983 by Hyrum W. Smith, Dick Winwood, Dennis Webb, and Lynn Webb; Senator Robert F. Bennett joined the company the following year as chairman of the board. However, the company was actually founded by Smith in 1981. The 37-year-old Smith, a graduate of nearby Brigham Young University, decided to start a business providing management seminars. He set up shop in his basement and was soon providing his homemade management courses to groups of business executives.

Benjamin Franklin served as the inspiration and guiding philosophy for the courses. In fact, Smith attributed his own achievements and the success of his company to Franklin's ideas about human values and quality of life. It was after reading Franklin's autobiography that Smith decided he would build his own time management program based on Franklin's proven self-improvement philosophy. Smith interpreted Franklin's philosophy to mean that peoples' happiness and inner peace do not come from owning things, but from identifying what is important to them and then making their lives conform with those goals.

"Time is the stuff life is made of," Franklin is quoted as saying, and few Americans have used time as effectively as Franklin. In his 84 years of living, Franklin rose from apprentice to statesmen, making valuable contributions along the way in the areas of science, social philosophy, education, and the arts. Franklin achieved greatness, in part, through his homemade self-improvement and time management system. The program was based on a checklist of 13 virtues, which included frugality, industry, sincerity, and temperance. "If you're not doing what you value, you don't value yourself, so you won't value your time and make good use of it," Smith posited in the December 1992 issue of *Success*.

Using Franklin's ideas, Smith developed a time management and motivational seminar program. The program's basic goal was relatively simple: to help people realize what they really want to accomplish, to help them do things for the right reasons, and to motivate them toward action. Although he targeted his courses primarily to corporate groups and business executives, he engaged in relatively little formal marketing after he started giving his seminars. Instead, he focused on creating an excellent product and allowing word-of-mouth to do the rest. Franklin Institute's guiding tenets became "How many people can we reach?" and "Do we have a product that works?"

After joining forces with Franklin Institute's co-founders in 1983, Smith and his team began giving their seminars all over the United States to just about anybody who would listen. In an effort to build a reputation, Smith accepted every opportunity to speak. Sometimes he found himself tutoring groups of only three or four people after expecting to work with a gathering of 30 or more. Smith would later calculate that between 1983 and 1990 he had spent four-and-a-half years either on a plane or in a hotel room. It was Franklin Institute's efforts in those early years that provided the foundation for its rapid rise during the late 1980s and early 1990s.

Franklin introduced the Franklin Day Planner in 1984 as a means of helping its seminar participants better implement the Franklin time management system. The Franklin Day Planner consisted of a ring-binder with paper planning aids, monthly and annual calendars, and various personal management aids. Besides boosting revenue from its seminars, the company then benefited by selling refill materials every year to its growing base of customers. In fact, the company estimated that approximately 90 percent of the people who purchased the planners through the seminar later bought refill materials or other products related to the Franklin Day Planner, an estimate that would continue to hold true into the year 2000.

In addition to offering the Franklin Day Planner to add value to its time management seminars, Franklin Institute also offered the Planner and several other related time management products beginning in 1984 through a catalog. The catalog represented Franklin's strategy of maintaining strict control over all distribution and customer service operations. By ensuring that its customers interacted only with trained Franklin employees, management reasoned that it could achieve much greater customer loyalty than it could if it sold its products through independent retailers.

Franklin's management seminars and Day Planner achieved immediate market penetration. By 1985, in fact, people who had heard about the Franklin System and wanted to try it provided a steady stream of walk-in traffic at Franklin's warehouse and catalog distribution facilities, demonstrating the company's growing reputation. As a result, Smith and his co-managers

decided to experiment by opening a local retail store that sold the Day Planner and a growing inventory of related Franklin merchandise. The initial success of the store prompted the company to initiate an aggressive outlet store program. Staffed by trained Franklin Institute employees, the stores would be situated in high-traffic areas, such as malls, that would attract walk-in customers. Because many of the new customers would be unfamiliar with the Franklin System, the stores would also serve as a marketing tool for the company's seminars.

Franklin Institute realized fast growth in its product sales during the early 1980s. However, its Franklin System training services remained the focus of its efforts during that period, only later giving way to the popularity of the Day Planner. Although the company relied heavily on word-of-mouth advertising, it also marketed its seminars by means of a direct sales force to institutions and the general public. Franklin, over time, developed a seminar entitled "Increasing Personal Productivity Through Effective Time Management." The "consultants" that administered the seminars were certified by Franklin only after a rigorous training program. Attendees received a Franklin Planner along with instructional materials and order forms for new filler materials.

Franklin often worked with institutional clients beforehand to create a tailored seminar that would emphasize the particular goals of that organization. During the 1980s, Franklin developed an impressive list of seminar clients, including MCI, Intel, Procter & Gamble, Eastman Kodak, and the Internal Revenue Service. The company also offered those customers its Franklin Flex Training (FFT) service, whereby employees of those institutions were trained and certified to give video presentations of Franklin's seminars to in-house employees. Franklin reached individuals and smaller companies through standardized public seminars that it offered in selected cities throughout the United States, and later in Hong Kong, Canada, and the United Kingdom.

The 1980s proved a perfect time for Franklin Institute to enlarge its fledgling time management company. Indeed, as U.S. corporations suffered from intense foreign competition and slowing domestic market growth during that decade, they began to search for ways to increase productivity and efficiency. In addition to laying off millions of middle managers, U.S. corporations and institutions turned to consultants like Franklin Institute to get more out of their decision makers. Franklin offered a seemingly perfect solution to much of what ailed corporate America. Through one or a series of simple seminars, it would essentially show a management team or group of individuals how to achieve a higher set of goals in a shorter span of time. Furthermore, it would boost their morale by helping them to focus on what they really wanted out of life. Franklin would even give them the tools they needed, such as the Day Planner, to make it happen.

By the end of the 1980s, Franklin Institute was garnering more than $10 million annually from its seminars. Most importantly, perhaps, sales of its Day Planner and related time management products had taken off. As seminar revenues swelled to $10.5 million in 1989, sales of Franklin's products reached an impressive $20.3 million. Although much of the growth in product shipments was a result of increased first-time catalog

<table>
<tr><td colspan="2">

**Key Dates:**

</td></tr>
<tr><td>**1981:**</td><td>Hyrum W, Smith begins home-based business providing management seminars.</td></tr>
<tr><td>**1983:**</td><td>Franklin Institute, Inc. is officially founded by Smith, Dick Winwood, Dennis Webb, and Lynn Webb.</td></tr>
<tr><td>**1984:**</td><td>Company introduces the Franklin Day Planner.</td></tr>
<tr><td>**1991:**</td><td>Franklin introduces its ASCEND personal information management software.</td></tr>
<tr><td>**1992:**</td><td>Company goes public as Franklin Quest Co.</td></tr>
<tr><td>**1997:**</td><td>Franklin acquires Covey Leadership Center Inc. and is renamed Franklin Covey Co.</td></tr>
<tr><td>**1998:**</td><td>Firm enters an alliance with At-A-Glance.</td></tr>
<tr><td>**1999:**</td><td>Robert A. Whitman becomes company chairman.</td></tr>
</table>

and retail sales, Franklin was also starting to benefit from its strategy of cultivating customer loyalty. While Franklin steadily attracted new customers through seminars, its old customers continued to purchase annual refills for their planners and to buy new Franklin offerings.

The strong growth of Franklin Institute and some of its competitors during the 1980s prompted many analysts to dismiss the popularity of time management systems as a corollary of the "go-go" 1980s. According to the critics, daily planners and motivational management seminars were simply a fad, destined to fade away when people realized the planners often consumed more time than they actually saved. Franklin rejected these appraisals outright, believing that its system offered a truly unique and effective method of giving greater meaning to the lives of its customers. Franklin's patrons supported their convictions; as the United States plunged into a deep recession during the late 1980s and early 1990s, Franklin's revenue and profit growth accelerated.

To augment sales from its profitable catalog and seminar divisions, Franklin decided to significantly expand its retail store operations in the early 1990s. It began opening stores, mostly in shopping malls, in areas that already had many Franklin clients, hoping that existing buyers would supplement new customer sales. The strategy was extremely successful. From just $710,000 in retail store sales in 1987, revenues vaulted to more than $34 million by 1993 from a chain of 28 outlets in 14 states. Furthermore, catalog sales grew at a record rate during that period, pushing total sales of Franklin products to $60.5 million in 1991 and to $130 million in 1993. Revenues from seminars gained at a slower though still healthy pace, reaching $35.5 million by 1993.

### 1992–96: Emergence as Franklin Quest, a Public Company

In 1992, Franklin Institute, Inc., went public, selling five million shares on the New York Stock Exchange at $15.50 per share. The company also changed its name to Franklin Quest Co., reflecting its ongoing diversification into markets other than training and seminars. The public offering was performed,

in large part, to raise $23 million in cash for Franklin's planned purchase of three separate companies that provided training, business communication, and various consulting services. Franklin expected the acquisitions, which would be completed in 1994, to enable it to penetrate a range of new markets and to bolster the presence of its existing divisions. The price of the shares nearly doubled by late 1993 to more than $30.

In addition to market diversification, Franklin's growth plan in the early 1990s included a steady stream of new product introductions. The new merchandise would allow it to capitalize on a loyal base of customers already comfortable with purchasing its goods. One of its most successful entries was the pocket planner. Introduced in 1992, the planner was designed to fit in a suit coat pocket or small purse while offering the same features as the popular Franklin Day Planner. After only one year Franklin had shipped more than 70,000 pocket planners for a gain of $7 million. Similarly, the company brought out a line of decorative filler pages for its planners; these were highlighted in floral patterns to coincide with the seasons of the year. Sales of that line topped a surprising $1.6 million during the first five months of 1993.

Perhaps Franklin's most notable new endeavor during the early 1990s was its foray into personal information management (PIM) computer software. In late 1991, Franklin unveiled its ASCEND software program, which was designed to be used in conjunction with the paper-based Day Planner or as a stand-alone time management system. The program was offered in a complete package with time management guide books and audio cassette tapes. ASCEND represented Franklin's effort to capture a piece of the burgeoning market for computer-based time management devices, such as personal digital assistants (hand-held electronic personal information devices).

Going into 1994, Franklin Quest continued to expand into new markets and to increase sales of its existing products and seminars. Since 1987, Franklin had trained more than one million people, including 280,000 during 1993 alone. The company had overseas sales offices in Taiwan, Great Britain, Hong Kong, Japan, and Australia, and was targeting several new foreign markets. Furthermore, during the first six months of 1994 Franklin opened 11 new retail stores and had developed plans to start several more before the end of the year. As if the company itself were a testament to the effectiveness of the Franklin System used by its managers, Franklin's sales and profit growth continued to accelerate into 1994. The three million people who were regularly using the Franklin System suggested a rich future for the company.

However, beginning in 1995 there were signs that some new strategies were necessary. For the first time in three years, there was a shortfall below the company's estimated earnings, sending Franklin Quest's stock into a 33 percent nosedive. The necessary growth in seminar attendance had begun to flatten out. To counteract the slowing down of growth in its seminar attendance, the company sought to increase its product line through additional acquisitions. In 1996, it purchased Productivity Plus, providers of planning materials for military customers, and the following year bought Premier Agendas, makers of student planners.

### *1997–2000: The Franklin-Covey Merger*

Perhaps its most important move, at a cost of $160 million, was a May 31, 1997 acquisition-merger with the Covey Leadership Center, a company that had been formed in 1980 by Stephen Covey, a former professor at Brigham Young University and author of motivational books, including the bestseller *The 7 Habits of Highly Effective People* (1989). Although the merger initially seemed very promising, the integration of the two firms proved much more difficult than the two parties had expected. Franklin and Covey maintained separate headquarters, which promoted an ''us-vs.-them culture,'' as Franklin Covey board member Robert H. Daines noted. Furthermore, keeping its personnel in Salt Lake City caused the sales force to lose touch with its customers, which not only violated Habit No. 5 of Covey's book (staying connected with customers) but also greased the competitive rails for rival companies. Other problems included Covey's reluctance to augment its rather cumbersome day-planners with alternative electronic planning devices, its failure to sell off its tangential assets in a timely fashion and eliminate redundant jobs, and its delay in achieving an equitable compensation system for the two staffs.

As a result of these problems, Franklin Covey did not fare well during 1997 and 1998. Overhead costs actually rose, climbing to 40 percent of its sales in 1998, up from a pre-merger figure of 35 percent in 1996. Although revenues increased from $433.3 million in 1997 to $546.6 million in 1998, the gross profit margin barely nudged less than one percent. The next year, although revenues increased to $554.9, the company reported a net loss of $8.8 million, down from a positive net income of $42.1 million in 1998.

Jon Rowberry, who had been promoted from CFO to CEO in March 1998, tried to counter the flat sales by divesting nonessential assets, including Covey's in-house printing operation and a 61-acre nutrition and fitness camp. However, these actions did nothing to heal the rift between the two merged companies. As a result, in July 1999, Rowberry resigned, and Robert A. Whitman, the new chairman, was made CEO as well, presumably on an interim basis. Whitman, former CFO of Trammell Crow Co. and an experienced troubleshooter credited with salvaging Forum Group Inc., a chain of retirement homes, had no prior connection with either Franklin or Covey until his investment group bought $75 million of Franklin Coveys preferred stock.

While hunting for a permanent CEO to replace him, Whitman was busy reorganizing the company. He shut down the Provo, Utah, office and developed major plans to set up eight regional retail sales offices, a restructuring strategy to put the company's sales force back in touch with its customer base. He also bought a major sales-training firm as well as a company that measured consulting effectiveness. At the same time, Whitman sought to reduce operating costs by cutting overhead, including a 600-job downsizing of the company's work force. With Whitman still at the helm, Franklin Covey opened the first of its regional retail stores and training centers—the Franklin Covey Effectiveness Center—in Irving, Texas, in September 2000.

### *Principal Subsidiaries*

Publishers Press Inc.

### *Principal Competitors*

Dale Carnegie Training & Associates, Inc.; Day Runner, Inc.; Fortune Brands, Inc.; Nightingale-Conant Corporation; Successories, Inc.

### *Further Reading*

Bonham, Nicole A., ''Hyrum W. Smith,'' *Alaska Business Monthly*, August 1999, p. 8.

Boulton, Guy, ''Utah-Based Franklin Covey to Raise Cash by Selling Stock,'' *Knight-Ridder/Tribune Business News*, May 13, 1999.

Covey, Stephen R., *Principle-Centered Leadership*, New York: Summit Books, 1991.

——, *The 7 Habits of Highly Effective People*, New York: Simon and Schuster, 1989.

Feldman, Amy, ''We'll Make You Scary,'' *Forbes*, February 14, 1994, p. 96.

Fest, Glen, ''Franklin Covey Opens Retail Store, Corporate Training Center in Irving, Texas,'' *Knight Ridder/Tribune Business News*, September 12, 2000.

''Franklin Quest's Acquisition Blend,'' *Mergers & Acquisitions*, May-June 1997, p. 48.

''Gurus Who Fail Their Own Course,'' *Business Week*, November 8, 1999, p. 125.

Marchetti, Michele, ''Stephen Covey's Win-Lose Merger,'' *Sales & Marketing Management*, March 1999, p. 20.

McDevitt, Kevin, ''Franklin Quest: Go Fly a Kite,'' *Financial World*, August 29, 1995, p. 20.

O'Laughlin, Lynette, and Karey Worton, ''A Look at Franklin Quest Corp.,'' *Daily Herald,* October 10, 1993, Bus. Sec.

''A Plan for Success,'' *Success,* December 1992.

Putnam, Richard, ''Franklin Quest Co. Acquires Shipley Associates, a Leading Business Communication Training and Consulting Firm,'' *PR Newswire,* December 21, 1993.

Smith, Hyrum W., *The 10 Natural Laws of Successful Time and Life Management*, New York: Warner Books, 1994.

''Sometimes Cooperation Works Better Than Competition,'' *Nation's Business*, July 1998, p. 14.

—Dave Mote
—updated by Jane W. Fiero

# The Gallup Organization

47 Hulfish Street
Princeton, New Jersey 08542
U.S.A.
Telephone: (609) 924-9600
Toll Free: (800) 888-5493
Fax: (609) 924-0228
Web site: http://www.gallup.com

*Wholly Owned Subsidiary of Selection Research Institute*
*Founded:* 1958
*Employees:* 3,000
*Sales:* $300 million (1999 est.)
*NAIC:* 54191 Marketing Research and Public Opinion
Polling

The Gallup Organization was created in 1958 by George Gallup, whose name worldwide is all but synonymous with public opinion polling. Although the Gallup Poll, which monitors political and economic trends, conducted since 1935, remains its most prominent enterprise, the company generates most of its revenues from marketing and management research. Gallup has offices in more than 25 countries.

### Polling Background

Although George Gallup did not invent public opinion polling, he virtually created the image of the "pollster." He helped to incorporate scientific methodology in the mid-1930s, but almost as important was his gift for promoting the field—and himself. The scores of pollsters that today work in politics, as well as market research, owe a debt of gratitude to his pioneering efforts.

Political polls were conducted in America long before Gallup. The first published presidential poll, based on a straw vote, appeared on July 24, 1824 in the *Harrisburg Pennsylvanian*. Newspapers at the time were little more than vehicles for the political parties, but as economic pressures forced publishers to become less partisan in order to expand readership, objectivity became a virtue. Straw polls were, by definition, objective; and

by the beginning of the 20th century they became a staple of newspapers.

The way straw polls were conducted, however, did not lend itself to accuracy. Some newspapers and magazines printed the ballot within its pages. Readers mailed in or hand delivered their votes, and they were encouraged to stuff the ballot box by purchasing more copies of the publication. Reliable results were willingly sacrificed for a spike in sales. A later technique, the mail ballot, selected names from such sources as telephone directories, registered voter lists, and automobile registrations. Then a "sample" was created by pulling names at certain intervals, such as every tenth one. It was more difficult to stuff the ballot box, but the sample had an inherent bias against the lower economic strata. The "personal canvass" proved to be the most reliable method for conducting straw votes. Under this method, "solicitors" would hand out pencils and ballots to people on the street and collect the votes on the spot. Some newspapers made an attempt to sample a cross section of voters by creating quotas for their solicitors, for example requiring a certain number of white-collar voters from one community and blue-collar voters from another. Although arrived at intuitively, this technique anticipated the scientific polling that Gallup and others would refine.

Most of the early newspaper polls were local or regional. The *New York Herald Tribune* and collaborating newspapers began to conduct wider pre-election polls in the 1890s. By 1912 they polled in over 35 states. The Hearst newspapers attempted nationwide polling in 1924. Forty-three states were covered, but the average error rate was a high six percent. In 1928, however, Hearst had an error rate of less than three points in 46 states.

By the 1930s the publication with the greatest reputation for accurate polling was the *Literary Digest*—the *Time* or *Newsweek* of its day. The *Digest* mailed out an incredible 20 million ballots and covered all 48 states. Although some critics questioned the sample, maintaining that the *Digest* overemphasized the higher income brackets, the results of the 1932 election silenced all doubters. The straw poll predicted a Franklin Roosevelt win with 59.85 percent of the popular vote. The election results gave Roosevelt the win with 59.14 percent of the vote. The straw poll also predicted that Roosevelt would win 41 states, totaling 474 electoral votes. The actual results were 42 states and 472 electoral votes.

The *Literary Digest* did not hesitate to crow about its accomplishment and was now more than a little confident in its ability to predict election results. Then in the summer of 1936, more than six weeks before the *Digest* began its massive mailing to poll for the winner of the Roosevelt–Alf Landon presidential race, a little-known pollster from Princeton, New Jersey, predicted that the *Digest* would be wrong, and he had the further audacity to predict their final numbers. That pollster was George Gallup.

### 1930s: George Gallup Devises a Poll

Gallup attended the University of Iowa, where he became editor of the campus newspaper. While working one summer for a St. Louis advertising agency that was researching reader satisfaction with the *St. Louis Post-Dispatch*, Gallup decided that there had to be a more efficient way to measure opinions than to go door to door, neighborhood after neighborhood. He wondered if he could use techniques similar to the ones employed by government inspectors who might test a crop of wheat or a supply of water by taking several small samples then extrapolate the quality of the entire amount.

While teaching journalism at Iowa, Gallup earned his M.A. and Ph.D. His doctoral dissertation, "A New Technique for Objective Methods for Measuring Reader Interest in Newspapers," outlined what would simply become known as the "Gallup Method." He began to conduct surveys and publish the results in trade magazines, drawing the attention of the newspaper world. In 1932 he was hired by the New York advertising agency of Young and Rubicam as director of research. He would work for the company until 1947.

It was also in 1932 that Gallup's mother-in-law was elected Iowa's Secretary of State, under unusual circumstances. She had been placed on the ballot in honor of her husband who had died during a run for governor in 1926. Despite running as a Democrat in a heavily Republican state, and without even mounting a campaign, she was swept into office with a Roosevelt landslide. Gallup began to wonder if his sampling methods could be used to forecast such drastic changes in public opinion. He used the Congressional elections of 1934 as a test and came within one percentage point of predicting the overall returns. A Chicago agent, Harold R. Anderson, recognized the potential to make money out of the technique and partnered with Gallup to create the American Institute of Public Opinion. They set up shop in Princeton, New Jersey, with the hope that the prestigious Princeton postmark might influence people to mail back their question-

naires to the "institute" that was in actuality a one-room office in which a handful of workers hand counted ballots.

In 1935 Gallup began writing a syndicated column using his poll results, titled "America Speaks." To sweeten his pitch to newspapers, Gallup offered a money-back guarantee that he would prove more accurate than the illustrious *Literary Digest* poll in predicting the presidential election of 1936. His partner was then able to place "America Speaks" with 42 newspapers. More than pride was now on the line. Given the cost of a poll sample of 15,000 respondents, ten times the size of what he would one day use, Gallup faced financial ruin. The *Digest,* suffering so much from the effects of the Depression that it was forced to reduce its mailing to ten million pieces, was more than eager to defend its franchise and to ridicule Gallup's charge that by drawing its sample mostly from the ranks of people who owned telephones and automobiles the *Digest* would undercount lower-income voters.

The final *Digest Poll* results were within one percentage point of Gallup's earlier forecast. The *Digest* gave the election to Landon with 57 percent of the vote. Gallup gave it to Roosevelt with 54 percent. In reality Roosevelt won another landslide victory, taking 61 percent of the popular vote. Gallup was off by seven points, much to his dismay, but at least he picked the winner. The *Literary Digest* put on a brave front, refusing to acknowledge its errors, but its reputation was shattered, and within a year the magazine folded.

The career of Gallup, as well as those of Elmo Roper and Archibald Crossley, who also predicted the Roosevelt victory, flourished. However, it was Gallup who became the best known of the new scientific pollsters. Eventually "America Speaks" would be carried by 200 newspapers. He founded the British Institute of Public Opinion, as well as polling operations in dozens of other foreign countries, making Princeton, New Jersey, the public opinion polling capital of the world. The Audience Research Institute, which Gallup founded in 1937, studied public reaction to movie titles, casts, and stories. He began to keep tabs on questions that are taken for granted today, but now provide a historical perspective on the American public and its officials. He kept track of Presidential popularity. He was the first to ask "Who would you vote for if the election was held today?" He asked Americans if they believed in God and how often they went to church. When Senator Joseph Lieberman was selected to run as the Democratic vice-presidential candidate in 2000, journalists could report how the country had changed in its willingness to vote for a Jewish American, because the Gallup Poll had been asking the question since the 1930s.

Gallup continued to refine his techniques, determined to avoid the large margin of error in his polling of the 1936 election. He no longer relied on mail ballots, because higher-income voters were more likely to return them, which he felt would favor Republican candidates. He sent his people into the field to interview respondents, with quotas based on demographic categories, such as age, sex, geography, and income. The interviewers, however, were given too much latitude. Rather than embarrass respondents by asking their age or income, they often guessed. Interviewers also tended to seek out respondents with whom they felt most comfortable, with the result that working-class interviewers and white-collar interviewers were getting different results. Overall, the Gallup Poll was displaying a systematic bias in favor of Republican positions over Democratic ones, enough to prompt Congress to call in Gallup to explain his election results of 1940 and 1944 that underestimated the Democratic vote in two-thirds of the states. A technical committee criticized him for using a quota system instead of "probability" sampling, a method that would give everyone a equal chance of being included in a poll. However, probability sampling was both complicated and extremely expensive. Gallup felt that the difference between quota and probability sampling was not large enough to justify the cost. Only in a very close election would it even matter. Unfortunately for Gallup such an election was at hand.

### 1948: Dewey Defeats Truman!

The presidential election of 1948 would prove almost as devastating to Gallup as the 1936 contest was to the *Literary Digest*. Because the Democratic Party was splintered, with Henry A. Wallace running for president on the Progressive party ticket and Strom Thurmond representing the Dixiecrats, Harry Truman appeared to have little chance to retain the White House against the bid of the Republican nominee, Thomas Dewey. Gallup and the other major pollsters believed that public opinion only showed dramatic change when responding to important events. Political campaigns were not considered important enough. A poll taken after the political conventions would surely predict the winner. Gallup stopped polling in mid-October, and although he noted a surge in support for Truman, he felt confident that Dewey would win the election. All the experts agreed with him. Truman did not stop campaigning, however; he beat the odds, and won the election.

"The pollsters became national laughingstocks," according to Michael Wheeler, author of *Lies, Damn Lies and Statistics*, "and Gallup, the most famous pollster of them all, took the hardest fall. Others were more graceful in their embarrassment, but Gallup was indignant. How, he sputtered, could scientific surveys be expected to take into account 'bribery of voters' and 'tampering with ballot boxes.'" Gallup was also accused of favoritism, a charge that could prove devastating to a man whose business depended on impartiality. Although Gallup vehemently denied that he rigged polls to favor Dewey, he admitted that he considered Dewey to be a close friend and had been in contact with him throughout the 1948 campaign.

There was no doubt, however, that Gallup's reputation had been tarnished. Many newspapers, unwilling to accept his ex-

planation that this was an election that would happen only once in a generation, threatened to cancel their contracts. Gallup managed to survive, became more scrupulous about maintaining distance from political candidates, and improved his polling methods. Still, the influence of political polling in America was diminished until the 1960s.

### Market Research in the 1950s

While other polling operations began to focus on the more profitable area of market research, Gallup maintained his academic approach. Finally in 1958 he created the Gallup Organization and moved his company into market research, but he never achieved a significant share of the business. Although in 1966 his son, George Gallup, Jr., became president of the Gallup Organization, the elder Gallup continued to serve as chairman of the board and was actively engaged in its day-to-day operations. He vowed that he would never retire, and he never did. He died in 1984 of a heart attack at his summer home in Switzerland.

Gallup's final years were not, however, without controversy. In 1968 two of Gallup's interviewers were discovered to have falsified data in a poll of Harlem residents conducted for the *New York Times*. More troubling were charges that Gallup's people maintained improper ties to the Nixon administration. Poll numbers were provided before publication, allowing Nixon to prepare the public and the put the best possible spin on the results. Nixon's aides also suggested questions for the Gallup Poll, thus influencing public opinion from the outset. The Nixon administration used both Gallup and rival Louis Harris, misleading the pollsters' associates into thinking that Nixon would not make improper use of early poll results. At the very least the pollsters were naive. The fact that Gallup officials only met with Nixon aides in a hotel rather than the White House was a tacit admission that if such contact were known to the public the company's reputation for objectivity would be compromised.

### New Leadership in the 1980s and Beyond

With the loss of its founder in 1984, the Gallup Organization struggled. According to George M. Taber writing for *Business News New Jersey*, "One of the most difficult transitions any corporation faces is to move away from the structure and style established by the founding father and become a company that has a life bigger than he. Corporations as large as the Ford Motor Company and as small as a country grocery store have faced that challenge. It was a transition, however, that the Gallup Organization did not successfully make."

The Gallup name did retain brand value, and in 1988, after discussing a merger for three years, the Gallup family sold its private company to the Selection Research Institute, a marketing research firm based in Lincoln, Nebraska. Gallup's data processing and interviewing operations were moved to Lincoln, but the company's headquarters remained in Princeton, considered the "epicenter of the polling world," according to a 1997 article in *Business News New Jersey*. The Gallup Organization continued to produce the Gallup Poll in conjunction with print and television news organizations, and became more aggressive in performing surveys for corporations and marketers.

Under its new parent, as well as the leadership of co-chairmen Alec Gallup and George Gallup, Jr., the founder's sons, The Gallup Organization saw increasing revenues in the late 1990s at an estimated annual rate of 30 percent. In a 1997 interview for *Marketing News,* the two men discussed the future of the research industry in an age of rapid technological advancement, agreeing that although the polling process has become quicker and more sophisticated, the "fine art of crafting a good question" remained integral to successful polling. Regarding Gallup's prominence in its field, one in which competition was heating up in the late 1990s, Alec Gallup noted, "We do have an advantage—and its an important one and we exploit the hell out of it—and that is the fact that the Gallup name is well-known and has credibility."

### Principal Competitors

McKinsey & Company; Harris Interactive Inc.; Opinion Research Corp.; Towers Perrin.

### Further Reading

Gallup, George Horace, *The Pulse of Democracy*, New York: Greenwood Press, 1968, 335 p.

Jacobs, Lawrence and Robert Y. Shapiro, "Presidential Manipulation of Polls and Public Opinion," *Political Science Quarterly*, Winter 1995/1996, p. 519.

McCullough, David, *Truman*, New York: Touchstone, 1992, 1,117 p.

Miller, Cyndee, "Gallup Brothers Analyze the Research Industry," *Marketing News,* January 6, 1997, p. 2.

Moore, David W., *The Super Pollsters*, New York: Four Walls Eight Windows, 1992, 388 p.

Pace, Eric, obituary, *New York Times*, July 28, 1984, pp. 1, 9.

Sussman, Barry, obituary, *Washington Post*, July 28, 1984, pp. A1, A7.

Smith, Richard D., "In Polling, It All Started with Gallup," *Business News New Jersey,* April 21, 1997, p. 5.

Taber, George M., "Gallup Polls Sells Out to a Nebraska Company," *Business News New Jersey*, October 11, 1988.

Wheeler, Michael, *Lies, Damn Lies and Statistics*, New York: Liveright, 1976, 300 p.

—Ed Dinger

# The General Chemical Group Inc.

One Liberty Lane
Hampton, New Hampshire 03842
U.S.A.
Telephone: (603) 929-2606
Fax: (603) 929-2404
Web site: http://www.genchem.com

*Public Company*
*Incorporated:* 1988
*Employees:* 1,041
*Sales:* $256.8 (1999)
*Stock Exchanges:* New York
*Ticker Symbol:* GCG
*NAIC:* 32518 Other Basic Inorganic Chemical
Manufacturing

The General Chemical Group Inc. is a leading producer of industrial chemicals, namely soda ash, both natural and synthetic, as well as calcium chloride. Soda ash is the raw material essential in making such staples as paper, glass, textiles, and foods. The company's soda ash, also the raw material for sodium bicarbonate, is sold to such manufacturers as Owens-Illinois, Church & Dwight, and TOSOH, and is used in products ranging from deodorants, toothpaste, and laundry detergent, to drinking glasses, insulation, and computer screens. Calcium chloride, on the other hand, a byproduct of synthetic soda ash, is perhaps best known for melting ice in winter and controlling road dust in summer. It is also used in petroleum refining, food processing, asphalt recycling, newsprint de-inking, water treatment, and construction. Chemical giant DuPont purchases General Chemical's calcium chloride for use in producing its Nomex brand fiber, which, in turn, is used in creating flame-resistant clothing. In April 1999, General Chemical underwent a dramatic reorganization in which a significant portion of its operations—namely, its performance products for the pharmaceutical, personal care, and environmental industries—were spun off as the independent GenTek Inc.

## The Early Years: 1899–1920

The General Chemical Group traces its roots to 1899 when The General Chemical Company was formed through the merger of 12 already well-established chemical producers, including the Nichols Chemical Company. Dr. William H. Nichols, a highly respected chemist, and his son, Charles W. Nichols, orchestrated the merger, and the elder Nichols became the new company's first chairman. Headquarters were located in New York City, and the company billed itself as "manufacturing chemists" selling "high grade sulphuric, muriatic, nitric, and acetic acids," as well as sulphate of alumina and mixed acid for explosives. Advertisements also highlighted the benefits of the newly merged organization: "by means of our works being located in all sections of the country, we can give buyers benefits of lowest freight rates."

In 1900, the new concern was producing about 15 chemicals in a fledgling industry rapidly shaped by new technologies; by 1920, the General Chemical product line would swell to over 100. The company pioneered many of the processes used in chemical manufacturing. In 1901, for example, the company established the world's first experimental contact sulfuric acid plant. The following year, it began to use bauxite in the production of alum, believed to be the metal's first such commercial application.

The company quickly expanded during the first decades of the 20th century. By 1903, two giant commercial sulfuric acid plants had been erected in Edgewater and Camden, New Jersey. General Chemical also built several other major production plants including, in 1909, its first West Coast plant, the Bay Point Works in the San Francisco Bay area. In 1912, the company's massive Delaware Valley Works in Claymont, Delaware, and Marcus Hook, Pennsylvania, opened. With its pervasive presence, General Chemical played an important support role in World War I, supplying Allied troops with critical ingredients for munitions and other supplies.

## The Allied Chemical Years: 1921–85

In 1921, General Chemical was one of five major U.S. chemical companies that came together to form Allied Chemical & Dye Corp. The merger, one of the largest to that date,

**Company Perspectives:**

*The General Chemical Group is a leading producer of soda ash and calcium chloride. Following the spinoff of its manufacturing and performance products businesses in 1999, General Chemical has become a smaller, more focused company committed to creating value as a low-cost, high-quality producer of its core industrial chemicals.*

included the Solvay Process Company (maker of alkalis), Semet-Solvay (builder and operator of coke ovens), the Barrett Company (maker of coal tar products), and the National Aniline & Chemical Company (supplier of aniline oils used in making dyes). General Chemical's founder, W.H. Nichols, was once again a leader in effecting the merger, and he was named chairman of Allied. As a diversified chemical producer, Allied was a dominant domestic and international chemical company throughout most of the 20th century. General Chemical retained its identify as a division within Allied during this period.

As part of Allied, General Chemical thrived, even during the Great Depression. Allied maintained large reserves of liquid assets, no debt, and paid dividends yearly. However, shortsighted management on the part of Nichols's successor at Allied, Orlando F. Weber, resulted in little to no budget for researching new products and applications. Weber's era as chairman was also characterized by intense secrecy; financial reports were kept vague and confidential, and Allied executives were forbidden to join trade associations or be featured in the media. Some speculated that Weber's autocracy created a knowledge vacuum at Allied, an intentional move to keep Dr. Nichols's son, Charles Nichols, from taking control of the company.

Despite managerial difficulties at Allied, General Chemical performed well, expanding its operations nationwide and building large production plants and renovating others. New products were introduced and processes for producing heavy chemicals, including alum, soda ash, and a spectrum of sulfur-based chemicals were improved and refined. During World War II, General Chemical facilities in Bay Point and Richmond, California, Claymont, Delaware, Point Pleasant, West Virginia, and elsewhere increased production to meet war efforts. Several company operations were awarded the Army-Navy "E" award for excellence four years in a row.

However, while it thrived filling war effort needs, General Chemical and its Allied associates experienced a general decline after the war; competition stiffened, and company policies and facilities were neglected and became outdated. Following years of uncertain direction and ever-changing leadership, Allied began a turnaround in 1985, when it merged with Signals Companies Inc. The new corporation, organized as a chemicals and aerospace company, was christened AlliedSignal Corporation.

### A New Company: 1986–96

The following year, AlliedSignal spun off 35 of the newly merged company's more marginal businesses in a then-record $1.2 billion initial public offering (IPO) to the newly formed Henley Group, Inc., headed by Wall Street merger and acquisi-

tion specialist Michael D. Dingman. Among these businesses were units from the original General Chemical Company, which reemerged later that year as a stand-alone company.

Christened "Dingman's Dogs," almost all of the Henley Group's troubled companies were turned around within 18 months and sold for a profit. "Followed by a trail of angry shareholders who claim he enriched himself at their expense," according to Charles P. Wallace, writing in *Fortune*, Dingman later moved to the Bahamas where he continued to make international investments and to serve as chairman of Fisher Scientific International, Inc., a world leader in supplying products and services to research and clinical laboratories.

Leading the turnaround in the fortunes of many of these companies was Paul M. Montrone, formerly executive vice-president of AlliedSignal Inc., who later became chairman and chief executive officer of Wheelabrator Technologies, Inc. as well as president of the Henley group. According to his official biography, Montrone "regrouped Henley's 35 disparate businesses into several successful public companies." In 1987, business columnist Tom Peters wrote that among the companies that saw a much-improved bottom line as a result of the Henley Group's activities were Fisher Scientific, "moving from a $99 million loss to a $99 million profit; Wheelabrator, from plus $10 million to plus $93 million; and General Chemical, from minus $4 million to plus $87 million."

By the turn of the 21st century, Montrone had become chairman and CEO of Fisher Scientific and chairman of GenTek Inc., ProcureNet Inc., and Prestolite Wire Corp. He was also chairman of The General Chemical Group, which had been formed in 1988 in Delaware. In 1999, Montrone owned just under half of General Chemical's equities, including all of its Class B stock, and, thus, had voting control of the company. According to a 1999 *Wall Street Journal* article, he did not take a salary from General Chemical.

Montrone was also a managing director of Latona Associates Inc., a private merchant bank. According to the *Wall Street Journal* (June 23, 1997), Latona provided " 'strategic guidance and advice' to General Chemical on financings and other matters. General Chemical pays Latona $5.6 million yearly and will pay additional fees at investment banking rates in the case of any acquisitions Latona advises on." All of the companies headed by Montrone, except ProcureNet, were headquartered on a spacious campus in Hampton Falls, New Hampshire.

### Going Public: 1996

In May 1996, The General Chemical Group went public with an initial public offering (IPO) of 7.5 million shares, with each share priced at $17.50 on the New York Stock Exchange. Salomon Brothers were the lead underwriters of the IPO, which raised $41 million for the company. Five million shares were sold on behalf of a single shareholder, the offshore Stonor Group, a Liberian corporation with a Cayman Island parent that at least one analyst believed represented Michael Dingman. Although 34 percent of General Chemical's equity was available for sale, its Class B shares were retained by its original owners. Less than five percent of the firm's voting rights were

## Key Dates:

**1899:** The General Chemical Co. founded.
**1921:** General Chemical Co. merges to form Allied Chemical & Dye, Corp.
**1985:** AlliedSignal Corporation formed.
**1988:** The General Chemical Group is incorporated in Delaware.
**1997:** Company acquires Peridot Holdings, Inc.
**1998:** Sandco Automotive Ltd. and Reheis, Inc. are acquired.
**1999:** General Chemical is split into two: The General Chemical Group and GenTek Inc., parent of the General Chemical Corporation.

available to new shareholders, with Montrone and the Stonor Group retaining control of 95.2 percent of voting rights.

### Acquisitions and Mergers: 1997–99

In the late 1990s, several acquisitions were actively pursued by General Chemical Group. In June 1997, for example, the company announced plans to acquire privately held Peridot Holdings, a manufacturer of sulfuric acid, water treatment chemicals, and aluminum sulfate products. At the time, Peridot had sales of about $43 million and operated plants in Wayne, New Jersey, and Augusta, Georgia. Terms of the deal were not disclosed.

The company also acquired Sandco, a Canadian manufacturer of engine parts for the North American auto industry. A producer of stamped automobile-engine components, principally rocker arms and roller followers, the company had 1997 sales of approximately $10 million. Sandco complemented another General Chemical subsidiary, Toledo Technologies, a major manufacturer of valve-train components.

In February 1998, General Chemical purchased another privately held company, Reheis Inc. of Berkeley Heights, New Jersey, again for an undisclosed price. Reheis, a producer of specialty chemicals, had 1997 sales of almost $60 million and was a leading supplier of the aluminum-based active ingredients in antiperspirant and antacid markets. The deal included two facilities in the United States and one in Dublin, Ireland.

A year later, in early 1999, General Chemical acquired Defiance, Inc., a major manufacturer of precision bearings for the auto industry. In March 1999, General Chemical acquired all outstanding shares of Toronto-based Noma Industries Ltd. With 1998 sales of approximately $265 million, Noma was a leading manufacturer of electrical wire and components for the automotive, appliance, and electronic industries.

### Spinoff of GenTek: 1999

In a major strategic move to consolidate its business focus on core industrial chemicals, particularly soda ash and calcium chloride, General Chemical announced in February 1999 that it intended to spin off its specialty chemicals and auto parts businesses into a new $440-million-a-year company, GenTek Inc. The new firm comprised aluminum chemicals, wet chemicals for electronics, Reheis, Peridot Holdings, and the company's subsidiaries related to the auto parts business. The spin-off was completed on April 30, 1999.

The *Wall Street Journal* reported on January 26, 1999, that Montrone believed the new company would be more highly valued by investors because, he noted, "it won't have the millstone of commodity chemicals." He also said that GenTek would embark on an active acquisitions course. In fact, GenTek did begin to acquire a string of related companies almost immediately. In August 1999, the new company purchased Krone AG from Jenoptik AG of Frankfurt for approximately $225 million. Krone was described at the time as a leader in quick-connection technology for voice and data networks. A year later, GenTek announced the pending acquisition of the Digital Communications Group of Prestolite Wire Corporation. Prestolite and Krone had previously worked together in developing products for the data communications market. The previous June, GenTek had acquired an 81 percent controlling interest in Con-X Corporation, an emerging leader in the development of automated cross-connect and loop management systems for DSL and other broadband service providers. The company also purchased Vigilant Networks for $12 million from LeCroy Corporation, a leading supplier of digital oscilloscopes. Vigilant provided products and services that used advanced signal acquisition technology. Finally, in October 2000, GenTek and Krone, by now its principal telecommunications subsidiary, announced a $40 million expansion plant for the company's copper and fiber optic cable manufacturing facilities in Sidney, Nebraska and North Bennington, Vermont.

Montrone, as chairman of GenTek, said that the expansion typified by the two fiber optic plants was essential to the company's growth strategy. That strategy appeared to be paying off. For the first six months of 2000, GenTek sales increased 86 percent to $642.1 million.

Meanwhile, due to higher energy costs, lower calcium chloride volumes attributed to wet spring weather, and lower soda ash prices, General Chemical posted a net loss of $1 million on sales of $120 million in the first six months of 2000. For the corresponding period of 1999, net income had been $3.3 million on sales of $130.6 million. According to General Chemical's 1999 Annual Report, the company received notice from the New York Stock Exchange (NYSE) on February 28, 2000, that it was no longer in compliance with NYSE requirements that a listed company have a market capitalization of not less than $50 million and total shareholders' equities of not less than $50 million. However, on June 21, 2000, General Chemical announced it would remain on the NYSE through September 2001, subject to quarterly monitoring. If the company proved unable to meet the exchange's financial requirements by September 2001, it faced delisting from the New York Stock Exchange.

Led by Chairman Montrone, Vice-Chairman Paul M. Meister, and President and CEO John M. Kehoe, Jr., management at General Chemical remained optimistic regarding the company's future. The company looked to focus on finding new uses for soda ash and calcium chloride, as well as new distribution channels for its products. Cost-reduction and improved efficiency in operations also became integral to the newly slimmed-down chemical company. In August 2000, General Chemical announced that, through its General Chemical Canada Ltd. subsidiary, it would establish a joint venture with Tangshan Sanyou (Alkali) Group Ltd. to produce, market, and sell calcium chloride throughout Asia. Capacity at the site was expected to be upgraded, using General Chemical's technology, from 30,000 metric tons/year to 100,000 metric tons of calcium chloride annually at a cost of about $10 million. The joint venture would also handle sales of Tangshan Sanyou's soda ash output, estimated at about 700,000 tons a year.

### Principal Subsidiaries

General Chemical (Soda Ash) Partners (51%); New Hampshire Oak; General Chemical Company; General Chemical Canada Ltd.

### Principal Competitors

Dow Chemical Co.; FMC Corporation; Solvay & Cie S.A.

### Further Reading

Bulkeley, William M., ''General Chemical Planning to Spin Off Its Specialty Chemical, Auto-Parts Lines,'' *Wall Street Journal*, January 26, 1999, B4.

Freedman, William, ''General Chemical IPO Offers Less Than 5% of Voting Rights,'' *Chemical Week*, May 1, 1996, p. 10.

Henry, Brian, ''General Chemical Completes Public Stock Offering,'' *Chemical Marketing Reporter*, May 27, 1996, p.26.

Peters, Tom, ''De-Scaling of America,'' November 2, 1987, at www.tompeters.com.

Vames, Steven, ''General Chemical Group to Buy Peridot Holdings,'' *Chemical Week,* June 4, 1997, p. 15.

Wallace, Charles P. ''The Pirates of Prague,'' *Fortune,* December 23, 1996, pp. 78+.

—Margery M. Heffron

# Gerald Stevens, Inc.

**301 East Las Olas Boulevard**
**Fort Lauderdale, Florida 33335**
**U.S.A.**
**Telephone: (954) 713-5000**
**Toll Free: (800) 333-8483**
**Fax: (954) 713-5020**
**Web site: http://www.geraldstevens.com**

*Public Company*
*Incorporated:* 1998
*Employees:* 3,775
*Sales:* $110.59 million (1999)
*Stock Exchanges:* NASDAQ
*Ticker Symbol:* GIFT
*NAIC:* 44422 Nursery and Garden Centers

Gerald Stevens, Inc. is the largest floral retailer in the United States. After rapidly consolidating the highly fragmented floral industry during the last years of the 1990s, the company operates more than 350 floral shops. In addition to its retail locations, Gerald Stevens also markets flowers, plants, and gifts through catalogs, direct mail, telegraph service, telephone orders, and via the Internet, offering same-day delivery throughout the nation.

## Origins

Gerald Stevens began with a single, albeit ambitious, goal: become the largest specialty retailer of flowers in the United States. At stake was the approximately $16 billion domestic floral market, an industry populated by 50,000 operators and dominated by no one. The industry was highly fragmented, representing an ideal opportunity for a company to act as a consolidator and, floral shop by floral shop, secure lucrative market share. Such was the objective of Gerald Geddis and Steven Berrard, two high-profile executives who founded Gerald Stevens in January 1998. Geddis and Berrard had worked together at Blockbuster Video, the giant video rental chain that had achieved its considerable mass by consolidating the video

rental industry. Geddis had served as the company's president and chief operating officer. Berrard had served as Geddis's superior, holding the title of chief executive officer. By 1997, Blockbuster, which had been purchased by Viacom Inc. three years earlier, was experiencing serious difficulties, convincing Viacom's chairman, Sumner Redstone, that wholesale changes were needed to protect his investment. As part of the company's reorganization, corporate headquarters were moved from Florida to Texas. Geddis and Berrard stayed behind, leaving the company in 1997. Although they conceded they knew nothing about running a floral business, Geddis and Berrard were intimately familiar with the riches consolidation could bring. The pair shied from the comparison, but industry analysts dubbed Gerald Stevens the Blockbuster Video of flowers.

"Our goal is to nationally brand our product," Geddis declared in a November 27, 1998 interview with *Business First-Columbus*. Although the company would fall short of making the Gerald Stevens name a national "label" for flowers during its first several years in business, it did score success in acquiring scores of florist shops, an inherent aspect of creating a national brand. Geddis and Berrard formed New River Capital, a venture fund, to serve as the financial vehicle to drive their acquisition campaign forward. The principle of economics underpinning Geddis's and Berrard's strategy was the economies of scale Gerald Stevens would realize as the umbrella organization for a national network of floral shops. As a group, Gerald Stevens floral shops would realize appreciable savings through volume buying and efficiencies in payroll, insurance, and administrative functions. As a group, the shops would benefit from increased advertising, eclipsing by far the marketing efforts the shops could afford independently. Further, the shops would benefit from any affiliations the corporate office forged with flower growers, adding to the incentive for floral shops to join Gerald Stevens.

Once Gerald Stevens started to expand, it did so with frenetic energy. After receiving a $20 million credit line from Nationsbank, the company raised $21 million in a private placement arranged by Allen & Company Inc., giving it the resources to embark on a prodigious acquisition campaign. The private placement of stock was completed in October 1998; the same month, the company acquired AGA Flowers, Inc., a floral import business based in Miami, Florida, the addition of which represented an important step toward the development of a same-day distribution system. During the next two months, Gerald Stevens dove headlong into the acquisition mode, purchasing 72 floral shops in ten domestic markets and entering into agreements to acquire an additional 41 stores in existing markets and in five new markets. Easily the most important acquisition agreement reached during this period occurred on December 10, 1998, when the company announced a reverse merger with Florafax International, Inc. The effect on Gerald Stevens' stature was profound.

### 1999 Merger with Florafax

Based in Vero Beach, Florida, Florafax was the fourth largest flowers-by-wire provider in the United States, having been founded in 1995. The company directed orders from consumers to its 5,300 member florists located in all 50 states, the Bahamas, Bermuda, Puerto Rico, and the U.S. Virgin Islands, serving as a powerful go-between. Through a wholly owned subsidiary named The Flower Club, Florafax also marketed flowers and gifts directly to customers. The merger provided ample evidence of Geddis's and Berrard's intent to develop a complete distribution infrastructure capable of serving customers wherever and however they wished to purchase and send flowers. The founders were striving to develop the capability to market flowers not only at retail locations, but also through catalogs, direct mail, the Internet, and through telephone orders.

In addition to its strategic importance, the merger with Florafax ushered Gerald Stevens into the public spotlight. According to the details of the transaction, publicly held Florafax in essence acquired Gerald Stevens and then changed its name to Gerald Stevens, making a new entity, with Geddis and Berrard in charge, that debuted on the NASDAQ National Market System. Based on the value of Florafax's stock price at the time of the announcement, the combined companies boasted a market capitalization of $350 million.

As Gerald Stevens entered 1999, company officials worked on finalizing the Florafax merger, which was not expected to be completed until March 1999. Meanwhile, the company adhered to its strategic plan, relentlessly pursuing expansion. In January 1999, the company acquired seven floral retailers that operated 21 retail stores. Significantly, the acquisitions moved Gerald Stevens into four new markets—Salt Lake City, Milwaukee, St.

Petersburg, Florida, and Savannah, Georgia—solidified the company's presence in existing markets, and provided the company with three new hub facilities that served satellite stores. In February 1999, the company acquired Internet Services, LP, the parent company of FlowerLink, which added another important distribution channel. FlowerLink, through its Internet commerce site, www.flowerlink.com., provided customers with access to nearly 1,000 floral shops throughout the country for delivery nationwide.

By May 1999, seven months after beginning its expansion campaign in earnest, Gerald Stevens held sway as the largest floral retailer and marketer in the country. The company operated 125 stores, most as free-standing units, acquiring floral shops at a rate of one every other day. In May 1999, the company continued with its development of a nationwide distribution infrastructure by announcing the acquisition of $20 million-in-sales Calyx & Corolla Inc. Based in San Francisco, Calyx & Corolla had been founded by Ruth Owades, a mail-order entrepreneur who developed Gardener's Eden into a $15 million-in-sales catalog enterprise before selling out to Williams-Sonoma in 1987. With Calyx & Corolla—ranked as the leader in Internet and telephone flower delivery—she opted for the same conclusion, but cashing out did not signal the end of her relationship with the business. Instead, she became part of the Gerald Stevens team, taking a seat on the company's board of directors and continuing to run Calyx & Corolla under its own name. Geddis and Berrard were the first to point out that they had little practical knowledge of how to run a floral business. Consequently, when Gerald Stevens acquired a floral business, it also absorbed the individuals who previously had managed the business, acquiring managerial expertise as its stature swelled.

By the fall of 1999, Gerald Stevens had earned two significant distinctions. The company ranked as the largest floral retailer in the country and as the fastest-growing concern in the industry. During the preceding year, the company had acquired more than 230 retail floral shops and established a presence in 28 states, with the total number of stores increasing by the week. By October, Gerald Stevens' corporate offices could no longer adequately house the company's staff, which, nationally, had increased from nine employees to 3,000 employees within a year. Office space was tripled, adding a new facility for the accounting and marketing teams and providing room for anticipated growth. According to the company's estimates, it controlled nearly 1.5 percent of the $16 billion market, leaving tremendous room for growth. Within the next five years, management expected to expand to at least 1,000 stores nationwide, to establish a presence in the 100 largest markets, and to develop 50 additional markets. Expectations were high, but as employees settled into the new building at Port Everglades, the feverish growth of the previous year began to produce worrisome results.

### Mounting Financial Losses in 1999

For Gerald Stevens, explosive growth through acquisitions delivered remarkable revenue growth and dismal profitability. During the third quarter of 1999, sales jumped from the $4.7 million registered during the third quarter of 1998 to $36.3 million, but the revenue increase also coincided with a net loss

**Key Dates:**

**1998:** Company is founded to consolidate the retail floral industry; reverse merger with Florafax International is announced.
**1999:** FlowerLink, an e-commerce floral concern, is acquired; Calyx & Corolla Inc. is acquired.
**2000:** Acquisition campaign is temporarily halted.

of $1.2 million. The loss was attributable to the overhead costs incurred from developing a corporate structure capable of managing a massive national chain, as Geddis and Berrard struggled to keep ahead managerially and administratively with the company's physical growth. At the time, analysts projected that the company would be profitable by February 2000.

Undaunted by the financial loss, Geddis and Berrard ended 1999 demonstrating the same aggressive behavior as they had shown at the start of the year. Late in the year, the company opened its first store under the Gerald Stevens brand name in Boca Raton, Florida. The development of the Gerald Stevens name into a national brand had been purposely slowed because most of the acquired stores enjoyed a loyal customer base— customers the company did not want to lose by quickly eliminating the local identity of the acquired stores. Instead, Gerald Stevens eased its stores through the transition. Concurrent with the opening of the Boca Raton store, the company began co-branding its others stores with the Gerald Stevens name in advertisements, seasonal catalogs, and direct mail deliveries. Additional Gerald Stevens branded stores were scheduled to open in Atlanta and Fort Lauderdale in February 2000, with other markets gained their own branded stores later in the year.

As the company took its first methodical steps toward fostering familiarity with the Gerald Stevens name, it also stepped beyond U.S. boundaries for the first time. In November 1999, the company gained access to the Toronto, Canada market in a month-long acquisition spree that added 51 floral and gift shops to its fold. Included within the month's purchases was the acquisition of Johnston The Florist, the largest chain in Pittsburgh and the fifth largest chain in the United States. By the end of the year, Gerald Stevens operated more than 300 retail locations, but as it entered the new century the mounting financial losses could not be ignored.

In 1999, Gerald Stevens posted a $12.3 million net loss. In the first half of 2000, the pattern of rapid escalating revenues and falling profits repeated itself. In the third quarter of 2000, revenues increased from $36.3 million during the same period in 1999 to $83.7 million, as the company's net loss increased from $1.2 to $3 million. The continuing losses and the inability of the company to meet analysts' projections translated into a declining stock price, serving as an unwelcomed catalyst for

change. By June 2000, the company's stock price had taken a 52-week plunge from $16 per share to $1.75 per share, forcing management to amend it expansion plans. The goal of reaching 1,000 retail locations by 2005 was shelved, primarily because of the depressed stock price, which was used as an acquisition currency. At the time, Gerald Stevens operated more than 350 stores, but with further acquisitions put on hold, the company focused on implementing cost-cutting measures. Said Geddis in a June 16, 2000 interview with *South Florida Business Journal:* "We built our corporate overhead to support a substantially larger company than we are today. Given our recent decision to temporarily suspend acquisitions, we have brought that overhead back in line with the needs of current businesses."

Considering the company's strengths, the future of Gerald Stevens was promising. The company controlled a nationwide network of stores, the ability to market flowers and gifts through every distribution channel, and was presided over by practiced corporate veterans. Much had been accomplished during the company's formative years in business, and much remained to be done, but assuming that management was able to turn Gerald Stevens' dominant market position into a profit-producing enterprise, the first decade of the 21st century promised to witness a single, unrivaled king of the retail floral industry.

### Principal Subsidiaries

Florafax International Inc.; Calyx & Corolla Inc.

### Principal Competitors

1-800-FLOWERS.COM, Inc.; Roll International Corporation; IOS Brands Corporation.

### Further Reading

Carlsen, Clifford, "Retailer Plucks Florist Calyx & Corolla," *San Francisco Business Times,* May 21, 1999, p. 5.
Duggan, Ed, "Flower Shop No Longer Blockbuster," *South Florida Business Journal,* June 16, 2000, p. 58.
"Gerald Stevens Adds 10 Sites, Expanding National Ordering," *South Florida Business Journal,* October 22, 1999, p. 18A.
"Gerald Stevens, Inc. Announces Two-Year Deal with Teleflora Wire Service," *Business Wire,* August 15, 2000, p. 294.
King, Julia, "Online Stores Add Off-Line Outlets, Back-End System Ties Key to Channel Links," *Computerworld,* August 9, 1999, p. 1.
Sayewitz, Ronni, "Flower Power: Gerald Stevens Takes More Room for Growth," *South Florida Business Journal,* October 8, 1999, p. 3A.
Showalter, Kathy, "Florida-Based Florist Chain with Local Ties Delivers New Products," *Business First-Columbus,* June 23, 2000, p. 1.
——, "Maple Lee, Connell's Join Florist Shop Consolidator," *Business First-Columbus,* November 27, 1998, p. 3.
Tanner, Lisa, "Firm 'Rolling Up' Florists," *Dallas Business Journal,* September 24, 1999, p. 1.

—Jeffrey L. Covell

# Gibraltar Steel Corporation

**3556 Lake Shore Road**
**Buffalo, New York 14219-0228**
**U.S.A.**
**Telephone: (716) 826-6500**
**Fax: (716) 826-1589**
**Web site: http://www.gibraltar1.com**

*Public Company*
*Incorporation:* 1993
*Employees:* 3,100
*Sales:* $621.9 (1999)
*Stock Exchanges:* NASDAQ
*Ticker Symbol:* ROCK
*NAIC:* 331221 Rolled Steel Shape Manufacturing;
  331513 Steel Foundries

Based in Buffalo, New York, the Gibraltar Steel Corporation is a leader in the intermediate steel processing industry, operating 52 facilities in 19 states and Mexico. Once highly dependent on its automotive customers, the company has in recent years engaged in an aggressive program of acquiring smaller businesses to become active in construction products, heat treating services, materials management, the manufacture and distribution of strip steel and steel strapping, as well as general consumer products such as mailboxes. Controlled by the second generation of the Lipke family, Gibraltar Steel went public in 1993.

### Dr. Ken Lipke buys Gibraltar Steel in 1972

Buffalo, with its access to the Erie Canal and Great Lakes, as well the power provided by Niagara Falls, was once a major center for the manufacture of steel. The industry in America was highly integrated, with companies controlling raw materials, manufacture, as well as the distribution of steel products, but some smaller businesses still found a niche. One such venture was the Gibraltar Steel Corporation, a marginally profitable, single facility, specialty steel processing company. Its modern history began in 1972 when Dr. Ken Lipke and two partners purchased the company for $1 million.

Although Gibraltar Steel posted modest annual earnings of $9 million, Lipke vowed to increase sales to $100 million within ten years. What to some seemed an unrealistic goal would be aided by changes in the steel industry. Steelmakers began to restructure their business to concentrate on manufacture. Likewise, major users of steel, such as automakers, eliminated facilities that processed steel to concentrate on the building of their final products. The result of this fundamental shift left a gap in processing, the preparation of steel for its actual use. A multitude of small companies like Gibraltar Steel were the beneficiaries.

Lipke came to the steel business by an unusual route. He was a chiropractor by training and ran a successful practice for 20 years. However, he was also a risk taker who enjoyed the competition of business. In the 1960s he established a stock brokerage, before raising the money to purchase Gibraltar Steel. His new business was a cold reduction strip mill that bought hot-rolled black steel, then produced sheet metal that was primarily used by automakers. Lipke's first major step in growing the business came in 1975 when he acquired another area cold-rolling operation, Seneca Steel. In that year he also added Buffalo's Beals, McCarthy & Rogers, as well as the Rochester firm of Follansbee Metals. In all, these transactions added $24 million in annual sales.

Lipke installed a management team that included two of his sons, Brian and Neil. By 1977 Gibraltar Steel posted sales in excess of $50 million dollars. By 1982 Brian Lipke was named corporate president. Although Dr. Lipke did not realize his ambitious sales goal for Gibraltar Steel, the company did reach the $100 million mark in 1984, in 12 years rather than ten. By 1987 he turned his attention to other interests, and sold the majority of the business to his four children. The management team he nurtured took over day-to-day operations of Gibraltar Steel. In addition to Brian Lipke as president, Neil Lipke was in charge of marketing; Walter Erasmus, finance; Joseph Rosenecker, commercial; and Carl Spezio, manufacturing. (In 2000 the team remained intact, providing stability during a period of exceptional growth for the company.)

Management quickly began to realize that it was too dependent on the often cyclical automotive industry. As much as 40

## Company Perspectives:

*Gibraltar's primary mission is to place the highest possible emphasis on quality, excellence, and continuous improvement, in a dedicated effort to exceed customer expectations and to maximize the total return to shareholders over the long term.*

percent of Gibraltar Steel's business came from General Motors alone. To begin the process of diversifying its risk, the company in 1987 acquired another cold-rolling operation, this mill located in Cleveland with customers in a range of industries. In 1989 Gibraltar Steel entered into a joint venture in Ohio with Samuel Steed for steel pickling (a finishing process). In 1990 Gibraltar Steel opened its first materials management facility, Integrated Terminals, that serviced a Buffalo Ford Motors plant.

### Gibraltar Steel goes Public in 1993

In 1992 Gibraltar Steel reached a turning point: Dr. Lipke passed away, and management realized that the company was still too dependent on automakers. In order to fuel growth, the company decided to convert from a Subchapter S corporation to a Subchapter C corporation and make a public offering of its stock. Not only would Gibraltar Steel shed $27 million in debt, it would be in a position to use its stock in order to acquire larger companies. Thus, on November 4, 1993, Gibraltar Steel sold 2.5 million shares of common stock at $11 per share, which began to trade on the NASDAQ exchange.

As Dr. Lipke had done when first purchasing the company, his son Brian announced an ambitious ten-year goal, this time to reach $1 billion in annual sales, a number that would require an average sales increase of 20 percent per year. As it formulated an acquisition strategy to make the goal a reality, Gibraltar Steel upgraded existing facilities as well as opening a new cold-rolling processing facility in Chattanooga, Tennessee, which gave the company a foothold in the rapidly expanding southeastern market. Sales in 1994 surpassed the $200 million mark.

Gibraltar Steel opted to grow more by acquisition than by starting new operations. According to Brian Lipke, ''If we were to build a brand new plant somewhere, it would take a year to design the plant, a year to build it, and a couple of years to build up the business to the point where you are making a profit. But if you make an acquisition, you get $60 million or $70 million worth of [annual] sales the day you close the deal; then you can refine the business and improve its profitability.'' Looking to diversify its product offering to make the company less dependent on the automotive industry, as well as broadening it geographic base, Gibraltar Steel established strict guidelines for potential purchases. First, the target had to be involved in the steel or metals industry, in order to best utilize management's experience and the company's infrastructure. The target also had to be profitable, with the clear potential for Gibraltar Steel to realize even greater revenues out of the business. A complimentary corporate culture was also a priority. Dr. Lipke had impressed on Gibraltar Steel management the concept of teamwork. In this regard, the company also looked to buy family-run

businesses with committed leaders who were willing to stay on after the purchase. Many steel businesses created after World War II were single facilities either run by aging founders or, like Gibraltar Steel itself, run by the founder's children, and now lacked the desire and means to expand at the rate necessary to properly compete in a contemporary environment. Unlike many corporations on acquisition sprees, Gibraltar Steel was not looking to cut work force in order to reduce costs. Its commitment to maintaining staff while gaining more business made it a desirable suitor to many companies looking to sell in an industry that was becoming increasingly more consolidated.

In 1995 Gibraltar Steel made its first acquisition employing these guidelines when for $39 million it purchased all of the stock of the Wm. R. Hubbell Steel Corporation, an Illinois processor. The move established Gibraltar Steel in the residential and commercial buildings industry. In addition to adding $70 million in annual non-car-related sales, Hubbell gained modern, well-maintained facilities in Illinois, South Carolina, and Florida.

The following year, Gibraltar Steel acquired Carolina Commercial Heat Treating (CCHT), based in North Carolina, for $25 million in cash. (Heat treating enhances the hardness and durability of steel products.) Whereas Gibraltar Steel was already involved in the business—heat treating coiled steel that it shipped to other firms for manufacture—CCHT gave the company a presence on the other end of the process. CCHT heat treated steel parts after manufacture, working for automotive, hand tool, construction equipment, and industrial machinery firms. Only 25 percent of its sales came from the auto industry. The purchase of CCHT added more than $20 million in annual sales to Gibraltar Steel, as well as adding to its presence in the South with plants in Tennessee, Georgia, South Carolina, and North Carolina.

In June 1996 Gibraltar Steel made a secondary public offering of two million shares of stock, raising an additional $34 million. Again, the purpose of the offering was to reduce debt and provide money for expansion and acquisition. Since going public in 1993, the company had grown from nine facilities to twenty-two, located in ten states and Mexico. Employment had increased from 470 people in 1991 to 682. Annual sales were also significantly ahead of the pace necessary to reach the $1 billion goal by 2003.

In 1997 Gibraltar Steel expanded its presence in the residential and commercial construction industry with the $40 million purchase of the Jacksonville, Florida-based Southeastern Metals Manufacturing Company. The deal was a direct result of the earlier acquisition of Hubbell, the executives of both companies being acquainted with each other. The two companies also complemented each other in product lines. Hubbell primarily sold prepainted, galvanized, and Galvalume steel to roofing and siding businesses, whereas Southeastern's 3,500 products included steel framing for buildings and sheds, metal roofing, storm panel systems, gutters, and metal trim. The acquisition contributed $90 million in annual sales, and customers in 20 U.S. states, Latin America, and the Caribbean. It also increased the Gibraltar Steel work force by 500, adding plants in Jacksonville, Miami, Tampa, San Antonio, Houston, Nashville, and Lyons, Georgia.

### *One of the Top 100 Fastest Growing Companies in 1997*

Gibraltar Steel increased its share of the heat treating business in 1997 with the purchase of an Athens, Alabama, facility from Specialty Heat Treating Inc. In addition to $2 million in annual sales, the new plant provided presence for Gibraltar Steel in a new state. The company, in the meantime, continued to upgrade existing operations, adding two annealing furnaces to its Cleveland plant, as well as beginning operation of the nation's widest cold-rolled strip mill that would by itself increase annual sales by $80 million. An auto strike hurt profits, prompting a steep drop in the price of Gibraltar stock, but it quickly rebounded, as analysts realized that the company was still enjoying a record-breaking year in sales. Management's effort to make the company less reliant on the automotive industry was already proving wise, despite the fact that sales to automakers still comprised 36 percent of annual sales. In September 1997 *Fortune* magazine recognized Gibraltar Steel by naming the company to its list of America's 100 fastest growing companies, ranking it 94th.

Gibraltar Steel increased its involvement in the building products markets with the March 1998 acquisition of the Mississippi-based Solar Group for $35 million in cash. Adding ventilation equipment to round out the line of construction products offered by the Southeastern Metals Manufacturing unit, Solar also brought with it the distinction of being the nation's leading manufacturer of mailboxes, made from galvanized steel as well as aluminum, brass, and plastic. The deal helped to make Gibraltar more involved in consumer product manufacturing, at the same time bringing an immediate $45 million in annual sales in the United States and from overseas.

The company continued to beef up its buildings product business with two more acquisitions in 1998. It purchased Wisconsin-based Appleton Supply Company for $28.5 million, followed two months later by United Steel Products Company for $35 million. United's Livermore, California, plant gave Gibraltar a West Coast presence, plus an additional $40 million in annual sales. Gibraltar Steel also augmented its heat-treating business with the acquisition of Harbor Metal Treating Company, allowing the corporation to service other types of customers, including tool and die manufacturing, medical equipment, and aerospace.

Gibraltar continued to acquire new companies at a steady pace in 1999. A heat-treating facility in Asheville, North Carolina, was added to the CCHT division. Hi-Temp Inc, an Illinois heat-treating company was also purchased, adding $23 million in annual sales and four more facilities. Yet another heat-treating company, Brazing Concepts of Coldwater, Michigan, added 200 employees and $14 million in annual sales, bringing the total of heat-treating sales to $80 million a year, well ahead of the $100 million goal for that portion of the business by 2003. Gibraltar Steel added to its share of the construction business by acquiring Weather Guard Building Products, a Denver-based manufacturer and distributor of gutters, roofing, and other related products. It also purchased Hughes Manufacturing, Inc., a Florida-based company that produced highly engineered steel lumber connectors, with $12 million in annual sales.

Despite generating $622 million in sales for 1999 and a net income of $25 million, which completed an impressive eight straight years of sales and earnings growth, the price of Gibraltar Steel stock lagged behind the rest of the rapidly escalating stock market. Whereas the company had increased sales since going public in 1993 by an average rate of 27 percent per year, and had increased profits by 22% per year, the value of its stock grew at an annual rate of only 15 percent. While many companies in the Standard & Poor's 500 were trading at more than 30 times earnings, and smaller companies in the Russell 2000 index at more than 60 times earnings, Gibraltar Steel traded at less than 12 times its annual earnings. Its many acquisitions of recent years may have saddled the company with $199 million in long-term debt, but the main reason that investors shied away seemed to be a preference for "growth" stocks over "value" stocks. Although management was confident that over time the long-term performance of the company would be reflected in the value of its stock, Gibraltar Steel announced in 1999 that it would begin to pay a modest dividend in an effort to lure institutional investors and individual investors who only purchased dividend-bearing stocks. Early in 2000 the company also hired an investment banker to find ways to boost the price.

In 2000 Gibraltar Steel sold a flat-rolled steel processing facility in Chattanooga, Tennessee, to Metals USA Inc. Citing that the operation simply did not fit its move to higher-profit operations, management insisted that no other divestitures were expected. In fact, later in the year the company made yet another acquisition, buying Milcor L.P., an Ohio-based manufacturer of building products, including registers, vents, bath cabinets, and doors for the residential, commercial, institutional, and industrial markets. Annual sales of $50 million were added to the balance sheet and increased Gibraltar Steel's presence in building products to seven companies, operating 23 facilities in 13 states.

Gibraltar Steel also made a move in 2000 to take advantage of business opportunities available through the internet. The company retained Xpedior to help it explore eBusiness opportunities, initially focusing on its construction products. The eventual goal was to improve operating efficiency, reduce costs, and strengthen sales throughout the corporation. Later in the year, Gibraltar Steel allied itself with FerrousExchange Inc., an internet-based service for the iron and steel industries, by making a minority investment and signing a multi-year commitment to purchase and offer significant quantities of steel products over the global on-line marketplace. Gibraltar Steel hoped to improve supply chain efficiency, as well as to broaden and diversify its supplier and customer base, in a continued effort to meet the aggressive goals that were a hallmark of the company ever since Dr. Lipke purchased it for $1 million in 1972.

### Principal Subsidiaries

Southeastern Metals Manufacturing Co.; Carolina Commercial Heat Treating; Wm. R. Hubbell Steel Corp.; Gibraltar Strip Steel.

### Principal Competitors

Cold Metal Products, Inc.; J&L Specialty Steel Inc.; Steel Technologies, Inc.; USX-U.S. Steel Group.

### Further Reading

Adams, Chris, "Aftershocks of Auto-worker Strikes Hit Stocks of Some Steel Service Centers," *Wall Street Journal,* September 15, 1997, p. A2.

"Gibraltar Acquires Milcor," *Metal Center News,* September 2000, p. 16.

"Gibraltar Increases Inroads into Construction Products," *Metal Center News,* April 1997, p. 16.

"Gibraltar Steel Expands in Heat-treating," *Metal Center News,* September 1999, p. 12.

Hartley, Tom, "Forging an Empire of Steel," *Business First,* August 21, 2000,

"Gibraltar Steel Diversifies in Value-Added Markets," *Metal Center News,* May 1997, pp. 106–15.

Linstedt, Sharon, "Gibraltar Steel Sells Processing Operation in Chattanooga," *Buffalo News,* February 15, 2000, p. D3.

Madore, James T., "Goal $1 Billion in Sales by 2003 Gibraltar Aims for 20% Annual Growth in Sales, Profits," *Buffalo News,* May 23, 1996, p. B6.

Robinson, David, "Sales Boom Expected by Gibraltar," *Buffalo News,* May 24, 1995, p. B7.

Robinson, David, "Gibraltar's Stock Continues to Lag Despite Firm's Steady Growth," *Buffalo News,* May 19, 1999, p. C1.

——, "Like Namesake Rock, Gibraltar Stock Withstands Nasty Jolt," *Buffalo News,* September 21, 1997, p. A15.

——, "Want to Buy a Company?," *Buffalo News,* January 23, 2000, p. D1.

"The Rock Makes Fortune 100 List," *Buffalo News,* September 14, 1997, p. B15.

Stouffer, Rick, "Costs of Stock Offering Cause Loss at Gibraltar," February 2, 1994, p. B1.

——, "Gibraltar Steel's Profits at Record High," April 30, 1996, p. E7.

Stundza, Tom, "Service Centers and Processors Bet Billions on Value Added," *Purchasing,* p. 41B1.

Williams, Fred O., "Gibraltar Steel Acquires Another Heat Treating Firm in North Carolina," *Buffalo News,* April 6, 1999, p. E3.

—Ed Dinger

# Global Industries, Ltd.

**8000 Global Drive**
**Carlyss, Louisiana 70665**
**U.S.A.**
**Telephone: (337) 583-5000**
**Fax: (337) 583-5100**
**Web site: http://www.globalind.com**

*Public Company*
*Incorporated:* 1973 as Global Divers
*Employees:* 2,044
*Sales:* $387.5 million (1999)
*Stock Exchanges:* NASDAQ
*Ticker Symbol:* GLBL
*NAIC:* 213112 Support Activities for Oil and Gas
    Operations; 23491 Water, Sewer, and Pipeline
    Construction; 332312 Fabricated Structural Metal
    Manufacturing; 333132 Oil and Gas Field Machinery
    and Equipment Manufacturing

Global Industries, Ltd., headquartered in Carlyss, Louisiana, is a major constructor of offshore oil and gas drilling platforms and pipeline systems. Although it principally serves the oil industry in the Gulf of Mexico, it has, as its name suggests, worldwide operations and has installed pipelines in the Pacific Rim, India, Mexico, West Africa, and the Middle East. In addition to installing and removing pipelines and platforms, Global provides diving and marine welding services for repair and salvage operations. William Doré, something of an oil-industry legend, founded Global and is still its CEO. He also owns about 31 percent of the business.

### 1973–74: William Doré's Risky Venture Pays Off

Global Industries traces its founding back to 1973 when Louisiana native William Doré bought a small business, Global Divers, from Ebb Lemaster. Global Divers, established in 1964 by Dick Evans, went to Lemaster after some company shuffling arrangements that started when Evans sold his parent company,

Dick Evans Divers, to a third party. Lemaster developed Global Divers into a small but successful firm specializing in offshore platform inspection, pipeline repairs, undersea construction, and oil drilling support. In 1970, he hired Doré, who, at the time, was trying to convince Lemaster to transfer his business profit-sharing funds from a bank certificate of deposit into mutual funds. Impressed by Doré's business savvy and determination, Lemaster hired him to head up Ebbco, a new diving-equipment rental company. Then, in 1972, when Ebbco grossed $500,000, Doré bought 49 percent of the company, using funds borrowed from his in-laws.

By 1973, Global Divers was hit with some serious reverses, in part because two major platform fires prompted regulations that discouraged new drilling in the Gulf of Mexico. The company's revenue plummeted to $200,000 from highs that at the end of the 1960s had reached $3 million. Faced also with equipment certification problems, Lemaster decided Global was about to fail, a view that Doré did not share. As a result, he offered Doré full ownership of Global in exchange for Doré's 49 percent interest in Ebbco. Despite the great risk involved, Doré agreed to the exchange and on May 3, 1973 became Global's sole owner.

With financial and logistical support from both family and friends, Doré began an energetic effort to turn Global once more into a viable, money-making operation. He badly needed equipment and personnel, and in both cases he had some initial good luck. He managed to rent an old broken down winch truck for a dollar a year and hired a former Lemaster employee, Joe Thornton, who proved to be a very versatile and dedicated worker. Doré's major problem was finding qualified divers and retaining them, and at the beginning he only had two who were committed to the company. He also needed to promote the company and find customers, tasks at which he excelled, even in the face of industry rumors that Global was teetering on the brink of insolvency. Within three months of taking over the company, he landed a $300,000 contract with Marathon Pipe Line of Findlay, Ohio, and shortly thereafter was able to land a Small Business Administration loan for $250,000. Those funds allowed Global to replace equipment that did not meet certification codes imposed by the Coast Guard.

### 1975–84: Global Grows at a Slow but Steady Pace and Begins Diversifying

Over the next decade, Global grew gradually but steadily. Its focus remained strictly on the oil industry in the Gulf of Mexico. In 1975, the company built a 10,000-square-foot operations and sales facility in Lafayette, Louisiana, where Doré had moved his family the previous year. Lafayette was rapidly becoming the hub for oil service companies providing logistical support for offshore drilling in the western Gulf. Global quickly began expanding its operations through the purchase of new equipment, allowing it to offer diving services for oil companies with platforms in deeper offshore water than it could initially manage. The company employed divers to help lay and repair undersea pipelines and install platforms as well as perform repair and salvaging operations.

In 1975, with its purchase of Pipelines, Inc., the company also began diversifying by laying pipelines using its own divers. Pipelines, Inc., using two pipeline barges, had been installing small-diameter pipe in shallow depths, up to 35 feet, for well over a decade. The opportunity to buy the company came after its owner, Eddie Lennard, suffered a heart attack. Lennard, who had contracted Global's services, was Doré's friend, and he wanted to sell him the business. Trusting his friend's business acumen, Lennard carried a note for Doré, who was not able initially to finance the buyout. Global moved the newly acquired business to a site on the Industrial Canal in Belle Chasse, just a few miles away from Doré's original office in Harvey, Louisiana.

Global also undertook to train its own divers for working in the deeper waters into which the offshore drilling companies were moving through the oil boom of the 1970s, although special training was also necessary in the shallower, muddier water, where visibility could be zero and much of Global's earliest diving services, in support of its own pipe-laying operations, were needed. Doré and his staff were well aware that future demands for Global's services, including pipelaying, would take their divers into deeper waters. Among other things, they added a third barge to Pipeline's small fleet. A converted Central Marine Service vessel dubbed *MAD III*, the new barge could lay pipe in depths of up to 100 feet. Following that, Global began building its own vessels, starting with the *GP 35*, designed with the help of Ivan L. Garzotto, an engineer who joined Global as executive vice-president in 1978. It soon added the *GP 37*, a vessel equipped with a crane capable of lifting 140 tons and laying pipe to a depth of 300 feet.

Meanwhile, Global's divers, contracted for offshore work for other companies, were going deeper and deeper. By 1978, when Global contracted for the construction of a saturation diving system allowing divers to work in depths up to 1,000 feet and maintain the pressure of that depth in a bell at the surface, the company had come up with its unique advertising slogan: "We've worked our way to the bottom!" Doré was also adding new, diversified services. In 1978 he incorporated Navigational & Safety Aids (NSA) to make, sell, install, and maintain navigational aids for offshore oil rigs, including domes for covering abandoned subsurface structures. Doré later sold NSA to his daughter and son-in-law.

It was also in the late 1970s that Global purchased a remote controlled vehicle (RCV) system nicknamed the "eyeball." It was basically a mobile video camera mounted on a frame. Equipped with thrusters and controlled from the surface, the eyeball could perform underwater reconnaissance and inspection without having to deal with such problems as diver decompression. So successful was the first of these units that by 1980, the year in which it computerized its operations in both Lafayette and Belle Chasse, Global added a second system. It also added a Honeywell Acoustic Tracking System (ATS), which, by using underwater acoustic beacons, permitted very accurate subsurface position tracking for use in tandem with RCVs.

Such new, state-of-the-art equipment helped Global position itself as an important and dependable diving company for construction, drilling, and production support at ever-increasing offshore depths. For example, it garnered important industry notice when, in the summer of 1982, it began helping Union Oil build an offshore oil platform at a Gulf site in almost 1,000 feet of water. Dubbed "Cerveza," the platform was built far more economically than a platform named "Cognac" that, some years earlier, Shell Oil had built at a similar depth. That same summer, using its saturation diving system and RCV, Global completed repairs on a pipeline for Columbia Gulf Transmission, working at depths of over 350 feet. It worked around the clock, saving that customer a considerable loss in revenue.

### 1985–92: Global Takes Advantage of the Oil Bust

When the oil bubble burst in the mid 1980s, all oil service and support companies had to undertake some belt-tightening measures, and some did not survive. Global managed to fare well despite the slowdown and recession. In fact, before the bottom fell out, Global had established itself in the Gulf of Mexico as a full-service diving company with the ability to lay pipe in up to 300 feet of water. Under Doré's prescient direction, the company proved willing to try new strategies for dealing with old problems and to invest in new equipment for future contingencies. For example, in 1985, as the industry was quickly tumbling, the company lost an opportunity for a major job with Shell Oil requiring the use of Global's saturation system. Global could not truck it to the Shell site in Texas because laws prohibited transport of oversized equipment over the weekend. As a result, Global procured a "mini" saturation system for jobs requiring an emergency response, even on weekends.

That sort of flexibility helped Global find and develop markets for its special services. In the mid-1980s, it became a major provider of wet welding services, something that other diving

---

### Key Dates:

**1973:** William Doré buys Global Divers and founds Global Industries.

**1975:** Company purchases Pipelines, Inc. and begins providing pipelaying services.

**1978:** Global builds barge ( the *GP 35*) to extend pipelaying services to intermediate water depths.

**1987:** Global buys Sea-Con Services and adds deepwater construction to its operations.

**1989:** Company begins installing and removing offshore drilling platforms and established Gulf of Mexico deepest dive (1,075 feet) in Jolliet project for Conoco.

**1990:** Acquires pipelaying and derrick vessels from Santa Fe Offshore Construction.

**1993:** Global purchases The Red Adair Company.

**1995:** Acquires ROV Technologies and buys *Hercules*, giving it heavy load lifting capabilities.

**1996:** Company buys Norman Offshore Pipelines, Inc., Divcon International, and a 49 percent share of CCC Fabricaciones y Construcciones; also acquires Mohawk pipelaying and derrick barge in Indonesia.

**1997:** Global acquires some assets of Sub Sea International from Dresser Industries Inc.

**1999:** Company opens Carlyss facility.

---

service companies were minimizing. In 1984, realizing that existing and future regulations would require considerable repair on the subsurface structures of existing production platforms, Doré hired C.E. "Whitey" Grubbs, former president of D & W Underwater Welding, to establish what became the country's most advanced underwater welding research facility. With the help of another man, Tom Reynolds, a welding engineer, Grubbs established a consortium with the Colorado School of Mines for developing subsurface welding techniques at various depths. At Global's Research and Development Center in Louisiana, divers learned the necessary wet welding techniques they put to practical use in the offshore oil patch.

Despite its growth and diversification, by the mid-1980s Global was still not competing with the much larger offshore construction firms like Brown & Root, J. Ray McDermott, and Santa Fe, all of which could lay large diameter pipes in depths up to 1,000 feet and had been growing very rapidly during the oil boom period of the late 1970s and early 1980s. Comparatively, Global was playing in a minor league, but in Bill Doré, the Coach, it had a team leader who knew a slump was inevitable and was positioning his firm to cope with it. He planned to take advantage of it when the downturn came and even at the height of the boom was creating a cash reserve while other firms were overextending. When the full collapse came in the winter of 1985–86, Global survived through an aggressive effort to find jobs, no matter how small, but it also began adding equipment it acquired from companies divesting assets in their own attempts to survive the hard times.

The major acquisitions that would transform Global into a major offshore, deepwater, turnkey contractor began in 1987

when, for $2.5 million, the company purchased the pipelaying assets of Sea-Con Services, Inc., including two barges, one of which, *Sea Constructor*, was capable of laying larger pipe at greater depths than any other vessels then owned by Global. The sale also gave Global a 15-acre site at the Port of Iberia in New Iberia, Louisiana, as well as important patents and exclusive rights to Sea-Con's wet welding technology.

It was also in 1987 that Global formed a partnership with Santa Fe, a major offshore drilling and construction company operating in international markets. Santa Fe, originally founded in Los Angeles in 1946, had been acquired by the Kuwait Petroleum Company (KPC) in 1981, at the height of the oil boom, and when oil prices bottomed out in the mid 1980s, KPC looked for ways to save its investment. Under the agreement, Global got a 49 percent share of the partnership and access to Santa Fe's equipment and markets.

In 1989, Global added *Sea Cat* to its fleet, a diving support vessel that improved its diving capabilities. Thereafter, in 1990, Doré acquired selected assets from Santa Fe at a bargain price of about $15 million. One major asset was the *Chickasaw*, a 270-foot pipelaying and construction barge that used a special reel technology which allowed it to lay pipe both quickly and efficiently. Two other acquired assets were the *Cherokee*, a 350-foot barge capable of laying large-diameter pipe in 800-foot depths, and another vessel, a dedicated bury barge named *Tonkawa*, which, though smaller, was still larger than the vessels used by Global before its partnering arrangement with Santa Fe. Also included in the sale were saturation diving systems (two capable of 1,500-foot depths) and an equipment yard in Houma, Louisiana. Altogether, these assets transformed Global into a company capable of laying pipe in depths up to 1,000 feet, a major turning point in its development. It was also in 1989 that Doré incorporated Pelican Trucking, a Global subsidiary created to reduce the cost of transporting Global's equipment to oil company docks on the Gulf Coast.

Although the purchase of Santa Fe's holdings and market slowdown led to problems in the first part of the 1990s, by June 1992 Global was again ready to invest in further expansion. At that time it bought Teledyne Movible Offshore's construction holdings, including three large derrick barges, two of which had a lifting capacity of 800 tons. Because new construction in the Gulf had come to a standstill, it was a risky venture that required some creative financing and some additional belt tightening. The company got help from an unexpected quarter, Hurricane Andrew, which roared across the Gulf oil patch in late August of 1992, leaving extensive damage. Suddenly Global had all the salvage and repair operations it could handle. The company also completed plans to go public in 1992, making its initial public offering in the winter of that year. The stock sale allowed Global to pay off its debt to Teledyne, which had agreed to carry the note financing the sale of its assets to Global.

### 1993–2000: Global Takes Its Operations Wider and Deeper

By 1993, the offshore oil industry had begun recharging, entering a deepwater revolution that was driven by technological breakthroughs that allowed drilling operations in ever increasing depths, moving far beyond the 1,000-foot limit established in the pre-bust boom in the early 1980s. Refinements in 3-D seismic technology permitted the pinpointing of promising formations at water depths of up to 10,000 feet, in turn calling for new or greatly modified drilling, diving, and construction systems.

Thanks to its earlier investments in equipment and its willingness to adapt to the demands of newer technologies, Global was ready to meet the deepwater challenge. It undertook extensive changes to vessels that it already owned, notably the *Chickasaw* and its reel-laying system. In 1994, Global invested about $9 million in upgrades that allowed the *Chickasaw* to lay pipe in depths up to 6,000 feet. Still, the company had to build or acquire other equipment, such as the *Hercules*, a very large, flat-bottom barge which Global purchased for $10.9 million from J. Ray McDermott in 1995 and retrofitted for deep water service at a cost of over $100 million. In 1998, with its final testing completed, *Hercules* began working as the most versatile and largest barge in Global's fleet, with a heavy load lifting capacity and ability to lay pipe up to 42 inches in diameter in depths up to 8,000 feet.

Throughout the 1990s, Global also built, commissioned, or purchased other important deep-water vessels and equipment. For example, in 1995 it bought the *Mohawk*, a 320-foot derrick and pipelaying barge operating in Indonesia. It also commissioned the building of the *Pioneer*, a 200-foot, semi-submersible dive-support vessel capable of working in 12-foot waves and staying on station in seas running up to 20 feet.

Throughout the 1990s, besides building, buying or modifying vessels in its fleet, Global was taking other important steps to both diversify its capabilities and hone its competitive edge. In 1993, it acquired The Red Adair Company, the high profile outfit made famous for its successful well-capping exploits throughout the world. To the well control services which that purchase provided, it added much improved deep-water, well-intervention services when, in 1995, it purchased ROV Technologies. By that time it had also purchased lift or jackup boats (self-propelled, self-elevating work platforms) for its growing fleet of specialized vessels, initially with a purchase of sixteen from Halliburton in 1994. In 1996, when it built two new liftboats capable of working in waters up to 180-feet deep, Global became the principal operator of liftboats in the Gulf of Mexico.

The expansion of Global greatly accelerated through the second half of the 1990s. Some of the technological advances that accounted for its ability to work at ever increasing depths led to a resurgence of shallow water drilling, notably the 3-D seismic technology. Global was in an enviable position to benefit, having the equipment and know-how to work at shallow depths, but because the company's focus had shifted to deeper water operations, Doré knew that the shallow-water pipeline division needed to be overhauled. In 1996, Global took a major step in that direction when it purchased Norman Offshore Pipelines, Inc. and created a new Coastal Division in New Iberia.

Partly as a result of its acquisitions, but also through careful planning, Global was also expanding into international markets, becoming truly global in its operations. To facilitate the deployment of its resources, Doré put together a management team, headed by Mike Buckley. Its main task, besides hiring experienced personnel, was to expedite operations outside the Gulf of Mexico. Then, beginning in 1995, Global commenced acquiring selected companies operating in various oil fields in widely spread locales. The company's first entry into foreign waters came in 1995, when it undertook two projects in waters off the coast of West Africa, using *Cheyenne*, a renovated derrick barge moved there from the Gulf of Mexico. The move proved to be very profitable; in fact, in 1997 *Cheyenne*, still operating off Africa, produced about 25 percent of Global's entire revenue. By that time the company had already acquired other assets that gave it a presence in both Asia and Mexico. It entered the Mexico market in 1996 when it purchased a 49 percent interest in CCC Fabricaciones y Construcciones, S.A. de CV. Although Global thereafter sold its interest in CCC, the deal allowed Global to acquire important equipment from J. Ray McDermott, including the *Shawnee* and the *Comanche*, both large derrick/pipelay barges. In the same year, the company also entered the Southeast Asian market when it bought the assets of Divcon International, an Australian company. Also, from Dresser Industries, at a cost of $102 million, it purchased several assets of SubSea International, including all assets in Pacific Rim Asia and the Middle East as well as those in the United States, with the exception of its ROV/engineering division.

Global's growth in the 1990s was close to phenomenal, especially between 1994 and 2000, both in terms of its revenue and its assets. Between 1994 and 1998, its revenue rose from $80.6 million to $379.9 million, a 471 percent increase. During the same period, Global's fleet grew from 15 to 80 vessels. In 1999, the year that Global opened its new headquarters and operational facility in Carlyss, Louisiana, crude prices plummeted, causing a temporary drop in Global's revenues and producing a net loss, but in 2000 prices quickly rose again, to new decade highs. In that year Global agreed to an asset exchange with Oceaneering International, whereby Global swapped some ROVs and support equipment in Asia and Australia for some of Oceaneering's diving and related assets. As the deal with Oceaneering suggests, one of Global's strengths has been its dynamic growth and change strategies. Although the oil industry's volatility can result in unanticipated, bottom-line havoc, over the years Global has demonstrated an uncanny ability to adjust to such conditions and even take advantage of them.

### *Principal Subsidiaries*

Global Industries Offshore LLC; Pelican Transportation; Global Offshore International, Ltd.; Global Offshore Mexico S. do R.L. de C.V.

### *Principal Competitors*

J. Ray McDermott; Stolt Comex Seaway S.A.; Cal Dive International; Torch, Inc.; Horizon Offshore, Inc.

### *Further Reading*

Bogle, Pegge, "The Giant: Growth of Global," *Oil and Gas Investor*, September 1993, p. A10.
"Global Industries Buys a Legend, Red Adair Co.," *Wall Street Journal*, January 5, 1994, pp. A8, C17.

"Global Industries Ltd. and Oceaneering International Inc.," *Oil and Gas Journal*, October 2, 2000, p 110.

Herold, Alan C., "Fourth Generation DP Set Up on Pipelay Unit," *Offshore*, March 1995, p. 42.

Lane, Randall, "Fire Sale," *Forbes*, January 31, 1994, p. 14.

Share, Jeff, "Firefighter Red Adair Caps Career with Sale of Company," *Oil Daily*, January 5, 1994, p. 2.

"Taking a New Angle Offshore," Interview, *Oil and Gas Investor*, July 1995, p. S10.

*Working Our Way to the Bottom: A History of Global Industries*, Dallas: Heritage Publishing Company, 1999.

—John W. Fiero

# GRANITE BANK
*The Power of Local Banking*

# Granite State Bankshares, Inc.

**122 West Street**
**Keene, New Hampshire 03431**
**U.S.A.**
**Telephone: (603) 352-1600**
**Toll Free: (877) 924-1224**
**Fax: (603)358-5707**
**Web site: http://www.granitebank.com**

*Public Company*
*Incorporated:* 1986
*Employees:* 281
*Total Assets:* $867.67 million (1999)
*Stock Exchanges:* NASDAQ
*Ticker Symbol:* GSBI
*NAIC:* 52211 Commercial Banking

Granite State Bankshares, Inc. is the holding company for Granite Bank, the largest independent bank headquartered in New Hampshire. Granite Bank is a New Hampshire chartered commercial bank and operates 18 branch banking offices throughout southern New Hampshire in Cheshire, Hillsborough, Merrimack, Rockingham, and Strafford counties. The bank serves its primary customers—individuals and small to mid-sized business customers—with retail banking services, including checking, savings, and money market accounts, NOW accounts, individual retirement accounts, and certificates of deposit. Lending activities include residential mortgages (approximately 63 percent of the bank's portfolio) and commercial real estate (24 percent), as well as construction, commercial, and installment loans. Mortgage loan products are provided by GSBI Mortgage, a nonbank subsidiary. In 1999, the bank introduced GRANITe-bank, an electronic banking service that combines the convenience of Internet banking with industry-standard security protection.

### At the Beginning: 1895–1900

On March 28,1895, seven prominent New Hampshire citizens, led by Obed C. Dort, gathered to form a bank in the small city of Keene, New Hampshire. Located just 15 miles from the Connecticut River, the state's boundary with Vermont, and 15 miles from Massachusetts, Keene was and would remain the economic hub for southwestern New Hampshire.

At the turn of the century, Keene was a bustling, forward-looking metropolis with a population of approximately 7,500. As the county seat for several surrounding rural communities in the shade of majestic Mount Monadnock, the city served as the cultural, social, and commercial center for the area. In the 1890s, for example, both Buffalo Bill's Wild West show and the Barnum and Bailey circus regularly came to town. The first motion pictures, presented with Edison's new "Vitascope," dazzled citizens as early as November 1896.

According to the bank's centennial history, "The First 100 Years," the Keene Savings Bank was "born in a time better suited to failure than success." Yet, the turn of the century seems to have been an auspicious moment to launch the fledgling bank. Innovative, new enterprises were springing up all over the city. The Keene Gas and Electric Company plant opened the year the new bank was incorporated, and the first commercial electric lights were installed in 1898. The city's first bus line, which featured a closed horse drawn vehicle, opened in 1896, and was eclipsed in 1900 by the installation of an electric railway through the commercial center of town. Railroads were a major factor in the city's economic life. The merger of the Cheshire Railroad with the Fitchburg Railroad in 1890 significantly expanded the ability of local manufacturers to reach new markets in Massachusetts and beyond. In the 1890s, a railway repair shop, which serviced engines and cars using the newly merged line, became one of Keene's largest employers.

The official city history, *Upper Ashelot: A History of Keene, New Hampshire,* reported six pail and pail stock makers, three box makers, two brick manufacturers, five chair makers, two carriage and two engine builders, a tannery, and a woolen mill among many other small and active businesses in Keene. A piano company and a toy company, the latter destined to put Keene on the map in the first half of the new century, were both started in 1892.

The Keene Savings Bank opened its first office on June 15, 1897, two years after incorporation, in the rear of a jewelry store on the corner of Washington Street and Central Square. After a

173

year in business, the bank showed assets of $16,957.67, no loans secured by mortgage, and a gross income of $85.36, according to a New Hampshire Bank Commissioner's report. In defense of its modest start, however, the city's newest bank faced significant competition. By 1900, Keene was home to eight other banks. The oldest, the Cheshire National Bank, had been in operation since 1804, and the Cheshire Provident Institution was established 1833.

### Solid and Steady Growth: 1900–1982

By its tenth anniversary, with deposits of more than $500,000, the bank was ready to move from the jewelry store backroom to an area known as Banker's Row on the west side of Keene's Central Square. At mid-century, Keene Savings Bank occupied two impressive adjacent buildings in the heart of Bankers Row. The Bank would remain on the square until 1976, when it built new headquarters.

Dr. Gardner C. Hill, who served as Keene Savings Bank's first president until his death in 1915, was a prominent physician and tireless public servant. He served on the Keene Board of Education for 31 years and was a Keene city councilor, county commissioner, and county treasurer. James Taft, the bank's first vice-president, was elected mayor of Keene for three consecutive terms, while Herbert Fay, the bank's first treasurer, served as mayor in 1914 and 1915. Following in the footsteps of these early leaders, later generations of bank officers and employees would also make a strong commitment to the communities in which they lived and worked. That this commitment proved advantageous to both the bank and its communities was reflected by the bank's consistent pattern of steady growth. By the end of its first quarter-century, total assets were slightly more than $1,000,000; 25 years later, assets would reach $4,222,000.

### The Smith Years: 1982 and On

The Keene Savings Bank pursued its successful strategy of steady growth throughout most of the 20th century. However, with the new leadership in 1982 of Charles W. Smith, the bank's eighth president and the first to hold the title of chief executive officer, the bank embarked on a period of significant change and extraordinary growth. In 1986, with assets of more than $87.5 million and earnings a record $901,476, Smith moved to form Granite State Bankshares, Inc. (GSBI). His purpose was to convert Keene Savings Bank from a mutual

savings institution to a New Hampshire chartered guaranty stock savings bank. The initial offering of 1,400,000 shares of common stock was sold in the subscription period and raised $17,074,000 in new capital. This capital would later enable the bank to diversify its markets through acquisition and expansion into other financial and geographical areas.

While he looked to expand the reach of the new bank holding company, Smith understood that the success of the Keene Savings Bank rested on its traditions as a community bank. In a 1991 interview in *Bottomline*, he said, "No matter how much this industry changes, there always will be a role for community banks. People want more than price. They want service. ... Even when larger banks move into a market, smaller banks have continued to thrive because bigger banks can't give the customer the same attention the community banks give them. You simply don't get the time and commitment from a bank that moves into an area substantially far away from its main base," Smith added.

Even as the bank began to expand into new communities, the tradition of service that had begun almost a century before in Keene, with the bank's first officers, remained a focus. The bank's 1989 annual report noted that employees had, in that year alone, contributed more than 1,500 hours of volunteer community service. Ten years later, the annual report emphasized the bank's sponsorship of community events, funding for regional development, support for the arts, and "a high level of volunteerism."

The bank's first venture beyond Keene occurred in 1987 when GSBI made New Hampshire banking history in becoming the first bank in that state to establish a *de novo* bank by purchasing an existing branch of another bank. This historic purchase was a branch of the Amoskeag Bank in Amherst, located in the economically booming central section of southern New Hampshire.

In 1988, the bank's name was changed from Keene Savings Bank to Granite Bank of Keene. More significant to the bank's new pattern of growth and development was its 1988 merger with the First Peterborough Bank Corp.(FPB) of nearby Peterborough. With the assumption of FPB's subsidiary, the First National Bank of Peterborough, GSBI gained assets of $46.9 million and a group of new staff members with their own strong tradition of community service dating back to 1865. The bank continued to grow in 1989 with the opening of new offices in Chesterfield and Milford. This expansion to both the east and west of Keene meant that Granite Bank now had offices in every major market from the Connecticut River in the west to the Merrimack River in the east.

"Financial opportunities are created in periods of economic downturn," wrote Smith in his message to stockholders in GSBI's 1991 annual report. That year saw more New Hampshire bank failures than any other year in the state's history. However, Granite Bank was able to turn the hard economic times to its advantage. With government assistance, GSBI purchased two banks that regulators had slated to close: First Northern Bank in Keene and Durham Trust Company in Durham and Portsmouth. This purchase gave Granite Bank a greater market share in Keene and extended the franchise to the seacoast.

These acquisitions were dwarfed, however, by the news, on October 31, 1997, that GSBI had acquired Peterborough-based Primary Bank through a merger with Granite Bank. As of March 31 of that year, Primary had total assets of approximately $430 million, ten branches located in Merrimack, Hillsborough, and Cheshire counties, and an extensive distribution of ATM locations throughout southern New Hampshire. The combination of these two banks resulted in Granite Bank's posting consolidated assets of $814 million.

Granite Bank completed the merger with Primary Bank and strengthened its financial position in the late 1990s. By the turn of the century, the bank had become the largest independent bank headquartered in New Hampshire. In 1999, Veribanc, a nationally-recognized rating service, gave Granite Bank a Blue Ribbon Award, its highest ranking for a financial institution and the oldest national recognition awarded to banks for financial safety and soundness. In October 2000, Smith announced that the bank had signed an agreement to purchase the two branch offices of Olde Port Bank in Portsmouth and Hampton, both in Rockingham County. The Olde Port branches brought with them approximately $47 million in deposits and repurchase agreements and $47 million in loans. The two branches employed 23 persons. The transaction was expected to become final by December 31, 2000. As a result of the purchase, Granite Bank was now represented in the economically vibrant seacoast region by five branches.

### Looking to the Future

Granite Bank was fully committed to remaining at the forefront in the swiftly changing personal and commercial banking environment. In 1999, in response to customer requests for Internet-based banking services, the bank launched GRANITe-bank, one of the first online services offered by a New Hampshire-based bank. Before designing the new service, the bank surveyed the opinions of more than 750 customers. GRANITe-bank, as a result, was developed with customer service and state-of-the-art security protection as high priorities. A fire wall of sophisticated technology, encryption, and confidential passwords protected confidential customer information. Individuals and small businesses appreciated the opportunity to access their own accounts at any time, and an added ability to see check images online differentiated GRANITe-bank from other Internet-based banking services. Customer response was overwhelmingly positive, and the service was expected to reach even more households and small businesses in the future.

In the first decade of the new century, Granite Bank planned to continue to offer customers the latest technology-based banking services available anywhere. The bank's Internet site had been designed to provide current and prospective customers with the information they needed to take advantage of the Granite Bank's many services from the comfort of their homes and offices. With assets of more than $860 million, and the purchase of the Olde Port Bank branches, Granite Bank had established a solid presence across southern New Hampshire from the Connecticut River to the Atlantic Ocean and appeared to be in a strong position to take advantage of further opportunities for growth and expansion.

### Principal Subsidiaries

Granite Bank.

### Principal Competitors

Andover Bancorp, Inc.; First Essex Bancorp, Inc.

### Further Reading

"Granite Bank Buys Olde Port Bank Branches in New Hampshire," *Prime Zone Media Network,* October 4, 2000.
"Granite Bank Earns Dividends from Tradition, Technology," *New Hampshire Business Review,* January, 14, 2000, pp. 15–16.
Hutnyan, Joseph D., "Rallying Around the Two Words that Sum It All Up," *Bottomline,* March/April, 1991, pp. 49+.
Keene History Committee, *Upper Ashelot: A History of Keene, New Hampshire,* Keene, N.H.: Author, 1968.
"What's the Biggest N.H. Bank? Try Looking in Keene," New Hampshire Business Review, November 7, 1997, p. 35.

—Margery M. Heffron

# Grupo Industrial Durango, S.A. de C.V.

Potasio 150, Ciudad Industrial
Durango, Durango
Mexico
Telephone: (521) 814-0078 or 814-1658
Fax: (521) 814-1275
Web site: http://www.gid.com.mx

*Public Company*
*Incorporated:* 1975
*Employees:* 7,600
*Sales:* 5.39 billion pesos ($554.9 million) (1999)
*Stock Exchanges:* Mexico City London New York
*Ticker Symbol:* GIDUSA (Mexico City); GID (New York)
*NAIC:* 321212 Softwood Veneer and Plywood Manufacturing; 32211 Pulp Mills; 322122 Newsprint Mills; 32213 Paperboard Mills; 322211 Corrugated and Solid Fiber Box Manufacturing; 322224 Uncoated Paper and Multiwall Bag Manufacturing; 322299 All Other Converted Paper Products Manufacturing; 551112 Offices of Other Holding Companies

Grupo Industrial Durango, S.A. de C.V. (also known as GIDUSA or Gidusa), is a Mexican holding company that, through subsidiaries, supplies high-quality packaging for a wide variety of consumer goods and industrial products, both in Mexico and the United States. It is the largest producer in Mexico of corrugated containers, containerboard, industrial paper, and molded-pulp egg cartons, and a leading producer of multiwall paper sacks and bags, plywood, particleboard, and lumber. In addition, Durango holds a half-share in a company that dominates the production of newsprint in Mexico.

### Private Company: 1975–93

Grupo Industrial Durango was founded in 1975 in the Mexican state of Durango from the combination of a forest products transportation company and a regional wholesaler of building products. It consisted at the time of a small sawmill and five

trucks, with annual revenue of $2 million. From its formation the company pursued a strategy of growth by acquisition and internal expansion, establishing plywood and particleboard plants during the following decade. Its transformation into one of Mexico's largest integrated packaging and forest products companies began in 1987, when it purchased about 75 percent of Grupo Industrial Atenquique, S.A. de C.V. from the federal government. (The remaining shares were purchased in 1996.) This company's principal products were containerboard, industrial paper, and corrugated containers. In 1988 Durango acquired Celulosicos Centauro, S.A. de C.V. from the conglomerate Grupo Industrial Alfa, S.A. de C.V. (later Alfa, S.A. de C.V.). This company, whose principal asset was a pulp mill, was producing virgin pulp and forest products. As part of the transaction, Durango purchased a high-capacity paperboard and industrial paper machine that was installed at a new company-owned paper mill in 1990. This machine was a 7.6-meter, twin-wire, state-of-the-art unit with a capacity of 240,000 metric tons a year of mottled white and white top-grade paper.

These two acquisitions, together with the installation of the Centauro machine, made Durango the largest containerboard and industrial paper producer in Mexico, in terms of capacity. In 1991, Durango acquired four independent multiwall sack and bag converters and purchased a group of plywood and particleboard companies. These purchases included Triplay Ponderosa de Durango, S.A. de C.V. and Maderas Moldeadas, S.A. and affiliates, producers of plywood, particleboard, and lumber, and Sacos y Envases de Mexico, S.A. de C.V., a producer of multiwall sacks and bags acquired from the Morodo group. In 1992 Durango's Atenquique operation opened corrugated container plants in Ciudad Guzman and Tuhitlan.

Durango, in 1993, acquired Carton Titan S.A. de C.V. from Alfa and Stone Container Corp. for about $155 million. Founded in Monterrey in 1936 by Eugenio Garza Sada to meet the growing needs of the beer, glass, and packaged snacks industries in the state of Nuevo Leon, Titan had evolved to become the largest Mexican corrugated container producer, in terms of capacity. It was also a leading Mexican producer of molded pulp products (primarily egg cartons) and a significant Mexican producer of containerboard and industrial paper. The

## Key Dates:

**1975:** Grupo Industrial Durango is formed.
**1991:** Acquisitions have made Durango the largest producer of containerboard and industrial paper in Mexico.
**1993:** Durango purchases Mexico's largest producer of corrugated containers.
**1994:** Grupo Industrial Durango becomes a publicly owned company.
**1997:** Durango makes its first U.S. purchase, of McKinley Paper Co. and related companies.
**1999:** The company assumes half-ownership of a Mexican newsprint operation.

Titan acquisition, which included paper mills producing medium, semi-chem kraftliner—both bleached and unbleached—also included a variety of other paper converting activities, including tubes and gummed paper. Also in 1993, Durango acquired Sacos Mexicanos, S.A. de C.V. from Cementos Apasco, S.A. de C.V. and three multiwall sack and bag companies from the Wellbanks group: Bolsas y Papeles de Mexico, S.A. de C.V.; Sacos de Tila, S.A. de C.V.; and Bolsas y Papeles de Jalisco, S.A. de C.V.

### Weathering the Recession: 1994–97

By mid-1994 Grupo Industrial Durango owned 11 corrugated box plants, seven multiwall bag plants, four molded-pulp plants, four paper mills, three lumber mills, two plywood plants, a particleboard operation, and 400,000 hectares (about one million acres) of forests. Containerboard and industrial paper, produced at the Atenquique, Centauro, and Titan mills, included linerboard and corrugating medium, used in the production of corrugated containers. Kraft paper, made from virgin pulp, was the raw material for the company's multiwall bags. Durango was producing about 100,000 tons per year of unbleached kraft pulp for its own use and also was supplying pulp to the company plants producing molded products such as egg cartons.

In July of that year, the company, formerly privately owned by the Rincon family, made an initial public offering at 30.61 pesos ($8.75) a share in Mexico and a concurrent offering of American Depositary Shares abroad at $18 a share. This reduced the Rincon family's shares of the firm to 70 percent. The proceeds of $117.5 million were used to repay most of the indebtedness incurred to finance the Titan acquisition, which included a $95 million loan from Chase Manhattan Bank coming due. Durango also secured an additional sum of about $150 million by issuing seven-year bonds at a yield of 12 percent. Before the year was out, Durango had acquired six companies from the Dabdoub family group Comercializadora Industrial Gusymex, S.A. de C.V., thereby adding to its production network three corrugated container plants and a small paper mill.

The sudden capital flight from the peso in late 1994 led to a deep recession in Mexico the following year, but Durango remained profitable, earning 295.51 million pesos (about $38.65 million) on net sales of 2.96 billion pesos (about

$387.18 million). Joel Millman of the *Wall Street Journal* later wrote that the "timely" Titan purchase had given Durango "the clout and customer base to attack the growing border market and provided a cushion of dollar-oriented sales during the recession that followed the 1994 peso devaluation." Also in 1995, the company purchased Cartones y Empaques del Sur, S.A. de C.V., a company whose principal asset was a corrugated container plant in Tapachula, from PIC International Inc.

In 1996 Durango purchased Productos Industriales Ponderosa, S.A. de C.V. from Empresa La Moderna, S.A. de C.V. and minority shareholders for $32 million. This acquisition gave the company access to important forest products resources in the state of Chihuahua, where it previously had no forestry operations. Because the Ponderosa companies operated in a region bordering the United States and, historically, had exported almost half of their production to the United States, the purchase significantly strengthened Durango's export sales of forest products, including plywood, particleboard, specialized wood products such as fine wood veneers, and resin. Also in 1996, Durango acquired Central de Envases y Empaques, S.A. de C.V. from Grupo Industrial Garcia Franco. Its principal asset was a corrugated container plant in Mexicali, allowing Durango to further expand its business among the 2,600 factories in this area assembling goods for export to the United States, mainly in the electronics, textile, and auto parts sectors.

Durango's export business and consequent dollar-denominated sales enabled it to overcome the weakness of the peso and continued Mexican recession. In 1996 it had net income of 1.08 billion pesos (about $106.36 million) on net sales of 3.40 billion pesos (about $429.29 million). In 1997 it made its first U.S. acquisition, purchasing McKinley Paper Co. and certain related companies from Amcor Paper US, Inc., a U.S. subsidiary of Amcor Limited, for about $70 million. These enterprises were operating a containerboard and industrial paper mill in New Mexico and two fiber recycling plants, in New Mexico and Arizona. This group was renamed Durango International, Inc. "Grupo Durango," its chairman, Miguel Rincon Arredondo, told Joel Millman, "has been able to outperform its global peers in a difficult business environment, because we take advantage of our integrated operations, especially in raw-materials supply, to cut costs."

### Further Acquisitions: 1998–2000

Durango, in early 1998, purchased, for about $20 million, plants in Houston and Dallas owned by Box USA Inc., plus a satellite facility in Nogales, Arizona, where cartons were being treated with wax for fruit and vegetable shippers from Mexico's Pacific coast. During the summer it signed a letter of intent to buy 23 box plants belonging to Four M. Corp. of Valhalla, New York, for $355 million, a transaction that would have included the assumption of $240 million in debt but would have made Durango North America's largest independent producer of corrugated packaging. Because of concerns over Durango's large long-term debt—which reached $557.5 million at the end of 1998—the deal was canceled in October. The company's depositary shares in New York were trading at less than $5 a share, compared with a high of $15.25 in early April. Durango recently had issued about $220 million in five-year bonds, leaving it with a ratio of 53 percent of total debt to capitalization.

The Wall Street investment community, according to one account, approved of Durango's efforts to turn its containerboard and industrial paper into value-added packaging products chiefly aimed at the border plants and export-oriented customers. It also approved of the company's greater vertical integration, evidenced by the high proportion of its containerboard production being utilized by its own converting plants. The company's network of recycled fiber collection centers throughout Mexico, its virgin pulp, and the efficiency of its plant operations were said to contribute to above-average profit margins. Nevertheless, analysts were worried that Durango's cash flow was not adequate, in view of its debt, the weak peso, and the declining price of paper in the international markets.

Durango moved into newsprint production in 1999 by purchasing the Mexican government's three newsprint mills from Grupo Productora e Importadora de Papel S.A. for $112 million. Only 49 percent of this acquisition was actually assumed by the group; the other 51 percent was purchased by the Rincon family's Corporacion Durango, S.A. de C.V. The acquired enterprise, formed into a new company named Pipsamex, was said to have annual sales of $240 million and monopolized the newsprint sector in Mexico, with a 90 percent market share. It had lost $24.6 million, however, during the first half of 1998, according to a Mexican financial daily. Pipsamex's mills had a combined capacity of 450,000 tons a year of newsprint and bond paper. Some 72,000 tons a year were being exported to Texas and New Mexico.

At the end of 1998 Grupo Industrial Durango had the capacity to produce 728,000 tons per year of containerboard and industrial paper (consisting of linerboard, corrugating medium, and unbleached kraft paper) at six mills, 601,000 tons per year of corrugated containers at 18 plants, and 70,000 tons per year of multiwall sacks and bags at three plants. It held two integrated pulp mills with the capacity to produce 200,000 tons per year of virgin pulp, of which it was Mexico's sole producer. The company also operated four molded-pulp egg carton plants and nine forest products plants producing plywood, particleboard, and lumber. Durango was supplying high-quality packaging for a wide variety of consumer goods and industrial products, including packaging used for consumer products, food, agricultural products, cement, and other industrial and construction products. By product, linerboard and packaging accounted for 89 percent of the company's sales in 1999. Approximately 45 percent of its revenues were derived from North American Free Trade Association (NAFTA) markets, with the remaining 55 percent from the Mexican market.

Durango's performance was poor in 1998, with net income of only 91.6 million pesos (about $13.5 million) on net sales of 5.58 billion pesos (about $523.7 million). In 1999 sales dipped to 5.39 billion pesos and increased only marginally in dollar terms (to about $554.9 million), but net income increased more than tenfold, to 1.01 billion pesos (about $102.3 million). The long-term debt fell slightly, to $543.2 million.

In January 2000 Corporacion Durango purchased Gilman Paper Co., a privately owned, New Jersey-based paper manu-facturer with 1998 revenues of $380 million, according to Durango. Gilman chiefly was producing bleached paperboard for folding cartons, printing bristols, and food service products; kraft paper for bags; bleached and unbleached envelope papers; and other fine papers and specialty packaging papers. The purchase included a paper mill in St. Marys, Georgia, and three converting facilities in Georgia, Tennessee, and Pennsylvania, manufacturing business forms, flexible packaging, and multiwall bags. The purchase also included a short-line railroad to transport raw materials to the mill and deliver finished products to major connecting railroads. Gilman was employing about 2,100 workers.

Management—which, effectively, meant the Rincon family—held 87 percent of Grupo Industrial Durango's common stock in 2000, through Corporacion Durango (59 percent) and Administracion Corporativa y Mercantil, S.A. de C.V. (28 percent).

### Principal Subsidiaries

Chapas Finas Ponderosa, S.A. de C.V. (50%); Durango International, Inc. (U.S.A.); Empaques de Carton Titan, S.A. de C.V.; Grupo Industrial Atenquique, S.A. de C.V.; Grupo Industrial Ponderosa, S.A. de C.V.; Grupo Pipsamex, S.A. (49%); Sistema Ambiental Industrial, S.A. de C.V. (26.2%).

### Principal Operating Units

Forest Products Group; Packaging Business Group.

### Principal Competitors

Georgia-Pacific Corp.; International Paper Co.; Kimberly-Clark de Mexico, S.A. de C.V.; Smurfit-Stone Container Corporation; Temple-Inland Inc.

### Further Reading

"Durango Delves into Newsprint Production," *Pulp & Paper International,* February 1999, p. 15.
"Grupo Durango Enters U.S. Debt Market," *Pulp & Paper,* September 1998, p. 27.
Marray, Michael, "Durango Overcomes a Little Local Difficulty," *Euromoney,* September 1994, "World's Best Credit" Supplement, p. 18.
"Mexico's Durango Buys Gilman Paper," *Pulp & Paper,* February 2000, p. 13.
Millman, Joel, "Mexico's Gidusa Cancels Deal to Acquire U.S. Box Maker Due to Market Turmoil," *Wall Street Journal,* October 29, 1998, p. A19.
——, "Mexico's Gidusa Plans to Buy 2 Plants in Latest Step to Dominate U.S. Niche," *Wall Street Journal,* January 14, 1998, p. A16.
"Rincon Durango Buy Pipsa Mills," *Pulp & Paper,* February 1999, p. 21.
Sickafoose, Keith, "Durango: An Exclusive Report," *International Paper Board Industry,* June 1994, pp. 65–66, 68.

—Robert Halasz

# Half Price Books, Records, Magazines Inc.

5803 E. Northwest Highway
Dallas, Texas 75231
U.S.A.
Telephone: (214) 360-0833
Fax: (214) 890-0850
Web site: http://www.halfpricebooks.com

*Private Company*
*Founded:* 1972
*Employees:* 1,100
*Sales:* $70 million (1999)
*NAIC:* 451211 Book Stores; 45122 Prerecorded Tape,
    Compact Disc, and Record Stores; 45331 Used
    Merchandise Stores

Through its chain of 64 stores in ten states, Half Price Books, Records, Magazines Inc. buys and sells nearly all used printed and recorded matter, including books, magazines, phonograph records, cassette tapes, eight track tapes, and computer software. The company is privately owned, in part by its employees; all stores in the chain are owned by the company, none are franchises. In addition to being a successful commercial venture, the company sees itself as a positive force for recycling and other important environmental concerns. In the words of founder Ken Gjemre, Half Price Books "has been a social, political, and environmental statement from the beginning. . . . I was upset at the waste in America." The company works with nonprofit organizations throughout the United States and contributes thousand of books annually to the poor and disadvantaged in the United States and the rest of the world.

## Origins

Half Price Books was the brainchild of Ken Gjemre. Gjemre was one of six children born to Norwegian immigrants who came to the United States around the turn of the century. They eventually settled on a farm in Indiana where they raised potatoes, onions, and peppermint. The frugality of farm life made a lasting impression on Gjemre. "[My parents] never threw anything away. If you took a worn-out piece of farm

equipment apart, you saved the bolts because you could use them later someplace else," he told the *Houston Chronicle* in 1988. That awareness of waste would become a principle upon which he later based his book business.

Gjemre received a degree in Chemistry from Purdue University and served with the American Army during the Second World War—he was with the first troops to meet Soviet forces at the Elbe in eastern Germany in 1945. After he left the service, he went to work in retail. In August, he moved to Texas to work as a vice-president for Zale, a chain of stores that specialized in jewelry, but which also sold a full line of housewares and appliances. As a buyer Gjemre was successful at what he was doing, however, he had recently become a Unitarian and he found it increasingly difficult to reconcile the nature of the work with his principles. "My ethic was of thrift and saving," he told *Publishers Weekly* in 1991. "I was a child of the Depression, but here I was selling things on credit to people who didn't need them and couldn't afford them. I was good at it, but I didn't like it."

In January 1972, with the Vietnam War still raging, Gjemre took a leave of absence to work for the New Party, a left liberal alternative party that counted among its supporters Dr. Benjamin Spock. Eventually he returned to Zale but was as unhappy there as ever. One day, though, he found himself in a secondhand bookstore in Dallas. Gjemre reflected a bit on the business. The busy bookstore bought books at ten percent of cover price and resold them at 50 percent of the cover price. That made its cost of goods 20 percent. Retail savvy Gjemre was amazed—normally retailers battle hard to keep costs at 50 percent. What's more, the store was selling product that people wanted, at a reasonable price, and they were goods that would otherwise have been thrown away with the trash.

It was the kind of retailing Gjemre, then 51 years old, could engage in with a clear conscience. He made the owner of the bookstore an offer to buy the business, but the deal fell through at the last minute. When it did, however, the other bookstore owner suggested Gjemre start a store of his own from the ground up. It was an attractive idea. However, at the time Gjemre was in the process of divorcing his wife and had less than $200 to his name. He was able to borrow $4,000 from a friend, 40-year-old Pat Anderson. That, together with 2,002

## Company Perspectives:

*Half Price Books is one of the only places where you can get cash for books you've already read. So if you have more books than shelves, bring your books to Half Price Books today and let our specialized trained buyers make you an offer. If you are unsatisfied with the offer, you may donate your books through Half Price Books. We work with several nonprofit organizations across the country through our A, E, I, O & YOU Program. And since our inventory changes daily, you will always find something new at Half Price Books.*

books from their own libraries, enabled them to open the first Half Price Books store in an abandoned laundromat in Dallas, Texas, on July 27, 1972. A local bookie who ran a shoe repair store in the same shopping center made book on how long their book business would survive. He gave them six months.

At the time the store opened, Anderson was making her way through the clinical psychology program at the University of North Texas. Within six months of opening Half Price Books, it was obvious to Gjemre that he would not be able to repay Anderson's loan as quickly as he had expected. He offered to make her his full partner in the business. She agreed and cancelled the loan. In keeping with Gjemre's philosophy of recycling, nearly everything in the store was either secondhand, like the cash register, or homemade, like the shelves the books were kept on.

### Innovative Approaches to Secondhand Retail

Secondhand bookstores were nothing new. However, from the beginning, Gjemre and Anderson designed Half Price Books to be very different from the others. First, at the time most other secondhand book dealers specialized in rare editions and collector's items—books that could easily cost hundreds of dollars each. Half Price Books, on the other hand, saw its audience as the general reader, interested in buying popular reading at a low cost, or looking for books that were hard-to-find or out-of-print, but not necessarily collectible. Consequently they made it a rule not to charge more than half of the cover price for any volume.

Unlike most other secondhand bookstores, Half Price Books would buy *anything* printed (except newspapers) from its customers, assuming it was still in good condition. The store stocked books from the ultraconservative John Birch Society despite the fact that Gjemre was a dyed-in-the-wool liberal; it sold old issues of *Gun Digest,* although Gjemre was a longtime pacifist. For many years, the store was the only one in Dallas with a section devoted to Marxist-Leninist thought. There was no censorship, even of material some people would consider obscene. Half Price Books bought and sold books and magazines such as *Playboy, Penthouse,* and *Hustler,* though they were displayed and sold in rooms off-limits to children. Later, when feminists criticized such materials as degrading to women, Gjemre allowed each Half Price Books store to decide on its own whether or not to deal in such merchandise.

It did not take Gjemre long to realize that the 1,000 square feet of floor space he had was not remotely sufficient. Within

three months of opening the first Half Price Books, he opened a new store in a shopping center that had five times as much space. From that time on, the business grew steadily. In fact, from the beginning, despite its steady expansion, Half Price Books never once had an unprofitable year. That was due in large part to Anderson's financial management. She was liberal politically, like Gjemre, but radically conservative when it came to borrowing—she refused to do it. "If we can't afford it, we don't do it," she told the *Dallas Morning News* in 1993. All growth was financed from Half Price's profits.

### Liberal Approaches to Employee Policies

Half Price Books found a willing and able work force that was often as unconventional as Gjemre and Anderson. In the early 1970s the local colleges around Dallas-Fort Worth were still graduating large numbers of liberal arts majors, people who Gjemre once told *Publishers Weekly* "couldn't or wouldn't work for Texas Instruments or GM or IBM. They were smart but into an alternative lifestyle." The company also attracted actors, musicians, and writers. By the time the 1990s rolled around, some 75 percent of these early employees were still with the company and many of them had become vice-presidents or board members.

This high degree of employee loyalty was due in large part to the progressive package of worker benefits that Half Price Books put together. Half Price Books was run as an industrial democracy, which Gjemre called "the hidden secret of how to solve strife in American industry." Its employees have participated in full profit sharing, based on the performance of the store they worked in and of the company as a whole. About 30 percent of the company's profits each year were returned to its employees and accounted for approximately 15 percent of an employee's annual salary. Salaries were structured so that executives did not earn more than about five times what an entry level employee made. The company instituted a policy of always promoting from within its ranks.

While remaining privately owned, Half Price Books distributed shares in the company to its upper management. By the end of the 1980s, about one-third of the company was employee owned. Responsibility was also shared. Whereas at most secondhand books stores only the owner and perhaps a trusted longtime assistant is allowed to purchase books from customers, most Half Price employees are trained to evaluate books people bring in. That means customers can brings books in any time during the day or evening and know they will be able to sell their books.

Anderson also inaugurated progressive policies that made life easier for working parents. Half Price Books employees were allowed to bring their babies to work until the children were able to move around on their own. In addition to the full package of paid holidays, vacation and sick time, mothers were given four weeks of paid maternity leave, plus twenty-three extra sick days that could be used during pregnancy of after the birth of their baby. New fathers were given two weeks of paid paternity leave.

### Growth and Profitability

By 1986, the chain had grown to include 23 stores, with nine in the Dallas-Fort Worth area alone. It had $17 million in annual sales. The company moved its flagship store four times in its first fourteen years. In 1986 it took over a building that had 17,000 square feet of space, a 20 percent increase over its previous store. Not only did expansion happen only when the company could afford to finance it on its own, it happened in ways other companies would shrink from in horror. In the early 1980s, one employee wanted to work and live in Seattle, Washington. So Half Price Books opened a store there in 1983. It turned out to be a shrewd move. The Seattle area was on the verge of tremendous economic and demographic growth. It became the company's most profitable area outside Texas. By 2000, it had seven stores in the Seattle area.

In addition to expanding its chain, it soon entered new product areas—frequently in just as serendipitous a manner as its chain expansion. A friend, for example, was selling Gjemre his library and asked him to take his record collection off his hands at the same time. Gjemre agreed, intending to have a one-time-only sale. He bought the records on Friday and by Sunday they had *all* been sold, persuading him to get into buying and selling recordings, too. By 1991, records accounted for about 15 percent of company sales. In 1986, noting the burgeoning popularity of computers, the company opened Half Price Software in a store it had vacated because it was too small to sell books in. The businesses were kept separate because the clientele were considered fundamentally different.

Gjemre was once upset when an employee purchased a lot of remainders—publishers' overstock and damaged stock. However he soon saw their sales potential—and how they fit his recycling philosophy. If he didn't sell them, they would probably end up in a landfill somewhere. Because Half Price Books bought *everything* it soon found it had large overstocks in certain items, for example encyclopedia missing a volume, Reader's Digest Condensed Books, and others with little conventional resale potential. To deal with these books, Half Price Books created Books By The Yard. For about $12.50 a linear yard, restaurants and decorators could purchase books, not to be read, but to create a specific ambience. Gjemre also began donating books to schools, libraries, prisons, and to the Peace Corps to distribute in the Third World.

By the end of the 1980s the company was hitting full stride. In 1988 it had 28 stores, all company owned, and annual sales of

about $10 million a year. By 1990 it could boast it was the largest buyer and seller of used books in the nation, with 34 stores in seven states and sales of $18 million. Then in August 1990, 70-year-old Gjemre collapsed from a stroke on the street in Hamburg, Germany. Anderson rushed to Europe to be with him in the hospital and to bring him back to the United States. Back home, he began a slow recovery and eventually resolved to retire from the company in November 1991. By the time he gave up the day-to-day management of Half Price Books—he remained as company chairman—the company had 40 stores in eight states, 400 employees and more than $25 million in annual sales. Its main store had 26,000 square feet of sales floor and 500,000 books in stock.

### New Leadership in the 1990s

Anderson, previously secretary and treasurer, succeeded Gjemre as CEO, and under her the company's impressive growth continued. By the end of 1993, it had 47 stores, mainly in the southwest but also in California, Washington, Iowa, Minnesota, Wisconsin, Indiana, and Ohio. It was opening new stores at a rate of about five a year when the company was thrown into turmoil in October 1995 after Anderson passed away unexpectedly of a heart attack. Anderson's 37-year-old daughter, Sharon ''Boots'' Anderson Wright, assumed the reins of leadership. Wright had started at the company shelving books when she was only 14 years old, and before her death Anderson had been grooming her to take over the company. When Wright took over a wave of anxiety swept through the employee ranks. Would Wright and her sisters decide to sell off Half Price Books to outsiders who would in all likelihood come in and do away with the company's unique corporate culture? Much to everyone's relief, Wright never considered such a step.

The company continued its steady, strong, well-paced growth under Wright. By February 1999 it had 61 stores in ten states and annual sales of $68 million. Opening a new store was also a collective endeavor at Half Price Books. To supply stock, existing stores contributed every fiftieth book on their shelves to the new location.

In early 1999, Half Price Books opened a new flagship store in Dallas. It was the first major innovation of Wright's tenure. With 55,000 square feet it was the largest store in the chain, and challenged the company to keep so much space full. The new building also included two special rooms for readings and art exhibits, and a rare book section, with first editions, autographed copies, and other collectibles as expensive as $500. Large windows were installed in the building to provide natural light. The building's concrete frontage was replaced with a ''green belt'' including trees. Half Price Books declined an offer from Starbucks to put a cafe in the new store. Unwilling to be like all the other bookstores, Half Price Books preferred to let a European restaurant from Dallas come in and provide a unique local touch.

The next hurdle for the company was to establish a presence on the Internet to challenge its nearest competitor, Powell's Books of Portland, Oregon. Computerizing its huge and constantly changing stock was seen as a complicated and expensive task, but one it was confident it would overcome.

### *Principal Divisions*

Half Price Software; Texas Bookman.

### *Principal Competitors*

Barnes & Noble Inc.; Borders Group Inc.; Follett Corp.; Powell's Books Inc.; Amazon.Com Inc.; Daedelus Books.

### *Further Reading*

"Chairman Plans Hiatus from Half Price Books," *Star-Telegram* (Fort Worth), November 8, 1991.

Chism, Olin, "His Profits and Politics are Liberal," *Dallas Morning News,* July 8, 1993, p. 8J.

Correa, Caleb, "Volumes of Success," *Arizona Republic,* October 1, 1998, p. EV10.

Edwards, Gary, "Half Price Books Sells Idea," *Houston Chronicle,* October 23, 1988.

"Half Price Books Hits Full Stride," *Publishers Weekly,* July 12, 1991, p. 38.

Halkias, Maria, "Dallas-Based Half Price Books Plans New Flagship Store, Headquarters, *Dallas Morning News,* February 18, 1999.

Hall, Cheryl, "Store Runs Counter to Corporate Culture," *Dallas Morning News,* November 3, 1993.

Hansard, Donna Steph, "A New Chapter for Half Price Books, *Dallas Morning News,* May 5, 1986, p. 6D.

Harris, Joyce Saenz, "High Profile Ken Gjemre: The Many Faces of Half Price Books' Enigmatic Founder," *Dallas Morning News,* May 26, 1991, p. 1E.

Hassell, Greg, "Half Price Books Succeeds by Not Going by the Book," *Houston Chronicle,* May 27, 1997.

Lane, Polly, "Used, But Still Useful–Bookstore Tears Out Pages of Tradition," *Seattle Times,* October 31, 1991, p. E1.

Macias, Anna, "Half Price Co-Founder Dies," *Dallas Morning News,* October 9, 1995, p. 15A.

Petzinger, Thomas, Jr., "Sharon Wright Follows Her Mother's Legacy Down to the Letter," *Wall Street Journal,* January 17, 1997, p. B1.

Ricketts, Chip, "Musty Bookshelves Offer Chain Big Profits," *Dallas Business Journal,* December 1, 1989, p. 1.

Rohde, Marie, "Owner Brings his Religion, Philosophy to Bookstores," *Milwaukee Journal,* July 21, 1990, p. A4.

Rothman, Andrea, "People: Ken Gjemre, The Ray Kroc of Used Books?," *Business Week,* January 15, 1998, p. 49.

Schaadt, Nancy, "Exec Takes a Page from Late Mom's Philosophy," *Dallas Morning News,* December 11, 1996, p. 5C.

Wascoe, Dan, Jr., "Success of Half Price Books is Only Half of the Story," *Star-Tribune* (Minneapolis), June 17, 1991, p. 3D.

—Gerald E. Brennan

The Harleysville
Insurance Companies

A National Network of Regional Insurers

# Harleysville Group Inc.

355 Maple Avenue
Harleysville, Pennsylvania 19438-2297
U.S.A.
Telephone: (215) 256-5000
Toll Free: (800) 523-6344
Fax: (215) 256-5799
Web site: http://www.harleysvillegroup.com

*Public Company*
*Chartered:* 1917 as Mutual Auto Theft Insurance
    Company/Mutual Auto Fire Insurance Company
*Employees:* 2,600
*Sales:* $824.8 million (1999)
*Stock Exchanges:* NASDAQ
*Ticker Symbol:* HGIC
*NAIC:* 524210 Insurance Agencies and Brokerages

The Harleysville Group Inc. oversees the operations of The Harleysville Insurance Companies, which offer a variety of insurance products to people and businesses in 32 eastern and Midwestern states. A *Fortune* 1000 company, Harleysville ranked 46th on A.M. Best's list of leading property/casualty insurance groups in the year 2000. Harleysville entered the 21st century by reaching the billion-dollar premium milestone, posting $1.07 billion in consolidated direct premiums. Commitment to people has been a hallmark of Harleysville's business strategy since it was chartered in 1917. When it was founded, Harleysville had little more than 100 insured members, mostly friends of the founder, and offered only automobile insurance. Today, the company's insurance products include personal and commercial auto, homeowners, commercial multi-peril, workers compensation, and life insurance. According to the company's breakdown, 27 percent of its business is personal auto insurance; 21 percent commercial multi-peril; 19 percent commercial auto, 15 percent workers compensation, and 11 percent homeowners. (These figures reflect the group's total consolidated operations.) As of 2001 the company has some 2,600 employees and 20,000 agents working through 3,000 independent agencies. *Forbes* magazine named Harleysville one of the ''200 Best Small Companies in America''

in 1989. Harleysville is a leader not only in the delivery of insurance but in its employment of technology to manage information, both internally and externally. It was honored by *Computerworld* magazine as one of the 100 best places for information technology professionals to work in the United States.

## A Community Grows Up: Harleysville's Background

Harleysville Insurance attributes part of its success to a company culture that provides a ''small town'' feel for its employees. This can be traced to the origins not only of the company but to the village of Harleysville itself. Originally part of the land settled by William Penn in the late 17th century, it took its name from Samuel Harley, a local businessman active before the American Revolution. The region was also heavily populated by the German immigrants commonly known as the Pennsylvania Dutch—a group that still has a strong presence in the community more than 300 years later.

In 1732, Friedrich Altdorfer arrived from Germany to work as an indentured servant. He eventually bought his freedom and later married the widow of the man who had held his indenture. In time the family became prosperous. It anglicized its name to Alderfer, a name that is still prominent in southeastern Pennsylvania. (Local businesses that bear the Alderfer name include a meat and dairy company and an auction house.) One of Friedrich's descendants, Alvin C. Alderfer, was an enterprising businessman who founded the Harleysville National Bank and Trust Company in 1909 and Harleysville Savings Bank in 1915.

Alderfer's decision to create what would become Harleysville Insurance stemmed from a problem not commonly associated with the early 20th century: car theft. The editor of the local newspaper brought the first automobile to the village in 1903, and the people were mesmerized. Those who could afford them began purchasing their own ''horseless carriages.'' Needless to say the cars were a source of envy, and some enterprising individuals from the surrounding areas began stealing them.

## Protecting the Public in the Early 20th Century

As the problem of auto theft grew, Alderfer decided something needed to be done. In 1915 he convened a meeting of the

## Company Perspectives:

*The Harleysville Group has three primary goals: to deliver superior insurance products and related services to its customers; to achieve consistent, profitable growth to enhance shareholder value; and to provide growth opportunities in a learning environment for those who contribute to the company's success.*

village's leading citizens at the local hotel and put forth his idea for an "association" that would protect its members against theft. His status as a business leader gave him the clout he needed to get his plan accepted.

Actually, the idea of this sort of protective association was hardly new; for generations, farmers had formed similar groups to minimize the costs incurred when a horse was stolen. Why not extend the same idea to automobiles, Alderfer reasoned. Each member would pay a membership fee of up to $5.00 (depending on the car's value), and the collected funds would be used to help members find or replace stolen cars. The initial group included 102 people, mostly friends of Alderfer.

Two years later, Pennsylvania's Department of Insurance informed Alderfer that his group would either have to charter itself according to state regulations, or else disband. The group obtained a charter on October 9, 1917. Actually, two groups were chartered: the Mutual Auto Theft Insurance Company and the Mutual Auto Fire Insurance Company. This was because at the time insurance companies were not allowed to sell more than one type of coverage.

Over the next few years the laws changed to accommodate a growing number of automobiles and drivers. By 1922, the Harleysville Mutual Casualty Company had been established; it merged with the Mutual Auto Theft Company 11 years later. Over the next few decades Harleysville continued to grow and expand; at the time of Alderfer's death in 1941 the company was quite different from the "association" he had originally formed with his friends and neighbors.

As the insurance industry changed to meet the increasingly complex needs of individuals, Harleysville adopted a long-term approach that allowed it to identify market trends and customer requirements. This included continued expansion. In 1956 the company changed its name to Harleysville Mutual Insurance Company. Harleysville branched into the life insurance market not long after that. By 1960, it had established Harleysville Life Insurance Company, which offered not only life insurance but also disability insurance and retirement plans.

### Further Growth in the 1960s–80s

In 1966, Harleysville underwent a corporate restructuring that is still reflected in the makeup of the current company. Harleysville Mutual was established as the parent company with several subsidiaries. Gradually, Harleysville began strengthening its presence in the consolidated commercial insurance market. The company had always focused primarily on personal lines, but by the mid-1970s the personal/commercial ratio had shifted. (In

the 1990s, commercial lines would account for around 60 percent of Harleysville's premium volume.) In 1979, Harleysville Group was formed to manage the growth–and the diversity–of the organizations' subsidiary operations. As of 2001, it owned 11 companies and manages an additional five.

One method of growth is acquisition of other companies. Harleysville saw acquisition as a way to increase not only the scope of its offerings but also its geographic reach. In 1982, Harleysville Group acquired McAlear Associates, which specialized in excess and surplus brokerage, as well as the related Huron Insurance Company. (McAlear was sold in 1986.) The Worcester Insurance Company, a 150-year-old firm that specialized in fire insurance, was acquired by Harleysville in 1983.

Perhaps the most important move Harleysville made during the 1980s was its decision to take the company public. For a long time, Harleysville had wanted to expand its operations to other states with the ultimate goal of creating a national network of regional insurance companies. To get started, it would take money. In 1986, Harleysville successfully sold 2,156,250 shares in its initial public offering.

### New Directions and Challenges in the 1990s and Beyond

Much of this growth was orchestrated by a management team headed by Harleysville chairman Bradford W. Mitchell. Mitchell joined Harleysville in 1976 as president and director. A year later he was named CEO, and in 1985 he was named chairman. He retired as CEO in 1993 but stayed on as chairman until his death in June 1998. It was during Mitchell's tenure that Harleysville developed its strategy of developing a national network that would extend to several states. Upon Mitchell's death, company president and CEO Walter R. Bateman was named chairman. Bateman joined Harleysville in 1988 as senior vice-president of field operations. He continued in that position until 1991 when he was named executive vice-president. He became president and chief operating officer in 1992, and was named chief executive officer in 1994.

As a company with a strong community base, Harleysville has been proud of its "small town" feel even among its 2,600-employee base. Part of this was reflected in a culture that valued employees and encouraged ongoing two-way communication between management and staffers. Commitment to the community extended beyond being a good employer, however, and Harleysville met what it felt was an important obligation through such programs as the Care Force. Created in 1993, the Care Force operated on the belief that people could make a difference by reaching out to those in need of support and who had no support network of their own.

As company literature explained, the Care Force "connects people who want to make a difference with those who so desperately need assistance." Employees who participated in the Care Force identified the kind of assistance they wished to provide and then joined individuals or group volunteer activities. Care Force volunteers might work in programs for the disadvantaged, the environment, neighborhood development, and education. A Care Force Council identified different groups and provided employees with information so that they could

## Key Dates:

**1915:** Alvin Alderfer forms "association" of 102 neighbors to insure against auto theft costs.
**1917:** Alderfer's company receives two state charters (for theft and fire insurance).
**1922:** Harleysville Mutual Casualty Company is founded.
**1933:** Harleysville Mutual Casualty merges with Auto Theft Company.
**1941:** Alvin Alderfer dies.
**1960:** Harleysville Life Insurance Company is founded.
**1966:** Companies are joined together under parent company Harleysville Mutual Insurance.
**1986:** Harleysville goes public; sells more than two million shares in IPO.
**1999:** Harleysville is named to Ward Financial's list of top 50 insurance companies in United States.

choose where they volunteer. The employees worked with the Care Force Council to identify specific activities and projects that they could work on.

The 1990s were a challenging decade for insurers, largely because of a series of expensive natural disasters including hurricanes Andrew in 1992 and Floyd in 1999. Such natural disasters wreaked havoc on local and regional communities, and they were hard on insurance companies as well. Harleysville minimized the impact of such disasters with a 1996 strategy aimed at reducing the company's overall exposure to homeowner losses. Whereas 91 percent of the claims in 1992 following Hurricane Andrew came from homeowner policies, only 35 percent came from similar policies after Floyd. Although Floyd's costs had an impact on insurance earnings, Harleysville's solid strategy helped lessen the blow; the success of the company's long-term strategy was evident as financials for 2000 showed stronger performance. Among the company's initiatives for improving performance were programs that would reduce future business costs while improving customer service, a reorganization of claims operations, a streamlining of field operations, and a commitment to advancing expertise in information technology. At a meeting of the Chartered Property Casualty Underwriters in September 2000, Harleysville chairman and CEO Bateman noted that he envisioned exciting times for the insurance industry. "The real winners," he added, "are not the trend watchers, but those who lay down the groundwork."

Nevertheless, the company faced some very real challenges with increased competition in the industry during good economic times in the United States. Insurance stocks as a whole fell an average of 15 percent in 1999, and Harleysville's stock fell along with them, though it fared better than many. In response to this trend, and believing its own stock to be undervalued, Harleysville initiated a stock repurchase plan in June 1999, authorizing the repurchase of up to one million shares, a move it hoped conveyed the confidence management had in Harleysville's future.

Harleysville's success was recognized professionally in 1999 when it was named to Ward's 50 Benchmark Group for "outstanding financial results in the areas of safety, consistency, and performance." The top 50 list was compiled annually by Ward Financial, a Cincinnati, Ohio-based firm specializing in insurer management consulting and investment banking. Ward measured corporate performance based on such criteria as surplus and premiums, adjusted net income, risk-based capital, and compound premium growth. Harleysville was named to the Ward's list again in 2000.

The predicted "Y2K" disaster of the late 1990s, which stemmed from the fear that computers would be unable to read the year "2000" accurately and thus be unable to run properly when the date changed, never quite materialized. The Y2K situation did mean, however, that Harleysville, like all companies, had to review its programs and systems, and in doing so it found a number of areas that required replacement or updating. The ultimate result was that Harleysville was able to streamline its computer systems and make them run more efficiently.

Such maintenance and improvements were particularly important for an industry like insurance, which lived and died by the quality of the information it could access and distribute. One of Harleysville's primary ongoing goals related to information was to constantly upgrade its information technology structure. A user-friendly and informative web site was launched in 1996 to provide easy access to information for clients and potential clients. The company also worked to make sure its internal technology structure allowed quick delivery of important information among company managers. Some of Harleysville's efforts were rewarded in October 2000, when it won an award for "E-Commerce Excellence," given by the Pennsylvania Chamber of Business and Industry. The state office recognized Harleysville's "significant transition to incorporate technological advancements in its day-to-day operations," as well as its "substantial contribution to electronic commerce."

### Principal Subsidiaries

Great Oaks Insurance Company; Harleysville-Atlantic Insurance Company; Harleysville Asset Management L.P.; Harleysville Insurance Company of New Jersey; Huron Insurance Company; Insurance Management Resources L.P.; Lake States Insurance Company; Mid-America Insurance Company; Minnesota Fire and Casualty Company; New York Casualty Insurance Company; Worcester Insurance Company; Harleysville Mutual Insurance Company; Harleysville Garden State Insurance Company; Harleysville Life Insurance Company; Pennland Insurance Company; Berkshire Mutual Insurance Company.

### Principal Competitors

The Allstate Corporation; The Chubb Corporation; State Farm Insurance Companies.

### Further Reading

Boone, Elisabeth, "Harleysville Insurance: National Network with a Hometown Flavor," *Rough Notes,* November 1, 1998, p. 34.
Drill, Herb, "Not Down on Main Street," *Focus,* February 28, 1990, p. 14.
"Harleysville Group and Harleysville Mutual Authorize stock Repurchase Plans," *PR Newswire,* June 23, 1999.

"Harleysville Group Inc. Captures Only Statewide Award Recognizing E-Commerce Excellence," *PR Newswire,* October 10, 2000.

"Insurer Harleysville Group Selects Unisys to Deploy and Manage Next-Generation Distributed Computing Systems," *Business Wire,* January 5, 1999.

"Largest Publicly Held Companies (in Philadelphia Area)," *Philadelphia Business Journal,* May 26, 2000, p. B10.

Leming, John, "Harleysville Group Positions Itself for New Strategic Directions," *Eastern Pennsylvania Business Journal,* September 20, 1999, p. 11.

Salvidge, Mariella, "Harleysville Group Rated a 'Hold' by Analysts," *Allentown Morning Call,* September 3, 2000.

——, "Harleysville Group Sees Lower Profit," *Allentown Morning Call,* April 27, 2000, Bus. Sec.

—George A. Milite

# Hibernia Corporation

**313 Carondelet Street**
**New Orleans, Louisiana 70130**
**U.S.A.**
**Telephone: (504) 533-3332**
**Toll Free: (800) 666-4417**
**Fax: (504) 533-2466**
**Web site: http://www.hibernia.com;**
**          http://www.hiberniabank.com**

*Public Company*
*Incorporated:* 1972
*Employees:* 5,211
*Sales:* $1,270.0 million (1999)
*Stock Exchanges:* New York
*Ticker Symbol:* HIB
*NAIC:* 52211 Commercial Banking; 551111 Offices of
    Bank Holding Companies

Hibernia Corporation, headquartered in New Orleans, is a holding company initially formed to serve as the parent company for what has since become Louisiana's largest bank, Hibernia National Bank, the Corporation's principal subsidiary. Along with its Texas counterpart, the Hibernia National Bank of Texas, the Louisiana bank has 255 offices located in 34 parishes in Louisiana and 15 counties in Texas, with total assets of about $15.8 billion. At 23 percent, Hibernia ranks first in Louisiana in its deposit market share and ranks at least within the top three banks in 31 Louisiana parishes and six Texas counties, where it commands an 11 percent deposit share. Its banks offer a full array of deposit services, including checking, savings, money market, CD, and IRA accounts. However, much of Hibernia National's focus has been on commercial lending to small and mid-sized businesses, and such loans still account for over 50 percent of its loan portfolio, while home mortgages and consumer loans together account for about 40 percent. In addition to Hibernia National Bank, under its corporate holding umbrella Hibernia has a loan production office in Mississippi and the Hibernia Rosenthal Insurance Company, the largest independent insurance broker in Louisiana. Other diverse operations of Hibernia include investment and brokerage services and on-line banking.

## 1972–84: From Origins to Competitive Position

Hibernia Corporation emerged in 1972 as part of a restructuring effort designed to promote the growth of the Hibernia National Bank. At the time, the bank was a venerable New Orleans landmark, already over 100 years old, having been founded by a group of Irish American investors in 1870 and given the ancient name of their native land. However, up until the early 1970s, it had been a very conservative "slumbering organization," content to keep financial pace with the slow development of Big Easy businesses, where, with its focus on commercial lending, its principal interest lay.

By 1972 it had become the third largest bank in New Orleans, but in size, with just over $500 million in assets, it was a distant third behind the city's premier, ultra-conservative bank, the Whitney, and the second-place First Commerce Corporation. Historically, it had been disinclined to invest much in growth. In fact, when Hibernia Corporation was formed as its holding company, Hibernia National only had ten branch banks and seemed determined to stay both small and safe, annually earning barely one-half of one percent on its assets. Although it had some strengths, including the only trust division in Louisiana in the top 300 nationwide, it simply continued to stir stagnant financial waters, lacking forceful, imaginative direction. It was what analyst Lisa L. Rogers termed "an also-ran wholesale bank." Its major innovation when it opened its 11th branch in 1973 was a cycle-up window for customers on bikes, toted as the first in the country—hardly a banking service milestone.

Through 1972 and 1973, there was a changing of the executive guard at Hibernia National. Under the holding company's umbrella, the new watch began transforming the bank into a major player, not just in New Orleans, but eventually throughout Louisiana and beyond. From the outset, the new managers of Hibernia National and its parent holding company were growth minded, even though they retained a reputation for fiscal conservatism, pursuing what Harlan S. Byrne in *Barron's* described as "aggressive but disciplined banking practices."

---

**Company Perspectives:**

*Hibernia's purpose is to help people achieve their financial goals and realize their dreams. Hibernia's Ten Commandments: 1. Make service matter; 2. Act empowered, like owners; 3. Make smart, quick decisions; 4. Sell ethically and aggressively, accept prudent risk and price accordingly; 5. Encourage continuous improvement; 6. Listen carefully, then communicate openly and quickly; 7. Create an environment where people can excel, be rewarded and have fun; 8. Win as a team; 9. Treat all others with respect; 10. Invest for long-term individual and company success.*

---

At the top, in 1973 Martin C. Miler replaced F. George Ramel as president and CEO of the Hibernia Corporation. Miler, a native of Iowa trained at the Wharton School, came to Hibernia from an executive post at the First Union National Bank in Charlotte, North Carolina, bringing a fresh perspective and a challenging motto: "Run scared, never got cocky." He faced major problems, the first being the seemingly impossible task of making any significant inroads with Whitney's extremely loyal clientele, which included the cream of the Crescent City's businesses. To break that bank's virtual monopoly, Miler began updating Hibernia National with a state-of-the art computer system and offering such new and popular services as discretionary fund management and Super Now accounts, services that the much more conservative Whitney disdained to extend to its customers.

A second major problem was that Louisiana law inhibited growth because it prohibited expansion across parish lines. Although that would change in 1985, Miler at first had to look beyond Louisiana for opportunities. He began by building strong correspondent ties with banks in other states, using them to purchase participation in out-of-state loans, some of which were made to large, well leveraged companies. It was an important strategy for two major reasons: it yielded high returns at a time when prime interest rates were very high, and it limited Hibernia's reliance on Louisiana's principal business–the energy industry. Even during the peak of the oil boom in the late 1970s and early 1980s, Hibernia's energy-related loans topped out at no more than seven percent of the total amount in its lending portfolio. In the same period, loans to out-of-state borrowers accounted for about 40 percent of its loan total.

Although more innovative than the managers of the Whitney, Miler was not inclined to take unnecessary risks. He was an excellent planner and very protective of Hibernia's clients. In 1979, when the Sandinistas overthrew the Somoza regime in Nicaragua, proving once again that overseas investments in developing countries was always a gamble, Miler appointed Thomas S. Mabon director of Hibernia's international banking division. Mabon's challenge was to create an overseas lending strategy that would provide investment security. As a result, Hibernia began limiting its third-world lending to the overseas operations of domestic companies with ties to Hibernia's regional, Gulf states customer base. It was a cautious policy, but one soon emulated by a growing number of U.S. banks.

Under Miler's leadership, Hibernia's profits continued to rise annually. He proved very adept at safeguarding the bank's

clients' principal through careful "market timing." Among other things, in the early 1980s, with interest rates near their peak, he invested extensively in high-yielding securities, including Ginnie Maes, and continued to diversify Hibernia's lending. By 1983, with $1.7 billion in assets, Hibernia National Bank had produced an average annual earnings growth of 22.8 percent per share over a ten year period, almost six percent higher than the average for the nation's top ten banks. Its performance prompted Keefe, Bruyette and Woods to rank it number one in the country for consistent growth of earnings. It was also running neck to neck with First Commerce for second place behind Whitney, still the big kid on the New Orleans financial block, though running out of competitive wind.

### 1985–89: Accelerated Growth Results in Louisiana's Largest Bank

It was in the first part of the 1980s that many Louisiana financial institutions went into an oil boom frenzy, overloading their portfolios with energy related loans, many of which were not adequately secured. Some of the less cautious banks took a bad beating in the hard recession that hit Louisiana when the oil bubble burst in the mid 1980s. These became attractive acquisition targets for Hibernia, which continued to report solid profits throughout the 1980s. Starting in 1985, after Louisiana removed its restrictions preventing banks from branching across parish lines, Hibernia began buying up some of the financially beleaguered in-state banks. By September 1989, it had acquired 15 of them and had moved into population centers like Baton Rouge, Shreveport, Alexandria, Lake Charles, Monroe, and Lafayette. Within a year, it also bought nine banks and thrifts in East Texas, establishing the Hibernia National Bank of Texas. The first of these, acquired in August of 1989 for $30 million, was First State of Pflugerville, located in an Austin suburb.

Many of these banks came to Hibernia at bargain prices. About half of them were banks in difficulty which, without watering down their shareholders' equity, Hibernia acquired through the cooperation of FDIC. Once getting a toehold in a new locale, Hibernia worked quickly to increase its market share. For example, before October 1987, Hibernia had no presence in Shreveport/Bossier City area, which had Louisiana's third largest market. By 1989, through buyouts and takeovers, it had established 35 branches in the area and owned a 20 percent share of its bank deposit market.

For 64 consecutive quarters, up to 1989, Hibernia increased its profits, augmenting its net income at a compound rate of 20 percent per annum, at the time an enviable and impressive performance for a Louisiana bank. Between 1973 and 1989, its assets rose from a paltry $500 million to $6.3 billion, its work force from 713 employees to close to 3,000, its banking offices from 12 in New Orleans to 150 in Louisiana and Texas. It had in fact become Louisiana's largest bank holding corporation.

### 1990–92: Hibernia's Fortunes Decline, Leaving it Vulnerable

However, midway through 1990 the corporation's financial worm started to turn. It had over-extended itself and, reportedly, undercapitalized its business, suffering an $11 million loss in 1990, the first in its history. Its out-of-state lending, which had

## Key Dates:

**1972:** Hibernia Corporation is formed as holding company for Hibernia National Bank.

**1973:** Martin C. Miler becomes president and CEO of Hibernia National Bank.

**1985:** Changes in Louisiana banking regulations allow Hibernia to begin acquiring other state banks.

**1989:** Hibernia, with the acquisition of First State of Pflugerville in Texas, becomes the first Louisiana bank holding company to expand across the state's boundaries.

**1990:** Company logs first annual loss in its history.

**1991:** Company sells credit card operation to First USA Inc. of Dallas.

**1992:** Miler resigns, and Stephen A. Hansel becomes Hibernia's president and CEO.

**2000:** Hibernia buys the Rosenthal Agency.

stood it in good stead through the 1980s, became a problem when, in 1990, the economy turned sluggish nationwide. Hibernia's real estate investments were especially hard hit. As a result, in the early 1990s it began some downsizing measures. Although it disclaimed a need for funds, in 1991 it sold its Hibernia National Bank credit card business to First USA Inc. of Dallas. At the time, Hibernia's credit card operation serviced 4,440,000 accounts and had outstanding loans of $315 million. The move was prompted by the increasing costs of processing credit card loans coupled with an increase in loan defaults and personal bankruptcies.

Hibernia's 1991 first-quarter net loss of $49.5 million fueled speculations that it might sell off its profitable Texas subsidiary, which in 1990 had net operating earnings of $5.9 million, performing better than expected. In 1991, with about $1.2 billion in assets, it clearly offered an enticing acquisitions plum. Not finding viable buyers or outside investments partners, Hibernia hung tough, despite a poorly performing real estate portfolio in Louisiana and ongoing bottom line problems that promoted fifty-fifty odds on Hibernia's financial collapse. To survive, Hibernia continued to tighten its corporate belt, selling off some $470 million in assets, cutting its work force by ten percent and reducing the ranks of its top executives. Among the departed was Miler, who resigned as Hibernia's president, CEO, and chairman. He was replaced by Stephen A. Hansel, a former CFO at Barnett Banks Inc., who took on the job in 1992. Also joining the top executive team as COO was C. Geron Hargon, who helped shaped new survival strategies, including a focus on lending within Hibernia's own markets rather than out of state and a bolstering of capital funds. It was a tough uphill fight. In 1991, despite a second-quarter bright spot resulting from an outsourcing of its data processing operations, Hibernia had had its worst year on record, with losses reaching $165.6 million. More losses followed in 1992, and although at $64 million they seemed less formidable, speculation about Hibernia's imminent collapse continued.

### 1993–2000: Phenomenal Turnaround

Hibernia's fortunes began improving after Hansel recapitalized the bank and renewed its focus, first on an improved

asset quality and then on business development initiatives. He also oversaw the upgrading of its technology, particularly its information-management and distribution systems. Late in 1993, he guided Hibernia into another acquisitions cycle that by the close of 1995 had substantially increased the corporation's assets and greatly improved its profitability. Between 1993, when Hibernias returned to the black at $48 million, and 1995, when its net income almost tripled, its assets grew from $4.8 billion to $7.2 billion, with 160 offices in Texas and 25 Louisiana parishes, or 12 more parishes than it operated midway through 1992. As Moody's senior analyst Nicholas Krasno observed, Hibernia's comeback had been "pretty extreme." Speculative doomsayers either grew silent, no longer predicting Hibernia's collapse, or spoke of it only as a likely target for a leveraged buyout.

In 1996, *US Banker* ranked Hibernia 5th among the nation's top 100 banks, noting that Hansel had "greatly expanded the bank's franchise territory and substantially altered its asset mix." Still, on paper it looked as if the runner had stumbled. Although its revenue increased to $736 million, up almost $70 million from 1995, Hibernia's net income declined by 16 percent and its earnings per share slid from $1.02 to 85 cents. In truth, Hibernia was still performing very well, but in 1996 it no longer had tax deferment benefits that it had enjoyed in 1994 and 1995, and it had to cough up more of its earnings to the IRS. Hibernia was still expanding, however, purchasing some banks and merging with others. It ended 1996 with almost 200 branches in Louisiana and Texas and assets of $9.37 billion.

Hibernia's impressive recovery and growth continued through the remaining years of the century. By 1999, its total assets had climbed to $15.3 billion and its net income to $175.1 million, and it was still expanding, both through acquisitions and diversification of its corporate portfolio. For example, in 1997, when legal and regulatory restrictions permitted, Hibernia began selling life insurance and fixed annuities through Tower Insurance Agency, which Hibernia had owned since 1991. In 1998, it bought two other agencies, gathering them under the banner of the newly named Hibernia Insurance Agency Inc. Two years later it made a major purchase, buying the Rosenthal Agency, Louisiana's largest independent insurance company, which, with $90 million in premiums, was more than four times the size of Hibernia's 1998 acquisitions combined.

By the summer of 2000, after purchasing three Texas offices from Compass Bank, Hibernia boasted 255 branches that spread across 34 Louisiana parishes and 15 Texas counties, with total assets of about $15.8 billion. Thanks to the strategies of its management team, it had not only grown but had stabilized through its risk reduction policies of diversifying it portfolio. Moreover, its future continued to look bright, despite continued speculation that, as a medium-sized fish, it might yet become fare for a much larger predator.

### Principal Subsidiaries

Hibernia National Bank; Hibernia National Bank of Texas; Hibernia Southcoast Capital.

### *Principal Competitors*

Acadiana Bancshares, Inc.; BANK ONE Corporation; Regions Financial Corporation; Union Planters Corporation; Whitney Holding Corporation.

### *Further Reading*

Byrne, Harlan S., "Hibernia Corp.: Conservative Lending, Acquiring Spell Bank Success," *Barron's*, August 2, 1989, pp. 36–37.

Dunaway, Kenneth W., "ABA Convention City: The Unique Nature of the New Orleans Banking Market," *ABA Banking Journal*, October 1985, p. 74.

Fink, Ronald B., "Lessons from New Orleans' Ills," *United States Banker*, February 1990, pp. 26–31, 88,

Greer, Jim, "Shrinking Hibernia Might Depart Texas," *Houston Business Journal*, June 17, 1991, p. 12.

Kimball, Allan C., "Hibernia Sells Its Credit Card," *Austin Business Journal*, March 18, 1991, p. 7.

Kreuzer, Terese, "At Hibernia, It's Mardi Gras All Year," *Bankers Monthly*, February 1990, pp. 21–24.

Mack, Toni, "The Battle of New Orleans," *ABA Banking Journal*, March 26, 1984, p. 62.

Milligan, John W., "Ranking America's Big Banks," *United States Banker*, April 1996, p. 37.

Reich-Hale, David, "Louisiana Purchase Is Hibernia's Biggest Ever in Insurance," *American Banker*, June 2, 2000, p. 7.

Zganjar, Leslie, "The Rise and Fall of Hibernia Corp.," *Greater Baton Rouge Business Report*," August 13, 1991, p. 12.

—John W. Fiero

# HOB Entertainment, Inc.

6255 Sunset Boulevard
Hollywood, California 90028
U.S.A.
Telephone: (323) 769-4600
Fax: (323) 769-4787
Web site: http://www.hob.com

*Private Company*
*Founded:* 1992
*Employees:* 2,029
*Sales:* $87.8 million (1998)
*NAIC:* 512220 Integrated Record Production/Distribution;
  512290 Other Sound Recording Industries; 514191
  On-Line Information Services; 722110 Full Service
  Restaurants; 711310 Promoters of Performing Arts,
  Sports, and Similar Events with Facilities; 711320
  Promoters of Performing Arts, Sports, and Similar
  Events without Facilities

HOB Entertainment, Inc. owns or operates several concert venues, with its primary involvements in blues music. The company's core operations are its House of Blues restaurant-concert hall venues in Cambridge, Massachusetts; Los Angeles; New Orleans; Chicago; Myrtle Beach, South Carolina; Orlando, Florida; and Las Vegas. The House of Blues offers a range of blues and blues-influenced music, such as the early, rural blues, gospel music, Cajun styles, reggae, contemporary blues, and rap. HOB Entertainment provides blues-oriented entertainment over the Internet, including live concert footage, and through its recording label. The company also promotes a variety of live music performances through concert venues nationwide.

## Isaac Tigrett's "Mission from God" in the Early 1990s

When Isaac Tigrett formulated the House of Blues restaurant and blues club concept, his intention was to bring something authentic to the world. Tigrett had been disappointed with the commercialism that developed as the Hard Rock Cafe, which he cofounded with Peter Morton in London in 1971, grew into an international chain of restaurants. The restaurants featured rock 'n roll music memorabilia, with Hard Rock Cafe t-shirts becoming a status symbol among fans of rock 'n roll music. Tigrett sold his interest in the company in 1988 and planned to lead a more spiritual life, but his spiritual teacher advised him to remain active in business. He conceived the House of Blues concept as a way to preserve blues music, as an art form with more than 100 years of continuous development, by providing a forum for live performance of traditional and contemporary blues. He also viewed education about the history and social influence of the blues as a way to cultivate multiculturalism, hence the company's slogan, "Unity in Diversity."

Some of the inspiration and momentum for the House of Blues came from the popular 1980 movie, *The Blues Brothers,* starring Dan Aykroyd as Elwood Blues and the late John Belushi as Jake Blues. Like the protagonists in the movie, Tigrett felt himself to be "on a mission from God" (*Los Angeles Times,* April 13, 1996). The original House of Blues logo featured the faces of Jake and Elwood Blues. Initial investors in the House of Blues included Aykroyd and Judith Belushi Paisano, widow of John Belushi, as well as the late John Candy and the late River Phoenix.

Tigrett opened the first House of Blues venue, a 280-seat concert hall and 200-seat restaurant, in Harvard Square in November 1992. The interior design of the restaurant-blues club presented a contemporary variation of the old southern juke joint like the ones Tigrett had enjoyed as a native of Tennessee. Artistic touches included African-American folk art and the plaster relief portraits of 80 renowned blues artists, such as Muddy Waters and B.B. King, embedded in the ceiling panels. A retail store—Take It Easy, Baby—offered recorded blues on audio and video, blues magazines, musical instruments, and a full line of clothing. In addition to live music nightly, the House of Blues offered a Sunday gospel brunch, with live gospel singers and three seatings, which sold out a week in advance.

The international menu offered dim sum, wood-fired pizza, and tandoori chicken, as well as classic southern dishes, such as jambalaya and baby back ribs with a choice of four barbecue sauces: spicy Jamaican, Smokey Joe, Tennessee Style, and

**Company Perspectives:**

*HOB Entertainment, Inc. is a Los Angeles-based global entertainment company committed to providing the best live concert entertainment both on-stage and on-line.*

Kansas City Style. Within a month the House of Blues served 200 to 225 lunches daily, with check averages at $8.50 person, and dinner checks that averaged $12.00 per person serving 175 to 200 meals per night.

Tigrett's plans for the company included House of Blues venues in New Orleans, Chicago, Los Angeles, and other major cities; syndicated radio and television shows; a record label; and a nonprofit educational organization on blues music. Through a joint venture with CBS Radio Network, HOB Entertainment launched the House of Blues Radio Hour in September 1993. Hosted by Aykroyd as his Elwood Blues character, the show emphasized the history of blues music. By December the show was syndicated in 35 markets.

To fund further projects Tigrett raised $32 million through a private placement of 71 percent interest in the company. Surprisingly, the Harvard University Endowment Fund invested $10 million, commending Tigrett's creative vision and previous success. Sir James Goldsmith, a wealthy British capitalist and an associate of Tigrett's father who had invested in the first Hard Rock Cafe, also invested in House of Blues. Other investors included James Belushi, brother of John Belushi, and members of the Aerosmith rock 'n roll band.

Tigrett formed the House of Blues Foundation to develop a curriculum on the history and culture of the blues and blues-based music from the plantation workers of the Mississippi Delta to present times. The Center for the Study of Southern Culture at the University of Mississippi and The Dubois Institute at Harvard University provided scholarly support. The first series of classes, offered three hours a week, three days a week took place at the House of Blues. The program proved to be very popular with local schools and Tigrett planned to offer it at other House of Blues venues as they opened.

The New Orleans House of Blues opened in the French Quarter in January 1994. The 27,000-square-foot facility housed a 1,000-seat concert hall and a 350-seat full-service restaurant. The interior featured a look similar to that of the Cambridge venue, with the plaster relief portraits on the ceiling by local artist Andrew Wood and folk art from the Mississippi Delta region. The grand opening featured renowned New Orleans blues artist Dr. John, and a newly formed Blues Brothers Band with Dan Aykroyd, Andrew Strong, Carla Thomas, and local bluesman Robert Jr. Lockwood.

Aerosmith played the March 1994 grand opening of the House of Blues on the Sunset Strip in West Hollywood. The $9 million project housed 1,000 seats in the concert hall, a $500,000 sound system, a 75-foot bar, and a movable wall on the second floor that could be raised for diner viewing when the concert hall was full. High-definition video monitors displayed information about the blues artist performing and about history.

Tigrett covered the front exterior of the three-story building with corrugated metal from a cotton mill in Clarksdale, Mississippi, where legendary blues singer-guitarist Robert Johnson supposedly gave his soul to the devil so he could play the blues.

The venue also housed the Foundation Room, a private club with membership based on a minimum donation of $2,200 to the educational foundation. The club featured a 70-seat luxury dining room and a lounge lushly decorated with East Indian fabrics, wood carvings, and art. Tigrett promoted the club by opening it to the entertainment elite, making the House of Blues the place to see and be seen. With the attraction of celebrities, the Hollywood House of Blues became overcrowded, but after a couple of years it settled into a credible blues night club, with performances that sold out regularly.

### House of Blues Expansion Through Related Businesses in the Mid-1990s

In August 1994 the House of Blues Music Company formed a new record label through a joint venture with Private Music, an imprint of BMG Music Group. Private Music handled sales and marketing, and HOB handled talent, recording, and publicity. House of Blues Music purchased and renovated a recording studio in Memphis, hiring David Z as producer and sound engineer. The company signed its first contract with ''Monster'' Mike Welch, a 14-year-old blues artist from Boston, and planned to produce a compilation of previously unreleased recordings by Albert King.

The House of Blues New Media group formed in January 1995 to utilize the capabilities of personal computers and the Internet toward the company's goals. HOB New Media planned to create interactive entertainment software for CD-ROM using live concert footage from HOB club venues. Electronic publishing projects included a blues magazine, the history of the blues, video games, and screen savers. The group's first main project involved a live gospel concert with the Five Blind Boys of Alabama and a show on blues history broadcast from the Hollywood club via the Internet on Martin Luther King Day. The successful project became an annual event. Only the most advanced computers could download the program, however, so HOB reprogrammed the show for general access. HOB Backstage Pass arranged similar reprogrammed, on-line concerts from House of Blues venues.

HOB Entertainment expanded and developed in a number of areas. The radio show expanded to 140 markets and attained worldwide syndication through Armed Forces Radio. ''Live! From the House of Blues'' began cable broadcast on Turner Broadcasting System (TBS) on network cable in early 1995, but it was canceled a year later after competition from major sports programming proved too formidable. House of Blues Records signed new gospel artists Blind Boys of Alabama and Cissy Houston. A compilation recording, ''Essential Blues,'' reached the top five on Billboard's list of Top Blues Albums.

HOB continued to successfully attract new capital for expansion. In mid-1995 Walt Disney purchased a 12 percent interest in the company in anticipation of the House of Blues opening near Pleasure Island at Walt Disney World in Orlando. A blues-themed hotel was under consideration for the Orlando site, as well as at proposed venues in Chicago and New York. Other new investors included Carly Simon, Isaac Hayes, and John Goodman. In May 1996 HOB obtained $55 million in financing from a consortium of venture capital firms.

HOB took the blues on the road with several temporary venues and its own concert tour in 1996. The "Barnburner" 30-city tour featured Joe Cocker and Buddy Guy and the Fabulous Thunderbirds. Participation in music festivals nationwide included company-sponsored stages at the Chicago Blues Festival and the New Orleans Jazz and Heritage Festival. Atlanta Mayor Bill Campbell invited Tigrett to stage a House of Blues venue during the 1996 Olympics. A 93-year-old Baptist Tabernacle church provided 2,200 seats for concerts held every day from July 19 to August 4. The Blues Brothers Band, with Aykroyd, Jim Belushi, and John Goodman, opened the events; other concert highlights included diverse, blues-influenced artists, such as Al Green, Johnny Cash, and Tito Puente and his Latin Jazz All-Stars. HOB also sponsored an outdoor stage and a food tent during the Olympics, with the rustic cabin where Muddy Waters was born on display next to the food tent. Mayor Campbell wanted Tigrett to open at a permanent location in Atlanta, but Tigrett declined, citing losses during the Olympics and lack of other development and a solid customer base near the proposed site. HOB also provided half-time entertainment for the Super Bowl in New Orleans in January 1997.

HOB Online continued to develop HOB's Internet presence with contests and live chats with blues artists through HOB's home page. HOBTours.com featured concert itineraries, artist biographies, sound clips, and merchandise. In a partnership with Progressive Networks HOB started LiveConcerts.com, the first web site dedicated to on-line concert programming. Progressive Networks had developed Real Audio, a technology that enabled real-time audio over the Internet, and continued to work on technology to provide live video in real time. HOB hoped to broadcast live concerts in real time via the Internet. The company planned to place computer monitors at restaurant tables, allowing customers at one House of Blues to watch a live show from a venue in another city.

Changes at House of Blues Music involved a change in ownership, with Private Music selling their interest in the joint venture to Platinum Entertainment in the fall of 1996. House of Blues Records became an imprint of Polygram, which took over sales and marketing responsibilities. While unknown artists had not done well, leading some evaluation of artists signed, compi-

lations sold well, as "Essential Blues 2" made Billboard's list of Top Blues Albums. Planned compilations included "Essential Southern Rock" and gospel artists on "Houses of God."

### New Venues and Internet Opportunities Becoming the Focus of the Late 1990s

By late 1996 HOB's expansion plans began to manifest themselves, with three new venues opening within a year. In November 1996 the Chicago House of Blues opened at the Marina City Towers. HOB modeled the 41,000-square-foot restaurant-night club on existing venues, with the addition of television production studios and multimedia and radio broadcast facilities. House of Blues venues opened in Myrtle Beach in May 1997 and in Orlando in September 1997. The 57,000-square-foot venue at Disney World, a warehouse-style juke joint, was set in a voodoo garden along a Louisiana-style bayou. The concert hall accommodated 2,000 people and the restaurant sat up to 500. New merchandise at the retail stores included pork-pie hats, like those worn in the 1940s, Louisiana hot sauce, and mojo bags, a voodoo love magic. Each House of Blues venue cost $15 million to $20 million to open.

Despite the opening of these new venues, the growth of the company was slower than expected, leading to conflicts between Tigrett and the board of directors. Tigrett wanted slow growth in order to build anticipation, but the board wanted rapid growth. Tigrett stepped down in October at the behest of the board, which also expressed concern about Tigrett's liberal spending habits and the company's poor financial performance. Tigrett remained on the board as emeritus, while COO and President Greg Trojan, who joined the company in 1996, became CEO.

Bob Dylan opened the seventh House of Blues venue in Las Vegas at the Mandalay Bay Resort & Casino in March 1999. Just off the casino floor, the House of Blues offered nightly live music at the 1,800-seat concert hall, Mississippi Delta cuisine at its 500-seat restaurant, a Sunday gospel brunch, and the 16,000-square-foot International House of Blues Foundation Room. In addition, one floor of the hotel featured guest rooms with House of Blues themes.

HOB's August acquisition of Universal Concerts from Seagram's for $190 million created a substantial shift in the scope of the company. Not only did HOB obtain the second largest concert promoter and venue operator, HOB gained some of the best and most experienced promoters in the business. Universal Concerts, renamed HOB Concerts, owned, operated, or controlled 20 concert venues of various sizes, and the acquisition included development plans for 12 new venues nationwide. The acquisition involved a record and home video label that provided a new source for on-line concerts, potentially beneficial for artists and HOB.

Through related agreements, Getmusic.com, an on-line venture by Universal Music Group (UMG) and BMG Entertainment, provided exclusive e-commerce opportunities for HOB on-line properties. In turn HOB provided support for Getmusic.com's introduction of the Digital Media Distribution (DMD) system. In addition, UMG artists received opportunities to play at HOB venues and to show concert footage on HOB web sites.

In early 2000 HOB expanded its presence on the Internet through its agreement with Internet providers. HOB's agreement with MTVi enabled live, pay-per-view concerts from House of Blues venues over the Internet at MTV.com, VH1 .com, and SonicNet.com. The two-year agreement involved MTVi's purchase of equity in HOB and HOB's commitment to promote the MTVi events at 27 concert venues. House of Blues Digital formed a partnership with Winfire, Inc., in June to provide HOB concerts on a pay-per-view basis and HOB's entertainment library archives on-demand to Winfire's FreeDSL subscribers. Under that agreement HOB.com became the preferred broadband content provider. Winfire provided high-speed Internet access on broadband delivery formats, such as cable DSL technology.

Through HOB's summer "Run of the House" promotion, the company sought to draw attention to House of Blues concert venues and the web site. The promotion gave away two ALL ACCESS passes to the seven House of Blues night clubs and 15 HOB Concerts venues. HOB distributed more than two million CD ROMs, which directed customers to the contest location on the web. The CD ROM highlighted the web site's audio and video download features and included concert archives and artist interviews. Winners of the promotion received unlimited entry to the 22 participating venues, including VIP parking and backstage access.

HOB planned to take the company public, registering with the Security and Exchange Commission in March 2000. HOB withdrew the offer in June, however, citing poor market conditions. HOB had hoped to raise $100 million to fund development of new venues and to expand its digital Internet presence. Cities targeted for new restaurant-concert hall venues included Paris, London, Tokyo, Rio de Janeiro, New York, Atlanta, and Denver.

### Principal Subsidiaries

House of Blues Club Venues; House of Blues Concerts; House of Blues Digital; House of Blues Music Company; House of Blues Media Properties; House of Blues New Media.

### Principal Competitors

Clear Channel Communications, Inc.; dick clark productions, inc.; Hard Rock Cafe International, Inc.; Launch Media, Inc.; Planet Hollywood International, Inc.; The MTVi Group; SFX Entertainment, Inc.

### Further Reading

Bessman, Jim, "Summertime Blues: Outdoor Venues Are 'In' for Artists and Labels," *Billboard,* June 15, 1996, p. 32.
Crowe, Jerry, "He's Happy to Have the Blues," *Los Angeles Times,* April 13, 1996, p. 1.
Ellis, Kristi, "House of Blues' Lucky Seven." *WWD,* March 1, 1999, p. 18B.
Evans, Rob, "HOB Goes Live on the Net," *Amusement Business,* September 9, 1996, p. 24.
Frumkin, Paul, "Tigrett's New House Built on Solid Foundation of Blues," *Nation's Restaurant News,* December 21, 1992, p. 17.
Gillen, Marilyn A., "House of Blues Stands at the Interactive Crossroads," *Billboard,* January 14, 1995, p. 6.
"HOB Entertainment, Inc. Announces Integrated Marketing Campaign for Summer 2000," *Business Wire,* July 3, 2000, p. 0048.
Hochman, Steve, "Opening the Doors to House of Blues," *Los Angeles Times,* December 17, 1993, p. 2.
"House of Blues Parent to Go Public, Raise $100M," *Corporate Financing Week,* April 24, 2000, p. 5.
"House of Blues to Break Ground on Disney World's Pleasure Island," *Travel Weekly,* December 14, 1995, p. F12.
Jordon, Catherine, "Club's Foundation Is a Blues Project," *Los Angeles Times,* July 29, 1994, p. 4.
Krueger, Jill, "Striking a Different Cord; Blues Man Meets Mouse House," *Orlando Business Journal,* August 29, 1997, p. 12.
Martin, Richard, "House of Blues Founder Tigrett Expected to Step Down as CEO." *Nation's Restaurant News,* October 27, 1997, p. 3.
Morris, Chris, "House of Blues Label Shifts," *Billboard,* September 21, 1996, p. 6.
——, "House of Blues Opening Two New Outlets," *Billboard,* December 25, 1993, p. 16.
"MTVi Takes Stake in House of Blues, Will Stream Live Music Events Online," *Los Angeles Times,* March 3, 2000, p. 6.
Muret, Don, "Chicago Fifth Home for House of Blues," *Amusement Business,* September 25, 1995, p. 6.
——, "Chicago House of Blues Restaurant Makes Strong Showing Its First Week," *Amusement Business,* December 16, 1996, p. 59.
Newman, Melinda, "House of Blues Label Signs First Acts," *Billboard,* August 6, 1994, p. 11.
Prewitt, Milford, "Former CPK Chief Trojan Finds New Home at House of Blues," *Nation's Restaurant News,* October 14, 1996, p. 7.
——, "House of Blues," *Nation's Restaurant News,* May 22, 1995, p. 116.
"Seagram Sells Universal Concerts to House of Blues Entertainment, Inc.; Acquisition Fuels House of Blues Digital Content Strategy," *Business Wire,* July 26, 1999, p. 0240.
Seigmund, Heidi, "$9 Million Sure Can Buy a Heap of Blues," *Los Angeles Times,* April 23, 1994, p. 5.
Seigmund Cuda, Heidi, "House of Dues, Paid," *Los Angeles Times,* May 8, 1997, p. 34.
Waddell, Ray, "HOB Newest Major Player in Concert Biz," *Amusement Business,* August 2, 1999, p. 1.
Wechsler Linden, Dana, "Spread the blues," *Forbes,* September 13, 1993, p. 90.
"Winfire and House of Blues Digital Form Partnership to Offer Rich-Media Internet Experience; Partnership to Deliver First Pay-Per-View and On-Demand Content to Winfire Users," *Business Wire,* June 13, 2000, p. 0197.
Zoltak, James, "Olympics' Impact Felt Industrywide; Both House of Blues Venues Strike Gold," *Amusement Business,* July 29, 1996, p. 3.
——, "Super Bowl Halftime to Have R&B Twist," *Amusement Business,* January 20, 1997, p. 1.

—Mary Tradii

# Horizon Organic Holding Corporation

**6311 Horizon Lane**
**Longmont, Colorado 80503**
**U.S.A.**
**Telephone: (303) 530-2711**
**Fax: (303) 530-2714**
**Web site: http://www.horizonorganic.com**

*Public Company*
*Incorporated:* 1997
*Employees:* 230
*Sales:* $84.8 million (1999)
*Stock Exchanges:* NASDAQ
*Ticker Symbol:* HCOW
*NAIC:* 112120 Dairy Cattle and Milk Production; 311421
    Juices, Fruit or Vegetable, Fresh Manufacturing;
    311511 Fluid Milk Manufacturing; 311513 Cheese
    Manufacturing

Horizon Organic Holding Corporation operates a dairy that provides fluid milk and more than 60 dairy products produced with raw milk from organically raised dairy cows. Horizon's products include yogurt, butter, cheese, and sour cream as well as eggs and fruit juices. Milk products include nonfat, low-fat, reduced fat, and whole milk, low-fat chocolate milk, and cream. Horizon products can be found in natural foods markets, conventional supermarkets, and health food stores in all 50 states.

The criteria for organic dairy certification involves the nourishment and treatment of dairy cattle. A cow is certified for organic milk production after feeding on organic feed for one year; chemical pesticides, herbicides, fungicides, or fertilizers cannot be used for growing animal feed for three years. For one year before certification the cows cannot be treated with antibiotics during sickness or with synthetic hormones to increase milk production. Restrictions for humane treatment include uncrowded pasture grazing and nighttime housing in barns. Organic certification requires that organic milk not be mixed or come into contact with conventional milk. Horizon's organic dairy farms produce about half of the company's supply of raw milk and more than 200 independent dairy farmers provide the balance.

### The Early 1990s: Finding a Niche in the Organic Foods Market

Two veterans of the natural foods industry started Horizon Organic Dairy in 1991: Mark Retzloff, cofounder of Alfalfa's chain of natural food grocery stores, based in Boulder, Colorado, and Paul Repetto, former president of Vestro Foods, national marketer of Westbrae, Little Bear, and other brands of organic foods. Retzloff and Repetto witnessed the growth of the organic foods industry in the 1980s and saw a potential market for organic dairy products. They each invested $100,000 and managed the company without pay for the first year and a half. Their vision was to produce and sell a national brand of organic dairy products. Mark Peperzak, owner of Aurora Dairy Corporation in Colorado, provided knowledge about the dairy industry as a silent partner.

Originally named Natural Horizons, the company launched its first product in April 1992, certified organic yogurt available in six flavors—plain, vanilla, strawberry, raspberry, peach, and cappuccino. Due to the higher cost of organically produced foods, Horizon sought to make its product accessible on a per-unit basis by offering the yogurt in six-ounce cups at a price comparable to conventional yogurt in the standard eight-ounce cups. A cooperative of 12 dairy farmers in southwestern Wisconsin provided organic milk to produce the yogurt. Certified organic fruit and a white grape juice concentrate sweetener came from organic sources in the Pacific Northwest. Processed at a facility in Madison, the equipment was thoroughly cleaned before making Horizon's organic yogurt. By the end of 1992, Horizon sold the yogurt to 2,000 stores, including Alfalfa's markets, as sales reached $460,000.

Whereas the dairy industry has handled milk as a commodity, combining milk from several regional sources into one tank, Retzloff and Repetto wanted Horizon to be a dairy with its own farm. In 1993 Retzloff and Repetto initiated a stock swap with Aurora Dairy as the first step toward integrating a dairy farm into the company. Pepezak leased an inactive dairy farm, in

Paul, Idaho, to Horizon during the transition to organic certification. At this time the company adopted the name Horizon Organic Dairy.

Horizon successfully introduced organic milk into the Los Angeles area through the Ralph's chain of supermarkets in September. The supply of nonfat and two-percent-reduced fat organic milk did not meet demand, however, even at 40 cents more per half gallon than conventional milk. Horizon's timing of the launch happened to occur a few months before the FDA approved a genetically engineered growth hormone, rBGH. Concerns about the possible dangers of the hormone to the health of milk drinkers stimulated sales of organic milk products. As the milk supply increased, Horizon introduced organic milk into natural food stores and supermarkets in Colorado, the Midwest, and the East Coast a few months later. The milk was processed and pasteurized at a facility in Des Moines and transported across the country in milk tankers.

Horizon secured $1.5 million in venture capital financing in 1994 and applied the funds toward the transition of the Idaho dairy farm, purchasing cows and organic feed. In July Horizon opened the organic dairy farm in Idaho with 1,000 head of Holstein cows. Unlike a factory farm, the cows grazed on pesticide-free pastures and spent the night in barn stalls; the cows were milked three times a day by special equipment for squeezing gentler than that of ordinary milking equipment. The 4,000-acre farm, the first organic dairy farm of its size in the United States, cost $5 million to bring to organic standards and held the capacity for 3,000 more cows.

With a new supply of organic milk, Horizon expanded distribution. By the end of the year Horizon milk, yogurt, and sour cream sold in 76 percent of King Soopers, Safeway, and Albertson's stores in metropolitan Denver, in five of the six major grocery store chains in the Los Angeles area, in areas of New York City, and in natural food stores across the country. Horizon became the first national brand of organic dairy products, garnering $3.7 million in sales in 1994.

### The Mid-1990s: Fantastic Growth But No Profits

Growth had its problems as Horizon tried to keep production in pace with demand. The farm in Idaho did not produce enough organic cow feed, so Horizon contracted with more local farmers. Originally, 19 organic farmers supplied pesticide-free feed; that number increased to 97 farmers on 50,000 acres in three states. Another problem involved finding enough facilities to process and pasteurize organic milk in Des Moines. In addition, most of the milk products sold on the West Coast, requiring long-distance travel in any weather to transport products

with limited shelf-life. Retzloff and Repetto solved the problem by building a plant in Petaluma, California, and at the farm in Idaho. The company also began to process milk at the Robinson Dairy in Denver, transporting raw milk in tankers from Idaho, to arrive at the facility 12 hours later. Robinson processed the milk after midnight, when the equipment was usually dormant. Horizon also contracted with processors in Minnesota, Nevada, and New Jersey. New processor contracts supported the introduction of butter, cream cheese, half-and-half, and 1% low-fat milk.

Additional processing capacity enabled Horizon to expand its sales territory to conventional grocery store chains in San Francisco, Seattle, Portland, Chicago, Atlanta, Boston, and New Jersey. The typical consumer of Horizon products tended to be an adventurous female, 20 to 50 years old, who had completed a course of higher education and who may have children. While many of Horizon's customers earned a higher than average income, education played a larger role in the decision to pay the higher price for Horizon products. Due to the costs of operating an organic dairy farm, Horizon priced a half gallon of milk at 25 percent to 50 percent more than conventional milk. Horizon's plans for advancement called for additional leadership and experience at the top. In October 1995, Horizon hired Barney Feinblum, former chairman of Celestial Seasonings tea company, as president and CEO of Horizon. Retzloff became vice-president of sales and Repetto became vice-president of operations. Venture financing provided $2.5 million for expansion.

In November 1996 Horizon launched a line of four organic cheeses with seven new products. Horizon introduced packages of eight-ounce, wax-dipped aged cheddar, reduced-fat aged cheddar, Monterey Jack, and low moisture/part skim mozzarella cheese. Shortly afterward, Horizon offered organic Parmesan cheese, available in wedges, shredded, or grated. Milk for the cheese came from organic dairy farms in Wisconsin and, later, from the Idaho farm, which doubled the herd to 2,000 cows.

With sales of $16 million and a loss of $5 million in 1996, Horizon had not made a profit yet. The transition to organic agriculture, public education about the benefits of organic foods, and the high cost of gentle milking equipment kept operating expenses high. Human labor involved one person for every 40 cows at Horizon's Idaho dairy farm, compared with one person for every 75 cows on a conventional dairy farm. Because Horizon did not use antibiotics on sick cows, the company implemented preventative health care measures to reduce the risk of infection, such as cleaning facilities 24 hours a day. Horizon employed homeopathic methods to treat sick cows and culled extremely ill cows from the herd. The company paid nearly 50 percent more for organic feed than conventional dairy farms paid for nonorganic feed; Horizon also devised its own feed mix, which included alfalfa hay, canola, and cottonseed meal. In addition, the company paid a high price for raw organic milk, at $18.00 per 100 pounds, compared with $12.00 for conventional milk.

With additional venture financing of $7.25 million, Horizon completed the three-year transition of the Idaho dairy farm to organic certification for animal feed in July 1997, allowing the company to increase the herd to 4,000 cows. Horizon bought the farm from Aurora Dairy at this time. The company also began to develop an organic dairy farm in Maryland to supply milk for the East Coast. With a herd of 556 cows, the Maryland dairy began to ship organic milk for processing in early 1998. Horizon expected the farm to be certified organic for animal feed in 2000.

Horizon continued to focus on growth along the East Coast, adding eggs to its list of products. A 1997 licensing agreement with Glenwood Farms of Jetersville, Virginia allowed that company to distribute eggs under the Horizon brand, using a happy chicken logo similar to the flying cow. The distribution area stretched along the East Coast from Virginia to New York. The April 1998 acquisition of Juniper Valley Farms in Roxbury, New York expanded Horizon's reach in metropolitan New York. Horizon planned to transfer brand products from Juniper Valley Farms to the Horizon name.

### 1998: The First Public Organic Foods Company

Horizon became the first publicly owned organic foods company with a June 1998 stock offering. Horizon expected to sell at $11.00 per share, but trading began at $13.13 per share. In a concurrent private placement, Brazilian conglomerate Suiza Foods acquired 1.1 million shares, a 12.5 percent ownership of the company. The offering raised $46 million, which Horizon used to pay debt, with $24 million available for acquisitions.

Horizon's corporate approach to organic food production drew criticism from small organic dairy farmers. Small dairy farms carried 40 to 80 cows, compared with Horizon's herd of more than 4,500, prompting the question of whether a large-scale farm can protect the animals and the environment as well as small organic dairy farms. Despite critics' concessions to the fact that the productivity of corporate farming met the demand for organic milk products, corporate farming entailed a different cultural attitude. Horizon countered that the productivity of the company had led many grain and dairy farmers to convert to organic methods.

In September 1998, Horizon introduced a line of organic fruit juices—Organic Orange Juice, with or without pulp, and Organic Ruby Red Grapefruit. Horizon used organic Valencia oranges and other oranges from Florida and California. Despite a retail price of approximately $4.79 per half gallon, sales were higher than expected. The juice containers featured the "Happy Cow" logo.

Horizon garnered its first profit in 1998—$486,000 from $49.4 million in sales, as lower operating costs improved profit margins. Horizon's association with Suiza facilitated distribution to the East Coast through Garelick Farms and processing of chocolate milk and cottage cheese at Suiza plants reduced overhead. Economies of scale through maximum use of Horizon's infrastructure and the maturity of the Idaho dairy farm also contributed to improved profit margins. Horizon products sold in 8,100 natural food and conventional grocery stores nationwide.

Horizon pursued international expansion through a licensing agreement for milk products in Japan and acquisition of an organic dairy in Wales. In April 1999 Horizon signed a distribution agreement to cobrand organic dairy products with Takanashi Milk Products Ltd. of Japan, beginning with organic yogurt. Horizon shipped organic feed and dairy ingredients to Japan until Takanashi developed its own supply of organic milk.

Expansion to the United Kingdom involved the acquisition of Rachel's Organic Dairy in Aberystywth, Wales, through which Horizon planned to introduce organic milk to the United Kingdom and Europe. Horizon retained the previous owners, Rachel and Gareth Rowlands, to act as liaisons between Horizon and local dairy farmers, assisting in the conversion to organic methods.

Horizon purchased the Organic Cow brand of dairy products from H.P. Hood for $10.9 million. Organic Cow of Vermont was the leading brand of organic milk products, with a strong customer base in Boston. Horizon intended to continue to sell dairy products under that brand.

Horizon used a variety of strategies to expand its reach as well as its product line. The company signed a licensing agreement with Nu-Cal Foods to distribute organic eggs under the Horizon brand. Horizon planned initial distribution for northern California, with later expansion to western states. A method of cobranding involved a coffee drink by Flavor Organics, which used Horizon milk; the packaging featured Horizon's "Happy Cow" logo. In October 1999 the company launched a line of yogurt flavors with added nutrients such as beta-carotene and vitamin C. Horizon began to sell some products in larger containers, with new gallon-sized jugs of milk and 24-ounce containers of yogurt in plain, vanilla, and honey flavors.

The successful expansion of organic dairy products increased competition for Horizon milk from some of the company's first customers. King Soopers supermarket launched a private label organic milk, followed by a Safeway grocery store brand. Whereas conventional grocers accounted for two-thirds of Horizon's sales volume, Retzloff thought the store brands were indicative of positive change and that the market niche had room for competitors. Nevertheless, Horizon increased its advertising campaign expenditure in 1999, involving in-store promotions and product sampling and continuing to advertise in parenting magazines. Horizon also sought to increase consumer awareness of the benefits of organic agriculture and of the Horizon brand through the company's web site.

Finding processors for its products continued to be a priority as the volume of fluid milk in 1999 increased 47 percent over 1998. With contracts for seven new dairy processors, Horizon attempted to expedite a faster pace of distribution, from cow to processor to grocery store shelves; in many places this often took place within 24 hours. Through a management and supply agreement with Aurora Dairy, Horizon augmented its organic dairy capacity with 1,150 cows at a farm in Platteville, Colorado.

### Leadership Changes Directed to the Future

Sales in 1999 reached $848 million, yet garnered a net profit of only $1.4 million. At the end of 1999 a spurt of growth increased revenues, but Horizon found it difficult to keep expenses down as the company's tracking techniques proved be outmoded for the higher level of activity. Other costly activities involved market expansion, new product launches, and integration of the Organic Cow brand. Horizon hired a consultant to assist with the organization of the business.

Organizational changes occurred naturally as Feinblum announced his intention to leave Horizon to seek new opportunities. The company named Charles Marcy as president and COO in November 1999 with the expectation of his succession to CEO. Previously employed with Sealright, Quaker Oats, Kraft, and General Foods, Marcy brought experience in brand promotion and management. Feinblum decided to leave early, placing Marcy in the position of CEO in January 2000. Retzloff took a new position, president of international operations; Repetto retired, but remained on the board of directors.

The company continued to expand its production capacity, winning the bid for a long-term lease of an 865-acre dairy at the U.S. Naval Academy in Gambrills, Maryland. Horizon planned a visitor and education center as well as a working dairy farm at the site. Horizon worked with state and local agricultural and wildlife organizations to develop programs that teach visitors about the relationship between agriculture and the natural environment. Named Horizon Organic Farm and Education Center, plans included the Organic Discovery Barn, a petting zoo, and a vegetable garden.

In March 2000 Horizon completed the acquisition of the George Dairy in cooperation with the Nature Conservancy of California, a nonprofit organization. The agreement between Horizon and the Nature Conservancy involved integration of the 605-acre dairy farm, located in south Sacramento County, into the 40,000-acre Cosumnes River Preserve. The plan protected the dairy farm from urban development or from becoming a vineyard, as many northern California dairy farms had in recent years. Dairy farms provided valuable habitat for sandhill cranes and other wildlife that cannot survive in a vineyard. Horizon sold conservation easements to the Nature Conservancy for $1 million, paid by state and federal grants, bringing the actual purchase price down to $1.5 million. Under the agreement, Horizon set aside a 110-acre freshwater marsh on the dairy farm as habitat for the endangered giant garter snake and for wastewater treatment. The previous owners had not used synthetic fertilizers so the land was already certifiably organic. The dairy included 350 cows and potentially supported 2,700 cows. Horizon planned to raze the milking facilities and build a modern plant.

Horizon began expansion of Rachel's Dairy, adding a new plant in Aberystywth to increase production capacity there by 75 percent. New Rachel's brand yogurt products included a rich, Greek-style yogurt with honey, whole milk yogurt with maple syrup, and a low-fat vanilla yogurt. Obtaining a supply of organic milk proved easy enough as a depressed agricultural market in the United Kingdom prompted farmers to change to organic practices, being persuaded by the premium price paid for organic milk and cow feed. Horizon also acquired two organic product makers: Meadow Farms in Devon, the largest supplier of store-brand milk in the United Kingdom; and Organic Matters, producer of a variety of organic dairy products.

With the company's products in more than 27 percent of supermarkets in the United States, Horizon set a goal to add another ten percent of the country's supermarkets to its customer list. Horizon hoped to raise brand awareness through increased marketing and public relations. New products in 2000 included a 64-ounce organic apple juice and lemonade, as well as orange-carrot juice from concentrate. Single-serving, 16-ounce organic fruit juices were offered in orange juice, orange-carrot juice, orange juice with added vitamin C, and lemonade. The company began to explore the possibility of introducing new cheese products, but did not plan to produce organic ice cream. In the future Horizon expected to provide organic dairy products to restaurants.

### Principal Subsidiaries

Rachel's Dairy Ltd. (U.K.)

### Principal Competitors

Dean Foods Company; Express Dairies plc; Organic Valley.

### Further Reading

"All-Organic Yogurt Idea for Start-up," *Boulder County Business Report,* December 1992, p. 10.

Clark, Gerry, "More Than Organic Growth: Small But Increasing Demand for Organic Products Provides National Market," *Dairy Foods,* April 1999, p. 72.

Croskey, Peter, "Organics: Pure But Not So Simple," *Grocer,* July 1, 2000, p. S15.

Cube, Christine, "New Visitor's Center Hires Marketing Firm," *Washington Business Journal,* April 7, 2000, p. 45.

Day, Janet, "Boulder Producer Gearing Up to Sell First U.S. Organic Milk," *Denver Post,* September 17, 1993, p. C1.

Doef, Gail, "Expanding Horizon," *Dairy Foods,* October 1995, p. 20.

"Flavor Organics, Inc.," *Beverage Industry,* June 1999, p. 14.

Hardcastle, Sarah, "Yogurt & Pot Desserts," *Grocer,* April 8, 2000, p. 43.

"Horizon Organic Juice—Apple Lemonade; Orange-Carrot; Orange; Super C.," *Product Alert,* May 8, 2000.

"Horizon Plans to Market Aggressively," *Food Institute Report,* May 29, 2000.

"Horizon Sets Scene for UK Sales Push," *Super Marketing,* June 23, 2000, p. 3.

Hudson, Kris, "CEO of Longmont, Colo, Organic Milk Company Departs Early," *Knight-Ridder/Tribune News Service,* January 9, 2000.

Lewis, Pete, "New Horizon for Dairy: IPO Creates First Public Organic Food Company," *Denver Business Journal,* February 26, 1998, p. 18B.

Locke, Tom, "Horizon Organic Milks the Competition and Moves into Other Natural Realms," *Wall Street Journal,* March 9, 1999.

"Making Milk Even More Wholesome," *Food Processing,* September 1999, p. 32.

"Organic Opportunity: Organic Cheese Becomes More Popular in the Rapidly Growing Organic Category," *Dairy Foods,* March 1997, p. 51N.

"Organic Overdrive," *Dairy Foods,* March 2000, p. 20.

Palmeri, Christopher, "New Age Moo Juice," *Forbes,* October 19, 1998.

"Rachel's Dairy Sold to Horizon," *Eurofood,* April 22, 1999, p. 10.

"Rachel's Expands Production Capacity at Aberystywth," *Dairy Markets Weekly,* June 15, 2000.

Romero, Christine, "Longmont, Colo.-Based Organic Dairy's Record Sales Fail to Win Wall Street," *Knight-Ridder/Tribune News Service,* October 28, 1999.

——, "Longmont, Colo.-Based Organic Milk Maker Expects Continued Growth," *Knight-Ridder/Tribune News Service,* May 13, 1999.

Smith, Jerd, "Horizon Grew with the Help of Investors," *Rocky Mountain News,* November 23, 1997, p. 14G.

——, "Making Organic Milk the Hard Way Boulder Entrepreneurs Provide the Spark for Idaho Operation That Pioneers New Methods," *Rocky Mountain News,* November 23, 1997, p. 13G.

——, "Organic Action Boulder-Based Horizon Dairy Milks Nationwide Market Sales Will Nearly Double to $30 Million," *Rocky Mountain News,* November 23, 1997, p. 1G.

Smith, Kerri, "As Demand for Organic Milk Rises, Companies Innovated to Meet Demand," *Denver Post,* November 8, 1996, p. C1.

"Suiza Foods Acquires Stake in Horizon Organic Dairy," *Dairy Markets Weekly,* June 25, 1998, p. 6.

Theodore, Sarah, "Organic Juice on the Horizon," *Beverage Industry,* September 1, 1998, p. 24.

Uhlnad, Vicky, "Expanding Organic Dairy Market Becoming 'Cash Cow' for Horizon," *Boulder County Business Report,* September 1, 1995, p. B2.

Vasquez, Beverly, "Horizon Says Cheese the Way to Double Sales," *Denver Business Journal,* November 1, 1996, p. 14A.

—Mary Tradii

# IBERIABANK Corporation

**1101 East Admiral Doyle Drive**
**New Iberia, Louisiana 70560**
**U.S.A.**
**Telephone: (337) 365-2361**
**Fax: (337) 364-1171**
**Web site: http://www.iberiabank.com**

*Public Company*
*Incorporated:* 1995 as ISB Financial Corporation
*Employees:* 565 (1999)
*Sales:* $108.8 million (1999)
*Stock Exchanges:* NASDAQ
*Ticker Symbol:* IBKC
*NAIC:* 52211 Commercial Banking; 551111 Offices of
    Bank Holding Companies

IBERIABANK Corporation has 25 branches in the New Iberia/Lafayette area of south central Louisiana, ten in northeast Louisiana, and eight in New Orleans and its environs. Strictly a savings and loan for much of its long history, IBERIABANK maintains its primary focus on single-family residential loans, but at all of its offices it offers a full range of banking services, including commercial loans, personal and commercial checking accounts, passbook and NOW accounts, certificates of deposit, and IRAs and Keogh accounts. Through Iberia Financial Services, LLC, IBERIABANK's wholly owned subsidiary, IBERIABANK Corporation offers securities and other financial products to meet its clients' investment needs. Iberia Financial's own subsidiary, Finesco, LLC, offers insurance premium financing to retailers and other commercial customers.

## 1887–1987: One Hundred Years of Stability and Conservative Banking

The grandsire of IBERIABANK, the principal subsidiary of IBERIABANK Corporation, was founded as Iberia Building Association, which opened its doors on March 12, 1887, in New Iberia, Louisiana. At the time, New Iberia was a farming community of about 3,000 inhabitants located in Iberia Parish, in the heartland of the Acadiana region of Louisiana. Its principal cash crops, then as now, were sugar cane and rice. The region's oil reserves, which would later spur New Iberia's population and economic growth, had yet to be discovered.

Although the Association was the first lending institution in the area, and one of only a handful in the entire state, it had a very unassuming start. It shared an office with William Robinson, one of its directors, and boasted assets of only $4,341. Like the sleepy Bayou Teche on whose banks New Iberia was located, the new thrift's business flowed serenely and slowly. It was a few weeks before it even made its initial loan, issuing a $600 mortgage. Its first officers were Fred Gates, president; J.W. Callahan, vice-president; and E.F. Millard, bank manager. According to Millard, the association was created to be "the wage earner's friend" in keeping with the stated aims of the association's first directors, which were "to help families in financing the purchase of homes and to encourage thrift." Those aims would remain in place for the next 100 years, during which the Association remained remarkably stable.

That stability was generally credited to two key figures: William G. Weeks and John W. Trotter. Weeks was a young lawyer when, in the summer of 1888, he was elected secretary of the Association. It was a post he held for the next 59 years. Trotter joined the bank in January 1947, serving as its managing officer for 30 years. He was succeeded by Emile J. Plaisance, Jr., who was president of the Association when, in 1987, it had its centennial celebration. By then its name had been changed to Iberia Savings & Loan Association (ISLA), and its assets had reached $294.6 million, up almost $100 million over the assets it had held in 1978. Its first mortgages and other loans totaled about $248.4 million. It also had branches in six locations and served not only New Iberia but also Jeanerette, Franklin, and Morgan City.

It was only a couple of years before ISLA reached its 100th year that regulatory agencies relaxed restrictions on savings and loan associations that had prohibited them from making business loans. Because the regulations had prevented the bank from lending money to oil companies and oil-related businesses, ISLA did not suffer the setback some Louisiana banks experienced when the oil boom ended and the state went into a fairly deep recession. ISLA had kept its focus on consumer-oriented services, following the philosophy of its founders. For years it had been providing loans for homes, automobiles, appliances, and such personal needs as college tuition. In 1987, when explaining ISLA's financial stability, Plaisance said, ''We have been profitable for many, many years because we run a very conservative type of operation.'' He added, ''And I don't see that philosophy changing, at least not in the next few years.''

### 1988–1996: IBERIABANK Begins Significant Growth and Restructures under ISB Financial, a Holding Company

Considering what happened in the next ten years, one might suspect that Plaisance had his tongue wedged firmly in his cheek. Although only on a small scale, ISLA had already started to grow. State restrictions on thrifts opening branches in more than one parish were dropped in 1985, allowing ISLA to open offices in Morgan City and Franklin, both in St. Mary Parish, to the south of Iberia Parish.

To grow significantly, ISLA had to cross more parish lines. Although Iberia Parish covered an area of 575 square miles, it remained fairly sparsely populated, despite the region's tremendous oil-industry growth in the second half of the 20th century. Even by 1995 it had only reached an estimated population of 70,742, considerably less than the population of Lafayette, a small but rapidly growing city some 20 miles to the north.

ISLA changed its name to Iberia Savings Bank in 1988, and in the next year it gained another toehold outside of Iberia Parish when it assumed the deposits of Acadia Savings & Loan, giving Iberia Savings branches in two more parishes—Acadia and Lafayette. Its new offices were located in the city of Lafayette as well as in the smaller towns of Crowley, Rayne, and Kaplan. Over the next two years it assumed additional deposits of troubled banks, first of First Federal Savings & Loan in September 1990, then of one branch of Louisiana Savings in October 1991. These mergers gave Iberia Savings additional branches in New Iberia, Lafayette, and Kaplan. They also moved the bank into St. Martinville in St. Martin Parish. Although eddying its way into parishes adjacent to Iberia Parish, the bank had not yet leapfrogged into other regions of Louisiana.

The regulatory changes made in 1985 had also permitted Louisiana-chartered, commercial bank holding companies to open branches anywhere in the state. By 1992, it also appeared that additional regulatory changes would soon permit Louisiana savings and loan banks to reorganize and convert to state-chartered commercial banks. Under the leadership of Larrey G. Mouton, who had succeeded Plaisance as president, Iberia Savings began preparations for the change, laying the

groundwork for forming a holding company to facilitate the transition and thereafter manage the business of Iberia Savings Bank, its wholly owned subsidiary. By then, too, Iberia Savings had begun broadening its services. For example, in 1992 it had organized Finesco, LLC as an affiliate of Iberia Financial Services, LLC, a subsidiary of Iberia Savings. Finesco was created to offer competitive rates on financing both commercial and personal insurance premiums.

In 1995, ISB Financial Corporation, the new holding company for Iberia Savings Bank, was formed and incorporated. Its immediate aim was to acquire all of Iberia Savings' capital stock issued by the bank in April of 1995 in its conversion to stock form. Iberia Savings then became the sole, wholly owned subsidiary of ISB Financial. Two years later, in December 1997, Iberia Savings was converted to a Louisiana-chartered commercial bank and renamed IBERIABANK.

In the interim, under the holding company's auspices, Iberia Savings continued to grow via further mergers and acquisitions. On May 3, 1996, through a multistep cash merger costing $9.1 million, ISB Financial acquired Royal Bankgroup of Acadiana, Inc. and the two branches of its Louisiana-chartered commercial bank and wholly owned subsidiary, Bank of Lafayette. The two offices in Lafayette continued to operate as branches of Iberia Savings. Next, on October 18, 1996, after entering into a complex interim agreement the previous May, ISB Financial completed a $47 million acquisition of Jefferson Bancorp, Inc. and its subsidiary, Jefferson Federal Savings Bank. Jefferson Federal was converted into a Louisiana-chartered stock savings bank operating as Jefferson Bank, which temporarily remained a separate subsidiary of ISB Financial. Jefferson was based in Gretna, Louisiana, and had six full-service branches in the greater metropolitan area of New Orleans. At the close of 1996, bolstered by these acquisitions, ISB Financial had total assets of $929.3 million and deposits of $760.3 million. It had also finally leapfrogged into another area of the state.

### 1997–2000: Becoming a Major Louisiana Company

With its 1997 renaming and conversion into a Louisiana-chartered, full-service commercial bank, IBERIABANK set out both to tap into new Louisiana markets and to increase and diversify its services. Even before the name change, Jefferson Bank was merged with and into Iberia Savings Bank. Thereafter, its offices became branches of IBERIABANK and began operating under that name. In addition to increasing operational efficiency, the move enhanced the bank's image. It both implied the bank's conversion into a commercial bank and removed any stigma of localism previously associated with ''Iberia.'' With total assets closing in on $1 billion, IBERIABANK had become much more than a regional institution; it had become a Louisiana bank.

That fact was made abundantly clear in 1998 when ISB Financial acquired 17 branch offices from select subsidiaries of the former First Commerce Corporation. The purchase opened up another market for IBERIABANK, giving it ten branch offices in the Monroe area of northeast Louisiana and a presence in a total of ten parishes. The acquisition also boosted the bank's assets to $1.4 billion and its total number of employees to 545.

## Key Dates:

**1887:** Bank is initially formed as Iberia Building Association.

**1956:** Bank changes name to Iberia Savings & Loan (ISLA).

**1971:** ISLA's assets reach $50 million mark.

**1988:** Iberia Savings & Loan becomes Iberia Savings Bank.

**1995:** Holding company is formed as ISB Financial Corporation to acquire the capital stock of Iberia Savings.

**1996:** ISB Financial purchases Jefferson Bancorp and Royal Bancshares, Inc., as well as their respective subsidiaries: Jefferson Federal Savings Bank and Bank of Lafayette.

**1997:** Iberia Savings Bank becomes IBERIABANK.

**1998:** ISB Financial acquires 17 branches of First Commerce Corporation.

**1999:** ISB Financial hires Daryl G. Byrd as president of both ISB Financial and IBERIABANK.

**2000:** ISB Financial is renamed IBERIABANK Corporation.

In the next year, ISB Financial also hired former First Commerce executive Daryl G. Byrd as its president, succeeding Larrey Mouton. Although Mouton did retain his post as CEO of ISB Financial, he passed operational control of the converted bank to Byrd because of Byrd's extensive commercial banking experience. Byrd had been with First Commerce since 1985 and had served in various executive positions. He had been in charge of commercial lending at the First National Bank in Lafayette, had served as president and CEO of Rapides Bank and Trust Co., and, in 1992, had been appointed executive vice-president in charge of the commerce and mortgage banking groups at the First National Bank of Commerce. After First Commerce was bought out by Bank One in 1998, he was named president and CEO of Bank One's Louisiana's New Orleans region.

Byrd immediately had to attend to some problems resulting from the company's aggressive acquisitions and Iberia Savings' conversion into a commercial bank, including what analyst Martin Friedman of Friedman, Billings, Ramsey & Co. of Arlington, Virginia, said was "the market's tendency to react negatively toward companies announcing restructurings." Fine-tuning in 1999 reduced ISB Financial's year-end assets from $1.40 billion to $1.36 billion and its net income from $10.1 million to $9.5 million. It began making further adjust-

ments in 2000, adding $1.6 million to its loan loss reserves and releasing 22 employees. It also made $190 million in securities available for sale instead of holding them to maturity, which reduced its equity by $4 million. Byrd claimed that these restructuring changes would result in savings of about $2 million starting in 2001.

IBERIABANK's make-over as a commercial bank involved providing new, up-to-date services designed to attract a wide range of customers, both private and commercial. Through 1998 and 1999, it added *Plus*Savings (accounts paying premium interest rates on high balances), *Plus*Pay (an Internet bill-paying service), *Plus*Banking (an account management service via the Internet), Ideal Business Checking (a checking product for small businesses with few monthly transactions), *50*Basic & *50*Plus (checking accounts for people 50 or older), *Business*Line & *Plus*Line (two lines of credit for businesses), and *Plus*Account (an interest-bearing checking account). Although such services were common enough in established commercial banks, to older customers of what was once Iberia Savings Bank they may have seemed nothing short of revolutionary. The conservative heritage of the old Iberia Savings & Loan Bank was fading fast, however. In fact, its last vestiges may have been expunged in 2000, when ISB Financial Corporation removed the "S" for Savings in its new name, IBERIABANK Corporation. That name change was made not to repudiate the past, of course; it was made to reflect where the corporation was and where it planned on going in the new century.

### Principal Subsidiaries

IBERIABANK; Iberia Financial Services, LLC.

### Principal Competitors

Acadiana Bancshares, Inc.; Bank One Corporation; Hancock Holding Company; Hibernia Corporation; Whitney Holding Corporation.

### Further Reading

"Iberia Unveils 10-Minute Automated Lenders," *Mortgage Marketplace*, June 24, 1996, p. 6.

Moran, Wilda B., "Cash Giveaway, Ceremony to Mark ISLA Centennial," *Daily Iberian*, February 19, 1987, p. 7.

Padgett, Tania, "Louisiana Woes Show Pitfall of Thrift-to-Bank Conversion," *American Banker*, January 3, 2000, p. 20.

Ptacek, Megan J., "Executive Changes," *American Banker*, May 18, 2000, p. 6.

——, "ISB Financial in La. Hires Bank One Exec to Be President," *American Banker*, July 22, 1999, p. 6.

—John W. Fiero

# Ibstock Brick Ltd.

Leicester Road
Leicestershire LE67 6HS
England
Telephone: (44) 1530 261 999
Fax: (44) 1530 257 457
Web site: http://www.ibstock.co.uk

*Wholly Owned Subsidiary of CRH plc*
*Incorporated:* 1899 as Ibstock Collieries Ltd.
*Sales:* not available
*NAIC:* 327331 Concrete Block and Brick Manufacturing;
    327121 Brick and Structural Clay Tile Manufacturing;
    327991 Cut Stone and Stone Product Manufacturing

Ibstock Brick Ltd. is a leading manufacturer of brick and paving products in the United Kingdom and operates manufacturing facilities in the United States and Europe as well. From its modest origins in early nineteenth-century coal mining, Ibstock grew to achieve a prominent and respected position in the brickmaking industry of the late 20th century. While Ibstock is perhaps best known for its clay facing bricks, the company also manufactures specially designed custom bricks, architectural terracotta, faience, and cast stone. In addition to manufactured products, Ibstock offers a building design service. The company was acquired by building materials conglomerate CRH plc in 1999.

### Early Years as a Colliery: 1825–1900

Ibstock was established in 1825 when William Thirlby, a farmer and lacemaker, started mining operations on his land at Ibstock, near Leicester. Within a few years his business was prosperous, serving local customers from a plentiful bed of coal. By the 1830s the mining site, which had grown to over 100 acres, was producing supplies of fire clay and clay suitable for making brick. Over the next ten years a primitive brickworks was developed, but bricks were strictly a by-product of the primary business of the colliery, with only the lowest-quality coal relegated to brickmaking. The sideline grew over the years as mechanization replaced the old, time-consuming processes by which brick was made. Nevertheless, brick's continuing low

status at the colliery was apparent in the company's sales figures for 1879: coal accounted for £27,000, brick for £2,991.

In the early years of its existence the colliery changed ownership several times. In 1875 Samuel Thomson became managing director, and the business soon became a family dynasty; under Samuel Thomson's son, also Samuel, Ibstock Collieries was incorporated as a private limited company in 1899.

### The Increasing Popularity of Brick: Early 1900s

Brickmaking began to assume a greater importance at Ibstock at the beginning of the twentieth century, as bricks became a popular choice of the building industry. By the start of World War I Ibstock was producing some three million bricks a year. After the war, coal mining became an increasingly problematic industry. Miners' coalitions were demanding better working conditions and higher pay, and were prepared to back up these demands with strikes. The government, which had taken control of the country's coal mines during the war (though Ibstock, due to its smaller size, had remained independent), continued to impose price controls on the industry. In 1921, when the government returned the mines to their owners, workers' wages dropped dramatically, prompting further labor unrest. In addition, foreign competition, particularly from Poland and Germany, was intense.

As a result of these internal and external pressures, in 1928 Ibstock decided to close the pits and elevate the company's sidelines of brick-, tile-, and pipemaking to center stage. An appraisal undertaken in 1933 showed that the company was capable of producing three million bricks and five million tiles and pipes per year, which was adequate for a subsidiary product, but not for a primary line of business.

Ibstock set about creating a more extensive works with modern equipment, including a Monnier kiln (the first such to be used in Britain), a novel tunnel kiln that fired bricks loaded on cars that moved through the kiln. Requiring a substantial investment of £8,000, the technological advance increased production capacity to nine million bricks a year. Reflecting its new direction, Ibstock Collieries changed its name to Ibstock Brick & Tile Company in 1935.

## Company Perspectives:

*The Ibstock Values describe the way we will work in Ibstock and the way we will behave towards our customers and colleagues. They are central to the type of culture we want to develop and are therefore essential to the achievement of our goals. They are: Promoting an environment of trust—a place where ideas are shared and contributions are welcomed; Responsiveness to customer needs—being seen as a company that will do everything it can to satisfy its customers; Measurement—making decisions based on fact, not just feeling and intuition; Ongoing improvement of all processes—to satisfy and delight the customer.*

World War II curtailed Ibstock's growth, and for a while after the war production was limited by shortages of labor and materials. By the 1950s, however, Ibstock was positioned for further expansion, which the company fueled with an aggressive sales strategy. Unlike other brick manufacturers, who sold their wares exclusively to building products merchants, Ibstock targeted brick users directly. By employing an active sales network to pinpoint architects, for example, and persuade them to use Ibstock bricks, the company was able to gain an edge on the competition.

Over the next few decades, Ibstock grew steadily by investing in further automation. In 1959 work commenced on a new 20-chamber Staffordshire kiln, bringing annual output to 41 million bricks, and the installation of yet another kiln soon afterward (bringing Ibstock's total to four) increased that number to 56 million.

### Rapid Expansion in the 1960s and 1970s

During the 1960s Ibstock began expanding rapidly. Led by a fourth-generation scion of the Thomson family, Paul Hyde-Thomson (the family surname had been modified years before to include an earlier chairman's wife's maiden name), and flush with capital from a stock market flotation in 1963, Ibstock acquired in quick succession several smaller firms, including Himley Brick, Aldridge Brick, Tile & Coal Company, Burwell Brick, Shawell Precast Products, and Superbrix. The aggressive acquisition strategy gave Ibstock a greater range of products, increased its geographical representation, and enlarged its production capacity: by 1967 the company had six manufacturing plants and an annual capacity of 130 million bricks.

Not all the acquisitions proved successful. Burwell was unprofitable and was retained only until 1971; Shawell, renamed Ibstock Precast, was abandoned in 1977; and Superbrix, makers of bricks from inferior grade sandline, rather than clay, was in retrospect a poor choice for a company that prided itself on producing quality products.

Nevertheless, Ibstock continued to thrive, and in 1970 the company effected an important merger with the privately owned international wood pulp agency Johnsen, Jorgensen and Wettre. While the two companies had virtually no common ground, Ibstock wanted Johnsen's healthy cash reserves to finance further expansion, and Johnsen believed that Ibstock

could invest that capital to the companies' mutual advantage. Thus the company became Ibstock Johnsen, with the two operating divisions kept separate.

Ibstock immediately embarked upon a new round of acquisitions, buying Roughdales Brickworks, North Eastern Bricks, Nostell Brick & Tile, and the Cattybrook Brick Company in 1971 and 1972. Because the company was reluctant to extend itself further domestically—fearing that in doing so it would compromise its position at the more exclusive end of the U.K. market—Ibstock looked abroad for further acquisitions.

The company's first overseas acquisition came in 1973, with the purchase of the Dutch facing brick manufacturer Van Wijcks Waalsteenfabrieken, followed closely by another Dutch company, Maatschappij tot Exploitatie van Steenfabrieken Udenhout, voorheen Weyers. These moves catapulted Ibstock to the position of sixth-largest brickmaker in the Netherlands.

The mid-1970s saw severe setbacks in Ibstock's home market, with labor unrest by British miners, OPEC's stranglehold on oil prices and the consequent energy crises, and the general economic downturn all having an adverse impact on Ibstock's domestic operations: profits were running approximately ten percent lower than normal. The company continued its overseas expansion, moving into Belgium in 1977 with the acquisition of Tuileries et Briqueteries d'Hennuyeres et de Wanlin and reinforcing its position in the Netherlands with the purchase of Steenfabriek De Ruiterwaard. With six factories in Holland, capable of producing 154 million bricks a year, combined with exports from its U.K. operation to fill Dutch orders, Ibstock controlled about seven percent of the Dutch market.

Ibstock next contemplated the potential rewards of the huge American market. In 1978 the company bought Marion Brick, based in Ohio, a significant purchase which boosted the company's turnover by a quarter and raised total production by one-half. Ibstock had an annual brick production of 400 million in the United States and Europe, and 250 million in the United Kingdom. The 1979 purchase of the Pennsylvania Glen-Gery Corporation increased the company's U.S. total to 500 million bricks a year and gave Ibstock approximately five percent of the U.S. facing brick market.

It quickly became apparent, however, that Ibstock's proud new empire was built on shaky foundations. Profits dwindled in Holland, evaporated in Belgium, and proved increasingly precarious in America. As Ibstock's chairman at the time, Paul Hyde-Thomson, later candidly explained: "In the U.K. we were doing well but the rest looked appalling, with Holland still hemorrhaging and the U.S. in a mess. ... We did not have sufficient resources and, on top of everything, the market collapsed on us. I had made a mess of it. We had been too bold in purchasing more capacity than we had in the U.K."

### Restructuring and Renewed Focus in the 1980s

Ibstock sold its Belgian operations in 1980, but conditions continued to worsen in the company's other markets. Faced with falling demand and stiff competition in the United States, Ibstock offset cost increases by charging higher prices to customers and carrying on with production as normal, stockpiling its unsold excess. This strategy was completely at odds with

**Key Dates:**

**1825:** Ibstock is founded in 1825.
**1899:** Company is incorporated as a private limited company and is named Ibstock Collieries Limited.
**1935:** Company is renamed Ibstock Brick & Tile Company Ltd.
**1963:** Ibstock offers company shares to the public.
**1970:** Ibstock merges with Johnsen, Jorgensen & Wettre Ltd. and becomes Ibstock Johnsen Ltd.
**1999:** CRH plc acquires Ibstock.

initiatives put into practice by Ibstock's American rivals, who drastically reduced prices and closed unneeded capacity. Ibstock's strategy only exacerbated an already grave situation. At the same time, sales levels in Holland were also dropping severely amid fierce competition. In 1981 Ibstock showed a profit of only £175,000 on revenues of more than £60 million.

It was a boost to the company's morale, if not to its bottom line, that it won the Royal Society of Arts Presidential Award for Design Management in recognition of the high standard of its brickwork, its varied spectrum of products, its marketing successes, and its design advisory service. The honor did not alleviate the company's financial difficulties, however, and it came as little surprise to observers that Ibstock found itself vulnerable to a takeover bid. The would-be buyer was London Brick, then the leader in the U.K. brick industry. While many within Ibstock were in favor of the alliance, others were opposed, making the proposal divisive within the company. Matters were then complicated by the appearance of a second bidder, the building materials group Redland. Both offers were subject to approval by the Monopolies and Mergers Commission (MMC), and while that body deliberated, Ibstock acted.

The company managed to divest itself of its unprofitable Dutch operations. At the same time, the U.K. side of the business began to show improvement, and while activities in the United States were still problematic, there was reason to believe the market might recover in the future. In short, Ibstock redeemed its flagging fortunes so far that by the time the MMC approved an alliance with London Brick (Redland had earlier withdrawn its offer), the larger company had to increase its bid from the £27 million it had proffered in December 1982 to £51.7 million in August 1983. By then, however, Ibstock was in a far stronger position and felt confident that it could proceed independently: the bid was rejected.

Freed of its disappointing European operations and with the U.K. business reassuringly steady, Ibstock turned its attention to the United States, where it set about revitalizing its affairs through a new, streamlined management structure, a renewed emphasis on an active, aggressive sales force, and the creation of a more visible public profile. In pursuit of the latter goal Ibstock opened a brickwork design center in Baltimore, an idea taken from the company's similar, successful centers in the United Kingdom. A kind of brickwork multimedia resource headquarters, the center provided designers with information about new brick technology and design innovation via a refer-

ence library, design equipment, brick samples, conference and audio-visual facilities, and staff experts in architectural design and structural engineering. Ibstock offered technical seminars for designers and users of brick. The company soon opened other, similar centers in Washington, D.C., New York, and Philadelphia.

In the United Kingdom Ibstock was expanding again, building new design centers, commissioning new kilns, and widening its range of available facing bricks with the introduction of new colors, shapes, and textures. The activity paid off: by the end of 1984 total revenues, split evenly between the United States and the United Kingdom, were up by 25 percent to £110 million, representing the sale of 653 million bricks. Pre-tax profits, nearly double those of the year before, reached £12.4 million.

Encouraged, Ibstock returned to a policy of expansion. Its U.S. subsidiary Glen-Gery acquired Hanley Brick, New Jersey Shale, and Midland Brick, diversified into clay paver products with the purchase of Capital Concrete Pipe Company, and moved further into concrete products with the acquisition of Kerr Concrete Pipe Company and Gomoljak, a concrete block and masonry distribution company. By the end of the 1980s, Ibstock's American operation was the fourth-largest brick producer in the United States and accounted for approximately 20 percent of the company's profits.

### New Challenges in the Early 1990s

From the relative triumph of the late 1980s, Ibstock moved to losses in the early 1990s; the company was £27.6 million in the red in 1992 and £18.7 million in 1993. Much of the losses was ascribed to reorganization costs and plant closures, particularly of the troubled Portuguese arm of the wood pulp business, Companhia de Celulose do Caima. The company began to divest itself of the wood pulp division, which had once been so lucrative that it could finance the rest of the group's expenditures. As late as the end of the 1980s the division was bringing in 30 percent of the group's profits, but by 1995 Ibstock had dropped "Johnsen" from its name and announced its intention to dispose of its by then 56.3 percent interest in Caima because of the extremely cyclical nature of the woodpulp business.

In 1994 Ibstock was back in the black again, expanding both through the acquisition of Centurion Brick and Scottish Brick and through increased production. The following year the company secured a deal to purchase the brick business of Tarmac, a construction and building materials group. The move was expected to give Ibstock control of approximately 19 percent of the U.K. market and move its rank in the U.K. brick market up to second, behind Hanson plc, which possessed a 30 percent share of the market, and ahead of Redland plc, which held a share of about 17 percent. Ibstock agreed to pay £65.4 million for Tarmac's clay brick and paving stone operations.

During the first half of 1995, Ibstock's pre-tax profits soared to £14 million, a 222 percent increase over the £4.36 million reported for the same period of 1994. Despite such a strong performance, however, Ibstock warned that the second half of 1995 would not repeat the achievements of the first half—efforts to sell wood pulp operation Caima had been unsuccessful, and the housing market in the United Kingdom was in a state of decline, negatively impacting demand for Ibstock's products. The company made plans to cut back production and lay off some workers temporarily until demand increased.

### Significant Changes in the Late 1990s

In spring of 1996 Ibstock announced plans to acquire the brick operations of building materials company Redland for £160 million. The deal, which involved 17 brick factories, four stone products facilities, and clay reserves to last 35 years, had the potential to catapult Ibstock into the lead in the U.K. brick market, with a market share of about 35 percent and the capacity to produce 1.3 billion bricks annually. The company's market share was knocked down, however, by the Office of Fair Trading, which asked Ibstock to sell or close factories that produced four percent of the market demand, amounting to about eight factories, in order to avoid a referral to the Monopolies and Mergers Commission. Still, Ibstock was able to maintain a market share of about 31 percent, placing it on equal footing with Hanson.

Though Ibstock became a market leader with its purchase of Redland's brick facilities, the company continued to face difficult times. In 1996 the prices of wood pulp declined significantly, demand for brick was at an all-time low, and Ibstock still had not managed to sell its stake in the Portuguese operation Caima. For the first half of 1996, Ibstock's pre-tax profits fell 82 percent, to £2.4 million. For the full year, pre-tax profits fell from £26.1 million in 1995 to £8.2 million. The company's shaky financial situation was accompanied by shakeups in management; both CEO Ian Maclellan and Anthony Hopkins, head of subsidiary Ibstock Building Products, were let go in November 1996.

The housing market began to improve the following year, and Ibstock's 1997 profits increased from £8.3 million in 1996 to £23.5 million. The construction market had not completely recovered, however, and the market slowed during the second half of 1997. Ibstock's brick sales improved only 4 percent over 1996 sales. The company was helped by a strong performance by subsidiary Glen-Gery as well as by cost-cutting measures.

Ibstock's future as an independent company appeared to be in peril in 1998 as large portions of the company's shares traded hands. In October Austria-based Wienerberger Baustoffindustrie, the largest brick manufacturer in Europe, acquired a 29.8 percent interest in Ibstock, fueling speculation of a takeover attempt. Wienerberger purchased the shares from Brierley Investments of New Zealand, which had first acquired a five percent stake in Ibstock in 1994. The following year it had increased its interest to 20 percent, and in 1997 Brierley upped its stake twice, to 25.1 percent in March and to 29.9 percent in July.

Then a white knight entered the fray, and Wienerberger suffered a blow in December 1998 when Irish building materials company CRH plc, with support from Ibstock, bought a 50.7 percent interest in Ibstock for £165.5 million. With little chance of acquiring Ibstock, Wienerberger agreed to sell its 29.8 percent stake to CRH in January 1999. CRH completed its full acquisition of Ibstock—CRH's largest purchase in its history—in early 1999. During 1999 Ibstock's head office in London was closed, and operations were managed from its Lutterworth,

Leicestershire, office. Ibstock was combined with CRH's Forticrete concrete masonry and rooftile operations.

Ibstock wasted no time setting about strengthening operations after its integration with CRH. Ibstock sold Caima Ceramic e Servicos, its Portuguese ceramics operations, to Caima's managers at less than book value in early 1999. Ibstock had unsuccessfully searched for a buyer for the ceramics business for two years. Portuguese wood pulp arm Caima, which Ibstock had been attempting to sell since 1995, was finally sold in mid-1998. In July 1999 Ibstock expanded its brick-making capacity once again by buying the brick operations of Hepworth plc, a British heating and building products company, for £10.8 million.

Though Ibstock had been in business for more than 170 years by the end of the 20th century, it celebrated its official 100th birthday as Ibstock Building Products in late 1999. The company had weathered the storms of many decades and continued to prosper as one of the leaders of the U.K. brick market. Looking toward the future, Ibstock faced many new challenges and changes as a member of the CRH family. Ibstock was confident it could meet these challenges and planned to continue manufacturing quality products and remain at the top of the brick industry.

### Principal Subsidiaries

Glen-Gery Corp. (United States); Ibstock Building Products Ltd.

### Principal Competitors

Hanson Bricks Europe; Wienerberger Baustoffindustrie AG

### Further Reading

Buckley, Christine, "Ibstock Hit by Shake-Up and Low Prices," *Times of London,* March 21, 1997, p. 30.

Cassell, Michael, *Dig It, Burn It, Sell It! The Story of Ibstock Johnsen, 1825–1990,* London: Pencorp Books, 1990, 193 p.

"CRH Pleased with Ibstock Acquisition," *Birmingham Post,* September 1, 1999, p. 20.

"Ibstock Builds Brick Sales but Chairman Wants More," *Birmingham Post,* March 19, 1998, p. 34.

"Ibstock to Sell Its Stake in Portuguese Forestry Group," *Financial Times,* March 15, 1995.

McIntosh, Bill, "CRH Acquires a 50.7% Stake in Ibstock for Cash," *Wall Street Journal Europe,* December 22, 1998, p. 3.

Pangalos, Philip, "Ibstock to Buy Tarmac Brick for Pounds 65m," *Times of London,* May 13, 1995.

"Reduced £19m Loss at Ibstock Johnsen," *Financial Times,* April 20, 1994.

Stevenson, Tom, "Ibstock Builds on Bricks with Redland Deal," *Independent,* April 26, 1996, p. 17.

——, "Ibstock in Brick Talks with Tarmac," *Independent,* April 7, 1995, p. 32.

Winnifrith, Tom, "Double Blow Sends Ibstock into a Dive," *Evening Standard* (London), September 25, 1996.

Wood, Martin, "Wienerberger Left in Dark As Ibstock Agrees to Pounds 326m Takeover," *Birmingham Post,* December 22, 1998, p. 17.

—Robin DuBlanc
—updated by Mariko Fujinaka

# Ilitch Holdings Inc.

2211 Woodward Avenue
Detroit, Michigan 48201-3400
U.S.A.
Telephone: (313) 983-6000
Fax: (313) 983-6494

*Private Company*
*Incorporated:* 1999
*Employees:* 8,000 (est.)
*Sales:* $800 million (1999 est.)
*NAIC:* 551114 Corporate, Subsidiary, and Regional
Managing Offices; 722211 Limited-Service
Restaurants; 711211 Sports Teams and Clubs; 722310
Food Service Contractors

Ranked 284 on the *Forbes* list of largest private companies, Ilitch Holdings Inc. was created in 1999 to manage the business interests of Mike Ilitch, whose Detroit-based private holdings include: Little Caesar Enterprises, Inc., the pizza chain that remains the family's core business; the Detroit Red Wings hockey team; the Detroit Tigers baseball team; Olympia Entertainment, devoted to management and concessions at sports stadiums; and Olympia Development LLC, which focuses primarily on real estate interests in downtown Detroit.

### Ilitch Builds an Empire

Michael Ilitch, a Detroit native and aspiring baseball player, who played for a Tigers' farm team until injury forced him to retire, founded Little Ceasars in 1959 with $10,000 in capital. He and his wife, Marian, opened their first business one year after Frank and Dan Carney opened the first Pizza Hut. Ilitch, then 29, started the establishment as a take-out restaurant in a strip mall in a Detroit suburb. In a style unusual for the time, the Ilitches's restaurant had no tables; it was purely a pick-up operation. His wife is credited with creating the new business's name, according to a 1995 *Los Angeles Times* article. She recalled: ''We were just married, and he was my hero, my Caesar. But he hadn't accomplished anything yet, so he was my little Caesar.''

In the late 1950s, pizza was considered a fad, much like Hula Hoops and coonskin caps, and few in the business world saw much potential for growth beyond mom-and-pop operations. They were wrong. A few years after Ilitch created Little Caesar, another Detroit native, Tom Monaghan, founded Domino's Pizza. Each of the three future pizza magnates unknowingly carved out a unique share of the future market. Pizza Hut pioneered sit-down restaurants; Domino's was first with home delivery; and Little Caesar initiated carryout. In the future, Ilitch and Monaghan would become rivals on another stage as well.

The Ilitches were ahead of their time in discounting, anticipating the pizza price wars of later years, as they undercut the price of their mom-and-pop competitors by 50 cents. Two years after opening the first Little Caesar, where Marian ran the counter and kept the books while Michael made the pies, the Ilitches opened a second outlet. In 1962 they began to expand by selling franchises of Little Caesars throughout the Detroit metropolitan area. They opened 50 franchises in the next ten years and went on to experience explosive growth in the 1970s.

### The 1970s and ''Pizza! Pizza!''

An economic slump caused by the Arab oil embargo of 1973 sent more married women into the workforce. One result was that families had less time to cook meals and needed a cost-effective solution that would replace some home-cooked meals. The Ilitches, with seven children, knew how expensive it was to feed a family. Their offer of two pizzas for one price found a ready market. Because a carry-out pizza operation was about four percent cheaper than home delivery, Little Caesars could undercut delivery rivals, such as Domino's.

In 1976 the Ilitches turned to Madison Avenue to pitch their one-price concept. Cliff Freeman, already famous for his Wendy's ''Where's the Beef?'' ad campaign, created the ''Pizza! Pizza!'' concept, backed by the slogan, ''Two Great Pizzas! One Great Price! Always! Always!'' As a regional company, Little Caesars had only 200 outlets in 1981. At that point, the Ilitches took the business nationwide, and by 1984 they had 500 outlets, a figure that had doubled within two years. Michael, a high-school graduate, and Marian, whose education

## Key Dates:

**1959:** Michael and Marian Ilitch open the first Little Caesar pizza restaurant.
**1962:** The Ilitches establish Little Caesar as franchise.
**1986:** The number of Little Caesars outlets reaches 1,000.
**1982:** The company purchases the National Hockey League (NHL) Detroit Red Wings hockey team.
**1987:** The company purchases the historic Fox Theater in downtown Detroit and relocates Little Caesar headquarters to a building adjacent to the Fox.
**1992:** The company purchases Detroit Tigers baseball team.
**1997:** Red Wings win their first Stanley Cup in 42 years.
**1999:** Ilitch Holdings Inc. is formed.

stopped after one year at a junior college, were now extremely wealthy entrepreneurs.

Michael never forgot his love for sports. In the mid-1970s he formed a local pro softball team, called the Caesars, and recruited the best players in the country. Although he lost $500,000 in three years, his team won two American Slo-Pitch titles. Ilitch was so successful that the other team owners changed the rules to restrict the Caesars, precipitating a row that ended up in court. Ilitch also sponsored numerous other amateur hockey, bowling, and softball teams. He encouraged his store operators to follow his example.

When his beloved Tigers came up for sale in the early 1980s, Ilitch was eager to purchase the team, but was thwarted when his crosstown rival, Domino's Tom Monaghan, was given an exclusive bid and purchased the team for $53 million. Still avid to own a major professional sports team, Ilitch turned his attention to the local NHL hockey club, the Detroit Red Wings.

Once a proud and winning franchise, four-time Stanley Cup winners from 1948 to 1955, the Red Wings had hit bottom after a long, slow decline. Only once in the previous 13 seasons had the team made the playoffs, at a time when 16 of the league's 21 teams qualified. Despite the attraction of watching games in three-year-old Joe Louis Arena, Red Wings' games were poorly attended. The season ticket base was reported to be a paltry 2,500, and according to Michael Ilitch, Jr., the number was actually closer to 1,500. Moreover, the team was saddled with debt and bereft of talent.

Ilitch purchased the Detroit Red Wings in June 1982 for $11 million. He improved every aspect of the organization, not only investing money in the recruitment of players from all over the world, but also upgrading the arena. Although the team's record did not improve much, attendance soon reached record levels, helped in part by Ilitch's marketing efforts that included giving away free cars during games. Season ticket holders swelled to 16,000, and after the team reached the Stanley Cup semifinals in 1987 and 1988, the Red Wings had become one of the league's most valuable franchises. Ilitch was now also one of the most respected owners, legendary for treating his players like family, often giving out spontaneous bonuses for good play.

The Ilitches became heavily involved in real estate in the mid-1980s. Their first major purchase was the Fox, an ornate 1920s 5,000-seat movie theater, once a jewel in a downtown Detroit that had seen decades of decline. Countering a 30-year trend of businesses fleeing the city, the Ilitches moved their Little Caesar headquarters from the suburbs to a ten-story office building adjacent to the Fox. Elected officials, eager to spark downtown development, helped them with the deal. The city council approved $18 million in city funds for the project.

After the Ilitches spent millions of dollars in renovations, the Fox reopened in 1988, offering a mix of concerts, theater, family shows, and restored classic films, and was quite profitable within a year. By the end of the 1990s it trailed only Radio City Music Hall in sales receipts among large theaters. Also in 1988 the Ilitches purchased a sports management company, Olympic Arenas, to handle events not only for the Fox, but also for Detroit's Joe Louis Arena, Cobo Arena, and other entertainment venues. In partnership with other businesses, the Ilitches helped to open restaurants and clubs in the revitalized theater district. The Ilitches also purchased the Detroit Drive arena football team and the Red Wings' farm team in Adirondack, New York.

To help run their businesses, the Ilitches enlisted the help of their grown children. All seven worked for the family concerns in some capacity at some time, and five became company executives. Often business would be hashed out around the kitchen table. According to *Detroit Free Press* columnist Doron Levin, the Ilitches were "a famously private clan. No one but their bankers and accountants know the inner workings of their companies. Since stock in their enterprises isn't publicly held, the family has no obligation to disclose sales figures or how much money their companies are making—or losing."

In 1990, however, there was no talk about losing money. Little Caesars and another Detroit-based corporation, Kmart, struck a deal to create Little Caesar Pizza Stations in more than 400 Kmart stores. Nationwide, pizza sales were so strong that the National Restaurant Association predicted in 1991 that within a few years pizza would supplant hamburgers as America's leading fast food—and attempts by McDonald's and Burger King to break into the pizza business never panned out. Little Caesar boasted more then 4,000 outlets and sales that continued to rise. Its rival, Domino's, was at the same time experiencing a number of reversals. Founder Tom Monaghan had taken a two-year leave of absence in 1989, and his business suffered as a result. In 1988 Domino's systemwide sales were double that of Little Caesar, but by the end of 1993 Little Caesar, with revenues of $2.3 billion, surpassed Domino's to become the second-largest pizza chain in the country, trailing only Pizza Hut and its $4.2 billion in U.S. sales. Monaghan, forced to retrench, began to sell off assets—including the Detroit Tigers.

### *Making the Big Leagues in the 1990s*

Ilitch finally realized his dream of owning the major league baseball team for which he played in the minor leagues. He purchased the Tigers from Monaghan for $85 million in July 1992, then gave up day-to-day control of Little Caesar to devote more time to his sports teams. The result was back-to-back

Stanley Cups for the Red Wings, a new stadium for the Tigers, and costly neglect of the core pizza business.

After several frustrating seasons during which the team failed to live up to its potential, the Detroit Red Wings finally returned to its former glory. Ilitch hired the NHL's most successful coach, Scott Bowman, in 1993. By 1995 the Wings reached the Stanley Cup Finals, losing to New Jersey. Two years later the team won its first Stanley Cup in 42 years, sweeping the Philadelphia Flyers in four straight, then backed it up the next season with another sweep, this time over the Washington Capitals. By the end of the decade, under Ilitch's ownership, the Detroit Red Wings were worth $184 million, according to *Forbes* magazine.

The Tigers, on the other hand, regressed. After challenging for a division title in 1993, the club finished last in its division in 1994, and by 1996 posted the worst record in baseball. On another front, however, Ilitch succeeded, accomplishing something at which the previous owner had failed: building a new baseball stadium to replace the decaying, however venerable, Tiger Stadium.

Ilitch had to overcome both political and community obstacles to reach his goal. He began his push for a new stadium by pledging to spend $175 million of his own money. Years of currying favor with local politicians, as well as the good will he had earned by moving Little Caesars from the suburbs to the city, now paid off. The city council repealed an ordinance banning the use of city funds to build a new stadium, pushed through by activists who wanted to preserve and renovate Tiger Stadium. When the matter became a ballot initiative, Ilitch and his political allies won an overwhelming victory, garnering 86 percent of the vote. A later vote authorizing the county to finance the stadium by a 1-percent tax on taxicab fares and hotel rooms was also approved by voters, this time by 82 percent of the countywide vote, as Ilitch and his allies outspent their opponents by about $700,000 to $20,000. Michigan's Governor John Engler then provided $55 million to cover the cost of clearing the land and providing infrastructure.

Comerica Park opened for the 2000 season, and the value of the Tigers franchise increased by a dramatic 32 percent, to $200 million, according to *Forbes*. The play of the team, however, continued to disappoint the fans, and attendance suffered accordingly; it was not at the level that other teams in the major leagues enjoyed with new ballparks.

While Ilitch devoted his time to running the Red Wings and Tigers, as well as shepherding through the stadium deal, his pizza business began to deteriorate. With a recession in the early 1990s, the relationship between Little Caesar and its franchisees turned confrontational. Members of the Association of Little Caesar Franchisees were unhappy with the high cost of ingredients charged by Little Caesar's subsidiary, Blue Line Distributing. What ensued was a lingering lawsuit that alleged the company violated antitrust laws. Franchisees also complained that the corporate parent lacked foresight and planning, changing from one strategy to the next in an attempt to spur flat sales. When pizza sizes were enlarged by two inches in the chain's "Big! Big! Pizza" initiative, franchisees were only given two weeks notice of the change and encouraged to get rid of their 12-inch pans. Later the 12-inch size was brought back by popular demand, and many of the franchisees were caught short. Other failed marketing attempts included football-shaped pizzas that never caught on, and spaghetti, frozen and heated in the ovens, which some owners said they couldn't give away. Little Caesar's move into the delivery business in 1996 also proved problematic. Franchisees complained that they did not receive proper training and that the $1 delivery charge alienated many customers. The taste of Little Caesar's pizza, baked on a conveyor belt system, also came under criticism. *Consumer Reports* found it "low in flavor, and the cheese can be so chewy it's almost rubbery." Cost-cutting efforts then brought lower grade ingredients to the product, according to franchisees.

Advertising budgets were slashed as sales slipped. Rather than challenging Pizza Hut for supremacy in the market, Little Caesar fell behind Domino's in systemwide sales. By the end of the decade, the company found its number-three position strongly challenged by newcomer Papa John's, with its emphasis on quality ingredients. By 1997 Ilitch was forced to refocus his attention on his pizza business. He eliminated 27 corporate management positions, followed a year later by a 25-percent cut of the chain's headquarters staff. In 1999 he closed 400 poorly performing restaurants to either remodel with drive-thru windows or to relocate. Little Caesar Enterprises looked to expand its overseas operations, totaling about 250 outlets in 18 foreign markets, by announcing in late 1999 that it would open 400 restaurants in Japan by 2003 and hoped to complete an agreement for 300 new stores in Latin America. In April 2000 the company also announced a co-branding arrangement with the Subway sandwich chain and the opening of a test unit that would offer the full menu boards of both restaurants.

Getting on in years and suffering from heart problems, Ilitch, along with his wife, had to face the task of transferring assets to their heirs. In 1999 Ilitch Holdings, Inc. was formed, and two outside executives were brought in to run it: Richard Peters, a Penske Corp. executive was named CEO, and Jim Weissenborn, from National Mortgage Corp., was made CFO. They lasted only six months before resigning. In June 2000 it was announced that two of the Ilitch children, Denise and Chris, would share the newly created job of president. While they would oversee day-to-day operations, Michael and Marian Ilitch would continue to serve as chair and vice-chair and assist in running the family businesses.

More than family interests were at stake. "A big part of downtown Detroit's future depends on the fate of the Ilitch businesses," wrote *Detroit Free Press* columnist Doron Levin, who then elaborated: "Detroit can benefit greatly from a smooth transfer of power—or suffer from a misstep. The next generation has lots of tough issues before it, chief of which is what to do about the faltering Little Caesars pizza chain. While the Ilitches have substantial non-pizza interests, Little Caesars has served as the linchpin for the whole empire."

### Principal Subsidiaries

Little Caesars Enterprises, Inc.; Blue Line Distributing; Olympia Entertainment; Olympia Specialty Foods; Olympia Development LLC; Detroit Tigers, Inc.; Detroit Red Wings.

### *Principal Competitors*

Pizza Hut Inc.; Domino's Pizza, Inc.; Papa John's International, Inc.

### *Further Reading*

Benezra, Karen, "Caesars' Fall," *Brandweek,* January 26, 1998, pp. 21–25.

Berss, Marcia, "A Tale of Two Strategies," *Forbes,* November 8, 1993, p. 198.

Carlino, Bill, "75 Years: The Odyssey of Eating Out," *Nation's Restaurant News,* January 1994, p. 11.

Diamond, Dan, et al., *Total Hockey.* Kingston, N.Y.: Total Sports, 1998.

Gave, Keith, "The Owners: Perseverance Pays Off for Ilitches," *Detroit Free Press,* June 9, 1997.

Henderson, Tom, "Profile: Mike Ilitch, Owner, Little Caesars, Detroit Red Wings," *Detroit Free Press,* August 9, 1982.

Howard, Theresa, "Attention, Shoppers: Retail Giant Hails 'Caesars' as a Big Buy," *Nation's Restaurant News,* January 1998, pp. 94–96.

Kapner, Suzanne, "Fifty: Profiles of Power," *Nation's Restaurant News,* January 1995, p. 105.

Krupa, Gregg, "Tale of this Tiger in Motor City, a Committed Owner Wins out over Beloved Ballpark," *Boston Globe,* May 2, 1999, p. C1.

Lam, Tina, "Ilitches Gives Reins to Daughter, Son," *Detroit Free Press,* June 20, 2000.

Levin, Doron, "Ilitches, 2 Top Execs Sever Ties," *Detroit Free Press,* September 16, 1999.

——"Smooth Power Transfer Vital to Detroit," *Detroit Free Press,* June 20, 2000.

"Little Caesars to Open 400 Stores in Japan," *Wall Street Journal,* December 9, 1999, p. 1.

MacArthur, Kate, and Jean Halliday. "More Changes Ahead for Post-FCB Little Caesars," *Advertising Age,* June 2000.

McGraw, Bill, "Fox Captures Little Caesars," *Detroit Free Press,* July 8, 1987.

——"Ilitch's Local Success is Legendary," *Detroit Free Press,* 20 June 2000.

Nauss, Donald W., "Pizza's Humble Giant Reaches for a Bigger Slice," *Los Angeles Times,* September 3, 1995, p. D1.

Pepper, Jon, "The Big Cheese," *Detroit Free Press,* February 26, 1984.

Stodghill II, Ron, "A Tale of Pizza, Pride and Piety," *Time,* October 26, 1998, p. 66.

Templin, Neal, "New Pizza King Set to Swallow Detroit Tigers," *Wall Street Journal,* July 30, 1992, p. B1.

Thorn, John, et al., *Total Baseball,* Kingston, N.Y.: Total Sports, 1999.

Zuber, Amy, "Little Caesars Cuts Staff, Fires 100+ Workers," *Nation's Restaurant News,* October 5, 1998, p. 1,171.

——"'Sub' Contracted: Little Caesars, Subway Try 1-Unit Marriage," *Nation's Restaurant News,* April 10, 1998, p. 6.

—Edward Dinger

# International Brotherhood of Teamsters

25 Louisiana Avenue N.W.
Washington, D.C. 20001-2198
U.S.A.
Telephone: (202) 624-6800
Fax: (202) 624-6918
Web site: http://www.teamster.org

*Labor Union*
*Chartered:* 1903
*Members:* 1.5 million
*NAIC:* 81393 Labor Unions and Similar Labor
Organizations

The International Brotherhood of Teamsters (IBT) is the largest labor union in the United States. In 2000, it had some 1.5 million members in 568 local unions in the United States, Canada, and Puerto Rico. Teamsters members included truck drivers, hospital workers, farm workers, airline pilots and flight attendants, police officers, custodians, toll collectors, and school principals. The IBT organized new members and negotiated with individual employers, such as United Parcel Service, and with employer groups to determine members' working conditions, wages, and benefits, including health coverage, paid vacation, and pension plans.

## *Early Roots: 1898–1902*

At the turn of the century, people depended on horse-drawn wagons to move produce and goods locally. Teamsters, who drove the teams of horses, generally worked 12–18 hours a day, every day of the week for an average wage of $2.00 per day. Not only was their pay low, they were held responsible when the merchandise was damaged or lost or when the shipper did not pay.

Individual teamsters began forming local groups to improve their working conditions. In 1899, the Team Drivers International Union (TDIU), composed of several local unions in the Midwest, received a charter from the American Federation of Labor, which was a loose confederation of national unions. The Team Drivers

membership numbered 1,700. Under the charter, anyone who drove a team for someone else or who owned up to five teams of horses and had others working for them could be a member.

Soon, the teams owners took control of the union. The two groups—the employees and the owners—often had different concerns, as might be expected. The drivers who owned no teams felt their issues were not being addressed. Many of these members belonged to local unions in Chicago, and in 1902 the Chicago locals pulled out of the Team Drivers and founded their own organization, the Teamsters National Union (TNU).

Membership in this union was limited to non-owner teamsters, teamster helpers, and owners of no more than one team of horses. The TNU pushed for higher wages and shorter hours, issues that attracted non-owners, and in a few months its membership was larger than TDIU. Another difference was that for TNU, a teamster was a skilled craftsman, and the unskilled immigrants and farmworkers coming to the cities were not welcome in the union. Finally, according to Arthur A. Sloane's *Hoffa,* the Chicago-based TNU colluded with employers and was considered a criminal association.

## *A Merger: 1903–07*

Samuel P. Gompers, the head of the American Federation of Labor, urged the two unions to get back together, and in 1903, at Niagara Falls, New York, they merged to create the International Brotherhood of Teamsters (IBT). The issue of owners versus non-owners was settled with the merger: no one owning more than one team of horses could belong to the IBT. Former TDIU head Cornelius Shea, of Boston, was elected president.

Four years later, with the loss of a bloody strike against Montgomery Ward Company and charges of racketeering, Shea lost his reelection bid. The new president, Daniel J. Tobin, was also from Boston, and would lead the union for the next four and one-half decades.

## *From Horses to Trucks: 1907–30*

Tobin's early years focused on organizing the ''skilled'' drivers, particularly beer wagon drivers and those delivering bakery

## Company Perspectives:

*Building better lives. Together. That's what the International Brotherhood of Teamsters is all about. To make life better for Teamster members and their families—and for all working families—the Teamsters organize the unorganized, make workers' voices heard in the corridors of power, negotiate contracts that make the American dream a reality for millions, protect workers' health and safety, and fight to keep jobs in North America. Today's Teamsters are a community of workers, fueled by a contagious spirit that is equal part passion, commitment, creativity, solidarity, and strength. Collectively, we are dedicated to the ultimate tenet of the trade union movement—the commitment to enhance the lives of our members all across North America . . . and to win justice for working families.*

and confectionery goods. The union was successful in improving working conditions for its members—reducing hours of work, winning the right to overtime pay, and standardizing contracts—but big changes were occurring within the industry. Motor trucks were replacing horses, and in 1912 the first transcontinental freight delivery by truck occurred. That same year, IBT's membership reached 40,000, and Tobin urged the organization of truck drivers as well as those delivering by wagon.

IBT membership hit 60,000 in 1915, and in 1920 the union expanded by affiliating with the Canadian Trades and Labor Congress, Canada's national confederation of unions. That same year Tobin convinced the members to double the per capita dues paid to the national union by all the locals. The increase, from 15 cents to 30 cents, strengthened the organizing efforts and raised benefits paid to workers striking to win a contract. By 1930, membership had reached 105,000, even though the IBT continued to ignore the drivers making long-distance hauls between cities.

### Organizing Over-the-Road Truckers: 1933–37

The Depression left thousands of drivers out of work, and in 1933 Teamster membership had dropped to 75,000. But the militant leaders of the Teamsters local in Minneapolis were about to change the power of the union. These men, who favored Leon Trotsky over Franklin Roosevelt, were Ray Dunne, his brothers Miles and Grant, and Farrell Dobbs. In organizing the city drivers, they ignored the national union's focus on skilled workers and worked to get any group of drivers into the union. They organized the city coal yard workers, following a bitter strike, and then turned to over-the-road drivers.

Farrell Dobbs, in particular, saw the importance of long-distance trucking as it replaced railroads as the means for handling freight. Their strategy was simple: Teamster members at the Minneapolis truck terminals would not unload any trucks unless they were driven by Teamster members. Out-of-town owners had to allow their drivers to join the Teamsters and then negotiate with the union. The new drivers would then go on to organize the next terminal. The leap-frog organizing of truck terminals was not limited to the Midwest. David Beck, in

Seattle, used it to organize almost all of the long-haul drivers from Washington to southern California. In Beck's opinion, "anyone who sleeps in a bed with movable castors" qualified as a Teamster.

Dobbs and the Dunnes were not organizing truck drivers only. They recruited loading dock and other workers by permitting Teamster drivers to deliver to and pick up only from warehouses where the Teamsters represented the workers. Once they had those workers in the union, the local negotiated contracts that allowed them to accommodate union-made goods only, thus bringing in many factory workers. By 1937, the IBT membership had jumped to 277,000.

### New Teamster Structures: 1936–38

Structurally, Teamster locals were strong, autonomous, and independent. Traditionally, they organized, provided services to, and negotiated bargaining agreements for people who worked in a specific trade in a specific city, such as the bakery truck drivers in Des Moines or the laundry truck drivers in Portland. The union would bargain with the employer or employers in that city who hired their members. Joint Councils were established where there were three or more locals, to coordinate Teamster activities in the area, especially organizing, and to decide certain jurisdictional matters.

The over-the-road drivers who joined the Teamsters as a result of the work of Dobbs and Beck did not live and work in one place. Both leaders realized how important it was to develop a means to negotiate area-wide contracts to ensure consistency in wages and benefits. If that did not occur, the owners could easily move a terminal to an area where the negotiated wages were low.

Beck negotiated the first area-wide trucking agreement in 1936, covering over-the-road drivers in Washington, Oregon, Idaho, and Montana. In 1938, Beck also introduced a new structure to the union, a multistate "conference" divided into trade divisions to provide specialized organizing help to joint councils and local unions. This new administrative entity would help expand Teamster membership and also provide regional power bases outside the control of the IBT president.

In the Midwest, Dobbs formed the North Central District Drivers Council in 1937, made up of 70 locals representing most of the several hundred trucking workers in the 12 midwestern states. One of the men working with Dobbs was a young Teamster organizer from Detroit, James Riddle Hoffa.

To negotiate a master regional agreement, Dobbs concentrated on Chicago, since almost all truck routes in the Midwest went through there, and then took the terms of that contract to the rest of the region. Because most trucking employers would have to abide by the terms of the Chicago agreement, they wanted to participate, and they set up the Central States Employers Negotiating Committee. The regional agreement was signed in 1938, granting road drivers 2.75 cents per mile and 75 cents per hour for lost time. It also established a grievance committee and made membership in the Teamsters a condition of employment for all drivers.

## Key Dates:

**1899:** Team Drivers International Union (TDIU) is chartered by American Federation of Labor.
**1902:** Breakaway Teamsters National Union is formed.
**1903:** Rivals merge to create International Brotherhood of Teamsters (IBT).
**1907:** Daniel J. Tobin is elected president.
**1912:** Organizing efforts turn from horse-drawn freight to motor truck.
**1934:** Minneapolis Local begins organizing over-the-road, long-distance drivers.
**1952:** Dave Beck is elected president.
**1957:** James R. Hoffa is elected president; AFL-CIO expels Teamsters on corruption charges.
**1964:** Hoffa negotiates National Master Freight Agreement.
**1975:** Hoffa disappears.
**1989:** Teamsters accept government's consent decree to conduct direct election of officers.
**1992:** Ron Carey is elected president in union's first national election.
**1998:** James P. Hoffa is elected president.

### Changing Labor Scene: The 1930s

The labor scene changed significantly during the 1930s. New federal laws established minimum wages and maximum hours of work for each industry, provided protection against management interference or intimidation aimed at union activity and established legal sanction for collective bargaining, the framework for the minimum wage, a 40-hour week, and overtime. Workers in the same industry, no matter what their actual jobs were, joined "industrial" unions. This approach was to counter the "skilled" trades organizing of the Teamsters, building trades and other "craft" unions. In 1934, John L. Lewis, head of the United Mine Workers, along with auto workers, garment workers, steel workers, and others founded the Congress of Industrial Organizations (CIO).

Meanwhile, in 1935, Congress passed the Motor Carrier Act, making regulation of the trucking industry a responsibility of the federal government. At the time, there were some 3.7 million registered trucks on the road, and the industry had revenues of about $500 million. In 1938, the Interstate Commerce Commission adopted the Motor Carrier Safety provisions, establishing maximum hours of driving and minimum hours of rest between driving shifts.

### Increasing Membership: The 1940s

By the beginning of the 1940s, IBT membership had reached 456,000. The trucking industry was considered essential to the war effort, and after World War II the industry grew tremendously.

By 1947, gross operating revenues of the motor carriers had risen to $2.2 billion. The union's membership grew to 890,000, and the Teamsters expanded their organizing efforts. While continuing to organize truck drivers, especially in the non-union

South, the Teamsters also moved into the auto industry food processing, dairy, and vending industries. During the decade, membership doubled to one million members.

### Leadership Changes: The 1950s

In 1952, Dan Tobin retired after 45 years as president and was succeeded by David Beck. The following year, Beck moved IBT's headquarters from Indianapolis to Washington, D.C., erecting a huge marble building across the street from the U.S. Capitol. From there, the union, along with the automobile, concrete, and rubber industries supported plans for a national highway construction program. The result was the beginning of the modern interstate highway system, a $41 billion, 16-year project that would cement trucking's supremacy over the railroad for hauling freight.

In 1955, the American Federation of Labor and the Congress of Industrial Organizations merged to form the AFL-CIO. Meanwhile, various committees in Congress were holding hearings on labor racketeering, particularly within the Teamsters. Although the early investigations ended with no findings, in 1957, the U.S. Senate created a bipartisan, special Select Committee on Improper Activities in the Labor or Management Field. The committee was chaired by Senator John McClellan, a Democrat from Arkansas. Its chief council was Robert F. Kennedy, and its first target was David Beck for misuse of Teamster funds. Beck eventually went to jail for falsifying income tax returns.

James Hoffa succeeded Beck as president in 1957, despite pending federal trials for perjury and wiretapping, 34 new charges from the McClellan committee, and a suit in federal court for improper selection of convention delegates. Three months latter, the AFL-CIO expelled the Teamsters, its largest affiliate with 1.5 million members, for corrupt leadership. It did not charter a rival union, however.

In 1959, the Teamsters created DRIVE (Democrat, Republican, and Independent Voter Education), one of the first political action committees, to educate members, to get them to the polls, and to make political contributions to campaigns.

### Changes in the Trucking Industry and Organizing Public Employees: The 1960s

The next decade saw the continuing centralization and standardization of bargaining for truckers and increased organizing of public employees. By 1961, the trucking industry directly employed more than seven million people and its carriers available for public hire had gross revenues of $7.4 billion. But the railroads were fighting to take back more of the freight hauling and air freight competition was accelerating.

In 1964, Hoffa negotiated the first national bargaining agreement for the trucking industry, covering 400,000 intracity and over-the-road drivers employed by some 16,000 trucking companies. According to Arthur Sloan, Hoffa was a realist as a negotiator and followed "an ability-to-pay" approach, protecting the industry as well as his members. As technology and innovations such as sleeper cabs and piggybacking changed the industry, his objective was to minimize displacement and ensure that the workers shared in whatever productivity gains resulted.

That same year Hoffa was found guilty of jury tampering, conspiracy, and mail and wire fraud. After appeals, he went to federal prison in 1967, and general vice-president Frank Fitzsimmons assumed control in his absence. Meanwhile, public employees, especially those working for state and local governments, were becoming more militant. Sanitation workers, teachers, nurses, and other hospital workers joined unions and made the concept of public employee collective bargaining more acceptable. By the end of the 1960s, the Teamsters had several hundred thousand members in the public sector.

### Growing Dissent: The 1970s

Frank Fitzsimmons was elected general president of IBT in 1971, and by 1975, the year James Hoffa disappeared, the union numbered 2.2 million members. The new members included local police, airline pilots, office workers, dental mechanics, and farm workers.

But some members, especially the truckers, were not happy with the union leadership and its priorities, and various dissident groups appeared to challenge the leadership— Professional Drivers Council (PROD), Teamsters United Rank and File (TURF), and Teamsters for a Decent Contract (TDC). Grass roots organizations, the groups built bases in local unions, electing reformers to leadership positions with the hope of eventually influencing national issues. In 1976, the various groups came together to establish Teamsters for a Democratic Union (TDU).

### Government Oversight: The 1980s

The 1980s were a turbulent time for the Teamsters. Four men served as general president during the decade, the union rejoined the AFL-CIO and membership dropped as a result of deregulation of the trucking industry.

By 1989, membership was down to 1.5 million. In March that year, the Teamsters signed a consent decree with the U.S. Department of Justice. The agreement settled a suit charging the union had allowed organized crime to infiltrate and dominate the organization. It called for a court-appointed panel to oversee the union's internal affairs for the next three years. It also required that top officers be elected by direct, secret vote of the membership, a long-time TDU demand. The suit was the first use of the federal Racketeer Influenced and Corrupt Organizations Act (RICO) against a national union and was brought originally by the U.S. Attorney in New York (and later Mayor) Rudolph Giuliani.

### New Leadership: The 1990s

Charges against Teamster officials resulting from the government investigations gave a boost to the dissidents and led to victories at the local level, such as that of Ron Carey, president of a New York local and former UPS driver. With promises to clean up the union and backing from TDU, Carey and his slate won the first direct election in 1991 and he was re-elected in 1996, defeating an attorney, James P. Hoffa, son of the former Teamster leader.

In 1997, the government invalidated Carey's win due to election finance illegalities. Hoffa won the new election in 1998. After taking office, Hoffa surprised many observers by building coalitions with environmentalists and other progressive groups on trade and human rights issues. He established the Respect, Integrity, Strength and Ethics (RISE) program to fight internal corruption, a move to encourage the end of government oversight.

In 2000, Hoffa announced that he would run for a full term in 2001. Although he had yet to mobilize and involve the membership as desired by TDU or to deal with the remaining old guard leaders, his future, as that of any labor leader, would depend on his ability to get his members good contracts and to attract more members to the union.

### Further Reading

Brooks, Thomas R., *Toil and Trouble: A History of American Labor,* 2nd ed., New York: Dell Publishing Co., Inc., 1971.

Butterfield, Bruce, "Teamsters Avert Trial by Accepting Reforms," *Boston Globe,* March 14, 1989, p. 1.

Cooper, Mark, "Where's Hoffa Driving the Teamsters?," *Nation,* July 24, 2000, p. 11.

Fitch, Robert, "Revolution in the Teamsters," *Tikkun,* March 1993, p. 19.

Hartson, Merrill, "Union Dissidents Asking Labor Department Assistance," *Associated Press,* August 9, 1985.

"Hoffa Case: Teamsters in Spotlight Again," *U.S. News and World Report,* August 18, 1975, p. 13.

Larkin, Jim, "Teamsters: The Next Chapter," *Nation,* January 4, 1999, p. 17.

"Low Gear for Teamster Reform," *Business Week,* December 3, 1979, p. 121.

Nicholson, Tom, et al., "Taking on the Teamsters," *Newsweek,* January 8, 1979, p. 54.

"Obituary of Dave Beck," *Daily Telegraph,* December 29, 1993, p. 17.

Slaughter, Jane, "Teamsters Reform Movement Survives Carey's Debacle," *Monthly Review,* April 1998, p. 1.

Sloan, Arthur A., *Hoffa,* Cambridge, Mass.: The MIT Press, 1991.

"The Teamster Century," International Brotherhood of Teamsters, AFL-CIO, 1999.

Yancy, Matt, "Teamsters Dissidents Seek Changes in Election Rules," *Associated Press,* May 19, 1986.

——, "Teamsters Union Seeks to Return to the Fold," *Associated Press,* October 23, 1987.

—Ellen D. Wernick

# International Total Services, Inc.

1200 Crown Centre
5005 Rockside Road
Cleveland, Ohio 44131
U.S.A.
Telephone: (216) 642-4522
Toll Free: (800) 456-4487
Fax: (216) 642-9235
Web site: http://www.itsw.com

*Public Company*
*Incorporated:* 1978
*Employees:* 15,000
*Sales:* $214.6 million (2000)
*Stock Exchanges:* Over the Counter Bulletin Board
*Ticker Symbol:* ITSW.OB
*NAIC:* 561612 Security Guard and Patrol Services;
488119 Other Airport Operations; 488190 Other
Support Activities for Air Transportation; 561210
Facilities Support Services; 561720 Janitorial
Services

International Total Services, Inc. (ITS) provides the world's airports and other public facilities with security services, security equipment, and support staff. The company's Aviation Staffing Services division, which represents the largest part of the company's business, contracts with airports to provide staff for roles as skycaps, baggage handlers, maintenance workers, and security screeners. Through its Crown Technical Systems, Inc. subsidiary, ITS supplies the equipment—including metal detectors, screening equipment, security systems, and other high-tech equipment—to help ensure safety at airports, museums, banks, government agencies, and other public places. Finally, ITS provides commercial security staffing for offices, hospitals, shopping malls, sports arenas, museums, airports, and other facilities. ITS serves more than 330 locations in the United States, Guam, the Philippines, and central Europe.

## 1970s Origins

Robert Weitzel and Richard P. Starke were executives at ITT Services Industries, when a British concern bought that company and brought in a new management team of its own. Suddenly without jobs, the two men decided to strike out on their own and establish their own business in the service industry. Based in Cleveland, International Total Services (ITS) was founded in 1978 and by the end of its first year was reporting $10 million in revenues providing janitorial services and a variety of airline services, such as baggage handling and the pre-departure screening of passengers for security reasons.

Pre-departure security soon became the company's major focus, as airport safety concerns made headlines nationally and abroad. ITS's security operations were considerably enhanced by its 1980 acquisition of the pre-board screening operations of American Airlines. Before long, ITS was the largest such operation in the United States. The company continued to provide janitorial services as well, serving airports and other service-oriented businesses. By 1984, ITS was reporting $40 million in annual revenues and had acquired Andy Frain Services, Inc., which specialized in providing ticket-takers and ushers for events at entertainment arenas. ITS was thriving and looking to expand into new markets, such as general staffing services. However, its fortunes were about to be reversed.

## Challenges in the Mid-1980s

While details on the case were never publicized, a legal dispute in the mid-1980s nearly ruined ITS. According to a 1988 article in *Crain's Cleveland Business*, the litigation involved one of the company's minority shareholders and proved costly to ITS. Though ITS prevailed in the case, Weitzel said that it "quite frankly brought us to our knees." ITS filed for bankruptcy and emerged in 1987, with Weitzel as CEO, a smaller, more focused company, having sold the Andy Frain subsidiary, which management regarded as seasonal and unstable. Annual revenues had suffered during this difficult period and were estimated at $25 million in 1987.

215

## Company Perspectives:

*It takes a lot of work and cooperation to run an airport, and it takes a team of dedicated people to make that happen. ITS works behind the scenes to help passengers get to their destinations comfortably and safely.*

Hoping to make a strong comeback, ITS was forced to address internal issues, one of which was improving efficiency of its airport operations. An estimated 65 percent of the company's business at that time originated with the airlines, and there ITS sought to control costs and provide better service through new methods of employee scheduling and tracking. One difficulty with scheduling involved the unproductive hours employees endured (or enjoyed) when waiting to serve delayed flights. A new method was devised under which employees clocked in at a central location and were dispatched to specific locations for specific jobs on an as-needed basis. This procedure allowed the company to keep track of its work force, be flexible with flight changes, and provide special services, such as wheelchair assistance for the elderly and disabled, more promptly. Moreover, an identification card with bar coding helped ITS keep track of employees, who used the card to check in at the airport locations where they had been assigned to perform a service.

Also, as airport pre-departure security screening continued as the company's main focus, employee training became integral to improving customer satisfaction. By 1990 ITS was serving 65 airports with 2,500 pre-departure security personnel, for a total of 4,500 employees in service positions nationwide. The company sought to ensure that these employees had the best training possible and toward that end stepped up its programs for new hires. To emphasize the importance of airport security, ITS offered a $50,000 reward to any pre-boarding screener, whether an ITS employee or not, who foiled a terrorist act on a flight within the United States.

Given its success in airport security, ITS next sought to expand the segment to include commercial security staffing for government facilities, business offices, factories, hospitals, museums, and sports arenas. After two years, the new operating unit accounted for 9.7 percent of annual revenue in 1994.

Moreover, through its Crown Technical Systems (CTS) subsidiary, ITS began offering security equipment, including walk-through and hand-held metal detectors, and closed circuit television monitors. In 1992 CTS introduced a new security system at Houston Intercontinental Airport, where the company was contracted to provide staffing. To existing metal detectors and x-ray devices in Houston, ITS's High Efficiency Screening System (HESS) added video cameras and monitors, audio recorders, modular walls, and porticoes. Secondary metal detectors rescreened passengers when the first detector tripped an alarm, allowing for faster movement of passengers through the first check.

CTS's first major contract, and the largest of its kind in the industry at the time, involved its deal for supplying 132 metal detectors to the Canadian government's transportation department. Transport Canada contracted to purchase the metal detec-

tors for $609,000, a price that would include employee training for 28 major airport locations. Transport Canada compared the products of ten companies and reported that Crown Technical Services had scored the best for price, performance, and maintenance. More good publicity came when the U.S. Secret Service began using Crown's metal detectors and recommended them to the Democratic National Committee for use at their 1996 national convention.

Also during this time, however, ITS began experiencing some bad press as well. After security breaches at several airports at which ITS was under contract, customers and the public began questioning the professionalism of ITS. In truth, personnel for airport pre-departure screening were difficult to hire; wages were low and turnover high. As a result, ITS lost some contracts for security at airports in Los Angeles, San Francisco, Ontario, Phoenix, Minneapolis, Detroit, and Boston. The company continued to serve these airports in other capacities, however, including some forms of pre-departure screening. To help improve the company's relationship with the airlines, ITS hired James O. Singer, formerly with American Airlines and an aviation industry consultant, as president and COO.

The company also expanded its business by purchasing service companies and contracts. In spring 1997, for example, ITS acquired contracts and goodwill from Intex Aviation Services, Inc. of Greenville, South Carolina, for $4.8 million. The contracts covered 30 locations nationwide and involved baggage handling, ground support, aircraft appearance, and aircraft lavatory cleaning services.

By the end of 1996 ITS provided pre-departure screening services to over 120 airports in 38 states for more than 60 domestic and international airlines. The company employed more than 4,400 pre-departure screeners, and approximately 50 percent of the company's revenues originated from this service. In Asian and European airports, where concern over terrorist activity was stronger than in the United States, ITS also provided document verification agents and passenger profiling services. Ramp and ground handling services accounted for over 14 percent of revenues, while passenger services, such as curbside skycap check-in, wheelchair assistance, and assistance with passenger problems accounted for approximately 20 percent of revenues. Commercial security comprised 11.7 percent of total revenues in 1996.

### Going Public in 1997

In 1997, ITS management decided to take the company public, selling over 2.8 million shares (about 45 percent of its total shares) on the NASDAQ exchange at $11.25 per share. The offering raised approximately $30 million, which the company used to pay down debt and fund further acquisitions. With the airport security market beginning to mature, and competition heating up, ITS set a goal of realizing $500 million in sales by the year 2000 through the expansion of service offerings.

In the six months that followed the stock offering, ITS doubled its revenues through several acquisitions. For $700,000 ITS acquired contracts from Curtis Security Systems, Inc. of San Francisco to provide commercial security services to 50 Fortune 500 companies in California, Nevada, and throughout the western

Key Dates:

**Key Dates:**

1978: Robert Weitzel and Richard Starke found ITS.
1980: Company acquires pre-departure screening operations from American Airlines.
1990: Company boasts pre-departure screening services at 65 airports.
1992: ITS enters business of commercial security staffing.
1997: Initial public offering of stock.
1999: Stock is delisted from NASDAQ after financial problems.
2000: New management team is hired in conjunction with organizational restructuring.

United States. ITS acquired aviation service contracts from ARC Security, Inc. of Atlanta for $9 million. Under the contracts ITS provided airline security, pre-departure screening, and aircraft appearance services for 12 major airlines in the south and east. Contracts purchased from ASI Inc. for $100,000 cash involved aircraft appearance and baggage handling services.

International expansion was a focus for ITS as well, and it made several acquisitions in England and Germany. Specifically, the company added to its service operations at London's three airports with the acquisition of White Lion Aviation Security Ltd. for $700,000. White Lion provided aviation security, baggage handling, and cargo delivery services, primarily at Stanstead Airport, a growing hub. The acquisition of Storehire UK Ltd. complemented existing services; that company provided secure, lockable storage units for commercial, professional, and personal use at Stanstead Airport. On the continent, ITS purchased OS Security Service GMBH, based in Frankfurt, Germany, for $300,000 cash. From its locations in Dusseldorf, Berlin, Hamburg, and Stuttgart the company provided aircraft guards, passenger profiling, and baggage and cargo screening services for eight major international airlines. ITS also initiated operations in Rome, under the name ITS Italia, which provided ground handling, supervisory, and administrative services.

The acquisitions continued the following year, when ITS purchased an aviation staffing service, Securex, Inc. of Tampa. Securex employed 1,200 people and provided staffing for commercial security, as well as skycap and aircraft cabin services in 30 Florida cities. The acquisition of contracts from Sky Valet, based in West Palm Beach, for $800,000 involved stations in South Carolina, Mississippi, Texas, Tennessee, Pennsylvania, and Massachusetts. ITS also acquired six contracts for $400,000 from Neptune Equipment and Facilities, Inc. which provided airport ground equipment maintenance, aircraft appearance, and janitorial services at Las Vegas International Airport and Denver International Airport.

ITS management created a new position, vice-president of marketing, to develop marketing programs in support of these acquisitions. Marketing concerns included developing brand name recognition and initiating a direct mail marketing program. In addition to sales and service skills, training for sales executives involved selling the company's services as a package. ITS planned to expand using existing infrastructure to offer a wider array of services. The resulting cost efficiency enabled ITS to offer airlines enhanced value on contracts which engaged the company for more than one service. ITS later created two operating divisions to improve cost efficiency related to selling integrated packages of aviations services. Charles P. Licata became president of Commercial Staffing Services, while Thomas M. Vaiden became president of Aviation Staffing Services.

At fiscal year end March 31, 1998, ITS reported $173.2 million in revenues and $5.7 million net income. Contracts with Delta Airlines comprised 26 percent of revenues, Continental Airlines contracts comprised 14.7 percent, and six other major airlines accounted for 57.3 percent of total revenues. During this time, ramp and ground handling services proved the fastest growing sector of the airline services business.

The company entered the market for high-level security personnel with the May 1998 acquisition of Gibraltar Protection, Inc. for $1.3 million. Rated one of the top security firms in Los Angeles and Orange Counties, the Torrance-based company provided commercial security for high rise office buildings, industrial facilities, and for executive protection. The company employed 350 people and generated $6 million in annual revenues in 1997. Other acquisitions involved Versatile Services, Inc., for $100,000, which provided skycap services in Hawaii. In June 1998 ITS acquired commercial security contracts from Security Coordinators, Inc., based in San Antonio.

### Financial Woes in the Late 1990s

Amidst this rash of acquisitions, in May 1998, ITS management announced that it had a banner fiscal year, with earnings of $5.7 million on sales that had increased 50 percent to $173.2 million. However, that June the company called for an outside audit of its books, which revealed lower earnings and eroding profit margins. The labor shortage had resulted in overtime wages and wage increases prior to contract renegotiation in order to attract and retain employees. Also, in an effort to discourage employee turnover, ITS had initiated an expensive employee health and medical benefits plan. Regardless of the reasons, Wall Street noticed the disappointing results, and ITS's stock value dropped to $6.31 per share, down from approximately $20 per share a month earlier and $24 per share in March. Interestingly, and for undisclosed reasons, over the course of the year two ITS executives left the company: vice-president of finance, Robert Schwartz, and president and chief financial officer, Singer. Such uncertainty in the leadership ranks was reflected in the declining stock price for ITS.

The following year, ITS moved to fill the leadership positions as well as to straighten out the financial morass left over from the year before. A payroll-related accounting problem was discovered during audits, and earnings again had to be restated, and again they were disappointing. In July 1999 NASDAQ moved to halt trading of the company's shares until ITS could answer some of the Exchange's questions regarding its finances. When ITS was unable to file a report as requested, NASDAQ debited the stock the following September. By November ITS traded on the over-the-counter Bulletin Board, at $1.13 per share.

In February 2000 ITS restated earnings from operations for 1997, 1998, and 1999 and hoped that the stock would be relisted. Changes in 1998's income involved a reduction from $5.2 million in profit, as reported after the previous audit, to $4.9 million. For 1999 the company had reported a net income of $1 million; the restated results showed a net loss of $7.3 million. At the time, the company's outside auditor questioned whether ITS could continue as a going concern.

Still, demand was for ITS services was high and management was cautiously optimistic. The company obtained a new executive management team which the board of directors hoped would reposition ITS for future profitability. After the retirement of Weitzel, Mark D. Thompson was named CEO, and in February 2000 ITS hired two new executive vice-presidents who, along with Thompson, had been instrumental in the turnaround of another company. Ronald P. Koegler managed financial reporting and tax functions, while Michael F. Sosh administered banking, insurance, cash management, accounts receivable and payable, payroll, information systems, and human resources functions. The new management team faced issues relating to high employee turnover and integration of the 25 acquisitions made by ITS since going public. Rather than continue to grow with acquisitions, the company sought to establish controls over finance and operations. In pursuing new business, ITS focused on opportunities with adequate profit margins. Potential areas of growth in airline services included passenger ticketing and cargo handling.

### Principal Subsidiaries

Crown Technical Systems, Inc.

### Principal Divisions

Aviation Staffing Services; Commercial Staffing Services.

### Principal Competitors

Borg-Warner Security Corporation; Burns International Services Corporation; International Aviation Security, Inc.; Globe Aviation Securities Corporation; Ogden Allied Support Services; Signature Flight Support Services; The Wackenhut Corporation.

### Further Reading

"$50,000 Reward Offered By ITS Airport Security Firm," *Business Wire*, August 21, 1990.

Bailey, Brandon, and Rodney Foo, "Suspected Gun Slips through Security at San Jose, Calif., Airport," *San Jose Mercury News*, April 1, 1997.

Beauprez, Jennifer, "ITS Amid Big Buying Spree," *Crain's Cleveland Business*, October 20, 1997, p. 1.

——, "ITS Asks Auditors to Re-Examine 4th-Quarter Books," *Crain's Cleveland Business*, June 29, 1998, p. 1.

——, "ITS Plans to Secure $30M in Public Sale," *Crain's Cleveland Business*, June 23, 1997, p. 1.

——, "ITS Silent on Latest Exec's Exit," *Crain's Cleveland Business*, November 9, 1998, p. 3.

Cook, Bob, "Heightened Safety Concerns Buoy ITS," *Crain's Cleveland Business*, August 12, 1996, p. 2.

"International Total Services Appoints New Management Team," *Business Wire*, February 10, 2000.

"International Total Services, Inc," *Going Public: The IPO Reporter*, July 14, 1997.

"International Total Services to Restate Past Three Fiscal Years." *Business Wire*, February 3, 2000, p. 1427.

Schwartz, Bonnie, "Role of Int'l Total Services is Servant of Service Firms," *Crain's Cleveland Business*, January 18, 1988, p. 14.

Serres, Christopher, "ITS Rushes to Answer NASDAQ Questions," *Crain's Cleveland Business*, July 5, 1999, p. 3.

Staklin, Jeff, "ITS Founder Yields Company Control; Weitzel Gives Voting Rights to New Trust," *Crain's Cleveland Business*, November 22, 1999, p. 3.

Winter, Ralph E., "International Total Services Expects Net In Fiscal Second Quarter to Miss Forecasts," *Wall Street Journal*, October 19, 1998, p. B15.

——, "International Total Services Plans Relisting on NASDAQ," *Wall Street Journal*, November 15, 1999.

—Mary Tradii

# The Jim Pattison Group

1055 West Hastings Street
Vancouver, British Columbia
V6E 2H2
Canada
Telephone: (604) 688-6764
Fax: (604) 687-2601
Web site: http://www.jimpattison.com

*Private Company*
*Incorporated:* 1961
*Employees:* 22,000
*Sales:* C$4.6 billion (2000)
*NAIC:* 551112 Offices of Other Holding Companies

The Jim Pattison Group is Canada's third-largest privately owned company, a multinational conglomerate with interests spanning a wide range of products and services, including grocery store chains, automobile dealerships, broadcasting and print media companies, packaging and signage operations, financial services, and other enterprises. The Vancouver-based company is owned by CEO and founder, Jim Pattison, who has directed every step of the company's growth, including impressive annual revenue increases from just over C$2 million in 1961 to over C$4 billion in 2000.

## Jimmy Pattison: Entrepreneur Extraordinaire

No history of the Jim Pattison Group is complete without discussion of its colorful, prominent, and controversial owner, President Jimmy Pattison. Pattison's influence on British Columbia has grown to such an extent that comedian Bob Hope once described British Columbia as a suburb of Jim Pattison. In a 1998 article for the *Financial Post,* Keith Damsell postulated: "It's virtually impossible to spend a Pattison-free day in the province."

Born in Saskatchewan, Pattison's family moved to British Columbia during the Great Depression. Pattison's entrepreneurial career began in 1935, when at age seven he sold seeds door to door. Other early jobs included bellhopping, washing cars, and delivering newspapers. On V-E Day in 1945, Pattison was called to work to deliver a special edition of *The Province* newspaper. Ever the entrepreneur, Pattison bought 100 copies himself and later sold them as souvenirs.

Later, while studying Commerce at the University of British Columbia, Pattison was distracted from his studies by his sideline of selling cars to his fellow students. Sensing a lucrative future in automotive sales, he dropped out of school a few courses short of his degree and went to work for a car dealership in Burnaby. Pattison's serious business activities began in 1961 with the purchase of the Burnaby dealership. By the turn of the 21st century, that little business would become a multinational empire covering several industries.

Pattison's business philosophy is said to be encapsulated by the tenet "no partner, no shareholders, no relatives." Analysts suggest that by keeping sole ownership of his ventures, Pattison is better able to keep his mistakes to himself and to maintain a long-term view of his enterprises. With a preference for moving quickly and acting independently, he has avoided the lure of the more rigid public market. Throughout Pattison's career, he has demonstrated a pattern of investing heavily in publicly traded companies, then buying out the shareholders.

Anecdotes about Pattison abound. One of the more widely told involved his unique tactic for motivating his sales force back in the days of his first car dealership. According to a *Business in Vancouver* special edition, "Business Leaders of the Century (1998)," the entrepreneur would simply fire the lowest achiever at the end of each month. Depending on the source, Pattison is either a ruthless business man or a "nice guy, devout Christian and family man." Those advocating the latter perspective point out that he has been generous to a fault, donating both time and money to good causes and public works. In the early 1980s, some even began to refer to Pattison as a pornographer, after he purchased a magazine distributorship called Mainland Magazines. Public outcry from the women's community erupted at the discovery that approximately 250 pornographic magazines were included among the thousands of publications that this company distributed to British Columbia retailers. Stating that the content could be distributed legally in British Columbia, but admitting to finding the magazines per-

---

## Company Perspectives:

*As we all know, things continue to keep changing faster than ever . . . and that's good for people like us . . . because with change comes opportunity—and that's what we really like. We as a company are focusing harder than ever in meeting our customers' ever-changing needs—and making sure that we are driving hard to lead the competitive market in every business we're in.*

---

sonally offensive, Pattison promised to sell the company. However, the sale did not go as quickly as the public had hoped. When it later became known that Pattison was negotiating to sell Mainland Magazines to a business associate, the outcry and personal attacks continued.

Pattison's pragmatic approach to business was also visible when a former CBC journalist, Russell Kelly, published a highly unflattering biography of Pattison. In a review of *Pattison: Portrait of a Capitalist Superstar* for the *Province* newspaper, Pamela Fayerman noted that the book "paints him as a greedy, porn-peddling hypocrite." After another book firm sold the first run of 6,000 copies very quickly, Pattison's Mainland Magazines decided to handle the book and took over its distribution. Pattison reported that he had not found time to read the book himself, adding that he left marketing decisions to his employees.

Regardless of its detractors, The Jim Pattison Group is among Canada's largest corporate donors, and one-tenth of the entrepreneur's personal income is directed to charities. Pattison is said to have slipped a C$1 million dollar check into the collection plate of the church he attended and also to have donated C$25 million to a private Christian school. In 1998, Pattison donated C$25 million to a New York Business Association to help clean up the area and also gave C$20 million to prostate cancer research. Moreover, the entrepreneur also became known for spending time and effort on good causes. In the 1980s, he accepted the position to chair Vancouver's World Trade Fair, Expo '86, for a fee of C$1 a year. At project's end, amid criticisms of his ruthless managerial style and well-publicized allegations of conflict of interest activities, Pattison brought the C$1.6 billion project in C$32 million under budget.

As Pattison and his family have learned, there is a price to be paid for public prominence. Shortly before Christmas, 1990, Pattison's adult daughter was kidnapped. Pattison paid a ransom of C$200,000 for his daughter's release. Shortly afterwards, eight kidnappers were arrested and convicted. Five years later, another man was charged for attempting to extort C$2 million from Pattison and of threatening death or bodily harm.

A person of many interests, including playing the trumpet and the organ, Pattison has also become notorious for his personal shopping sprees, which have included the purchase, for US$4.6 million, of Frank Sinatra's former home in Palm Springs, California, complete with furniture and Lionel model train collection. (The home was later designated for business use.) At an auction sale, Pattison bought John Lennon's psychedelic Rolls Royce for US$2.3 million. The Rolls was installed in

the British Pavilion at Expo '86 and later donated to the Royal British Columbia Museum in Victoria. Other purchases have included a US$1 million selection of Marilyn Monroe memorabilia, later included in the holdings of Pattison's Ripley's Believe It Or Not! entertainment and museum chain. The memorabilia included a traveling makeup case and color snapshots of Monroe's dog, Mafia.

However one views Pattison's approach to business, no one can deny the success of his enterprises. *Business in Vancouver* described Pattison as "The quintessential West Coast entrepreneur," concluding that, "At the end of the century, Pattison is easily the most recognized and influential business leader in the province."

### History of an Canadian Conglomerate

The roots of Jim Pattison Group stem back to the late 1950s when Pattison ran a car lot for a man named Dan McLean. In addition to setting sales records, Pattison convinced McLean to invest in the largest neon sign in North America. The sign proved significant, not only because it stood for almost 40 years, but also because it set the wheels in motion for what later was to become Pattison's Signage Group.

In 1960, Pattison was offered the chance to go in on a business deal with McLean's son-in-law. The deal would have made him a million almost immediately, but Pattison turned it down. Instead, he took out a C$40,000 loan against his mortgage and his insurance, and bought the troubled GM dealership he was working at, changing the company's name to Jim Pattison Lease. The bank loan was repaid within one month, and the dealership went on to become one of the largest in western Canada.

Pattison went on to acquire more companies in rapid order. First came the purchase of local radio station CJOR. Two years later, in 1967, he purchased Neon Products, the signmaker that had created the dealership's huge neon sign.

The entrepreneur began operating on a philosophy of ploughing most of what he earned back into the business, and he also believed strongly in diversification. As his success grew, and his acquisitions became larger, a personal style emerged that *Financial Post* writer Damsell described as "the creeping takeover." Under this method, Pattison took his time learning about a prospective takeover target, and gradually began buying shares in the company, before taking it over outright.

Not all of Pattison's investments were successful. In 1969, one of his holdings, a company called Neonex, unsuccessfully tried a takeover of Maple Leaf Mills Ltd. of Toronto. Pattison was almost bankrupted in the process. The Maple Leaf Mills takeover resulted in a series of lawsuits that took 13 years to settle. At the same time, Neonex incurred losses from a carpet company it had taken over. Neonex shares went from a high of C$45 to a low of 80 centers a share. Suddenly, Pattison was in financial trouble and his credibility had suffered considerable damage. When the entrepreneur rebuilt his fortune in the late 1970s, he took Neonex and another company, Great Pacific, private. Experts speculated that Pattison's experience with publicly held corporations had scarred him for life. A few other unsuccessful forays included involvement with the World

Hockey Association and bids for such sports teams as the Vancouver Canucks and the British Columbia Lions.

Nevertheless, Pattison persevered and continued to expand his company. In time, he acquired grocery store chains, fish canning plants, and aviation companies, and, by 1970, the foundation of the Pattison empire was in place. In one of his better-known deals of the time, the entrepreneur purchased the maker of Orange Crush soda and sold it within six months at a C$44 million profit. Pattison's holdings in 1970 were generating over C$100 million in annual revenues, and the company employed over 2,000.

By 1979, Pattison had 44 profit centers, and the Jim Pattison Group was Canada's 11th largest company. It was the only privately held firm among the top 500. In 1980, the company reported annual sales of C$500 million and employed a work force of some 6,000. During these boom years, before the recession of the early 1980s, according to *Vancouver Sun* writer Der Hoi-Yin, "Pattison had the incredible foresight to veer against the going takeover trend and instead liquidate the bottom 20 percent of his assets." These assets, an estimated C$140 million in cash and liquid money market instruments, would later be used for new acquisitions after the recession ended.

In the early 1980s, a recession in Canada let to cutbacks and layoffs. Concerned over a myriad of challenges, including high interest rates, government deficits, high unemployment, low productivity, and the potential for an international banking collapse of a third world nation, Pattison cut back on expenditures and acquisitions. Still, during this time Pattison agreed to chair the world trade fair, Expo '86, for the fee of C$1 a year. He somehow managed to look after his own interests and manage the Expo project as well.

In 1884, Pattison drew upon his cash reserves and began aggressively acquiring new holdings, perhaps the best know of which was Ripley International Ltd., operator of Ripley's Believe It or Not! museums. At an estimated cost of C$17 million, Pattison acquired 13 wholly owned museums in Canada, the United States, and Europe, real estate properties, royalties to a Believe It Or Not! board game that was then the number two

seller in the United States, license arrangements to Believe it Or Not! novelties, and comic strips that were running in approximately 300 newspapers. Also during this time, Pattison added the Jim Pattison Yacht Leasing division to his business empire. It was the only leasing program for boats in Canada.

In the early 1990s, the entrepreneur overhauled and revamped many of his companies. By way of setting an example, Pattison pledged to cut his costs at the head office by 25 percent. Cuts included staff layoffs, cancelled publication subscriptions, elimination of travel and hotel expense accounts, and even efforts to reduce telephone bills. "We have to get our costs down if we're going to continue to grow. We're cutting loose the non-performers and the businesses we don't think can make it in a borderless society," Pattison was quoted as saying.

The 1990s brought about many new acquisitions and new markets. In 1990 the Jim Pattison Group acquired the Foodservice Packaging Group and the Flexible Packaging Group, as well as Coroplast and Montebellow Packaging. In 1991, the Jim Pattison Trade Group was established, as was a new Financial Services Division. By the mid-1990s, the Jim Pattison Group was generating annual sales of C$3.3 billion. In 1994, Pattison was involved in restructuring the debt of the Westar Group and became the majority shareholder, as well as acquiring Westshore Terminals, a British Columbia-based coal-export terminal facility. The following year, the Pattison Group acquired Buy-Low Foods, and in 1997, Pattison started Select Media Services. In 1999, he acquired Cooper's Foods.

Throughout his career, Pattison continued to support a theory of streamlined management. In 1997, the corporate empire, with C$3.4 billion in sales and 17,000 employees, was run with fewer than ten executives. After buying control of the Westar Group, Pattison closed down the head office and reduced staff there to one person. *The Globe & Mail* reported, "When Mr. Pattison buys a company, its staff go into shock when they are presented with his management style, but workers who survive generally emerge as part of a healthier company."

Surviving employees were often well rewarded for years of good service. The late Bill Sleeman first met Pattison back in 1961 when he worked for the GM dealership that Pattison managed. Sleeman later joined the Pattison empire and eventually retired in 1990 after 21 years of service. The *North Shore News* reported that Pattison gave him a red Rolls Royce convertible, saying, "We gave that to him as a goodbye present. If there was anything better, we would have done that." In his role as vice-chairman of the Jim Pattison Group, Sleeman acquired more than 50 private companies for his employer. At the end of 1999, the Jim Pattison Group had 22,000 employees and sales of C$4.6 billion, and the company showed no signs of slowing down.

### Principal Subsidiaries

Jim Pattison Developments Ltd.; Canadian Fishing Co.; Merchant Media Ltd.; Ski Media Ltd.; Great Pacific Capital Corp.

### Principal Divisions

Jim Pattison Trade Group; Food Group; Sign Group; Out-Of-Home Media Group; Automotive Group; The News Group;

Communications/Entertainment; Broadcast Group; Financial Services; Flexible Packaging Group; Food Service Packaging Group; Specialty Packaging Group; Export Service.

### *Principal Operating Units*

Buy-Low Foods; Save-On Foods; Overwaitea Foods; Giant Foods; Associated Grocers; Shop N' Save; Kanaway Seafoods; Ripley Entertainment; Guinness Attractions; Louis Tussaud's Waxworks; Beautiful British Columbia; Genpak; Purity Packaging; Fibracan; Montebello Packaging; Coroplast; Westshore Terminals; Strout Plastics; Continental Extrusion; Progressive Packaging; CFJC-AM/CIFM-FM Radio; CFJC-TV; Jim Pattison Toyota; Jim Pattison Lease; Jim Pattison Chevrolet Oldsmobile; Gould Outdoor Advertising; Hook Outdoor Advertising; MétroBus; Seaboard Advertising; Neon Products; Claude Neon.

### *Principal Competitors*

Empire Company Ltd.; George Weston Ltd.; Canada Safeway Ltd.; Quebecor Inc.

### *Further Reading*

"The Billionaires," *Forbes Global,* July 5, 1999.

Damsell, Keith, "Deep Pockets, Broad Vision," *Financial Post,* February 2, 1993, p. 8.

Hoi-Yin, Der, "One Man's Chips Another's Comeback," *Vancouver Sun,* December 15, 1984.

"Jim Pattison: Quintessential Entrepreneur," *Business In Vancouver: Business Leaders of the Century,* 1998, pp. 98–99.

Kelly, Russell, *Pattison: Portrait of a Capitalist Superstar,* Vancouver: New Star Books, 1986.

Mackie, "Pattison Splurges on Monroe Memorabilia," *Vancouver Sun,* November 2, 1999, p. A4.

"Pattison Group Freezes Wages," *Globe & Mail,* March 17, 1982.

Schreiner, John, "The Private Style of Jim Pattison," *Financial Post,* May 22, 1997.

—June Campbell

# LaBranche & Co. Inc.

1 Exchange Plaza
New York, New York 10006-3006
U.S.A.
Telephone: (212) 425-1144
Fax: (212) 344-1469
Web site: http://www.labranche.com

*Public Company*
*Incorporated:* 1999
*Employees:* 264
*Sales:* $201.04 million (1999)
*Stock Exchanges:* New York
*Ticker Symbol:* LAB
*NAIC:* 52311 Investment Banking and Securities Dealing;
52312 Securities Brokerage; 551112 Offices of Other
Holding Companies; 52232 Financial Transactions
Processing, Reserve, and Clearing House Activities

LaBranche & Co. Inc., a holding company, is one of the oldest and largest specialist firms on the New York Stock Exchange (NYSE). As a specialist, or "broker's broker," it enjoys a monopoly on trading the securities of certain firms on the exchange. In return, it is obligated to act as a barrier in a rising market or a support in a falling market, using its own capital when necessary to minimize an actual or reasonably anticipated short-term imbalance between supply and demand in such securities. Formerly a private partnership, LaBranche became, in 1999, the first specialist firm to turn itself into a publicly owned corporation. It ranked first in trading volume and second in listings among Big Board specialist firms in July 2000.

### LaBranche & Co.: 1924–98

George Michel Lucien LaBranche was born in New York City in 1875 and went to work for a stockbroker in 1897. He became a member of the New York Curb Market (which later became the American Stock Exchange) in 1912 and purchased a seat on the New York Stock Exchange in 1917. Along with a son (also George M.L. LaBranche), who also bought a seat on the exchange, in 1923, he founded LaBranche & Co. LLC, a partnership, in 1924. The firm was a specialist in trading the securities of three listed companies at the time. It became a specialist in the stock of the American Telephone & Telegraph Co., one of the most heavily traded securities, in 1929.

LaBranche & Co. survived the Wall Street crash of 1929, although the *New York Times Index* for 1933 records that a George M.L. LaBranche was suspended from the New York Stock Exchange in October for two years on a charge of violating rules governing stock specialists. The elder LaBranche retired in 1946 and was succeeded as senior partner of the firm by his son. In 1973 LaBranche & Co. was a specialist for the stock issues of 28 companies, including AT&T, Atlantic Richfield Co., McDonnell Douglas Corp., and E.F. Hutton & Co.

As a private partnership and "broker's broker" (as opposed to a retail broker), LaBranche pursued its presumably profitable business outside of the public gaze. Like other firms in the field, it no longer faced any internal competition; in 1933 there were 466 stocks traded by more than one specialist, but by 1968 there were none at all. But the role of the specialist, according to some observers, was no longer necessary because floor traders frequently made transactions without their help, and outsiders such as mutual and pension funds, insurance companies, and bank trust departments were taking an increased share of their business to regional exchanges and over-the-counter dealers.

The sharp stock market decline of 1970 resulted in increased, although short-lived, scrutiny of specialist firms, which had three sources of revenue: broker's commissions, trading profits, and capital gains from long-term investment accounts (as distinct from trading accounts). A Securities and Exchange Commission (SEC) study that considered only the first two revenue sources estimated the gross return on capital for specialists at between 84 and 192 percent a year. These figures did not, however, take operating costs into consideration. In any case, the SEC left the New York Stock Exchange to deal with complaints against specialists; these grievances fell into two categories—practical matters of sufficient liquidity and ethical questions involving conflict of interest. Although the Big Board's governors rarely took a stock away from a specialist, they sometimes refrained from awarding lucrative, actively

## Company Perspectives:

*LaBranche remains committed to providing expert trading, unparalleled customer service and a forward-thinking vision that continues to define our business. We strive to provide consistently superior markets for the stocks that we trade so shareholders, whether individual or institutional, can be assured of getting the best price possible. We view the relationship with our listed companies as a partnership, in which we serve as their eyes, ears and agent on Wall Street and offer superior services to the executives who have their shareholders' best interests in mind.*

traded new stocks to specialists whose performance in handling market fluctuations had been deemed unsatisfactory.

### Going Public in 1999

By 1999 the volume of stock trading, both within and outside the New York Stock Exchange, had grown so great that numerous specialists had merged in order to pool the necessary capital needed to stay in business. There were only 29 specialist units left on the exchange at midyear, compared with 39 at the end of 1994. LaBranche & Co. ranked third, handling about 280 stocks listed on the Big Board, but it was first in dollar volume traded on the exchange. Among the stocks for which it was acting as specialist were 47 of Standard & Poor's 500 and five of the 30 comprising the Dow Jones Industrial Average— AT&T, Chevron Corp., Exxon Corp., Merck & Co., and Minnesota Mining & Manufacturing Co. In 1999 the stocks for which LaBranche acted as specialist accounted for 14.5 percent of the dollar volume of common stock traded on the exchange. In addition, with about 50 foreign listed companies, LaBranche was trading more American Depositary Receipts than any other specialist. Some 73 seats on the NYSE were controlled, financed, or leased by LaBranche.

LaBranche's revenue grew considerably during the bull market of the late 1990s, from $37.17 million in 1995 to $201.04 million in 1999. Its net income increased even more dramatically, from $1.13 million in 1995 to $29.03 million in 1999. The firm, which had been in fifth place among NYSE specialists at the end of 1995, handling 125 stocks, solidified its position in 1997 by acquiring a portion of the specialist operations of Stern Bros., LLC and the specialist Ernst, Homans, Ware & Keelips. In 1998 it added another specialist firm, Fowler, Roenau & Geary, LLC. These acquisitions added 131 new common stock listings. To acquire still more firms and to buy out, for $90 million, the 14.2 percent stake in LaBranche held by the Dutch specialist firm Van der Moolen Holding NV, the firm elected in 1999 to become the first New York Stock Exchange specialist to go public. This decision was not well received by LaBranche's rivals. "You've got this parochial industry that's used to holding its cards close to the vest," a source said to be well acquainted with the firm told Marcia Vickers of *Business Week*. "LaBranche has upset the gentleman's club."

When LaBranche & Co. issued its prospectus, the public learned how lucrative specialist operations could be. In 1998 the firm—including its recent acquisitions—had a pretax profit margin of 45 percent, compared with, for example, 25 percent for the financial services firm of Goldman Sachs & Co. and 12 percent for Merrill Lynch & Co., the world's largest brokerage. In 1998 LaBranche's 36 managing directors received $60.2 million in compensation—an average of $1.7 million each. George M.L. (Michael) LaBranche IV and the other 35 managing directors collectively owned about 70 percent of the firm. LaBranche, president, chairman, and chief executive officer, was also a governor of the New York Stock Exchange.

In transforming LaBranche from a partnership, the firm established LaBranche & Co. Inc. as a holding corporation with two subsidiaries. LaBranche & Co. became a limited partnership, with LaB Investing Co. L.L.C as the general partner of LaBranche & Co. The members of the latter agreed to exchange their interests in this partnership for 34.8 million shares of the holding corporation's common stock and $9 million in cash. The offering barred them from selling their stock for between three and five years. In August 1999 LaBranche sold another 10.5 million shares to the public at $14 a share. The price fell short of the $15 to $17 anticipated, however, and a million shares offered went unsold.

The cool response to LaBranche's offering was motivated in part by fears that its revenues and profits would slide sharply once the bull market came to an end. In 1999 the firm received 75.1 percent of its revenue from trading in specialist stocks and 18.5 percent from commissions. Unlike many other brokerage businesses, it was not engaged in investment banking, bond trading, or money management. "By having to support an orderly market, maintain inventory positions and refrain from trading under some favorable conditions," the prospectus noted, "we are subjected to a high degree of risk." The new holding company structure allowed LaBranche to incur $115.82 million in long-term debt as of the end of 1999, with interest on this sum to be paid each year.

### Foreseeing a More Competitive Future

Some observers believed that LaBranche and other specialist firms would become obsolete as investors turned to alternative trading systems. A number of electronic trading networks, such as Instinet and Island, had become serious competitors to the New York Stock Exchange itself as well as the NASDAQ market and regional exchanges. "The changes in financial services are coming faster than everybody anticipated," an investment analyst told Terzah Ewing of the *Wall Street Journal* during the summer of 1999. "Traditional investment banks, commercial banks and even exchanges have to adapt and adapt quickly because technology is reshaping the competitive landscape."

LaBranche & Co. was reported in early 2000 to be planning to expand its scope by beginning to trade in NASDAQ stocks before the end of the year and forming alliances with electronic communications networks. It also was said to be planning to increase its presence after trading hours on the Big Board and to be developing an e-platform to trade foreign stocks in the hours before markets opened in the United States. The company would then no longer be a New York Stock Exchange specialist but, according to Michael LaBranche, a "trading corporation" and "a market maker in different markets."

## Key Dates:

**1924·** LaBranche & Co. is founded by George M.L. LaBranche.

**1973:** LaBranche is the specialist for 28 New York Stock Exchange listings.

**1999:** LaBranche is the first NYSE specialist to become a public company.

**2000:** Two acquisitions expand LaBranche's number of stock listings to 413.

In March 2000, LaBranche & Co. acquired Henderson Brothers Holdings, Inc., owner of Henderson Brothers, Inc., a New York Stock Exchange specialist firm, for about $230 million in cash. This purchase included the company's clearing operations. Founded in 1861, Henderson Brothers became a NYSE specialist in 1948 and was the eighth largest at the end of 1999, with 113 listings. Its revenues came to $82.1 million that year. Also in March 2000, LaBranche acquired Webco Securities, Inc., another NYSE specialist firm, for 2.8 million shares of common stock, $10.9 million in cash, and $3 million in senior promissory notes. Founded in 1981, Webco had $13.7 million in revenue in 1999 and 34 stock listings at the end of the year. The acquisitions of Henderson Brothers and Webco Securities made LaBranche the specialist for 413 common stock listings, including 75 of the S&P 500 and seven of the 30 companies included in the Dow Jones Industrial Average. One year after the initial public offering, LaBranche's stock was trading at more than double the original price.

### Principal Subsidiaries

Henderson Brothers, Inc.; Henderson Brothers Futures Corporation; Henderson Brothers Holdings, Inc.; LaB Investing Co. L.L.C.; LaBranche & Co.

### Principal Competitors

Fleet Specialists, Inc.; Speer, Leeds & Kellogg; Wagner Stott Mercator L.L.C.

### Further Reading

Ewing, Terzah, "Not So Special: 'Specialist' IPO Fails to Impress," *Wall Street Journal,* August 20, 1999, pp. C1, C7.

Ip, Greg, "LaBranche IPO Shows Gilt Side of 'Specialists,'" *Wall Street Journal,* June 21, 1999, pp. C1, C2.

"LaBranche, George Michel Lucien," in *The National Cyclopedia,* Vol. 46, New York: James T. White & Co., 1963, p. 321.

"People and Business," *New York Times,* March 28, 1973, p. 75.

"Specialists Lose Their Old-Time Grip," *Business Week,* December 4, 1971, pp. 72–75.

Thomas, Dana L., "Throwing Out the Book?," *Barron's,* July 6, 1970, pp. 3, 8, 10, 12, 14.

Vickers, Marcia, "Getting Off the NYSE Floor," *Business Week,* February 7, 2000, pp. 80–81.

Willoughby, Jack, "Offerings in the Offing: Double Play," *Barron's,* June 28, 1999, p. 51.

—Robert Halasz

# Laura Ashley Holdings plc

**The Chambers, 3rd floor**
**Chelsea Harbor**
**London SW10OXF**
**United Kingdom**
**Telephone: 44-20-7880-5100**
**Fax: 44-20-7880-5200**
**Web site: http://www.lauraashley.com**

*Public Company*
*Incorporated:* 1954
*Employees:* 2,725
*Sales:* £276,264,900 ($400 million)(2000)
*Stock Exchanges:* London
*Ticker Symbol:* LARAY
*NAIC:* 6711 Holding Companies; 315232 Women's and
    Girls' Cut and Sew Blouse and Shirt Manufacturing;
    315233 Women's and Girls' Cut and Sew Dress
    Manufacturing; 315999 Other Apparel Accessories
    and Other Apparel Manufacturing; 32551 Paint and
    Coating Manufacturing

Laura Ashley Holdings plc is an international designer and retailer of clothing and home furnishings. Invariably described as ''quintessentially English,'' the Laura Ashley name conjures up images of pretty, romantic women and rooms draped in tasteful, gracious dresses and soft furnishings. To financial analysts and shareholders, however, the Laura Ashley name conjures up another, less pleasing image: that of a company that, strangely, seems unable to translate its popularity into profits. Laura Ashley markets a dream of English gentility and elegance, as well as countryside wholesomeness and purity, which can be purchased in the urban centers of Britain and around the world. According to the company's former marketing director, the typical Laura Ashley shopper is ''romantic, feminine . . . caring, environmentally aware . . . , family orientated, cultured, well-traveled and educated.'' Laura Ashley (North America) is 70 percent owned by Regent Carolina Corporation, which is 49 percent controlled by Malaysia United Industries. The other 30 percent is owned by management officials.

## *A Family Business Experiences Steady Growth: 1953–85*

''I trust my feelings implicitly in my work. I look at fabrics and I need to feel they've got life and animation; they've got to have character to work for me.'' Thus Laura Ashley's eponymous founder described the inspiration for her work. Laura and her husband Bernard started their business in 1953. Working from the kitchen table in their London home, the two used the hand silk screen method to print textiles. Laura designed small items such as linen napkins and tablemats, and Bernard's specialty was furnishing prints. Design inspiration came from many sources, particularly nature and 19th-century prints by artists such as William Morris.

So favorable was the initial reaction to the Ashleys' work that within a year they had formed a private limited company and hired more employees. Laura Ashley products were sold in London in the stores John Lewis, Heal's, and Liberty's, and almost from the beginning, were shipped to Paris, Amsterdam, the United States, and Australia. Operations continued to grow, and by 1957, when the first Laura Ashley showroom was opened in London's Burlington Street, domestic and overseas customers numbered about 500.

In 1961, the company introduced its first item of apparel—gardening overalls—and within five years clothing accounted for a significant proportion of Laura Ashley's revenues. Another, larger London showroom was opened in 1966, and two years later the first Laura Ashley shop debuted, in Pelham Street, Kensington, London. A year later, a second shop opened, in Fulham Road, London, and it became apparent that the company was moving from being a design-based business to become a retailer in its own right. From this juncture, the company grew very quickly, with profits recycled back into research, design, more factories, and a rapidly increasing number of Laura Ashley outlets.

Along with domestic expansion came overseas growth: the first foreign shop opened in Geneva in 1972, followed two years

## Key Dates:

**1953:** Laura Ashley and her husband Bernard start their business in their kitchen.
**1957:** The first Laura Ashley showroom opens in London's Burlington Street.
**1972:** Laura Ashley begins international operations.
**1985:** Laura Ashley dies weeks before the company's first stock flotation.
**1991:** Jim Maxmin becomes chief executive officer.
**1994:** Maxmin resigns.
**1995:** Ann Iverson becomes chief executive officer.
**1997:** The board dismisses Iverson and names David Hoare chief executive officer.
**1998:** The board appoints Victoria Egan chief executive officer and Michael Appel chief executive for its North American operations; the company sells Laura Ashley Japan; Malayan United Industries purchases 40 percent of Laura Ashley's stock.
**1999:** Ng Kwan Cheong becomes chief executive officer; MUI management purchases Laura Ashley North America.

later by stores in Paris, Dusseldorf, and San Francisco. Success followed success, and it seemed that the global appeal of Laura Ashley's pretty floral designs would result in a retail empire.

### The Move to Become an International Retail Chain: 1985–92

Then in 1985, with 30 years of steady, solid success to their credit, and every expectation that expansion would continue, Laura and Bernard Ashley decided to float the company on the stock market. Sadly, Laura died in an accident just weeks before the flotation. The validity of the somewhat melodramatic conclusion later reached by the *Sunday Times*—"with her death, the company lost its essence"—is arguable, but it is certainly true that the new plc was soon engulfed in severe difficulties.

The flotation itself was an undeniable triumph, with shares oversubscribed 34 times. Yet only five years later, in 1990, the company had plummeted sharply into the red and was at serious risk of a takeover bid. What had gone wrong? Part of the trouble arose from the general economic situation—many British companies suffered in the economic recession of the late 1980s—and part from the prevailing fashions of the times: Laura Ashley's trademark of graceful, floral, feminine apparel was at odds with the vogue for sharp-suited power dressing.

Probably much more damaging than the recession or contrary fashion trends, however, was what the *Independent on Sunday* understatedly labeled Laura Ashley's "rather naive management." Flush with success and plenty of capital after the flotation, Laura Ashley plunged into enthusiastic expansion. By 1987, the company was operating in 13 different countries but not operating all that well in most of them. The company's performance in the North American market was particularly troubled, bedeviled as it was by an unnecessarily complicated, top-heavy structure, excessive overhead and inventory costs, and an inadequate allocation and distribution system that was exacerbated by deficient communications methods.

Laura Ashley's management team appeared to have little control over a decentralized, haphazard, and inefficient corporate structure. Further, rather than reining back when it began to find itself in financial trouble, the company spent even more; borrowing reached unmanageable proportions, and profits first dwindled, then disappeared. Perhaps the *Economist* described it best: "For decades Laura Ashley made money by selling a vision of Englishness: flowing, flowery frocks and furnishing fabrics in polite, pastel tones. But it also came to indulge in a very English failing—mismanaging the transition from a successful family business to an international retail chain." In 1990, Laura Ashley posted a loss of £11.5 million and was saved only by the intervention of the Japanese retailer Aeon, whose welcome infusion of cash, in exchange for a 15 percent stake, bailed the company out.

### A Series of Management Teams: 1992–99

For 13 months during this crucial time, to the amazement of financial analysts, the company operated without a chief executive. Finally in 1991, an American manager, Jim Maxmin, was brought to the position. Maxmin, who later stated starkly that the company had been "heinously mismanaged," embarked on a program of cutbacks, reorganization, and realignment. Believing that Laura Ashley's real strength lay in its quality as a brand, rather than its status as a retailer, Maxmin sought to concentrate on the company's strengths—creating popular designs in clothing and furnishings—and to extricate it from those activities in which its record was less favorable. To this end, he contracted out most manufacturing and distribution operations. The latter was achieved via an alliance with Federal Express, in a move to reduce expensive inventories and improve stock movement (a perennial problem area for Laura Ashley, which had on one occasion shipped its winter stock to the United States two months late). Staffing levels were cut and managers were encouraged to take a more hands-on approach to retailing operations. They were required, for instance, to periodically visit shop floors and endure stints on the customer complaint line. Maxmin's strategies were successful, and Laura Ashley worked its way back to a slight profit in 1992–93 after several years of losses. Recovery continued steadily, though it was slowed by lingering difficulties in the American market.

It came as something of a surprise, then, when it was announced in 1994 that Maxmin was to leave the company after a boardroom "disagreement over investment levels." No further explanation was forthcoming, and no new chief executive was actively sought to replace Maxmin. He left with a compensation package of £1.8 million in a year when the company's entire profits totaled £3 million.

After Maxmin's departure, Laura Ashley continued its course of rationalization. Laura Ashley, commented *The Times*, still retained "an absurdly large infrastructure plagued with overmanning." Further jobs were cut, particularly in senior management and administration, in which employee numbers were slashed by a quarter. From 1990 to 1995 some 1,500 jobs were eliminated and six factories closed. "Non-core" products were axed from the Laura Ashley line, and renewed efforts were made to reduce overheads. The head offices in North America and Europe were pared down, bringing them under the jurisdiction of the U.K. head office. In the United States, the company closed down some stores and amalgamated others, and the firm began pulling out of Australia completely. The company also focused on improving its information systems to help alleviate the self-confessed "dysfunction and confusion which has inhibited our past development and held back profitability." Most significantly, Laura Ashley continued to concentrate on its strengths: creative design, a popular brand, a readily identifiable and appreciated image. Still, the company experienced losses in 1990, 1991, and 1992.

Laura Ashley remained an irony of British business. The quality and desirability of the product it sold were not—and never had been—in doubt. Promoted as a "lifestyle" brand, Laura Ashley scored consistently high in terms of customer recognition and appreciation. "Life," as Laura Ashley's lyrical annual report noted, "is often an assault on the mind." Laura Ashley aimed to soften the blow for its customers by offering products that are "unselfconsciously graceful and soothing" and evoke "a timeless mood of peace and serenity." Somehow, though, while Laura Ashley's creative philosophy might have been popular globally, the company's bottom line remained strangely depressing: on a 1994 turnover figure of £300 million, Laura Ashley's profits were a disappointing £3 million. By 1995, the company was in the red for £31 million.

In June 1995, the company once again determined to get on the right track when it hired Ann Iverson, who arrived from Mothercare, a company that she had successfully turned around. Iverson, who had also been the chief executive of Kay-Bee Toys in the United States, led the company into a four-year restructuring and recovery program aimed at trimming sales outlets in North America, curtailing operations in England and the Netherlands, and centralizing marketing and finance at its world headquarters. The company cut 200 jobs, half of them in Britain, 50 at its U.S. headquarters, and 50 at its European head office in the Netherlands. It simultaneously made its manufacturing operations into a stand-alone business.

Within ten months, Iverson had restored dividend payments for the first time since 1989. By 1996, the company was back in the black as Iverson announced an ambitious expansion program aimed at overhauling the company's image and changing its marketing strategy. Iverson closed 40 of the 200 outlets in the United States and in their place opened ten larger stores that sold home furnishings as well as women's and children's apparel. Laura Ashley introduced new designs that used new colors, softer fabrics, and lighter patterns.

Seven months later, the difficulty of transforming the group's fortunes hit home. Management had overestimated the strength of the brand in the United States and did not have the resources in place to back up the expansion with marketing and promotions. The stock ordered to fill the new, larger stores instead filled warehouses. The company froze its operating program in the United States while belatedly introducing a £2 million advertising campaign to support its expansion. Things worsened in May 1997 when the company's director of merchandise and finance director resigned a month after Laura Ashley warned that its 1998 profit would not meet expectations because supplies of unsold merchandise would force it to cut prices.

That same month, at the company's annual shareholder meeting, some were calling Iverson's management style into question. Despite her ability to articulate strategy in down-to-earth language, according to a 1997 *Financial Times* article, Britain's highest paid businesswoman had shocked colleagues by publicly chastising an employee and was preoccupied with details normally left to individual department managers. In addition, she had chosen an unorthodox recovery team that included a city analyst in charge of merchandising. Iverson herself recognized that problems were still afoot at the company at that meeting, when she announced amid news of a sales slowdown that, "We will get a few things wrong, but we will get many more things right."

By July 1997, however, shares of the company were at their lowest in more than six years and Iverson's design director also had resigned. The company hired outside consultants to help it "rediscover its distinctiveness" in August, while analysts were beginning to attribute the failure of Iverson's strategy to bad recruitment, bad merchandising, and over-aggressive expansion. The board of directors also hired David Hoare, a management consultant turned venture capitalist, as chief operating officer and assigned him the responsibility of day-to-day purchasing, distribution, and stock control. Hoare was described by colleagues as a man who erred on the side of caution. In November, the board, led by Sir Ashley, dismissed Iverson and named Hoare chief executive officer. In January 1998, it named a new chief executive for its North American operations, Michael Appel, a former merchandising director for Bloomingdale's, and posted losses of £25.5 million.

During Hoare's brief tenure as chief executive, he halted Iverson's aggressive expansion program and began plans to sell the company's four factories in Wales and one in the Netherlands. In March 1998, the company sold Laura Ashley Japan, which had continued to earn profits, to Jusco, while still maintaining a 27 percent share of the company. In April 1998, Malayan United Industries (MUI), which ran the Malaysia department store chain, Metrojaya Bhd, entered into an agreement to purchase 40 percent of Laura Ashley. In return for its purchase, MUI appointed four new board directors. Sir Bernard Ashley left the board, replaced by his son, in June 1998.

Victoria Egan, the former head of an MUI Group mall in the Philippines, took over as chief executive of Laura Ashley in August 1998. Under her administration, the company restructured, devolving much of its administration to three headquarters—one in Europe, one in North America, and a third in east Asia—and closed ten of the 30 larger North American stores. Egan's tenure was even briefer than Hoare's; in January 1999, she was replaced by Ng Kwan Cheong, an executive of MUI.

When the company's bankers threatened to end their financial support if Laura Ashley did not shed its North American operations, MUI stepped in again. This time, the company's North American management bought the 100 U.S.-based stores, headquarters, and warehouse for $1 and agreed to write off their $34.4 million debt in April 1999. Laura Ashley North America had lost $64 million in 1997 and 1998. The new Laura Ashley,

Inc., headquartered in Boston, began remodeling almost immediately to turn its large stores into intimate boutiques. As part of its strategy, the company began to beef up its brand-licensing program in home furnishings and planned to increase this category of products from 45 to 60 percent.

After disposing of its North American franchise, Laura Ashley Holdings raised £25 million in a rights issue that enabled it to eliminate its bank borrowings. Ng Kwan Cheong then led the company to restructure its product and price range and to carry out a study on customer expectations. Examining the company's supply chain, he expanded its number of suppliers. Looking at advertising, he branched out from promotional to brand advertising. By the end of 1999, Laura Ashley had posted a solid rise in sales and gross margins over the Christmas period. In 2000, the group expanded its home furnishings units in many of its stores and began plans to open additional stores in France and Germany and to develop an online shopping facility.

### Principal Subsidiaries

Laura Ashley Ltd.; Laura Ashley Investments Ltd.; Laura Ashley B.V. (Netherlands); Laura Ashley Manufacturing B.V. (Netherlands); Laura Ashley Distribution B.V. (Netherlands); Laura Ashley Investments B.V. (Netherlands); Laura Ashley Trading B.V. (Netherlands); Laura Ashley N.V. (Belgium); Laura Ashley Gmbh (Germany); Laura Ashley Gmbh (Austria); Laura Ashley Srl (Italy); Laura Ashley Espana S.A. (Spain); Laura Ashley Shops Ltd. (Ireland); Laura Ashley Shops Ltd. (Canada); Laura Ashley, Inc. (United States).

### Principal Competitors

Next plc; Oasis; Guccio Gucci SpA; Polo/Ralph Lauren Corporation; Chanel S.A.; Debenhams plc; Marks and Spencer plc.

### Further Reading

Abdullah, Saiful Azhar, "Turning Around Laura Ashley," *New Straits Times (Malaysia),* March 3, 2000, p. 27.
Bain, Sally, "Life Begins at 40 for Laura Ashley," *Marketing,* May 13, 1993, pp. 18–21.
Baharuddin, Zety Fazilah, "Laura Ashley Seen Profitable in Two Years," *Business Times (Malaysia),* June 19, 1999, p. 5.
"Chief's Design Out of Style at Laura Ashley," *Sunday Times,* April 17, 1994.
Gilchrist, Susan, "Followers Need Faith in Fashion of Laura Ashley," *London Times,* February 7, 1995, p. 27.
——, "Laura Ashley Cuts Jobs," *London Times,* February 7, 1995, p. 23.
Hollinger, Peggy, "UK Company News: Minimum Reasons Maximise Puzzle," *Financial Times,* April 15, 1994.
——, "Unflattering Figures Invite Questions About Style," *Financial Times (London),* May 31, 1997, p. 16.
"Knifework in the Shrubbery," *Economist,* April 16, 1994.
"Laura Ashley," *London Times,* February 7, 1995, p. 26.
"Laura Ashley Axe Falls on Managers," *Daily Telegraph,* February 7, 1995.
"Laura Ashley Draped in the Colour of Money," *Daily Telegraph,* June 8, 1994.
"Laura Ashley Fails to Bloom," *Independent,* September 23, 1994.
"Laura Ashley Follows the Same Old Pattern," *Independent on Sunday,* April 17, 1994.
*Laura Ashley: History,* Maidenhead, England: Laura Ashley Holdings plc, n.d.
"Laura Ashley Needs a Heavyweight," *Independent,* April 13, 1994.
"Laura Ashley on Course with Pounds 3m," *Daily Telegraph,* April 15, 1994.
Merrill, Ann, "Laura Ashley About to Open New Concept Store in Rosedale," *Star Tribune,* May 22, 1996, p. 1D.
"The New Pattern for Laura Ashley," *Sunday Express,* April 17, 1994.
"Out of Fashion," *London Times,* April 15, 1994.
Price, Christopher, "A Retailer Out of Fashion in the 1990s," *Financial Times,* August 20, 1997, p. 19.
"Shears Snip Away at Cumbersome Laura Ashley," *Guardian,* February 7, 1995.
"Signature Laura Ashley: Selling a Lifestyle," *HFN,* April 27, 1998, p. 12.
Snowdon, Ros, "Fashion Retailers Dress to Impress," *Marketing Week,* February 11, 1994, p. 24.
Stevens, Larry, "A Perfect Fit," *Bobbin,* November 1992, pp. 88–91.
"UK Company News: Further Cuts at Laura Ashley," *Financial Times,* February 7, 1995.

—Robin DuBlanc
—updated by Carrie Rothburd

# Logica plc

Stephenson House
75 Hampstead Road
London NW1 2PL
United Kingdom
Telephone: (20) 7637-9111
Fax: (20) 7468-7006
Web site: http://www.logica.com

*Public Company*
*Incorporated:* 1969
*Employees:* 8,115
*Sales:* £847.4 million (2000)
*Stock Exchanges:* London
*Ticker Symbol:* LOG
*NAIC:* 541511 Custom Computer Programming Services;
   541512 Computer Systems Design Services; 54169
   Other Scientific and Technical Consulting Services

London-based Logica plc provides information technology services, including management consulting, software development, systems integration, product innovation, and managed services, to clients around the world. Though Logica is involved with a number of industries, including energy and utilities, financial services, and industry and transport, the company has its strongest presence in the telecommunications sector. Growth through acquisitions and continued expansion are among Logica's focuses in the early part of the 21st century.

### Late 1960s: Entrepreneurial Beginnings

Logica was founded as a private company in London in 1969 by Len Taylor and Philip Hughes, who left their employment at Scicon, a subsidiary of British Petroleum, to start their own enterprise. Building their original team largely from other former employees of Scicon, Taylor and Hughes soon established the fledgling Logica as a company known for its technical excellence in computer services. The company's first big coup came in the 1970s, when it was awarded a contract to design S.W.I.F.T., a transference network for the international banking community. Thereafter Logica's growth was quick and consistent, and it built a portfolio of well-known and influential clients. Logica recognized the importance of an international approach from the beginning, establishing its first overseas subsidiary in 1973 in the Netherlands and quickly expanding into the rest of Europe, North America, and the Pacific Rim.

Logica had entered the computer services market at an ideal time, getting in on the ground floor of what was to become the phenomenal growth industry of information technology. Others saw the potential as well, and many similar firms were created at around the same time as Logica. Over the years, however, most of these rivals foundered or were absorbed into large, often foreign, companies, leaving Logica as one of the few, and certainly the dominant, independent U.K. computer services firms.

### Rough Times in the 1980s and Early 1990s

Since its flotation in 1983, Logica struggled with its bottom line, and the company's share price remained static for the next ten years. Logica's weakness was such that it was nearly scooped up by the American company Electronic Data Systems in 1985. The takeover was avoided, but conditions worsened in the late 1980s. An unwise acquisition in 1988 of the American banking and telecommunications company Data Architects, intended as a foothold in the American market, turned out instead to be what *Financial Times* bluntly termed a "financial black hole." This setback, combined with the recession that swept the United Kingdom and elsewhere, damaged Logica, and matters were not improved by the departure of the firm's two founders.

Perhaps Logica's most severe drawback, however, was its own mix of corporate strengths. Noted since its inception for its technical excellence, Logica was less well-endowed with business acumen. Financial commentators delighted in painting an amusing picture of Logica as a company populated by absent-minded computer nerds so immersed in the arcane joys of information technology that they neglected the "real world" of sound business principles and competitive spirit. In any case, it was an irrefutable and uncomfortable fact that Britain's largest independent computer services company, highly respected though it was, did not even figure in the European top 50 such companies.

**Company Perspectives:**

*People who work for Logica are people with a real flair for technology. People who aren't just fascinated by intellectual problems, but who strive to find solutions to help businesses perform better. From our beginning, Logica has broken technical barriers to help people and organizations make a quantum leap in what they can achieve.*

### Innovation and Growth in the Mid- to Late 1990s

In 1993 new chief executive Martin Read appeared, intent on what *Financial Times* described as "injecting a cool measure of market realism into Logica's technological hot-house culture." Read immediately set about dramatically realigning and restructuring the company. "Logica is 25 years old," commented Read, "and could be described as having a mid-life crisis." One high priority was to transform Logica into a truly international concern. Although Logica had operated in international markets for years, with subsidiaries and representative offices worldwide, each country's Logica functioned as a separate entity; Read aimed to convert this system to a seamless, global whole, whereby technical expertise and staff experience could be accessed as, where, and when needed.

Unusual for a company in the throes of restructuring, Logica did not shed staff, although management layers were simplified and administrative functions trimmed. (Indeed, the company maintained—as it had maintained, even throughout the recession—a substantial annual intake of recent graduates: one key, many believe, to Logica's continued position at the forefront of technological advancement.) In the new global Logica, staff could expect to be assigned to any country where their skills would be most useful.

Another of Read's first moves was to beef up Logica's sales and marketing team, a needed effort, as the *Sunday Times* commented: "Logica can be a difficult firm to identify. It does almost no advertising. . . ." The company was also thought to suffer from a lack of focus, which promoted a tendency to become involved in too many small or dead-end projects when it should have been considering each project as a stepping-stone to other opportunities. Logica had pursued a short-term consulting job or single installation project with enthusiasm equal to that with which it greeted, say, a several-year contract involving customized applications and complex systems integration. Under Read's direction, the company began to refocus its priorities—for example, axing its involvement with healthcare in Italy, but making a push into new geographical areas such as eastern Europe and the Middle East, where opportunities for future growth were likely to arise.

Part of the new plan involved a policy of strategic acquisitions, and Logica made its first significant purchases in a number of years. In 1994 alone the company acquired Precision Software Corp., a Virginia-based provider of commercial loans systems to prominent banks; the software division of Houston's Synercom Technology Inc.; and the Dutch company Fray Data International. The acquisitions were designed to further Logica's goal of widening its product offerings and consolidating its place in chosen geographical markets.

Logica's new strategies calculated to promote a happy marriage of Logica's traditional technological distinction with a new, sharpened business instinct, soon showed signs of paying off. In 1994 the company's pre-tax profits were up 50 percent. Activities in the United States, unprofitable for years, returned to a small but heartening profit. Operations in the United Kingdom and continental Europe showed continued improvement.

In the mid-1990s, the range of market sectors to which Logica lent its expertise was extremely diverse. The company prided itself on a cross-market, "multi-disciplined" approach, and over the years had built up specialties in several areas, most notably banking and finance, defense and civil governments, energy and utilities, telecommunications, space, transport, computing and electronics, and manufacturing.

Banking and finance traditionally provided Logica's largest market (generating 32 percent of revenues in 1994), with the company's experience in the sector extending back to its earliest years. Logica was much in demand for payment systems and network services, an area in which the company had excelled since the pioneer days of S.W.I.F.T. The company was also credited with the creation of CHAPS, the network for the United Kingdom's Clearing House Automated Payment System. Logica worked on trading and settlement systems for prominent international securities houses, clearing banks, fund and investment managers, and stock exchanges. Stock exchanges themselves were another area of expertise for the company, with Logica being called in to improve and streamline existing systems in London, Hong Kong, Switzerland, Norway, Denmark, Australia, and Italy, and involved in the development of new exchanges in Trinidad and Tobago, Hawaii, Kuala Lumpur, Chicago, and Kuwait.

Retail banking proved a busy and lucrative field for Logica; retail institutions had long been acutely aware of the advantages of increased automation but were not always sufficiently knowledgeable about information technology to implement the most effective system—or, crucially, to be able to integrate a new system with other systems in use. Logica completed some 300 projects harnessing information technology capabilities for retail banking use, including customer information, deposits, credit and debit cards, loans, and branch automation. Logica was also active in the financial sector in the areas of commercial loans and insurance.

Logica's work in the fields of defense and civil government ranged from fairly standard administrative and operational systems to specialized intelligence, weapon, and sensor systems. The company undertook projects in communications, data processing, pattern recognition, image and signal processing, computer simulations, machine intelligence, monitoring, and surveillance for its government clients, which included the United Kingdom, Australia, Belgium, the Netherlands, and the European Commission.

Logica also developed a specialty in energy and utilities. Many of the company's contracts in these fields arose from the needs of newly privatized companies in the United Kingdom and elsewhere, which recognized the need for improved efficiency in a more competitive environment. For clients in the oil, gas, electricity, and water industries, Logica worked to supply and install systems for better customer service, asset management, maintenance, materials, logistics, and assessment of environmental concerns.

Logica's expertise in the telecommunications sector, which began in the 1970s when the company developed the software for the first teletext system, grew steadily, and in the mid-1990s Logica offered services and products in broadcasting and video technology, digital image storage media, data communications, control systems, intelligent scheduling, and studio automation. Among the company's more ambitious projects was a long-term venture with Ameritech began in the early 1990s. Logica was charged with developing an interactive, multimedia information and entertainment service that would allow Ameritech's six million customers to access shopping, games, news, education, movies-on-demand, and travel arrangements through their television sets.

In the field of space exploration, Logica created sophisticated experimental space systems for such clients as the British National Space Centre and the European Space Agency. The company's commercial applications included satellite control centers to provide information about the weather, forecasts of crop yields, and earth observation programs.

In transportation, Logica was involved in projects relating to traffic control systems via air, road, rail, and water. Speedwing Logica, established jointly with British Airways in 1990, was a provider of applications software and services to the international air transport industry. In addition, Logica helped with a number of high-profile transport projects including the Channel Tunnel, the London Underground, the Dutch highway network, and Bologna's public transportation service.

Logica found natural clients in computer companies such as IBM, Digital, AT&T, Tandem, and Microsoft, developing systems and applications software for use with those companies' hardware systems. In industry, Logica's experience encompassed the manufacturing, pharmaceutical, and automotive markets. Here the company supplied help with business applications including customer service, streamlined procedures, and systems integration for business operations from stock ordering through to distribution.

To each sector it serviced, Logica offered expertise in three areas: consulting, software, and systems integration. Some 25 percent of the company's revenues derived from consulting. Logica enjoyed a solid reputation for its consulting work, the result not only of years of experience in the field of information

technology itself, but also of the company's thorough understanding of the business nature of the specialist sectors its served.

Detailed knowledge of its clients' particular business environments also aided Logica in providing software: many of the company's software applications, originally developed for a specific use by a particular customer, became available as generic packages which, depending on the individual case, could either by used as they came or modified to meet individual needs. Alternatively, Logica could supply products for entirely new applications, either developed in-house or by other computer companies.

Systems integration played an increasingly important role in Logica's business as clients, already possessing a computerized infrastructure, sought to make use of the latest technology to expand their automation. Logica's role was to harmonize new hardware, software products, systems applications, and developing technologies with existing capability, and serve as project manager for the whole operation.

Logica occupied a unique position as an independent computer services firm. Tied to no computer product vendor but conversant with the attributes of all, Logica was free to offer advice and aid in the implementation of the most suitable combination of hardware, software, and systems applications available.

Continuing research and development was obviously vital to maintain Logica's position in the forefront of information technology. The company's technology center in Cambridge, acting as consultant to the rest of Logica as well as directly to clients, fulfilled the allied functions of formulating new technologies and developing practical applications for these innovations. In 1994 the company's spending on research and development was £5.7 million.

Heading into the second half of the 1990s, Logica continued to concentrate on growth through acquisitions to position itself strategically as the dominant information services provider. In late 1996 Logica acquired Paris-based Axime Ingenierie, a software consulting firm, from parent Groupe Axime for about £18.4 million. Axime had a staff of about 1,000 and became Logica's biggest overseas subsidiary. The deal prepared Logica for the anticipated increase in computer systems spending in Europe as the information technology field continued its rapid growth.

In August 1997 Logica made another significant buy when it purchased Aldiscon, an Irish telecommunications software company, for about £57 million. Aldiscon provided network systems and services, including systems for mobile phones, to the telecommunications industry worldwide. A year later Logica purchased French information technology consultancy Delog Conseil for about £3.7 million. Delog catered to the financial services and insurance markets. A month later, in July 1998, Logica made two additional acquisitions. The company bought Belgian information technology consultancy Administra/CIM-Hardi. The company also provided systems development and enterprise resource planning (ERP) services and served multinational industrial customers. Logica's second acquisition in July was of the Quaestor product and development team. Based in Bangalore, India, the Quaestor team focused on the development of electronic retail banking solutions.

Continuing its flurry of acquisitions, Logica closed the 1998 year with four more purchases. In October Logica paid about $35 million for the Carnegie Group, a U.S.-based consultancy and designer of customized software systems primarily for the telecommunications sector. Carnegie Group's clients included US West and BellSouth. In December Logica acquired FCC Folprecht, a software and services company in the Czech Republic, for about £6.3 million. FCC Folprecht focused mostly on the utilities, finance, and industrial markets. Also in December Logica purchased Aethos Communication Systems, a provider of calling solutions for mobile operators, and DDV Group, a European telecommunications and new media consultancy. Logica paid about £47.6 million for Aethos and £15 million for DDV Group. During fiscal 2000, which ended June 30, Logica acquired consultancy Team 121 as well as the Dutch information technology project management firm Contigo.

In addition to growth through acquisitions, Logica focused on strengthening operations and building business through lucrative contracts. In the late 1990s Logica boosted its energy and utilities operation with several new contracts, including one with the New Electricity Trading Arrangements (NETA) in England and Wales worth more than £50 million. Logica was also awarded a two-year contract, worth about £60 million, with British gas utility company Transco, and a contract with utility company Electricité de France. In the United States, Logica secured a five-year contract to provide a Market Data Clearing-House (MDCH) service to support American Electric Power, which had operations in eleven states.

The rapidly growing telecommunications arena proved beneficial to Logica, and the company enjoyed a 69 percent growth in sales in its telecommunications division during fiscal 2000. Logica worked with more than 200 telecommunications companies in more than 60 countries at the end of the century and continued to offer innovative solutions and technologies to clients. The company, for instance, introduced a wireless Internet gateway designed to support mobile services. Logica won contracts with Cable & Wireless Communications in the United Kingdom and with Bahrain-based telecommunications operator Batelco, among others.

Fiscal 2000 marked the seventh consecutive year of record profits for Logica, and the company hoped to continue the streak. Logica's revenues of £847.4 million in fiscal 2000 marked a 28 percent increase over the previous year. Profits before tax reached £97.4 million, a 54 percent rise. Logica planned to continue its acquisitive strategy, which it demonstrated in October 2000 with the purchases of MITS, an Australian information technology services company focused primarily on the utilities market, and PDV Unternehmensberatung GmbH, a German information technology services firm.

As Logica ventured into the 21st century, the company remained confident in its ability to provide its customers with cutting-edge, technological solutions. With more than 90 offices in 24 countries and a work force numbering more than 8,000, Logica hoped to dominate the global information technology sector and solidify its leadership position in what was increasingly becoming a digital world.

### Principal Subsidiaries

Logica U.K. Limited; Logica Mobile Networks Limited; Logica Mobile Networks Inc. (U.S.A.); Logica SA (France); Logica S.a.r.l. (Luxembourg); Logica BV (Netherlands); Logica Consulting BV (Netherlands); Logica GmbH (Germany); Logica Consulting AG (Switzerland); Logica SA/NV (Belgium); Administra-Cim/Hardi SA (Belgium); Logica Svenska AB (Sweden); Logica s.r.o. (Czech Republic); Logica Inc. (U.S.A.); Logica Carnegie Group Inc. (U.S.A.); PT Logica Indonesia; Logica Pty Limited (Australia); Logica (Malaysia) Sdn Bhd (Malaysia); Logica Pte Limited (Singapore); Logica Limited (Hong Kong); Logica Synectics Private Limited (India); Team 121 Holdings Limited.

### Principal Competitors

Cap Gemini Ernst & Young; Misys plc; Sema Group plc.

### Further Reading

*About Logica,* London: Logica plc, 1994, 8 p.

''All Systems Go in Software,'' *Independent,* September 16, 1994.

''Bearbull,'' *Investors Chronicle,* June 17, 1994.

''Doing It the Logica Way,'' *Independent,* March 23, 1995.

Head, Beverley, ''After France, Logica Looks At Australian Takeover Targets,'' *Australian Financial Review,* December 9, 1996, p. 34.

''Kudos for Read as Logica Scales £7m,'' *Observer,* March 12, 1995.

''Logica Embraces Corporate Positivism,'' *Observer,* April 23, 1995.

''Logica Learns to Sell Itself,'' *Sunday Times,* April 3, 1994.

''Logica on a High Note,'' *Evening Standard,* July 15, 1994.

''Logica Profit Surges, but Stock Can't Keep Up,'' *Wall Street Journal Europe,* February 25, 1999, p. 7.

''Logica Revamp Costs £2m,'' *Independent,* March 11, 1994.

Mathieson, Clive, ''Logica Stretches Run of Profits,'' *Times of London,* September 7, 2000, p. 25.

Newman, Michael, ''Carnegie Group Bought for $35 Million,'' *Pittsburgh Post-Gazette,* October 2, 1998, p. D1.

O'Keeffe, Barry, ''Shareholder Windfall As Logica Buys out Aldiscon,'' *Irish Times,* August 1, 1997, p. 60.

''People: Mann's Long Stint at Logica Comes to an End,'' *Financial Times,* February 25, 1994.

''Shopping-Mad Logica Grabs £13.5m Profit,'' *Daily Mail,* September 16, 1994.

''UK Company News: Logica Advances to £13.5m,'' *Financial Times,* September 16, 1994.

''UK Company News: On Course against the Odds,'' *Financial Times,* May 31, 1994.

—Robin DuBlanc
—updated by Mariko Fujinaka

# Longview Fibre Company

**300 Fibre Way**
**Longview, Washington 98632**
**U.S.A.**
**Telephone: (360) 425-1550**
**Fax: (360) 575-5934**
**Web site: http://www.longviewfibre.com**

*Public Company*
*Incorporated:* 1927
*Employees:* 3,650
*Sales:* $774.3 million (1999)
*Stock Exchanges:* New York
*Ticker Symbol:* LFB
*NAIC:* 11311 Timber Tract Operations; 11331 Logging;
    321113 Sawmills; 321912 Cut Stock, Resawing
    Lumber, and Planing; 32211 Pulp Mills; 322121
    Paper (Except Newsprint) Mills; 32213 Paperboard
    Mills; 322211 Corrugated and Solid Fiber Box
    Manufacturing; 322224 Uncoated Paper and Multiwall
    Bag Manufacturing

Longview Fibre Company owns and operates a pulp and paper mill as well as 16 container and bag plants in 11 states. The company also manages a sawmill and owns more than 570,000 acres of timberlands in Oregon and Washington, which produce logs for sale. Longview Fibre's plants make a number of paper products, including corrugated shipping containers and merchandise bags, and its paper mill uses wood waste, wood chips, and sawdust to produce pulp to produce kraft paper and containerboard.

## Paper Products from Waste Wood: Late 1920s–30s

Longview Fibre Company was first conceived in the mind of Monroe Wertheimer of Thilmany Pulp and Paper Company, based in Wisconsin. Wertheimer had noted the waste wood being produced by a new sawmill overseen by the now defunct Long-Bell Lumber Company. The idea was to utilize that waste wood at a paper mill in Longview, Washington. The first concern was whether or not the wood produced by the Northwestern saw-mill—which came from Douglas fir trees—would make suitable paper. After experimenting in Wisconsin with wood shipped from Longview, Wertheimer collected a group of investors and launched the new paper mill. Elected as president was H.L. Wollenberg, formerly an oil company executive. Wertheimer's son, R.S. Wertheimer, became Longview Fibre's vice-president and resident manager. Wertheimers and Wollenbergs remain among the company's directors and corporate officers.

Longview's beginning sparked the company's tradition for utilizing waste wood fiber. Wood from the Douglas fir tree, a dominant species in the Northwest, was formerly wasted; it had been burned before Longview decided to utilize its wood chips in the production of kraft paper. The method was a cornerstone on which Longview Fibre was built, and it continued into the 1990s. Longview was also the first to utilize sawdust in the manufacture of paper.

Once arrangements were made with Long-Bell to provide a plant site, waste wood, steam, and electricity, all the newly formed Longview Fibre Company needed was a pulp mill and a containerboard machine, which were constructed within a year. When Longview Fibre first opened its doors in 1927, there was one containerboard machine and 300 committed employees. The company's goal was to produce high-quality paper products. The total output at that time was 100 tons per day.

A second paper machine was up and running by 1928. The following year, Longview acquired General Fibre Box Company, which had a large container plant in Springfield, Massachusetts. Despite the financial difficulties of the Great Depression, earnings throughout the 1930s were good enough for Longview to expand considerably. In 1933 a third paper machine was installed at the Longview mill. Also during the 1930s, the first electrostatic precipitators were installed in Longview's recovery furnaces to enhance air emission control. Longview's box plants were enlarged in 1934. Then a fourth paper machine was purchased, followed by the fifth machine in 1941. By 1948 a newly constructed container plant in Los Angeles began operations. Another newly built plant was opened in Oakland in 1950.

## Expansion and Growth: 1940s–60s

At the same time that the company was expanding its production capacities, it was acquiring timberlands. Its first purchase was in 1941, and through the years a number of acquisitions of small parcels of timberlands in Oregon and Washington grew into the 525,000 acres Longview owned by the early 1990s. The lands were purchased because the company recognized the importance of having its own timber supply. Timberlands provided the company with a wood supply for its own use in making paper if faced with an extreme wood fiber shortage, a condition that began to appear alongside of environmental pressures that surfaced in the late 1980s. The majority of Longview's timberlands were in Oregon. They were managed for timber harvest and the logs sold to independent solid-wood products manufacturers. Since 1951 the company has engaged in a full-scale, sustained-yield forest management program.

A sixth paper machine was installed at the Longview mill in 1951. Business was profitable enough for the Los Angeles and Oakland, California, plants to double their capacity in 1955 in an effort to keep pace with growth on the Pacific coast. Longview took a leading role around that time of converting wooden boxes—used for such things as transporting fruits and vegetables—to fiber or paperboard boxes. This conversion brought so much business to Longview that they built a new container plant in Seattle, Washington, in 1955. The following year a seventh paper machine was helping the Longview mill meet demands. Whenever a paper machine was added to the equipment fold, it required other additions as well, such as pulp machines and recovery equipment. These were all signs of growth.

Longview Fibre acquired Downing Box Company in 1960. Downing produced both corrugated and solid-fiber boxes and added four plants to the Longview fold. The plants were in Milwaukee, Wisconsin; Minneapolis, Minnesota; and Cedar Rapids, Iowa. That same year, the company started running its eighth paper machine. In 1961, the ninth was added. A new container plant near Minneapolis was constructed from scratch in 1963 in order to serve the Twin Cities area. In 1966 Longview Fiber acquired Waltham Bag Company, a producer of grocery bags out of a Massachusetts-based factory and owner of warehouses in other locations in the East. A tenth paper machine was put into operation that year, and another newly constructed container plant was completed in Amsterdam, New York, in 1967.

### Challenges and Restructuring: 1970s–80s

The industry was in flux during the 1970s. While sales dipped and energy costs soared, many companies concentrated on investing in updating existing equipment. Longview pursued the development of its profitable converted products business and continued its capital investment programs. During this time,

two more container operations were built, one in Yakima, Washington, and another in Twin Falls, Idaho. Another paper machine was added to the Longview mill in 1974. The economic slump of the late 1970s impacted Longview in much the same way that the economic downturn of the late 1980s would: depressed purchases—such as fewer appliance sales—meant fewer boxes sold. In addition, the housing slump hurt lumber sales.

In 1980 Longview suffered its worst earnings drop—a staggering 97 percent plunge after 53 years in business. Not only was the company suffering from the housing slump that was pummeling the entire lumber industry, but Longview was hit doubly hard because it was then buying wood chips from independent lumber mills in order to make paper. The independent mills were down because of the collapsed housing market; the price of wood chips more than doubled in a few months' time, from $60 per ton to $130. Fluctuations in the lumber business had always been balanced for Longview by its paper business, especially since most of its paper business was in grocery bags and containers, a fairly recession-proof market. With the severe crunch in the late 1970s and early 1980s, Longview was in a bind: it had to meet its paper commitments despite the pounding it would take on wood chip prices.

Another contributor to that year's dip in earnings was the Mt. St. Helens eruption; the resultant pollution obliged Longview to purchase a water clarifier it had not previously needed. This was added to $6 million worth of other unanticipated repair bills that year. Financially conservative like his father, Longview president Dick Wollenberg invested approximately $35 million back into the company's paper business. This included $5 million for two new chipping plants so Longview could reduce its dependency on outsiders. This would prevent a repeat of the painful month of April Longview had in 1980, when the company was forced to shut down its paper mill for two weeks because of a shortage of chips. The overall strategy was to focus more on high-margin items such as bleached papers and lighter-weight papers. Despite paper-making being a highly capital-intensive business, it had long been a profitable one for Longview Fibre.

Over the next two years, many modifications were made in Longview Fibre's paper machine, pulping, power, and recovery areas in order to save on energy costs and increase efficiency. This was part of the company's overall upgrading. Energy costs were substantial in an operation the size of Longview's. Still, the continuing recession rocked the industry. The price of 1,000 board-feet of logs dropped nearly 28 percent in 1982 from its high in 1979. By 1984 Longview's margins on logs was only 23 percent.

Longview continued its capital improvements agenda, investing close to $100 million in its pulp and paper mill and converting plants by 1987. This translated into gains in output and quality; reduction in energy costs; and improved product mix and mill utilization. Fourteen converting plants were at work making corrugated and solid-fiber shipping containers and paper bags in Washington, California, Idaho, Minnesota, Wisconsin, Illinois, Iowa, and Massachusetts, while Longview's primary paper grew to maximum capacity. Longview also acquired a site for a box plant in Spanish Fork, Utah, and closed down an unprofitable bag plant in Kansas City.

Prices rose on all four of Longview Fibre's product lines in 1987, as domestic and export markets revived. In 1986 about 40 percent of the company's timber production was sold in Japan, China, and Hong Kong. The company-owned 487,000 acres of tree farms looked well poised to profit from a decline in competition from Canada and the South, as well as from government-owned timber in the Northwest.

More expansion projects were announced in 1988, including a 12th paper machine to produce lightweight bag and specialty kraft paper grades and a new recycling plant to process old corrugated containers and new kraft clippings. Between 1983 and 1988, improvements had been made on every paper machine at the Longview mill, greatly increasing production rates. Other changes alongside the mill modernization program was Longview's handling of raw material. Whereas previously close to 90 percent of the company's materials arrived by rail, by 1989 truck dumps had been rebuilt to accommodate larger rigs, and 274 trucks, four barges, and 60 railcars were handled daily. Also in 1989, the company built a new used-box recycling plant. The used-box recycling plant, recognized as state-of-the-art in its field, reflected the growing public demand for recycled fibers, but was also built, according to Longview, because of reduced wood supply brought about by environmental pressures—particularly the issue of the northern spotted owl—in the timberlands.

### Ups and Downs in the 1990s

The northern spotted owl, threatened with extinction, had a native habitat in the Pacific Northwest. To protect the bird, restrictions were placed on harvesting and foresting within its habitat circles. That habitat encompassed private as well as public lands, and restrictions impacted the industry. A wood shortage due to reduced harvesting drove up the price of wood chips—they more than doubled between 1990 and 1993—in the Pacific Northwest, and owl protection restricted Longview's managing of its timberlands. Longview was still buying nearly half of its wood chip supply from independent saw mills in 1993, and as the major wood source for independent mills was federal forests, costs soared. The best use for timber was not to grind up entire trees for making paper, but to use the residual from trees cut for lumber.

The Pacific Northwest had been in the center of the spotted owl/ancient tree controversy and also the worldwide dioxin/water quality controversy, which came to a full boil in the early 1990s. While the world was overcutting forests from Scandinavia and Canada to Africa and South America, demand for tree products kept growing, particularly in foreign markets. The forest-rich Pacific Northwest became a prime base for export, which intensified the struggle for its preservation. Longview was considered the most conservative of loggers in the region; in fact, it was said to be the only lumber company in the region that could accelerate its timber harvesting. Profits in all product lines inched upward as the battles raged on. The spotted owl issue became a point of war between the lumber industry and environmentalists, and with the change of administration in 1993, the shift of focus in Washington, D.C., went from industry to environment.

Meanwhile, Longview Fibre's healthy cash flow brought about talk of leveraged takeovers and, by the spring of 1990, the Robert Bass Group owned 8 percent of Longview. Just over a quarter of the company was owned by officers, directors, descendants of the company's founding families, and employees. While log prices improved somewhat, prices for wood chips remained high and earnings low. Takeover rumors peaked, then calmed when the Bass Group lowered its stake in the company to less than five percent. In the summer of 1990, a strike was averted when pulp mill workers approved a new four-year contract that had been in dispute. That same year, the company's 12th paper machine started producing lightweight paper.

Fire weather caused some concern in 1992, when a long west coast drought threatened to limit log production. Nonetheless, Longview Fibre officials said demand and prices were strong in the log market. Prices for paper and paperboard products declined during that same time. While earnings improved by 93 percent in 1992, the mill production was still down due to lagging paper markets and industry over-capacity. In 1992 Longview Fibre started the first ever solid wood products mill; the central Washington mill utilized very small logs and included special equipment from Finland. The mill produced dimension lumber and timbers in both standard and metric sizes for markets at home and abroad. Meanwhile, Longview Fibre Company's main pulp and paper mill maintained a daily production capacity of 3,000 tons, in addition to three container divisions and bag plants.

Struggles continued in 1994, and the company's earnings fell 17 percent for fiscal 1994, dropping to $33.4 million from $40.3 million in 1993 and marking Longview Fibre's sixth consecutive year of poor results. Longview blamed unsatisfactory earnings on a weak market that forced the company to run at about 87 percent of capacity. Despite the problems, however, the company managed to have some bright spots—paperboard demand was on the rise, the paper market saw improvement, and the prices of corrugated boxes increased. In addition, Longview was in the midst of constructing a cogeneration plant for long-term energy supply and a corrugated sheet plant in Utah.

Longview Fibre refused to let poor market conditions take over operations, and to combat the fluctuations of the pulp and paper market, the company spent the mid-1990s searching for more stable alternatives. One option Longview explored was to offer more niche products, such as high-end, multicolored boxes designed to hold specialty items such as software or wine. Another new item offered by Longview was a new kind of extensible paper, called Tea-Kraft. Extensible paper was used to construct bags for holding products such as cement. Longview also planned to introduce pallets manufactured with corrugated material. The company also continued its effort to modernize its plants and equipment, which it began at the beginning of the decade.

In 1995, in the wake of restored trade relations with Vietnam, Longview exported 2,000 metric tons of kraft paper to Vietnam. The following year the company announced plans to expand its three plants in Utah. Longview's largest Utah plant, Spanish Fork, was expanded considerably, with more than 90,000 square feet added to the plant. This marked the fifth expansion effort of Spanish Fork since its construction in 1988. Longview's Cedar City plant was doubled in size, and its container distribution warehouse in Logan was also expanded, gaining a new design center to better assist customers with box design. In 1997 Longview began building a corrugated sheet plant in Grand Forks, North Dakota, to meet growing box demand in the North Central region. Also that year the company upgraded its printing and labeling equipment.

Despite efforts to improve operations, Longview continued to perform poorly. Though net earnings in fiscal 1995 improved an impressive 128 percent over fiscal 1994 earnings, the following year earnings declined 26 percent and revenues fell 17 percent. Longview's plants ran at about 82 percent of capacity in fiscal 1996, and the company suffered from declines in timber, paper and paperboard, and converting operations. In fiscal 1997 Longview reported a six percent drop in sales and a 77 percent decline in net earnings, falling from $56.4 million to $12.7 million, the lowest in a decade. Oversupply of containerboard was partly to blame, and Longview also felt the effects of the economic crisis in Asia—about 22 percent of the company's sales in 1997 came from Asia.

Longview felt confident that a recovery was forthcoming, and in early 1998 company officials cautiously indicated that a turnaround was imminent. Though the paper and paperboard and converting divisions suffered from declines in fiscal 1997, Longview's timber operations had operating profits of $101 million. Industry analysts agreed that Longview had most likely hit bottom in the winter of 1997–98 and that the company's outlook was more positive.

Unfortunately for Longview, the worst came in 1998, when it reported a net loss of $6.65 million on sales of $763.2 million, a drop of three percent compared to sales in 1997. Plants operated at 75 percent of capacity, and the Asian economic crisis created lower demand for containerboard, causing an oversupply of containerboard and thus lower prices. Longview discontinued manufacturing grocery and carry bags at its Spanish Fork plant because of poor results, and a lack of profitability forced the company to close its Rockford box plant in Illinois. In 1998 Longview Fibre announced plans to exit the grocery bag business to focus more attention on higher priced merchandise, such as color print bags, and handle shopping bags.

Longview began its long-awaited turnaround at the end of the decade. In fiscal 1999 it posted net earnings of $19.9 million on revenues of $774.3 million, and by the close of the fiscal year Longview's plants were running at 97 percent of capacity. The company's three divisions also fared better, with operating profits for timber operations increasing 12 percent, and operating losses in paper and paperboard falling from $13 million in fiscal 1998 to $4.1 million. Operating losses in the converted products division also fell, from $39.9 million in fiscal 1998 to $11.5 million the following year. Longview began construction of a corrugated sheet plant in Seward, Nebraska, to accommodate industrial and agricultural packaging demands in the region. In October of 2000 Longview began building a corrugated container plant in Bowling Green, Kentucky.

For the first nine months of fiscal 2000, Longview continued to show improvements. Sales reached $642,506, up from $547,342 for the first nine months of fiscal 1999, and net income increased 255 percent, from $7,975 in the first nine months of 1999 to $28,303 for the comparable period in 2000.

Still, the company struggled with a poor timber market, which affected profits in the timber division during the third quarter of 2000. Having been in business for more than 70 years, however, Longview had learned to weather the cyclical nature of the timber and paper markets. Longview Fibre remained confident and hopeful that it would survive and succeed well into the next millennium.

### Principal Subsidiaries

Longfibre Ltd.; Longtimber Company of Oregon.

### Principal Competitors

Boise Cascade Corporation; Smurfit-Stone Container Corporation; Weyerhaeuser Company.

### Further Reading

''Bass Group Cuts Stake in Longview,'' *New York Times,* November 2, 1990, p. D4.

''Box Plants Learn Ink is the Key Link,'' *Paperboard Packaging,* November 1986, p. 32.

Denne, Lorianne, ''Longview Fibre Gears Up For a Fight,'' *Puget Sound Business,* January 29, 1990, p. 14.

Drapeau, Jacques, ''Longview Fibre Lowers Steam Use by Reducing PV Air Temperatures,'' *Pulp & Paper,* September 1983, pp. 167–69.

Ducey, Michael, ''Longview Fibre Modernization Plan Shifts to Pulp Mill, Recovery Block,'' *Pulp & Paper,* July 1989, pp. 96–97.

Erb, George, ''Longview Fibre Takes Long View of Rebound; Worst Seems Over for Wood-Products Firm,'' *Puget Sound Business Journal,* January 23, 1998, p. 4.

——, ''Outlook Is Improving for Longview Fibre,'' *Puget Sound Business Journal,* January 21, 2000, p. 6.

Guide, Robert, ''Mill-Wide Process Changes Reduce Energy Use at Longview Fibre,'' *Pulp & Paper,* March 1982, pp. 114–16.

Harris, William, ''Catch-22,'' *Forbes,* September 14, 1981, p. 214.

''Long Longview,'' *Barron's,* December 10, 1990, p. 44.

''The Long View on Longview,'' *Forbes,* March 5, 1990, p. 176.

''Longview Expands in Utah,'' *Paperboard Packaging,* July 1996, p. 12.

''Longview Fibre Co.,'' *Business Journal-Portland,* July 30, 1990, p. S33.

''Longview Fibre Co.,'' *Insiders' Chronicle,* August 20, 1990, p. S37.

''Longview Fibre Co.,'' *Wall Street Journal,* August 20, 1992, p. B4.

Maturi, Richard, ''Logging Profits,'' *Barron's,* June 22, 1987, p. 56.

Shaw, Monica, ''Aggressive Strategy, Flexibility Boost Product Performance at Longview Fibre,'' *Pulp & Paper,* July 1, 1999, p. 42.

Shortt, Lee, ''Condensate Treatment Program at Longview Fibre Reduces Corrosion,'' *Pulp & Paper,* September 1986, p. 166.

Stepankowsky, Paula L., ''Longview Fibre Chief Sees Possible Signs of Improvement in 1999,'' *Dow Jones Business News,* December 23, 1998.

Stepankowsky, Paula L., ''Longview Fibre's Chief Is Uncertain Company Can Meet Analyst Estimates,'' *Wall Street Journal,* December 22, 1995.

Wilma, D.D., ''Press Rebuild Improves Mullen, Output of Linerboard Machines,'' *Pulp & Paper,* February 1982, pp. 57–58.

''Woodsman's Song,'' *Forbes,* April 6, 1987, p. 194.

—Carol I. Keeley
—updated by Mariko Fujinaka

# LTU Group Holding GmbH

**Flughafen, Halle 8**
**D-40474 Dusseldorf**
**Germany**
**Telephone: (49) (211) 9418-888**
**Fax: (49) (211) 9418-881**
**Web site: http://www.ltu.de**

*Private Company*
*Incorporated:* 1955 as Lufttransport-Union
*Employees:* 5,236
*Sales:* DM 3.97 billion ($2.02 billion) (1998–99)
*NAIC:* 481111 Scheduled Passenger Air Transportation;
481112 Scheduled Freight Air Transportation; 72111
Hotels (Except Casino Hotels) and Motels

LTU Group Holding GmbH is Germany's third-largest leisure travel tour operator and one of Europe's leading charter airlines, assisting over 2.25 million customers with their travel needs annually. Based in Germany, the group consists of the airline LTU Lufttransportunternehmen GmbH, the organized travel group LTU Touristik GmbH (LTT), the catering company LTC, and the hotel group LTI International Hotels. The LTU Group also includes the Swiss-based LTU Destination Management AG and several incoming-agencies in Spain, the Dominican Republic, Mexico, and Thailand. LTU Lufttransportunternehmen GmbH is Germany's third largest airline, with service from 12 airports in Germany, Salzburg, Austria, and Zurich, Switzerland, to over 70 destinations worldwide. LTI International Hotels owns 41 hotels in 13 countries with more than 22,700 beds. The catering company LTC, headquartered in Dusseldorf, with a subsidiary in Frankfurt/Main, provides over 22,000 meals daily to LTU and other airlines. The travel agency LTU Touristik oversees the operations of several travel agencies, including Meier's Weltreisen, Tjaerborg, Jahr Reisen, Marlboro, THR Tours, and smile&fly. Swiss SAir Group owns a 49.9 percent stake in the LTU Group.

## LTU Takes Off: 1955–63

When Germany regained sovereignty on May 5, 1955, ten years after World War II had ended, the country also regained sovereignty over its air space. Five months later German star architect Kurt Conle, who also had his own construction business, and his business partner Ernst-Jürgen Ahrens founded a new airline: the Lufttransport-Union. Soon thereafter, Ahrens became CEO of the Frankfurt/Main-based company and successfully led it through the first 20 years of its existence. LTU's fleet consisted of one—and later three—British Viking aircraft with two motors and 36 seats. On March 2, 1956, the first LTU charter flight took off from Frankfurt. With 340 kilometers-an-hour maximum speed, the flight to the Italian island of Sicily took over eight hours. The Jungfernflug turned into an adventure for the 36 passengers when the machine was forced to stop in southern French harbor town of Marseille to be repaired. Right from the beginning, the Spanish island Palma de Mallorca turned out to be the German's favorite holiday destination. By the end of its first year of operation, LTU served 58 destinations in Europe, Asia, and Africa.

In 1957 LTU's fleet was upgraded with two more Vikings, an advanced version of the Britain's Wellington Bomber. In addition, a Bristol 170 aircraft with 44 seats and a Douglas DC4 with 72 seats were purchased in 1958. LTU's seating capacity more than doubled from 108 in 1956 to 260 two years later. When the European Economic Community (EEC) was founded in 1958, competition among airlines became fiercer. LTU's airplane construction plants in Cologne won the German air force as a customer in the second half of the 1950s, after Germany's NATO membership required the country to establish an air force. Another business segment for LTU was air transportation of such freight as newspapers, machinery, and livestock. When shipping magnate Aristotle Onassis, who owned his own airline, chartered an LTU Viking in 1960 for a medium distance flight, the machine was equipped in luxurious style. However, the VIP passenger was reportedly disappointed when LTU was not able to satisfy his desire for a Frankfurter sausage.

Because the company's name was easily confused with another airline, it was renamed Lufttransport-Unternehmen in 1959. However, the company continued using the abbreviation LTU. In 1960 LTU moved its headquarters to Dusseldorf. A ruinous airline fare war broke out in the same year, causing a 30 percent decrease in flights and passenger count for

LTU. The crisis year resulted in slimming LTU's fleet and work force. However, the remaining 50 employees under the leadership of Ernst-Jürgen Ahrens were ready to take on the challenge. In 1962 LTU's fleet consisted of only two machines, a Viking and a Fokker Friendship 27. However, the company consolidated its finances and the number of passengers began to rise again.

### The Innovative Period: 1963–70

LTU's early years, up until 1964, were characterized by CEO Ahrens as "the intuitive phase." This was followed by a period of creativity in which new ideas put the company on its future success track, and Ahrens dubbed the era "the innovative period." One of these ideas was to add organized travel packages to LTU's services. In 1964 the company founded its air travel subsidiary TRANSAIR. Five years later another LTU travel agency, THR TOURS, was founded. Its travel service Caravelle-Club offered LTU holiday charter flights as well as trips via scheduled flights to North America, Central Africa, and the Far East. Another subsidiary, the Interregionale Fluggesellschaft (IFG), was founded in 1968. IFG offered regional private charter and scheduled flights within Germany via some smaller aircraft of the German airline Lufthansa.

In 1966 LTU founder Kurt Conle died at age 48. The visionary had not only made his idea of affordable holiday flights for everyone come true under his motto "Fliegen ist für alle da"—"Flight is for everybody," but the socially-engaged entrepreneur had also helped build affordable housing as an architect and through his construction business. Conle's place at LTU was taken by Wolfgang Krauss, who had already acted as a shareholder trustee for the company founder.

In the second half of the 1960s, LTU constantly upgraded its fleet. Two new aircraft, the French "Caravelle", were added in 1967. That year the number of passengers LTU carried jumped to 250,000, a 40 percent increase over the year before. The air carrier conducted 7,577 flights to 20 destinations worldwide. To gain a competitive advantage over other airlines, LTU used only brand-new airplanes, and reduced the number of seats per aircraft to make the trip more comfortable. Bolstering its image as new and innovative, LTU flight attendants were dressed in the latest fashions. By 1970 LTU was the only airline that also offered fully organized travel service. The airline was popular among such high ranking German politicians as Willy Brandt and Hans-Dietrich Genscher.

### LTU Flies High With Jumbo Jets: 1971–79

In 1971, LTU began offering scheduled flights to about 50 sunny destinations, in addition to its charter holiday flights. Two years later the company pioneered a new industry area when it became the first European charter airline to operate the wide-body airplane with two aisles, a Californian three-stream jet known as the Lockheed TriStar. Although two Fokker 28s were eliminated from its fleet, LTU's capacity increased to 899 in 1973. However, for several reasons, the airline could not reap immediate results from this move. First, a strike by German air traffic controllers that lasted several weeks brought turmoil to the industry. Second, the oil crisis of 1973 and subsequent economic downturn was pushing costs up. Third, political unrest and assassinations in several holiday travel regions had a devastating effect on the travel industry, causing industry-wide losses far into the year 1974. LTU reacted by putting the last two Fokker 28s out of service, cutting capacity back by 30 percent. Also during this time, IFG, the regional arm of LTU, filed for bankruptcy.

By 1975, the year LTU celebrated its 20th anniversary, the company's fortunes were turning around again. LTU's new TriStar jet achieved popularity as the "whispering giant" and was the first charter aircraft to meet the strict guidelines of the International Civil Aviation Organization (ICAO). In 1975 LTU invested in a second TriStar jet, which replaced one of the Caravelle aircraft. One year later LTU's numbers soared again. That year, 770,000 passengers used the service of the airline—200,000 or 25 percent more than in the year before. In 1977 LTU enlarged its fleet again with two more of the jumbo jets. All together the company now operated three Caravelles and four TriStars. New destinations were also added, including New York, the Bahamas, and Sri Lanka. On a sad note, 1975 also marked the year that CEO Ernst-Jürgen Ahrens died, leaving the company well on its way to becoming one of Europe's leading airlines and travel businesses.

In 1977 LTU's top management proclaimed three rules as basic to the company's further success. The first was that LTU should never operate the same type of aircraft used by its competitors. Second, LTU should never give more than 20 percent of its capacity to a single travel agency. The third rule stated that business decisions should always be put into practice in big steps. In 1978 LTU invested in a fifth TriStar jet and got rid of its remaining Caravelles. As the first European charter airline to operate only wide-body jets with quiet engines, LTU received several awards.

At the end of the 1970s, LTU's passenger count had begun to rise again, reaching one million for the first time in 1978. That same year the exchange rate for the American dollar dropped below DM 2 for the first time and holiday trips to the United States and to the Far East came into reach for more people. In 1979 LTU offered a new chain-flight service for organized travel businesses with scheduled times and routes. On long distance flights, the airline offered a luxury First-Class Lounge area. By the end of the 1970s, 60 percent of all European flight passengers were tourists who used charter flight services, and intercontinental flights were in rising demand. In 1979, LTU gave financial support to the establishment of ABC Worldwide, which emerged as a recognized German travel agency chain.

### Traveling Farther: 1980–86

In 1980 another travel agency chain, Meier's Weltreisen, was established with a focus on marketing trips to locations farther away; LTU had invested in a long-distance aircraft for nonstop flights, the TriStar L-1011-500. One of the new destinations added to LTU's schedule was Brazil. Another acquisition followed in 1981 when LTU bought a majority share in travel agency TJAEREBORG, the German subsidiary of a Danish travel agency with the same name. In 1982 LTU acquired the Munich-based travel firm JAHN-Reisen. As a result, the company's revenues rose again, reaching DM 600 million for the first time in 1983.

In 1984 LTU founded another subsidiary, Lufttransport Süd (LTS). Like JAHN-Reisen, the new airline was based in Munich and served the southern German region, especially Bavaria. By 1986, LTU's fleet consisted of nine wide-body TriStar jets with 3,000 seats. LTS flew the new Boeing 757, an aircraft for middle distance flights that was very advanced technologically and more environmentally friendly. The three Boeing 757s had a total capacity of 597 seats.

In the mid-1980s, as oil prices fell, the cost of jet fuel dropped by 30 percent compared to the early 1980s. This made trips to exotic, sunny locations, such as the Caribbean and the Far East, more affordable for Germans, and LTU's business thrived.

The company was also gaining a worldwide reputation. LTU made headlines during this time when NASA officer O'Dwyer flew LTU to Germany, bringing with him some moon rock samples that were later displayed at the Herrman Oberth-Museum in Nuremberg/Fürth. In the same year, the island republic of the Maldives published a postal stamp with an LTU-TriStar its as major motif. In 1986, 92-year-old German professor Dr. Herman Oberth—regarded as the father of modern space travel—flew LTU to Washington, D.C., to an audience with then-president Ronald Reagan.

### New Services and New Destinations: 1987–94

In the late 1980s and early 1990s, LTU continued to grow and expand into new markets. The planned liberalization of the European market posed a strategic challenge for the company's upper management. They decided to expand into new markets such as catering and cruises, as well as to step up efforts to promote the company internationally.

In 1987 Munich-based subsidiary LTS was renamed LTU-Süd (LTU-South). The same year, the company's first foreign airline subsidiary, LTE, was founded, with headquarters in Mallorca, Spain. One year later the company's new catering subsidiary LTC was established. LTC operated from a new office building at the Dusseldorf airport and supplied food and duty-free products to several airlines with its own truck fleet. In 1990 LTU's hotel subsidiary LTI took over a luxury cruise liner on the river Nile. It was an overwhelming success, and soon more ships were cruising the Nile under the LTI flag. In 1991 LTI was the first German business to invest in Cuba when the company took over the management of the first-class hotel LTI-Tuxpan on the beach of Varadero. In 1994 LTU established a new concern, Worldwide Destination Services, which offered contract management with local agencies for all LTU travel businesses.

At the same time the airline continuously expanded its reach and added new destinations. After the Berlin Wall fell in 1990, LTU charter flights began departing from Schönefeld airport in East Berlin to Palma de Mallorca. In 1990 LTU became a member of the International Air Transport Association (IATA) and started offering scheduled flights to four cities in the United States as well as domestic flights from Dusseldorf to Hamburg, Frankfurt, and Munich. In 1991 the company received the right to make scheduled flights to Thailand and began making three flights a week.

Another target area for LTU was the Caribbean. Beginning in 1991 LTU flew to Isla Margarita in Venezuela, Santo Domingo and Punta Cana in the Dominican Republic, and Holguin, Cuba. Another new path for LTU was its winter schedule with flights to Orlando, Florida, and Atlanta, Georgia, in the United States, Eilat in Israel, Rio de Janeiro in Brazil, Acapulco in Mexico, and San José in Costa Rica. Beginning in 1994, LTU also included Bali, Sumatra, and the Caribbean island Curaçao in its roster. The winter schedule proved a success with 394 flights per week from nine German airports and Salzburg in Austria to about 70 destinations.

LTU made German headlines again when, on New Year's Eve 1992, Germany's public TV station, ARD, broadcast a live concert given by pianist Justus Frantz and a 53-piece orchestra on board LTU's brand-new McDonnell Douglas MD11. That same year, 75 newly married couples started their honeymoons on a single LTU flight, all dressed in their wedding dresses and suits, the winners of a competition of German wedding photographers. In 1993 the first female captain, 36-year-old Sabine Trube, began flying a Boeing 767 for LTU. In 1993 the number of LTU passengers reached five million for the first time.

### A Period of Reorganization: 1995–2000

By 1995 LTU had invested more than DM 1 billion in its fleet. Moreover, that year the airline invested in the new Airbus

A330-300, the first airplane of its kind registered in Germany. Over the following years a total of six of these new airplanes with 387 seats gradually replaced the TriStar jets. By 2000 the airline flew about 7.2 million passengers in 29 aircraft to 70 destinations, with 96 percent of all flights scheduled. In 1996 LTU founded its first cargo office in Dusseldorf, followed by additional offices in Frankfurt, Munich, and Hamburg, which added a considerable stream of revenue.

However, in the second half of the 1990s LTU was challenged by problems with its reservation system, ruinous price competition, and deleterious analyst speculation. The company's value declined suddenly, resulting in restructuring and cost reduction efforts. In 1996 LTU merged its travel agencies to form the tourism holding company LTU Touristik GmbH (LTT); all brand names of the former travel agency subsidiaries were kept under LTT's corporate umbrella. In November 1998 Swiss SAirGroup, parent company of Switzerland's airline Swissair, became LTU's new majority shareholder. SAirGroup bought a 49.9 percent stake in LTU from Westdeutsche Landesbank and four private shareholders and then transferred it to the new holding company LTU Group Holding. By 1999 LTU was Germany's number three airline and the country's third largest leisure travel tour operator. However, the latter segment of the operation was deeply in the red. At the end of 1999 LTU announced a rigorous cost-cutting program called ''Fit for the Future,'' which was followed by one even more rigorous three months later. The program aimed at cutting personnel cost by ten percent and reducing passenger capacity by 20 percent, as well as taking advantage of synergy between LTU and SAirGroup. In 2000 German Rewe Group agreed to take over LTU's organized travel arm (LTT) and to buy 40 percent of the airline's capital (Rewe, Germany's giant grocery retailer, had ventured into tourism beginning in the early 1990s.) The deal was subject to approval of several groups and authorities. Whether LTU's efforts to streamline and better manage its holdings would prove successful or not would be answered in the 21st century.

## Principal Subsidiaries

LTU Lufttransport-Unternehmen GmbH; LTU Touristik GmbH; LTI Hotelbeteiligungs- und Investitionsgesellschaft mbH; LTU Destination Management AG; LTC Catering GmbH; LTU Aircraft Maintenance GmbH; LTU Aviation Handling GmbH; LTE Fluggesellschaft (Spain); RAS Fluggesellschaft m.b.H.

## Principal Competitors

Lufthansa AG; TUI Group; Condor & Neckermann Group.

## Further Reading

Borchardt, Alexandra, and Scheherazade Daneshkhu, ''UK: Round Two as Airtours and Rewe Eye LTU Leisure Groups Set to Clash Again,'' *Financial Times*, May 9, 2000 p. 30.

Doyle, Andrew, ''SAirGroup buys 49% of LTU and Eyes Full Access to EU Market,'' *Flight International*, November 18, 1998, p. 10.

Fairlie, Rik, ''LTU, Bank to Buy U.K. Thomas Cook,'' *Travel Weekly*, June 22, 1992, p. 43.

*LTU Story: Das Wichtigste Aus 40 Jahren Fernweh*, Dusseldorf, Germany: LTU Lufttransport-Unternehmen GmbH, 1995, 10 p.

Needham, Paul, ''LTU Merging Brands to Cut Back its Costs,'' *Travel Trade Gazette Europa*, February 22, 1996, p. 9.

''Pan-European Charter Alliance Set to Take Off,'' *Travel Trade Gazette Europa*, November 26, 1998, p. 1.

''Rewe Touristik schliesst mit Einstieg bei der LTU zu den beiden Marktfuehrern auf,'' *Frankfurter Allgemeine Zeitung*, August 23, 2000, p. 20.

''Speculation over LTU Touristik Sell-Off Plans,'' *Travel Trade Gazette UK & Ireland*, September 20, 1999, p. 7.

''Wir können das,'' *Focus Magazin*, August 28, 2000, p. 192.

—Evelyn Hauser

# McDermott International, Inc.

**1450 Poydras Street**
**New Orleans, Louisiana 70112-6050**
**U.S.A.**
**Telephone: (504) 587-5400**
**Fax: (504) 587-6153**
**Web site: http://www.mcdermott.com**

*Public Company*
*Incorporated:* 1946 as J. Ray McDermott & Company
*Employees:* 17,000
*Sales:* $1.89 billion (1999)
*Stock Exchanges:* New York
*Ticker Symbol:* MDR
*NAIC:* 213112 Support Activities for Oil and Gas
    Operations; 221113 Nuclear Electric Power
    Generation; 23331 Manufacturing and Industrial
    Building Construction; 333132 Oil and Gas Field
    Machinery and Equipment; 48611 Pipeline
    Transportation of Crude Oil; 48691 Pipeline
    Transportation of Refined Petroleum Products; 48699
    All Other Pipeline Transportation

McDermott International, Inc. and its subsidiaries have operations in three main areas: marine oil field construction, power generation construction services, and management of nuclear power plants and other government projects. Its Babcock & Wilcox unit has been hit hard by asbestos-related lawsuits; this and investigations of McDermott's overseas competitive practices helped sour analysts on the company in the late 1990s.

## Origins

What is now known as McDermott International originated in 1923, when 24-year-old R. Thomas McDermott received a contract to build 50 wooden rigs to drill for oil. The contract came from an east Texas wildcatter, or oil prospector. McDermott asked his father, J. Ray McDermott, to supervise construction of the rigs, and named the business after the elder McDermott.

Over the next two decades the firm expanded, establishing itself in Texas and following exploration to southern Louisiana. In 1923 J. Ray McDermott & Company moved its headquarters from Eastland, Texas, to Luling, Texas, after a boom in oil exploration in the area. McDermott continued to grow during the Depression. In the early 1930s the Houston area enjoyed an oil boom, and in 1932 J. Ray McDermott & Company moved to Houston. McDermott first opened a New Orleans, Louisiana area office in 1937—across the Mississippi River from McDermott's present headquarters. Some years later, McDermott moved its headquarters to Louisiana.

McDermott became associated with the J.G. McMullen Dredging Company in 1938 and bought that company in 1939, branching into dredging. The Olsen Dredging Company was established in 1939 as a result of this purchase. The company remained a small, regional concern during World War II. In April 1946 J. Ray McDermott & Company was reorganized and incorporated in Delaware. By this time, the company was supplying services to support oil and natural gas production in the marshlands.

### Offshore After the War

In the late 1940s oil and gas companies became interested in exploiting fields beneath the Gulf of Mexico. McDermott, with its floating equipment for marshland work, formed joint ventures and made acquisitions that enabled it to pioneer the construction and installation of platforms and pipelines to support drilling and development near shore. In August 1947, McDermott set the world's first steel template platform in 20 feet of water in the Gulf of Mexico, for the Superior Oil Company. Prior to this, the few offshore platforms in existence had rested on wooden pilings. Steel was stronger and more durable than wood, and the template design of these new platforms distributed weight better. Soon after, a second platform was installed in 50 feet of water, and the offshore marine construction business was launched. McDermott formed its contracting division—the major operating segment during its early years—in 1947.

With the 1948 purchase of all of the assets of the Harry F. Allsman Company, its joint venture partner for several contrac-

## Company Perspectives:

*Today, McDermott companies provide an array of products and services. Some of our customers may be developing hydrocarbons far below the surface of the ocean. Others may be bringing electricity that will bring light and power to new areas of the world. Our customers depend on our products to defend the United States, to clean the environment, to efficiently refine petroleum into other useful products and to complete numerous others tasks that help the world create and use energy. No matter where we work or what we do, whether supplying traditional services in marine construction and power generation or developing future technologies such as fuel cells, McDermott companies are committed to quality, innovation and technological leadership.*

ting jobs in the Gulf of Mexico, McDermott boosted its efforts in the offshore construction area. This acquisition included equipment assets that helped McDermott meet the new demand for offshore construction.

In 1949 McDermott commissioned the world's first derrick barge, which was built specifically for offshore use. The barge significantly increased the kind of work that could be performed offshore. By 1953 McDermott had built another derrick barge, with a lifting capacity of 250 tons.

In 1950, to handle numerous customer requests for pipeline construction, J. Ray McDermott & Company established a pipeline department. That same year, McDermott constructed the first Gulf of Mexico pipeline and also created an oil division.

In 1953 DeLong-McDermott—a joint venture formed that year by McDermott and the DeLong Engineering Company—built the first mobile air-jack rig using a jacking, or elevating, device patented by L.B. DeLong. Later in 1953, DeLong-McDermott merged with Southern Natural Gas Company to form The Offshore Company, a drilling contracting firm. McDermott held a one-third interest in The Offshore Company. The Offshore Company became a major competitor of McDermott in the deep-water drilling business, and McDermott gradually sold its interest in Offshore, completing the divestiture in 1971.

J. Ray McDermott & Company went public in 1954. It was listed on the New York Stock Exchange in January 1958. In 1956 Bayou Boeuf Fabricators became McDermott's fourth division, and the world's largest offshore structure fabrication yard. The division's name was changed to McDermott Fabricators in May 1958.

In 1957 McDermott established a subsidiary, J. Ray McDermott (Venezuela), C.A., to fabricate the world's first aluminum platforms for the highly corrosive waters of Venezuela's Lake Maracaibo. In 1958 McDermott acquired Associated Pipeline Contractors, to supplement its domestic pipeline business and provide international expansion opportunities. Associated Pipeline Contractors was involved in the laying of large-diameter, cross-country oil and natural gas transmission lines. In 1959 McDermott sold Associated Pipeline to Reading and Bates in exchange for common stock.

In 1959 McDermott acquired Dupont Fabricators, to supplement the light fabrication capabilities of McDermott Fabricators, which eventually absorbed the new unit. That same year, McDermott Fabricators created a marine department primarily for the repair of the company's heavy construction equipment. The marine department repaired McDermott's own equipment and that of other companies. In 1962 the department became a separate operating division, McDermott Shipyard division.

McDermott continued to move into the international sphere, establishing an office in Beirut in 1960. In 1962 McDermott installed the first platform placed in Cook Inlet, Alaska. In 1963 McDermott Overseas, McDermott Far East, McDermott Enterprises France, and Oceanic Contractors were established as subsidiaries of the company. In March 1964, McDermott had eight direct subsidiaries that operated under five divisions: contracting, oil, McDermott Fabricators, Harvey Lumber and Supply Company, and McDermott Shipyard.

In 1965 the first 500-ton derrick barge was introduced. By 1967, however, new methods were required to install the increasingly large skeletal outer structures—called jackets—that supported the platform decks. Prior to 1967, derricks on barges lifted the jacket from a cargo barge and set it in position. In the summer of 1967 McDermott first executed what is now the common method of launching large jackets. At that time a jacket that McDermott was to install in 340 feet of water was too heavy for the derrick to raise. Therefore, the jacket was fabricated on its side and slid onto a barge. At the installation site, it was slipped off the cargo barge and into the water. As it floated horizontally in the water, the jacket was gradually ballasted until it turned upright and then it was guided into place.

In 1968 the oil and natural gas exploration and production operations handled by the oil division of McDermott were transferred to a newly formed company, TransOcean Oil. In 1969 McDermott acquired the stock and subsidiaries of Hudson Engineering Corporation. Hudson had a background in petrochemical process engineering and in offshore engineering facilities. Another key acquisition during this period was the purchase in November 1971 of Ingram Corporation's foreign marine construction equipment business. This purchase expanded McDermott's operations into three new areas: Australia, Trinidad, and Brazil.

### Rapid Change in the 1970s and 1980s

R. Thomas McDermott died in 1970, after serving as chairman for nearly 25 years. Edward J. Hudson succeeded McDermott as chairman, serving from July 1970 until August 1974.

McDermott changed significantly from 1969 to 1979. McDermott's growth and expansion continued with major acquisitions—including The Babcock & Wilcox Company, purchased in 1978. The addition of the established power generation company was McDermott's first diversification outside the marine construction business.

James Cunningham, chief executive officer and chairman from 1979 until 1988, was instrumental in the 1978 acquisition of Babcock & Wilcox, for which McDermott paid a total of approximately $748 million. The acquisition was meant to provide balance against the cyclical marine construction business. The two engineering firms shared some common ground. Both were in the energy business and both worked in steel formation. The similarity in basic technologies and engineering and the fact that both firms served the same markets paved the way for the Babcock & Wilcox acquisition. Babcock & Wilcox had interests in the manufacture of equipment such as process controls, boiler-cleaning products, and metal tubing. In the 1950s the firm became a leader in the development of nuclear power and had become a key part of the United States Navy's nuclear program. By the time it was acquired by McDermott in 1978, Babcock & Wilcox was a major supplier of products and services to the electrical power and other industries throughout the world.

In acquiring Babcock & Wilcox, McDermott became a much larger, diversified company. To reflect its growth, J. Ray McDermott & Company became McDermott Inc. in 1980. In 1983, with McDermott's international business growing in stature, the company was reorganized again. McDermott International, McDermott's wholly owned Panamanian subsidiary since 1959, became the parent company of McDermott Inc. and its subsidiaries. McDermott International had been established as the international subsidiary of J. Ray McDermott & Company. McDermott's reorganization as a Panamanian company allowed it to avoid paying income tax on most of its operations.

In the 1970s new technologies in marine construction permitted offshore structures to grow quickly in size. In 1978, McDermott installed Shell Oil's Cognac structure in 1,025 feet of water in the Gulf of Mexico. Cognac was the first jacket installed in more than 1,000 feet of water.

In 1978 a federal grand jury returned indictments alleging conspiracy among some officers of McDermott and of its competitor Brown & Root to restrain or eliminate competition in marine construction. McDermott and Brown & Root each pleaded no contest to the antitrust charges and were fined $1 million each.

Dependent on the oil economy, McDermott's problems were compounded when the bottom fell out of the energy business during the early 1980s. As profits dropped, oil companies cut back on capital spending, and marine construction also took a beating. Starting in the early 1980s, there was less demand for boilers, as a result of power generating overcapacity, and the

generating market shrank as well. McDermott did not make a profit in 1988 or in the following two years.

In 1979, James E. Cunningham became chairman. Cunningham, a chemical engineer and 30-year McDermott employee, was credited with keeping the firm afloat when the marine market shrank from more than $2 billion in 1982 to $500 million in 1989. Cunningham implemented a financial restructuring that streamlined the company.

McDermott shrank by 57 percent between 1979 and 1988. Most of the employee reductions were made at Babcock & Wilcox. A number of plants were closed or sold.

Robert Howson took over as chairman of the board and CEO in August 1988. McDermott had grown since Howson, a civil engineer, came to the company in 1957. Although the 1980s were difficult for McDermott, Babcock & Wilcox was a bright spot on the McDermott balance sheet. Babcock & Wilcox, which offered services such as design, construction, and maintenance of steam-generating equipment, had not had a losing year since its sale to McDermott and had, in effect, carried the parent company since the early 1980s. For the fiscal year ending March 31, 1990, McDermott's business overall consisted of about 75 percent power generation work and 25 percent marine construction, compared with about 65 percent and 35 percent, respectively, ten years before.

### Struggling Through the 1990s

The oil business began to recover in 1988, and by mid-1988 McDermott's fortunes had begun to improve. Chairman Howson consolidated operations, focusing on McDermott's five core businesses, and reduced the company's debt. Revenues for fiscal 1990 were $2.64 billion, up from $2.16 billion in 1989. Babcock & Wilcox contributed $1.7 billion in revenues.

McDermott still lost $10.2 million in fiscal 1990, less than net losses of $91.7 million in 1989 the year before. The improvement was mainly the result of gains from the sale of McDermott's Bailey Controls operations for $295 million and half of its commercial nuclear services operations for $51 million to form a new commercial nuclear service joint venture. Funds from these sales helped McDermott reduce short-term debt. McDermott's marine backlog—the number of orders received—grew two and a half times, from $650 million to $1.6 billion in fiscal 1990.

McDermott still performed all facets of marine construction. It took about one year to fabricate a large—at least 400 feet high—fixed offshore platform. Although McDermott had competitors in each segment—design, engineering, and fabrication—it was the only worldwide contractor that could handle all phases of the process from beginning to end. McDermott had constructed most of the world's drilling platforms.

McDermott's real strength in marine construction lay in its fleet of very powerful offshore equipment, which allowed more work to be completed onshore. With 200 vessels, McDermott had the largest fleet of marine equipment used in major offshore construction. Technological advances have paved the way for diversification in marine construction for McDermott, which had long constructed high-horsepower tugboats, pushboats, and offshore supply vessels. It branched into the construction of ships for the U.S. Navy, including prototype small waterplane area twin hull ships and torpedo test craft.

The company vied for additional work in government markets. About one-fifth of McDermott's business in fiscal 1989 was government related. During the early 1990s a continued shortage of equipment propelled a surge in power equipment sales. McDermott expected its boiler business to expand significantly between 1990 and 2000. Babcock & Wilcox was the nation's top boilermaker.

McDermott wanted to grow in core-related areas, but it first had to further reduce debt. McDermott also hoped to expand its overseas operations, including those in the Pacific Rim, where McDermott began doing business in the mid-1960s. McDermott was building boilers in China as part of a joint venture and was also involved in offshore marine construction work there.

The J. Ray McDermott (JRM) unit merged with its main competitor, Offshore Pipelines, in 1995. The combined companies were poised with a dominant market position at the beginning of an oil exploration cycle. The Babcock & Wilson subsidiary, in spite of impressive gains in the Far East, was weathering a serious downturn in the domestic power generation market. The Asian market would wither within a few years as well.

CEO Robert E. Howson resigned in September 1996; James L. Dutt became interim chairman and CEO. In October, after two quarters of losses, McDermott announced a plan to cut noncore businesses—this would be a familiar refrain for the rest of the decade.

Losses mounted through the end of the 1996–97 fiscal year, totaling some $192 million in the last quarter alone. McDermott posted a net loss of $214 million for the year. The J. Ray McDermott subsidiary lost money because of lower barge use in the Gulf of Mexico and unfavorable exchange rates. Asbestos-related lawsuits were taking a toll on the underinsured Babcock & Wilcox subsidiary. McDermott also managed nuclear power plants; eight cancer victims filed a lawsuit, later settled, alleging that McDermott had contaminated them with stray radioactive dust.

In April 1997, McDermott announced that it was probing serious, yet unspecified allegations of employee misconduct in its international units. Share prices fell sharply at the news. Three months later, a federal grand jury was investigating anticompetitive activity at J. Ray McDermott and HeereMac, a JRM joint venture with the Dutch construction company Heerema. A joint venture with ETPM SA of France was added to the probe in December 1997.

By this time, McDermott had sold off its 50 percent interest in HeereMac. Divestment would be another common theme. McDermott sold off its 50 percent stake in offshore construction company Unifab International when the unit went public in September 1997.

McDermott announced earnings of $207 million for 1997–98, up from the previous year's $214 million loss. The promising recovery was slowed by low oil prices in the 1998–99 fiscal year. An unusual setback came in December 1998 when a platform deck worth $70 million sank in the Gulf of Mexico as it was being lifted by a JRM barge.

McDermott's power generation division was showing strong results at the time, though that market would soon flatten in the next two years. McDermott's oil-related backlog, however, steadily shrank in the persistently depressed oil market, leading to layoffs and other cost-cutting measures from 1997 to 1999. The company put more resources into its information technology (IT) infrastructure, awarding AT&T a contract worth $60 million a year to manage it in March 1999.

Roger Tetrault was named CEO in February 1997. He sold off the company's shipyards and focused the company on three core areas: marine oil field construction (particularly deepwater), power generation construction services, and management of nuclear power plants and other government projects. Within two years, a newly profitable McDermott was looking to expand again.

Tetrault also set about simplifying McDermott's corporate structure. A bid for the remaining 37 percent of JRM was tendered in March 1999. This offer, however, seemingly fell through within a few weeks over a price dispute. A few weeks after that, the deal was in fact sealed, at a price of $513 million in cash, a third more value than the stock swap originally offered. The purchase gave McDermott access to $600 million in cash controlled by JRM.

In spite of newfound profits and a recovery in the oil industry, McDermott's stock price continued to trail behind that of its peers. An investigation into bidding practices in Indonesia unsettled some investors, but a new development in a lingering problem would cause the most damage on Wall Street.

Asbestos claims continued to burden Babcock & Wilson, which settled 26,000 asbestos-related claims from former employees or subcontractors in the 1998–99 fiscal year alone. In November 1999, McDermott's market valuation was cut in half in one 48-hour period after it increased its estimate of its asbestos-related exposure.

Babcock & Wilcox filed for bankruptcy protection in February 2000, with 45,000 asbestos claims pending. Executives blamed a wave of increases in the damages sought by plaintiffs' attorneys. McDermott had bought Babcock & Wilcox in 1978 and had spent $1.6 billion since 1982 to settle more than 340,000 claims.

Although Tetrault was credited with getting the company in shape operationally, his handling of the investment community during times of trouble was roundly criticized. Bruce Wilkinson, a specialist in corporate turnarounds, was hired as president and chief operating officer in April 2000 and replaced Roger Tetrault as CEO four months later. The company announced that it would stop paying dividends on its stock and planned to cut costs at its headquarters further.

### Principal Subsidiaries

BWX Technologies, Inc.; The Babcock & Wilcox Company; J. Ray McDermott, S.A.; McDermott Technology, Inc.; Hudson Products; Delta Catalytic; Delta Hudson.

### Principal Operating Units

BWX Technologies; Babcock & Wilcox; J. Ray McDermott; Industrial Operations.

### Principal Competitors

Global Industries; Gulf Island Fabrication; Hyundai Heavy Industries.

### Further Reading

Biers, John M., "Asbestos News Jolts Stock by 25 Percent; McDermott Could Face More Claims," *Times-Picayune,* November 12, 1999, p. C1.

——, "McDermott Earnings Take Dip; Weak Oil Market Means Job Cuts," *Times-Picayune,* January 28, 1999, p. C1.

——, "McDermott Has Tough Job Ahead, Analysts Say," *Times-Picayune,* February 24, 2000, p. C1.

——, "McDermott Merger Falls Through; Parent, Subsidiary Stocks Fall on News," *Times-Picayune,* April 21, 1999, p. C1.

——, "McDermott Moves to Simplify; CEO Seeks Respect on Wall Street," *Times-Picayune,* May 16, 1999, p. K19.

——, "McDermott Reports Strong Profit, But Low Oil Prices Slowing Business," *Times-Picayune,* October 31, 1998, p. C1.

——, "McDermott Stock Decline Prompts Major Changes," *Times-Picayune,* August 3, 2000, p. C1.

——, "McDermott Stock Takes a Plunge; Asbestos Scare Hurts Market Confidence," *Times-Picayune,* November 13, 1999, p. C1.

——, "McDermott Subsidiary Declares Bankruptcy; Babcock & Wilcox Cites Asbestos Litigation," *Times-Picayune,* February 23, 2000, p. C1.

——, "Oil Stock Gushing, But N.O. Firm Lags; McDermott Execs Still Confident," *Times-Picayune,* October 17, 1999, p. F1.

*Deepwater: Marine Construction's Frontier Technology,* New Orleans, La.: McDermott International, 1985.

Ewing, Terzah, "McDermott Inquiries by Grand Jury, SEC Are Expanded to a Joint Venture," *Wall Street Journal,* December 22, 1997.

——, "McDermott Says It Will Post Loss, Probe Wrongdoing," *Wall Street Journal,* April 29, 1997, p. C21.

——, "McDermott Says Unit, Joint Venture Are Under Inquiry," *Wall Street Journal,* July 16, 1997, p. B9.

——, "McDermott Shares, Units Take Plunge in Wake of Probe," *Wall Street Journal,* April 30, 1997, p. B7.

Judice, Mary, "Merger of N.O. Firms Likely; McDermott Deal Awaiting OK," *Times-Picayune,* May 8, 1999, p. C1.

Mishra, Arnab, "McDermott International: Ready to Recover," *Financial World,* July 18, 1995, p. 22.

"Pipeline Contract Gets Heat; N.O. Firm Is Caught Up in Indonesian Dispute," *Times-Picayune,* June 22, 1999, p. C1.

*The Story of Oil and Gas Offshore,* New Orleans, La.: McDermott International, n.d.

Waxler, Caroline, "Up from the Depths," *Forbes,* December 2, 1996, p. 258.

—Gwen M. LaCosse
—updated by Frederick C. Ingram

# Milwaukee Brewers Baseball Club

201 South 46th Street
Milwaukee, Wisconsin 53214
U.S.A.
Telephone: (414) 933-4114
Fax: (414) 933-5474
Web site: http://www.milwaukeebrewers.com

*Private Company*
*Incorporated:* 1970
*Employees:* 130
*Sales:* $60.8 million
*NAIC:* 711211 Sports Teams and Clubs

The Milwaukee Brewers Baseball Club oversees the operations of the Milwaukee Brewers, a Major League baseball team competing in the National League's Central Division. The Brewers have been searching for the right combination of players and coaching to field a consistently winning squad, but have only once made it to the World Series, which they narrowly lost in 1982. The privately held team is headed by President and CEO Wendy Selig-Prieb, the only woman to hold such a position in the majors. Her father, team founder Bud Selig, stepped down from those roles in 1998 to become Commissioner of Baseball. The team is scheduled to move into newly built Miller Park in 2001, which will offer a domed roof to protect against the chilly Wisconsin weather, as well as luxury skyboxes for use by corporations.

### Roots

The Milwaukee Brewers' beginnings can be traced to 1964, when the Milwaukee Braves announced that they would be moving to Atlanta. Attempts to prevent the move failed, and in 1965 four prominent Milwaukeeans founded Teams, Inc. to bring Major League Baseball back to their city. Among the four were one-time Braves director Edmund Fitzgerald and car dealer Allen "Bud" Selig, who was named president of the company. Attempts over the next several years to purchase expansion teams in both the National and American leagues, and even to entice the Chicago White Sox to move to Milwaukee, failed. Teams, Inc. did secure 21 regular season White Sox

games and several exhibition games for Milwaukee's County Stadium, the former home of the Braves.

In 1969 the American League announced that it was sanctioning new franchises for Seattle and Kansas City, leaving Milwaukee in the lurch yet again. The newly formed Seattle Pilots' 1969 season was a disappointing one, however, hampered by a weak team, a 25,000-seat stadium (about half the average size), and a disinterested fan base, which never once sold out the stands during the year. At the end of the season a group of 15 Milwaukee businessmen, led by Selig and Fitzgerald, made a $10.8 million offer to buy the franchise. As had happened with the Braves, a number of measures were taken to stop the team from moving.

In the spring of 1970 the Pilots declared bankruptcy, which enabled the purchase to finally go through. Just one week before the regular season was to start, the players were told that they would be moving to Milwaukee. The season was so close to starting that there was not even time for new uniforms—they simply had the word "Pilots" removed and "Brewers" sewn on. The new name was chosen as a tribute to the city's long association with beer production. Although the first season in Milwaukee was only slightly more successful than the one in Seattle had been, attendance improved by 38 percent, and the fans showed great enthusiasm for their new team.

Following another lackluster season in 1971, newly appointed General Manager Frank Lane made a major trade with Boston, getting six new players in exchange for four Brewers. The team also shifted divisions, moving from the Western to the more competitive Eastern. The move was occasioned by the relocation of the Washington Senators to Texas, but Brewers management also felt that ticket sales would be boosted by the increased number of games against that division's powerhouse teams. These included the New York Yankees, Boston Red Sox, and Baltimore Orioles.

Personnel changes continued in 1972, when original manager Dave Bristol was fired and replaced by Del Crandall. G.M. Lane himself was subsequently replaced by Jim Wilson. By this time, only one of the original Brewers players was left. The year 1973 saw a slight improvement, with a final tally of 74 wins and

## Company Perspectives:

*Commitment—That one word captures the essence of the Milwaukee Brewers' mission on and off the field. The Miller Park era is beginning soon, and with it a renewed vitality for Major League Baseball in Wisconsin. Accordingly, we are committed to bringing a championship to Wisconsin. Our fans will enjoy a world class ballpark, and also deserve a rewarding game experience. We are fortunate to live and work in a giving, caring community. Our region is recognized for its philanthropic spirit, and it is the Brewers' privilege to be a component of this regional partnership. We are proud of our community accomplishments, and are committed to the club's tradition of proving positive impact for young people and those less fortunate. The Greater Milwaukee area and the state of Wisconsin have supported and encouraged the Brewers for thirty years. We take pride in that special relationship, which serves to grow the Brewers' resolve in sharing our unique resources to make Wisconsin a better place.*

88 losses, culminating in fifth place in the division. Attendance went back up, topping a million. After another losing season the following year, the struggling team hired baseball legend Hank Aaron as a designated hitter, a move that brought out more fans but did not produce a significant improvement in the standings. Aaron, who had started with the Braves in 1954, finished his playing career in Milwaukee after two seasons.

In 1976, following a loss of player confidence in his leadership, the team replaced Del Crandall with Alex Grammas, assistant coach of the Cincinnati Reds. Grammas imposed strict rules that limited hair length and banned beards, mustaches, and other "facial adornments." His tenure was also to be short. In November of 1977 Selig fired Grammas, new General Manager Jim Baumer, and several other members of the coaching staff. Grammas was replaced by Baltimore pitching coach George Bamberger and Baumer by Harry Dalton from the California Angels. Dalton immediately secured several new players, including free agent Larry Hisle for a six-year, $3 million deal.

### Success at Last in the Late 1970s

The changes brought about a turnaround in fortunes. The 1978 season saw the Brewers, now sporting new uniforms and a new logo, finish above .500 for the first time. They led the American League in home runs and six other offensive categories, and one of the team's key players, infielder Paul Molitor, was named Rookie of the Year. The final tally of 93 wins and 69 losses was only good for third place in the tough division, however. A record 1.6 million tickets were sold for the year.

The next season was even better, with 1.9 million in attendance, and a second place finish to the Baltimore Orioles. Gorman Thomas's 45 home runs led the league, and the team racked up more multiple base hits of every type than the previous year. These statistics improved again in 1980, although the season was hampered by injuries to several key players as well as by Manager Bamberger's mid-season heart attack. The team installed a new, high-tech scoreboard during the year and also

completed a postseason trade that brought in much-needed pitching strength, including famed Oakland A's reliever Rollie Fingers. He delivered the goods in his first season, leading the majors in saves and being named both the Cy Young Award winner and Most Valuable Player.

In 1981 came the first Major League Baseball players' strike, which occurred in the middle of the season and resulted in the year being divided into two halves. The Brewers won the second half-season, but lost the division title to New York in the playoffs. Despite new coach Buck Rodgers's winning ways, he lacked the support of many of his players. In early 1982, with the team off to a lackluster start, Dalton replaced him with batting coach Harvey Kuenn. The Brewers quickly caught fire, finishing the season on top of their division and then taking the pennant. Although they lost the World Series in the seventh game, they were greeted as heroes upon their return to Milwaukee. The following season saw the team's best attendance ever, with nearly 2.4 million tickets sold.

Unfortunately, the Brewers' fortunes began to slip after their pennant win, with a fifth place finish the following year, then 67 wins against 94 losses in 1984, last place in the division. Kuenn had been fired before that season, and his successor Rene Lachemann was replaced by George Bamberger within a year. Rebuilding with a number of new, younger players, the team's record slowly improved, reaching 91 wins for 1987, and third place. By this time Bamberger, too, was gone, having given way to Tom Trebelhorn.

For once the Brewers stuck with a manager; Trebelhorn stayed at the helm for the next four seasons. The team's performance was still only fair, however, with final rankings during those years between third and sixth place. Trebelhorn ultimately was dismissed in October of 1991 and replaced by Phil Garner. The next season was the best since 1983, with the team taking second place in the division. The next year, however, the Brewers dropped to last place once again.

At this time the Brewers were one of only four teams in the majors with no cable broadcasting contract, and one of only three without corporate "skyboxes" in their stadiums. An attempt to form a sports cablecasting venture with the Milwaukee Bucks basketball team in the mid-1980s had gone under after only one year. The Brewers' ticket sales and broadcast revenues were now second worst in the majors. A primary reason for the Brewers' lowly status was the team's inability to compete in terms of player salaries, which had been rising steadily since the early 1970s. The team's $15 million payroll was the lowest in the major leagues. The biggest problem for the team was the limited size of its market area, which had a population base of only 1.3 million.

In 1994 the Brewers were moved into the newly created American League Central Division. The strike-shortened season served to lessen the team's misery, as it found itself in the cellar once again. A fourth place finish in 1995 gave way to a third place result in 1996, but the team was back in fifth the following year.

### New Leagues and Stadiums in the Late 1990s

At the end of the 1997 season, the Brewers made an historic move from the American League to the National, a switch

## Key Dates:

**1965:**  Teams, Inc. is founded to bring a new Major League Baseball team to Milwaukee.
**1970:**  The Brewers are born when the Seattle Pilots franchise is purchased.
**1972:**  Brewers change from Western to Eastern Division in the American League.
**1979:**  First season with more wins than losses.
**1982:**  The Brewers win their first pennant, but lose the World Series in the final game.
**1983:**  Attendance reaches an all-time high of nearly 2.4 million.
**1994:**  Brewers move to the newly created A.L. Central Division.
**1996:**  Ground is broken on a new $250 million stadium.
**1998:**  Brewers switch from A.L. to the National League; Wendy Selig-Prieb is named CEO.
**1999:**  An accident kills three workers at the new stadium, delaying its opening until 2001.

was broken in November of 1996, with a projected completion date of spring 2000. A 1999 crane accident killed three workers, however, raising the stadium's cost and delaying its completion by a year.

The months following the accident saw several major personnel changes. Selig-Prieb fired Manager Phil Garner near the end of his seventh losing season with the club, replacing him with Davey Lopes. G.M. Sal Bando also was given a different assignment within the organization and replaced by Dean Taylor. Once again, new uniforms were designed, this time in preparation for the move to Miller Park.

As the Brewers completed their last season in County Stadium, they were still searching for the right combination of elements to field a championship team. The new domed stadium was expected to give a sizable boost to ticket sales, and the anticipated upward spike in revenues would facilitate increasing player salaries to a competitive level. This, along with Bud Selig's inter-team revenue sharing agreement, was the team's best hope to date for a return to winning form.

### Principal Competitors

Chicago National League Ball Club, Inc.; Chicago White Sox Ltd.; Cincinnati Reds; Houston Astros Baseball Club; Minnesota Twins; Pittsburgh Baseball Club; St. Louis Cardinals, L.P.

### Further Reading

Adomites, Paul D., "Seattle Pilots-Milwaukee Brewers," in Bjarkman, Peter C., ed., *Encyclopedia of Major League Baseball Team Histories—American League,* Westport, Conn. and London: Meckler Publishing, 1991.
Cooper, Geoff, "Swimming Against the Revenue Stream," *Business Journal—Milwaukee,* June 6, 1992, p. 1.
Dewey, Donald, and Nicholas Acocella, *Encyclopedia of Major League Baseball Teams,* New York: HarperCollins Publishers, 1993.
Dries, Mike, "Brewers, District Board Actually Agree," *Business Journal—Milwaukee,* March 21, 1997, p. 3.
——, "History Helped Shape Brewers, Miller Park Contract," *Business Journal—Milwaukee,* April 27, 1996, p. 4.
Hoeschen, Brad, "Changes Pose Challenges for Selig-Prieb, Brewers," *Business Journal—Milwaukee,* November 12, 1999, p. 16.
——, "Fever Pitch: Brewers Use Transition Years to Boost Season Ticket Sales," *Business Journal—Milwaukee,* March 6, 1998, p. 1.
——, "Get Up! Get Up!," *Business Journal—Milwaukee,* March 24, 2000, p. 3.
Jagler, Steven, "Miller Park's Premium Seats Virtually Sold Out," *Business Journal—Milwaukee,* November 19, 1999, p. 5.
Kass, Mark, "A Game of Political Hardball," *Business Journal—Milwaukee,* April 9, 1994, p. 1.
King, Bill, "Chip off the old Bud," *Business Journal—Milwaukee,* October 2, 1998, p. 12.
Millard, Pete, "Stadium Mishap Leaves Brewers' Marketing Plans in Disarray," *Business Journal—Milwaukee,* July 23, 1999, p. 4.
Muret, Don, "Miller Brewing Pours Out $41.2 Mil for Naming Rights to Brewers Stadium," *Amusement Business,* April 1, 1996, p. 29.
Thorn, John, et al., eds., *Total Baseball* (6th ed.), New York: Total Sports, 1999.
Whiteside, Kelly, "This, Bud, Is for You," *Sports Illustrated,* May 8, 1995, p. 24.

—Frank Uhle

necessitated by the uneven number of teams in the two leagues. Research by the team showed fan preference for the move, as the Braves played in that league and Milwaukeeans still had fond memories of their years in the city. The Brewers' first game after the switch was in fact played against them in Atlanta. The team's new division was the N.L. Central, home to the St. Louis Cardinals and Chicago Cubs. These teams fielded top sluggers Mark McGwire and Sammy Sosa, respectively. The sizable number of games the Brewers would play against them was expected to boost ticket sales.

Since the team's founding, Bud Selig had gradually acquired majority ownership. In 1992, following the forced departure of Fay Vincent, he started to work part-time as interim commissioner of baseball. When he was officially appointed to serve in that role six years later, he handed ownership duties to his daughter Wendy, putting his own shares of the club in a trust. The well-respected Selig was able to help the Brewers and other struggling teams by creating a revenue-sharing plan that required the more successful teams to share their broadcasting income with the rest of the league. Thirty-seven-year-old Wendy Selig-Prieb, who was married to the Brewers' vice-president of corporate affairs, had grown up with the team and had gone to law school before hiring on as the Brewers' general counsel in 1990. Her work on the negotiating team during the 1994 players' strike had earned her the respect of her peers, and her move to the role of owner was a natural one.

During the mid-1990s the team began seeking municipal assistance in building a new domed stadium that would keep the cold Wisconsin weather from hampering attendance. The new park would also feature luxury skyboxes in which corporations could entertain. The $250 million project was set to receive $90 million in funding from the Brewers and Miller Brewing, whose name would be given to the facility in exchange for a $41.2 million investment. The remainder was to come from taxpayers. After a number of hurdles were overcome, including a close vote in the state senate, public funding was approved. Ground

# MITROPA AG

---

**Michaelkirchstrasse 17**
**D-10179 Berlin**
**Germany**
**Telephone:** (49) (30) 3024744-5
**Fax:** (49) (30) 3024744-999
**Web site: http://www.mitropa.de**

*Wholly Owned Subsidiary of DB Reise & Touristik AG*
*Incorporated:* 1916 as Mitteleuropäische Schlafwagen
    und Speisewagen AG
*Employees:* 6,500
*Sales:* DM 805 million ($410 million) (1998)
*NAIC:* 72211 Full-Service Restaurants; 722211 Limited-
    Service Restaurants; 722213 Snack and Nonalcoholic
    Beverage Bars; 72231 Food Service Contractors

---

German-based MITROPA AG is Germany's fourth largest restaurant chain and one of Europe's leading caterers for people on the road. MITROPA operates throughout Europe in three major market segments: catering services on trains; snack bars, restaurants and convenience stores in train stations; and highway restaurants. For Germany's national railroad company Deutsche Bahn AG MITROPA operates 750 sleepers and dining cars and serves snacks and beverages to train passengers. In train stations MITROPA operates various brand name restaurants and stores such as InterCity Treff and nimm's mit, as well as international franchises such as Segafredo and Pizza Hut. Located mostly in eastern Germany, MITROPA owns and operates highway restaurants in 30 locations. MITROPA Schiffs-Catering GmbH provides food and other product sales on board of the big ferries between Germany and Denmark or Sweden for Scandlines Deutschland GmbH. MITROPA has foreign subsidiaries in Switzerland, Austria, and France. The company is wholly owned by DB Reise & Touristik AG, a subsidiary of Germany's privatized railroad company Deutsche Bahn AG.

## World War I Origins

Before World War I there was only a handful of regional operators of railroad dining cars in Germany. Most of Europe,

however, was served by one company, the Compagnie Internationale des Wagons-Lits et des Grands Express Européens. Founded in 1876 by George Nagelmacker, Wagons-Lits was legally registered in Brussels, Belgium, but in fact was managed from its headquarters in France. Wagons-Lits's sleepers and dining cars ran from western Europe to the Balkans, Constantinople, and Vladivostok. The company also had long-term general contracts with the railroad authorities of many German states.

An exception was the Prussian railroad authority, the Königlich Preussische Eisenbahn-Verwaltung (KPEV), which, after a wave of nationalization of private Prussian railroad companies, was the largest organization of its kind in Germany. KPEV did not renew its contracts with Wagons-Lits in the mid-1880s and began setting up its own sleeping and dining car operations. To gain access to the Prussian dining car market Wagons-Lits founded a subsidiary in Berlin—the Deutsche Eisenbahn-Speisewagen-Gesellschaft (DESG). Before World War I the Prussian-Hessian railroad administration operated sleepers on 49 lines, while Wagons-Lits served on 38 long-distance lines in Germany. Wagons-Lits also catered on 43 German lines, while its DESG subsidiary served 41 lines with its 116 dining cars. The five private dining car companies served on 37 lines with 70 dining cars.

Four weeks after World War I started, in September 1914, Wagons-Lits's manager in Berlin sent a letter to the Prussian minister for public works proposing transferring all Wagons-Lits's assets to a German public company with a maximum share of 30 percent retained by Wagons-Lits. In the following months all contracts with Wagons-Lits were canceled. Then, after German troops occupied France and Belgium, Wagons-Lits was put under German administration. In August 1915 the Prussian minister wrote to the German chancellor Theobald von Bethmann Hollweg, describing as an "intolerable situation" the fact that a company of Belgian-French origin dominated the German, Austrian, and Hungarian market for catering and sleeping car services. He suggested forcing Wagons-Lits out of Germany, Austria, and Hungary. Not only were France and Belgium at war with these countries, he noted, but the likely expansion of the German Empire eastwards meant good growth potential in the Balkan states, which were connected with western Europe only by some major railroads.

## Company Perspectives:

*MITROPA bears its destiny in its name: Middle European Sleeping and Dining Car Company. This description is, we admit, a bit too narrow, considering our many activities in addition to the railroad. But it shows that MITROPA was already seen as an internationally active enterprise when it was founded more than 80 years ago. Today we continue to emphasize our presence throughout Europe. Our newly founded subsidiaries, thus far successful, demonstrate that, reaching to the stars, we are on the right path.*

After long negotiations between the German, Austrian, and Hungarian governments, ten railroad authorities, and several banks, the parties agreed to transfer rights to operate sleeping and dining cars in their territories to a German company. Deutsche Bank and Dresdner Bank used the Akt. Ges. Kaliwerk Neu-Bleicherode, a company founded in 1905, as a vehicle for the transaction. First the company was renamed Mitropa AG für Erwerb und Verwertung von Eisenbahnmaterial in May 1916. Then, the Mitteleuropäische Schlafwagen- und Speisewagen-Aktiengesellschaft (MSG) was officially founded on November 24, 1916, at a meeting held in Berlin by the two banks. Soon abbreviated as MITROPA from ''mitteleuropäisch'' (middle European), the company was to be engaged in buying and operating sleepers, dining cars, and luxury coaches and trains. Two-thirds of its capital was held by German banks, one-fifth by Austrian banks, and the rest by Hungarian banks.

According to the plan that had been worked out, Wagons-Lits would surrender all dining car and sleeper lines in Germany and in the occupied territory to MITROPA by January 1, 1917. Wagons-Lits was also obliged to sell its sleepers and dining cars to MITROPA, which also took over Wagons-Lits's staff and lease agreements, as well as its stock of food, beverages, tobacco products, and other supplies in the coaches and warehouses. The five regional operators of dining cars in Germany were also merged with MITROPA.

### Progress and Setbacks Until 1925

In its first year of business MITROPA operated about 250 sleepers and dining cars throughout Germany and areas occupied by German troops. However, because of the war, securing food supplies was becoming more and more difficult. Finally, at the war's end in November 1918, Germany signed the Versailles Treaty which went into effect on January 10, 1920. Article 367 of this treaty stipulated that Germany reimburse Wagons-Lits for all losses and damage by the war and surrender all international rail lines to Wagons-Lits.

Germany's defeat, the political unrest after the war, and the restrictions of the Versailles Treaty were a major setback for MITROPA. All foreign rail lines which the company served during the war—including Austria and Hungary—were lost. By June 1920 all Austrian and Hungarian shareholders returned their MITROPA shares to the Deutsche Bank and left the company's board of directors. At the same time its competitor Wagons-Lits tried successfully to win back the German markets it lost during the war. Wagons-Lits refused to communicate with MITROPA directly, claiming that MITROPA was a war creation and hence illegal. Wagons-Lits also filed about 20 lawsuits against the German Reich and its railroad administration, demanding that MITROPA be dissolved, that all Wagons-Lits's prewar contracts within Germany from 1914 be reactivated, and that MITROPA reimburse Wagons-Lits for all losses and damages it had suffered. Later, in June 1922, a court ruled that the liquidation of Wagons-Lits's German subsidiary DESG was not considered an act of war but had been based on legal business agreements. That meant that MITROPA was not required to return the 116 DESG dining cars it had purchased from Wagons-Lits.

While these lawsuits made their way through the legal system, MITROPA sought a way to establish itself on a solid foundation and start expanding once again. In November 1919 MITROPA director Hermann Witscher met with Sir Henry Worth Thornton in London. Thornton, an American by birth, was general manager of England's Great Eastern Railway Company (GER) and also represented Canada Trust Limited, a consortium of GER, the Canadian Pacific Railway (CPR), and Barclay Bank. GER was interested in expanding to continental Europe while the trust envisioned controlling the sleeping and dining car business in Europe by means of a holding company based in England. As a result of ongoing negotiations between the parties, in October 1921 the Societé Anonyme Transcontinent—based for political and tax reasons in Geneva, Switzerland—was founded. Prior to that transaction, Canada Trust had secured the rights to MITROPA's foreign contracts, and these were then transferred to the newly founded London-based Trans-European Company Limited. Trans-European also acquired 40 percent of MITROPA's share capital. Trans-European held 80 percent of the Swiss holding company's share capital while MITROPA was issued 20 percent. However, the deal finally went against MITROPA's interests. By 1924 there were no leading figures of the Canadian Trust left on MITROPA's board of directors. In that year Swiss banker Felix Somary joined the board. He represented Blankart, a financial group which by that time owned the other 80 percent of the Transcontinent shares.

Article 367 of the Versailles Treaty was scheduled to expire on January 10, 1925, and Wagons-Lits had a vital interest in settling its yet outstanding issues with MITROPA. In early 1925, when negotiations had almost been finalized, Somary offered Wagons-Lits the Transcontinent shares of the Blankart group. This would have given Wagons-Lits 40 percent of MITROPA's share capital and 26 percent of the voting rights. The German railways company Deutsche Reichsbahn-Gesellschaft had already acquired a 17 percent share in MITROPA in 1921. MITROPA itself would have owned only a 43 percent minority share.

In April 1925 the ''Peace Treaty'' between Wagons-Lits and MITROPA was finally reached. It regulated the relationship of the two companies concerning international railroad traffic with and through Germany. In general, Wagons-Lits served in all transit trains through Germany from all other European countries and from Germany to other European countries, with some exceptions. MITROPA served on all domestic trains in Germany, as well as on trains from Germany to the Saar, Danzig, Scandinavia, the Netherlands, and popular destinations in Switzerland, Austria, and Bohemia.

## Key Dates:

**1916:** MITROPA is founded in Berlin, taking over many of the dining cars and assets of French-Belgian concern Wagons-Lits.

**1924:** MITROPA sets up headquarters at the "Hermes" trading house in Berlin.

**1925:** A "Peace Treaty" between Wagons-Lits and MITROPA is reached; Germany's public railroad company becomes MITROPA's majority shareholder.

**1944:** MITROPA's central food warehouse is completely destroyed by bombs.

**1949:** DSG is founded in Frankfurt/Main.

**1954:** Agreement between MITROPA and DSG concerning "Inter-Zone Travel" is reached.

**1990:** MITROPA and DSG sign cooperation agreement after Germany's reunification.

**1994:** The two German service companies are reunited as MITROPA.

**1997:** MITROPA's subsidiaries in Switzerland and France are founded.

After Wagons-Lits's agreement with MITROPA went into effect, Wagons-Lits announced that it had no interest in buying the Transcontinent shares. However, in November 1925 Deutsche Reichsbahn wrote to MITROPA's board of directors that they had acquired the shares and thereby owned a 57 percent majority in MITROPA. Transcontinent tried to bring MITROPA new business abroad, for example in Italy, Spain, and even the Soviet Union, but failed. As a result of this adventure, MITROPA lost its independence to the growing influence of its new parent company, the Deutsche Reichsbahn.

### The 1920s through World War II

MITROPA initiated several attempts to modify the terms of the agreement with Wagons-Lits during the second half of the 1920s. However, just the business it was allowed to conduct enabled the company to experience a remarkable upswing. Deutsche Reichsbahn, which owned almost 90 percent of MITROPA's share capital, transferred a large part of its sleeping car business to MITROPA but requested the company to not expand into foreign countries. Due to the growing transportation needs in Germany, MITROPA ordered new sleepers and dining cars. By the end of 1926 MITROPA was operating 565 dining cars and sleepers. To maintain these cars it established a second repair and maintenance workshop in Berlin-Falkensee. From 1928 on, MITROPA's railroad cars featured a new red and gold corporate logo.

MITROPA also became involved in several side businesses. The company acquired vineyard Franz O. Klein in Traben-Trarbach and served its own MITROPA Gold, MITROPA Silber, and MITROPA Kupfer brands of wine. MITROPA also provided catering services on a ferry line from Sassnitz, Germany, to Trelleborg, Sweden, as well as on cruise ships on the Danube and Havel rivers. In 1927 MITROPA acquired a majority share in Elite Autofahrt GmbH, a company that organized

sightseeing trips through Berlin and to popular destinations nearby, such as Potsdam, Wittenberg, and Wörlitzer Park. A year later MITROPA bought Siesta GmbH from Deutsche Reichsbahn; this company rented travel pillows at train stations for one German Mark. In addition, MITROPA started operating train station restaurants, and in 1928 MITROPA also landed a catering deal with two-year-old German airline Luft Hansa. The first meal on a Luft Hansa plane was served by a MITROPA waiter on a flight from Berlin to Paris in that year. The catering deal included a supply of white table cloths, china, silverware, and fresh flowers. In 1931 MITROPA became responsible for the telephone service on Deutsche Reichsbahn trains. In the late 1930s the company equipped baggage wagons with kitchens, for catering on trains without dining cars.

When the National Socialists came to power in Germany, they began exploiting MITROPA for their own aggressive expansion plans. MITROPA's board of directors was aware of this "favorable situation" and declared that the company could be a "valuable propaganda tool for the German economy." The Nazis were open to this idea and used MITROPA's services for their subsidized "Kraft-durch-Freude" (Strength through Joy) holiday trips for low income residents, as well as for the 1936 Olympic Games in Berlin, where MITROPA served over 700 special rail lines. Before the outbreak of World War II in July 1939, MITROPA operated about 298 dining cars and 244 sleepers daily.

However, once World War II began, the situation changed completely. At first, the whole business came to a halt. Later, after all contracts with Wagons-Lits were canceled once again, MITROPA served on all trains traveling into the countries occupied by the German army. Purchasing food and supplies became more and more difficult, and the German military requested a increasing part of MITROPA's capacity. In the early 1940s MITROPA was asked to run a growing number of restaurants in train stations in and outside Germany. However, when the fronts were pushed back, and the war came back into Germany, over 40 percent of MITROPA's staff was called to serve in the German army. In May 1944 bombs destroyed MITROPA's central food warehouse in Berlin. As Russian troops were approaching Berlin, MITROPA's headquarters was moved in the dead of night, April 12, 1945, from Berlin to Hamburg on a train with 14 sleeping and dining cars.

### Divided and Reunited after 1945

By the end of World War II, 50 percent of MITROPA's cars had been destroyed. Like Germany itself, the company was divided into four, with one division for each of the sectors occupied by the Allied Powers of France, Great Britain, the United States, and the Soviet Union. After the Federal Republic of Germany was established in 1949 in the three Western German sectors, the former MITROPA divisions were merged into a new company, the Deutsche Schlafwagen- und Speisewagen-Gesellschaft (DSG) headquartered in Frankfurt/Main. In 1954 an agreement between MITROPA and DSG went into effect, regulating the so-called "Inter-Zone Travel" between the two German states. MITROPA, in the meantime, maintained the legal form of an Aktiengesellschaft, which was very unusual in East Germany. However, the company was more and more integrated into the centrally planned economy of the German Democratic Republic (GDR). As such, MITROPA's CEO received orders from the GDR's Minister for Transportation, including an annual plan for sales and profits, a percentage of which was transferred to the government budget.

In the following years MITROPA was able to significantly expand its business again. In 1954 MITROPA was awarded a catering contract for the Weisse Flotte, a fleet of pleasure and sightseeing ships, first in Berlin and two years later in Dresden. From 1958 onward, MITROPA operated all the airport restaurants in East Germany and three years later the highway restaurants as well. In 1969 MITROPA's first hotel opened in Sassnitz on Germany's biggest island Rügen. In the meantime DSG was expanding in West Germany. In 1972 the company opened its first InterCity restaurant in Frankfurt/Main. Two years later it took over the catering on the ferries from Germany to Scandinavia. In the early 1970s the relationship between the two German states improved, resulting in several agreements on transit travel, including the Berliner Abkommen of May 24, 1973, which regulated the relationship between the two railroad companies and their caterers on the basis of international law. The relationship between MITROPA and DSG remained cooperative through the 1970s and 1980s.

In 1989, the year when the Berlin Wall came down, MITROPA employed 15,000 people, and DSG employed 5,000. On January 24, 1990, MITROPA and DSG signed an agreement of cooperation. Four years later the two German service companies were reunited under the name MITROPA, headquartered in Berlin. In the first years after its reunification, the company reorganized and streamlined its business. In 1994 a new wage agreement was reached, cutting wages by about 14 percent. At the same time, the number of MITROPA's employees was reduced by over 7,000. In 1995 the subsidiary of the also reunited Deutsche Bahn AG employed 6,393 people and served about 25 million travelers in 760 dining and sleeping cars. In addition to its core business, MITROPA also operated 270 restaurants and convenience stores in train stations, catered on seven ferries, and ran 27 highway restaurants.

In the late 1990s MITROPA started focusing on international expansion again. In 1997 it founded subsidiaries in Switzerland and France and won international catering contracts from the Swiss and French railroad companies Schweizerische Bundesbahnen (SBB) and Société Nationale de Chemin de Fer Français (SNCF). Another subsidiary was founded in Austria. Looking back at MITROPA's history it seemed that—finally—the company was in a position to reach its goal to become a European player—in times of peace.

### Principal Subsidiaries

MITROPA Schiffs-Catering GmbH; MITROPA Suisse SA (Switzerland); MITROPA France S.A.S. (France; 99.9%); MITROPA Austria Handels- und Gastronomie GmbH (Austria); EURO-MOTEL Rheinische Hotel GmbH (50%); Werkstätte Neuaubing OHG (50%); ComforTable Gesellschaft für Catering und Logistik GmbH (33%); ICHG-InterCityHotel GmbH (4.5%).

### Principal Competitors

McDonald's Deutschland Inc.; Lufthansa Service GmbH; Autobahn Tank & Rast Raststaetten AG.

### Further Reading

"Aus zwei mach eins / Fuenf Jahre nach der Verschmelzung von DSG und MITROPA," OTS Originaltextservice, September 8, 1999.

"Der erste Lufthansa-Steward war ein Oberkellner der Mitropa," Frankfurter Allgemeine Zeitung, October 17, 1997, p. 31.

Gummich, Karl-Heinz, Johannes Puschmann, and Rolf Horstmann, MITROPA zwischen gestern und morgen, Berlin: Transpress VEB Verlag für Verkehrswesen, 1966, 286 p.

Krüger-Wittmack, Gottfried, and Johannes Puschmann, "75 Jahre MITROPA," Eisenbahn Journal (special issue), February 1992.

Mühl, Albert, 75 Jahre MITROPA, Freiburg, Germany: EK-Verlag GmbH, 1992, 286 p.

Scherer, Brigitte, "Die Mitropa wird achtzig und ist auf dem Weg zum 'European Player,'" Frankfurter Allgemeine Zeitung, November 21, 1996, p. R1.

Sieger, Heiner, "BUNDESBAHN; Zurück in die Zukunft," Focus Magazin, May 16, 1994, p. 222.

—Evelyn Hauser

a legendary gaming experience

# Mohegan Tribal Gaming Authority

**One Mohegan Sun Boulevard**
**Uncasville, Connecticut 06382**
**U.S.A.**
**Telephone: (860) 204-8000**
**Fax: (860) 204-7167**
**Web site: http://www.mohegansun.com**

*Private Company*
*Incorporated:* 1995
*Employees:* 5,703
*Sales:* $682.1 million (1999)
*NAIC:* 713210 Casinos; 722110 Full Service Restaurants;
  722213 Snack and Non-Alcoholic Beverage Bars;
  711310 Promoters of Performing Arts, Sports, and
  Similar Events with Facilities

The Mohegan Tribal Gaming Authority operates the Mohegan Sun casino for the Mohegan Tribe of Indians of Connecticut. The Mohegan Sun casino offers a variety of gaming options in a spectacular setting of Native American motifs. With 176,000 square feet of gaming space, the casino provides more than 3,000 slot machines, high-stakes bingo, and 150 game tables, including blackjack, craps, roulette, baccarat, Caribbean stud poker, pai gow, and 42 poker tables. Mohegan history and culture infuse the casino's interior design and place names. Natural elements inside the casino include a 30-foot waterfall and flaming urns as well as lifelike animals, trees, and rocks. The casino is set along the tribe's traditional trading cove on the Thames River in southeastern Connecticut. In the tribe's native language, "Mohegan" translates into "wolf people" and "sun" translates into "rock."

### The Endurance of the Mohegans

The development of the Mohegan Sun casino rested on U.S. government recognition of the Mohegan Tribe of Indians of Connecticut as a sovereign people. The Mohegans began the petition process in 1978, but the government rejected the petition in 1989. Although the Mohegans traced their history to

cooperation with English settlers during the 1630s, lack of evidence of tribal activities during the 1940s and 1950s led to federal rejection of sovereignty. The Mohegan system of female authority that dominated that period had been overlooked by federal employees who had focused their research on male leadership. Under Chief Ralph Sturges, elected in 1992, the tribe reinvigorated its campaign to gain federal recognition. That same year RJH Development and LMW Investments of Connecticut and Slavik Suites, Inc. of Michigan proposed the idea of developing a casino with the Mohegans. The three companies formed Trading Cove Associates (TCA), which provided the Mohegans with financial support, tribal attorneys, and advisors to assist in the effort to gain official recognition.

While the petition process continued, TCA and the Mohegans addressed the issue of obtaining state approval for development of the casino as well as obtaining more land for the small reservation. The Mohegans had partially terminated their reservation in 1861, because Mohegan overseers had permitted the theft and desecration of tribal land. By 1872 only the burial grounds and the Mohegan Church remained on the reservation roles, preserving approximately 150 acres. The Mohegans claimed the State of Connecticut had ignored the 1790 Trade and Intercourse Act, which protected Mohegan land rights.

In negotiations with the state in 1993, TCA and the Mohegans settled these centuries-old land disputes. The Mohegans dismissed its land claims and the state conceded the right of the Mohegans to seek economic independence on their traditional reservation through their choice of development. The Mohegans and TCA secured the option to purchase the 240-acre site of the United Nuclear Corporation (UNC), a dormant nuclear manufacturing facility located on part of the tribe's original reservation, and began to plan and design the casino.

The Mohegans gained federal recognition as a sovereign people in March 1994, opening the way to casino development. Sol Kerzner, head of Sun International, became involved with a 50 percent interest in TCA, bringing a certain savvy from that company's world-renowned casinos and resorts. The tribe and TCA settled issues related to development of the casino with the nearby town of Montville. The Mohegans agreed to pay $3 million toward infrastructure improvements and usage and to pay $500,000 annually in lieu of other tax arrangements. In a compact with the State of Connecticut the Mohegans pledged a Slot Win Contribution of 25 percent of annual slot revenue to the State.

The Mohegan Tribal Council, the tribe's governing body, constituted the Mohegan Tribal Gaming Authority (MTGA) in July 1995 to represent the tribe in the development and management of the Mohegan Sun casino, including oversight of the fair and proper operation of the games. MTGA hired TCA to oversee development and construction of the casino. MTGA's Business Board handled day-to-day operations and legal issues related to the development of the casino; the board consisted of two representatives from the tribe and two representatives from TCA. MTGA later changed the structure to a Management Board, composed of nine members of the Tribal Council. Once the casino opened, management arrangements between TCA and MTGA involved a 14-year contract for operations management and marketing and a seven-year contract (a legal limit) for gaming management, with TCA receiving a management fee and up to 40 percent of profits.

Financing for construction of the $280 million casino came from two sources, through the capital market and a debt-investment from Sun International. MTGA obtained $175 million through a private placement of Senior Notes, which guaranteed a 13.5 percent return on investment and a share of future profits. Sun International loaned $90 million in Subordinated Notes to MTGA to purchase the UNC land and to secure financing for equipment. MTGA obtained approval from the National Indian Gaming Commission and the Bureau of Indian Affairs and broke ground in November 1995. The Mohegans celebrated the event with a ceremonial blessing of the ground and traditional dancing.

Intending to complete construction of the casino within one year, the Mohegan Sun employment office opened in January 1996. In April the company began one of several employee education programs with the Slot Technician School. By summer, training was under way for craps, blackjack, and other table games. From more than 25,000 applicants the Mohegan Sun hired more than 5,000 employees, including many former employees of UNC. Employee uniforms incorporated buckskin aprons and vests bearing tribal symbols.

The interior design of the casino reflected the Mohegan's cultural heritage. The main center of the building replicated a wigwam, being circular in shape with aluminum poles covered in bark-colored spackle to represent tree trunks. The four entrances to the casino corresponded with the four compass directions, with each section of the structure correlating to tribal themes on the four seasons. For instance, the east corresponded with spring, so traditional spring motifs dominated the eastern portion of the casino. The carpet pattern of colorful wildflowers not only evoked the feeling of spring, but helped patrons identify their location within the casino. Pictures on the ceiling banshells included strawberries, dogwood blossoms, and fish (spring being the tribe's traditional season for fishing). Giant canvas wall hangings, made to look like animal skins, also portrayed the season's cultural associations, such as hands holding corn for planting, giving thanks to the Spirit of the Corn. The 13 lunar moons were depicted in their appropriate places throughout the casino; the Maple Sugar Moon represented the first moon of spring when the ice thaws and maple syrup flows from the trees. *The Secret Guide* offered an interpretation of the cultural symbols found throughout the facility.

The Mohegans planned to use the profits from the casino to preserve their tribal heritage and to care for the 1,100 members of the tribe. They hoped to reclaim sacred artifacts and to revive their language. They planned to build housing and a medical center for elderly members of the tribe, to give scholarships to young members, and to provide health insurance for all members. Many young Mohegans returned to the reservation with development of the casino. Contrary to J. Fenimore Cooper's 1826 novel, *The Last of the Mohicans,* the Mohegans had not disappeared but had endured and discovered a means of rebirth.

### 1996 Grand Opening and Immediate Success

When the Mohegan Sun opened on October 12, 1996, gaming facilities at the casino included a high-stakes bingo hall, 2,500 slot machines, including high-limit slots, and 170 game tables. The bingo hall converted to an 1,800-seat events center, hosting its first major boxing event in December. The Wolf Den, a 24-hour lounge in the center of the casino, featured live music every night and seating for 350 people. The Mohegan Sun catered to families with a 6,000-square-foot KidsQuest Family Entertainment Center, which provided hourly child care for children four to 12 years of age while parents gambled; children's activities included nonviolent video arcade games, a Kiddie Theater, and Barbieland, a master-planned community for Barbie dolls.

After its first 20 days in business, the Mohegan Sun counted $21.2 million in slot revenues alone. First-year profits, for fiscal year September 30, 1997, reached $36.9 million with an average daily slot win of $327. The casino counted more than 20,000 customers daily and more than 30,000 patrons on weekends.

The Mohegan Sun's promotional campaign involved grand events designed to attract a diverse customer base. Musical entertainment at the events center included Al Jarreau, Ringo Star, Pam Tillis, and Tony Bennett. The Wolf Den, featuring state-of-the-art sound and light technology, hosted Grover Washington, Jr., Duran Duran, Blondie, and other popular recording artists. "The Biggest Wedding Under the Sun" took place in the Wolf Den on Valentine's Day 1997, when 95 couples exchanged wedding vows and received a Mohegan tribal blessing. With the addition of six Let It Ride-The Tournament tables, the Mohegan Sun became the fourth venue to offer the game, holding its first tournament during the summer of

---

### Key Dates:

**1992:** Development, hotel interests approach Mohegan Tribe with casino idea.

**1994:** Federal recognition of tribe's sovereignty accelerates development.

**1995:** Mohegan Tribal Gaming Authority (MTGA) is formed to represent tribe in casino development, management.

**1996:** Mohegan Sun casino opens less than one year after construction begins.

**1998:** MTGA announces plan to expand with luxury hotel, convention facilities, and arena.

**2000:** MTGA assumes management of Mohegan Sun.

---

1997. The Mohegan Sun also sponsored Hartford's annual Fourth of July Riverfest celebration and other local events. In January 1998, the casino hosted a ten-day series of culinary classes given by 15 chefs from the Mohegan Sun and Sun International resorts.

Television advertising focused on the casino's interior ambiance, the friendly staff, and the glamor and excitement of gaming. After showing a collage of images from the casino, a chauffeur stated, "You'll find it easy to get here, but very hard to leave." A dealer followed, "We keep the lines short and the action non-stop. It's the Mohegan Sun way." The advertisements targeted audiences in New York, Massachusetts, Connecticut, and Rhode Island. Cities within 125 miles of the casino included New York City, Boston, Providence, and Hartford, as well as many wealthy suburbs.

In February 1998 the MTGA announced changes to its relationship with TCA in conjunction with the announcement of the Mohegan Sun's expansion plans. The two organizations agreed to terminate TCA's management contracts effective January 1, 2000. The Mohegans agreed to pay TCA five percent of gross profits for 15 years beginning on that date. TCA and MTGA announced a new partnership agreement involving a $450 million expansion of the casino into a hotel and casino resort destination. Expansion plans included a 1,500-room luxury hotel, 100,000 square feet of casino and entertainment space, and a meeting and convention center.

The MTGA continued to expand gaming and services within existing facilities at the Mohegan Sun. In May 1998 the company added 500 new slot games, with 100 machines replacing existing slots; customer and technology-driven changes required an unusually early adjustment. A state-of-the art RaceBook opened on Labor Day for wagering on live Jai-Alai and horse and greyhound racing from Florida, California, Illinois, Kentucky, and New York. In addition to 300 wall-to-wall televisions, RaceBook provided 200 personal wagering terminals with 13-inch television monitors and computerized, self-service betting. The Micro-Brew Pub opened adjacent to the RaceBook area, featuring Sachem's Ale and Matahga Lager, both named for past Mohegan Chiefs. The new Uncas Pavilion, a temporary structure holding 5,000 seats, hosted several events in 1998, including a Heavyweight Title boxing match,

Oktoberfest activities, and concerts by Lynyrd Skynyrd and The Steve Miller Band. A 16-pump Citgo gas station and convenience store opened on the reservation in December.

Advertising for the Mohegan Sun continued to focus on the ambiance and service. In "Winning," the camera followed an elegantly dressed couple from their limousine, through the casino, to a blackjack table. The voiceover stated, "The Mohegan Sun. . . . Nothing even comes close." In "Details," a montage of images accompanied the voiceover, "To make a big impression, it helps to remember that the little things really aren't so little. . . . Experience the difference the Mohegan Sun way." Print advertisements in New York and New England supplemented the television advertisements.

The MTGA continued to update its slot offerings at the existing casino. In May 1999 the company installed Wolf Den Hits, a link-progressive slot game. Custom designed for the Mohegan Sun, the slot game featured lifelike replicas of wolves on a rock outcropping. Howls emanated from the wolves when a patron hit the jackpot. Slots played an important role in rising revenues at the casino, as average daily slot win increased from $361 per day in fiscal 1998 to $430 per day in 1999.

Revenues for fiscal year ended September 30, 1999 increased to $682 million, from $583.2 million in 1998, but the Mohegan Sun's financial activities resulted in a loss of $39 million. This was actually an improvement over a loss of $332 million in 1998. Both years' losses related to agreement relinquishment payments to TCA, and 1999 losses also stemmed from debt extinguishment fees. MTGA expected to be profitable in the future as operating margins continued to improve. Players Club, which offered points based on game play toward food, merchandise, day care, and gasoline, counted more than 1.2 million members at the end of fiscal 1999.

### Into the Future with Project Sunburst

The MTGA reorganized its financial debt in preparation for expansion of the Mohegan Sun, dubbed "Project Sunburst." The company paid its original development debts and secured lower interest debt with the issuance of $200 million in Senior Notes and $300 million in Senior Subordinated Notes. Construction began in May 1999 when the MTGA broke ground on a parking garage and a $30 million Employee Center.

The Mohegans hoped to lure quality employees for the new resort with progressive employee benefits, including the Employee Center. The facility provided covered parking, a state-of-the art fitness center, a wellness center, a post office, a dry cleaning service, a banking facility, and a computer and training center. Tribal themes extended into the interior design of the Employee Center.

In February 2000 the Mohegans unveiled final plans for expansion, which had itself expanded into an $800 million project. Hoping to attract business and leisure travelers as well as gamblers, Project Sunburst involved a 34-story luxury hotel with 1,200 guest rooms, including 175 suites. Convention and meeting space included a 40,000-square-foot ballroom (the largest in New England), 30 meeting rooms holding up to 5,300 people, and a business center with computer workstations and electronic equipment rental. To 2,300 square feet of existing retail space, Project Sunburst added 275,000 square feet of premium space. MTGA planned a world-class spa with a 16,000 square-foot swimming pool and a 12,500-square-foot sun terrace. Staff at the spa, salon, and fitness center included personal trainers and nutritionists. KidsQuest added a 10,000-square-foot adventure arcade and accommodations for children as young as six weeks old. New gaming space housed 2,000 slot machines, Keno, and 75 game tables. The ambitious plan included more than 20 new dining options and a 10,000-seat arena with retractable seating for exhibition space. Construction on the arena began in February 2000 and MTGA expected the arena to be completed in the fall 2001.

Design elements of Project Sunburst extended from the Mohegan tribal motifs of the original casino, expressing elemental and celestial themes. A Tree of Life at the walkway between the two facilities represented the past, present, and future of the Mohegan tribe. The roots symbolized the tribe's ancestors and the branches, with sparkling beaded canopies, signified the future generations. Thus the original Casino of the Earth connected to the new Casino of the Sky, with its 115,000-square-foot planetarium, the largest working planetarium dome in the world. Wombi Rock, at the center of the casino, was to be made of translucent alabaster and onyx and to house a three-story lounge with a dance floor. Restaurant designs incorporated water, earth, sun, and air motifs as did the interior of the 300-seat cabaret. The hotel, with reflective glass and towers bursting from the center tower, exemplified the celestial dimension of Project Sunburst. MTGA expected Project Sunburst to be completed in April 2002 during the Moon of the Peeping Frogs, a time of rebirth in the Mohegan tribal calendar.

### Principal Competitors

Harrah's Entertainment, Inc.; Mashantucket Pequot Gaming Enterprise, Inc.; Trump Hotels & Casino Resorts, Inc.

### Further Reading

Barberi, Kelly, "Mohegan Sun to Include $10 Mil Arena as Part of $800 Million Expansion Plan," *Amusement Business,* March 13, 2000.

Cassidy, Tina, "Connecticut Casinos Lure Gamblers from Massachusetts," *Knight-Ridder/Tribune Business News,* March 1, 1999.

Chapman, Mark, "New Mohegan Sun Shines, Growing Foxwoods Glitters as Southeast Becomes the Not-So-Quiet Corner," *Boston Herald,* October 24, 1996, p. T1.

Coleman-Lochner, Lauren, "Connecticut Building on its Casino Economy," *New Jersey Record,* October 20, 1996, p. 8.

Eichelberg, Sandra J., ed., *Mohegan Sun: The Secret Guide,* Uncasville, Conn.: Little People Publications, 1998.

Fawcett, Melissa Jayne, *The Lasting of the Mohegans,* Uncasville, Conn.: The Mohegan Tribe, 1995.

Gaines, Judith, "High Stakes Mohegans, Others Betting on Casino to Brighten Future," *Boston Globe,* June 19, 1996, p. T1.

Green, Marian, "The New Slot Market," *International Gaming and Wagering Business,* May 1998, p. 1.

Jones, Sarah, "Mintz & Hoke Debuts Casino Spots, Picks Up Two Assignments," *ADWEEK New England Advertising Week,* June 23, 1997, p. 3.

———, "Mohegan Sun Gambles on Glamor," *ADWEEK New England Advertising Week,* January 25, 1999, p. 2.

Kaplan, David, "Connecticut Mohegans Push Back Casino Debt's Tender Offer Deadline," *Bond Buyer,* February 25, 1999, p. 3.

Longmore-Etheridge, Ann, "Casinos Face a Tough ID Challenge," *Security Management,* April 1998, p. 65.

Pederson, Mark, "Massive Mohegan," *Leisure Travel News,* February 21, 2000, p. 1.

Selwitz, Robert, "New Casino Is First of the Mohegans," *Hotel & Motel Management,* September 16, 1996, p. 18.

Sinclair, Sebastian, "Go-go Times Roll on for Foxwoods, Mohegan Sun," *International Gaming and Wagering Business,* May 1998, p. S8.

"Sun Casino Plans $450 Million Expansion," *Knight-Ridder/Tribune Business News,* February 15, 1999.

Wolfson, Bernard J., "Mohegan Sun Slots Pull in $21.2M in First 20 Days," *Boston Herald,* November 6, 1996, p. 37.

—Mary Tradii

# Mr. Bricolage S.A.

1 rue Montaigne
45380 La Chapelle Saint Mesmin
France
Telephone: (+33) 02.38.43.50.00
Fax: (+33) 02.38.43.11.58
Web site: http://www.mr-bricolage.fr

*Public Company*
*Incorporated:* 1968 as ANPF (Action nationale des
   promoteurs du faites-le vous-même); 1995 as Mr.
   Bricolage S.A.
*Employees:* 4,859
*Sales:* EUR 916 million ($900 million)(1999)
*Stock Exchanges:* Euronext Paris
*Ticker Symbol:* 7568.PA
*NAIC:* 444130 Hardware Stores

Mr. Bricolage S.A. has all the right tools for building France's fourth-largest chain of do-it-yourself hardware stores. As the publicly listed holding company for the cooperative network of 326 independently operated Mr. Bricolage stores, Mr. Bricolage S.A. was originally known as the ANPF (Action nationale des promoteurs du faites-le-vous-même). The ANPF was a cooperative organization that, as a holding company, converted its status in 1995 to that of a limited liability company in order to be able to raise outside capital. Since then, Mr. Bricolage S.A. has built its own network, in addition to continuing in its capacity as purchasing and distribution center for the entire Mr. Bricolage network of stores. In addition, it has been responsible for coordinating the group's strategy, marketing and communications program, and employee training. Mr. Bricolage S.A. also coordinates the group's range of some 5,000 Mr. Bricolage brand label products—a number expected to double by 2004. The company also produces and distributes its own magazine, with a circulation of some 80,000 per issue.

## Do-It-Yourself Club in the 1960s

The origins of Mr. Bricolage lay in the stirrings of France's do-it-yourself (DIY) market in the 1960s. The extended eco-nomic expansion in France as the country rebuilt after World War II had also brought more leisure time to the people—and a new spirit of leisure activities. More and more people were turning to a new hobby—that of 'bricolage,' a term which quickly encompassed every level from the simple tinkerer to full-scale home renovation and construction projects, including interior decorations and fittings. More and more traditional hardware stores began to cater to this new breed of customer, expanding both their product range and their level of customer assistance. Many stores, such as Castorama (later a market leader), looked toward their American counterparts for inspiration and imported the so-called ''category killer'' concept (vast warehouse stores with extensive product ranges) to France.

During the 1960s, a number of France's hardware stores catering to the DIY market started an association to encourage the growing DIY market. Created in 1964, the group operated more or less informally, and consisted primarily of individual and small groups of stores operating under various names such as Kit, Leroux & Fils and Tout Pour le Bricoleur (''Everything for the DIY'er''). But by the end of the decade, the group had formalized their association as the cooperative ANPF, or Action Nationale des Promoteurs du Faite-le-vous-même, the direct French translation of 'do-it-yourself.'

The ANPF had originally formed as an information exchange, and the cooperative quickly transformed into a centralization force for the group's individual members and their stores. The ANPF began coordinating purchases—obtaining better prices with larger orders—while the individual stores continued operating under their former store names. Among those joining the cooperative was Maurice Vax, himself owner of two DIY stores.

If the DIY market had flourished as a leisure market in the 1960s, it took on new steam in the 1970s. The Arab Oil Embargo and the resulting worldwide recession ended some 25 years of economic expansion in France. The tightening economy was to lead still greater numbers of people into the DIY market—not simply as a leisure pursuit, but also as an economic necessity. Before the end of the decade, many were referring to the DIY market as France's national hobby.

The country's retail market was also changing. Where France had once relied on its small, independent merchants, the new retail scene featured growing numbers of regional and national chains and large-scale store formats. These included the so-called 'hypermarkets,' which functioned as combined grocers and department stores. As the French shopper became used to the extended range of products found in the large-scale format, most retailers were forced to follow suit, developing warehouse-style and category killer concepts for most retail segments. The DIY market was among the fastest growing sector, and by the end of the 1970s a number of national chains—including Leroy Merlin, Castorama and Lapeyre—had begun to dominate the marketplace, crowding out the country's smaller independent merchants.

The members of the ANPF had also come to feel the threat of the new competition. While their larger competitors fought for the country's large urban markets, the ANPF members saw the benefits of specializing on the country's small and mid-sized markets, with populations ranging from 20,000 to 80,000. Yet the cooperative had also started to feel the need to create a more unifying and recognizable brand in order to compete against its larger, national rivals, which were quickly attracting consumers away from their local markets to a growing number of vast retail parks located on the outskirts of the country's urban centers.

### Call Me "Mr." in the 1980s

In 1980, the members of the ANPF cooperative decided to group their stores under a single, nationally identifiable brand name. While maintaining their independent status, the retailers sought to introduce not only a unifying brand, but also a national advertising and marketing strategy as well. The ANPF looked for a name for their proposed network, scouting the existing retail landscape. As Vax explained to *Capital:* "The furniture retailers had created Mr. Meuble. So why not Mr. Bricolage?"

So the title became Mr. Bricolage—and during the 1980s, the new national chain quickly built a national brand reputation, making it one of the country's best-known brands. The ANPF membership was also growing quickly, as more and more independent retailers turned to the group—with its centralized purchasing and marketing and communications programs—in order to compete against the growing number of large-scale chains. Still, the members retained their independence, to an extent.

During the mid-1980s, the ANPF's role in the Mr. Bricolage network expanded to include employee training initiatives. Indeed, the Mr. Bricolage name was soon to become synonymous with its highly trained sales staff offering a high-degree of personalized assistance to its customers. In this way, the network

was able to set itself apart from its competitors. The company's training program became one of the country's most ambitious, with employees—most often themselves dedicated DIY'ers—with total man hours reaching nearly 9,000 hours by the beginning of the new century. Mr. Bricolage also served to train store managers, to serve the growing number of ANPF members who operated multiple stores. The Ecole Mr. Bricolage formed the partnership in the Ecole Nationale de Distribution Spécialisée, to extend its training program to other retail groups.

The success of the Mr. Bricolage brand led to the creation of a second brand—Bricotruc—in order to place the cooperative's smaller stores under the same banner. Serving the country's rural and agricultural towns and villages, with populations ranging from 4,000 to 7,000 residents, and with store formats averaging less than 600 square meters, the Bricotruc stores featured the same product categories as the larger Mr. Bricolage stores. Launched in 1989, the Bricotruc chain added to the ANPF's growing membership of some 300 total stores at the beginning of the 1990s.

At the same time, the cooperative had also begun to export its brand name. In 1990, the first foreign Mr. Bricolage opened in Lisbon, Portugal, and was directly owned by the ANPF. Two years later, the group decided to enter the Spanish market as well. This time, however, the ANPF formed a local partnership, taking a 51 percent share in the newly created ANPF Espagne, and opened its first Spanish store in Malaga. Through the 1990s, Mr. Bricolage turned to other European markets, including Belgium and Turkey, and then looked farther abroad, licensing the Mr. Bricolage name and concept to independent retailers in Azerbaijan and Uruguay.

### Obstacles in the 1990s

The housing crisis of the late 1980s, and the beginning of an economic recession in France that extended deep into the mid-1990s, led to a shakeup of the French retail market—and the DIY market in particular. Companies entered a period of consolidation, and before long the market narrowed to a reduced number of clear leaders. Mr. Bricolage had managed to maintain its independence throughout this period, capturing the number four position in the French DIY market. Aiding the group's growth during this time was the highly successful rollout of a range of products featuring the Mr. Bricolage name. Launched in 1993, the Mr. Bricolage product line grew to some 5,000 products by the end of the decade.

Meanwhile, the tightening competition in France during the 1990s—especially as a growing number of French were developing a taste for other leisure pursuits, to the detriment of the DIY market—forced Mr. Bricolage to seek further expansion in order to gain greater economies of scale. At the same time, growing numbers of the ANPF's original members were looking forward to retirement, but, finding no successors, the future of their stores were placed in doubt. The ANPF itself was faced with buying their stores—some 21 stores in all by the end of the 1990s, with the purchase of another 40 member stores appearing likely before the year 2005.

The growing Mr. Bricolage format also played a role in a transformation of the ANPF. After converting the Bricotruc

---

## Key Dates:

**1964:** An information exchange group is organized among independent hardware stores in France.
**1968:** The cooperative ANPF is formed.
**1980:** Mr. Bricolage brand name is launched.
**1989:** The Bricotruc store format is introduced.
**1990:** First foreign store opens in Portugal.
**1992:** Store opens in Spain.
**1993:** Launch of Mr. Bricolage branded product range.
**1995:** ANPF converts to Mr. Bricolage S.A.
**2000:** Public offering on Euronext Paris secondary market; launch of new large-scale store format.

---

stores to the Mr. Bricolage banner in the mid-1990s, the ANPF began to define a new expanded store format for the future. The cooperative was preparing to meet its competitors on their large urban area turf, and a new Mr. Bricolage format was developed for stores larger than 3,000 square meters—with some stores reaching up to 11,000 square meters. The flexibility of the Mr. Bricolage format—redefined into four store-size ranges—helped the company continue to boost its share of the national DIY market. Because of these new factors, the company needed an influx of capital.

Yet ANPF's cooperative status prevented it from raising outside capital. In order to circumvent this limit, the group decided to 'empty' the ANPF and form a new central organization, Mr. Bricolage S.A. As a limited liability company, Mr. Bricolage S.A. was able to pursue outside investors, and quickly sold a 25 percent share to capital risk firm 3I. By then, the total Mr. Bricolage network sales had topped the FFr 4 billion mark.

### Growth in a New Millennium

The group's expanded store formats and continued international growth, as well as its strong brand name, helped send sales soaring in the late 1990s. While sales increased to FFr 5 billion in 1997, they soared to reach an expected FFr 6.7 billion (EUR 916 million) by the end of 2000. Aiding the company's growth was a return to vitality for the French economy. In order to take further advantage of this, the group—through Mr. Bricolage S.A.—prepared to make a public offering. The listing, placing the

company's stock on the Euronext Paris secondary market, was completed at the beginning of the year 2000, coinciding with the 20th anniversary celebration of the Mr. Bricolage brand. As part of that celebration, the group launched a new store format, placing a new emphasis on home decoration.

Mr. Bricolage S.A. announced ambitious growth plans for the first five years of the new century, proposing to build out the company's network to more than 560, including 350 in France, thereby multiplying by six its international stores, to reach 150 stores. Mr. Bricolage itself, which by then owned 26 stores, expected to continue buying up other Mr. Bricolage stores. At the same time, there were plans to open new stores, particularly as the costs of opening new large-format Mr. Bricolage stores, estimated at some FFr 15 million, had become too heavy a burden for the group's independent retailers. As such, Mr. Bricolage S.A., which continued its central role to the network, also intended to become a major retailer in its own right, with 60 company-owned stores by the year 2004.

Led by president Maurice Vax and CEO Hervé Courvoisier, Mr. Bricolage S.A., set its sights on increasing expansion in the first half of the first decade of the new century. The company was beginning to depart from its traditional focus on smaller cities of populations less than 80,000 to meet its competition—the French DIY market leaders Castorama and Leroy Merlin—head to head in the larger urban centers. Mr. Bricolage's flexible store configuration—four formats ranging from less than 1,000 square meters up to 11,000 square meters—was enabling it to tailor its stores to the specific needs of each local market.

### Principal Competitors

Leroy Merlin S.A.; Groupe Castorama-Dubois Investissements; Carrefour-Promodes S.A; Lapeyre S.A.

### Further Reading

Besses-Boumard, Pascale, ''Mr. Bricolage bouleverse son statut pour entrer en Bourse,'' *Les Echos,* November 10, 1999, p. 25.
Bialobos, Chantal, ''Monsieur Bricolage fait son trou,'' *Capital,* June 2000, p. 66.
Lupieri, Stephane, ''Mr. Bricolage s'emancipe,'' *Enjeux Les Echos,* April 1, 2000, p. 78.

—M.L. Cohen

# MTS Inc.

**2500 Del Monte Street, Building C**
**West Sacramento, California 95691**
**U.S.A.**
**Telephone: (916) 373-2500**
**Fax: (916) 373-2434**
**Web site: http://www.towerrecords.com**

*Private Company*
*Incorporated:* 1960
*Employees:* 7,500
*Sales:* $1.02 billion (1999)
*NAIC:* 45122 Prerecorded Tape, Compact Disc, and
    Record Stores; 451211 Book Stores; 443112 Radio,
    Television, and Other Electronics Stores

MTS Inc., the little-known corporate name of the much more widely recognized Tower Records, is the second largest music retailer in the United States. In addition to CDs, cassette tapes, and music videos, MTS outlets sell movie videos, books, magazines, and newspapers, as well as its own line of designer clothing. In mid-2000 MTS had a chain of more than 183 stores that it owned and another 61 stores that were operated as franchises. Tower Records stores are located in some 20 countries on four continents. In contrast to many other large chains, Tower does not order for its branch locations centrally. The corporate philosophy is that each store knows best what its own local demand is and thus each store decides for itself what it will stock and how its stock will be merchandised.

## Company Origins

Tower Records, the international chain of record, book, and video stores run by MTS Inc., traces its origins to a small drugstore in Sacramento, California. For much of the 1940s, young Russ Solomon sold records from the store, which belonged to his father. In the 1950s Solomon took a chance, left retailing, and tried his hand at distributing records. It was a miserable failure. He borrowed heavily to finance the business and in 1960, after eight years of struggle, he went bankrupt.

The experience left a somewhat bitter taste in Solomon's mouth and it would be many years before he looked for outside financing help.

The experience did not dampen Solomon's ambition, however. A month after the failure of his distribution business, with a $5,000 loan from his father, Russ Solomon opened a record store of his own. It was located in Sacramento's famous old Tower Theater, which gave Tower Records its name. The Tower concept—"supermarket-style" record stores open until midnight with an incredibly deep selection of merchandise— developed through the 1960s. Fueling the store's success was the skyrocketing popularity of rock 'n roll and other recorded music. That trend hit its full stride in 1967 with the Summer of Love in San Francisco and the definite emergence of rock as a pervasive cultural, social, and political phenomenon. That same year, Russ Solomon met by chance a person who knew of a vacant supermarket on Columbus Street in San Francisco.

One year later, a Tower Records store opened in the former supermarket. It was significant for two reasons. First, the new store pioneered the Tower "large-store concept"; it had 5,000 square feet of sales space, minuscule by later Tower standards, but twice as much as any other Tower store at the time. Second, it was the first Tower store outside Sacramento, and it represented the chain's first step in an expansion that would eventually reach four continents.

At first, Tower grew in California. The chain built a store in Los Angeles on the Sunset Strip in 1969. The location became Tower's flagship site for many years. Its location in the music capital of the United States put Tower on the map for the first time. The company expanded quickly beyond Los Angeles, though, to Berkeley and San Diego in 1972, to Chico and Stockton, California in 1974, and to Anaheim in 1975. It burst the bounds of its home state in 1976, opening stores in Seattle, Washington and Phoenix, Arizona.

## Moving into Japan in 1980

Most companies would have set their sights on eastward expansion into other American cities. However, a combination of savvy, seduction, and serendipity took Tower into the market

```
┌─────────────────────────────────────────────┐
│              Company Perspectives:            │
│                                               │
│  With a keen eye on the future Tower Records' │
│  commitment to introducing its customers to   │
│  the latest trends in new product lines is    │
│  paramount to the organization's retail       │
│  philosophy. Tower forges ahead with the      │
│  development of exciting shopping environ-     │
│  ments, espousing diverse product ranges,     │
│  cafés, artist performance stages, personal   │
│  electronics departments, digital centers;    │
│  stores that celebrate the unique interests   │
│  and needs of the local community. At the     │
│  same time Tower's strong presence online     │
│  continues to add significant value to the    │
│  company and to provide online customers      │
│  with the world's largest selection of music  │
│  and more.                                    │
└─────────────────────────────────────────────┘
```

that would prove to be one of its most lucrative: Japan. In 1979, Solomon was approached by a group of Japanese businesspeople who proposed opening Tower franchise stores in Japan. Despite the rosy outlook, things began going poorly almost from the start. First, at the last minute it developed that Tower's Japanese partners, who had promised to finance the deal, had far less cash than they had let on. A badly thought-out distribution company foundered. A fact-finding trip by a Tower executive led to a company decision to set up and run a store in Japan itself, without any middlemen. That decision barely was made when the company discovered there was *already* a Tower store in the Japanese city of Sapporo. Its owners later told Tower people that they had used the name because they were so impressed by Tower's Sunset Strip outlet. In the end, Tower took over the Sapporo store and began doing business there in April 1980.

Just one year later, the company opened stores in the Japanese cities of Shibuya and Yokahama, and by the end of 1993 there were 16 Tower Records locations in Japan. Significantly, except for a few restaurants such as McDonald's, Tower Records was the first foreign retailer to crack the Japanese market. It contributed to the growth of the Japanese indie record scene by becoming the first chain in the country to stock records released by independent Japanese labels. In March 1986, Todd Rundgren performed at a Japanese Tower Records store, the first foreign artist to make an in-store appearance in a Japanese record store.

### Expanding in the 1980s

Tower was already well-established in its first overseas market before it cracked New York City in 1983. The discovery of the store's site at Fourth and Broadway was due to another of Solomon's chance encounters. That store would encompass three stories with 30,000 square feet of sales floor. That Greenwich Village store was the anchor of Tower's east coast expansion and would long be the chain's flagship location in that part of the country. It would later lead the National Association of Recording Merchandisers to name Tower its "Merchandiser of the Year."

In addition to broadening its base of stores, MTS Inc. also increased Tower's product line steadily. In 1963, the company opened the first Tower Books location. "It was a way for me to

get books cheap," Russ Solomon once told *Billboard* magazine. In 1989, at a time when the rest of the record industry viewed video with suspicion, Tower made a significant commitment to selling that product. The decision was primarily Solomon's, who realized early on that videos were collectible.

Contrary to rumors in the music industry that Boston would be the next eastern city invaded by MTS, Tower instead set its sights on Washington, D.C. It was attracted by the fact that competition among record retailers was less fierce in the capitol, and that there was a large market for classical music there that was not being served. Tower did eventually reach Boston, however, in 1987. By that time, the chain had crossed the Atlantic, opening its first stores in Great Britain. One year after Tower opened a small store in Kensington, England, it opened a huge, 25,000-square-foot outlet on London's Piccadilly Square. That move—like so many in Tower's history—was, in large part, unplanned. An acquaintance from the Hard Rock Cafe phoned Russ Solomon to tell him that the location was becoming available. It turned out to be ideal. By 1992 Tower had five stores in the United Kingdom, including sites in Glasgow and Kingston-on-Thames. Tower's growth in the United Kingdom was slow compared with that in Japan, and industry observers speculated that Tower had found the English market much more difficult that it had anticipated. Real estate prices were much higher than Russ Solomon expected. Tower also was said to have been hurt by a fine levied by British authorities for Tower's violation of laws barring Sunday hours of operation. Tower's losses were said to be significant, especially since it did 25 percent of its weekly business on Sundays.

### Introducing New Products in the Early 1990s

Tower added stores in Dublin, Ireland and Tel Aviv, Israel in 1993. It began expanding its Far East presence in 1992, opening its first store in Taiwan. The following year it announced that it would open a second store in Taipei, along with stores in Hong Kong and Singapore. As in Japan, Tower confronted a company in Singapore that was already using the name, "Tower Megastore." It was a paper company with ties to Tower's competitor, Virgin. Other problems faced by Tower in Asia and Southeast Asia included strict government censorship of music that could be sold, laws that strictly limited parallel imports that would compete with releases by labels in the host country, and widespread record piracy that enabled rival record stores to undercut Tower by selling CDs and cassette tapes at grossly reduced prices. Tower expressed its commitment to sell only legitimately manufactured recordings in its stores. It soon discovered that its level of service and the variety of music it sold enabled it to compete without becoming involved in price wars.

By 1992, Tower had about $650 million in annual sales, which increased to more than $700 million in 1993. More than $500 million of those were from the United States; Asia accounted for approximately $120 million. The chain had 77 record and video stores, 15 bookstores, and three art galleries in the United States; it had five stores in the United Kingdom and Ireland and 16 stores in Asia. At the same time Tower was working hard to implement a new point-of-sale system linked to computers in individual stores that would make ordering and restocking more efficient.

## Key Dates:

**1960:** First Tower store opens in Sacramento, California.

**1968:** Tower opens its first out-of-town store, in San Francisco, California.

**1970:** Showcase store on Sunset Boulevard in Hollywood opens.

**1979:** Tower establishes a base of operations in Tokyo, Japan.

**1981:** First Tower video store opens.

**1983:** Tower opens its first East Coast store in Greenwich Village in New York City.

**1985:** Piccadilly Circus store in London, England opens.

**1992:** First Taiwan store opens; Tower acquires Bayside Record Distributing.

**1995:** Tower opens store in the Shibuya district of Tokyo, Japan, which is the largest record store in the world.

**1996:** TowerRecords.com is launched on the Internet.

**1999:** Acquisition of franchise locations throughout Israel; first store opens in Quito, Equador.

**2000:** First Tower 2 concept stores open within Good Guys automotive stores locations in Las Vegas.

Tower made its first venture into the clothing business in the summer of 1993. It introduced a line of streetwear, hip-hop, and grunge fashion that included jackets, shorts, and shirts, designed by The Lab, Inc. Announcing the new clothing line, Tower pointed out the "synergy" that had always existed between music and clothing, remarking in *Billboard,* "Clothing is a visual extension of what this company is about." The clothing line was first presented in 30 Tower stores.

Tower sent a wave of panic through independent labels and distributors in September 1993 when it announced that it was consolidating its vendors. Henceforth, it would purchase approximately 70 record labels exclusively from a single distributor, INDI. Other distributors handling those labels would lose business they had previously done with Tower. The announcement led to a scramble among distributors of other labels to form a loose national network, hoping to remain in Tower's good graces. Although all Tower stores did their own purchasing, many regional distributors feared they could lose Tower business completely.

### International Focus in the Mid-1990s

The year 1995 was marked by more milestones for Tower Records. In March it opened its Bangkok store, the first western-style music store ever in that city. The same month it opened an enormous new store in Tokyo's Shibuya district, bringing its total outlets in Japan to 22. Billed as the world's largest record store, the Shibuya Tower—a megastore if there ever was one—filled an eight-story building and boasted more than 52,000 square feet of sales floor. The store set a sales record on its first day of business—$450,000—four and a half times more than Tower's previous best opening day. Some industry observers questioned the wisdom of the mammoth store, speculating that it could mean Tower had overextended itself in a market where it was already well-represented and where thousands of other record stores were already doing business. The Shibuya store proved itself a star performer for the company for the rest of the 1990s, however.

Tower was the second largest record retailer in the United States by 1995, trailing only Musicland. Its annual sales exceeded $800 million. In April of that year it began selling records through America Online on the Internet, aided by the chain's new on-line magazine, *Addicted to Noise.* In August Tower teamed up with The Good Guys, a retail chain that sold consumer electronics, in the first WOW superstore in Las Vegas. It was the first time two chains ever shared a single store, down to the cash registers, without merging completely.

Tower had established a solid beachhead in South Korea by spring 1996. It opened a 10,000-foot-store in Seoul in June 1995 and, later, a smaller one in Taegu. In May 1996, it opened a second large Seoul store. As in other Asian countries, import restrictions and government censorship presented challenges to getting and keeping Tower's Korean stores stocked with music. Tower's three stores in Israel, in Tel Aviv, Haifa, and Jerusalem, also were thriving by 1996 and the chain was planning to add five more there by the end of the decade.

The year 1997 saw Tower expand its international activities significantly. It enlarged its presence in Singapore in 1997 when it took over the music departments of three stores at the Singapore airport. It began negotiations for a second Singapore franchise store that year as well. It extended its base in Southeast Asia into new territories as well. In September 1997 it became the first international music retailer to enter the Malaysian market. In January 1999, after nearly a year and a half of delays, it launched its first store in the Philippines. In October, it was the first international record retailer to enter the South American market, when it opened stores in Buenos Aires, Argentina and Bogota, Columbia. Previously, Tower had not ventured further south than Mexico City. By 1998 at least one-third of all Tower's sales came from stores outside the United States.

### Planning for the Future

For most of the 1990s MTS Inc. was the object of speculation: When would it finally go public? Tower Records had always managed to finance expansion without the help of outside capital. Russ Solomon's early overextension of credit and subsequent bankruptcy also may have helped make him immune to IPO fever. In May 1998 Tower did not make a public offering. The company did, however, sell $110 million worth of seven-year subordinated notes intended to finance further international growth—into the Middle East, South Africa, India, and South America. At the same time, the issue won MTS $275 million in revolving credit from a group of banks headed by Chase Manhattan.

A year later MTS Inc. may have begun to question the wisdom of the note offering. In June 1999 it reported a loss of $2.6 million for its third quarter as well as for the nine months ending in April. Despite a gross profit of $76 million, it was forced into the red by sizable interest payments. MTS paid $4.5 million in interest during its third quarter of 1999 and $13.1 million for the nine months.

As 2000 turned to 2001, Tower Records continued to make wide-ranging plans for its future. Russ Solomon hoped to finally realize a lifelong dream of starting his own record label. A potential source of artists, he felt, could be Tower's own workforce, which included a sizable number of musicians or people who knew musicians. He also looked forward to the day when Tower had full department stores that would sell electronics, videos, books, photographic equipment, and clothes in addition to music. Solomon hoped to create a kid-in-a-candy-store atmosphere with such Tower department stores. Another ambitious program was a plan to begin selling records in a supermarket chain in Texas. Further expansion throughout the United States, into cities such as Memphis, Miami, and Houston, was also in the works.

### Principal Subsidiaries

Tower Books.

### Principal Competitors

Musicland Group Inc.; Virgin Retail Group Ltd.; HMV USA Corp.; Barnes & Noble Inc.; Borders Inc.

### Further Reading

Callaway, Erin, "Wow: Superstore Opens with a Twist; Retailers Merge POS Systems in Joint Business Strategy," *PC Week,* September 4, 1995, p. 1.

Christman, Ed, "Tower Shuffle Has Indies Scrambling; Distribs May Form Alliances, Go National," *Billboard,* September 4, 1993, p. 1.

Jeffrey, Don, "Tower's Solomon Weighs Expansion, Stock Offering," *Billboard,* May 27, 1995, p. 3.

Johnson, Kelly, "Solomons Still Feel That Tower Power," *Sacramento Business Journal,* April 16, 1999, p. 1(2).

Mayfield, Geoff, "The Flowering of Tower," *Billboard,* March 14, 1998, p. 73.

——, "Founder Russ Solomon Remembers the Decision to Take Tower Overseas," *Billboard,* September 4, 1999, p. 74.

McClure, Steve, "Selling: Across the Pacific," *Billboard,* September 4, 1999, p. 71.

——, "Tokyo Tower Has Record Sales," *Billboard,* March 25, 1995, p. 44.

White, Adam "Tower Continues U.K. Expansion, Crowns Kingston Site," *Billboard,* January 9, 1993, p. 57.

Wright, J. Nils, "Tower Expands in Megastores and Cyberspace," *Business Journal Serving Greater Sacramento,* March 20, 1995, p. 3.

—Gerald E. Brennan

# National Rifle Association of America

11250 Waples Mill Road
Fairfax, Virginia 22030
U.S.A.
Telephone: (703) 267-1000
Toll Free: (800) NRA-3888
Fax: (703) 267-3938
Web site: http://www.nrahq.org

*Nonprofit Organization*
*Incorporated:* 1871 as the National Rifle Association
*Employees:* 450
*Sales:* $131.3 million (1998)
*NAIC:* 81394 Political Organizations

The National Rifle Association is a nonprofit organization promoting gun safety and lobbying for its interpretation of the second amendment, the right to bear arms. (The amendment in full, subject to various modern interpretations, reads: ''A well-regulated militia, being necessary to the security of a free State, the right of the people to keep and bear arms shall not be infringed.'') Long respected by some and feared by others on Capitol Hill, the Association's impressive influence extends beyond its three million members. The NRA reaches one million young men and women through educational programs, including 40,000 in its young hunters program. Moreover, 6,000 marksmen compete nationally in the Association's shooting competitions.

## Yankee Origins

The NRA traces its origins to the 1870s, when two former Union Army officers—Colonel William Conant Church and General George Wingate—formed the National Rifle Association (NRA) to foster marksmanship. The NRA was chartered in the state of New York on November 17, 1871. Another well-known Civil War veteran, General Ambrose Burnside, served as the group's first president. Burnside had been a U.S. Senator and governor of Rhode Island. Although he lobbied very effectively for funding, he was not otherwise actively involved in the fledgling group and resigned within a year.

Through the founders' efforts, the state of New York granted the NRA $25,000 to create a practice ground on a 100-acre lot on Long Island. The Creedmoor range opened there in 1873 and hosted the Irish Rifle Association in a two-entrant international shooting competition held the next year. The event drew 8,000 spectators. Even in those early days, however, the NRA faced anti-gun sentiment in the cities, and in 1892 the land grant was rescinded and the range was moved to Sea Girt, New Jersey.

New York governor Alonzo Cornell, predicting a long age of peace, cut the NRA's funding in 1880. However, technological innovations and events overseas soon made weapons training relevant again. Dutch South African farmers demonstrated the effectiveness of new, highly accurate rifles in the Boer War, which led to a renewed interest in marksmanship and military preparedness in the British Empire and in America.

A revitalized NRA began setting up programs at colleges and military schools in 1903; within three years there were more than 200 young men competing at the shooting contest in New Jersey.

NRA headquarters moved to Washington, D.C. in 1907. According to Osha Gray Davidson's book, *Under Fire,* the NRA persuaded Congress and the War Department to first sell, then give away, surplus rifles and ammunition to NRA-sponsored shooting clubs. Between World War I and World War II, 200,000 rifles were reportedly distributed at cost to NRA members, whose ranks were ballooning. The NRA also received federal money and army assistance for its shooting competitions during this time.

The Association's Legislative Affairs Division was created in 1934 to disseminate information to its members regarding pending gun control legislation. Among the vehicles of communication was the group's flagship publication, *The American Rifleman,* published sporadically at first and later gaining a large and regular readership. A huge NRA letter-writing campaign helped temper one wave of gun control sentiment so that the National Firearms Act of 1934 would extend only to regulating machine guns and sawed-off shotguns. In 1938, the NRA supported provisions to limit the sale of guns across state lines and prevent the sale of guns to fugitives and convicted felons.

At the dawn of World War II, the NRA collected 7,000 guns to aid Great Britain's defense. When the United States was drawn into the war, the NRA offered its facilities and encouraged its members to guard factories.

In the postwar years, the NRA focused on hunting issues, developing a pioneering hunter education program with the state of New York. The Association also began a program for instructing policemen in marksmanship; it would introduce the country's only national law enforcement certification program in 1960. Membership in the NRA reached nearly 300,000 and employment 140 in the 1950s.

### The Controversial 1960s and 1970s

The assassination of President John F. Kennedy in November 1963 prompted the nation to rethink the availability of guns in the United States, which ultimately led to the Gun Control Act of 1968. This act banned the sale of guns through the mail; Lee Harvey Oswald had ordered his infamous rifle from the pages of *American Rifleman* for just $19.95.

A new NRA shooting range, Camp Perry, had been constructed in Ohio on the Lake Erie shore, and during this time it became home to the NRA's National Matches. The U.S. government supplied $3 million a year and the use of 5,000 troops a year for these tournaments. Opposition to such government aid to the NRA was challenged; Senator Edward Kennedy attempted to cut off the financial aid in the late 1960s and routinely fought NRA-backed bills in Congress throughout his career.

The NRA launched a new magazine, *The American Hunter*, in 1973, addressing hunting issues only. Two years later, it formed the Institute for Legislative Action (ILA), designed specifically as a lobby for second amendment rights. The ILA was headed by Harlon Bronson Carter, a Texan controversial for his involvement in the shooting murder of a Mexican youth, for which he was convicted and later cleared. The goals of the NRA during the 1970s had become two-fold. Sportsmanship and safety, embodied in *The American Hunter,* competed for attention with the role of the ILA as a gun lobby.

During this time, the NRA acquired 37,000 acres of land in the New Mexico wilderness. Controversy in the organization arose, according to Davidson's *Under Fire,* when some proposed that the New Mexico lands be designated as a shooting center, while others favored an outdoor center, dedicated to camping, wilderness survival, environmentalism, and other wide-ranging concerns, in addition to marksmanship and safety. The rift in the NRA—between those supporting the single issue of second amendment rights and those hoping to broaden the scope of the NRA— culminated, according to Davidson, at the NRA national convention of 1977 in Cincinnati. Led by Carter, the so-called "hard-liners" took over the convention in what became known as the "Cincinnati Revolt." In short, Carter and his supporters, fervently opposed to any form of gun control, wrested control of the NRA from the existing leaders (whose concerns included sportsmanship and environmentalism), turning the NRA into a single-issue gun lobby, according to Davidson. Carter was named executive vice-president, the most powerful position in the organization.

### Strength in the Reagan Years

With newly reorganized management and purpose, the NRA entered the 1980s on more cohesive footing. Energies were focused on opposing gun control. When a few local communities, such as Morton Grove, Illinois, enacted city ordinances to ban handguns all together in 1981, the NRA fought the ban unsuccessfully in court. The group then battled similar legislation on the state level, helping defeat Proposition 15 in California, which called for a ban on the sale of new handguns. However, the NRA was unable to overturn a new ban on handguns in Maryland in 1988.

A national print advertising campaign launched in January 1982 gained wide attention. With the tagline "I am the NRA," a variety of individuals—including an eight year-old boy, former astronaut Wally Schirra, former Dallas Cowboys cheerleader Jo Anne Hall, actor/singer Roy Rogers, and others—highlighted the group's diverse member base. While several magazines refused to run the ads, particularly those ads depicting handguns, some 45 magazines did run them, and they were credited with raising the NRA's profile considerably. The NRA had more than one million members in 1977; its ranks would reach 2.6 million by the time Ronald Reagan became the first U.S. president to address the group in 1983. Reagan's address to the NRA was regarded as an important affirmation of NRA principles; the president averred that "we will never disarm any American who seeks to protect his or her family from fear or harm."

G. Ray Arnett was picked to succeed Carter in 1985. Surrounded by scandal, however, Arnett lasted only until May 1986, when ILA leader J. Warren Cassidy became the next executive vice-president.

In 1986, the NRA had three million members and income of about $66 million a year. During this time, the group was sponsoring the McClure-Volkmer Act, which amended restrictions in the Gun Control Act of 1968 and was eventually passed. The group also fought to temper legislation banning Teflon-coated "cop killer" bullets. By this time, the issue of gun control in the United States had become highly fragmented and charged with emotion. In fact, the Association was beginning to find itself on different sides of gun control issues with much of the country's police force. In the late 1980s, the NRA ran

## Key Dates:

**1871:** The NRA is chartered in New York.
**1903:** Shooting programs for students is set up.
**1907:** National headquarters moves to Washington, D.C.
**1934:** The Legislative Affairs Division is created to organize political action.
**1949:** NRA launches a hunter education program.
**1968:** First significant gun control legislation in 30 years passes.
**1975:** Institute for Legislative Action, the NRA's lobbying unit, is created.
**1983:** Reagan becomes the first U.S. president to address the NRA.
**1994:** The Brady Bill, calling for waiting periods and background checks, is passed.
**1995:** A new headquarters building is constructed.
**1998:** NRA hosts its largest convention ever and names actor Charlton Heston president.

political ads and direct mail campaigns against several police chiefs who favored regulating handguns.

Although many of its members were Democrats, the NRA spent an estimated $7 million to defeat Democratic candidate Michael Dukakis, a staunch supporter of gun control, in the 1988 presidential campaign. Republican George Bush broke ranks with some in the NRA while campaigning for the presidential nomination, calling for a ban on "plastic" handguns. Still, as an avid hunter, veteran, and NRA member, he appealed to the group and won its approval.

### New Challenges in the 1990s

As the U.S. public became ever more aware of increases in violence involving firearms, the NRA again sought to address issues beyond gun ownership. The NRA Foundation was created in 1990 to raise tax-exempt funds for gun education. The Eddie Eagle Gun Safety Program, started two years earlier, taught elementary and middle school children to avoid guns and report them to adults. Moreover, Refuse to Be a Victim seminars, introduced in 1993, lectured women on personal safety issues. According to the NRA, three out of four women would suffer through a violent crime in their lifetimes.

The early 1990s were difficult years financially for the organization. According to NRA figures cited by *Fortune* magazine, the NRA lost $10 million in 1991, $38 million in 1992, and $22 million in 1993. In 1991, the board replaced Warren Cassidy—whose reputation was tainted by a sex scandal, less than stellar financial results, and diminishing popularity due to what some perceived as a willingness to compromise the Association's mission—with long-time politico Wayne LaPierre, another former leader of the group's lobbying arm, the ILA.

The NRA then faced several challenges to its mission. Efforts to overturn New Jersey's ban on semiautomatic weapons and Virginia's gun-rationing program in 1993 both failed. In the late 1980s, the NRA had lobbied unsuccessfully against a national ban of certain semiautomatic assault rifles. Moreover,

after several years of struggle, in 1994 the Brady Bill passed. Named for White House press secretary Jim Brady, who was shot and partially paralyzed during an attempt on Reagan's life, the bill mandated a five-day waiting period and a background check for gun purchasers. (This process would replaced by a computerized verification system run by the FBI in 1998.) However, the Brady Bill did not apply to flea markets and gun shows, and gun sales at these venues boomed.

Annual revenues for the NRA approached $150 million in 1994 as the group attracted a more active and high profile membership. The group spent $15 million on a new headquarters in Fairfax, Virginia, in the mid-1990s and also invested in a new computer system.

To address issues of increasing violent crime in the country, the NRA called for more prisons, tougher sentences, and more law enforcement officers. However, the Association continued to struggle with public relations issues and alienated certain law enforcement groups. Congressman John Dingell, an NRA board member, had called the U.S. Department of Alcohol, Tobacco, and Firearms (ATF) a "jackbooted group of fascists" in one of the group's promotional films in 1981. The NRA repeated the rhetoric in a 1995 fundraising letter, prompting former president George Bush to rescind his life membership.

In October 1997, nine firearms manufacturers, including Smith & Wesson, announced they were voluntarily adding child safety locks to their products. The unprecedented break from NRA policy was prompted by a litigious climate that had cities such as Chicago and New Orleans filing lawsuits similar to the ones that had been launched against the cigarette industry. The gun makers risked a boycott by NRA members who opposed compromise of any kind. According to *Newsweek,* the publicly-traded Sturm, Ruger firm had faced such a boycott earlier in the decade after it came out in favor of limiting high capacity ammo clips for assault weapons.

In 1997, in the face of such challenges, the NRA began publishing *The American Guardian,* designed to appeal to a more general audience, with less emphasis on technical subjects and more on self-defense and sporting uses for firearms. Membership in the NRA, after reaching at 3.5 million, had fallen by about a million in the mid-1990s. Still, the group held the largest convention in its history in 1998, attracting 41,000 attendees. In the same year, the NRA elected as its president the actor Charlton Heston, perhaps best known for his performance as Moses in the epic film *The Ten Commandments.* Another famous actor, Tom Selleck, appeared in a new round of magazine advertising for the NRA.

In the late 1990s, following several highly publicized incidents of violence involving guns among American teenagers, some polls indicated that 70 to 80 percent of Americans favored stricter gun control laws. However, *Newsweek* reported, the fear of political retaliation from the NRA killed a new round of gun control bills in June 1999. NRA membership climbed again late in the decade. By May 2000, the Association reported 3.7 million members fighting challenges to the right to bear arms.

### Principal Divisions

Institute for Legislative Action; NRA Foundation.

### Principal Competitors

Handgun Control, Inc.

### Further Reading

Bai, Matt, "Caught in the Cross-Fire," *Newsweek,* June 28, 1999, pp. 31–32.

——, "Clouds Over Gun Valley," *Newsweek,* August 23, 1999, pp. 34–35.

Birnbaum, Jeffrey H., "Under the Gun," *Fortune,* December 6, 1999, pp. 211–18.

Davidson, Osha Gray, "Guns and Poses," *New Republic,* October 11, 1993, p. 12.

——, *Under Fire: The NRA and the Battle for Gun Control,* New York: Henry Holt, 1993.

Drake, Donald C., "NRA Made Anti-Gun Lawmakers Pay in Election; Group Targeted Oklahoma Race," *Times-Picayune* (New Orleans), December 4, 1994, p. A8.

Fineman, Howard, "The Gun War Comes Home," *Newsweek,* August 23, 1999, pp. 26–32.

France, Mike, William C. Symonds, and Seanna Browder, "Can Gunmakers Disarm Their Attackers?," *Business Week,* November 10, 1997, p. 94.

Gilmore, Russell S., *Crack Shots and Patriots: The National Rifle Association and America's Military-Sporting Tradition, 1871–1929,* Ph.D. dissertation, University of Wisconsin, 1975.

Graham, George, "US Gun Group Returns to Clinton Offensive: NRA Chief Defends Fund-Raising Letter," *Financial Times,* May 22, 1995, p. 6.

"Gun Control: Bang Bang, You're Dead," *Economist,* September 30, 2000, pp. S26–S27.

"Guns in America: Arms and the Man," *Economist,* July 3, 1999, pp. 17–19.

Hornblower, Margot, "Have Gun, Will Travel," *Time,* July 6, 1998, pp. 44–46.

Leddy, Edward, *Magnum Force Lobby,* Lanham, Md.: University Press of America, 1987.

Novak, Viveca, "Picking a Fight with the NRA," *Time,* May 31, 1999, p. 54.

Smolowe, Jill, and Andrea Sachs, "The NRA: Go Ahead, Make Our Day," *Time,* May 29, 1995, p. 18.

Trefethen, James, and James Serven, *Americans and Their Guns: The National Rifle Association's Story Through Nearly a Century of Service to the Nation,* Harrisburg, Pa.: Stackpole Books, 1967.

"Wounding the Gun Lobby," *Time,* March 29, 1993, p. 29.

—Frederick C. Ingram

# New Dana Perfumes Company

470 Oakhill Road
Mountain Top, Pennsylvania 18707
U.S.A.
Telephone: (570) 474-7500
Fax: (570) 474-5704
Web site: http://newdana.com

*Private Company*
*Incorporated:* 1994 as Renaissance Cosmetics Inc.
*Employees:* 1,000
*Sales:* $150 million (2000 est.)
*NAIC:* 32562 Toilet Preparations Manufacturing

New Dana Perfumes Company sells perfumes and cosmetics, principally through mass market retailers such as Sears and Walgreens. The company was known as Renaissance Cosmetics Inc. until 1999. Its specialty is buying up classic perfume brands that have fallen on hard times and reviving them. The company owns more than 100 trademarks and sells such well-known perfumes as Chantilly, Love's Baby Soft, Canoe, and English Leather. Many of its brands had heydays in the middle decades of the 20th century. The company is able to capitalize on the nostalgic appeal of these older scents. New Dana also operates a cosmetics subsidiary, Nat Robbins, and sells a line of artificial nail products through its Cosmar division.

### Harvard Professor Builds a Company in 1994

New Dana Perfumes Co. started out in 1994 as Renaissance Cosmetics Inc., the pet project of Thomas Bonoma, the former head of Harvard's MBA program and a well-known marketing expert. Bonoma was trained as a psychologist and began teaching marketing somewhat by accident. Although he became a tenured professor at Harvard's business school, he had no business degree. He wrote or co-authored several influential marketing texts, including *Industrial Market Segmentation* (1983), *Managing Marketing* (1984), and *Marketing Edge* (1985). He had a clever and colorful approach to his adopted field. In a July 22, 1991 interview with *Adweek's Marketing Week*, he declared that marketers "have taught their consumer

that they lie about their products. Consumers have learned to believe nothing." He scorned much traditional marketing as busy work that kept marketing departments happy.

In the mid-1980s, his pronouncements caught the ear of Peter Harf, the chief executive of an old, established German firm, Benckiser Group. Benckiser dated back to 1823, and it had made its fortune selling chemicals. In the 1970s the company underwent a transformation. The Reimann family, who owned the firm, hired Peter Harf, a management consultant with a Harvard business degree, to revive the slumbering company. Harf at first acted as a consultant for Benckiser, then joined the firm in 1981. He took the company on an acquisition binge that brought it a large stable of brand-name consumer goods, including Spanish and Italian soaps and cleaners, and American brands such as Cling Free fabric softener and Calgon bath beads.

Harf first contacted Bonoma in 1986 and persuaded him to lend his talents to managing the company's rapid growth. Bonoma followed Harf's path, first consulting, then joining the company. Bonoma eventually became head of Benckiser's U.S. operations, a $200 million-a-year division that handled cleaners and soaps such as the dishwasher detergent Electrasol and Clean & Smooth liquid hand soap. Bonoma the Harvard marketing professor then had some real-life successes. Electrasol, for example, grew in market share under his management, from less than three percent to more than ten percent. He did this by concentrating on price. He positioned the detergent as the low-cost alternative to leading brands, thereby attracting customers.

Benckiser entered the perfume and cosmetics market in 1991, acquiring the Germaine Montiel cosmetics line from Revlon and the Jovan perfume line from Quintessence Inc. Bonoma became interested in perfumes, believing that his company could do with fragrances what it had done with many other brands, building up market share by aiming at the low end of the market. Unfortunately, Benckiser's board wished to pursue the opposite strategy and move into high-end cosmetics and perfumes. This made Bonoma unhappy. Benckiser also wanted Bonoma to take over its worldwide cosmetics operations, a job that required constant international travel. Bonoma, who had four children, was unwilling to take the position. Benckiser's management also refused to take any part of the company public, fearing it would not be advantageous for the family that had owned the firm for generations. So Bonoma had no lucrative stock options. In May 1993, he resigned from Benckiser, but immediately set to work launching his own company, Renaissance Cosmetics.

### New Growth from Old Brands in the Mid-1990s

Bonoma formed a group with five other executives from Benckiser; together, they raised $65 million from institutional investors. Bonoma also approached a leveraged buyout firm called Kidd, Kamm, which put up $26.5 million in equity. Bonoma's vision was to buy up cosmetics and perfume companies that traditionally sold to the low end of the market. Most of these small firms did not have the marketing clout to promote their products, so many strong brands had fallen out of favor. Bonoma believed that he could acquire these "Mom-and-Pop" companies and build a marketing giant. By his estimate there were close to 1,200 small companies in the beauty business. By skillful acquisition of these little firms, Bonoma thought he could build Renaissance Cosmetics into a $1 billion company in three to five years.

Renaissance Cosmetics Inc. began in 1994, buying a nail care company called Cosmar Corp. Soon after, it bought a line of 12 fragrances from Houbigant, one of the oldest perfume companies in the world. Houbigant had made perfume for Napoleon and had many famous scents in its library. One of its best-known was Chantilly. Introduced in 1941, Chantilly had sales of $60 million in 1960, but declined steadily thereafter. By 1992, Houbigant's total volume was just $41 million. The struggling company was forced into bankruptcy in 1993, and Renaissance was eager to snap up a portion of it. The Chantilly brand was just the thing Bonoma had imagined when he began his company. The name still had considerable cachet, but it had not been seriously advertised since 1986. It sold mostly in lower-end department stores such as J.C. Penney and Montgomery Ward. Renaissance revamped the packaging and began advertising the scent with television commercials and the slogan "the spray lingerie." Another bestseller Renaissance acquired from Houbigant was Parfums Parquet's French Vanilla.

In early 1995, Renaissance made another major acquisition, Dana Perfumes Corp. Dana was similar to Houbigant in that it had some classic scents that lacked a recent marketing push. Dana's Tabu dated to 1932, and it sold another long-standing men's fragrance, Canoe. After only six months in business, Renaissance Cosmetics had bought three companies, giving it a sales volume of around $150 million. This put it in third place in the mass market perfume and cosmetics market. It had a much smaller market share than the leading companies Coty and

Procter & Gamble, but Bonoma was confident his strategy would pay off and the company would grow quickly.

Renaissance pushed its new brands in several ways. The same strategy applied to Chantilly, Tabu, Canoe, and others the company acquired. The scent was repackaged to give it a slightly updated look, and the scent itself was sometimes adjusted. Canoe, for example, was changed so that it still smelled like the 1958 original scent, but also like what Bonoma called a "Nineties citrus." The brands were pushed with television and print ads, with catchy new slogans. In addition, to make the old brand appeal to younger buyers, the brand was extended. Chantilly, for example, spawned White Chantilly, a lighter version meant for women aged 18 to 34. Tabu was marketed to younger women as Dreams by Tabu. Renaissance also offered its marketing expertise to retailers, sending its agents to analyze a store's perfume counter and find ways to increase overall volume. Renaissance also tried to push its brands year-round, getting away from holiday specials that customers often returned.

Renaissance's strategy of reviving old fragrances seemed to be working beautifully after only two years in business. By 1996, sales of Chantilly had risen by about a third, and sales volume of Tabu had doubled. The company also launched a new scent, Classic Gardenia, which had been set for release by Dana when that company was acquired. Classic Gardenia had estimated sales of from $8 to $10 million in its first year.

Although sales at Renaissance were growing, the overall low-end perfume market was stagnant. Thomas Bonoma hoped to influence retailers toward better ways of marketing scents. He especially emphasized the idea of taking the product out from glass cases, so consumers could test and sample. Bonoma also wanted to get away from seasonal discounted promotions, which were often time-consuming for stores to set up. Bonoma thought these seasonal promotions hurt basic year-long sales. The company also looked for ways to expand its presence in international markets. By 1996, about 15 percent of the company's business came from overseas, and it hoped to double this.

Meanwhile, Renaissance continued its acquisitions strategy. In late 1996, it spent $41.5 million to buy rights to 11 perfumes from Procter & Gamble. These included Navy, Navy for Men, Toujours Moi, and Jaclyn Smith's California. Almost simultaneously with the Procter & Gamble deal, Renaissance acquired the men's fragrance line of a company called MEM. The MEM scents included the classic English Leather, as well as Heaven Scent, Love's, and British Sterling. The MEM and Procter & Gamble scents were sold to more than 1,000 mass market retailers at approximately 25,000 stores across the United States. Renaissance also believed that Procter & Gamble's scents in particular could enjoy greater sales internationally. The company had to refinance its debt to bring off these two 1996 acquisitions. That year Renaissance also bought a cosmetics company, Nat Robbins. Nat Robbins had a line of color cosmetics that were sold in mass market outlets like the ones that featured Renaissance's perfumes.

An overlooked goody emerged from Renaissance's deal with MEM. This was Tinkerbell, a line of perfume, makeup, toys, and accessories designed for girls ages four to nine. Tinkerbell came on the market in 1952 and had peak sales in the early 1980s of around $30 million. But by the mid-1990s, sales were less than half that, from $10 to $15 million annually, and MEM had not put much energy into promoting the line. Tinkerbell differed from Renaissance's other perfume acquisitions, since it was not merely a scent but a line of slippers, toys, and princess crowns as well as brushes and combs, lipsticks, and nail polish. The cosmetics were nontoxic and spill-proof, and so would appeal to parents whose children liked playing with adult makeup. Renaissance planned to revive the line with new advertising and packaging and to expand its appeal to older girls. Tinkerbell also had strong international sales, and the company hoped to expand on that.

Renaissance was proceeding according to plan, buying strategically and building up its new brands. Sales were close to $300 million in 1997, impressive growth for a company that had started at zero only three years earlier. But Thomas Bonoma, the company's founder and visionary, died suddenly at age 50 in May 1997. Norbert Becker, a former Benckiser executive who had joined Renaissance in 1996, succeeded Bonoma as president and chief executive officer. Becker declared that the company would continue to follow the path that Bonoma had laid out. Although the loss of Bonoma was unexpected, Renaissance had a long-term strategy in place, and there were to be no major changes with the new leadership.

Nevertheless, despite Becker's optimism, the company soon stumbled. Disappointing sales in the third quarter of 1997 led to red ink in the neighborhood of $14 to $16 million. CEO Becker managed to secure additional credit for the company, and Renaissance began 1998 by announcing ambitious new plans to revive another scent it had acquired from MEM two years earlier, Love's Baby Soft. Love's Baby Soft was a classic teenage scent. Renaissance hoped to revive the brand and boost it with many line extensions. The company also pursued the teen market through a bath and body line that spun off of Fetish, one of the nail products of its Cosmar division.

## Turnaround and New Name in the Late 20th Century

In late 1998, Renaissance Cosmetics hired a turnaround specialist, William A. Brandt, Jr., to get the company in order. Its acquisitions had led to heavy debt, the death of Bonoma had been a blow, and the perfume market was shrinking. Brandt became acting CEO, and he worked to streamline the company. He announced that something would have to be sold to keep Renaissance going, perhaps the Tinkerbell brand. But despite Brandt's efforts, less than a year later, Renaissance filed for bankruptcy. The company's total assets were valued at only $50 million, and debt stood at around $200 million. The failing company went on the auction block. Within a month, the entire company had been bought by a Pompano Beach, Florida firm, Fragrance Express Inc. Fragrance Express had several lines of business, including telemarketing and catalogs, and import and export of gift items like chocolates and perfume. Fragrance Express paid just $29 million for Renaissance. Also contributing to the purchase was a Pennsylvania investment company, Dimeling, Schreiber & Park.

The new owners merged Renaissance with their existing operations and named the resulting firm New Dana Perfume Corporation. Renaissance's divisions also were renamed, from Nat Robbins to New Nat Robbins, Cosmar to New Cosmar, etc. The company retained the Tinkerbell brand as New Tinkerbell.

The new chief executive was Robert Bartlett. With the new name, the company did not change drastically. From 70 to 90 percent of Renaissance's executives stayed on, and the basic business strategy was the same. New Dana went ahead with the repackaging of some of its men's scents and planned to update some others. The company now owned more than 100 trademarks, and it planned to continue Bonoma's strategy and develop them all. Fetish, the body, bath, perfume, and cosmetics line that had grown out of Cosmar shortly before the bankruptcy, was relaunched in 2000 under the auspices of teenage pop star Christina Aguilera. The world-famous Aguilera not only lent her name to the product line, but served as image consultant, suggesting changes to the packaging and personally reviewing and approving the products.

New Dana's new owners seemed confident that they could continue the company's growth. Sales were projected at around $150 million for 2000. Sales from Fetish and other new promotions were expected to add another $50 million the next year. New Dana seemed certain that Bonoma's basic vision was a winner and that the classic perfume brands it owned could be made to perform again in the coming years.

### Principal Subsidiaries

New Nat Robbins; New Cosmar; New Tinkerbell; New Dana.

### Principal Competitors

Revlon, Inc.; The Procter & Gamble Co.; L'Oréal SA; Avon Products, Inc.

### Further Reading

Auerbach, Jonathan, ''Houbigant Seeking Ch. 11 Reorganization,'' *WWD*, November 30, 1993, p. 15.

Berman, Phyllis, ''The Spray Lingerie,'' *Forbes*, November 7, 1994, pp. 102–08.

Berman, Phyllis, and Michael Schuman, ''Globaloney,'' *Forbes*, November 22, 1993, pp. 44–45.

Bonoma, Thomas V., ''The Instant CEO,'' *Across the Board*, October 1992, p. 16.

Brookman, Faye, ''Renaissance Aims to Rejuvenate Dana,'' *WWD*, January 20, 1995, p. 10.

——, ''Renaissance Moves on with New Credit,'' *WWD*, February 13, 1998, p. 7.

——, ''Renaissance: Show Must Go On,'' *WWD*, June 13, 1997, p. 9.

——, ''Renaissance's Goal of Brand Rebirth,'' *WWD*, January 26, 1996, p. 12.

——, ''Renaissance's Rebirth,'' *WWD*, October 23, 1998, p. 7.

——, ''Tinkerbell Set to Fly Again,'' *WWD*, February 14, 1997, p. 7.

Kagan, Cara, ''Chantilly Beckons Youth,'' *WWD*, May 19, 1995, p. 8.

Klepacki, Laura, ''Renaissance Redux,'' *WWD*, September 3, 1999, p. 8.

——, ''What Fetish Needs: Aguilera,'' *WWD*, June 30, 2000, p. 10.

Monahan, Julie A., ''Houbigant Takes a Classic Approach,'' *WWD*, September 11, 1987, p. S42.

Naughton, Julie, ''New Dana Breathes Life into Old Brands,'' *WWD*, June 30, 2000, p. 10.

Ramey, Joanna, ''Reawakening Sleeping Giants,'' *WWD*, July 28, 1995, p. 8.

Warner, Fara, ''Benckiser Who?,'' *Adweek's Marketing Week*, July 22, 1991, p. 16.

—A. Woodward

# Newman's Own, Inc.

Shameless exploitation in pursuit of the common good.

# Newman's Own, Inc.

246 Post Road East
Westport, Connecticut 06880
U.S.A.
Telephone: (203) 222-0136
Fax: (203) 227-5630
Web site: http://www.newmansown.com

*Private Company*
*Incorporated:* 1982
*Employees:* 18
*Sales:* $100 million (1999)
*NAIC:* 311421 Fruit and Vegetable Canning; 312111 Soft
   Drink Manufacturing

Since its founding in 1982 by veteran actor Paul Newman and writer A.E. Hotchner, Newman's Own, Inc., has grown from a small salad dressing producer into a highly successful specialty prepared foods company. After initial success with salad dressings, the company added pasta sauce, salsa, steak sauce, popcorn, and lemonade to its food line, each bearing Paul Newman's famous face on the label. Newman's Own Organics: The Second Generation, an organic food division headed by daughter Nell Newman, was established in 1993. All the company's products are made without artificial ingredients or preservatives, and are distributed in major U.S. grocery chains as well as in Canada, Europe, Israel, Japan, and Australia. Paul Newman, founder and president of Newman's Own, donates 100 percent of after-tax profits from Newman's Own to charitable and educational organizations. As of November 1999, he passed the $100 million mark in charitable giving from the proceeds of Newman's Own, benefiting over 2,000 charities. Of note among his many philanthropies is The Hole in the Wall Gang Camp in Ashford, Connecticut, which was founded by Newman in 1988 for children with serious illnesses, and five affiliate camps in the United States and Europe. Paul Newman remains closely involved as high-profile company spokesperson and philanthropist, and Newman's Own, Inc., continues to thrive. He personally approves all new products and recipes.

## 1982: Newman's Own Begins on a Whim

For several years, Paul Newman and his long-time friend, author A.E. Hotchner, were in the habit of giving bottles of their homemade salad dressing to friends as holiday gifts. They would mix up a batch in Newman's basement and hand out old wine bottles filled with the dressing while Christmas caroling in their Westport, Connecticut, neighborhood. The response was favorable, and their "limited edition" bottled dressing became a sought-after item in neighborhood gourmet shops.

Newman and Hotchner reasoned they might attempt to market their dressing. They were told to expect to spend $400,000 on test marketing, but instead they simply invited a group of friends to choose from among a few salad dressing samples, and then selected the favorite. The two men each contributed $40,000, and a private manufacturer agreed to bottle the dressing. Thus, in 1982, Newman's Own, Inc., created its first product: Olive Oil & Vinegar Salad Dressing. As a joke, Newman put a likeness of his own face on the label, deciding to give any after-tax profits away because he had no need or desire to make money from the business. He convinced his friend Stew Leonard of the famous Stew Leonard's grocery store in Norwalk, Connecticut, to take 10,000 cases, though Leonard cautioned Newman not to expect much from a celebrity food product.

Marketing experts also had their doubts, warning Newman to expect $1 million in losses during the first year. Instead, Newman's Own Olive Oil & Vinegar Salad Dressing was wildly successful, generating after-tax profits of nearly a half million dollars in the first year, which was all donated to charity. Quoted in a company press release, Newman stated, "If we'd followed the experts' advice, we'd probably still be bottling dressing in our basement, wondering if Newman's Own was a worthwhile business venture." Hotchner went on to become Newman's partner, vice-president, and treasurer of Newman's Own, Inc., based in Westport.

## 1983–99: Growing A Business;
## Increasing Philanthropy

What had begun as a lark quickly took on a life of its own. The Olive Oil & Vinegar dressing was soon followed by New-

272

man's Own salad dressings in varieties including Caesar, Creamy Caesar, Balsamic Vinaigrette, Italian, Ranch, and others. Success inspired Newman and Hotchner to branch out into other food items, and the Newman's Own product lines grew to include pasta sauce in seven varieties, steak sauce, Bandito salsa in three strengths, Old Fashioned lemonade, and Picture Show popcorn. By 1987 the company was growing at about 20 percent per year. Only five years after the company's inception, *Grocery Marketing* reported that the success of Newman's Own appeared to be due to the combination of the popular Paul Newman image on the product labels, a strong public relations effort, and quality products that inspired repeat sales. Each year the company showed increased earnings, grossing $36 million in 1988. The next year the company realized a reported 16 percent pre-tax profit, about five times the 3.4 percent food industry average.

The company's finances remained an internal affair, while manufacturing and distribution were subcontracted out to various concerns around the United States. The pasta sauces were manufactured in Rochester, New York; the popcorn was packaged in Iowa and Illinois; the salad dressing was bottled in Fullerton, California, and Framingham, Massachusetts; and the lemonade was created in various locations throughout the country. Supermarkets and giant chain stores such as Wal-Mart and Kmart were responsible for 90 percent of all sales. As the company grew, opportunities for increased profits and visibility were sought. One such opportunity came with an alliance between Newman's Own and Burger King Corporation, with good results. In 1990, the fast food chain reported that by adding Newman's Own salad dressings to its offerings, the company doubled its salad dressing sales for the month of July.

A notable aspect of Newman's Own's success was the company's lack of advertising. However, the food labels themselves—printed with an illustration of actor Paul Newman's face smiling out at the consumer—served to create an easily identified brand identity. The Newman image on the label was often cleverly customized to illustrate the product, for example, putting the actor in a sombrero on the salsa labels, adding steer horns to his head on the steak sauce bottle, or translating his image into a ''Roman'' bust for the Caesar dressing. The witty, tongue-in-cheek marketing copy on the labels, which seemed almost to poke fun at the Newman's Own enterprise, added to the products' appeal. The company said that the label and promotional copy were written by Paul Newman and A.E. Hotchner themselves, who imbued it with their distinctively offbeat sense of humor. For example, the Sockarooni spaghetti sauce label claimed that it ''delivers a zesty twist that will knock your socks off,'' while the ''Virgin'' lemonade label said it was ''made from lemons that have never been squeezed.'' This irreverent marketing approach seemed to wink at the con-

sumer while promoting a line of high-quality all-natural food products.

For publicity, the company turned to charitable events. In 1990, Newman's Own and *Good Housekeeping* magazine began sponsoring an annual national recipe competition. To be eligible, every recipe entry needed to include a Newman's Own food product among the ingredients. The recipes were chosen from thousands of submissions from around the United States, and the final judging was held at prestigious venues such as New York City's Rainbow Room or the Waldorf Astoria hotel. Each year, several recipe semi-finalists were chosen, and a professional chef prepared the recipes. To lend excitement to the event, Newman and Hotchner personally tasted the resulting creations, with Newman's wife, actress Joanne Woodward, sometimes joining in. The top prize of $50,000 was given to a worthy cause of the recipient's choice, with smaller prizes given to the runners-up, as well as to favorite charities of selected supermarkets that sold Newman's Own products. The contest judging and *Good Housekeeping* received good publicity, helping to market Newman's Own products while promoting a high-profile charitable event.

With the steady growth and increasing success of Newman's Own the company remained fully committed to charity, with Paul Newman continuing to give away 100 percent of after-tax profits in the form of grants to non-profit organizations. At the end of each year, Newman and Hotchner sat down together to review grant applications personally and divide the year's profits among educational and charitable organizations that they deemed most in need of assistance. As Paul Newman's charitable giving became more widely known, more and more organizations began to apply for aid. As early as 1993 there was a notable increase in applications, from 1,500 up to 2,500. In that year alone, 460 applicants were given aid.

Perhaps the most well known of the Newman's Own philanthropies was The Hole in the Wall Gang, a charitable association founded by Newman to operate a group of six camps for gravely ill children. Named for the outlaw-heroes in Newman's celebrated film *Butch Cassidy and the Sundance Kid,* the first Hole in the Wall Camp—inspired by letters to Paul Newman from children with life-threatening diseases—was founded in Ashford, Connecticut, in 1988. A nonprofit residential camp, The Hole in the Wall Gang Camp offered free lodging, medical care, counseling, and recreational activities for children with cancer and other serious diseases. Subsequently, five affiliated camps were added, all partly funded by Newman's Own: The Painted Turtle Gang Camp (California), The Boggy Creek Gang Camp (Florida), The Double ''H'' Hole in the Woods Ranch (New York), L'Envol (France), and The Barretstown Camp (Ireland).

In 1993 a new division, Newman's Own Organics: The Second Generation, was established. The brainchild of Nell Newman, the third of Newman's five daughters, it was created to develop products using certified organic ingredients, marketed with the slogan: ''Great products that just happen to organic.'' According to a 1998 *New York Times* report, Ms. Newman convinced her father to start the division after impressing him with an all-organic Thanksgiving dinner she prepared. The division was based in Aptos, California, where Nell

---

### Key Dates:

**1982:** Newman's Own, Inc., is founded by Paul Newman and A.E. Hotchner.
**1988:** The Hole in the Wall Gang Camp is founded and built in Ashford, Connecticut.
**1990:** First annual recipe award co-sponsored with *Good Housekeeping* magazine.
**1993:** Newman's Own Organics division is launched.
**1998:** Two Newman's Own cookbook titles are published.
**1999:** $100 million in lifetime charitable giving is reached.
**2000:** Paul Newman makes significant donation to Oprah Winfrey's Angel Network ''Use Your Life'' award.

---

Newman lived, and was headed by herself and her business partner Peter Meehan. The first product, seven-grain organic pretzels, was followed by organic chocolate bars and fat-free Fig Newmans.

Plans for a major marketing push of Newman's Own products were set in motion in the United Kingdom in 1993. It was reported in *Marketing* that a budget of £500,000 was set aside for the first advertising campaign, planned for print ads in the women's press. It was hoped that the appeal of the famous actor combined with the company's policy of donating profits to children's charities would be a draw for consumers. Fisher Quality Foods, Newman's Own's sole importer in the United Kingdom since the brand launched there in 1989, was set to become the brand's sole manufacturer, in anticipation of the new marketing campaign. At the time of the reported expansion, Newman's Own pasta sauce had a two percent U.K. market share, while the salad dressing enjoyed a five percent U.K. market share.

Newman's Own's unorthodox success caught the attention of several business schools. In 1995, Newman and Hotchner's offbeat company became the focus of a hands-on business course at Fairfield University's School of Business in Fairfield, Connecticut. With the cooperation of a group of management, finance, and marketing professors, Newman's Own invited teams of students to run focus groups, brainstorm about new products, and plot marketing strategies for the Westport company. At the end of the course, the student teams reported their findings, with the top two teams receiving $2,500 to be donated to their favorite charities. Three years later, Newman addressed a group of students at the Harvard Business School, joking that he was planning a ''hostile takeover'' of the H.J. Heinz Company, according to the student newspaper *The Harbus*. Newman mesmerized his audience with his unusual approach to business. James Austin, chairman of the schools Initiative on Social Enterprise, said, ''Newman's Own reveals the synergistic relationship between the social purpose and the commercial operations.''

As the company continued to evolve, Newman's Own acknowledged the need for a more directed marketing approach. Thomas Indoe, a former executive with Del Monte Foods and RJR Nabisco, was brought on board in 1997. His first big change was to include a line of copy on the actual product packaging advertising the philanthropic mission of Newman's Own, since focus group research had determined that less than 25 percent of consumers knew that after-tax profits went to charity. Indoe also instituted the practice of using newspaper inserts to advertise Newman's Own products with a headline reading ''Over 90 Million Given to Charity by Paul Newman,'' aimed at improving public awareness of the company's charitable goals.

1998 was a busy year for the company. *Retail World* noted plans to increase Newman's Own's range in Australia, with four new pasta sauces to be introduced in that country in the second half of the year, and new salad dressings to follow. The same year, *Frozen Food Age* reported the launching of Newman's Own Ice Cream. Though it was manufactured and packed by Ben & Jerry's Homemade of Waterbury, Vermont, the line of all-natural premium ice cream was to be marketed apart from Ben & Jerry's ice cream, without that company's identification printed on the packaging. Ben & Jerry's retained the license to produce, distribute, and sell the five-item Newman's Own ice cream line, which bore such humorous flavor names as Pistol Packin' Praline, Milk Chocolate Mud Bath, and Obscene Vanilla Bean.

Two Newman's Own-inspired cookbooks were published in 1998: *The Hole in the Wall Gang Cookbook: Kid-Friendly Recipes for Families to Make Together* (Fireside), with an introduction by A.E. Hotchner, and *Newman's Own Cookbook* (Simon & Schuster). Both well-received cookbooks contained recipes using Newman's Own products, as well as recipes contributed by such famous friends as Whoopi Goldberg, David Letterman, and Julia Roberts. In keeping with the company's charitable spirit, all proceeds from the sale of the two cookbooks went to The Hole in the Wall Gang Fund.

### Into the New Millennium

As the year 2000 approached, most Newman's Own products were still in production and going strong, with only the Newman's Own ice cream line discontinued. Organic cookies were added to the organic food line, and the seven-grain pretzels had become the natural food industry's best-selling organic pretzels. Most important for Newman and Hotchner's unique enterprise, however, was the announcement in November 1999 that Paul Newman had passed the $100 million mark in charitable giving since his company began, to over 2,000 charitable and educational organizations. In April 2000, talk show celebrity Oprah Winfrey highlighted Paul Newman and Newman's Own's charitable efforts on her television ''Angel Network.'' Winfrey announced the establishment of a weekly ''Use Your Life'' award of $50,000, funded in part by Paul Newman, to be given to an honoree chosen for his or her work on behalf of the betterment of others.

For his part, Paul Newman remained actively involved in the company: working as spokesperson, writing ad copy, tasting new food products, judging recipes, and personally choosing and approving charitable and educational donations. As he once told a *New York Times* reporter, ''If we stop having fun, we're closing up shop.''

### Principal Divisions

Newman's Own Organics: The Second Generation.

## Principal Competitors

Kraft Foods, Inc. (salad dressing); Lipton (salad dressing, pasta sauce), Campbell Soup Company (pasta sauce); Nabisco, Inc (steak sauce); The Coca Cola Company (lemonade); The Pillsbury Company (salsa); Conagra Grocery Products Company; General Mills, Inc. (microwave popcorn).

## Further Reading

Allen, Mike, "Making His Own Charity an Acquired Taste," *New York Times,* November 18, 1998, p. G2.

"Brand Building," *Marketing,* July 15, 1993, p. 7.

Brozan, Nadine, "Chronicle," *New York Times,* January 19, 1993, p. B2.

——, "Chronicle," *New York Times,* October 29, 1997, p. B10.

Dagnoli, Judann, et al, "Food Brands Team with Fast-Food," *Advertising Age,* July 22, 1991, p. 40.

Driscoll, Lisa M., "How to Succeed in Business Without Knowing Nothing," *New England Business,* September 1989, pp. 22–26.

Fabricant, Florence, "New Salsa Is True to Newman's Own Taste," *New York Times,* April 3, 1991, p. C7.

Fenn, Donna, "Star Quality," *CFO,* May 1987, pp. 102, 104.

Ferretti, Fred, "Charity's Leading Man," *Gourmet,* April 1997, p. 82.

Fitzpatrick, Jackie, "Newman's Own as a Business Course," *New York Times,* December 31, 1995, Section 13CN, Connecticut Weekly Desk, p. 11.

"Newman's Own Ice Cream to Debut in Five Flavors," *Frozen Food Age,* March 1998, pp. 8, 40.

Henry, Jim, "Newman's Own Organics Enters Chocolate Market," *Candy Industry,* September 1995, p. 16.

"A Hollywood Good Guy Talks Tough," *New York Times,* November 22, 1998, Sec. 3, p. 2.

Hume, Scott, et al, "Burger King Attacks Big Mac with Brands," *Advertising Age,* July 16, 1990, pp. 3, 39.

Klein, Alvin, "The Way It Really Was, Hotchner Style," *New York Times,* September 5, 1993, Connecticut Weekly Desk, p. 12.

Markgraf, Sue, "Indulgence Supreme, *Dairy Foods,* March 1998, pp. 82–84.

McNeil, Liz, "A New Twist on Pretzels," *People Weekly,* August 14, 1995, p. 75.

Nelton, Sharon, "Creating a Hit of Her Own," *Nation's Business,* December 1994, p. 63.

"Newman's Own," *Publisher's Weekly,* October 1998, p. 75.

"Newman's Own Daughter," *Vegetarian Times,* April 1999.

—Kathleen Paton

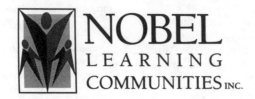

# Nobel Learning Communities, Inc.

**1400 North Providence Road**
**Media, Pennsylvania 19063**
**U.S.A.**
**Telephone: (610) 891-8200**
**Toll Free: (888) 996-6235**
**Fax: (610) 891-8200**
**Web site: http://www.nobeleducation.com**

*Public Company*
*Incorporated:* 1984 as Rocking Horse Child Care Centers
    of America Inc.
*Employees:* 3,800
*Sales:* $109.76 million (1999)
*Stock Exchanges:* NASDAQ
*Ticker Symbol:* NLCI
*NAIC:* 61111 Elementary and Secondary Schools; 62441
    Child Day Care Services

Nobel Learning Communities, Inc. operates private schools that serve students from preschool through high school. The company runs approximately 150 schools in 14 states, including its largest school operation, the California-based Merryhill School system, which comprises 30 preschools, elementary schools, and middle schools. The company builds and acquires its educational facilities in clusters, thereby creating a network within a community that can accommodate a child throughout his or her primary and secondary education. Nobel schools are generally open between 6:30 AM and 6:00 PM, providing child supervision for the company's target customers, single-parent and double-income families. Nobel schools operate under various names, including Merryhill School, Chesterbrook Academy, Evergreen Academy, Paladin Academy, and Another Generation Preschool.

### Origins

It took roughly a decade before Nobel arrived at the strategy, the corporate structure, and the leadership capable of achieving consistent success. The years in between were difficult, a period when Nobel operated under a different name and pursued a different corporate mission. Nobel began operating in 1984 as Rocking Horse Child Care Centers of America Inc., a Cherry Hill, New Jersey-based operator of private child-care centers.

Rocking Horse began modestly, with a single child-care center that recorded $48,000 in revenue during its first year of operation. Rocking Horse did not expand until April 1986, but once it began developing into a chain of day-care centers, the company did so with fervor. By the end of 1986, the company's revenue total had increased mightily, swelling to nearly $3 million as it began an aggressive acquisition campaign. Between April 1986 and October 1987, Rocking Horse acquired 31 child-care centers and constructed two new facilities, extending its operating territory to an eight-state area. The company's energetic growth, however, did not translate into profitability. Rocking Horse posted a net loss of $3.2 million in 1986, $300,000 more than it collected in revenue.

Despite the loss, the company continued to expand into the late 1980s. Rocking Horse raised $5 million in a public offering of stock in October 1987, the capital from which was used, as its president, John W. Quaintance, told the *Philadelphia Business Journal* in the October 12, 1987 issue, "to continue our acquisition strategy." By the end of 1988, the company operated 41 of what it called "preschool learning centers." There were ten in each Georgia and Florida, eight in South Carolina, four each in Illinois and Pennsylvania, three in New Jersey, and one each in Maine and Massachusetts. Rocking Horse held licenses to accommodate 5,538 children, allowing an average of 135 children per center. The company charged between $43 to $140 per week for its child-care services, the nature of which represented the hidden and unexploited strength of the chain. To distinguish itself from the scores of other child-care companies in existence, Rocking Horse used professionally developed educational and recreational programs administered by trained supervisors and teachers. By tailoring itself as more than a traditional day-care provider, the company's management hoped to attract parents and their children away from the competition, but the strategy never worked, at least not financially. By the end of the decade, Rocking Horse was a company suffering from profound financial problems.

## Company Perspectives:

*The company's mission is to create unique educational environments built on sound research, qualified instruction, and local communities of learning that foster academic excellence, instill a love of active learning, and provide experiences that enable all students to acquire a foundation of skills for lifelong achievement . . . increasing value to our families, our shareholders, and our employees. We nurture creativity and exploration in learning; respect children, parents, employees, and the environment; foster collaboration in our community of learners; meet the needs of children and the expectations of their parents; provide educational programs that consistently meet quality assurance criteria; develop and improve instructional delivery of our programs; demonstrate accountability and effectiveness to our constituencies; build and maintain our learning communities on a foundation of integrity and high standards.*

As Rocking Horse entered the 1990s, the signs of financial distress were alarmingly abundant. Saddled with an extremely large bank loan it could not pay, Rocking Horse had difficulty convincing its bank to approve a lease on a company vehicle. The company had a negative net worth of $3.8 million and was reeling from the effects of successive annual loses. After Rocking Horse defaulted on its loans, the accounting firm of Coopers & Lybrand issued a statement based on the child-care provider's 1991 results, stating that it was unsure if Rocking Horse had the capacity to survive.

### Clegg Leads Revival in 1992

The task of rescuing Rocking Horse fell to a new management team headed by A.J. "Jack" Clegg, whose arrival marked the beginning of a new and decidedly more successful era. Clegg's professional background included the 1979 founding of Empery Corporation, an operator of cable television and printing business. At Empery, Clegg served as chairman, president, and chief executive officer from 1979 to 1992, but his duties at Empery represented only a fraction of his business background in the decade preceding his arrival at Rocking Horse. Between 1983 and 1993, Clegg served as chairman and chief executive officer of TVC, Inc., a distributor of cable television components. During the same period he also held identical titles at Design Mark Industries, a manufacturer of electronic senswitches. Clegg served as chairman and chief executive officer of Globe Ticket and Label Company from 1984 to 1991 and was on the board of directors of Ferguson International Holdings, PLC. In the academic world, he was a member of the Advisory Board of Drexel University, an honor bestowed on the then 50-year-old Clegg in 1989.

When Clegg joined Rocking Horse in May 1992, he inherited a company that had lost $10.2 million during the previous two years. The losses were out of control, delivering staggering blows to a company that only generated roughly $30 million in annual sales. Clegg worked quickly to trim the company's liability, reducing Rocking Horse's debt by nearly $7 million within a year. He raised money for much-needed restructuring

through private placements, initially raising $2 million by selling stock and private holdings and raising another $2.5 million in 1993. Thanks to Clegg's restorative efforts, Rocking Horse reversed its losses, going from losing $3.8 million in 1991 to posting a profit of $1.8 million in 1992. Revenues slipped during the first stages of the turnaround, dropping from $34.7 million in 1991 to $33.5 million in 1992—a consequence of having to divest several child-care centers—but the company was on the mend. After the restructuring and divestitures, the company operated 44 child-care centers in 11 states, with the most significant addition in northern California where Rocking Horse operated 29 schools called the Merryhill County Schools. As Clegg looked beyond the immediate need to arrest the company's money-losing ways, the Merryhill system would serve as his blueprint for the future.

Aside from Clegg's focus on financial matters, the survival of Rocking Horse depended on another contribution from its new chairman, president, and chief executive officer. In the course of inspecting Rocking Horse's properties, Clegg visited one of the company's Merryhill schools, then operating as a division of Rocking Horse. During his visit, Clegg noted of the focus on offering curriculum-based programs to the children. Rather than merely offering custodial care, Rocking Horse—Clegg realized—was offering something beyond the services of baby sitter. "The company never really took advantage of the fact that it had something relatively unique," Clegg told the *Philadelphia Business Journal* in a May 23, 1997 interview. Educational programs represented Rocking Horse's distinguishing mark, a specialty that Clegg intended to use as the emphasis underpinning Rocking Horse's expansion.

With a clear vision of what the company should become, Clegg began making wholesale changes. He began converting the company's child-care centers into curriculum-based preschools, a shift in strategy that called for a new corporate title. In 1993, Rocking Horse Child Care Centers of America was dropped in favor of Nobel Education Dynamics, Inc. Once the company's financial health was restored, Clegg also began acquiring and expanding preschools, elementary, and middle schools, a mode of expansion that touched off in 1994. An integral aspect of the company's expansion strategy involved grouping its properties around each other. Clegg did not try to establish a presence in a wide geographic area; instead, he only moved into new territory if he was able to acquire additional nearby properties, a strategy he likened to playing the board game Monopoly. "If we go into a brand-new area," Clegg explained in his May 23, 1997 interview with the *Philadelphia Business Journal,* we will buy [an existing] school and use that school base to build clusters." According to the plan, the acquisition or construction of a preschool was followed by the addition of other preschools within the same vicinity. After establishing a network of preschools in a given area, the company next built centrally located elementary and middle schools, thereby creating a system that could accommodate the same pupil through his or her preschool, elementary, and middle school years.

Adhering to its blueprint for expansion, Nobel began acquiring facilities within roughly the same geographic area that Rocking Horse had penetrated. By the end of 1995, the company had 101 facilities in operation within an 11-state region. The process of acquiring and converting preschools into accred-

**Key Dates:**

**1984:** Rocking Horse Child Care Centers of America is founded.

**1988:** Following the company's first acquisition campaign, there are 41 Rocking Horse child care centers in operation.

**1992:** A.J. Clegg is hired as chairman and chief executive officer.

**1993:** Rocking Horse changes its name to Nobel Education Dynamics, Inc.

**1998:** Renamed Nobel Learning Communities, Inc., the company acquires three schools catering to the learning-challenged.

**1999:** Nobel Learning acquires five specialty high schools from Houston Learning Academy.

ited private elementary schools was in full swing, as Clegg targeted the children of single-parent families and two-income families to fill his growing number of educational facilities. Nobel schools provided child supervision from 6:30 AM to 6:00 PM, a schedule that conformed to the work schedule of most parents. Public schools, by contrast, typically provided child supervision 8:30 AM to 3:00 PM, which generally required single parents or double-income parents to pay for after-school child-care services. The savings partially offset Nobel's average tuition of $5,500, a fee that was 17 percent below the average $6,630 tuition at private nonparochial schools. Educationally, Nobel schools also compared favorably to other private schools, with Nobel students scoring one to two grades above their grade level, according to the Stanford Achievement Test, a standardized reading and math test.

Nobel's operating hours, its curriculum, and its tuition fees distinguished the company from many of its competitors. The company presented itself as an intriguing alternative to a specific sector of the market, leading one industry analyst to remark, "Noble is the first private educator to provide solutions at a price the middle class can afford," as quoted in the January 1996 issue of *Money* magazine. Importantly, Clegg's approach to education operated on sound financial footing as well. The company's primary schools earned 22 percent profit margins, a figure that was achieved largely because Nobel operated with minimal overhead and without burdensome bureaucracy. Nobel's facilities were modest structures without the manicured lawns and architecturally elegant buildings found at the most expensive private schools. Nobel schools typically employed fewer support personnel that their private and public counterparts, and teachers' salaries averaged 41 percent less than the $37,000 average salary of public school teachers. Despite the lower pay, teachers welcomed the opportunity to work at Nobel, where average class sizes were smaller than at public schools—17 students per class versus 24 students per class—and where the pupils were generally more committed to learning, largely because the schools had the ability to turn away children with disciplinary problems.

With a proven business model, Clegg entered the latter half of the 1990s ready to expand his concept by creating clusters of

Nobel communities. By the beginning of 1996, 13 of company's properties in California had been converted to elementary schools catering to students from kindergarten through the eighth grade. Clegg intended on nearly tripling the number of converted schools during the next two years, as well as converting approximately 70 percent of Nobel's 51 preschools to kindergarten through second grade schools. Clegg also announced aggressive acquisition plans, endeavoring to dramatically increase the $44 million in sales the company recorded at the end of 1995.

### Late 1990s Diversification

As Clegg pursued his ambitious expansion plans, another change in the company's corporate title was needed to more accurately reflect the strategy driving it forward. In 1998, the company adopted the name Nobel Learning Communities, Inc., indicative of Clegg's desire to serve the educational needs of all children within a given community. Toward this end, the company's acquisition campaign enabled Clegg to create a more entrenched position within Noble communities—between 1994 and 1999, 68 schools were acquired—but the last years of the decade also saw Nobel target other segments of a community's student base. In 1998, the company formed a joint venture with Developmental Resource Center, Inc. (DRC), owned by Dr. Deborah Levy, a developer of special education programs. Under the terms of the agreement, Paladin Academy, LLC was formed, a joint venture project 80 percent owned by Nobel and 20 percent owned by DRC. The joint venture gave Nobel control of three schools in Florida that specialized in full day programs, summer camps, testing services, and clinics for kindergarten through 12th grade students challenged by learning disabilities such as dyslexia and attention deficit disorder. In 1999, Nobel added three more Paladin Academy locations, offering the specialized educational programs in the classrooms of existing Noble schools. Based on the performance of the new Paladin Academy schools, the company planned to open additional schools in areas where Nobel schools were clustered.

Nobel also moved in several other new directions in 1999, as Clegg shaped the company into a comprehensive education facility for the next century. Late in 1999, Nobel began offering tutorial and diagnostic programs under the name Nobel Learning Advantage. The programs, the company planned to market to Nobel students and non-Nobel students both, were offered at two of Nobel's schools in 1999, with a company-wide rollout scheduled to begin in January 2000. Nobel entered the charter school market in 1999 as well, facilitating a nonprofit entity's application for a charter from the School District of Philadelphia. Under the terms of a five-year management contract, Nobel agreed to provide administrative and construction management services to the charter school, which funded its own operations through payments from the School District of Philadelphia. The last year of the decade also saw Nobel acquire the Houston Learning Academy, an operator of five specialty high schools in Houston, Texas. The schools offered half-day curriculum programs focused on individualized attention.

As Nobel prepared for further expansion in the 21st century, the achievements of the 1990s suggested energetic growth lay ahead. The company eclipsed the $100-million sales mark in 1999, recording $109 million in sales, more than twice the total collected five years earlier. With the additions to the company's operating scope made in 1999, the opportunities for growth increased commensurately, positioning Nobel to attract students of all ages and abilities within a given community. After righting a floundering enterprise, Clegg demonstrated the ability and willingness to expand aggressively and strategically, a behavior he promised to display in the years ahead.

### Principal Subsidiaries

Merryhill Schools, Inc.; Merryhill Schools Nevada, Inc.; Nedi, Inc.

### Principal Competitors

KinderCare Learning Centers, Inc.; Bright Horizons Family Solutions, Inc.; Edison Schools, Inc.

### Further Reading

Abelson, Reed, "Rocking Horse Offering Aimed at Expansion," *Philadelphia Business Journal,* October 12, 1987, p. 10.

Davis, Jessica, "Venture Firm Invests in For-Profit School Company," *Philadelphia Business Journal,* September 2, 1994, p. 3.

Ellis, Junius, "A Potential 48% Gain Puts These Education Stocks at the Head of the Class," *Money,* January 1996, p. 25.

Geiger, Mia, "Nobel's ABCs of Private Schooling," *Philadelphia Business Journal,* May 23, 1997, p. B1.

——, "Rocking Horse Changes Image after Quick Financial Turnaround," *Philadelphia Business Journal,* June 28, 1993, p. 6B.

Gubernick, Lisa, "Midmarket Schools," *Forbes,* July 31, 1995, p. 46.

"Rocking Horse Child Care Centers of America Inc.," *Philadelphia Business Journal,* December 12, 1988, p. 26.

Woodall, Martha, "Media, Pa.-Based Education Firm Plans Philadelphia Charter School," *Knight-Ridder/Tribune Business News,* November 11, 1998.

—Jeffrey L. Covell

# NorthWestern Corporation

125 South Dakota Avenue
Sioux Falls, South Dakota 57104
U.S.A.
Telephone: (605) 976-2908
Fax: (605) 978-2910
Web site: http://www.northwestern.com

*Public Company*
*Incorporated:* 1923 as Northwestern Public Service
  Company
*Employees:* 7,965
*Sales:* $3 billion (1999)
*Stock Exchanges:* New York
*Ticker Symbol:* NOR
*NAIC:* 221112 Fossil Fuel Electric Power Generation;
  221122 Electric Power Distribution; 22121 Natural
  Gas Distribution

One of the United States' fastest-growing companies, North-Western Corporation is a diversified holding company with operations and customers in all 50 states. For most of its history, the company (previously known as the Northwestern Public Service Company) was an electric and natural gas distributor operating in South Dakota, North Dakota, and Nebraska. But the deregulation of the electric utilities in the 1970s and 1980s spurred NorthWestern to expand its holdings into new service-related niches. Most of NorthWestern's sales are derived from its 30 percent stake in Cornerstone Propane Partners, L.P. which distributes propane through a network of local stores, repairs and maintains propane heating systems, and sells propane-related supplies and wholesale propane. NorthWestern also owns Exp@nets, a telecommunications and data networking services provider for small and mid-sized businesses; Blue Dot Services, a heating, ventilation, air conditioning, and plumbing services provider; and NorthWestern Energy and Communications Solutions (formerly the Northwestern Public Service utility). In addition, NorthWestern acquired the electric and gas distribution business of The Montana Power Company in 2000.

## Roaring Twenties Origins

Northwestern Public Service Company was incorporated on November 27, 1923, when three investors associated with the Albert Emanuel Company of New York purchased several small electric utilities in rural Nebraska and South Dakota from the Omaha, Nebraska-based Union Power & Light Company. Northwestern, like many other electric utilities of this era, was controlled by a giant utility holding company—the Albert Emanuel Company—which owned utilities in Ohio, Michigan, and Pennsylvania.

Backed by Emanuel's considerable resources, Northwestern went on an acquisition spree in 1924, purchasing ten local utilities, including South Dakota's Huron Light & Power Company, which became Northwestern's headquarters. In 1925, Emanuel reorganized its corporate interests and formed the National Electric Power Company, which subsumed Northwestern along with dozens of utilities in Delaware, Florida, Georgia, Kansas, Maryland, Michigan, North Carolina, Ohio, Pennsylvania, South Dakota, Virginia, and West Virginia. After this restructuring, Northwestern continued to acquire local electric companies. By the end of 1927, the company served 68 towns and had gross earnings of more than $2 million.

In 1928 National Electric was swallowed by an even larger holding company, Middle West Utilities Company, which incorporated Northwestern into its Wisconsin-based Northwest Utilities Company. Owned by Samuel Insull, Middle West was a sprawling concern that reached into 19 states. Under Insull's aegis, Northwestern bought two North Dakota utilities and the Knife River Coal Mining Company in 1929. These acquisitions marked Northwestern's first penetration into North Dakota and encompassed consumers in 53 new towns. In addition, the Knife River facility provided Northwestern with a constant, low-cost supply of coal to feed its power plants.

## Dark Days: Turmoil in the 1930s

Northwestern's fortunes soon changed dramatically. The stock market crash rocked the entire utility industry, and Insull compounded Northwestern's problems by making a disastrous bet on further expansion in the belief that the downturn would be temporary. The financial market remained in free-fall, and Middle West went with it, going bankrupt in 1932. After three years in bankruptcy court, Insull's far-flung holdings were reorganized and Northwestern, along with Insull's other utilities, were transferred to a newly created corporate entity, the Middle West Corporation.

Local conditions hurt Northwestern as well. South Dakota was devastated by both the Great Depression and the Dust Bowl, leading to a massive population exodus. Northwestern stayed afloat by cutting electric rates and trimming salaries, but Franklin Delano Roosevelt soon worsened Northwestern's situation when he made the breakup of utility holding companies the centerpiece of his 1932 presidential campaign (even singling out Insull as a particular example of rapacious corporate greed). The public (which was becoming increasingly accustomed to cheap, plentiful electricity) agreed, and Roosevelt was able to push the Public Utility Holding Companies Act (PUHCA) through Congress in 1935. The act dramatically changed the landscape for electric utilities, as it mandated the breakup of all holding companies within five years unless the Federal Power Commission certified that a holding company was necessary for the operation of an economic unit in contiguous states. (The implementation of this law eventually was delayed until after World War II.)

In this new environment, Northwestern recognized that its survival depended on "building load," or encouraging consumers to use more power. To this end, the company aggressively sold appliances, lights, and light bulbs to consumers. By 1939 this strategy proved effective. That year the company served more than 50,000 customers in 190 communities across three states, and its revenues exceeded $3 million, regaining the ground that had been lost since 1929.

Northwestern suffered a setback in 1940 when it was forced out, essentially, of Nebraska's electric market. Nebraska had established a state-owned power system in the late 1930s and ultimately forced Northwestern—along with all other private utilities operating in the state—to sell out. Northwestern challenged the move in court but lost, finally, in the U.S. Supreme Court. The company was able to retain its Nebraska natural gas business, though.

### Growth and Change in the 1940s and 1950s

World War II had a minimal effect on Northwestern, but the postwar years brought considerable change. As the United States demobilized in 1945, the Securities and Exchange Commission began to enforce the PUHCA and required Middle West to dispose of its holdings in Northwestern. Middle West turned Northwestern into a publicly traded company and sold its interest in it in 1946. As part of this process, Bear Stearns & Co., a New York investment banking house, took control of the company for one year.

Newly independent, Northwestern found new opportunities. The end of World War II unleashed a flood of demand for electric power as Americans hungered for labor-saving appliances that had been underproduced during the war years (factories had had to devote their resources to military rather than consumer uses). The sale of electrical appliances quadrupled between 1945 and 1946 alone, and factories ran around the clock to meet this demand—consuming even more power in the process. Farms undertook major electrification projects as well. Northwestern's revenues soared to more than $4 million in 1946.

In the midst of these boom years, however, Northwestern was confronted with two distinct challenges. In 1946 the Montana-Dakota Utilities Co. (MDU) filed suit against Northwestern. MDU had purchased a pair of North Dakota utilities and the Knife River coal plant from Northwestern in 1945, and subsequently charged that Northwestern had looted the accounts of the three companies before the sale. Although Northwestern eventually was exonerated (the U.S. Supreme Court dismissed the case in 1951), it was forced to spend thousands of dollars on legal fees. The suit also was a major distraction for Northwestern during what was otherwise a time of phenomenal growth for the utility industry as a whole.

The second major factor affecting Northwestern in the postwar era was the entrance of the federal Bureau of Reclamation into South Dakota's electric market. In the wake of severe flooding on the Missouri River in 1943, Congress enacted the Flood Control Act in 1944, which empowered the Bureau of Reclamation and the Army Corps of Engineers to construct five major hydroelectric dams on the Missouri River in South Dakota. Congress ordered the Bureau to sell the hydroelectric power from these dams to "preference" customers, typically publicly owned electric utilities. Northwestern feared that it would not survive if it had to compete with public power utilities awash in cheap, federally funded hydroelectric power, and it pleaded for relief throughout the 1940s. It had little success, but the company's bottom line remained strong. Revenues for 1950 exceeded $7 million.

Northwestern's concerns were treated more sympathetically after Republican Dwight D. Eisenhower was elected to the presidency in 1952. Fred Aandahl, Eisenhower's Assistant Secretary of the Interior for Water and Power, believed that the government should not be competing with private utilities, and championed the rights of private power companies in South Dakota. In 1953, Aandahl enabled the Bureau to sell excess power to "nonpreference" customers—private electric utilities. Northwestern signed a contract with the Bureau in 1953 to purchase heavily discounted power under the condition that it

## Key Dates:

**1923:** NorthWestern Public Service Company is incorporated.
**1925:** NorthWestern becomes an operating utility of National Electric Power Company.
**1928:** Middle West Utilities acquires National Electric Power Company.
**1932:** Middle West Utilities enters bankruptcy proceedings.
**1935:** Congress passes the Public Utilities Holding Companies Act.
**1944:** Congress passes the Flood Control Act.
**1945:** The Securities and Exchange Commission orders Middle West to dispose of its holdings in NorthWestern.
**1953:** NorthWestern begins to purchase power from Missouri River dams.
**1956:** Company brings natural gas to South Dakota.
**1957:** NorthWestern joins the Upper Missouri Power Pool.
**1969:** NorthWestern joins with other utilities to build Big Stone Steam Electric Generating Plant.
**1994:** NorthWestern forms the Northwestern Growth Corporation.
**1998:** NorthWestern Public Service changes its name to NorthWestern Corporation.
**2000:** Company purchases The Montana Power Company's energy distribution and transmission business.

pass along savings to customers. For the next 25 years, the Missouri River dams provided the vast majority of Northwestern's power generation (freeing the company from having to invest in generating plants of its own).

The 1950s brought rapid economic growth to South Dakota, and Northwestern invested in new plant facilities, as well as substations that connected it with the Bureau's dams, to keep up with burgeoning demand. The company also achieved a long-standing goal in 1956 when it introduce natural gas into South Dakota. Northwestern had been a major natural gas distributor in Nebraska since the early 1940s, but had been stymied by its efforts to expand northward. In 1952, however, Northern Natural Gas of Omaha had begun to study the feasibility of running a pipeline to the Dakotas and eventually opted to do so. Northwest jumped at the opportunity to distribute Natural's gas to individual customers. By 1959, Northwestern had more than 71,000 customers and revenues of nearly $12 million, with almost as much of that amount generated by natural gas as by electricity.

### Reorganization and Turbulence in the 1960s and 1970s

In 1961 the company made the biggest acquisition in its history to date when it purchased ten electric franchise towns in South Dakota, thereby gaining a firmer foothold in the more prosperous eastern half of South Dakota. As this part of the state was more industrialized, Northwestern was now less dependent on the vagaries of agriculture for its revenues.

But in the mid-1960s Northwestern faced a unique set of problems posed by its customers' ever-increasing demand for electric and gas power. While the company's swelling sales were obviously welcomed (revenues had reached $16.5 million by 1964), Northwestern struggled to get enough power across its lines. The company was not alone in this predicament. Demand for power had become so great nationwide that system overloads began to cause widespread power outages. To alleviate this problem, utilities begin to interconnect their electric transmission networks. In 1963, Northwestern joined with 21 power suppliers from nine states to form the Mid-Continent Area Power Planners (MAPP—later renamed Mid-Continent Area Power Pool), whose goal was to develop integrated regional planning.

As demand for power continued to rise, Northwestern encountered a more serious hurdle. The number of public preference customers for the federal hydropower allocations on the Missouri River had grown in the 1960s, and by 1970 Northwestern recognized that it would soon be unable to purchase discounted power. Therefore, it needed to return to the generation business. To this end, Northwestern, along with Otter Tail Power Company and Montana-Dakota Utilities, agreed in 1969 to build a new coal-fired plant. But by the time this Big Stone Steam Electric Generating Plant was completed in 1975, it proved so expensive (costs ran to more than $160 million, with Northwestern alone contributing $52 million) that Northwestern had to raise its rates. Customers were undaunted by the new prices, though, and when Big Stone failed to slake the region's thirst for power, Northwestern entered into more joint ventures to construct new generating plants. In 1975 Northwestern, Minnesota Power & Light, Minnkota Power Cooperative, Otter Tail, and Montana-Dakota built the Coyote I Generating Station near Beulah, North Dakota. This $385 million project went on line in 1981.

Unfortunately for Northwestern—and much of the electric utility industry—demand eventually slackened. The Organization of Petroleum Exporting Companies' (OPEC) 1973 oil embargo put a premium on energy conservation. At the same time, energy companies such as Northwestern faced natural gas shortages. Responding to pressure from both industry and consumer groups, Congress took the first steps toward deregulating the gas and electric industry in 1978. But deregulation brought its own set of challenges. For instance, although natural gas distributors such as Northwestern were free to buy their gas from any supplier (not just from pipelines that had served them in the past), customers could also choose to bypass their local distributors (such as Northwestern) and purchase natural gas directly from pipelines and natural gas brokers.

### The Deregulation Era: 1980s and Beyond

The early 1980s were not kind to Northwestern. With a downturn in demand and an enormous debt load from construction projects that suddenly seemed superfluous, the company suffered from a cash-flow crunch. To cope, Northwestern—like many of its competitors—sought to diversify its assets and investments to protect itself from the vicissitudes of the gas and electric industry. In the mid-1980s, for example, Northwestern began to sell its computerized Customer Service System to other utilities, and in 1986, the company invested in the Satellite Movie Company, which provided in-room movies to hotel chains.

Northwestern's diversification efforts gained greater momentum in the mid-1990s. In 1994 the company formed Northwestern Growth Corporation, a strategic development and private investment arm. Northwestern Growth advised the company to complement its current holdings in the energy business, which Northwestern did by venturing into the propane distribution business. In 1995 the company acquired Synergy Group Inc., a propane distributor with 152 retail branches in 23 states. Northwestern increased its presence in this new niche the following year with the purchase of another propane distributor, Empire Energy Corp. Also that year, Northwestern took a stake in Cornerstone Propane Partners, L.P., one of the leading propane retailers in the country. Cornerstone was also a wholesale propane marketer through its own subsidiary, The Coast Energy Group. Through Cornerstone, Northwestern was able to expand beyond the geographic confines of its electric and gas holdings. By 2000, Cornerstone was the fifth largest propane distributor in the United States with 460,000 customers in 43 states.

Northwestern Growth also prompted its parent company to explore business areas wholly unrelated to energy. In 1997, Northwestern founded ServiCenter USA, a provider of value-added heating, air-conditioning, plumbing, and related services. ServiCenter quickly conducted a spate of acquisitions, making it a leader in this sector. In 1998, Northwestern changed ServiCenter's name to Blue Dot. By 2000, Blue Dot boasted 600,000 customers in 25 states.

Also in 1997 Northwestern created Communication Systems USA (renamed Exp@nets in 1998), which became a force in the telecommunications and data communications industries. Exp@nets designed networked communications solutions—call centers and messaging, web enablement, data network design and engineering, and systems installment and support—for mid-sized business customers. In 2000, Exp@nets acquired the Enterprise Network Group from Lucent Technology. With 750,000 customers in 29 states, Exp@nets was the country's largest integrated communications solutions provider for small and mid-sized businesses.

Northwestern was well positioned for future growth and development. The company transformed itself from a regional utility company into a leading provider of energy, telecommunications, and related services nationwide. Reflecting its new and diversified identity, the company renamed itself the NorthWestern Corporation in 1998. But the company had not abandoned the electric and natural gas utility sector. Northwestern Public Service—re-christened NorthWestern Energy and Communications Solutions in 2000—remained a key part of the company. In 2000, NorthWestern expanded its utility operations by acquiring The Montana Power Company's electricity and natural gas distribution business. For $1.1 billion, NorthWestern gained an additional 493,000 electric and natural gas customers in Montana as well as the capacity to build further into the west. With more than two million customers, NorthWestern was named to *Forbes'* "Platinum List" and to *Fortune's* list of "America's most admired companies" in 2000.

### Principal Subsidiaries

Blue Dot Services; Exp@nets; NorthWestern Growth Corporation; NorthWestern Energy and Communications Solutions; Cornerstone Propane Partners, L.P. (30%).

### Principal Competitors

AmeriGas Partners, L.P.; At&T Corp.; Ferrellgas Partners, L.P.; Suburban Propane Partners, L.P.

### Further Reading

Beck, Bill, *Light Across the Prairies,* Huron, S.D.: Northwestern Public Service Company, 1989.
Byrne, Harlan, "Big Sky Telecom," *Barron's,* October 9, 2000.
"CEO Interview: Northwestern Public Service Company," *Wall Street Transcript,* June 27, 1994.
Hannon, Kerry, "A Few Utilities with Staying Power," *US News & World Report,* March 24, 1997.
"New Kid in Town: Northwestern Subsidiary," *Computer Re-Seller News,* May 25, 1998.
Nguyen, Pham-Duy, "Silicon Valley Propane Company Keeps Pace in High-Tech World," *San Jose Mercury News,* September 18, 2000.
Smith, Rebecca, "Montana Power to Sell Pipes Unit to NorthWestern," *Wall Street Journal,* October 3, 2000.
"South Dakota Utility Pursues Energy Alternatives," *Gas Daily,* September 17, 1996.

—Rebecca Stanfel

# Nutraceutical International Corporation

1400 Kearns Boulevard, Second Floor
Park City, Utah 84060
U.S.A.
Telephone: (435) 655-6000
Fax: (435) 647-3802
Toll Free: (800) 669-8877
Web site: http://www.nutraceutical.com

Public Company
Incorporated: 1993
Employees: 550
Sales: $106.8 million (1999)
Stock Exchanges: NASDAQ
Ticker Symbol: NUTR
NAIC: 325411 Medicinal and Botanical Manufacturing

Nutraceutical International Inc. develops, manufacturers, and markets a wide variety of vitamin, mineral, herbal, and nutritional supplements that are sold in the United States and many other nations. Over its short history, the company has acquired several other companies to fulfill its original goal of consolidating a fragmented industry. Unlike some supplement firms that sell their products in supermarkets and other mass and discount retail outlets, Nutraceutical sells its brand-name products to about 7,000 health food stores in the United States. It offers some 1,600 supplements sold under the brand names of Solaray, KAL, NaturalMax, VegLife, Premier One, Solar Green, Natural Sport, and Action Labs, and also sells ActiPet supplements for pets. The company also makes bulk nutritional products that are used in its own products, as well as being sold to other supplement companies under the trade names Monarch Nutritional Laboratories and Great Basin Botanicals. Nutraceutical International is one of the numerous natural products firms that make Utah the leader in an industry that grew dramatically in the 1990s.

## The Early Years

Nutraceutical's beginnings date to 1993, when Bain Capital, Inc.—a Boston-based private equity company—paired with senior management to organize Nutraceutical and consolidate what its leaders thought was a very divided nutritional supplements industry. Bain Capital's leader was Mitt Romney, the Mormon Republican who tried in vain to defeat Democratic incumbent Senator Edward Kennedy of Massachusetts. Later, Romney became the head of the Salt Lake Organizing Committee preparing for the 2002 Winter Olympics.

Nutraceutical's first acquisition in 1993 was Solaray, Inc. of Ogden, Utah. The company had begun making capsules of herbal products in 1973 under the company name Solar Products, Inc. The following year, the company was incorporated as a Utah entity known as Solaray.

According to the Nutraceutical Web site, Solaray was "a pioneer in formulating and marketing blended herbal products that contain two or more herbs with complementary effects." By 1984, Solaray had added vitamins and minerals to its product lines. Later, in 1990, Solaray received funds from the Utah Department of Agriculture to work with Weber State College's Department of Chemistry to develop new products made from whey—a byproduct of cheese making that normally was discarded.

When Nutraceutical was founded in the early 1990s, it joined a natural products industry in Utah that had a long and colorful history. For example, in a 1979 article, writer Elaine Jarvik said that six Utah herbal companies were not only "the first companies in the world to put herbs in capsules, but they now account for 85 percent of the nation's herb business." Other Utah herbal firms in the 1990s included Murdock Madaus Scwabe, Nature's Herbs (part of Twin Labs), Nature's Sunshine, Enrich International, USANA, NuSkin, Weider Nutrition, E'Ola, Morinda, and Neways. In addition, Sunrider had started in Utah, but later relocated to Torrance, California. Unlike Nutraceutical, many Utah herbal products firms used multilevel marketing to distribute their products.

In 1998, the Los Angeles Times ran a four-part series on alternative health. The third article focused on how Utah became what writer David R. Olmos called the "Silicon Valley of herbs." He pointed out that the state's herbal and supplement industry was "bigger even than the skiing trade." In addition to entrepreneurship, Olmos credited Utah's Mormon culture. Although the LDS church had long accepted modern scientific medicine, many of its members used herbs and other forms of alternative healing, partly due to the church's ''Word of Wisdom'' found in founder Joseph Smith's *Doctrine and Covenants.* Thus, herbalism, capitalism, and religious factors all took part in creating the history of Utah's herbal products industry.

The early years of the herbal and supplement industry were tough, but times had improved by the time Nutraceutical was founded. ''It wasn't always easy to be in this business,'' said Grace Rich, marketing director for Nature's Herbs in the August 16, 1998 *Salt Lake Tribune,* noting ''There were plenty of people out there who thought we were all quacks trying to take their money.'' Ken Murdock, chairman of Utah's Nature's Way, said the growing emphasis on preventive care and individuals taking responsibility for their own health had helped to end what he called ''the Dark Ages of health care when doctors had all the answers.'' A new federal law helped the vitamin and herbal industry, however. Sponsored by Utah's Republican Senator Orrin Hatch, the 1994 Dietary Supplement Health and Education Act prevented what the industry considered to be over regulation by the U.S. Food and Drug Administration (FDA). Following the passage of the new law, the nutritional supplement industry rapidly expanded. According to the Marketing Intelligence Service as reported in the September 1998 *Utah Business,* in 1993 the industry added 633 new items, but in 1996 that had increased to over 800 new products.

### Acquisitions and Other Developments in the Mid-1990s

In October 1994, Nutraceutical acquired Premier One Products, Inc., a Nebraska corporation. Premier One had been founded in July 1984 in Omaha, Nebraska, as one of the first companies to sell items made completely from bee products. Nutraceutical stated in its 1998 Stock Prospectus that it believed ''by 1995 the Premier One Royal Jelly products had become the best-selling royal jelly products'' sold in health food stores.

Nutraceutical's third acquisition came in January 1995, when the company acquired the California-based Makers of KAL, Inc. Nutraceutical also acquired Healthway Corporation, a company that had been founded in 1958, as part of its KAL acquisition.

KAL's beginnings dated to 1932, when the company was formed in Southern California as a pioneering firm providing supplements. Soon after its start, it switched from selling powdered products to tablets. According to Nutraceutical's Web site, one of KAL's ''innovative product introductions was 'Beyond Garlic,' which remains a popular garlic product in health food stores and was the first 'enteric coated softgel' garlic product.'' It also claimed that KAL was ''the first nutritional supplement marketer in health food stores to introduce pycnogenol and melatonin,'' two popular items.

In early 1995, Nutraceutical's subsidiary Solaray announced its plan to purchase 12 acres of land in Mountain Green—a bedroom community ten miles from Ogden—and to move its most of its operations there by the end of the year. Also in 1995, Nutraceutical started VegLife as a separate brand, following its previous origin in 1992 as a line of products marketed under the Solaray brand. VegLife was comprised of strictly vegetarian products, including encapsulated items and two beverages: Peaceful Planet—a soy protein drink, and Peaceful Kava, which contained Kava—used originally by Pacific islanders.

To sell its products overseas, Nutraceutical in fiscal year 1995 organized a wholly owned subsidiary called Au Naturel, Inc. Operating as a separate business, Au Naturel reformulated some Nutraceutical products and labels to meet the regulatory demands of the foreign nations where it operated.

A couple years later, in April 1997, Nutraceutical introduced a new line of supplements called Solar Green. The product line included tablets containing different kinds of algae and cereal grasses, and also a drink mix used to prepare a beverage supplement.

By early 1998, Nutraceutical products were being sold through Au Naturel in about 30 foreign countries. Foreign sales accounted for just 6.3 percent and 6.5 percent of Nutraceutical's total net sales in 1996 and 1997 respectively, however. Nutraceutical saw this area as a great opportunity for future growth, due to the fact that its foreign sales had increased 21.4 percent in 1997.

A 1997 survey sponsored by *Health Supplement Retailer* found that Solaray ranked as the top selling brand of nutritional supplements, and the second best selling line of herbal products. The survey also found that Solaray's St. John's Wort was the best selling herbal product, and Nutraceutical had the best customer service. By 1998, Nutraceutical employed 450 individuals, including 70 at its Park City, Utah headquarters.

### Company Additions and Innovations in the Late 1990s

In the summer of 1998, Nutraceutical acquired Action Labs Inc. for about $13.7 million cash. Started in 1988, Action Labs marketed and distributed some 65 brand name nutritional supplements sold mainly in health food stores, so it fit well with Nutraceutical's general distribution strategy. The acquisition of the Long Island, New York company gave Nutraceutical ''additional market penetration in the eastern United States,'' said Nutraceutical Chairman and CEO Bill Gay in the August 3, 1998 edition of *The Enterprise,* a Salt Lake City business newspaper. Within a year, Nutraceutical was making its own Action Labs products instead of buying them from other manufacturers.

In September 1998, Nutraceutical introduced a new brand of products called Natural Sport. Designed for athletes and avid exercisers, the Natural Sport line included two beverages called Pre-Burn and Post-Up, a soy protein beverage supplement called ProSoy, creatine monohydrate, and Phyto Sport multivitamins.

## Key Dates:

**1993:**  Nutraceutical International is founded.
**1993:**  The company purchases Solaray, Inc.
**1994:**  Acquisition of Premier One Products, Inc.; Nutraceutical Newco, Inc. is incorporated in Delaware, renamed Nutraceutical Corporation.
**1995:**  Acquisition of the Makers of KAL, Inc.; acquisition of Monarch Nutritional Laboratories, Inc.
**1997:**  The Solar Green brand is introduced in April.
**1998:**  Stock is first sold on the NASDAQ; July acquisition of Action Labs, Inc.; August acquisition of Nutraforce (Canada) International, Inc.
**1999:**  Nutraceutical acquires Woodland Publishing, Inc. and Summit Graphics, Inc.
**2000:**  The company buys Thompson Nutritional Products.

The following year, Nutraceutical purchased Woodland Publishing, Inc., a pioneering publisher of books and other literature for the natural products industry. Based in Lindon, Utah County, Utah near many large herbal products manufacturers, Woodland had been started in 1975 to publish the writing of some of Utah's well-known herbalists, such as John Christopher. In 1985, Woodland published *Today's Herbal Health*, of which over 750,000 copies had been sold by 1999. On August 20, 1986, Louise Lisonbee, David Lisonbee, and Josie Palmieri had incorporated Woodland Health Books under Utah law. The name was changed to Woodland Publishing, Inc. on August 30, 1993. In 1995, Woodland began publishing its popular specialized booklets for sale mostly in health food stores. By 2000, Woodland had published over 160 titles.

On May 26, 2000, Nutraceutical announced that it had purchased a division of Rexall Sundown, Inc., called Thompson Nutritional Products. For over 60 years, Thompson had been making nutritional supplements. Upon acquiring Thompson, Nutraceutical planned to expand the company's brand name line of products. Nutraceutical had acquired numerous companies, folding most of them into the company and retaining their recognized names as brands.

### Business in a New Millennium and Beyond

Meanwhile, the herbal and supplements business was evolving. For many years, consumers had been able to buy herbal products in health food stores, but not in grocery stores or other outlets. In the late 1990s, however, large supermarket chains and mass retailers like Wal-Mart realized the consumer demand, and thus opened new sections for supplements. ''Paced by positive press,'' wrote Renee M. Kruger in the January 1999 edition of *Supermarket Business,* ''once strange-sounding herbal supplements such as St. John's Wort, echinacea and gingko biloba have now moved into the mainstream as viable health enhancers, especially to aging baby boomers who are trying to maintain a higher quality of life.''

By the year 2000, a seven-member Board of Directors oversaw Nutraceutical International Corporation. Frank W. Gay II had served as board chairman since the company began, and had also been its CEO since 1994. Other directors were Robert C. Gay, Ph.D., a managing director of Bain Capital, Inc.; J. Steven Young, J.D., the former star quarterback of the San Francisco 49'ers; EOTT Energy Corporation President/CEO Michael D. Burke; James D. Stice, Ph.D, a Brigham Young University accounting professor; Matthew S. Levin, a Bain principal; and Jeffrey A. Hinrichs, a former Solaray executive who since 1994 had served as Nutraceutical's executive vice-president and chief operating officer. Bruce R. Hough, former chair of the Utah State Republican Party, served as Nutraceutical's president.

Under these leaders, Nutraceutical faced a challenging future. Although the demand for herbal products and nutritional supplements was increasing, an increasing number of corporations, including some much larger than Nutraceutical, competed for market share.

### Principal Subsidiaries

Nutra-Force (Barbabdos) International, Inc.; Nutra Corp.

### Principal Competitors

Twinlab Corporation; Solgar Vitamin and Herb Company; Rexall Sundown Inc.; NBTY, Inc.; Melaleuca, Inc.; Nature's Sunshine Products Inc; Murdock Madaus Scwabe; General Nutrition Companies, Inc.

### Further Reading

Carricaburu, Lisa, ''The Changing Nature of Supplements,'' *Salt Lake Tribune,* December 20, 1998, pp. E1, E4.
——, ''Utah's Natural-Products Firms Blossom from Need,'' *Salt Lake Tribune,* August 16, 1998, pp. E1–E2.
Campbell, Joel, ''Nature's Own,'' *Deseret News,* June 28, 1998, p. M1.
Greenwald, John, ''Herbal Healing,'' *Time,* November 23, 1998, pp. 58–68.
Hills, Bruce, ''6 Utah Firms Win Grants to Help Boost Agriculture,'' *Deseret News,* January 25, 1990, p. D8.
Jarvik, Elaine, ''Underground Health,'' *Utah Holiday,* November 1979, pp. 24–36.
Kruger, Renee M., ''High Time for Herbals,'' *Supermarket Business,* January 1999, pp. 65–68.
Olmos, David R., ''Herbal Medicine Sets Firm Roots in Utah,'' *Los Angeles Times,* September 1, 1998, p. 1.
''Park City Firm Buys Laboratory Assets for $13.7 Million Cash,'' *The Enterprise* (Salt Lake City), August 3, 1998, p. 15.
Repanshek, Kurt, ''Powders, Pills + Profits,'' *Utah Business,* September 1998, pp. 38–40.
''Solaray Announces Plans to Buy 12 Acres in Mountain Green for its New Headquarters,'' *Deseret News,* January 5, 1995, p. E3.

—David M. Walden

**Offshore Logistics, Inc.**

# Offshore Logistics, Inc.

**224 Rue de Jean**
**Lafayette, Louisiana 70505**
**U.S.A.**
**Telephone: (337) 233-1221**
**Fax: (337) 235-6678**
**Web site: http://www.olog.com**

*Public Company*
*Incorporated:* 1969 in Louisiana, 1988 reincorporated in
 Delaware
*Employees:* 3,131
*Sales:* $420.6 million (2000)
*Stock Exchanges:* NASDAQ
*Ticker Symbol:* OLOG
*NAIC:* 481211 Nonscheduled Chartered Passenger; Air
 Transportation 481212 Nonscheduled Chartered
 Freight Air Transportation

Offshore Logistics, Inc., with headquarters in Lafayette, Louisiana, provides a variety of services to the petroleum industry, including air transportation and oil production management. Through a network of subsidiaries and affiliates, it operates one of the largest fleets of commercial helicopters in the world. Although it principally operates in the Gulf of Mexico, the North Sea, and Alaska, over its history it has provided logistical services in close to 100 countries. It is the only helicopter operator in the world to serve both the Gulf and North Sea oil markets. Its consortium of subsidiaries and partially owned affiliates includes Air Logistics, Air Logistics of Alaska, Inc., AirLog International, Inc., Grasso Production Management, and Bristow Helicopter Group Limited. Air Logistics provides helicopter transportation services for the offshore petroleum industry in the Gulf of Mexico, while its counterparts, Bristow Helicopters and Air Logistic Alaska do the same for oil production sites in, respectively, in the North Sea and Alaska. As of the end of March 2000, Air Log and Bristow operated 380 aircraft, 78 of which were under the control of unconsolidated entities. In addition, OLOG provides support services in other parts of the world, including Africa, Asia, the Pacific Rim and Central and South America. Grasso Production

Management, Inc., operating in the Gulf of Mexico, is a major provider of oil production services. It offers contract personnel plus medical and engineering services to the Gulf's oil and gas industry and is a wholly owned subsidiary of OLOG. The company is not solely dependent on the petroleum industry, however; it also offers emergency services and support to agriculture and forestry industries.

### 1969–83: Offshore Logistic Gets Off and Running in the Oil Boom

Burt Keenan started up Offshore Logistics in 1969, after studying Business Administration at Tulane University, where he earned both his B.A. and M.B.A. and developed his interest in capital investment in middle market companies. As Offshore Logistics' name implies, its purpose was to provide support services to the rapidly expanding offshore oil industry, then on the verge of a major boom. Initially, Keenan's company used boats to transport workers and materials down Louisiana's bayous out to offshore drilling platforms in the Gulf of Mexico "oil patch."

Although crew boats and supply vessels continued to meet many of the needs of the offshore oil industry, such as rotating the "seven on, seven off" crews working on the rigs, a quick response capability mandated the use of helicopters for some tasks, and Offshore started using them in 1972, competing with such established companies as Petroleum Helicopters Inc. (PHI), which by 1970 had already logged over one million flight hours.

Keenan slowly built up the company's fleets of vessels and helicopters, faring well through the 1970s when offshore drilling in the Gulf of Mexico got into high gear. Management did face a few problems. For example, in 1975 the Teamsters Union mounted a campaign to unionize OLOG's pilots, something they had done at Petroleum Helicopters as early as 1970. However, the unionization efforts failed and would continue to fail for another two decades. A greater challenge for Keenan was to make significant inroads in a market dominated by PHI.

In the 1970s, Keenan also hired some key personnel, men who would survive his 1986 resignation and rise to important executive positions. Among others that Keenan hired as pilots in 1972

## Company Perspectives:

*Our Company's mission is to provide the safest, most cost-effective and most reliable service to customers in a diverse community of markets including the Gulf of Mexico; Alaska; the North Sea region, including England, Scotland and Europe; and a number of international markets including Brazil, Mexico, Colombia, Australia, Nigeria, China and others.*

was Hans J. Albert, who would become OLOG's executive vice-president of international operations in 1999. In 1976, James B. Clement joined the company as controller. (He would become Keenan's successor as president and CEO in 1986–87.) In the next year, 1977, George M. Small also joined on as company controller. In 1997, when Clement became chairman, Small became the company's president, director, and COO.

In 1980, Offshore floated a public issue of 800,000 shares of $2.4375 convertible preferred stock that sold out at $25 per share. The proceeds of the sale were used to reduce debt as well as fund the purchase of needed equipment. The largest investor in Offshore was Atwood Oceanics, Inc., which purchased a 7.25 percent stake in the company in 1983, then increased it to 20 percent when OLOG hit troubled times with the deflation of oil prices.

### 1984–89: OLOG Survives the Deep Oil Industry Recession

Offshore Logistics was hit very hard in the oil bust. In 1984, it was forced to suspend its common and preferred stock dividends. In the next year, when its short-term debt climbed to over $71 million, the company sold its corporate office building and some aviation and marine equipment. It also cut employee salaries by ten percent and reduced paid vacations. Then, under pressure from creditors, it also restructured its principal and interest payments. In an additional move to remain viable, it transferred title to its fleet of 24 domestic supply boats and ships to the U.S. Maritime Administration in exchange for $50 million in loan guarantees. The debt service on the 24 vessels had cost the company about $14 million between 1983 and 1984, an expense that by 1985 it could no longer offset from the declining revenues produced by them. Offshore's agreement with the Maritime Administration reduced its long term debt of about $120 million to about $75 million. The company kept only its fleet of helicopters and international vessels.

In 1986, with the company struggling to survive, Keenan resigned, swapping his interest in OLOG for the cancellation of a personal $3.6 million loan he had floated with the company in 1982. He would eventually join the firm of Chaffe & Associates, Inc., a New Orleans corporate service company. With Keenan's departure, operational control of Offshore Logistics passed to senior vice-president Clement, who took on the posts of president and COO. At the time, OLOG was still in deep trouble. In the fiscal quarter that had just been completed in March, it logged a $2.9 million loss from revenues that had dropped to $19.1 million from $26.9 million in the same quarter the previous year.

For the remainder of the 1980s, under Clement's leadership the company continued following its strategy of selling its ships and boats and buying some of the assets of companies that were also using helicopters for offshore support services. By January 1987, the company also completed a recapitalization and debt restructuring that gave it some breathing room. By trading 31 percent of its stock, the company was able to lower its minimum annual debt service from $22 million to $8 million and free some capital for equipment purchases. Its chief acquisition was made in 1989, when it bought helicopters from a unit of Omniflight.

### 1990–2000: Some Early Obstacles and a Strong Finish

Although the offshore oil industry was still depressed at the start of the 1990s, up until the later part of fiscal 1991 the demand for OLOG's helicopter services continued to grow, helped some by the fact that some its smaller competitors stopped providing helicopter services altogether, leaving a vacuum that Offshore and its major competitor, Petroleum Helicopters, were quick to fill. Meanwhile, OLOG made its commitment solely to air support services, selling off the remnants of its marine fleet in 1991 and closing down its Marine Division altogether. Proceeds then went into the purchase of new helicopters. Its air fleet grew to 145 aircraft by March of 1991, at which time it had another 15 helicopters on order, with plans for adding 12 more in fiscal 1992.

With a 25 percent market share, second only to Petroleum Helicopters' 50 percent share, Offshore had emerged as a major provider of helicopter services in the Gulf and had doubled it revenue between 1989 and 1991. It appeared to be positioned to raise its earnings by about 20 percent per year. Even when Iraq's invasion of Kuwait brought a steep increase in aircraft fuel cost, OLOG was able to add fuel-cost surcharges to its rates without complaints from its principal customers. Also, because 60 percent of its revenue came from servicing existing production platforms, it was fairly well buffered against swings in the riskier oil industry enterprise—exploration drilling. It had also begun tapping into more markets abroad. In 1990, in a partnership with a Norwegian company, it formed H.S. Logistics, which soon landed contracts for providing helicopter services in New Guinea, India, and Brazil. It also had a 25 percent interest in a helicopter service operation with the Egyptian government and a sideline business providing training and maintenance services to helicopter operators in Indonesia and Mexico.

However, the industry's downswing in the early 1990s worsened, and by the end of 1991 new construction and drilling fell sharply, driving the rig count in the Gulf of Mexico to its lowest point in four years. It remained stagnant throughout 1992. To deal with the problem, Offshore's management imposed stringent cost controls over its domestic operations and attempted to compensate for the drop in domestic flight hours by increasing the company's international operations, which, at the end of 1991, had been using only ten of OLOG's 154 helicopters.

Although the rig count in the Gulf improved in 1993, which led to a rebound in contracted helicopter services through 1995, Offshore had already begun following through on plans for diversification of its operations that it had made in 1992. Convinced that the instability of the industry was forcing some

The following year, OLOG increased the size of its helicopter fleet, purchasing 23 new aircraft, 18 of which it bought outright. These were to be added to its fleet of helicopters and fixed-wing planes that by May 1997 had already climbed to 307 aircraft.

Prospects for increasing contracted flight services seemed very good in 1998. Among other things, Bristow landed a seven-year contract with Shell Exploration UK. However, a temporary setback came in 1999 when depressed oil prices slowed down North Sea exploration activities and forced OLOG to curtail some of its operations. That proved to be a brief lull, however, and in the summer of 2000 crude prices soared up again. In any case, thanks to its diversification in the 1990s, the company seemed most unlikely to be derailed on any oil-price roller-coaster ride provided courtesy of OPEC. It was also doing well enough by the decade's end let the unionization of some of its personnel roll easily off its corporate back.

### Principal Subsidiaries

Air Logistics of Alaska Inc.; Air Logistics LLC; Airlog Part Sales Inc.; Offshore Logistics Management Services; Grasso Production Management Inc.

### Principal Competitors

CHC Helicopter Corporation; Petroleum Helicopters, Inc.; Rowan Companies, Inc.

### Further Reading

Albright, Sam Z., "Offshore Logistics Inc.," *Oil & Gas Investor*, May 1997, p. 68.
Byrne, Harlan S., "Offshore Logistics Inc.: Its Helicopter Force Wins Big in Gulf Engagements," *Barron's*, March 18, 1991, pp. 45–6.
"Companies Agree to Merge," *Oil Daily*, April 19, 1994, p. 5.
"Firm Will Buy Helicopters from Unit of Omniflight," *Wall Street Journal* [Western Edition], September 11, 1989, p. A9.
Ivey, Mark, "Offshore Logistics: Flying High over the Oil Patch," *Business Week*, September 16, 1991, p. 66.
Kreuger, Gretchen, "Offshore Logistics Chairman Resigns," *Daily Advertiser* [Lafayette, Louisiana], May 22, 1986, p. 10.
"Offshore Logistics Inc.," *Insiders' Chronicle*, April 25, 1983, p. 2.
"Offshore Logistics Inc. Sells Issue of Preferred," *Wall Street Journal*, March 14, 1980, p. 37.
"Offshore Logistics Says Debt Payments to Be Restructured," *Wall Street Journal*, August 30, 1985, p. 31.
"Offshore Logistics Inc. Gives 24 Ships to U.S. for Loan Guarantees," *Wall Street Journal*, November 12, 1985, p. 26.
"Offshore Logistics Cancels Loan to Chief, Who Quits Position," *Wall Street Journal*, May 15, 1986, p. 22.
"Offshore Logistics Inc. Completes Revamping," *Wall Street Journal*, June 7, 1987, p. 27.
Palmeri, Christopher, "After the Fall," *Forbes*, 153 (January 3, 1994), p. 268.
"Stake in Helicopter Firm is Bought for $155 million," *Wall Street Journal* [Eastern Edition], December 20, 1996, pp. B6.

—John W. Fiero

restructuring of the nation's oil and gas industry, the company began a new phase of development. In 1993, it purchased a 50 percent interest in Seahawk Services Ltd. and for the first time began offering oil production management services for offshore drilling and production rigs. Seahawk was proffering these services as well as providing offshore medical support services and temporary personnel to the petroleum industry. In October of 1993, OLOG took additional steps to expand its oil and gas production management services by trading its share in Seahawk for a 27.5 percent interest in Grasso Corporation, a Dallas-based oilfield services company whose wholly-owned subsidiary, Grasso Production Management (GPM), was providing similar services to the oil industry in the Gulf. Like Seahawk, GPM provided contract personnel and medical and engineering services to offshore sites. OLOG's investment in Grasso at that juncture amounted to about $4.13 million. The investment grew in September 1994, when, through a merger agreement, OLOG acquired the remaining 72.5 percent interest in Grasso Corporation by issuing a 0.49 share of common share for each share of stock held by Grasso's shareholders. The merger, treated as a purchase for accounting purposes, turned Grasso Production Management (GPM) into a wholly-owned OLOG subsidiary.

In October of that same year, OLOG bought 75 percent of Cathodic Protection Services (CPS), a company that provided oil companies with corrosion control services. CPS, headquartered in Houston, Texas, was established in 1946. It was the nation's first commercial engineering company exclusively devoted to using cathodic corrosion control in pipelines, oil and gas casings, offshore rigs and platforms, storage tanks, and other steel structures. However, OLOG did not keep its majority interest in CPS, electing to sell it in 1997, in part to offset the cost of its 1996 purchase of a 49 percent share in Bristow Aviation Ltd., a British helicopter company that served the oil industry in the North Sea with operations parallel to those of OLOG in the Gulf of Mexico.

It was in also in 1997 that Clement retired, and CFO George Small succeeded him as Offshore's president and CEO.

# O'Melveny & Myers

400 South Hope Street, Suite 1060
Los Angeles, California 90071-2899
U.S.A.
Telephone: (323) 669-6000
Fax: (323) 430-6407
Web site: http://www.omm.com

*Partnership*
*Founded:* 1885 as Graves & O'Melveny
*Employees:* 1,450
*Sales:* $372.5 million (2000)
*NAIC:* 54111 Offices of Lawyers

O'Melveny & Myers is one of the largest law firms in the world, with more than 700 lawyers working from its Los Angeles home office and several other offices in the United States, Europe, and Asia. Formed in 1885, it played a key role in making Los Angeles and Southern California one of the world's population and business centers. It has important clients in the entertainment and media industries, including Walt Disney, Sony Pictures Entertainment, and Time Inc. It represents corporations in many other fields and government agencies in the United States and abroad. At the beginning of the 21st century, O'Melveny & Myers plays an important role in the globalization of the world economy and the major changes occurring due to the Information Age and electronic commerce.

### Origins and Early Impact on Southern California

Founder Henry William O'Melveny was born in Central City, Illinois in 1859 and moved with his family to Los Angeles ten years later. There his father became a prominent lawyer and judge. The son graduated from the University of California at Berkeley in 1879 and two years later was admitted to the state bar after studying the law on his own and serving as an apprentice.

On January 2, 1885 Henry W. O'Melveny joined in partnership with Jackson A. Graves. The firm played a crucial role in much of the land title work associated with the population and real estate boom that lasted until 1888, when the railroads brought in up to 1,000 people a day. That transformed Los Angeles from a small Mexican community to a bustling American city.

Many prominent individuals and businesses in Southern California used the services of the small but growing law firm, including Newton Van Nuys, Farmers and Merchants Bank, The First National Bank, James B. Lankershim, and the Los Angeles Board of Trade. In 1891 O'Melveny began representing William G. Kerckhoff, a long-term client who played a major role in developing the area's hydroelectric capacity. Near the end of his life, O'Melveny "concluded that the most important work he had done in his professional career was in the development of hydro-electric power," according to William W. Clary in his history of the law firm.

In 1892 the partnership began representing the Chino Valley Beet Sugar Company, later acquired by Henry T. Oxnard's American Beet Sugar Company. Later renamed the American Crystal Sugar Company, it retained the O'Melveny law firm for advice on water litigation, labor and water matters, and other concerns. Although its Chino and Oxnard factories had been closed, the sugar company in the 1960s still used the law firm as it sold its lands for residential and industrial developers.

The law firm also represented the Home Telephone Company when it was incorporated and gained a necessary franchise from the Los Angeles city government in 1897. Henry O'Melveny served the telephone company for several years after the turn of the century. The Home Telephone Company was a predecessor of the Pacific Telephone & Telegraph Company.

After oil was discovered in 1886 near Puente only about 20 miles east of Los Angeles, the O'Melveny law firm gained considerable work in that developing industry. It drafted oil leases, incorporated new oil companies, and provided litigation and other services for companies such as the Puente Oil Company (later acquired by Shell Company of California) and the Westlake Oil Company.

Meanwhile, the partnership assisted individuals in resolving conflicts over estates that involved valuable Southern California lands. A good example was its representation in the 1890s of

## Key Dates:

**1885:** The law firm of Graves & O'Melveny is founded in Los Angeles
**1888:** J. H. Shankland joins the firm.
**1903:** Partnership is dissolved, and O'Melveny begins solo practice.
**1906:** Partnership of O'Melveny & Stevens is started with Henry John Stevens.
**1926:** With more partners, the firm becomes O'Melveny, Millikin & Tuller.
**1931:** Firm adopts permanent name of O'Melveny & Myers following death of Tuller.
**1935:** Firm begins its labor relations practice soon after Congress passes the Wagner Act.
**1937:** A Tax Department is established at the firm.
**1938:** A small branch office in Hollywood is opened.
**1964:** An office in Paris is opened, and then later closes.
**1976:** A presence in Washington, D.C., is established.
**1983:** The firm opens its New York City office.
**1985:** The London branch office is opened.
**1987:** The Tokyo office is launched.
**1996:** The firm's Shanghai office is started.

heirs to the estate of Jose Diego Sepulveda and Rancho Palos Verdes. Some of that land eventually became part of San Pedro, California and Sepulveda Boulevard, which runs from San Pedro to West Los Angeles and San Fernando.

By 1900 more persons became lawyers to meet the challenges of a growing state that was rapidly industrializing. Gordon Bakken analyzed a sample of 1,168 California lawyers admitted to the bar through 1900 to track the profession's trends. Not surprisingly, he found about half of those identified practiced in either San Francisco or Los Angeles where most of the business growth had been developing. Only 18.5 percent of the lawyers sampled were specialists. To help lawyers like Henry O'Melveny and others gain access to law books, the Los Angeles Bar Association was organized to fund a new law library. Just one year after the O'Melveny firm was started, the Law Library of Los Angeles was incorporated in 1886.

After the turn of the century, the O'Melveny law firm continued to represent local banks and also assisted California Governor Hiram Johnson as he worked with the dominant Progressive Party to pass a new state banking law in 1913. In 1914 the partnership prepared the incorporation papers for the new Kaspare Cohn Commercial & Savings Bank.

For years the O'Melveny law firm was involved with water companies and water-related litigation. For example, the flooding of the Colorado River in 1905 and 1906, which created a huge inland lake called the Salton Sea that threatened to destroy Imperial Valley crops, resulted in considerable litigation. The law firm successfully represented the plaintiff in *Title Insurance and Trust Company v. California Development Company, et al.*

During World War I, the firm's younger attorneys joined the military, while Henry O'Melveny played a major role in encouraging Los Angeles residents to buy Liberty Bonds and

promoting other patriotic causes. In 1917 O'Melveny became a director of the Los Angeles Morris Plan Company, one of 88 Morris Plan companies across the nation designed to help people get loans who otherwise were not eligible for regular bank loans. For more than 30 years the First Industrial Loan Company, owner of the Morris Plan license rights, was a client of the O'Melveny law firm.

After World War I, the law firm gained two new clients: the Goodyear Tire & Rubber Company of California and the Pacific Cotton Mills Company. Since those two companies were among the first outside national companies setting up branch operations in Southern California, the O'Melveny law firm began to expand beyond its historic area.

In 1919 Henry O'Melveny became president of the Wilshire Boulevard Hotel Company, financed by the Chicago company S.W. Straus & Company. After the hotel company changed its name to the Ambassador Hotel Corporation in 1920, it provided much of the legal work for the law firm in the 1920s. Meanwhile, the law firm's partners provided legal counsel and served on the boards of many major organizations, including the California Institute of Technology, Security First National Bank, Northwestern Mutual Life Insurance Company, Northrop Corporation, Arrowhead Lake Company, the Union Oil Company, the Shell Company of California, and several Bing Crosby corporations.

When the firm moved in 1928 to new offices in the new Title Insurance Building, it employed 53 persons, including nine partners, 13 staff attorneys, and other clerks and staff members. Soon the Great Depression hit the nation. Although many businesses collapsed, many lawyers prospered as they served bankruptcy clients. The O'Melveny firm thus expanded in the 1930s, serving clients such as the Guaranty Building and Loan Association, which collapsed in 1930. The firm in 1931 also helped write a new state law to charter building and loan associations, later called savings and loan associations.

The firm continued to grow during the Great Depression, hiring 17 new lawyers just out of law school from 1934 through 1939. Much of this new manpower worked on the major receivership cases, including Paramount. In the 1930s many law firms, including O'Melveny, Tuller & Myers, started labor practices after the unions expanded following the passage of the famous Wagner Act or National Labor Relations Act in 1935. Many companies needed more legal assistance following the creation of the Securities and Exchange Commission and other New Deal legislation of the 1930s.

In 1939 the firm adopted the permanent name of O'Melveny & Myers after Tuller died of a heart attack. Although some partners favored adding and deleting name partners as the firm had done in the past, they voted unanimously for the permanent change as a way to eliminate confusion. In 1941 Henry O'Melveny died at age 81 after a sudden illness. Typical of other Southern California newspapers, the Los Angeles *Examiner* on April 16, 1941 said, "It is seldom indeed that the life of one man can be so completely and intimately connected with the life of a great city." With the 1939 adoption of a permanent name and the 1941 death of its founder, the law firm of O'Melveny & Myers marked a major turning point in its history.

## World War II and the Early Postwar Years

The firm's practice increased in World War II due to increased government regulations over many aspects of business and also the growth of Southern California's industrial and military establishment. The law firm's growth continued in the postwar period under the leadership of John O'Melveny, a son of the founder Henry W. O'Melveny. The firm's expansion was influenced by the booming population of Los Angeles and the increase in value of goods manufactured in Los Angeles from about $2 billion in 1947 to more than $9 billion in 1962.

The firm's Litigation Department, its largest department with five lawyers in 1946, became involved in numerous antitrust lawsuits in the postwar era. For example, it represented Paramount Pictures, Twentieth Century-Fox Film, Warner Brothers, and Universal Pictures in a number of antitrust suits.

In February 1964 the law firm started its branch office in Paris, mostly to serve clients with Paris offices, including Hughes Aircraft Corporation, Lockheed Aircraft Corporation, and Northrop Corporation. Although most of the firm's international work was in Europe, its Entertainment Law Department did some work in Malaya, Hong Kong, Ceylon, Tahiti, and other places. The firm also represented the Brown Citrus Machinery Company in its dealings in Mexico, Argentina, and Australia, and the Suburban Gas Corporation and Garrett Corporation in Latin America. Other international work was conducted in Japan, Nigeria, Algeria, and Saudi Arabia.

As of September 1, 1965, O'Melveny & Myers employed a total of 102 lawyers, including 37 partners, three of counsel, and 62 associates. At that point, no women had ever become partner, and the firm previously had employed just three women associates—the first two in 1943, and just one in 1965. This was typical for most law firms, for it was not until the 1970s that many firms began hiring more women lawyers.

## Practice in the Late 20th Century and Beyond

In the late 1970s the legal profession began a major transformation to become much more competitive and business oriented. First, the U.S. Supreme Court ruled that professional association restrictions on advertising violated the First Amendment's guarantee of free speech. That led to more advertising by lawyers, doctors, dentists, and other professionals.

Second, lawyers learned much more about comparative finances and management practices in large law firms with the start of two new periodicals, the *National Law Journal* and the *American Lawyer*. Previously, many large law firms were more or less secret organizations due to bar rules that discouraged any contact with the press or historians. Within a few years many firms approached the new periodicals to make sure they were included. Both soon ranked the nation's largest law firms based on the number of their lawyers, annual sales, and other financial statistics. That knowledge facilitated lateral hiring of experienced lawyers from rival firms. With the growth of the economy, new government regulations, the start of high-tech industries, and many more mergers and acquisitions in the 1980s, law firms grew by leaps and bounds.

In the 1970s O'Melveny & Myers opened two new branches. In 1976 it became one of the first West Coast firms to open a branch in Washington, D.C. In 1979 it started its Newport Beach, California office to serve clients in the rapidly growing areas south of Los Angeles, mainly in Orange County and San Diego.

Further expansion followed. For example, in the 1980s the law firm opened four new branch offices, including ones in New York City in 1983, Tokyo in 1987, and San Francisco in 1989. In 1985 O'Melveny opened its London office, which served clients in many nations. Some of the London office's representative clients at the end of the century were Advanced Micro Devices, Inc.; Bankers Trust Company; Bankers Trust International PLC; Goldman Sachs International; Dresdner Kleinwort Benson; and Korn/Ferry International.

Other offices were started in the 1990s, including the Hong Kong office in 1994. Two years later the law firm gained approval from the People's Republic of China to start a registered law office in Shanghai. The firm's web site claimed in 2000: "O'Melveny is only one of a few international law firms to be granted this status, and our Shanghai office is now the largest foreign law office in the city."

The firm also operated an office in Century City in West Los Angeles that originated with the firm's Hollywood office started back in 1938. In 1999 the Los Angeles Board of Education sued O'Melveny & Myers, which had represented the school district for about 30 years. The law firm was sued for malpractice because it allegedly downplayed the environmental concerns at the half-completed Belmont Learning Complex. The O'Melveny law firm was defended by Gibson, Dunn & Crutcher, one of its long-term rivals based in Los Angeles.

One of O'Melveny & Myers's most important lawyers in the late 20th century was Warren Christopher. He had served President Lyndon Johnson as deputy attorney general, President Jimmy Carter as deputy secretary of state, and President Bill Clinton as his secretary of state. He led the international growth of the law firm as its chairman from 1982 to 1992. As O'Melveny & Myers's senior partner, he was chosen as one of California's ten most influential lawyers, according to a *California Law Business* survey of 200 California attorneys.

The *American Lawyer* in July 2000 ranked O'Melveny & Myers as the country's 18th largest law firm, based on its 1999 gross revenue of $372.5 million. That made it the third largest law firm in Los Angeles, behind Latham & Watkins, ranked number four with $581.5 million, and Gibson, Dunn & Crutcher, ranked number 14 with $418 million in 1999 gross revenue.

### Principal Competitors

Gibson, Dunn & Crutcher; Latham & Watkins; Skadden, Arps.

### Further Reading

Bakken, Gordon Morris, ''Industrialization and the Nineteenth-Century California Bar,'' in *The New High Priests: Lawyers in Post-Civil War America,* ed. Gerald W. Gawalt, Westport, Conn.: Greenwood Press, 1984, pp. 125–49.

Clary, William W., *History of the Law Firm of O'Melveny and Myers, 1885–1965,* Los Angeles: privately printed, 1966.

Goldgaber, Arthur, "Gibson Dunn & Crutcher Maintains No. 1 Ranking on Law Firms List," *Los Angeles Business Journal,* November 19, 1990, p. 29.

Platt, Pearl I., "A California Icon," *California Business Journal,* September 28, 1998, p. 13.

——, "The Top 100," *California Business Journal,* September 28, 1998, p. 16.

Smith, Doug, "In Suing Law Firm, District Takes Risks," *Los Angeles Times,* September 18, 1999, p. 1.

"Solid Growth—But Little Crowing from L.A. Firms," *Recorder/Cal Law,* January 11, 2000.

—David M. Walden

# Outlook Group Corporation

**1180 American Drive**
**Neenah, Wisconsin 54956**
**U.S.A.**
**Telephone: (920) 722-2333**
**Fax: (920) 727-8529**
**Web site: http://www.outlookgroup.com**

*Public Company*
*Incorporated:* 1977 as Mailing and Printing Services Inc.
*Employees:* 600
*Sales:* $71.3 million (2000)
*Stock Exchanges:* NASDAQ
*Ticker Symbol:* OUTL
*NAIC:* 323112 Commercial Flexographic Printing; 56191
    Packaging and Labeling Services

Outlook Group Corporation is a leading printing and packaging company with special expertise in flexographic printing and laminating for the food industry, in the printing and packaging of promotions such as the cards and trinkets found in cereal boxes, and in printing sports cards and other collectible cards. The diversified company also provides a broad range of services to its clients. It prints brochures, reports, catalogs, and promotional materials for many commercial customers. Its flexible packaging division prints on plastic films, papers, and foil used for food packages. The firm also has expertise in packaging of promotional items. For example it can print coupons, wrap them in plastic, and insert them in the finished package. Additionally, the company handles mailing or distribution of packages for its clients. Beyond packaging, Outlook Group also sells its logistical prowess, offering information management, warehousing, inventory control, and order fulfillment services to clients.

### Looking for Niche Markets in the 1980s

Outlook Group began in 1977, the project of four longtime friends in Neenah, Wisconsin. David Erdmann, Charles Thompson, John Wiley, and Elton Beattie, Jr., had known each other since high school. When they were in their early 30s, they

decided to go into business together providing bulk mailing service for a local printer, Banta Corp. A fifth investor in the new company, called simply Mailing and Printing Services Inc., was Beattie's father Elton Beattie, Sr., Erdmann took the post of president and chief executive officer, and Thompson became executive vice-president. The company gradually expanded beyond its first mission of working for Banta, and became more of a printer itself. Erdmann's marketing strategy was to look for specialty jobs it could do for customers, and then try to persuade the clients to let the company do other jobs as well.

Business was up and down, but Mailing and Printing seized a few lucky opportunities. In 1984 the company found work printing, cutting, and wrapping cards for a trendy board game called Trivial Pursuit. This work took the company into an area that would be crucial for it, printing specialty cards. The company expanded rapidly in the mid-1980s, adding as many as 100 new employees a year. In 1986, Mailing and Printing got another card printing job, this one printing and wrapping recipe cards. The company gained valuable experience in both printing and packaging these items, enough so that it stood out as one of only a few entities in the nation that could handle this type of work.

Meanwhile, the collectible sports card market was growing. Baseball cards had long been popular, and their printing was done almost entirely by a company called Topps. The National Football League (NFL) wondered if kids might also buy cards with images of professional football players. In 1989 a marketing branch of the NFL called National Football League Properties Inc. began granting licenses to entrepreneurs who wanted to get into the football card business. However, before it could get this project off the ground, it needed to find a printer who could produce the cards. Very few companies had the necessary equipment and know-how, and the NFL turned to Mailing and Printing, by then known as Outlook Graphics. Outlook took the NFL's business, and soon garnered other sports card clients.

Outlook followed up other niche markets as well. When a manager at Procter & Gamble complained to an Outlook sales representative about the time-consuming handwork the company did stuffing its Bounce fabric softener sheets into cartons, Outlook determined that it could do the job automatically. It got a contract from Procter & Gamble, and became the company's

## Company Perspectives:

*Our mission is to be "the best" by exceeding all others in performance through profitably satisfying the needs of our clients for the goods and services that are derived from core competencies in printing, packaging, and mailing in a safe and quality working environment.*

source for all the Bounce it sold through laundromat vending machines. Outlook levied this contract into more work from the company. Eventually Outlook printed the Bounce packages, as well as filled them. Outlook's sales grew rapidly in the late 1980s, leaping from $7.7 million in 1986 to over $30 million in 1990. Earnings did not rise quite so steadily, dipping in 1987, but they began to rise steeply after 1989 with the addition of the sports card business.

### High Flyer in the Early 1990s

Outlook Graphics made an initial public offering in 1991. The company had attracted a reputation in the Midwest and beyond for its specialty printing products, and it seemed to have an extraordinary touch for developing profitable niches. The public offering went exceptionally well. Shares started out in April 1991 at $11.50, and one year later the price had more than doubled. Outlook had prominent clients, such as Procter & Gamble, cereal manufacturer Kellogg, and food giant Kraft. *Fortune* magazine picked Outlook as a company to watch in a January 13, 1992 column, noting "the company can do just about anything to turn a plain piece of paper or plastic into an alluring consumer product."

The company built much of its growth on picture cards. From football cards it went on to produce cards for other sports, and also made cards for entertainment companies, including Marvel Comics. Outlook formed a joint venture with another company to make and market picture cards based on the Berenstain Bears series of children's books in 1991. The company was the primary producer of cards for three major companies: Fleer Corp., Liggett Group Inc., and Upper Deck Co.. However, as the trading card market grew, many companies tried to get in on the boom. The glut in the card market led to a collapse. In 1992, the trading card industry as a whole brought in around $2 billion. Outlook was getting about 60 percent of its revenue from its card printing and packaging. However, signs that the card market was in decline were clear. Producers were asked to turn over orders in just two to three weeks, instead of the usual six weeks. With the shortened lead time, Outlook couldn't handle all the work, and ended up outsourcing some of the work to area printers. This cut into Outlook's profit margin. The company had too much invested in cards, and it struggled to diversify into other areas before the market fell apart. By 1992, Outlook had cut its dependence on trading cards to 50 percent, and aimed to lower this as a percentage of sales in coming years.

### Diversification Efforts in the Mid-1990s

Outlook struggled to find another market as profitable as trading cards to protect itself from being dragged down as the

trend faltered. Late in 1992, Outlook spent $5.4 million to acquire a powdered food mixing and packaging plant in Oconomowoc, Wisconsin. The plant was owned by Nestle Beverage Co., and packaged foods like powdered gravy, hot cocoa mix, and malted milk. Outlook named the company Outlook Foods, and operated it as a subsidiary. It began by operating the plant under contract to Nestle, keeping the same employees and machinery. But within a year, Outlook was adding new customers of its own. The plant was expected to bring in from $25 to $35 million in revenue. The company hoped the added income would cushion it from stagnation in its trading card business. Several months after the Nestle deal was settled, Outlook made another acquisition. It bought up a Milwaukee-area flexographic printing and laminating company named Sunrise Packaging Inc. Outlook renamed this company Outlook Packaging. The new purchase broadened Outlook's food packaging capabilities. It already had contracts from major manufacturers like Oscar Mayer Foods Corp. and General Mills for work at its Oconomowoc plant, and it hoped to be able to offer more services to food industry customers.

The diversification strategy brought Outlook work in a more stable industry—food packaging—as opposed to the boom-and-bust work of printing trading cards. The company hoped to grow at a more modest rate of 20 percent annually in the mid-1990s. Although this was less than the explosive growth the company had seen when it first gained all its trading card business, the company executives hoped this rate was sustainable. One more acquisition in the mid-1990s added depth to the firm's packaging division. It bought Barrier Films in 1995, a company which turned resins into the filmy plastic used to wrap food products such as prepackaged salads.

### Falling Profits in the Late 1990s

Outlook repositioned itself as a broad-ranged packaging and printing company in order to get away from its dependence on trading cards. Nevertheless, the firm was unable to recapture the profit margins it had in the early 1990s, when the trading card market was still growing. Earnings in fiscal 1992 were $5.8 million on sales of $64 million. In 1995, sales had almost doubled, to $120 million, but profits were only $1.3 million. The company had continued to print trading cards, even though the market was no longer growing. But the failing trading card market took another chop in the neck with the baseball players strike of 1995. The whole sports card industry suffered as a result. In late 1995, Outlook lost its major trading card contract when it was dropped by Fleer Corp.. The company lost money for the next two years, and as the company's profitability vanished, its stock price tumbled. By 1996 Outlook shares were going for approximately $5, less than half what they had cost at the 1991 public offering.

In 1997 Outlook announced that it would sell off two of its divisions, Barrier Films and Outlook Foods, the Oconomowoc dry food packaging plant. Barrier, which was based in Sparks, Nevada, was sold in February 1997 to World Class Film Corp. of Yonkers, New York. Then in August, Outlook announced that it had agreed to be acquired by a Minneapolis-based leveraged buyout group, a private company called Goldner Hawn Johnson & Morrison. Goldner Hawn agreed to pay $8.25 a share for Outlook, which came to about $38 million. Outlook was to remain headquartered in Neenah, and the deal did not include its Outlook Foods subsidiary, which was to be sold to a company in Illinois. Goldner Hawn was founded in 1990, and specialized in buying up midwestern manufacturing companies. Outlook's management considered the deal the best it could do for its shareholders. Goldner Hawn said it would continue to operate the company, and retain its employees.

But the deal did not come off. In November 1997, Outlook announced that it was making a new acquisition, buying the packaging division of a California company called R.P. Packaging. Outlook bought R.P.'s general converting division, a plant in Emeryville, California. It planned to move production to its Oconomowoc facility, but retain the California sales force. This gave Outlook increased capacity for flexographic printing and laminating, and an entrance into the West Coast market. But the Oconomowoc food processing division had been scheduled for sale to a company in Hinsdale, Illinois. In December 1997, the division did find a new owner, but it was Outlook's president David Erdmann. He bought Outlook Foods and left the company he had founded. The new principals were Richard Fischer, chairman, and Joseph Baksha, president.

In June 1998, Fischer and Baksha announced that the acquisition deal with Goldner Hawn had been cancelled. The buyout had been pending for almost a year, while Outlook sold off its Barrier Films and Outlook Foods divisions. But in the time since the deal was first announced, Outlook made a surprising return to profitability. By June 1998, the company had had four straight quarters of profits. Fischer and Baksha refrained from discussing details of why they pulled out of the buyout, but it was clear that Outlook seemed in better shape financially in 1998 than it had in 1997.

Under its new management, Outlook trimmed down, shedding unprofitable customers. It continued to improve slowly,

earning $753,000 in 1998 and then around $1.4 million in 1999. Sales that year were close to $67 million. Earnings were rising at a faster rate than sales. The company was now profitable, and showing modest growth. But what Fischer and Baksha really wanted was a new buyer. In late 1999 they told shareholders that they still wanted to sell, preferably to a larger company who would continue to run the business. But there were no takers. Into the year 2000 Outlook's managers were still hoping for a buyer. Yet even without a merger, the company seemed to be doing better. By the third quarter of 2000, Outlook was able to report that earnings were up almost 60 percent over the same period a year earlier, and sales too were rising.

### *Principal Competitors*

Banta Corporation.

### *Further Reading*

"Appleton, Wisconsin, Printing, Packaging Firm Reports Earnings Growth," *Knight-Ridder/Tribune Business News,* July 12, 1999.

Boardman, Arlen, "Despite Recovery, Buyer Eludes Neenah, Wisconsin, Printing, Packaging Firm," *Knight-Ridder/Tribune Business News,* October 24, 1999.

——, "Neenah, Wisconsin-Based Firm Ends Talks with Investment Group," *Knight-Ridder/Tribune Business News,* June 10, 1998.

——, "Outlook Group Finds Buyer for Barrier Films," *Knight-Ridder/Tribune Business News,* February 21, 1997.

——, "Wisconsin Sports Trading-Card Firm Outlook Group Peaked in Early 1990s," *Knight-Ridder/Tribune Business News,* September 2, 1997.

Martin, Chuck, "Investors Don't Like the Outlook," *Milwaukee Journal,* September 26, 1993.

——, "Outlook Promising," *Milwaukee Journal,* January 19, 1992, pp. 1, 10.

Mullins, Robert, "Outlook Graphic's Area Acquisitions Fuel Diversification Drive," *Business Journal-Milwaukee,* February 12, 1994, p. 10A.

Neumeier, Shelley, "Outlook Graphics," *Fortune,* January 13, 1992, p. 65.

"Outlook Group Agrees to Acquisition; Shares Up," *Wisconsin State Journal,* August 30, 1997.

Romell, Rick, "Wisconsin's Ailing Outlook Group Corp. to Sell Two Subsidiaries," *Knight-Ridder/Tribune Business News,* September 27, 1996.

Rondy, John, "Packaging Deals May Mean Whole New Ballgame for Outlook," *Business Journal-Milwaukee,* June 26, 1993, p. 4A.

"Wisconsin's Outlook Group Acquires California Packaging Maker," *Knight-Ridder/Tribune Business News,* November 26, 1997.

—A. Woodward

# P.F. Chang's China Bistro, Inc.

5090 North 40th Street, Suite 160
Phoenix, Arizona 85018
U.S.A.
Telephone: (602) 957-8986
Fax: (602) 957-8998
Web site: http://www.pfchangs.com

*Public Company*
*Incorporated:* 1996
*Employees:* 5,000
*Sales:* $153.3 million (1999)
*Stock Exchanges:* NASDAQ
*Ticker Symbol:* PFCB
*NAIC:* 72211 Full Service Restaurants

P.F. Chang's China Bistro, Inc.'s 40-plus restaurant chain, operating in 19 states, owes much of its success to founder Paul Fleming's unique idea of pairing oriental cuisine with American-style service. At the outset, when he opened the first of the restaurants in Scottsdale, Arizona, Fleming broke with the traditional Chinese restaurant format. With his collaborator, chef Philip Chiang, he devised a comparatively limited menu that featured far fewer dishes than the menus of typical, full-service, Chinese restaurants. Incorporating an American steak house dining style and a formidable selection of wines and cheeses, P.F. Chang's offers such additional oriental restaurant anomalies as espresso and cappuccino. Although P.F. Chang's China Bistros are stylish in decor, displaying motifs from the Ming and T'ang Dynasties and hand-painted murals, the dishes are moderately priced, partly because one of Fleming's aims was to provide high quality but affordable Chinese food for "the masses." Fleming, who still owns about 12 percent of the chain, serves as a consultant, as does Chiang. The company is managed by an executive team headed by CEO and president Richard Federico, CFO and secretary Bert Vivian, and COO Greg Carey.

### 1993–95: The First Five P.F. Chang's China Bistros

Fleming, a native of Louisiana who had worked in the oil business, entered the restaurant business in the early 1980s when the global oil glut devastated the petroleum industry in the Gulf of Mexico and sent Louisiana into a deep recession. He managed to gather together enough funds to open a franchise of New Orleans-based Ruth's Chris Steak House in Beverly Hills, California. Fleming had immediate success in a tough business. Eventually, he would acquire the franchise rights for Ruth's Chris Steak Houses in California, Arizona, and Hawaii, and he would also purchase other restaurant franchises, including four Z'Tejas Grills and one Nola's Mexican Restaurant. But it was not until he opened P.F. Chang's China Bistro in Scottsdale, Arizona, in 1993 that he began his own, rather unique chain. As president of Fleming Chinese Restaurants Inc., he started up and managed the first four restaurants in the fledgling enterprise. Fleming claimed that his principal motivation was his fondness for Chinese food, which he wanted to make available to all comers at reasonable prices in a less intimidating format than that of most Chinese restaurants.

As Fleming himself noted, the new restaurant chain did not just spring up overnight. Three years went into conceptualizing and planning, and two more into convincing Philip Chiang, chef and owner of the Mandarin, a popular Beverly Hills restaurant, to serve as Fleming's principal collaborator. He needed Chiang's expertise because, although he loved oriental cuisine, he had no experience in the Chinese restaurant market. Chiang's major role was to help create the recipes for the base of about 60 dishes on the restaurant's menu. His name, less one letter, became the "Chang" of the restaurant's name.

The original restaurant quickly caught on. Although it took no reservations, it became a haunt for media and sports celebrities, who were soon helping to attract patrons willing to wait up to two and a half hours just to get seated. By 1995, the shopping mall restaurant, with just 6,000 square feet of space and 175 seats would be generating $4 million in sales, with about 70 percent coming from evening meals and 30 percent from lunches. During this time, Fleming had already decided to begin expanding the operation into a chain. He opted to test markets outside Arizona, first taking on the California market, where *nouveau cuisine* and novelty played well but competition for a market niche could be fierce. Fleming chose Newport Beach as the locale for his second P.F. Chang's China Bistro, which opened in 1994. The next year he opened two other California units, one at the Irvine Entertainment Center and the other in La Jolla.

Fleming knew that effective management and further planning for future growth would require more time than he could give to the tasks. Even in 1995, with the opening of the P.F. Chang's China Bistro in Newport Beach, he had begun thinking about new possibilities. At the time he owned 13 restaurants, located as far apart as Texas and Hawaii, with an array of ethnic cuisines. His solution to the problem of the company expansion was to hire a team of professional managers. Although he would retain a minority 12 percent ownership of the company, he decided he would step down and let P.F. Chang's China Bistro become a separate entity outside of his control. His future role would be that of consultant and advisor.

### 1996–2000: Rapid Expansion under New Management

Early in 1996, the company was incorporated as P.F. Chang's China Bistro, Inc., which acquired the four units making up the chain. Fleming found the man to head the new executive team, Richard L. Federico, who, in a partnership arrangement with Fleming, took on the presidency of P.F. Chang's. He joined the company after leaving his posts as president of Brinker International's (BI) Macaroni Grill 65-unit chain and president of BI's Italian concepts. Like Fleming, he came to the Chinese restaurant market with no experience in oriental foods. In fact, unlike Fleming, he had never really acquired a taste for it. He did bring managerial experience, however. He was a cofounder of the Grady's Goodtimes concept, which originated in Knoxville, Tennessee, and was bought by Brinker International in 1988. Joining Federico in major executive positions were Bert Vivian, who served as CFO, and Greg Carey, who took on the job of COO. Vivian, who signed on in April of 1996, also came to the company from Brinker International, where he had been vice-president of investor relations. Carey joined Federico and Vivian two years later, in 1998, coming over from his post as COO at Rainforest Café.

With venture capital provided by out-of-state backers, the company began accelerating its growth near the end of 1996, when it opened restaurants in Las Vegas, Houston, and Denver. The managers were testing new markets, moving into new locales after careful demographic analyses of their prospective customer pools. They wanted to avoid the fate of the China Coast, a chain of Darden Restaurants which tried to expand too rapidly and failed. In fact, P.F. Chang's had some early growth pains, logging a net loss of $1.7 million in 1997 with revenues of $39.8 million. In part to pay down its $11.6 million debt to

$2.6 million and finance the chain's growth, the company decided to go public.

The company made its IPO in December of 1998. By that time, its fiscal picture had improved; its revenue of $32.9 million for the first six months of fiscal 1998 was almost double its sales of the same period in the previous year. Moreover, to the surprise of many analysts, the company's stock fared extremely well. It grossed $49.8 million for the company when it almost immediately climbed from $12 to $18.50 per share, producing an unexpected windfall encouraging further expansion.

Of course, the chain had already been growing. It had begun a major eastward expansion in 1997, with openings in New Orleans; Dade County, Florida; Charlotte, North Carolina; and McLean, Virginia. It had also opened its second Arizona restaurant in Tempe. By the summer of 1998, when it announced plans to make its IPO later in the year, it had grown to 15 units. In that year, P.F. Chang's also emerged from the red, though barely. Its sales surged to $78.0 million, up from $39.8 million in 1997, but its debt obligations held its net profit down around $100,000.

The 1998 stock windfall allowed the company to begin accelerating its growth as well as pay down its debt. Plans called for adding an additional 21 new restaurants by the close of 1999, bringing its total to 36 units, and an additional 15 openings in 2000. They also called for new, untapped market incursions, in, for example, large metropolitan areas like New York, Washington, D.C., Chicago, and Atlanta.

The company stayed on target for the most part. Although in 1999 it actually put just 13 new units into operation, by July of 2000 it was running 39 restaurants, with a geographical spread over 30 states, and was still planning to reach a goal of 54 units by the end of the first quarter in 2001. All added restaurants, as in the past, would be company owned. With systemwide sales of $153 million in 1999, or an average unit sale of $5.15 million, prospects for realizing company goals for 2000 looked good. One problem did loom on the horizon, at least for the company's very successful restaurant in Santa Monica, California, where a public ordinance setting a minimum hourly wage of $10.69 was about to go into effect. Such an ordinance would force the restaurant to double the pay of some its staff, which would either cut deeply into its profits or, alternatively, force it to raise its prices or downsize its staff. "Living wage" ordinances, already in place in some 41 U.S. cities, were likely to spread, hitting the restaurant industry hard since it has a history of running on low wages. If P.F. Chang's China Bistro were to up its prices to counteract increased labor costs, it would certainly erode its "oriental-food-for-the-masses" customer base to which founder Fleming hoped to make his appeal.

Perhaps addressing that problem had something to do with the company's decision to develop a new concept—a casual, quick-service variation on its base restaurant, known as Pei Wei's Asian Diner, the first of which was scheduled for opening in late 2000, at Chandler, in the company's home state, Arizona. At a start-up cost of about $500,000, Pei Wei's would involve a much smaller investment than its China Bistro counterpart. Although it would include sit-down service, it would also appeal to take-out customers. Most importantly, its menu,

## Key Dates:

**1993:** Paul Fleming opens first P.F. Chang's China Bistro in Scottsdale, Arizona.

**1995:** Fleming opens three new P.F. Chang's China Bistros in California.

**1996:** Company incorporates and new management team is brought in, headed by Richard L. Federico; restaurant chain is named one of the year's "Hot Concepts" by *Nation's Restaurant News* but company records first net loss.

**1998:** Company goes public and returns to profitability.

**1999:** Chain increases to 29 restaurants by year's end.

**2000:** Company plans to open its first Pei Wei's Asian Diner.

though featuring some of the same dishes as its bigger brother, would scale down both their prices and their portions.

### Principal Competitors

Advantica Restaurant Group, Inc.; Benihana, Inc.; Darden Restaurants, Inc.; Carlson Restaurants Worldwide Inc.; Panda Management Company, Inc.

### Further Reading

Carlino, Bill, "P.F. Chang's: Far East Meets West at Chinese Bistro," *Nation's Restaurant News*, May 20, 1996, p. 80.

——, "Richard L. Federico: Fusing Authenticity with the Contemporary Inspires the P.F. Chang's Chef," *Nation's Restaurant News*, January 1997, p. 62.

Coeyman, Marjorie, "Orient L'Express: Chinese Food with . . . Cappuccino? P.F. Chang's Brings a European Touch to Traditional Asian Food," *Restaurant Business*, June 15, 1997, p. 33.

Ferguson, Tim W., "Enacting Wealth," *Forbes*, November 29, 1999, p. 64.

Gonderinger, Lisa, "Venture Capital Backs P.F. Chang's Expansion," *Business Journal—Serving Phoenix & the Valley of the Sun,* November 29, 1996, p. 5.

Heimlich, Cheryl Kane, "Hot West Coast Eatery Sings Deals in Dade," *South Florida Business Journal*, January 31, 1997, p. 1A.

Houten, et. al., "Follow the Leaders," *Restaurant Business*, April 15, 1998, p. 28.

Lape, Bob, "Stirring Together Sinatra, Szechuan: Upscale Chain Expands into N.Y.; Succinct Menu Taps 5 Regions of China," *Crain's New York Business*, June 14, 1999, p. 38.

Overstreet, James, "China's Culture Visible at New East Memphis Restaurant," *Memphis Business Journal*, June 2, 2000, p. 4.

Papiernik, Richard L., "Old Acquaintance Is Forgot as the 'Chicken' Chokes, Chang's Smokes," *Nation's Restaurant News*, December 21, 1998, p. 3.

Ruggless, Ron, "P.F. Chang's Chain Plans Initial Public Offering in Later Part of This Year," *Nation's Restaurant News*, August 17, 1998, p. 3.

——, "P.F. Chang's Founder Brings Far East to the West," *Nation's Restaurant News*, April 10, 1995, p. 1.

——, "P.F. Chang's Prexy Frederico Charts Cautious Growth Pace," *Nation's Restaurant News*, February 12, 1996, p. 3.

——, "P.F. Chang's Readying Pei Wei's Fast-Casual Offshoot," *Nation's Restaurant News*, February 7, 2000, p. 8.

—John W. Fiero

# PC Connection, Inc.

**730 Milford Road**
**Merrimack**
**New Hampshire 03054-4631**
**U.S.A.**
**Telephone: (603) 423-2000**
**Fax: (603) 423-5766**
**Toll Free: (800) 800-5555 (PC Connection);**
**(800) 800-2222 (Mac Connection)**
**Web site: http://www.pcconnection.com;**
**http://www.macconnection.com**

*Public Company*
*Incorporated:* 1982
*Employees:* 1,400
*Sales:* $1.06 billion (1999)
*Stock Exchanges:* NASDAQ
*Ticker Symbol:* PCCC
*NAIC:* 454110 Electronic Shopping and Mail-Order
Houses

PC Connection, Inc. was founded by Patricia Gallup and David Hall as a direct marketer of business computer solutions to small and medium sized businesses (SMBs), educational and government institutions, and individual consumers. Headquartered in Merrimack, New Hampshire, this rapid-response provider of information technology (IT) offers a broad selection of over 100,000 brand-name products (such as computer hardware, software, peripherals, and networking equipment) at competitive prices in conjunction with award-winning service and support. PCC has more than 730,000 active customers in its database. At its Wilmington, Ohio-based Distribution and Custom-Configuration Center, the company receives and ships inventory overnight, configures computer systems, and processes returned products. PCC consistently wins praise for customer service and recognition of its outstanding business acumen. For example, in the year 2000 *Business Week* magazine cited PCC as having "scored big by offering all the computer gear a small business might need," and ranked the company as seventh on its list of the world's leading IT companies. Like-

wise, *Yahoo! Internet Life* magazine named PCC "the best place to shop for computers," and listed the company's Web sites among the "100 Best Sites on the Internet." *PC Magazine* included the company among its list of the "100 Technology Companies That Are Changing the World;" *PC Computing* magazine named the company "Best of the Best;" and for nine times over the past 11 years PCC won *PC World* magazine's "World Class Award for Best Online Computer Store." At the end of 1999, PCC's five-year compound growth rate was 96 percent, a percentage that placed the company among an elite group of the fastest-growing companies in America; the company's share price increased 96 percent during 1999.

### 1970–82: Applying Age-Old Wisdom to Marketing Computers

According to the Winter 1998 issue of *Finance* magazine, Patricia Gallup's creativity was nurtured from her earliest years. "She grew up in a household where her father, a carpenter [union organizer and mediator] would present a situation at the dinner table and the family would engage in mini-debates on current events and other issues of the day," wrote Anita Burroughs. Patricia paid her way through the University of Connecticut, where she majored in anthropology. She worked as a field archaeologist for the Public Archaeology Survey Team, "a for-profit business that surveyed lands to ensure their compliance with laws protecting cultural resources," according to Ilan Mochari's article in the October 1, 1999 issue of *Inc.* magazine.

From the study of tools our ancestors used some 30,000 years ago, Gallup and the Survey Team learned not only to determine the age and use of the tools, but also how and why they evolved. The work helped Gallup develop her creative problem solving skills, and she was later able to apply her understanding of the past and relationships between items to ideas such as cultural changes, business operations, and technological innovations.

Still another experience prepared Patricia for her future business role. While hiking on the Appalachian Trail in 1976, she met David Hall; together, they served as a support crew to endurance hikers on the Trail. "Our function was to anticipate

## Company Perspectives:

*PC Connection will be a high-growth, profitable, world class leader in providing the best solutions, products, communications, and services to our customers.*

the arrival of the hikers at different points and to take care of whatever needs they might have,'' Gallup explained in an article published in the May 15, 1998 issue of *Inc.* magazine. ''From the beginning,'' she wrote, ''David and I shared a belief in trying to put ourselves in other peoples' shoes. We learned how to work together to come up with solutions to get tasks accomplished.''

Then, in 1980, Hall recruited Gallup for Audio Accessories, Inc. (Audio), his father's Marlow, New Hampshire-based company that operated in an abandoned woodworking mill in the small rural town. Audio made high quality broadcast and recording equipment, published a catalog, provided customers with over-the-phone service, and shipped products by UPS.

At about this time, IBM introduced and began to market its personal computer (PC). Eager to know how PCs could contribute to the efficiency of their company, Gallup and Hall studied business and technical magazines, called companies that were developing PC products, tried to make a purchasing decision . . . and discovered that the closest PC retailer was in Connecticut—more than two hours from Marlow. Realizing that their case was like that of many other Americans deprived of easy retail access, the two business partners decided to launch a direct-marketing company that ''could create stronger customer-service support and provide more thorough information to consumers . . . than [could be offered by] in-store sales representatives with no technical training or PC experience,'' according to an interview reported in the December 1998 issue of *Chain Store Age* magazine.

In July 1982, Gallup and Hall pooled their entire savings of $8,000 and launched PC Connection, Inc. (PCC). They placed a small ad in the back cover of *Byte* magazine, installed two phones, and waited for *Byte's* on-sale date. There were no bites for two days after the magazine's release, but on the third day, the phones began to ring and the fledgling company was off to a flying start. PCC's business requirements for phone lines and power increased so rapidly, actually, that additional wires and telephone poles had to be installed over the 15 miles separating Marlow (population 600) from Keene, the nearest ''urban'' center. Initially, PCC carried only 12 products designed to run on the IBM PC, including an AST multi-function board, Peachtree business software, and several highly publicized computer games.

### 1983–97: The Evolution of the Computer and a Focus on Customer Needs

First-year net sales reached $233,000. Initially, Gallup and Hall made up the entire staff: during the day, they answered the phones, and at night they shipped orders and stocked inventory. To recruit help willing to drive to Marlow (known as the Icebox of Cheshire County in New Hampshire), the young entrepre-

neurs enticed future employees by giving them studded snow tires and ice-breaker windshield wipers. As orders and sales multiplied, Gallup developed the company's marketing approach while Hall—an audio engineer—took care of technical matters and kept an eye on developments in the computer industry.

In 1982, PCC was the first direct-marketing company to offer toll-free technical support to callers before, during, and after a sale—even if they requested help for computers and products that had been bought elsewhere. Thus, from its earliest days, PCC differentiated itself from other direct-marketers by offering its customers superior support and value: a combination of product knowledge, consistent and reliable service, and leading products at competitive prices. In 1988, when David Hall suggested overnight delivery, PCC's in-house professionals said that it was an unheard of idea. Prior to that, mail-order products were typically shipped to customers in four to six weeks. Undeterred, Hall presented some schemes for cost reduction to five next-day carriers, and managed to turn their laughter into a consideration of his proposal. None came up to match his initial wish of overnight shipping at ''A buck a pound the world around,'' but Airborne won the contract, which introduced the ''Everything Overnight'' program.

From that point on, except as noted, any order placed by 8:00 p.m. was received the following day. In *Inc.* magazine's May 1989 issue, Robert Mamis gave the following example of the new program's efficiency: at 7:54 p.m. one evening, a medical-equipment distributor in Pennsylvania sent PCC an urgent request for a fax device for his Macintosh. ''The plug-in board was packed and ready to be picked up at 9:07 p.m.'' and the distributor received the component at 9:00 the next morning. The total freight was $3—''exactly what Sears, Roebuck would have charged for express freight to Pennsylvania in 1902,'' Mamis noted.

Soon, the deadline for ordering was extended to 2:00 a.m., making it possible for customers in the continental United States to receive same-day delivery. Also, custom-configured systems loaded with the requested software and peripherals, if ordered by midnight, were usually delivered by noon the next day. Even before the introduction of Caller ID, PCC worked with Telecom and IBM to develop applications for Caller ID technology. This resulted in a 1991 application—named ''One Minute Mail Order''—that enabled customer account information to appear instantaneously on a PCC salesperson's screen when a call came in, thereby expediting sales.

PCC received and shipped inventory, configured computer systems, and processed returned products at its approximately 102,000 square-foot distribution and fulfillment center (expanded to 205,000 square feet by the end of 1999) in Wilmington, Ohio. The company also maintained a related 25,700 square-foot warehouse for inventory in nearby Xenia, Ohio. After credit approval, orders were transmitted electronically from the company's New Hampshire sales facilities to the Wilmington distribution center, where packing documentation was printed automatically and order fulfillment took place.

In November 1996, PCC launched an Internet web site that included a complete product catalog, and in July 1997 began to

## Key Dates:

**1982:**  Business partners Patricia Gallup and David Hall found PC Connection, Inc. (PCC), the first computer direct-marketing company to offer toll-free technical support.

**1988:**  PCC pioneers "Everything Overnight" delivery program.

**1989:**  PCC introduces Money-Back Guarantees.

**1996:**  PCC launches Internet web site that includes a complete product catalog.

**1997:**  PCC introduces online ordering from its web site.

**1998:**  Company goes public and is traded on NASDAQ; moves headquarters to Merrimack, New Hampshire.

**1999:**  PCC acquires its first subsidiary: ComTeq Federal, Inc.; introduces its Epiq line of desktop business personal computers; net sales pass $1 billion mark.

**2000:**  PCC restructures into a holding company; announces a three-for-two common stock split.

accept electronic orders placed through this site. At a customer's request, the company customized management information systems (principally software running on IBM AS/400, RS6000 computers, and Microsoft NT-based servers). PCC also integrated key elements of its advanced telecommunications equipment with its computer systems in order to support its sales and customer-service operations, ship orders to customer on a same-day basis, and adjust quickly to changes in the industry. The company configured almost half of the computer systems it sold. Typically, configuration consisted of installing memory, accessories, and/or software. In 1996 PCC relocated its headquarters to Milford, New Hampshire.

The company recorded rapid growth in sales, profitability, number of orders, and size of average orders. By year-end 1997, PCC was a leading direct-marketer of brand-name computers and related peripherals, software, and networking products. Some of the 15,000 competitively priced items targeted for business use included products from Compaq, Hewlett-Packard, Toshiba, IBM, Microsoft, Sony, Hitachi, and Apple. PCC sold products through two direct mail catalogs: *PC Connection* focused on personal computers and compatible products, and *MacConnection* focused on Macs and compatible products. In 1994, PCC had distributed 16.9 million catalogs and entered 803,000 orders—each having an average price of $282. In 1996, those numbers rose to 18.6 million catalogs distributed, and 910,000 orders averaging $453. By 1997, PCC distributed 33.8 million catalogs and entered 1,252,000 orders having an average price of $524.

Outbound telemarketing, the PCC Web site, and advertisements on the Internet and selected computer magazines also stimulated increases in sales. For fiscal years 1994, 1996, and 1997, the company posted net sales of $196.7 million, $333.3 million, and $550.6 million, respectively. The effectiveness of PCC's growth strategy was described in many industry publications and highlighted by multiple awards. For example, in 1997—for the seventh time in eight years—*PC World* magazine gave PCC the "World Class Award for Best Mail-Order Company," and in July 1997, *PC Magazine* awarded PCC the highest ranking of only two direct resellers included in the first-ever ranking of the "100 Most Influential Companies in the Computer Industry."

PCC was soon the largest private employer in New Hampshire, but relinquished that distinction in November 1997 when it filed with the Securities and Exchange Commission for a proposed initial public offering of its common stock. Then, in December of that year, PCC decided to move to Merrimack, New Hampshire "in order to be closer to a larger pool of skilled workers," that were needed to continue the company's rapid growth, according to Gallup's interview with Eileen Kennedy in the July 31, 1998 issue of *The Telegraph*.

### 1998–99: Explosion of Internet-Related Business

Without having recourse to venture capital funds, in early 1998 PCC completed its initial public offering—thereby obtaining the financial flexibility necessary for future growth, and the funds needed to institute an employee stock-purchase plan. In March 1998, PCC went public and was traded on NASDAQ under the ticker symbol PCCC. From its earliest days, the company "kept a low profile and lived frugally," wrote reporter Tim McLaughlin in his July 1998 article for the *Concord Monitor*. "PCC grew from within as Patricia Gallup and David Hall paid themselves $100-a-week salaries for several years. The $57.3 million raised in the initial public offering allowed the company to reward shareholders in a big way.... 'Creating wealth is not what drove us,' Gallup said. 'What drives entrepreneurs is changing the way people think. We wanted to change the way people buy computer products. That was the kick, changing the buying environment.' "

Furthermore, PCC changed its entire business environment by saving and/or revitalizing the buildings and locations where it located its headquarters. "In the past," wrote *The Telegraph's* Eileen Kennedy, "PCC redid a Victorian inn, a former Moose lodge, an old wood-working mill, a former produce warehouse, a distribution center and an old house trailer. The trailer served as construction headquarters for PCC's new Merrimack headquarters in an old strip mall—Post Road Plaza (locally known as Ghost Road Plaza after the 1990 recession)." Kennedy went on to quote New Hampshire's Governor Shaheen as saying that "PC Connection has invested in its people and in the community everywhere that it has been." PCC moved to its completed Merrimack facility in November 1998.

One of PCC's innovative 1998 programs was a two-pronged, Internet-based service called "Smart Selectors," consisting of "System Selector" and "Memory Selector." On the company's Web site, customers used System Selector in a simple three-step process to compare up to five computer systems and over 20 corresponding peripheral features; they then could customize their choices to their special specifications. With Memory Selector, customers followed the same three steps to take the guesswork out of upgrading computer-system memory. PCC continued to focus on synergistic growth of its three marketing channels: catalogs, telemarketing, and e-commerce. By year-end 1998, PCC reported a 33 percent increase in net revenues of $732.4 million, net income of $18.6 million, and earnings of $.98 per share.

During 1999, the SMB market—as well as government and educational organizations—invested aggressively in Information Technology (IT). PCC's high-quality customer service and technical support, its efficient and innovative delivery programs (especially the continuous Everything Overnight program), and its competitive prices and reasonable return policies established the company as the middle market's premier rapid-response supplier of IT products and solutions. Increased earnings served as a platform for the execution of PCC's core business and growth strategies: focus on acceleration of the Outbound Sales Managed Account Program; expansion of products and services; leveraging of IT power; and pursuit of acquisitions and alliances. Result: for the first time in the company's history, net sales crossed the $1 billion mark, with an increase of 44 percent over the preceding year.

In May 1999, PCC launched its Epiq (pronounced epic) line of business desktop PCs; by September they had expanded this business, and the Epiq line was among the company's top-selling lines. Epiq PCs were manufactured by a third party ISO 9002-certified manufacturer, and built according to PCC's direct experience in serving the needs of SMBs. Additionally, PCC built relationships with potential high-volume customers by assigning them to individual account managers. Introduction of the Internet Business Accounts program for corporate customers brought the number of Outbound Account Sales Managers to 345, compared to the 1998 team of 200 Account Managers. This service gave customers access to special pricing and allowed them to view their purchasing history and online purchase orders. By year-end 1999, PCC had mailed approximately 47 million catalogs to over 2,800,000 current and potential customers on its mailing list, of which 732,000 had purchased products from the company within the last year. Internet-sourced sales increased 85 percent in 1999.

The company's fastest growing customer segments included businesses that invested aggressively in early-stage web-based marketing programs in order to compete more effectively with the so-called "dot com" companies and other high-growth organizations increasingly dependent on distributed-data and communication networks. The virtual explosion of Internet-related business gave rise to a significant demand for networking infrastructure services and products, such as PC servers, routers and switches. PCC's sales of these products increased more than 150 percent in the fourth quarter of 1999, compared to 1998 fourth quarter sales.

In June 1999, PCC strengthened its government-sales platform by acquiring its first subsidiary—Maryland-based ComTeq Federal, Inc. Founded in 1993 as a private company, ComTeq had been successfully serving the expansive and growing needs of computer equipment and services to key government agencies.

The last year of the 20th century capped all records for PCC. Net sales surged 44 percent to $1.06 billion, compared to $732.37 million for the preceding year. Net income peaked at $22.73 million, or $1.41 per share, compared to 1998 net income $15.27 million, or $.98 per share. In her 1999 Annual Report, Chairman and CEO Patricia Gallup commented that "our five-year compound growth rate in operating earnings was 96 percent, ranking PC Connection among an elite group of the fastest growing companies in America."

### *2000 and Beyond: Into a New Millennium*

On January 3, 2000, PCC formed and became a holding company—named PC Connection, Inc.—consisting of PC Connection Sales Corp., Merrimack Services Corp., and ComTeq Federal, Inc. The next day, PCC negotiated the acquisition of a call-center facility from Marlborough, Massachusetts-based Merisel Inc., a leading full-line distributor of technology products. In January, PCC also launched its proprietary Networking Sales Specialist Program, and in February the company won IBM's "Personal Systems Group Business Partner Award for the Top North American Computer Reseller to SMBs." This award program acknowledged sales performance on behalf of IBM Business Partners worldwide.

In March 2000, PCC expanded its Smart Selector service by adding computer monitors, printers, and digital cameras. Two months later, in May, the company announced a three-for-two common stock split. In a news release dated July 24, 2000, PCC reported that "According to Forrester Research, by 2003, the average company will be storing 150 terabytes of data, a ten-fold increase over today's storage needs. Because of the increased data storage demands, International Data Corporation predicts the storage area network (SAN) market will grow from $1 billion in 1999 to more than 11 billion in 2003." Remaining in the forefront of this industry trend, PCC in July 2000 formed an alliance with EMC Corporation to sell the EMC CLARiiON midrange storage systems and was the first in its sector to sell these storage products. The CLARiiON Fibre Channel storage systems, capable of storing up to 3.6 terabytes of data, provided information consolidation for highly distributed, critical stand-alone server environments and could store up to 3.6 terabytes of data.

Computer dealers serving large corporations were once "the kingpins of the corporate PC market," and paid little attention to smaller markets, wrote Gary McWilliams in the July 13, 2000 edition of the *Wall Street Journal*. "The mail-order houses were the also-rans," he said. PC Connection was the first company to tap the neglected market by developing a sales model that was "right for the times. Small and medium companies . . . [were] the least penetrated, the most rapidly growing and the least price-sensitive," said Robert P. Anastasi, director of research at James & Associates, as quoted in the *Wall Street Journal* article. The PCC founders' insight into the needs and growth possibilities of SMBs and the potential of the Internet did change the buying environment for computers, realizing the hope expressed above when the company went public.

PC Connection's outstanding record also supported Chairman/CEO Patricia Gallup's forecast for the future: "In the new millennium, we'll see rapidly changing technology that will shape the way we work. Computers with speeds of 1 gigahertz and beyond are in the pipeline. . . . Whatever the new millennium brings, PC Connection will be at the forefront of direct marketers, delivering to our customers the technology they need, backed up with the best service in the industry."

### *Principal Subsidiaries*

ComTeq Federal, Inc.; Merrimack Services Corp.; PC Connection Sales Corp.

### *Principal Competitors*

CDW Computer Centers, Inc.; Compaq Computer Corp.; CompUSA, Inc.; Dell Computer Corporation; Gateway, Inc.; Insight Enterprises, Inc.; Micro Warehouse, Inc.

### *Further Reading*

Burroughs, Anita, "Connecting With Patricia Gallup," *Finance Magazine,* Winter 1998, pp. 33–34.

Coles, Barbara, "The Recipe for Sweet Success: A Handy Dandy Guide to Getting Rich in NH," *New Hampshire Magazine,* February 2000.

Gallup, Patricia, "You, Me, and All Those Others Just Like Us," *Inc.,* May 15, 1998.

Garfield, Charles, "PC Connection Inc.," *Executive Excellence Magazine,* November 17, 1994, p. 17 ff.

"Information Technology 100," *Business Week,* June 19, 2000, p. 140.

Kennedy, Eileen, "Computer Firm Connects in Merrimack," *The [Nashua] Telegraph,* July 31, 1998, pp. 13–14.

Mamis, Robert A., "Real Service," *Inc.,* May 1989.

McLaughlin, Tim, "Gallup Connected With the Computer Industry," *Concord Monitor,* pp. A1, A3.

McWilliams, Gary, "Big Computer Dealers Feel Mail-Order Bite," *Wall Street Journal,* July 13, 2000, pp. B1, B6.

Mochari, Ilan, "In a Former Life: Patricia Gallup, 45, Chairman and CEO of PC Connection, Inc.," *Inc.,* Oct. 1, 1999, p. 90.

Parets, Robyn Taylor, "Computer Seller Taps Into New Sales Channels," *Investor's Business Daily,* August 24, 1998.

"Retail Entrepreneurs of the Year: Patricia Gallup," *Chain Store Age,* December 1998, p. 94.

Rossa, Jerry, "Service Sells Online," *Computer Reseller News,* January 10, 2000, pp. 31, 33.

Spring, Tom, "Connected," *PC World Online,* February 19, 1999, pp. 1–2.

—Gloria A. Lemieux

# Philadelphia Eagles

Veterans Stadium
3501 South Broad Street
Philadelphia, Pennsylvania 19148-5201
U.S.A.
Telephone: (215) 463-2500
Fax: (215) 339-5464
Web site: http://www.eaglesnet.com

*Private Company*
*Founded:* 1933
*Employees:* 120
*Sales: $102.5 million* (1998)
*NAIC:* 711211 Sports Teams and Clubs

The Philadelphia Eagles, a privately owned football team in the National Football League, is an enduring symbol of sports in the Delaware Valley region. The Eagles are not among the powerhouse teams in the NFL; they made one appearance in the Super Bowl and during the 1990s ranked last or near-last. Their playing field at the much-maligned Veterans Stadium, built in the 1970s, was considered dated only 25 years later. Yet Philadelphians have always treated the team with genuine affection, and Eagles fans are arguably among the most stalwart.

### Early Days: The Yellow Jackets

The team that eventually evolved into the Eagles first appeared in a Philadelphia suburb in 1919, when a group called the Frankford Athletic Association founded the Frankford Yellow Jackets. The team played semi-professional football with neighboring teams until it joined the recently formed National Football League in 1924. The Yellow Jackets built a 10,000-seat field to accommodate fans.

At that time, many states, including Pennsylvania, had what were known as "blue laws" on the books; these laws, which had their origins in colonial times, prohibited certain activities on Sundays that could be considered disrespectful of the Christian sabbath. Sporting events were among those prohibited activities. This created a double problem for many fledgling pro

teams. Not only could they not play on Sundays, but if they played on Saturdays they often had to compete for an audience with college football games, which were often more popular. Teams like the Yellow Jackets found a partial solution to the problem by playing home games on Saturdays and scheduling away games with teams not subject to blue laws on Sundays.

The Eagles came into existence in 1933 when De Benneville "Bert" Bell and Lud Wray purchased the franchise then known as the Frankford Yellow Jackets for $2,500. The Bell name was a venerable one in Philadelphia; Bell's grandfather had served in Congress and his father had been state attorney general. Bell himself played college football at the University of Pennsylvania, where he later coached; he also coached at nearby Temple University.

The Yellow Jackets franchise was up for sale in 1933 and Bell was eager to acquire the team. He and his family had suffered huge financial losses during the stock market crash in 1929, but he had recently married a former Ziegfeld Follies actress who had managed to save some of her earnings. Bell and his partner Wray (who was bought out in 1936) got the franchise for $2,500.

Almost immediately Bell moved the team to Philadelphia and he chose a new name, the Eagles, to honor the symbol of Franklin D. Roosevelt's new National Recovery Act. The first Eagles game was played on November 12, against the Chicago Bears. (The game ended in a tie, 3–3).

Bell, who would later become NFL commissioner, took a long-term view of professional sports. It was Bell who in 1935 initiated the practice of an annual college draft, which he believed would spread talent evenly across all the teams in the league. In his book *Pigskin: The Early Years of Pro Football,* Robert Peterson described Bell as "a jack of all trades." He was at various times a coach, scout, contract negotiator, press agent, ticket seller, janitor, and "gateman" for the team. He moved the team to Municipal Stadium, where it would remain for the next four years.

Even in the 1930s, the Eagles were not among the stellar teams of the NFL. In 1939, they signed Davey O'Brien, an All-

American quarterback from Texas Christian University, for the then sizable sum of $12,000 per year salary (plus a percentage of the gate). The Eagles achieved a now largely forgotten but nonetheless groundbreaking achievement that year; on October 22, they played in the first game ever televised. They played against the Brooklyn Dodgers at the famed Ebbets Field. (At that time team names and playing locales were commonly shared by more than one sport.) The score of the first TV game was 24–13, with the Dodgers winning.

In 1940, Pittsburgh Steelers owner Art Rooney sold his franchise to Alexis Thompson, a 30-year-old businessman and heir to a steel fortune. Rooney then purchased a half-interest in the Eagles; he and Bell then arranged to swap franchises with Thompson. Thompson soon hired Earl "Greasy" Neale to serve as the Eagles' head coach. Neale proved to be an auspicious choice; during his nine-year tenure the Eagles would win three Eastern Division crowns and two NFL championships. A year later saw the beginning of regular radio broadcasts of NFL games, a move that helped popularize the sport. The NFL also launched something of a publicity campaign that offered a number of guidelines for teams and players; among the recommendations were restrictions on endorsing cigarettes and liquor, and limits to commercial messages over stadium public address systems.

### The 1940s: Progress During and After the War

The U.S. entry into World War II in 1941 altered the progress of professional sports. Able-bodied men—the natural choice for athletic teams—were entering the U.S. Armed Forces. Many football fans actually found out about the Pearl Harbor bombing while at one of the many NFL games taking place, since December 7 was a Sunday. This left a shortage of players, and the teams felt the loss. During the war years 638 active NFL players served in the war, and the NFL gave generously to war relief agencies.

During the World War II, many of the young men who would normally be playing professional football were either enlisting in the armed forces or getting inducted. This created a severe shortage of players. In some cases, retired players were asked to come back; some teams simply suspended activity. One innovative way several teams employed as a means of solving the manpower shortage was to combine teams. During the 1943 season, the Eagles and the Pittsburgh Steelers joined forces as the "Steagles." (The following year, the Steelers joined forces with the Chicago Cardinals as the "Card-Pitts.") Eagles head coach Greasy Neale was so discouraged during the 1944 season that he insisted on cutting his salary of $12,000 by 75 percent.

Neale's pessimism turned around after the Eagles signed Steve Van Buren, a halfback who had been a star player at Louisiana State University. Van Buren had both strength and speed (he could run 100 yards in 9.8 seconds) and in his rookie year he managed to help lead the Eagles to second place in the Eastern Division. Van Buren would prove to be one of the key players for the Eagles for the next half dozen years.

In 1946, when Bell became NFL commissioner, he moved NFL headquarters from Chicago to Bala Cynwyd, a small town just outside Philadelphia. (Bell remained NFL commissioner until his death in 1959.) The Eagles continued to improve their performance; by now they had come in second in the Eastern Division three years in a row, and in 1947 they won their first Eastern Division title, losing the championship to the Chicago Cardinals. The following year marked the beginning of a two-year period during which the team dominated NFL football.

### Back-to-Back Champions

By 1948, the war was over and many of the young men who had served had gotten their bearings. This was good for professional football in general and the Eagles in particular. Although there had been challenges to the NFL's role as the dominant professional organization for the past couple of years, there was no doubt that the Eagles were a strong, talented, and determined team. They played well during the season, finishing with a 9–2–1 record and winning the Eastern Division for the second straight year. The championship game, against the Cardinals, was held in Philadelphia during a terrific snowstorm. Despite blinding conditions, the teams played on, and Steve Van Buren scored the game's only touchdown. The Eagles had won their first championship. On a different note, 1948 also marked the debut of the Eaglettes, a cheerleading squad. They were briefly known in the 1970s as the Liberty Belles before settling on the far simpler moniker The Eagles Cheerleaders.

In 1949, the Eagles won the Eastern Division for the third straight year with an 11–1 record, and played against the Los Angeles Rams for the championship. This time it was torrential rain instead of snow that fell, but once again the Eagles prevailed. Van Buren slogged through rain and mud at the Los Angeles Coliseum and rushed 196 yards. The Eagles won the game 14–0. Other players who were important in the late 1940s included center/linebacker Chuck Bednarik and end Pete Pihos, both of whom, like Van Buren, were later named to the Eagles Honor Roll.

There was activity in the back offices as well in 1949. Thompson had decided to sell the Eagles to a group of 100 investors, each of whom paid $3,000 for a one percent share. They came to be know as the "Happy Hundred" and the "One Hundred Brothers" and would retain ownership of the franchise for the next 13 years.

Meanwhile, the Eagles continued to do well, although not as well as they had in 1948 and 1949. In 1950, Greasy Neale's last season as coach, the Eagles finished third in the American conference. Over the next decade, the Eagles would sometimes finish second in their division, and several players distinguished themselves. Bobby Watson was named Rookie of the Year in 1951 and led the NFL in scoring in 1954 with 114 points. Other

## Key Dates:

**1919:** Frankford Yellow Jackets team established outside Philadelphia.

**1933:** Bert Bell and Lud Wray purchase Yellow Jackets franchise and rename team Eagles.

**1935:** Bell proposes annual NFL college draft to help equalize talent within league.

**1943:** Eagles and Pittsburgh Steelers temporarily merge to form "Steagles" to accommodate shortage of players during World War II.

**1948:** Eagles win first NFL championship against Chicago Cardinals.

**1951:** End/placekicker Bobby Watson named NFL Rookie of the Year.

**1958:** Eagles begin playing at University of Pennsylvania's Franklin Field.

**1971:** Veterans Stadium opens as home of Eagles and Phillies baseball team.

**1980:** Eagles make Super Bowl but lose to Oakland Raiders 27–10.

**1992:** Eagles have first post-season victory since 1981 but lose in divisional playoff game to Dallas Cowboys.

**1994:** Movie producer Jeffrey Lurie purchases Eagles for $185 million.

**1999:** Eagles unveil plans for new stadium.

key players included Bobby Thomason, Adrian Burk, and Sonny Jurgensen. Still, the Eagles continued to fall short of championship status. In 1958 the team moved to the University of Pennsylvania's Franklin Field, which doubled attendance from around 18,000 to nearly 36,000.

### Ups and Downs in the 1960s–80s

In 1960, the Eagles won back some of their magic with the aid of such players as Chuck Bednarik and Norm Van Brocklin. The team won the Eastern Division championship—the first in 11 years. The following year the Eagles did well but won no championships. In 1962, however, several players were out with injuries and the Eagles won a mere three games; they fell to last place in the league.

In 1963 the remaining members of the "Happy Hundred" (several had sold their shares to other members) put the franchise up for sale. The asking price was $4.5 million, but in a bidding war Washington, D.C. business executive Jerry Wolman paid just over $5.5 million. The following year the Eagles named Joe Kuharich, former coach of the Cardinals and the Washington Redskins, as the new head coach. Kuharich worked to rebuild the problematic team. His efforts paid off; the Eagles had a winning season in 1966, with a 9–5 record. Injuries marred the Eagles' performance in 1967.

In 1969, trouble of a different sort hit the Eagles. Jerry Wolman, the owner, suffered a financial setback that forced the sale of the franchise. The buyer was Leonard Tose, a trucking executive, and the price was a reported $16.1 million (at that time a record for professional athletic teams).

An even more momentous development was the Eagles' 1971 move to their new home, Veterans Stadium in South Philadelphia. Owned by the city of Philadelphia, the new stadium (capacity 65,352) was shared by Philadelphia's baseball team, the Phillies. One amenity at the "Vet" that did not please players was its playing surface, which was not real grass but the synthetic known as AstroTurf. AstroTurf was durable, but also hard on knees and elbows, and it made it easier for injuries to occur.

The Eagles continued their lackluster performance until 1973 when newly named coach Mike McCormick began to turn the team around. The team was still unable to boast a winning season, and in 1976 Leonard Tose named UCLA coach Dick Vermeil as head coach. Vermeil made visible progress with the team, which had its first winning season since the 1960s in 1978. The following year, they tied the Dallas Cowboys for first place in the NFC East division and earned a wild card spot in the playoffs. They lost to the Tampa Bay Buccaneers, but their strong showing made them a force to contend with once again. Vermeil was voted NFL Coach of the Year at the end of the season.

In 1980, the Eagles won the NFC East championship with a 12–4 record; they then beat the Minnesota Vikings and the Dallas Cowboys to win their first spot in the Super Bowl. They played the Oakland Raiders, and lost 27–10. Key players won accolades, however, including wide receiver Harold Carmichael and quarterback Ron Jaworski (voted NFL Player of the Year).

Although the Eagles got off to a good start in 1981, they trailed off in the second half of the season. A players' strike in 1982 cost the league eight weeks, and the Eagles were unable to gain any real momentum. Over the next few years, the Eagles' record was mediocre. Despite the strong performance of several players, such as Randall Cunningham, Reggie White, and Mike Quick, the team was unable to capture its former strength. The team was sold in 1985 to businessmen Norman Bramans and Ed Leibowitz for a reported $65 million. Bramans bought out Leibowitz in 1986 and held the team until 1994.

In the late 1980s the Eagles began to do better, with winning seasons from 1989 to 1992. In 1992, they had their first post-season victory, against the New Orleans Saints, but lost a divisional playoff to Dallas. The Eagles had been poised for a particularly strong season, but the pre-season accidental death of defensive tackle Jerome Brown cast a tragic shadow over the team.

### New Challenges in the 1990s and Beyond

In 1994, Bramans sold the Eagles to movie executive Jeffrey Lurie for an estimated $185 million. Lurie understood the city's attachment to the Eagles, but he also wanted the team to give back in other ways. In 1995, he and his wife initiated the Eagles Youth Partnership, a non-profit group that provides assistance to disadvantaged families in the greater Philadelphia area. The program includes free eye exams for children, asthma management training for children and their parents, and a program that distributed books to low-income children.

Performance-wise, the 1990s turned out to be less than stellar. The Eagles had winning seasons in 1995 and 1996, but 1997 was disappointing and 1998 left the 3–13 Eagles with the worst record in the league. With the arrival of new head coach Andy Reid in 1999, the team began to show promise. The team finished the season 5–11, but with a decidedly more positive attitude, and the 2000 season got off to a strong start.

Veterans Stadium, the city-owned complex that had been home to the Eagles and the Philadelphia Phillies baseball team since 1971, began to show definite signs of wear in the 1990s. The desire on the part of players for a modern facility—coupled with the fans' desire to be able to watch games in comfort if not luxury—spurred a number of new sports complexes across the country.

In 1999 the Eagles unveiled plans for a new stadium, to be built near the Vet. With a capacity of 66,000, the state-of-the-art building would offer all the amenities that have become essential in today's arenas—including more comfortably appointed luxury boxes. The City of Philadelphia became embroiled in a protracted debate over where a new stadium should go, whether there should be two separate stadiums for the Eagles and the Phillies, and how much should be spent. In November 2000 Philadelphia mayor John Street announced a tentative deal pending approval of the City Council. Under this deal, two stadiums, one for baseball and one for football, would be built near the Vet. The total cost was set at roughly $1.01 billion, with funding coming from the teams, the city, and the state of

Pennsylvania. Meanwhile, the city also announced that in the interim it would make a much-desired improvement at the Vet: replacement of the dreaded AstroTurf.

## *Principal Competitors*

Washington Redskins; The Dallas Cowboys Football Club Ltd.; New York Football Giants.

## *Further Reading*

Anastasia, Phil, *Broken Wing, Broken Promise: A Season Inside the Philadelphia Eagles,* Philadelphia: Camino Books, 1993.

Benson, Clea, et al, "$1 Billion Deal Reached for Stadiums," *Philadelphia Inquirer,* November 17, 2000, p. 1.

Bowden, Mark, *Bringing the Heat,* New York: Knopf, 1994.

Cunningham, Randall, with Steve Wartenberg, *I'm Still Scrambling,* New York: Doubleday, 1993.

Kim, Albert, and Mark Mravic, "Philly Turf War," *Sports Illustrated,* November 13, 2000, p. 26.

Peterson, Robert W., *Pigskin: The Early Years of Pro Football,* New York and Oxford: Oxford University Press, 1997.

Rothaus, James R., *The Philadelphia Eagles,* Mankato, Minn.: Creative Education, 1981.

White, Reggie, *Reggie White in the Trenches: The Autobiography,* Nashville: Thomas Nelson, 1996.

—George A. Milite

# Premcor Inc.

8182 Maryland Avenue, Suite 600
St. Louis, Missouri 63105
U.S.A.
Telephone: (314) 854-9696
Fax: (314) 854-1580
Web site: http://www.premcorinc.com

*Private Company*
*Incorporated:* 1932 as Clark Oil & Refining Corporation
*Employees:* 2,000
*Sales:* $4 billion (2000 est.)
*NAIC:* 32411 Petroleum Refining

Premcor Inc. is one of the United States' leading privately owned oil refiners. It operates four refineries, which primarily produce gasoline and diesel fuel. Its largest refinery is in Port Arthur, Texas, a historic facility that began operating in 1901 following the first discovery of oil in Texas. This facility produces jet fuel as well as diesel and gasoline and is one of the most technologically advanced refineries in the world. Premcor also owns a refinery in Lima, Ohio, which produces nearly a quarter of the gasoline bought in that state. Of its two Illinois refineries, one is located in Hartford, Illinois, just across the Mississippi from Premcor's St. Louis headquarters, and the other is in a suburb of Chicago, Blue Island. Combined capacity at Premcor's four refineries is 547,000 barrels per day. The company purchases crude oil for its refineries from petroleum producers worldwide. It has no oil production capacity itself. Premcor began as Clark Oil, a leading refiner and marketer of gasoline. It sold its product at thousands of Clark gas stations in the Midwest and bordering states. Premcor sold all of its retail business and the Clark brand name in 1999 and is no longer affiliated with Clark gas stations and stores. The company changed its name in 2000 to reflect its severance with Clark. Premcor is now owned by two major groups of shareholders. The largest stake is held by affiliates of the Blackstone Group, a New York City-based investment bank. The second largest stake is owned by Occidental Petroleum. Premcor operates four subsidiary companies. Port Arthur Coker Company L.P. and Port Arthur Finance Corp. are also affiliated with Occidental.

Premcor's other major subsidiaries are Premcor USA Inc. and The Premcor Refining Group Inc.

## Early History

Premcor Inc. began its life as a gasoline refiner and marketer named for its founder, Emory T. Clark. Clark moved from his native Georgia to Milwaukee, Wisconsin, and worked in the construction business. During the Depression, it was hard for Clark to find enough construction work to get along. So in 1932 he made an investment of $14 and took over a one-pump gas station in Milwaukee at the corner of 60th and Greenfield Streets. Clark named the station Clark's Super Gas and began investing in more stations in the area. Clark built his brand around premium gasoline. Clark stations sold premium gas exclusively and did not offer some of the other services, such as tire changing and engine repairs and maintenance, available at competitors' stations. The idea behind Clark was that the customer could drive up, get filled with the best gas, and drive away in a hurry.

Clark Oil built up its market through Wisconsin, Illinois, and surrounding Midwestern states. In 1943, the company began refining oil, taking over a refinery at Blue Island, Illinois. The Blue Island refinery was connected by pipeline with automated terminals, and it could also ship its finished product via water using the Cal-Sag canal and the Great Lakes. This was convenient to markets throughout the Midwest. By the mid-1950s, the company operated close to 500 gas stations, located in Ohio, Indiana, Michigan, Illinois, Wisconsin, Minnesota, Iowa, and Missouri. In 1957 the company broadened its scope further, moving from marketing and refining into oil exploration and production. In 1964 Clark opened a plant to produce petrochemicals and began selling acetone and phenol.

By the late 1960s, Clark Oil & Refining was one of the most profitable oil enterprises around. It stuck to its marketing formula of providing only high-octane premium gas and not offering any repair services. Its stations were built primarily at high-traffic intersections or highway off-ramps and boasted speedy, efficient service. Its refinery at Blue Island was able to produce a higher proportion of premium gas than almost any other in the industry. The company was publicly traded on the New York Stock Exchange.

Clark's growth in the 1960s was impressive. Its revenues tripled between 1959 and 1969, while its profits went up by a factor of six. Sales surpassed $200 million for the first time in 1968, and Clark continued to add gas stations. It acquired a chain of 117 Owens Oil stations in 1969, and it began building up its Ohio market as well as moving beyond the Midwest into bordering states.

### Changes in the 1970s

By 1970, Clark operated 1,489 stations, and its two refineries, the one at Blue Island and a second at Woods River, Illinois, acquired in 1968, were refining almost 100,000 barrels a day combined. The Milwaukee-based company was the largest independent oil refiner and marketer in the Midwest, and one of the most successful in this competitive market. The average amount of gallons sold per Clark station was twice the national average, and its emphasis on premium gasoline gave it a high profit margin. Emory Clark stepped down as president of Clark Oil & Refining in 1970, although he stayed on as chairman and was the firm's principal stockholder. Leadership of the company passed to Owen Hill, a former accountant.

The oil industry began to go through significant changes in the 1970s. Clark was forced to give up selling only premium-grade gasoline when pollution concerns brought about the industrywide conversion to unleaded gas. It began selling unleaded gas in 1974. Clark's oil exploration had not gone well, and it continued to buy its crude on the open market. The OPEC oil embargo of 1973–74 led to increased crude oil costs for Clark. In the 1970s Clark's profitability often was determined by complex regulations governing the crude oil market.

In the late 1970s, the company embarked on a plan to make its marketing operations more efficient. The plan was carried out under the auspices of Clark's new chairman and CEO Robert G. Reed III. Emory Clark, who retained almost a quarter of the firm's stock, was still chairman of the company's executive committee. Reed began by assessing the profitability of each of the company's nearly 2,000 stations. Over the next two years, almost 400 were closed down. He also reorganized the firm into a less complex corporate structure. While it shut some stations, Clark began building so-called Superstations, which were larger format stations, and began converting most of its stations to self-service. It also began adding "grocerettes" to some of its stations, offering 24-hour fast food. In 1981 Clark spent $15 million on a marketing push that converted stations in ten major metropolitan markets to a more competitive format.

The company began competing on price, shedding its old image of the purveyor of high-priced premium gas. Clark hired an executive who had worked for 7-Eleven and Stop-N-Go, the convenience store chains, to head a new division of convenience store operations. The company seemed to be moving aggressively to get the most out of its retail empire as the costs associated with its refinery operations grew more uncertain.

### Under Apex in the 1980s

In early 1980, Emory T. Clark had briefly floated the idea that Clark Oil might be for sale. The company's stock went up, and then down, as Clark announced that acquisition talks with an unnamed suitor had broken down. Later that year, a St. Louis-based company called Apex Oil began buying up Clark stock. Clark's chairman, Robert Reed III, initially wrote Apex a letter asking it to cease. The company was not for sale. But by the middle of 1981, Clark Oil had accepted an offer from Apex to buy out the Clark family for $37 a share. Apex shelled out more than $483 million for the family's shares and prepared to invest another $100 million for other outstanding shares. By August 1981, the publicly traded Clark Oil had become a subsidiary of Apex, a privately held and mysteriously closed-mouth conglomerate run by two men, Samuel R. Goldstein and P.A. "Tony" Novelly. At the time of the sale, Clark had revenues of $1.6 billion. The relatively unknown Apex had gross sales of $6.25 billion. To buy Clark, Apex got a consortium of 12 banks to put together a $740 million line of credit.

Apex was founded in the 1930s by Charles Mintz. It began as a small company that stored oil at a terminal near St. Louis on the Mississippi. Samuel Goldstein, Mintz's son-in-law, entered the business in the 1940s. Goldstein bought out his family's shares in the 1960s and began buying up more oil storage space. During the oil shortage caused by the embargo of 1973, Apex profited handsomely on the oil it had in storage, and the company began to grow exponentially.

Goldstein took on Tony Novelly around that time. Novelly seems to have had an explosive personality, and the quick rise of Apex was usually attributed to his drive and acumen. Apex began the 1970s with revenues of about $10 million. By 1980, the company had become a behemoth, with revenue of $6.25 billion, which soon leapt to $10 billion with the addition of Clark Oil. It owned 25 sea-going tankers and 38 barges, had two million barrels of storage space, plus more than 11 million more that it leased, many subsidiary companies in the oil business, as well as a real estate subsidiary and ownership of a Colorado ski resort. Apex was one of the nation's biggest oil traders, and it made gargantuan deals in oil futures, though not always successfully. In 1982 Apex lost $32 million selling oil futures. Soon after Apex acquired Clark, oil prices began to fall, and Apex had trouble getting credit. Short of cash, Apex decided to sell Clark. By 1985, Apex had hired Merrill Lynch & Co. to negotiate a sale, but the company then rejected the offers it received as too low. In 1986, Apex again lost badly in the oil futures market, eventually throwing away $96 million. Declining oil prices meant that the oil in Apex's inventory was worth less. The efforts to keep Apex afloat were generally attributed to Tony Novelly, but he apparently had trouble keeping his temper when arranging matters with Apex's bank. In one meeting he was said to have stormed out after calling the banks "stupid."

When a sale of Clark to Getty Petroleum was arranged in 1987, Novelly again stomped out of the meeting room after finding that the stock he was getting in the deal was to be nonvoting. Novelly quickly set up another deal for Clark, this time with a Chicago financier named Samuel Zell, but this also fell through. In December 1987, Apex's banks called in the company's loans. Apex declared bankruptcy, and Clark also went Chapter 11. At the time, it was one of the largest bankruptcy petitions ever for a privately held company.

### The 1990s and Beyond

Clark Oil & Refining was then bought by a unit of Horsham Corp., a Toronto investment firm. Horsham offered $454 million for 60 percent of Clark, the revenues of which had risen to $3.5 billion under Apex and then fallen to around $2 billion at the time of the bankruptcy. Clark's assets included its two Illinois refineries and about 1,000 gas stations. Horsham eventually acquired 100 percent of Clark in 1992. The company changed its name to Clark Refining and Marketing in 1993. It was still run out of St. Louis.

In the early 1990s, Clark invested in its remaining gas stations, now clustered in eight Midwestern states. It seemed to pick up where it had left off before the acquisition by Apex, remodeling old stations, expanding its convenience store offerings, and stepping up its investments in key competitive markets such as Chicago. Under Horsham Clark also updated its logo, changing the colors for a more 1990s look. Clark invested some $300 million in its two refineries, updating equipment and redesigning to conform to new environmental regulations.

In the mid-1990s, Clark began expanding through acquisition. The company purchased its Port Arthur, Texas refinery from Chevron in 1995, and then in 1998 bought a refinery in Lima, Ohio from BP Oil. The two acquisitions quadrupled the company's refining capacity. Meanwhile, ownership of the company changed. Horsham Corp. had changed its name to TrizecHahn. This company sold 80 percent of its stake in Clark to a New York-based investment company, the Blackstone Group. Occidental Petroleum acquired another large stake. Clark had been working on its retail marketing, selling off gas stations in some territories and trying to step up its presence in others through the late 1990s. In 1999, Clark Refining and Marketing announced that it would sell all of its retail opera-

tions, and remain only in the refining business. Clark's remaining 700 gas stations and 200 convenience stores were sold in December 1999, along with the Clark brand name. These were then operated by a company that took the name Clark Retail Enterprises Inc. Clark also sold its product distribution terminals in 1999. The company was pared down to running only its four refineries. It changed its name to Premcor in 2000, a name that was put together from "premier" plus "corporation." Premcor stood as the fifth largest independent oil refiner in the United States, and the eleventh largest overall. The company planned to concentrate exclusively on its refinery business in the future, making significant investments in upgrading and expanding its existing facilities.

### Principal Subsidiaries

Premcor Refining Group, Inc.; Port Arthur Coker Company L.P.; Port Arthur Finance Corp.; Premcor USA Inc.

### Principal Competitors

BP Amoco plc; Ultramar Diamond Shamrock.

### Further Reading

Bailey, Jeff, "Apex Oil Prevents Massive Liquidation with Filing for Chapter 11 Protection," *Wall Street Journal,* December 29, 1987, p. 4.

"Clark Oil—On the Move," *Financial World,* November 26, 1969, p. 7.

Dwyer, Steve, "Back on Course, Clark Pushes Retail Expansion, Station Upgrades," *National Petroleum News,* October 1991, p. 14.

Geary, Cornelius, "Retail Revival," *National Petroleum News,* July 1981, pp. 51–53.

"Horsham Agrees to Buy Remaining 40% Stake of Its Clark Oil Unit," *Wall Street Journal,* December 15, 1992, p. A6.

Kovski, Alan, "Clark Oil & Refining Announces Plan to Sell Operations in Kansas, Kentucky, Minnesota," *Oil Daily,* January 20, 1993, p. 2.

——, "Clark Pursues Independent Marketers to Spread Brand in Competitive Midwest," *Oil Daily,* February 12, 1997, p. 3.

Lamphier, Gary, "Court Approves Sale of Clark Oil to Horsham Unit," *Wall Street Journal,* November 8, 1988, p. C15.

"Missing Leg," *Forbes,* June 1, 1973, pp. 22–23.

Moore, Rob, "Clark to Spend $300 Million on Refineries," *St. Louis Business Journal,* October 28, 1991, p. 1A.

"Over a Barrel," *Forbes,* February 1, 1971, pp. 18–19.

Sandler, Linda, "Peter Munk Bets Horsham Corp. Can Match the Success of American Barrick Resources," *Wall Street Journal,* April 17, 1989, p. C2.

Shaner, Richard, "Apex Oil: Midwest's Mystery Giant Casts Bold Shadow in Buying Spree," *National Petroleum News,* October 1981, pp. 76–79.

Sherrid, Pamela, "Don't Squeeze This Bear, He Will Sue," *Forbes,* May 24, 1982, pp. 58–59.

"Specialist Diversifies," *Financial World,* June 19, 1968, pp. 56.

Wall, Wendy, "How a Bold Executive Made Apex Oil Grow, and How It Collapsed," *National Petroleum News,* April 1988, p. 49.

—A. Woodward

# Qwest Communications International, Inc.

**1801 California Street**
**Denver, Colorado 80202**
**U.S.A.**
**Telephone: (303) 992-1400**
**Toll Free: (800) 899-7780**
**Fax: (303) 992-1724**
**Web site: http://www.qwest.com**

*Public Company*
*Incorporated:* 1988 as SP Telecom
*Employees:* 70,000
*Sales:* $3.92 billion (1999)
*Stock Exchanges:* New York
*Ticker Symbol:* Q
*NAIC:* 513310 Wired Telecommunications Carriers;
513322 Cellular and Other Wireless Telecommunications; 514191 On-Line Information Services

From its origins as a fiber-optic network-building subsidiary of Southern Pacific Transportation Co., Qwest Communications International, Inc. has grown through acquisitions to offer local and long-distance telephone services, as well as a range of Internet, multimedia, data, and voice services that are sold to business, consumer, and government customers. The company completed construction of its 18,500-mile national fiber-optic network in 1999, and then added 4,300 route miles in Canada and Mexico. At the end of the century, it was also building fiber-optic rings in Europe. In the year 2000 it completed its acquisition of regional Bell operating company (RBOC) US West.

## SP Telecom Builds Telecommunications Lines: 1988–95

Qwest Communications International originated as a subsidiary of the giant railroad company Southern Pacific Transportation Co. In 1988, reclusive Denver billionaire Philip Anschutz acquired Southern Pacific from Sante Fe Industries, after the Interstate Commerce Commission ruled that the 1983 merger of the Atchison, Topeka & Santa Fe Railroad with Southern Pacific was anticompetitive. Anschutz, who had gained much of his wealth in the oil industry, first entered the railroad industry with the 1984 purchase of the Rio Grande Railroad for $500 million. His company, Anschutz Corp., paid about $1.8 billion for Southern Pacific, with much of it being leveraged debt.

SP Telecom was established in San Francisco in 1988 as a subsidiary of Southern Pacific Transportation Co. It was founded to construct telecommunications lines along Southern Pacific's 15,000 miles of railroad right-of-way. It was part of the company when Anschutz acquired it, but he later reorganized it as a subsidiary of Anschutz Corp. In 1992, Anschutz negotiated an easement agreement with Southern Pacific to lay fiber-optic cable along 11,700 miles of its tracks.

It should be noted that SP Telecom was not the first successful telecommunications spin-off from Southern Pacific. Earlier, the railroad giant had created and sold another subsidiary that later became Sprint Corp. (the first two letters in Sprint were taken from its parent's name).

By 1993, the privately-held SP Telecom had annual revenue of more than $50 million, and employed 410 people. During the early 1990s SP Telecom built fiber-optic linkups for other carriers, sold space on its fiber-optic network, and introduced commercial products—including a video teleconferencing system. In mid-1993 it began offering commercial services such as long-distance, 800-number, calling-card, and debit-card products.

## Becoming Qwest and Going Public in the Mid-1990s

In 1995, SP Telecom moved to Denver, after acquiring the Dallas-based firm Qwest Communications Corp. and taking over its name and facilities. Anschutz also expanded his telecommunications holdings in 1995 with the purchase of Interwest Communications C.S. Corp. Around this time he also agreed to sell his interest in Southern Pacific to the Union Pacific Corp. for about $1.6 billion worth of stock, which made him Union Pacific's largest shareholder.

In May of that year, Qwest reached an agreement with CSX Transportation Inc. to use its rail corridors to install a high-speed, high-volume fiber-optic network. CSX owned 19,000 miles of track in 20 eastern states. Qwest already had a strong presence in the West through agreements with Southern Pacific Rail Corp. and Santa Fe Railway. The agreement with CSX would enable Qwest to build a fiber-optic network from coast to coast.

In laying its fiber-optic cables, Qwest would bury four to six high-density polyethylene pipes at a time, each capable of carrying a separate system. It used a $1 million, 76-ton rail-mounted plow that laid the pipe next to the rail line at a depth of four to five feet. The machine was capable of laying about eight miles per day.

That year, Qwest completed a fiber link between Sacramento and Los Angeles. Other projects ongoing in the first half of 1995 included links between Denver and El Paso, Dallas and Houston, and St. Louis and Kansas City. The company soon planned to build a national fiber-optic network. Four other companies were in the process of doing the same: AT&T, MCI Communications, LDDS WorldCom, and Sprint (WorldCom would acquire MCI in 1997). Later in 1995, Qwest gained permission to link several Mexican cities, including Mexico City, Monterrey, and Guadalajara, with about 5,000 miles of fiber-optic cable. This network was later linked to U.S. long distance carriers at the U.S.-Mexican border.

In 1996 Qwest was negotiating with other long distance providers to buy or lease part of its fiber-optic network. Some analysts felt that the United States already had more fiber-optic cable than it needed. Later in the year, Frontier Corp. joined with Qwest in building its $2 billion fiber-optic network. Lucent Technologies agreed to supply its True Wave fiber cable to the multi-ring SONET-based network, which would connect nearly 100 cities and have more than 13,000 route miles.

The company initiated an IPO on June 23, 1997, renaming itself Qwest Communications International, Inc. The offering raised $297 million on the sale of 13.5 million shares. Only 14 percent of the company was offered to the public, however; the rest was held by Philip Anschutz. The IPO gave the company a market capitalization of $2.1 billion. Joseph Nacchio became Qwest's new president and CEO in 1997, after leaving the No. 3 post at AT&T, where he had been head of AT&T's consumer services until late 1996.

Qwest's strategy in building its nationwide fiber-optic network was that a ground-based network would be more reliable for the transmission of data than satellite-based networks. Demand for high-speed networks that could transmit data as well as audio and video were set to explode over the next five years, and this demand would be led by banks and other financial institutions. In addition, deregulation would bring other companies—including the regional Bell operating companies

(RBOCs)—into the long-distance market. Also, costs for fiber and equipment were expected to drop dramatically.

At the time it went public, Qwest had already negotiated for nearly 90 percent of the right-of-ways it needed to complete its 13,000-mile network. It planned to complete construction on the fiber-optic network in 1998, and would then reach into 92 cities—representing 65 percent of all long-distance traffic in the United States. Qwest had reached agreements with Frontier Corp., the fifth-largest long-distance carrier in the United States; WorldCom Inc., the fourth-largest long-distance carrier and the largest Internet access provider with its acquisition of UUNet; and GTE Corp., the largest non-Bell local telephone company. Those three companies would together lease about half of the capacity of Qwest's network for an investment of about $1 billion. Qwest also received $90 million in vendor financing from Nortel. Other potential revenue streams were expected to come from the RBOCs and from Internet service providers (ISPs), for whom Qwest planned to install sophisticated switching equipment.

Later in 1997, Qwest acquired Colorado's largest ISP, SuperNet Inc., for $20 million. SuperNet was also the state's oldest ISP, having been originally founded by the Colorado Advanced Institute of Technology and other local universities as a nonprofit venture. Qwest also introduced the first advertising campaign—developed by ad agency Bright Sun Consulting—for its fiber-optic telecommunications network. The print campaign, estimated to cost $5–10 million, employed the tagline, "Ride the light." Qwest's network was now projected to reach 125 U.S. cities and several cities in Mexico, have 16,000 miles of fiber-optic cable, and be completed in mid-1999. For 1997, Qwest reported revenue of $697 million.

### Acquisitions and Expansion in the Late 1990s

With Internet usage increasing dramatically in 1997, Qwest made plans to take advantage of the expansion of voice-over-Internet protocol (IP) services. In December 1997 Qwest announced it would offer IP-based services to users in nine Western cities. The service was expected to resolve voice-quality problems associated with IP-based telephone services. It was initially offered as a consumer long-distance package at 7.5 cents per minute, with business customers to follow.

In March 1998, Qwest announced it would acquire the Mc-Lean, Virginia-based long-distance carrier LCI International Inc. for $4.4 billion. The deal would create the fourth-largest long-distance carrier in the United States behind AT&T, MCI Worldcom, and Sprint Corp. The combined companies would have about 5,800 employees and revenue of $2.3 billion. The acquisition gave Qwest two million long-distance customers and a well-established sales force. In the same month, Qwest also announced that it would purchase EUNet, a European ISP based in Amsterdam with about 60,000 customers and 1997 revenue of $55 million, for $154 million.

A month later, Qwest activated the portion of its fiber network that connected Los Angeles, San Francisco, and New York, giving the company more than 5,400 route-miles of its network in service. The company also joined with Cisco Systems Inc. and Nortel to create a new IP backbone network called

---

**Key Dates:**

**1988:** SP Telecom is established as a subsidiary of Southern Pacific Transportation Co.
**1995:** SP Telecom assumes the name of Qwest Communications Corp. and goes public later in the year as Qwest Communications International, Inc.
**1998:** Qwest acquires long-distance carrier LCI International for $4.4 billion.
**1999:** Qwest receives a $3.5 billion investment from Bell-South; initiates takeover bids for US West and Frontier Communications.
**2000:** Qwest completes acquisition of US West.

---

Internet2 for use by the academic community. The project was conceived by the University Corporation for Advanced Internet Development (UCAID), which was a consortium of 130 universities. Qwest contributed capacity on its fiber network, while Cisco contributed $4.5 million worth of switch routers and Nortel contributed products used in its SONET interface technology. The project was announced by Vice President Al Gore in a White House Press conference, where he praised Qwest for donating $500 million worth of bandwidth to the project. Later in 1998, Qwest planned to roll out its own ATM, frame relay, and virtual private network (VPN) services at lower costs than its long-distance competitors AT&T, MCI, and others.

Soon thereafter, RBOC Ameritech (which was in the process of being acquired by SBC Communications Inc.—formerly Southwestern Bell) announced that it would begin offering long-distance service through an alliance with Qwest. The plan was challenged by other long-distance carriers, however, who pointed out that the Telecommunication Act of 1996 required the RBOCs, which had virtual monopolies on local phone markets, to prove their local market were open to competition before they could offer long-distance services. Qwest and US West had reached a similar agreement earlier in 1998 that was also challenged. Later in the year the Federal Communications Commission (FCC) ruled against the agreements.

In mid-1998 Qwest announced it would offer long-distance service in Europe. While the acquisition of ISP EUNet gave Qwest data services, it planned to offer voice services by making deals with established carriers in Europe. Meanwhile, back in the United States Qwest sold bandwidth on its fiber network to competitive local exchange carrier (CLEC) Electric Lightwave for $122 million. Qwest also sold $60 million worth of bandwidth to Digital Broadcast Network Corp. for IP-based ATM services.

In September 1998 Qwest acquired Icon CMT of Weehawken, New Jersey, for $185 million in stock. Icon CMT provided Internet-based services, such as web hosting, intranets, online stock trading, and online publications for larger corporations. Qwest also formed a three-year alliance with Netscape Communications to provide Netscape's web portal, NetCenter, with a range of telecommunications services including Internet access. Qwest was in the process of building 10 CyberCenters around the United States to offer a range of web hosting and multimedia applications to Internet customers. Four centers would open in 1998 in Los Angeles, New York, San Francisco, and Washington, D.C., with six centers slated for 1999.

Before the end of the year, Qwest snared another AT&T executive when John McMaster, acting head of AT&T's consumer markets division, left the firm to join Qwest and take control of its international operations. At the same time, Qwest announced it would build a fiber-optic network in Europe with Dutch telecommunications company KPN. Qwest's European network would soon link with its North American network.

In December 1998 Qwest and Microsoft Corp. announced an agreement whereby Microsoft would invest $200 million in Qwest, taking a 1.3 percent minority interest in the company. Qwest, in turn, would use the Microsoft Windows NT Server OS as the basis of its electronic commerce, Web hosting, streaming media, managed software, and virtual private networking services to be introduced in 1999. Qwest's 1998 revenue was reported at $2.2 billion.

As part of its national fiber network, Qwest had completed local fiber optic rings in 10 cities in 1998, and planned to add nine more by 2000. The company's Seattle ring ran through Microsoft's Redmond, Washington, campus, giving Qwest the ability to provide broadband connectivity directly to Microsoft.

At the beginning of 1999, Qwest invested $1.5 million in CLEC Covad Communications Group Inc. In exchange, Covad provided Qwest customers with high-speed digital subscriber line (DSL) service in 22 markets. Covad also agreed to purchase network capacity from Qwest to interconnect its high-speed local networks. It was Qwest's first investment in DSL local networks.

Also in January of that year, Qwest introduced its first Internet services for consumers and small businesses, offering flat-rate service for $19.95 a month. Qwest's long-distance customers, however, would only pay $14.95 a month for the service, which was called Q.home. Qwest also announced it would offer paging, conferencing, and faxing services from its web site. In a move to increase its bandwidth, America Online Inc. selected Qwest to provide it with national Internet connectivity services in a deal valued at $13 million.

Qwest's first national branding campaign, created by advertising firm J. Walter Thompson, was launched in March 1999. The 30-second television ads opened with a voiceover that said, "The promise of the Internet is not in the future. It is now." The ads also featured the tagline, "Ride the light," which was created by the company's previous agency, Bright Sun Consulting.

Also in March, Microsoft and Qwest teamed to introduce Q-Commerce-Retail, an online storefront service that included Web hosting services, high-speed Internet access, hardware and software, consulting, design and graphics, direct merchandising assistance, and site promotion. The applications ran on Windows software and were hosted on servers on Qwest's network. Pricing began at $150,000, with a monthly fee of about $10,000.

The following month, Qwest announced it would be able to expand its high-speed DSL services into more markets through a $15 million agreement with Rhythms NetConnections Inc., a local DSL provider. The agreement involved 31 cities, with some overlap with the 22 cities serviced under Qwest's agreement with Covad Communications.

A consortium of banks and financial institutions, led by Bank of America, agreed to provide Qwest with a $1 billion revolving credit facility starting in April 1999. Also in April, Bell South Corp. agreed to purchase a 10 percent interest in Qwest for $3.5 billion. The investment would enable BellSouth to bolster its digital data services and use Qwest as its wholesale provider, while Qwest would use BellSouth for local service where possible. The funds also enabled Qwest to reduce the debt it took on for overseas expansion, and helped the company finance construction on the rest of its fiber-optic network.

In May, Qwest president and CEO Joseph Nacchio gave up his title of president to Afshin Mohebbi, who also became Qwest's chief operating officer in charge of day-to-day operations. Nacchio would remain as CEO and focus on overall corporate performance, development, and long-term strategies. Prior to the change, had most recently been the president and managing director of U.K. markets for British Telecom.

Soon thereafter, Qwest and a group of investment funds put together a $251 million investment in Advanced Radio Telecom Corp. (ART), which was in the process of building a high-speed wireless network. ART planned to build in 40 of the top 50 U.S. during the two years following the deal. Qwest's share of the investment was $90 million, and the investment gave it a foothold in the broadband wireless market.

By May 1999, Qwest had completed 16,2000 miles of its planned 18,500-mile fiber-optic network. It was planning to introduce more hosted applications, including electronic commerce services that would allow a company to completely outsource its Web sales operations. The company had signed application hosting service agreements with SAP America Inc., Seibel Systems Inc., Hewlett-Packard, and Oracle Corp.

A month later, Qwest teamed with KPMG to launch Qwest Cyber.Solutions, a joint application service provider (ASP) in which Qwest would own 51 percent. The ASP would offer application hosting and application management services. Also, Qwest and Cisco Systems announced a partnership under which they would co-develop applications for Internet-based data, phone, and image services to be sold to businesses and consumers.

Rumors soon surfaced that Qwest might be a long-term acquisition target for BellSouth, which had a 10 percent interest in the company. Those rumors, however, were quickly overshadowed when Qwest announced hostile takeover bids for US West—a RBOC with local phone customers in 14 Western states, and Frontier Communications—the fifth-largest U.S. long-distance carrier. At the time, US West was already the subject of a $52 billion takeover proposal from Global Crossing Ltd., a Bermuda-based company that was building an undersea fiber-optic network. Wall Street reacted to the announcement by driving Qwest's stock down more than 20 percent.

At first, US West rejected Qwest's bid and reaffirmed its commitment to Global Crossing. Qwest responded by increasing its offer to $68 a share for Frontier and $69 a share for US West, or about $48 billion in all. Global Crossing's offer

amounted to about $11 billion for Frontier and $30 billion for Qwest. Following the new offer, both Frontier and US West agreed to discuss the proposal with Qwest. Qwest and US West quickly reached an agreement whereby Qwest would acquire US West for an amount estimated between $35 and $50 billion, according to various sources. As part of the purchase, Qwest agreed to forego providing long-distance service in US West's territory. Qwest's acquisition of US West also had the effect of diluting BellSouth's interest in the new company from 10 percent to about 3.5 percent. Qwest subsequently withdrew its offer for Frontier, and Frontier agreed to be acquired by Global Crossing for $10.9 billion.

By the summer of 1999, Qwest had about 8,700 employees, while US West had 55,000 employees. The acquisition not only gave Qwest a huge workforce, but also 25 million US West local phone customers in 14 western states. Before the acquisition was finalized in 2000, US West CEO Solomon Trujillo announced he would not remain with the new company, leaving Joseph Nacchio in charge.

Qwest's acquisition of US West had to pass several regulatory hurdles, including approval from the U.S. Department of Justice (DOJ), the Federal Trade Commission (FTC), the Federal Communications Commission, and public service commissions in seven of the 14 states served by US West.

Qwest continued to offer new services, enter into new partnerships, and strengthen existing ones in the latter half of 1999. Together with Microsoft it announced the Qwest Business Partner Program, which would offer a wide range of Internet services using the Windows 2000 platform as well as other platforms. Qwest also introduced DSL service for businesses in 13 markets through Rhythms NetConnections and Covad Communications. Qwest also bundled Internet access with long distance services in a package priced at $24.95 a month for consumers. To strengthen its application service provider (ASP) program, Qwest added revenue-sharing incentives to attract national systems integrators and distributors and increase the number of participants from 300 to 1,000 during 2000. One of the applications it would introduce in 2000 was a practice management application for small doctors' offices.

Meanwhile, the US West acquisition received approval from the U.S. DOJ and the FTC in September. Shareholders of both companies approved the merger in November. State public service commissions were expected to bring up US West's poor service record during hearings on the merger over the next six months.

Qwest completed its national fiber-optic network with 18,500 route miles in September 1999. In December it added 4,300 route miles in Canada and Mexico. In the first two months of 2000 the company experienced service problems due to the rapid expansion of its customer base, including frame relay service slowdowns and circuit outages lasting up to 11 days. Qwest's 1999 revenue was $3.92 billion, with net income of $458 million.

### Acquisition of US West: 2000

Several developments in the US West acquisition occurred in March 2000. The FCC gave its approval, but six state public service commissions had yet to rule on the merger following Colorado's approval in 1999. US West CEO Sol Trujillo had announced he would leave once the merger was completed, and rumors surfaced that Deutsche Telekom AG—Europe's largest telecommunications company—had made a $100 billion bid for both companies. Qwest announced that talks with Deutsche Telekom would not continue, however, following objections from US West.

In April 2000 Qwest announced a new development in its CyberCenter program. The company joined forces with IBM to open 28 CyberCenters, which would provide end-to-end control of applications, services, and network infrastructures in a hosted environment. Qwest would build and own the centers and act as the network provider, while IBM would provide operational support and buy hosting space for its e-commerce clients.

In addition, Qwest was in the process of selling part of its long-distance business to Touch America, a subsidiary of the Montana Power Co. Under federal rules Qwest would not be able to offer long-distance service within states served by US West. In July 2000 the FCC approved the sale of Qwest's long-distance assets in US West territory to Touch America for $193 million. About 250,000 Qwest subscribers, 1,800 miles of fiber, and 170 Qwest sales agents were involved in the transaction. The operations that were sold represented about six percent of Qwest's customers and accounted for about $300 million in annual revenue.

By July, the merger with US West had received approval from the state public service commissions and was a "done" deal. In many cases, state approval was gained by agreeing to negotiate new service quality standards. Estimates of the price of the merger ranged from $35 billion to $80 billion. The new company would lose the US West name and continue using the Qwest name. Qwest immediately held a meeting for about 10,000 employees at the Pepsi Center in Denver, where it announced that it was dropping some 17 lawsuits US West had brought against various state public utility commissions. Altogether, the merged companies had about 70,000 employees worldwide. Later in the year Qwest announced it would streamline its workforce by cutting about 11,000 employee positions and 1,800 contractor positions by the end of 2001.

With the acquisition of US West completed, Qwest announced it would make quality of service its top priority for the local telephone customers it had gained. Other announced goals included doubling its DSL users from 250,000 to 500,000; doubling the number of wireless users from 800,000 to 1.6 million; and doubling its web-hosting space—all by the end of 2001. The company also planned to improve access to its network in order to be able to re-enter the long-distance market again in the 14 western states formerly served by US West.

### Principal Competitors

AT&T; MCI Worldcom Inc.; Sprint Corp.; IXC Communications Inc.; Level 3 Communications Inc.; Williams Communications Solutions LLC; Cable & Wireless plc.

### Further Reading

Andreoli, Teresa, "Peter Kim's Bright Sun Breaks First Qwest Communications Ads," *Adweek Eastern Edition,* October 13, 1997, p. 5.

Barrett, William P., "Working over the Railroad," *Forbes,* October 31, 1988, p. 51.

Bryer, Amy, "Hurdles Ahead for US West Merger," *Denver Business Journal,* March 17, 2000, p. 1A.

——, "Qwest Forges Identity as Phone Provider," *Denver Business Journal,* July 7, 2000, p. 1A.

Carter, Wayne, "Qwest + LCI = IXC Powerhouse?," *Telephony,* March 16, 1998, p. 1.

"Download: Qwest Rumbles Again: Trujillo Will Resign, Acquisition Rumors Surface," *Telephony,* March 6, 2000.

Dubroff, Henry, "Anschutz Keeps Deals Turning at Qwest," *Denver Business Journal,* June 4, 1999, p. 1A.

Edwards, Marcelene, "Qwest Promises New Name, New Reputation after Merger with US West," *Knight-Ridder/Tribune Business News,* July 18, 2000.

Engebretson, Joan, "The Rise of the Carrier's Carrier," *Telephony,* September 7, 1998.

Gerwig, Kate, "Carrier's Qwest for Users," *InternetWeek,* December 22, 1997, p. 12.

——, "IXC, Qwest Spread Fear and Fiber," *InternetWeek,* April 27, 1998, p. 39.

Goldblatt, Henry, "Qwest's Latest Fashion Makeover," *Fortune,* August 16, 1999, p. 30.

——, "Wild, Wild Qwest," *Fortune,* June 8, 1998, p. 255.

Hawn, Carleen, "No Ordinary Joe," *Forbes,* August 7, 2000, p. 82.

Kleinbard, David, "US West, Frontier Agree to Discuss Qwest Deals," *InformationWeek,* July 5, 1999, p. 16.

Lucas, Sloane, and Hank Kim, "JWT Bows Qwest Work," *Adweek Eastern Edition,* March 1, 1999, p. 8.

Mack, Toni, "Empty Pipes," *Forbes,* November 30, 1998, p. 76.

——, "Stark Raving Rich," *Forbes,* February 26, 1996, p. 44.

McCarthy, Jack, "Cisco, Qwest to Partner on Major IP Network," *InfoWorld,* July 5, 1999, p. 38.

Metcalfe, Robert M., "Qwest Buries Fibers of Huge Packet Bandwidth to Unbog the Internet," *InfoWorld,* January 5, 1998, p. 87.

Olgeirson, Ian, "Behind Qwest's Big Bid," *Denver Business Journal,* June 18, 1999, p. 1A.

——, "Qwest Reaches Overseas, Prepares Service in Europe," *Denver Business Journal,* June 9, 1998, p. 5A.

Pereira, Pedro, "Qwest Seeks Partners for Hosting Service," *Computer Reseller News,* November 22, 1999, p. 1.

"Qwest Cuts Back to Go Forward," *InformationWeek,* September 18, 2000, p. 125.

"Qwest for Flexibility," *Electronic News (1991),* April 12, 1999, p. 6.

"Qwest for the Masses," *Telephony,* February 1, 1999.

"Qwest's Lucky $13 Million Deal," *Content Factory,* January 28, 1999.

Rauber, Chris, "SP Telecom Puts its Fiber-Optics Network to Work," *San Francisco Business Journal,* June 11, 1993, p. 6A.

Rendleman, John, "Qwest Gets US West for $35B," *PC Week,* July 26, 1999, p. 49.

——, "Voice over IP Moves Ahead," *PC Week,* January 12, 1998, p. 113.

Rooney, Paula, "Pro-Windows 2000 Deals Unveiled," *Computer Reseller News,* August 2, 1999, p. 26.

Russo, Ed, "US West Rejects Qwest," *Knight-Ridder/Tribune Business News,* June 23, 1999.

Ryan, Vincent, "Download: A Smooth End to a Rocky Road," *Telephony,* July 3, 2000.

Svaldi, Aldo, "Qwest Inks Pact with CSX," *Denver Business Journal,* May 12, 1995, p. 9A.

Thyfault, Mary E., "Microsoft, Qwest Launch Online Service," *InformationWeek,* March 8, 1999, p. 30.

Torode, Christina, and Jennifer Hagendorf, "Qwest, IBM Team up in Hosting Deal," *Computer Reseller News,* April 3, 2000, p. 32.

"US West, Qwest Hit Snag," *InformationWeek,* June 8, 1998, p. 24.

Vogelstein, Fred, "In Telecom, Bigger May No Longer Be Better," *U.S. News & World Report,* November 17, 1997, p. 64.

Wallace, Bob, "Qwest Pays Price for Rapid Growth," *InformationWeek,* February 14, 2000, p. 113.

Wells, Garrison, "Anschutz Co.," *Denver Business Journal,* April 2, 1993, p. 21S.

——, "Anschutz: Now Ex-Billionaire?," *Denver Business Journal,* June 5, 1992, p. 1.

Zelger, Dinah, and Henry Dubroff, "Qwest's Game Plan Unveiled," *Denver Business Journal,* July 4, 1997, p. 3A.

—David P. Bianco

# Racing Champions Corporation

**800 Roosevelt Road**
**Building C, Suite 320**
**Glen Ellyn, Illinois 60123**
**U.S.A.**
**Telephone: (630) 790-3507**
**Fax: (630) 790-9474**
**Web site: http://www.racingchamps.com**

*Public Company*
*Incorporated:*
*Employees:* 519
*Sales:* $231.36 million (1999)
*Stock Exchanges:* New York
*Ticker Symbol:* RACN
*NAIC:* 339932 Game, Toy, and Children's Vehicle
  Manufacturing

Racing Champions Corporation is one of the largest die-cast collectible companies in North America, a position it reached in 1999 when it acquired The Ertl Company, which had over 50 year's experience in making farm toys, model kits, and die-cast collectibles. Through its various subsidiaries, the Racing Champions holding company produces such popular brands in die-cast collecting as Ertl Preschool, American Muscle, Agriculture and Construction, AMT Model Kits, Racing Champions, Press Pass, and Wm. Britains. The key to Racing Champions' success has been quality, attention to detail, and licensing agreements, most notably from the National Association for Stock Car Auto Racing (NASCAR).

### Seeing Opportunity in a Growing Sport

Robert Dods, met Boyd Meyer in the 1980s when Dods was a sales representative for several toy manufacturers, and Meyer was a buyer for a chain of five-and-dime stores. The two men eventually formed a partnership, Dods-Meyer, Ltd., to serve as an agency representing manufacturers in the sale of product lines to mass merchandisers.

Soon Dods and Meyer were looking beyond the partnership to create a product of their own. As racing fans, both men were aware of the surging popularity of the sport, especially in the NASCAR racing circuit. They also knew that race fans were loyal, buying and collecting merchandise endorsed by their favorite drivers. Looking for an untapped market, the men decided to go into the die-cast collectible area. First they had to decide where and how to make the cars, and then they had to secure licensing agreements with NASCAR and with individual drivers.

Overseeing the manufacturing side of the business, Dods traveled to Hong Kong and set up agreements with local entrepreneurs to have the cars made in China. By 1994, Racing Champions had an office in Hong Kong with 40 employees in engineering, graphic design, shipping, and quality control. The cars were made at 11 manufacturing sites in China.

Arranging licensing deals was a little tougher. Sanctioning bodies, such as NASCAR, had to be convinced to sign with Dods and Meyer first. Then the fledgling company had to approach car owners and drivers, automobile manufacturers (such as Ford and General Motors), and corporate sponsors. Ultimately Dods and Meyer were successful, making their case and signing exclusive deals with NASCAR, Indycar, World of Outlaws sprint cars, and IROC (International Race of Champions). The deals not only enabled the company to approach the drivers but also added credibility to their pitch.

Auto makers were next up, as Racing Champions needed permission to duplicate the cars driven by the race teams. Corporate sponsors were then pitched, enabling Racing Champions to duplicate the corporate decals on the cars, which made them authentic and collectible.

Once Racing Champions had the manufacturing and licensing deals in place, Dods and Meyer turned their attention to distribution. Both men had years of contacts in the industry built up, and distribution to retail outlets, such as departments stores, toy stores, hobby shops, and discount stores, were quickly set.

### Vintage Replicas and Special Cars in the 1990s

Not long after Racing Champions began business, Richard Petty, the so-called King of NASCAR, drove in what was to be his final season. In 1992, the Richard Petty farewell tour was a boon to Racing Champions, which made 30 different die-cast cars to commemorate each of the 30 races during the 1992 NASCAR season. Racing Champions sold over one million Richard Petty cars that season. Seeing how fans reacted so positively to the Richard Petty cars, Racing Champions began offering a line of vintage die-cast cars, to capitalize on the popularity of some of NASCAR's past stars. The company made replicas of 1970 Plymouth Superbird driven by Richard Petty as well as Cale Yarborogh's 1969 Ford Talledega.

Racing Champions signed a deal with Ford Motor Company in early 1999 to build a collection of 1:18 scale cars. Called the Ford Precision Collection, the cars would reflect Ford's history in the automobile market, beginning with the 1964 Mustang in the third quarter of 2000. The die-cast models were to be sold through some Ford dealerships, hobby stores, and specialty retailers, with a new car released every quarter through Ford's 100th anniversary in 2003. Racing Champions hoped to go beyond the anniversary year, continuing to release a new model every quarter until the company produced 100 different models.

### Collectibles for the Masses

As many people associated collectibles with high prices and specialty stores, Racing Champions believed in the niche market for mass-produced, mass-merchandised collectibles. Thus, in addition to producing die-cast cars for use mainly as children's toys, the company produced limited-edition, yet inexpensive, collectible models every year. In racing, drivers changed teams and teams changed sponsors frequently, so Racing Champions offered an inexpensive means by which fans could keep pace with their favorites. Moreover, Racing Champions did not limit itself to the production of racing-sanctioned die-cast models; its die-casts also sported the images of popular cartoon and television characters and theme-based cars, appealing to collectors from a broad range of interests.

Research indicated that the market for Racing Champions products ranged from three years to 90 years, the prime collecting age range being 35–64. As the demand for inexpensive collectibles grew, so too did available floor and shelf space in mass-market retail stores. In 1996 the die-cast car and replica model market rose 28.7 percent, accounting for $513.5 million of the $9.1 billion adult collecting market.

According to Racing Champions, the key to retaining the adult market was to constantly offer new merchandise. Toward that end, the company seized opportunities to offer new prod-

ucts based on well-publicized anniversaries, farewell tours, and changes in drivers/sponsors. The company also created a demand among collectors by limiting the number of die casts it issued for each model, particular with its series of models commemorating NASCAR's 50th anniversary.

### Increasing Competition in the Late 1990s

In 1996, Racing Champions was still a private Illinois company, while foreign operations were overseen by Racing Champions Ltd. in Hong Kong. In April of that year, a group of investors joined with the Chicago-based venture capital firm Willis Stein & Partners LP in arranging a $96 million recapitalization of the company. This resulted in the Delaware incorporation of Racing Champions as a holding company for the concern's foreign and domestic operations. Under the new arrangement, the investor group retained a 54.4 percent stake in the company, while management, including founders Dods and Meyer, held a combined 45.6 percent share. The following year, Racing Champions was ready to make an initial public offering (IPO) on the New York Stock Exchange.

Just as management was taking Racing Champions public, two large toy makers decided to enter the racing replica market. Industry giants Hasbro, Inc. and Mattel, Inc., for example, noted the enormous increase in demand for both die-cast toys and the scale models favored by collectors. Hasbro entered into an agreement with Action Performance Companies, Inc., one of Racing Champions competitors, to create a line of Hasbro die-cast cars for mass-market retailers.

Competition in the market was not just over shelf space at retail chains. Perhaps more importantly, die-cast car makers competed for licensing agreements, and during this time, Racing Champions met with further challenge by Action Performance over exclusive contracts with drivers. Racing Champions had a licensing deal with popular driver and Winston Cup champion Jeff Gordon, but this deal expired in September 1995, and he eventually signed with Action Performance. Moreover, the equally-popular driver Dale Earnhardt went with Action Performance as well; Racing Champions' rival had long-term agreements with NASCAR's most popular drivers. Unquestionably, not being able to produce replicas of NASCAR's two most popular drivers hurt Racing Champions.

Nevertheless, Racing Champions enjoyed strong sales, particularly in 1988. With NASCAR celebrating it's 50th year, Racing Champions had a host of commemorative cars and other memorabilia ready for the collectors market. Once following year, however, the market dipped, as Racing Champions found the demand for its products weakening. Analysts suggested that collectors had gorged themselves during NASCAR's anniversary year. Moreover, the anticipated release of the new "Star Wars" movie as well as the mania for the Pokéman animated characters had collectors' money diverted towards other products.

To bolster its sales and reputation, in April 1999, Racing Champions made an acquisition, purchasing The Ertl Company of Dyersville, Iowa, from U.S. Industries, Inc. Ertl, a 50-year-old company specializing in farm-related toys, die-casts, and model kits, was larger than its purchaser, with about $25 million

## Key Dates:

**1989:** Racing Champions is founded.
**1996:** Company introduces a line of custom and classic vehicle collectible die-cast models.
**1998:** Company produces a new line of die-cast replicas to be sold exclusively through hobby shops; Wheels Sports Group, Inc., is acquired and renamed Racing Champions South, Inc.
**1999:** The Ertl Company is acquired and renamed Racing Champions Ertl, Inc.

more in sales than Racing Champions in 1998. While Racing Champions thus added the popular Ertl brand name to its holdings, it also gained in the deal that company's manufacturing facilities in Mexico, which incurred relatively high production costs. Racing Champions soon planned to shut down the Mexican plant and move production of Ertl products to Racing Champions manufacturing plants in China and Hong Kong.

Revenues at Racing Champions for 1999 had increased some 47.9 percent over the previous year. However, net income had plunged dramatically, as the company took a $6.4 million restructuring charge against earnings to help defray the cost of the Ertl acquisition. Wall Street took notice of the earnings reversal, and Racing Champions stock dropped from $17.88 per share in the second quarter of 1999 to just $3.56 per share in the fourth quarter. With shareholders wondering just what had happened to the lucrative company, a lawsuit was filed against the company by a New York law firm, alleging misrepresentation and breach of fiduciary duty. By the third quarter of 1999, Racing Champions found itself the target of takeover bids. Tower Hill Holdings reportedly made an offer, but then withdrew it when it wasn't welcomed; then the Enna Corporation made an offer that was also rejected by Racing Champions' board of directors.

In an effort to reverse the downward trend, Racing Champions management planned to reduce the company's dependency on mass retailers, by selling only 45 percent of its merchandise through the retailers. The rest of Racing Champions merchandise was slated for sale through specialty stores and directly to the customer via a revamped web site. The company signed an agreement with the Bradford Exchange in mid-1990, allowing Racing Champions to sell new collectibles via direct-response advertising.

In 2000, Racing Champions entered the market for a hot new product on the collectors market: memorabilia cards. Offering more than just a picture of a sports hero and a list of his stats, the most coveted among these trading cards were actually embed-

ded with a memento, for example, a piece of a player's uniform or a small piece of a game ball; the valuable cards were then randomly inserted in packs of regular trading cards. Collectors bought entire packs, hoping to be lucky enough to find a memorabilia card. Naturally, the memorabilia cards were difficult to make, requiring precision cutting and application by hand of the actual memento, which was typically less than one-inch square. Racing Champions made the trading cards, including memorabilia cards, under its Press Pass brand name.

As Racing Champions entered a new century, the market for collectibles in general, and die-casts as well, remained soft. However, with part of its reputation staked on the enduring appeal of NASCAR and its loyal fan base, and part on the expanded product lines brought to the company by the Ertl acquisition, the company remained optimistic. Responding to industry trends, as well as successfully integrating the operations of the newly acquired Ertl, offered Racing Champions some challenges in the early 2000s.

### *Principal Subsidiaries*

Racing Champions Inc.; Racing Champions Ertl, Inc.; Racing Champions Ltd. (Hong Kong); Racing Champions International Ltd.; Racing Champions South, Inc.

### *Principal Competitors*

Action Performance, Inc.; Hasbro, Inc.; Mattel, Inc.

### *Further Reading*

Cummings, Randy, "Action Packs," *Boys' Life*, July 2000, p.56.
"Ertl Adds Muscle," *Car Craft*, July 2000, p. 22.
Fitzgerald, Kate, "Racing Champions Corp.; Rank: 133," *Crain's Chicago Business*, June 7, 2000, p.74.
Jacobson, Jim, "Illinois Firm to Acquire Iowa's Ertl Toy Company, Inc.," *Cedar Rapids Gazette*, February 8, 1999.
Mandernach, Mark, "Their Race Cars Are Way Out In Front," *Chicago Tribune*, January 30, 1994.
"Margin Magic: Collectibles," *Discount Store News*, February 9, 1998, p. 63.
Mateja, Jim, "Ford Puts Focus On Production Boost," *Chicago Tribune*, March 9, 2000.
Merrion, Paul, "No Checkered Flags Yet for Toy Car Maker," *Crain's Chicago Business*, March 31, 1997, p. 4.
Murphy, H. Lee, "Flying Under Radar: Fewer Options; Financing Alternatives Shrink When a Stock Dips Below $5," *Crain's Chicago Business*, June 19, 2000, p. 17.
——, "Second Quarter Skid Puts Dent in Racing Champions' Stock: Collectibles Firm Hopes New Lines Put It Back On Track," *Crain's Chicago Business*, September 20, 1999, p. 51.

—Lisa Musolf Karl

# Razorfish, Inc.

**107 Grand Street, 3rd Floor**
**New York, New York 10013**
**U.S.A.**
**Telephone: (212) 966-5960**
**Fax: (212) 966-6915**
**Web site: http://www.razorfish.com**

*Public Company*
*Incorporated:* 1995
*Employees:* 1,355
*Sales:* $179.2 million (1999)
*Stock Exchanges:* NASDAQ
*Ticker Symbol:* RAZF
*NAIC:* 541512 Computer Systems Design

Created out of an apartment in the East Village of New York City in 1995, Razorfish, Inc. is a leading internet consulting company that in its brief history has expanded into a global concern through an aggressive pattern of acquisitions and mergers. A separate entity, Razorfish Studios, was created to develop new media products—such as Web sites, screensavers, and Internet games—as well as old media products such as books, films, and music. The start-up went public in 1999, quickly becoming a darling of investors. The company's stock actually soared to such incredible heights that Razorfish was once valued at more than $4 billion, before a market correction and other concerns about the company in 2000 sent the stock plummeting. Despite such setbacks, in the beginning of the new millennium, Razorfish was one of the few internet companies that could actually boast that it had turned a profit.

### A 1994 Chance Encounter Leads to Razorfish

Razorfish founders Jeffrey Dachis and Craig Kanarick were childhood friends in Minneapolis. Kanarick studied computer science at the University of Pennsylvania and earned a Masters degree in visual studies from the Massachusetts Institute of Technology, but Dachis took a less obvious path to becoming a new media mogul. He studied dance and dramatic literature at SUNY-Purchase in New York, and then earned a Masters degree from the college of education at New York University. His background in business was limited to his childhood, when he reportedly broke up packs of Bubble Yum to sell the individual pieces to classmates at a profit, as well as later scalping tickets to University of Minnesota football games. Dachis dabbled as an actor, disc jockey, and model. He then ventured into "guerrilla-marketing" when he founded In Your Face, an events firm.

In his late twenties, Dachis was freelancing at a record company in 1994 when he ran into Kanarick on a Manhattan street corner. Kanarick showed him the Mosaic Web browser, the first viable graphic interface to the internet. Before Mosaic, the only way users could navigate the internet was through a text-only environment using arcane programming language. The possibilities of combining pictures, text, and sound excited Dachis. "After that," he was quoted as saying, "it was sort of a zealot-like focus. The revolution was about to happen, and we were not going to miss it."

Dachis and Kanarick mapped out their plan for a business on a napkin while sitting in the kitchen of Dachis's East Village apartment. Their concept, according to Dachis, "was a mixture of some technology, some business modeling, some one-on-one direct marketing communications, and some branding and visual identity." Supposedly the two partners coined the company's name by randomly selecting words from a dictionary, as well as other forms of brainstorming. Dachis went to the bank with a list of ten possible names and only decided on Razorfish when he opened the company's checking account.

Working out of Dachis's apartment, Razorfish began to do freelance Web design work, although on occasion Dachis had to wait tables to pay the bills. It was when Razorfish created Blue Dot—an online art gallery, which Dachis said was done "for our souls" rather than direct commercial gain—that the company really began to take off. Using a beta version of Macromedia's Shockwave software, the site utilized visual effects that were a radical departure from what the Web had been offering. Razorfish attracted the attention of Omnicom Group. The New York advertising organization bought a stake in the start-up, allowing the company to set up shop in a SoHo loft. Dachis served as CEO for Razorfish, and Kanarick as chief scientist.

The company's first major project was a $20,000 assignment to create a virtual garden for the New York Botanical Society, commissioned by Time-Warner's Pathfinder business unit. From the beginning, Razorfish went beyond providing mere graphic design. The site was, in essence, an experimental e-business that allowed Time-Life to sell its list of gardening books.

After generating sales of $300,000 in 1995, Razorfish took in $1.2 million in 1996 and earned a profit of $300,000, a feat that precious few internet start-ups could claim. The company also brought attention to the creative work being done in the fast growing "Silicon Alley" section of Manhattan. Razorfish quickly outpaced Agency.com, the leading internet advertising agency at the time. Its list of powerful clients included CBS, IBM, America Online, Charles Schwab & Co., and Sony. After posting sales of $3.6 million in 1997, Razorfish was poised for even more rapid growth.

### 1998: Razorfish Goes National, then Global

In the late 1990s, Razorfish was at a crossroads: to keep pace with demand for its services, the company either had to hire new talent or acquire it. Razorfish chose the latter course, and was systematic in its approach to expansion. First, it solidified its position in New York City by merging with Avalanche Systems. Avalanche could also boast brand name clients—Cosmopolitan, Warner Music Group, and Carnegie Hall, among others—but it was an independent shop that was finding it increasingly more difficult to survive in an environment in which its competitors were partly owned by larger conglomerates. With great expectations, in September 1997 Avalanche had moved into larger offices, and had then overspent its budget on several projects which forced it to lay off staffers. Other disenchanted employees soon left the troubled company, and Avalanche began to field offers from potential suitors. Razorfish made the highest offer, instantly gaining a reputation as a player to watch. The move more than doubled the size of Razorfish's staff, to approximately 150, and increased its revenue by 400 percent.

In May 1998, Razorfish gained a presence in the Silicon Valley market by acquiring the San Francisco-based Plastic, an interactive ad agency. Via the newly named "Razorfish San Francisco" office, clients Joe Boxer, Computer City, and Microsoft were added to the fold. Later that month, Razorfish staked a claim overseas by acquiring London-based CHBi, another interactive agency whose clients included British Aerospace and Virgin Cola. While allowing the company to better serve its multinational clients, the move also provided Razorfish with a gateway to the rest of Europe.

Two months later, Razorfish continued its rapid growth by tapping into the entertainment and media clients of Los Angeles by purchasing Tag Media and its ten full-time staff members—and by renaming it "Razorfish Los Angeles." Tag had gained notice by creating a parallel web show of FOX's "The Visitor." Tag CEO and president Richard D. Titus had been approached by other agencies, but went with Razorfish because he believed Dachis shared his vision of parallel media on the Web. Clearly, Razorfish was positioning itself for a future role that would transcend the confines of a graphics company or interactive advertising agency. Tag also brought with it more traditional business. Its roster of clients included NASA, Intel, and Metropolis Entertainment—the producer of such major films as *Independence Day* and *Godzilla*.

The following month, Razorfish made its biggest acquisition with the addition of Spray, a Stockholm-based interactive agency with offices throughout Scandinavia as well as in Germany. The move made Razorfish a truly global business, with more than half of its 350 employees located in Europe. Razorfish and Spray had already enjoyed a working relationship throughout the brief history of both companies, having conducted an exchange program in which every six months two employees traded places. Aside from adding more prominent clients, such as Ericsson and Nokia, the acquisition of Spray also made sense for Razorfish on a financial level. Europe already boasted the highest internet usage in the world, and the potential for future business on the continent was tremendous. Furthermore, with the national monetary systems of Europe poised to complete a transition to the Euro currency by 2000, the exchange rate for the dollar was considered advantageous for U.S. buyers. It was also expected that the adoption of the Euro would stabilize markets.

### Razorfish goes Public in 1999

In April 1999 Razorfish made an initial public offering of its stock. After completing what was described as a seventy-one stop IPO road show, Razorfish raised $48 million at $16 a share. Trading on the NASDAQ Stock Market, Razorfish stock exceeded a price of $80 within seven months, a period during which many internet start-ups achieved values completely out of keeping with their earnings. Sales in 1998 for Razorfish were $13.8 million, but the company showed no profit after its spree of acquisitions. Sales then ballooned to $170 million in 1999, but the company posted a loss of $14.5 million as it continued to expand at an incredible pace and solidify its reputation as a cutting edge company.

Razorfish Studios began to produce traditional media products in 1999 when it published a book of photographs by Danny Clinch, featuring famous musicians, titled *Discovery Inn.* Razorfish also delved into music by releasing an album, Ticklah's *Polydemic,* which could be purchased over the Web as a CD, vinyl LP, or mp3 file, or in traditional stores as a CD or LP.

Generally regarded as a Web graphics and advertising agency, Razorfish now rejected the limitations of such a definition. According to Dachis, "The agency of the future isn't an agency. The agency model doesn't provide the strategic benefit that it should and could." Razorfish preferred to view its primary business as helping a client to establish a brand in an

## Key Dates:

**1995:** Razorfish formed, working out of New York apartment.
**1996:** Funding from Omnicom Group allows Razorfish to move to SoHo loft.
**1998:** Avalanche Systems becomes first major acquisition.
**1998:** Razorfish goes global with acquisition of Swedish company, Spray.
**1999:** Razorfish makes initial public offering of its stock.

increasingly digital world, either in traditional or new media. To bolster that position, Razorfish continued to acquire properties in 1999. It purchased Santa Monica-based broadcast design firm Fuel and its commercial production arm Tonga, bringing to Razorfish traditional production and broadcast design capabilities. It also bought I-Cube—a Cambridge, Massachusetts company—to provide back-end Web expertise, the technical support that drives a Web business, which is invisible to the consumer on the front end. Rather than merely designing a client's Web site, Razorfish could now offer what Dachis called "end-to-end solutions."

The company also opened a laboratory in Helsinki to research and develop wireless applications. Wireless, already with deep penetration in Europe, promised the potential of huge growth in the United States. All of these strategic acquisitions positioned Razorfish to promote a client's brand across platforms, whether that be over the broadcast medium of television, print, on the internet via broadband, or through wireless devices such as cell phones, hand held computers, or future laptop computers.

Razorfish also positioned itself to provide content that could be delivered across these platforms. No possibility for future applications was dismissed. For example, Razorfish worked with CIEOS, a New Jersey consulting firm, to develop a flat-panel display screen that could be held on the lap of dental patients, to allow them to watch pay-per-view movies or surf the Web while having work done on their teeth. The dentist would also be able to show the progress of the work on a similar screen.

In addition to its vision of a digital future, Razorfish was also gaining a reputation in other areas. Like many other internet companies, it embraced a non-traditional work culture that critics called cult-like and others called fun. Instead of traditional business cards that measure 3.5 inches across by 2 inches down, Razorfish turned to cards that measured 1.5 inches across by 3.5 inches down. Employees were encouraged to bring their dogs to work. The company shut down operations for a weekend so that 1,200 employees could fly to Las Vegas for a three-day party it called a FishFry. The company spent another three days whitewater rafting in Oregon.

Razorfish also gained a reputation as arrogant. It was reported to turn away half of the customers that approached the company because of a "wrong fit." At a time when labor was hard to find, Razorfish rejected 80 percent of its job applicants for similar reasons. Clients were also showing some concerns about the company. Joe Boxer discontinued its e-commerce business, after executives complained that Razorfish had failed to meet deadlines.

Investors' euphoria over internet companies in general began to wane in 2000. Many, like Razorfish, were so inflated in value that analysts were not surprised when on April 14, 2000, the NASDAQ lost 355 points. Although Razorfish stock began a steady decline, the company continued its aggressive pattern of growth. In the first half of 2000, Razorfish opened offices in Melbourne, Australia and Milan, Italy, as well as expanding its Mobile Solutions units to all of its European offices to take advantage of the expanding mobile Internet business. In August 2000, Razorfish acquired the German e-business company Medialab. In September the company opened an office in Chicago, despite the level of competition heavily entrenched in the market.

Throughout much of 2000, rumors swirled around president Michael Pehl, who had joined the company after selling I-Cube to Razorfish. The *Wall Street Journal* reported that former Razorfish employees suggested that Pehl did not mesh with other top managers. What was certain, however, was that in February he had begun to sell off shares of Razorfish stock. When he announced in August that he was leaving the company to spend more time with his family, he had cashed in $6 million worth of stock. Shares immediately dropped 6 percent, and investors expressed concerns about the company's stability.

The price of Razorfish stock continued to slide as autumn arrived. When in early October the company announced that it expected lower than projected third-quarter earnings because of a seasonal impact in Europe and a strong dollar, the stock plunged another 40 percent, dipping below $5 a share. Razorfish, however, was still much better off than most internet companies. The steep decline in the NASDAQ forced many start-ups to cut staff or to simply cease operations altogether. Razorfish was now worth only a fraction of the $4 billion it had been worth only months earlier, but it remained a global company with many assets ready to take advantage of a rapidly changing media landscape. Considering that the company was only six years removed from its origins in an un air-conditioned East Village apartment, Razorfish remained a huge success story.

### Principal Subsidiaries

Razorfish San Francisco; Razorfish Los Angeles; Spray Media Agency; Razorfish Studios.

### Principal Competitors

Agency.com; IXL Enterprises; MarchFIRST.

### Further Reading

"Australian Entertainment Nets Hook Razorfish," *News Bytes News Network,* April 12, 2000.
Bunn, Austin, "Bigger Fish," *Village Voice,* December 23, 1997, p. 31.
Doyle, T.C., "Inside the Fish," *VAR Business,* February 7, 2000, p. 13.
——, "Masters of the E-Channel," *VAR Business,* June 7, 1999, p. 46.
——, "New Economy, New Culture," *VAR Business,* July 10, 2000, p. 26.
Feuerstein, Adam, "Hollywood Deal Clears Way to 'Reel.com: The Sequel,'" *San Francisco Business Times,* August 14, 1998, p. 11.

Germain, Arthur H., III, ''Razorfish Ignites a Powerhouse,'' *VARBusiness,* August 16, 1999, p. 11.

Gilbert, Jennifer, ''Agencies Eye Potential in Wireless Apps,'' *Advertising Age,* March 6, 2000, p. S46.

Jastrow, David, ''Razorfish Turns to Japan for Next Integrator Venture,'' *Computer Reseller News,* May 22, 2000, p. 131.

Johnsson, Julie, ''Web Developer Fishes for Biz in Busy Waters,'' *Crain's Chicago Business,* September 11, 2000, p. 6.

Kaufman, David, ''Razorfish Finds New Fish to Fry,'' *SHOOT,* May 29, 1998, p. 26.

Mand, Adrienne, ''Razorfish,'' *Adweek,* October 18, 1999, p. 88.

——, ''Razorfish Captures Tag Media,'' *Adweek,* July 27, 1998, p. 24.

——, ''Razorfish Dives into Spray, Acquiring Stockholm Shop,'' *Adweek,* August 10, 1998, p. 35.

Ostertag, Krista, ''Overseas Opportunities Abound for Start-Ups Like Razorfish,'' *VARBusiness,* August 17, 1998, p. 15.

——, ''Razorfish Bites into Another Company,'' *VARBusiness,* May 25, 1998, p. 17.

Rewick, Jennifer, ''Departure of Razorfish's President Spurs Concerns About Management's Stability,'' *Wall Street Journal,* August 28, 2000, p. B6.

Riedman, Patricia, ''Sharp Anglers,'' *Advertising Age,* October, 1996, p. 19.

Sabatini, Joanna, and Kipp Cheng, ''Razorfish,'' *Media Week,* February 14, 2000, p. 40.

''Shadowram,'' *Computer Reseller News,* June 6, 2000, p. 298.

Smith, Dawn, ''The Downtown Crowd,'' *Marketing Computers,* July/August, 1995. p. 16.

Snyder, Beth, ''Razorfish Acquires Avalanche Systems,'' *Advertising Age,* January 26, 1998, p. 38.

Snyder, Gabriel, ''Wall Street Lays an Egg,'' *The New York Observer,* October 11, 2000, p. 5.

Torode, Christina, ''The Channel Mavericks,'' *Computer Reseller News,* November 15, 1999, p. 135.

Walsh, Mark, *Crain's New York Business,* January 31, 2000, p. 20.

Woodward, Sarah, ''Fueling Convergence,'' *SHOOT,* November 19, 1999, p. 64.

——, ''Razorfish Buys Fuel, Tonga,'' *SHOOT,* July 30, 1999, p. 1.

—Ed Dinger

# RENK AG

**Gögginger Strasse 73**
**D-86159 Augsburg**
**Germany**
**Telephone: (49) (821) 5700-0**
**Fax: (49) (821) 5700-573**
**Web site: http://www.renk.de**

*Public Company*
*Incorporated:* 1873 as Mechanische Werkstatt von
    Johann Renk
*Employees:* 1,510
*Sales:* DM 442 million ($226 million) (1998–99)
*Stock Exchanges:* Frankfurt/Main
*Ticker Symbol:* RENK
*NAIC:* 333612 Speed Changer, Industrial High-Speed
    Drive, and Gear Manufacturing ; 333613 Mechanical
    Power Transmission Equipment Manufacturing; 33635
    Motor Vehicle Transmission and Power Train Parts
    Manufacturing; 336322 Other Motor Vehicle
    Electrical and Electronic Equipment Manufacturing

RENK AG is a leading German firm for the engineering and manufacture of the power transmission components, gear units, and couplings used in industry, ships, motor vehicles, and tanks. In addition to its three German production plants in Augsburg, Rheine, and Hannover, the company has production subsidiaries in France, Romania, and the United States. French subsidiary Systèmes et Mécanismes (SESM) makes gearboxes for tracked vehicles and brake systems. RENK Corporation in Duncan, Oklahoma, assembles and markets slide bearings and flexible couplings. RESITA-RENK S.A. in Romania, of which RENK holds 51 percent, makes industrial and marine gear units and rail bound vehicle transmissions. The German MAN Group owns a 76 percent share of RENK AG.

## From Mechanical Workshop to Public Company in the 1890s

Johann Julius Renk, the founder of RENK AG, was born on April 1, 1848. While a young man he worked as an apprentice at the machine-building factory Maschinenfabrik Augsburg. In 1866 Renk started working as a lathe operator at another company that manufactured machines, Maschinenfabrik L.A. Riedinger. When he was 25 years old, Renk set up his own workshop in the German town Augsburg and began making cogwheels of all kinds. He had realized that the specially shaped cogwheels that he designed ran much more smoothly than the other ordinary models available at that time. Because at the time no machines were available that could manufacture such cogwheels, Renk first concentrated on developing a machine that could do so. The current technology was to produce roughly shaped cogwheels by machine and then shape them by hand with the help of stencils, a process that was very time-consuming. In 1877, after numerous experiments, Renk constructed a machine that could manufacture conical-shaped cogwheels with teeth that were arranged in a mathematically precise way. Two years later Renk was awarded German patent DRP 8000/79 for his invention. The new machine was well received in the industry, and Renk's factory started to develop a reputation both within Germany and elsewhere. After several moves to larger sites, Renk built a new factory, which included a foundry for iron and bronze, at Göttinger Strasse.

The small factory grew quickly and worked continuously in two shifts to fill orders on time. By 1888 Renk owned machinery that included 15 self-produced plane machines for cogwheels and employed 37 people. In 1890, the foresighted entrepreneur initiated a company health care plan, and six years later, he died at the young age of 48. By that time he had built his company into a leading manufacturer of cogwheels with more than 100 employees. The annual output—some 12,000 cogwheels—was shipped to many factories that built different machines. One year after Renk died, the company was legally made a public company. Its new name was Zahnräderfabrik Augsburg, vorm. Johann Renk (Act.-Ges.).

## RENK in the First Half of the 20th Century

The business continued to grow, production facilities were expanded, and a railroad connection was established. At the same time RENK engineers developed new technologies for cogwheel manufacture. In 1916 RENK manufactured the largest gear-cutting machine of the time, a piece of equipment that

## Company Perspectives:

*In 1873, RENK was founded by Johann Renk as a gear production facility in Augsburg, the town where 20 years later Rudolf Diesel registered the patent for his engine. Years of experience and our own research work enabled us to become one of the trend-setters in power-transmission engineering. RENK is now a globally renowned manufacturer of high-grade gear units and power transmission components at several production locations and together with associated companies in Germany and abroad.*

was seven meters in diameter. In 1923 the company ceased to be independent, becoming part of the German iron works conglomerate Gutehoffnungshütte (GHH), which would later become MAN AG. However, RENK's new parent company was able to provide raw material for cogwheel production and to market them more widely. In 1926 RENK introduced a novelty: the first cogwheels with a ground tooth profile.

Beginning in 1930 RENK began manufacturing gear transmissions. The new product line soon increased its share of the company's total sales. The company's engineers designed all RENK gear transmissions. At the same time the production of cogwheels for other firms that manufactured machines became less important. However, the company advertised in one brochure that it would be willing to connect cogwheels to a functioning mechanism for any customers who preferred to submit their own wheels to RENK. The largest gear transmissions were made for turbines and steelworks.

RENK survived the World War I and the chaotic Great Depression and became a crucial supplier for the German war industry. Just before World War II began in 1939, the company made the world's fastest gear transmission—36,000 revolutions per minute—to be used in aircraft. In 1943 RENK engineers invented the principle of hydrostatic superimposition steering systems for tanks.

### RENK Writes Engineering History After World War II

In the three decades after World War II, the cogwheel remained one of the most important and most difficult elements in machine building. RENK's smallest cogwheel weighed only half a kilogram, while its heaviest weighed 35 tons. During that period, RENK engineers continuously produced innovations in the field of gear transmissions. In 1956 the company manufactured a turbine gear unit that had the highest pitch circle velocity at that time—185 meters per second. Five years later RENK developed the first electronic control system for an automatic vehicle transmission in the world. In 1965 the company introduced another pioneering technology—the hydrostatic/hydromechanical steering drive for track-laying vehicles, which made it possible to steer such vehicles just like a car. The list goes on. In 1971, the company introduced the first vehicle-braking system with a friction brake and retarder that was integrated into a vehicle gear transmission and also worked as an operating brake. RENK achieved another record in 1976: as

the world's first drive system manufacturer, the company was able to harden and grind gear wheels that measured more than 30 meters in diameter. All these achievements in research and development were made possible by RENK's ongoing efforts to lead the industry. One of the company's main research focuses was on securely running gear transmissions that produced little noise pollution. To optimize the geometry of its toothed wheels, RENK established as early as the 1970s a test laboratory and used computer-aided calculation and design methods. The company worked also closely with German technical universities.

In the 1970s RENK offered three main product lines. The first was turbo gear transmissions and "Planetengetriebe" for heavy industry use. They were used in turbines for power production in factories, refineries, cement mills, facilities of the chemical industry, pumps, and water power stations. For industrial use the importance of standard gear transmissions faded while the market called for more and more customized solutions. One of the biggest gear transmissions RENK ever made for a steelworks weighed as much as 180 tons. It was connected to four electric motors and contained two transmission units with two gears each.

RENK's second hallmark was its gear transmissions for ships. For fast and slender container ships running on a diesel motor, RENK manufactured so-called "Planetengetriebe." Bigger, slower container ships ran on RENK two-motor transmissions. To optimize the power supply on ships, the company included so-called power-take-off's that enabled the use as electricity on board of some of the energy produced by the ship motors. This was even possible when the ship's propeller shaft wasn't moving, which was especially useful in harbors when freight, such as oil, needed to be moved with the help of huge pumps.

The third major market for RENK was special gear transmissions for track-laying vehicles such as tanks, which were manufactured in serial production. In addition to these three main areas RENK also made gear transmissions for the electronic manipulation of radio telescopes and huge satellite dishes. Because electronics was becoming more and more important in gear transmission technology, RENK ventured into that area. The result was the "RENK Checker," an electronic control system for gear transmissions that could, for example, be integrated into a ship's central control system.

In 1974, Willy-Werner Schwarz, who had served at RENK's Executive Management Board from 1947 on and as the company's CEO since 1971, resigned. In 1975 the company took a chance and acquired the slide bearings and coupling division of Hannover-based Eisenwerke Wülfel. That marked the end of RENK's post-war period.

### Reorganization and International Expansion in the 1980s

A decade later RENK entered a period of reorganization. The market for marine and industrial gear transmissions had changed. Industrial construction was not flourishing as much as it had during the reconstruction and economic boom years. Ship building as an industry had migrated to Asia. Over-capacities in both markets led to fierce price competition. To be able to compete, RENK spun off its industrial and marine gear division and organized it under the umbrella of the new RENK TACKE

## Key Dates:

**1873:** Johann Renk founds a mechanical workshop in Augsburg, Germany.
**1897:** Company becomes an Aktiengesellschaft (public company).
**1916:** Renk builds the then-largest gear-cutting machine, which is seven meters in diameter.
**1923:** The company is acquired by the German GHH concern.
**1961:** RENK develops the world's first electronic control system for an automatic vehicle transmission.
**1986:** RENK TACKE GmbH takes over the industrial and marine gear transmissions division.
**1987:** Company becomes RENK AG.
**1998:** RENK AG forms partnership with German manufacturer ZF Friedrichshafen AG.

GmbH, in partnership with German manufacturer F. Tacke KG, in 1986. In the same year a new division was founded to pursue the growing market for control and test systems for motor vehicle manufacturers. In 1987 the entire company was re-named RENK Aktiengesellschaft. It had three remaining product divisions: automatic vehicle transmissions, drive elements and test systems. To reduce its dependence on orders from the German military, RENK developed prototypes of gear transmissions for heavy vehicles such as fire engines, special transport vehicles and heavy construction vehicles.

As early as 1973 RENK had founded a joint venture in Eastern Europe, RESITA-RENK S.A. in Romania, in which the company held a 49 percent share. In 1980 RENK founded their first subsidiary overseas—RENK Corporation, based in Duncan, Oklahoma—which mainly assembled and distributed components for bus and other heavy road vehicle transmissions, such as "Doromat," its automatic gear transmission for city buses. By 1988 RENK was also present in the United Kingdom, Spain, Switzerland, and South Africa. In 1989 RENK acquired a 90 percent stake in French gear transmission manufacturer Société Européenne d'Enprenages (SEE), based in Sens.

### Struggling in the 1990s

RENK's entrance into the 1990s was a bumpy one. Caused first by stagnating demand from defense and international markets and then by another company reorganization program enacted in 1990, sales dropped by over 9 percent. At the same time, severance payments and money for the company's pension funds to finance early retirement, among other factors, put higher financial strain on the company. However, parent company MAN subsidized RENK and the company kept its independent shareholders happy with a dividend. In the following years RENK continued to produce losses, but managed to lower them significantly. For fiscal year 1992–93, the company was DM 2 million in the red, one year later it reported a slight profit, but carried losses from the previous years into that period, ending up with DM 31 million in losses on its balance sheet. One of the consequences was the reduction of RENK AG's work force by 15 percent in 1992–93 and by another three percent the following

year. In fiscal year 1994–95, RENK managed to pull out of the red, reporting a small profit of DM 5.8 million from DM 349 million in total sales. It was the first year in the 1990s that RENK was not subsidized by its parent company. Orders started increasing again that year, spurred by an upswing in the economic cycle, including rising demand from the military. In October 1995, CEO Heinz-Ludwig Schmitz left the company to become CEO of German Kloeckner-Werke AG. Dr. Manfred Hirt became the new speaker of RENK's Executive Board while Ulrich Sauter, former director at MAN's B&W Diesel AG, joined RENK's Executive Management Board.

The second half of the 1990s didn't look much brighter for RENK. At that time, the company's French subsidiaries reported losses of DM 12 million, and RENK once again ended up with a loss on its 1995–96 balance sheet. However, the company's fate seemed to turn around again in the late 1990s. Beginning in its 125th anniversary year, RENK started producing profits again and was able to pay back its debt to its parent company MAN. In fiscal year 1998–99 RENK paid its shareholders their first dividend in seven years. During the same period the company sold off one of its French subsidiaries, Société Européenne d'Engrenages (SEE), a manufacturer of small gear transmissions for ships and brake pads for rail vehicles, to Padua, Italy-based ZF Marine. RENK's Romanian subsidiary didn't seem to promise many business opportunities for the future, and RENK questioned it's further involvement in the country.

As the 1990s ended, RENK's future prospects again looked promising. In fiscal year 1998–99, the vehicle transmission division received three major orders from abroad. The Spanish Army ordered over 200 gear transmissions for its "Leopard 2" tanks, a contract worth DM 150 million. RENK's French subsidiary SESM received an order for 90 transmissions to be built into the French "Leclerc" tanks. Another DM 44 million order came from Austria for transmissions used for medium-duty track-laying vehicles. To secure its leadership in the field of military vehicle transmissions, RENK signed an contract with ZF Friedrichshafen AG, another German manufacturer in that market. As part of the deal, the companies agreed to exchange their respective product lines.

RENK's marine gear division also received a rising number of orders, the result of the fact that demand for mechanical gear units was not depressed by increased use of diesel-electric propulsion units, as had been forecast. RENK's products were still built into diesel and gas turbine-powered high-speed ferries. Demand for industrial gear units was driven by a growing market for gas turbine- and wind-powered energy generators, especially in the United States. Another promising sign was the large number of new orders for the testing rigs division, especially from the commercial vehicles sector and helicopter manufacturers. Due to a new wave of automation in the automobile industry, the use of testing rigs was expected to grow further. Another prospective market for testing rigs was the testing of high-speed railroad vehicles.

### Principal Divisions

Vehicle Transmissions Division; Drive Elements Division; Marine Gear Units Division; Industrial Gear Units Division; Couplings Division; Testing Rigs Division.

### Principal Subsidiaries

Société d' Equipements, Systèmes et Mécanismes (SESM) (France); RENK Corporation; RESITA-RENK S.A. (Romania; 51%).

### Principal Competitors

Preussag AG; A Friedr Flender AG; Johann A Krause Maschinenfabrik GmbH; Lohmann and Stolterfoht GmbH.

### Further Reading

*100 Jahre RENK*, Augsburg, Germany: Zahnräderfabrik RENK Aktiengesellschaft, Augsburg, 1973.

''Die Mutter muss Renk unter die Arme greifen,'' *Süddeutsche Zeitung*, October 23, 1991.

''Die Renk AG kann auf den Mutterschutz verzichten,'' *Süddeutsche Zeitung*, October 31, 1995.

''Ergebnissprung bei Renk,'' *Frankfurter Allgemeine Zeitung*, September 2, 1999, p. 29.

''Getriebehersteller Renk wieder mit Verlusten,'' *Süddeutsche Zeitung*, November 30, 1996.

''Jahresüberschuss für Getriebehersteller Renk,'' *Frankfurter Allgemeine Zeitung*, October 4, 1995, p. 23.

''Renk arbeitet wieder rentabel,'' *Frankfurter Allgemeine Zeitung*, September 1, 1998, p. 25.

''Renk-Getriebe arbeiten sich aus den roten Zahlen,'' *Süddeutsche Zeitung*, October 17, 1994.

''Renk verringert den Verlust,'' *Frankfurter Allgemeine Zeitung*, October 19, 1993, p. 25.

—Evelyn Hauser

# Rock of Ages Corporation

772 Graniteville Road
Graniteville, Vermont 05654
U.S.A.
Telephone: (802) 476-3121
Toll Free: (800) 875-7353
Fax: (802) 476-3110
Web site: www.rockofages.com

*Public Company*
*Incorporated:* 1885
*Employees:* 1,078
*Sales:* $96.52 million (1999)
*Stock Exchanges:* NASDAQ
*Ticker Symbol:* ROAC
*NAIC:* 327991 Cut Stone and Stone Product
    Manufacturing

Rock of Ages Corporation is an integrated quarrier, manufacturer, distributor, and retailer of granite and products manufactured from granite. The company owns and operates 13 active quarry properties and ten manufacturing and sawing facilities in North America, principally in Vermont, Georgia, and the Province of Quebec. The quarry division sells granite blocks to the manufacturing division and outside manufacturers as well as to distributors in Europe and Japan. The principal manufactured product is granite memorials, which the company's sales force sells wholesale to approximately 2,100 independent memorial retailers in the United States and Canada. Rock of Ages is widely recognized for its personalized granite memorials and for the very large memorials it can produce. The retail division primarily sells granite, bronze, and marble memorials directly to consumers. Rock of Ages operates 100 company-owned, retail-sales outlets in 15 states. The company markets its memorials under four separate brand names: Rock of Ages Signature, Rock of Ages Sealmark, Golden Rule by Rock of Ages, and Stone Eternal by Rock of Ages. A seal bearing the Rock of Ages name is placed on each of the branded memorials, which are supported by a perpetual warranty. The company believes that its Rock of Ages trademark is one of the oldest and best-known brand names in the granite memorialization industry.

## The Birth of Granite to the Birth of an Industry

According to the theories expressed in Rod Clarke's *Carved in Stone: A History of the Barre Granite Industry*, the story of Rock of Ages granite goes back to shortly after the dawn of time, millions of years ago, when planet earth was "a swirling mass of gas and liquid hurtling through the cosmos." The new planet shrank as it cooled, building up enormous pressure at its core and forming an outer crust. During this process—in a complex succession of violent contractions—pent-up gasses and rocks rose to form the surface of the earth while the molten rock deep in the earth's core continued to cool and solidify to form granite (igneous rock), marble (metamorphic rock) and sedimentary rock. Marbles of many kinds were created when pre-existing rocks underwent changes (that is, metamorphosed) brought on by intense heat and pressure. "The mountains of New England, born about 500 million years ago, were among the first to be formed," wrote Clarke. Then during the Ice Age, about 25,000 years ago, rain and the ice sheets wore off the higher points of the mountains and exposed the granite that had been formed possibly two billion years before.

Todd Paton, in his 1992 edition of *The Rock of Ages Story*, noted that the Massachusetts Institute of Technology estimated Rock of Ages granite to be approximately 340 million years old. He quoted geologists as estimating the deposit of Barre granite "to be four miles long, one to two miles wide, and ten miles deep." Crystallized grains of granite—formed from the slow melting of the molten substance during the prehistoric period—assembled into the "interlocking network of crystals that gave Barre granite its hard, uniformly granular texture, capable of enduring centuries of exposure to the elements without crumbling," Paton explained. Indeed, Barre granite was a hard, durable substance that had been exposed to the vicissitudes of New England weather for over 10,000 years without crumbling.

By the early decades of the 19th century, Wildersburgh, Vermont—as Barre was first called—had been permanently settled by emigrants from New Hampshire, Massachusetts, and Rhode Island. The granite outcroppings that the early settlers removed from their fields were manufactured into doorsteps, fence posts, and boundary markers. Robert Parker—a veteran of the Revolutionary War and of the War of 1812—settled in Barre in 1812 and, as a professional quarryman, was quick to recognize the economic potential of Barre granite; he opened the town's first commercial quarrying and finishing business.

The most significant event in Barre's budding granite industry was a contract won by Pliny Wheaton—who had opened a quarry on Cobble Hill—to furnish Barre granite for the pillars, foundation, window caps, sills, and cornices for Vermont's new State House, completed in Montpelier in 1838. Despite this initial boost, however, the granite industry began to stagnate and then to decline because draft animals had to be gathered throughout the area to haul the chunks of granite. Rod Clarke related the story of "a massive granite block of fifty tons being moved from the 'hill' to the city on rollers at the rate of one mile a week."

### 1875–54: Transportation, Influx of Workers, New Technologies, National Markets

The transportation of granite was partially solved in June 1875 when the last spike was driven to connect Barre to the Montpelier line of the Central Vermont Railroad. Quarrymen still had to haul granite blocks from Millstone Hill down to the Barre depot. The Montpelier and Wells River Railroad offered to build a spur between the main railroad line and Millstone Hill if Barre residents bought $40,000 worth of railroad stock to fund the project. The offer was quickly accepted and filled. The "Barre Quarries Spur" (also called the "Sky Route") had a grade of 250 feet per mile from the Barre Terminus to the quarries on Millstone Hill. To solve the problem of running the rails from Barre to the Hill (1,025 feet above the town), the quarry line was built using smooth rails with switchbacks to circumvent gravity. This rail system, completed in 1888, remained in use until the 1950s, when it was replaced by trucking. The town and the granite industry were energized. News of what was going on in Barre reached master quarrymen and artisans in foreign lands.

By 1910 skilled sculptors, stonecutters, and other hopeful laborers had come from Canada, Scotland, Italy, Scandinavia, Spain, Greece, Ireland, and England—to name but a few of the emigrants' home countries—to pursue the American Dream. Barre reached a population of over 12,000 people. Among the early newcomers was George Barron Milne, a visionary Scot gifted with keen business acumen. By 1885 he had saved enough money to buy a quarry of his own and in a few years partnered with another frugal quarry owner—Montpelier-born James M. Boutwell, a railroad engineer by trade—to form a new company. The two partners recognized the engineering skills of another Vermonter, Harvey W. Varnum, who had played a key role in diverting the river that ran through Barre and in developing many railroad lines in Vermont, thereby greatly improving traveling and business opportunities. In 1905, the three men founded Boutwell, Milne and Varnum Granite Company (BMV) and, according to historian Clarke, "concen-

trated on selling their stone to local manufacturers. But they quickly recognized the need for diversification and built a large, modern plant near their quarries."

The coming of the railroad triggered the growth of the granite industry in Barre but "it was the advent of new labor-saving technologies that propelled the town headlong into the twentieth century; veteran quarryman, innovator and entrepreneur Emery L. Smith led the way," Clarke wrote. As early as 1871, Smith was the first Barre quarry operator to set up a permanent derrick by anchoring it to trees and stones on Cobble Hill. He improved the derrick by installing a gearing system that doubled its capacity to five tons. Smith also pioneered the use of electric batteries to detonate explosive charges. He put the first steam drill to use in his quarry, adopted the pneumatic plug drill, and used compressed air for drilling. Furthermore, the coming of electricity to Barre in 1885 made possible the use of power-cutting and polishing lathes, surfacing equipment, and the first band saw for cutting stone.

In 1905 there were no fewer than 42 operating quarries in Barre, owned by about two dozen firms—a few large, many small. Clarke noted that as the Barre granite industry grew, so did the number of people dying from "the occupational disease silicosis, caused by breathing large quantities of free silica contained in granite dust." A breakthrough did not occur until 1937 when dust and silicosis were put in check via $300,000 worth of ventilating equipment in 80 plants.

Initially, BVM was engaged in quarrying activities and sold its granite to manufacturers in Barre. In 1915, however, the company decided to enter national markets and turned to a Burlington advertising agency for advice on a more effective way of marketing granite. The result was the suggestion for using "Rock of Ages" as a trademark that emphasized the strength and durability of Barre granite. BMV published a small pamphlet with the picture of a monument praising the quality of Rock of Ages granite and changed the company's name to Rock of Ages Corporation in 1925. As the years sped by, new technology made it relatively less expensive to quarry and transport granite, and demand for granite increased. For example, the 1930 introduction of detachable drill bits revolutionized the drilling process by allowing for the replacement of dull bits, thereby prolonging the life of drills. Furthermore, wet-drilling methods used in the quarries protected the workers' lungs from granite dust.

In 1930 Rock of Ages acquired ten granite-manufacturing plants in Barre and began to compete with the approximately 125 monument manufacturers in that area. Then Rock of Ages launched a growth-by-acquisition strategy that led to its becoming the best-known name in the granite industry. Barre granite's uniformity of crystal structure and unique proportions of quartz and feldspar made it unusually durable, moisture-resistant, and thermally stable. This granite was—and remained—eminently suitable for family memorials and monuments. The original Rock of Ages Quarry yielded a dark shade of gray granite ideally suited for monumental use. Through the 1940–86 acquisition of four other quarries in Barre, Rock of Ages created a five-quarry complex considered to be the largest granite quarry in the world. This complex included the E.L Smith quarry where Smith had pioneered many innovations that increased the productivity of granite and helped to keep quarrymen healthy. These quarries yielded both dark-gray and light-to-medium gray Barre granite. Acquisition of the Wells-Lamson Quarry and adjacent saw plant made Rock of Ages the owner of the oldest, continually operating quarry in the United States and established it as the only granite quarrier in Barre.

### 1955–97: Expansion and Reorganizations

In 1955, the company built the Rock of Ages Craftsman Center, at that time one of the largest and most modern granite-manufacturing plants in the world. In 1956 the company purchased the Ezra White granite firm and its patent rights to the Rosary cutting process. In 1957 the Bethel, Vermont-based quarry was reactivated to provide the white stone popular as building material in western Europe and highly prized by architects. The purchase of Iberville, Quebec-based Brodie's Limited gave Rock of Ages access to pink granite; the acquisition of Beebe, Quebec-based Stanstead Granite Quarries Co., Ltd. made Rock of Ages the owner of one of the top manufacturers of granite. In 1984, the two Canadian companies were consolidated and renamed Rock of Ages Canada.

During 1969, Rock of Ages itself was purchased by Rhode-Island based Nortek, Inc., a mini-conglomerate with diversified holdings. That same year, Rock of Ages installed a custom-designed 160-foot steel derrick that allowed for the quarrying of rough granite blocks weighing over 150 tons. This was the first of many other steel derricks that replaced the wooden derricks then in use. Rock of Ages continued to upgrade its procedures; for example, use of the jet-channelling machine. The jet channeling torch used small, individual pipes to feed fuel oil and oxygen under pressure through a nozzle to create a channel in granite. A third pipe provided water as a cooling agent. When the flame of over 4,000 degrees Fahrenheit was placed near the granite to create a channel, about one-eighth inch of the granite

surface expanded and flaked away, leaving a smooth face on the sides of the channel. This method, although expensive because of the cost of the oxygen and fuel oil, was efficient, flexible and the most cost effective means of channeling and of obtaining a smooth face on the stone.

Sculptors, artists, and engravers produced many a work of art on memorials and on granite blocks used for other purposes. According to Nortek's *1975 Annual Report*, Rock of Ages "was particularly proud of the unique 27- by 30-foot bas-relief granite sculpture completed for installation on the facade of the giant Libby Dam in Montana."

During 1977, harsh winter weather severely impacted Nortek subsidiary Rock of Ages's quarrying operations but in 1979, Rock of Ages more than doubled its operating revenue to $3.7 million; net sales of $20.7 million were up 25 percent from 1978, according to an article published by the *Boston Globe* on April 20, 1980. Large investments in housing and construction, however, made Nortek vulnerable to higher prices for supplies and raw materials, rising wage levels, and other costs that severely impacted total net earnings. In 1984 Nortek sold Rock of Ages to Concord, New Hampshire-based Swenson Granite Company, Inc., a family-owned granite firm established by John Swenson in 1883, two years before the founding of Rock of Ages.

As a subsidiary of Swenson Granite, Rock of Ages acquired quarries in other states and expanded its production of granite headstones. In 1988 Rock of Ages built a 24,00 square-foot facility in Barre and produced precision granite press rolls and large machine bases. By 1991, Rock of Ages was the only granite quarrier in Barre and had purchased an interest in 14 Canadian quarries, a granite manufacturing plant in Quebec, and 14 granite quarries in the state of Georgia. In 1997, the company owned and operated 13 active quarries and 12 manufacturing and sawing facilities in North America, principally in Vermont, Georgia and the Province of Quebec. Rock of Ages marketed and distributed its memorials on a wholesale basis to some 1,835 independent memorial retailers in the United States and Canada, including approximately 495 independent authorized Rock of Ages retailers that were the primary outlet for the company's branded memorials.

### 1997–2000: Entry into Retailing

Rock of Ages estimated that in North America 80 percent or more of all granite memorials were manufactured in Barre, Vermont; Beebe, Quebec; Elverton, Georgia; and the "Northwest" (an area encompassing Milbank, South Dakota; Cold Spring, Minnesota, and Wassau, Wisconsin), Rock of Ages continued to implement its growth strategy through acquisition of additional quarries and major granite manufacturing companies in these regions. In June 1997, Rock of Ages entered into a definitive agreement to acquire Childs & Childs Granite Co., the second-largest manufacturer of granite memorials in Georgia. Then in July, Rock of Ages made its first significant entry into memorial retailing by entering into an agreement to acquire Keith Monument Co. and its affiliated companies; Keith, an authorized Rock of Ages dealer for over 50 years, was one of the largest retailers of granite memorials in the United States.

On August 13, 1997, Rock of Ages entered into a merger and reorganization agreement with Swenson Granite, whereby the name Rock of Ages Corporation was retained as the name of the company and Kurt M. Swenson, a fourth-generation descendant of John Swenson, became Rock of Ages's President and CEO. The reorganized company went public in October 1997 and was traded on NASDAQ under the symbol ROAC. Some $19 million of the proceeds from Rock of Ages' initial public offering (IPO) went to the purchase of Childs & Childs and of Keith Monument and their affiliated companies. John E. Keith, a principal owner and the president of Keith Monument, was retained to head Rock of Ages's expansion into retailing by means of other acquisitions and through strategic alliances with funeral home and cemetery owners.

For fiscal 1997, Rock of Ages posted sales of $54.21 million and net income of $2.65 million, compared to 1996's sales of $44.67 million and net income of $1.91 million.

In order to continue building a fully vertically-integrated organization, in 1998 Rock of Ages acquired 13 memorial retailers with 40 locations in eight states and additional quarries. Rock of Ages reported fiscal 1998 as an outstanding year: net sales rose to $82.75 million and net income to $7.24 million. The principal product from quarries was granite blocks of various colors: gray, black, gray, pink, white, brownish red, and grayish pink. The blocks were sold for memorials, building and other uses. Granite pieces not of a shape or size for manufacturing were sold as rip rap for embankments, bridges, or piers—among other uses—or crushed for sale as crushed stone. Rock of Ages' principal manufactured product was granite memorials sold to retailers of granite memorials. These memorials—whether markers, hickeys, slants, standard uprights or mausoleums—were placed in cemeteries. Some retailers sold other granite products, such as benches and steps, that were not necessarily placed in cemeteries. Other manufactured products included precision granite items, such as surface plates, machine bases, coordinate measuring devices, and other products manufactured to exacting dimensions. The company's retail division marketed and sold granite, bronze, and marble memorials.

Also in 1998, analysts started to take note of Rock of Ages. Referring to the company as the "leader in the tombstone business," *Business Week* reported that several asset management firms—including Wellington Management, Goldman Sachs, and Fidelity—were acquiring shares in Rock of Ages. Writer Gene Marcial noted that Rock of Ages had a virtual lock on its industry and thus was well positioned to withstand market fluctuations.

In 1999 the retail division of memorials reported a loss of $2 million before taxes. The loss was attributed, in part, to a gradual growth in the number of families that chose cremation as an alternative to traditional methods of burial and installation of headstones. According to a source from the Cremation Association of North America (CANA), cremations represented approximately 22 percent of the United States burial market in 1996, compared to approximately ten percent in 1980; CANA expected this rate to rise to 29 percent by 2010.

In the company's *1999 Annual Report,* Chairman/CEO Kurt Swenson explained that consolidation of retail operations had taken longer than expected. Furthermore, Swenson commented

that it was necessary "to completely re-brand the company with the addition of 300 product lines, new warranties, all new point-of-sale materials, new retail price books, advertising and other support materials." During fiscal 1999, Rock of Ages acquired 15 companies. Swenson remained upbeat when he commented on the total financial situation of the 1999 fiscal year: "Being part of a fully vertically integrated memorial business—quarrying, manufacturing and retailing—was truly a record change for everyone in our company . . . and it took time to adjust," he emphasized.

By the end of fiscal 1999 Rock of Ages had completed the formation of its new business strategy as a fully integrated granite company. Pricing problems had been corrected in manufacturing operations. "The quarry team delivered record revenue and earnings that enabled us to earn a profit . . . despite the growth-related problems in our manufacturing and retail operations," Swenson reported. The poor earnings performance was offset by the highest cash flow from operations in the company's history: over $9 million or $1.17 per share, compared to about $3.7 million or $0.46 per share in 1998 when the company reported earnings of $0.91 per share.

At the end of the third quarter of 2000, Rock of Ages's total debt had declined 21 percent to $21.11 million from $26.86 million at year-end 1999. Improvements in quarrying and retail operations boded well for a fourth quarter in which earnings were expected to increase about 50 percent. Thus, at the beginning of a new millennium, a reorganized Rock of Ages Corporation was ready not only to experience a profitable fourth quarter but also to reach its goal of providing its customers "with superior value, personal service, and honest dealing for years to come."

### Principal Subsidiaries

Associated Memorials Inc.; Autumn Rose Quarry, Inc.; Carolina Quarries, Inc.; Childs & Childs Granite Company Inc.; Childs & Childs Trucking Co., Inc.; Kabushiki Kaisha Rock of Ages Asia (Japan; 50%); Keith Monuments Company LLC; Keystone & Childs Inc.; Pennsylvania Granite Corp.; Rock of Ages Canada, Inc. (Canada); Rock of Ages International Corp. (Japan); Rock of Ages International, Ltd. (Virgin Islands); Rock of Ages Memorials Inc.; Sioux Falls Monument Co.

### Principal Competitors

Matthews International Corp.; Service Corporation International; Stewart Enterprises Inc.

### Further Reading

Clarke, Rod, *Carved in Stone: A History of the Barre Granite Industry*, Barre, Vt.: Rock of Ages Corp., 1989.

Marcial, Gene G., "Critical Mass at Rock of Ages," *Business Week,* November 9, 1998, p. 166.

Patton, Todd, ed., *The Rock of Ages Story*, Barre, Vt.: Rock of Ages Corp., 1992.

"Special to the Globe," *Boston Globe*, April 20, 1980.

—Gloria A. Lemieux

# RolandBerger
## Strategy Consultants

# Roland Berger & Partner GmbH

Arabellastrasse 33
D-81925 Munich
Germany
Telephone: (49) (89) 9223-0
Fax: (49) (89) 9223-202
Web site: http://www.rolandberger.com

*Private Company*
*Incorporated:* 1967 as Roland Berger GmbH
*Employees:* 1,341
*Sales:* DM 680 million ($347 million) (1999)
*NAIC:* 541611 Administrative Management and General
Management Consulting Services; 541613 Marketing
Consulting Services; 541614 Process, Physical
Distribution, and Logistics Consulting; 541612
Human Resources and Executive Search Consulting
Services; 54191 Marketing Research and Public
Opinion Polling

German-based Roland Berger & Partner GmbH is among the leading management consulting firms in Europe. With an emphasis on strategy consulting the company also offers advice in the fields of administrative, process, information technology (IT) and e-commerce, human resources, and marketing management. While Roland Berger & Partner is the company's executive search arm, it also operates its own market research institutes, the Roland Berger Institute for International Marketing Research GmbH and the IJF Institute for Youth Research GmbH. About half of Roland Berger's revenues come from industrial clients and about one-third from clients in the services sector. Roland Berger maintains 30 offices in 21 countries worldwide. International clients account for about 45 percent of the company's sales, and some 57 percent of the roughly 950 consultants are not German. Since a management buyout in 1998 Roland Berger is owned by the company's 120 partners and associate partners. Founder and CEO Roland Berger holds a 9.9 percent stake in the company.

## Origins in 1967

The founder of Roland Berger & Partner GmbH International Management Consultants was born in Berlin, Germany, in 1937, two years before World War II broke out. Roland Berger grew up in a well-to-do family with Bavarian roots: His father was a director-general and ministerial counselor. As a high school student in Nuremberg, Berger studied humanities, Latin, and Greek and he graduated in 1956. Afterwards, Berger studied economics and business in Hamburg and Munich. As a student he completed several internships at industrial, bank, and insurance companies. During his time as a student Berger also got his first experience as an entrepreneur. Registered under his mother's name until his 21st birthday, Berger established and managed a laundry business which, because modern washing machines were not widespread at that time in German households, became quite successful. In 1962 Berger received a degree in business administration from Munich's Ludwig-Maximilian University and his high grades ensured him a position as the best student of the year.

Berger's future aspirations had a more intellectual focus than running a laundry business required. He envisioned a job that would be theoretical, but also pragmatic, and that would allow him to work at a variety of tasks, while also contributing to the public good and meeting interesting people along the way. One day, while delivering fresh laundry to a client, he became involved in a conversation about this topic. The woman to whom he was delivering the laundry told Berger about her son, who worked in Milan for an American consultancy; she recommended Berger visit him there. Berger, who spoke Italian well, was intrigued by the idea. After running the laundry for three years, Berger decided to sell the business which by then employed 15 people. He traveled to Italy and was hired on the spot by the Boston Consulting Group, one of America's leading management consultancies. For a few months Berger worked at the Boston office before he returned to Italy. For four years Berger worked as a consultant at the Milan office and finally became a partner.

Following his strong desire to be independent and stand on his own two feet, Roland Berger, at age 29, founded his own consulting business in 1967. Starting out with one secretary in Munich's upscale Bogenhausen neighborhood, his business

## Company Perspectives:

*Today we are already the leading globally active top-man-agement consultancy of European origin. Our roots are in the center of Europe, and its diversity of languages, cultures, legal and market structures. European management culture for us means being able to handle diversity: Not thinking in patterns and methods, but sensibility for different cultures, flexible adoption to changing rules and the ability to operate worldwide without losing sight of regional peculiarities. This turned out an advantage especially in global competition. We feel committed to this management culture and it determines our consulting philosophy: individually tailored concepts instead of standardized solutions, created in close teamwork with the client, and the facilitation of their practical realization. Creative strategies that work!*

soon employed three people. Consulting was perhaps a unique undertaking for a man of Berger's age and station; his peers were heavily involved in the ideological discussions of the late 1960s, and becoming a social revolutionary fit the Zeitgeist more than giving advice to capitalist enterprises. Moreover, management consulting was a very uncommon business in Germany at that time. Berger spent an estimated one-third of his time evangelizing for this "new" profession, which was already big in the United Kingdom and the United States.

### Renown in the 1980s

While most German management consultants in the late 1960s focused on cost-cutting strategies and offered primarily administration and operations consulting, Roland Berger positioned himself as a marketing and strategy consultant. Berger's first client was an advertising agency owned by one of his classmates. His first big challenge followed when the travel firm Touropa asked the 30-year-old Berger to help them solve a marketing problem. Berger's solution, which eventually was enacted, was the merger of Touropa with three other mid-sized German companies, Scharnow, Hummel, and Dr. Tigges. This took place two decades before merger-mania broke out worldwide. Together these companies formed the new travel giant TUI, which in the following decades would become one of the world's leading players in that industry. Other assignments for Roland Berger included a market introduction strategy for Goretex, a new textile fiber brand, and a marketing strategy for a large German bank. Other large corporate clients were German chemical giant Hoechst AG and German food industry conglomerate Dr. Oetker.

In the early 1970s Roland Berger evolved from a one-man consulting business to a partnership with a growing number of partners. The company established its own market research subsidiaries, one for general marketing research and one aimed specifically at the youth market. Another subsidiary was founded for executive search services. All these subsidiaries were organized under the Roland Berger & Partners Holding GmbH corporate umbrella.

Roland Berger's revenues experienced explosive growth during the 1970s and 1980s. Between 1967 and 1970 revenues

doubled every year. Three years after its founding, Berger's consultancy generated DM 5.6 million in revenues. From 1971 to 1972, while expanding his business, Berger also made a name for himself teaching marketing and advertising at the Munich Technical University. New partners came on board, and the range of services was continuously broadened. By 1974 Roland Berger was number three in the German consulting market, bypassed only by McKinsey & Co. and Kienbaum. The company had become a full service consultancy, whose product line included general management consulting, human resources consulting, logistics, and IT consulting.

About half of the strategies developed by Roland Berger dealt with increasing profits, while the other half dealt with strategies for growth, mergers, and diversification. More than 40 percent of Roland Berger's sales derived from big corporations, about 40 percent came from mid-sized companies—especially breweries—while about 20 percent originated from clients in small businesses and public administration. Another area that Roland Berger focused on was acquiring high quality, well-paid staff. As a result, Roland Berger made about DM 120,000 revenues per employee, while other management consultancies in Germany brought in sales, on average, of DM 70,000 to DM 80,000 per employee.

In 1981 Roland Berger organized its strategic consulting subsidiary, the Gesellschaft für Strategische Planung. However, when strategic consulting accounted for almost 70 percent of all business, the company reintegrated that business back into Roland Berger & Partner. In 1987 Roland Berger's sales passed the DM 100 million mark for the first time. By then Roland Berger had become the largest German management consultancy, with 180 consultants and 70 administrative staff. Eighteen of the 20 largest German companies from the nation's industrial sector were on Roland Berger's client roster, as were eight of the ten largest German banks and six of the top ten German transportation firms. The Roland Berger had come to signify management know-how and professionalism in Germany.

At this point Berger began looking for a business partner with the financial background to help his company ensure continued growth and international expansion. The size and importance of his company attracted Frankfurt-based Deutsche Bank, which acquired a 24 percent share in the company. This stake was upped to 75.1 percent a year later. though Berger retained a veto right and owned the remaining shares. As part of the agreement with Deutsche Bank, Berger was required to stay in his position as CEO until at least 1995. Roland Berger Verwaltungsgesellschaft mbH was founded as the new holding company which owned the majority of all Roland Berger companies while 19 partners held minority shares.

During this time Roland Berger became the first German consultancy to introduce annual press conferences. Because of the rather modest size of his company, balance sheet figures were not the main focus of these events. Instead, a national or international economic issue was discussed.

### Shifting Gears in the Early 1990s

Right from the beginning, Roland Berger paid close attention to foreign markets. As early as 1969 the company's first

## Key Dates:

**1967:** Roland Berger founds a consultant business
**1969:** First foreign office is established in Milan, Italy.
**1976:** Office in Sao Paulo, Brazil, opens.
**1987:** Deutsche Bank becomes major shareholder.
**1990:** Expansion into Eastern Europe begins.
**1991:** The company acquires Japanese consultancy Vaubel & Partners.
**1994:** First office in China is established.
**1998:** The company becomes independent again after a management buyout.
**1998:** Offices in New York and in Detroit, Michigan, are established.

foreign presence was established in Milan, Italy. In 1976 Roland Berger opened its first office in Latin America, in Sao Paulo, Brazil. One year later the company co-founded The International Group Consultancy and Research (TIG), a consortium that consisted of management consulting firms from the United Kingdom, France, Italy, Switzerland, and the Netherlands. In 1979 Roland Berger started cooperating with the Japan Management Association, one of Japan's largest top management consultancies. In the following year Roland Berger became the first European company to join the oldest and most reputable trade organization of consultant companies in the United States—the Association of Consulting Management Engineers (ACME). By 1986 more than 20 percent of Roland Berger's revenues came from abroad. A first endeavor to break into the U.S. market via a joint venture with the consultancy of Hayes Hill ended in 1986, but Roland Berger was planning to set up his own office in New York. In the same year an office was set up in Spain, followed by branch offices in Vienna, Paris, Lisbon, London, and Buenos Aires in the late 1980s.

The fall of the Berlin Wall in 1989 and the following disintegration of the Soviet Union opened new international markets for Roland Berger, and the company's expansion into Central and Eastern Europe began. In Russia Roland Berger organized management training programs for managers of the old government-owned companies. In China the consultancy developed a strategic plan for the tool and die industry. In 1991 Roland Berger acquired 100 percent of the shares in Japanese consultancy Vaubel & Partners, a firm in which it had held an interest for several years. The ten-year-old consultancy was founded by German CEO Dirk Vaubel and offered services mainly to German companies which were expanding into the Japanese market. The company was renamed Roland Berger, Vaubel & Partners Ltd. and employed about 15 consultants and 15 staff. Roland Berger's foreign sales climbed from 22.8 percent of its total sales in 1987 to 27.7 percent in 1991. In 1994 Roland Berger's first office in China was established in Shanghai. A second one opened in Beijing in 1995.

While the company expanded into Central Europe and Asia, its Western European branch offices reached critical mass with between 15 and 50 employees. A new office was opened in Brussels in 1993. Five years later Roland Berger expanded with new offices in India and Malaysia. In the United States the

situation was more complicated. The Federal Reserve Bank did not allow commercial banks and their subsidiaries to become involved in consulting activities. With the Deutsche Bank as major shareholder in Roland Berger, this rule precluded the latter from establishing its own U.S. presence; however, the company continued to work cooperatively with a few American partners.

By 1997 Roland Berger employed about 800 consultants, and revenues had climbed to over DM 500 million. About one-third of the company's sales came from abroad, as did about half of Roland Berger's consultants. Besides the traditional clientele from private companies, Roland Berger's roster of clients from governments, non-profit organizations, and public administrations continued to grow.

### Targeting the United States in 1998 and Beyond

In 1998 Roland Berger became independent again, as the company's managers staged a buyout of 90 percent of Deutsche Bank's shares in the consultancy. The other 10.1 percent were then acquired from Deutsche Bank by January 1, 2000. The transaction cleared the way for Roland Berger to enter the United States—the world's largest market for consulting services. A branch office was set up in New York City. Another office was established in Detroit, Michigan, where Roland Berger targeted suppliers to automotive suppliers—companies such as TRW Inc, Lear Corp., and Johnson Controls Inc.

However, competing in the United States would be no easy task for Berger; the U.S. was the land of top management consulting firms and home to 14 of the world's 15 largest strategy consultancies, according to a Kennedy Information Research Group study from 1999. Berger was also forced to enter the battle for the best talent from U.S. business schools, and the Roland Berger name was not as familiar to young grads as the names of the major U.S. players. Among the questions Roland Berger planned to address in the 21st century was that of whether to achieve a critical mass of consultants through the its own growth or to consider a merger with another mid-sized U.S. strategy consultancy. Regardless, the company planned to set up a Silicon Valley office by 2001.

In the meantime Roland Berger was looking for new areas in which to specialize. The company had positioned itself as the leading European strategy consultancy for the "e-transformation" of large clients hoping to be ready for a much-heralded Internet economy. At the same time, however, recruiting capable consultant talent for that area was becoming more difficult than ever as many were leaving to work for independent Internet startups. Roland Berger responded to this challenge by sponsoring a professorship for e-business at the Technical University in Munich and by establishing a new chair in "E-Business and Information Technology" at INSEAD, the renowned business school in Fontainebleau near Paris.

Another strategy for generating growth at Roland Berger was to further promote the idea of "consulting for equity," which meant being paid with shares in startup companies rather than in cash, which such new companies always lacked. To help finance these activities Roland Berger formed a strategic alliance with German venture capital firm bmp AG; the venture went public in July 1999 and financed about 62 startup companies in the fields of e-commerce, media, entertainment, software, biotech, and other high-tech markets. Roland Berger also planned to establish the first German "turnaround fund" with German bank HypoVereinsbank; the fund would buy companies with growth potential, restructure and make them profitable again, and then sell them to interested investors for a profit.

In terms of international expansion, a branch office in Warsaw was added to Roland Berger's network of branch offices of Eastern Europe in June 2000; existing locations there included Moscow, Riga, Kiev, Prague, Budapest, and Bucharest. On November 22, 2002, the man who created *the* German consultancy and reached the status of a media darling in his home country will turn 65. Needless to say, he has already put together a strategic plan for the company when his leadership is over.

### Principal Subsidiaries

Roland Berger & Partner S.R.L. International Management Consultants (Italy); Roland Berger & Partner GmbH International Management Consultants (France); Roland Berger & Partners Ltd. International Management Consultants (United Kingdom); Roland Berger & Partner Lda. International Management Consultants (Portugal); Roland Berger S.A. International Management Consultants (Spain); Roland Berger AG International Management Consultants (Switzerland); Roland Berger & Partner, LLC International Management Consultants; Roland Berger & Partners S/C Ltda. (Brazil); Roland Berger y Asociados S.A. International Management Consultants (Argentina); Roland Berger & Partner International Management Consultants Sp.zo.o. (Poland); Roland Berger (Shanghai) International Management Consultants Ltd.; Roland Berger & Partner Ltd. International Management Consultants (Japan); Roland Berger & Partner GmbH International Management Consultants (Russia).

### Principal Competitors

McKinsey & Company; Andersen Consulting; Boston Consulting Group.

### Further Reading

Freitag, Michael and Wilfried Krüger, "Sein Rat ist gut und teuer," *Frankfurter Allgemeine Zeitung Magazin*, May 26, 1989.

Fröhlich, Thomas, "Ein Unternehmer, der Erfolg schafft," *Süddeutsche Zeitung*, August 8, 1997.

"Management Consultant Roland Berger Talks About Incomes, Jobs and Creativity," *Deutschland-Magazin*, August 1996, p. 53.

Richter, Konstantin, "German Consulting Guru Seeks U.S. Audience," *Wall Street Journal Europe*, August 17, 1999.

"Roland Berger will Auslandsgeschäft stärken," *Frankfurter Allgemeine Zeitung*, January 25, 1996.

Swat, Wolfgang, "Ohne Gefühle gibt es keinen Erfolg," *Lausitzer Rundschau*, July 8, 2000.

"Unternehmensberatung Roland Berger expandiert in Japan," *Frankfurter Allgemeine Zeitung*, March 12, 1991.

"Unternehmensstrategie steht im Vordergrund," *Handelsblatt*, October 8, 1974.

—Evelyn Hauser

# Roll International Corporation

**11444 West Olympic Boulevard, Tenth Floor**
**Los Angeles, California 90064-1060**
**U.S.A.**
**Telephone: (310) 966-5700**
**Fax: (310) 914-4747**

*Private Company*
*Incorporated:* 1993
*Employees:* 7,500
*Sales:* $1.57 billion (1998)
*NAIC:* 551112 Offices of Other Holding Companies

Roll International Corporation, a private company, is made up of a collection of companies owned by husband-and-wife team Stewart and Lynda Resnick. The biggest and best known of the operations are the Franklin Mint, the world's largest collectibles company, and Teleflora LLC, the world's largest florist network. The other Roll subsidiaries are pistachio producer Paramount Farming Co., citrus grower and packer Paramount Citrus, processor and marketer Paramount Farms, and Bundy Properties, which owns and manages commercial properties in Los Angeles and Pennsylvania.

## Forming a Holding Company in the 1960s

The Resnicks started their empire by buying Teleflora, a flowers-by-wire company. They then bought American Protection Industries Inc. (API), a security company. API Alarm Systems, which started in the 1960s, provided both patrols and alarm systems. The alarms, installed in retail, office, and industrial buildings as well as in houses, were connected to monitoring centers. If an alarm went off, an operator at the center could summon the closest police or fire department. By 1987, it was the largest alarm company in California.

The Resnicks made API their holding company, with API Alarm Systems another subsidiary. In 1989, they sold the subsidiary to the British company Automated Security Holdings plc (ASH) for $105 million. At that time, API Alarm Systems served some 21,000 customers and had seven central stations. The Resnicks, however, kept the API name. In 1993 they

renamed their holding company Roll International after an agricultural company they had acquired.

## Late 1970s Addition of Teleflora LLC

Sending out-of-town flower orders by wire began in 1910 when two U.S. florists agreed to telegraph each other orders and then settle up on costs. Thus was born Florists' Transworld Delivery Association (FTD). In 1934, attorney Edwin S. Douglas founded a rival service. Originally called Telegraph Delivery Service, the name was changed to Teleflora. The Resnicks bought the California-based company in 1979 after it had changed hands several times.

A year after the purchase, Lynda Resnick introduced the concept of keepsake containers and revolutionized the floral delivery business. Instead of just wiring a flower arrangement or a dozen flowers, people could order their flowers in a special vase or basket that the receiver could use after the flowers died.

In 1987, the company set up its Teleflora Technologies division, providing retail members a computer system with software specifically designed for florists, and Creditline, which allowed members to process credit card purchases immediately. The company also published an award-winning magazine for the retail floral business.

But by the early 1990s customers had options other than wire services for out-of-town orders. Toll-free telephone numbers were the biggest competition, although catalogs and online delivery services added to the problem. In 1993, Roll made the first of its three bids for FTD. A year later, the FTD board rejected Roll's final bid of $175 million, which consisted of $140 million in cash and taking over FTD's debt of $35 million. The merger would have positioned Roll to dominate the industry, but FTD announced it would instead accept a lower bid from Perry Capital Inc. The nonprofit florist cooperative became essentially a trade group representing member florists. The business ventures became part of FTD Inc., a for-profit corporation. One of the first initiatives of the new owners was the establishment of FTD.com, an online service for order flowers.

Teleflora continued to look for acquisitions. In 1997, the company became the largest florist network in the country with the

## Key Dates:

**1979:** Stewart and Lynda Rae Resnick buy Teleflora, LLC; Resnicks buy American Protection Industries and set it up as holding company.
**1984:** Resnicks buy Franklin Mint from Warner Communications Inc.
**1985:** Resnicks begin adding agriculture subsidiaries Paramount Citrus and Paramount Farming.
**1989:** Resnicks sell API Alarm Systems; form Paramount Farms.
**1993:** Resnicks rename holding company Roll International Corporation.

purchase of Redbook Florist Services. The next year it acquired Daisy Systems, which provided computerized shop-management systems to retailers. Building on those systems, Teleflora introduced its "Teleflorist Online" service in October 2000. The new service offered Teleflora's 27,000 members professionally designed and managed web sites with e-commerce support such as credit card processing, e-mail gift reminders, and an online address book for customers. Unlike competitor FTD.com, Teleflora's approach was to help its members establish their own online businesses (with their own web sites) and to keep their own customers along with 100 percent of their revenue.

### 1980s Entry into Agricultural Subsidiaries

The Resnicks moved into agribusiness in the mid-1980s. They first bought a citrus growing and processing operation near Bakersfield, California, which became Paramount Citrus Association. Paramount Citrus grew and packed fruit for both the retail and wholesale markets, selling oranges, lemons, apples, and grapefruit. The company sold much of its juice as Alpha-Beta.

In 1986, they purchased Apex Orchards from Mobil Oil for $30 million. The 12,000-acre pistachio and almond farm near Bakersfield was renamed Paramount Farming Co. The next year the Resnicks bought Texaco's central California farming operations, adding some 77,000 acres of farmland, also in the San Joaquin Valley.

In 1989 the Resnicks formed Paramount Farms, a processing and marketing group that sold pistachios and almonds under its own label as well as wholesale. Paramount Farms' nuts were soon selling across the country and internationally, primarily to cereal and candy manufacturers, including Cadbury, Nestle, Hershey, Carnation, and Kellogg. Over the years, Paramount Farms expanded its processing and marketing operations to include citrus, olives, and pomegranates. In 1993, Paramount Farms and the Pistachio Producers of California (PPC) formed a marketing co-op called Cal-Pure Pistachios and began offering pistachios under the Sunkist name. By 1996, Paramount Farms was the largest grower, processor, and marketer of almonds and pistachios in the world.

By the late 1990s, Paramount Citrus had become one of the state's largest citrus producers. In 2000, the company bought 3,912 acres and several packing houses from Dole Food Co. for $55 million. The purchase, which brought its total acreage of

citrus to nearly 27,000, made Paramount Citrus the largest grower, packer, and marketer of fresh citrus in the country.

### Addition of The Franklin Mint

In 1964, Joseph Segal founded General Numismatics, a company devoted to producing and marketing commemorative coins, medals, and other metal objects. The company's first coin was a commemorative of General Douglas MacArthur. Segal, who paid a medal manufacturer $10,000 to make the MacArthur coin, advertised his product in collectors' magazines and was soon making $10,000 a month. Segal set up his own production facility and in 1965 took the company public and changed the company's name to Franklin Mint. Within two years, Segal had built a new headquarters and a modern mint and foundry near Media, Pennsylvania, a Philadelphia suburb. When Segal retired in 1973, Franklin Mint had sales of nearly $113 million and earnings of over $9 million as well as its own post office. Sales during the 1970s peaked in 1975 at $233.9 million. After that, sales dropped, although they remained in the $150–$200 million range throughout the decade.

Warner Communications (now Time Warner) purchased The Franklin Mint and its Franklin Mint Museum in 1981, paying some $250 million for the operation. At that point, Franklin Mint became a subsidiary of Warner. In 1984, Warner sold a majority interest (70 percent) to the Resnick's American Protection Industries for $167.5 million. It retained the administration building, minting facilities, library, mailing center, and a retail store. Stewart Resnick became chairman and Lynda vice-chairman. In its first year of operation under the Resnicks, Franklin Mint had sales of about $250 million, but it lost money from 1988 through 1990. In 1991 it earned $9.1 million, about what its profits were when Segal retired in 1973.

As the Resnicks expanded Franklin Mint's offerings, they also set about making Franklin Mint Museum a tourist destination. The museum, which opened in 1973, contained about 7,000 square feet of exhibit space. A visitor could find the major items from the Franklin Mint offerings and trace popular tastes—pewter during the American Bicentennial, the growth of fantasy, and dolls, dolls, dolls. In the museum's gift shop, visitors could buy any of the items they had just viewed.

In 1992, the Resnicks were considering taking Franklin Mint public. They hoped to raise $100 million and use most of it to repay bank debt and interest owed to Time Warner. However, the stock sale was canceled. Allan Sloan, writing about the proposed public offering in *The Washington Post*, noted that Franklin Mint spent $140 million to make its products in 1991 and $184 million to market and promote them. Sales for 1991 were $538 million, more than 250 percent over its cost of goods.

The company the Resnicks proposed taking public was very different from the one they had bought from Warner Communications. It now manufactured collectibles, not commemoratives. In 1993 it promoted over 950 products: jewelry, Christmas ornaments, plates, dolls, games, religious sculptures, miniature cars, Arthurian swords, Faberge-type eggs, scale model replicas of the Harley-Davidson Heritage Softail. There was also a magazine for collectors, *Almanac*. Coins represented less than three percent of the company's total business. Franklin Mint retail stores were opening and there were plans for catalogs, clothing, cosmetics, and perfume. By 1994, Franklin Mint had expanded to a 187-acre campus, and was housed in a facility larger than ten football fields. It also had employees in 20 countries.

### The 1990s and Beyond

While Stewart Resnick was seen to be the financial and organizational genius behind the transformation of Franklin Mint, Lynda Resnick was acknowledged as the marketing and aesthetic genius. Art collectors themselves, the Resnicks understood that people are passionate collectors. What they learned from their experience at Franklin Mint is that people collect by theme, such as wildflowers or dogs or movie stars, and by form—dolls, plates, games. With that knowledge, they saw the potential for crossover sales.

Lynda Resnick also had a keen feel for cultural trends, which she augmented with equally talented staff around the world. In the mid-1990s she began establishing licensing agreements, first with museums, including the Vatican Museum and the Louvre, and then with celebrities (or their estates), including Elvis. She added fashion designers, then moved to agreements with corporations, including Coca Cola, Campbell Soup, and Parker Bros., as well as movie companies. One reason the corporations found an agreement with Franklin Mint attractive was the company's advertising budget ($120 million in 1995) and range. Their ads in *Parade, TV Guide,* and *USA Weekend* magazines reached more than 70 million households each week.

However, collectible sales were beginning to shift from direct marketing to retail and TV shopping. In 1995, top management from several companies left the collectible business. This included Tom Dorovsik, president of Franklin Mint, who joined U.S. Healthcare. Sales were strong but profits were weak and there appeared to be a need for more products.

Lynda Resnick's response was to buy Jackie Kennedy Onassis' faux pearls for $211,500 when Southeby's auctioned the former first lady's possessions in 1996. At the Franklin Mint, a replica of the pearls sold for $195 and was an immediate hit. Resnick also bought one of Princess Di's evening dresses, and displayed it in the museum. A version of the gown clothed the Mint's Princess Diana porcelain doll, which also sold for $195. As Resnick explained to David Richards in his 1998 article in *The Washington Post,* "Nothing lasts. What the Franklin Mint does is create a permanence about the memories we have of the past." Meanwhile, the company had expanded its retail operations to 50 stores.

Franklin Mint began having some problems in 1997, when Tiger Woods sued the company after it produced a commemorative medal of his win in the 1997 Masters tournament. Franklin Mint paid Woods an undisclosed amount of money to settle the case. In May 1998, the estate of Princess Diana filed a lawsuit to keep Franklin Mint from profiting from the sale of commemorative Princess Di merchandise. In addition to the Diana porcelain doll and a commemorative plate, Franklin Mint sold a jeweled tribute ring and a diamond pendant. The case was not settled until January 2000, when the judge ruled in favor of Franklin Mint. In reality, Franklin Mint had donated over $4 million to charities supported by the late princess. The legal battles led to rumors that the Resnicks were considering selling Franklin Mint. The company quickly denied the reports.

For over 30 years, the Resnicks have been buying and building companies. In almost each case, their purchase has become the nation's or the world's largest operation in its specific field—pistachio production, processing and marketing; manufactured collectibles; flowers by wire; citrus production. With such an amazing record, Roll International was poised for continued success at the start of the new century.

### Principal Subsidiaries

The Franklin Mint; Paramount Farms; Paramount Farming Company; Paramount Citrus Association; Teleflora LLC; Bundy Properties.

### Principal Competitors

Collections; Bradford Exchange; Danbury Mint; FTD Inc.; 1-800-FLOWERS Inc.

### Further Reading

Carr-Brown, Jonathon, "The Princess of Sales," *Ottawa Citizen,* June 1, 1999, p. A14.
"Franklin Mint is Going Public," *New York Times,* March 13, 1992, p. D3.
Hodges, Jane and Laura Loro, "Collectibles Cut Budgets," *Advertising Age,* November 13, 1995, p. 4.
Littman, Margaret, "A Thorny Side to FTD.com IPO," *Crain's Chicago Business,* July 12, 1999, p. 1.
Loro, Laura, "The Marketing 100; Lynda Rae Resnick," *Advertising Age,* June 26, 1995, p. S22.
Lubove, Seth, "King of the Startups," *Forbes,* November 8, 1993, p. 186.
MacNeil, V. "American Protection Industries Inc.: Enterprise Collects Sweet Smells and Heirlooms," *Los Angeles Business Journal,* February 5, 1990, p. 6.
Mehren, Elizabeth, "Objects of Desire," *Los Angeles Times,* June 8, 1993, p. E1.
"Mint Conditions," *Guardian,* January 7, 2000, p. 5.
"Paramount Farms to Drop Sunkist Growers as Marketer of Nut Brands," *Bakersfield Californian,* February 28, 1996.
Piskora, Beth and John Crudele, "A Sale Worth a Mint," *New York Post,* August 10, 1998, p. 024.
Richards, David, "Don't Say Tchotche! Why America Loves the Franklin Mint," *Washington Post,* January 25, 1998, p. G1.
Rodriguez, Robert, "Paramount Ripens with Recent Dole Land Purchase," *Fresno Bee,* October 3, 2000, p. C1.
Salley-Schoen, Gwen, "A Peek Inside the Franklin Mint," *Sacramento Bee,* November 28, 1992, p. CL11.
Serdahely, Franz, "Will Franklin Mint Regain Lost Luster?," *Focus,* September 11, 1985, p. 44.
Sherefkin, Robert, "FTD Expected to Approve Perry Bid," *Crain's Detroit Business,* November 7, 1994, p. 1.
Sloan, Allan, "Don't Rush to Add Franklin Mint to Your Stock Collection," *Washington Post,* May 19, 1992, p. C3.
"State's Largest Alarm Service," *Southern California Business,* October 1987, p. 8.
"Tiger Woods Settles Lawsuit Over Franklin Mint Medal," *Sports & Entertainment Litigation Reporter,* May 1998, p. 5.
"Warner Communications Sells Major Stake in Franklin Mint," *American Metal Market,* December 17, 1984, p. 19.
Warner, Susan, "Owners Deny Philadelphia's Franklin Mint for Sale," *Philadelphia Inquirer,* August 11, 1998.

—Ellen D. Wernick

# Royal Numico N.V.

P.O. Box 1
2700 MA Zoetermeer
The Netherlands
Telephone: +31-79-3539-000
Fax: +31-79-3539-620
Web site: http://www.numico.com/uk/english-set.html

*Public Company*
*Incorporated:* 1896 as N.V. Nutricia
*Employees:* 18,853
*Sales:* EUR 2.29 Billion (US$2.31 billion) (1999)
*Stock Exchanges:* Euronext Amsterdam
*Ticker Symbol:* Numico
*NAIC:* 422490 Other Grocery and Related Products Wholesalers; 311422 Specialty Canning; 311230 Breakfast Cereal Manufacturing; 311514 Dry, Condensed, and Evaporated Dairy Product Manufacturing

Fast-growing Royal Numico N.V. (Koninklijke Numico N.V.), based in Zoetermeer, the Netherlands, has nearly tripled in size in the last five years to become one of the world's leading companies devoted solely to the manufacture and distribution of nutritional products. Numico, best known for its Nutricia, Milupa, and Cow & Gate infant formulas in Europe, has become a North American nutritional heavyweight through its acquisitions of Rexall Sundown, General Nutrition Companies, and Enrich International, placing Numico at the top of the United States' market for vitamins and other nutritional supplements. In addition to baby formulas, Numico is also a leading producer of medical nutrition products, including enteral (direct-to-stomach) clinical nutrition products, intravenous supplements, disease-specific nutrition programs, and other special-needs dietary products, such as for diabetes and other chronic health conditions. In its home Benelux base, Numico is also well known for its chocolate and other flavored-milk products, such as Chocomel and Fristi, and coffee milk substitute Nutroma, and for its infant foods products marketed under the Olivarit and other labels. Numico, which changed its name in 1998 from Nutricia to avoid confusing the corporate entity with its food label, is listed on the new Euronext Amsterdam stock exchange. In 1999, the company posted EUR 2.29 billion in sales.

## Infant Formula Pioneer in the 1890s

As the 19th century neared its end, infant mortality rates remained shockingly high—one in five children did not live to see its first birthday. Advances in medical research had, however, made it possible to identify causes for the high mortality rates, and by the end of the century lack of proper nutrition was widely recognized as a chief factor in infant death. Researchers began to seek means for producing nutritional supplements for children, especially supplements based on cow's milk. Because cow's milk placed too much stress on a child's system, methods were sought to produce more easily digestible "formulas" from milk. In 1896, Martinus van der Hagen, who had founded the Steam Dairy Factory in what later became known as Zegwaard, acquired the exclusive rights to develop formulas using the so-called Backhaus method.

Van der Hagen named his company's formula Nutricia, and then incorporated that operation under the N.V. Nutricia name. The company quickly expanded its focus beyond infant nutrition, as medical advances discovered key links between nutrition and certain illnesses. As such, the Nutricia company was among the first to develop special milks with low-sugar contents for diabetic patients and iodine-fortified milk for goiter sufferers. Nutricia by then had already distinguished itself for its close collaboration with the medical community and its commitment to food and nutrition research. The company was one of the first to adopt a new method of processing milk proteins—normally indigestible by infants—developed by Finkelstein in 1909.

By then, the Nutricia brand name already had begun to become known across Europe, and it quickly grew to become one of the world's top-selling infant formulas. The company's expansion targeted especially the Flemish-speaking market in Belgium, before spreading through the rest of the later Benelux region. In 1924, Nutricia boosted its international presence with the purchase of a dairy production facility in Cuijk, Belgium.

## Company Perspectives:

*At Koninklijke Numico N.V. we are in the business of supporting health. Our vision is to be a profitable and growing worldwide leader in specialised nutrition. We want our products to help people lead healthy and rewarding lives. We accept and welcome the challenges and responsibilities that accompany our ambitions.*

While continuing to focus on dairy-based nutritional supplements and special medical products, Nutricia's research and development department continued to search for new outlets for the company. In the 1930s, Nutricia stepped into the consumer products category with the introduction of Chocomel, a chocolate milk product with a long shelf life—one of the first milk products to offer extended storage times. The company also began developing a new type of milk especially formulated for mixing with coffee. By the end of the 1940s, the company was able to launch its highly successful Nutroma coffee milk.

By then, Nutricia had decided to focus still further on its so-called "scientific" food products. As part of this new focus, the company built a new research laboratory in 1946, complete with prototype manufacturing capacity. Nutricia's researchers worked closely with the medical and research communities at large. Although many of the company's products remained dairy-based, Nutricia began to expand into other food categories. In 1946, the company launched its own line of baby foods, under the Olivarit brand, featuring prepared vegetables. The Olivarit brand was to remain a top-seller for the company through the end of the century and see its range expanded to include a wide variety of food types and preparations.

### "Scientific" Foods in the 1950s

Nutricia's new research focus enabled the company to introduce a number of new products in the 1950s. Among these were one of the first "humanized" milk products, that is, infant milk formula that more closely resembled the makeup of human breast milk. Nutricia also introduced its Almirige line of infant formulas for premature babies and babies with special feeding needs. At the same time, Nutricia increased its marketing focus, hiring dieticians to market its product specifically to doctors and nurses. Meanwhile, sales of the company's infant formulas boomed as the medical community encouraged women to abandon breast feeding and adopt formula-based feeding.

In the 1960s, the company enhanced its international position with the purchase of a new production facility in Bornem, Belgium. Nutricia also extended its nutritional array to the medical community, when it brought out a new range of intravenous and other nutritional products for use in a hospital environment. To support the company's research and development efforts, and its international expansion, Nutricia re-incorporated as Verenidge Bedrijven Nutricia, taking a listing on the Amsterdam stock exchange.

The company's medical research culminated in a new product, dubbed Nutri 2000, during the 1970s. Nutri 2000 represented a full feeding system for chronically ill patients, based on the newly developing enteral method, that is, direct-to-stomach feeding methods. The company also developed its Nutrison product line, for intravenous drip feeders.

The company continued to grow through the 1980s. Yet a growing number of mothers and fathers had begun to challenge the focus on infant formulas at the expense of breast feeding. As more and more people became convinced of the benefits of mother's milk over infant formula, the company also was tainted by a number of formula contamination scares among its own and other brands. Meanwhile, declining birth rates in the company's core European base was cutting deeply into infant formula sales.

The sagging formula market opened a new opportunity for Nutricia, when it bought Cow & Gate, a leading maker of infant formulas for the United Kingdom market. That acquisition helped the company gain a solid position as a leading European formula maker.

### Nutritional Leader in the 21st Century

While birth rates and formula demand continued to decline in much of Western Europe throughout the 1980s and early 1990s, Nutricia recognized new growth opportunities in the newly opening Eastern European countries. During the early part of the 1990s, the company began making acquisitions and establishing distribution networks in the former Eastern Bloc countries. Other international markets for the company were found in Turkey, Indonesia (the company became market leader in the former Dutch colony), and South America. Attempts to enter the North American market, with the acquisition of the Loma Linda brand, among other moves, proved less than successful. In the early 1990s, the vast Asian market became a company priority, especially the huge market in China, which the company entered through a distribution agreement.

Meanwhile, the company was rocked by two food contamination scares. The first occurred in 1989, when cans of Cow & Gate formula were discovered to have been contaminated during shipping. The second scandal hit the company's Olivarit brand in 1993, when traces of a cleaning solvent were detected in some of the Olivarit baby jars. The company promptly recalled more than 14 million jars of baby food. Nonetheless, the rapid renewal of the company's market—every two years, as a new population of women give birth—enabled the company to come through these food scares (the company was hit again in 1997) without suffering too much damage to its reputation or sales.

By 1995, the company's sales had topped NFl 1.5 billion. In that year, however, Nutricia doubled in size when it acquired struggling German formula rival Milupa for some $560 million. Milupa, which had gotten itself into trouble through an ill-timed expansion into the former eastern region of the newly reunified Germany, nevertheless allowed Nutricia to take the place of European leader in the infant formula market, with an average per-country share of some 35 percent. The Milupa acquisition also allowed the company to head off looming threats of a hostile takeover. Meanwhile, the company's medical side also was enjoying success, particularly with the launch of the company's Nutrison Pack drip-feeding system.

## Key Dates:

**1896:** Martinus van der Hagen acquires exclusive rights to Backhaus formula production method; incorporates formula production operations as N.V. Nutricia.

**1905:** Production of diabetic milk products and iodine-enriched milks begins.

**1911:** Company begins production of protein milks using Finkelstein method.

**1924:** N.V. Nutricia acquires dairy product production facility in Cuijk, Belgium.

**1930:** Chocomel chocolate milk is introduced.

**1945:** Nutroma coffee milk is introduced.

**1950:** Company hires dietitians to market products to doctors and nurses.

**1966:** Reincorporation as Veringde Bedrijven Nutricia and listing on Amsterdam stock exchange.

**1970:** Nutricia launches Nutri 2000.

**1981:** Company acquires the Cow & Gate formula manufacturer of the United Kingdom.

**1997:** Company is granted "Royal" title, becoming Koninklijke N.V. Verenigde Bedrijven Nutricia.

**1998:** Company's name is changed to Koninklijke Numico N.V., or Royal Numico N.V.

**1999:** General Nutrition Companies, of the United States, is acquired.

**2000:** Enrich International and Rexall Sundown (both of the United States) are purchased.

In 1997, the company's contribution to the Netherlands' society was recognized by the granting of use of the royal title to the company's name. Now known as Koninklijke N.V. Verenigde Bedrijven Nutricia, the company was then faced with a new food contamination scare. The new scare led the company to change its name, to disassociate its individual brands from the corporate entity, and avoid allowing one label's food scare to "contaminate" the other Nutricia names. Using the beginnings of its three core brand names, the company became Royal Numico N.V. at the beginning of 1998.

By then, Royal Numico, which had built up its European leadership to capture some 40 percent of the total European infant formula market, as well as leadership status in its hospital nutrition products market, sought to build on its research and development expertise to expand into a new and fast-growing market, that of vitamins and nutritional supplements. For this, the company turned to the United States, by then the world's largest market for this product category.

In 1999, Royal Numico entered the United States with a bang—in July of that year, the company reached agreement to acquire General Nutrition Companies, well known for its 4,200-strong chain of GNC and other retail stores, and one of the world's leading makers and distributors of vitamins and nutritional supplements. Worth some US$2.5 billion, the acquisition gave Royal Numico a nearly 13 percent share of the estimated US$9 billion market. At the same time, Royal Numico gained access for its products to GNC's manufacturing and distribution network, including its vast retail empire, while GNC's own development efforts were strengthened by its new parent company's research expertise.

With sales now boosted to nearly EUR 2.3 billion, Royal Numico returned to its newfound growth drive in 2000. After buying up multilevel vitamin supplement marketer Enrich International, Royal Numico solidified its newfound position as the world's leading vitamin maker when it paid US$1.8 billion for Boca Raton-based Rexall Sundown. The Rexall Sundown purchase, which added that company's catalog of more than 1,300 products, also gave Royal Numico access to a number of Rexall Sundown's major customers, including the Wal-Mart and Publix retail chains.

The Rexall Sundown acquisition gave Royal Numico a commanding 21 percent of the fast-growing U.S. vitamins and supplements market, which was expected to top US$16 billion in the year 2000. Royal Numico's own sales were expected to top EUR 4.5 billion for the year. The company's future appeared vitamin-enriched indeed.

### Principal Subsidiaries

Çarmosan A.S. (Turkey); Efamol Ltd. (United Kingdom); Enrich International Inc. (United States); General Nutrition Companies, Inc. (United States); Hindustani Lever (India); Kasdorf S.A. (Argentina); Larkhall (United Kingdom); Milupa S.A. (Switzerland); Mococa (Brazil); Northfield Laboratories Pty Ltd. (Australia); Nutricia Australasia Ltd. (New Zealand); Nutricia Nederland B.V.; N.V. Galenco (Belgium); Ovita Nutricia Sp. z.o.o. (Poland); Pack-o-Med Medical Supply Systems B.V. (Netherlands); PT Sari Husada Tbk (Indonesia); Qihe Dairy Corporation Ltd of Heilongjiang (China); Rexall Sundown, Inc. (United States); Scientific Hospital Supplies Ltd. (United Kingdom); Szabolcstej (Hungary); Vitamex AB (Sweden).

### Principal Competitors

Bristol-Myers Squibb Company; NBTY, Inc.; Danone; Nestlé S.A.; Heinz; Novartis; Leiner Health Products; Perrigo Company; Milnot Company; Sunrider Corporation; Nature's Sunshine Products, Inc.; Twinlab Corporation.

### Further Reading

Jonas, Ilaina, "Royal Numico Buys GNC," *Reuters,* July 5, 1999.

Murawski, John, "Dutch Company to Buy Rexall for $1.8 Billion," *Palm Beach Post,* May 2, 2000, p. 1a.

Newman, Anna, "Booster Shot for a Vitamin Maker," *Business Week,* May 15, 2000, p. 56.

Onstad, Eric, "Numico's Rexall Buy Cements US Position," *Reuters Business Report,* May 1, 2000.

Smit, Barbara, "Nutricia Growing Fast and Hungry for More," *European,* October 5, 1995, p. 19.

—M.L. Cohen

# The Ryland Group, Inc.

**2425 Park Sorrento, Suite 400**
**Calabasas, California 91302**
**U.S.A.**
**Telephone: (818) 223-7500**
**Fax: (818) 223-7667**
**Web site: http://www.ryland.com**

*Public Company*
*Incorporated:* 1967 as The James P. Ryan Company
*Employees:* 2,130
*Sales:* $2 billion (1999)
*Stock Exchanges:* New York
*Ticker Symbol:* RYL
*NAICs:* 23321 Single Family Housing Construction;
    52231 Mortgage and Nonmortgage Loan Brokers

A leading homebuilder in the United States, The Ryland Group, Inc., has operations in about 21 markets in 14 states and Washington, D.C. With an average selling price of about $190,000, the company's homes are geared toward entry-level buyers and first- and second-time move-up buyers, as well as active retirees. The Ryland Group also offers mortgage-related services, ranging from escrow and title search services to homeowners insurance. The majority of loans handled by the company are for homes constructed by The Ryland Group.

### Early Years As a Homebuilder: Late 1960s–70s

What became The Ryland Group was originally named after its founder, James P. Ryan, an energetic real estate entrepreneur who established the James P. Ryan Company in Columbia, Maryland, in 1967. Columbia was a new, planned community of 220 single-family-homes situated midway between Washington, D.C., and Baltimore, Maryland. Ryan created the name "Ryland Homes" when he chanced upon a sign that was supposed to say "Maryland," but on which the first two letters had been covered; "Ryland" struck him as the ideal name for his homes.

Operating in a dynamic and highly volatile housing market, Ryland developed a marketing strategy targeted toward the middle class or up-and-coming middle class: homes were built with only brand-name construction materials and appliances and sold in the middle range, starting at $20,000. Ryland sought to be a highly focused home building business rather than a development company speculating in land dealing or the development of "raw" land. In its first year of operation, the company concluded 48 sales and made a modest profit of $12.7 million.

In 1970 the company changed its name to The Ryland Group, Inc., and the following year the company went public. That same year Ryland broke ground on another planned community, Peachtree City, outside of Atlanta, Georgia. Here Ryland Homes, with their careful attention to detail, frequent inspections at crucial phases of building, and use of only premium brand name materials and appliances (Anderson windows, Armstrong floor coverings, Owens Corning Fiberglass, General Electric stoves and refrigerators), struck a balance between cost, quality, and choice that was extremely popular with consumers. The customer could select from 15 different floor plans and from a variety of different housing styles that often reflected regional tastes. Ryland also was building a variety of homes, from single-family dwellings to townhomes (the "townhome" concept was pioneered by Ryland) to condominiums, just as the last was growing in popularity. Ryland's building venture prospered, and more than 75 percent of its employees became stockholders.

The next several years saw further expansion into Texas. Ryland manufacturing centers, initially called Ryland Building Systems (later integrated into the Ryland Homes division in 1992), were also constructed at this time, providing preassembled, factory supervised home building components to the home site. By 1977 Ryland had penetrated the Midwestern market as well as the Philadelphia area, and had completed its 10,000th home. A mere eight years later, in 1985, Ryland celebrated the completion of its 50,000th home.

### Diversification and Continued Growth: Late 1970s–Early 1990s

The purchase in 1978 of Crest Communities in Cincinnati, Ohio, launched Ryland's mortgage operations, modestly begun through Crest's subsidiary Crest Financial Services. From there Ryland Mortgage Company grew to become one of the nation's largest mortgage-finance companies, offering a full range of mortgage financing with branches in 18 states. In 1981, with the acquisition of Guardian Mortgage Company, RMC introduced full loan servicing. By the early 1990s, RMC was handling more than $2 billion in mortgage loans on an annual basis. In 1982 RMC formed Ryland Acceptance Corporation (which became a wholly owned subsidiary of RMC in 1987), an administrator and distributor of mortgage-backed securities.

During the 1990s Ryland entered the booming Florida and California home building markets. In the latter, the M.J. Brock Corporation, with divisions in Los Angeles and Sacramento, was acquired in 1986. Ryland homes were marketed in California under the Brock or Larchmont Homes labels, and by the early 1990s 40 percent of the company's business derived from southern California. At that time, however, the savings and loans scandal and the recession of the early 1990s struck California especially hard and moderated returns from land investment in the Golden State.

Fortunately, at the same time Ryland was expanding in California, it was also vigorously penetrating markets in Arizona, Colorado, Georgia, and North and South Carolina. In 1987 Ryland crossed the $1 billion mark in revenues; that same year founder James P. Ryan retired from the board of directors. In 1989 Ryland established the Cornerstone Title Company, a wholly owned subsidiary of RMC in Columbia, Maryland, that administered real estate closings.

Market analysts gave Ryland credit for its geographical diversity, which enabled the company to compensate for difficulties in California and other local markets experiencing periodic difficulties. Ryland expanded into the Midwest as well as expanding its activities in the Southwest.

With mortgage interests declining during the recession, Ryland Mortgage Company had record profits, derived largely from entering the "spot loan" origination market. The savings and loan crisis, which culminated in the federal government taking over the ailing financial institutions and selling off their assets one by one, also became an advantage for RMC. Ryland's powerful mortgage servicing division, one of the largest in the country, benefitted from the federal government's assumption of mortgage servicing contracts when S & L home mortgages were taken over by the government; by the early 1990s, they comprised approximately 50 percent of RMC's mortgage servicing portfolio.

With the worst of the recession over by 1993, the company was stronger than ever. The housing market had recovered completely, with the exception of California and Florida. Thanks to Ryland's geographical diversity and its conservative business philosophy, it had not only weathered the recession (earnings climbed a phenomenal 191 percent between 1991 and 1992) but, unlike many of its competitors, company finances were in the black. Annual revenues still topped $1 billion. The company's four manufacturing centers, which produce the basic materials (lumber and trim) for all Ryland homes except those in the western states, were working over capacity. Ever attuned to the marketplace, the company shifted its marketing strategy in the 1990s to larger homes that did not necessarily cater to first-time home buyers. The average price of a Ryland home climbed to more than $150,000, with resulting larger profit margins.

In February 1991, Ryland Homes was asked to build single-family housing units in Israel because of that country's massive influx of immigrants from Russia. Unlike Israeli stone houses, which take an average of 18 months to build, Ryland homes could be assembled in a matter of weeks. Eventually, 1,300 housing shells were carefully packed in crates for assembling in Israel. In so doing, Ryland became the biggest American manufacturer of Israeli homes, earning a profit of $13 million.

Also in 1991 the company formed a new subsidiary, Ryland Trading Ltd., to specialize in building Ryland homes for the overseas market, with a particular eye toward market opportunities in Eastern Europe and the former Soviet Union. The federal government even contributed $400,000 in two grants to Ryland Trading Ltd. to encourage it to study housing-market opportunities and the construction of housing factories in the former Soviet Union.

The result was the first U.S. housing project in newly renamed St. Petersburg, Russia, which had not seen the completion of new private housing in more than 70 years. In 1992 Ryland, in a joint venture with Russian companies, began a housing settlement outside of the city consisting of American-style homes priced at $150,000 and up. The homes were targeted toward the increasingly large contingent of foreign businessmen and women in Russia. In a very short time Ryland Trading Ltd. had also expanded its joint-venture portfolios with Mexico, Spain, Turkey, and Senegal.

### New Directions in the Mid- to Late 1990s

Though Ryland appeared to be on track, the company struggled with the effects of its expansion efforts and the economic recession, and Ryland posted a net loss of $2.7 million for fiscal 1993. R. Chad Dreier, who joined Ryland in November 1993 as president and CEO and became chairman in 1994, implemented a restructuring strategy that turned Ryland's efforts back to its core business of building homes. Dreier planned to de-emphasize Ryland's mortgage banking operations, believing that over the long term, the company would meet with the highest profits and the most success by concentrating on home construction, managing costs more effectively, and establishing a strong national

<table>
<tr><th colspan="2">Key Dates:</th></tr>
<tr><td>1967:</td><td>James P. Ryan Company is formed.</td></tr>
<tr><td>1970:</td><td>Company is renamed The Ryland Group, Inc.</td></tr>
<tr><td>1971:</td><td>The Ryland Group goes public.</td></tr>
<tr><td>1978:</td><td>Ryland Mortgage Company is founded.</td></tr>
<tr><td>1983:</td><td>The company's stock moves to the New York Stock Exchange.</td></tr>
<tr><td>1987:</td><td>The Ryland Group's revenues surpass the $1 billion mark.</td></tr>
<tr><td>2000:</td><td>Corporate headquarters are relocated from Maryland to California.</td></tr>
</table>

profile. Ryland also intended to increase customer satisfaction, which had declined from a high of about 85 percent in the late 1980s to less than 70 percent in the early 1990s, by introducing new home models and allowing more customer customization.

In 1995 Ryland sold its Institutional Financial Services division, which handled a $46 billion portfolio, to Norwest Bank Minnesota. The divestment of the division, a leading private issuer and administrator of mortgage-backed securities, was in keeping with Ryland's strategy to concentrate on home-building and retail mortgage finance services. The following year Crestar Financial Corp. acquired Ryland's wholesale mortgage banking operations, known as Ryland Funding Group.

Ryland's streamlining began to pay off in 1996, when the company reported net earnings of about $16 million, up from a net loss of $2.6 million in fiscal 1995. Still, the company faced many challenges, including a relatively slow housing market that led to declines in both Ryland's number of homes built (8,388, a decline of 6.2 percent compared to closings in 1994) and new home orders (7,838, a fall of 14.2 percent). In 1997 Ryland upped its net income to $22 million, but the number of closings was flat, at 8,377 houses built.

Continuing to improve operations and sticking with its focus on the business of home construction, Ryland sold $2.7 billion in mortgages to PNC Mortgage Corp. of America in 1998, leaving Ryland with a loan servicing balance of about $800 million. The company planned to continue offering home loans to buyers of Ryland homes but felt increasing competition in the home financing business made remaining in the business risky and potentially unprofitable. While shedding some mortgages, Ryland also made some gains—the company acquired Regency Communities, a Florida homebuilder, and Thomas Builders of Baltimore. The Regency purchase provided Ryland with a strong foothold in the growing retirement market in Florida.

Net earnings for fiscal 1998 nearly doubled to $40 million, up from $22 million in fiscal 1997. The number of homes built rose to 8,994 homes, and Ryland appeared securely back on track. Earnings during the first quarter of 1999 jumped 116 percent compared to first-quarter earnings in 1998, marking the sixth consecutive quarter of increased earnings. 1999 was certainly proof that Ryland could do better, as the company reported record earnings of $66.7 million on revenues of $2 billion for the full year. The number of houses built surged 13 percent to 10,193 homes, and new orders increased by 10 percent.

The company made a major change in 1999 when it decided to move its mortgage subsidiary to southern California. Corporate headquarters soon followed, completing the relocation in 2000. California was known as a leader in homebuilding innovation, and Ryland hoped to capitalize on the connection and keep a closer eye on homebuilding trends. The move apparently did not affect Ryland's bottom line, and the company continued to report recording earnings and strong sales. For the first nine months of 2000, Ryland reported consolidated net earnings of $50.7 million, up from $45.9 million for the first nine months of 1999. The company planned to keep the momentum going in the 21st century by keeping in tune with customers' lifestyles and wishes, which included the possibility of building more townhouse communities and retirement communities targeted toward "active adults" and expanding into new housing markets, such as the rapidly growing markets of Las Vegas, St. Louis, Detroit, and Nashville. "We're proud of our product now, of what we're doing," CEO Dreier told the *Baltimore Sun,* adding, "We've had bumps in the road and bad days, but we've now created a pride that we know we're going to do better in the future."

### *Principal Subsidiaries*

Ryland Mortgage Company; Cornerstone Title Company; RH of Indiana LP; RH of Texas LP; Ryland Homes of Arizona, Inc.; Ryland Homes of California; Ryland Homes of Florida, Inc.

### *Principal Competitors*

Pulte Corp.; Centex Corp.; Kaufman & Broad Home Corp.; D.R. Horton, Inc.; Lennar Corp.

### *Further Reading*

Blumenthal, Robyn G., "Ryland Group Inc. Indicates Net Rose in Third Quarter," *Wall Street Journal,* October 12, 1992, p. B6.

Fink, Ronald, "Ryland Group: the Contracyclical Developer?," *Financial World,* March 3, 1992, p. 15.

Henry, Kristine, "Ryland Homes' Earnings Leap 128%," *Baltimore Sun,* July 24, 1998, p. 2C.

Kaplan, Peter, "Ryland Leads Home Builders in Work Abroad," *Baltimore Business Journal,* February 21, 1992, p. 3.

Kyriakos, Marianne, "Getting Focused at Ryland," *Washington Post,* December 13, 1993, p. F8.

McQuaid, Kevin L., "Ryland Group Announces Sale of $2.7 Billion in Mortgages," *Baltimore Sun,* April 4, 1998, p. 12C.

——, "Ryland Posts Another Gain," *Baltimore Sun,* February 4, 1997, p. 1C.

——, "Ryland Raises Roof after Turnaround," *Baltimore Sun,* April 18, 1999, p. 1D.

——, "Ryland Undergoes Alterations," *Baltimore Sun,* January 15, 1995, p. 1D.

Salmon, Jacqueline L., "Ryland Group's Tough Year," *Washington Post,* November 15, 1993, p. F5.

Snow, Katherine, "Russian Houses to Carry 'Made in USA' Label," *Business Journal Charlotte,* September 21, 1992, p. 1.

Wells, Melanie, "Builders Still Falling as Market Hits Bottom (Washington Area Residential Real Estate Market)," *Washington Business Journal,* September 2, 1991, p. 13.

—Sina Dubovoj
—updated by Mariko Fujinaka

# SAGEM S.A.

6, avenue d'Iena
75783 Paris Cedex 16
France
Telephone: (+33) 1 40 70 63 63
Fax: (+33) 1 47 20 39 46
Web site: http://www.sagem.com

*Public Company*
*Incorporated:* 1924 as Société pour l'Application
    Générale de l'Electricité et de la Mécanique
*Employees:* 15,600
*Sales:* FFr 22.37 billion (EUR 3.4 billion; US$3 billion)
    (1999)
*Stock Exchanges:* Euronext Paris
*NAIC:* 334220 Radio and Television Broadcasting and
    Wireless Communications Equipment Manufacturing;
    334511 Search, Detection, Navigation, Guidance,
    Aeronautical, and Nautical System and Instrument
    Manufacturing

French high-tech company SAGEM S.A. has carved out a commanding position for itself among the world's top electronics companies, despite its relatively modest size. France's second largest maker of telecommunications equipment, and one of the world leaders, SAGEM produces GSM and WAP mobile telephone handsets, a market in which SAGEM's products account for more than one-half of total market sales, fax machines, networking systems, and digital set-top boxes for Internet, cable, and satellite transmissions. The communications division accounts for more than 56 percent of the company's fast-rising sales, which topped FFr 22 billion (EUR 4.3 billion) in 1999. SAGEM is also Europe's number two leading electronics group manufacturing for the defense and security industries. Within its special product categories, SAGEM has built up European and global leadership positions, such as inertial guidance systems, optronic systems, and helicopter flight controls. Through its SAGEM Morpho subsidiary, the company is the world leader in automatic fingerprint recognition systems, used by police forces and other agencies throughout the world. SAGEM also produces optics systems for the space and astronomy industries. The Defense division accounts for 22 percent of total company sales. SAGEM's third product segment is the automotive market, where the company specializes in automotive electronics systems, such as engine management, body electronics, injection and ignition systems and sensors, and cockpit electronics. The company's automotive division adds another 22 percent to the company's sales. SAGEM's global interest is reflected in the growing share of international sales in its overall sales. More than 46 percent of SAGEM's revenues were generated outside of France in 1999. Led by Chairman and CEO Pierre Faurre, the company has more than doubled its annual sales in ten years, and continued growth is forecasted, by as much as 30 percent, for the year 2000. Quoted on the Euronext Paris stock exchange, the company's shares remained, in large part, owned by its employees.

### Turning to High Technology in the 1980s

Marcel Môme founded the Société pour l'Application Générale de l'Electricité et de la Mécanique (SAGEM) in Paris in 1924. Formed initially to produce tools and other equipment for French tire maker Michelin, Môme, who remained at the head of the company until 1962, soon turned to the defense industry. After the end of the Second World War, the company became still more closely involved in the country's defense and aeronautics industries. The company continued its defense focus through the leadership of its second president, Robert Labarre, who took over the lead of the company from Môme and remained in place until 1987.

Although SAGEM remained primarily a defense contractor, the company also branched out into the telecommunications sector, perfecting a line of telex machine products to become the world's number two manufacturer in the category. SAGEM's emphasis on research and development enabled it quickly to capture the world leadership in the next generation of screen-based telex machines, which appeared in the early 1980s. By then, however, a new type of communications product was appearing on the market, threatening SAGEM's position.

346

## Key Dates:

**1924:** Marcel Môme founds the Société pour l'Application Générale de l'Electricité et de la Mécanique (SAGEM).
**1940s:** Company begins production of telex machines.
**1962:** Robert Labarre is named president and CEO.
**1985:** Pierre Faurre leads management buyout of company.
**1987:** Faurre is named president and CEO; launch of first company-made fax machine.
**1990:** Launch of new generation fax machine.
**1995:** Company enters automobile electronics market.
**1999:** SFIM Industries is acquired.
**2000:** SFIM and other subsidiaries are consolidated as SAGEM operating divisions.

The arrival of the first facsimile machines, a technology developed in Japan, promised a new means of communication—and the end of the dominance of the costlier telex machine. The facsimile machine, though still mostly confined to businesses, promised to become a household appliance by the early 1990s. Caught by surprise, most of the European electronics community, including heavyweights such as Alcatel and Siemens, found itself outpaced by such Asian rivals as Matsushita, Samsung, and Canon.

Rather than attempt to enter the head-to-head competition for the facsimile market, yet eager to save the market position built up through its telex sales, SAGEM took an approach different from that of its larger European competitors. Instead of risking its own resources on developing the technology to produce its own facsimile machines, particularly given the high cost of developing first-generation technology, SAGEM entered a distribution agreement with Japan's Murata, in which the French company took over the marketing of two of Murata's low-end and mid-level facsimile machines in Europe. The agreement also called for SAGEM to adapt the fax machines to the various specifications of the European market—an area in which the company's long leadership of the telex machine market had given it ample experience.

By the mid-1980s, the competition to produce the first generation of fax machines had exhausted many of SAGEM's would-be competitors. SAGEM, which had used its Murata distribution deal as a stepping stone to developing and perfecting its own facsimile machine technology, now prepared to enter the fray. By then the company was also boasting new management, as Pierre Faurre, leading a management buyout of the company in 1985, prepared to take over the reins from Robert Labarre.

Faurre was to be credited with reshaping SAGEM into one of France's and Europe's leading high-technology specialists. Graduating at the top of his class at the elite French university Polytechnique, Faurre had earned a Ph.D. at Stanford University, before joining the prestigious Corps des Mines in 1967. At the same time, Faurre joined in establishing the French Research Institute of Computer Science and Automation (INRIA), while serving as a technical consultant for SAGEM. Faurre formally joined SAGEM in 1972, first as the company's general secretary, then as its general manager in 1983.

### High-Technology Leader in the 1990s

Faurre had immediately grasped the importance of the new facsimile machines and the need for SAGEM to compete in this new arena—particularly as it threatened to render the telex all but obsolete. At the same time, the dethawed political climate, as the Soviet Union introduced new liberties—and prepared to collapse by decade's end—spelled the end of the era of huge defense budgets, placing SAGEM in the position of seeing the collapse of its primary market as well.

In 1987, after Faurre was named chairman and CEO of the company, SAGEM entered the battle for the fax machine manufacturing market. During the company's distribution agreement with Murata, its own research and development component—nearly one-third of its workforce—had not only allowed the company to catch up to its competitors, but to surpass them with cutting-edge innovations. As such, the first SAGEM fax machine was also the smallest to feature the A4 format size. SAGEM continued to post innovations in the category, adding screen menus to its fax machines in 1988. In 1989, the company helped to revolutionize the fax machine market when it introduced the first machine capable of printing on standard paper, instead of the expensive thermal paper used by earlier machines. The company also saw rising sales, topping the FFr 10 billion mark in 1990, with communications products taking a growing share against the company's defense sector revenues.

The new machine helped boost SAGEM to the ranks of the world's leading facsimile machine manufacturers—and enabled the company to capture the European leadership early in the 1990s. The company also extended its product range, which allowed it to end its distribution agreement with Murata. SAGEM's experience in the European market gave it a competitive edge against its Japanese competitors, who tended to introduce standard models that then had to be adapted to each of the various country-specific norms then in place throughout the continent. SAGEM was able instead to produce its models for each specific market, which placed the company's machines in high demand among such third parties as France Telecom, British Telecom, Telefax, Impronta, Alcatel, and Siemens. By the early 1990s, less than one-third of SAGEM's production actually bore the company's own name.

In 1991, SAGEM helped again to revolutionize the fax machine market when it launched the first machines destined not to corporations, but to individual consumers. The new generation of machines, sold in department stores, also became a significant part of a growing movement toward home offices, even before the appearance of widespread Internet access. The movement into the consumer market encouraged the company to strengthen its mass production facilities, as SAGEM began building a manufacturing network into such countries as Germany, Brazil, Spain, the United States, and the Czech Republic by the end of the decade.

By controlling almost the totality of its production—from the design to production of components—SAGEM had given itself a strong high-technology foundation. The company's excellence in communications technologies was to stand it in good stead as the years leading up to the new century quickly proved to be the inauguration of a new era in communication. The perfection of mobile telephony to the new digital television technologies and the debut of the so-called "net-economy," as well as the refinement of electronic automotive and other systems, all represented potential bonanzas for SAGEM. By the mid-1990s, SAGEM had developed a reputation as a highly successful high-tech niche player, with communications products ranging from its fax machines, credit card readers, and digital set-top boxes.

The company entered the automotive market in the mid-1990s. Adapting its technology to automotive control systems and other automotive components enabled the company quickly to place itself among the top ranks of European automobile electronics suppliers. The company also started an acquisition drive to expand its technology reach, buying up Souriau Diagnostique, a maker of engine controls, and Eyquem, which manufactured more than 75 million spark plugs per year. Meanwhile, the company made a foray into televisions, purchasing Kaïsui. In addition, SAGEM was making a mark in the race to provide digital set-top boxes and decoders for satellite television, especially in the United States, providing decoders for the Echostar system.

By the mid-1990s, SAGEM's revenues had climbed to more than FFr 15 billion. The company had easily weathered the extended economic crisis as well, posting steady increases in net profits, which neared FFr 550 million in 1995. The company's international sales also were taking an increasingly prominent place in SAGEM's balance sheet, reaching one-third of total sales. By then, too, the company's communications products had outpaced, in large part, its defense sector activity, which accounted for only 22 percent of its sales. SAGEM's automotive branch, launched in the mid-1990s, quickly grew to match the size of the company's defense division. Yet communications products continued to provide the fuel for the company's growth.

The company had placed itself, meanwhile, in prime position to reap the benefits of the coming explosion in the mobile telephone market. Although the mobile telephones at first were restricted for the most part to a corporate market, the definition of a European-wide GSM mobile telephony standard, the deregulation of Europe's telephone markets, and the introduction of competition as former national telephone monopolies were shattered, helped bring the mobile telephone to the mass market. Beginning in 1997, with the appearance of affordable mobile telephones and consumer-oriented subscription plans, sales of mobile telephones skyrocketed. SAGEM quickly became one of the world's leading manufacturers of GSM telephones, and the undisputed French leader, with some 50 percent of the market.

Even as SAGEM's fortunes soared with the mobile telephone booming, it also was reaping the rewards of strong investment in Internet and networking technologies, as the world's economies began a shift toward the Net-based economy. At the same time, SAGEM benefited as France and other countries stepped up their levels of defense spending, replacing aging equipment with new, cutting-edge systems. By 1999, the company sales leaped by more than 19 percent from the year before, topping FFr 22.3 billion. SAGEM also was eminently profitable, with net profits nearing the FFr 1 billion mark. In that year, the company helped boost its defense division with the acquisition of defense technology company SFIM, formerly held by French investment bank Paribas and nuclear powerhouse Framatome.

In the year 2000, SAGEM hoped to improve on its already strong performance, forecasting rises in revenues of as much as 30 percent. After turning around the money-losing SFIM operation, that subsidiary and others were consolidated as operating divisions of SAGEM. Much of the company's hopes lay in the adoption of the next-generation WAP (Wireless Access Protocol) telephones. The rollout of that technology, however, did not meet with the anticipated acceptance by mid-2000. Nonetheless, the convergence of the Internet with the mobile telephone seemed a near certainty as the new century got under way. SAGEM's position at the technology center promised strong growth for the future.

### Principal Subsidiaries

Sagem CR; SAGEM Morpho Inc. (United States); Sagem Inc. (United States); SFIM Industries; AVIAC; CERME; REOSC; SCI Minerve.

### Principal Competitors

Alcatel; Digital Biometrics Inc.; Nokia Corporation; Pace Micro Technology PLC; Robert Bosch GmbH; Siemens AG; Tyco International Ltd.

### Further Reading

Gallard, Philippe, "Comment SAGEM a conquis le fax Européen," *Le Nouvel Economiste,* November 25, 1994, p. 66.

Jacquier, Jean-François, "SAGEM, l'empire des niches," *L'Expansion,* June 11, 1995, p. 62.

Lamm, Patrick, Philippe Escande, and Vincent Collen, "Interview: Le président de SAGEM, Pierre Faurre," *Les Echos,* January 11, 2000, p. 16.

——, "Premiere World Orders Digital TV Decoders from SAGEM," *European Report,* September 2, 2000.

——, "SAGEM Embellishing European Market Position," *Wireless Today,* October 15, 1999.

—M.L. Cohen

# Santa Barbara Restaurant Group, Inc.

3938 State Street, Suite 200
Santa Barbara, California 93105
U.S.A.
Telephone: (805) 563-3644
Fax: (805) 563-3844
Web site: http://www.sbrg.com

*Public Company*
*Incorporated:* 1986 as GB Foods Inc.
*Employees:* 5,000
*Sales:* $114.4 million (1999)
*Stock Exchanges:* NASDAQ
*Ticker Symbol:* SBRG
*NAIC:* 72211 Full-Service Restaurants

Santa Barbara Restaurant Group, Inc. (SBRG) owns or franchises three different restaurant chains: La Salsa (which specializes in moderately priced "fresh mex" cuisine and of which there are about 100); Timber Lodge Steakhouses (in 20 locations); and Green Burrito restaurants (roughly 40 stand-alone eateries). SBRG also operates 214 dual-concept restaurants with the fast food chain Carl's Jr. (which is owned by CKE Restaurants, Inc.). In 2000, SBRG was in the process of divesting its 52 JB's Family Restaurants and six Galaxy Diner establishments. William Foley, the restaurant mogul who presides over CKE, is SBRG's chairman and exerts considerable influence over the company.

## Humble Beginnings: 1980–85

SBRG's roots date back to 1980, when a Puerto Rican-born social worker named Ruben Rodriguez paid $40,000 for a small Mexican restaurant—The Green Burrito—a few blocks from his house in the Los Angeles suburb of Hawaiian Garden. Dissatisfied with the eatery's heavy menu, Rodriguez took night classes in cooking and invented new recipes that were fresher and lighter. He wanted his establishment to occupy a market niche between fast food Mexican chains such as Taco Bell and more expensive sit-down Mexican restaurants. His strategy was validated as sales at the Green Burrito began to soar.

In 1985 Rodriguez met Gary McArthur, a more experienced restaurateur who was familiar with owning, operating, and developing franchises (though his previous venture in franchise building had resulted in bankruptcy). McArthur was enchanted by Green Burrito's potential, and he pushed Rodriguez to franchise the concept.

## Franchising and Growth: 1986–92

Rodriguez and McArthur joined with attorney Robert Gibson in 1986 and founded GB Foods Inc., which owned the rights to the Green Burrito name and oversaw the building of new restaurants (both company-owned and franchised). The troika ran the fledgling company as an executive committee: Rodriguez (with an 18.8 percent share in the venture) dealt directly with the franchisees; McArthur (who controlled 17.4 percent of GB Foods) administered the company; and Gibson (with a 4.4 percent stake) provided legal counsel.

For the next four years, GB Foods rolled out new company-owned stores and franchises in the Los Angeles area. The company differentiated itself from rival chains in a number of ways. Rather than pay a premium for roadside real estate, GB Foods built Green Burrito restaurants in less expensive strip malls. Green Burrito also abjured the plastic booths, drive-thrus, and multiple cashier stands characteristic of most fast food establishments in favor of real tables and long wooden order counters. In addition, its diverse menu featured an assortment of traditional Mexican dishes, such as tacos, burritos, tostados, chile rellenos, and flan.

What truly distinguished Green Burrito from its counterparts, though, was its centralized food preparation and high-quality ingredients. GB Foods insisted that all proprietary menu items be prepared at the company's commissary. Less than a dozen cooks created dishes for all Green Burrito eateries. The dishes were delivered twice a week to individual restaurants, which then put the finishing touches on them. This method ensured a consistent quality of food and also helped keep costs down by allowing the company to pay its managers less (as they had fewer supervisory responsibilities). These lower labor costs enabled the company to buy more expensive ingredients; GB

Foods spent 38 percent more than the average fast food establishment on its ingredients, using items such as Grade A white chicken meat and 95 percent lean pork not generally found at its competitors' restaurants.

The company blossomed during the late 1980s. Between 1985 and 1990, GB Foods built a network of nine company-owned and 23 franchised Green Burrito restaurants. Low start-up costs made the franchises attractive to prospective owners. GB Foods sold its franchises for $25,000, and without the need for heavy cooking equipment or drive-thru technology, start-up costs to the franchisee ranged from $209,900 to $312,500 in 1990 (compared with the $400,000 needed simply to purchase a lot to construct a Taco Bell restaurant). GB Foods' revenues tripled between 1987 and 1990, while its profits grew twelvefold. Between 1989 and 1990 alone, the company's net revenue soared from $3.66 million to $5.08 million. This rate of growth—GB Foods' sales rose 39 percent in 1990 alone—was particularly impressive as the rate of increase industry-wide during the same period was only one percent. "We have no limits," an ebullient Rodriguez told the *Orange County Business Journal,* adding, "I think we can be the McDonald's of the 1990s."

Buoyed by such optimism, GB Foods sought to expand more rapidly. In 1990, Rodriguez, McArthur, and Gibson merged GB Foods Inc. with GB Foods Ltd. (which they had founded in 1989) to form GB Foods Corp. Soon thereafter, they took their company public, selling off roughly 39 percent of their holdings, in the hope of generating capital to fund future growth. The $2.9 million they raised was immediately used to begin construction on four new company-owned stores. In December of 1990 GB Foods leased a larger commissary capable of preparing food for more than 300 individual Green Burrito restaurants.

By September of 1992, 44 Green Burrito restaurants existed, all in the Los Angeles area. Rodriguez opted to locate some of his newest restaurants in less-traveled areas such as La Verne and Temecula so that Green Burrito could beat the "majors" (the likes of Taco Bell and McDonald's) in establishing new markets. "They're going to wake up to our stores out there and hear our salsa; the salsa music we play in our stores," Rodriguez averred in the September 7, 1991, *Los Angeles Times.* Despite his bravado, there were indications that GB Foods was overextended. The company reported a net loss in 1991 (although sales rose to $8.5 million).

### Ups and Downs: 1992–96

In April of 1992 GB Foods signed an agreement with KFF Management, a 62-unit Arby's franchise in Los Angeles, to convert ten underperforming Arby's restaurants into dual-concept stores that offered both Green Burrito and Arby's menus. The first such establishment opened in September. Within weeks, sales at that store nearly doubled. But GB Foods lacked sufficient capital to continue to expand (it had, in fact, reported losses for every quarter but one since it had gone public in 1990). To improve its financial picture, the company sold about 20 percent of its common stock (one million shares) for $3.1 million to William Theisen in November of 1992. In return, Theisen gained a seat on GB Foods' board of directors, as well as voting control of a majority of the company's common stock.

Theisen was the wildly successful founder of Godfather's Pizza, which he had launched as a single restaurant in 1973. Within ten years the chain had grown to 950 units and Theisen sold it to the Pillsbury Co. But Green Burrito's potential brought him out of semi-retirement. Theisen's enthusiasm stemmed from his belief that he could make a Godfather's Pizza-style triumph out of Green Burrito. He planned to transform the regional chain into a national powerhouse of 3,000 restaurants by adding 500 stores each year.

To meet his ambitious expansion goals, Theisen aimed to graft Green Burrito franchises onto existing fast food restaurants. GB Foods' dual-concept success at Arby's restaurants showed that the idea was a viable one, and that offering two distinct menus could boost sales at stagnant fast food restaurants. Moreover, since almost all of Green Burrito's menu was precooked off-premises, fast food chains would need to make only minimal changes to accommodate Green Burrito.

Theisen immediately began to cast about for a partner to implement his dual-concept restaurants, settling on Carl N. Karcher, the chairman of CKE Restaurants, Inc. (which was the parent company of Carl's Jr.). Although Karcher was supportive of the idea (and of the loan Theisen was prepared to make him), the rest of CKE's board was not. After a boardroom battle, Karcher was dismissed as CKE's chairman.

With prospects of partnering with CKE dimming, GB Foods looked for other ways to leverage the Green Burrito brand and drive expansion outside the southern California region. In April of 1993 GB Foods signed an agreement with D.I. Manufacturing Inc., the parent company of Deli International, for that concern to distribute Green Burrito products through its system of grocery stores, convenience stores, and warehouse clubs. In September GB Foods joined with Eagle Distributing Co. (the snack food arm of the Anheuser-Busch Companies, Inc.) to market Green Burrito frozen snacks in bars, convenience stores, supermarkets, and restaurants. Despite these steps, GB Foods continued to lose money.

Matters worsened in May of 1993, when GB Foods was sued by 13 Green Burrito franchisees. The plaintiffs claimed that GB Foods had overstated the sales volume of typical Green Burrito restaurants to lure franchisees, had improperly directed start-up franchisees to subcontractors who were relatives of the company, and had concealed the fact that company founder Gibson had been sanctioned by the Securities and Exchange Commission and that McArthur had declared bankruptcy. The franchisees demanded repayment of their start-up costs. GB Foods denied the allegations but eventually settled the suit in May 1994, agreeing to give the franchisees $280,000 in cash and 400,000 shares of stock.

The following month, another round of Green Burrito franchisees made identical claims. (The case settled on similar terms.) Rodriguez and Gibson resigned shortly thereafter, though they denied that their abrupt departure was related to the lawsuits. Theisen assumed Rodriguez's position as chairman and chief executive officer, while Gibson was replaced as chief financial officer by Madeline Cline.

GB Foods' fortunes revived in June of 1994, when CKE reversed its earlier opposition to dual-concept restaurants and agreed to introduce Green Burrito menus at six Carl's Jr. locations. CKE's about-face was due in large part to a change in leadership. (After Karcher's ouster in October of 1993, William Foley II led a team of investors who took control of Karcher's stock. Early in 1994, Foley was named CKE's chairman, and he negotiated Karcher's return to the company as chairman emeritus.) If the dual-concept restaurants proved successful, CKE would exchange warrants for up to 20 percent of GB Foods' stock, and GB Foods would purchase up to 2.5 percent of CKE stock.

Unfortunately, the agreement was temporarily jeopardized in 1995, when CKE began to test its own Mexican fast food chain, Picante Grill, in Carl's Jr. GB Foods immediately filed suit against CKE, alleging breach of contract. The dispute blew over in May 1995 when CKE agreed to convert at least 140 Carl's Jr. restaurants to dual-concept stores with Green Burrito. That same month, Rally's Hamburger Inc., a chain with 500 restaurants in 23 states, also announced that it would incorporate Green Burrito franchises into some of its restaurants. These arrangements seemed to offer benefits to all parties. Green Burrito hoped to profit from both the national exposure and the franchising fees it would collect (a $7,500 development fee for each burger unit, as well as a four percent royalty on all Green Burrito sales). Carl's Jr. was plagued by flattening sales and wanted to boost its tired brand image.

In the end, the dual-concept system assisted CKE far more than GB Foods. The incorporation of Green Burrito into Carl's Jr. was a huge success (some stores reported sales increases of up to 25 percent after the changeover), bolstering CKE's bottom line. GB Foods, on the other hand, lost $4.5 million on sales of $6.3 million in 1994, and its gross revenues continued to trend downward, dropping to $6.2 million in 1995 and $4.5 million in 1996. To stanch the bleeding, Theisen closed GB Foods' company-owned restaurants to devote more resources to joint branding efforts.

### Changing Direction: 1997 and Beyond

In July 1997, CKE Chairman Foley shocked the industry when his Fidelity National Financial Inc. (which owned seven title insurance companies) paid $5.8 million for a 41 percent stake in GB Foods. Theisen resigned and was replaced as chairman by Foley and as CEO by Andrew Puzder (a former executive vice-president at Fidelity). Although most analysts speculated that Foley took control of GB Foods primarily to buttress the Carl's Jr. revival, Foley proved such rumors wrong in 1998 when he led GB Foods into new sectors of the restaurant business.

In April of 1998 GB Foods announced plans to acquire JB's Family Restaurants from CKE (a deal that included 62 company-owned JB's restaurants, 20 franchisee-owned JB's restaurants, and six Galaxy Diners). GB Foods also sought to purchase Timber Lodge Steakhouse Inc., a chain of 18 family-style restaurants concentrated in Minnesota, South Dakota, and Wisconsin. To facilitate these massive transactions, GB Foods formed a strategic alliance with Franchise Finance Corp. of America. Under the terms of the deal, Franchise would provide the money for GB Foods to acquire land or property, but would lease the restaurants back to GB Foods. The two acquisitions transformed GB Foods ''from a company with annual sales of $5.3 million into one with about $100 million,'' the *Orange County Register* reported on August 22, 1998. GB Foods' board approved the various facets of the arrangement in September. The company re-christened itself Santa Barbara Restaurant Group (SBRG) to reflect the new diversity of its holdings. By the close of 1998 SBRG controlled 343 restaurants, which generated $35.6 million in sales.

SBRG continued to grow in 1999. In July the company completed the purchase of La Salsa Holding Co., the parent company of 50 company-owned and 48 franchised La Salsa Fresh Mexican Grill Restaurants. Soon after, SBRG announced that it would sell JB's to focus more heavily on ''fresh Mex'' restaurants and steakhouses. Fresh Mex represented an upscale, quick-service alternative to traditional Mexican fast food. Made from high-quality ingredients (often displayed for customers), fresh Mex restaurants were taking the industry—especially in the western United States—by storm. SBRG planned to expand fresh Mex La Salsa beyond California, into regions where Taco Bell dominated the Mexican food market.

SBRG was forced to pursue fresh Mex in another arena as well. The company's freestanding Green Burrito restaurants (those not attached to a Carl's Jr.) successfully sued SBRG for cheapening the Green Burrito brand by SBRG's association of it with fast food restaurants. In 2000, SBRG agreed to provide $1.2 million in loans to its 42 freestanding Green Burrito franchisees for remodeling. Ruben Rodriguez emerged from retirement to take charge of the overhaul. In an effort to distinguish themselves from the dual-concept Green Burritos, the freestanding restaurants planned to focus more on fresh Mex and to rename themselves The Grill by Green Burrito.

In June 2000, Puzder left the SBRG to become the new CEO and president of Hardee's (which CKE had acquired in 1997). Although his post as SBRG's CEO was left unfilled for some time in 2000, and SBRG struggled to integrate its latest far-flung holdings, the company was on solid ground. Sales in 1999 topped $114 million, and the company continued to concentrate on its multifaceted efforts to develop its dual-concept restaurants, to build its presence in the lucrative fresh Mex market, and to expand Timber Lodge Steakhouse.

### Principal Subsidiaries

Timber Lodge Steakhouse, Inc.; La Salsa Holding Company.

### Principal Competitors

Advantica Restaurant Group, Inc.; CBRL Group, Inc.; Metromedia Company; Outback Steakhouse Inc.; Pancho's Mexican Buffet, Inc.; Ryan's Family Steakhouse, Inc.; Taco Bell Corp.

### Further Reading

Barron, Kelly, "Burrito Banditos: Bucking Industry Norms Works for Fast Food Upstart," *Orange County Business Journal,* May 27, 1991.

Chow, Elaine, "The Whole Enchilada," *Orange County Register,* January 10, 1991.

Hardesty, Greg, "GB Gets a Major Helping of Funds," *Orange County Register,* August 22, 1998.

——, "Green Burrito Parent Likes Taste of La Salsa," *Orange Country Register,* June 9, 1999.

Martin, Richard, "CKE Board Reverses Dual-Brand Decision," *Nation's Restaurant News,* July 11, 1994.

Mouchard, Andre, "Furor Over Franchises," *Orange County Register,* May 7, 1993.

Rasmussen, Jim, "Green Burrito Coming to Omaha Soon, Theisen Says," *Omaha World-Herald,* January 21, 1993.

——, "Theisen Tosses His Sombrero into Food Ring," *Omaha World-Herald,* November 25, 1992.

Reyes, David, " 'Burrito King' Masters Recipe for Success," *Los Angeles Times,* September 7, 1991.

Taylor, John, "Agreements with Theisen Mean 'Pass the Burrito,' " *Omaha-World-Herald,* May 31, 1995.

Yoshitake, Dawn, "Founders of Green Burrito Parent Firm to Resign July 1," *Orange County Register,* June 22, 1994.

——, "Green Burrito, Carl's Jr. in Suit," *Orange County Register,* January 6, 1995.

—Rebecca Stanfel

# Sensory Science Corporation

**7835 East McClain Drive**
**Scottsdale, Arizona 85260**
**U.S.A.**
**Telephone: (480) 998-3400**
**Fax: (480) 951-4404**
**Web site: http://www.sensoryscience.com**

*Public Company*
*Incorporated:* 1984 as Go-Video, Inc.
*Employees:* 97
*Sales:* $72.14 million (2000)
*Stock Exchanges:* American
*Ticker Symbol:* VCR
*NAIC:* 33431 Audio and Video Equipment Manufacturing

Sensory Science Corporation designs, develops, and markets electronic video and audio products, concentrating on high-performance digital televisions, DVD players, CD players, VCRs, home-theater systems, and portable MP3 players. Sensory Science's products are sold in major retail outlets and through catalogues. Until 1999, the company operated as Go-Video, Inc., the embattled pioneer of dual-deck VCRs. Diversification into other product lines during the late 1990s prompted a change in the company's name and led to an encouraging change in the company's financial performance.

### *Origins*

When a company called Go-Video, Inc. changed its name to Sensory Science in 1999, one of the most controversial business names in the consumer electronics industry made its exit. At the time of the name change, the company was celebrating its 15th year of business, but only its ninth year of actually producing a product. During the years in between, Go-Video awaited approval of patent application for a product whose potential existence drew the ire of immensely powerful forces. Fighting on the behest of Go-Video was its founder, R. Terren Dunlap. At stake in the legal battle was a $4.5 billion antitrust lawsuit, upon which Go-Video's existence depended.

Dunlap, a native of Tucson, Arizona, who left his law practice and a part-time teaching job at Scottsdale Community College to become an entrepreneur, founded Go-Video in 1984. The formation of the company coincided with the filing of a patent application for a dual-deck videocassette recorder, the VCR-2. The implications of Go-Video's patent application were profound, at least to the Japanese VCR manufacturers who thoroughly dominated the U.S. market. As a bloc—grouped within The Electronics Industry Association of Japan—the Japanese manufacturers had purposefully refrained from manufacturing a dual-deck VCR that would be capable of duplicating videotapes and enabling the viewer to watch one taped program while recording another. The motivation for their stance was the powerful pressure exerted by the Motion Picture Association of America, an organization that was opposed not only to dual-deck VCRs but also to the advent of the VCR itself. Accordingly, to appease the content owners in Hollywood, The Electronics Industry Association of Japan, through a press release, declared that its members would neither produce nor supply the parts for dual-deck VCRs, thereby easing its members' entry into the conventional, single-deck VCR market.

After filing for a patent for a dual-deck VCR, Dunlap prepared for the production of Go-Video's prototype VCR-2, doing what he could until the U.S. Patent Office delivered its verdict. It was during this period, according to Dunlap's allegations, that Go-Video suffered from the tacit agreement between the Japanese and Hollywood. Dunlap claimed he was unable to get access to the licenses covering the patents for basic VCR parts such as the head and drive assembly, without which he could never hope to manufacture Go-Video's dual-deck VCR. By 1987—a year in which 13 million VCRs were sold in the United States; none manufactured by an American company—Dunlap's frustration manifested itself in a $4.5 billion antitrust lawsuit. Fighting against what he perceived as an international cartel, Dunlap's lawsuit named 25 leading Japanese VCR manufacturers and American entertainment companies.

The lawsuit, filed in June 1987, included some of the most powerful companies in Japan: multibillion-dollar corporations such as Sony, Toshiba, Mitsubishi, and Victor Co. of Japan, owner of the JVC brand. At the time the lawsuit was filed,

## Company Perspectives:

*We believe that a company's intellectual capital will be a key measure of its future success, especially in our industry. Our intellectual capital can be found in our people and in our products, which combine to create the Sensory Science experience. The Sensory Science experience puts the consumer at the center of the revolution sweeping our industry by offering superior product choices at key points on the analog-to-digital spectrum. The essence of the Sensory Science experience is fingertip delivery of unparalleled performance, award-winning industrial design and world-class engineering, backed by customer support that we hope will become legendary in our business.*

Dunlap presided over a company that had yet to collect $500,000 in annual revenue. Dunlap accentuated the disparity between his tiny company and some of the largest multinational corporations in the world, doing whatever he could to keep the lawsuit in the public eye. He appeared on the television show "Today," and proclaimed in a November 1988 interview with *Inc.* magazine, "We could be the last hope for the domestic consumer electronics industry." For Go-Video, the antitrust lawsuit meant everything to the company's survival, providing the company's chief source of revenue and representing its sole means of gaining access to basic VCR parts. Without a settlement or the ability to market a product, the company would financially deteriorate. During its first five years in business, Go-Video registered revenues of $1.5 million, but accumulated $3.5 million in losses.

### Patent for the Dual-Deck VCR Is Approved in 1988

Go-Video's patent application was approved in August 1988; a victory dulled somewhat by the formidable opposition the company still faced. The trial was scheduled to begin in the spring of 1989, but before the case went to court Go-Video's opposition began to lessen. By late summer 1988, five of the defendants—companies such as Mitsubishi, Akai, and Toshiba—had settled, promising to provide Go-Video with access to some of the suppliers of the necessary parts. By November 1988, the Motion Picture Association of America had also agreed to withdraw its opposition to the VCR-2, its fears of piracy quelled by Dunlap's promise to add a circuit that would prevent illegal copying of videotapes.

After the events of 1988, Dunlap was much closer to bringing the VCR-2 to market, but he still had a major hurdle to clear. Finding a manufacturer willing to produce the product proved a daunting task. Zenith refused Go-Video's proposal to manufacture the dual-deck VCR domestically, presumably because of the controversial nature of the product. "What price heroism?," a Zenith executive reportedly remarked to Dunlap, according to the November 1988 issue of *Inc.* One possibility was a joint venture with Mitsubishi, which had been granted limited first rights of manufacturing refusal in exchange for supplying basic parts, but the deal never materialized. Eventually, in February 1989, a deal was struck with Samsung Corporation, which agreed to manufacture Go-Video's VCR.

After entering into manufacturing and licensing agreements with Samsung, Go-Video still had more than a year to wait before it officially ended its drawn-out development phase. Sales of the company's revolutionary VCR, introduced as the Dual-Deck VCR, began in June 1990, formally ending six years of preparatory work. The long wait had been costly, resulting in financial losses that the company had difficulty in overcoming. To make matters worse, the long wait proved to be in vain, ending with discouraging failure. In 1991, Go-Video lost its lawsuit, sending the company's stock price tumbling downward.

After its first full year as a company with a product on the market, Go-Video generated $12.5 million in sales, nearly $5 million of which came from litigation settlement revenues, but it was unable to turn a profit. In 1991, the company posted a $1.3 million loss and repeated the discouraging feat the following year, registering another $1.3 million loss.

### Hackett Takes Over in 1993

After eight years of unprofitability, Go-Video was desperately in need of changes. Late in 1992, the company gained the individual who would be responsible for sparking a turnaround. In December 1992, Roger B. Hackett was elected to Go-Video's board of directors. The following month, he was named president and chief operating officer, with Dunlap serving as chief executive officer and as chairman of the board. Hackett faced several fundamental tasks when he took over day-to-day control of the company in January 1993, one of which was leading Go-Video's evolution from an entrepreneurial organization into an industrial concern. Hackett also had to try to lower the manufacturing costs of the company's Dual-Deck VCR. The machine retailed for approximately $650, with some models reaching $1,000, which by far eclipsed the $250 price tag for a typical single-deck VCR. Additionally, Hackett wanted to diversify the company's product line, a move that would lessen Go-Video's complete dependence on the Dual-Deck VCR and utilize the company's existing distribution channels.

Progress was slow, but by the end of Hackett's first year with the company the perennial annual losses came to a stop. Go-Video posted a modest $116,706 in profit for 1993, a level the company's net income would hover around for the next several years. Progress with Hackett's other objectives—reducing manufacturing costs and embarking on diversification—occurred after his control over the company increased. In March 1994, he was also named to the posts of chief executive officer and chairman, earning the trust of the board of directors and the confidence of Dunlap, who assumed the title of special projects coordinator for the company. Several months after taking on the added positions of power, Hackett steered the company toward its first product line expansion, introducing the 8mm/VHS format Dual-Deck VCR in July 1994. The machine enabled users to make copies of their 8mm tapes in VHS format, but not many consumers were interested in such capabilities. Go-Video recorded negligible success in marketing the machine and stopped producing them not long after their introduction. By the beginning of 1996, the company's only involvement in the product line consisted of attempting to exhaust its inventory of the 8mm/VHS Dual-Deck VCRs.

Despite the ill-fated venture, Hackett was able to convince Go-Video's board of directors to approve a more adventurous diversifying move. The decision led to the company's first acquisition, the purchase of Dublin Companies in April 1995. Dublin, under the Private Eye label, was a distributor of home and business video security and surveillance products. The acquisition led to the formation of Go-Video's security products division, which competed within the closed-circuit television market. The division marketed products such as black-and-white cameras, time-lapse VCRs, monitors, and related items designed to be used in commercial and residential settings.

Diversification represented an important part of Hackett's plan to reshape Go-Video, but arguably a greater achievement followed the acquisition of Dublin Companies. For years, Hackett had been trying to lower the manufacturing costs of the company's signature dual-deck VCRs, an arrangement he had been unable to broker with the company's sole manufacturer, Samsung. In January 1996, however, he reached a manufacturing agreement with a second supplier, Shintom Company Ltd. and Talk Corporation. The agreement led to the introduction of the GV60xx series of dual-deck VCRs, a product line that debuted in June 1996 with significantly lower manufacturing costs than the models manufactured by Samsung.

Following the new manufacturing agreement, Go-Video began to flesh out its presence in the consumer electronics industry. In 1997, the company entered a development, marketing, and distribution agreement with Loewe Opta GmbH, a German manufacturer of televisions and home audio consumer electronics. Under the terms of the agreement, Loewe and Go-Video began developing a line of high-performance televisions to be distributed in North America by Go-Video. Also in 1997, Go-Video collaborated with Prolux Corporation and began developing a prototype LCD (liquid crystal display) projection televi-

sion. Go-Video anticipated launching the distribution of the projection televisions in 1997, the same year distribution of the Loewe televisions was expected to begin.

The next addition to the company's growing roster of consumer electronics product lines arrived in 1998. In April, Go-Video acquired California Audio Labs, a designer, manufacturer, marketer, and distributor of high-performance audio, video, and projection television products. The acquisition greatly increased Go-Video's product line in the home entertainment segment, adding DVD players, CD players, and front projection television products to the company's product lines.

With the diversification and expansion of 1997 and 1998, Go-Video represented a much more broadly-based consumer electronics company. The changes to the company's profile were dramatic, taking a company dependent on one main product line and reshaping it into a multifaceted concern capable of churning out dozens of new products each year. Although the Go-Video name would remain a brand name, the company decided a new corporate title was needed to signify the profound changes that were occurring. In March 1999, Go-Video changed its name to Sensory Science Corporation, the same month the company decided to focus its efforts exclusively on the consumer electronics market. The decision meant the end of the company's involvement with security and surveillance products, leading to the closure of the security products division. More in line with the company's focus was a new business area it entered in July 1999, when it introduced the first in a line of Internet audio (mp3) players, which were used to download, store, and replay music from the Internet. Sales of mp3 players were expected to increase from one million units in 1999 to 8.5 million units by 2002.

As the company exited the 1990s, evidence of its product diversity was on display. Dual-deck VCRs, which historically had accounted for 98 percent of the company's sales, were joined by 30 new products, all introduced in 1999. As a result of the product line expansion, the percentage of total sales derived from dual-deck VCRs fell to 81 in 2000, a decline that was expected to continue as Sensory Science broadened and strengthened its product lines, particularly in digital televisions. "This has been a total renaissance for this company, a rebirth," Hackett remarked in a February 28, 2000 interview with *Knight-Ridder/Tribune Business News*. The transformation appeared to be working, producing 25 percent annual revenue growth and freeing the company from utter dependence on a single product line.

In the fall of 2000, the company introduced the DVR5000, a combination DVD/VCR player that plays DVDs, CDs, including those with mp3 files as well as videocassettes. Retailers have been unable to keep the DVR5000 in stock.

As Hackett prepared for the future, he hoped to continue building on the favorable trends established in the late 1990s and to secure a future of financial consistency in the digital age.

### *Principal Subsidiaries*

Go-Video Productions, Inc.; California Audio Labs, LLC.

### *Principal Competitors*

Matsushita Electric Industrial Co., Ltd.; Koninklijke Philips Electronics N.V.; Sony Corporation.

### *Further Reading*

Barrett, William P., "A Roll of the Dice," *Forbes,* February 20, 1989, p. 81.

Brown, Ken, "People the Focus at Go-Video," *The Business Journal— Serving Phoenix & the Valley of the Sun,* September 4, 1998, p. 17.

Creno, Glen, "Profit Rises at Scottsdale, Arizona-Based Sensory Science," *Knight-Ridder/Tribune Business News,* January 24, 2000.

"Go-Video Buys California Audio," *Television Digest,* January 5, 1998, p. 12.

Mattern, Hal, "Scottsdale, Arizona-Based Firm Diversifies Home Entertainment Products," *Knight-Ridder/Tribune Business News,* February 28, 2000.

Plotkin, Hal, "Do Not Pass Go," *Inc.,* November 1988, p. 14.

Slovak, Julianne, "Go-Video Inc.," *Fortune,* November 7, 1988, p. 64.

—Jeffrey L. Covell

# Simco

## Simco S.A.

34, rue de la Federation
75015 Paris
France
Telephone: (+33) 1 40 61 66 20
Fax: (+33) 1 40 61 65 06
Web site: http://www.simco.fr

*Public Company*
*Incorporated:* 1956 as CEFI; 1967 as Simco (Société
    d'Investissements Immobiliers et de Construction)
*Employees:* 335
*Sales:* EUR 144.8 million ($123.16 million) (1999)
*Stock Exchanges:* Euronext Paris
*Ticker Symbol:* 12180.PA
*NAIC:* 53 Real Estate and Rental and Leasing; 531311
    Residential Property Managers; 531312 Nonresidential
    Property Managers

Simco S.A., an acronym for Société d'Investissements Immobiliers et de Construction (which translates roughly as Company of Real Estate Investment and Construction), is one of the top three property groups in France and one of the top seven in all of Europe. The company's Paris focus has given it a number of prime locations in that city, one of the world's top real estate markets. At the end of 1999, Simco held title to 217 buildings and building parks, including more than 800,000 square meters of rental space across 11,200 apartments, 48,000 square meters of commercial real estate, 197,000 square meters of office space, and 15,900 parking spaces. This total of more than 1.3 million square meters was worth an estimated EUR 2.48 billion. The acquisition of fellow Parisian real estate group Société des Immeubles de France (SIF), announced in the summer of 2000, was expected to further boost Simco's holdings to more than EUR 3.6 billion. The acquisition of SIF, which specialized in office space, complemented Simco's focus on residential rentals—generally some 60 percent of Simco's portfolio, with a large number of high-end Haussmann-era apartments—at a time when the market for office space was growing strongly. The company's largest shareholder has long been insurance giant Axa, which held more than 45 percent of the real estate group's stock in 1999.

### Renting Paris in the 1950s and 1960s

The beginnings of Simco S.A. date back to the formation of CEFI S.A.R.L. in 1956, which was formed with capital of just FFr 120,000. CEFI was formed to respond to a growing housing crisis in Paris. At the end of the Second World War, legislation enacted to protect apartment renters—including caps on rent increases—resulted in a near stoppage of new apartment building construction. By the mid-1950s, the shortage of affordable housing had reached crisis proportions; the severe winter of 1954 in particular had exposed the vulnerability of lower income groups and the lack of proper housing. Pressure was placed on the government to enact new legislation to encourage the construction of rental apartment buildings for the lower and middle-income groups. The resulting construction boom transformed Paris, particularly the outskirts of the city.

One of the factors leading to the construction of new buildings was the creation, in 1958, of a new class of real estate companies. This class was the Société Immobilières Conventionnée, or SIC, and provided tax advantages for the construction of housing for middle-income populations. These tax advantages thereby compensated real estate groups for their loss of income due to the rent control that was enacted a decade earlier.

As the Paris building market began to grow, CEFI grew as well. In the early 1960s, the company prepared to take advantage of new legislation to be enacted that was to create a new type of real estate group, with its own set of financial and tax advantages. In 1963, CEFI renamed itself Union Immobilière d'Investissement UNIFIMO S.A., with a capitalization of FFr 1 million. The company anticipated the passage of new legislation creating the Sociétés Immobilières d'Investissment, or SII, which allowed real estate groups to raise capital by making public offerings on the stock exchange. UNIFIMO converted to SII status in November 1967 and retained that status until the early 1990s. This status marked the company's growth, particularly as the law creating the SII category stipulated that all buildings constructed by SII-type real estate companies were required to adhere to a strict proportion of 75 percent residential rental apartments and 25 percent commercial rental space.

Meanwhile, the building boom that had begun at the end of the 1950s took on new vigor in the 1960s, especially outside of Paris

## Company Perspectives:

*Growth has always been the company's objective, through increasing profitability, improving the quality of property holdings, and favoring the stock's liquidity. This objective is more important than ever in a quickly consolidating economic environment. For Simco, growth must be "chosen" with respect to the "fundamentals" of the business: remain concentrated on the "savoir-faire" of the group, developing and exploiting the building park concept through investment, rentals, management and sales, in blocks or parcels; focus on Paris and the Paris region, a high quality market where the group is well implanted; diversify the nature of holdings along two lines—a dominant share of lodgings (which stabilize the group's business and assure it of recurring revenues in the long term) and a significant share of office buildings, which boost profits in growth periods through reactions to market conditions.*

as the city saw the rise of a huge new suburban ring. The opening of the RER train network serving these new areas helped relieve the housing congestion of Paris itself, and gave new opportunities to the real estate industry. Another boost to the real-estate market—if not to the beauty of Paris itself—came in 1967, when changes were made to a number of the city's long-held building codes. In particular, one 19th century code had limited building height to 20 meters (five stories), while another required the alignment of buildings to the street. The new changes allowed building heights to reach 37 meters—some new buildings reached ten stories—and buildings were allowed to break from the alignment with the street. Thus, the housing market saw the rise of a whole new type of building complex, often containing hundreds of apartments in several linked buildings. The new modern buildings became highly sought after among Parisian renters.

The opening real estate market provided by the new building codes encouraged UNIFIMO to expand not only its holdings but also it capital. In 1967, the company acquired two of its rivals—Simco and IFF—and in order to emphasize its growing commitment to new building construction, took on the name of its Simco acquisition, which stood for Société d'Investissements Immobiliers et de Construction ("Real Estate Investment and Construction").

### Growth by Acquisition in the 1970s–80s

It soon became apparent that acquisitions would be an important part of Simco's growth. The company made another important purchase in the mid-1970s, when it took over rival SAGIMO in 1975. By that time, Simco had built up a strong portfolio of modern apartment complexes, including a number of buildings in the western suburbs of Paris. Yet the company's primary focus remained on the Parisian market proper. The adoption of a new building code in 1977 once again tightened construction requirements, renewing the requirement that buildings be aligned to the city's streets, while instituting new height requirements based on the width of the new sites' streets.

Building code changes were just one factor in the rapidly slowing new construction market in Paris, however. Another

significant factor was the impact of an economic recession, which had begun with the Arab Oil Embargo in the early 1970s and lasted in France through the late 1980s. The depressed economy not only discouraged new building construction and lead to new housing shortages, but also encouraged the consolidation of the city's real estate groups. Simco was to prove a leader in this trend, making a series of significant acquisitions in the 1980s and 1990s.

Instead of simply boosting its real estate holdings with each acquisition, Simco used an acquired company's portfolio of buildings to balance and re-orient its own portfolio. As such, an important part of Simco's activity became its arbitrage of its own and newly acquired buildings. This enabled Simco to increase the value and scope of its properties, while also maintaining the 75–25 split of residential/commercial properties required by regulation governing its SII status.

Among Simco's most important acquisitions in the 1980s were those of UPH in 1984 and IMMINDO in 1988. The first of these, UPH, gave Simco some 1,500 residential apartments and 38,000 square meters of retail and office space, including a number of residential buildings in Lyon and other provincial cities. From this acquisition, Simco kept more than 400 residential apartments, including two buildings in Paris's 15th arrondissement, as well as several of UPH's province locations. Simco also kept an important part of UPH's non-residential portfolio, including its 16,000 square meter office and retail space in the Gamma towers near the Gare de Lyon train station. This space was located in what was later to become an important financial district. Almost all of UPH's buildings that were kept by Simco dated either from the 1960s or the mid-1970s, giving the company a relatively large increase in its modern building portfolio.

The IMMINDO acquisition presented similar opportunities for Simco. Focused on Paris and the immediate surrounding area, IMMINDO brought a portfolio of 16 buildings representing more than 800 residential apartments and some 13,500 square meters of offices and retail space, almost all of which had been constructed since the 1970s. Of the 16 buildings acquired with IMMINDO, Simco kept 12, including a building still under construction and not completed until 1989. Once again, Simco rebalanced its assets, maintaining the 75–25 split (both UPH and IMMINDO had been oriented more along a 61 percent residential/39 percent non-residential proportion) required by SII status.

### Changes in the Early 1990s

The late 1980s had seen a brief but intense building boom that was to result, as was the case elsewhere in the world, in a glutted office building market as the worldwide economy shrunk back in the early 1990s. In France, and in the Paris area in particular, the resulting extended recession depressed the building market into the late 1990s. Simco took a three-prong approach to its development in the new decade.

First, In 1992 the company made another large scale acquisition, this time of COGIFI, whose holdings included 27 building complexes containing 2,400 residential apartments and more than 44,000 square meters of office and retail space. In detail, COGIFI's holdings included a largely modern park of buildings, most of which had been built in the late 1960s and early

## Key Dates:

**1956:** Founding of CEFI, the precursor to Simco.
**1963:** Company changes its name to Union Immobilière d'Investissement UNIFIMO S.A.
**1967:** Company acquires Simco and IFF, and adopts the name Simco.
**1984:** Simco begins an acquisition spree.
**2000:** Simco becomes the seventh-largest European real estate group.

1970s, as well as a focus on the Parisian suburbs. There were also five buildings in the provinces and a strong portfolio of central Parisian buildings. Simco sold many of the buildings acquired through COGIFI, but kept some 70 percent of the Paris center locations, adding another 16,000 square meters of prime Paris office space to its holdings.

At the same time, Simco prepared to abandon its status as an SII company in order to rebalance its holdings to take advantage of the new economic situation in its sector. Freed of the requirements placed on it as an SII, Simco was able to change the balance of its park, shifting closer toward a 60–40 split of residential and non-residential properties.

More than ever, arbitrage became the company's central focus, as it stepped up its long-held policy of building acquisitions and building sales in order to maintain a portfolio reflecting current market demands. This third part of the company's 1990s development played an important part in the transition of Simco's holdings from a largely middle-income residential group to a more high-end of the Parisian market. By 1996, Simco had built itself into the largest of the real estate groups quoted on the Paris stock exchange, and one of the largest in the overall Paris market.

### A Real Estate Giant for the 21st Century

As the economic and building crisis finally eased toward the end of the 1990s, Simco prepared to take on another scale. In 1997, the company bought up rival group Compagnie des Immeubles de la Plaine Monceau (CIPM), the second-largest quoted real estate company. CIPM was worth some FFr 6.8 billion in market capitalization and boasted a portfolio of 114 buildings, equaling nearly 680,000 square meters of space. In addition to 55,000 square meters of office space, CIPM controlled nearly 4,000 apartments—nearly 40 percent of which were so-called "Haussmann" apartments.

The "Haussmann" designation referred to Baron Haussmann—named as prefect by Napoleon III in 1853—who had transformed Paris by instituting a new street grid and defining a new building code. The Haussmann-style buildings, constructed mainly in the second half of the 19th century, came to evoke Paris itself, and, by the end of the 1990s, were among the city's most expensive rental locations. Simco's acquisition of CIPM gave it more than 50 Haussmann-era buildings and expanded its presence into nearly every one of Paris's arrondissments. Among CIPM's other holdings had been a number of other prestigious buildings as well, some of which dated to the 17th century.

The merger of CIPM into Simco took most of the following year. Upon completing the integration of CIPM's operations with its own, Simco began looking for new acquisition possibilities. The rebounding French economy had thrust the office space sector in full gear, and Simco moved to take advantage of these developments. At the same time, the Paris market was seeing a rapid consolidation—a trend driven especially by the appearance of foreign investment capital (particularly British and American) eager to gain footholds in the highly sought-after Parisian real estate market.

Simco was frustrated in its next two acquisition attempts, however, after its targets—Sefimeg and Immobilière Batibail—were both snapped up by rival Gecina. Gecina also took Simco's place in the top three of Parisian real estate groups. It was not until mid-2000 that Simco was at last able to announce its next successful acquisition. This time the company agreed to acquire Société des Immeubles de France (SIF), a company which was at that time classified as the 20th-largest European real estate group. Prior to the merger, Simco was classified as the 11th-largest European real estate group; adding SIF to Simco, however, allowed the company to move into the number seven spot. The company then boasted a capitalization of more than EUR 2.1 billion, and a portfolio estimated at nearly EUR 3.7 billion.

The SIF acquisition was most likely not to be Simco's last, as the company moved to protect its position in the rapidly consolidating European real estate market. Indeed, at the same time that the company announced its SIF acquisition, it also announced its agreement to purchase three office buildings, for a price of EUR 240 million. Meanwhile, Simco remained committed to maintaining the high quality of its building portfolio, earmarking some FFr 2 billion in assets that it was preparing to sell off in the first years of the new century.

### Principal Subsidiaries

SCI Franco-Russe; GIE Gessi; Locare S.A.; Parigest S.A.; SCI Paris St. Michel; SCI Ternes-Opéra; SCI Vouillé-Nanteuil.

### Principal Competitors

Gécina S.A.; Klépierre S.A.; Unibail S.A.; Société Foncière Lyonnaise S.A.; Foncière Euris S.A.; Rue Impériale de Lyon S.A.

### Further Reading

Bériot, Frédéric, "Interview, Jean-Paul Sorand, vice-président de Simco," *Journal des Finances,* June 10, 2000.
Bériot, Frédéric and Kempinski, Michel, "Interview, Jean-Paul Sorand, vice-président de Simco," *Journal des Finances,* October 31, 1998.
Besses-Boumard, Pascale, "La société foncière Simco décidée à renouer avec la croissance externe," *Les Echos,* December 10, 1999, p. 32.
Chevallard, Lucile, "Le nouvel ensemble Simco-SIF se hisse au 7e rang des foncière européenes," *Les Echos,* July 20, 2000, p. 20.
Jacquin, Jean-Baptiste, "OPA, fusions et acquisitions secouent le secteur de l'immobilier," *L'Expansion,* August 21, 1998.

—M.L. Cohen

# Sonic Corp.

**101 Park Avenue**
**Oklahoma City, Oklahoma 73102**
**U.S.A.**
**Telephone: (405) 280-7654**
**Fax: (405) 280-7568**
**Web site: http://www.sonicdrivein.com**

*Public Company*
*Incorporated:* 1959
*Employees:* 227
*Sales:* $257.61 million (1999)
*Stock Exchanges:* NASDAQ
*Ticker Symbol:* SONC
*NAIC:* 722211 Limited-Service Restaurants

Sonic Corp. franchises and operates the United States' largest chain of drive-in restaurants and the fifth largest hamburger chain. As of August 31, 2000 there were 2,172 Sonic restaurants, of which 1,860 were owned and operated by independent franchisees; the remainder were majority-owned by Sonic Corp. Company-owned restaurants averaged $702,000 a year in 1999; franchised restaurants took in about $842,000 each. Under the slogan "America's Drive-In," a Sonic restaurant features fast service by roller-skating carhops and a limited menu of cooked-to-order items, including hamburgers, hot dogs, French fries, tater tots, and onion rings, and a wide variety of soft drinks and frozen desserts. Sonic restaurants operate in 27 states in the Bible Belt and Sun Belt.

### Oklahoma Origins

The Sonic concept originated in Shawnee, Oklahoma in the early 1950s. Troy Smith, a World War II veteran, operated a small diner called the Cottage Cafe, which, with only four booths and 12 counter seats, could not support him and his family. Smith sold the diner and opened a larger restaurant, called Troy's Panful of Chicken. His attempts to expand into multiple locations were not successful, and by 1953 Smith's chicken restaurants had failed.

Smith next dreamed of running an upscale steakhouse. In 1953 he purchased land on the edge of Shawnee, a five-acre property that held a log cabin and included a root beer stand called the "Top Hat." Smith's original intent was to operate his steakhouse in the log cabin and to tear down the root beer stand to make more room for parking. In the meantime, the root beer stand, which sold hot dogs and hamburgers, was averaging sales of $700 in cash per week. Customers would park, walk up to the stand to get food, and eat in their cars.

The postwar boom in automobile purchases created an increasingly mobile public, and businesses developed to serve this new population. Fast food restaurants began to appear across the country; in California, many operated as "drive-ins," with covered parking spaces and a wait staff that roller-skated to customers' cars. The drive-in concept soon spread across the country, particularly in the warm-weather states. While traveling in Louisiana, Smith stopped at one of these new restaurants. It had an intercom system with homemade speakers that allowed customers to remain in their cars while they placed their order. Smith contacted the inventor of that system and ordered intercoms for his Top Hat root beer stand. Smith also constructed parking canopies, which allowed him to control parking in the root beer stand's lot, and hired carhops to serve his customers. Sales at the stand jumped to $1,750 in the first week after the intercom system was installed, and Smith quickly lost interest in his steakhouse.

The Shawnee restaurant remained the sole Top Hat until 1956. In that year, Smith met Charles Pappe, a manager of a Safeway supermarket in the Oklahoma town of Woodward who was interested in starting his own restaurant. Pappe, visiting Shawnee, met Smith, and, as the two discussed Pappe's restaurant plans, Smith convinced him to dub his drive-in a Top Hat as well. They began to operate their restaurants under the slogan "Service at the Speed of Sound" and developed paper goods with the Top Hat name. By 1958 two more Top Hats opened, in Enid and Stillwater, Oklahoma.

### "Sonic" in the Jet Age

Smith and Pappe made plans to step up their franchise business. They soon discovered, however, that the name Top

Hat had already been copyrighted. The pair consulted the dictionary, where they found the word "sonic." The term fit neatly with their slogan. New signs and paper goods were developed, and in 1959 the Stillwater restaurant became the first to adopt the Sonic name.

The partners soon received requests from other entrepreneurs to open their own Sonic Drive-ins. Smith and Pappe assisted these new owner-operators with choosing locations and designing the restaurant layout and operations. Formal franchise agreements were drawn up for the new restaurants. The new owners paid a royalty fee of one penny per sandwich bag, purchased through a central supplier. These franchise agreements contained no provisions for advertising, territorial rights, or fixed menus. Instead, Smith and Pappe's business operated mostly on handshake deals. Sonic operators were still most likely to be local businessmen, owning in part or in full their restaurants, and restaurants were often family-run.

Sonic grew modestly through the 1960s. By 1967, the year of Charles Pappe's death, there were 41 Sonics in operation. Smith brought in two long-time Sonic restaurant franchisees, Matt Kinslow and Marvin Jirous, to run Sonic Supply, the company's supply and distribution division, while Smith continued to develop the company's franchise operations. Franchises appeared in Texas and Kansas, and, by 1972, there were 165 Sonic Drive-ins.

### Over-the-Counter in 1973

The company had grown too large for Smith, Kinslow, and Jirous to run alone. So, in 1973, Sonic restructured as a franchise company under the name Sonic Systems of America. Shortly thereafter it became Sonic Industries, Inc., which was a company composed of ten key franchise owners who served as officers and directors of the new company. Smith became chairman of the board and Jirous was named president. Sonic purchased the rights to the name, logo, trademark, and slogan from

Smith, and the supply company from Kinslow and Jirous. Each owner also was offered 1,250 shares at $1 per share, and the volume of shares pushed the company to become an over-the-counter, publicly traded company. By year-end 1973, there were 200 Sonic Drive-ins. An additional 75 opened in 1974, and by 1975 Sonic was operating in 13 states.

The 1970s saw a dramatic growth in the number of Sonic restaurants. This growth was attributable to Sonic's second generation of owner-operators. Employees, many the sons and daughters of the original franchisees, were encouraged to become managers and supervisors and to open stores of their own. The company's franchise structure became increasingly complex. As former CEO and President C. Steven Lynn related to *Restaurant Business*, "[Troy Smith] would perhaps sell a one-unit franchise to a small town man. That man might train his high school buddy. . . . When he knew the business, another franchisee might recruit him to manage a second unit. All three might own a piece of the unit. . . . Nearly all of our franchisees own pieces of each others' stores, which were often structured as general partnerships."

Between 1973 and 1978 more than 800 new restaurants opened—during one two-year period, more than one new Sonic Drive-in opened each day. The rapid expansion of the chain created a shortfall in the number of trained managers. Despite the establishment of a Sonic School manager training program in the mid-1970s, a number of restaurants began to fail. Rising inflation rates and higher gasoline prices as a result of the Oil Crisis of 1973 also placed pressure on the drive-in restaurant business. In addition, the company lacked a systemwide advertising program through most of the 1970s.

To boost advertising, the company established the Sonic Advertising Trust, requesting drive-ins to contribute 1.5 percent of their gross. Participation, however, was voluntary, and the first Sonic television commercials did not appear until 1977. By 1979 profits began to fall nonetheless. A new advertising campaign, budgeted at only $5 million, could not reverse the decline, and by 1980 the company posted a net loss of almost $300,000. Overall revenues and per-store sales were down. In that year, 28 company-owned stores were closed, and by 1981 300 stores had closed.

### Cooperating in the 1980s

Jirous, Kinslow, and other original directors and officers left the company to focus on their own franchises. A new president was hired in 1981 but was replaced by Troy Smith in 1982. The following year, C. Stephen Lynn, formerly with Kentucky Fried Chicken and Century 21, took over the leadership of the company. Lynn identified a number of problems facing Sonic. Its licensing agreements—there were as many as 20 different agreements throughout the chain—did not bring in the revenue the company needed to provide support services across a system that had spread through 19 states. Many of the drive-ins were two decades old and had become shabby, and many were losing money. Most important, the restaurants continued to operate more or less independently, with little cooperative purchasing and advertising.

Lynn worked to unify the company. By promising to cut food costs by three percent and to increase sales by 15 percent, he convinced 200 restaurants to consolidate their purchasing and to contribute one percent of sales to an advertising program. A new franchise agreement in 1984, adopted by nearly 90 percent of the franchisees, provided the company with ascending royalties, beginning at one percent of gross sales and rising to three percent, depending on store volume. By 1986, more than one-third of the stores in the chain were working cooperatively. Per-store sales grew to an average of $350,000 per year, with new stores averaging up to $550,000.

In 1986, Lynn, along with a group of investors, performed a leveraged buyout for approximately $10 million and took the company private. Calling franchisees ''partners,'' Lynn was able to increase chainwide cooperation, forming advertising groups focused on key markets. Sonic put together a low-cost remodeling package, initially priced at $20,000, to encourage older restaurants to revitalize their image. At the same time, the new structure price was set at around $140,000. Lynn also moved to fix the Sonic menu to a limited number of basic items and regional specialties. Soon, Sonic was once again growing. In 1987 it built its 1,000th restaurant.

### Public Again in 1991

Sonic's growth continued into the 1990s. It went public again in 1991, raising $52 million in its initial public offering. Lynn had increased cooperative advertising participation to 93 percent of the restaurants, which by then contributed an average of 2.25 percent of gross sales. Between 1990 and 1994 Sonic added nearly 400 new restaurants, tagging on more than 120 in 1994 alone. Systemwide sales rose from $454.6 million to $776.3 million; same-store sales rose from $446,000 to $585,000; and company revenues grew from $45.8 million to $99.7 million. In 1993, Sonic's market value was estimated at $200 million. Sonic had grown to the fifth largest hamburger chain in the United States and the top drive-in chain.

Sonic's growth remained relatively flat after 1992. After reaching a high of $33, its stock price slipped to around $23 per share in 1995. Per-store sales seemed stagnated between $515,000 and $585,000. Sonic, which traditionally owned its rural and suburban southern markets, was facing increasing competition from drive-through chains such as Checkers and Rally's

(these two would merge in 1999), while the giants of the industry—McDonald's and Burger King—with their ability to discount, began to invade its territory. Meanwhile, despite discussion of acquiring a Northern-based partner, Sonic clung to its traditional market, making few inroads outside of the warm-weather Southern areas. The company faced additional trouble in 1994 when it was forced to take a $3.9 million writedown charge for discontinuing its five company-owned properties, including two closed restaurants in South Florida that had suffered as a result of the hurricane that devastated the area in 1992.

In 1994, after more than a year of often bitter talks with franchisees, Sonic renegotiated its franchising contracts. The new contract, good for 20 years with a ten-year option to renew, raised graduated royalties to four percent and increased advertising contributions to a fixed 2.5 percent while granting Sonic control over a systemwide advertising program. It also fixed a sole soft drink supplier. In addition, Sonic collected conversion fees from franchisees signing new contracts. In return, the company agreed to give up its first right of refusal for franchisees wishing to turn over restaurants to their heirs or partners, and agreed to fewer audits of franchisees' books. Franchisees also gained wider territorial protection guarantees, with a protected trade radius of 1.5 miles in larger cities, and up to three miles in rural areas. About two-thirds of Sonic franchisees accepted the new contract.

The terms gave Sonic increases of $5 million in royalties and conversions and allowed it to raise its advertising budget to $20 million. With the discontinuation of its Florida operations, Sonic saw its total revenues rise by 24 percent, to $123.75 million in 1995. At the beginning of that year, Lynn, who owned approximately 12 percent of the company, named J. Clifford Hudson, former executive vice-president and COO, to take over as president of the company. When Lynn left Sonic to become chief executive officer and president of the beleaguered Shoney's restaurant chain, Hudson was appointed chief executive officer as well.

The typical Sonic restaurant of the mid-1990s remained true to the 1950s-style carhop concept: customers drove up to one of an average of 24 covered parking spaces, placed orders through an intercom, and were served at their car. Restaurants also offered drive-through service, with some restaurants operating as drive-throughs only. The absence of indoor dining allowed the company to maintain one of the highest margin restaurant operations in the country, with a new construction package costing less than $515,000 per unit and first-year sales of more than $700,000. Average per-store sales were around $585,000 per year in 1995.

The company owned and operated, often through various franchise and partner agreements, 178 restaurants going into 1995. Company restaurants, together with franchise royalties and conversion fees, generated $123.75 million in revenues. Growth in the number of units was averaging 26 percent for franchised restaurants and 106 percent for company-owned restaurants over the five years from 1990 to 1994. Approximately two-thirds of franchisees were represented by the National Association of Sonic Drive-in Franchisees, which operated entirely separately from the company. Sonic entered the late 1990s with a new executive team, including former executives from Coca-Cola Co., Taco Bell, McDonald's, and Wendy's, and plans for 125 new franchised and company-owned restaurants in 1996.

In September 1995, Sonic Corp. restructured its holdings into two subsidiaries, Sonic Industries Inc., which handled franchising, and Sonic Restaurants, Inc., which handled company-owned restaurants. Sonic's equipment sales unit was sold off to Columbus, Ohio-based N. Wasserstrom & Sons, Inc. in February 1996.

Sales boomed in the mid-1990s, with the company opening 100 to 150 new restaurants a year. Sonic's large variety of drinks and a new line of ice cream desserts won repeat business, and the chain added a grilled chicken sandwich for health-conscious diners.

### A Brand New Look in 1998

Sonic updated its image as it entered the late 1990s. The novelty of a 1950s drive-in was not enough to keep people coming back. In fact, a 1995 survey indicated people identified the company most strongly not with its unique food items but with Frankie Avalon, the icon of 1960s beach films who pitched Sonic in television ads from 1987 to 1993.

The company began to develop the Sonic brand as never before. Its new advertising focused on the signature carhops and food offerings that differentiated Sonic from other national fast food chains, items such as hot dogs, tater tots, and cherry limeades. Through its Sonic 2000 retrofit program, in 1998, the chain set out to redesign all of its 1,750 stores in neon-illuminated "retro-future" mode. Soon, Sonic was leading all other fast food restaurants, including McDonald's, in customer frequency rates—between eight and nine visits a month.

In 1998, *Nation's Restaurant News* and *Inc.* magazine each profiled the D.L. Rogers Group, a Bedford, Texas-based Sonic franchisee that operated 54 drive-ins generating $42 million in annual sales. Its founder, Don Rogers, an Oklahoma oilman, had opened his first Sonic Drive-In in 1962. The group was credited with introducing the ice cream concept to the Sonic system after proving it at its own restaurants.

Jack Hartnett, president since 1983, led the Rogers Group to more than a dozen years of record profits and the highest unit volumes of any Sonic franchise. His style of "extreme managing" included a great deal of interpersonal contact and early morning phone calls. Eight terse, old-fashioned rules including "If I have to do your job, I want your money" and ending with "I will only tell you one time" contained the essence of his managing philosophy. In spite of Hartnett's authoritarian style, *Inc.* writer Marc Ballon credited his success with the stable, predictable environment he created for his managers—or "owner-operators," as Hartnett called them. They were in fact required to buy 25 percent shares in the drive-ins they managed. Hartnett, a demanding, "larger than life" figure, paid his managers as much as three times the industry average. Turnover at the Rogers Group was a fraction of that at other fast food restaurants.

Feeling its stock undervalued, Sonic Corp. began to buy back shares in March 1998. The press agreed with its valuation. In April 1999, *Investor's Business Daily* included Sonic in its list of the country's 200 best stocks. In November, *Forbes* called Sonic one of the 200 best small companies in America. By August 2000, the company had bought back $53 million of its stock and had authorized another $20 million for that purpose.

The updates in menu and image were working. Sonic Corp.'s revenues rose 18 percent in 1999 to $257.6 million. Seasonal offerings like the Chocolate Cream Pie Shake, complete with graham cracker crumbs, kept repeat business up. Still, a new restaurant expected to have the most business during its "honeymoon." Omaha's first Sonic Drive-In served 4,000 customers in its first two days. Sonic planned to open 200 restaurants in 2001.

### Principal Subsidiaries

Sonic Industries Inc.; Sonic Restaurants, Inc.

### Principal Competitors

Burger King; Checker's Drive-In Restaurants, Inc.; International Dairy Queen, Inc.; McDonald's Corp.; Wendy's International; Whataburger, Inc.

### Further Reading

Alva, Marilyn, "Season of the Switch," *Restaurant Business*, February 10, 1995, pp. 56–64.

Ballon, Marc, "Extreme Managing," *Inc.*, July 1998, p. 60.

Bunn, Dina, "It's a Sonic Boom: New Drive-Ins on Way," *Denver Rocky Mountain News*, June 24, 1999, p. 2B.

Fuller, Jennifer Mann, "Being Different Is Paying Off for Sonic Corp. Analyst Says," *Kansas City Star*, November 3, 1996, p. F6.

Gindin, Rona, "Everything Old Is New Again," *Restaurant Business*, February 10, 1987, pp. 150–59.

Hassell, Greg, "Fresh Ways to Get Folks to Drive In," *Houston Chronicle*, Bus. Sec., May 13, 1998, p. 1.

Hogan, Gypsy, "Drive-Through Restaurant Chain Squeezes into Prime Space in Oklahoma City," *Daily Oklahoman*, June 24, 1999.

Keenan, John, "Carside Service: Sonic Drive-In Finds Diners Willing to Wait for a Stall," *Omaha World-Herald*, Bus. Sec., August 10, 2000, p. 20.

King, Ronette, "Meals on Wheels—Sonic Makes a Comeback with a Dash of Nostalgia," *Times-Picayune*, October 25, 1996, p. C1.

Lynn, C. Stephen, *Sonic: 40 Years of Success 1953–1993*, Oklahoma City: Newcomen Society, January 12, 1993.

Robertson, Nancy Love, "The Long and Winding Road: Sonic Turns 40," *What's Cookin': Sonic Industries News Magazine*, Spring 1994, pp. 9–16.

Ruggless, Ron, "D.L. Rogers Group: Sonic Drive-Ins Franchisee Succeeds by Putting Its People First," *Nation's Restaurant News*, NRN Fifty Special Issue, January 1998, p. 68.

"Sonic Escapes Frankie's Shadow," *Houston Chronicle*, Bus. Sec., February 16, 2000, p. 1.

Wood, E. Thomas, "Shoney's New Chief Hungry for a Rebound," *Chicago Sun-Times*, Financial Sec., April 30, 1995, p. 37.

—Mickey L. Cohen
—updated by Frederick C. Ingram

# Spacehab, Inc.

**300 D Street S.W., Suite 814**
**Washington, DC 20024**
**U.S.A.**
**Telephone: (202) 488-3500**
**Fax: (202) 488-3100**
**Web site: http://www.spacehab.com**

*Public Company*
*Incorporated:* 1984
*Employees:* 831
*Sales:* $105.71 million (2000)
*Stock Exchanges:* NASDAQ
*Ticker Symbol:* SPAB
*NAIC:* 51334 Satellite Telecommunications; 54171
Research and Development in the Physical,
Engineering, and Life Sciences; 92711 Space
Research and Technology; 336419 Other Guided
Missile and Space Vehicle Parts and Auxiliary
Equipment Manufacturing

Spacehab, Inc. is the only private company to own and operate space vehicles; namely, pressurized modules used to house experiments on board space shuttles and the international space station. Clients include various governmental space agencies, private corporations, and research institutions. The company has moved to become less dependent on NASA by acquiring a satellite services company and an astronaut training firm, and establishing a media company.

### Smithsonian Origins

The idea for what would become Spacehab, Inc. originated in 1983 with Robert Citron, a former scientist with the Smithsonian Institution. According to the *New York Times*, Citron, who then lived in Seattle, conceived of a pressurized container for tourists to be carried in the cargo bay of the space shuttle. Round-trip airfare would be $1 million. NASA turned down this proposal, but voiced interest in a similar module for manned experiments.

Spacehab's name was created as a contraction of ''Space Habitat.'' The company's new mission was to provide a commercial supplement to the similar-sounding Spacelab, which was NASA's version of the mobile laboratory that flew inside the space shuttle beginning in 1983. Spacelab was limited by funding and ultimately flew on only five flights between 1983 and 1992.

Unlike other government contractors, Spacehab would own its product and would seek service contracts for the use of it. The company raised $2 million before the explosion of the Challenger in January 1986. NASA suspended shuttle launches for two years following the accident.

During that time, Spacehab began looking for a CEO, and signed on Richard Jacobson in February 1987. Prior to his appointment, he had led the McDonnell Douglas Delta rocket program. He was preparing to retire when McDonnell Douglas offered to become the prime contractor for Spacehab. Spacehab's chairman, James Beggs, also had long ties to the space industry, championing the commercialization of space while an administrator at NASA. In 1987, Spacehab's offices were relocated opposite NASA's in Washington, D.C., near the Smithsonian Institution's National Air and Space Museum.

In the spring of 1988, the government of Taiwan offered to finance the Spacehab project's entire $75 million estimated cost. Taiwan had been excluded from NASA's space projects because the United States did not officially recognize its government. Unfortunately for Spacehab, however, the president of Taiwan died before their deal could be consummated. (Spacehab did receive about $10 million from private Taiwanese investors in 1989, though.)

Later in 1988, Spacehab landed a major contract from NASA. The agency authorized Spacehab to develop a 1,000 cubic foot pressurized space habitat module for the cargo bay of the space shuttle. The company would pay NASA $28 million for each of six flights to cover transportation costs and other expenses, and would lease space for up to 50 scientific experiments on the space shuttle.

Encouraged by the NASA contract, more investors— including Chemical Bank, Mitsubishi Trust Bank, and Industrial Bank of Japan—committed another $150 million to the project in 1989. The Industrial Bank of Japan dropped out within a year, however, to be replaced by Banque National de Paris and Paribas.

### A Big Sale in 1990

By the fall of 1990, Spacehab had four contracts worth $50 million for space on its ten-foot by 13.5-foot aluminum module, which multiplied the space shuttle's manned experiment capacity by a factor of four. In November, NASA bought 200 of Spacehab's 300 available slots on six shuttle flights for $184 million. Spacehab had been the only company to respond to NASA's request for bids for research space in March 1990. Commercial operations like Spacehab offered NASA's research centers a less cumbersome administrative means to get experiments into orbit than the traditional procurement process.

Because Spacehab had only eight employees in 1991, the company farmed out the design and manufacturing work. McDonnell Douglas Space Systems Company became the prime contractor for the module. Aeritalia (later Alenia SpA) designed and built most of it, while the Mitsubishi Corporation of Japan acted as its home country's sales agent. By this time, Spacehab had $40 million committed to the module, mostly from its manufacturing partners and overseas investors. The module was expected to cost $92 million to build, plus more than $5 million a year to insure.

The buyback arrangement with NASA enabled Spacehab to secure $64 million in financing from Chase Manhattan Bank in March 1991, a deal that took two years to complete. Although the Bush administration was generally sympathetic to the space program, NASA remained subject to the whims of the federal government, with every contract subject to Congress's annual appropriations process. A group of 150 insurers led by Lloyd's of London provided unique insurance against these risks, while McDonnell Douglas guaranteed against cost overruns. All told, the modules cost $150 million to build.

By the middle of 1991, Spacehab had a backlog worth $250 million. Its two 1,100-cubic-foot modules, with 25 lockers each, were capable of carrying 50 experiments in all. The company was renting each locker for $1.8 million a flight—the first of which was scheduled for December 1992, but later postponed.

The Spacehab module took its first flight on the space shuttle Endeavor in July 1993. The mission lasted ten days. The Discovery then carried the module in February 1994 and February 1995. The *Washington Post* recorded that these three missions were backed by 46 corporations, 27 universities, and eight research institutes, as well as NASA. They studied the possibility of growing protein crystals (used in drug synthesis) or assembling semiconductors in space. In July 1995, Spacehab won a $54 million, four-mission contract to resupply Russia's Mir space station.

### Public in 1995

Spacehab launched an initial public offering on the NASDAQ exchange in December 1995. This act presented people with a rare opportunity to invest in a company solely dedicated to the commercialization of space. The company's lack of consistent revenues, however, made it a purchase for the long term. The share price fell from $12 to $8 within a year.

By this time, there had been a change in the executive ranks. Dr. Shelley A. Harrison became chairman, while Richard P. Hora—formerly with General Dynamics Corp.—became president. Prior to these changes, Harrison had co-founded Cymbal Technologies, the company that developed bar code scanners. He had taken over Spacehab through his venture capital firm, had been on the board of directors since August 1987, and became chairman in August 1993 and CEO in April 1996.

In 1996, Spacehab was building a new module double the size of the original to help meet NASA's massive demand for experimentation space. NASA reportedly found it cost only a tenth as much to hire Spacehab's module as it would have to maintain its own. In 1997, NASA awarded Spacehab a Research and Logistic Mission Support (REALMS) contract that allowed the agency more flexibility in ordering Spacehab's services.

Spacehab changed its conservative accounting practices in 1997 to allow it to report revenues earned before missions were completed. The company acquired Astrotech Space Operations, L.P., a provider of satellite processing services, from Northrop Grumman Corporation in February 1997. This became another factor keeping zeroes out of the company's quarterly income reports and making it less dependent on NASA. Spacehab bought another NASA contractor, Johnson Engineering Corporation, in July 1998. This unit (renamed Spacehab Engineering Services) conducted training for astronauts at the Johnson Space Center in Houston. All of these occurrences led to Spacehab's reporting of a net income of $9.6 million on revenues of $64 million for the 1998 fiscal year.

In May 1999, the Spacehab module was used to resupply the first elements of the long-awaited international space station (ISS) under construction. Spacehab bought the first option on commercial space aboard the ISS from the Canadian Space Agency in August 1999. By this time, David A. Rossi was serving as Spacehab's president.

In December 1999, Spacehab contracted with RSC (Rocket Space Corporation) Energia of Korolev, Russia to build a manned, pressurized module (dubbed "Enterprise") to attach to the ISS for commercial purposes. The two companies were sharing the cost of building the $100 million module, which was expected to launch via a Russian rocket in 2002 (later rescheduled for 2003).

Microgravity experiments similar to those performed on the space shuttles were also scheduled for the ISS module. Spacehab formed a joint venture (Spacehab Canada, Inc.) with the Canadian telecommunications company EMS Technologies, Inc. to market its commercial space on the ISS.

### New Horizons in a New Millennium

Spacehab planned to make the first independent television and Internet broadcasts from space, mostly centering on activities aboard the ISS. Its tiny TV studio aboard the Enterprise module would have two cameras, remote controlled from Earth. Spacehab set up Space Media, Inc. to handle the Enterprise's multimedia applications. "Sharing the excitement and wonder of space exploration with everyone, everywhere," was its mission, according to Harrison. Broadcasts were scheduled to begin in late 2000. Space Media also acquired an e-commerce site, The Space Store, which offered space-related items, including a $2 million used Soviet space capsule (the Soyuz TM-26).

Spacehab won contracts for second and third ISS resupply missions via space shuttle in 2000. These missions ferried food and equipment needed by the first permanent crew, and were scheduled for that October. By this time, Spacehab's long-term strategic partners included Daimler Chrysler Aerospace (or DASA, which merged with Matra Marconi to form Astrium) and the Mitsubishi Corporation.

Spacehab prepared to debut its Research Double Module (RDM) on a space shuttle flight in early 2001. Part of the mission involved the company's Space Technology and Research Students (STARS) program, which carried experiments from students in five different countries. The STARS program's experiments included one from China to see how well silkworms produce silk in zero gravity. Spacehab hoped to have up to a million students involved as the company moved into the future.

### Principal Subsidiaries

Astrotech Space Operations, L.P.; Johnson Engineering Corporation; Space Media, Inc.; Spacehab Canada Inc.

### Principal Divisions

Spacehab Flight Services; Spacehab Engineering Services; Astrotech.

### Principal Competitors

Boeing Co.; Lockheed Martin Corp.; Spaceport Systems International; United Space Alliance.

### Further Reading

Bradford, Michael, "New Policy for Space Lab; Lenders Covered if Government Grounds Program," *Business Insurance,* July 8, 1991, p. 1.

Dunlap, Craig, "Canaveral Trade Zone Focuses on Space Niche," *Journal of Commerce,* November 5, 1992, p. 4A.

Feder, Barnaby J., "Searching for Profits in Space," *New York Times,* February 11, 1990.

——, "Talking Deals; Chase Financing of Spacehab Plan," *New York Times,* March 14, 1991, p. D2.

Guida, Tony, and Bob Beard, "Spacehab Business Update," *Entrepreneurs Only, CNNfn,* April 28, 2000.

Hinden, Stan, "Arlington Space Firm Readies Wall Street Landing," *Washington Post,* October 23, 1995, p. F33.

"Interview with Shelly A. Harrison," *Wall Street Transcript,* July 17, 2000.

Knight, Jerry, "For Some, Spacehab Still Carries a Lot of Weight," *Washington Post,* September 9, 1996, p. F33.

Metaxas, John, "Interview of Shelley Harrison," *Entrepreneurs Only, CNNfn,* March 2, 1999.

Schafer, Sarah, "A Tether with Some Stretch; Spacehab's Fortunes Are Still Tied to NASA but Other Worlds Beckon," *Washington Post,* November 2, 1998, p. F5.

Segal, David, "With NASA Its Only Client, Spacehab Shoots for the Moon," *Washington Post,* March 11, 1996, p. F8.

Sugawara, Sandra, "Flight of Frustration; Spacehab's Commercial Venture Has Trouble Getting Off the Ground," *Washington Post,* July 8, 1991, p. F1.

Webb, Margaret K., "Shuttle Commercial Venture Gets a Big Lift from NASA; Agency Buys Room on Spacehab's Module," *Washington Post,* December 10, 1990, p. F6.

—Frederick C. Ingram

# Stanadyne Automotive Corporation

**92 Deerfield Road**
**Windsor, Connecticut 06095-4200**
**U.S.A.**
**Telephone: (860) 525-0821**
**Fax: (860) 683-4500**
**Web site: http://www.stanadyne.com**

*Private Company*
*Incorporated:* 1989
*Employees:* 2,204
*Sales:* $281.6 million (1999 est.)
*NAIC:* 333911 Pump and Pumping Equipment
Manufacturing; 332911 Industrial Valve
Manufacturing; 33361 Engine, Turbine, and Power
Transmission Equipment Manufacturing

Stanadyne Automotive Corporation is a leading manufacturer of fuel injectors and pumps for diesel engines and hydraulic valve lifters for gas engines. Diesel products account for about 85 percent of sales with most customers being original equipment manufacturers like Daimler Chrysler, Deer & Co., and Ford Motor Co. More than nine out of ten farm and industrial tractors produced in the United States are diesel powered and many come equipped with a Stanadyne fuel system.

### 19th Century Origins

The company traces its roots back to 1876 when the Hartford Machine Screw Company was formed. The Connecticut legislature granted a charter to the Hartford Machine Screw Company in May of 1876. Nineteen years later the company became one of six screw companies that were part of the holding company known as Standard Screw Company. Standard Screw's first printed stockholders report appeared in 1902 showing sales of $900,000 and earnings of $67,500 according to a 1985 history of the company by Ellsworth S. Grant.

The company's first outstanding leader came from Chicago. Walter B. Pearson, an inventor, sold his small screw machine company to Standard Screw on July 9, 1900. From 1904, when Pearson took over as president, until his death in 1917, he was the architect of Standard Screw Company's rise to prominence in its industry. By doubling the company's subsidiaries to eight, Pearson gained an edge in the industry in the form of increased facilities and know-how. Along with two other early company leaders (Edwin H. Ehrman and Charles E. Roberts), Pearson introduced the "new Standard Automatic," a machine that reduced the cost of making screws nearly 40 percent. In February 1904 the company also reduced prices by 45 percent, a move that gave it the inside track with fledgling automobile manufacturers.

### A Steady Stream of Profits Broken in 1931

World War I brought the company contracts from the British and U.S. governments for millions of bullets and fuses. In 1916 the company's profit of $2.2 million was ten times higher than the preceding year's, and 1917 saw another 340+ percent increase to $7.5 million. Although it could boast few proprietary products, Standard Screw dominated the screw machine products industry during the early decades of the 20th century. It succeeded through sophisticated job shops that churned out specialized, complex parts for manufacturers in many industries.

The company delivered a steady stream of profits until 1931, one of the Great Depression years. By 1934 the company rebounded, invested in modernization, and began to solidify its reputation for design as well as manufacturing. Rather than blindly following customer specifications, company engineers tried to create ways to improve the product and production process.

In 1935 the Chicago Screw subsidiary developed a mechanical type of tappet, the intricate, noise-reducing lifter device for engine valves. Tappets released oil in precise amounts to lubricate rocker arm assemblies and they provided an ideal surface for cam action. The company saw a tremendous business opportunity if it could meet the precision requirements of tappet customers like International Harvester and automobile manufacturers. By 1971 the Chicago operation would become a leading supplier of hydraulic tappets, producing more than 30 million a year.

## Company Perspectives:

*Stanadyne has worked hard to develop lasting relationships with its employees, customers, and suppliers. Our product innovation and manufacturing leadership brings the knowledge, skills and expertise of our people to the marketplace through our Diesel Systems Group, Precision Engine Products and Precision Components and Assembly businesses. We will continue to strive to be our customers' supplier of choice by providing high quality, innovative products and services, and on-time delivery performance to assure a stable future for all of our employees while providing adequate returns to continue investments in new products and process technologies.*

### Changing Market Brought a Dramatic Turn

World War II brought a deluge of challenges to Standard Screw. Every company facility was overwhelmed with the need for vital components for airplanes, engines, tanks, bulldozers, shells, cartridges, and other munitions. At the war's end the screw machine products industry was a changed landscape. The strong need for metalwork had spawned small, well-equipped shops with low overhead and few labor burdens. From 1939 to 1947 competition quadrupled to 1,200 shops. Standard Screw's competitors could buy government surplus machines at ten percent of their value. And some manufacturers, including many automotive companies, began making their own parts.

Perhaps no one influenced Standard Screw's history as much as its fourth president, Webster D. Corlett. He joined the company during World War I and by 1925 was responsible for all manufacturing. He became president in 1945 and retired as chairman of the board in 1964. For four decades he dictated manufacturing policy. Corlett could also claim responsibility for the Chicago operation's specialization in engine tappets and for acquiring the Moen single-handle faucet.

In 1949 Corlett announced a dramatic turn in company direction. Standard Screw would de-emphasize the highly competitive general screw machine products to concentrate more on a new type of injection pump for diesel engines, textile spindles, a new line of furniture fasteners, and automotive valve tappets.

### Research and Development in 1950s

Since 1900 the company was a conglomeration of skilled job shops with no special resources allotted to research and development. The move into fuel injection pumps, plumbing, and tappets changed that. In 1961 the company established a $500,000+ annual research and development budget. In 1967 the company built an Advanced Products Technical Center in Windsor, Connecticut, to build and test products for the fuel injection business. (In 1982 Stanadyne doubled the size of the facility and renamed it the Vernon Roosa Engineering Center after the inventor of the diesel engine pump.)

The diesel pumps and tappets would prove particularly important to Standard Screw's future. In May 1947 the company convinced Long Island inventor Vernon D. Roosa to join its Connecticut operating company, Hartford Machine Screw, and perfect his diesel engine injection pump. Diesel engines had always been more economical and powerful than gasoline-fueled engines. They weren't used often because of a cumbersome power plant that did not fit well into vehicles. The diesel engine required a pump for each cylinder. Roosa's invention employed a single, small pump that reduced engine bulk and weight.

The first few years proved unprofitable, and Standard Screw nearly gave up on the project. Four years later, however, sales had eliminated all development costs. The pump's versatility, flexibility, and low cost made it popular with farm equipment manufacturers like Allis-Chalmers, Ford, International Harvester, and John Deere. In March 1953 the diesel fuel injection product company, CAV, Ltd. of London, contracted to manufacture and distribute the Roosa pump in Europe.

### Operating Companies Combine in 1955

Standard Screw's structure as a holding company with separate operating companies eventually led to internal competition that created damaging rivalries among its Hartford, Connecticut; Elyria, Ohio; and Chicago screw machine products operations. In 1955 management dissolved the subsidiaries and made them divisions. However, nothing stopped the decline of the overall fastener and job shop business. The close business relationships Standard Screw had with many customers came to be less important, as the value of a dollar gained overriding prominence in the customer's mind. Marginal pricing created havoc in the industry. New distribution methods allowed customers to skirt around Standard Screw. And foreign competition intensified. The company reacted by consolidating its standard fastener sales and selling nationally under a new trade name, "Stanscrew" in 1961.

While continuing to struggle in the screw products machine business, Standard Screw's business in tappets grew. Early in the 1950s Corlett and Carl Voorhies created a hydraulic lifter with tolerances held to 35 millionths of an inch that won contracts from Chrysler and other manufacturers. In 1956 Corlett signed a deal, with Ravenna Metal Products of Seattle, to acquire the single-handle faucet technology developed by Al Moen. The Moen faucet became the company's first consumer product. After several years of development, the company perfected the Moen faucet for mass marketing.

### A New Name in the 1970s

For the first time, in 1966 the company instituted formal divisional planning, in an effort to further develop and market its own products. Company Chairman James A. Taylor acknowledged in 1969 that although Stanscrew fasteners were still important, the company would not base its future on them. To further signal the shift in company product, Standard Screw changed its name to Stanadyne, Inc. in 1970.

The old screw machine products and fasteners still acted as an anchor on company progress. In the 1970s that portion of Stanadyne's business had to weather two energy crises, more aggressive foreign competition, and the decline in general of the U.S. manufacturers.

## Key Dates:

**1876:** Hartford Machine Screw Company is established.
**1900:** Standard Screw Company is incorporated in New Jersey.
**1952:** Company receives its first production order for 500 Roosa Master Pumps.
**1956:** Technology for the Moen single-handle faucet is acquired.
**1963:** Company introduces the first major injector design change in 30 years, the Pencil Nozzle.
**1967:** The one-millionth Roosa Master Pump is produced by Hartford Division.
**1970:** Standard Screw changes its corporate name to Stanadyne.
**1980:** An International Division is established.
**1984:** The Slim Tip Pencil Nozzle line debuts.
**1991:** Company introduces the Fuel Manager line of pumps.
**1997:** Company begins introducing environmentally friendly pump systems for diesel engines.

### *Rising Fortunes in Pump, Faucet, and Tappet Markets*

Fortunately, the Roosa pump, the Moen faucet, and the tappet business rose at about the same time that the screw products machine business fell. The 1970s oil crisis propelled the pump sales beyond all company expectations. In 1976 General Motors first contracted for Roosa pumps annually for its light trucks and passenger cars. As GM's orders grew from 75,000 to about 300,000 annually, Stanadyne opened plants in North Carolina. In 1988 the pump joined the likes of the San Francisco cable cars and Pitney Bowes' postage meter when the American Society of Mechanical Engineers recognized its revolutionary impact. By that year nearly 30 million rotary type fuel pumps had been produced by Stanadyne and its licensees. Before Roosa's invention the diesel engine powered five percent of farm tractors, construction equipment, and commercial trucks, while the gasoline engine powered 95 percent. By 1988 the reverse was true.

In the late 1960s and early 1970s the company tried diversifying to protect itself from loses in its core business and to take advantage of its strong, debt-free financial position. It purchased the Chicago Starter Company in 1969 to complement the Roosa Pump product. In March 1970 the company bought Capewell Manufacturing Company of Hartford, a maker of saw blades and parachute buckles. To supplement Moen's line of plumbing products, Stanadyne bought the outstanding stock of Ziegler-Harris, a small sink manufacturer in January 1973.

Next, the company sought to capitalize on the growing interest in powdered metallurgy. Using this new technology for making hydraulic tappets would reap considerable savings. It would eliminate machining as a step in the formation and fusing of certain parts. Powered metallurgy might also be useful in pump production. In January 1977 Stanadyne bought the Supermet Division of TRW Inc. The investment in Capewell even-

tually required Stanadyne to choose to either get further into the industrial saw market or abandon it. It chose to sell Capewell in 1980. A year later, when it became clear the Chicago Starter Company did not fit in with the company's strategic direction, it was sold to Sycon Corporation.

The Moen faucet showed great sales growth throughout the 1970s. By 1979 Moen's annual sales topped $100 million, or 25 percent of the parent company total. Semi-proprietary valve train line and cold-drawn steel operations also proved profitable.

Transition from a fastener and job shop was completed by 1980 when the company liquidated its entire screw machine products and fastener business. At that time the company competed in four main businesses: diesel fuel injection systems, valve trains, cold-finished steel, and powdered metal parts.

### *Going International*

As early as 1958 Stanadyne had a worldwide network for distribution and service of the Roosa Master Pump. Agreements included a 1961 license granted to a West German company to use Moen patents to produce some faucet parts and a 1964 agreement with Moresa, S.A. in Mexico to make tappets.

Engineering innovations helped keep the company moving into markets worldwide. The 1963 introduction of the Pencil Nozzle was a major design change that reduced manufacturing costs and helped spur worldwide sales. In 1984 Stanadyne introduced the Slim Tip Pencil Nozzle that allowed Ford U.K. and the Japanese farm equipment manufacturer, Kubota, to reconfigure combustion chamber designs for higher horsepower and lower emissions.

May 1972 saw the opening of Stanadyne of Canada to promote Moen products in that country. The company's first branch office in Trappes, France was established in 1975. By 2000 it served Europe, Africa, and Asia through 52 distributors and 400 dealers.

In 1980 Paul Mongerson, chief executive officer, established the company's International Division. During that decade Stanadyne targeted the U.S. and European on-highway diesel engine market, becoming the sole supplier of fuel pumps for General Motor's 6.2L diesel engine and Navistar's 6.9 diesel engine. To better serve Europe, Stanadyne acquired a fuel injector manufacturing plant in Brescia, Italy.

During the 1980s Stanadyne also began creating ancillary products for the diesel market. These included a diesel engine timing kit and the development of fuel additives.

By the beginning of the 21st century the company had seven manufacturing plants as well as five engineering and technical centers worldwide. Locations included Windsor, Connecticut; Jacksonville, North Carolina; Tallahassee, Florida; Elmhurst, Illinois; Washington, North Carolina; Brescia, Italy; Huntingdon, U.K.; Trappes, France; and Curitiba, Brazil. More than 33 percent of the company's $282 million annual sales were in markets outside North America.

### Ownership Changes and New Products in the 1990s

In the late 1980s and the 1990s ownership and makeup of the company continued to change and evolve. Early in 1988 a private New York investment firm, Forstmann Little, bought Stanadyne. At the time, the company had four operating groups: 1) Moen plumbing products; 2) the automotive products group; 3) Supermet, a powdered metal group; and 4) the Western Cold-drawn Steel group. All four operations were quickly sold. KSP, another private New York investment firm, bought the automotive products group and the rights to the Stanadyne name in February 1989. KSP renamed the company, Stanadyne Automotive Corp. In 1997 American Industrial Partners purchased Stanadyne and owed nearly 95 percent of the company in 2000. The company had two independent business segments, the diesel systems division, which accounted for more than 80 percent of sales, and the precision engine division, which designed and manufactured hydraulic valve lifters, primarily for automotive gasoline engines.

A continuing theme throughout the 1990s was product development. Several innovations arose from Stanadyne's efforts to help manufacturers meet stricter worldwide emissions regulations. In 1991 Stanadyne developed the Fuel Manager, a product using a completely modular system with interchangeable components for fuel filtration, water detection and removal, in-unit heating, and hand priming. In 1994 the company introduced its Model DS electronic fuel injection pump. The pump provided electronic control of both fuel quantity and the start of injection timing. The precision engine division developed a new roller rocker arm assembly and expanded into Brazil to support Tritec, a joint venture between Daimler Chrysler and BMW.

As it moved into a new century, Stanadyne's focus was on innovation and new markets for its precision components. As the United States stepped up regulations on emissions levels for diesel engines, the company was exploring new, environmentally sound products to aid in fuel economy and air quality. With a long tradition of quality and reliability, Stanadyne seemed assured of a secure place in the automotive industry of the future.

### Principal Subsidiaries

Precision Engine Products Corp.; Stanadyne Automotive S.p.A. (Italy); Precision Engine Products Ltda. (Brazil).

### Principal Divisions

Diesel Systems Group; Precision Components & Assembly.

### Principal Competitors

Robert Bosch GmbH; Federal-Mogul Corp.; Eaton Corp.

### Further Reading

Grant, Ellsworth S., *Stanadyne: A History*, Windsor, Conn.: Stanadyne, Inc., 1985.

Murphy, Robert F., "Diesel Pump a Landmark," *Hartford Courant,* April 19, 1988, p. B1.

Rasie, Lawrence B., "Forstmann Little Decided Quickly on Stanadyne Buy," *Hartford Courant,* February 10, 1988, p. C1.

—Chris John Amorosino

# Steven Madden, Ltd.

52-16 Barnett Avenue
Long Island City, New York 11104
U.S.A.
Telephone: (718) 446-1800
Toll Free: (888) 697-4632
Fax: (718) 446-5599
Web site: http://www.stevemadden.com

*Public Company*
*Incorporated:* 1990
*Employees:* 709
*Sales:* $162.04 million (1999)
*Stock Exchanges:* NASDAQ
*Ticker Symbol:* SHOO
*NAIC:* 316214 Women's Footwear (Except Athletic)
   Manufacturing; 44234 Footwear Wholesalers; 44821
   Shoe Stores

Steven Madden, Ltd. designs, markets, and sells style-conscious contemporary footwear and related products for women and girls. Its core constituency consists of teenagers intrigued by platform shoes in a variety of far-out designs, but the company also designs a wide range of other footwear, including boots, sneakers, slippers, sandals, and evening shoes at prices ranging from $48 to $150 and creates styles for women and for girls younger than teenagers. Steven Madden also owns and operates retail stores, licenses a variety of women's wear under the Steve Madden trademark, and, under license, markets and sells the footwear of other companies.

## Steven Madden to 1995

Steve Madden's entry into the shoe business began in 1974, when in his late teens the Long Island resident took a job in a shoe store. "It was a time of Elton John and David Bowie's Ziggy Stardust," he later recalled, according to Elaine Underwood of *Brandweek.* "It was a tremendously exciting time in the shoe business. Everything was platform. It affected me." The son of a textile company owner, he enrolled at the University of Miami, where, he told Suzanne C. Ryan of the *Boston Globe,* he "majored in girls and drugs." After two years, Madden's exasperated father yanked him out of school. He took a job as a shoe salesman near his Long Island home in 1978 and two years later moved over to New York shoe wholesaler L.J. Simone Footwear. While there, Madden began designing shoes aimed at the teenage market, such as white fringe boots and penny loafers in pink and white.

After nearly a decade in design, Madden was successful enough to negotiate a deal in 1988 with M.C.S. Footwear, where he designed, developed, and marketed the "Souliers" line of footwear for women. They put his name on the shoes he designed and gave him 10 percent of the profits. In 1990 he struck out on his own, renting a small office in the Long Island City neighborhood of New York City's borough of Queens with a $1,000 grubstake and one employee. Borrowing money from friends, Madden began manufacturing his own designs and selling them to small and trendy Manhattan stores, where they attracted clothing designers such as Betsey Johnson and Jill Stuart, who used them in their fashion shows. The chunky platform look reportedly was inspired by a 15-year-old customer who added a higher platform to the sole of a pair of his shoes. Steven Madden, Ltd. had revenues of $134,424 in fiscal 1991 (the year ended June 30, 1991), $759,856 in fiscal 1992, and $1.38 million in fiscal 1993. It made a small profit in 1992 but lost $98,351 the following year, which the company attributed to amortization of deferred financing costs and factor interest expenses.

By the summer of 1993 Steven Madden, Ltd. had moved its offices to lower Broadway in Manhattan's SoHo neighborhood, where it also operated a retail store. The company had 13 employees. Its footwear, including boots, clogs, and sandals, was being manufactured in Brazil, Mexico, and New York City, and was being sold in department stores and footwear specialty stores, mostly in the New York metropolitan area, California, and Florida. The company went public in 1993, raising about $5.6 million in net proceeds by selling 1.725 million shares at $4 each. Revenues rose to $5.33 million in 1993 and $8.45 million in 1994. Development costs resulted in a loss of $878,630 in 1993 and $736,988 in 1994. Steven Madden moved its headquarters and warehouse facility back to Long Island City in 1994 and acquired

Marlboro Leather, Inc., a marketer of finished leather to manufacturers of shoes, apparel, and accessories.

The public offering was made through Stratton Oakmont Inc., a Long Island-based investment bank and brokerage house that specialized in raising capital for start-up companies. Danny Porush, a childhood friend of Madden, was one principal of the partnership; the others were Jordan Belfort and Kenneth Greene. In return for an earlier $100,000 loan, Madden had agreed to give the partners 40 percent of the stock of Steven Madden, Ltd. However, Stratton Oakmont had a reputation for noncompliance with securities laws. Since a NASDAQ listing for the Steven Madden, Ltd. stock was not possible as long as the partners held so much control, the shares were transferred to BOCAP Corp., a Florida-based company personally owned by Madden, in return for a promissory note of $5.1 million. In 1997 Belfort demanded BOCAP shares equivalent in value to the note and thereby claimed ownership of 15 percent of Steven Madden through an escrow account. In a 1998 settlement, Belfort agreed to abandon his claims to the stock in return for $4.1 million in cash from BOCAP.

### Taking Giant Strides: 1995–99

In 1995 Steven Madden acquired Adesso Shoes of Roslyn Heights, Long Island, which, as Adesso-Madden, Inc., became a subsidiary serving as a buying agent for the manufacture abroad and import to the United States of private label shoes. The parent company's sales reached $38.74 million that year and rose to $45.82 million in 1996, when it acquired the David Aaron brand for older, more sophisticated, career- and fashion-oriented women. By 1997 Madden's styles, which included leopard print platforms, zebra print loafers, chunky four-inch heels, and satin prom night shoes, were hits with young women such as "first daughter" Chelsea Clinton and centerfold Jenny McCarthy. Madden's Long Island City headquarters included a facility for turning out samples—at a rate of 10 to 15 a week—by his young designers for testing in the company's four stores. Successful designs then were shipped abroad for mass production, followed by nationwide distribution. The Madden stores also introduced Takeout Tees, cotton T-shirts packed in take-out food containers with a picture of a porno actress on the lid, and Ice Tees, summer styles packed in cans reminiscent of Nestea.

Also in 1997, Steven Madden signed its first licensing agreements for handbags, sunglasses, hosiery, outerwear, and jewelry. In November of that year, Winer Industries was chosen as the licensee for Steven Madden sportswear and jeans. (This license subsequently lapsed.) The chain of Madden stores grew

to 17, including units in Miami and Los Angeles, and the David Aaron division opened its first outlet, just across the street from Madden's flagship 1,200-square-foot SoHo store. Moreover, in April 1998 Steven Madden obtained the l.e.i. license from R.S.V. Sport, Inc. This trademark was well known for jeanswear in the junior marketplace and footwear for young girls and teenagers.

Now past 40, Madden did not resemble the average chief executive officer. Ryan observed him at company headquarters in blue jeans (with a gaping hole in the seat), a baseball cap atop wavy red hair, and white gym socks in black Gucci loafers. Saturday afternoons would find him trolling his stores to find out what shoppers were wearing and query them about their tastes. Insecurity, he claimed, was the motivation for his continuing search for new concepts and trends in the shoe trade. "I never think I'm good enough," he confessed to Amanda Plotkin of *Footwear News*. "You have to keep updating. The worst thing that happens is you get comfortable in your success and stand around and tell yourself how great you're doing, and then you're not doing so great anymore."

Steven Madden, Ltd. kept doing great in 1998 and 1999. Net sales rose to $85.78 million and then nearly doubled to $162.04 million in 1999. Net income doubled to $5.45 million in 1998 and more than doubled to $11.45 million in 1999. Early that year the company began selling Jordache footwear under license, primarily to girls ages 10 to 16. An affiliate of Jordache Enterprises, Inc. also agreed to manufacture, market, sell, and distribute sportswear and jeanswear under the Steve Madden trademark to better department stores and specialty shops. By the end of 1999 Steven Madden's own roster of licensed products now also included belts, hair accessory products, and intimate apparel.

In January 2000 Steven Madden announced the creation of its new Stevies brand of footwear for girls ages 6 to 12. The brand, with styles created by spinning off variations on designs of the Steve Madden brand, was to be sold in department and specialty stores but not in Madden's own stores. Instead a Stevies accessories concept shop for retailers was established. By the end of March the company had signed licensing agreements for a wide range of Stevies accessories: hair and fashion accessories such as hats, ponchos, and neckwear; jewelry; sunglasses; belts; and handbags and backpacks. "Apparel will be my next step," licensing director Corinne Moroney told Claude Solnik of *Footwear News*. "The whole focus right now is to develop Madden from head to toe in both Steve Madden and Stevies."

The Steve Madden line of shoes at the end of 1999 included a wide range of footwear, including boots, sneakers, evening shoes, slippers, casual and tailored shoes, and sandals, designed to appeal to girls and women ages 16 to 25. They typically sold at retail for prices ranging from $48 to $70 for shoes and up to $99 for boots. The David Aaron line, aimed at women ages 26 to 45, generally was priced at $70 to $85 for shoes and up to $150 for boots. L.e.i. footwear was being targeted to attract girls and young women ages six to 20.

Steven Madden, Ltd. owned and operated 41 retail stores under the Steve Madden name at the end of 1999; by mid-2000 that number would increase to 58. The company also fielded one store under the David Aaron name and six outlet stores at the end of 1999. Forty one stores were located in major shopping malls in 15 states. Four stores were in Manhattan. The remaining three were in highly traveled urban street locations in Philadelphia, Washington, D.C., and Coconut Grove, Florida. Each was designed to appeal to young, fashion-conscious women by creating a "nightclub"-type atmosphere. Retail sales accounted for 30 percent of the company's total sales in 1999.

The remaining sales of Steven Madden, Ltd. in 1999 came from creating, sourcing, selling, and marketing the company's brands to major department stores, better specialty stores, and shoe stores in the United States and Canada. The Steve Madden wholesale division alone accounted for about 48 percent of the company's total sales. The l.e.i. wholesale division accounted for about 17 percent and the David Aaron wholesale division for about 5 percent. The private label division was manufacturing women's footwear for large retailers and was also sourcing and selling footwear under the Soho Cobbler and Jordache trademarks. The private label division generated commission revenue of $2.56 million in 1999.

### Founder's Arrest in 2000

Madden's ties with Stratton Oakmont came back to haunt him in 2000, when he was accused of receiving shares below the offering price in many of the companies for whom the firm underwrote initial public offerings. Madden, it was alleged, would then reap a substantial profit once the offering had been completed. Following the demise of Stratton Oakmont, Madden allegedly established a similar relationship with another such firm, Monroe Parker Securities, paying back a portion of these prearranged "flip" trades. A former Monroe Parker executive testified in 1999 that Madden gave him $80,000 in a brown paper bag as part of the stock-manipulation scheme.

In June 2000, federal prosecutors indicted Madden on charges of securities fraud, conspiracy, and money laundering in 22 initial public offerings of stock, including the IPO of his own company. The frauds were alleged to generate about $7 million for Madden and others. Shares of Steven Madden stock fell 40 percent on the news. Clad in jeans, cap, and a white polo shirt, Madden, who pleaded not guilty and was released on bail, temporarily relinquished his position as chairman of the company but continued as chief executive officer. Wellington Management Co., the largest shareholder in the company except for Madden himself, reduced its holdings by about two-thirds between the end of April and the end of June. A share of Madden stock, which reached a high of $22.70 in April, dipped as low as

$5.50 during the summer of 2000. Steven Madden owned 18 percent of the shares in May 2000.

### Principal Subsidiaries

Adesso-Madden, Inc.; Diva Acquisition Corp.; Steven Madden Retail, Inc.

### Principal Divisions

The David Aaron Wholesale Division; l.e.i. Wholesale Division; Private Label Division; Steven Madden Retail Division; Steven Madden Wholesale Division.

### Principal Competitors

Kenneth Cole Productions Inc.; Nine West Group Inc.

### Further Reading

Barron, Kelly, "Sole Man," *Forbes,* November 1, 1999, pp. 264, 266.

Butler, Simon, "It's a Madden, Madden, Madden World," *Footwear News,* May 26, 1997, pp. 14–15.

Emert, Carol, "Steven Madden Hopes IPO Will Raise $4.5 Million," *Footwear News,* August 30, 1993, pp. 2, 37.

Feigenbaum, Randi, "Taking the Next Step," *Newsday,* July 14, 1997, p. C6.

Gasparino, Charles, and Terzah Ewing, "Penny-Stock Ties Entangle Shoe Mogul," *Wall Street Journal,* February 18, 2000, pp. C1–C2.

Harrigan, Susan, "The Shoe Magnate and the Broker," *Newsday,* August 10, 1998, pp. C8–C11.

Kern, Beth Sever, "Madden Will Enter Unbranded," *Footwear News,* September 11, 1995, pp. 2, 23.

"Madden Signs Key Agreement to Market l.e.i. Footwear," *Footwear News,* April 27, 1998, p. 7.

Paar, Karen, "Steven Madden Launches Juniors," *WWD,* November 13, 1997, p. 15.

Plotkin, Amanda, "King of Cool," *Footwear News,* December 6, 1999, p. 16.

Ryan, Suzanne C., "For Madden, Fashion Starts with the Feet," *Boston Globe,* February 18, 1998, pp. D1, D5.

Solnik, Claude, "Steve Madden Builds Brand for Lollipop Set," *Footwear News,* January 17, 2000, p. 10.

——, "Stevies Aims for 'Tween' Brand Status by Accessorizing," *Footwear News,* March 27, 2000, p. 2.

Underwood, Elaine, "Off the Wall Display," *Brandweek,* March 3, 1997, pp. 18–19.

Young, Vicki, and Claude Solnik, "Madden Remains CEO: Company Shifts into Damage Control," *Footwear News,* June 26, 2000, pp. 1, 8, 33.

—Robert Halasz

# Stock Yards Packing Co., Inc.

340 North Oakley Boulevard
Chicago, Illinois 60612
U.S.A.
Telephone: (312) 733-6050
Toll Free: (800) 621-1119
Fax: (312) 733-0738
Web site: http://www.stockyards.com

*Wholly Owned Subsidiary of U.S. Foodservice*
*Incorporated:* 1893
*Employees:* 115
*Sales:* $78.20 million (1998)
*NAIC:* 311611 Animal (Except Poultry) Slaughtering

Stock Yards Packing Co., Inc. is one of the largest suppliers of choice and prime cuts of beef to restaurants, resorts, hotels, and private clubs. The company also supplies lamb, poultry, pork, and desserts in the United States and worldwide. Through the years, Stock Yards has pioneered such distribution concepts as shipping by train, offering meat as specified by the customer, offering hand-cut individual portions, and vacuum-packing. The largest concentration of customers are in Chicago, Las Vegas, and Atlantic City, but the company supplies meats to the world market and to individual customers via mail order and the Internet. Owned by the Pollack family for five generations, the company was sold to U.S. Foodservice in 2000.

## The Early Years

In the early 1890s, Chicago was known throughout the United States, and the world, as the butcher capital. In 1893, Bernhard Pollack opened a retail butcher shop on Halstead Street. He took inspiration for the stock yards of the area to name his shop Stock Yards Packing Company. With his son, Gus, as an assistant, Pollack expanded the business to include the wholesale markets of restaurants, hotels, and clubs. Gus took over the company in 1902 and moved the shop to Wells Street as business increased. The younger Pollack felt the potential from wholesale business was so great that when he moved the company, he discontinued the retail portion of the business.

Just as World War II was breaking out, Gus's son Bernie joined Stock Yards in 1939. Father and son moved the company yet again, to the Fulton Market area of Chicago. The war years were difficult for Stock Yards, as the U.S. government instituted rationing. During those years, the company covered the display windows of the coolers with paper, so people in the streets could not see the large quantities of meat that, because of rationing, the company would be unable to sell them.

## Postwar Growth

The end of World War II saw the push for Stock Yards to become a national company. Bernie Pollack headed the company and brought on his two brothers-in law, Harry Katz and Stanley Katz. With each man overseeing his specialty—Bernie, administration and sales; Harry, merchandising and sales; and Stanley, purchasing and production–the company's sales outside of the Chicago area began to grow. Harry Katz began to drive throughout the Midwest, Texas, and Oklahoma, visiting restaurants, clubs, and hotels to push for business. Many customers were gained with the company's promise to deliver meat that met the customers' selection for specifications and aging. In fact, Stock Yards was one of the first meat companies to allow customers to order specific grades and cuts of meat. Stock Yards shipped its orders outside the Chicago-metro area in wooden barrels and ''church containers'' packed with dry ice.

In the early 1950s, Stock Yards continued to look for new and innovative ways to provide customer service. The company hired sales people outside of the Chicago area—first in Texas and Louisiana—so they could offer hands-on service for customers. Stock Yards began shipping customers individual portion-sized cuts of their meats at this time, again becoming one of the first companies to do so. When the USDA designated grades of meats and required that they be cut in separate rooms during this time, Stock Yards designed two different rooms at their facilities, for U.S. Choice and U.S. Prime, and became one of the first companies to win approval from the USDA for such labeling.

It was at this time that Stock Yards re-entered the retail business. As one of the first wholesalers to offer meat directly to consumers, Stock Yards began selling meats via mail-order in

374

**Key Dates:**

**1893:** Stock Yards Packing Company is founded by Bernhard Pollack as a retail butcher shop in Chicago.
**1902:** Gus Pollack takes over and concentrates on the wholesale side of the business.
**1939:** Gus's son, Bernie Pollack, extends sales to Wisconsin and Michigan.
**1948:** The company begins shipping meat in barrels packed with dry ice.
**1964:** With new USDA grading requirements, Stock Yards has its beef cut in separate rooms.
**1970:** A permanent facility is opened in Las Vegas.
**1982:** A cooler-freezer distribution center is built in Atlantic City, New Jersey.
**1990s:** Stock Yards cultivates business in the Caribbean, Mexico, and Asia.
**2000:** Stock Yards is sold to U.S. Foodservice, a national food distribution company.

gift packs and for home consumption. The retail business took off and Stanley Katz produced a newsletter, *Prime Times,* for mail-order customers. The newsletter offered recipes (later put together in a cookbook) and showed the best of what Stock Yards had to offer consumers.

Pushing westward, Harry Katz made some sales trips to Las Vegas. After World War II, the tourism industry in Las Vegas grew rapidly, and the city became that area's largest employer. The postwar period saw immense growth in the hotel industry, as casinos were built and resorts and restaurants sprang up to accommodate out-of-town visitors. The tremendous growth in the Las Vegas market soon resulted in Stock Yards sending refrigerated trucks to the area twice a week. Over the next two decades, business grew at such a rapid clip that Stock Yards built its first non-Chicago area distribution facility in Las Vegas in 1970.

Due to growth in the late 1940s and early 1950s, and with an eye towards future growth, Stanley Katz located and purchased a new site for Stock Yards in 1953. Located three miles from the Fulton Market area, the Oakley Boulevard headquarters would continue in use through the 1990s. Originally encompassing some 30,000 square feet, the new site was the first meat packing plant designed specifically for customers in the hotel, restaurant, and resort business. Through the 1970s, several expansions were made to the plant, the first being a 10,000-square-foot addition in 1960, which was used for coolers that dried aged beef. Demand for dried aged beef fell during the 1980s, and the coolers were converted to cryovac age beef. The last addition to the Stock Yards plant was in 1978, bringing total freezer, storage, and office space to 60,000 square feet.

In 1965 the fourth generation of Pollacks joined the company. Bernie's son, Dan, first spent ten years working in all departments, learning every aspect of the business. He then concentrated on sales, working under Stanley Katz. Recalling the boon the casino resorts in Las Vegas had been to the company, Dan Pollack made sales trips to the Atlantic City, New Jersey, casinos in the early 1980s. By the end of 1982, business in Atlantic City had grown to the point that Stock Yards built a distribution center in the area.

### International and Internet Expansion in the 1990s

Not content with a growing and thriving U.S.-based business, Stock Yards began branching out internationally. By the early 1990s, restaurant and resort sales had been made in Jamaica, the Bahamas, Japan, Mexico, and Hong Kong. To develop more island-based business and to better service existing customers, Stock Yards hired a Caribbean sales person.

The fifth generation of Pollacks came on board in 1994. Dan Pollack's son, Matthew, joined the company after a brief stint working for an insurance company after college. By 1997, at age 27, Matthew took over the running the company's day-to-day operations from his father. His goal in the first years was to reorganize and modernize the company. To that end, he expanded on the retail side of the business, by establishing a web site for customers to order their gifts and meats. By early 2000, four percent of sales were coming through Internet orders. The company also signed up with some portals on the Internet, considering it an important part of its Internet strategy. About one-third of Stock Yards' Internet sales came from portals. Net sales for the company in 1999 was approximately $108 million.

In the late 1990s, the challenge facing the beef industry was primarily one of nutrition. Health experts had been telling consumers for years that too much red meat was bad for their health, and the message was getting across. By 1997, the consumption of beef was down 30 percent from 20 years earlier. Other meat producers were quick to offer their meats in convenience packages and in pre-cooked, individual portions to consumers. Beef producers were behind the curve in that regard.

A Beef Forum held by the Cooperative Research Farms in 1997 defined the problems and explored solutions to the industry's problems. Cattle feeders were encouraged to raise high-quality meat, as most packers paid a premium for higher-quality meat. It was also suggested that producers needed to focus on international marketing, as demand for beef was higher internationally than in the United States.

The third quarter of 1999 saw good times for meat packers, as the price of beef soared. Cattle feeders, responding to demand, raised the price of cattle, and packers, in turn, passed along higher prices to restaurants. In October 1999, the wholesale price of tenderloin was $10.55 per pound, up from a price of $7.50 to $8 per pound. Increased demand was attributed to the continued growth of the U.S. economy, leading to higher demand for better-quality meats, and to the upcoming millennial New Year's Eve celebrations.

In February 2000, Stock Yards Packing was sold to U.S. Foodservice, one of the largest food distributors in the United States. With annual sales of about $8 billion, U.S. Foodservice supplied over 143,000 restaurants, hotel, cafeterias, and sports arenas in the United States. The company distributed national, private label, signature brand items—over 143,000 of them.

U.S. Foodservice owned seven other custom meat cutters at the time and wanted to add a company with a solid reputation to its mix. Other pluses in acquiring Stock Yards were that company's strong management and labor force; their excellent customer service; reputation for high-quality products; and the fact that Stock Yards was a Certified Angus Beef distributor. Dan Pollack stated at the time of the acquisition that he hoped to use Stock Yards's expertise to streamline and standardize the meat cutting operations of U.S. Foodservice.

### Principal Competitors

IBP, Inc.; Moyer Packing Company; Rymer Foods, Inc.

### Further Reading

Chiem, Phat X., and George Gunset, "Beefed-Up Prices a Tender Restaurant Subject, Year 2000 Spurs Surge in Demand for Better Cuts," *Chicago Tribune,* October 21, 1999.

"Our 100th Anniversary," Chicago: Stock Yards Packing Co., Inc. 1993.

Pankaskie, David, "Beef Industry is Suffering from 'Growing Pains'," *Agway Cooperator,* Fall 1997.

Russis, Martha, "An Open Window," *Crain's Chicago Business,* February 4, 2000.

"U.S. Foodservice Announces the Acquisition of Stock Yards Packing," *PR Newswire,* February 16, 2000.

Waters, Jennifer. "Rare Start for Third-Generation Stock yards Manager," *Crain's Chicago Business,* November 24, 1997, p. 15.

—Lisa Musolf Karl

# The Stride Rite Corporation

191 Spring Street
P.O. Box
Lexington, Massachusetts 02420-9191
U.S.A.
Telephone: (617) 824-6000
Fax: (617) 824-6549
Web site: http://www.strideritecorp.com

*Public Company*
*Incorporated:* 1919 as Green Shoe Manufacturing
    Company
*Employees:* 2,300
*Sales:* $572.7 million (1999)
*Stock Exchanges:* New York
*Ticker Symbol:* SRR
*NAIC:* 316219 Other Footwear Manufacturing; 42234
    Footwear Wholesalers; 44821 Shoe Stores

Founded in 1919 as Green Shoe Manufacturing Company, The Stride Rite Corporation has become a major designer and manufacturer of shoes and casual footwear for both children and adults. Stride Rite markets its products under its own brand names: Stride Rite, Pro Keds, Keds, Sperry Top-Sider, Munchkin, Street Hot, and Grasshoppers. It also markets footwear under the licensed brand names of Tommy Hilfiger and Nine West Kids. Besides wholesaling its line, Stride Rite sells its shoes through about 120 company-owned stores as well as about 50 leased departments in major department stores and some 30 Stride Rite Family Footwear outlets. It also manufactures and markets a limited line of adult and children's sports and casual wear. Although headquartered in Lexington, Massachusetts, most of Stride Rite's footwear is made through contract arrangements with manufacturers in the Far East. Even though it markets its products in more than 30 countries, about 96 percent of its annual revenue comes from domestic sales. Stride Rite has also been recognized in the United States for its innovative, socially-conscious programs.

## 1919–24: Partners Slosberg and Green Start Company

In 1919, Jacob A. Slosberg founded a small shoe manufacturing company with his partner, Philip Green. Initially set up in converted stables in the Roxbury section of Boston, the Green Shoe Manufacturing Company specialized in making stitchdown shoes (also called welt shoes) for children. The company, employing nearly 100 people, was able to produce between 800 and 1,000 pairs of shoes each day.

Slosberg, who came to the United States from Russia in 1887 at the age of 12, had almost 30 years of experience in the shoe manufacturing industry when he co-founded Green Shoe. Beginning in 1892 he had worked for a series of shoe and shoe machinery manufacturers in Lynn and Beverly, Massachusetts. In those factories he had spent long hours stitching shoes and later dismantling and reassembling shoe machinery. He had then become a foreman at the Thomas Plant Company, a manufacturer of shoe machines, and when Thomas was sold to United Shoe Machinery, he joined the Greenberg-Miller Company, a manufacturer of children's shoes in New York. He put the money he had been able to save and the experience he had been able to garner into Green Shoe.

In the early 1920s a disagreement emerged between Philip Green and Slosberg. Some sources say that it involved the quality of the product, which Slosberg was determined to maintain, while others say it was about whether to produce children's shoes or, as Green favored, women's shoes. In any case, in 1924 Green sold his share of the enterprise, which was bought up by Charles B. Strecker, a banker, and his son Seymour.

## 1925–44: Green Shoes Fares Well Through the Depression and War Years

Green Shoe grew rapidly under Slosberg's direction. The main brand names were Green-flex and Mo-Debs. Because of overcrowding in the converted stables, Slosberg built a new manufacturing facility. Seymour Strecker sold his share of Green Shoe to Slosberg ten days before the stock market crash of 1929. However, even during the Depression, Green Shoe continued to grow. By the mid-1930s, the company was manu-

## Company Perspectives:

*The Stride Rite Corporation is the leading marketer of high quality children's footwear in the United States and is a major marketer of athletic and casual footwear for children and adults. Our business was founded on the strength of the Stride Rite children's brand, but today includes a portfolio of great American brands addressing different market segments within the footwear industry. . . . The company is predominately a wholesaler of footwear, selling its products nationwide to independent retail stores, department stores, sporting goods stores, and marinas. We market our products in countries outside the United States and Canada through independent distributors and licensees. The Company imports substantially all of its products from independent resources in the Far East who manufacture footwear according to each brand's specifications and quality standards.*

facturing about 3,000 pairs of shoes per day. During hard times, the company gained a reputation for reliability and value.

In 1933 Green Shoe, already seeking a brand name that could unite its entire line, hired Tom Lalonde, a manufacturer of children's shoes, to work in sales. Lalonde owned the name Stride Rite, and Green Shoe bought the name for $1,000 from him, using it for a line of extra support shoes. By 1937 the name was extended to all shoes manufactured by the company.

Jacob Slosberg had two sons, Sam and Charles, who began work at Green Shoe in the early 1920s. Sam eventually went into sales, and Charles took over manufacturing. Charles visited shoe factories in the United States and Europe in order to find ways of streamlining production and distribution without sacrificing quality. He was particularly concerned that the company be able to deliver shoes to outlets in a timely fashion with a minimum of mistakes. To this end, he developed a highly efficient in-stock system. Incoming orders were analyzed immediately. If the items requested were out of stock, production lines were switched over to that product as needed. Workers known as "expediters" hand-carried these orders through the production process. In this way, the company was never "out of stock." This enabled Green Shoe, and for some years Stride Rite, to guarantee that 100 percent of an order would be delivered within 24 hours of the placement of the order.

During World War II, Green Shoe helped develop and manufactured the nurse's field boot and the WAC boot for the Army. Slosberg, who was a member of the War Production Board, used the opportunity to encourage retailers to buy Stride Rite, with the result that the business boomed. It was also during the war that the company began selling shoes to department stores such as Jordan Marsh, Filene's, and the J.L. Hudson Co. in Detroit, all under private store labels.

### 1945–70: Rapid Expansion, Going Public, and Becoming Stride Rite

The years between 1945 and the late 1950s saw the most rapid expansion in the company's history, partly as a result of the postwar baby boom. One of the hallmarks of the company came

to be multiple widths in children's shoes. Daily production rose to about 25,000 pairs in 1959. The work force quadrupled, and factory floor space increased seven-fold. In fact, the Stride Rite factory was at the time the largest factory in the United States manufacturing all of a company's products under one roof.

When Jacob Slosberg died in 1953, his sons and son-in-law, Martin Landay, assumed the management of the company. Samuel became president and Charles treasurer, with the additional duties of managing production, maintenance, and in-stock operation. Landay was named vice-president. Charles Slosberg died unexpectedly in 1960.

The 1960s and 1970s saw great changes in the way Green Shoe did business. The company went public in 1960. Then, in 1962, the first of several acquisitions greatly expanded the company. That year, Green Shoe acquired the Weber Shoe Company in Tipton, Missouri. Weber became a Green Shoe manufacturing facility. A second factory was built in 1969 in Hamilton, Missouri, to augment Weber's capacity. The Weber acquisition was followed in 1964 by that of the R.J. Potvin Company, in Brockton, Massachusetts. A new warehouse was built there in 1965.

In 1966, with increased capacity and public recognition of its name, Green Shoe became the Stride Rite Corporation. In that year, the company acquired the H. Scheft Company and Stone Shoe Company in Boston and in 1967, Blue Star Shoes, Inc., in Lawrence, Massachusetts. Arnold Hiatt, Blue Star's president, became the first non-family member to become president of Stride Rite in 1968. The same year, Orange Shoe Co., in Orange, Massachusetts, was added to Stride Rite. The shoe company that began in 1919 with a capacity of 1,000 pairs per day was producing 30,000 in 1969.

This period also saw great changes in the work force at Stride Rite. During the 1960s, African American women in particular joined the Stride Rite work force in great numbers, reflecting the changing population of Roxbury, the neighborhood in which the Boston factory was located. Many of the new employees could work only if they had day-care services for their children. Thus, in response to its employees' needs, Stride Rite opened the first company-run day-care center in the United States in 1971. The idea for the center, conceived by Arnold Hiatt, was initially seen as a charitable gift that would serve the surrounding community only. As Hiatt explained, "The company had had a charitable foundation for some time, but it had limited itself to the traditional kinds of gifts–hospitals, universities, and other very visible community organizations–and had played a relatively passive check-writing role. I felt it was time for us to do something in a more targeted way . . . in our community. At the time our offices and our plant were located in Roxbury, and I thought we ought to do something right there."

Shortly after the center opened in the spring of 1971, it began enrolling employees' children. Hiatt commented: "We're given credit for being a pioneer in employer-supported day care, but our aim was to provide child care for the community, for children of welfare mothers and single-parent households. Shortly after we started, one of our workers approached me and said, 'You're willing to do this for the children in the neighborhood. Why don't you do the same for our children?'

## Key Dates:

**1919:** Company founded in Boston by partners Slosberg and Green as the Green Shoe Manufacturing Company.

**1924:** Green sells his share of the company to Charles B. Strecker and his son, Seymour.

**1929:** Seymour Strecker sells his share to Philip Green.

**1933:** Green Shoe buys the name Stride Rite from Tom Lalonde, manufacturer of children's shoes hired by the company as a sales person.

**1960:** The company goes public.

**1962:** The company acquires the Weber Shoe Company.

**1966:** Green Shoe Manufacturing Company becomes Stride Rite and acquires the H. Scheft Company and Stone Shoe Company

**1968:** Arnold Hiatt, Blue Star's president, becomes the first non-family member president of Stride Rite; company buys the Orange Shoe Co.

**1971:** Stride Rite opens the first company-run day care center in the United States.

**1979:** The firm opens its first Overland Trading Company and purchases Keds and Sperry Top-Sider from Uniroyal.

**1983:** Company headquarters moves to Cambridge, Massachusetts.

**1993:** Bob Siegel is named company president and CEO.

**1997:** Siegel retires and Jim Eskridge succeeds him as president.

**1999:** Eskridge resigns and is succeeded by David M. Chamberlain.

And I said fine. And from that day forward we tried to maintain a balance at the center between children from the community and the children of our employees.''

Although company headquarters were moved to Cambridge, Massachusetts, in 1983, and the original site was turned into a warehouse, the day-care center continued to service the same number of children as before. (In 1993, the company announced that the Roxbury warehouse would close. However, grants were made available to community groups to continue providing day-care services.) In addition, a day-care center was opened in Cambridge. The Stride Rite day-care centers, which were modeled in part on the Head Start program, have been studied and adapted by hundreds of companies all over the United States. Stride Rite looked into providing day-care services to employees at its production and distribution facilities outside of Massachusetts, but it plans were hindered by complications resulting from state regulations regarding child care. Abroad, the company had fewer problems, and by 1993 had opened a day-care center at a Stride Rite factory in Bangkok, Thailand.

### Continued Expansion through Acquisitions in the 1970s–80s

During the 1970s, faced with stalled profits due to skyrocketing leather prices and competition from low-priced imports, the company decided to explore new territory, entering the market for the outdoorsy, sporty shoes gaining popularity among young people and children. The company opened its first Stride Rite Bootery in 1972 and its first Overland Trading Company in 1979. In addition, the company purchased Keds and Sperry Top-Sider from Uniroyal in 1979 for $18 million and $5.7 million respectively. Keds, which had been losing money for Uniroyal, achieved a full turnaround by 1982, and Sperry also became very popular as a result of the "preppie look" fad of the 1980s. In fact, in the early 1980s, Sperry grew at a rate of 80 percent, a rate described as "unmatched at the moment in the shoe industry" by *Footwear News* in 1982. The ultimate decline in the popularity Top-Siders emphasized what at the time was a basic Stride Rite marketing approach: in general the company did not try to hitch onto every fad and did not try to associate its name with high profile athletes as did some of its competitors. The success of Top-Siders was unplanned and unexpected; thus the downturn was also unexpected.

During this time, Stride Rite benefitted most perhaps from its reputation as a maker of high-quality children's shoes. Parents looked for reliable quality and value for their children, and the company appeared not to stray too far from their expectations. Moreover, studies began to appear in the 1980s indicating that toddlers learned to walk better in shoes than in sneakers, and these findings fueled a 31 percent increase in sales of baby shoes in 1986 over 1985. Several of Stride Rites' baby shoes were granted the Seal of Acceptance by the American Podiatric Medical Association in 1989, the only baby shoes to hold that seal. As children's apparel became trendier in the 1980s, Stride Rite responded by changing its marketing, while retaining the basic look and quality of the line itself. By early 1989, Stride Rite had 715 retail units, 70 percent of which were owned by independent dealers, and the 25 Overland Trading Companies were spun off as an independent entity in 1988. Also in 1989, Keds brought out a line of natural fiber sportswear for children, under the name Keds Kids Clothes. Two years later, in 1991, Stride Rite founded Stride Rite International as a vehicle for marketing its products in foreign countries. The division marketed Stride Rite shoe lines in Europe, Asia, and Latin America. In 1992, the company also began to market a domestic line of women's clothes, Keds Apparel.

During this flurry of marketing activity, Stride Rite also started a new social program. Hiatt, who was then chairman of the company, had read an article in 1986 in the *Wall Street Journal* which detailed problems encountered by families with both child care and elder care responsibilities. After several years of research and with funding from the Stride Rite Charitable Foundation and input from several social agencies and Wheelock College, the company opened its Intergenerational Day-Care Center in 1990. The Center, which was housed at the company's headquarters, had separate areas and activities for seniors and children as well as common areas. According to Karen Leibold, the director of the center, "The relationship between the children and the elders has really exceeded our expectations. We thought we'd need to bring them together very slowly, with a lot of staff direction and with specific projects to do. What we've found is that they're like magnets with each other. . . . Sometimes it can be five minutes at the beginning or the end of the day. . . . Sometimes it's waving across the lunchroom at each other. Sometimes it can be an extended period of time, reading books together, or cooking, or making things with blocks or Play-Doh.''

Stride Rite demonstrated that socially conscious policies and profitability could go hand in hand. Net income rose by $5 to $10 million each year between 1984 and 1991—from $5.4 million to $66 million—and its return on equity exceeded 30 percent between 1989 and 1991. Both of these figures were down slightly in 1992; net income dropped to $61.5 million and equity return to 23.6 percent even though net sales increased. Still, the company appeared to understand the employees and customers who make such growth possible. At the time, Arnold Hiatt summarized the Stride Rite philosophy: "We don't live in a vacuum. We live in a community. And that community has needs. It is people from the community who buy our products and support our business. It doesn't seem too far-fetched to have an interest in the well-being of that community. We're just broadening the definition of our self-interest."

### 1993–2000: Ups and Downs and Revamped Product Lines for the New Century

After Bob Siegel was named Stride Rite's CEO in 1993, the company began updating its product line, partly in response to the great popularity of the variety of athletic shoes being marketed by such competitors as Nike and Reebok. The need to do so had become obvious, mostly because the thicker-soled, training and running footwear had by then replaced the old style tennis shoe as the casual footwear of choice in America. Bottom-line figures for Stride Rite showed that its market share of casual footwear sales was nosediving. In 1994 its net income dropped to $19.8 million, down from $58.3 million the previous year, and in 1995, with its total revenue falling off to $496 million, the company recorded a $8.4 million net loss. Siegel responded by closing more than 80 company-owned, underperforming retail stores, which by 1996 put the company back in the black, but just barely. Sales in that year continued to fall, dropping to a low of $448.3 million, down from an average total revenue of $556.6 million for the five year period between 1990 and 1994.

The market realties forced Stride Rite to adopt a more fashion-conscious philosophy. In 1997, the company commissioned Todd Oldham to design a new line of Keds. It also partnered with London Fog to develop a Sperry clothing line, with Nine West for a line of children's shoes, and with Tommy Hilfiger for a line of adult footwear. Also, in 1998, the year in which Siegel retired, using its poor sales record as the principal reason, Stride Rite severed the licensing ties with Levi Straus that had been agreed to in April 1997.

Former Mattel executive Jim Eskridge succeeded Siegel as Stride Rite's CEO. During his tenure, which was less than a year, Stride Rite continued to rally, with revenues climbing to $539.4 million in 1998, and $572.7 million in 1999, with net income figures, respectively, of $21.1 million and $26.4 million. The financial gain was achieved at some cost, notably in the cutting down of the company's work force, which fell from 3,500 in 1996 to 2,300 in 1999, way below the 1990 figure of 5,600.

Over disagreements with the board about the company's direction, Eskridge resigned in July 1999. Temporarily, his place was taken by Myles J. Slosberg, board member and grandson of Stride Rite's founder. Thereafter, David M. Chamberlain, former Genesco chairman, was named both CEO and chairman. Under his watch, Stride Rite's profits again dove, partly because Keds, Sperry, and Tommy Hilfiger footwear did not perform as hoped. Nevertheless, Chamberlain claimed that the company was strengthening its product line and would rally in the Spring 2001 selling season.

### Principal Subsidiaries

The Keds Corp.; Sperry Top-Sider, Inc.; Stride Rite Children's Group, Inc.; Stride Rite Intl. Corp.; Stride Rite Sourcing Intl., Inc.

### Principal Competitors

adidas-Salomon AG; Brown Shoe Company, Inc.; Converse Inc.; Genesco Inc.; NIKE, Inc.; Reebok International Ltd.

### Further Reading

Chabrow, Eric, "Supply Chains Go Global," *Information Week*, April 3, 2000, p. 50.

*From Green Shoe to Stride Rite,* Cambridge, Mass.: Stride Rite Corp.

Gonsalves, Antone, "Stride Rite Gets E-Com Footing: Outsourcing Design and Upkeep of Apps Brings Shoe-Selling Online, on Time," *PC Week*, September 27, 1999, p. 31.

Keegan, Paul, "Doing the Rite Thing," *Boston Magazine,* July 1991, p. 22.

Laabs, Jennifer, "Family Issues Are a Priority at Stride Rite," *Personnel Journal*, July 1993, p. 48.

Morgan, Hal, and Kerry Tucker, *Companies That Care,* New York: Simon and Schuster, 1991.

Moukheiber, Zina, "They Want Mules, We'll Sell Mules: Robert Siegel's Management of Stride Rite Corp.," *Forbes*, September 12, 1994, p. 42.

Olivieri, David, "Progressive Company Profits from Its Steady Pace," *Business Journal,* May 25, 1992, p. 4A.

Reidy, Chris, "Lexington, Mass.-Based Shoe Maker Hopes for Rebound under New CEO," *Knight-Ridder/Tribune Business News*, November 4, 1999.

Solnik, Claude, "Recharged Stride Rite Seeks to Give Keds Sales More Voltage," *Footwear News*, February 4, 2000, p. 7.

Stone, Nan, "Building Corporate Character: An Interview with Stride Rite Chairman Arnold Hiatt," *Harvard Business Review*, March-April 1992, p. 94.

Tedeschi, Mark, "Stride Rite Corp. Selects David Chamberlain as Chairman/CEO," *Sporting Goods Business*, December 10, 1999, p. 30.

Van Tuyl, Laura, "Day Care Program Bridges Generations," *Christian Science Monitor,* April 15, 1991.

Wilson, Marianne, "Through a Child's Eyes," *Chain Store Executive with Shopping Center Age*, September 2000, p. 156.

—Kenneth F. Kronenberg
—updated by Jane W. Fiero

# Ticketmaster Group, Inc.

3701 Wilshire Boulevard
Los Angeles, California 90010
U.S.A.
Telephone: (213) 639-6100
Fax: (213) 386-1244
Web site: http://www.ticketmaster.com

*Wholly Owned Subsidiary of USA Networks, Inc.*
*Incorporated:* 1982 as Ticketmaster Corporation
*Employees:* 6,355
*Sales:* $341 million (1998)
*NAIC:* 561599 All Other Travel Arrangement and
    Reservation Services

Ticketmaster Group, Inc. is the largest ticket distribution company in the United States, completely dominating its market niche. The company distributes tickets for more than 4,000 clients whose events range from professional wrestling matches and rock concerts to Broadway shows and operas. Tickets are sold at more than 3,400 outlets nationwide, over the telephone, and through the Ticketmaster Online-CitySearch web site, which is run by a publicly traded affiliate of the company. Ticketmaster also has been branching out into international markets, making moves into Australia, Europe, and Latin America. Barry Diller's USA Networks, Inc. owns 100 percent of the company.

### Early Years

Ticketmaster was started by two Arizona State University students who were looking for a solution to a problem they encountered when buying concert tickets. At the time, the buyer of a ticket was forced to select from the seats that had been allotted to the particular vendor from whom he or she was purchasing the ticket. If the vendor was nearly sold out, the buyer might be forced to buy bad seats even though better seats were available through other ticket sellers. Melees occasionally erupted when ticket buyers, after standing in line for hours at one place, found that the vendor was sold out or that better seats

were available elsewhere. The system also was inefficient for promoters and owners of venues, who often had difficulty selling all of their tickets, despite unmet demand.

In 1978, the two budding entrepreneurs developed a solution to the problem. They created an innovative computer program that networked several computers in such a way that a person buying an event ticket at a box office could quickly select from the total reserve of seats available. Thus efficient computerized ticket vending was born, and Ticketmaster—the company that sprouted from student innovation—became one of several small vendors in the late 1970s and early 1980s that pioneered the industry. When it was starting out, in fact, Ticketmaster was just one of many small ticket-vending companies competing for a small share of the industry; the business had come to be dominated by ticket distribution giant Ticketron. Nevertheless, Ticketmaster, with its unique computer-based vending system, managed to increase its ticket sales to about $1 million annually by 1981. That amount was still less than one percent of the business controlled by Ticketron, however.

Ticketmaster's fate was changed in 1982, when Chicago investor Jay Pritzker purchased it. Pritzker, the wealthy owner of the Hyatt Hotel chain, paid $4 million for the entire company. He immediately brought in Fred Rosen as chief executive to manage the operation. Rosen, an attorney and former stand-up comic, brought energy and vision to the enterprise. He believed that the future of the ticket industry was in concert sales, rather than sporting events, in part because sporting event-goers often were able to circumvent service fees charged by ticket sellers by purchasing season tickets. But his feeling also arose from his observations about the dynamics of the concert industry. Indeed, if concert fans wanted to see a show badly enough, they would buy on impulse and would be willing to pay higher prices for tickets. Furthermore, the giant lines that formed at box offices for rock concerts indicated a great need for Ticketmaster's computerized service.

Aside from new computer and information technologies, other forces were at work in the ticket industry in the early 1980s that boded well for an innovator like Ticketmaster. In fact, the rock concert industry, among other entertainment businesses, was becoming much more complicated. Prior to the

1970s, bands were paid a lump sum—usually in cash just a few minutes before they went on stage—by the promoter of the concert. The promoter would agree beforehand to pay the band, say, $20,000, and any money left over would be used to pay the promoter's expenses and profit.

In the 1970s, however, bands started demanding more. They started charging minimum appearance fees, for example, and wanted a cut of the money generated from concessions and parking. The demands, in part, were the result of a feeling by top bands that promoters were taking advantage of them. But the increased cost of traveling and putting on a show also contributed the bands' desire for better compensation; fans came to expect much more in the way of expensive sound systems and special effects, for example.

One result of the new demands was that, after a concert, the band's manager and the promoter typically negotiated, or argued, about exactly how much the promoter and other involved parties would be paid. The new system increased the bargaining power of the bands, eventually boosting their take to 75 percent or more of the gross receipts. Meanwhile, the promotion industry was pinched. Many promoters saw their profit margins deteriorate to as little as one percent, despite the fact that they were still bearing much of the risk of a failed concert. To get the big name bands, however, promoters had to be willing to accept that risk and honor many of the group's requirements.

### A New Strategy in the Late 1970s and the 1980s

That was the environment still evolving when Rosen took the helm at the fledgling Ticketmaster. Realizing the folly of trying to compete with the mammoth Ticketron using conventional industry tactics, he devised a strategy that exploited the frustrations of the promoters. He effectively offered to limit inside charges—the money taken from promoters and facility owners—thus reducing the promoter's risk. He would accomplish this by raising service charges on individual ticket sales and giving promoters a percentage of the proceeds. In return, the promoters agreed to give Ticketmaster the exclusive rights

to ticketing for their shows. To boost service fees, Rosen implemented new sales techniques, particularly telephone sales service, which gave customers an alternative to standing in line. For the convenience, Ticketmaster was able to charge as much as a 30 percent premium, or higher in some instances.

Many promoters gave exclusive rights to Ticketmaster. Indeed, aside from guaranteed fees, the promoters benefited from Ticketmaster's state-of-the-art ticketing system. The company's computers could sell 25,000 tickets in just a few minutes, if necessary, which substantially reduced the promoter's advertising and related costs and improved customer satisfaction with the overall event. The arrangement worked so well that Ticketmaster eventually was able to secure long-term contracts with several major promoters for handling ticketing for all of their events. Promoters also viewed Ticketmaster as preferable alternative to the giant Ticketron, which many promoters believed had become arrogant and sloppy.

Despite steady gains, Ticketmaster lost money in the late 1970s and early 1980s as it scrambled to implement its expensive strategy. By the mid-1980s, though, the company was posting profits. To boost sales and market share, Ticketmaster began buying out smaller competitors in an effort to broaden its reach into major cities. It acquired Datatix/Select-A-Seat in Denver, for example, and SEATS in Atlanta. As it bought up more companies and drove others out of business, the number of competitors in the industry declined. At the same time, Ticketron's supremacy was rapidly waning. Aside from complacency, part of Ticketron's problem was that it lacked the investment capital afforded by Ticketmaster's deep-pocketed owner. Its ticketing systems soon became obsolete in comparison with those in use at Ticketmaster.

By the late 1980s, Ticketmaster had become a top player in the ticketing business and Ticketron was scurrying to duplicate Rosen's successful revenue-sharing strategy. But it was too late; Ticketmaster had mastered the recipe and was rapidly increasing the number and size of its contracts. In fact, Ticketmaster's relationship with, and control over, its promoters had evolved to the point where Ticketmaster was deeply entwined in the promotion business. That involvement was evidenced by a relationship in Seattle that finally ended in a lawsuit. In 1989, Ticketmaster made a loan and credit line guarantee valued at $500,000 to two of the area's top promoters. The promoters used the money to start a new operation promoting concerts in The George, a facility in central Washington. In that same year, one of the promoters launched another venture, PowerStation, to sell tickets in competition with Ticketmaster. Enraged Ticketmaster executives responded by withholding cash from the promoter's ticket sales through Ticketmaster. The promoter sued and finally settled with Ticketmaster out of court, but the PowerStation was shuttered and both promoters left the concert business.

### Market Dominance in the Early 1990s

By the end of the 1980s, Ticketmaster was selling more than $500,000 worth of tickets annually. Ticketron was still considered an industry power, but its status was diminished and its long-term prospects were dismal. The only other competition consisted of a smattering of local and regional companies struggling to combat Ticketmaster. Ticketmaster finally delivered the crowning blow to Ticketron in 1991, when it purchased some of the company's assets and effectively rendered the company no more than a lesson in corporate history. Questions were raised about whether or not the buyout would give Ticketmaster a monopoly on the industry, but the U.S. Department of Justice approved the deal. With Ticketron out of its way, Ticketmaster was virtually dominant and its sales began rising rapidly toward the $1 billion mark.

Because it had so much control in the ticket industry, Ticketmaster came under fire from numerous critics following the demise of Ticketron. Some fans complained that Ticketmaster was raising its fees, reflecting a monopoly on the industry. Similarly, some promoters argued that Ticketmaster wielded too much power and that it was willing to abuse that power to get its way. Finally, some rock bands complained that Ticketmaster was gouging their profits with excessive fees, knowing that the bands had nowhere else to turn. Ticketmaster countered, citing rising operating costs and relatively modest overall company profits. Still, criticism continued.

Band discontent with Ticketmaster's tactics culminated in one of the most visible disputes with Ticketmaster on record: a complaint filed with the Justice Department by the popular rock band Pearl Jam, alleging that Ticketmaster engaged in monopolistic practices. Pearl Jam wanted Ticketmaster to drop its service fees to $1.80 per ticket, but the company refused to drop below $2.50. Pearl Jam rejected the offer and threatened to work without Ticketmaster. The band planned to find venues, such as fairgrounds and racetracks, that were not subject to Ticketmaster's exclusive contracts. Their efforts eventually failed and their concert tour fell apart. It was then that the band filed the complaint, and the Justice Department launched an investigation.

Ticketmaster argued that from about $1 billion worth of tickets sold in 1993, it generated revenues of $191 million in 1993, only $7 million of which was earned as net profit. That amounted to less than ten cents in profit per ticket. Critics complained that Ticketmaster was simply concealing the profitability of the business, but Rosen and his fellow executives were adamant that the industry was still competitive. "Fifteen years ago, there was another company everybody said had a monopoly—Ticketron," said Larry Solters, Ticketmaster spokesperson, in the July 31, 1994 *News & Observer*. He added, "Ticketmaster did ticketing better. And I wouldn't be surprised if somebody else comes up with a better system someday. There are a million ideas out there. . . . It's not that tough."

After posting record sales and profits in 1993, Ticketmaster's fate was changed again when Paul Allen beat out several big media players in a bid to purchase controlling interest in the company. The 40-year-old Allen, who had gained fame as the cofounder of Microsoft, paid an estimated $300 million for his stake. Following his departure from the software giant, he had assembled an interesting portfolio of investments, many of which were related to the emerging information highway. He also owned the Portland Trailblazers basketball team and a charitable foundation, among other interests. Allen retained Rosen as CEO, but he had new plans for the company. In fact, he wanted to increase its sales threefold to fivefold within five years and expand into different distribution avenues.

Ticketmaster sold a whopping 52 million tickets to entertainment and sporting events in 1994 and captured about $200 million in revenues. Having nearly cornered the ticket market, it was setting its sights on several other media-related ventures. The company already was distributing a regional monthly events guide to about 600,000 customers, and it planned to use that as a base for creation of a new entertainment magazine. Ticketmaster also was working on a new online service, hoping to position itself as a one-stop shopping center for entertainment and event needs.

The company launched its new magazine, *Live!*, in February of 1996. Critics saw the publication as a thinly veiled attempt to brighten Ticketmaster's tarnished image. The magazine field was definitely a difficult one to break into, and *Live!* lost money from the start, costing its owners $11 million in the first two years. Other ventures introduced during 1996 included a hotel and airline reservation service, Ticketmaster Travel and Ticketmaster Online. The latter was an instant success, topping $3 million a month in revenues within a short time.

### 1996 IPO and Bright Prospects for the 21st Century

The biggest story for Ticketmaster in 1996 was its decision to go public. Paul Allen kept his stake, retaining control of 54 percent of the company after the IPO. The initial offering price had been considered high by many analysts, and it soon fell off. Within a year it recovered, however, rising to nearly double the original figure.

On April 28, 1997, Ticketmaster filed suit against Microsoft over that company's practice of "deep linking" from its web site to an inner page of Ticketmaster's site, bypassing the company's home page and its logo and advertising content. To some users, it could appear that the Ticketmaster page was generated by Microsoft, rather than Ticketmaster. The suit was later settled out of court, with Microsoft agreeing to link only to Ticketmaster's home page. The year also saw the company's online ticket service merge with CitySearch's entertainment guide web site, and new investments in Australian and French ticketing companies. A joint venture with Jack Nicklaus's Golden Bear Golf to market golfing reservations was launched as well.

In May of 1997 Barry Diller's HSN, Inc. (soon to be known as USA Networks, Inc.) announced plans to buy out Allen's stake in Ticketmaster. The following year the company became a subsidiary of USA Networks when the remainder of its stock was acquired. After the acquisition, Fred Rosen stepped down as CEO, allegedly due to clashes with Diller. He was replaced by Terry Barnes. At about this time Diller acquired City Search, Inc., merged it with Ticketmaster's online operation to form Ticketmaster Online-CitySearch, Inc., and spun it off as a public company, retaining 60 percent ownership. In December a contract was signed with event promotion giant SFX Entertainment that guaranteed Ticketmaster exclusive ticketing rights for seven years. Diller and SFX Chairman Robert F.X. Sillerman had earlier engaged in a very public battle of words, but were able to bury the hatchet when it came time to do business.

A lawsuit over Ticketmaster's alleged monopoly on ticket distribution reached the Supreme Court in 1999. The court let a prior ruling, which was in Ticketmaster's favor, stand. Also during the year, an attempt to merge Ticketmaster Online-CitySearch with Lycos and USA Networks failed when Lycos shareholders rebelled.

In late 1999 and early 2000, Ticketmaster acquired several more of its competitors. These included Alabama-based TicketLink, multilingual ticketer Admission Network, Inc. of Canada, and ETM Entertainment Network, Inc., which had contracts with the Los Angeles Dodgers and New York Mets, among others. The company also sued Tickets.com, in conjunction with Ticketmaster Online-CitySearch, over alleged deceptive practices involving its web site. The appeal of buying tickets online was growing steadily, with 40 percent of some events' seats selling over the Internet. As a result, Ticketmaster's telephone operators were taking fewer orders, and the company shut down several of its call centers. Tickets purchased on-line were still mailed to customers, but new technology was being tested that would allow them to be printed at home, further streamlining the process.

At the start of a new century, Ticketmaster's dominance of the ticket distribution business in the United States looked unassailable. With its exclusive agreement to sell tickets for SFX Entertainment events, its successful co-venture with Ticketmaster Online-CitySearch, and the favorable resolution of antitrust allegations, the company's future seemed bright.

## *Principal Subsidiaries*

Ticketmaster Ventures, Inc.; Ticketmaster Corp.; TMC Realty Holdings, Inc.; Ticketmaster Publications, Inc.; Ticketmaster Travel Corp.; TM/Video International, Inc.; Ticketmaster Advertising, Inc.; TMC Consultants, Inc.; Ticketmaster Tell Ltd.; Ticketmaster-Direct, Inc.; Cinema Acquisition Corp.; Ticketmaster Cinema Group, Ltd.; TM Movie Tix Holdings, Inc.; TM Marketing, Inc.; Ticketmaster Merchandising Corp.; Ticketmaster-Golf, Inc.; MFG Management Corp.; TM Flowers; TM National Flora LLC.

## *Principal Competitors*

LM Loyalty Management; Neighborhood Box Office; NEXT Ticketing; Prologue Systems; Tickets.com, Inc.

## *Further Reading*

Andrew, Paul, "Paul Allen's Ticket to Future," *Seattle Times,* November 23, 1993, p. E1.

Balzer, Stephanie, "That's the Ticket," *Business Journal—Serving Phoenix & The Valley of the Sun,* August 25, 2000, p. 1.

Corr, O. Casey, "Big-Ticket Troubles: Concert Industry Rolls in Money, But Where Is It All Going," *Seattle Times,* August 21, 1994, p. A1.

Francis, Mike, "Paul Allen Slowly, Surely Steps into Public Light," *Oregonian,* August 14, 1994, p. F1.

Gaulin, Jacqueline, "Consumer Groups Go After Ticketmaster," *Washington Times,* March 22, 1995, p. B7.

Helm, Leslie, "Ticketmaster IPO Set at $14.50 a Share," *Los Angeles Times,* November 19, 1996, p. D2.

Menconi, David, "Ticketmaster's Money Tree—A Giant With It Made in the Shade," *News & Observer* (Raleigh, N.C.), July 31, 1994, p. G1.

Philips, Chuck, "Ticketmaster Cleared; Justice Department Drops Antitrust Probe," *Washington Post,* July 6, 1995, p. C2.

Reilly, Patrick M., "Ticketmaster Gears Up to Launch a New Entertainment Magazine," *Wall Street Journal,* October 25, 1995, p. B5.

"Rosen Reflects on Ticketmaster," *Amusement Business,* May 25, 1998, p. 1.

Saylor, Mark, "Ticketmaster's Tough CEO Ready for the Next Act," *Los Angeles Times,* November 30, 1997, p. D1.

Shapiro, Eben, and Bruce Orwall, "Roadshow Spurs Battle of SFX, Ticketmaster," *Asian Wall Street Journal,* August 4, 1998, p. 13.

Sloan, Allan, "Scalped at Ticketmaster? Paul Allen Leaves Investors in the Lurch," *Newsweek,* June 16, 1997, p. 76.

Spring, Greg, "Ticketmaster Sets Sights on New Ventures," *Los Angeles Business Journal,* February 13, 1995, p. 6.

Stooksbury Guier, Cindy, "Ticketmaster Changed the Face of Live Entertainment," *Amusement Business,* July 27, 1998, p. A10.

—Dave Mote
—updated by Frank Uhle

# Tidewater Inc.

**601 Poydras, Suite 1900**
**New Orleans, Louisiana 70130**
**U.S.A**
**Telephone: (504) 568-1010**
**Toll Free: (800) 678-8433**
**Fax: (504) 566-4582**
**Web site: http://www.tdw.com**

*Public Company*
*Incorporated:* 1956 as Tidewater Marine Service, Inc.
*Employees:* 6,100
*Sales:* $574.8 million (2000)
*Stock Exchanges:* New York
*Ticker Symbol:* TDW
*NAIC:* 336611 Ship Building and Repairing; 33612 Boat
   Building; 48833 Navigational Services to Shipping;
   532412 Construction, Mining, and Forestry Machinery
   and Equipment Rental and Leasing

Tidewater Inc. has grown from one small boat operating in the Gulf of Mexico to a fleet of more than 680 vessels ranging from the waters of the Caspian Sea to the Gulf of Tonkin off the Vietnam coast. With offices located in New Orleans, Louisiana, the company's marine division runs the world's largest fleet of vessels serving the international offshore gas and oil industry, although its home market, the Gulf of Mexico, still accounts for about one third of its sales. It provides an array of logistical services, including crew and materiel transportation, mobile drilling rig towing and placement, cable laying, and 3-D seismic operations. In addition to its offshore marine support and transportation services, Tidewater operates two shipyards that build, repair, retrofit, and dry-dock marine vessels.

## 1954: Industry and Company Origins

Tidewater's development parallels the discovery of oil in the Gulf of Mexico and the development of the offshore oil industry. The first offshore oilfield in the Gulf of Mexico was found in 1938, a little more than one mile from Cameron Parish, Louisiana. By the mid-1940s, petroleum geologists were estimating that there was between 10 and 12 billion barrels of oil waiting to be recovered in the Gulf. After fixed platforms were built and large-scale drilling operations started in 1946, a new industry developed around what was termed an "oil rig."

Oil rigs were manned 24 hours a day, with living and eating facilities, a galley, and even recreation areas. Although they seemed self-sufficient, the rigs were entirely dependent on the supply boats that brought food, water, and drilling equipment, and transported crews back and forth from the mainland. The first vessels to serve the oil rigs were old Navy boats and reconfigured shrimp boats. It soon became clear, however, that a special type of boat designed specifically for supplying offshore oil rigs was needed.

Alden J. "Doc" Laborde, a retired Navy officer who was chairman and president of Ocean Drilling and Exploration Company (ODECO), one of the first firms to drill for oil in the Gulf, was convinced that the offshore oil industry needed a specialty supply boat with a revolutionary design. His own design put the boat's pilot house forward, and the crew's quarters and wheelhouse forward in the bow. The boat's deck was entirely flat in order to easily lay various piping and supplies, yet still had a clear afterdeck for any towing that was required. Laborde organized a meeting with nine other men—including his older brother, C.E. Laborde, Jr., as well as a marine operator, an owner of a towing business, an engineer, an accountant, and a few of his closest personal friends—and sought their support in forming a marine supply service for offshore oil rigs. Contributing $10,000 each toward the construction of the first boat, the men incorporated the Tidewater Marine Service Corporation in Louisiana on July 8, 1954.

Tidewater's first boat, the steel-hulled Ebb Tide, was built and launched in 1955. A request from ODECO to lease the boat resulted in Alden Laborde's decision to withdraw from involvement in Tidewater to avoid an apparent conflict of interest. Authority for all company decisions was left up to Laborde, Jr., Ed Kyle, and Don Durant. When the Shell Oil Company heard about the new boat and contacted Tidewater to charter a similar vessel, Laborde, Jr., decided to form a second corporation for the purpose of constructing and operating another supply boat. A

## Company Perspectives:

*Tidewater owns hundreds of service vessels, all of which are operated and managed by thousands of employees worldwide. . . . Tidewater vessels can be found in virtually every area of the world where there is significant oil and gas exploration, development or production. These provide a wide range of services including transporting crews and supplies between the mainland and offshore locations; towing and positioning mobile drilling rigs; assisting in offshore construction projects; and a variety of specialized services including cable laying and 3-D seismic work. . . . At Tidewater, quality is an ethic that commands not only what we do, but how we do it. Our philosophy is to invest the time and effort necessary to fulfill each customer's objectives, while maintaining high standards of safety and providing cost effective services.*

third corporation was also formed when Phillips Petroleum wanted to charter a boat. As the demand for its vessels grew, the initial investors in Tidewater began to discuss an expansion program and the possibility of additional financing. Arrangements were made through Rheinholdt & Gardner, an investment firm with close ties to the offshore oil industry, and Whitney National Bank of New Orleans to provide the necessary funding, including loans and an initial public stock offering. On February 7, 1956, a parent organization, Tidewater Marine Service, Inc., was incorporated under the state laws of Delaware.

### 1956–66: Near Disaster and a Decade of Growth

Throughout its initial period of development, Tidewater's management was informal. There was no main office, records were kept haphazardly, business commitments were made by any one of the original ten investors without regard to formal contracts or agreements, and the company's only employee worked out of his own home. Realizing that Tidewater's rapid expansion necessitated a professional management team, Laborde, Jr., consulted with the other investors and agreed to ask his younger brother, John, to accept the position of president. The younger Laborde, a graduate of Louisiana State University Law School who had served as an adjutant on the staff of General Douglas MacArthur during World War II, accepted the offer. Although he knew absolutely nothing about boats, John Laborde was very familiar with the oil industry and its operations in the Gulf of Mexico.

Laborde went to work immediately; he rented office space, hired secretarial and bookkeeping help, sorted out the little documentation there was on the company, and met with the original investors, convincing them it was his responsibility alone to make agreements and arrange contracts for Tidewater. Not long after he started, Laborde was notified by the U.S. Coast Guard that one of Tidewater's vessels was in violation of marine regulations. The fine amounted to nearly $168,000. Knowing that Tidewater faced bankruptcy if the full amount of the fine were paid, Laborde explained the circumstances of the violation, which was due to a lack of knowledge on the part of the crew, and negotiated a settlement of $2,000 with the Coast

Guard. This exchange with the Coast Guard led Laborde to educate himself on all aspects of marine laws and regulations so that he could formulate operating procedures for Tidewater.

During its first fiscal year, Tidewater recorded a loss of $10,027. Yet Laborde remained optimistic, largely because of a gross revenue amounting to over $400,000. The company's fleet expanded to 11 vessels. Near the end of 1957, Tidewater became the first offshore marine transportation business located in the Gulf of Mexico to make a foray into foreign waters. Laborde reached an agreement with a small boat company, Semarca, to transport supplies for an over-water oil and gas firm operating on Lake Maracaibo in Venezuela. By the end of the second fiscal year Laborde's optimism was rewarded; Tidewater doubled its gross revenues to $851,156, while net earnings jumped to over $97,000.

Tidewater grew rapidly during its first decade of operation. In 1961, just five years after the company's first boat was launched, Tidewater had already made a major acquisition by purchasing the Offshore Transportation Corporation. By taking over OTC's fleet, Tidewater increased the number of its revenue-producing vessels to 56. The Venezuelan venture was contributing nearly 40 percent of the company's total earnings. Individual stockholders in the company had grown from under 50 to over 800. Most importantly, the company reported gross revenues of $4.88 million for 1961, and net revenues of $584,444, an increase of 59 percent over the previous year.

In 1962, Tidewater suffered a small decrease in revenues from the previous year, but the Venezuelan venture continued to be very profitable, and the company expanded its operations to include the coastal waters off California and Trinidad. One year later, Tidewater continued the development of its American West Coast operation by initiating business in Alaska and by locating a base at Santa Barbara, California. In 1964, the company's fleet of vessels was working regularly in the Red Sea, the Gulf of Suez, the North Sea, Lake Maracaibo in Venezuela, the Gulf of Mexico, off the coastal waters of Trinidad, and along the entire U.S. Pacific coast. Having purchased T.J. Falgout, a Galveston, Texas-based competitor in the Gulf of Mexico, Tidewater's fleet amounted to 104 vessels. That same year, Tidewater passed one of its most important milestones; it increased profits to over $1,000,000. Gross revenues were reported at $7.62 million, a leap of almost 50 percent over the previous year.

By the end of its first decade, company operations had expanded to the Persian/Arabian Gulf, and plans were being implemented to provide marine services to Nigeria, Iran, Canada, and Australia. More boats were added to the Tidewater fleet, some newly constructed and some purchased used, which brought the total to 180 vessels. Not surprisingly, revenues and profits continued their upward spiral. In 1966, Tidewater revenues soared to $19,733,881, an increase of 90 percent over the previous year. Profits jumped 30 percent over the previous year, and were now close to $3 million.

### 1967–83: Acquisitions, Restructuring, and the Oil Boom

In order to capitalize on its success, during the following years Tidewater's strategy was to concentrate on diversifying

## Key Dates:

**1951:** Alden J. "Doc" Laborde and nine others found Tidewater Marine Service Corporation.
**1955:** Company builds and launches first boat.
**1956:** Company is incorporated in Delaware as Tidewater Marine Service Inc. and is reorganized as a public company with John Laborde as president.
**1961:** Tidewater acquires the Offshore Transportation Corporation.
**1964:** Company purchases T.J. Falgout.
**1968:** Company merges with Twenty Grand Marine Services, Inc. and buys Sandair Corporation.
**1969:** Firm purchases Hamer Hammer Service, Inc. and South Coast Gas Compression Company, Inc.
**1971:** Tidewater acquires interest in offshore oil production in Indonesia, Java, and Sumatra; creates Pental Insurance Company, Ltd.
**1977:** Firm buys Hilliard Oil and Gas Company, Inc.; company changes name to Tidewater, Inc. and reorganizes.
**1984:** Company faces hostile takeover by corporate raider, Irwin L. Jacobs.
**1989:** Firm defeats Jacobs' last attempt to buyout company.
**1992:** Tidewater purchases Zapata Gulf Marine Corporation.
**1994:** John Laborde retires after serving 38 years as president and CEO and is succeeded by William O'Malley.
**1996:** Company acquires Hornbeck Offshore Services.
**1998:** Company sells its natural gas compression division.
**2000:** Tidewater sells 40 percent interest in National Marine Service.

and expanding its operations. In 1968, Tidewater merged with Twenty Grand Marine Services, Inc., its closest competitor in the Gulf of Mexico. This acquisition brought in Twenty Grand's tugboats and other vessels, and Tidewater's fleet increased to a total of 358. Tidewater also purchased Sandair Corporation, a leader in the air and gas compressor market; entering the air and gas compressor business was regarded by Tidewater management as a logical extension of its specialized services for the offshore oil industry. Foreign partnerships were established in the Netherlands and Iran. In 1969, the company acquired Hamer Hammer Service, Inc., a firm that supplied both equipment and personnel for the onshore and offshore driving of oil well casings, and South Coast Gas Compression Company, Inc., a provider of natural gas compression equipment and services for the offshore oil industry.

The 1970s were just as successful for Tidewater as the company's early years. In 1970, Tidewater reported revenues of over $50 million, and over $5 million in profits. In May of the same year, Tidewater joined the select list of 1,300 companies listed on the New York Stock Exchange. In 1971, Tidewater acquired interests in offshore oil production in Indonesia, Java, and Sumatra. At the same time, the company created Pental Insurance Company, Ltd., a Bermuda-based firm insuring all of Tidewater's vessels. The company was soon providing services in the Adriatic Sea, and its large supply and towing-supply vessels were commanding higher and higher rates wherever they operated. Hilliard Oil and Gas Company, Inc., an American oil and gas exploration firm, was purchased in 1977, the same year the board of director's decided to change the name of the Tidewater Marine Services to Tidewater, Inc. Tidewater, Inc., reorganized to function as a parent organization for its many subsidiaries, formed six divisions, including Marine Services, Compression Services, Oil & Gas, Insurance, Real Estate, and Contractor Services. By 1979, total revenues shot past the $200 million mark, and profits exceeded $30 million.

### 1984–91: A Reversal of Fortunes and an Attempted Corporate Raid

Revenues and profits continued their meteoric rise during the early 1980s. However, when the oil and gas industry was sent into an historic decline by plummeting oil prices, Tidewater's fortunes went spinning downward. The company's position was exacerbated by an inundated supply boat market, and a sudden decrease in day rates for its vessels. The most significant threat to Tidewater, however, came from hostile takeover attempts. In 1984, Irwin L. Jacobs, a corporate raider, purchased enough Tidewater stock to attempt to take control of the company. When Jacobs's first offer was rejected by Tidewater's board of directors, he engaged in a complicated series of corporate and legal maneuvering over the next five years to wrest control of the company from the directors. Frustrated by his inability to acquire Tidewater by legal means, in 1989 Jacobs made another offer to purchase Tidewater at $11 per share. With John Laborde still providing sound leadership, Tidewater's board of directors sidestepped Jacobs by agreeing to facilitate the sale of Jacobs's stock and arranging a registered secondary stock offering. As a result, Jacobs withdrew his offer to acquire Tidewater and disposed of his shares with a handsome profit.

The takeover attempts and the continuing slump in the oil and gas industry had deleterious effects on Tidewater. In 1985, the company reported it first loss since 1957, and by 1987 losses amounted to a record $56 million. With losses continuing to mount, John Laborde proved his leadership with a calm, confident demeanor and astute decision-making skills. Although Tidewater was losing money, Laborde's earlier decision to enter the natural gas compression business seemed prescient. During the worst years of the oil and gas industry recession, Tidewater's compression business provided a steady flow of revenue that kept the company afloat. Laborde also decided to sell all of the company's Indonesian oil interests. In 1987, Laborde restructured debt payments with Tidewater's primary lenders and by 1990 had pared downed over $60 million of the company's senior debt. During the same year, Laborde convinced Tidewater's board of director's to make a public offering of over five million shares of common stock. With revenues starting to increase, Laborde thought it best to continue expanding Tidewater's international operations by placing 41 pieces of towing equipment in and around West Africa.

### 1992–2000: Emerging as World Leader in Marine Support Services

Perhaps most important of Laborde's decisions involved the acquisition of Zapata Gulf Marine Corporation in 1992. Tidewater's biggest rival, Zapata was an amalgamation of the company's four most important competitors. By consolidating Zapata's vessels with its own, Tidewater doubled its marine fleet. For Laborde, the timing of this acquisition could not have been better; after one of the worst freezes of the century in the Gulf of Mexico, a spring thaw led to a doubling of day rates for workboats. With the largest fleet in the Gulf, Tidewater took advantage of this opportunity to put all of its newly acquired vessels from Zapata into service.

By the end of fiscal 1994, Tidewater had completely recovered from the recession of the offshore oil industry, increased its fleet to 594 vessels, and expanded its overseas ventures. Over 70 percent of Tidewater's fleet operated in foreign waters. With nearly 85 percent of its revenues from marine operations and the remainder from compression operations, Tidewater reported total revenues amounting to $522 million. A good cash flow and increasing offshore marine contracts from around the world enabled the company to eliminate its entire debt. In October 1994, confident that he was leaving the company in good financial condition, John Laborde stepped down as CEO and president and was replaced by William C. O'Malley, the former chief executive officer of Sonat Offshore Drilling Inc. In consultation with Laborde, O'Malley immediately directed Tidewater's expansion of its compression services through a $240 million acquisition of Brazos Gas Compressing Co. (a unit of Mitchell Energy & Development Corp.) and the Haliburton Compression Service.

Over the following year, Tidewater made some changes in its corporate structure in order to improve its profit margins, increase its cash flow, and build its revenues in core marine and compression services. To that end, Tidewater eliminated about one-third of the work force at its company headquarters, saving an estimated $3.3 million annually.

In 1996 and 1997, following its restructuring and slimming down, Tidewater purchased two major companies. The first was Hornbeck Offshore Services, acquired in a trade in which Tidewater swapped nearly 8.8 million shares of it common stock for the 13.2 million shares of Hornbeck's outstanding common stock. The deal added 61 vessels to Tidewater's domestic fleet operating in the Gulf of Mexico. The second major acquisition was O.I.L. Ltd., a part of the U.K.-based Ocean Group, which added 100 vessels to Tidewater's overseas fleet. In 1998, in order to help offset the $535 million price tag on the O.I.L. purchase, Tidewater sold its compressor unit to the merchant bank Castle Harlan for $360 million.

These moves prompted significant gains by Tidewater. In the fourth quarter of 1998, the company's net income, on sales of $278.6 million, climbed to $126.5 million, up $81 million over the previous year. It was the best performance in the 42 years of Tidewater's history as a public entity. O'Malley indicated that high per diem rates, strong world markets, and the expansion of the company's fleet fueled the impressive performance.

Although a slump in the oil industry in 1999 slowed exploration and production, negatively impacting all oil service companies, Tidewater was looking beyond the inevitable potholes inherent in the industry and concentrated on plans for future expansion. In October 2000 it sold its 40 percent holding in National Marine Services for $31 million in order to channel its resources into the purchase of additional vessels, thereby increasing the company's offshore service capabilities. At that time it announced that it had agreed to buy two 236 foot UT755L platform supply vessels at a cost just under the $31 million it received for its share of National Marine Services. The company also revealed plans to invest $300 million in building new support vessels for servicing oil platforms constructed in depths up to 10,000 feet. Clearly, Tidewater was positioning itself to go wherever the offshore oil industry was headed at the start of the new century.

### Principal Subsidiaries

Quality Shipyards Inc.

### Principal Competitors

Global Marine Inc.; Nabors Industries, Inc.; R&B Falcon Corporation; Schlumberger Limited; Trico Marine Services, Inc.

### Further Reading

Bradford, Michael, "Program Causing Ebb in Lost-Time Accidents," *Business Insurance*, September 27, 1999, p. 3.

Fletcher, Sam, "Tidewater Earnings Rise Despite Weaker Market for Supply Vessels," *Oil Daily*, July 22, 1998.

Hartley, Lynn, "U.S. Service Sector Follows Majors Abroad," *Platt's Oilgram News*, July 2, 1992, p. 3.

Mack, Toni, "Shipshape," *Forbes*, January 2, 1995, p. 158.

Sheets, Ken, and Gregory Spears, "Drilling for Dollars," *Kiplinger's Personal Finance Magazine*, February 1997, p. 63.

"Tidewater Has Buoyant Quarter, Best Year Ever," *Oil Daily*, May 5, 1998.

"Tidewater Sells National Marine," *Oil Daily*, October 11, 2000.

"Tidewater to Sell Hilliard Oil Interests to Graham Resources Affiliates," *Oil Daily*, December 3, 1985, p. 4.

—Thomas Derdak
—updated by Jane W. Fiero

## TOM BROWN, INC.

# Tom Brown, Inc.

555 17th Street, Suite 1850
Denver, Colorado 80202-3981
U.S.A.
Telephone: (303) 260-5000
Toll Free: (888) 829-3408
Fax: (303) 260-5001
Web site: http://www.tombrown.com

*Public Company*
*Incorporated:* 1971 as Tom Brown Drilling Company,
   Inc.
*Employees:* 360
*Sales:* $212.7 million (1999)
*Stock Exchanges:* NASDAQ
*Ticker Symbol:* TMBR
*NAIC:* 213111 Drilling Oil and Gas Wells; 211111 Crude
   Petroleum and Natural Gas Extraction; 213112
   Support Activities for Oil and Gas Operations

Tom Brown, Inc., is one of the leading independent oil and gas firms in the United States. Headquartered in Denver, Colorado, Tom Brown primarily performs the following oil- and gas-related services: exploration for, and acquisition, development, and production of, natural gas and crude oil; marketing, discovering, gathering, processing, and selling of natural gas; and drilling of gas and oil wells. Tom Brown performs exploration and development primarily of gas-prone basins of the Rocky Mountains. The company leases a substantial quantity of land in key basins and owns a drilling company that provides services to its consulting division. In 1999, Tom Brown produced 130 million cubic feet per day (Mcfd) of oil and natural gas liquids, while the company's proved reserves totaled 524 billion cubic feet of gas equivalent (Bcfe).

### 1950s Origins

Tom Brown, Inc. traces its origins to the 1955 founding of the Scarber-Brown Drilling Company. Prior to that time, founder Tom Brown was working as salesman of wellheads, the structures built atop oil wells. During a fishing expedition to the Brazos River in north-central Texas, Brown reportedly mentioned to some clients from the Walker-Near Rig Manufacturing Company that he wished he could own his own drilling rig. They took his remark seriously, made some contacts, and a week later Brown was heading up his own one-rig drilling operation, known as the Scarber-Brown Drilling Co. Brown's one employee at that time was Joe Roper, from Henrietta, Texas, who had been working on oil rigs since he was a teenager.

While Brown took responsibility for procuring business, Roper oversaw the drilling projects. The combined expertise and complementary styles of Brown and Roper proved a successful formula. Among their first projects was drilling in the Permian Basin of West Texas and southeastern New Mexico. Brown was particularly adept at explaining the oil drilling process to potential investors from Wall Street as well as to interested corporate investors. Once Brown and Roper had funding, analysts noted, they used it efficiently and effectively. In fact, the two are considered major influences on the economic development of the Permian Basin area.

In a 1999 article in the *Midland Reporter-Telegram*, Joe Liberty, a Midland, Texas, stockbroker, and Ted Collins, president of Collins & Ware, each recalled Tom Brown's and Joe Roper's pioneer spirit in the early years of Texas oil exploration. "They were nuts and bolts oil men," said Liberty, "They were true pioneers, and probably did more in the early days to create jobs and energize the Permian Basin oil industry than another oil company. Brown was instrumental in obtaining capital for the drilling crew." Collins agreed, "They helped pave the way and bring hundreds of millions of dollars to the Permian Basin over the past 40 years. There is no doubt that they paved the way for much of what is happening today in the Permian Basin today. They were true pioneers."

In 1959, Tom Brown bought out the Scarber interests in Scarber-Brown Drilling and made Joe Roper a full partner, rechristening the concern Tom Brown Drilling Company. By this time they had added another rig to their operations, and they continued to drill, usually successfully, in the West Texan Permian basin. In 1968, the company went public by merging with Gold Metals Consolidated Mining Company, the "corporate

## Company Perspectives:

*Tom Brown, Inc., is an independent energy company engaged in the domestic exploration for, and the acquisition, development, production, and marketing of, natural gas, crude oil, and natural gas liquids with core areas of activity in the Rocky Mountains and Texas. Tom Brown focuses it operations in areas where it has developed significant geologic expertise and established critical mass through the strategic accumulation of large, continuous acreage positions. The Company's principal exploration, development, and production activities are conducted in the Rocky Mountains and Texas, including the Wind River and Green River Basins of Wyoming; the Piceance and Paradox Basins of Colorado and Utah; and the Val Verde and Permian Basins of Texas.*

shell'' of a company founded in the 1930s, based in Nevada. In 1971, the company shortened its name to Tom Brown, Inc., reflecting its intentions of expanding beyond drilling activities into exploration and production. In the 1970s, the company began exploration and drilling in the Rocky Mountain region, which would later become its primary base of operations.

### Early 1980s Challenges

In the early 1980s, the rapidly expanding company experienced a dip in its financial picture. It had purchased a drilling tool company called Encore Corp., and the new subsidiary promptly began losing money. Moreover, Tom Brown was debt-laden, and, in order to pay down some of this debt, it was forced to sell many of its assets. Encore was jettisoned to the Hughes Tool Company, while some of Tom Brown's interests in oil fields were sold off as well. Finally, a restructuring of the company was necessary. Donald L. Evans was brought in to manage Tom Brown, while founder Tom Brown continued an active role as a member of the company's board.

The company then spun off its drilling operations into the newly created TMBR Drilling, which was managed by Brown and Roper. Challenges continued in the mid-1980s, when oil prices crashed, and the drilling industry in particular suffered. Rather than exiting that segment of the industry, however, the TMBR merged with the Sharp Drilling Company, an operating unit of Pioneer Natural Gas. Sharp brought some 52 rigs to the merger, many of which were fitted to drill gas wells. When the oil market righted itself, TMBR/Sharp Drilling Inc., became an independent company, its shares trading on the NASDAQ Exchange, with Brown as CEO and Roper as president. It would eventually become one of the largest drilling companies in the Permian Basin area.

### The Late 1980s–90s Growth Through Acquisition

From the mid-1980s on, Tom Brown Inc. was strictly a production and exploration company. Toward that end, from 1986 to 1990, Tom Brown acquired substantial interests in central Wyoming's Wind River Basin. In March 1994, the Eastern Shoshone and Northern Arapaho tribes signed a lease

option agreement with Tom Brown for 400,000 acres in the centrally located Wind River Indian Reservation in Wyoming. Under terms of the agreement, Tom Brown agreed to pay the tribe for leasing each time it explored one of the four blocks included in the lease. The lease option agreement brought Tom Brown's interest in the Wind River Basin to approximately one million gross acres. Tom Brown had also already been operating the Muddy Ridge and Pavillion fields in the Wind River Basin on the Windy River Reservation.

Using a technique that was new to the industry in 1994, Tom Brown began performing three-dimensional seismic testing. With the three-dimensional equipment, drillers ''shot'' more than 100 square miles in each block. During the same ''shoot,'' Tom Brown would drill one exploratory well in each block. The company looked for relatively small geological structures using the more advanced three-dimensional seismic testing techniques. Previously, drillers used two-dimensional seismic equipment that limited the detail that was shown. According to CEO Don Evans, during its exploratory activities within the Wind River Basin on the reservation, Tom Brown was able to ''look at all of the producing horizons'' or formations.

In December 1996, Tom Brown finalized a major acquisition when it bought Presidio Oil Co., which had filed for bankruptcy court protection in Delaware. Tom Brown acquired Presidio for approximately $202 million in cash, stock, and assumed liabilities. By the end of 1996, Tom Brown's assets totaled $406 million; the company's assets the previous year had totaled $164 million.

In January 1998, Tom Brown acquired complete rights to W.E. Sauer Companies, LLC, of Casper, Wyoming. The $8.1 million acquisition included five drilling rigs. In July 1999, Tom Brown acquired the Rocky Mountain oil and gas assets of Unocal Corporation. It paid a total purchase price of $68.5 million—5.8 million shares of common stock and $5 million in cash. The assets in the Paradox Basin of southwestern Colorado and southeastern Utah enhanced Tom Brown's existing 163,000 net undeveloped acres there.

This was one of many 1999 acquisitions made by Tom Brown. The company purchased certain Rocky Mountain assets in Wyoming from an undisclosed seller in September 1999. For $7.7 million, this deal included 9.7 Bcfe of proved reserves and 34,000 net acres in the Greater Green River Basin in Wyoming. In October 1999, Tom Brown acquired Genesis Gas and Oil, LLC, assets in the Piceance Basin in western Colorado for $35.5 million. This acquisition increased Tom Brown's acreage position in the basin to 68 percent in 500 potential development locations.

In June 2000, Tom Brown acquired an estimated 22 Bcfe in the Pavillion field, located in the Wind River Basin of Wyoming. The company paid $16.2 million to an undisclosed seller for this working interest. Tom Brown then operated the Pavillion field, which had a current net daily production of approximately eight million cubic feet of equivalent gas. This acquisition brought Tom Brown's interest in the Pavillion field to 90 percent, up from approximately 50 percent. ''This acquisition consolidates our interest in an area in which the Company has a long history of success. We continue to believe that our com-

## Key Dates:

**1955:** Tom Brown sets up the Scarber-Brown Drilling Company in Midland, Texas.
**1959:** Company changes name to Tom Brown Drilling Company.
**1968:** Company goes public.
**1971:** Company shortens name to Tom Brown, Inc.
**1999:** Tom Brown relocates its headquarters and executive offices to Denver, Colorado.
**2000:** Founders Brown and Roper receive Hearst Newspapers *Midland Reporter-Telegram* Lifetime Achievement Award.

mitment to the Rocky Mountain gas basins has positioned us well for the future and we are aggressively adding to that position as appropriate opportunities are defined,'' stated Jim Lightner, Tom Brown's president.

In addition to its presence in Texas and Colorado, Tom Brown also began exploring acreage in several midwestern and western states. By the end of 1999, Tom Brown had expanded to include interests in the following states: Colorado, Kansas, Louisiana, Michigan, Mississippi, Montana, Nebraska, New Mexico, North Dakota, Oklahoma, Texas, Utah, West Virginia, and Wyoming. Moreover, the company was exploring numerous basins throughout the United States. Still, the company's focus remained on the basins in Colorado.

Tom Brown's marketing operations were handled by a wholly owned subsidiary called Retex, Inc., based in Midland, Texas. In addition, in 1995, Wildhorse Energy Partners, LLC, was created by Tom Brown and KNE, a marketing partner of Tom Brown. Tom Brown owned a 45 percent stake in Wildhorse, which performed gas gathering and processing functions in the Rocky Mountains. An additional subsidiary, Sauer Drilling Company, provided drilling services to oil and gas operators in the central Rocky Mountains and drilling for Tom Brown company-wide.

### The Late 1990s and Beyond

In 1999, Tom Brown moved its corporate headquarters to Denver, Colorado, from Midland, where it had been situated from its inception in 1955. In a December 1999 *Denver Rocky Mountain News* article, CFO Dan Blanchard remarked, ''We are principally an oil and gas exploration and production company. We have probably 70 to 80 percent of our gas reserves located here in Wyoming, Colorado and Utah. We are really a Rockies company, so Denver was a logical fit in terms of location and corporate headquarters.'' The company's end of the year 1999 total assets totaled $536 million, up from $441 million at the end of 1998.

In December 1999, company founders Brown and Roper (gradually retiring from the business though Brown remained

on the board), were recognized for their contributions to the Permian Basin economy when they received the Hearst Newspapers, Reporter-Telegram Lifetime Achievement Award. As the company entered a new century, its leadership included Don Evans as chairman and CEO; James D. Lightner as president and director; and Thomas W. Dyk as executive vice-president and chief operating officer. The company's board of directors once included presidential-hopeful George W. Bush, and CEO Evans served as a top advisor in Bush's 2000 campaign.

As the company grew, so did its market share. Elaborating on the company's future in its annual report, CEO Evans noted, ''The strategy we put in place over ten years ago is really beginning to bear fruit in today's high commodity price environment. Our large undeveloped land position and exploration portfolio, combined with our multi-year development drilling inventory, has Tom Brown well positioned for the months and years ahead.''

### Principal Subsidiaries

Retex, Inc.; Sauer Drilling Co.; Tom Brown Resources Ltd. (Canada); Wildhorse Energy Partners, LLC (45%).

### Principal Competitors

Barrett Resources Corp.; Basin Exploration, Inc.; KCS Energy Inc.; Prima Energy Corp.; BP Amoco plc; Dominion Resources, Inc.

### Further Reading

BeDan, Michael, ''Oil Company Seeks 12 Employees in Denver After Move from Texas,'' *Rocky Mountain News,* December 26, 1999, p. 3J.
Jefferson, Elana Ashanti, ''Oil, Gas Panel Rejects Spacing Protest,'' *Denver Post,* July 1, 1997, p. C2.
''Colorado Earnings Watch,'' *Denver Rocky Mountain News,* May 10, 2000, p. 6B.
Lofholm, Nancy, ''As Oil, Gas Prices Drop, Rigs Go Silent,'' *Denver Post,* January 28, 1999, p. B3.
Miller, Ellen, ''Local Rules on Drilling Urged, Landowners Seek Mitigation,'' *Denver Post,* February 21, 1998, p. B-03.
Pitts, John Paul, ''Tom Brown, Joe Roper Honored,'' *Midland Reporter-Telegram: Permian Basin Oil & Gas Report,* December 26, 1999, pp. 1–2.
''Presidio Oil Files for Bankruptcy, Agrees to be Sold,'' *Denver Post,* August 6, 1996, p. C2.
Rebchook, John, ''Oil Company Returns to Downtown: Exploration Company Tom Brown Inc. Leases Two Floors of Anaconda,'' *Rocky Mountain News,* May 15, 1997, p. 6B.
Smith, Kerri S., ''Gas Firm Fetches $180M Highlands Deal Extends Consolidation,'' *Denver Post,* June 10, 1997, p. C1.
Williamson, Norma, ''Mineral Lease Agreement Waiting to be Signed Soon,'' *Wind River News,* March 31, 1994, p. 1.
Williamson, Richard, ''Shortages on Equipment, Capital, Crews Hurting Some Oil Producers,'' *Rocky Mountain News,* July 2, 2000, p. 1G.

—Peggy Hazelwood

# The Tranzonic Companies

670 Alpha Drive
Highland Heights, Ohio 44143
U.S.A.
Telephone: (440) 449-6550
Fax: (440) 449-0256
Web site: http://www.tranzonic.com

*Wholly Owned Subsidiary of Linsalata Capital Partners Fund II, L.P.*
*Incorporated:* 1946 as Ace Cigarette Service Co.
*Employees:* 1,027
*Sales:* $150 million (1998 est.)
*NAIC:* 322291 Sanitary Paper Product Manufacturing; 31321 Broadwoven Fabric Mills; 31323 Nonwoven Fabric Mills; 325611 Soap and Other Detergent Manufacturing

The Tranzonic Companies manufactures personal care products, wiping and cleaning goods, safety products, and washroom supplies and distributes its products to industrial and institutional clients. Tranzonic makes both private-label and brand-name goods, including Bottoms Up diapers and Tampax and Maxithins feminine hygiene products, and, through subsidiary CCP Industries, distributes industrial textiles, such as restroom supplies, disposable work clothing, floor mats, industrial wiping materials, and cleaning chemicals.

### Early Years as a Cigarette Vendor: 1930s–1950s

The business was founded in 1933 by Louis B. Golden, who emigrated to Cleveland, Ohio, from Russia in 1892 at the age of 17. Golden earned a bachelors degree from Case Western Reserve University and a law degree from the John Marshall Law School but eschewed a legal career to found the Golden Tobacco Co. in 1931. With the help of wife Miriam and an $800 initial investment, Golden ran the business—renamed Ace Cigarette Service Co. in 1933—from his kitchen table.

Ace Cigarette was incorporated in 1946, by which time it was already one of America's largest cigarette vendors. From this early foundation the company expanded into candy and soft drinks. A registered dietitian and longtime company executive, Miriam probably influenced the firm's move into automatic food service. In the late 1950s, the company acquired a half-interest in the Industrial Vending Co. and began to sell food prepared at its Cleveland headquarters through vending machines in local factories. Annual sales surpassed $6.5 million by 1957, when profits totaled about $83,750. While sales remained flat through the remainder of the 1950s, profits multiplied to $174,500 by 1959. The family took the company public and changed its name to Ace Vending Co. to reflect its broadened activities in 1961. A 1962 name change to American Automatic Vending Corp. anticipated an acquisitive push that took the firm nationwide.

### Expansion and Diversification in the 1960s and 1970s

American Automatic Vending (AAV) used the proceeds of its initial public offering to fund a decade-long spate of acquisitions that expanded its business interests beyond vending into personal care products and manual food service. Before its first fiscal year was out, the company had purchased Cincinnati's American Vending Service Inc. and Detroit's Market Vending Co. In 1962, the company acquired Consumers Cigarette Service Co., Seaway Vending Co., and Hospital Specialty Co., a business that would prove key to AAV's long-term growth. At the time it was purchased, Hospital Specialty had over 80,000 vending machines in all 50 states and brought with it valuable contracts to vend leading Kotex and Tampax brands of feminine napkins and tampons, as well as its own Gards, She, and Soft n' Thin labels. Hospital Specialty had been founded by the Ensheimer family, called "pioneers in the vending industry" in a 1962 *Cleveland Plain Dealer* article. Swifty Food Commissaries, Inc., a Cleveland catering company, was acquired in 1963, by which time AAV ranked as "Ohio's largest operator of vending equipment."

The ensuing years brought a relative lull in the pace of acquisitions. AAV bought Deegan-Denham Candy and Tobacco Co., a distributor of tobacco, candy, and over-the-counter drugs, in 1965 and expanded its vending reach into Kentucky and Indiana with the acquisitions of Southern Automatic Music Co.,

Wagg Vending Co., and Toledo Music and Novelty Co. in 1968. AAV rounded out the busy 1960s with the purchases of Nursing Homes Council, Budd, Inc., and Catering Management Inc. Renamed American Nursing Home Consulting Company, Nursing Homes Council formed the core of AAV's institutional food service division, which also catered to schools and factories.

Fueled by the growth of the overall vending industry, which doubled from $3 billion in 1963 to $6 billion in 1970, as well as its string of acquisitions, AAV's sales increased from $14.3 million in 1962 to $37.67 million in 1969. During that same period, net income nearly tripled, from $392,000 to $1.2 million. By 1971, American Automatic Vending boasted over 20,000 vending machines in Ohio, Michigan, Indiana, Kentucky, and Florida and ranked among the top ten players in the industry. In 1972, the company formally abbreviated its name to AAV Cos. to reflect its expansion beyond vending. Having surpassed many of his growth goals, Golden moved to Florida in 1970 and was succeeded by his son-in-law, Robert S. Reitman, that same year. Golden continued as chairman until 1973, when Reitman assumed that title as well.

Reitman continued his father-in-law's acquisition strategy into the early 1970s, purchasing Scan-O-Vision, a closed-circuit television security service, in 1971; Standard Cigar & Tobacco Co., a Washington, D.C. distributor, in 1972; and Beaver Falls Candy and Tobacco Co., a Pennsylvania distributor, in 1974. AAV's sales burgeoned over the course of the decade, from $40 million in 1970 to $73.8 million in 1979. But while the company's profits grew steadily to $1.8 million in 1976, AAV endured three consecutive annual earnings declines from that point through 1979, by which time net income had halved to $834,000. Mitchell Gordon, an analyst for *Barron's* magazine, blamed the erosion of AAV's profits on "the deteriorating industrial economy in the upper Midwest region, where its vending and distribution activities were located."

### Shifting Focus in the 1980s

CEO Reitman must have concurred. In 1981, he began to execute a reorganization strategy that shed two-thirds of his company's operations and created an entirely new corporate focus. That year's $9.5 million acquisition of Cleveland Cotton Products Co. was a pivotal factor in the new corporate scheme. Founded in 1921, this family owned firm had grown to lead the industrial wiping cloth business by the late 1970s. Industrial

wiping cloths, which Reitman called "new rags" in a 1988 *Crain's Cleveland Business* article, were tailored to customers' requirements for strength, absorbency, and texture. The disposable cloths were used in health care, food service, auto repair and auto body, oil-drilling, and electronics. When Cleveland Cotton Products' second-generation company leaders died within six months of one another in 1979, the private firm became an asset of their estate, and executor Larry L. Wymor sold Cleveland Cotton Products to AAV in 1981. Wymor went on to become president of Cleveland Cotton Products, which formed the core of the parent company's Industrial Wiping Division, contributing over half of total annual revenues by 1983.

In 1982, Chairman and CEO Robert S. Reitman decided to sell off AAV's traditional vending machine business, as well as its tobacco and candy wholesaling and food service operations. *Crain's Cleveland Business* called the spun-off businesses "regional cash cows that in recent years drained each other." Reitman's original deal with Edwin M. Roth's Electronic Theatre Restaurants Corp. fell through, but before the year was out, AAV sold the businesses to Crescott, Inc., a New York firm, for $5.6 million in cash and $6.3 million in notes. In order to keep its bond payments coming, Reitman's firm continued to provide Crescott with support such as public and shareholder relations and financial services through the ensuing few years.

Reitman retained the Personal Care Division and expanded its product line from the core feminine hygiene goods into elastic-leg disposable diapers, sterile obstetrical pads for hospitals and nursing homes, and an adult incontinent diaper. While AAV's share of the disposable diaper market stood at less than 1 percent, CEO Reitman told *Crain's Cleveland Business* that he expected the company's own-label diapers under the "Best Buy," "Precious," and "Happy Bottom" names to "come into their own" in the 1980s. Indeed, the $1.9 billion private-label disposable diaper market was advancing at about 8 percent each year during the early 1980s, and this became "one of AAV's fastest-growing segments" mid-decade.

Reitman changed his company's moniker to Tranzonic Companies in 1983. Flush with cash from the divestment, the CEO started aggressively seeking out acquisition candidates, eyeing at least six companies from 1983 to 1985. Left with two core businesses, industrial textiles and personal care, the company hoped to focus its future efforts on other "low-cost, repeatable goods." In 1987, Reitman told *Barron's* reporter Richard J. Maturi that Tranzonic was "looking for a complementary firm with growth opportunities and a reasonable price." Although the firm had trouble finding a good takeover target, its stock was one of *Forbes* magazine's 100 best-performing stocks for 1987, ranking 66th on that year's list.

After suffering a net loss during the transition from vending to industrial wiping, Tranzonic's sales increased steadily from $43 million in 1983 to $58.6 million in 1987. Profits grew erratically, from $1.2 million in 1983 to a high of $4.1 million in 1986, then declined to $2.4 million in 1987.

### Rapid Growth and Change: Late 1980s–90s

Tranzonic made its first post-reorganization acquisition the following year, a transaction that heralded a rash of corporate purchases in the late 1980s and early 1990s. American Homeware Inc. was a Dallas company whose line of personal travel organizers, garment bags, sweater drying racks, clothes hampers, and other storage items were made overseas and shipped directly to retailers, thereby eliminating warehousing expenses. American Homeware became the nucleus of Tranzonic's Housewares Division. The 1989 purchase of J.C. Baxter Co. formed the core of Tranzonic's industrial packaging division, which made spiral-wound paper tubes and cores for industrial and consumer markets.

In 1992, Tranzonic bought Tambrands Inc.'s Maxithins sanitary pad business, giving the company a nationally recognized addition to its line of feminine hygiene products. The parent increased its holdings in the household goods business with the purchase of Ever-Ready Appliance Manufacturing Co., a top producer of ironing boards and step stools, the following year. Tranzonic then combined its three laundry care companies—American Homeware, Pressing Supply, and Ever-Ready—into one company known as Design Trend, Inc.. The 1995 acquisition of Plezall Wipers & Cleaning, Inc., complemented Tranzonic's Industrial Textiles Division.

These acquisitions fueled a 113 percent increase in sales, from $69.7 million in 1988 to a record $149 million in 1995. Profits slid from $3.9 million in 1988 to $2.8 million in 1994, then reached a record $5.3 million in 1995. Tranzonic's fiscal 1995 annual report laid out CEO Reitman's plan to more than triple annual sales to $500 million by fiscal 2001. While the corporate leader expected internal growth to contribute to the realization of this "admittedly ambitious" objective, his 1995 letter to shareholders acknowledged that the firm "will not achieve [its] growth goal without acquisitions, given the slow-growth nature of our existing markets."

Working toward its goal to increase sales, Tranzonic announced the sale of its housewares division in spring of 1996. The sale of subsidiary Design Trend, Inc., allowed Tranzonic to focus on its divisions that served the wholesale and institutional sectors, markets that had traditionally generated a higher rate of return. Buyer Whitney Corr-Pak International, Inc., paid about $10 million for Design Trend, which by 1996 ranked second in the $255 million U.S. laundry care industry.

Due to the sale of Design Trend, Tranzonic recorded a loss from discontinued operations of $7.2 million during the fourth quarter of fiscal 1996. For the full fiscal year Tranzonic reported sales of $137.2 million, up 8 percent from the prior year, and a net loss of $2.4 million, compared to a net profit of $5.3 million in fiscal 1995. Fiscal 1997 proved kinder to Tranzonic's bottom line as the company reported record sales and earnings. Sales totaled $139.7 million and earnings from continuing operations reached $7 million, up from $4.4 million in 1996. Tranzonic attributed the improved margins to lower costs of raw materials and increased operating efficiency. CEO Reitman commented on Tranzonic's goals in a prepared statement and said, "Going forward, our emphasis continues to center on being the most efficient provider of products and services to customers, and to promote growth within our existing businesses through acquisition, product line extension, and the targeting of new market segments for current product lines."

During fiscal 1997 Tranzonic demonstrated its growth strategy by acquiring First Step from Dailey's, Inc. in July of 1996. First Step, a seller and distributor of safety, first aid, and infection control products, joined subsidiary CCP Industries. Also in July Tranzonic purchased the business and assets of Supply Line, Inc., which converted and distributed nonwoven and woven textile wiping and polishing cloths. Several months later, in October, Tranzonic bought three divisions—Midwest Disposable Products Division, Chicago Sanitary Division, and Globe Cotton Mills Division—from Cook & Riley, Inc. These divisions, like Supply Line, converted and sold industrial wiping cloths and also joined CCP Industries.

Tranzonic acquired Unity Paper Tubes from Wyndeham Press Group plc in March of 1997. Unity, based in England, was a maker and distributor of spiral-wound paper tubes and cores serving clients in the United Kingdom. Unity joined subsidiary Baxter Tube Company. The acquisition significantly extended Tranzonic's reach, but Baxter remained smaller than Tranzonic desired, and in September Tranzonic sold Baxter Tube Company to Caraustar Industries, Inc. for approximately $13 million. The sale left Tranzonic with two remaining operating divisions—Hospital Specialty Company and CCP Industries.

In a significant move, Tranzonic was purchased by Linsalata Capital Partners Fund II, L.P., in early 1998 for more than $100 million. Tranzonic had been seeking a buyer beginning in the mid-1990s in order to increase shareholder value. Linsalata was known for purchasing middle-market businesses and assisting management in developing strategies to fuel growth and expansion. Linsalata planned to accelerate growth at Tranzonic through new products and new management approaches. Upon completion of the sale, Tranzonic's senior vice president and president of CCP Industries, Richard J. Sims, was appointed president of Tranzonic, and Robert Reitman stayed on the board of directors as chairman emeritus. Alayne Reitman, Reitman's daughter and chief financial officer, left Tranzonic. Linsalata's Frank Linsalata became chairman and CEO. Sims was confident that Tranzonic was a wise buy for Linsalata and explained in the *Cleveland Plain Dealer,* "We have a clear strategy for growing this company's profitability. . . . We are working to establish firm foundations and accelerate growth at a faster rate than in the last few years."

In the late 1990s Tranzonic concentrated on strengthening operations and sought acquisition targets. In April of 1999 Tranzonic, through subsidiary CCP Industries, acquired

Spintex, a California-based maker and distributor of cleaning chemicals, washroom supplies, work apparel, and wiping cloths. The Spintex buy significantly boosted Tranzonic's presence in the West. As Tranzonic headed into the new millennium, the company hoped to realize its long-term strategy for growth and expansion and worked to strengthen its two primary divisions.

### Principal Subsidiaries

Hospital Specialty Co.; CCP Industries Inc.; Plezall Wipers & Cleaning Inc.; Gamco General Accessories Mfg.

### Principal Competitors

Kimberly-Clark Corporation; Playtex Products, Inc.; Steiner Corporation.

### Further Reading

Barnes, Jon, "More Good Changes Are Tranzonic's Goal," *Crain's Cleveland Business,* May 9, 1988.

Bryan, John E., "Vending Firm Buys Hospital Specialty," *Cleveland Plain Dealer,* August 2, 1962.

Datzman, Cynthia, "Brothers Let Family Heritage Set Firm's Course," *Crain's Cleveland Business,* September 1, 1986, p. 2.

Gleisser, Marcus, "Tranzonic Buys Maxithins Business," *Cleveland Plain Dealer,* June 26, 1992, p. 2G.

——, "Tranzonic to Hike Prices to Improve Earnings," *Cleveland Plain Dealer,* June 13, 1995, p. 3C.

——, "Tranzonic's New Owner Has a Mission," *Cleveland Plain Dealer,* March 6, 1998, p. 1C.

Gordon, Mitchell, "Well-Disposed: Tranzonic, Formerly AAV, Narrows Focus After Sale of Big Operations," *Barron's,* January 9, 1984, p. 52.

Kapner, Bill, "Tranzonic is Looking for an Opportunity to Unload Some Cash," *Crain's Cleveland Business,* May 27, 1985, p. 14.

Maturi, Richard J., "Clean Shot: That's What Tranzonic Cos. Has at Record Earnings," *Barron's,* June 8, 1987, p. 51.

Sabath, Donald, "Small But Mighty Tranzonic Set to Grow," *Cleveland Plain Dealer,* July 19, 1988, p. 1D.

Schiller, Zach, "The Quiet Dealmaker: President of Fund Buying Tranzonic Cos. Keeps a Low Profile but Makes Money from His Deals," *Cleveland Plain Dealer,* November 7, 1997, p. C1.

Ward, Leah, "AAV: 'Detoured But Not Derailed'," *Crain's Cleveland Business,* July 11, 1983, p. 2.

——, "AAV Now Disposed to National Market," *Crain's Cleveland Business,* May 30, 1983, p. 1.

Wyatt, Edward A., "Smiles on Chagrin Boulevard: Tranzonic Shrugs Off Cyclical Dips," *Barron's,* April 13, 1992, p. 15.

Yerak, Becky, "Investor Group Buys Tranzonic; Company Plans to Remain in Cleveland with No Job Cuts," *Cleveland Plain Dealer,* October 18, 1997, p. C1.

—April Dougal Gasbarre
—updated by Mariko Fujinaka

# Travis Boats & Motors, Inc.

**5000 Plaza on the Lake, Suite 250**
**Austin, Texas 78746**
**U.S.A.**
**Telephone: (512) 347-8787**
**Fax: (512) 329-0480**
**Web site: http://www.travisboats.com**

*Public Company*
*Incorporated:* 1979
*Employees:* 708
*Sales:* $182.30 million (1999)
*Stock Exchanges:* NASDAQ
*Ticker Symbol:* TRVS
*NAIC:* 441222 Boat Dealers

Travis Boats & Motors, Inc. is one of the leading boat retailers in the United States. The company has aggressively acquired independently owned operations as well as opening new superstores, a strategy that has allowed the company to expand from just one location in 1979 to about 40 in 2000. Retail outlets are located in the southern states of Alabama, Arkansas, Florida, Georgia, Louisiana, Mississippi, Oklahoma, Tennessee, and Texas. Unlike MarineMax, a larger competitor that specializes in Sea-Ray brand boats that start around $40,000, Travis Boats starts at a lower price point ($15,000) and offers boats from a variety of manufacturers. Because it has no competitors of similar size in its niche of the retail market, Travis Boats has been able to pursue a plan to consolidate the industry while keeping its acquisition costs low. Selling an array of brand-name fishing, water-skiing, and recreational boats, Travis Boats offers a variety of options at a posted price, thus eliminating the haggling that many customers dislike about the boat-buying experience. Travis Boats also takes advantage of its volume purchasing power with manufacturers by creating Travis Edition ''packages'' that allow the company to add features that smaller competitors are unable to match. At a lower price Travis Boats can include such options as a trailer, boarding ladder, more powerful motor, depth finder, stereo, upgraded interiors, as well as extended service contracts and insurance. In addition, Travis Boating Centers include a multi-bay service department plus a large stock of parts and accessories.

Travis Boats was founded in Austin, Texas, in 1979 by Mark Walton. While a student at the University of Texas, majoring in business, he cleaned boats at a local shop. It was there that he recognized that customers were uncomfortable negotiating every option when buying a new boat. That simple insight led him into the boat-selling business that began with a single store named after the county of its location, Travis.

During the 1980s Travis Boats was slow to expand. Its first foray outside of Austin was San Antonio, Texas, where a new outlet was built. Travis then bought existing Texas operations at Midland, Dallas, and Abilene. While the company learned how to manage a multi-store operation before attempting further expansion, the boating industry underwent significant turmoil, which would have a significant impact on Travis Boats in the 1990s.

## 1990 Luxury Tax: Crippling of Boating Industry

Boat sales in the United States peaked at $7.9 billion in 1988. A downturn in the economy then hurt the industry, adversely affecting sales and triggering a significant number of layoffs. The situation, however, would soon turn much worse with the imposition of a luxury tax in 1990.

To many, the 1980s was a decade of help-the-rich Reaganomics, and both Democrats and Republicans began to sense an anger in the electorate about the state of the sluggish economy and the mounting budget deficit. According to the Congressional Budget Office, from 1977 to 1988 the total tax burden on the wealthiest one percent of Americans fell by six percent, whereas the poorest ten percent paid 1.6 percent more. The budget package of 1990 was prepared at a time in which there was a widespread perception that the rich were not pulling their weight. Congressional Democrats insisted that any tax increase should target the rich, but Republicans were averse to raising income tax rates that had just been cut for the wealthiest taxpayers in 1988. In an attempt to reach a compromise, Congress looked to the luxury tax that had been imposed by the federal government during World War II and not phased out until 1965. The Treasury also had examined the concept during the Reagan administration, but it was never proposed. Defining what constitutes a ''luxury'' was considered too difficult, and overcoming resistance from the affected industries was even more problematic.

After much give and take, Congress decided in 1990 on a bipartisan budget plan that called for a ten percent luxury tax on the purchase of furs and jewelry in excess of $5,000, autos in excess of $30,000, and boats and yachts in excess of $100,000. The National Marine Manufacturers lobbied against the proposal, pointing out that a weak economy already had cost the boating industry 100,000 jobs. Jim Schaefer of Miami boat builder Richard Betram & Co. was quoted at the time as saying, ''The unfortunate thing about a rich man's tax is they're going to put a lot of poor people out of work.'' No matter how persuasive the economic arguments against the luxury tax, however, political considerations prevailed.

Almost as soon as the tax went into effect, the boating industry complained bitterly about the harm it was causing. Although the sale of boats costing more than $100,000 accounted for less than two percent of units sold in 1990, they generated about 22 percent of total revenue and sustained much of the industry's overhead costs. In the first half of 1991 after the luxury tax went into effect, sales of boats priced at $100,000–$300,000 dropped 61 percent, and sales of boats priced in excess of $300,000 fell 87 percent. The tax also depressed sales for boats priced at less than $100,000, as many customers mistakenly thought the tax applied to all boat sales. To avoid the tax, people turned to used boats, or purchased from a foreign builder and registered their boats in Canada, Mexico, the Bahamas, or other Caribbean islands. The downturn in boat sales also had a ripple effect on the businesses that serviced and supported the boating industry. The country's balance of payments also were adversely affected. In 1990, $792 million worth of pleasure craft were exported, as opposed to $265 million worth of imports. Furthermore, it was becoming apparent that the luxury tax would take in far less than what it would cost in lost revenue and unemployment benefits.

Six months after the luxury tax went into effect, the Senate Finance Committee held hearings to consider proposals to repeal all or part of the tax. Critics of the repeal effort claimed that retailers spiked sales at the end of 1990 by encouraging people to avoid the tax by buying early. Others blamed the downturn in sales on the recession that was affecting even the sale of used boats. The Bush administration took the position that it was simply too early to tell what effect, if any, the luxury tax had on the boating industry.

The reality was that the industry went into a freefall. Revenues dropped and jobs were lost. It would take another two years and a change in presidents before the luxury tax would finally be repealed as part of the Clinton economic plan that passed the House and Senate in August 1993. Within a year, boat sales, as well as the economy in general, began a healthy rebound.

### Travis Boats in the 1990s: Expansion Beyond Texas

Although many boat dealers went under during the rough times of the early 1990s, Travis Boats seized the opportunity to grow by picking up weaker competition. Having already expanded to more Texas cities in the later 1980s, Travis Boats now began to move into other Southern markets, such as Louisiana and Arkansas. During the period 1995–97, the company added outlets in Tennessee, Alabama, Florida, Georgia, and Oklahoma. A pattern of aggressive acquisition was established: The best dealer in town was the desired target. Walton describe his approach of ''friendly persuasion'' in a 1997 article in *Forbes*: ''We make it clear, not in a mean way, that we sure like that market and we would like them to join us, but if they elect not to, that we would be friendly competitors, but— nonetheless—competitors.'' When competing against established retailers, Travis Boats used its size to full advantage. The company could command a better wholesale price, and a wider variety of boats, by offering to take delivery of one-third of its orders in the off-season, a time when manufacturers normally would have to suspend operations. Travis Boats also was able to arrange financing for its customers. Even though smaller rivals joined purchasing co-ops, they were unable to match Travis Boats' competitive edge. When acquiring a local dealership, Travis Boats also was sensitive to established customer relationships, generally taking a year to phase in the Travis Boats name. In the meantime, the company provided employee training in the Austin headquarters.

With 12 outlets in operation, Travis Boats made a public offering of its stock in 1996, selling 46 percent of the company, or 1.88 million shares, at $9 per share. With this infusion of cash, Travis Boats began a period of accelerated growth. Its five-year goal was to reach $300 million in revenues and expand to 17 Southern states, a region that accounts for 57 percent of the continental shoreline and 43 percent of all inland water, as well as 35 percent of all domestic boat-related sales in the United States.

By 1999 Travis Boats doubled its outlets to 24 and was recognized by *Forbes* as one of the ''200 Best Small Companies'' of 1998, based on benchmarks such as profitability, sales growth, earnings per share, and return on equity. Travis Boats ranked #25 on the list. In early 1999 the company acquired six more existing dealerships and opened one new store. Florida was a particular target area, as outlets in the state doubled. Travis Boats then opened two new Florida stores in early 2000. By the fall of 2000, Travis Boats outlets numbered 39, fully a third of which were located in Florida. The company's home state of Texas was now second, with eight stores.

The rapid expansion of Travis Boats was not without complications. Its stock, after reaching a high of $29.125 in April 1998, dropped steadily over the next two years. During the summer of 2000 Travis Boats dipped below $4 per share. In July of that year, the company's board of directors expressed confidence in its stock by announcing a Limited Stock Repur

## Key Dates:

**1979:** Travis Boats is formed.
**1988:** U.S. boat sales peak.
**1990:** Luxury tax cripples boating industry.
**1993:** With repeal of luxury tax, boating industry rebounds.
**1996:** With 12 outlets, Travis Boats makes public stock offering.
**1999:** Travis Boats expands to 24 outlets.
**2000:** Travis Boats acquires The Boatworks; outlets number 39; begins internet sales.

chase Program. During the same week, Travis Boats released information that revealed a mixed financial situation for the company. While sales increased during the previous year, profits fell. Nevertheless, Walton claimed that the company was well positioned for going forward.

### Meeting the Challenge of a New Century and the Internet

The coming of the new century posed challenges for all retailers, let alone the boating industry. Selling boats via the internet became an area of concern for Travis Boats in 2000. With financial backers that included the founder of CarsDirect, a company that had already made an impact by selling cars over the Web, BoatsDirect.com threatened traditional marine dealerships, even as large a player as Travis Boats. BoatsDirect allowed consumers to research, review, and purchase boats online, as well as arrange for financing and delivery. Although the internet company maintained that it would purchase boats through a network of dealers, traditional retailers feared that they would lose money, with the result that many small dealers would be forced out of business. Whereas car dealers enjoyed some legislative protection to prevent encroachment on their markets, boat dealers were fearful that manufacturers would simply bypass them for direct sales to consumers through the internet. BoatsDirect made it clear that its intent was to be a volume seller and ultimately to offer every boat line possible.

Travis Boats' response to the internet challenge was to introduce a new line of boats to be sold exclusively over its Web site. The Travis e.dition line was intended to be low-cost fishing boats, pontoon boats, and family runabouts targeted at the first-time or value-driven buyer. Several weeks later another player, pcBoat.com, announced that it had signed a deal with the largest boat retailer in North America, West Marine, Inc. Despite already having its own Web retailing operation, West Marine agreed to co-brand its site with pcBoat. The Atlanta-based internet company also purchased the *Powerboat Guide* and *Mauch's Sailboat Guide* to provide research content for its customers. Yet another internet competitor, San Francisco-based Boats.com, announced plans to launch its Web business.

Aside from the changing dynamics of the boat retailing business, Travis Boats still had the traditional problems with which to contend. First, sales tend to be seasonal. Second, with any downturn in the economy, boats are among the first luxury items to suffer. Finally, there is the weather. Hurricanes along coastal territories of Travis Boats could disrupt sales, while inland, drought conditions or excessive rains could have similar adverse effects. By continuing to expand throughout the southern United States, the management of Travis Boats hoped, at least, to lessen the regional threat of bad weather. With so many uncontrollable variables in its future, the company came to see the virtue of continued growth as a business necessity.

### Principal Competitors

Holiday RV Superstores; MarineMax; West Marine, Inc.

### Further Reading

Aguayo, Jose, "We're Gonna Consolidate This Industry," *Forbes,* August 11, 1997, p. 65.

"Budget Fallout," *Wall Street Journal,* October 2, 1990, p. B1.

Denn, James, "Boat Dealers Faced with Challenge from Dot-coms," *Boating.*

Hampton, Phil, "Boating Casts Off Bad Times," *USA Today,* August 19, 1994, p. 1B.

Hiestand, Michael, "Tax Sinks Luxury Sales to Rock Bottom," *USA Today,* October 10, 1991, p. 5C.

Johnson, Sharen Shaw, "Tax Debate: Who 'Should Take the Hit,' " *USA Today,* October 9, 1990, p. 1A.

"Management's Discussion and Analysis of Financial Condition and Results of Operations," SEC Form 10-Q, May 19, 2000.

Manor, Robert, "Ahoy! Boating Industry on the Lookout for a Fair Wind," *St. Louis Post-Dispatch,* February 12, 1992, p. 1B.

Moran, Brian, "Rival Makes Waves for Travis Boats' Net Plan," *Austin Business Journal,* July 3, 2000.

"Sales Jump, Profits Fall for Travis Boat Dealer Chain," *Boating,* July 26, 2000.

Weil, Jonathan, "Travis Boats Appears to Have Its Motor Running for a Rebound," *Wall Street Journal,* January 27, 1999, p. T2.

Wessel, David, "Consideration of Luxury Tax Is Touching Off an Old Debate," *Wall Street Journal,* September 11, 1990, p. A2.

Wessel, David, and Jackie Calmes, "Momentum Grows Against Luxury Tax As Critics Complain It Enriches No One," *Wall Street Journal,* June 12, 1991, p. B1.

—Ed Dinger

# United Industrial Corporation

**570 Lexington Avenue**
**New York, New York 10022**
**U.S.A.**
**Telephone: (212) 752-8787**
**Fax: (212) 838-4629**
**Web site: http://www.unitedindustrial.com**

*Public Company*
*Incorporated:* 1959 as Topp Industries Corporation
*Employees:* 1,600
*Sales:* $216.98 million (1999)
*Stock Exchanges:* New York
*Ticker Symbol:* UIC
*NAIC:* 333319 Other Commercial and Service Industry
Machinery Manufacturing; 335999 All Other
Miscellaneous Electrical Equipment and Component
Manufacturing; 336411 Aircraft Manufacturing;
485112 Commuter Rail Systems; 562213 Solid Waste
Combustors and Incinerators

United Industrial Corporation (UIC) is a diversified holding company. It once owned a leader maker of surgical gloves; in 2000 its subsidiaries manufactured waste incinerators (Detroit Stoker) and computer-controlled firefighter training systems (Symtron). AAI Corp., long UIC's largest contributor of revenues, makes unmanned aerial vehicles (UAVs), ordnance, and training and simulation systems for defense forces. Electric Transit, Inc., a joint venture with the Czech SKODA Group, makes electric trolley cars.

## Origins

In the 1950s, Bernard Fein, a retired lawyer and an early HAM radio buff, built up a large holding in United Industrial Corp. (SEC records indicate that the company was called Hayes Manufacturing Corp. until 1966.) United Industrial Corp. (UIC) merged with Topp Industries, a West Coast electronics firm, in 1959. Fein reportedly opposed the union. Within a few months

of the merger, Fein told *Forbes,* Topp management went on a buying spree, acquiring a cement aggregate company, a road-building company, an Ohio-based rubber company, and Phoenix-based U.S. Semiconductor. Further, Topp had carried certain R&D costs as inventory, which led to UIC posting a $6.4 million loss the year after the merger. It also led to the New York Stock Exchange suspending the company's stock from trading in January 1961 and delisting it that September. As Fein had helped turn around several other firms, he was called upon to do the same at UIC, which was $10 million in debt and had a negative net worth approaching $500,000.

Fein did not file for bankruptcy protection, as many expected. Three troubled subsidiaries were sold off, which reduced debt, and the workforce was reduced by 500 to about 3,000 employees. Fein increased production and sales at UIC's remaining subsidiaries. UIC was able to post a $3 million profit in 1962. Annual sales reached the $60 million range in the mid-1960s.

The Perry Rubber Company tripled its production and doubled its market share of surgical gloves in five years, while simultaneously expanding its product line. To complement UIC's most profitable enterprise, in October 1964 UIC acquired an 85 percent interest in Shampaine Industries, Inc., a privately owned manufacturer of medical equipment and furniture based in St. Louis. At the time of the purchase, Shampaine was losing about $1.5 million a year on annual sales of $11 million. UIC announced the purchase of a 28.5 percent stake in the I.B. Kleinert Rubber Company for $2 million in August 1966. Kleinert was profitable on $18 million a year in sales of rubber and plastic goods such as shower caps and shower curtains.

Another major UIC subsidiary, Baltimore-based Aircraft Armaments, Inc. (AAI), provided the U.S. military with ordnance and training devices. Former engineers at Glenn Martin Co. (later part of Martin Marietta) had started the company in 1950. UIC also built this line of business by acquisition. AAI bought a 51 percent interest in Burtek, Inc. of Tulsa, Oklahoma in August 1963 for a reported $1 million. Burtek produced missile and aircraft training systems and had sales in excess of $3 million a year.

In the early 1960s, UIC reduced its dependence on government contracts from 90 percent to 25 percent of business, according to *Financial World*. Other holdings included venerable incinerator manufacturer Riley Stoker, aggregates and concrete supplier Southern Pacific Milling, and road equipment maker Trucks & Equipment, Inc. In December 1964, the revitalized UIC became the first company in the history of the New York Stock Exchange to have its stock relisted.

### Record Growth in the 1970s and 1980s

Profits reached $4.7 million on sales of $92 million in 1976. Several consecutive years of record profits followed. UIC averaged earnings growth of more than 20 percent a year at the end of the decade.

In the late 1970s, AAI (now formally named AAI Corp.) branched out beyond its traditional research and development activities into manufacturing. Electronics systems such as simulators, test equipment, and weapons systems accounted for most of AAI's business, although it continued to develop new munitions and ordnance. AAI was the prime contractor for most of its manufacturing projects, but it also supplied Ford Aerospace and Harsco Corp. UIC revenues reached $165 million in 1980, with a net income of $8.3 million. AAI accounted for half of each. This unit was developing a RDF light tank that could be readily airlifted and cost a fraction of the price of a conventional tank.

By this time, the Perry Rubber business had transformed into Affiliated Hospital Products Inc., a publicly traded company in which UIC held a 72.1 percent interest. It had a sales volume of $48 million in 1980. As the country's leading supplier of surgical gloves, the unit had suffered from an increase in rubber prices in the late 1970s.

UIC sold its money-losing Carrom Division, which made furniture for patient waiting rooms, in December 1980. There were also difficulties at Detroit Stoker, where United Steelworkers staged a strike in October 1981.

In spite of these problems, UIC's consolidated revenues continued to rise, reaching $283 million in 1983. *Barron's* noted that by 1984, UIC had posted a dozen years of record sales and profits. Defense contracting and a new line of generic drugs fueled growth in the early 1980s, while Detroit Stoker's combustion equipment business slowed.

Powered by Cold War demand, AAI then accounted for two-thirds of UIC's revenues. It was the leading producer of simulators and training equipment for electronic warfare. It also was developing new kinetic energy artillery shells. In August 1984, AAI contracted to adapt Israeli-developed Mastiff drone aircraft for the U.S. market. At its peak, AAI employed 3,500 workers. Manufacturing accounted for 60 percent of its revenues in the mid-1980s.

At this time, Affiliated Hospital's surgical glove sales were falling due to reduced Medicare and Medicaid budgets, though its new line of generic drugs allowed the unit to continue to grow. In January 1985, UIC announced that it was selling its share in Affiliated Hospital to Smith & Nephew for $58 million.

### A Slow-Down in the 1990s

UIC's sales reached $315 million in 1988, with earnings of $17 million. The company was debt-free. The end of the Cold War, a slow economy, and bad luck, however, made the early 1990s a difficult period for UIC.

UIC bought Microflite for $16 million in 1991, a purchase that proved to be disastrous. Microflite made flight simulators for commercial aircraft; it was bought to make AAI less dependent on government contracts. CAE-Link Corp. sued Microflite for patent infringement soon after the deal, however. The Persian Gulf War and a global recession crippled the aviation industry, leading to mass lay-offs of pilots and little market for flight simulators. UIC unloaded Microflite after three costly years.

Among UIC's diversified holdings was the Spectrum Group, which marketed Hot Shot and Rid-A-Bug pesticides. AAI accounted for 80 percent of UIC's revenues, however, and it was dependent on defense contracts and civil aviation—both struggling industries. AAI lost $20 million on sales of $216 million in 1993, and parent company UIC lost $11 million on sales of $253 million.

AAI, which had grown rapidly under the defense buildup of the Reagan years, shed more than 2,000 jobs in the early 1990s. UIC hired Richard E. Erkeneff, formerly with McDonnell Douglas Corp., to turn around AAI in the fall of 1993. A restructuring was announced the next spring. AAI was divided into four segments: defense systems, fluid test, transportation, and weather. There were few jobs left to trim by that time, although AAI also exited a joint venture to build a simulated ride for a Las Vegas resort. A venture to produce simulators for U.S. Navy helicopters was also unprofitable. UIC finally was allowed to leave the contract in November 1996.

AAI had begun to take a loss on fire trainers, which were expensive to build. These devices electronically controlled fires in buildings, aircraft, and ships in order to train firefighters. In early 1994, UIC bought AAI's main fire trainer competitor, New Jersey-based Symtron Systems Inc. The purchase left AAI with a 75 percent market share in the fire trainer business. All of this work was shifted to Symtron.

In February 1994, AAI entered into a joint venture to launch the first American electric trolley bus company in nearly 40 years: Electric Transit Inc.. AAI's partner was SKODA, a Czech industrial manufacturing company founded in the 1860s.

```
┌─────────────────────────────────────────────┐
│              Key Dates:                      │
│                                              │
│  1950:  AAI Corp. established by former       │
│         Martin engineers.                    │
│  1959:  UIC merges with free spending Topp    │
│         Industries.                          │
│  1961:  UIC is delisted from the New York     │
│         Stock Exchange; Bernard Fein takes    │
│         over.                                │
│  1964:  UIC is allowed back on the Big Board. │
│  1972:  A dozen years of sales and earnings   │
│         growth begins.                       │
│  1985:  Surgical glove business is sold to    │
│         Smith & Nephew.                      │
│  1993:  UIC posts a loss as defense and civil │
│         aviation industries suffer.          │
│  1994:  Symtron Systems is acquired; Electric │
│         Transit venture is launched.         │
│  1995:  A management shake-up ends with       │
│         Fein's resignation as chairman.      │
└─────────────────────────────────────────────┘
```

UIC had been producing electric trolleys at its Dayton, Ohio facility and maintained and overhauled transit vehicles for the state of Maryland.

### Management Shake-Up in 1995

Corporate turnaround specialist P. David Bocksch was hired as CEO in April 1995. He was credited with turning around New York container maker Flexi-Van Corp. and overseeing a fourfold increase in business at the leading security firm, Pinkerton's Inc. At UIC, Bocksch planned to sell off Detroit Stoker Co., Neo Products Co., and other marginal business. According to the *Baltimore Sun,* he also felt that Fein, then 87, was too old to function effectively as chairman. Further, Bocksch wanted to bring more outside directors into the board dominated by Fein's relatives and friends.

The *Baltimore Sun* reported that Bernard Fein's daughter, Susan Fein Zawel, plotted against Bocksch to protect her own job as counsel and secretary. Needing an experienced hand to implement his strategy of acquisitions and divestments, Bocksch tried to replace her with AAI's head of legal affairs, Robert W. Worthing. Zawel refused to accept the consulting contract Bocksch offered. She also maintained that there was no power struggle. There was, however, a major shake-up in UIC's executive ranks in October 1995. Bocksch resigned; the chief financial officer, Thomas J. Carmody, was fired. Bernard Fein resigned as board chairman a few days later, although he remained a director. In fact, a third of the board was replaced.

Harold S. Gelb, formerly a senior partner with the Ernst & Young accounting firm, was designated Fein's successor in November 1995. (He was also a friend and neighbor to Fein, according to the *Sun.*) AAI's CEO, Richard Erkeneff, was named president and CEO at UIC in January 1996 after filling that role on an interim basis.

The instability at the top seemed to have an effect on financial performance. UIC managed only a $880,000 profit on sales of $227 million in 1995. Westport, Connecticut-based COMPO Consulting Group was brought in after the management upheaval to evaluate UIC's various lines of business. Prospects for the company's Pioneer UAV (unmanned aerial vehicle) program appeared promising. AAI was the only company producing the drones in quantity. Simulation and testing programs remained active. In May 1997, Romania bought a Shadow 600 UAV and a Moving Target Simulator from AAI for $20 million.

Other high-tech projects under development included the Objective Individual Combat Weapon and the Advanced Boresight Equipment system. UIC also was pursuing logistics support contracts with other aerospace companies and end users. In July 1997, AAI's engineering unit landed a $35 million Air Force contract to upgrade devices used to train mechanics for the C-17 transport aircraft.

UIC sold Neo Products Co. in September 1997. The thermoplastics unit had contributed just one percent of UIC's earnings the year before. The sale to a group of private investors garnered about $1.5 million plus a share of earnings for a couple of years. UIC's weather systems subsidiary, AAI Systems Management, Inc., was sold the next month to All Weather, Inc. for about $20 million. Weather Systems had contributed a quarter of UIC's pretax earnings.

UIC was announcing improved results by the end of 1997. Electric Transit won a $174 million contract to supply San Francisco's MUNI program, although UIC later was forced to cover partner SKODA's share of financing. There was also strong interest worldwide in AAI's various training simulators at the end of the decade.

In late 1999, AAI won a $42 million Army contract for Shadow 200 UAVs to evaluate. If chosen for production, the contract had a potential value of more than $300 million over five years.

### Principal Subsidiaries

AAI Corporation; Detroit Stoker Company; ETI (35%); UIC Products Co.; UIC International, Ltd. (Barbados).

### Principal Divisions

Commercial and Defense Simulation and Test Systems; Unmanned Air Vehicles; Engineering and Maintenance Services; Transportation Systems; Energy Systems.

### Principal Competitors

DRS Technologies; ECC Group plc; General Atomics Aeronautical Systems Inc.; Lockheed Martin Corporation; Northrop Grumman Corporation; Racal Defense Systems; Reflectone Inc.; Smith Group.

### Further Reading

Dorfman, John, ''Look, Ma, No Hands,'' *Forbes,* October 11, 1982, pp. 139–40.

Gordon, Mitchell, ''Defense and Drugs: They're Big Ingredients in United Industrial's Gains,'' *Barron's,* September 24, 1984, pp. 54–56.

——, ''On the Beam: United Industrial Is Targeted for Fresh Earnings Growth,'' *Barron's,* November 23, 1981, pp. 50–51.

Marcial, Gene G., "This Armsmaker Is 'A Sitting Duck,'" *Business Week,* March 22, 1999, p. 94.

Martin, Ellen James, "Gelb Is Named Chairman at United Industrial Corp.," *Baltimore Sun,* November 4, 1995, p. 13C.

Shelsby, Ted, "AAI Corp. Restructuring to Cut Costs, Few Jobs," *Baltimore Sun,* June 28, 1994, p. 13C.

——, "AAI Parent to Buy Chief Competitor in Fire Training Simulators," *Baltimore Sun,* January 25, 1994, p. 12C.

——, "AAI's Parent Attributes Profit Drop to a Contract; No Chief at the Moment at United Industrial Corp.," *Baltimore Sun,* November 1, 1995, p. 4C.

——, "Rescue Attempt Rattles UIC," *Baltimore Sun,* May 13, 1996, p. 11C.

"United Industrial to Win Relisting," *Financial World,* November 18, 1964, pp. 14, 21–22.

—Frederick C. Ingram

# Unitil Corporation

**6 Liberty Lane West**
**Hampton, New Hampshire 03842-1720**
**U.S.A.**
**Telephone: (603) 772-0775**
**Fax: (603) 773-6605**
**Web site: http://www.unitil.com**

*Public Company*
*Incorporated:* 1984
*Employees:* 328
*Sales:* $172.37 million (1999)
*Stock Exchanges:* American
*Ticker Symbol:* UTL
*NAIC:* 551112 Offices of Other Holding Companies;
        221122 Electric Power Distribution; 22121 Natural
        Gas Distribution

Unitil Corporation is a public utility holding company system. It is the parent company of eight wholly owned subsidiaries, known as the Unitil System, in New Hampshire and Massachusetts. These subsidiaries form a fully integrated system of energy and service companies that supply some 100,000 customers in New Hampshire and Massachusetts. Unitil's principal business is the purchase, transmission, distribution, and sale of electricity, as well as the distribution and sale of natural gas through its three retail subsidiaries, Concord Electric Company, Exeter & Hampton Electric Company, and Fitchburg Gas and Electric Light Company. Unitil Power Corp. provides wholesale power and transmission services to the system's retail subsidiaries. Unitil Resources Inc. (URI) markets energy, consulting, and other energy-related services to nonaffiliates. Unitil Corporation owns real estate to support the utility business of its affiliates. Until Service Corp. provides centralized support to the system's companies. Usource L.L.C. (a subsidiary of URI) Internet-based energy procurement supplies services to large commercial, industrial, and institutional customers throughout New York and New England. In 1999, *Electric Light & Power* magazine ranked Unitil's three distribution subsidiaries as first (Exeter & Hampton Electric Company), seventh, and 17th in its list of the nation's 100 lowest-cost distribution companies.

### 1852–75: Pioneering Electric and Gas Services

Unitil's history is rooted in its three retail distribution utilities—Fitchburg G&E, Concord Electric, and Exeter & Hampton—three independent, investor-owned utility systems formed through a significant ownership by the Tenney family. More than 100 years after the founding and development of these companies, Unitil emerged as the holding company of a retail electric and gas distribution utility in Massachusetts and of two retail electric distribution utilities in New Hampshire.

In 1852, before the Civil War, the Fitchburg Gas Company began to supply customers in central Massachusetts. Shortly a practical version of the incandescent lamp was invented, Fitchburg Gas bought the Wachusett Electric Light Company and in 1895 changed its company name to Fitchburg Gas and Electric Light Company (Fitchburg G&E).

Concord Land and Power Company—incorporated in Concord, New Hampshire in 1892—became the Concord Electric Company (Concord Electric) in 1901 and acquired Penacook Electric Light Company in 1918. Exeter and Hampton Electric (Exeter&H)—established in 1908—began by serving customers in 13 towns in Rockingham County, New Hampshire, and then extended its lines to Hampton Falls, Newton, East Kingston, and South Hampton. These companies functioned as private, investor-owned firms to supply electricity in their respective New Hampshire markets. Fitchburg G&E, also a private, investor-owned company, supplied its Massachusetts market with electricity and gas.

Electricity was relatively inexpensive, but the need to save energy would soon arise. While serving as a minister to France, Benjamin Franklin had suggested Daylight Saving Time (DST) as a way of conserving the cost of lighting for shops. Although close to 150 years passed before his suggestion was adopted, when England became involved in World War I, Parliament responded to the need to save energy with the 1916 act that introduced British Summer Time. The act mandated that clocks be advanced one hour during the summer months. During

403

**Company Perspectives:**

*We will be a leader in the innovative and efficient management of a growing distribution business and in meeting customers' delivery service needs. We will be a leader in providing customers with control over their energy procurement process through our Internet-based marketplace for energy commodities and services. We will be a leading provider of integrated utility-management services by forming strategic alliances with smaller public and private power systems.*

World War II, England again recognized the saving aspects of British Summer Time and instituted Double Summer Time, which was two hours ahead of Greenwich Mean Time.

In 1918, to conserve resources for the war effort, the U.S. Congress placed the country on DST for the remainder of World War I. The law was observed for seven months but proved to be so unpopular—especially with farmers—that President Woodrow Wilson had it repealed in March 1919. What had become obvious, however, was that DST did save energy and fuel. When America entered World War II, Congress reinstated DST year-round basis, which remained in effect until September 30, 1945. For the next 21 years, no U.S. law enforced DST. States and localities were free to choose whether they would observe DST; any area could exempt itself from DST by passing a local ordinance. The resulting confusion was not resolved until Congress passed the Uniform Time Act of 1966. Following the 1973 Arab Oil Embargo, Congress put most of the country on extended DST in hopes of saving additional energy. The experiment worked, but opposition, mostly from the farming states, caused Congress to end the experiment in 1975. The Uniform Time Act of 1966 was amended in 1986. From then on, DST began the first Sunday of April and ended the last Sunday of October.

### 1935–84: Regulation, Deregulation, Re-Regulation

During these early years, Fitchburg G&E, Concord Electric, and Exeter&H operated in a relatively unregulated environment; they competed mostly on the basis of price and personal service, especially during the economic depression of the 1930s.

During the 1980s research economists realized that the early electricity market "was remarkably competitive." Across America, consumers could choose from more than one electric company. In that environment, production quadrupled and prices fell 26 percent." When competition began to erode their profits, the oldest companies considered the advantages of consolidation. "States passed laws guaranteeing exclusive franchises to those utilities and propping up their prices," Ryan Oprea reported in a study published in *Reason.* "The federal government's response was passage of interstate legislation, known as the 1935 Public Utility Holding Company Act, which kept utilities from entering other energy-related businesses and seriously limited their capacity for expansion."

In 1935, Congress also founded the Federal Power Commission (later restructured as the Federal Energy Regulatory Commission), which established "the complex rate and merger regulations that delayed and contorted changes within the industry." In 1936, the three independent public utilities that eventually became subsidiaries of the Unitil System—Fitchburg G&E, Concord Electric, and Exeter&H—began to test the advantages of cooperation when Charles H. Tenney opened an office in Boston to offer centralized services to these companies.

Concord Electric extended its services to Concord, New Hampshire, and the greater Concord area. Fitchburg G&E converted to natural gas in 1952 and in 1969 acquired the Gardner, Massachusetts-based Gardner Gas Company. The three retail utilities continued to accept shared services from an office based in Bedford, New Hampshire. "In the late 1970s," Oprea wrote, "the new Department of Energy wanted to develop environmentally sound, renewable resources. To that end, Congress passed the Public Utility Regulatory Policies Act (PURPA), which required utilities to purchase a portion of their electricity from environmentally friendly producers." PURPA forced the dominating, vertically integrated electric firms to let small, independent nonutility generators sell energy to other producers over the large companies' transmission grid (vast networks of electric lines). Suddenly, the wholesale market was available to hundreds of companies that could produce and sell their electricity.

### 1984–97: Birth of the Unitil System, Competition, Development Strategy

In 1984 Concord Electric and Exeter&H agreed on a stock-exchange plan that became effective in 1985 for the creation of the Unitil Power Corporation, a wholesale electric power utility. They became subsidiaries of Unitil Corporation (Unitil) in 1985; Fitchburg G&E merged into Unitil in 1992. Unitil Service Corporation (Unitil Service) was established in 1984 to provide, at cost, centralized management, accounting, planning, procurement, and other services to the Unitil System companies. Unitil Realty Corporporation was established in 1986 to own and manage the company's corporate office building and property. Thus, the three independent retail electric and gas distribution utilities that had been sharing centralized administrative services became wholly owned subsidiaries of Unitil Corporation.

The management of Unitil System developed a growth strategy based on foresight, dependability, stability, and sophistication. According to Unitil's *1994 Annual Report,* the Unitil companies' historic strategy had been "to preserve efficiencies and enhance cost savings through strategic alliances." This strategy allowed the distribution utilities to maintain the lowest per-customer operating costs of all major investor-owned utilities in New England. About 75 percent of total costs for Unitil's distribution companies were related to energy supply. Unitil focused on finding the best wholesale terms and prices and made it a point to participate in the market at regular intervals to participate in the latest products and services.

Unitil was dependable in that it provided its customers with quality energy services at competitive prices. During the system's first ten years of operation, its distribution utilities were in the mid-to-low range among their peers. Unitil's ability to maintain its competitive position was based on conservative financial management practices and a diversified power-supply portfolio. As the need arose, Unitil could quickly realign its

## Key Dates:

**1852:** Fitchburg Gas Company is founded; name changes to Fitchburg Gas and Electric Company (Fitchburg G&E) in 1895.

**1892:** Concord Land and Power Company is incorporated and becomes Concord Electric Company (Concord Electric) in 1901.

**1908:** Exeter & Hampton Electric Company (Exeter&H) is founded.

**1916:** British Parliament introduces Daylight Saving Time (DST) to save energy during World War I.

**1918:** U.S. Congress mandates DST when the nation enters World War I.

**1935:** U.S. Congress passes the Public Utility Holding Company Act.

**1936:** Charles H. Tenney opens Boston office to provide centralized services to Fitchburg G&E, Concord Electric, and Exeter&Hampton.

**1952:** Fitchburg G&E converts to natural gas.

**1978:** Congress passes the Public Utility Regulatory Policies Act (PURPA).

**1984:** Unitil Power Corp. and Unitil Service Corp. are established.

**1986:** Unitil Realty Corp. is established.

**1993:** Unitil Resources Inc. is founded to provide energy-consulting services.

**1996:** Unitil moves corporate headquarters to Hampton, New Hampshire.

**1998:** Governor signs New Hampshire House Bill 1392 for mandatory implementation of full, open retail electric competition.

**1999:** Unitil launches Usource L.L.C. to provide Internet-based energy procurement services.

power-supply resources through selected contract terms and conditions. Years of shared services had brought Unitil's distribution companies to a level of marketing sophistication that few other investor-owned utilities employed.

Additionally, for more than a decade, the three Unitil retail utilities benefited from the company's pursuit of power supply solicitations, bidding and negotiation programs. Consequently, when Order 636 of the Federal Energy Regulatory Commission became effective during 1993 and revolutionized the way gas distribution companies were to buy their natural gas, Unitil welcomed the prospect of open access as an opportunity for growth. Although many in the industry were upset by the coming of competitive bidding in gas supply, Unitil found itself in an improved competitive position. Indeed, Unitil had been among the first in the industry to purchase almost all its electrical power by competitive bid from a wide variety of suppliers. The company could readily adapt its expertise to the natural gas industry.

Unitil Resources Inc. (URI) was established in 1993 as Unitil's wholly owned nonutility subsidiary to engage in business transactions as a competitive marketer of electricity, gas, and other energy commodities in wholesale and retail markets. URI was also meant to provide energy brokering, consulting, and management-related services within the United States. Unitil's earnings were $1.83 per average common share outstanding for fiscal 1994, compared to 1993's record earnings per share of $1.75; 1992's earnings of $1.50 per share; 1990's earnings of $1.26 per share; and 1985's earnings of $.26 per share.

Unitil intensified its focus on customers' needs and on meeting these needs with appropriate products and services, dependably, and at the lowest price possible. By the end of fiscal 1997 Concord Electric's principal business was the distribution and sale of electricity at retail prices to approximately 26,400 customers in the City of Concord and 12 surrounding towns, all in New Hampshire. The State of New Hampshire's government operations were within Concord Electric's service area, including the executive, legislative, judicial branches and offices, and facilities for all major state government services. Concord Electric's service area was also a retail trading center for the north-central part of the state and for more than 60 diversified businesses relating to insurance, printing, electronics, granite, belting, plastic yarns, furniture, machinery, sportswear, and lumber.

Exeter&H was engaged principally in the distribution and sale of retail electricity to approximately 38,400 customers in the towns of Exeter and Hampton and in all or part of 16 nearby towns in New Hampshire. This utility's diversified customer base included retail stores, shopping centers, motels, farms, restaurants, apple orchards, and office buildings, as well as manufacturing firms that produced sportswear, automobile parts, and electronic components. An estimated 150,000 daily visitors came to Exeter&H's territory, which included several popular resorts and beaches along the Atlantic Ocean.

Fitchburg Gas&E distributed and sold both electricity and natural gas in Fitchburg, Massachusetts, and in several nearby communities. The company's service area encompassed close to 170 square miles in north-central Massachusetts. Electricity was supplied to some 27,200 residential and commercial customers; industrial customers included paper manufacturers, fabricators of rubber and plastics, chemical products companies, and printing and publishing companies, among others.

### 1998 and Beyond

Restructuring consisted of reorganizing three components: *generation*, which referred to the creation of electricity; *transmission*, which referred to the wires and associated facilities that transported electricity at high voltage levels from power plants to distribution substations; and *distribution*, which referred to the wires and associated facilities that transported electricity at lower voltage levels from distribution substations to customers' facilities and homes. Originally, electric companies offered these three components as bundled services, but new legislation obliged the industry to change its mode of operation. Restructuring of the electric industry became law in New Hampshire in May 1996 when the governor signed House Bill 1392 to establish principles, standards, and a timetable for the New Hampshire Public Utilities Commission (NHPUC) to implement full and open-access retail electric competition as early as January 1, 1998, but no later than July 1, 1998. The law also directed the NHPUC to set interim access charges for the recovery of above-market ''stranded'' power supply costs and to make a final determination on these access charges within two years of implementation of full competition. (The words *stranded costs* refer to financial obligations that became unduly expensive as a result of restructuring; for example, investments in generation facilities, contractual obligations for power supplies, and the like.)

Unitil had in place transition plans to move its utility subsidiaries into this new market structure. The plan ensured fairness in the treatment of the company's assets and obligations and, at the same time, allowed customers to choose. The company positioned its competitive market subsidiary, Unitil Resources Inc., to pursue growth areas both within and beyond the company's traditional franchises in the emerging, competitive electric energy market. However, pending resolution of key restructuring policies and issues—especially recovery of "stranded costs"—slowed the reconstruction of process for Concord Electric and Exeter&H. Meanwhile, taking advantage of the New Hampshire Retail Competition Pilot Program mandated by law in June 1996, Unitil Resources, Inc.—the company's non-utility subsidiary not subject to utility regulations—began selling. As of March 1, 1999, Unitil Resources marketed energy competitively to over 700 customers outside the Unitil companies' traditional franchise territories.

Unitil's third retail-distribution subsidiary, Fitchburg Gas and Electric Light Company, completed the divestiture of its electric generation and power supply portfolio, complied with legislatively mandated rate discounts for all customers, and provided systems and information for customers to choose their electric energy supplier. The company also expanded programs for energy efficiency and the protection of low-income customers.

By year-end 1999, Unitil had decided to abandon the business of competitive energy supply at the retail level. Energy marketing was a low-margin, high-risk business, and the retail level—due in large part to the hesitation of many regulators and policy-makers to trust competitive market forces—was developing more slowly than Unitil had anticipated. Unitil opted to act as an energy-procurement specialist; in March the company acquired a minority interest in Enermetrix.com, a Massachusetts-based technology company that had established a business conducting Internet-based energy-supply acquisitions for large gas consumers. Enermetrix.com also set up the country's first retail electricity transactions over the Internet.

In June 1999 Unitil launched Usource L.L.C. as a subsidiary of URI, its unregulated business unit. Usource ran on the transaction-based software and energy commodity Exchange (developed and licensed by Enermetrix.com.) and provided Internet-based energy procurement services to large commercial, industrial, and institutional customers throughout New York area and New England. Usource was launched in Philadelphia under the URL [www.phillyenergy.com]. Other customers soon included MI Energy, L.L.C., a consortium of many of the largest industrial firms in New York State, and the New York City Housing Authority.

For fiscal 1999, total operating revenues rose to $172.37 million, compared to $166.68 million in 1998. The 1999 diluted earnings per share were $1.74, compared to $1.72 in 1998. The small gain was a major achievement, considering Unitil's transition into an unregulated market, New England's third consecutive warm winter, and severe summer storms—among other challenges. At the beginning of a new millennium, Unitil Corporation stood out as one of a small number of utility companies capable of repositioning its business to prosper in a changing marketplace.

Historically, innovation came from entrepreneurs and small companies that prospered by challenging the "bigger is better" conventional wisdom: it was relatively easier for small entities to be swift and nimble enough to capitalize on emerging trends. Unitil was one of the swift and nimble small companies sensitive to a quickly changing market. As Unitil Chairman and Chief Executive Officer Robert B. Schoenberger said in the company's *1999 Annual Report*, Unitil Corporation had positioned itself "to take advantage of the far-reaching changes in one of the largest industry sectors of our national economy." The company's future was bright with opportunities—and Unitil was ready to capitalize on them.

### *Principal Subsidiaries*

Concord Electric Company; Exeter & Hampton Electric Company;Fitchburg Gas and Electric Light Company; Unitil Power Corp.; Unitil Realty Corp.; Unitil Service Corp.; Unitil Resources, Inc.; Usource L.L.C.

### *Principal Competitors*

Bangor Hydro-Electric Company; CMP Group Inc.; National Grid USA; Northeast Utilities; NSTAR.

### *Further Reading*

Donker, Peter P., "Unitil Buys Into Internet Electronic Auction Firm," *Telegram & Gazette* (Worcester, Mass.), March 31, 1999.

"FlexFinancials Powers Unitil," *Institute of Management Accountants*, December 1998.

Kalt, Joseph P., and Frank C. Schuller, eds., *Drawing the Line on Natural Gas Regulation: The Harvard Study on the Future of Natural Gas*, Westport, Conn.: Greenwood Publishing Group, Inc.

Lyons, Barry, "How the Concord Monitor Selected an Electric Supplier: A Strategy for Dealing With Competition," *Business & Industry Association [Forum] of New Hampshire*, 1998.

McLean, Bethany, "Still Think Utility Stocks Mean Worry-Free Dividends? Not Anymore. Deregulation Means Figuring Out Which ones Will Fade—and Which will Surge, Here's How," *Fortune*, September 29, 1997.

Oprea, Ryan, "Electric Visions: Unleashing the Market for Power," *Reason*, January 2000.

—Gloria A. Lemieux

# Valassis Communications, Inc.

19975 Victor Parkway
Livonia, Michigan 48152
U.S.A.
Telephone: (734) 591-3000
Toll Free: (800) 437-0479
Fax: (734) 591-4994
Web site: http://www.valassis.com

*Public Company*
*Incorporated:* 1992
*Employees:* 1,679
*Sales:* $794.6 million
*Stock Exchanges:* New York
*Ticker Symbol:* VCI
*NAIC:* 323110 Commercial Lithographic Printing

Valassis Communications, Inc. is a relatively young corporation, but it has the distinction of having created the industry of freestanding inserts, the four-color coupon booklets distributed in newspapers. The company's coupons are added mechanically to papers throughout the week, but are carried most prominently in Sunday newspapers, where as many as a dozen separate inserts are common. These appear in single or multiple folded sheets, printed in full color. As the first and largest company in the business, Valassis controls nearly half of the freestanding insert market. Valassis coupons are distributed to more than 60 million American households in more than 530 different newspapers. Three-fourths of its income comes from this area. The company also produces specialized promotional materials and has stakes in firms that provide Web-based coupon distribution, data warehousing, and direct mail advertising services.

### Beginnings

The company had its origin in 1969, when George Valassis opened a small sales agency in his home in suburban Detroit. He handled contract printing for numerous products, including computerized form letters. After purchasing his own printing press in 1971, however, he found it difficult to keep the machine in operation due to a lack of business.

In 1972, Valassis decided to solicit coupon advertising from a variety of retail product companies. After locating merchandisers who wished to promote their products with cents-off coupons, he then printed the coupons and purchased distribution arrangements with local newspaper publishers that would insert the coupon sheets in their papers. The business proved to be highly successful, as product manufacturers discovered the advantages of cooperative coupon advertising. The inserts were effective at enticing consumers to try virtually any product and, unlike advertising, their influence on buying patterns was highly measurable.

The inserts developed by Valassis were freestanding sheets containing bold four-color promotions. Because each sheet could be divided into 8, 10, 16, and even 24 or more different coupons, each a small advertisement, Valassis could piggyback several different companies' promotions on the same printing. This created a need to assign coupon spots carefully, since competing colas or brands of raisin bran, for example, could not be satisfactorily run on the same page. Valassis's solution was to encourage large manufacturers to purchase several coupon spots at once. These companies would place coupons for several nonrelated products, from breakfast cereal to cleanser, thereby creating demand for additional sheets from competitors.

Valassis immediately won business from companies such as General Foods, Procter & Gamble, General Mills, Nabisco, and Kellogg, but, still unable to purchase newspaper distribution rights on an efficient scale, the company lost money for several years as it pioneered a path in the new industry. Undeterred, George Valassis purchased additional printing machinery and increased his sales and production staff to 46 employees. By 1974, circulation of his freestanding inserts had grown to 25 million households on sales of $5.7 million. Finally, in 1976, with virtually the same circulation, sales rose to $11.8 million, nearly double the 1974 circulation. This confirmed to Valassis that manufacturers placed a high value on coupon advertising and encouraged him to continue efforts to expand the business.

## Company Perspectives:

*Our vision is to be the world's leader in the marketing services industry. This means we will provide our customers with proven, effective solutions to a wide range of marketing challenges. This also means listening to their need and creating solutions where they currently don't exist. We want to partner with our customers to help them grow their businesses. Our vision will be achieved through the efforts of the people working at our company. We will strive to provide our employees with fulfilling career opportunities, listen to their suggestions, and recognize their accomplishments. We believe that if we focus on our customers and value our people, our shareholders will benefit from growth in their investments.*

### Upgrading and Expanding in the Late 1970s and Early 1980s

He began replacing his older equipment with newer, state-of-the-art machinery that featured added functionality. This included large, eight-page inserts and an oversized "super page." To house the operation, Valassis purchased a new production facility at Livonia, in west suburban Detroit. With sales growth at nearly 40 percent per year, Valassis marked sales of $23.5 million on a circulation of 27.8 million in 1978, and $33.7 million in sales on a circulation of 30 million a year later.

The company's employee roll grew to 193 people in 1979, and additions to staff included a young marketing manager from Procter & Gamble named Dave Brandon. Brandon, who played football at the University of Michigan, found employment at Procter & Gamble after graduation through a recommendation from coach Bo Schembechler. Brandon remained in touch with a former teammate, Larry Johnson, who joined Valassis after marrying George Valassis's daughter. Brandon brought to Valassis a powerful personal style. Although he began in the company performing some low-priority jobs, his potential was quickly appreciated. As he ascended to higher levels of management, he developed an open, folksy style within the company, giving personal attention to the human, as well as the business, aspects of Valassis. This atmosphere later won Valassis inclusion in a publication that identifies the best 100 companies for which to work. One component of that atmosphere is an across-the-board employee profit-sharing plan that can augment annual salaries by as much as 15 percent.

By 1982 circulation had grown to 38 million (50 percent more than in 1977) and sales had increased to more than $90 million, representing a fivefold increase over the period. This expansion led Valassis to build a second plant at Durham, North Carolina, in 1983, which would enable the company to more easily distribute its materials in southeastern markets. The following year, a third plant was established in Wichita, Kansas.

With the expansion of printing capacity, Valassis's sales more than doubled in 1984, to $200 million. Now in a position to consolidate its market, Valassis bought out its largest competitor, Newspaper Co-op Couponing (NCC). In an effort to streamline operations, Valassis dissolved NCC's freestanding insert operation and added two new printed promotional products to the operation. Nearing saturation of the freestanding insert business, in large part as a result of good expansion and a rise of upstart competitors, Valassis began run-of-press advertising, in which coupon space is reserved on pages of the newspaper itself. The primary market for run-of-press coupons was the typical weekly food section of daily newspapers, again featuring cents-off coupons for a variety of products.

A second extension was specialty printing, including production of brochures, catalogs, posters, and magazine inserts that concentrated on food service and fast food promotions. More sophisticated specialty printing included scratch and sniff and lottery-style rub-off contests. Primary customers included Pizza Hut, Arby's, McDonald's, and Lens Crafters.

Run-of-press and specialty printing were aggressively promoted as complements to the standard freestanding insert promotion. The success of the formula also propelled Valassis into a new function, that of promotional consultant. Now advertisers could retain Valassis much as they did ad agencies or public relations firms and receive advice on specific campaigns.

### Acquisition by Consolidated Press Holdings in 1986

The consolidation of NCC also made Valassis an attractive takeover target. With an extremely strong record of sales growth and a favorable position in a market that included competition only from much smaller companies that lacked the finances of a larger operation, Valassis was discovered by Kerry Packer, chair of Consolidated Press Holdings, an Australian publishing conglomerate. The Australian publishing industry, dominated by a handful of media barons, had been exhausted of virtually all of its independents. With few investment opportunities in Australia, Packer and other barons such as Rupert Murdoch and Robert Holmes à Court began shopping for deals in the American and British markets. The acquisition of Valassis in 1986 represented an unusual departure for Packer, who had confined his takeovers mostly to magazines and other periodicals. Rupert Murdoch's company, News Corp, was evidently on the same track as Packer. Valassis's principal competitor in the freestanding insert market in the early 1990s was News America, a subsidiary of News Corp.

After the takeover by Consolidated Press Holdings, George Valassis left the company for retirement. His company, however, benefited from numerous press arrangements made possible by its association with Packer. Sales increased by nearly $100 million by 1987, to $381 million. Packer placed David Brandon in charge of Valassis. The arrangement, in which Packer maintained a hands-off approach from 12,000 miles away, suited Brandon well. He maintained his folksy style, insisting on personally meeting each new hire. But with the added responsibility came larger compensation. When the private Mr. Brandon's million-dollar-plus salary became known, his relationship with employees suffered somewhat.

Brandon kept Valassis on track and ensured that all sales and growth targets were met. For the most part, this kept Packer content and in Australia, but by 1992, Packer decided the time was ripe to reap the benefit of his investment in Valassis. In March of that year, he engineered the sale of 51 percent of the

## Key Dates:

**1969:** George Valassis founds a small printing sales agency in a suburb of Detroit.

**1972:** Valassis introduces first "freestanding inserts" of newspaper ads.

**1970s:** Company grows with success of inserts, moves operations to Livonia, Michigan.

**1982:** Durham, North Carolina plant is opened.

**1983:** A Wichita, Kansas facility is added.

**1986:** Acquisition of Newspaper Co-Op Couponing; Kerry Packer buys Valassis.

**1989:** Valassis Impact Productions is formed to produce specialized promotional items.

**1992:** Valassis goes public on the New York Stock Exchange.

**1995:** Purchase of Canadian marketing company McIntyre & Dodd.

**1997:** Packer sells his stake in Valassis; new corporate headquarters is completed.

**1999:** Valassis begins investing in companies that distribute coupons on the Internet.

company's shares to the public. More than 22 million shares were issued through the New York Stock Exchange, yielding Packer's Consolidated Press Holdings a profit of about $900 million. The company continued to trade publicly, but was dominated by Consolidated's 49 percent interest.

Meanwhile, Valassis's business continued to expand. Because more than three-quarters of American households used coupons, they were proven sales aids. In Brandon's words, Valassis's coupon business is analogous to printing money. "We bring it to your home and lay it on your doorstep and say 'use whatever you will.' " But manufacturers' customers are always retailers, rather than consumers. Retail grocery stores stock, on average, 18,000 items, all of which compete for shelf space. As the coupons drive up consumer demand for a product, retailers are "pushed" into distributing—and giving favorable shelf display—to that product.

In 1995 Valassis acquired McIntyre & Dodd, a Canadian company that produced freestanding inserts and sold mail-order gifts. It was subsequently renamed Valassis of Canada. Two years later Valassis's new corporate headquarters in Livonia was completed. The building featured a gym, salon, cafeteria, and in-house physician, keeping intact the company's commitment to its employees' well-being. Also that year Kerry Packer sold his shares of the company, and Valassis's Mexican operations and a French joint venture were shuttered.

CEO David Brandon stepped down in 1998 to make way for Alan F. Schultz, who had been serving as executive vice-president and chief operating officer. Under his leadership Valassis began to invest in a variety of new ventures. In 1999 the company purchased a majority stake in Independent Delivery Services, Inc., a provider of home-shopping software products for supermarkets. Valassis also bought 30 percent of Relationship Marketing Group, Inc., a company that utilized retailers'

frequent shopper card data to send direct mail offers to consumers. Late in the year the company restructured its Canadian operations, eliminating mail-order subsidiary Carole Martin Gifts due to poor performance.

Valassis also entered the world of cyberspace in 1999. An investment in Merge, LLC, subsequently renamed Save.com, gave the company a 52 percent stake in an online coupon distributor. In October Net's Best LLC, an Internet marketing company, was acquired. This was followed in 2000 by the purchase of a minority stake in Coupons.com, which offered coupons on-line. Save.com also purchased MyCoupons.com and Direct Coupons.com, further expanding the company's presence on the Internet. CEO Schultz described Valassis's intentions as follows: "Valassis will be the leader in online promotions."

In August of 2000 the company's Valassis Data Management subsidiary acquired 80 percent of PreVision Marketing, Inc. for $30 million plus 145,000 shares of stock. PreVision was a Massachusetts-based customer relationship management firm. Valassis was also actively buying back its stock, announcing that it would devote half of its free cash to this purpose.

At the start of the 21st century, Valassis remained the pioneer and leader in its field, annually printing inserts containing more than 300 billion money-saving coupons. In addition to providing insert and other promotional printing, Valassis offered a range of value-added services in the marketing area, including promotion consulting, design services, sweepstakes planning, and industry research. Valassis was also one of the nation's largest purchasers of newspaper space, maintaining its dominant position in the market through long-standing relationships with publishers, who frequently gave volume discounts. Looking to the future, the company had begun making investments in technologies that complemented, and looked beyond, its print-based products.

### Principal Subsidiaries

VCI Enterprises, Inc.; Valassis International, Inc.; Promotion Watch, Inc.; VCI Electronic Commerce, Inc.; Valassis Retail Connection, Inc.; VCI Direct Mail, Inc.; Valassis Data Management, Inc.; Save.com (52%).

### Principal Divisions

Valassis FSI; Valassis Impact Promotions; Valassis Sampling; ROP Solutions; Valassis of Canada; Promotion Watch.

### Principal Competitors

ACG Holdings, Inc.; Acxiom Corporation; ADVO, Inc.; Big Flower Holdings, Inc.; Catalina Marketing Corporation; Grey Global Group, Inc.; Harte-Hanks, Inc.; Mosaic Group, Inc.; The News Corporation, Ltd.; Norwood Promotional Products, Inc.; Outlook Group Corporation; Quebecor, Inc.; Queens Group, Inc.; R.R. Donnelley & Sons Company; Snyder Communications, Inc.; SPAR Group, Inc.

### *Further Reading*

Adams, Cheryl, "King of Coupons," *Printing Impressions,* April 1, 2000, p. 26.

Gallagher, Kathleen, "Multiyear Contracts Provide Marketer with Growth Potential, Analyst Says," *Milwaukee Journal-Sentinel,* June 6, 1999, p. 3.

Gargaro, Paul, "After a Great Quarter, Valassis Wants Growth," *Crain's Detroit Business,* August 24, 1998, p. 3.

Hunter, George, "Valassis Ready to Roll: Pennies Add Up for Livonia Coupon Company," *Detroit News,* May 29, 1997, p. D1.

Keeton, Ann, "Valassis Sees $1 Billion Internet Opportunity," *Dow Jones News Service,* May 12, 1999.

Markiewicz, David A., "Clip Job," *Detroit News,* March 14, 1993.

Pachuta, Michael J., "Valassis Looks for New Ways to Stuff Bargains into Papers," *Investor's Business Daily,* May 27, 1997, p. B12.

Palm, Kristin, "Perks (and Pooches) Can Help Keep Your Employees in Place," *Crain's Detroit Business,* May 24, 1999, p. E-19.

Roush, Matt, "Don't Discount Valassis," *Crain's Detroit Business,* February 19, 1996, p. 2.

——, "Valassis Takes a Clipping: But Analysts Expect '97 to Be a Cut Above," *Crain's Detroit Business,* February 3, 1997, p. 2.

Stoffer, Jason, "Valassis Communications, Inc.," *Crain's Detroit Business,* September 6, 1999, p. 18.

"Valassis Communications," *The 100 Best Companies to Work for in America,* 1992.

"Valassis Communications, Inc.: Leading the Way," Livonia, Mich.: Valassis Communications, Inc.

—John Simley
—updated by Frank Uhle

# Viessmann Werke GmbH & Co.

Viessmannstrasse 1
D-35108 Allendorf
Germany
Telephone: (49) (6452) 70-0
Fax: (49) (6452) 70-2780
Web site: http://www.viessmann.de

*Private Company*
*Incorporated:* 1917 as Johann Viessmann, Hof
*Employees:* 6,700
*Sales:* DM 1.7 billion ($867 million) (1999)
*NAIC:* 333414 Heating Equipment (Except Warm Air
Furnaces) Manufacturing; 333415 Air-Conditioning
and Warm Air Heating Equipment and Commercial
and Industrial Refrigeration Equipment Manufac-
turing; 22133 Steam and Air-Conditioning Supply

Viessmann Werke GmbH & Co., based in Allendorf, Germany, is one of the world's leading manufacturers of furnaces,
boilers, and heating systems and equipment. In Germany
Viessmann leads the market of ground-based furnaces with a
share of about 38 percent, while it maintains a market share
between 10 and 20 percent for wall-based heaters. Viessmann
has 11 production facilities in Germany and abroad, and 22
foreign subsidiaries. About one-third of Viessmann's sales
come from exports, and ten percent of export sales are generated in Eastern Europe. Viessmann products are also manufactured under license agreements in Japan and Korea.

### Viessmann Origins in 1917

The founder of the Viessmann Werke, Johann Viessmann,
was born in 1879 in the German town of Kulmbach. He worked
there as a master locksmith until World War I. Thereafter, he set
up his own small locksmith business in Hof on the river Saale.
At first Viessmann's business concentrated on repairing farm
machinery. However, he didn't hesitate to help when a machine
in a local textile factory broke down or when one of the early
automobiles, fashionable but sensitive, didn't run the way it was
supposed to. Possessing a creative mind, Viessmann also invented new machinery, such as vulcanizing chambers for the
re-treading of old tires and automatic targets for himself and
other members of his gun club.

Inspired by suggestions from local gardeners Johann
Viessmann started building furnaces in 1928. At that time most
furnaces were made from cast iron. Recognizing the potential
for improvement of the prevailing technology Viessmann developed a new generation of furnaces. Sturdy steel pipes were
welded together, giving overall construction much more stability under pressure. Viessmann's furnaces also used less fuel and
produced heat more quickly than other models. Within a short
period of time, Viessmann had begun manufacturing these new
furnaces in his own workshop. Because of their cost-saving
advantages, they became popular among greenhouse farms in
and around Hof as well as in nearby Leipzig.

During the 1930s central heating systems became a dominant technology and the market for furnaces was constantly
expanding. At the same time electrical welding technology
increased the speed and quality of their manufacture.
Viessmann began experimenting again and developed a new
furnace design whereby steel pipes were replaced by sheet
metal. The new design allowed him to build furnaces which
were smaller but still effective and economical. Viessmann was
also able to customize his furnaces for certain industries. For
restaurants he designed a very cost-effective warm water circulating heating system with heating pipes mounted along the
walls under the benches on which people sat, rather than under
the windows. For a shoe factory, Viessmann built combined
furnaces in which coke as well as leather, paper, and carton
waste from the factory could be used as a fuel. For public
buildings, factories, and residential buildings, Viessmann developed special low-pressure steam furnaces. He received patents for his inventions and worked with a sub-contractor based
on a license agreement for a while. However, in 1937 he moved
his business to Allendorf on the river Eder, where he set up a
new factory with 30 employees.

### Son of Founder Takes Over in 1947

During World War II, Viessmann Werke continued to produce steel furnaces for the German war economy. Hans

411

## Company Perspectives:

*Within our company we see strengthening the self-reliance of our employees as a major task. ... With the help of suitable measures of human resources development our employees will become entrepreneurs. That is the only way besides utilizing the full market potential to achieve the increase of efficiency that is crucial for a positive and sustainable development of the company in the future. Facing fierce competition and increasing price pressure we are forced to boost our productivity.*

Viessmann, the son of the company's founder, served as a soldier in Greece. However, in his spare time he took law classes at the Athens University and designed new furnace models. In 1945 after Germany's defeat, he came back home with a thick folder full of drawings, plans, and ideas. Two years later Hans Viessmann took over the family business from his father. It employed 35 people at that time. At first, the younger Viessmann focused on modernizing the production facilities to enable substantial growth and on new product development. By 1949 the number of employees at the Viessmann Werke had almost tripled.

The German economic boom of the 1950s created an expanding market for heating systems. At the same time, as Europe was flooded with less expensive Arab oil that started replacing coal and especially coke as a fuel, the industry underwent a substantial change. Oil, in turn, spurred the development of new technologies which allowed for fully automated heating systems based on circulating warm water. Their low maintenance contributed greatly to the growing popularity of these heating systems in all kinds of buildings. Viessmann responded with the development of oil-based furnaces. However, the company also pioneered another technology that enabled the system to be converted from coke to oil with very little effort. The innovative Viessmann Triola furnace was presented at the Hannover Trade Fair in 1957. The new model also contained a powerful water boiler made out of copper pipes.

This new generation of Viessmann steel furnaces was eventually able to gain considerable market share in comparison with the traditional cast-iron models. The optimal design, and the possibility of including an appliance for heating water in particular, won the acceptance of many customers. Automated heating systems based on burning oil also required the development of new automated control systems which Viessmann Werke added to its product range. At the end of the 1950s, the company employed about 350 people and produced 5,000 furnaces annually.

### Viessmann Heating Technology in the 1960s

In the 1960s oil and gas replaced coal as primary fuel on a large scale. The use of oil to heat residential buildings increased from 15 percent in 1960 to 45 percent at the end of the decade. In big cities, in particular, gas generated as a byproduct of making coke from coal—so called *Stadtgas*—became more and more important for central heating systems. Viessmann's

new furnaces—Imperator-Duo and Imperator-Triola—were in high demand. To keep up with production, welders were replaced by automated production systems at the company's manufacturing facilities.

Another development of the 1960s was a new generation of heating systems for tap water. The older systems collected deposits of calcium in their pipelines which couldn't be cleaned without chemicals and which therefore had to be replaced periodically. In 1962 Viessmann introduced a new system that used pipelines made from nickel-bronze which could be cleaned mechanically.

In 1965 Viessmann used that same material for its water boilers that were built into furnaces, to protect them from corrosion as well. Due to the decreasing demand for furnaces that could be run with coke Viessmann developed a new product generation that was solely based on the use of oil or gas— the Parola series. The new design was optimized for low emissions and high energy-efficiency, and the water boiler was placed on the bottom of the furnace instead of on top. The Viessmann product range of the 1960s also included a new range of control systems called 4-Way-Mixers. The new systems included electrical regulation of the furnace based on room or outside temperature along with electronic systems that lowered the temperature automatically at night.

In the late 1960s Viessmann's annual output amounted to 40,000 furnaces per year, while its work force had increased to 1,400. In 1969 a new production facility was erected in Battenberg, Germany. By the end of the 1960s, steel furnaces, with a market share of 65 percent in Germany, had successfully defeated cast-iron furnaces.

### Oil Crisis and Expansion in the 1970s

In winter 1973 a sudden increase in oil prices shocked the world economies and caused crises in many countries. For the first time in 30 years, world energy consumption dropped. Like many countries, Germany reacted with special programs to cut energy use. At the same time, legislation was passed to limit environmental pollution. The two most important laws—the Bundes-Immissionsschutz-Gesetz of 1974 and the Energie-Einsparungsgesetz of 1976—had a direct impact on the demand for heating systems. One resulting trend was toward the increasing use of natural gas. Within a decade, the market share of natural gas as a primary energy source almost tripled, from 8 percent up to 22 percent by the end of the 1970s. German municipal heating systems were switched over to natural gas because that fuel was less harmful to the environment than the *Stadtgas* produced from coal.

Despite the oil crisis, the 1970s marked a decade of significant expansion for Viessmann. In Germany new production facilities started operation in Oberkotzkau and Unterkotzkau, near Hof, with metal and other materials processing, furnace production, and assembly units put into operation. Existing factories in Battenberg and Allendorf were modernized and enlarged. Other production sites were taken over in Hamburg and Berlin. An important step for Viessmann was the acquisition of the foundry Weso-Aurorahütte. In 1972 the first Viessmann production plant outside Germany was opened in

Faulquemont, France; the first Viessmann subsidiary outside Europe was established in Waterloo, Canada, in 1978.

One of Viessmann's strategies for coping with the structural changes in the energy market was new product development. In 1972 the company presented the world's first furnace made from stainless steel. The novelty had several advantages in comparison to other models. It was lighter than other furnaces; it was highly effective in terms of the ratio of fuel input and heat output; it was easy to clean; and it contained a larger water boiler. The innovation was successful and Viessmann began using stainless steel on a broad scale in its heating technology products. The oil crisis of 1973 spurred research and development on the energy efficiency of furnaces. As a result, Viessmann introduced two new furnace models both of which were able to use either oil or gas as fuel. One of them—the symmetrical Rotola model—was the first furnace that could be turned upside down to be used as an upper or lower hot water tank. Beginning in 1976 Viessmann started making solar energy collectors as an alternative to conventional heating technology. Two years later, the company introduced its first heat pump and the first microprocessor-based control systems. A significant innovation of the late 1970s was the introduction of new low-temperature water-based heating systems. Instead of keeping a constantly high water temperature of about 70 degree Celsius, the new technology allowed for adjusting the temperature according to current needs. The water temperature could be as low as 40 degrees Celsius, which saved about 30 to 40 percent of the energy used by the older heating systems.

### Environmentally Friendly in the 1980s

Growing concerns about the greenhouse effect and the possibility of a significant climate change caused by burning fossil fuels influenced the heating system industry in the 1980s. Viessmann responded with a low-temperature furnace that was very energy-efficient. The Vitola series used a combination of two heating surfaces that were linked together. More than one million of the two models—Vitola-biferral with a combined cast-iron and steel heater and Vitola-uniferral with a steel-steel heating surface—were sold during the 1980s. Beginning in 1984 the new technology was also used in furnaces with a higher performance of between 70 and 5900 kilowatts (kW). In 1989 Viessmann introduced the Paromat-Triplex model, the first furnace with three combined heating surfaces.

To reduce environmental pollution Viessmann also developed new burner-systems, after research had shown that an optimal combination of furnaces and burners had a great impact on emissions of pollutants. Beginning in 1981 Viessmann Vitola furnaces were equipped with a Unit-oil-burner that was pretested and preset for best results. In 1984 Viessmann used the results of research done in the United States to develop the Renox-System, which achieved lower nitric oxide emissions through cooling the burning flames. The technology was soon adopted by other leading European manufacturers of heating systems.

Another trend of the 1980s in heating technology was the replacement of electronic control systems with digital ones. The main feature of the new systems was self-diagnostic systems and the ability to communicate with other control systems. With these features, it was possible to directly control heating systems that were connected to a furnace. Viessmann introduced two of these control systems, the Viessmann Trimatik-MC in 1988 and the Dekamatik system in 1990.

In 1989 company CEO Dr. Hans Viessmann was named a Fellow of the American Society of Heating, Refrigerating and Air-Conditioning Engineers (ASHRAE), a membership grade that recognized distinction in the arts and sciences of environmental technology. At that time Hans Vießmann held 62 German patents, five U.S. patents, six Canadian patents, and 75 patents in other countries. Of more than 50,000 ASHRAE members throughout the world, only about 400 held Fellow ASHRAE honors at that time.

### International Expansion and a Lawsuit in the 1990s

The year 1991 marked one of the best years for German producers of heating systems. The major reasons were the construction boom caused by the German reunification, along with a new law linking a tax break to the modernization of buildings that would go into effect at the end of the year. Viessmann's sales in that year jumped to DM 1.8 billion, DM 700 million more than in the year before. However, after that the market normalized again.

In January 1993 Martin Viessmann, son of Hans Viessmann, took over the family company as CEO. He had received his Ph.D. for a dissertation on the adjustment of corporate strategy and culture, and at Viessmann he made it a priority to improve communication among employees on all levels.

In 1995 the German market for furnaces shrank by 15 to 20 percent, caused partly by a slump in the construction industry. Competition in Germany turned fierce, and Viessmann decided to focus more on markets abroad. By that time, Viessmann's main foreign markets were in France, Austria, Belgium, Switzerland, and Italy. In addition to its Canadian subsidiary, the company had established another one in the United States, in Warwick, Rhode Island, in the early 1990s. Eastern Europe was a high priority for Viessmann because it promised high growth potential and low production cost. In 1994 the company was planning to build a production facility in the Czech Republic where production costs were DM 3 an hour compared with DM 43 in Germany. The plan threatened many of Viessmann's German jobs. When German Viessmann workers agreed to work three hours more per week without any extra compensation in spring 1996, the company dropped its plans to move. However, the most powerful German union, IG Metall, sued Viessmann for breaching the agreement that had been worked out between the union and the industry. In September 1997 the Landesarbeitsgericht in Frankfurt/Main ruled that both parties should negotiate a special complementary contract, which was finalized in March 1998.

Another strategic market for Viessmann was Poland, where in 1991 the company had established a subsidiary in Breslau. By 1998 Viessmann employed over 100 people in five Polish sales offices. In the same year new subsidiaries were opened in Moscow, Russia, and Bejing, China. As a result, Viessmann's export sales grew by 12 percent in 1998 and reached one-third of total sales.

### Principal Subsidiaries

Viessmann Belgium B.v.b.a.; Viessmann China Ltd.; Viessmann A/S (Denmark); Viessmann S.A. (France); Viessmann Ltd. (United Kingdom); Viessmann S.r.l. (Italy); Viessmann Manufacturing Company Inc. (Canada); Viessmann Manufacturing Co. (United States) Inc.; Viessmann Hrvatska d.o.o. (Kroatia); Viessmann Nederland B.V.; Viessmann Ges.m.b.H. (Austria); Viessmann Sp.z o.o (Poland); Viessmann SRL (Rumania); Viessmann OOO (Russia); Viessmann Värmeteknik AB (Sweden); Viessmann (Schweiz) AG (Switzerland); Viessmann s.r.o. (Slovakia); Viessmann d.o.o. (Slovenia); Viessmann SL (Spain); Viessmann Spol.s r.o. (Czech Republic); Viessmann Isi Teknikleri Ticaret A.S. (Turkey); Viessmann Fütéstechnika Kft. (Hungary).

### Principal Competitors

Vaillant Corp.; Buderus AG.

### Further Reading

"ASHRAE Honors 18 New Fellow Members," *Air Conditioning, Heating & Refrigeration News*, February 20, 1989, p. 40.

"Berichte von der ISH '93 Frankfurt: Nach dem Ausnahmejahr wieder ein normaler Heizungsmarkt," *Frankfurter Allgemeine Zeitung*, March 26, 1993, p. 20.

"Das Unternehmergespräch," *Frankfurter Allgemeine Zeitung*, January 9, 1995, p.12.

"Viessmann baut ein Werk in Tschechien," *Frankfurter Allgemeine Zeitung*, December 14, 1995, p. 22.

"Viessmann beklagt fehlende Impulse für Heizungsmodernisierung," *Frankfurter Allgemeine Zeitung*, March 25, 1999, p. 25.

*Viessmann Chronik: 75 Jahre Viessmann Werke, 1917–1992*, Allendorf, Germany: Viessmann Werke GmbH & Co., 1992, 16 p.

"Viessmann investiert in Polen," *Frankfurter Allgemeine Zeitung*, May 5, 1998, p. 28.

"Viessmann und die IG Metall einigen sich gütlich," *Frankfurter Allgemeine Zeitung*, March 18, 1998, p.17.

—Evelyn Hauser

# Villeroy & Boch
## 1748
# Villeroy & Boch AG

Postfach 11 20, D-66688 Mettlach
Germany
Telephone: (49) (6864) 81-1293
Fax: (49) (6864) 81-2692
Web site: http://www.villeroy-boch.com

*Public Company*
*Incorporated:* 1836
*Employees:* 9,818
*Sales:* DM 1.63 billion (1999)
*Stock Exchanges:* Frankfurt
*Ticker Symbol:* VIB3
*NAIC:* 327212 Other Pressed and Blown Glass and
   Glassware Manufacturing; 327122 Ceramic Wall and
   Floor Tile Manufacturing; 327111 Vitreous China
   Plumbing Fixture and China and Earthenware
   Bathroom Accessories Manufacturing; 327112
   Vitreous China

Villeroy & Boch AG has been one of Europe's top names in household and architectural ceramic goods for more than 250 years. The company's three divisions produce goods in 36 plants in 20 countries. The tile division produces ceramic tile for floors and walls, with an annual output of nearly 25 million square meters of tile. The bathroom and kitchen division manufactures high-quality ceramic plumbing fixtures, such as sinks, bathtubs, and toilets. The tableware division produces a broad line of dishes. Its DM 1.63 billion in 1999 sales represented an increase of eight percent over 1998, and the first half of 2000 saw a 15 percent rise over the same period a year earlier. The company made more than 87 percent of its 1999 sales in the European market, and nearly half of those were in Germany, where the company brand has established a strong presence. According to a study by Gruner + Jahr, out of 325 brands of household goods, Villeroy & Boch had the fifth-highest name recognition among German consumers. Nonetheless, the company sees itself not so much as a brand manufacturer, but as a "lifestyle supplier," a "seller of ideas" for stylishly furnished

bathrooms, for beautifully laid tables, and accessories used elsewhere in the house.

### 18th-Century Origins in Ceramic Tableware

Villeroy & Boch's beginnings date back to the summer of 1748 when François Boch, an iron founder in the village of Audun-le-Tiche in Lorraine, began manufacturing ceramic dishes. Until that time almost all the porcelain in Europe originated in the Far East and sold for prices only the wealthy could afford. Boch's dishes cost significantly less than that produced in China and Japan, but was also of such high quality that his reputation soon spread through the surrounding regions and into Luxembourg. So successful did his business become that, in addition to his three sons, he was able to hire six other villagers. Perhaps out of gratitude, the village elected him mayor.

In 1766, Boch received a license from the Austrian empress, Maria Theresa, to build a new earthenware factory in Septfontaines in Luxembourg, call it the "Imperial and Royal Manufactory," and display the imperial coat of arms. Boch worked at improving the quality of the ceramics at his new facility and introduced various innovative cost-cutting measures, including primitive mass production and more energy-efficient kilns. By the end of the 18th century the Septfontaines factory employed some 300 workers. Much of the factory was destroyed in 1794 by troops of the French Revolution. Within a few years, however, the youngest Boch son, Pierre-Joseph Boch, had returned and rebuilt the factory. In the wake of the revolution, few people could afford the ceramic dishes. However, the demand for Boch ceramics rose rapidly after Napoleon closed continental European markets to popular English porcelain.

Pierre-Joseph Boch was a highly talented artist who designed stunningly beautiful ceramic products for the Boch company. He was also a forward-looking businessman. In 1812, out of gratitude to the workers who had helped him rebuild his business—sometimes without pay—he instituted an early insurance program, which he named the Antonius Guild, after St. Anthony of Padua, the patron saint of potters. It included disability insurance, health insurance, a pension fund, even burial insurance. The Antonius Guild eventually became a

415

## Company Perspectives:

*Having been in existence for 250 years, Villeroy & Boch is one of the oldest industrial enterprises in Europe. Being totally devoted to ceramic, decisive technical achievements were made in this area which serve as an example for the whole branch of industry—from late baroque times up to the present day. There have always been different challenges, but principles have remained the same; principles which have ensured the continued existence of a family business to this very day namely, entrepreneurial flexibility, artistic expertise, technical innovation and social commitment. Over a period of 250 years eight generations of Villeroy & Boch families, as well as their employees, have worked to create a tradition of progress. They have always felt obliged to the people of their time. This support gives us, and generations to come, both the self-confidence and freedom to shape the future—every day.*

model for the social welfare programs inaugurated by German Chancellor Otto von Bismark at the end of the 19th century.

Jean-François Boch, Pierre-Joseph's son, invented techniques that revolutionized the production of ceramics. He built a state-of-the-art factory in an abandoned abbey he acquired in the town of Mettlach in the Saarland. It incorporated a kiln that burned coal instead of wood, and that ventilated the fumes in a way that enhanced the firing of the clay and burned off as many fumes as possible. He took advantage of the water power provided by a nearby brook. More importantly, he invented a pyrometer that enabled his craftsmen to regulate the temperature in the kiln—long a problem for European porcelain-makers. The process made it possible to achieve standardized high quality across different batches of ceramics. Mass production was also advanced by means of machines that automatically cut pieces of clay into uniform pieces that could then be assembled quickly into a particular design. In 1824, Jean-François Boch founded a copperplate-engraving studio in Mettlach. The method permitted both mass-producing of ceramic pieces, but also the pictorial designs on the ceramic, which previously had to be painted on by hand.

Another earthenware factory, which since 1798 had been owned and operated by Nicolas Villeroy, was producing ceramic ware in Wallerfangen, just a few miles from Boch's in Mettlach. Villeroy achieved much of his success by attracting the most talented ceramics specialists to his company, including English experts whom he found imprisoned in Napoleon's prisoner-of-war camps. But Villeroy could be as innovative as Boch: he had introduced coal-burning kilns even earlier than had Boch and was also experimenting with copperplate printing of designs. He established his own Antonius Guild five years after Boch. In 1836, faced with increasing competition from English porcelain manufacturers, Boch and Villeroy merged their businesses, a union that was made even stronger when Eugen Boch, Jean-François' son, married Nicolas Villeroy's granddaughter, Octavie. The first joint project of the new firm was the Cristallerie, a crystal manufacturing facility in the town of Wadgassen.

The company continued its innovations in tableware, developing new formulas and production processes for the ceramics. Earlier, in 1829, Jean-François Boch had developed feldspathic ware, a stoneware that used feldspath. Feldspathic ware had a brilliant whiteness similar to Chinese porcelain and was a remarkably strong, durable material. The company began to produce bone china at the Wallerfangen plant in 1847. Around the same time, it began experiments using color lithography to imprint patterns on china, and also shifted much of the tableware production to a new factory, more centrally located in the city of Dresden. Beginning operation in 1856, the new facility produced simple, everyday tableware that most families could afford, was of the highest quality. Although near important rivers, the Dresden factory also took advantage of the latest medium of transportation, the railroad. By 1900 it was the largest of all Villeroy & Boch's production facilities.

### New Products/Sales Organization Turns Company International

Under Eugen Boch, Villeroy & Boch developed new products and a sales and marketing organization that eventually extended across the globe. The company began to manufacture terra cotta ornamentation for buildings at Mettlach in 1856. Inspired by the discovery of well-preserved mosaic floors built by the ancient Romans, Boch developed architectural tiles that were durable, attractive, and could be mass-produced. He introduced them at a point of rapid, global urban growth. The new division was founded to produce architectural ceramics, and by the end of the 19th century, millions of square yards of the company's tiles had been used as ornamentation in churches, post offices, theaters, railway stations, official buildings, hospitals, and other buildings throughout the world. The company's most prestigious commission was to produce the tile floor for the newly completed Cologne Cathedral.

So successful were the tiles that throughout much of Europe the name *Mettlacher Platten*—or "tiles from Mettlach"—became a generic expression for any architectural ceramic tile, no matter who produced it. Villeroy & Boch had to build a separate factory, the first in Europe that specialized in tile production, in the late 1860s specifically to handle demand for the *Mettlacher Platten*. In addition to producing the actual tiles, Villeroy & Boch trained its own crews of tiling specialists who traveled worldwide to oversee installation. By 1870, Mettlach tiles accounted for a full 60 percent of the company's sales. By the end of the 1870s Villeroy & Boch was the most successful ceramics company in the world and employed nearly 7,000 workers.

Another area that became important for Villeroy & Boch was so-called hygienic ceramics. Until the 1900s, homes had a washstand that consisted of a washbasin, a jug, a soap dish, and a chamber pot, all made by hand. These products were made throughout the latter half of the 19th century at Villeroy & Boch's Dresden works. Around 1900, however, as indoor plumbing spread, the company developed a successful process that automated the production of hygienic ceramics. A mold filled with liquefied ceramic mass guaranteed the uniform thickness of finished product, permitting the precise control of the dimensions of bathtubs, toilets, and washbasins. Ceramic sanitary ware, which included household tiles for bathrooms and kitchens, became the third pillar in the Villeroy & Boch product

## Key Dates:

**1748:** François Boch begins manufacturing ceramic tableware

**1766:** Boch receives a license from the Austrian empress to build an earthenware factory in Septfontaines, Luxembourg.

**1795:** Nicolas Villeroy becomes sole owner of the Fabrique de Faïence in Wallerfangen.

**1812:** Pierre-Joseph Boch founds the Antonius Guild, an insurance program for his workers.

**1812:** Jean-François Boch starts work on a state-of-the-art ceramics factory in Mettlach in the Saarland.

**1824:** Jean-Francois Boch introduces copperplate engraving to print designs mechanically on ceramics.

**1836:** Jean-François Boch and Nicolas Villeroy merge their ceramics businesses into Villeroy & Boch.

**1869:** Villeroy & Boch begin operating the first factory that specializes in architectural tile.

**1892:** 84-year-old Eugen Boch is ennobled by the German emperor in recognition of his work as a businessman and philanthropist.

**1902:** Villeroy & Boch begin operating Europe's first gas-heated kiln at Mettlach.

**1918:** Company is divided among French, German, Polish, and Baltic state territory as a result of World War I surrender accords, leaving some factories without access to German markets and only two in German territory.

**1945:** Dresden factory is destroyed in bombing raids; occupying Russian forces dismantle other eastern facilities.

**1951:** Company establishes its first foreign subsidiary in Argentina.

**1982:** Previously autonomous product lines are established as company divisions.

**1987:** Villeroy & Boch converts from a family limited partnership into a public limited company.

**1990:** The company begins trading on the Frankfurt stock exchange.

line, with tableware and architectural tile. Within 20 years, they were being manufactured at three Villeroy & Boch locations, Wallerfangen, Merzig, and Dresden.

In 1902, Villeroy & Boch introduced a new concept in kiln design. First, the new ovens were heated by natural gas instead of coal. Second, several kilns were linked, forming a so-called "tunnel kiln." Materials moved on tracks through the series of kilns, being fired in the first, gradually cooling off in later kilns, and emerging completely cooled at the end of the line. Because kilns no longer had to be heated before goods could be inserted, nor completely cooled before they could be removed, the design lowered energy costs. The technology was so sophisticated that it remained in use until well into the 1980s.

The company was also a pioneer in worker safety. By the end of the 19th century, although lead was essential to ceramics production, the danger of lead poisoning was well known. At the impetus of René von Boch-Galhau, the son of the ennobled Eugen von Boch, fans, air humidifiers and dust extractors were installed in the company's factories. Workers could not take food in work areas and had to change clothes when they left work. Boch-Galhau also forbade the use of pure lead in company workshops, replacing it with the considerably less hazardous lead oxide. In the meantime, company scientists looked for safer substitutes.

The Boch family had highly refined aesthetic sensibilities. Eugen von Boch, as well as his niece Anna Boch and nephew Eugène Boch, were accomplished painters. They opened their company to the most advanced artists and designers of the day. Especially important to Villeroy & Boch was the concept of *Jugenstil*, a philosophy that even the most mundane objects—dishes, coffee cups—should be carefully and beautifully designed. Beginning in the late 19th century, the company commissioned leading *Jugenstil* artists, including Henry van der Velde, Peter Behrens, and Richard Riemerschmidt, to create washstand sets, tableware, and—most successfully—ornamental tiles. The designs were frequently far ahead of their time and, as a result, were not among the company's most popular products. Today, however, they are recognized as belonging to the most advance designs of Arts and Crafts school of artists. Later, in the early decades of the 20th century, the company offered a similar outlet to artists from the Bauhaus.

### War, the Great Depression, and the Rise of Nazism

When René von Boch-Galhau died in 1908, his company had reached a pinnacle of success. It operated a total of nine factories in Germany and Luxembourg, employed more than 8,000 workers, and made washbasins, bathtubs, ceramic tile for floors and walls, dishes, tiled stoves, decorative objects such as vases and flower pots, sewage pipes, terra cotta figures and architectural ornamentation—virtually everything that could be made of ceramics. The second decade of the 20th century, however, massively disrupted Villeroy & Boch, like much of the rest of the world, caught in World War I.

In 1912, a factory in the Black Forest town of Schramberg was forced to close so a state railway could be built across the land. During the war, Roger von Boch, one of the company's co-managers, was killed on the eastern front. When peace finally came at the end of 1918, the Saarland, site of two Villeroy & Boch factories, was ceded to France as part of the surrender. The Wallerfangen and Mettlach works no longer had access to important German markets, while the French ones were, as yet, relatively underdeveloped. Other factories were in territory taken over by Poland and the Baltic states—only two remained within the borders of Germany, a factory in Dresden and one in Lübeck-Dänischburg. Within two years, however, the company had built and begun operating new facilities in Bonn and Breslau. The Breslau site, in the countryside with considerable space to expand, was particularly promising.

The 1920s were a time of ups and downs for the company. The Saarland branch made steady inroads into French markets, and production at the Dresden plant rapidly returned to pre-war figures. However the highly charged political situation in which the company found itself after the war, with its facilities scattered among countries, led it to reorganize into two largely independent company groups. The facilities in Germany were organized into a public limited company, while those in the Saarland became a limited partnership.

The catastrophic inflation that hit Germany in the early 1920s resulted in a radical simplification of most Villeroy & Boch designs—to keep them affordable. In August 1921, company headquarters and the stoneware plant in Mettlach went up in flames. The Great Depression affected Villeroy & Boch as profoundly as it did the rest of the economy. In 1930, the Dresden factory was forced to closed down for months and reopened with a workforce reduced by 40 percent. The plants in Bonn and Wallerfangen closed in 1931.

The rise of the Nazis and the shift toward a war economy directly affected Villeroy & Boch. In the latter half of the 1930s, the government declared the company nonessential for the war effort and closed its factory in the Saarland—in the meantime returned to Germany through a popular plebiscite. When it resumed production in 1940, its product line was severely restricted to floor tiles and tableware of the most Spartan design. The war itself was catastrophic for the company. Its factories in eastern Germany were lost completely, either destroyed in Allied bombing raids or dismantled and shipped off to the Soviet Union by the Russian occupation forces.

After World War II, France once again took over the Saarland, cutting the company's headquarters in Mettlach off from the rest of Germany. Company head Luitwin von Boch, who was given political responsibilities by the Allies, worked at reducing tensions between Germans and the French occupation. He co-founded the bilingual French-German University of the Saarland, He also lobbied for the Europeanization of the Saarland—establishing it as an autonomous region that was neither French nor German. The movement was dashed when the area's population voted in 1955 to be German, but his efforts anticipated the more united Europe of the 1990s.

By the late 1940s, the company had resumed production of its three lines, tiles, tableware, and bathroom fixtures. It established its first foreign facilities in 1951 in Argentina and in 1959 in Canada. In 1972, after having run Villeroy & Boch for 40 years, Luitwin von Boch stepped down and turned the reins over to his son Luitwin Gisbert von Boch Galhau. The 1970s saw the company faced with increasing competition from abroad: mosaic tile produced in Japan and wall tile in Italy, for example. But Villeroy & Boch was able to start successfully cultivating foreign markets itself, in particular the Far East and North America.

As global markets evolved into new forms, however, it became obvious that Villeroy & Boch would have to adapt. In 1982 the company began a far-reaching reorganization. The three product lines, which had always been run as decentralized profit centers, were united as centrally managed company divisions: Tiles, Tableware, and Sanitary Ware. Three years later, in a more radical move, management of the company was broadened from a single general manager to a six-person executive board. An administrative oversight board was also founded that including outsiders as well as members of the Boch and Villeroy families—unprecedented in company history. In May 1987,

Villeroy & Boch was converted from a family limited partnership into a public limited company. In 1990 the company commenced trading on the Frankfurt stock exchange. In 1995 a family member once again assumed leadership of the company when Wendelin von Boch was appointed chairman of the executive board. As the 21st century began Villeroy and Boch operated 36 facilities in 20 countries in Europe, North America, Asia, and Australia.

### *Principal Divisions*

Tile Division; Bathroom and Kitchen Division; Tableware Division.

### *Principal Subsidiaries*

Fliesenhandel an der Cristallerie GmbH; Villeroy & Boch Creation GmbH; Villeroy & Boch S.A.S. (France); Boch Frères S.A.S. (France); Comar S.A. (France); Ceramica Ligure S.r.l. (Italy; 70%); Villeroy & Boch Ungarn Rt (Hungary; 99.78%); Das Bad Gesellschaft m.b.H. (Austria; 50%); S.C. Mondial S.A. (Romania; 99.04%); Villeroy & Boch (USA) Inc.; Villeroy & Boch S.à.r.l. (Luxembourg); Villeroy & Boch Arts de la Table S.A. (France); Villeroy & Boch Arti della Tavola (Italy); Villeroy & Boch CreaTable AG (Switzerland); Villeroy & Boch Sverige AB (Sweden); Villeroy & Boch Wooncultuur B.V. (Netherlands); Villeroy & Boch Tableware Ltd. (United States); Villeroy & Boch Tableware Ltd. (Canada); Villeroy & Boch Australia Pty. Ltd. (Australia); Villeroy & Boch Tableware (Far East) Ltd. (China); Villeroy & Boch Tableware Japan K.K.; Ucosan Holding B.V. (Netherlands); S.D.P.C. S.A. (France); Villeroy & Boch United Kingdom Ltd.; Villeroy & Boch Hogar S.L. (Spain); Villeroy & Boch Austria Handelsgesellschaft m.b.H.; Villeroy & Boch Denmark A/S (Denmark); Villeroy & Boch Belgium S.A.

### *Principal Competitors*

Waterford Wedgwood plc; Rosenthal AG; Porzellanfabrik Schönwald; Hutschenreuther AG; Porzellanfabrk Waldsassen; Carl Schumann; Schirnding Porzellan Fabrik A.G; W Goebel Porzellanfabrik; Porzellanfabrik Langenthal AG; Porzellanfabrik Mittertcich AG.

### *Further Reading*

Cartigny, Georgette, "New Flair in German Ceramics," *Gifts & Decorative Accessories,* October 1985, p 92.

McAlister, Liane, "New U.S. Directions for German China Firms," *Gifts & Decorative Accessories,* July 1990 p. 72.

Pouschine, Tatiana, "We Will Remove the Cobwebs," *Forbes,* August 22, 1988, p. 56.

Thau, Barbara, "Villeroy & Boch Cookware to Reach U.S. Shelves in 2000; Licensing Deal Brings Tabletop Company's Designs to New Category," *HFN—The Weekly Newspaper For The Home Furnishing Network,* December 20, 1999, p. 20.

*Villeroy & Boch: 250 Years of European Industrial History,* Villeroy & Boch Aktiengesellschaft, 1998.

*Villeroy & Boch: Where the Future has Been a Tradition Since 1748,* Villeroy & Boch, 1998.

—Gerald E. Brennan

# Wind River Systems, Inc.

500 Wind River Way
Alameda, California 94501
U.S.A.
Telephone: (510) 748-4100
Toll free: (800) 749-2010
Fax: (510) 749-2010
Web site: http://www.windriver.com

*Public Company*
*Incorporated:* 1983
*Employees:* 818
*Sales:* $171.1 million (2000)
*Stock Exchanges:* NASDAQ
*Ticker Symbol:* WIND
*NAIC:* 541511 Custom Computer Programming Services;
541512 Computer Systems Design Services

Wind River Systems, Inc. is a leading provider of embedded software and services for ''smart'' devices. The company's technology is found in products—such as laser printers, automotive braking systems, robots, cellular phones, and traffic signals—that have computer-enhanced capabilities. Organized into five distinct business units (Platform Engineering, Consumer, Networks, Services, and Transportation/Defense/Industrial), Wind River creates the operating systems and development tools for the computer chips (comprising more than 90 percent of all microprocessors sold) that enable such devices to operate intelligently. A key to Wind River's success is its relationships with technology leaders. The company's clients include Cisco Systems, Inc., Hewlett-Packard Co., Intel Corp., International Business Machines Corp. (IBM), and Sun Microsystems, Inc. In fact, more than 30,000 developers across the high-technology industry incorporate Wind River technology in some 30 million devices. In recent years, Wind River has concentrated on developing the software and infrastructure required to connect products and appliances to the Internet. The company also made two significant acquisitions in 2000 when it purchased Embedded Support Tools Corporation and Integrated Systems Inc.

## Company Origins

Wind River Systems cofounder Jerry Fiddler did not set out to enter the computer industry. Rather, after graduating with a degree in music from the University of Illinois, he hoped to pursue a musical career, applying for a position as the resident composer at the University of Illinois' dance department. He discovered, however, that an advanced degree was required for the post so he re-enrolled at the university. Instead of studying music, he pursued a master's degree in computer science because he was interested in the field of computer-generated music. But after obtaining his master's, Fiddler had difficulty finding meaningful work in Illinois, so he headed for California in 1977.

With his computer background, Fiddler was hired by the University of California's Lawrence Berkeley Laboratory. There he wrote software that enabled computers to control large systems, such as linear accelerators. In addition to formulating systems that operated in real-time (as opposed to the interrupt-response times that are common to most personal computers), he learned to write programs using coding conventions (techniques that allow programmers to re-use chunks of code). He would later apply these lessons to Wind River.

In 1981 Fiddler quit his job at the lab to pursue his interest in computer-generated music. But to pay the bills, he launched a consultancy business focused on real-time. (His early clients included the National Football League and film director Francis Ford Coppola, for whom he designed a unique film editing system.) Also in 1981 Fiddler took an extended vacation and asked David Wilner, a former colleague at Berkeley, to oversee his business. Wilner was enchanted with Fiddler's work and, upon Fiddler's return, they formed a partnership called Wind River Systems (named after Wyoming's Wind River mountain range where Fiddler had vacationed). They officially incorporated their consultancy in 1983, with each partner contributing $3,000 and a desk to the business. They flipped a coin to determine who would serve as CEO; Fiddler won.

## Manufacturing Software Beginning in 1987

For the next four years, Wind River continued to specialize in consulting about real-time software for complex applications. In

## Company Perspectives:

*Wind River's embedded real-time operating system, VxWorks, introduced in 1987, has become an industry standard for performance and sound operation. The success of VxWorks, now part of the company's revolutionary Tornado environment for embedded development, has made Wind River a premier supplier in this market. Factors that contribute to the company's future growth include market growth, technology leadership, customer support and partnerships.*

1987, though, the company shifted gears dramatically and began to manufacture its own software. VxWorks was the company's first offering. A real-time operating system designed for embedded microprocessors, VxWorks was part of what was then a fledgling and esoteric field. But, as the *Red Herring* put it, Wind River recognized that "future computing would take place not on a desktop PC, but inside the myriad appliances of everyday life."

Embedded microprocessors "hidden" in a variety of products make everyday appliances and systems "smart" by giving them computing ability. Just like a microchip inside a personal computer, an embedded microprocessor requires an operating system to direct its operations. Unlike a PC's microprocessor, however, embedded computer chips typically perform only one task (such as activating a car's anti-lock brakes when certain conditions are met or regulating the temperature of a refrigerator). Timing is the most important factor in embedded technology. If an operating system needs to initiate the anti-lock breaks in a car, for example, that operating system must be able to manage and choreograph myriad activities in microseconds. In other words, it must work in "real time" with no delays or lag times. Wind River's VxWorks held the distinction of being the first real-time operating system that worked for different (and unrelated) products. The result was that product manufacturers no longer had to devise a unique embedded operating system for each specific application.

VxWorks quickly became an industry standard. Wind River's sales grew rapidly—rising from $8.02 million in 1991 to $17.09 million in 1992—as demand for its software boomed. In the early 1990s Wind River also developed business relationships with companies that would drive the future course of technology development. In 1993, for example, Wind River designed software for Motorola, Inc.'s high-performance microprocessor unit, which would play a key role in the burgeoning field of wireless communications. Despite such initial successes, though, Wind River needed additional funding to expand its product offerings. To this end, Fiddler and Wilner took their company public in April of 1993, generating $15 million to fuel Wind River's expansion. That same year Wind River introduced WindView, a productivity tool for embedded software that permits developers to watch the dynamic behavior of their applications.

### New Leadership and Growth in the Mid-1990s

Although it had obtained its desired investment capital, Wind River slumped in 1994. Hampered by its nonhierarchical

management style, Wind River was adrift, especially after David St. Charles (who had served as Fiddler's top adviser) abruptly left the company in 1993 to lead Wind River's top competitor, Integrated Systems Inc. In 1994 Wind River's stock hit an all-time low, its profits sank to nearly zero, and sales for the year flattened to $27.3 million. Fiddler recognized that his company would need the leadership of a business veteran to recover. In March of 1994 he stepped down as chief executive officer and turned the day-to-day operations over to Ronald Abelmann, who had served as CEO of Vantage Analysis Systems prior to joining Wind River.

*Investor's Business Daily* credited Abelmann with "engineering a dramatic turnaround" in his first year at Wind River. He quickly restructured the company's business model, cut personnel by ten percent, and bolstered the company's reach by launching operations in Europe and Japan. With Abelmann running the business side of Wind River, Fiddler could concentrate on what he did best: designing new software for embedded systems. Under Fiddler's guidance, Wind River introduced the Tornado development tools package in 1995. Tornado included an updated version of VxWorks as well as a complete set of tools that ran in both Microsoft and Unix environments. But Tornado's greatest strength was its flexibility. It could be integrated with either home-grown or third-party tools, and it had applications across a number of different industries. Tornado won *Electronic Design News'* "Embedded Development Software Innovation of the Year" award in 1995. Wind River also debuted its TakeFive SniFF+ 2.0 that year.

After reporting its strongest year to date in 1995 (revenues rose to $32.1 million), Wind River made a secondary stock offering in 1996. The $50 million raised by this sale was used to fund future acquisitions as well as ongoing research and development. Wind River also began to invest its money in technology start-ups. The company hoped that these nascent firms, who were creating products incorporating embedded microprocessors, would develop into long-term customers and partners relying on Wind River's software. The company's products also received a great deal of attention in 1997, when VxWorks was chosen as the operating system for NASA's Pathfinder mission. Boosted in part by this distinction, Wind River's sales for the year hit a new high of $64 million, $11.3 million of which was net income.

By 1998 it was obvious that Wind River's market niche was booming—nine out of ten microprocessors sold in 1998 were destined for embedded applications. As the *San Francisco Chronicle* noted, "The market for embedded systems [was] growing much more rapidly than the PC market, and many [saw] it as the next great frontier for software companies." Fiddler described the significance of this shift to the *San Jose Mercury News:* "Microprocessors are all around us. The world is becoming embedded. They're hidden in the walls and they're in cars. The microprocessors aren't just in computers; they're controlling our infrastructure, they control our transportation, our communications, our energy systems, our medical systems." Industry analysts at International Data Corp. confirmed Fiddler's observations and predicted that between 1998 and 2003, the embedded systems market would increase 76 percent (compounded annually) to reach $7.9 billion in 2003. Technology watchers predicted a not-too-distant "post-PC" era, in

```
┌─────────────────────────────────────────────────┐
│                  Key Dates:                      │
│                                                  │
│  1981:  Jerry Fiddler and David Wilner found     │
│         Wind River Systems.                      │
│  1983:  Company is formally incorporated.        │
│  1987:  Wind River introduces VxWorks.           │
│  1993:  Wind River becomes a publicly traded     │
│         company.                                 │
│  1995:  Tornado development tools package is     │
│         launched.                                │
│  1997:  Company's VxWorks is chosen as the       │
│         computer operating system for the        │
│         Mars Pathfinder space mission.           │
│  2000:  Wind River acquires Embedded Support     │
│         Tools Corporation and Integrated         │
│         Systems Inc.                             │
└─────────────────────────────────────────────────┘
```

which consumers would no longer purchase cumbersome, expensive, but all-purpose PCs. Instead they would acquire an array of specific tools for particular tasks, such as "smart" cellular phones that could surf the web or kitchen refrigerators that could inventory their contents and order more food when supplies ran low.

Two factors were driving the rapid growth of the embedded systems market. First, computer chips were constantly becoming more powerful and less expensive and, therefore, could be included feasibly in countless products. Second, the blossoming of the Internet led to a vast array of new opportunities. "Until now, we have only scratched the surface of products and appliances that will be connected to the Internet for a wide variety of yet-untold reasons," Fiddler declared in a column in the July 5, 1999 *Electronic Engineering Times*. Digital cameras and recorders, set-top boxes, and Internet-based communications became increasingly popular (and virtually essential) to consumers. For Fiddler, the changes wrought by the Internet were profound. "We are moving into a . . . world where the Internet will no longer connect just computers but will connect people and things in all different ways . . . not only on a desktop but in our kitchens and living rooms and cars and bedrooms and through telephones and everywhere else," he said on the CNBC news show, "Power Lunch."

Wind River was not the only company to notice the potential embedded systems offered. In 1998 the European firms Nokia Corp., Psion PLC, and Telefonaktiebolaget Ericsson LM launched Symbian, a joint venture that produced an operating system called EPOC, which enhanced the functionality of cellular phones and other wireless devices. Wind River's closest domestic rival was Integrated Systems Inc., whose pSOS embedded operating system had a cadre of loyal followers among product developers. Microsoft Corp. also sought to leverage its dominance in the PC operating systems realm into strength in the embedded systems market. In April of 1998, the Redmond, Washington-based technology giant announced that it was revamping its embedded operating system, Windows CE, to include real-time features. Microsoft particularly touted Windows CE's compatibility with its standard Windows System (which enabled consumers to transfer data easily between an embedded product and a PC). Although analysts paid a great deal of attention to Microsoft's entry into the market, Fiddler remained sanguine. After all, the embedded systems market was

extremely fragmented, and Wind River controlled a 35 percent share of the market. "Let's be realistic, one should never ignore Microsoft," Fiddler told the *Red Herring*, "but Microsoft doesn't want to control elevators and cars."

### Challenges in the Late 1990s and Promising Prospects for the 21st Century

To bolster its market position, Wind River made a couple of strategic acquisitions in 1998, purchasing Internet connectivity technology from Network Computer Inc. (later renamed Liberate Technologies) as well as Zinc Software. The pace of Wind River's activities escalated in 1999, as the company made further inroads into the market for Internet-based embedded devices. After purchasing switching technology from Xact Corporation, Wind River acquired RouterWare, Inc., a leading supplier of portable source code. RouterWare expanded Wind River's "offering of high-value, integrated software solutions for data communication and telecommunication equipment manufacturers," noted *EDGE*. Wind River also shipped its next generation development platform—Tornado II—that year.

But 1999 was not without its challenges, as CEO Abelmann resigned unexpectedly in April. Analysts speculated that he had wanted to make Wind Rivers an acquisition target, a course that Fiddler opposed. In any event, Fiddler took charge as interim CEO after Abelmann's departure. Fiddler set an ambitious $1 billion revenue target for the company to meet by 2004 and reorganized Wind River's structure into five business units—Platform Engineering, Consumer, Networks, Services, and Transportation/Defense/Industrial. In September of 1999, Wind River hired Tom St. Dennis, a former executive for semiconductor manufacturing equipment specialist Applied Materials, to be its new CEO.

Wind River made its most significant acquisition to date in 2000 when it closed a deal to buy Integrated Systems and its subsidiaries (which included Doctor Design, DIAB-SDS, and TakeFive). With 1999 sales exceeding $143 million, Integrated Systems was the second largest real-time software producer in the industry. After finalizing the purchase, Wind River reshuffled its executive roster. Fiddler continued to serve as chairman, while Integrated Systems' founder Narend Gupta was named Wind River's vice-chairman. Wind River, however, earned the ire of some equipment manufacturers when it announced that it would phase out Integrated Systems' popular pSOS System in favor of its own VxWorks. "At the end of the day, you've got to have one platform, otherwise you're not running your company properly," Fiddler explained to *Electronic Engineering Times* on March 6, 2000. Later in the year, Wind River purchased Embedded Support Tools Corporation, which provided hardware and software tools for the programming, testing, and debugging of embedded systems.

Wind River's prospects for the new century were quite promising. Wind River's clients included some of the brightest stars in American industry: Agilent Technologies, Inc., Lockheed-Martin Corp., Motorola, and Sony Corp. While serving its existing customer base, Wind River also continued to develop future clients. To this end, the company established Wind River Ventures, a $25 million venture capital fund in June of 2000. "Wind River intends to jump-start the early-stage innovators and entrepreneurs behind these products and technologies, acting as an active catalyst of industry growth,'' Fiddler declared in a company press release.

### Principal Subsidiaries

Embedded Support Tools Corporation.

### Principal Competitors

Applied Microsystems Corporation; Be Incorporate; Microsoft Corporation; Microware Systems Corporation; Sun Microsystems, Inc.; Symbian Ltd.

### Further Reading

Cole, Bernard, ''Change Is Music to His Ears,'' *Electronic Engineering Times,* December 28, 1998.

Fiddler, Jerry, ''Smart Solutions for Post-PC,'' *Electronic Engineering Times,* July 5, 1999.

Fost, Dan, ''Taking On Microsoft,'' *San Francisco Chronicle,* November 3, 1998.

Fuller, Brian, ''Wind River Sinks pSOS as ISI Takeover Plays Out,'' *Electronic Engineering Times,* March 6, 2000.

Quinlan, Tom, ''Alameda, Calif.-Based Firm's Operating System Has the Right Connections,'' *San Jose Mercury News,* September 20, 1999.

Stubbs, Christina, ''Wind River Goes on the Defensive Against Microsoft,'' *Red Herring,* August 1, 1999.

Turner, Nick, ''Software for Sophisticated Chips,'' *Investor's Business Daily,* January 2, 1996.

''Wind River Systems Acquires RouterWare, Inc.,'' *EDGE,* July 5, 1999.

—Rebecca Stanfel

# The Yankee Candle Company, Inc.

102 Christian Lane
Whately, Massachusetts 01093
U.S.A.
Telephone: (413) 665-8306
Toll Free: (800) 243-1776
Fax: (413) 665-4815
Web site: http://www.yankeecandle.com

*Public Company*
*Incorporated:* 1973
*Employees:* 3,300
*Sales:* $256.57 million (1999)
*Stock Exchanges:* New York
*Ticker Symbol:* YCC
*NAIC :* 339999 All Other Miscellaneous Manufacturing;
    442299 All Other Home Furnishings Stores

The Yankee Candle Company Inc. is the leading maker of scented candles. Yankee Candle sells its candles through approximately 130 company-owned retail stores and through wholesale gift store customers who operate approximately 12,500 stores nationwide. The company's products are available in more than 160 fragrances and are marketed as Yankee Candle branded products bearing the trade names Housewarmer, Country Kitchen, Aroma Formula, Flickers, and Frosted Favorites. Yankee Candle's main store is located in South Deerfield, Massachusetts, where the company also operates Chandler's Restaurant and the Yankee Candle Car Museum, both of which are adjacent to the store. In addition to its retail and wholesale sales, the company also sells its candles through direct mail catalogues and its Internet web site. Manufacturing operations are in Whately, Massachusetts, where the company maintains a 300,000-square-foot production facility. Internationally, Yankee Candle sells candles through overseas distributors, and it operates a distribution center in Bristol, England. The investment group Forstmann Little & Co. controls Yankee Candle. Together with Yankee Candle management, the investment firm owns 74 percent of the company's stock.

## Yankee Candle's Origins

Growing up in western Massachusetts, Michael J. Kittredge led the life of a typical teenager. In the mid-1960s, when he was 12 years old, he formed his own rock band. For the next several years, Kittredge divided his time between school and playing guitar in front of a loyal local audience. By the end of the 1960s, Kittredge, like most teenage musicians, saw his dream of rock stardom evaporate. His band broke up in late 1969, dashing any hope of Kittredge's music career extending beyond the confines of his native South Hadley. Worse still, Christmas was near, and Kittredge was strapped for cash. "I was a 16-year-old kid," Kittredge reflected in an April 1997 interview with *Gifts & Decorative Accessories* magazine. "My rock band had just broken up, I had no money, and I needed a gift for my mother." Kittredge's solution to the problem unexpectedly launched his career as an entrepreneur, marking the beginning of Yankee Candle's existence.

Lacking the money to buy his mother a gift, Kittredge relied instead on his resourcefulness. He looked around his family's house and grabbed some used milk containers, old metal bowls, and used crayons. Kittredge melted the crayons and experimented with various fragrances, eventually producing his first candle. Kittredge's gift dilemma was solved in time for Christmas, but his mother never received the candle. The entrepreneur in Kittredge prevailed over the anxiety of a teenage son unable to offer his mother a gift for Christmas. Kittredge sold the candle to a neighbor for $2, and from that moment forward, his life would be devoted to selling candles.

After selling his first creation, Kittredge made another candle for his mother's gift, but turning a profit was already on his mind. He began devoting his spare time to his new business, a venture that had all the trappings of sidewalk lemonade stand. Kittredge hired his cousin Ken, paying him $1 an hour to help make candles in the Kittredges' South Hadley garage. The pair made their candles for friends and family, with each making an extra effort to drink as much milk as possible so they could replenish their supply of empty milk cartons. Initially, Kittredge used the name Candles by Michael Kittredge for his enterprise, but he eventually settled on The Yankee Candle Company because he believed "a stodgier-sounding name would be better,'' as he explained in his April 1997 interview with *Gifts & Decorative Accessories.*

### 1973: Yankee Candle Stands on Its Own

As Kittredge matured, so did his burgeoning candle-making business. After finishing high school, Kittredge enrolled at the University of Massachusetts, but he continued making candles in his parents' home. By 1973, it was hard to discern whether the Kittredges' house was a home or a candle factory. The family furniture was lost amid piles of finished and unfinished candles, and the Kittredges had had enough. They asked their son to move his bustling candle-making business elsewhere, prompting Kittredge to move his manufacturing and warehousing operations to Holyoke, Massachusetts. The relocation marked the promotion of Kittredge's candle-making pursuits from hobby to legitimate business. The site of the company's new home strained the meager resources supporting the former garage-based business. Kittredge could only afford a run-down, abandoned mill. The facility had no electricity and no running water, yet "the business expanded slowly but steadily from there," Kittredge remembered in a December 1996 interview with *Chain Store Age Executive* magazine.

With no clear idea of how to run a manufacturing operation, Kittredge learned by his mistakes. He performed a full range of tasks at the Holyoke plant, leading the candle-making efforts, acting as the company's marketing chief, and sweeping and mopping the factory's floors at the end of the day. Yankee Candle subsisted largely by word-of-mouth advertising, as one Holyoke neighbor told another Holyoke neighbor about the fragrant, long-burning candles being made at the dilapidated mill. The news filtered beyond Holyoke, and within months, lines of customers were waiting outside Yankee Candle's manufacturing plant. A few short years after occupying the old mill, Kittredge had completed the transformation from a home-based sidelight venture into a full-time, genuine business. By the mid-1970s, Yankee Candle had 30 employees, and its manufacturing space had doubled from the area first occupied in 1973.

Having gained his business footing, Kittredge followed his initial burst of expansion by slowly nurturing his company's growth. The production and retail aspects of the company's operation were intertwined at the Holyoke site, an arrangement that existed until Yankee Candle reached its first financial milestone. In 1983, after a decade of production at the Holyoke site, Kittredge's company recorded $1 million in sales. By this point in the company's development, the old mill in Holyoke, like the South Hadley house before it, could no longer adequately accommodate Kittredge's booming business. Another move was needed, precipitating Yankee Candle's relocation to

South Deerfield, Massachusetts, where, for the first time, the company's production and retail operations were separated. Near the company's new production facility, a 2,000-square-foot store was established, an addition that Kittredge credited for greatly increasing the pace of Yankee Candle's growth in subsequent years.

A year before the move to South Deerfield, an important new member of the Yankee Candle's management joined the fold. Michael D. Parry was hired by Kittredge to serve as the company's general manager. As Yankee Candle evolved from regional concern into a national force, Parry would serve as Kittredge's most influential advisor.

Once settled in South Deerfield, the 14-year-old company prospered, generating sufficient profits to fuel more ambitious expansion. Yankee Candle's flagship store flourished during its first several years in business, encouraging Kittredge to add a second retail unit in 1986, when he opened a store in Sturbridge, Massachusetts. Shortly thereafter, a small chain of Yankee Candle retail outlets made its debut, beginning with a third store in Lenox, Massachusetts, and followed by a spree of store openings scattered throughout the New England area. As the scope of Yankee Candle's operations widened, Parry's responsibilities increased, culminating in his promotion to vice president in 1989. The company exited the 1980s with Parry in charge of all the wholesale and retail functions, as well as the company's manufacturing and distribution activities.

### 1990s: The Rise of the Nation's Premier Candle Maker

Yankee Candle's third decade of existence proved to be a decisive era in the company's history. The company branched out into new areas, exploring different ways to display its candle-making talents, and it expanded its retail arm aggressively, particularly late in the decade. Yankee Candle's accelerated growth mirrored that of its industry, as the scented candle segment of the giftware industry recorded lively revenue growth in the 1990s. Driven by annual revenue increases of between 10 percent and 15 percent during the decade, the domestic market for scented candles blossomed into a $2.1-billion-a-year business by the end of the 1990s.

Kittredge seized the opportunities made available in the fertile business climate, assuming an aggressive posture that dramatically increased the size of his company. In the early 1990s, he moved his production site again, relocating to nearby Whately, Massachusetts, where Yankee Candle's manufacturing operations occupied a sprawling 300,000-square-foot facility. The South Deerfield store remained in place, although it too was increasing its square footage year by year. At roughly the same time, the company opened its first store tailored exclusively for the Christmas season, a theme that would be expanded upon in 1993 when Yankee Candle opened a Bavarian Christmas Village. Kittredge then applied the company's resources in two entirely new directions, establishing Chandler's Restaurant and the Yankee Candle Car Museum, which housed a collection of antique and classic automobiles and motorcycles. Both the restaurant and the museum were adjacent to the company's South Deerfield store, adding to the drawing power of the Yankee Candle complex. By the end of the decade, the

**Key Dates:**

**1969:** Using melted crayons, 16-year-old Michael Kittredge makes his first candle.
**1973:** Upon outgrowing the space available in his parents' house, Kittredge moves his candle-making operations to an old mill in Holyoke, Massachusetts.
**1983:** Manufacturing and retail operations are relocated to South Deerfield, Massachusetts; sales reach $1 million.
**1986:** A second store is opened in Sturbridge, Massachusetts.
**1993:** The opening of Yankee Candle's Bavarian Christmas Village leads to the development of the Yankee Candle Car Museum and the opening of Chandler's Restaurant in South Deerfield.
**1996:** Annual sales pass $100 million.
**1998:** Yankee Candle enters into a partnership agreement with investment firm Forstmann Little & Co.
**1999:** Yankee Candle completes its initial public offering of stock.

company estimated that it received more than 2.5 million visitors each year at its South Deerfield site, ranking the store as the second-largest tourist destination in Massachusetts.

By the mid-1990s, shortly after the restaurant and the museum began operating, Yankee Candle had long distanced itself from its modest beginnings. The company eclipsed $100 million in sales in 1996, collecting $112 million, a total generated by the company's 32 freestanding stores and 15,000 wholesale accounts nationwide. Since moving production from the old mill 13 years earlier, sales had increased robustly, swelling nearly 30 percent each year. The company's flagship South Deerfield store, originally a 2,000-square-foot shop, occupied 60,000 square feet by 1996, serving as the anchor of a retail chain on the verge of exponential growth. Kittredge planned to open between 10 and 17 new stores in 1997, but, as he plotted the company's strategic development, he began to delegate greater responsibilities to Parry. Kittredge ceded day-to-day control over Yankee Candle's operations to Parry in July 1996, naming him president. Kittredge remained chief executive officer and chairman, but he would soon relinquish further control as Yankee Candle entered the most ambitious expansion period in its history.

Yankee Candle's expansion during the late 1990s more than doubled its size, far outdoing the achievements of the previous 25 years. After launching www.yankeecandle.com on the Internet in 1996 for informational purposes, the company enhanced the web site in 1997 to accommodate online purchases. The primary focus, however, was on greatly expanding the company's chain of retail stores, an objective that could only be fulfilled with far greater capital than the company had at its disposal. Consequently, Yankee Candle entered into a recapitalization agreement with Forstmann Little & Co., a New York investment firm that acquired a 90 percent equity interest in Kittredge's company for approximately $500 million. The agreement, brokered in March 1998, was a tremendous boon to

Yankee Candle's ability to accelerate the expansion of its retail chain, an infusion of capital that added "fuel to the ship and captain and crew of Yankee Candle in order to reach the destination sooner," according to a company executive quoted in the July 5, 1999 issue of *Investment Dealers' Digest*.

As Yankee Candle set its sights on expanding aggressively, control over the company shifted hands. After its sizable investment, Forstmann Little gained the power to elect Yankee Candle's entire board of directors and to control the company's management, policies, and strategic direction. Further, Parry's ascension within the company's executive ranks continued as Kittredge's influence waned. Parry was named chief executive officer in November 1998, gaining control of Yankee Candle at a decisive juncture in the company's history. The objective was to blanket much of the country with Yankee Candle shops, focusing primarily on establishing a greater retail presence in shopping malls, as opposed to the freestanding stores that constituted the majority of the existing Yankee Candle chain.

Yankee Candle concluded the 1990s with a flourish of activity, setting the tone for the company's further expansion in the 21st century. On the wholesale side, the company bolstered its overseas business by establishing a 27,000-square-foot distribution center in Bristol, England, which began operating in January 1999. By the end of the year, the company had forged business relationships with more than 500 United Kingdom-based accounts and roughly 30 accounts on the European continent. In pursuit of a European candle market estimated at $1 billion, Yankee Candle also had agreements with 14 distributors whose territory of service covered 17 countries. Yankee Candle's retail chain drew considerably more attention from industry observers, as the company used the capital from the Forstmann Little investment and from its debut on the New York Stock Exchange in July 1999, which yielded $97 million in proceeds. The company entered ten new states in 1999, opening 40 stores primarily in shopping malls. By the end of the year, the Yankee Candle chain comprised 102 retail outlets in 30 states, helping the company collect $256 million in sales three years after passing the $100 million in sales mark.

Yankee Candle's expansion in 1999 represented the model of growth for the company's immediate future. Parry announced plans for opening 40 additional stores in 2000, a target number the company anticipated reaching each year for the next several years. If Yankee Candle's expansion efforts unfolded as planned, exponential sales growth appeared likely, ensuring that Kittredge's creation would continue to hold sway in the fast-growing scented candle market in the decade ahead.

### *Principal Subsidiaries*

Yankee Candle Holdings Corp.; Yankee Candle Company (Europe), Ltd. (England); Chandler's Tavern, Inc.; Yankee Candle Car Museum, Inc.

### *Principal Competitors*

Lancaster Colony Corporation; Intimate Brands, Inc.; Blyth, Inc.

### *Further Reading*

Armand, Maria E., "Michael J. Kittredge: Founder, Chairman, and CEO, Yankee Candle Company," *Gifts & Decorative Accessories,* April 1997, p. 168.

Crowley, Aileen, "Order? What Order?," *PC Week,* March 8, 1999, p. 8.

Donovan, Doug, "Out of Magnitude," *Forbes,* February 7, 2000, p. 116.

Garrity, Brian, "Forstmann-Backed IPO," *Investment Dealers' Digest,* July 5, 1999.

"Industry News," *Gifts & Decorative Accessories,* June 1999, p. 12.

Parker, Tom, "S. Deerfield, Massachusetts," *American Demographics,* August 1992, p. 37.

"Yankee Candle Adds Two More Stores," *Gifts & Decorative Accessories,* August 1999, p. 172.

—Jeffrey L. Covell

# Zoltek Companies, Inc.

3101 McKelvey Road
St. Louis, Missouri 63044
U.S.A.
Telephone: (314) 291-5110
Toll Free: (800) 325-4409
Fax: (314) 291-8536
Web site: http://www.zoltek.com

*Public Company*
*Incorporated:* 1976
*Employees:* 1,650
*Sales:* $68.52 million (1999)
*Stock Exchanges:* NASDAQ
*Ticker Symbol:* ZOLT
*NAIC:* 335991 Carbon and Graphite Products

Zoltek Companies, Inc. manufactures carbon fibers, a material renowned for its combination of strength and light weight—but not widely used because of its high cost. Zoltek is trying to increase the use of carbon fibers by reducing manufacturing costs. Rather than use custom-made acrylic fibers to make carbon fibers, the company uses textile-grade acrylic fibers that are less expensive. Zoltek operates seven factories in the United States, the United Kingdom, and in Hungary.

## Origins

Zoltek's self-declared revolutionary role in the development of the carbon fibers business was led by Zsolt Rumy, who was himself no stranger to revolution. A native of Hungary, Rumy grew up in a time of profound divisiveness, with his country struggling to free itself from Soviet dominance and his father jailed as a political prisoner. At the age of 14, Rumy threw Molotov cocktails at Soviet tanks patrolling Budapest during the Eastern European country's 1956 uprising. The overthrow failed and the Communist forces tightened their grip, but not before the Rumy family escaped.

A decade later, after settling in the United States, Rumy had earned a degree in engineering from the University of Minnesota.

In 1975, he took out a second mortgage on his house to start his own business, using $8,000 in start-up money to form Zoltek. Beginning with his wife, Mary, as his only employee, Rumy began his business as a distributor for the local chemical industry in St. Louis, Missouri. This was the origin of Zoltek's equipment and services division that supplied industrial process equipment, aftermarket components, and repair services for the chemical, petrochemical, food processing, and power generating industries.

For the next 13 years, Zoltek was supported solely by the acts of selling, installing, and servicing industrial process equipment. Later, Rumy took a gamble and steered his company in a new direction; the decision eventually cast Rumy as a pioneer, promoting a revolutionary cause in the advanced materials industry. If successful, Rumy's second revolution promised to make Zoltek one of the country's leading industrial concerns.

The event that triggered a new era in the company's history was Zoltek's $750,000, 1988 acquisition of Massachusetts-based Stackpole Fibers—a financially troubled manufacturer of specialty carbon fibers. Although Stackpole Fibers was ailing at the time of the acquisition, Rumy was attracted by the technology the company employed, which at the time was being used in the manufacture of jumbo jet aircraft. Beginning in 1985, carbon fibers were used to make airbrakes for jumbo jets due to the fact that, unlike steel brake pads, the material did not soften when subjected to the friction and resultant heat caused by stopping a 280-ton airplane. Further, at the time of the acquisition, Stackpole Fibers appeared to be close to securing a lucrative contract with the National Aeronautic and Space Administration (NASA) as a supplier of carbon fibers for rocket nozzles. After completing the acquisition, in 1990 Rumy moved Stackpole's operations to St. Louis, establishing manufacturing, research, and development facilities near Zoltek's industrial process equipment business.

## Early Roadblocks to Success

Zoltek's two operating divisions operated side by side, but it soon became apparent that the gamble on Stackpole Fiber had not paid off—certainly not in the short term. The Zoltek division failed to land the NASA contract and found itself anxiously

427

---

**Company Perspectives:**

*We expect to lead a revolution in the advanced materials business. Revolutions in materials are slow to develop, but they become unstoppable once they have gathered momentum. The coming revolution in carbon fiber composites is based on the material's unquestioned technological advantages. We at Zoltek have set our sights upon becoming a much, much larger company. We believe we must attain a large critical mass if we are to fulfill our potential and truly make the future happen for big customers in major industries.*

---

awaiting the development of the carbon fibers aircraft brake business, a process that was proceeding at a dishearteningly slow pace. By the early 1990s, the foray into carbon fibers had proven to be a frustrating disappointment and a strategic misstep for Zoltek, at the least.

No one doubted the qualities of carbon fibers as a material used in industrial applications—carbon fibers were exceptionally strong and exceptionally light in weight—but also exceedingly expensive. Manufacturers who otherwise would have wholeheartedly embraced carbon fibers could not look past the cost. Other widely used materials such as steel (selling for $.35 per pound), and fiberglass (available for $.80 per pound), were by far less expensive than carbon fibers (selling for as much as $12 per pound). Accordingly, companies such as Zoltek who competed in the carbon fibers market were forced to consign themselves to catering to aerospace customers. Because of this, the carbon fibers business was characterized by a low volume of output and high prices. Rumy, unable to penetrate into the exclusive community of carbon fiber end-users, faced a dilemma.

Rebuffed initially, Rumy actually decided to delve deeper into the carbon fibers business. Instead of divesting his interests in carbon fibers, he assumed the role of a pioneer, intent on revolutionizing the industry much like the proponents of aluminum and plastics had done decades before. He conducted pilot studies, hoping to discover that carbon fibers could be manufactured at a significantly lower cost. Rumy theorized that once costs were reduced substantially, the applications for carbon fibers would increase exponentially, thus creating an ideal business opportunity for a company poised to take advantage of the rush towards carbon fiber use. When the Zoltek's investigations revealed that carbon fibers could be manufactured from inexpensive acrylic fibers typically made by the textile industry, Rumy decided to risk more than he had with the acquisition of Stackpole Fibers. He diverted all of the company's resources toward duplicating the properties of the carbon fibers used by aerospace customers and producing them at a substantially lower cost. At that time, the industrial equipment and services aspect of Zoltek was phased out, leaving the company and Rumy entirely dependent on the potential of carbon fibers.

### 1992–94: An Emerging Strategy

Rumy's new corporate mission was formally launched with Zoltek's debut as a publicly traded company. In November 1992, he completed an initial public offering (IPO) of Zoltek

stock, raising $4 million to develop the company's first continuous carbonization line for prototype acrylic-based carbon fibers. Zoltek's equipment and services division was still in operation at this time, delivering steady—albeit modest—revenue and profit growth. But the company's future was in carbon fibers. One year after the IPO, Zoltek posted $567,000 in net income, compared to a net loss of $206,000 during the previous year. Revenue was up as well, rising from $9.6 million to $12.3 million in 1995 primarily due to a 70 percent increase in sales from the carbon fibers business.

In 1994, Zoltek began using its proprietary acrylic-based system to manufacture lower-cost carbon fiber composites. The practicality of the company's product received an encouraging boost in 1994 as well when TRW Vehicle Safety Systems Inc. awarded Zoltek a three-year contract, naming the company as the exclusive supplier of carbon fibers for the propellant systems in vehicular airbags. The TRW contract, rumored to be worth $5 million in sales annually, typified the new, broader-based applications for carbon fibers that Rumy was pushing for. It was an indication that those outside the aerospace industry would find the willingness to pay for the remarkable qualities of carbon fibers.

Aided by increased manufacturing efficiencies and the successful commercialization of the material, Rumy believed he could transform a high-price, low-volume industry into a low-price, high-volume industry. In his mind, Zoltek was poised to reap the financial benefits. Toward this end, Rumy made an important addition to the company's operations in 1995, an acquisition that took Rumy back home—that of Magyar Viscosa.

### 1995 Acquisition of Magyar Viscosa Spurs Growth in Mid-1990s

In November 1995, Rumy turned to Wall Street for another infusion of cash, selling 1.85 million shares in a secondary offering that raised $26.3 million. With the proceeds raised from the offering, he purchased Magyar Viscosa, a Hungarian producer of acrylic and nylon fibers that were purchased by the European textile market. The acquisition, completed in December 1995 for $17.4 million, represented a significant step toward vertical integration, providing the company with a supply of acrylic fiber produced within the Zoltek organization. The purchase of the Hungarian plant also gave the company control over a fundamental aspect of producing carbon fibers, which enhanced Zoltek's potential to achieve manufacturing efficiencies and drive down manufacturing costs. The acrylic fibers manufactured by Magyar Viscosa were textile-grade, considerably less expensive than the custom-made acrylic fibers generally used to make carbon fibers

Investors were evidently in favor of Rumy's 1995 acquisition, voicing their approval by sending the value of Zoltek's stock price soaring in late 1995 and 1996. At that point, the company was ranked as the fifth-largest carbon fibers manufacturer in the world, a position that Rumy was intent on improving. In the wake of the Magyar Viscosa acquisition, Rumy laid out plans for his company's future objectives: during the next five to seven years, Rumy wanted to increase Zoltek's annual revenue to $200 million and increase the company's carbon fiber production by 30 million pounds. This represented a massive increase that exceeded "the entire current world capacity of carbon fiber," according to Rumy in a January 29, 1996 interview with the *St. Louis Business Journal.* For comparison, Zoltek produced approximately 3.5 million pounds of carbon fiber a year during the mid-1990s; thus, his projection represented a tenfold capacity increase.

Although much work remained to be done before Zoltek reached the lofty targets set by Rumy, there soon were indications that the company was making promising progress. Sales in 1996 ballooned from $12.6 million to $68.9 million, invigorated primarily by the company's acrylic fiber plant in Hungary. A bigger cause for celebration occurred at the beginning of 1996, when the company introduced a new price point of $8 per pound for high-volume orders of carbon fiber. Said Rumy in his January 29, 1996 interview with the *St. Louis Business Journal,* "this price is revolutionary in the industry because it is sufficient to attract new cost-sensitive, broad-based applications, such as large ocean-going shipping containers and automotive components." The reduced price was also creating viable applications in a broad assortment of products, ranging from hip implants, to fire-retardant materials, to conductive coatings. Rumy knew he had to drive down production cost further, however, and set a target price of $5 per pound to be reached by the end of 2000. At $5 per pound, industry analysts projected that the carbon fiber market would begin to open up substantially.

Rumy's objectives, which were part of a five-year strategic plan called Zoltek 2000, served as the compass point directing Zoltek's actions during the latter of the 1990s. To accomplish one of the company's fundamental goals—the exponential increase of its production capacity—a fresh supply of capital was needed. As he had done before, Rumy turned to Wall Street, completing two more secondary offerings of stock in 1996 and 1997. The stock offerings raised more than $95 million, providing the money needed to install new continuous carbonization lines in Hungary and at the company's plant in Abilene, Texas.

### Obstacles in the Late-1990s

In late 1997 and early 1998, the heady days when Zoltek's stock value had escalated month by month came crashing to an end. Being a publicly-traded company had its advantages—it had enabled Rumy to raise more than $100 million through stock offerings, for instance—but it also had its disadvantages. Namely, public ownership required a company to meet analysts' quarterly expectations or suffer immediate consequences. Zoltek experienced the downside of the public ownership equa-

tion in 1998, when its earnings plunged and analysts, previously enamored of the company's potential, began to distance themselves from it. Between October 1997 and August 1998, Zoltek lost $780 million of its market value, or 75 percent of its projected worth.

The cause of the company's anemic profit performance was an inherent aspect of its plan to dominate the carbon fibers market. To position itself as preeminent global leader in a market that was filled with potential yet largely unproven, Zoltek's production capacity was being increased, but not being fully used. Rumy's expansion of production capacity was based on the future, dependent on a lower production cost of carbon fiber and the development of new markets for carbon fiber. It was a plan predicated on a situation that did not exist in 1998, which meant idle plants and weak profit performance. Rumy was pursuing a vision, however—one that necessitated short-term sacrifices to fulfill long-term objectives. "We have had depreciation costs because of the over-capacity, but we don't mind" he explained in a January 31, 2000 interview with the *St. Louis Business Journal.*

### Acquisitions and Optimism for the Future

Due to Rumy's insistence on increasing capacity, Zoltek reported a substantial loss for the fiscal year ending in September 1999. The company posted a $2.6 million loss, as it was unable to overcome the estimated $4 million in losses stemming from idle factories. The announcement of the loss, however, occurred at approximately the same time that Rumy announced a string of acquisitions that again buoyed analysts' regard for Zoltek's prospects. In October and November 1999, Zoltek completed the acquisition of four companies: Structural Polymer Holdings Ltd., Cape Composites Inc., Engineering Technology Inc., and Composite Machines Company Inc.

The acquisitions more than doubled the size of Zoltek, adding profitable businesses and managerial expertise that decidedly strengthened the value of Rumy's organization. Perhaps more importantly, though, the acquisitions promised to help Zoltek in one area where the company needed help most. The acquired companies were "downstream," or closer to the end-user, enabling Rumy to take an active role in the development of markets for carbon fiber composites. For instance, the largest of the acquisitions, U.K.-based Structural Polymer, was designing a 50-meter blade for a windmill that incorporated roughly 3,000 pounds of reinforcing carbon fiber. Structural Polymer was scheduled to begin producing the blades in 2001 for sale to Europe's wind-powered electricity generating industry. As one industry analyst noted in a January 31, 2000 *St. Louis Business Journal* article, referring to the importance of the downstream acquisitions, "they don't have to just sit there and be carbon fiber salesman. They can help the development process along."

As Zoltek entered the 21st century, its success depended on the future development of carbon fiber markets. Although widespread demand for carbon fiber composites had yet to materialize as the company celebrated its 25th anniversary, Rumy was optimistic. One news item that supported his sanguine perspective was an announcement by Delphi Automotive Systems in early 2000; the automotive parts manufacturer said it wanted to use carbon fiber in several new automobile safety features. If

Delphi followed through with such plans, new automobiles could contain roughly 20 pounds of carbon fiber, which Rumy estimated would increase global demand from 35 million pounds annually to more than 600 million pounds annually. "I'm looking down the road five or 10 years from now, when carbon fiber is an important material," Rumy explained in his January 31, 2000 interview with *St. Louis Business Journal,* "Then we will be a premier company."

### Principal Subsidiaries

Zoltek Corporation; Zoltek Intermediates Corporation; Zoltek Properties, Inc.; Zoltek Rt. (Hungary).

### Principal Competitors

Hexcel Corporation; Toray Industries, Inc.; SGL Carbon AG.

### Further Reading

Desloge, Rick, "Here's a Switch: a CEO Passes on Bonus Take; Zoltek's Rumy Declines $125,000 Increase," *St. Louis Business Journal,* January 20, 1997, p. 3A.

Gotthelf, Josh, "Short-Sellers Gobble Up 29% of Zoltek's Available Shares," *St. Louis Business Journal,* June 9, 1997, p. 5A.

Herrick, Shera, "Zoltek Companies Inc.," *St. Louis Business Journal,* March 7, 1994, p. 24A.

Holyoke, Larry, "Rumy Stages a Comeback," *St. Louis Business Journal,* January 31, 2000, p. 1.

McLaughlin, Tim, "Zoltek Invests $5 Million, Hoping to Cut Fiber Costs," *St. Louis Business Journal,* January 29, 1996, p. 9A.

——, "Zoltek Stock Defies Gravity," *St. Louis Business Journal,* August 14, 1995, p. 1A.

——, "Zoltek Reaps Benefits from Moving to Research Park," *St. Louis Business Journal,* January 2, 1995, p. 25.

Morganson, Gretchen, "A Penny Here, a Penny There," *Forbes,* June 2, 1997, p. 60.

Song, Kyung M., "St Louis' Zoltek Cos. Denies Early Warning to Brokerage," *Knight-Ridder/Tribune Business News,* August 20, 1998.

"SP Systems Acquired by Zoltek," *Advanced Materials & Composites News,* December 6, 1999.

"Zoltek Makes Four Strategic Acquisitions, More than Double Size of Company," *Advanced Materials & Composites News,* December 6, 1999.

"Zoltek Shifts to Profit as Sales Climb 28.5%," *American Metal Market,* November 24, 1993, p. 4.

"Zoltek's Strategy after String of Acquisitions," *Advanced Materials & Composites News,* December 6, 1999.

"Zsolt Rumy, Zoltek Corp.," *St. Louis Business Journal,* June 24, 1996, p. 6B.

—Jeffrey L. Covell

# INDEX TO COMPANIES

# Index to Companies

Listings in this index are arranged in alphabetical order under the company name. Company names beginning with a letter or proper name such as Eli Lilly & Co. will be found under the first letter of the company name. Definite articles (The, Le, La) are ignored for alphabetical purposes as are forms of incorporation that precede the company name (AB, NV). Company names printed in bold type have full, historical essays on the page numbers appearing in bold. Updates to entries that appeared in earlier volumes are signified by the notation (upd.). Company names in light type are references within an essay to that company, not full historical essays. This index is cumulative with volume numbers printed in bold type.

Environmental Industries, Inc., 31 182–85

Environmental Planning & Research. See CRSS Inc.

Environmental Research and Technology, Inc., 23 135

Environmental Systems Corporation, 9 109

Environmental Testing and Certification Corporation, 10 106–07

Environmentals Incorporated. See Angelica Corporation.

Envirosciences Pty. Ltd., 16 260

Envision Corporation, 24 96

Enwright Environmental Consulting Laboratories, 9 110

Enzyme Bio-Systems, Ltd., 21 386

Enzyme Technologies Corp., I 342; 14 217

Eon Productions, II 147; 25 328

Eon Systems, III 143; 6 238

l'Epargne, 12 152

EPE Technologies, 18 473

EPI Group Limited, 26 137

Les Epiceries Presto Limitée, II 651

Epiphone, 16 238–39

Epoch Systems Inc., 9 140; 12 149

ePOWER International, 33 3, 6

Eppler, Guerin & Turner, Inc., III 330

Eppley, III 99

Epsilon Trading Corporation, 6 81

Epson, 18 386–87, 435

Equator Bank, II 298

EQUICOR-Equitable HCA Corp., III 80, 226

Equicor Group Ltd., 29 343

Equifax, Inc., 6 23–25; 25 182, 358; 28 117–21 (upd.)

Equilink Licensing Group, 22 458

EquiStar Hotel Investors L.P. See CapStar Hotel Co.

Equitable Bancorporation, 12 329

Equitable Equipment Company, 7 540

Equitable Life Assurance Society of the United States, II 330; III 80, 229, 237, 247–49, 274, 289, 291, 305–06, 316, 329, 359; IV 171, 576, 711; 6 23; 13 539; 19 324, 511; 22 188–90; 23 370, 482; 27 46

Equitable Resources, Inc., 6 492–94

Equitable Trust Co., II 247, 397; 10 61

Equitas, 22 315

Equitec Financial Group, 11 483

Equitex Inc., 16 431

Equity & Law, III 211

Equity Corp. Tasman, III 735

Equity Corporation, 6 599; 37 67–68

Equity Group Investment, Inc., 22 339

Equity Marketing, Inc., 26 136–38

Equity Title Services Company, 13 348

Equivalent Company, 12 421

Equus Capital Corp., 23 65

Equus II Inc., 18 11

Eramet, IV 108

ERAP. See Entreprise de Recherches et d'Activités Pétrolières.

Erasco Group, II 556; 26 58

EraSoft Technologies, 27 492

ERCO Systems Group, 16 461–63

ERDA Inc., 36 160

Erdal, II 572

Erdölsproduktions-Gesellschaft AG, IV 485

Erftwerk AG, IV 229

Ericson Yachts, 10 215

Ericssan, AB, 11 501

Ericsson, 9 32–33; 11 196; 17 33, 353; 18 74. See also L.M. Ericsson.

Eridania Béghin-Say S.A., 14 17, 19; 36 185–88

Erie and Pennyslvania, I 584

Erie County Bank, 9 474

Erie Indemnity Company, 35 167–69

Erie Railroad, I 584; II 329; IV 180

Erie Scientific Company, 14 479–80

Eritsusha, IV 326

erizon, 36 264

ERKA. See Reichs Kredit-Gesellschaft mbH.

ERLY Industries Inc., 17 161–62; 33 30–31

Ernest Oppenheimer and Sons, IV 21, 79

Ernst & Young, I 412; 9 198–200, 309, 311; 10 115; 25 358; 29 174–77 (upd.), 236, 392

Ernst, Homans, Ware & Keelips, 37 224

Erol's, 9 74; 11 556

ERPI, 7 167

Ersco Corporation, 17 310; 24 160

Erste Allgemeine, III 207–08

The Ertl Company, 37 318

Erving Distributor Products Co., IV 282; 9 260

Erving Healthcare, 13 150

Erwin Wasey & Co., I 17, 22

Erzbergbau Salzgitter AG, IV 201

ES&A. See English, Scottish and Australian Bank Ltd.

Esanda, II 189

Esaote Biomedica, 29 298

ESB Inc., IV 112; 18 488

Esbjerg Thermoplast, 9 92

Escada AG, 14 467

Escalade, Incorporated, 19 142–44

Escambia Chemicals, I 298

Escan, 22 354

Escanaba Paper Co., IV 311; 19 266

Escaut et Meuse, IV 227

Escher Wyss, III 539, 632

Eschweiler Bergwerks-Verein AG, IV 25–26, 193

ESCO Electronics Corporation, 17 246, 248; 24 425

Esco Trading, 10 482

Escoffier Ltd., I 259

Escotel Mobile Communications, 18 180

Esdon de Castro, 8 137

ESE Sports Co. Ltd., V 376; 26 397

ESGM. See Elder Smith Goldsbrough Mort.

ESI Energy, Inc., V 623–24

Eskay Screw Corporation, 11 536

Eskilstuna Separator, III 419

Eskimo Pie Corporation, 21 218–20; 35 119, 121

Esmark, Inc., I 441; II 448, 468–69; 6 357; 12 93; 13 448; 15 357; 19 290; 22 55, 513

Esperance-Longdoz, IV 51–52

Espírito Santo. See Banco Espírito Santo e Comercial de Lisboa S.A.

ESPN Inc., II 131; IV 627; 19 201, 204; 24 516

Esporta plc, 35 170–72

Esprit de Corp., 8 169–72; 29 178–82 (upd.)

La Espuela Oil Company, Ltd., IV 81–82; 7 186

Esquire Education Group, 12 173

Esquire Inc., I 453; IV 672; 13 178; 19 405

ESS Technology, Inc., 22 196–98

Essanelle Salon Co., 18 455

Essantee Theatres, Inc., 14 86

Essef Corporation, 18 161–63

Esselte Pendaflex Corporation, 11 100–01

Essence Communications, Inc., 24 153–55

Essener Reisebüro, II 164

Essex International Ltd., 19 452

Essex Outfitters Inc., 9 394

Essilor International, 18 392; 21 221–23

Esso Petroleum, I 52; II 628; III 673; IV 46, 276, 397, 421, 423, 432–33, 439, 441, 454, 470, 484, 486, 517–19, 531, 555, 563; 7 140, 171; 11 97; 13 558; 22 106; 24 86; 25 229, 231–32. See also Imperial Oil Limited and Standard Oil Company of New Jersey.

Estat Telecom Group plc, 31 180

Estech, Inc., 19 290

Estee Corp., 27 197

The Estée Lauder Companies Inc., 30 187–91 (upd.)

Estée Lauder Inc., I 696; III 56; 8 131; 9 201–04; 11 41; 24 55

Estel N.V., IV 105, 133

Esterline Technologies Corp., 15 155–57

Eston Chemical, 6 148

Estronicks, Inc., 19 290

ETA Systems, Inc., 10 256–57

Etablissement Mesnel, I 202

Etablissement Poulenc-Frères, I 388

Etablissements Badin-Defforey, 19 98

Etablissements Braud. See Manitou BF S.A.

Etablissements Economiques du Casino Guichard, Perrachon et ie, S.C.A., 12 152–54; 16 452

Etablissements Pierre Lemonnier S.A., II 532

Etablissements Robert Ouvrie S.A., 22 436

Etam, 35 308

Eteq Microsystems, 9 116

Ethan Allen Interiors, Inc., III 530–31; 10 184; 12 307; 12 155–57

Ethical Personal Care Products, Ltd., 17 108

Ethicon, Inc., III 35; 8 281; 10 213; 23 188–90

Ethyl Corp., I 334–36, 342; IV 289; 10 289–91 (upd.); 14 217

Etienne Aigner, 14 224

Etimex Kunstoffwerke GmbH, 7 141

L'Etoile, II 139

Etos, II 641

EToys, Inc., 37 128–30

ETPM Entrêpose, IV 468

Euclid, I 147; 12 90

Euclid Chemical Co., 8 455–56

Euclid Crane & Hoist Co., 13 385

Euralux, III 209

Eurasbank, II 279–80; 14 169

The Eureka Company, III 478, 480; 12 158–60; 15 416; 22 26. See also White Consolidated Industries Inc.

Eureka Insurance Co., III 343

Eureka Specialty Printing, IV 253; 17 30

Eureka Technology, 18 20

Eureka Tent & Awning Co., III 59

Eureka X-Ray Tube, Inc., 10 272

Euris, 22 365

# INDEX TO INDUSTRIES

# Index to Industries

## CONGLOMERATES

## FINANCIAL SERVICES: BANKS

## FINANCIAL SERVICES: NON-BANKS

## FOOD PRODUCTS

## HEALTH & PERSONAL CARE PRODUCTS

## HEALTH CARE SERVICES

## INSURANCE

## LEGAL SERVICES

## MANUFACTURING

## MATERIALS

## MINING & METALS

## PAPER & FORESTRY

## PERSONAL SERVICES

## PETROLEUM

## PUBLISHING & PRINTING

## RUBBER & TIRE

## TELECOMMUNICATIONS

## TEXTILES & APPAREL

## WASTE SERVICES

# GEOGRAPHIC INDEX

# Geographic Index

# *NOTES ON CONTRIBUTORS*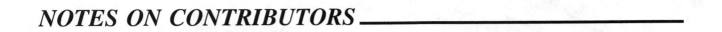

# Notes on Contributors

**AMOROSINO, Chris John.** Connecticut-based freelance writer.

**BIANCO, David.** Freelance writer, editor, and publishing consultant.

**BRENNAN, Gerald E.** Freelance writer based in California.

**CAMPBELL, June.** Freelance writer and Internet marketer living in Vancouver, Canada.

**COHEN, M. L.** Novelist and freelance writer living in Paris.

**COVELL, Jeffrey L.** Seattle-based freelance writer.

**DINGER, Ed.** Brooklyn-based freelance writer and editor.

**FIERO, Jane W.** Freelance writer and editor.

**FIERO, John W.** Freelance writer, researcher, and consultant.

**FUJINAKA, Mariko.** Freelance writer and editor based in California.

**HALASZ, Robert.** Former editor in chief of *World Progress* and *Funk & Wagnalls New Encyclopedia Yearbook*; author, *The U.S. Marines* (Millbrook Press, 1993).

**HAUSER, Evelyn.** Freelance writer and marketing specialist based in Northern California.

**HAZELWOOD, Peggy.** Freelance writer and editor in Denver, Colorado.

**HEFFRON, Margery M.** Freelance editor and writer living in Exeter, New Hampshire.

**INGRAM, Frederick C.** South Carolina-based business writer who has contributed to *GSA Business, Appalachian Trailway News,* the *Encyclopedia of Business,* the *Encyclopedia of Global Industries,* the *Encyclopedia of Consumer Brands,* and other regional and trade publications.

**KARL, Lisa Musolf.** Editor for LifeServ.com; freelance editor, writer, and columnist living in the Chicago area.

**LEMIEUX, Gloria A.** Freelance writer and editor living in Nashua, New Hampshire.

**MILITE, George A.** Philadelphia-based writer specializing in business management issues.

**PATON, Kathleen.** Freelance writer based in New York City; contributor to *Contemporary Fashion.*

**ROTHBURD, Carrie.** Freelance technical writer and editor, specializing in corporate profiles, academic texts, and academic journal articles.

**STANFEL, Rebecca.** Freelance writer and editor based in Montana.

**TRADII, Mary.** Freelance writer based in Denver, Colorado.

**UHLE, Frank.** Ann Arbor-based freelance writer; movie projectionist, disc jockey, and staff member of *Psychotronic Video* magazine.

**WALDEN, David M.** Freelance writer and historian in Salt Lake City; adjunct history instructor at Salt Lake City Community College.

**WERNICK, Ellen.** Freelance writer and editor.

**WOODWARD, A.** Freelance writer.